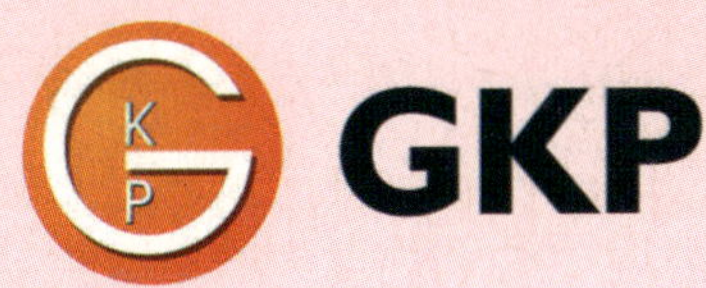

Unravelling

Indian Culture

The Essence of Bharat

Modern India

MADHUKAR KUMAR BHAGAT

Title : Unravelling Indian Culture : The Essence of Bharat – Modern India

Language : English

Author : Madhukar Kumar Bhagat

Typeset & Published by :

Career Launcher Infrastructure (P) Ltd.

A-45, Mohan Cooperative Industrial Area, Near Mohan Estate Metro Station, New Delhi - 110044

Marketed by :

G.K. Publications (P) Ltd.

Plot No. 63, Sector-27A, Near Sector - 28 Metro Station, Faridabad, Haryana-121003

ISBN : **978-93-56814-76-9**

Printer's Details : Printed by Druck Media Private Limited, Greater Noida.

DISCLAIMER

This book may not be construed as a statement or documentation of history. It is based on the facts cited in various books and publications referred to, as also highlighted in the Bibliography. While best efforts have been made by the author and the publisher to verify the facts from the accredited sources, some inadvertent or typographical mistakes if noted, may be brought to the knowledge of the publisher or the author to facilitate improvements in future editions. The views expressed are personal of the author. The author or the publishers do not claim any copyright over the photographs of various government agencies or the copyright-free images of Wikipedia, published in this book with due acknowledgement.

Acknowledgements & Thanks

Government Departments, Museums and Art Galleries

- Department of Posts, Government of India
- Department of Tourism, Bihar
- Department of Tourism, Odisha
- Department of Tourism, Rajasthan
- Department of Tourism, West Bengal
- Directorate of Uttar Pradesh Tourism
- Karnataka State Tourism Development Corporation
- Madhya Pradesh Tourism Board
- Maharashtra Tourism Development Corporation
- National Film Development Corporation (NFDC) - National Film Archives of India
- Sangeet Natak Akademi
- Tamil Nadu Tourism Development Corporation
- Bihar Museum, Patna
- Chatrapati Shivaji Maharaj Vastu Sangrahalaya, Mumbai
- Government Museum, Chennai
- Nagpur Central Museum
- National Crafts Museum & Hastkala Akademi, New Delhi
- National Gallery of Modern Art, New Delhi
- National Museum, New Delhi
- Patna Museum, Patna
- State Museum, Bhopal
- The Government Museum, Bangalore

The Publishers

- **Vinod Bhan** – *Business Head*
- **Kannath Prakash** – *Editorial Coordinator*
- **Brijesh Jha** – *Text Layout & Design*
- **Bhagwan Das** – *Cover Design*

Excerpts on Indian Culture from the **author's book**

UNRAVELLING INDIAN CULTURE ANCIENT INDIA

Featured in the 'Invite Section' of

Hindustan Times

Scan to read

[BY INVITATION]

Religion, culture distinct elements of civilisation with a deep connection

Madhukar Kumar Bhagat

NEW DELHI: At times used synonymously with culture, the word civilisation is said to have its origin in the Latin word Civitas, meaning a city. Thus, it was originally meant to distinguish the human settlements, particularly the more complex urban settlements from the nomadic, transitory or rootless people or those with a rudimentary society and negligible form of institutional governance. In the modern context, civilisation refers to a fairly advanced stage of human development of a people, which encompasses social, urban, technological as well as cultural development.

The presence of organised urban settlements, with diversity of human activity hierarchical society, distinct form of governance, social stratification, development of economic systems, technological growth, evolution of ethical traits and cultural elements, all can be said to be distinct features ascribable to an evolved civilisation. Thus, civilisation can truly be said to be a milestone of human evolution, encompassing within its fold all elements of growth and transformation of a society. The Indus Valley, Egyptian, Mesopotamian and Chinese were the earliest of ancient civilisations that prospered and left a mark on the sands of time.

[BY INVITATION]

Inclusivity and evolution are inherent traits of Indian culture

Madhukar Kumar Bhagat

Dedicated to

Maa, Papa,

Bhaiya,

Garima,

Pranshu and Prabhav,

for family is

the fountainhead

of values and culture.

Preface

It is sheer joy to see a work of more than four years come to fruition. The third and final volume of this series on Indian culture is now with you, while the first two volumes (Ancient India & Medieval India) have already made their space on the bookshelves and received positive responses from dear readers. With the publication of this third volume, a journey that took me through thousands of pages of diverse texts covering several millenniums of India's rich and dynamic cultural history has culminated. Reading copious publications on multifarious and intricate topics, reflecting on the varied perspectives of numerous thinkers and then writing bit by bit, to encapsulate their ethos through the prism of my comprehension in a simple yet lucid manner, has been the essence of this endeavour. As a gratifying journey nears its close, it becomes difficult to let it go despite its inevitable end. But then one must do so and so do I. As I pen the lines of this preface, there is a sense of satisfaction that I could attempt to make a humble contribution, to foster an appreciation of the rich Indian culture. If to 'give' is a higher form of human fulfilment, then this work marks my modest, albeit gratifying offering to this quintessential element of Indianness.

The ambit of the subject of Indian culture and this entire work is indeed vast and complex. The three books (Ancient India, Medieval India & Modern India) take the readers through the different cultural waves that have swept this vast land and its people. It highlights the cultural confluences and the emergence of the diverse, inclusive and ever-evolving Indian culture. While an analytical appreciation of the different cultural phases is an integral element of this work, the various chapters also identify the macro and micro elements of Indian culture. These are covered in the three books, of the ancient, the medieval and the modern Indian culture.

It is said that a picture is worth a thousand words. Taking inspiration from this idiom, this work in three volumes has included nearly 1700 photographs. In certain chapters, an exclusive picture gallery has also been appended that provides a visual complement to the narrative. These pictures encompass different phases of cultural history and varied subjects. Many of the photographs are those taken by me over several years. Some of the images are sourced from the different state tourism departments and government agencies. These are high-quality images taken by professional photographers. Some are also sourced from Wikipedia. These pictures, taken by common folks are thus, a contribution to this common cause of Indian culture. Pictures are indeed integral to the primary concept of this project which is to offer to the reader, a lucid understanding of the intricacies of the glorious Indian culture. The photographs also take these three volumes into the category of illustrated works on Indian culture.

This book (volume 3) covers the cultural elements of modern India. It comprises 11 chapters making it the most voluminous among the three books, despite it covering a relatively shorter period of less than three centuries of cultural history. 'The Cultural Eras: Modern India'(chapter 14; the first chapter of volume 3), traces the course of Indian culture, beginning from the late 18th century and over the next 250 years. It analyses the emergence of European influence on Indian Culture with the rise of the sceptre of colonialism that later metamorphoses into the growing and dominating influence of British Culture. The rise of Indian nationalism, the phase of socio-cultural regeneration and the post-independence Indian culture are also analysed from the perspective of different macro and microelements. Chapter 15 takes a closer look at the socio-religious reforms, the numerous reform movements, the eminent reformists and the socio-cultural regeneration that ensued in its wake. Indeed, its impact was enduring and continues to nourish Indian society.

'Paintings in Modern India', Chapter 16, takes the reader through a colourful journey tracing the evolution of Indian paintings from the medieval to the modern. It also showcases the salient works of eminent artists like Raja Ravi Varma, the Bengal School of Art and other modern art movements, that had a salutary influence on Indian art. Folk paintings of India, which are the cultural repositories of the traditional societies, also find a special mention. The next chapter, 'Music in Modern India' brings out the categories of Indian music, the exponents of classical music-instrumental and vocal, and also highlights some traditional musical instruments. Folk music from different states as well as popular film music and the playback singers, are some other interesting domains of this chapter. Chapter 18 takes one through the story of the evolution of Indian classical dances, their ancient roots and medieval interconnect. It also showcases the folk and tribal dances of different states, bringing out their intricate bond with popular culture and the daily lives of common people.

The account of Indian textiles and handicrafts (chapter 19) highlights the important fabrics of India and the traditional textile techniques and handicrafts. It also showcases numerous handicrafts of India and their tradition including; gems and jewellery, pottery work, terracotta handicrafts, traditional leather products, glass works, wooden handicrafts, metal handicrafts, stonecrafts, papier mache works and even traditional toys and puppets. The Languages and Literature of Modern India, (chapter 20) traces the evolution of modern Indian languages and literature. It succinctly brings out the milestones of literature in modern India, the eminent litterateurs in Hindi and regional literature and how intricately has Indian literature been weaved with our culture, society and national ethos. The next chapter is the story of folk theatre of India and the evolution of modern theatre. It identifies the traditional roots of theatres seeped into the regional and folk culture which is deeply influenced by elements of religion, festivals, mythology and literature besides the concurrent influences of the society.

Indian Cinema (chapter 22) is an exciting account of the century long journey of this relatively nascent medium of cultural and artistic expression. It traces the journey of Indian movies from the very first display in the late 19th century, to the first Indian silent movie in the early 20th century and the mega blockbusters of the 21st century. How movies transitioned from mythological and historical to social and contextual, the different genres ranging from parallel to commercial, from art to masala, and how the silver screen mirrored the changing facets of Indian society and culture is brought out through the lens of dynamic Indian cinema. Festival and Fairs of India, the next chapter brings out the diversity of Indian culture showcased through its numerous religious, social and secular festivals. Besides weaving the very fabric of Indian society and being a bridge between the diverse communities, festivals and fairs have a unique social and economic facet seeped in age-old traditions. The last chapter carries the story of the evolving modern Indian architecture. The account traces the numerous colonial influences which have shaped this socio-cultural element. It also brings out as to how the administrative and social demands, technology, economy and need of the common folks have influenced architecture, one of the most visible and changing cultural element.

Over the centuries, Indian culture has experienced several winds of change. It has been dynamic and evolving, with fresh waves of socio-cultural influences sprouting diverse cultural milieus. In the numerous hues of culture and its myriad of elements, these three books bring out some. Its chapters are akin to those windows in a large mansion, where each window offers a unique glimpse of the outside world, and each glimpse through these windows representing a macro element of the grand Indian culture. No book on culture can claim to be comprehensive and nor does this. But it sincerely endeavours to bring out the salient elements of Indian culture and their essence.

I am thankful to the publishers for believing in this project from the outset and sustaining their interest and hard work throughout these years. A special thanks is due, to different state tourism departments and other government agencies who have contributed numerous photographs, and to the different museums across the country and their officials, whose guidance has been invaluable. Some of the unsung contributors whose photographs have found a place through the pages of Wikipedia, also deserve my thanks. And of course, a big thanks to you readers, for sparing your time in going through this book and evincing interest in this profound and yet fascinating subject.

Our family remains the repository of the social culture and the primary teacher and transmitter of values. I am thankful to my family. A special thanks to my father, who painstakingly went through the first draft of all the chapters and corrected me as he has always done with me. To my wife and children who had to bear with me in these years, a thank you will not suffice. Above all, I pray to the Divine, to continue to bestow His grace as He has always done.

Om!

Madhukar Kumar Bhagat

September 2024

New Delhi

Contents

Ancient India is the first book of the **three-book series** titled *Unravelling Indian Culture : The Essence of Bharat* and **comprises seven Chapters**.

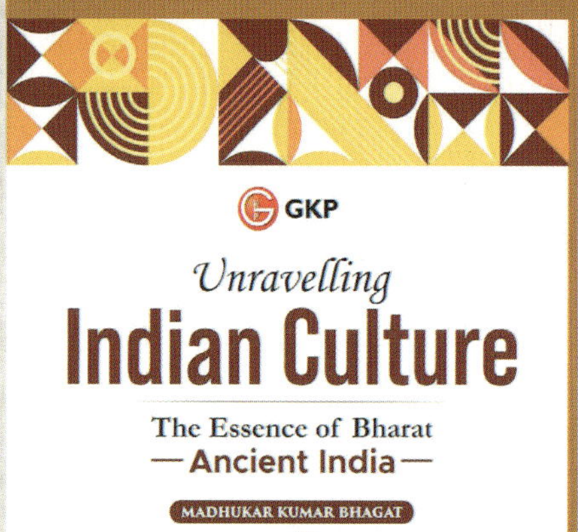

ISBN : 978-93-56815-24-7

1. Culture Eras: Ancient India
2. The Indus Valley Civilisation and Harappan Culture
3. Hinduism: A Way and View of Life
4. Buddhism: The Middle Path
5. Jainism: The Theology and Practice of Ahimsa
6. Tangible & Intangible Elements of Culture in Ancient India
7. Temples in Ancient & Medieval India

Medieval India is the Second book of the **three-book series** titled *Unravelling Indian Culture : The Essence of Bharat* and **comprises six Chapters**.

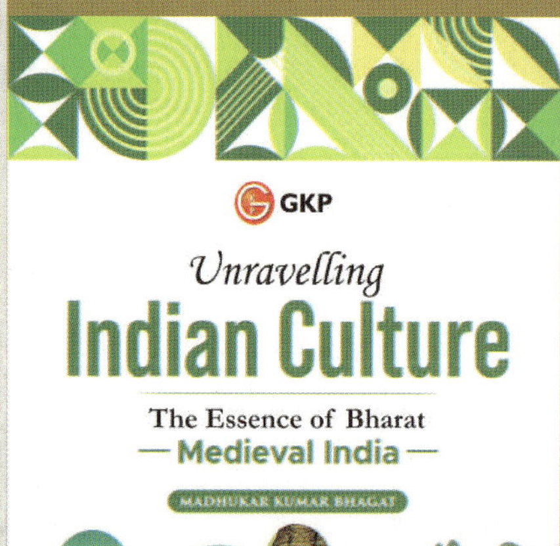

ISBN : 978-93-56816-43-5

8. The Cultural Eras: Medieval India
9. Bhakti Movement and Sufism
10. Architecture in Medieval Age: Palaces, Forts and Other Monuments
11. Medieval India –Visual Arts: Indian Paintings & Bronze Sculptures
12. Literature in Medieval India
13. Music & Dance in Medieval India

Cultural Eras: Modern India

> *A nation's culture resides in the hearts and in the soul of its people.*
>
> — Mahatma Gandhi

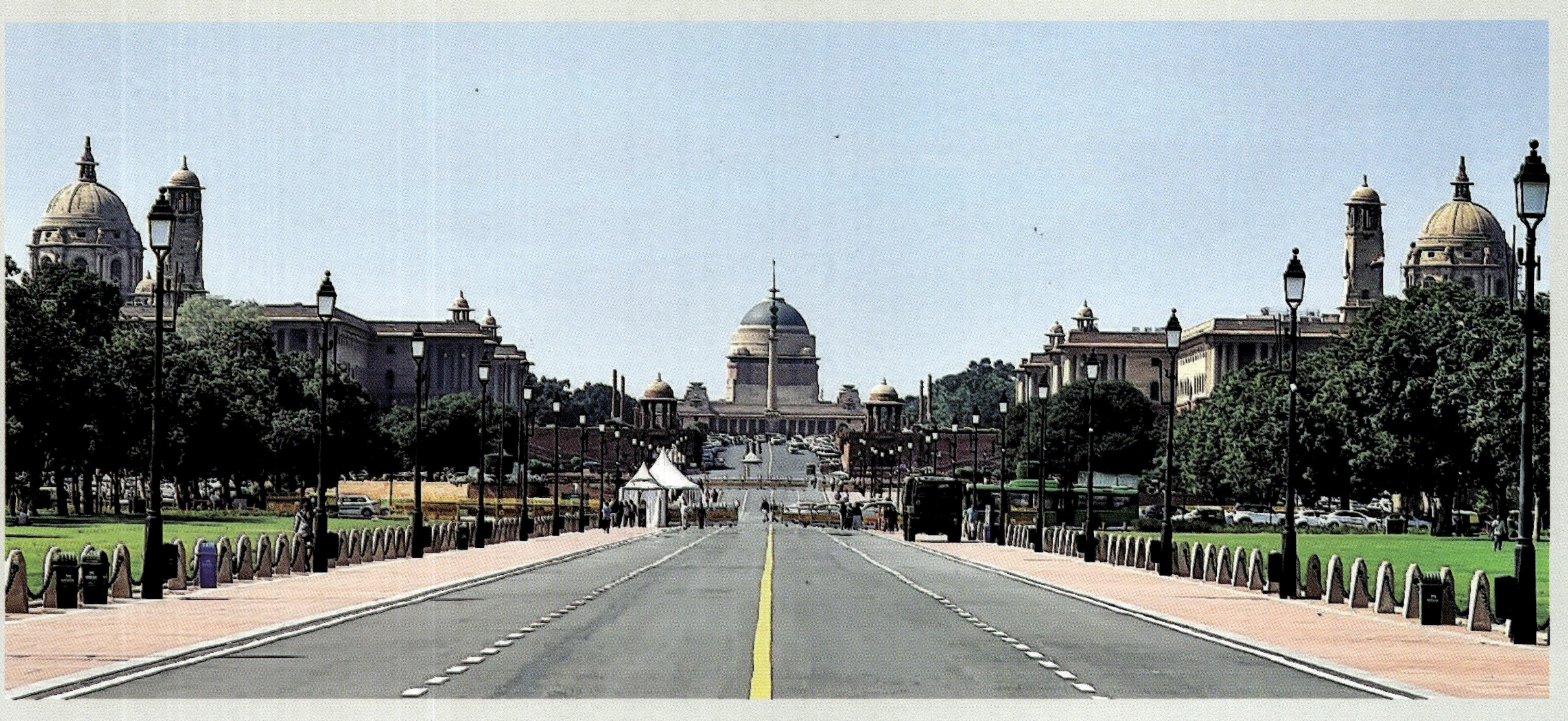

14.1: Rashtrapati Bhavan and the two secretariats, North Block (right image as seen in the picture) and South Block (left image), a view from Kartavya Path before Vijay Chowk — photograph by Madhukar K Bhagat

INTRODUCTION

Another wave of cultural influence, which had a considerable impact on the culture, society and polity of India, emerged in the late 18th and early 19th centuries. This was a wave that arose owing to the **colonisation of India.** Politically, socially and culturally, this was a phase of great tumult and drastic transition. It was a period unlike any other in the past several centuries of India's political and cultural history. The span of the next two centuries shook Indian society, wrenched its very fabric, and jolted it from the socio-cultural stupor induced by centuries of orthodoxy, dogma, complacency and inward look. It was indeed also a period of great pain and suffering. There were phases of abject despair, darkness and gloom. The socio-political edifice of the medieval era which had been entrenched for centuries, crumbled. It compelled the people to question the status quo, to reform their socio-religious and cultural practices, to challenge the inimical and exploitative political system and eventually, after nearly a century and more of struggle, to remould themselves into a new nation. But this was not without great sacrifices, acute tribulations and irreparable losses. However, there did emerge a new dawn, and with it the hope of peace, prosperity and cultural regeneration.

DIFFERENT PHASES OF EMERGENCE OF MODERN CULTURE

The culture of India transitioned over a period of time, from the medieval Hindustani culture- a confluence of Indo-Islamic elements, to the **modern Indian culture** — an assimilation of different cultural streams with indigenous roots. The period of transition oversaw the **decline of the Mughal Empire** in the 18th century. The **early European influence** of the 18th century was marked by the rise of different colonial powers which were competing to protect their mercantile interests and had clandestine designs that were beyond their ostensible trade and commercial interests. **The growing phase of British/English culture** of the late 18th century and the 19th century was a phase of growth and consolidation of the authority of the British. It was a period synonymous with economic despair and degeneration and marked by the complete erosion of the Indian political authority and the decay of the indigenous culture. The **rise of Indian nationalism in** the late 19th and early 20th century eventually leading to India's independence, besides being a period of creation of political and national consciousness, was also a period of increasing cultural consciousness.

The **post-independence culture** and the first few decades thereafter, were not only harbingers of a new hope, but also a period of great struggle. The division of the country, the communal bloodshed in its wake, and the multifarious challenges of an emergent nation struggling to find its feet, all had a profound impact on its culture. The following phase of economic and political reconstruction of the nation was characterised as well by a search for cultural identity and cultural regeneration. The last, but not the least can be said to be the period of the three decades after economic liberalisation, and in particular the quarter century of the new millennium. This is the phase of a **modern assimilative and inclusive culture**, which is marked by the economic buoyancy of a growing country and the confident strides of a nation effusing self-belief. Its changing demography, rising aspirations of its human resource, technological prowess and global interconnect, are redefining Indian culture. Now, while the country is proud of its ancient roots, it is also embracing modernity in full measure. It has hope. It has challenges. It is the harbinger of a culture where its ancient philosophy of *Vasudhaiva Kutumbakam* (all world is a family) has the space to grow and be a beacon of universal interconnect and inclusiveness.

THE EARLY EUROPEAN INFLUENCE

The European powers arrived in India as merchants in the 16th and 17th centuries in search of spices. This marked a direct contact between the Indian civilisation and the Western world on Indian soil. This, however, was a phase of limited European influence on Indian culture as the colonial trading companies had minimal interconnect with the masses and lacked socio-political authority to cast any meaningful influence. But in a century, the Portuguese, the Dutch, the British, the French and the Danish managed to establish their respective presence and pockets of their stronghold. The political chaos of the 18th century gave space to the colonial powers to make deeper inroads within the country. The Mughal empire was on a steady decline post the reign of Aurangzeb. The Maratha and Sikh empires provided brief periods of strong regional Indian authority. But in the latter half of the 18th century, amidst sweeping political changes, the British emerged as the singular most powerful political authority.

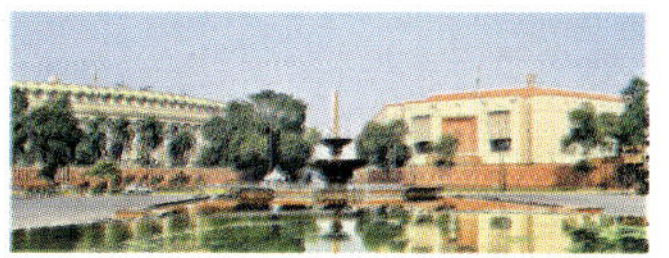

The victory of the British East India Company forces in the Battle of Plassey in 1757 over the Nawab of Bengal, Siraj-ud-Daulah, gave them sizeable territorial rights. Later, the acquisition of *Diwani* of Bengal in 1765 from the Mughal emperor, endowed them with the right to collect revenue. In the Carnatic Wars (1744-1763), the British East India Company had emerged victorious over the French East India Company, their most powerful European rival in India. The Portuguese, once having a powerful presence in South and West India, by now had their authority limited to regions such as Goa and some regions in present-day Gujarat (including Daman, Diu, Dadra and Nagar Haveli). The influence of the French was curtailed to small regions of Pondicherry on the Coromandel coast, Mahe on the Malabar coast and Chandernagore in Bengal. By this time, the Dutch had negligible political authority in India and neither did the Danish. Thus, by the mid-18th century, the British had wrestled and established a significant presence and reasonable political control in India. Their authority in India had grown from mere trading rights to territorial rights. With this, also came the **European or Western influence on Indian culture**.

Socially and culturally, the European influence up to the 18th century was restricted only to certain regions and certain segments of Indian society and was not as profound as it would become in the 19th century. By this period, the colonial companies' major interest was mercantile. This necessitated a certain degree of military presence and even fortification. At times, the colonial powers asserted their authority and established political control in the adjoining regions as in the case of the Portuguese in the 16th century. This also brought them and other colonial powers into conflict with the regional rulers and the Mughal dynasty. This did have a socio-political impact; however, their cultural impact was limited. The adversarial position of the colonial companies, which was initially bereft of any political authority, allowed for limited interaction with the common folks and for cultural interchange. At times, the local population was suspicious or opposed to the foreign powers, and in some instances, at the receiving end of their excesses and cruelty.

The early European cultural influences in the late 17th and 18th were not as geographically widespread as they were to become later. Further, except in certain regions of a political stronghold as that of the Portuguese in Goa and others, they could not cast a deep social influence. The majority of the Indian society, entrenched in its age-old cultural traditions was largely aloof of the European influence. However, this period did witness the introduction of some European cultural elements to the Indian landscape.

Architecture was the foremost of the European cultural influences which struck roots in India. This was borne out of the need of the colonial traders to protect their merchandise and personnel. There was also the need to have a place of residence, worship and other structures in the European settlements. The Portuguese, among the earliest of the colonial powers, had a significant presence in Goa. Some examples of the architecture of the 17th and 18th centuries can be witnessed in the churches and forts of Goa. Old

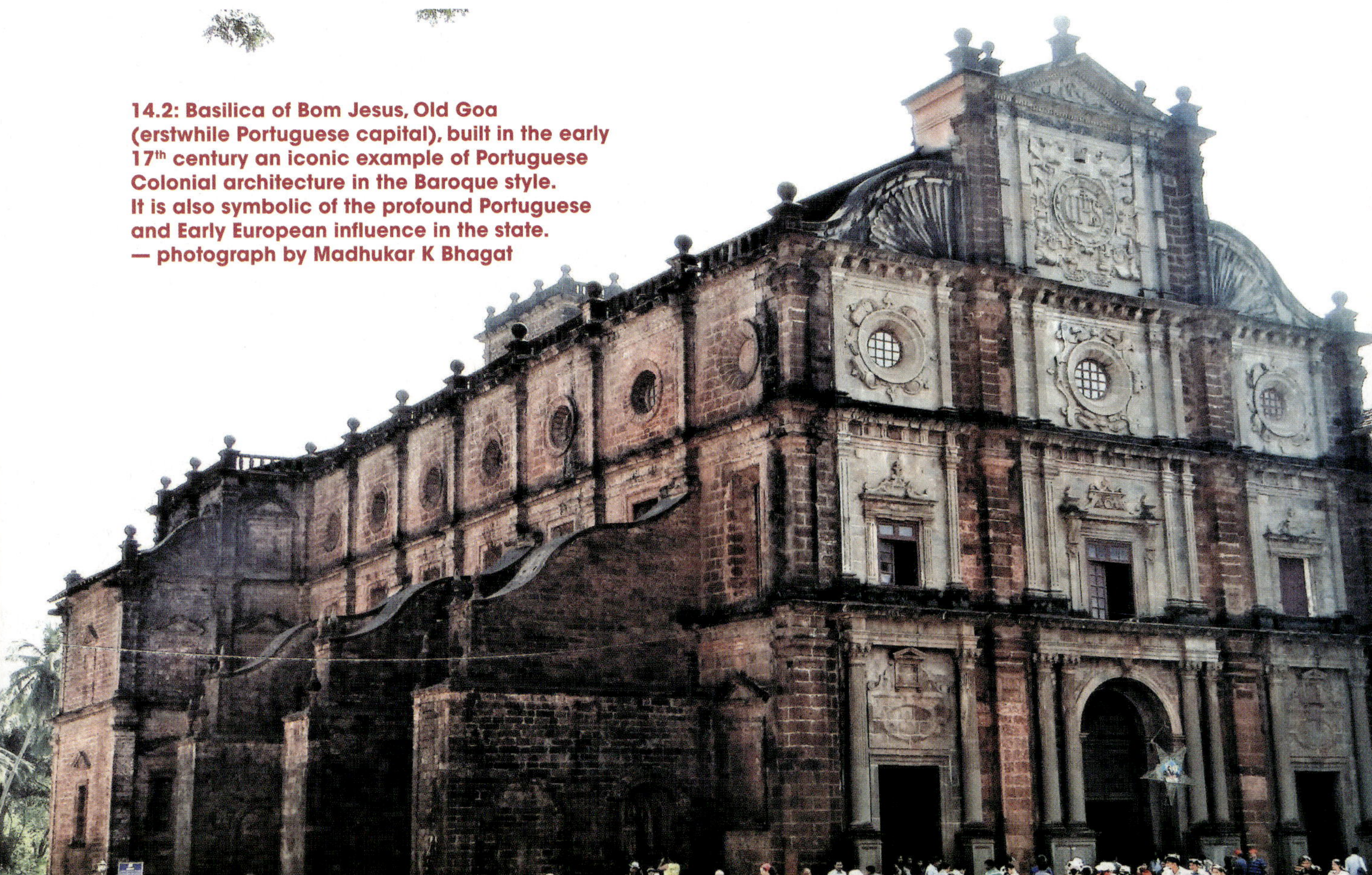

14.2: Basilica of Bom Jesus, Old Goa (erstwhile Portuguese capital), built in the early 17th century an iconic example of Portuguese Colonial architecture in the Baroque style. It is also symbolic of the profound Portuguese and Early European influence in the state. — photograph by Madhukar K Bhagat

mansions and houses of Goa are also reflective of the Portuguese architectural influence. Similarly, the Dutch architectural influence of this period can be seen in the areas colonised by them in Ahmedabad, Surat, Bharuch, and Kochi. Puducherry (Pondicherry), a French stronghold, reflects the cartesian grid plan of the old city referred to today as the French Quarters' which has the old colonial-style villas. A variety of British structures came up in the port cities and presidency towns of Madras, Calcutta and Mumbai. Fort St. George in Madras (built 1639-1644) is the oldest British structure in India. Fort William in Calcutta (built 1696-1706 & 1758-1781) and Fort in Bombay (first built in 1665 and expanded in 1715-1722) were other centres of British East India Company which were witness to the early British architecture.

Religious Beliefs and Christian Missionary Activities

Although Christianity had come to India in the first millennium, and as per some scholars, in the very first century CE, it had a limited presence in India, restricted largely to the Malabar Coast. Post the arrival of the Portuguese and their establishment of political authority in Goa and some other regions, Christian missionary activities increased. With this, came up the establishment of new churches in different parts of Malabar and Goa region and the conversion of the local population to Christianity. The Portuguese, who also married the local women in Goa, are believed by scholars to have started the conversion of these women to Christianity. This intermingling of the populations also had a deeper cultural impact, whereby the Portuguese culture, besides the Christian religion, was entrenched in the region. Later, the arrival of the Dutch, the English and the French, further enabled the spread of Christian missionary activities to different parts of the country and in particular to the Madras, Bombay and Bengal regions. While the St. Thomas Christians who were settled in the Malabar region since the first millennium were the earliest practitioners of Christianity in India, with this 'wave' of European influence in the 17th and 18th centuries, other sects of Christianity, including the Catholic and the Protestants, established their presence and churches in India. These were the harbingers of the Christian faith and traditions that grew in India in the next couple of centuries.

While, with the exception of the Portuguese, the other European powers remained largely aloof from the local population, it was the missionary activities that brought some degree of people-to-people contact between the Europeans and Indians. However, this interconnect too was marked with animosity and suspicion to begin with. Another fringe effect of the missionary activity was also felt in the **Indian languages**. The missionaries had to converse with the local population to explain the philosophy, precepts and practices of Christianity. They learned the local languages and published the Bible and other religious publications in these languages. Scholars believe that for this they also understood and wrote the basic grammar of those languages, brought out the primer of Indian and European languages and started a trend of writing prose in these languages. The development of the first printing press also happened in Goa in the 16th century to print material for missionary activities and this trend continued in the subsequent centuries.

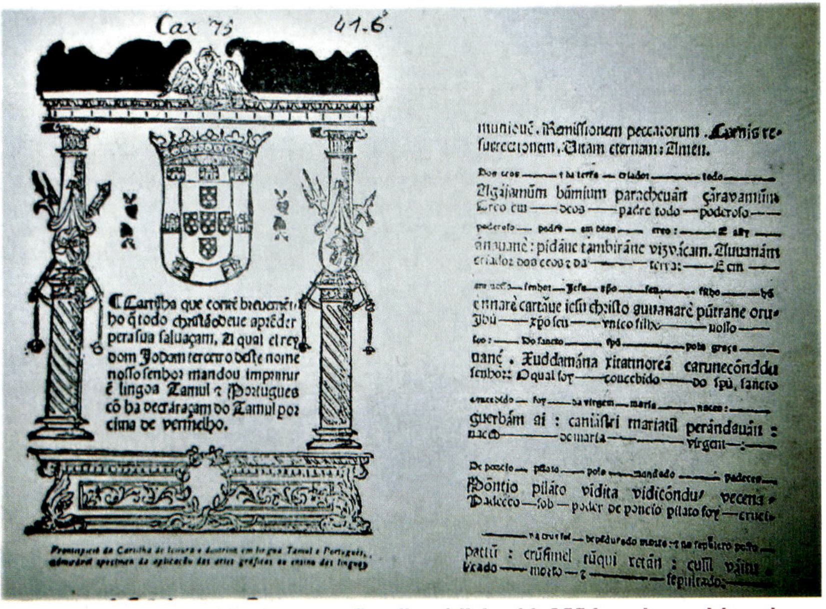
Cax 75 41.6

Carinha que contẽ breuemẽte ho q̃ todo christão deue aprẽder pera sua saluaçam. A qual el rey dom Joham terceiro deste nome nosso senhor mandou imprimir ẽ lingoa Tamul e Portugues cõ ha decraraçam do Tamul por cima de vermelho.

muniõẽ. Remissionem peccatorum. Carnis resurrectionem. Vitam eternam: Amen.

Algájamũm bámium parachcuán çáravamũm
Creo em — deos — padre todo — poderoso —

ánauané: pidáue tambiráne vizváçam. Aluuanám
criador dos ceos e da — terra: — E em —

ennaré cartáue iesu christo guiranare pútrane oru
Jhũ — xpo seu — unico filho — nosso —

nanç. Xuddamána xitannoreá carunecónddu
senhor: O qual foy — concebido — do spũ. sancto

guerbám ai: caniáshri mariatil perándauán:
naceo — de maria — virgem —

Pôntio piláto vidita vidicóndu vecena
Padeceo — sob — poder de poncio pilato foy — cruci

pattũ: crúsimel túqui xetán: cull váitu
ficado — morto — e — sepultado

14.3: A primer of Portuguese-Tamil published in1554 and considered to be one of the earliest known Christian books in an Indian language — Wikimedia Commons

European Languages and Their Influence

European languages and their introduction in India happened in this phase. The earliest of the European languages to be understood was the Portuguese. Marrying with the local women in Goa, interaction

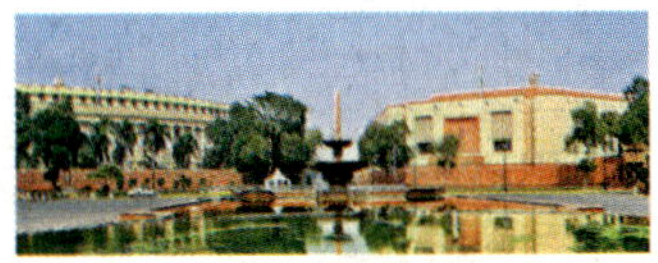

with the local population elsewhere, and the needs of trade and commerce necessitated the learning of the Portuguese language to be learnt by some section of the Indian population. The Portuguese were the unrivalled colonial power of the 16th century and thus had an early bird advantage. As this was the European language somewhat understood by a few in the Indian population, it for some time served as a bridge language for other European powers in the later period. As per scholars, Lord Clive who is credited with defeating the forces of Siraj-ud-Daulah (in the battle of Plassey-1757) and thus laying the foundation of the British empire, understood a bit of Portuguese which helped him to communicate with the local population, by whom this language was partly understood. The influence of this language can be seen in the fact that several words in Hindi/Urdu/ Hindustani having Portuguese origin, have entered the local language lexicon since then and fully become a part of vocabulary. This includes words such as अलमारी (*almari:* cupboard)-*armário* (in Portuguese), इस्पात (*ispat:* steel, sword)-*Espada* (in Portuguese); कमरा (*kamara:* room)- *câmara* (in Portuguese), गिरजा (*girija:* church)- *igreja* (in Portuguese), बाल्टी (*balti*: bucket)- *Balde* (in Portuguese) साबुन (*sabun*: soap)- *sabao* (in Portuguese) besides several others. The entry of such words of common usage in the vocabulary of Hindi and other languages reflects people-to-people contact and the cultural influence it casts.

However, in the 17th century, the Portuguese were largely displaced by the Dutch. Thus, the cultural influence of the Portuguese remained limited to certain pockets such as Goa and a few others, while in other regions it waned over a period of time. The Dutch in turn were uprooted by the French and British in the 18th century. Each of these colonial powers introduced their respective languages in their region of political authority. Thus, in this phase, India witnessed exposure to a variety of European languages. Through them occurred a certain degree of social intercourse and hence certain European cultural influences permeated the country. But as the British were the colonial powers that outlasted the other rivals, it was the English language that had a profound and indelible impact on the Indian culture and society. The other European linguistic and cultural influences gradually faded from most parts of the country over the next couple of centuries.

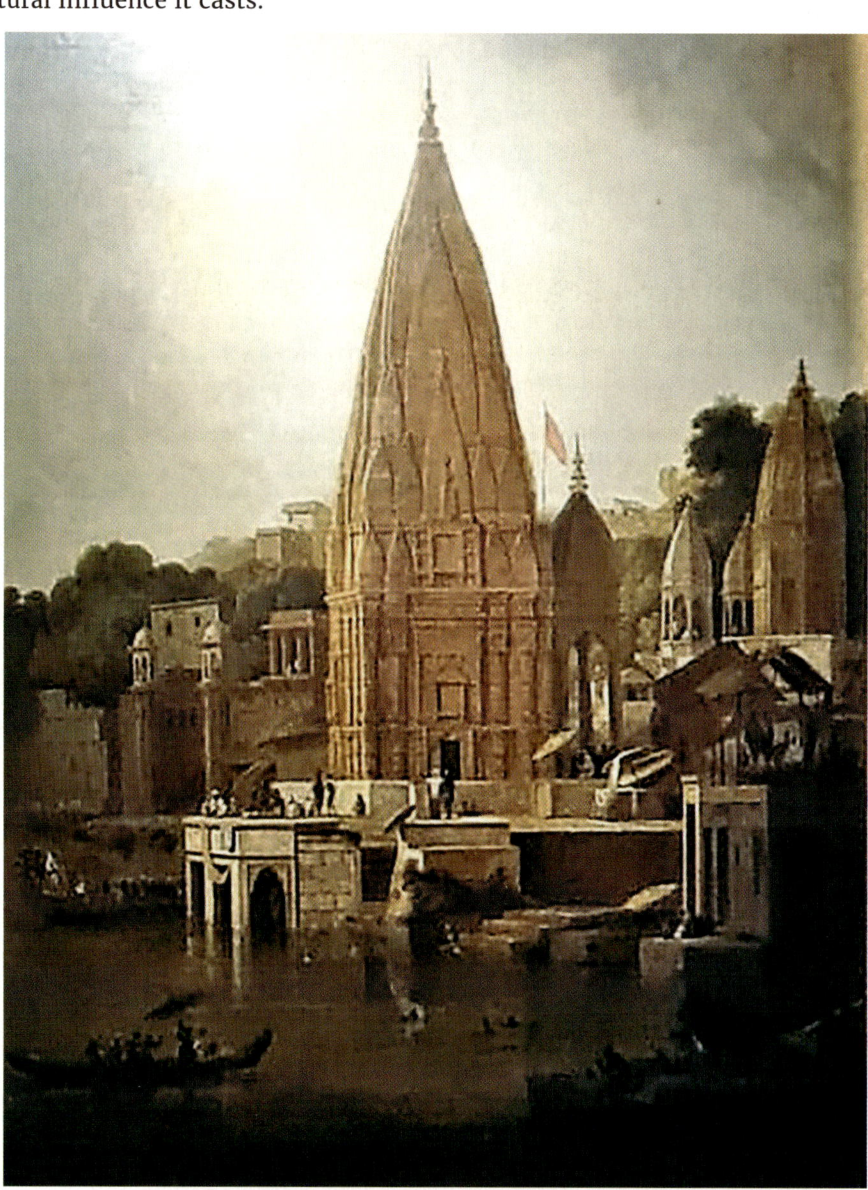

14.4: Manikarnika Ghat, Varanasi; oil on canvas by Thomas Daniel; National Gallery of Modern Art, New Delhi — photograph by Madhukar K Bhagat

Art and Other Influences

Paintings were one of the art forms that experienced European influence in this early phase. The presence of European powers enabled many European painters to explore India and paint Indian landscapes, Indian

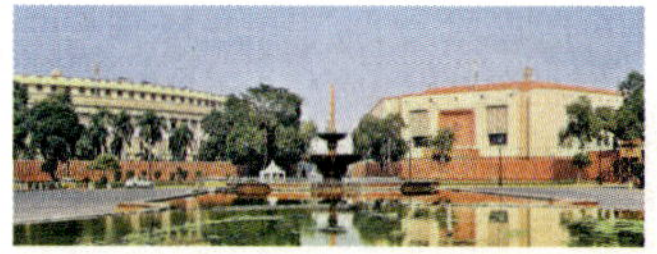

subjects and portraits. Among the prominent European painters in India of this period were; **Tilly Kettle** (the first prominent English painter in India, late 18th century) **Johan Zoffany** (German Neoclassical painter; late 18th century), **William Hodges** (English, landscapes and portraits, late 18th century) **Thomas Daniell** (English, landscape painter late 18th century) and **William Daniell** (English, landscape painter late 18th century), **George Chinnery** (English, portrait and landscape painter, late 18th & early 19th century), besides others. Many of these paintings were in oil medium. Further, their perspective and style were Western. Hence, European techniques and styles of painting were introduced in India.

European paintings were among the few art forms that had a confluence with the Indian genre of painting. In the later years, the mingling of the Indian art style with the Western influence brought out what was referred to as the **Company style** of painting; as it emerged during the period of influence of the British East India Company. It was a set of paintings done by Indian painters usually working under British patrons, or hired by them temporarily, to capture indigenous subjects/topics in the form of a portfolio. Such paintings were popular with the British and other European travellers who wanted to take back images of the country. However, the Indian painters had to adopt some of the techniques of the European school, as this was the genre with which the European patrons and buyers were familiar and such paintings were valued by them. This led to the emergence of the Company style which was a blend of the European/British influence and also the extant Mughal, Rajput and other traditional styles of painting. Subsequently, this style spread to other centres in Calcutta (now Kolkata), Murshidabad, Patna, Benares, Agra, Lucknow, Delhi, and parts of western India, thus developing into regional and local Schools.

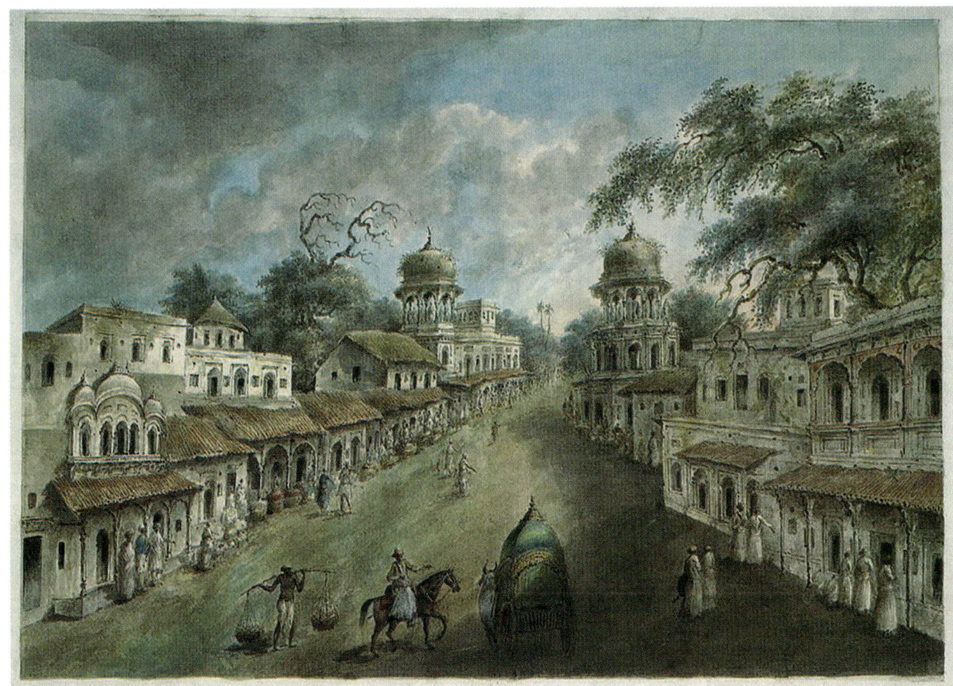

14.5: Chowk and the main street of Patna, 1814-15, by Sita Ram; a Patna Kalam painting, a regional school influenced by the Company style and local traditions; British Library — Wikimedia Commons

European presence also touched Indian society and people in other aspects of life. Several new **food items** were introduced. These include vegetables considered now to be a staple part of Indian cuisine such as potatoes, sweet potato, cauliflower, tomato, cabbages, red chilli, capsicum, cashew nuts and fruits like guava, papaya pineapple, sweet lime and oranges. These were brought by the Portuguese to Goa from where they spread to other parts of the country. The baking of *pao* (a form of bread) now popular in Goa and western India was also introduced by the Portuguese and so was the cultivation and use of tobacco. **Tea**, now a ubiquitous and pan-Indian drink, was introduced by the British in the early 19th century. In the decades to come, India was to become a major producer and consumer of tea.

THE GROWING PHASE OF ENGLISH CULTURE

The period of around 100 years since the last quarter of the 18th century was indeed a period of the growing phase of English culture in India. This cultural phase was accompanied by and was a direct consequence of the establishment of British political authority in India. Post the **Battle of Plassey** (1757) and the **Battle of Buxar** (1764) the British East India Company had acquired the *diwani* of Bengal-Bihar (which included the undivided Bengal and the States of Bihar and Odisha). Thus, the Company had transitioned from being a commercial trading venture in India to a collector of revenue and the de facto ruler of the region. The success in different wars of the 1750s and 1760s and the ensuing political

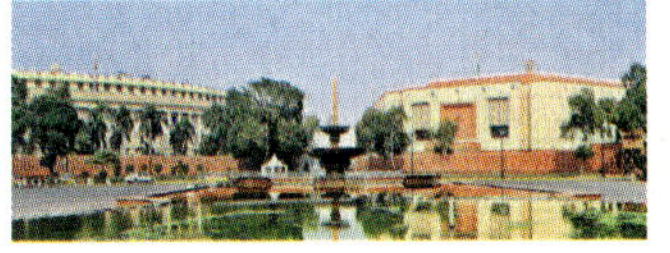

events helped to lay the foundations of British rule in India through its agent, namely the British East India Company. The **Anglo-Maratha Wars** (1772-1818) enhanced their political authority considerably. Meanwhile, with the British Parliament's **Regulating Act** of 1773 and the **Pitts Act** of 1784, there was greater parliamentary control over the Company and its administration in India. With the annexation of the Sikh empire post the **Anglo-Sikh war** of 1845-1846, the British, hegemony extended to a larger part of India. The **Doctrine of Lapse** of Lord Dalhousie (1848-1856) was the proverbial last straw on the camels' back. It culminated in the annexation of many of the states under the Indian rulers, thus making the British East India Company the undisputed ruler of India.

This period of around a century was marked by increased economic exploitation by the East India Company. Its oppressive policies, misrule and considerable drain of Indian wealth had impoverished a large section of Indian society. It brought a transition of the country from a medieval economic powerhouse to a distressed economy. Undoubtedly this had a profound impact on Indian society and cultural life as well. There was growing resentment in the masses and antagonism, particularly of the Indian nobility and zamindars. This combined with other socio-political factors culminated in the **First War of Independence** in **1857** (considered by the British as a Sepoy Mutiny). The use of the cartridges greased with cow and pig fat, which had to be bitten to be used, was a **religious-cultural** trigger for the revolt of the soldiers of the Hindu and Muslim communities in the ranks of the army of East India Company. The brutal suppression of the revolt in 1858 marked a turbulent and bloody period of Indian history. The rule of the Company ended and henceforth all the powers of it were taken over by the British Crown vide the **Government of India Act** of 1858. Hence began the direct rule of the Crown.

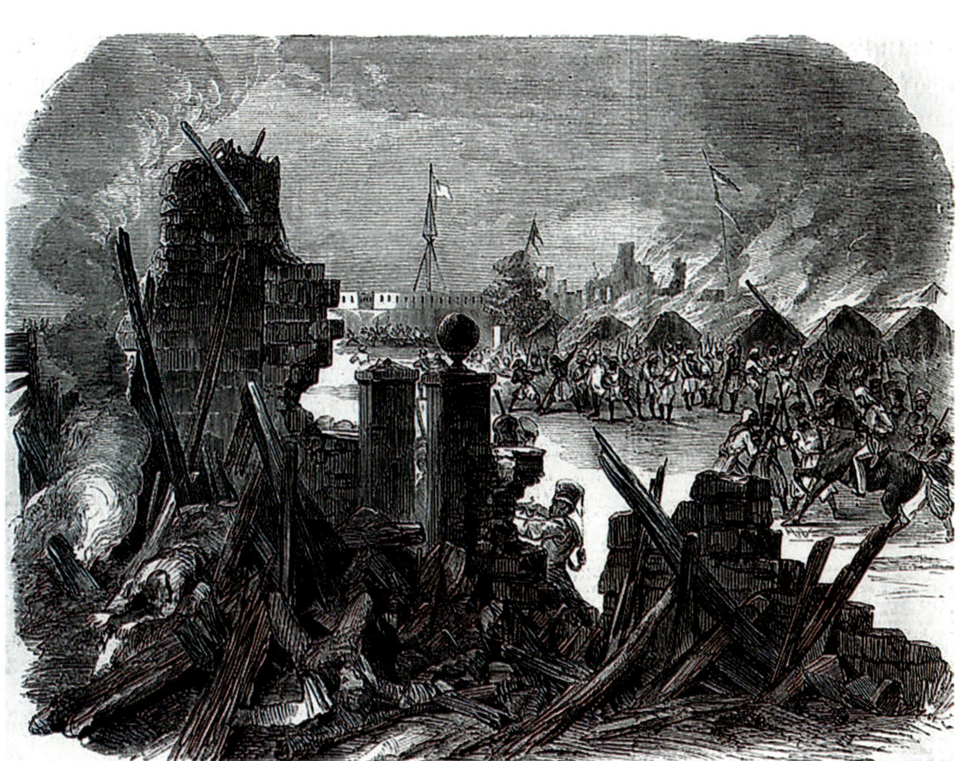

14.6: "The Sepoy revolt at Meerut", wood-engraving from the *Illustrated London News*, 1857 — Wikimedia Commons

An Impoverished India - A downtrodden India : A Perspective of Derozio

By the early 19th century, the rule of the British East India Company had substantially impoverished the country. The days of its past glory were over. India was culturally degenerating and the self-belief of the people was flagging. Henry Vivian Derozio (1809–1831) a young poet, and radical thinker who inspired a generation of students at Hindu College, Calcutta has best expressed the plight of India in his poem 'To India My Native Land'. He bemoans how India a land of riches and glory now lies in the dust. Although the poem in itself is not an account of the economic distress of the country or the region, it is emblematic of the perspective of cultural despondency and demoralisation of the common man of this country at that point in history.

To India – My Native Land" –

by Henry Louis Vivian Derozio

My country!
In thy days of glory past
A beauteous halo circled round thy brow
and worshipped as a deity thou wast—
Where is thy glory, where the reverence now?

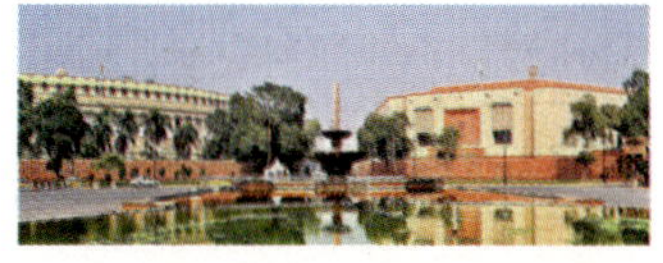

Thy eagle pinion is chained down at last,
And grovelling in the lowly dust art thou,
Thy minstrel hath no wreath to weave for thee
Save the sad story of thy misery!
Well—let me dive into the depths of time
And bring from out the ages, that have rolled
A few small fragments of these wrecks sublime
Which human eye may never more behold
And let the guerdon of my labour be,
My fallen country! One kind wish for thee!

In this period of 100 years since the establishment of the political control of the British, numerous facets of socio-political life were significantly impacted. Unlike the earlier period of European influence, the administration of the land was in the hands of the British and thus there was an unavoidable contact and interconnect between the two civilisations and cultures. **The 'growing phase of English culture' deeply influenced the Indian consciousness and the very cultural identity of the land and its people.** The transition was a rude shock to the Indians who after successive losses to the British, seemed to have lost their very self-believe. The concept of the **White man's burden**, a facile moral justification for the British rule that rubbed their racial superiority had demoralised the Indian masses. Indian cultural identity was fading, self-worth was eroding, and gradually at least a section of Indians, were looking up to their colonial masters for deliverance. The solution to India's socio-political, economic and cultural woes was now being searched in the English culture and political system believing in its inherent superiority. The very cause seemed now to have become the panacea.

The period was also marked by the beginning of the **English education** and exposure to **Western concepts of state**, **systems of governance** and the **study of sciences**. This was to bring a substantial shift in the Indian thought process in the coming decades. The Indian traditional and local systems of education were adversely affected and began to collapse. There was a relook and questioning of the socio-religious orthodoxy and ills by the Indians. This was instrumental in ushering in a wave of social reforms. The era of printing and publication came and hence emerged newspapers, journals and press. The launch of railways and the beginning of the Industrial Age marked a new epoch. The new means of transport enabled the movement of people over large distances, raw materials from the Indian hinterland and British goods from the ports. It provided for quicker connectivity to the different parts of the country. The industries were later to become the engines of economic growth which attracted the manpower from the villages, drew the raw material from the hinterland and caused the development of new cities. A new urban culture emerged and with it the migration of people and the attendant socio-economic challenges. A rich social class was to gradually replace the old nobility and create economic disparities like never before. The industries and railways were also becoming the apparatus to suck out the economic wealth of the nation and reduce the country to an impoverished market. This had far deeper socio-cultural as well as political and economic consequences.

Different streams of culture were also influenced in this phase. Some elements like **writing of proses** came up as a new trend and enriched the regional languages and literature. On the literary horizon of India there also emerged **English literature** and in the later years, even some Indian authors took up writing in English. **British colonial architecture**, which had a limited presence in the previous century, now spread to different parts of the country through some more imposing and majestic structures, and gradually replaced the other European styles. The **European Proscenium theatre** emerged, gained popularity and took deep roots in the coming decades. The traditional Indian painting including the Mughal, Rajasthani, Pahari and other medieval styles, took a back seat with the **European Academic art** occupying centre stage. There was little growth in Indian music, and Indian dances declined, many of which were banned by the British.

With the growing influence of English culture over decades, there came a realisation that Indian salvation could not be sought as a part of the British political system or within the English culture. A singular political authority over a larger swathe of the land that was patently inimical to the people had fired their imagination as to their own identity. This brought in a growing realisation of the need for **Indian consciousness**, a realisation that was to usher in the next cultural phase.

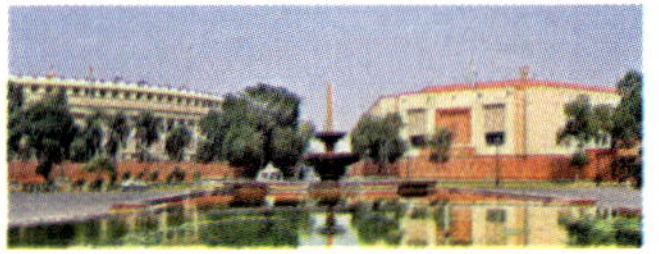

The Growth of English Education in India

English Education was a crucial element of this phase of cultural confluence. Till now India had its system of traditional education which was based on the *pathshalas* and the *madrasas*. It had served well in the preceding centuries. These were distributed throughout the country and provided education in orthodox subjects through the medium of Persian, Sanskrit and other languages. Although the distribution of schools was wide and these existed even at the village level as per the reports of those times, they lacked more contemporaneous education and a study of modern disciplines. These schools laid emphasis on learning of traditional streams of language, grammar, regional literature, astrology, philosophy and basic arithmetic. Furthermore, there existed centres of higher learning which imparted higher standards of education for similar disciplines with the addition of ayurveda, ancient treatises and other disciplines. Contemporaneous disciplines of education in vogue in Europe such as modern maths and geometry, natural sciences, geography and modern medicine etc. were however not in vogue. However, the extant system of education served the masses for ages.

The divergent schools of thought on Indian education

The British wanted European education and modern sciences to be brought to the Indians. The motives of different thinkers and authorities were different. The belief in the superiority of European race and civilisation and the philosophy of the **'white man's burden'** was one school of thought. At the other end of the spectrum, there were some orientalist thinkers and administrators like **Mountstuart Elphinstone** (Governor of Bombay Presidency, 1819-1827) and **Thomas Munro** (Governor of Madras Presidency 1820-1827) who had some degree of interest in the general well-being of the Indians and believed education to be a tool of emancipation of the masses. Christian missionaries were another set of players for whom English education and its spread could aid in their objective of the spread of Christianity. However, the interest and intent of all three sections, were in a way, instrumental in starting schools in different places which brought English education to India.

There was also a section of Indians like **Raja Ram Mohan Roy** who were completely dejected by the orthodoxy and decay in the social set-up and valued the Western sciences, the system of learning and the spirit of enquiry. He sincerely believed that these could be accessed by Indians only through English education. He and other Indians also opined for the beginning of English education in India. They also felt that there was no dearth of vernacular education, and that the British further supplementing it would not make much of a value addition to the Indian society. English education to them meant a liberal and contemporaneous education that could enable the Indians to participate in the administration. However, there were orthodox sections of Indians that were opposed to this view.

Thomas Munro: A Proponent of Vernacular Education

The advocates of improvement do not seem to have perceived the great springs on which it depends; they propose to place no confidence in the natives, to give them no authority.... but they are ardent in their zeal for enlightening them by the general diffusion of knowledge. No conceit more wild than this was ever engendered in the darkest ages.

— **Sir Thomas Munro**, *December 31, 1824*

Sir Thomas Munro the Governor of Madras Presidency (1820-1827) was the earliest of the British officers to look into the educational needs of the Indians and also start educational reforms. He conducted a wide range of educational surveys to ascertain the status of schools and educational institutions in the region. He was also the author of the "Minutes of the Native Education' (1822 and 1826) which shed valuable light on the status of education in the region at that time and recommended grassroots educational reforms.

As per these Minutes, the Madras Presidency had 11758 schools as well as 740 centres of higher education at that time. Most of these schools and their expenses were managed at the level of the community. The number of boys and girls in these schools and institutions was 157644 and 4023 respectively. These represented 1in 6 boys of school age as compared to 1 in 8 boys of school age of the Bombay Presidency. In this minute, Munro also suggests the construction of new schools by the company with the provision of textbooks and payment of stipends to the teachers to supplement the existing system of education in the region.

Munro was a proponent of vernacular education and of supporting the native effort. Munro's proposal was accepted by the Board of Directors of the Company. Several higher schools at the level of collectorates and lower level tehsildari schools were created, where vernacular education was provided. The study of English was confined to a central collectorate school and was elementary in nature. However, post the decision to impart English education as per the proposal of Macaulay in 1835, these schools were abolished.

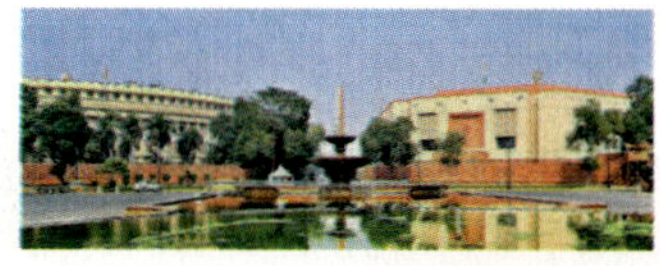

The early educational institutions

The earliest educational institutes established by the Company were the **Calcutta Madrasah** (1781) by Warren Hastings and the **Benares Sanskrit College** (1791) by Lord Cornwallis. However, these institutions provided traditional education in the extant languages of Persian and Sanskrit. One of the earliest to moot the idea of English education was Sir Charles Grant, who in 1892, moved a proposal to the Directors of the Company in this regard; however, it remained unimplemented. In 1813, the renewed charter of the Company had provision for spending of Rs. 1,00,000/- exclusively on education. However, this also remained unimplemented for the want of clarity as to the format of education to be adopted. The dilemma was whether the amount was to be spent on oriental education or the teaching of the English language and Western sciences. In 1823, the company opened **Delhi College** and **Agra College** to provide oriental education and made provision for translation of English books in the oriental languages. However, for a variety of reasons the endeavour did not become popular with the Indians. Meanwhile, with the private initiative of Englishman David Hare, Sir Hyde East, Raja Ram Mohan Roy and other Indians, **Hindu College** was established in Calcutta in 1817. Here English was taught, besides Persian and Bengali, and it soon became popular. This was later to become the Presidency College of Calcutta.

Besides the above, there were some other initiatives, but no major change in Indian education happened till 1835. This year proved to be a watershed in the educational history of India. Lord Macaulay who was the Chairman of the 'Committee on Public Instructions', wrote his famous note on Indian education which was later to become the permanent policy of British education in India. Macaulay recommended teaching Western sciences in the English language in schools and colleges, with English not only as a compulsory subject but also as a medium of instruction. This was accepted by the Governor General of India Lord William Bentick. With this, the other schools of thought that espoused the cause of oriental education or education of Western sciences in Indian languages were completely shut.

Early English education and its impact

The decision to impart English education to Indians had far-reaching consequences. Over the years, a number of schools and colleges were opened that imparted English education. These started to become popular among the masses. The prospect of securing a job with the Company and later with the British government in India, was a major allurement for the young Indians to take up English education. The language and the education were also becoming windows for the impressionistic young minds to understand the English culture and the sciences. These were begun to be looked upon by different sections of the society. Post the decision of 1835 of William Bentick, efforts were also made to open a school in every district. Later, more schools also came up. Many colleges and universities were also started including the **Calcutta Medical College** (1835), **Madras Medical College** (1835), **Bombay Grant Medical College** (1845), **College of Civil Engineering, Roorkee** (1847), **University of Calcutta** (1857), **University of Bombay** (1857), **University of Madras** (1857), **Central College Lahore** (1864), **University of Punjab** at Lahore (1882) and **Allahabad University** (1887). This was the phase of the beginning of the modern education system in India.

Impact of English Education in India

The introduction of English education broke the barrier which had hitherto effectively shut India from the Western world. The great Muslim scholar, Al-Biruni, remarked about 1000 AD that the Hindus kept themselves aloof from the outer world and were ignorant of the arts and sciences of the West. This glaring defect of Hindus was equally evident eight hundred years later. But a great change came over them at the beginning of the 19th century A.D. English education opened the floodgates of Western ideas which almost overwhelmed them at the beginning. 50 years of English education brought greater changes in the minds of the educated Hindus of Bengal than the previous thousand years.

The principal reason for this is that India came into contact with Western ideas at the most opportune moment. It was the age of French illumination when the spirit of rationalism and individualism dominated Europe and thought. It proclaimed the supremacy of reason over faith, of individual conscience over outside authority, and brought in its train new conceptions of social justice and political rights. A new ideology suddenly burst forth upon the static life, moulded for centuries by a fixed set of religious ideas and social conventions. It gave birth to a critical attitude towards religion and a spirit of enquiry into the origin of state and society with a view to determining their proper scope and functions.

To put it in a concrete form, the most important result of the impact of Western culture on India was the replacement of blind faith in current traditions beliefs and conventions- characteristics of the mediaeval age- by a spirit of rationalism which seeks to enquire and argue before accepting anything....

R.C Majumdar and K.K. Datta in *The History and Culture of the Indian People, British Paramountcy and Indian Renaissance*, part II, chapter II (page 106)

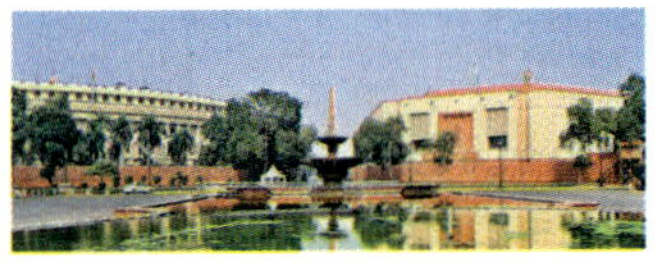

Over the years traditional oriental education started to collapse. The local schools and high schools which were run based on community support were finding fewer takers. The support from the Indian rulers for some schools which was there in the early part of the 19th century had already ceased. This created a void in the educational apparatus of the country. The demand for education could not be met by the schools and colleges set up by the Company and later the British Government. Further, English education had its limitations, to the extent it could spread despite its contemporaneous nature. Although private initiatives of the likes of Raja Ram Mohan Roy or other Englishmen did open some schools and colleges, these were insufficient. A part of the education institutional space was also taken up by the missionary educational institutions which had a reasonable presence in different parts of the country. However, overall there remained a dearth of schools and colleges in India. English education was largely limited to the upper section of the society. The British expectation of the trickle-down effect taking Western sciences and English education to the masses did not materialise in the 19th century. Further, English education had little focus on vocational education and preserving Indian values.

The education system despite the reforms brought by **Wood's Despatch** (1854) and **Hunter Commission report** (1882-1883) broadly functioned in the same direction, with English as the medium of education and some other relevant improvements. Macaulay's efforts had also earlier helped in replacing Persian with English as the language of administration. Now the British needed more Indians who could understand the language, communicate with the masters and fill the lower rungs of bureaucracy. English education served this well. It was also creating a new generation of Indians who believed in English culture, dressed, ate, and conducted themselves like the English. They believed in the inherent superiority of the English and owed allegiance to the colonial masters.

However, English education did have some significant and positive impact on Indian society. It provided for a modern education infrastructure ranging from schools and colleges to technical institutes and universities. It created awareness of the western thought and sciences in a section of the Indian society. Indians of the richer section, who could afford the English education and in particular the costlier higher and overseas education, were not only exposed to the British pedagogy of learning, the Western sciences and other disciplines, but also to the modern systems of governance. India and the Indian political establishment, in the late 18th and even in the early 19th centuries, had largely been aloof of the wave of democracy sweeping the Western world post the French Revolution of 1789 and the emergence of democracy in the United States of America in the late 18th century. With the arrival of English education, there was exposure to the concepts of democracy and representative governance which once had birth in India but was long forgotten thereafter.

The consciousness towards the country and society began to evolve. Equally significant was that the exposure to English education also fired up some of the Indians, a spirit of questioning the status quo and inquiry, which seemed to have become dormant in the past centuries. There was questioning of the orthodoxy. The culture of rationalism was revived. This was to prove crucial in ushering in a wave of educational and social reforms by Indians and later in creating a national consciousness.

The Press: The harbinger of change

The advent of the press and the printing of newspapers and periodicals in India was an outcome of the British presence in India. In the coming two centuries, the press had a pioneering role to play. The printing press had already made its appearance in some parts of India in the 16th-17th century. By the late 18th and the early 19th century, some newspapers were also printed in India. **Hicky's *Bengal Gazette***, started in Calcutta, in 1780 by James Augustus Hicky was the first newspaper in India. This was followed by; *The Indian Gazette* (Calcultta, 1780), *The Calcutta Gazette* (Calcutta, 1782), *Bombay Herald* (Bombay, 1789), *The Bombay Gazette* (Bombay, 1791), *The Madras Gazette* (Madras, 1795), *Samachaar Darpan* (Calcutta, 1818), *Sambada Kaumudi* (Calcutta, 1821), *Bombay Samachar* (Bombay, 1822) etc. The earliest newspapers and periodicals were started by private English individuals and catered largely towards the Anglo-Indian community in India. Later, there emerged the vernacular press which was started by the Indians.

These newspapers, including the English papers, owed little allegiance to the Company and were at times critical of the Company and its policies. Accordingly, the Company officials looked at the press suspiciously. They frequently adopted the policy to muzzle it, despite protests and appeals from many quarters, including eminent Indians like Raja Ram Mohan Roy. The **Press Ordinance of 1823** introduced stringent regulations against the Indian press. It was only after **The Press Act** was passed in 1835, that the Indian vernacular press (in particular) received the essential liberty. It was henceforth that the growth of the press and newspapers started to take place. **Sir Charles Metcalfe** the acting Governor-

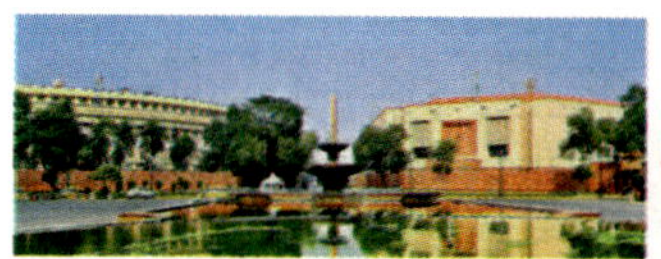

General (1835-1836) who brought this ordinance sincerely believed that it was through the freedom of the press that true knowledge could be disseminated among the masses, and it was their duty to spread the knowledge and civilisation and the arts and sciences of Europe over the land. His views were only to prove prophetic, and the press was to play a yeoman's role in heralding the social change and national consciousness in the coming decades.

Freedom of the Press and the Perspective of the English in the Early 19th Century

As a matter of fact, the real grounds of opposition to a free press in India had always been the fear that it would alienate against the British government, not only the people but, what mattered more, the Indian Army on which rested the main strength of the British in India. The Court of Directors actually expressed the fear that "free discussions of political questions in newspapers might goad the sepoys to revolt".

Sir Charles Metcalfe made this argument in a few words which deserve to be placed by the side of the more well-known speech of Macaulay in the same tenor. "If their argument be", said he, "that the spread of knowledge may eventually be fatal to our rule in India, I close with them on that point". He expressed his hope that the increase of knowledge in India would strengthen and not destroy the British Empire. But he maintained that "whatever may be the consequence, it is our duty to communicate the benefits of the knowledge". Then he observed:

"whatever however, be the will of the Almighty Providence respecting the future government of India, it is clearly our duty, as long as the charge be confided to our hands, to execute the trust to the best of our ability for the good of the people. The promotion of knowledge – of which the liberty of the press is one of the most efficient instruments – is manifestly an essential part of that duty. It cannot be that we are permitted by the divine authority to be here merely to collect the revenues of the country, pay the establishment necessary to keep possession, and get into debt to supply the deficiency. We are doubtless here for higher purposes; one of which is to pour the enlightened knowledge of civilisation, the arts and sciences of Europe, over the land and thereby improve the condition of the people. ***Nothing surely is more likely to conduce to these ends than the liberty of the press."***

R.C Majumdar and K.K. Datta in *The History and Culture of the Indian People, British Paramountcy and Indian Renaissance*, part II, chapter II

In the coming years the press, and in particular the vernacular press, played a stellar role in highlighting the emerging social issues as well as critiquing the government and its policies. The movements in social reforms spearheaded by Raja Ram Mohan Roy, and Keshub Chandra Sen in Bengal were highlighted through the press and so were the works of other reformers and educationists in later years. **Raja Ram Mohan Roy** established and was editor of **Samvad Kaumudi** (established in 1821), which was launched to campaign against the practice of Sati. **Keshub Chandra Sen**, a leading reformer in Bengal wrote articles for the **Indian Mirror**, a weekly journal of the Brahmo Samaj in Calcutta in the 1860s. He also wrote for the **Hindoo Patriot**, a leading Bengali journal in the 1850s and 1860s. **M.G Ranade**, who was associated with Prarthna Samaj, which led to socio-religious reforms within Hinduism, particularly in the Maharashtra region, was the editor of **Bombay**, an Anglo-Marathi daily paper. He also founded **Induprakash**, a bi-weekly Anglo-Marathi paper that championed the cause of social reforms and later criticised the British policy and supported the Indian national movement. **Rast Goftar** (literal meaning 'the truth-teller'), an Anglo-Gujarati journal, was started by **Dadabhai Nauroji** and others in Bombay (in 1854) to pioneer social reforms amongst the Parsis in western India. Later, it also echoed political views. **Sir Syed Ahmed Khan**, an eminent educationist and Islamic reformer started the journal, **Mohammedan Social Reformer** (1870) to promote liberal ideas among the Indian Muslims.

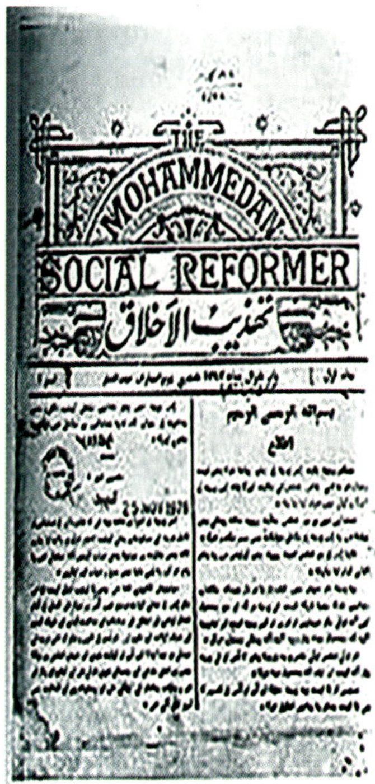
THE MOHAMMEDAN SOCIAL REFORMER

14.7: The First Edition of Mohammedan Social Reformer dated 24th December 1870 brought out by Sir Syed Ahmed Khan — Wikimedia Commons

During the revolt of 1857, the regional and local press played a significant role in highlighting the Indian perspective and also spreading disaffection towards the Company government. While the English press, post 1857-1858, was very critical of the revolt and its comments were bitter and acrimonious, the vernacular press despite the fear of retribution and government restrictions, portrayed the Indian perspective boldly. On socio-economic issues the Indian press was unrelenting. The *Hindoo Patriot* had staunchly denounced the indigo planters and highlighted the plight of the oppressed cultivators who were being subjected to terrible miseries. *Amrita Bazaar Patrika*

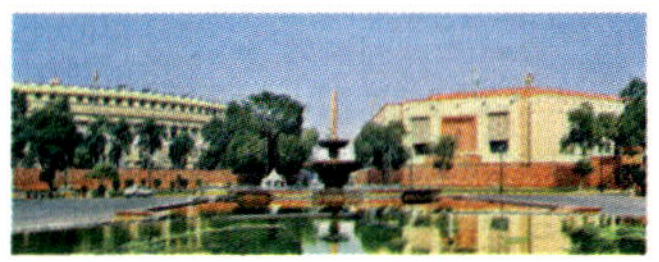

also wrote extensively about the Indigo revolt of the Bengal. **G. Subramania Iyer**, a social reformer and nationalist, founded ***The Hindu*** (English newspaper) and ***Swadesamitran*** (Tamil newspaper) in 1878 and 1882 respectively. **Lokmanya Bal Gangadhar Tilak**, a leading figure of the Indian nationalist movement in the late 19th century, launched *Kesari*, a Marathi newspaper and *Mahratta*, an English newspaper in 1881. Both newspapers were crucial in the expression of the political views of Tilak, in furthering Indian consciousness and taking the idea of Indian nationalism amongst the masses. In later years, press also played a stellar role in the growth of Indian nationalism.

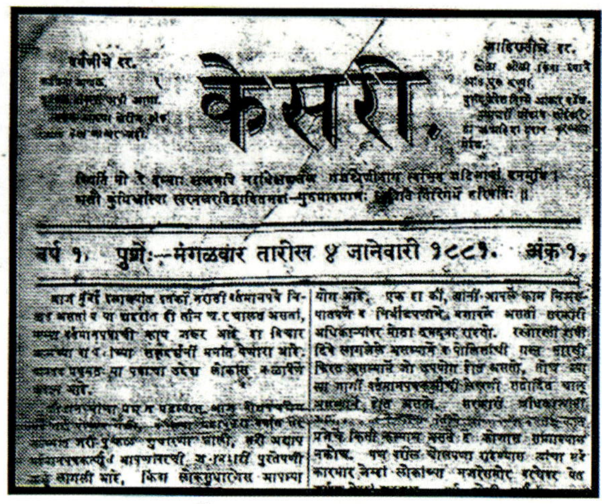

केसरी.

वर्ष १. पुणें:-मंगळवार तारीख ४ जानेवारी १८८१. अंक १.

14.8: The first edition of *Kesari* newspaper dated 4th January, 1881 — Wikipedia

The growth of the press also aided the growth of **Indian literature** which prospered in the second half of the 19th century. As many vernacular newspapers and journals were established, journalistic writing grew. It also afforded space to the literary as well as non-literary articles. The art of writing **prose** developed. An eminent author like Bankim Chandra, a towering figure of Bengali literature, had his earliest of publications in a weekly newspaper **Sangbad Prabhakar**. His much-acclaimed novel *Anand Math* first appeared in the public domain in a serial form in the literary magazine ***Bangadarshan*** founded by him (in 1872). Like him, for many other authors, newspapers and journals were the first medium of literary expression. Further, while the books had their reach and specific market, newspapers and magazines could penetrate deeper into the Indian hinterland and could connect better even with the villages. Thus, they opened the world of literature to the common man.

The advent and growth of the press touched the Indian life deeply. It was a powerful instrument for the diffusion of ideas and knowledge. The rationality and reasoning induced in Indian thought as a result of European influence and English education were further disseminated through the press. Diverse issues ranging from social reforms to economic policy of the government, were discussed and analysed in it, which enabled the formation of public opinion. This enabled the launch as well as sustenance of many social and nationalist movements. While the vernacular press criticised the exploitation of the Indigo cultivators, it also criticised the social evils like *sati* and untouchability and raised public awareness about it. The role of the press in the growth of nationalism can hardly be overemphasised. The press aided in the growth of literature. It also helped in the creation of awareness about other elements of regional culture that were neglected or looked down upon. It was undoubtedly the most important means of public communication and provided a connection between the people in different parts of the country as perhaps never before. Even in the 20th century, the writings of eminent nationalist leaders like Lokmanya Tilak in *Kesari* and Mahatma Gandhi in *Young India* and of others, was to serve as a beacon of light for Indian nationalism and culture.

Social Reforms-Heralding an Indian Renaissance

The confluence of European rationality, English education and the Indian society of the 19th century, heralded a phase of social reforms, at times considered by scholars as the Indian Renaissance. This was a phase of reform that influenced our very thoughts, permeated different aspects of our social life, and helped our art forms, literature and other elements of Indian culture to evolve. It was an age of 'introspection', whereby the questioning of the dogmatic socio-religious traditions and customs, exposed the rot and the dead wood within the Indian society. A rational enquiry of the myriad of social beliefs and practices ensued. This was followed and supported by decades of hard groundwork. Sustained campaigns to oppose the social evils, support the reforms, and create public awareness, which was aided by some strict laws, helped to stem this rot. Gradually, a positive change began in the Indian society. The century witnessed a number of socio-religious reforms which included; the Brahmo Samaj, the Young Bengal Movement, Arya Samaj, Prarthana Samaj and the Theosophical Society, among others.

Many of these early reform movements were against evil practices like *sati*, child marriages and female infanticide. The earliest among these was the **Brahmo Samaj,** established in 1828 by **Raja Ram Mohan Roy**, a modern-thinking scholar and a great visionary. The movement and its name denoted a society of

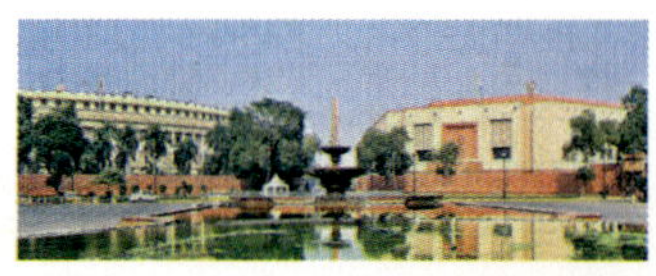

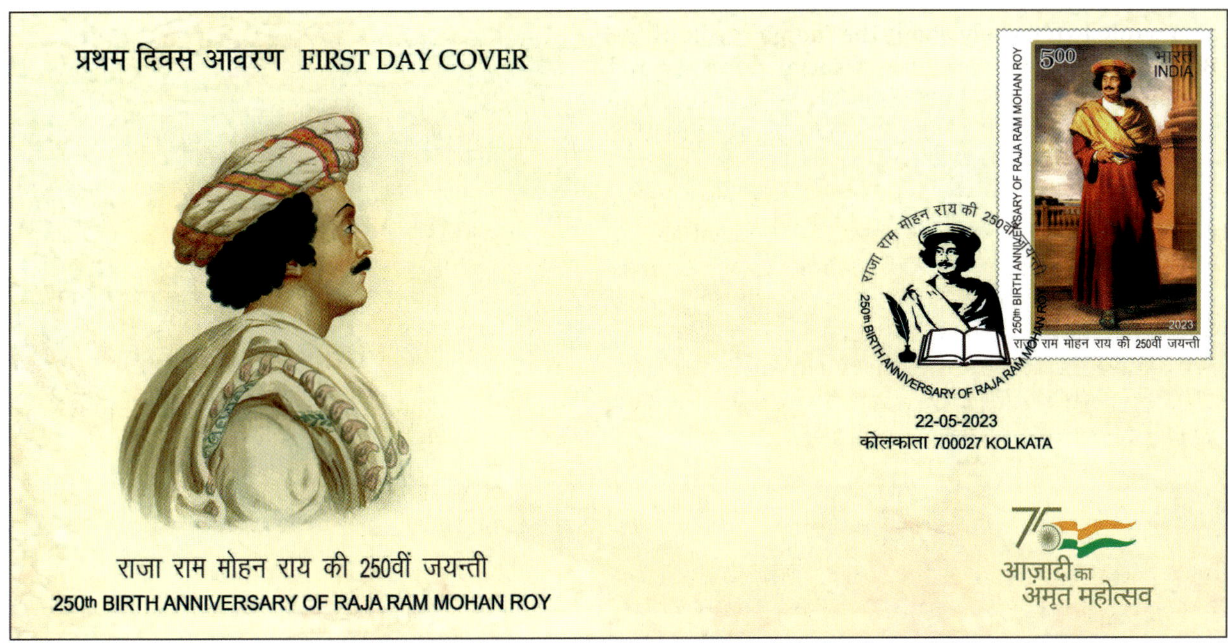

14.9: Raja Ram Mohan Roy, a social reformer, an eminent scholar and the father of the renaissance of modern Bengal; first-day cover and stamp released in 2023 on the occasion of his 250th Birth Anniversary — Courtesy, Department of Post

the worshippers of the Brahma-the Ultimate Reality and the Supreme Consciousness. While it preached the principles of monotheism and the universality of the godhead, it also worked against child marriage, caste system and Brahmanical orthodoxy. Its relentless efforts culminated in *sati* being declared a punishable offence in 1829.

The various movements also emphasised upon education for women and supported widow remarriages. Inter castes, marriages removal of the purdah system etc. were some other social reforms they pursued. **Bharatiya Brahmo Samaj** or **Naba Bidhan Samaj**, a sect established by **Keshub Chandra Sen** (in 1866) was a champion of these issues. **Ishwar Chandra Vidyasagar**, an eminent educator and reformist worked tirelessly for the education of the girl child and the emancipation of women and started many schools for them. He was opposed to child marriages and supported widow remarriages, which were legalised by the Widow Remarriage Act of 1856. His efforts were also instrumental in passing of the Age of Consent Act of 1860, fixing the minimum age of consummation of marriage at 10. **Dhondo Keshav Karve** established the **Widow Remarriage Association** (in 1883) and the **Hindu Widows Home** (in 1896). He also worked against the Devadasi system and was a pioneer of women's education in Maharashtra.

Besides, the reforms were also opposed to the caste system, Brahmanical orthodoxy, and untouchability and worked for the emancipation of the downtrodden. **Veda Samaj,** established by **Kandukuri Veeresalingam** (in 1864) opposed caste discrimination. He also opposed child marriage and the dowry system. **Satya Shodhak Samaj** founded by **Jyotiba Phule** (in 1873) opposed untouchability, caste system and Brahmanical supremacy. He also worked for the education of women and the oppressed caste of the region.

Some of these movements emphasised upon the Vedantic philosophy and spiritual regeneration of the Hindu society. **Arya Samaj,** started by **Swami Dayananda Saraswati** in 1875, was one such movement. Its socio-religious reforms were based on the principles of monotheism, with its teachings centred on the Vedas. But unlike the earlier monotheistic movements such as Brahmo Samaj, it considered the Vedas to be infallible. It also exerted a wider ambit of social influence beyond the reforms by including work and issues like providing Vedic education and setup of educational institutions, working to prevent conversion of the Hindus and establishing a deeper connection with the people.

The Ramakrishna Mission, founded by **Swami Vivekananda** (in 1897) to spread the teachings of his guru **Swami Ramakrishna Paramahamsa**, started as a religious and spiritual organization. The philosophy of the movement was based on the principles of Vedanta and aimed at the spiritual rejuvenation of Indian society. It also created a monastic order of *sanyasis* (renunciates) and a *math* at Belur (Howrah), which became the focal point of the 'Mission'. While the Mission's aims were spiritual attainment and realisation of God, renunciation and humanitarian service were considered to be the ideals to be pursued for the attainment of its goals. Along with spiritual regeneration and doing invaluable work in the humanitarian field, it also actively pursued education as a goal in the coming century.

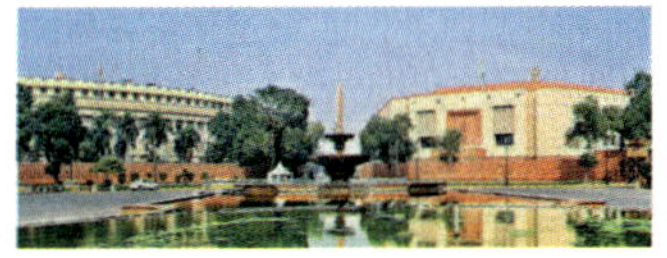

Besides these reform movements within Hinduism, this phase also witnessed the emergence of movements in other religious communities. These brought educational reforms within those communities and emphasised upon the revival of their socio-religious character. In 1851, **Dadabhai Nauroji**, **Naoroji Furdoonji** and **S.S. Bengalee** launched the **Religious Reforms Association of the Parsis** (Rehnumai Maz'dayasan Sabha). It strived to reform the Zoroastrian religion to its pristine purity as well as to bring social reforms among the Parsis. The **Aligarh Movement** started by **Sir Syed Ahmad Khan**, worked for the education and social upliftment of the Muslims. He firmly believed that Muslims should be broadminded and not be secluded from modern ideas and that this could be attained through modern and scientific education. In 1866, he started the Muhammadan Educational Conference and in 1875 he founded the Mohammedan Anglo-Oriental College at Aligarh which became the centre of the reform activities and lent the name 'Aligarh Movement' to the reforms initiated by him. The **Ahmadiya Movement** was a revivalist Islamic and messianic (based on a messiah) movement started in 1889 by **Mirza Ghulam Ahmad**. It aimed to usher in the true intent of Islam and emphasized upon the universality of religion, principles of peace, brotherhood, justice and other salient aspects of Islam. Similarly, among the Sikhs, the **Namdhari movement** (in the early 19th century) and the **Nirankari movement** (in the latter half of the 19th century) strived to revive the true Sikh religion and reform it of corrupted practices.

The social movements of the 19th century were both **reformative** and **revivalistic.** The former challenged the traditions and rejected some of the popular doctrines that had been accepted for ages. The Brahmo Samaj, Prarthana Samaj, the Parsi reforms, the Aligarh Movement, the Ahmadiya Movement, the Wahabi Movement, etc. are often considered in this category. The Ramakrishna Mission, which did not completely reject idolatry and ritualism, but synthesized it with the deeper Vedantic traditions and the Theosophical movement, can be considered among the latter category. The Arya Samaj, which rejected idolatry, but aimed at reviving the Vedic traditions while considering the Vedas to be infallible, can be considered to combine the traits of both. Irrespective of the categorization and their approach, they all left a significant mark on the socio-cultural milieu.

These social movements were spread in different parts of the country. Bengal, which spearheaded the reform movement also inspired similar movements in different parts of the country, be it Maharashtra, Punjab or the Deccan region. Over a period of time, these movements imbued Indian society, particularly the religion, culture and social thought, with liberalism and modernity. They were also instrumental in invoking a sense of Indian identity which had been dormant for centuries. In the later decades of the 19th century, in the wake of the anti-colonial sentiments simmering in the land, they also aided in the emergence of nationalistic fervour and thus channelled our socio-cultural identity into Indian nationalism.

Literature and Indian Nationalism

In the latter half of the 19th century, the resurgence of Indian nationalism and the growth of literature complemented each other. This phase was marked by a reformistic and nationalistic fervour. A variety of social issues, especially those related to women, child marriage, education of women, and prohibition of widow remarriage, emerged as the main theme of many early Indian novels. *Bishabriksha* (1873), by **Bankim Chandra**, *Indulekha* (1889), the first novel in Malayalam by **Chandu Menon**, and later *Chokher Bali* (1901), *Ghaire Baire* (1915) by **Rabindranath Tagore**, were some of the novels of this genre. These engendered a larger social and cultural consciousness which also paved the way for Indian nationalism.

The rise of nationalism and the critique of British misrule were also the themes of many literary works of this period. *Neel Darpan* (play) by **Dinabandhu Mitra** (*Bagala* 1859-60) highlighted the plight of indigo farmers condemned to indigo plantations; a demand of the then flourishing British looms. *Chakar Darpan* (Mirror of Tea-Planters, 1875) by **Dakshina Charan Chattopadhyay** also highlighted the oppression of the tea planters. *Bharat Durdasha* (Hindi, 1875) written by **Bharatendu Harishchandra** succinctly brings out the reasons for India's economic plight. Amongst its major causes, besides the social and internal factors, he highlights British misrule. He identifies the destruction of the rural economy and cottage industries as an instrument of British policy to enrich its mills and economy. *Andher Nagari* (Hindi 1889), was another satirical play by Bharatendu on the perils of misrule and was metaphoric for India's condition. **Bankim Chandra Chatterjee's** *Anand Math* hails the motherland. Its song *Bande Mataram*, was an inspiration to the people during the partition of Bengal (1905) and continued to inspire several generations of nationalistic leaders. *Devi Chaudharani* (1884), another novel by Bankim Chandra made a call for patriotic struggle against the British, especially inspiring women. It was banned by the British and only post-independence of India the ban was lifted. *Poverty and Un-British Rule in India* (1901) a book by Dadabhai Naoroji, brings out the theory of the drain of wealth from India, and how India was being systematically impoverished.

Besides the above, the writings of Gokhale (in *Hitavaad*, a weekly newspaper) of Tilak (in *Kesari*) and other leaders like Tagore, Aurobindo, Mahatma Gandhi and others were instrumental in the evolution of a pan-India consciousness and nationalistic fervour.

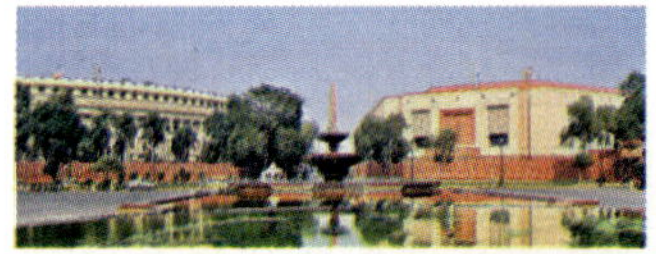

British Architecture: New Influences and Confluence of Styles

Growth of British Architecture

By the last quarter of the 18th century, the British authority was firmly entrenched in India and by the beginning of the 19th century their influence had spread in a large part of the country. As with their spreading influence, British architecture also spread to different parts of the country. Indeed, their architectural style was a new influence on the Indian landscape and perhaps one of the significant and visible elements of the British tangible culture. This was an element that evolved squarely out of the needs of the colonial masters as well as their desire to stamp a mark of the ruler on the land on which they established their political authority.

British colonial architecture developed in different phases and in different cities and towns. Among the earliest to develop were the port cities. To begin with, the need for constructing various structures arose on account of practical and security considerations in the port cities from where the British carried their trade. The Company and its officials needed structures to fulfil the requirements of, trading, basic administration, security, housing and other social needs. Accordingly, in the early phase of the East India Company in the 17th-18th century, colonial architecture emerged in form of the warehouses, residential houses, churches and other monuments. These were however largely limited to the forts of Madras (Chennai), Calcutta (Kolkata) and Bombay (Mumbai) where the Company's settlements, factories and mercantile offices were fortified as protection against the other competing colonial powers and the local rulers.

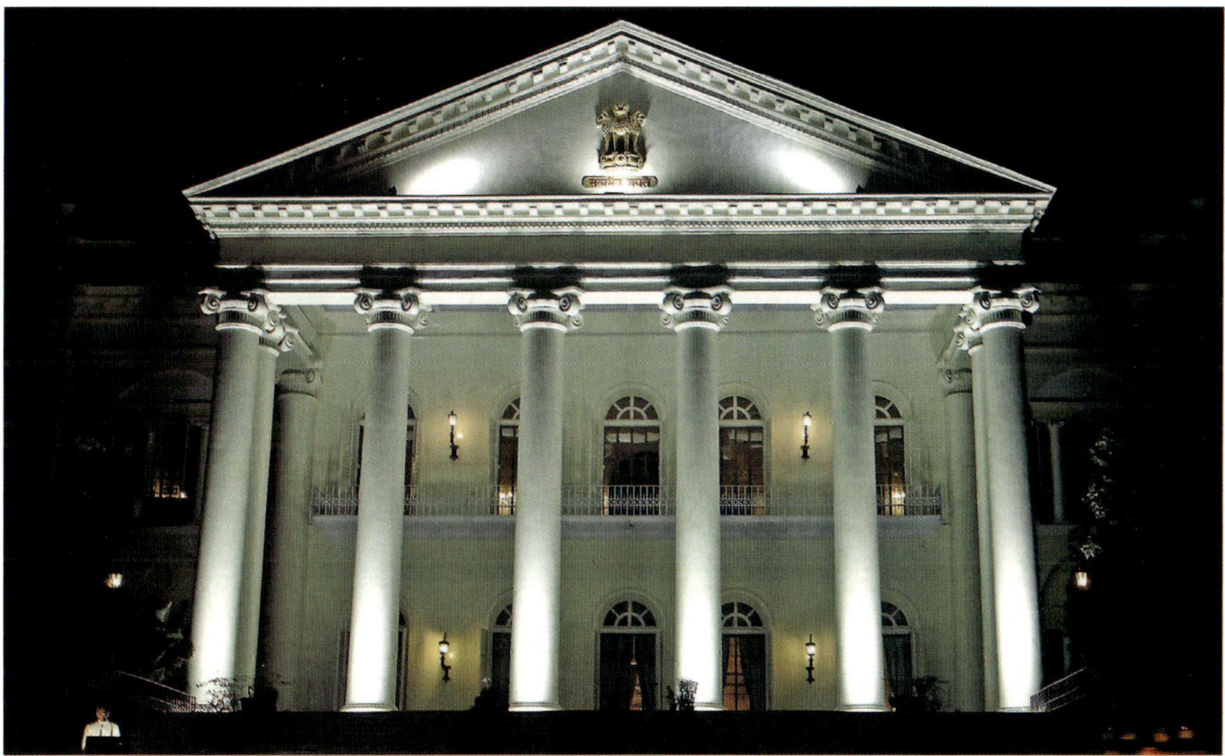

14.10: Raj Bhavan, Kolkata, a mid-19th century example of British architecture in India which incorporated elements of neo-classical style; erstwhile Government House; in view, the front façade and the entrance with a majestic portico and Ionic pillars — Courtesy, Department of Tourism, West Bengal

In the 18th and 19th centuries, the Company had taken over the administration of several provinces. Henceforth, the demands of administration and thus of the infrastructure requirements, became more complex. This marked the next phase of British architecture which came out of the forts and manifested in the Presidency cities of Calcutta, Madras and Bombay and the adjoining regions. While the fort areas were the exclusive preserve of the British, other areas also developed around it for the settlement of the native population. This catered to the needs of the merchants, artisans, workers and others who dealt with the Company and the British merchants. In the vicinity, came up the houses of the rich Indian merchants, agents and middlemen. These were large traditional courtyard houses, particularly in the vicinity of the *bazaars.* Such native settlements were referred to as the **Black town** while the British settlement was referred to the **White town**, a segregation which remained as sharp even in the times to come. Thus, the landscape of our towns and cities changed.

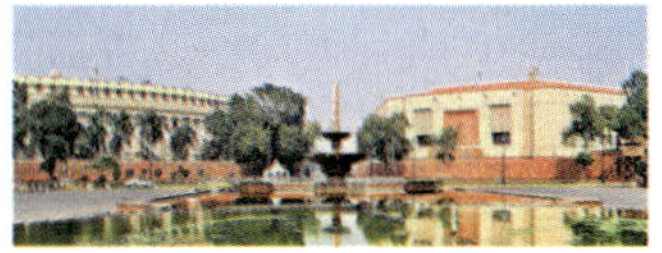

Post the rebellion of 1857 and the British crown taking over the administration, the British became extremely wary and security conscious. There was a growing realization to better defend the towns. The British cleared the pastures/grasslands and agricultural fields around older towns and built areas called **'Civil Lines'** which were urban spaces exclusively/substantially for the British. **Cantonments** were also developed in many towns which were areas where the Indian troops were stationed under the command of European officers and were considered as a safe enclave. These areas were characterized by wide roads/streets, large bungalows with gardens, space for the barracks, parade grounds and churches. They were also seen as the models of urban settlements as compared to the dense and crowded Indian towns. Thus, came up new standards of urban town planning and infrastructure.

In the latter half of the 19th century and later in the 20th century, new cities and towns developed further. Rail lines were laid to connect different parts of the country. This was essential to establish administrative control of the British as well as to transfer the raw materials and finished goods from the hinterland to the ports and vice-versa. There was an increasing need for the establishment of government administrative complexes, military complexes, large residential complexes, public infrastructure, railways and transport infrastructure, besides commemorative monuments and other structures. This was reflected in the changing landscape, emerging monuments and evolving architecture which penetrated even smaller towns and cities. This was the final phase of British architecture in India which continued in the 19th and 20th centuries till India's independence.

British architectural styles

The British Colonial architecture was not a singular style but a mix of different styles of European architecture which flourished in different phases of their presence in the country. These included Gothic, Renaissance, Baroque, Neo–Classical, Neo-Gothic, and Victorian styles. While the **Viceregal Lodge** in Shimla (now referred to as the *Rashtrapati Niwas*) was a classic example of **British Renaissance**

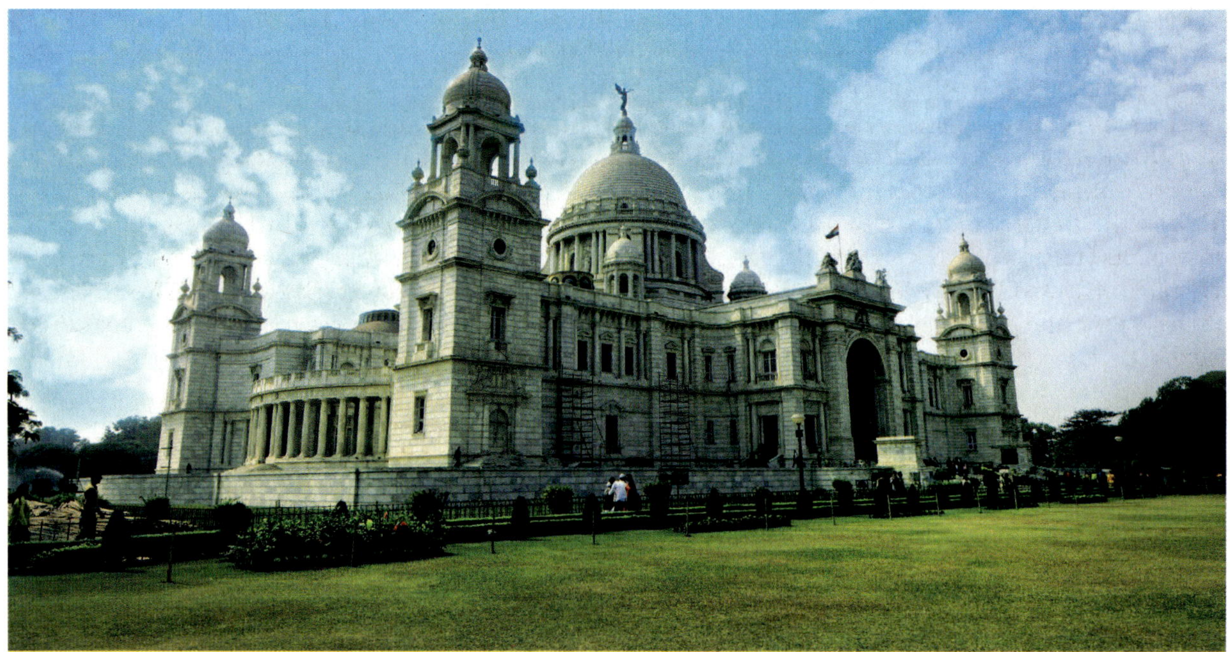

14.11: Victoria Memorial, an iconic monument of the early 20th century and glowing example of Indo-Saracenic architecture — Courtesy, Department of Tourism, West Bengal

architecture, the **Government House** (1803) the **Indian Museum** (1875) in Kolkata, the **Town Hall** (1833) and the **Elphinstone Circle** in Mumbai (1869) are some glorious examples of **Neo-Classical architecture. Neo-Gothic or Victorian Gothic** became popular in India in the mid and late 19th century. Some of its spectacular examples are the **Chhatrapati Shivaji Terminus building** (1887), the **Municipal Corporation building** and the **Maharashtra Police Headquarters building** (1872-1876) in Mumbai. The **Calcutta High Court** (established 1862), is another example of Neo-Gothic architecture.

British architecture could not remain untouched by indigenous architecture and by the demands placed on it by environmental and social-political factors. By the late 19th and beginning of 20th centuries, it incorporated elements of Mughal architecture and other indigenous Indian elements. It evolved into a fusion of British style with Indian elements and was referred to as **Indo-Saracenic architecture.** The **Victoria Memorial** in Calcutta (1921) is an exquisite example of this style. The **Senate House**, the

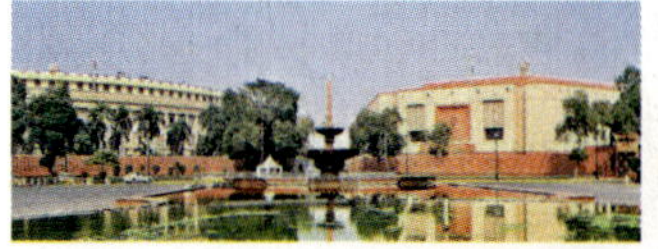

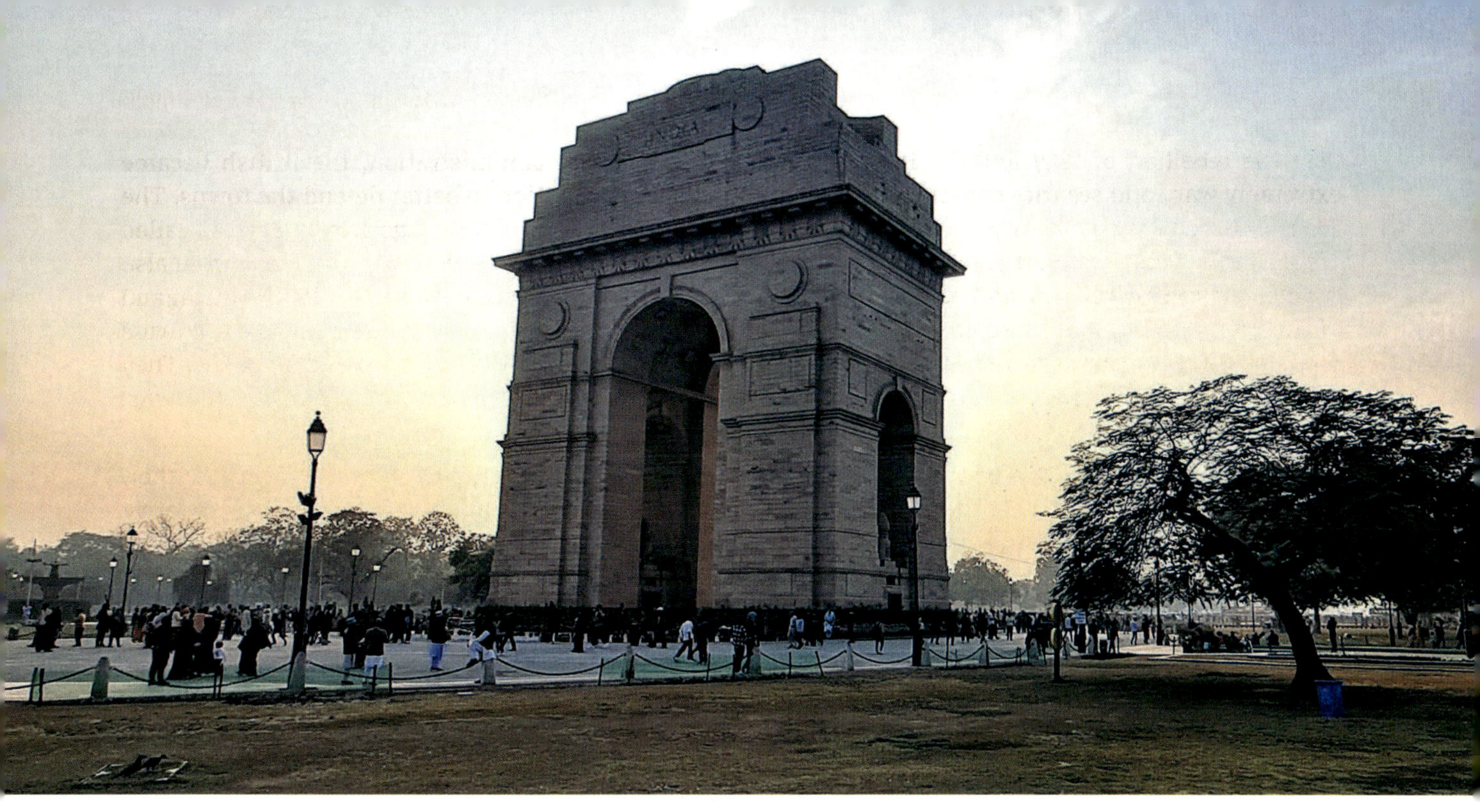

14.12: India Gate (1921), an iconic monument, symbolic of the 20th century British architecture of India; established as a war memorial; a sunset view from the lawns — photograph by Madhukar K Bhagat

National Art Gallery, (1906), and **Egmore Railway Station** (1908) in Chennai are some other prominent examples. The structures of the new capital city of New Delhi which included the **Viceroy's House** (now the *Rashtrapati Bhavan*: completed in 1927) and the Secretariat complex of **North** and **South Blocks** and other structures are some of the grandest examples of this style.

British architecture marked a transition from the erstwhile medieval architecture and manifested itself across the length and breadth of the country. Its presence was visible not only in the stately and grand structures of the new capitals the British built and in the Presidency towns, but also in numerous minor official and residential structures in smaller towns and cities. It brought in more contemporaneous construction techniques with modern materials. The concept of city planning and municipal functions was also instituted. Railways and industrial structures came up and so did roads and bridges. These changes were indeed a necessity for the British to sustain their administration in India, but then they also deeply influenced Indian architecture.

Socio-cultural Impact of Railways and the Growth of Industries in British India

Railways and industrialisation were other factors that had a considerable impact on society, people and culture. The period of the first few decades of the 19th century had been characterised by a considerable erosion of the export of cotton textiles and cotton piece goods from India. **While till the late 18th century India had the status of the world's major exporter of cotton, by the middle of the 19th century India itself became a major importer of cotton piece goods from Britain**. As per certain accounts, in 1811-12 export of cotton piece goods constituted nearly 33 per cent of India's exports, but by 1850-51 this was reduced to a paltry three per cent. While at the turn of the century, there were hardly any imports of cotton piece goods in India, by the 1850s, this figure had reached nearly 31%. The British policy of taxation of imports from India (import substitution), control of the ports and trade and pumping the machine-made cheaper products from the Manchester mills, had crippled the cotton industry and weaving in India, and thus the Indian economy.

The mills of Britain also needed access to Indian raw materials and to the markets. With the arrival of the railways in the 1850s, this link was established. The raw material from the hinterland could now move through the rails to the ports controlled by the Company and then to the mills in Britain. The finished goods could move through the same channel of ports and rails to the cities and smaller towns.

With the coming of the Industrial Revolution in Europe and machines replacing manual labour, the advent of machines and mills was not very far for India. By the 1850s, cotton mills in Bombay and jute mills in Bengal had been set up. By the 1860s, cotton mills had come up in Ahmedabad and Kanpur and by 1870s in Madras. Many of these mills were built by Indian entrepreneurs and traders.

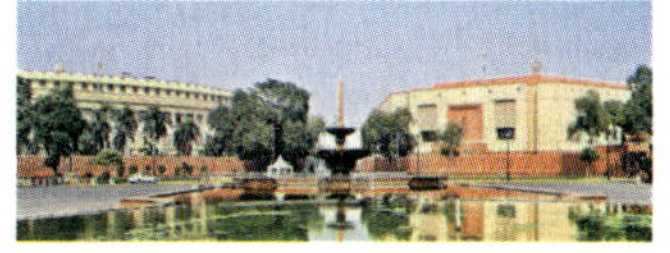

With the collapse of the market and traditional weaving, the source of revenue that sustained the rural economy for centuries dried up. People in different communities in the villages were becoming paupers as the pressure on agriculture also piled up. The villages were impoverished. The coming up of the mills, ports, railways and other establishments and with it more opportunities made the cities richer creating an unparalleled rural-urban divide. The growth of large cities also offered economic opportunities to the rural poor and this resulted in a **migration** of people from the villages and smaller towns to the larger cities. From weavers and peasants in their ancestral lands, they now became labourers in the mills in distant cities. They were uprooted from their society and culture and became rootless in their new environment in the cities.

Society changed in villages as well as in the cities and so did their culture. Villages were no longer, the reasonably self-sufficient centres of production. They had become impoverished end consumers dependent to an extent on the cities and production centres. The economic distress and the increasing dependency had a telling impact on the people. Besides, their weakening economic status and even their self-belief started to wane. Resentment against the company and the administration was on the rise.

The migration of villagers was not limited to the ports and industrial cities in India but migration also occurred to several **British plantations** in different parts of the world. This was a part of the indentured labour system through which nearly 16 lakh migrants were taken to work in the British and European plantations in the Caribbean, South Africa, East Africa, Mauritius, Malaysia, Myanmar, Fiji, Singapore and other places. These migrants hoped to return to their native villages after earning sufficiently to tide over their economic distress, but for many this return never materialised. The migrants to distant foreign lands took with them their traditions, religion, language and culture which got implanted in their new environs. Decades later, this intermingling of cultures was to blossom in new hues.

The industries, and in particular the Railways, were an instrument of British administration brought to establish their control over the economy and the territory of command. However, both had other unintended effects. Both proved to be places where the people of different communities could not keep their social segregation or religious and caste-based aloofness intact. Such distinctions had to be eschewed perforce. Thus, they became **melting pots of people from diverse backgrounds and regions**. Railways also connected different parts of the country and brought the people closer. It was responsible for making the three ports of Bombay, Calcutta and Madras into large cosmopolitan cities, a growth which continued to propel in the next century. Thus, **Railways integrated the country by interconnecting the regions and connecting the people**. This interconnect was crucial in later decades in the rising phase of Indian nationalism.

British Influence on Dress, Food and Other Elements of Micro-Culture in India

This was also a period in which the Indian population assimilated other elements of European culture, in particular, dress, food, and lifestyle. The influence on dress was substantial and visible especially in the aristocratic and the upper class. The British believed in their cultural superiority and so did a section of Indians which looked upon the British culture. They adopted British costumes and copied their lifestyle. One of the ostensible factors for this would have been that this could give them a greater connect with those who mattered then. This adoption of the new attire was reflected in men wearing a British/ European upper garment such as a shirt or a coat. This would go with their traditional lower garment such as *dhoti/ mundu/lungi,* a practice that is still popular in parts of South India. Some men started wearing *sherwani* or an *achkan* which fused with the British Frock coat. Some adopted the complete European wear of a pantsuit and a hat. Tie and shoes were also introduced and adopted by some Indians. The dress of women also underwent assimilation of the British elements. Although the *saree* continued to remain the traditional attire, the concept of a petticoat and a blouse was adopted by Indian women from the British women's attire.

Michael Madhusudan Dutt and Western Culture

The European influence on Indians in particular on dress and lifestyle is best exemplified by Michael Madhusudan Dutt (1824-1873), an eminent poet and litterateur in English and Bengali, who adopted the European lifestyle, early in his life. Dutt who studied at Hindu College in Calcutta, was a part of a generation of students who were stipulated to dress in Western clothing, eat European food using cutlery, speak in English and learn British culture. This was intended to anglicise a section of Indians who could work in the colonial administration. They were representative of a section of Indians who looked upon the British/European culture and emulated it. Dutt developed a yearning for European culture, converted to Christianity and also completely adopted Western outfits. In one of his poems, he writes about this yearning as below;

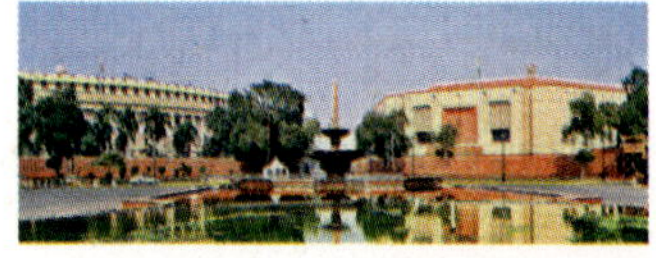

Where man in all his truest glory lives,
And nature's face is exquisitely sweet;
For those fair climes, I heave impatient sigh,
There let me live and there let me die

Michael Madhusudan Dutt and like him other Indians who adopted European lifestyles in part or substantial measure were in a way harbingers of a cultural confluence. However, this adoption was hardly ever complete, and was in part or at most in a substantial measure with elements of indigenous culture residing in the individual. This was responsible for producing an admixture of cultures and lifestyles. Dutt, in the later part of life after his long stay in Europe and England, was himself apparently disillusioned with European culture. It is believed that he wrote to his friend from France as below and in his later years took up writing in Bengali in a substantial way. 'If there be anyone among us anxious to leave a name behind him, and not pass away into oblivion like a brute, let him devote himself to his mother tongue. That is his legitimate sphere, his proper element.'

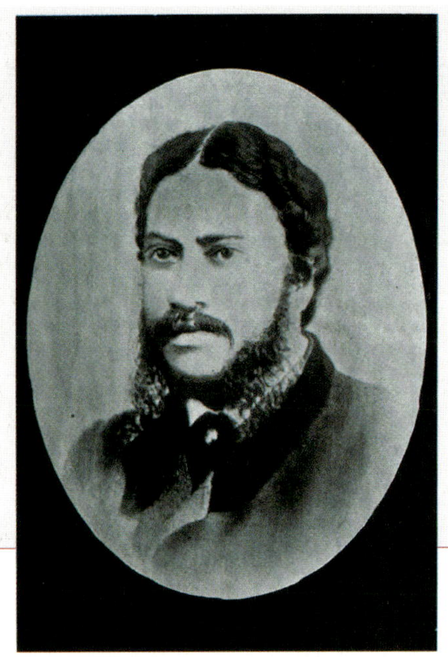

14.13: Michael Madhusudan Dutt, a portrait from 1907 — Wikimedia Commons

The confluence of cultures at the people-to-people level also affected the **culinary traditions** of both cultures. New items of foods, dishes and styles of cooking were introduced. Baking and items of food referred to as 'New World' vegetables (those brought in from the Americas) were introduced by the Portuguese and later popularised by the British. These included items such as potato, sweet potato, tomato, chilli, peanuts, amaranth etc. The long British presence and administrative control in different parts of the country were especially significant in popularising these items and also in their geographical spread. The introduction of tea in India and its popularity as a ubiquitous drink also can be traced to the introduction by the British in this period. Bread, toast, boiled eggs and some other items of food that gained popularity later with the Indians were other influences on the Indian food habits. The impact of Indian food on British cuisine also occurred. The Britishers often employed Indians as cooks and therefore the English meals began incorporating Indian dishes. Items of food such as curries, and chutneys, became popular, albeit in a modified form or with lesser spiciness.

Indian lifestyle and **habits** could not remain aloof from the British influence either. Indians were exposed to European music, Proscenium theatre, a culture of clubs, games like cricket, dining tables and chairs, the use of cutlery, the supply of piped water in households etc. Many of these were adopted by the Indians and by the end of British rule had become ubiquitous in India and completely ingrained with the Indian lifestyle. The use of the British form of greetings and salutations also got introduced in Indian society and later became common. However, the British influence on social life also exposed the Indians to **British racism**. The creation of 'white towns' of the British, 'black towns' for Indians, exclusive public spaces for the British, the exalted status of the English and the denigration of Indians, were the demeaning social influences that the Indians experienced.

Thus, the rising phase of English culture touched upon almost every aspect of Indian life and profoundly influenced many.

Mahatma Gandhi: Social Influences, British Superiority and Meat Eating

In his autobiography (*My Experiments With Truth*), Mahatma Gandhi recounts candidly as to how as a teenager he took to meat eating for a while. He attributes this to the negative influences of his friend and to the belief that it would make him strong and superior as were the British, who were so as they were meat eaters. It was a perception, he also recounts, which was in vogue then. It also succinctly brings out the general yearning of the vanquished (Indians) to be stronger, the complex of inferiority that seems to have seeped into the common folks and their desire to emulate their rulers at the cost of shedding their own strong traditions. It is indeed a pointer to the British social influences. The relevant excerpts are as below.

......A wave of 'reform' was sweeping over Rajkot at the time when I first came across this friend. He informed me that many of our teachers were secretly taking meat and wine. He also named many well-known people of Rajkot as belonging to the same company. There were also, I was told, some high-school boys among them. I was surprised and pained. I asked my friend the reason and he explained it thus: 'We are a weak people because we do not eat meat. The English are able to rule over us, because they are meat-eaters. You know how hardy I am and how great a runner too. It is because I am a meat-eater........

All these pleas on behalf of meat-eating were not advanced at a single sitting. They represent the substance of a long and elaborate argument which my friend was trying to impress upon me from time to time. My elder brother had already fallen.

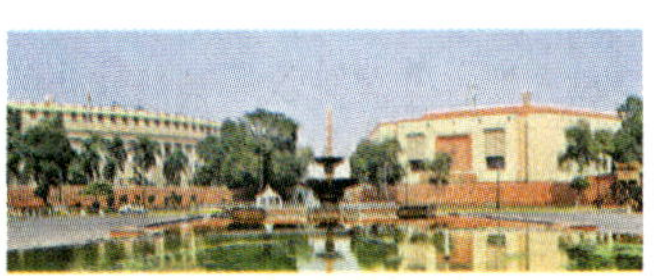

He therefore supported my friend's argument. I certainly looked feeble-bodied by the side of my brother and this friend. They were both hardier, physically stronger, and more daring. This friend's exploits cast a spell over me.......

Moreover, I was a coward. I used to be haunted by the fear of thieves, ghosts, and serpents. I did not dare to stir out of doors at night. Darkness was a terror to me. It was almost impossible for me to sleep in the dark, as I would imagine ghosts coming from one direction, thieves from another and serpents from a third. I could not therefore bear to sleep without a light in the room. How could I disclose my fears to my wife, no child, but already at the threshold of youth, sleeping by my side? I knew that she had more courage than I, and I felt ashamed of myself. She knew no fear of serpents and ghosts. She could go out anywhere in the dark. My friend knew all these weaknesses of mine. He would tell me that he could hold in his hand live serpents, could defy thieves and did not believe in ghosts. And all this was, of course, the result of eating meat. A doggerel of the Gujarati poet Narmad was in vogue amongst us schoolboys, as follows:

Behold the mighty Englishman
He rules the Indian small,
Because being a meat-eater
He is five cubits tall.

All this had its due effect on me. I was beaten. It began to grow on me that meat-eating was good, that it would make me strong and daring, and that, ***if the whole country took to meat-eating, the English could be overcome****. A day was thereupon fixed for beginning the experiment. It had to be conducted in secret. The Gandhis were Vaishnavas. My parents were particularly staunch Vaishnavas. They would regularly visit the Haveli. The family had even its own temples. Jainism was strong in Gujarat, and its influence was felt everywhere and on all occasions. The opposition to and abhorrence of meat-eating that existed in Gujarat among the Jains and Vaishnavas were to be seen nowhere else in India or outside in such strength. These were the traditions in which I was born and bred. And I was extremely devoted to my parents. I knew that the moment they came to know of my having eaten meat, they would be shocked to death. Moreover, my love of truth made me extra cautious. I cannot say that I did not know then that I should have to deceive my parents if I began eating meat. But my mind was bent on the 'reform'. It was not a question of pleasing the palate. I did not know that it had a particularly good relish. I wished to be strong and daring and wanted my countrymen also to be such so that we might defeat the English and make India free. The word Swaraj I had not yet heard. But I knew what freedom meant. The frenzy of the 'reform' blinded me. And having ensured secrecy, I persuaded myself that mere hiding the deed from parents was no departure from truth....*

Excerpts from Chapter-6 of, 'The Story of My Experiments with Truth' an autobiography of Mahatma Gandhi

THE RISE OF INDIAN NATIONALISM AND CULTURAL CONSCIOUSNESS

The Rising Indian Nationalism: Tracing its Course

The period since the last few decades of the 19th century leading to India's independence in 1947, was a phase of the rise of Indian nationalism. It was a period where our cultural consciousness was also driven by our nationalistic fervour. The growth of Indian nationalism experienced different phases of resurgence and suppression and different elements of Indian culture and social life remained closely interlinked with it.

By the middle of the 18th century, economic despair and misrule had already resulted in the alienation of the masses. Combined with a variety of other socio-economic and political factors, Indian nationalism was on the rise. This culminated in the First War of Independence in 1857. However, the brutal suppression of the revolt and later the takeover of the administration directly by the British crown and other factors had a dampening effect on the growth of Indian nationalism. The debacle of different Indian powers in the previous 100 years had a demoralising effect on the Indians and then with the crushing of the revolt, Indian self-belief also seemed to have vaporised. In the subsequent decade, there also emerged a belief in a section of Indians about the inherent superiority of the political masters, their society, governance, technology and even culture. Some Indians even looked upon the British and began to emulate them. The period 1860s and 1870s were the decades in which the British had fully and firmly established their political authority and to an extent pushed back Indian nationalism.

However, in the last quarter of the 19th century, Indian nationalism and consciousness of our socio-cultural identity grew again. The social awakening also affected the evolution of the political consciousness and both complimented each other. The exposure to the ideas of democracy and a representative system of government, which arose on account of the influence of Western culture and British education, had already kindled a national consciousness among Indians. The above factors induced a sense of rational inquiry which began in the socio-religious domain but transcended well into the political realm. There gradually emerged a section of Indians, who questioned the status quo. The culture of dogmatic acceptance of things or compliance to the status quo, driven merely on account of tradition and faith, had started to wane. The socio-cultural reforms and revivalist movements were gradually awakening our

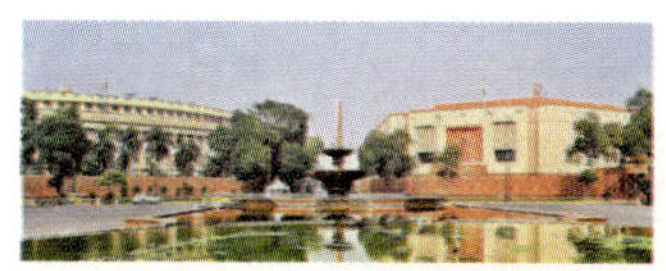

self-belief and belief in our socio-cultural identity. These continued well in the late 19th and early 20th centuries and created an environment for the growth of Indian nationalism.

Indian National Congress and Early Nationalism

The formation of the Indian National Congress in 1885, provided a platform for the growth of nationalism. Over the decades since its formation, several political events and movements unfolded many of which were launched by it and its leaders, and some supported by it, which fuelled Indian nationalism. To begin with, the Congress was envisaged as a 'safety valve' against a nationalist upsurge. It was meant to be a platform to voice the public opinion. It did serve as an early platform to this effect but also aided in the formation and shaping of the socio-political views of the Indians. The early leaders of the Congress like Dadabhai Naoroji, Surendranath Banerjee, Pherozshah Mehta, Badruddin Tyabji, W.C. Bonnerjee, Gopal Krishna Gokhale and others, adopted the approach of submitting memorandums and petitions to the Government to press for their social, economic, and administrative demands. This was what the political masters envisaged them to do. This was the generation of the '**Moderates**' who believed in the '**constitutional process**' and working with the governmental institutions. They played a significant role in establishing a discourse with the government and at times criticising it for its discriminatory laws and detrimental policies. In his book *Poverty and Un-British Rule in India* (1901), **Dadabhai Naoroji** brings out the **theory of the drain of wealth from India** and how pernicious the economic policies and British rule had been to the Indian economy and its people.

By the turn of the 20th century, the futility of the approach of appealing to the government had started to become apparent to a section of Congress leaders. A new generation of leaders like Bal Gangadhar Tilak and others had emerged who did not believe in improvements through petitioning but in '**direct action**'. Referred to as the 'Extremist' group within the Indian National Congress, the troika of Lala Lajpat Rai, Bipin Chandra Pal and Lokmanya Tilak (popularly known as Lal Bal Pal) engendered a new political ethos. The culture of Indian nationalism transitioned from petitioning for greater rights to the demand for *swaraj* (self-rule/self-governance). The subsequent partition of Bengal, the protest against it and the movement of *Swadeshi* etc., marked a closure of the 'moderate chapter' and announced the arrival of a new period of Indian nationalism.

The Partition of Bengal: A New Chapter of Indian Nationalism

In the first decade of the 20th century, Indian nationalism took a new direction and grew by leaps and bounds. The partition of Bengal and the ensuing mass movements kindled a nationalistic fervour not only in Bengal but also in the rest of the country. The British strategy to curb the growing nationalism in Bengal and sow a divide by partitioning Bengal on communal lines completely backfired. The mass protests against the partition were unprecedented. These cut across the classes and communal lines with Hindus as well as Muslims opposing the partition vehemently. Opposition was seen even from the *nawabs* and the nobility besides the commoners. The press, and Congress, all were completely against it. Eminent personalities like Rabindranath Tagore were highly critical of it. He exhorted the people of Bengal to tie *raksha bandhan*/ *rakhi* on each other's hands as a mark of solidarity on the day when partition was to be implemented. A unanimous rejection and persistent protest against the partition followed. Thousands of public meetings and protest marches in Bengal and elsewhere were organised. *Bande Mataram* (composed by Bankim Chandra) became a virtual anthem of the protests in Bengal. The movement unified the people of Bengal and India.

The entire movement opposing the partition was also accompanied by a movement for ***Swadeshi***. This meant the promotion and purchase of Indian goods as well as the boycott of foreign goods. This was a measure of last resort adopted when the other constitutional measures of written appeals, petitions, criticism by the press (including a section of Anglo- Indian press), vocal protests and mass meetings had failed. The Manchester-made cloth was the chief target of the boycott protests along with foreign-made salt, sugar and other luxury goods. The demand for swadeshi and emphasis on the use of Indian products also provided some impetus to local production, especially of cloth, a product whose industry had been ruined by the cheaper machine-made Manchester cloth.

The movement eventually resulted in the annulment of the partition in 1911. But this was also accompanied by a shift of the capital from Calcutta to New Delhi (a new capital that was later formed). The measure was considered a rebuttal of the movement and a means to contain the growing nationalism of Bengal. However, as time was to prove, the shift in the capital was insufficient to dampen the nationalistic fervour which had been evoked sufficiently. The partition of Bengal inspired a culture of nationalism

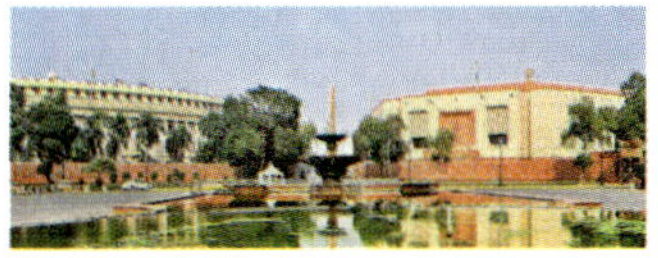

permeating every aspect of the social life including art and culture, trade and commerce. It integrated the socio-religious and economic dimensions with political nationalism thus engendering a new phase of our nationalistic culture.

The British constitutional reforms and disillusionment

The early 20th century also witnessed some measures of constitutional and legal reforms. However, they were far too little for Indian aspirations and too late in the day. There was already great disillusionment among the leaders and people from the inimical political developments and grossly inadequate measures of British policy. Then the proposed constitutional reforms such as the **Morely-Minto Reforms,** the **Indian Councils Act of 1909**, the **Montagu Chelmsford Reforms** (1918) and the subsequent **Government of India Act of 1919** etc. came. However, these were insufficient to fulfil the nationalistic aspirations as these were perceived as little more than 'lip service' and hardly sufficient to meet the genuine interest of the people. It convinced Indians that their salvation and hopes for a better future could not materialise under the exploitative British Rule or the legal framework set up by them.

The partition of Bengal on communal lines (1905), had already inflamed the masses and fired Indian nationalism. The two reforms had failed to inspire any confidence among Indians. Following it, came the **Rowlatt Act** of 1919 which authorised the police to arrest any person for any reason, to curb the rising Indian nationalism. This was sufficient to add fuel to the fire. Protests were organised by the Indian National Congress which now under the leadership of Mahatma Gandhi asked the people to oppose it by means of peaceful *Satyagraha*. In the wake of one such peaceful protest against the Rowlatt Act, the brutal **Jallianwala Bagh Massacre** (1919) took place. This completely exposed the British designs, eroding all faith in the British Government. The remnants of hope, if any, in British Constitutional reforms as a means for India's upliftment, were by now completely extinguished and gave way to the growth of Indian nationalism.

Mahatma Gandhi and the socio-political culture of ethics and principles

The arrival of Mahatma Gandhi in the Indian political scene and subsequent movements launched by him were crucial in **galvanising the masses and revitalising the Indian freedom struggle**. Till now Indian nationalism and the freedom struggle were led by educated Indians, intellectuals, professionals like lawyers and the upper-class elite. It was Mahatma Gandhi's leadership, ideology and conduct that enabled the freedom struggle to be a movement with which the peasants, the workers, the artisans and a common Indian could identify themselves and be a part. This changed our national consciousness.

14.14: Stamps depicting Mahatma Gandhi's Dandi yatra and the Salt Satyagraha released in 1980 and commemorating 50 years of the watershed moment of Indian nationalism — Courtesy, Department of Post

Post the launch of **Champaran Satyagraha** in 1917 by Mahatma Gandhi, the period of the next 25 years witnessed several mass movements. These included the **Non-cooperation movement** (1921), the **Civil Disobedience movement**, **the Salt Satyagraha** (1930) and the **Quit India movement** (1942), among others. These movements were not only crucial in further awakening the political consciousness but also awakening and evolving our socio-cultural consciousness.

Mahatma's firm belief in the tenet of *Ahimsa* infused the movement and the people with moral authority and vitality. His entire socio-political conception was built on the unshakeable bedrock of non-violence and ethical principles. Now India's freedom struggle was not merely concerned with the ouster of an unjust ruler and the termination of British imperialism, but also with the awakening of those moral principles in the Indians that could enable them to be a worthy free people. A path of freedom that treaded through the woods of violence was completely unacceptable to him, for the ends would not justify the means. ***Satya* (truth) and *Ahimsa* (non-violence) were two cardinal principles of his**

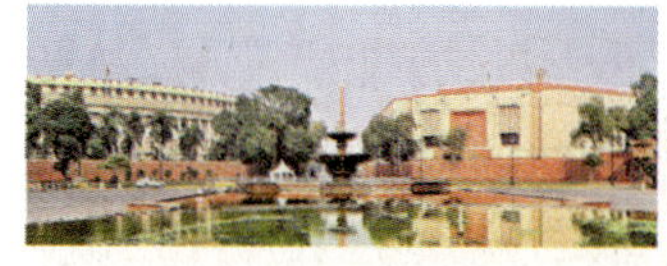

socio-political conduct which were inspired by the deep-rooted Indian cultural ethos. Thus, violence became antithetical to Indian freedom and its struggle. It had to be eschewed at all costs even if it meant to call off the movement of non-cooperation in 1922, post the Chauri-Chaura incidence of violence perpetrated by the Indians.

The principle of *Ahimsa* called for the inculcation of self-discipline and self-restraint and the Indians had to rise to a higher call to tread this path. This was reflected in these movements, where Indians who protested against the British policies without resorting to any mass violence bore the brunt of police *lathis* (batons) and suffered years of imprisonment. Thus, Mahatma Gandhi's leadership not only integrated the commoners with the freedom struggle, while imbuing the masses with nationalistic fervour, but more significantly, **infused in our social and national culture, a view of higher ideals and principles**. This vision of Mahatma gradually became integral to modern Indian national culture and continues to serve as a beacon of light for our socio-political culture transcending time and even societies.

Besides the infusion of the principles of truth and nonviolence in the political realm and integrating the common people with Indian nationalism, Mahatma Gandhi's efforts were also instrumental in **forging a greater Hindu and Muslim unity** at least in the early decades of the 20th century. His endeavour was also crucial in creating greater awareness about the **plight of Indian women**, promoting their rights, and their greater inclusion in Indian society, particularly in the national movement. Equally significant was his emphasis on the rights of the **marginalised communities** of India referred to by him as *Harijans* and bringing them into the mainstream of Indian society. Thus, this phase of Indian nationalism was also a witness to the emergence and growth of **Gandhian nationalism** of truth and non-violence and a larger **Gandhian culture** that permeated different elements of life and society, transcending the barriers of time, region and society.

Gandhi's View on Women

To call women the weaker sex is a libel; it is man's injustice to women. If by strength is meant brute strength, then, indeed, woman is less brute than man. If by strength is meant moral power, then a woman is immeasurably a man's superior. Has she not greater intuition, is she not more self-sacrificing, has she not greater powers of endurance, has she not greater courage? Without her, man could not be. If nonviolence is the law of our being, the future is with women. Who can make a more effective appeal to the heart than a woman?

Mahatma Gandhi in *Young India*, October 4, 1930

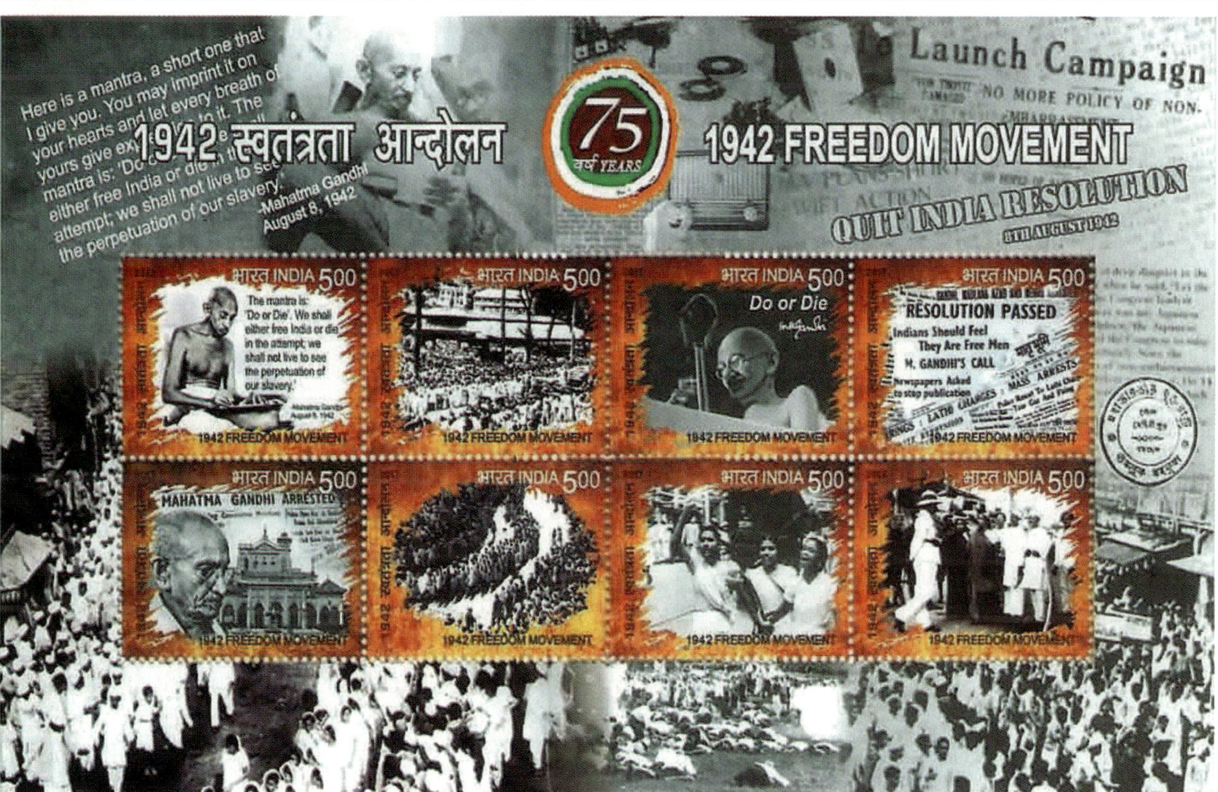

14.15: The Quit India Movement of 1942, wherein Mahatma Gandhi gave a clarion call of 'Do or Die', a culmination of India's rising nationalism; a stamp sheet commemorating 75 years, released in 2017 — Courtesy, Department of Post

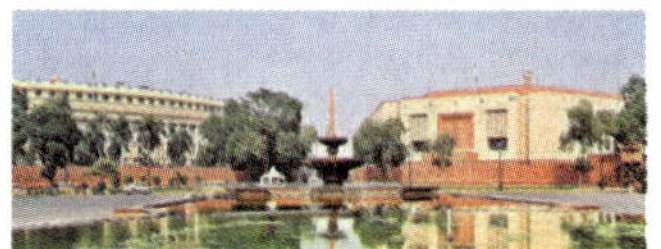

Social Harmony: The Change with the Times

The growing phase of Indian nationalism was also a phase that tested the communal character and social resilience of Indian society. Hindus and Muslims, the two large communities in the country, had lived together for nearly 700 years and evolved a shared culture. The social intercourse emanating from living together on the same land had generated at times social friction between the two communities; however, these were not socially disintegrative or destabilising. The approach and response of Hindus and Muslims had also been largely similar to the inimical British rule. Its tyrannical policies, economic exploitation and interference in the personal laws had brought the two communities together against a common enemy.

In the 19th century and early part of the 20th century, there was a definite convergence of views of the two communities on national issues and opposition to British rule. In the War of Independence in 1857, the two communities presented a united face. Bahadur Shah Zafar, the last Mughal, became an unwitting leader, of the rebellion and both the communities. The 'Partition of Bengal' in 1905 on communal lines (purportedly on grounds of administrative efficiency) saw stiff opposition to this 'divide and rule policy' from both communities. Mass movements of both communities followed, eventually leading to the annulment of partition in 1911. The arrival of Mahatma Gandhi on the political horizon and his efforts to cement the unity of the two communities were particularly successful in the 1920s. This culminated in the cooperation of the two communities in the **Khilafat movement**.

However, the later years saw a divergence of views on issues like governance of Muslim-majority provinces, abolition of *zamindari* (which was a touchy issue for the Muslim upper and middle class) and other matters. There was a fissure in the Indian National Congress on the above and other issues concerning the two communities. Hence, there emerged a communal divide, with the Indian Muslim league and right-wing Hindu parties each professing to be the champions of the causes of the respective communities. With the notion of a separate Islamic state emerging in the 1930s and the demand for a Pakistan crystalising and becoming shrill in the 1940s, our communal integrity was tested like never before. The emergence of the two-nation theory resulting in the unfortunate division of the country, revealed the deep communal fault lines.

Historians and scholars have different views as to whether the 'divide' had existed in the past and been dormant, or was it instituted by the British policy of 'divide and rule', or both. Some even opine that it was just a spate of uncontrolled factors and events that culminated in the partition of the undivided India but there was no underlying chasm between the communities. Irrespective of the root cause, the 'divide' deeply impacted the communal character of the country and proved to be a socio-cultural disaster despite the bond of growing nationalism. The horrendous communal riots that accompanied the decision of partition tore asunder the social and communal fabric. Indeed, overcoming the pangs of partition, the sorrow of lost lives and uprooted communities, was a daunting task at a critical juncture of a nation. Overcoming the social chasm and stitching together the communal fabric remained one of the most imposing socio-cultural challenges of the decade of the 40s and of the independent India.

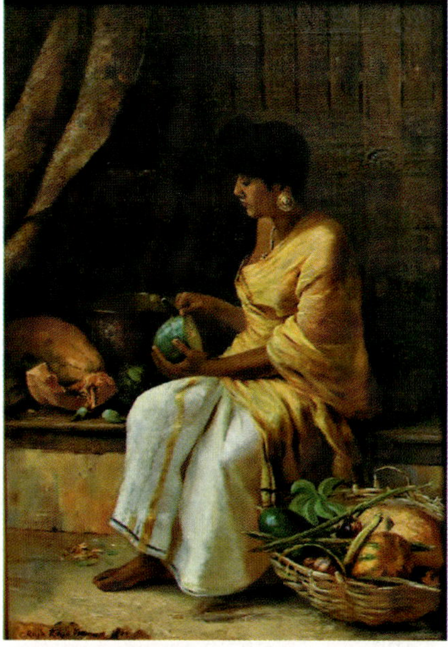

14.16: "Mother preparing vegetables"; oil on canvas; a painting by Raja Ravi Varma depicting the indigenous subject in the European Academic Art style; late 19th century, location Government Museum, Chennai — photograph by Madhukar K Bhagat

The Growth of Indian Art Forms and Literature in Pre-independence India

This rise of Indian nationalism in the 19th and 20th centuries permeated deeply into Indian culture as well. The Bengal Renaissance which had started in the early 19th century and engendered a wave of socio-religious reforms also witnessed a new wave of art and cultural reforms. Eminent personalities such as Bankim Chandra Chatterjee, Rabindranath Tagore, Sarat Chandra, and Nandalal Bose, ushered new movements and infused new life in Indian literature, poetry painting and other art forms. The revival of Indian art and literature was not just limited to Bengal but also witnessed in other parts of the country. There was a growing search for Indian roots and identity which was reflected in this cultural revival manifested in the entire

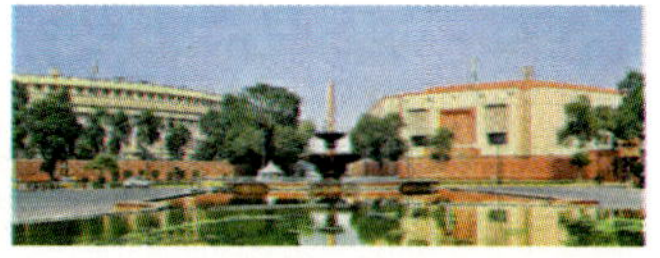

country and cut across the social hierarchy touching Indian life very deeply. The theme of nationalism, the search for Indian identity and the gradual emergence of social realism has been a characteristic of this period and resonated in different forms of cultural expression be it literature, paintings, music and dance or theatre and cinema.

Indian paintings

The **Indian painting** of the middle of the 19th century was dominated by the European Academic art movement. It imbibed the style of European realism with its subjects being a mix of portraiture and Indian panorama. The advent of Raja Ravi Varma, in the latter half of the 19th century, ushered in a tradition of Indian painting wherein the subjects and ethos were uniquely Indian. His artworks were also significant as they brought in a confluence of Western/European painting techniques with Indian sensibility and subjects. It inspired a generation of Indian artists.

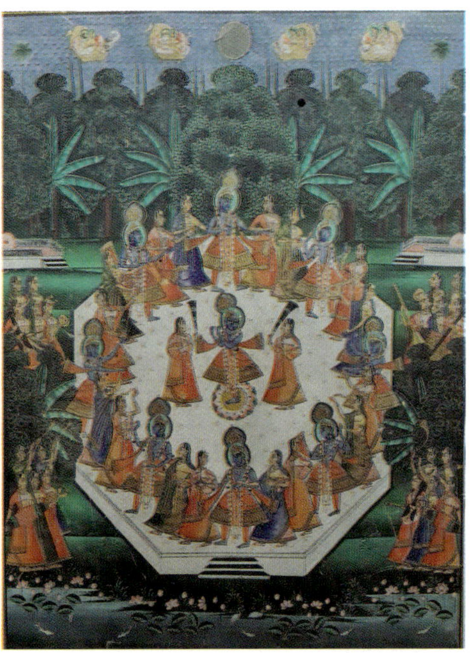

14.17: "Sri Krishna in *raas krida* with *gopikas*", opaque watercolour on paper, a Nathdwara painting, Rajasthan, late 19th century; depicting a class of indigenous school of painting which survived in this period in the wave of European Academic art movement; location Chhatrapati Shivaji Maharaj Vastu Sangrahalaya Mumbai — photograph by Madhukar K Bhagat

In the early 20th century, Indian art progressed a step further. The **Bengal School of Art** ushered in a new era of **revivalist nationalism** in paintings. This art movement was started by **Abanindranath Tagore** (nephew of Rabindranath Tagore) along with **E.B. Havell** (Principal of Government Art School, Calcutta) and **Sister Nivedita** (an associate of Swami Vivekananda). The paintings of this school were connected to the Indian roots in terms of style as well as the subject. It aimed to regenerate Indian art heritage by recognising and bringing alive its ancient and folk traditions of painting as well as by connecting the art with the people and their lives. It drew inspiration from the murals of the ancient period and the work of folk painters and artists as well as the indigenous schools. Among the other greats associated with the Bengal school were, **Rabindranath Tagore, Abanindranath Tagore, Gaganendranath Tagore, Nandalal Bose, Jamini Roy, Sunayani Devi, Ram Kinker Baij**, **M.R. Chugtai**, besides others.

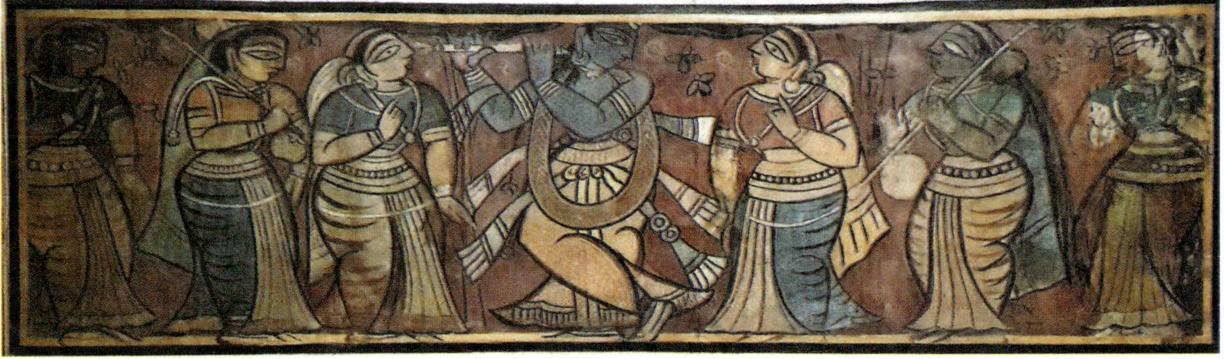

14.18: "Krishna and Gopiyan"; tempera on cloth, a painting by Jamini Roy, one of the iconic artists of Bengal School of Art; in the early 20th century National Gallery of Modern Art, New Delhi — photograph by Madhukar K Bhagat

Indian Literature

The late 19th century was also witness to resurgence in Indian literature. **Mirza Ghalib** (1797-1869) was already a celebrated name in Urdu poetry at the beginning of the decade of 1850s. He and other poets of the age made an invaluable contribution to Indian poetry. But this phase is especially significant for the growth of **Indian prose**. Several works of novels and plays were written heralding a remarkable chapter of Indian literature in the next 100 years.

The works of prose, *Neel Darpan* (play) by **Dinabandhu Mitra,** *Durgesh Nandini* and *Anand Math* by **Bankim Chandra**, and *Andher Nagari* (Hindi play) and *Bharat Durdasha* (Hindi play) by **Bharatendu Harishchandra,** were indeed milestone literary works. Many greats of regional literature and prose emerged including; **Lakshminath Bezbarua** (Assamese literature), **Fakir Mohan Senapati** (Odia literature), **Narmadashankar Lalshankar Dave** (Gujarati literature), **Samuel Vedanarayan Pillai**, (Tamil literature), **Kandukuri**

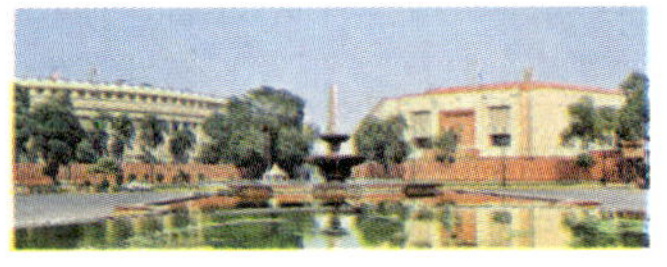

Veerasalingam Pantulu (Telugu novelist), **Oyyarathu Chandu Menon** (Malayalam novelist,), **Krishnamma Chetty** (Malayalam novelist).

The advent of **Rabindranath Tagore** on the Indian literary landscape in the late 19th century was indeed a watershed in Indian literature. In a literary career spanning nearly five decades, he wrote several momentous works of prose and poems, including novels, short stories, plays, essays, and travelogues and became the first and the only Indian to receive a **Nobel Prize for Literature**.

The 20th century was witness to another colossal of Indian literature. **Munshi Premchand**, considered a *upanyas samrat* (an emperor amongst novelists), authored 14 novels and nearly 300 short stories, besides essays and translations of literary works from other languages. Among other eminent writers of Hindi prose in this period were; **Acharya Mahavir Prasad Dwivedi** (editor of the esteemed Saraswati magazine), **Acharya Ramchandra Shukla** (critique, essayist and literary historian), **Vrindalal Verma** (dramatist and novelist), **Rahul Sankrityayan** (great travel writer), **Bhagwati Charan Verma** (novelist), **Hazari Prasad Dwivedi** (a novelist and literary historian), **Yashpal** (novelist and short story writer) besides others.

The coming decades were also a golden phase of **Hindi poetry**. *Chhayawaad,* a new genre of romanticism in Indian poetry blossomed. **Maithali Sharan Gupta**, **Jaishankar Prasad**, **Suryakant Tripathi 'Nirala'** and **Mahadevi Verma** considered the four pillars of the *Chhayawaad* movement, contributed richly to Indian poetry and literature. **Ayodhya Singh Upadhyaya 'Harioudh'**, **Makhan Lal Chaturvedi**, **Subhadra Kumari Chauhan**, **Ramdhari Singh Dinkar**, **Harivansh Rai Bachchan** and **Nagarjun** were some other Hindi poets of this period who are considered doyens of Indian literature.

Regional literature bloomed. **Sharat Chandra Chatterjee** and **Kazi Nazrul Islam** were celebrated Bengali novelists and poets respectively. **Subramania Bharati,** an eminent Tamil poet, is deemed the father of modern Tamil literature. **Vishnu Sakharam Khandekar** (Marathi novelist) is reckoned as a great of Marathi literature. **Bhai Veer Singh** (Punjabi poet) heralded modern Punjabi poetry. **Puran Singh** (Punjabi poet) was considered the 'Tagore of Punjab'. **B.M. Srikanthaiah, D.R. Bendre** (poet), and **K.V. Putappa** (poet and novelist) were eminent Kannada litterateurs. In Malayalam literature, the triumvirate of **Vallathol Narayan Menon**, **Kumar Asan** and **Ulloor S. Parameswara Iyer** ushered a new chapter.

Urdu literature, especially poetry, continued to flourish in this phase. Eminent poets like **Hasrat Mohani**, **Muhammad Iqbal**, **Yaganaa Changezi**, **Jigar Moradabadi**, **Firaq Gorakhpuri**, **Josh Malihabadi**, **Faiz Ahmad Faiz** and **Sadaat Hasan Manto** ushered a golden age of Urdu poetry. Many Indian litterateurs of English gained wide recognition. This included **Sarojini Naidu** (an eminent poet), and novelists like **Mulk Raj Anand**, **R.K. Narayan**, **Raja Rao** and others.

Different genres of literature evolved. The literature of reformism and revivalism of the late 19th century transitioned into nationalistic literature in the 19th and early 20th centuries. Spiritualism and philosophy found expression in the works of Vivekananda, Aurobindo, Dr. Radhakrishnan and others during these decades. The genre of poetry came up with romanticism in *Chhayawaad* and became popular in the 1920s and 1930s. Then came the wave of 'realism' in Indian literature which was best evident in the works of Premchandra and Sarat Chandra Chatterjee. The decade of the 30s also witnessed 'progressive' literature in the growth of the *Pragativaad* movement in Hindi literature. Thus, Indian literature evolved from strength to strength changing with the times. It was also symbolic of the wave of cultural revivalism sweeping the country even in the politically turbulent and challenging times.

Music and Dance

Indian music came out from the shadows of post-medieval decline and witnessed unprecedented growth in the late 19th and 20th centuries. At the turn of the century, among the greats of Indian classical music who laid the foundation of new trends in music and inspired a generation of musicians, were **Alladiya Khan**, **Vishnu Narayan Bhatkhande**, **Abdul Karim Khan** and **Vishnu Digambar Paluskar**. **Allaudin Khan** was another doyen of Indian classical music of this period who nurtured the next generation of music greats. In the first half of the 20th century, some of the stalwarts of classical music came into prominence. This included vocalists such as; **Bade Ghulam Ali**, **Siddheshwari Devi**, **Mallikarjun Mansur**, **Gangubai Hangal**, **Begum Akhtar**, **M.S. Subbulakshmi**, **D.K. Pattamal**, **Bhimsen Joshi**, **Kumar Gandharava** and **M.L Vasanthakumari**. A galaxy of classical instrumentalists too came into prominence, including masters of their craft such as; **Allauddin Khan**, **Bismillah Khan**, **Pandit Ravishankar**, **Allah Rakha**, **Ali Akbar Khan**, **V.G. Jog** and **Vilayat Khan**, among others.

Indian classical dances also underwent revival and resurgence in this phase. In the 18th and early 19th centuries, many of these dance forms had withered or they were confined to the narrow domain of arts practised by the courtesans and temple *devadasis*. In the 19th century, dances such as Kathak, Odissi and

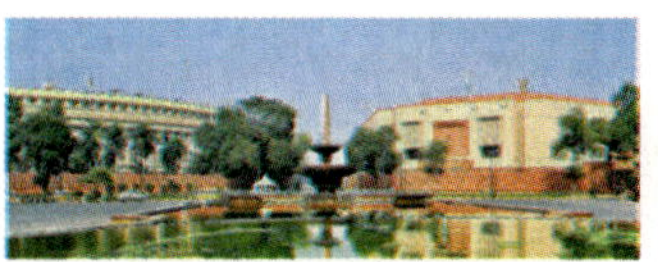

Bharatanatyam were looked down upon by the Britishers and even banned at times. In the late 19th and 20th centuries, Kathak was revived due to the efforts of **Bindadin Maharaj**, **Kalka Prasad**, **Uday Shankar**, **Shambhu Maharaj** and **Birju Maharaj** among others. Similarly, **Pankaj Charan Das** (considered *adiguru* of Odissi in the 20th century), **Kavichandra Kalicharan Pattanayak** and **Kelucharan Mahaptra**, helped to revive the traditions of Odissi dance.

The centuries-old tradition of Manipuri dance declined post the annexation of Manipur by the British. In the 20th century, a new life was infused in it due to the efforts of **Rabindranath Tagore** and other exponents and gurus of this art form, including **Naba Kumar**, **Senarik Singh Rajkumar**, **Nileshwar Mukherji** and **Atomba Singh**, amongst others. Bharatanatyam, a temple dance of ancient origin, suffered due to the prohibition of the temple *devadasi* system, wherein the art form remained reposited. However, in the 20th century, it was refashioned and resurfaced as a theatre art. Further, due to the efforts of **Meenakshisundaram Pillai**, **E. Krishna Iyer**, **Rukmini Devi Arundale**, and **T. Balasaraswati**, this art was preserved and even popularized. Kuchipudi was another classical dance to be revived in the early 20th century. Some prominent names associated with it in this phase were; **Vempati Venkatanarayan**, **Chinta Venkataramayya** and V. **Lakshminarayan Shastry**. Kathakali and Mohiniattam were two other great art forms and classical dances of Kerala that made a comeback in the 1930s and 1940s due to the efforts of **Vallathol Narayana Menon**, a Malayali poet. Thus, the 20th century not only revived the tradition of classical music and dances, but also took it to new heights and ushered in a period of cultural renaissance.

Indian theatre and cinema

The tradition of **Indian theatre** traces its roots to ancient times. The modern Indian theatre, and in particular the Proscenium theatre came to India in the late 18th century, and by the next 50 years, was popular in Bengal. By the latter half of the 19th century, commercial theatre was popular in the country, particularly in the presidency towns of Calcutta, Bombay, Madras and the adjoining regions. *Buro Shaliker Ghare Ro* (1860) by **Michael Madhusudan Dutt**, *Nil Darpan* written by **Dinabandhu Mitra** (1858-1859), and its production in 1872 by **Girish Chandra Ghosh**, were some early commercial theatre productions. *Bharata Durdasha (1875), Satya Harishchandra* (1876), and *Andher Nagari* (1881) by **Bharatendu Harishchandra** were some prominent plays of Hindi theatre. *Jhansichya Raniche Naatak* (1870), and *Afzal Khan Chaye Mrutyuche Naatak* (1871) by **Vishnu Das Bhave**, were some of the eminent Marathi plays that were commercially produced.

But Indian theatre also passed through a phase of trials and tribulations, experienced because of the political tumult. In 1872, **Girish Chandra Ghosh** founded the **National Theatre**, the first Bengali professional theatre company, which took the performance of *Nil Darpan* to different parts of the country. The play brought out the tyranny of the British indigo planters over the peasants and farm labour. It was banned by the British. *Chakar Darpan* (Mirror of Tea-Planters, 1875) by **Dakshina Charan Chattopadhyay** which highlighted the oppression of the tea planters was also banned by the British government. Soon the *Playwrights Dramatic Performance Act 1876* was passed, empowering the government to prohibit public dramatic performances that it found seditious, obscene or defamatory. Henceforth the playwrights adopted historical figures and mythological contexts to depict concurrent issues thus creating a genre of plays such as *Andher Nagari*, where the British misrule was conveyed in a veiled manner.

By the late 19th and the beginning of the 20th century, Indian theatre and its narrative took the next leap. Its genre was now not restricted to the epic tales of the gods or the heroic deeds of the great kings but centred on the common man, the social lives and the national problems as well. *Bharat Durdasha* by Bharatendu Harishchandra succinctly brought out the reasons for the deprivation of India in colonial rule. *Andher Nagari*, *Nil Darpan* and *Chakar Darpan* were categoric in their nationalistic themes, thus integrating Indian theatre with the **rising nationalism**. The element of nationalism, albeit in the historical context, was also brought out in plays like *Mir Qasim* (1906), and *Sirajuddaulah* (1909) by **Girish Chandra Ghosh** which elucidated the fall of dynasties on account of betrayals. Others like *Chhatrapati* (1907) by Girish Chandra Ghosh, and *Mebar Patan* (The Fall of Mewar), *Shahjahan* (1910), and *Chandragupta* (1911) by **D. L. Roy** also explored elements of nationalism.

A genre of plays that portrayed social evils and were reformistic also came up. *Naba Natak* and *Kulina Kulasarbasva* by **Ramanarayana Tarkaratna** opposed polygamy. *Kanyasulkam* (Telugu) by **Gurajada Apparao**, succinctly portrayed the evil practice of marrying young girls to much older brides for a fee. *Raktakarabi* by **Rabindranath Tagore** was centred on the theme of the demeaning influence of our greed in human lives. *Parapare* and *Babganari* by **Dwijendralal Ray** portrayed the evils of the caste system. Thus the plays of this period introduced an element of **social realism**. By this time Indian theatre had also transitioned to a commercial avatar. They were now not just a means of entertainment exclusively for the elite but accessible to all who could afford it.

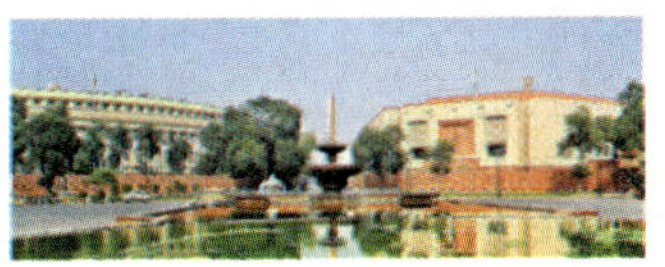

Coming to the 20th century, and particularly around and after the First World War, Indian theatre again experienced the winds of change. This was influenced by the socio-political environment, rising nationalism and parallel movements in the world of art and literature. In the 1920s and 30s, experimental and amateur theatre movement emerged. This was evident in the works of Gujarati playwrights like **Chandravardan Chimanlal Mehta** whose play *Aag Garhi* (Fire Engine) had a theme of social realism. *Sarjanhar* (in Gujarati), inspired by Gandhian ideology, dealt with the issue of untouchability and was another important play of a social genre.

With the emergence of the Bengal revivalist school, the founding of the **Progressive Writers Movement** (1936) and the growth of the communist movement, Indian theatre also became more people-centric. This was reflected in the birth of the **Indian People's Theatre Association** (IPTA). In 1944 *Nabanna*, written by **Bijon Bhattacharya**, a drama about the Bengal famine highlighted the great tragedy of the man-made famine which killed nearly three million people. The play was staged in various parts of the country by IPTA and later by the *Bohurupee Theatre* of Sombhu Mitra. This was truly the coming of age of the Indian theatre. Changing with the times, it now evolved to become a medium that was not limited to bringing a cultural awakening and infusing a sense of nationalism in the masses, but also to be a platform that could succinctly portray the society and the people at the very grassroots level and could identify with their causes. This was a long journey for Indian theatre having its origin in folk theatre, moving to professional theatre, graduating to commercial theatre and then evolving to grassroots theatre.

Indian cinema had its birth in the last decade of the century. This was within a few years of the Lumiere Brothers making their first public screening of cinema in Paris (in 1895) and later in Bombay (in 1896). **Sakharam Bhatwadekar Harishchandra**, who was one of the witnesses to the Lumiere Brothers' show in Bombay, produced in 1899, a series of six short films based on day-to-day activities. The first of these was *The Wrestlers*, which was shot during a wrestling match in Bombay (now Mumbai). Thus began the dawn of the age of movies in India, which, a century later, was to become among the biggest film industries of the world.

The first feature film of India, *Raja Harishchandra* by **Dada Saheb Phalke**, a silent movie came out in 1913. Within the next few decades, Indian movies reached great heights. By 1931, when the first talkie movie *Alam Ara* by **Ardeshar Irani** came, over 200 movies were being produced annually. Thus, Indian movie-making had become an established industry within just two decades of its fledgling start with a few movies in the silent era.

Cinema as an art shares many skills and attributes essential to the theatre, and in a way, theatre was a precursor to Indian cinema. Initially its growth and in particular the genre of movies also mimicked the theatre. But over a period of time, it emerged as a distinct art form, substantially overtaking theatre in popularity, reach and versatility of artistic expression. The films in the early phase of the silent era, as in the case of theatre, were often based on religious and mythological characters or devotional themes. These included movies such as *Raja Harischandra* (1913), *Mohini Bhasmasur* (1913), *Lanka Dahan*

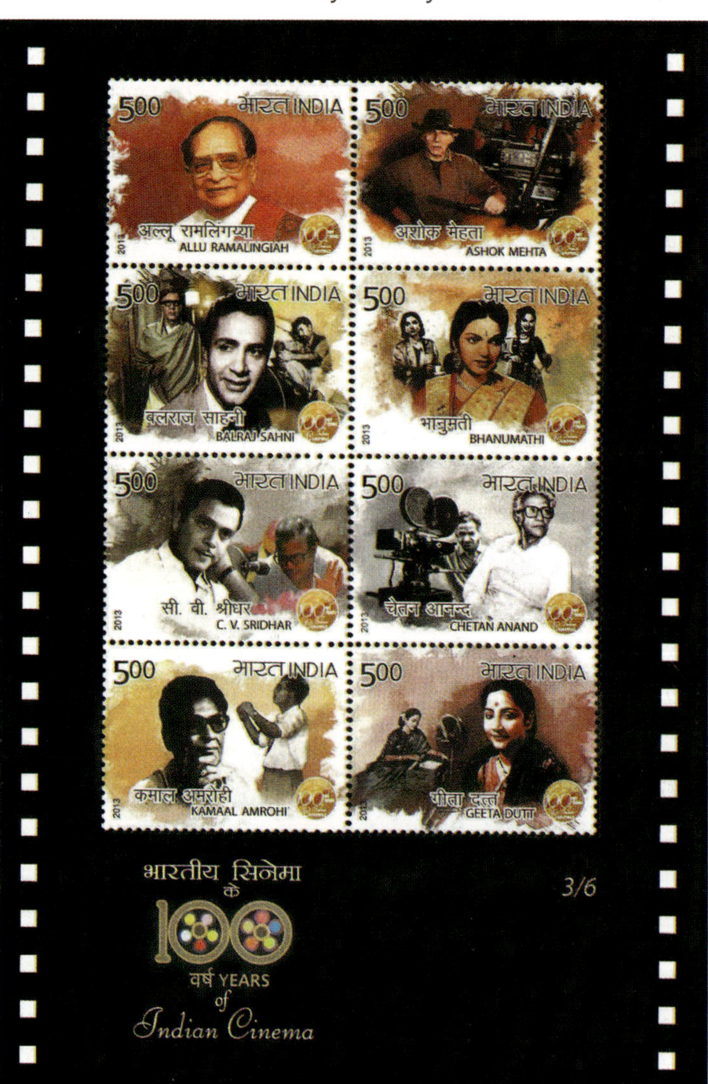

14.19: A stamp sheet released in 2013 to commemorate the hundred years of Indian cinema, depicting some early stalwarts of Indian movies — Courtesy, Department of Post

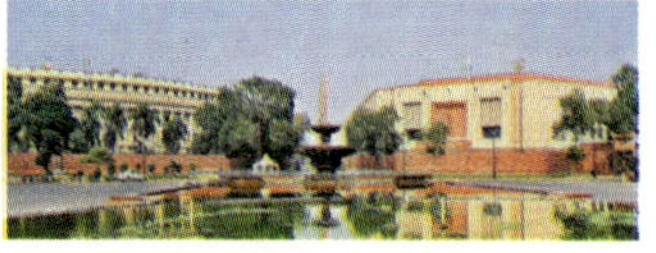

(1917), *Nala Damayanti*, *Sri Krishna Janam* (1918), *Keechaka Vadham* in Tamil (1918), *Kaliya Mardan* (1919), *Buddha Dev* (1923), *Bhakta Prahalad* (Malayalam), *Sant Tukaram* etc. Some movies were also based on historical characters, such as Kalidas, Sati-Padmini, Noor Jahan, Anarkali, etc. These early movies were essentially in the nature of cinematic retelling of stories of the epics and the Puranas, or those drawn from the pages of history.

Coming to the late 1920s, 1930s and 1940s, the Indian movies diversified substantially and highlighted a range of social issues. Women-related issues were the subject of acclaimed works such as *Achhut Kanya* (1936), *Joymoti* (in Assames-1935), *Duniya Na Mane* (1937) and *Manoos* (1939). Some movies also broached on the subject of nationalism and India's freedom struggle but were banned by the British government. *Bhakt Vidur* (1921), *Wrath* (1930) and *Raithu Bidda* (1938-Telugu) were some such productions. The song in the movie *Kismet* (1942), *door hato ae duniya walon Hindustan Hamara haye* (O' people of this world, get away, Hindustan is ours) became a song of inspiration and protest during the Quit India movement.

Movies of the entertainment genre were also quite popular in this period. *Shirin Farhad*, produced as early as 1931, was structured like an opera with nearly 42 song sequences. *Inder Sabha*, produced in 1932, had a whopping 69, the most in any film ever, thus ushering in a culture of songs in Indian movies. Social dramas were also quite popular in this period. A series of movies of Wadia & Wadia productions such as *Hunterwali*, *Toofan Mail*, *Punjab Mail*, and *Flying Rani* featuring Australian-Indian actress Mary Evans, were based on a female protagonist and were of the category of an outright entertainer.

With the birth of the Indian People's Theatre Association (IPTA), the Bengal famine, and plays such as *Nabanna* (1944) gaining substantial traction with the masses, came a genre of movies like *Dharti Ke Lal* (*Children of the Earth* in 1946). Produced by **Khwaja Ahmad Abbas** and directed by him and Bijon Bhattacharya, the film received critical acclaim for its bold and realistic portrayal of the disastrous Bengal famine (1943). *Neecha Nagar* (1946) directed by **Chetan Anand** (an Indian adaptation of Maxim Gorky's *Lower Depths*) starkly portrayed the gulf between the lives of the rich and poor and won the Palme d'Or at the Cannes Film Festival (1946). Thus, the genre of social realism which had already swept Indian literature and embraced the modern theatre also permeated in the Indian movies. This was a precursor to what a few decades later were to emerge as a 'parallel cinema'.

The regional film industry also flourished along with Bollywood which had taken the mantle of mainstream industry. Among the earliest regional language films was *Shree Pundalik*, (Marathi 1912). Made by **R.G. Torney and N.G. Chitre**, this movie, however, was in the nature of a recording of a play and accordingly was not accorded the status of a feature film. As such, *Keechaka Vadham* produced in 1917-1918 by **R. Nataraja Mudaliar** in Tamil is considered the first regional language cinema of India. Among other important regional films of the silent era were; *Bhishma Pratigyna* (1921: Telugu) by **Raghupati Venkaiah Naidu**, *Vigathakumaran* (1928: Malayalam) by **J.C. Daniel**. In the era of the talkies, after Alam Ara was produced in 1931, **Ardeshar Irani** also produced *Kalidas*, a bilingual Tamil-Telugu movie in 1931. Closely following it was the Marathi movie *Ayodhyecha Raja* (1932) produced by **Shantaram Rajaram Vankudre** (V. Shantaram), which was based on the story of Raja Harishchandra. Another regional talkie of this period was *Sati Savitri*, a Telugu film produced by **C. Pullayya** in 1933. *Joymoti*, produced in 1935 by **Jyotiprasad Agarwalla**, was among the earliest of Assamese movies.

Indian movies in this phase witnessed phenomenal growth. They integrated various art forms and were assimilative of the numerous movements witnessed in the fields of art, literature and theatre. Ranging from pure entertainment to social reforms from nationalism to realism, the movies of this period projected all the genres. But their crucial contribution to society was in their reach and connecting with the masses to the farthest of regions of the country and cutting across the classes. Thus, they were reflective of the changing society and in a way integrative of it in the turbulent times of a nation.

CULTURE OF POST-INDEPENDENT INDIA

Significant Elements of Influence on Indian Culture Post-Independence

Post-independence began a new chapter of Indian culture. Several factors played a significant role in shaping Indian culture in this phase. The **independence** of the country in itself was the most crucial influence on Indian culture. India now had the opportunity to reflect on its continuous cultural legacy of over 5000 years. It also had the freedom to change and evolve as per the need of time and the call of its soul, hitherto suppressed for centuries. Independence paved the way for the creation of a new **Constitution** and making India a sovereign, democratic republic. The Constitution heralded a new phase

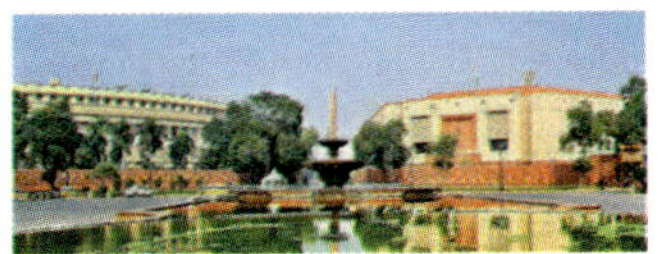

in national polity and society which had a profound influence on culture as well. While the independence of the nation was the culmination of the growing nationalism of the past two centuries, the Indian Constitution was emblematic of the unity and integrity of the geographically vast and culturally diverse country. Hence, there also came several **institutions of governance** in the country, which harnessed our diversity into a **national unity**, thus adding another base to our national culture. The different elements of culture blossomed in the coming decades under the patronage of several **cultural organisations** set up by the governments and through social initiatives. As culture reposits in people, it was the **peace**, **progress** and endeavour of **people** which were undoubtedly the most significant factors in the evolution of Indian culture.

Emergence of the Indian Nation and the New Constitution

The independence of the country ushered in a new **cultural** epoch in India. To begin with, the freedom of the country was met with a tumultuous phase. It was a phase marked by rejoicing at the advent of a new era of Indian history and culture. It was a phase that ushered hope. It was also a phase marred by the division of the country and by the accompanying communal riots. The displacement of millions, the flow of refugees, and the cry of the hungry and homeless took the sheen off India's joy and celebrations. The initial turbulence was followed by a phase of reconstruction, regeneration and growth.

A new **Constitution** was framed which marked a departure from several centuries-old traditions of monarchy, which had later given way to colonialism. Power now rested with people rather than with monarchs and despots and this was to be exercised through the elected representatives of the people. Universal adult suffrage was enshrined in our Constitution and thus the country took a giant leap in creating a democracy and building **institutions of democracy**. This indeed was a turning point in the history and culture of the country.

Besides the daunting economic and political challenges several **cultural challenges** were witnessed by the country, in the first few years post-independence and the decades ahead. What could integrate such a large and diverse country? The harmonisation of several regions in the new Indian nation, each having a sub-national culture of its own; the challenge of integration of nearly 500 princely states that had experienced a different socio-political trajectory, the problems posed by numerous languages, each representing a people and their socio-cultural identity; the communal divide that bifurcated the nation; the ugly riots that followed; a society fragmented by caste divide; the issue of untouchability which was a slur on the society; the plurality of races and tribes; all raised questions as to the viability of the envisioned nation. The poor economic condition of India on the eve of independence, and the mammoth population to feed and find a livelihood for all of these, did not make the situation any easier for the country.

The **socio-cultural-political challenges** were aplenty. The demand for linguistic organisation of states was one of the major stumbling blocks for the pan-Indian national identity in the early years of independent India. However, the subsequent reorganisation of several states based on linguistic identity helped to quell the language-based and region-based separatist demands and kept intact the integrity of the emerging nation. Communal challenges which had already divided the country were far from over. The issue of reservations for the scheduled castes and scheduled tribes highlighted another socio-cultural disquiet within the country. Despite these and other sectarian forces, **India emerged stronger**.

What kept the integrity of the country intact in post-independence India and what has been the basis of the unity of this new nation? Was it that the very forces that tended to carve out a separate identity for the groups and regions were in a way acting as a counterforce to the other factors that could be divisive? In a given region where the plurality of religion, communities and castes could be perceived as forces tending to pull in separate directions, could the commonality of language and regional culture be the integrating influence? This could perhaps be seen in the similarity of the culture of the families, in the food and the dress etc. which all had distinct regional traits.

Religion could transcend inter-regional differences and could create a bond cutting across the boundaries of the new states. For the majority Hindu community spread in different parts of the country, could the belief in a common religious culture with commonality of gods, religious practices, pilgrimage sites and temples, been a factor that helped to tide the regional dissimilarities? And could similar sentiments be a factor for other religious communities to form a bond cutting across languages and regions?

On the surface, these may appear to have an element of truth. However, these factors and differences have been the characteristics of the land not only in the post-independence cultural phase, but also in its recorded history in the past 2500 years. Unity in diversity has been a cultural trait of the land, and its people since time immemorial despite it being besieged by seemingly divisive forces. In a way, this

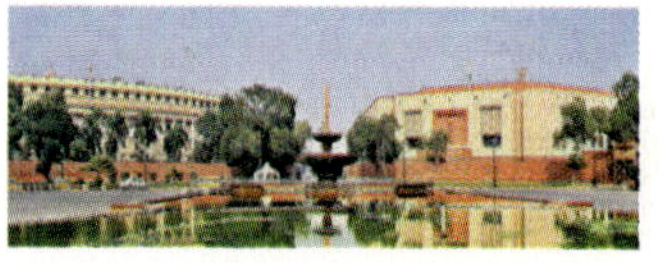

was true for the post-independence phase also. While individuals and communities aspire for freedom to practise and preserve their own culture, in the Indian context they are largely non-interfering and to an extent respectful of the identity and culture of others, till it becomes inimical to their own identity and cultural practices. This in itself is a culture that has evolved with the common and symbiotic living together of centuries. The socio-economic need for each other, tolerance of the angularity of others and to an extent respect for others, has kept the inter-community bonds intact. The centuries of living together have blunted to a certain measure, the cultural angularities of communities and the fusion of practices have led to the creation of new and common cultures. Thus, the **confluence of cultures** has been a crucial basis of communal bonds and this has also been the basis of India's unique ethos of plurality and inclusivity. The **inheritance of this culture** which we all are justifiably proud of helped to keep the nation together in a post-independent turbulent India.

But socio-cultural conflicts do arise. The bonds are then strained. The resolution to conflicts may or may not be feasible in the cultural traditions itself. At times, even the age-old bonds may prove insufficient to keep the communities bonded. The communal disharmony of pre-independence leading to the division of the country and the demand for the linguistic organisation of states post-independence were some significant examples of the divisive forces that the country experienced in the previous century. While the former could not be successfully resolved and resulted in the disastrous division of the country, the latter was relatively amicably settled post-independence with the creation of some more linguistic states. There was a vital change in the country within the few years that separated the two occurrences and this was crucial in building a new culture of India.

India had become an independent nation with a **written constitution** of its own. As a democratic republic, the law of the land became integrated with the aspirations of its people. The resolution of the conflicts and fulfilment of people's aspirations were a part of the law of the land within the **framework of the Constitution**. Thus the creation of a nation-state, with a written Constitution enshrining the philosophy of republican democracy and vital principles of governance, accompanied by the emergence of **organs and national institutions of governance**, marked a salient departure from the past and led to the advent of a **new phase of Indian culture.** This phase inherited the cultural legacy of the past but also evolved a culture based on the firm foundation of a nation, national identity and national institutions that integrated the country and people.

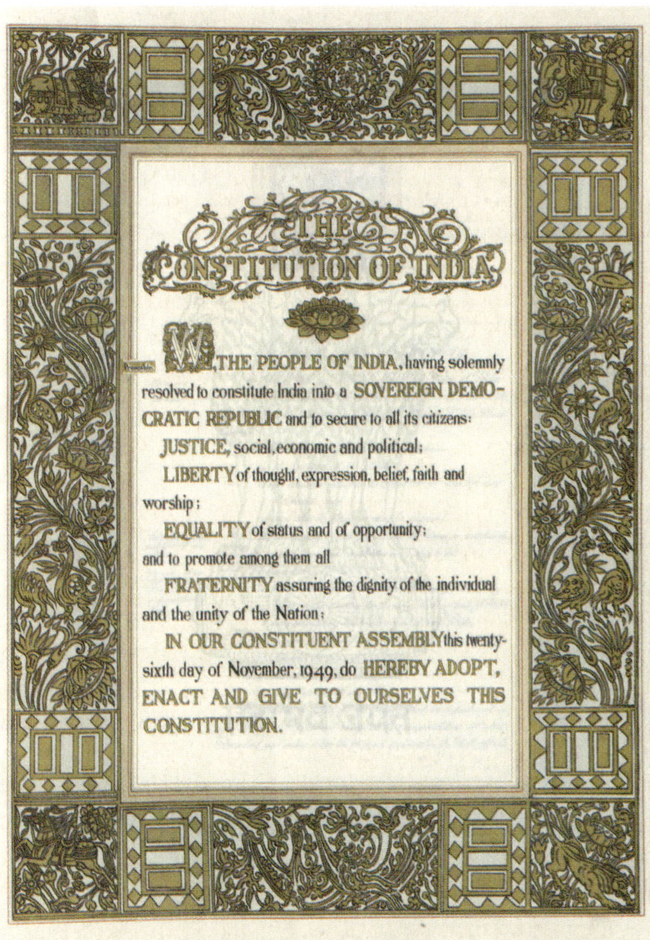

THE CONSTITUTION OF INDIA

WE, THE PEOPLE OF INDIA, having solemnly resolved to constitute India into a SOVEREIGN DEMOCRATIC REPUBLIC and to secure to all its citizens:

JUSTICE, social, economic and political;

LIBERTY of thought, expression, belief, faith and worship;

EQUALITY of status and of opportunity;

and to promote among them all

FRATERNITY assuring the dignity of the individual and the unity of the Nation;

IN OUR CONSTITUENT ASSEMBLY this twenty-sixth day of November, 1949, do HEREBY ADOPT, ENACT AND GIVE TO OURSELVES THIS CONSTITUTION.

14.20: Preamble of the Constitution symbolising a new beginning in the life of a nation — Wikipedia

The **Indian Constitution**, the **national symbols**, the **common judiciary**, the **Indian parliament**, the **organs of the executive**, the **common defence forces**, and the **various other institutions of democracy**, which all transcend the regional identities helped to create an identity of an Indian nation. The concept of **federalism** enshrined in the Constitution created the federation of states with a unitary bias. Thus, our Constitution and the institutions of governance provided an environment for preserving individual, social and national identities and even harmonising them. The aspirations of the people, the expression of the diverse regional cultural identities and the unity of the nation, all were integrated into a living and dynamic whole. Thus, the new cultural phase draws upon the **national identity** apart from the **regional culture** or the sub-national culture and the centuries-old shared **cultural heritage**.

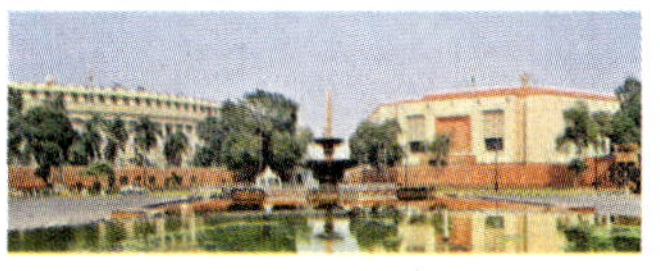

Evolution of cultural institutions as patrons of cultural elements

The independence of India ushered in the growth of several institutions that were crucial in preserving and promoting the diverse elements of Indian culture. While some cultural institutions like the **Asiatic Society** (established 1784), the **Archaeological Survey of India** (1861), the **National Archives of India** (1891), the **All India Radio** (1936) and the **Anthropological Survey of India** (1945) were established in the pre-independence period, many new institutions also came up in the 1950s and 1960s, particularly through the governmental effort and as autonomous bodies. The **Indian Council of Cultural Relations** (1950) was formed to promote Indian culture on international platforms. **Sangeet Natak Akademi** (1952), or the 'national academy of music, dance and drama' was established for the promotion of the performing arts. The **Lalit Kala Akademi** (1954) or the 'national academy of fine arts', was established to promote and propagate understanding of Indian art both within and outside the country. The **Sahitya Akademi** (1954), or India's 'national academy of letters', had the objective of promotion of the constitutionally recognized Indian languages and literature therein.

The **National Gallery of Modern Art,** established in 1954 has emerged as a premier institution of the country for the preservation and promotion of contemporary Indian art and houses more than 17000 works of nearly 2000 eminent Indian artists. **National Book Trust** (1957) was another autonomous organisation established to encourage the production of good books and literature at a low cost and for wider dissemination amongst educational institutions, libraries, students etc. The **Film and Television Institute of India** (FTII- established-1960) has come up as a leading institute of the world in the field of training personnel in the art and craft of productions in these domains. The **National School of Drama** (1959) was established by **Sangeet Natak Akademi** to promote Indian theatre and to train artists. Eventually, it became an independent school in 1975. The latter two organisations have had a significant role in the revitalization of Indian theatre, television and films.

In the subsequent decades there too came up some institutions of eminence. The **Indian Council of Historical Research** (ICHR) was established in 1972 to promote and preserve Indian history. It formulates and implements a national policy for the writing of historical research and scientific history. The **Directorate of Film Festival** was set up in 1973, as a part of the Ministry of Information and Broadcasting. It organised the national and international film festivals of India and presented the National Film Awards including the prestigious Dada Saheb Phalke Award. The **Centre for Cultural Resource & Training** (CCRT), an autonomous organisation under the Ministry of Culture was founded in 1979 for wider dissemination of Indian art and culture. It conducts training programmes for in-service teachers to enable them to get a deeper understanding of the Indian culture, besides other activities. **Indira Gandhi National Centre for Art** (IGNCA) came up in 1985 with the objective of research, conservation, display and dissemination of various art forms. In the new millennium came the **National Mission for Manuscripts** (2003) to locate, document and preserve (physical as well as digital preservation) different manuscripts and enable access to the documents.

Some cultural institutions also emerged with the efforts of social groups and non-governmental organisations. SPIC MACAY, or the *Society for the Promotion of Indian Classical Music and Culture Amongst Youth* is a non-governmental organisation and voluntary movement founded in 1977. In the last five decades, it has promoted, Indian classical music, classical dances, folk music and the tradition of yoga, besides other intangible cultural elements, among the students and younger generation. The **Indian National Trust for Art and Cultural Heritage** (**INTACH**) founded in 1984 has played a significant role in the field of preservation of cultural heritage, especially in creation of awareness and preservation and management of monuments. Besides the above, the role of the large network of national and state museums and libraries, the cultural centres of different zones of the country, international organisations like **UNESCO** and **Aga Khan Trust for Culture** and others have played a crucial role in the preservation and promotion of culture.

The above and other institutions gave a fillip to different elements of Indian culture, art and heritage. Thus, Indian culture and its elements which had been reposited, preserved and promoted primarily by the private individuals and social groups, now had the backing up of eminent institutions and professional organisations. Truly, these have rendered yeoman's service in advancing the cause of Indian culture in the post-independence phase.

Evolution of Macro Elements of Culture in Post-Independence

Different elements of culture flourished in the post-independence phase. Despite this cultural period being relatively short and of just a few decades, nurtured by the people and groups and patronised

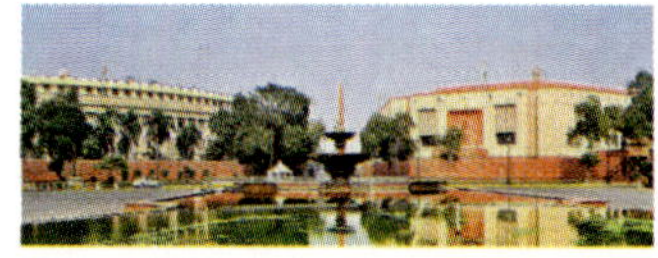

by the Government and other organisations, different elements of Indian culture have truly come of age in this period. Be it Indian literature, performing arts like Indian music and dance, visual arts like painting, sculpture and architecture, or other tangible and intangible elements of Indian culture, they all experienced a period of unprecedented growth and enrichment. They made a mark not only at the national level but even on the international stage, with many elements receiving recognition from UNESCO and other international fora. In this bouquet of cultural elements, the growth of a few is highlighted here as representative of this short but dynamic cultural phase.

Literature

Post-independence Indian literature began on a fresh note. The nationalistic and progressive literature of previous decades waned as they were no longer contextual. In the early years of independence, Indian literature was influenced by the new hope of freedom, but the pain of partition and the anguish over the communal bloodbath was also reflected in it. In the decade of the 1950s and 1960s, the works of many eminent litterateurs in different languages enriched Indian literature. These include the likes of **Amrita Pritam** (Punjabi poetry), **Khushwant Singh** (English prose), **Faiz Ahmad Faiz** (Urdu poetry), **Kartar Singh Duggal** (Punjabi, English Hindi; novels short stories), **Premendra Mitra** (Bengali poet writer), **Bhai Veer Singh** (Punjabi poet & author), **Bhisham Sahni** (Hindi novelist & playwright), **Yashpal** (Hindi novelist & playwright), **Manohar Malgonkar** (English prose) besides others. A new generation of Hindi poets came up with many inspiring works. This included several celebrated poets like **Nagarjuna**, **Ramdhari Singh Dinkar**, **Sohan Lal Dwivedi**, **Bhavani Prasad Mishra**, and **S.H. Vatsyayan Agyeya**.

New trends and new genres of literature emerged with the upcoming writers and poets, some of whom believed in the traditional Indian values while some borrowed from the Western values of rationality and modernism. This brought in an element of experimentalism in Indian literature. This was also referred to as the ***Prayogvaad*** in Hindi literature and was analogous to the worldwide modernist or avant-garde movement. S.H. Vatsyayan Agyeya was one of the pioneers of *Prayogvaad* in Hindi poetry and is said to have ushered the ***Nayi Kavita*** (new poetry) Hindi literary movement along with other poets. Another genre of poetry around this time was the ***Pragateesheel*** Hindi poetry of which the prominent patrons were **Nagarjun**, **Dinkar** and others. Both genres were prevalent in the pre-independence period and continued to flourish even in the 50s. Similarly, a ***Nayi Kahani*** movement based on *Prayogvad* was ushered with the works of **Nirmal Verma**, **Bhisham Sahni**, **Mohan Rakesh**, **Rajendra Yadav**, **Amarkant** and others.

In the period of growth of experimental literature, some litterateurs were of the view that Western materialism and ideals could not provide all the solutions to the Indian challenges. Hence, a genre of literary works emerged that questioned these principles and their relevance in the Indian context. Thus came forth a phase of Indian literature in the late 1950s and 1960s which was sharply divided between the Western ideal of materialism and Indian traditional values. This eventually led to a state of crisis of identity in Indian literature which was also referred to by some scholars as a phase of **Dark Modernism**.

Among other subgenres were works espousing the cause of marginalised and downtrodden sections. This was also referred to as the ***Dalit*** and **tribal literature**. **Mahashweta Devi** was one of the foremost Bengali authors in this genre. Yet another subgenre explored the depiction of mythology, folk legends and mythic thoughts in a modern-day context. **C. Rajagopalachari** (English prose and novels), **Vishnu S. Khandekar** (Marathi novelist) **U.R. Ananthamurthy** (Kannada novelist), **Girish Karnad** (Kannada novelist & playwright), **Badal Sircar** (Bengali playwright), **Mohan Rakesh** (Hindi novelist), **Ramakanta Rath** (Oriya novelist) and **Sitakant Mahapatra** (Oriya novelist) were some others who explored this category of literature.

Satire was another sub-genre that attained popularity amongst readers as well as literary acclaim. **Sharad Joshi** is among the most notable writers in this category. **Harishankar Parsai** (Hindi poetry, short story writer, humorist and satirist), **Kaka Haathrasi** (poet, humorist and satirist), **Ashok Chakradhar** (poet, humorist and satirist), **Shail Chaturvedi** (poet, humorist and satirist), **Pradeep Chaube** (poet, humorist and satirist) were others who attained fame in the category of satire. *Hasya Kavita* (poems of wit and humour) which was also laced with satire was another complimentary subgenre with eminent poets like Gopal Prasad Vyas, Surender Sharma, Hullar Muradabadi and others.

Post-independence **regional literature** also witnessed some stellar contributions from eminent authors and poets. These included the works of **Birendra Kumar Bhattacharya** (Assamese novelist), **Abdur Rehman** (Kashmiri poet), **Qurratulain Haider** (Urdu novelist short story writer), **Shankha Ghosh** (Bengali poet), **Satya Vrat Shastri** (Sanskrit scholar and poet), **M.T Vasudevan Nair** (Malayalam author, screenplay writer), **Ravuri Bhardwaj** (Telugu novelist), **Bhalchandra Nemade** (Marathi novelist and

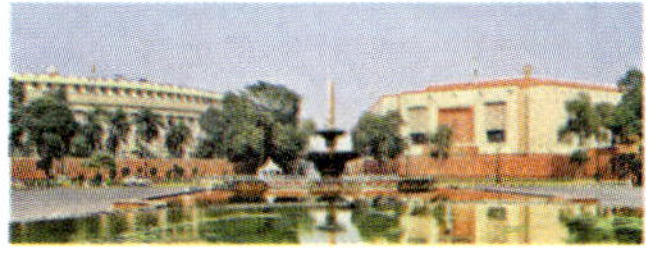

poet), **Raghuveer Chaudhari** (Gujarati novelist and poet), **Pratibha Ray** (Odia novelist), **Maimoni Raisom Goswami** (Assamese writer and poet), **Damodar Mauzo** (Konkani novelist), besides others. English literature in particular had phenomenal growth in this phase, particularly in the new millennium. It includes works of some much-celebrated authors and icons of modern English literature such as **R.K Narayan**, **Nirad C. Chaudhari**, **Mulk Raj Anand**, **Khushwant Singh**, **Ruskin Bond**, **Nissim Ezekiel**, **Nayantara Sehgal**, **Vikram Seth**, **Amitabh Ghosh**, **Arundhati Roy**, **Arvind Adiga** and others.

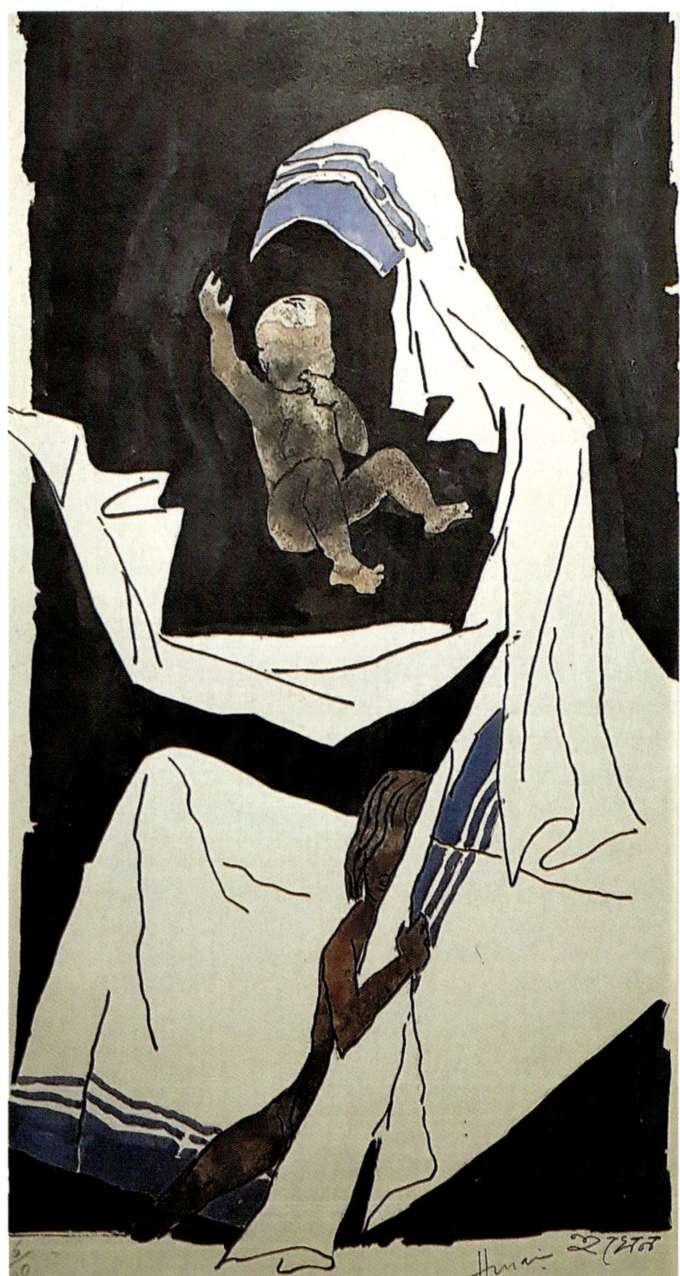

14.21: "Mother and Child", lithograph on paper, MF Hussain; National Gallery of Modern Art, New Delhi — photograph by Madhukar K Bhagat

The literature since the 80s and beyond reflects the new genre of **Post-modernism**. It is characterised by proximity to the life of a common man. Unlike the past phases, it may not bear the burden of being a harbinger of a social message or a philosophical ideology but reflects what it witnesses. The truth and reality that the writer perceives and which the reader can identify with usually form the substance of the work. Language may be bereft of the ornamentation of the past and be marked with pointedness and simplicity. This phase is also referred to as the *Uttara Adhunik* in the Hindi literature.

In the post-independence phase, Indian literature evolved and also flowed along with the world trends in literature. From the nationalism of the early 20th century, it moved to Experimentalism, Modernism and then to Post-modernism. It has explored different subgenres as well. It has changed with the times and also reflects the change in the society and Indian culture with times.

Paintings

A **'new modernism'** in **Indian paintings** emerged in the post-independence phase. The early decades post-independence assimilated the influences of the extant Indian art, the trends of the world art movements and the tastes of the changing Indian society. This ethos was typically reflected in the style and subjects in the works of the artists of the **Progressive Artists' Group of Bombay**. This group which came up post-independence in 1947, comprised many pioneering artists who were later to become celebrated names of Indian art. While it was formed with famous painters, **F.N. Souza**, **S.H. Raza**, **M.F. Hussain**, **K.H. Ara**, **H.A. Gade**, and **S.K. Bakre** (a sculptor) as its founders, later, other eminent painters and artists such as **Tyeb Mehta**, **Gaitonde**, **Manishi Dey**, and **Akbar Padamsee** joined it. Though eventually disbanded in 1956, even in this short period, it made a significant mark on Indian art.

The work of these artists had a distinctness of their own in both subject and style. Souza's paintings, particularly the nudes of women, had exaggerated proportions, as if wanting to break from the conventions of beauty of the extant artistic traditions. The works of Hussain endeavoured to explore modernism in the Indian context. It mixed the brush strokes and certain elements of cubism of the West with the

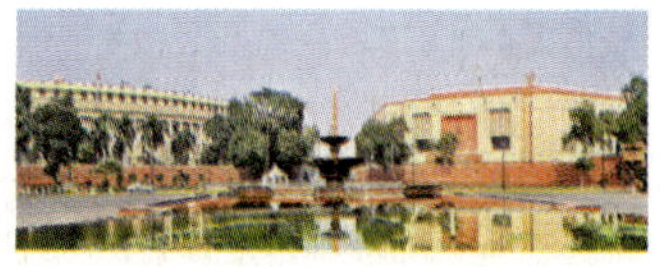

bright colours of the Indian art tradition. Raza who began with landscapes, moved towards abstraction while incorporating the use of *mandala* and *yantra* in his art. His later paintings incorporated a *bindu* (a point) representing the spiritual unity of Indian philosophy. **Gaitonde** was another artist pursuing abstraction through the representation of translucent beams of light. Many other artists of this period like **Tyeb Mehta**, **Akbar Padamsee**, **K.K. Hebbar** and others worked between abstraction and figurativeness. Thus, these painters broke away from the revivalist nationalism of the Bengal Art movement and set the path for **modern** and **abstract art** which synthesised Indian art tradition with 'European Modernism'. In the later years, many new artists have also come up with different genres such as new figurative art, new media art, digital art etc., while the older art forms of abstraction, folk art, washes, oil and easel art continued to be practiced.

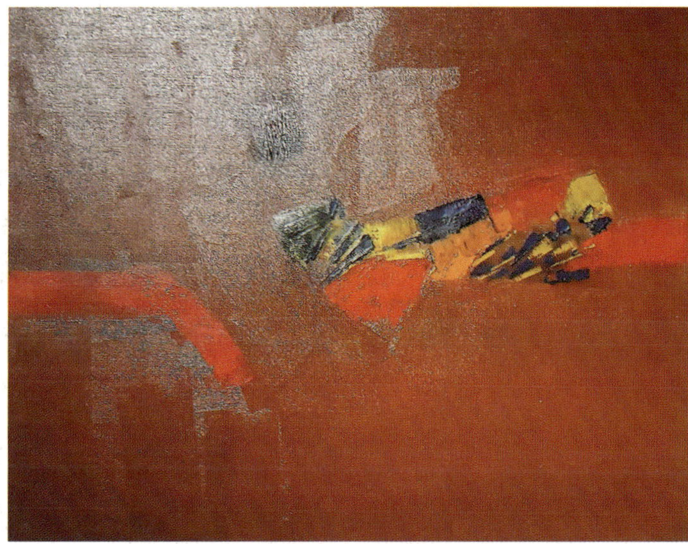

14.22: Composition in red, Vasudeo Gaitonde; an abstract art; National Gallery of Modern Art, New Delhi — photograph by Madhukar K Bhagat

Music and Dance

Music in modern India evolved and grew exceptionally in the post-independence chapter. The institutions set up to promote Indian music, means of public transmission like radio and television, the vibrant and successful film industry, the works of a generation of musical stalwarts and most importantly the demand for diverse genres of music by the Indian public, took Indian music to new heights The traditional classical musical forms of Hindustani Classical and Carnatic music attained greater acceptance and popularity within the country as well as abroad. Musical maestros like; **Bismillah Khan** (Bharat Ratna), **Ravi Shankar** (Bharat Ratna), **Allah Rakha**, **Ali Akbar Khan**, **V.G. Jog**, **Vilayat Khan**, **Lal Gudi Jayaraman**, **Hari Prasad Chaurasia**, **Shiv Kumar Sharma**, **Amjad Ali Khan**, **L. Subramaniam** and **Zakir Hussain**, redefined Indian music bringing international recognition and acclaim. Classical vocalists like **M.S. Subbalakshmi** (Bharat Ratna), **D.K. Pattamal**, **Bhimsen Joshi** (Bharat Ratna), **Kumar Gandharva**, **Pandit Jasaraj**, **M.L. Vasanthakumari**, **Balamurali Krishna**, **Dagar Brothers**, **Bhupen Hazarika** (Bharat Ratna) amidst others inspired generations of singers in modern India.

New musical forms came up in a big way. **Indian film music**, a potpourri of different musical genres was indeed the most popular and visible form of musical expression in the country. It transcended the boundaries of the various regions and cut across the barriers of language and regional culture to garner popularity not only within the country but even a considerable international following. *Thumri*, *ghazals*, *bhajans*, *qawwali*, disco, rock music, pop music, Indipop, *sufi*, folk and others found expression in Indian film music and prospered over decades. An industry of singers, musicians, song lyric writers, and others flourished in tandem with the film industry, making this musical expression, widespread, deep-rooted and also commercially institutionalised. While light music as characterised by film music has been like a pillar of Indian music, other forms like folk music, devotional music, remixes, private albums, musical bands and troupes have also flourished.

The renditions of playback singers like **Lata Mangeshkar**, **Asha Bhonsle**, **Mukesh**, **Geeta Dutt**, **Mohammed Rafi**, **Manna Dey**, and **Kishore Kumar** have transcended the regional divide and cultural diversity to bring the melody of Indian music to millions of parched souls. In the later decades, a new generation of eminent singers such as **S.P. Balasubramanyam**, **Yesudas**, **K.S. Chitra**, **Kumar Sanu**, **Alka Yagnik**, **Anuradha Paudwal**, **Udit Narayan**, **Sonu Nigam**, **Shankar Mahadevan**, **Sunidhi Chavan**, and others enthralled the audience. **Arijit Singh**, **Shaan** and **Shreya Ghoshal** represent the millennial generation of successful singers who have held aloft the banner of playback singing and Indian music.

In the last seven decades, a bevy of film music composers have imparted melody to Indian music. **Naushad Ali**, **S.D. Burman**, **Madan Mohan**, **Shankar-Jaikishan** (duo), **O.P. Nayyar**, **Salil Chowdhury**,

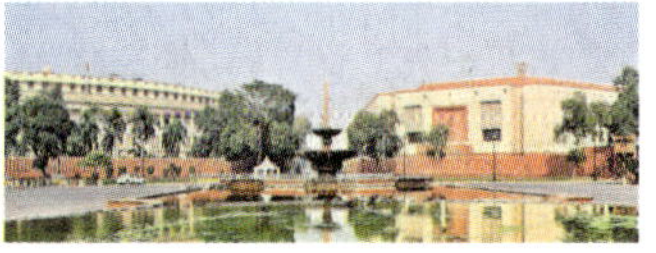

Hemant Kumar, **Khayyam**, **Laxmikant-Pyarelal** (duo), **Kalyanji-Anandji** (duo) and **Roshan,** were some among the renowned music directors of the 50s and 60s. The eminent music directors of later decades included **R. D. Burman**, **Rajesh Roshan**, **Bappi Lahiri**, **Anu Malik**, **Anand-Milind**, **Nadeem Shravan**, **Jatin Lalit**, **Shankar-Ehsan- Loy**, **Illayaraja**, **A.R. Rahman**, amongst others.

The film music has also changed with the times. The decades of the 1950s and 1960s to the early 70s have been referred to by critics as the **golden phase** of film music. The classical base had a strong influence on it, with the melody being the soul of music. Bollywood in the late 70s and 80s saw a transition in the music genre. Melody of earlier years gave way to the fast-paced music and the disco beats of the 80s in the film world. The economic liberalisation of the 90s and global interconnect again brought a transition. Pop and other forms of Western music gained increasing popularity. In the new millennium, the genre of soulful *Sufi* music and *ghazals* made a comeback. The trend of Indian rock and pop was also on the rise. Thus, film music and its genres have been quite dynamic. It has mirrored the changes in society, the trends in the world and consequential changes in the tastes of the people.

Classical dances too have grown in this phase. They came out of the temples and houses of the courtesans where many of these remained centred for centuries, to the public arena and even national stages. The institutional support, particularly of the Sangeet Natak Akademi in this phase, helped not only revive the dances but also helped it acquire international acclaim. Traditional dances associated with festivals and folk dances also prospered. Some of these such as **Chhau**, **Kalbelia**, **Muddiyettu** and **Garba** dance forms acquired the status of intangible cultural heritage of the world under the aegis of UNESCO. Several dance and music festivals have come up in different parts of the country that showcase the depth and diversity of this art form to national as well as international audiences.

Cinema

Indian cinema which had its genesis in the early 20th century, emerged in the next 50 years as a succinct reflection of Indian society and its changing culture. By post-independence, it had also become a platform that integrated different tangible and intangible cultural elements including, theatrical performance, acting, music, dance, script and songwriting, besides other arts and crafts. It emerged not only as a medium of entertainment and a seller of dreams that provided succour to a population struggling with the challenges of their daily lives but also as a powerful means of social communication and portrayer of social realism and idealism. Cinema transcended regional boundaries and thus became a medium to showcase, reposit and integrate the diverse Indian culture. Gradually, cinema in itself became a significant cultural element of society.

In post-independence, Indian cinema evolved to include diverse genres ranging from popular entertainment to parallel cinema and from regional movies to award-winning international movies. While some early movies like *Awaara* (1951), *Shree 420* (1955); *Pyaasa* (1957), *Chaudavi Ka Chaand* (1960), *Parineeta* (1953), *Devdas* (1955) got commercial success, movies like *Do Aankhen Barah Haath* (1957), *Naya Daur* (1957) and *Mother India* (1957), besides being popular, also won critical acclaim. In the first few decades after independence, the growth of '**parallel cinema**' ushered some greatest works ever of Indian cinema by maestro movie makers like; **V. Shantaram**, **Satyajit Ray**, **Ritwik Ghatak**, **Tapan Sinha**, **Mrinal Sen**, **Shyam Benegal** and **Adoor Gopalakrishnan**. In the coming decades, the works of **M.S. Sathyu**, **P. Lankesh**, **Grish Karnard**, **Govind Nihlani**, **Aparna Sen**, **Shyam Benegal** and **Saeed Akhtar Mirza** carried forward the tradition. This category of cinema, inspired by cinematographic realism and naturalism, pushed the boundaries of art in an otherwise commercial domain and brought international fame and recognition to Indian movies.

The mainstream Indian movies have also changed over the decades. The romantic musical genre of the 60s gave way to the dark and violent crime thrillers of the 70s. While Dilip Kumar came to personify tragedy in the 50s and 60s, stars like Dev Anand, Rajesh Khanna and others became the quintessential face of romance in the 60s and early 70s. Exemplified by Amitabh Bachchan, an angry young man, a generation of movies came up in the 70s and 80s. While romance, comedy, drama and thrillers continued to find cinematographic space, *masala* movies which combined these diverse flavours, were perhaps an invention of the 70s and continued to rule the roost even in the later decades.

The decade of the 80s witnessed the emergence of India as the largest film production centre and earning its major centre, Bombay (now Mumbai) the epithet of 'Bollywood'. The production of art movies continued in this decade also, although the genres of action, romance and *masala* continued to dominate the industry. In the sweeping wave of disco gripping the country in the 80s, a poignant but short-lived sub-genre of movies was those with disco-based themes and songs. Some of these were not only

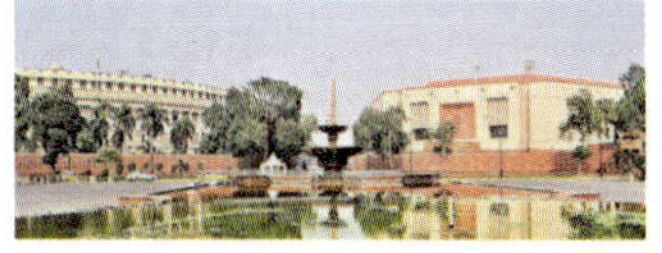

commercially successful within the country but also enjoyed international popularity. But the decade is also remembered for its stereotyped movies which were indeed a dampener to the growing culture of movies. Adding to the woes of the industry in this period, was the rise in home video viewership, video piracy and a relentless decline in theatre footfall; a trend which continued in the early 90s, even affecting the quality of movies produced.

With the economic liberalisation in the 90s and the arrival of satellite TV, there was a greater interconnect of the Indians with the world and with movies from around the world. New genres of movies were in demand by the new generation, but this was rather conspicuous by its absence in production. Even the art cinema of the early decades had dried up by this time. However, romantic musicals and action movies which were the staple productions, continued to churn commercial successes. A noticeable change in the movies of this decade was the transition of the backdrop of the movies to urban settings, urban characters and at times even to international locales. The rural landscape was rarely seen any more, nor was portrayed the themes of economic struggles and social challenges of the 50s, 60s and 70s. The villains who personified the antagonist, a poignant aspect of the Indian movies, were no more the wily *sahukars* of the villages (village money lenders), the marauding dacoits of Chambal ravines, or even the dangerous smugglers operating in the dark alleys of the cities. They had transitioned from the specific classes and categories to generic characters and even to anti-heroes. This was also a reflection of the changing character of the society, the demographic profile of the country and the culture of the people.

In the new millennium, Indian movies moved from strength to strength, be it in terms of the volume of production, the quality of movies, or the genre of themes. A salient feature of Indian cinema in this period was its burgeoning international appeal. With their commercial distribution reaching as many as 90 countries, and the popularity of Indian films and stars soaring in the foreign markets, Indian movies had their best international presence. The large Indian diaspora abroad also fuelled the international demand.

The most significant feature of the new millennium is indeed the rise of the regional film industry. This is best exemplified by the movies of South India which have recorded phenomenal success. Another noticeable feature is the merger of genres of social realism and commercial cinema which no longer stand as separate productions. New-age cinema tends to integrate both art and commerce rather than produce exclusive art movies. With the changing technology and coming of the digital age, Indian movies have not been left untouched. Modern technology and the change it has ushered in society, are redefining the movie culture of the country and its various dimensions.

Folk Culture in Post-independence

Folk culture is another salient element that has come into prominence in the post-independence period. Art and crafts of the common folks, their rituals, fairs and festivals, folk theatre, folk music and dance are among the numerous elements that the large canvas of folk culture encapsulates. These draw from and reflect the aspects of the daily lives of the common people, communities and tribes. Thus, they are true manifestations of culture at the very grassroots of a society.

Folk music and dance are ancient traditions of this grassroots culture of India. These arts have flourished in the hinterland, in the villages, in the tribes and in diverse communities. As traditional music and dance forms, it is infused into the very micro-culture of the population and is also integrated with the daily lives of people. Besides being a form of entertainment, a means to overcome the routine and drudgery of daily work, it is also an expression of joys and sorrows of people which are practised on the occasions of childbirth, betrothal, marriage or other events of life. Fairs, festivals religious ceremonies, agricultural activities, harvests etc. are some other occasions of their expression. While communities and their cultural practices have been the traditional repository of these art forms, in the post-independence period, government institutions, non-governmental organisations and other private initiatives have helped to provide a platform, for these art forms and also aided in their propagation and preservation for future generations.

Emblematic of the regional and local culture, each state and region of India has a bewildering variety of such folk music and dance traditions. Among the **folk music** forms that enjoy wide popularity include; *Chakri* of Jammu and Kashmir, *Tappa* of Punjab, *Laman* of Himachal Pradesh, *Alah* of Haryana, *Barahmansa* of Kumaon, *Basanti* of Garhwal, *Pankhida* of Rajasthan, *Rasiyageet* of Uttar Pradesh. Amongst the states of Eastern India, some popular folk music forms include, *Sohar* of Bihar, *Jhumair* of Jharkhand, *Baul* of West Bengal, *Bihu* of Assam, *Lai Haroba* in Manipur, *Saikut Zai* in Mizoram, *Tamang Selo* of Sikkim, *Daskathia* of Odisha. In central and western India, some popular forms of folk music include; *Pandavani*

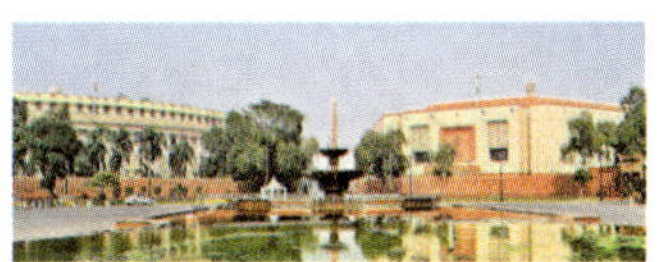

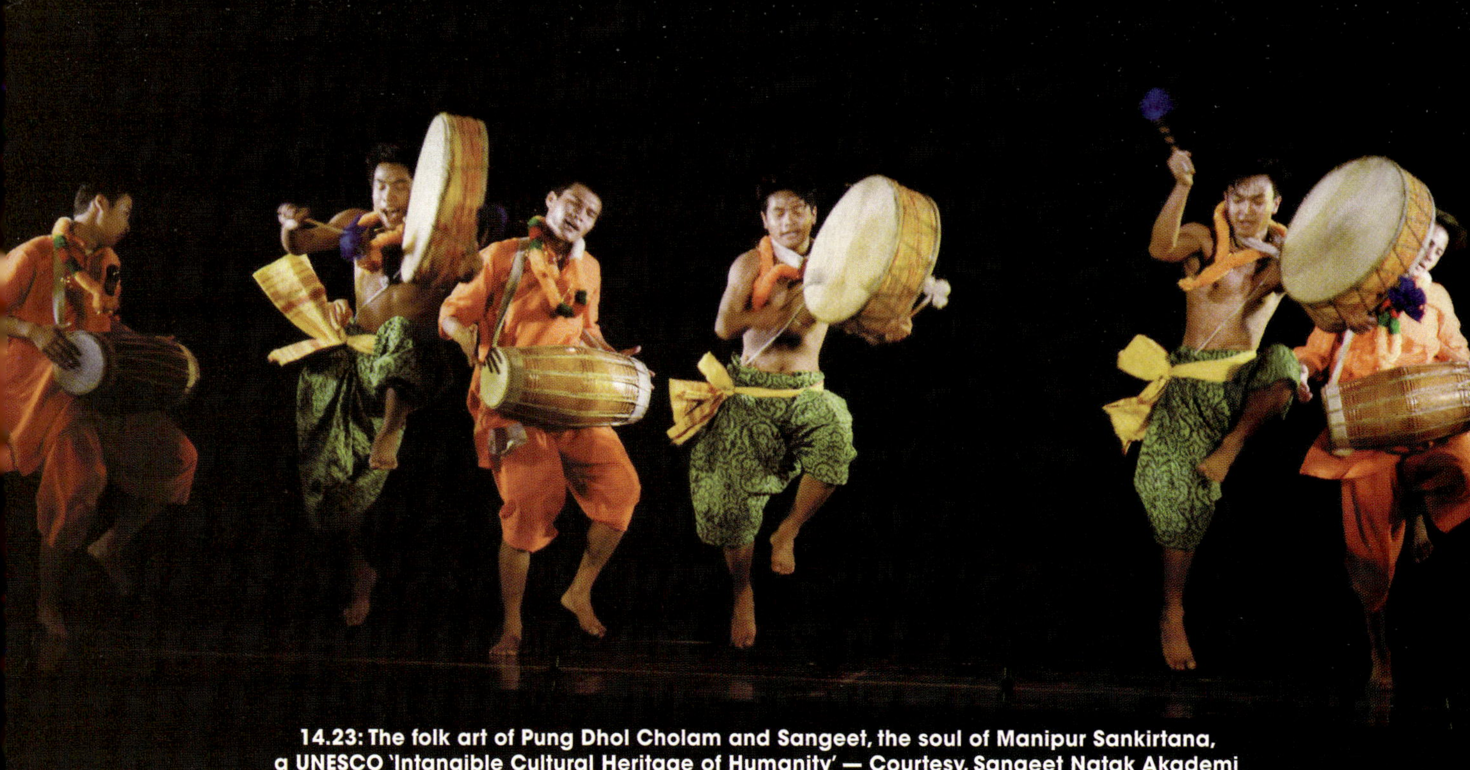

14.23: The folk art of Pung Dhol Cholam and Sangeet, the soul of Manipur Sankirtana, a UNESCO 'Intangible Cultural Heritage of Humanity' — Courtesy, Sangeet Natak Akademi

of Chattisgarh, *Alha* of Madhya Pradesh, *Powada* of Maharashtra, *Sugam Sangeet* of Gujarat and *Mando* of Goa. In the South the popular folk music forms are; *Burrakatha* in Andhra Pradesh and Telangana, *Janpad Geethe* in Karnataka, *Villu Pattu* in Tamil Nadu and the *Sopana Sangeetham* in Kerala, among some others. ***Sankirtana***, the ritualistic singing, drumming and dancing of the Vaishnava people of Manipur is also recognized by UNESCO as an 'Intangible Cultural Heritage of Humanity', thus exemplifying the richness of this folk art.

Folk and tribal dances too have an amazing diversity and spread. Each is associated with different occasions, has a different purpose and even expresses different moods. *Rouf* of Jammu and Kashmir, *Nati* of Himachal, and *Choliya* dance of Uttarakhand are symbolic of the diverse dances and unique culture of the hills. *Bhangra* and *Gidda* of Punjab, and *Ghoomar* of Rajasthan are dances of energy and liveliness. *Raas Leela* popular in Haryana and Rajasthan is inspired by the legends of Lord Krishna and the love of the *gopikas* for him. *Garba* and *Dandiya* of Gujarat are associated with the religious festival of *Navaratra* and the worship of Goddess Durga. *Jawara* of Budelkhand region of Madhya Pradesh is associated with agricultural harvest. *Raut Nacha* and *Gaur Maria* of Chattisgarh are some of the popular tribal dances and so are *Chaau* and *Paika* of Jharkhand. *Purulia Chhau* of West Bengal is known for its vivid masks depicting various deities. *Kajari* of Bihar is a dance celebrating the arrival of the rains.

The colourful *Bihu* dance of Assam is associated with the Bihu festival and agricultural harvest. *Thang-Ta* of Manipur is a traditional martial arts form of dance, while *Hozagiri* of Reang tribes of Tripura is a dance of great skill and balance performed while standing on earthen pitchers and balancing a bottle on their head with a lit earthen lamp on it. *Goti Pua* is a unique dance tradition of Odisha that is performed by young boys who dress up as girls. *Lavani* of Maharastra, performed by women, is a dance of beauty and sensuousness. *Dekhani* of Goa is another folk dance performed by women and is associated with beauty. *Burrakatha* of Andhra Pradesh and Telangana region is a form of ballad dance and singing. *Kunitha* folk dances of Karnataka which include the popular *Dollu Kunitha* is a class of ritualistic folk dances. *Mayilattam*, popular in Tamil Nadu, is a dance of women who are dressed as a peacock. *Theyyam* is a popular ritual form of dance and worship in Kerala.

Thus, folk dances, very much like folk music, are associated with different occasions which are connected with the life, of the people, social events, festivals and other occasions. Both forms of art and the culture associated with it were nurtured for ages by the communities and their social practices. With migration displacing the people from their sociocultural roots, and the modern lifestyle leaving less time for these performing arts, both have experienced a weakening of their cultural roots. Institutional support from Lalit Kala Akademi and other organisations has helped these art forms to get a platform as well as due recognition. However, their practice and preservation will eventually depend on the survival of the communities in their traditional environment and eco-system and the interconnection of the migrated communities with their traditional culture.

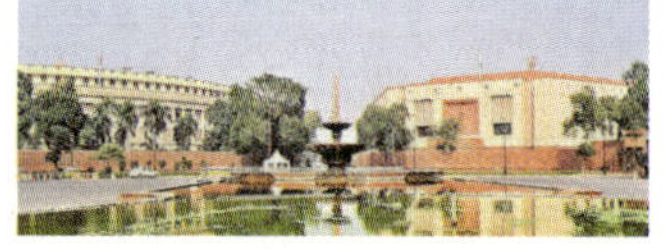

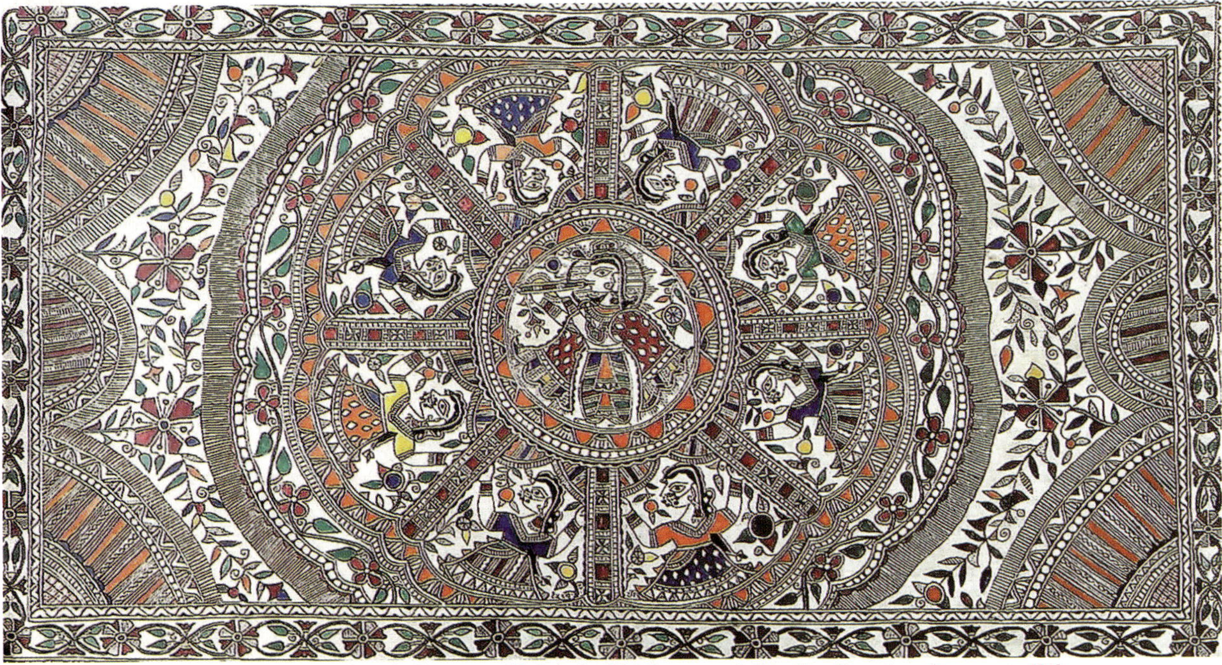

14.24: Madhubani painting on silk fabric, 'Krishna and Gopika Raas', unknown artist, private collection — photograph by Madhukar K Bhagat

Folk paintings, a part of the diverse folk culture of India, have seen increasing popularity in the post-independence period. **Madhubani paintings** (Bihar), **Pattachitra** (West Bengal & Odisha), **Kalighat paintings** (Kolkata-West Bengal), **Pichwai paintings** (Rajasthan), **Phad paintings** (Rajasthan), and **Kalam Kari** (Andhra Pradesh) are some examples of the many folk paintings practised today. Tribal art is another wide domain of folk art that has grown and now enjoys increasing social visibility. **Warli paintings** (Maharashtra), **Gond paintings** (Madhya Pradesh), the **Santhal paintings** (West Bengal; Jharkhand) the **Bhil paintings** and the **Paitkar paintings** are some prominent examples of tribal art.

These paintings are based on the local culture and tradition and include diverse subjects. These may include; scenes from community life as in Warli paintings, or scenes of Ramayana, Mahabharata, and Indian mythology as in the Madhubani, Pattachitra, and Pichwai paintings. While day-to-day happenings of rural life are captured in the Kalighat paintings, Paitkar paintings often depict the rituals and ceremonies of the community. The canvas of these paintings is the walls, the floor of the house, paper, scrolls, and even fabric. Events like birth, marriage ceremonies, festivals, rituals, etc. are often the

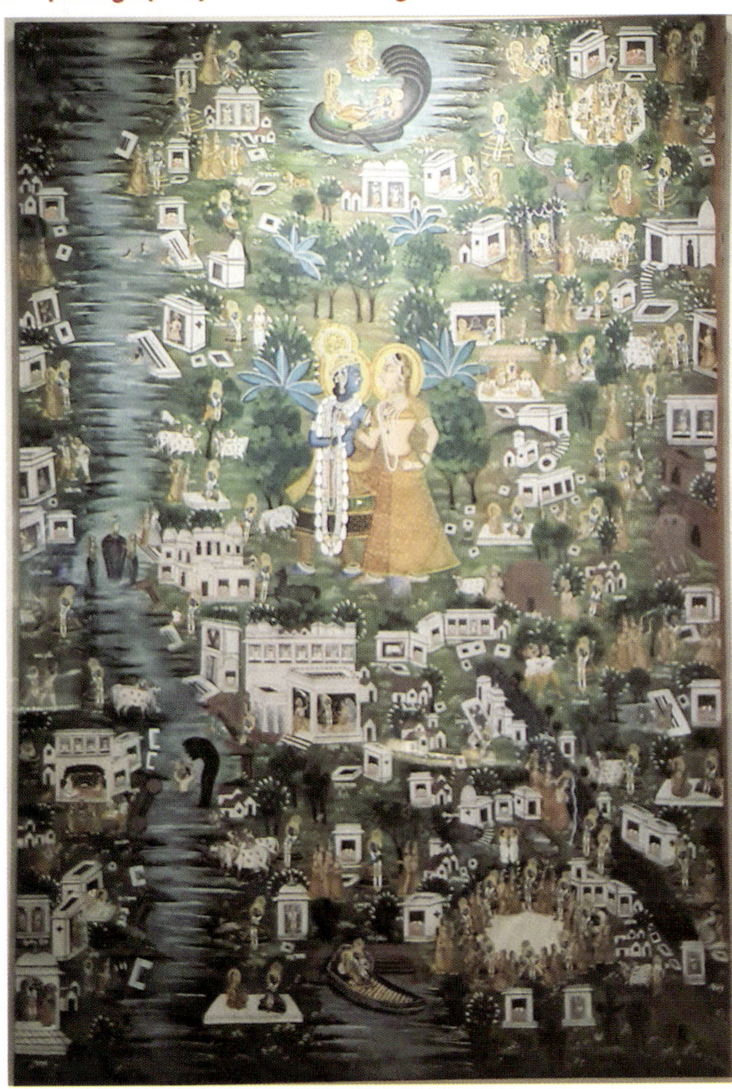

14.25: A Pichwai painting of Nathdwara representing Vraja Yatra, painting on cloth, late 20th century; location Chhatrapati Shivaji Maharaj Vastu Sangrahalaya, Mumbai — photograph by Madhukar K Bhagat

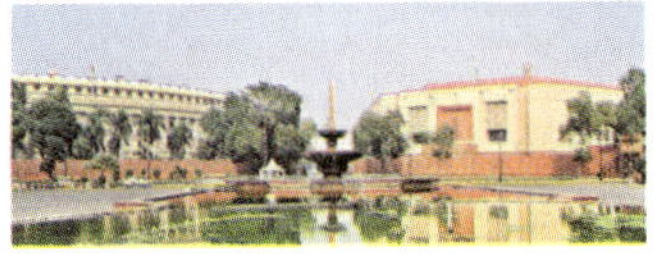

occasions for such art. A unique aspect of these paintings is the use of natural and earthy colours that are available locally. This integrates them with the local environment and also reflects the indigenous ethos and culture. Like other folk arts, they remain reposited in the folk knowledge and often have a tradition of several centuries. They too face the headwinds of change in societies experiencing the transition to modern lifestyle.

Folk theatre is another salient element of our grassroots culture and a centuries-old enduring and living tradition. It is a fusion of different elements of performing arts including dances, singing and music, besides literary arts like poetry/writing of verses. Arts of pantomime and ballad recitation are some of its other elements. Numerous traditional crafts like puppetry, costume making and others are also integrated with folk theatre. The uniqueness of folk theatre lies in its expression of the creativity and spontaneity of the common people who are not bound by the rules of classical theatre. Some prominent forms of folk theatre which have survived to modern times include **Ramlila**, **Krishna Lila**, **Nautanki**, **Jatra**, **Tamasha**, **Bhavai**, **Yakshagana**, **Bhand Pather** and **Swang**. These theatre arts are practised in different regions of the country. In the post-independence period, besides performing traditional epic tales, local legends and ballads, the folk theatre also diversified into communicating social messages and became a means of popular entertainment. However, in recent times and the 21st century in particular, folk theatres are on the decline. The arrival of modern theatre, the dominance of Indian cinema later as a means of entertainment, and the recent spurt in the electronic and digital means of entertainment have limited the presence of this once-popular form of grassroots theatre. However, with some institutional and governmental support, there is hope for the preservation of these art forms.

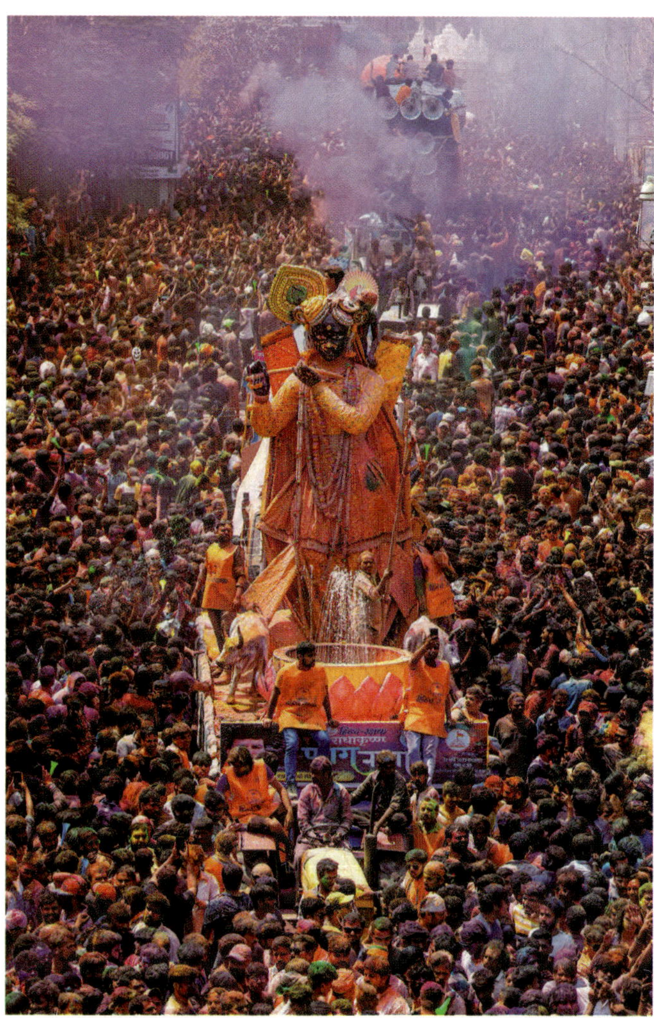

14.26: Festivals are an ancient, ubiquitous and salient cultural tradition of India. A large idol of Sri Krishna and the crowd of revellers, celebration of Rangpanchami at Indore — Courtesy, Madhya Pradesh Tourism Board

Besides the above, several other elements of Indian culture have witnessed considerable change and evolution. **Indian theatre** has moved from strength to strength. Although cinema became stronger and other digital means of entertainment appeared from time to time, theatre has held on its own and carved a social niche. **Indian architecture** has endeavoured to come out of the colonial hangover and find an Indian identity rooted in its culture and ethos. The changing tastes, technology, modern demands and environmental considerations have played an important role in shaping modern Indian architecture. **Arts and crafts** of India have made their presence felt at the global scale, especially Indian fabric. GI-tagged crafts of today represent a confluence of the local culture, social practices and the associated commerce. **Fairs and festivals**, be it religious, social, agricultural or of any other genre, have always been a crucial element of Indian culture and occupy a position of pride in modern-day Indian culture. **Food** and **dress** are among other elements of micro-culture which have uniqueness of their own and also witnessed considerable change. Each region and state has a vibrant diversity of food and dress in a way symbolic of the pluralism of Indian culture itself.

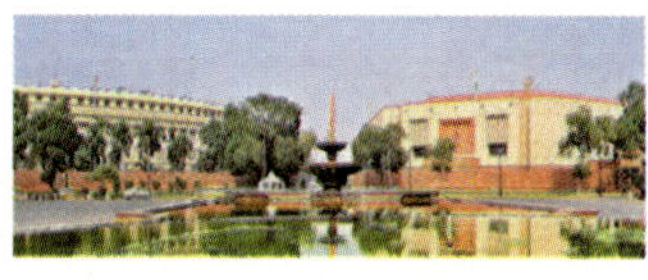

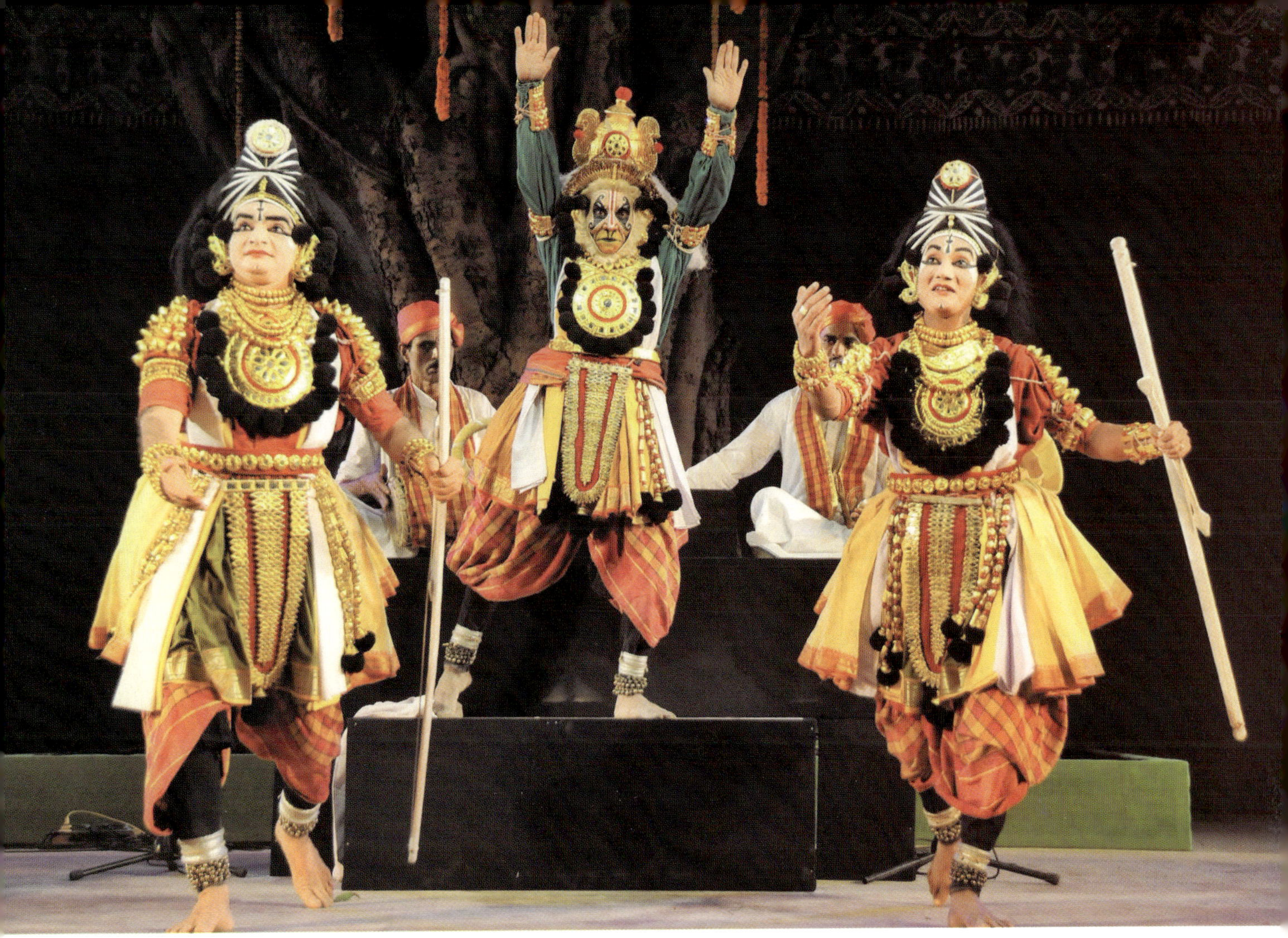

14.27: A Yakshagana performance with elaborate makeup headgear and costumes; a folk theatre of Karnataka — Courtesy, Sangeet Natak Akademi

DRIVERS OF CHANGE IN INDIAN CULTURE IN THE NEW MILLENNIUM

With the various macro and micro elements changing over time, the broad contours of the culture itself change. This is evident in the Indian context, especially in the last 25 years of the new millennium. The change in the economic policy of the 90s and the global interconnect, ushered in a period of economic growth, bringing a change in consumption and material aspirations of the Indians. The economic and other opportunities generated by the metropolitan cities attracted an increasing population to them and other urban centres. They spawned a new social culture that was more cosmopolitan breaking the social and caste rigidities of the erstwhile traditional rural society. But at the same time, it also uprooted a population from its cultural ecosystem.

New cultural trends emerged. Elements of material culture prospered. Greater emphasis on material gains also changed cultural tastes and perceptions as to the appropriate elements of culture. Tangible elements of culture grew. Changes in elements like food and clothing took place, which was as much influenced by the growing urbanisation, and also inspired by the global culture and materialism. Many other macro elements like art and literature followed similar trends. Platforms like entertainment which integrate the diverse elements of culture reflected this change and at times ushered new trends. The cultural elements of India were also significantly influenced by the changing population profile and social demography. With a younger population (median age of 28.7 in 2022) emerging in the new millennium, cultural tastes have changed and so has the demand, particularly for popular culture. Fast-paced music, action genre of cinema, fast food, emerging fashion, digital entertainment, culture of sports and other lifestyle trends are reflective of this influence.

Perhaps the most significant driver of cultural change in this phase has been technology which has also profoundly influenced other aspects of modern society and human civilisation. Like the industrial age, the digital age in the new millennium has caused socio-cultural upheavals and changed the very face of

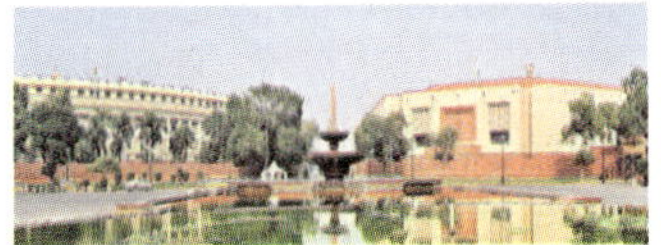

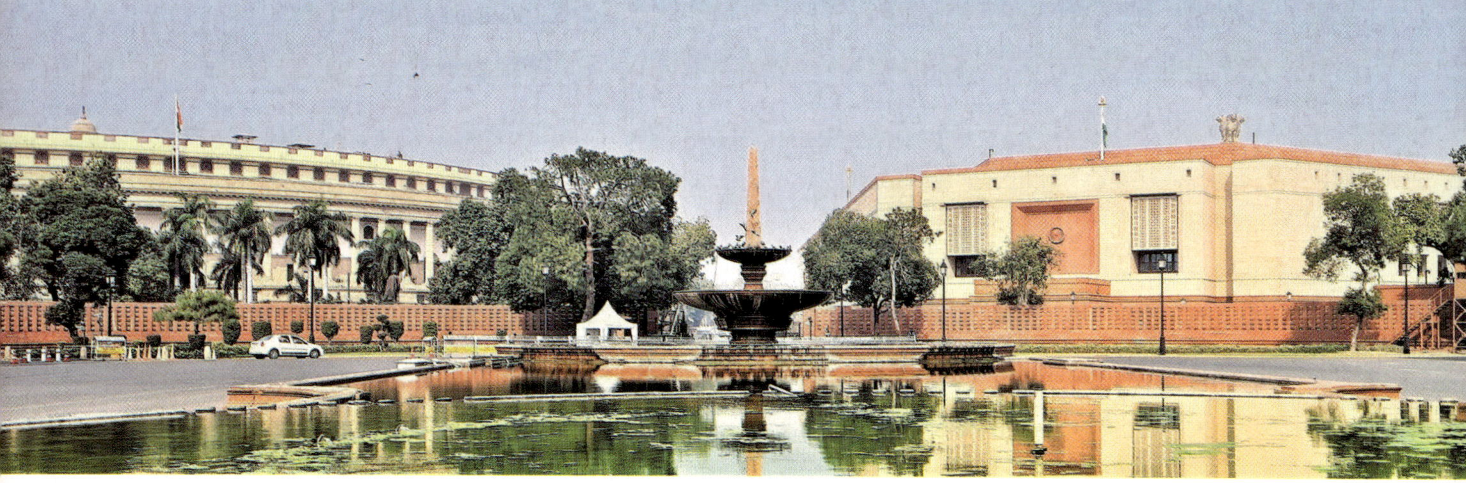

14.28: A view of the erstwhile and the new parliament from the Vijay Chowk, coexisting side by side, the past and the present and the promise of a new future — photograph by Madhukar K Bhagat

society. India and its society have been abreast of this change and have embraced the numerous facets of digital technology in full measure. E-commerce, e-education, online entertainment, 'work from home', digital social media, crypto currencies, net meetings, 'over the top entertainment', and 'home delivery industry', among others, are some recent products of digital technology. These are changing the society and social discourse. These are also influencing certain subtle aspects of human society and influencing culture itself. In the coming decades, with emerging technologies such as artificial intelligence and others ruling the roost, how much they influence creative arts, literature, entertainment, and other aspects of human society and culture is yet to be seen. However, change they certainly will bring.

The changing environment is yet another factor of the socio-cultural change. India with its vast and diverse geography and sensitive ecology is particularly vulnerable to it. As global and local weather patterns change, it is eventually affecting the human habitat and society. Agriculture, commerce, industry and other aspects of human civilisation are beginning to be impacted and culture will not be able to remain aloof. Large cities have become vulnerable to urban flooding while unstable hills are now unable to cope with human pressure and changing environment. Rising sea levels are a threat to the coastal habitations. To adapt to and mitigate the adverse effects of the changing environment, traditional settlements and lifestyles are also beginning to change. These are likely to see disruptive changes in future, particularly in India. Will some of these cities meet the same fate as those of the ancient cities like Dholaveera of the Indus Valley civilisation? Those cities flourished for hundreds of years but perished due to the changing environment leading to the loss of their civilisation and culture. Or whether we have learnt from our history and past culture? Time will only tell.

Energy technology and fossil fuels have brought human civilisation into a sharp clash with the biotic and abiotic world, to the peril of all. However, technology also has the wherewithal to pull the world out of this quagmire. Whether and how much of the salvaging would eventually be done, would depend, as much on the culture we adopt as on the technology we develop and adopt. Whether materialism would remain the mainstay of human civilisation; whether universalism would prevail over utilitarianism; and whether the political systems can harmonise the elements of democracy (read people), ecology and technology; all would cast crucial influence on the world of tomorrow. India and India's culture would surely be affected by it as well. In a way, it is India's culture with its abiding emphasis on universalism and inclusiveness (*sarve bhavantu sukhinah* – may all be happy) and ancient heritage of living in harmony with nature as reflected in the wider philosophy of *ahimsa*, which offers hope and shows the way forward to this world in peril.

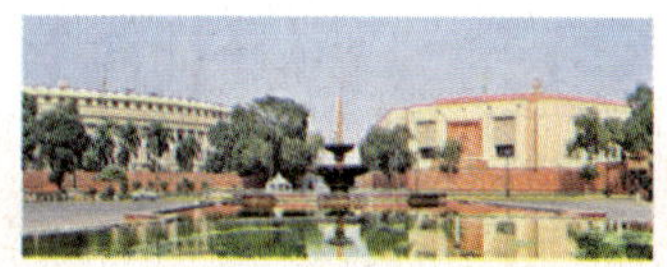

15

Socio-Religious Reforms and Reformers in Modern India

Arise, awake and stop not till the goal is reached.

— Swami Vivekananda

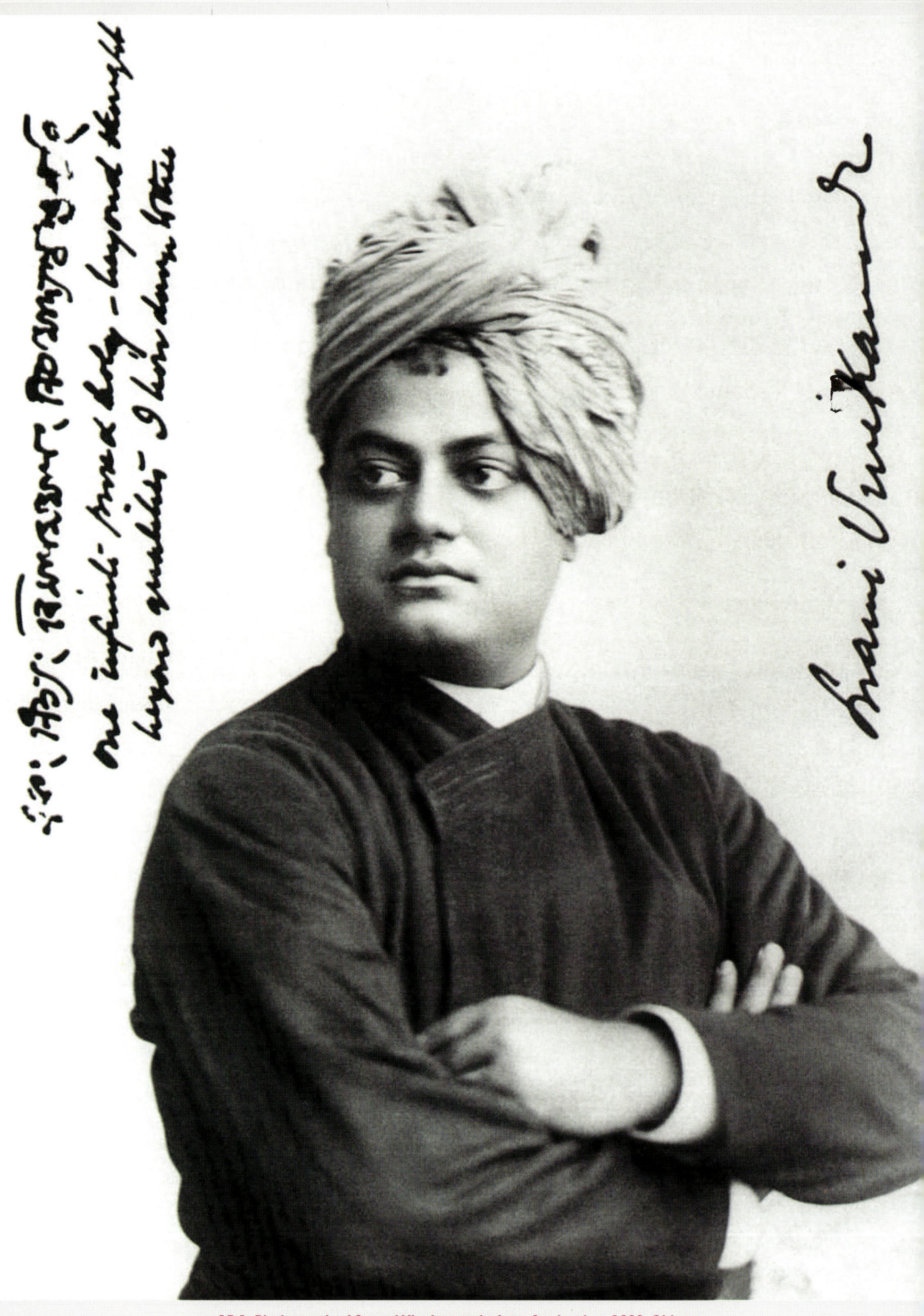

15.1: Photograph of Swami Vivekananda from September, 1893, Chicago; on the left a note by Vivekananda in his handwriting: "One infinite pure and holy - beyond thought beyond qualities, I bow down to thee." — Wikimedia Commons

SOCIO-RELIGIOUS MOVEMENTS AND THEIR OBJECTIVES

The 19th century saw the emergence of a number of socio-religious reform movements which had a transforming effect on the socio-cultural life of the people. The **Brahmo Samaj** spearheaded by Raja Ram Mohan Roy, the **Young Bengal Movement**, **Arya Samaj, Prarthana Samaj, Theosophical Society** and **Ramakrishna Mission** were amongst the most prominent of them. These reforms in the socio-religious and spiritual realm ushered a change in Hindu society. At times, this entire movement is even referred to as the **Modern Hindu Renaissance.**

This was also a period of **Bengal Renaissance**, a socio-cultural and artistic movement which permeated the region in the early 19th to the early 20th centuries. It inspired similar movements in different parts of the country, and over a period of time, it imbued the Indian society, particularly the religion, culture and social thought, with liberalism and modernity. In the course of the anti-colonial sentiments simmering in the land, it also aided in the emergence of nationalistic fervor.

Among many of the reforms these movements ushered was the **education for women**, support for **widow remarriages**, and **emancipation of the downtrodden**. Besides, they opposed the **caste system, Brahmanical orthodoxy, untouchability** and evil practices like *sati* and **child marriages.** Some of these also emphasised on the **Vedantic philosophy** and **spiritual regeneration** of the Hindu society. Thus, these movements were both reformative and revivalistic.

However, these reforms were not limited to Hinduism alone, but this phase of cultural regeneration also witnessed **Islamic movements** such as the **Aligarh Movement**, the **Ahmadiya Movement**, the **Deoband School Movement**, the **Sikh reforms,** and the **Parsi reforms**. The various social movements were spread in different parts of the country, be it Bengal, Maharashtra, Punjab or the Deccan region. Together, they had a profound impact in preserving the strained socio-religious character of the Indian society and purging it of many evils plaguing it for centuries. They were also instrumental in invoking a sense of Indian identity which had been dormant for centuries, and thus channelizing our socio-cultural identity into **Indian nationalism**. Accordingly, this phase of cultural history is also identified as a period of **Indian renaissance**.

IMPORTANT MOVEMENTS AND THEIR FOUNDERS

Brahmo Samaj

The **Brahmo Samaj** (or the Brahma Samaj) established in 1828 by **Raja Ram Mohan Roy**, was the earliest of the reform movements. The movement and its name literally denoted a society of the worshippers of the Brahma or the Ultimate Reality, and the Supreme Consciousness.

It preached the principles of **monotheism** and the **universality** of the godhead and endeavoured to bring reforms in the Hindu society based on these principles. It also emphasised on the immortality of the human soul, the belief in goodness of the different holy scriptures and respect for other religions. Its principles of monotheism were based on the **teachings of the Upanishads** and it was against idol worship, religious sacrifices and other ritualism of the extant Hinduism.

It also worked against the evil practices of *sati*, female infanticide, child marriage, caste system and Brahmanical orthodoxy. Raja Ram Mohan Roy, the founder of the movement, was an exponent of many languages including English, Sanskrit, Arabic, Persian, French, Latin, and Greek and was a modern thinking scholar. His efforts enabled William Bentinck to declare *sati* as a punishable offence in 1829 (vide the Abolition of the Sati Act of 1829). For his efforts, he is also referred to as the **Father of Bengal Renaissance** whose ideas and works inspired several generations of reformists and leaders.

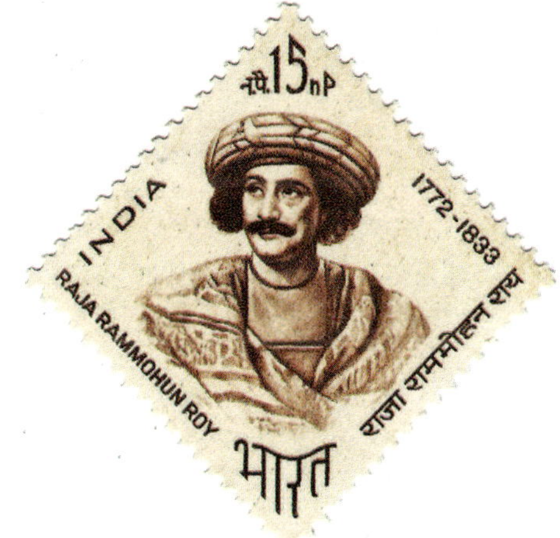

15.2: An Indian postage stamp of Raja Ram Mohan Roy released in 1964 — Courtesy, Department of Post

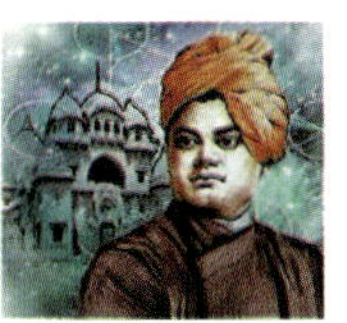

Earlier, Raja Ram Mohan Roy had also founded **Atmiya Sabha** in 1815. This Sabha promoted free thinking and philosophical discussions on a wide range of topics from Vedantism to social reforms, and served as a precursor to the Brahmo movement. After the death of Raja Ram Mohan Roy in 1833, the Brahmo Samaj entered a phase of decline with elements of idol worship seeping in its traditions. Later, a revival in the Brahmo Samaj happened under **Debendranath Tagore**. It reemerged as a dynamic movement, with leaders like Keshub Chandra Sen emerging on the horizon, but later split into different sects on account of difference of opinion.

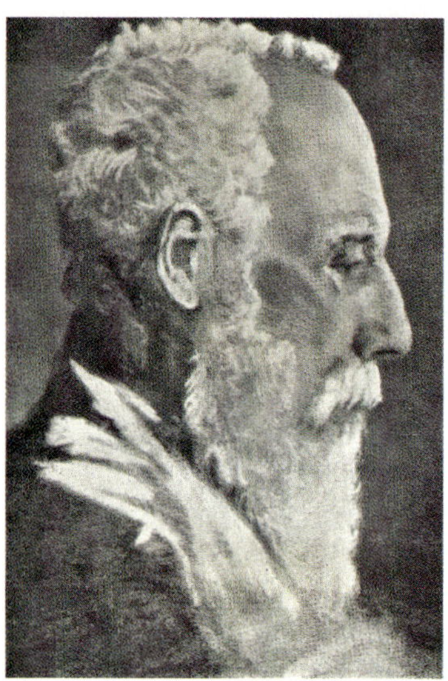

15.3: A portrait of Debendranath Tagore — Wikimedia Commons

It was through the efforts of Debendranath Tagore that **Tattvabodhini Samaj** was created in 1838, which later merged with the Brahmo Samaj (1843) and thus marked the revival in it. Eschewing ritualism and idolatry, and following the Vedantic principles, were emphasisied. Specific tenets for worship were laid to be followed by the members. With the joining of new reformists like **Keshub Chandra Sen, Akshay Kumar Datta** and others, the work of the Samaj was again on ascendancy in the period of the 1850s and early 60s. Newer areas of reforms, viz. education and improvement of the condition of females, education of the working class etc. was taken upon. However, a split occurred in the Samaj in 1866 and the sect under Debendranath Tagore was referred to as **Adi Brahmo Samaj.** This sect continued to emphasise on following the principles of monotheism and teachings from the Upanishads.

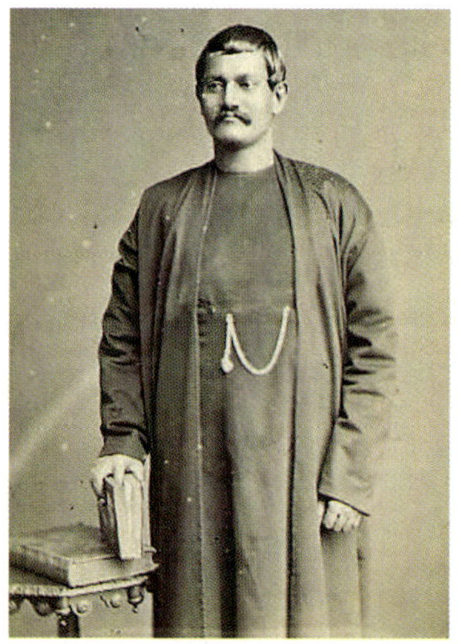

15.4: Keshub Chandra Sen; photograph from 1870 — Wikimedia Commons

Bharatiya Brahmo Samaj or **Naba Bidhan Samaj** was another sect established by **Keshub Chandra Sen** (in 1866).The differences on issues of active pursuance of other social reforms like inter-caste marriage, widow's remarriage and removal of *purdah* system for women, which the latter and younger followers of the Samaj wanted to follow, was the primary reason for the split. Keshub Chandra Sen also tried incorporating Christian ideals and theology of more rationalistic ideals in the Hindu thoughts. In 1878, another split occurred in the Brahmo Samaj when **Pandit Shivnath Shastri** founded the **Sadharan Brahmo Samaj**.

Thus, the Brahmo Samaj and the works of Raja Ram Mohan Roy, Debendranath Tagore and Keshub Chandra Sen, besides others, **heralded a relook at the Hindu religion and inspired people to believe in the principles of monotheism** and **Vedanta** and work for eradicating the many evils which plagued the society. Among many of the leaders inspired by this movement was a young Narendranath, later to be known as Swami Vivekananda, a champion of Vedanta and revivalism in subsequent decades.

Young Bengal Movement

Founded by **Henry Vivian Derozio**, this movement comprised a group of **free thinkers** who professed **free spirit** and **thought,** questioned authority, and opposed the old traditions and decadent customs. Henry Vivian Derozio taught in the Hindu College in Calcutta. His followers were known as Derozians. The movement inspired by him also supported **rights and education of women** and **opposed caste system, idol worship** and **superstitions**. He died at an early age (24 years) due to cholera in 1833 and with him the movement extinguished. The scholars consider the movement to be too radical for its time and the social environment not ready to accept it. As such, the movement had limited mass connect or an enduring impact.

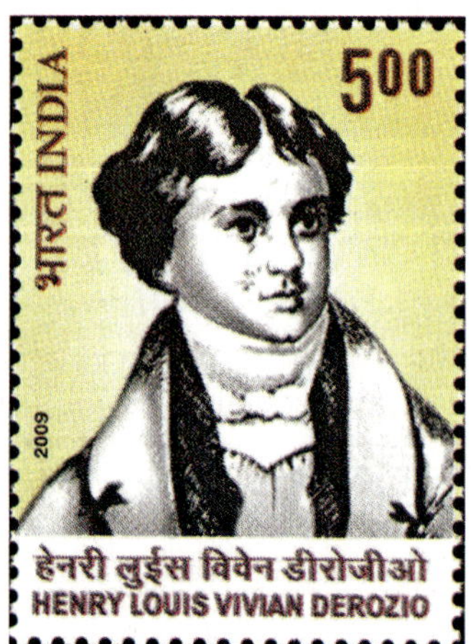

15.5: An Indian postage stamp of Henry Louis Vivian Derozio released in 2009 — Courtesy, Department of Post

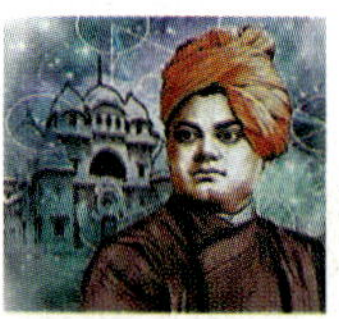

Prarthana Samaj

Prarthana Samaj, which literally means 'a prayer society', was a movement for bringing socio-religious reforms within Hinduism, particularly in the Maharashtra region. The movement was established in 1863 by **Atmaram Pandurang**, during the Bombay tour of Keshub Chandra Sen. Later, the Samaj gained popularity when **Justice M.G. Ranade** and **R.G. Bhandarkar** joined the movement. (Justice Ranade had earlier founded the **Widow Remarriage Association** in 1861 and also started the **Deccan Education Society)**. The Prarthna Samaj movement was also propagated in South India by noted Telugu writer and reformer **Kandukuri Veerasalingam**.

The main planks of the Prarthna Samaj were theistic worship and social reform. It advocated belief in one God, and in pursuance of its philosophy, it drew upon the ancient Vedic texts, besides the traditions of the Marathi bhakti poets such as Namdev and Tukaram. In the ambit of its social reforms was the opposition to idol worship (which it considered a sin), the caste system and dominance of priests. It worked for education of women, prohibition of child marriage and abolition of purdah in women. Further, it promoted inter-dining and inter-marriage amongst different castes. It also supported widow remarriage and worked for the general upliftment of women and the marginalised sections.

Arya Samaj

Started by Swami Dayananda Saraswati in 1875, Arya Samaj (literally meaning; 'society of noble men') was a **socio-religious reform movement** based on the principles of **monotheism** with its teachings centred on the **Vedas**. But unlike the earlier monotheistic movements such as Brahmo Samaj, it considered the **Vedas** to be **infallible** and also believed in the transmigration of the soul. Further, its ambit was much wider; including social reforms, education, preventing conversion of the Hindus and establishing a bigger connect with the people. The rationalism of the west, as adopted by the earlier movements, too was missing. Arya Samaj appealed to the emotion of the masses as it adopted veneration of the cow and rituals of sacrifice of butter in the fire hearth.

The realm of its social reforms included opposition to idolatry, caste system, Puranic ritualism, Brahmanical orthodoxy, child marriage and support to inter- caste marriages. Its views on religion and philosophy were brought out as a lecture series of Swami Dayananda and published as *Satyarth Prakash* (meaning; 'the light of the truth'). He also authored *Veda Bhashya Bhumika* (an introduction to Vedic commentary) and *Veda Bhashya* (a commentary on Yajurveda and Rigveda). Swami Dayananda had himself started a number of Vedic schools to impart the *gurukul* system of education. This trend continued even after his death in the form of Dayanand Anglo Vedic (DAV group) of schools and other educational institutions.

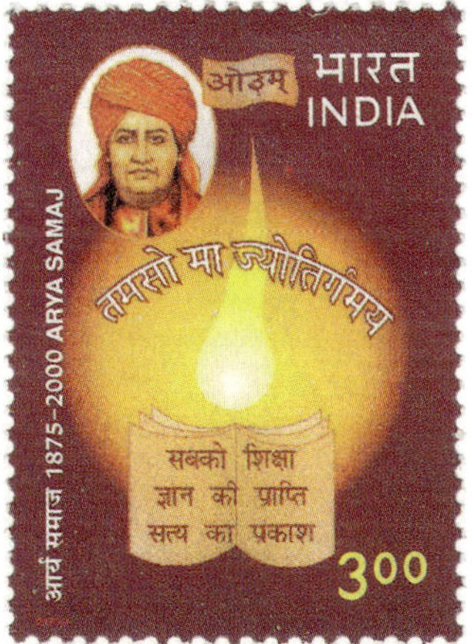

15.6: A postage stamp released in 2000 dedicated to Arya Samaj — Courtesy, Department of Post

The Samaj and its later leaders, and in particular Swami Shraddhanand, opposed the conversion of Hindus to other religions. It also started the *Shuddhi* movement for bringing the Hindus who converted into other religions, back into the fold of Hinduism. This brought Arya Samaj and its followers in confrontation with some of the leaders of other communities, particularly the Muslims and Christians.

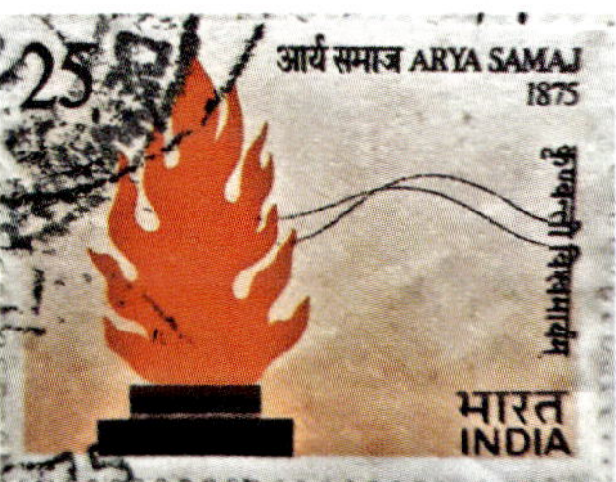

15.7: A postage stamp released in 1975 to mark 100 years of Arya Samaj; — photograph (personal collection) by Madhukar K Bhagat

The Arya Samaj movement had a profound impact in India, particularly in the Punjab region where its teachings based on the infallibility of the Vedas, and social reforms, brought a new vigour in the Hindu society. It even inspired nationalistic zeal as seen in some of the leaders such as Lala Lajpat Rai who followed its ideals.

Ramakrishna Mission

The Ramakrishna Mission was founded by **Swami Vivekananda** in 1897 to spread the teachings of his guru **Swami Ramakrishna Paramahamsa** (1836 to 1886). It started as a religious and spiritual organisation with the philosophy of the movement being based on **Vedanta** and aimed at **spiritual rejuvenation** of the **Indian society**. It also created a **monastic order of *sanyasins*** (renunciates) and a *math*/*muth* at Belur (Howrah), the focal point of the Mission.

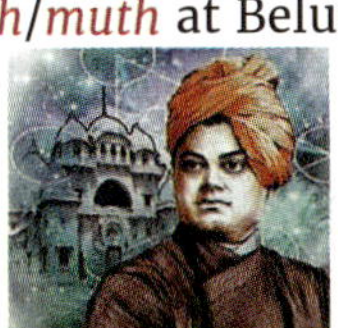

Swami Vivekananda (1863-1902) himself came into prominence after his famous speech at the **'Parliament of Religions'** held in Chicago (USA) in 1893. Over the period of next decade (till his death in 1902), he engaged in several lecture tours in different countries, propagating the ideals of his guru and the principles of Vedanta, thus bringing the Vedantic philosophy and Hinduism to a **world stage.** He founded the order of *sanyasins* as the Ramakrishna Mission, determined its guiding principles, rules of conduct and goals of the organisation.

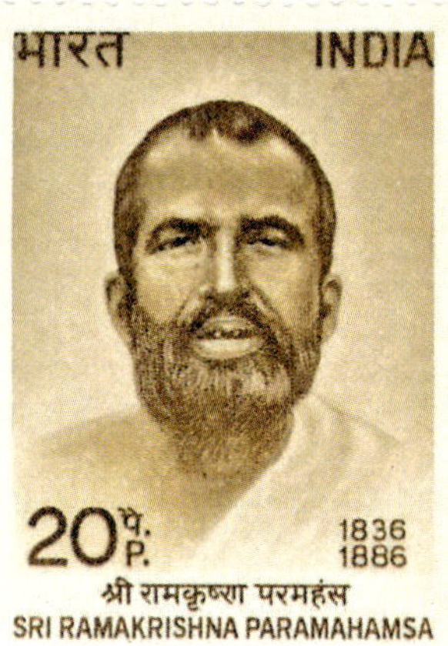

15.8: An Indian postage stamp of Ramakrishna Paramahamsa released in 1973 — Courtesy, Department of Post

While the mission's aims were **spiritual attainment** and **realisiation of God**, **renunciation** and **humanitarian service** were considered to be the ideals to be pursued for attainment of its goals. 'The God resides in the living' (*Jiva* is Shiva), the message of Ramakrishna and 'identify the lord in poor' (*Daridra Narayan*) the message of Vivekananda, remains the cornerstone of its activities, thus exemplifying that service to poor is the service to God. To see divinity in humanity and to serve the needy was the crucial message of the Mission's great masters, which over a period of 125 years the Mission has assiduously observed.

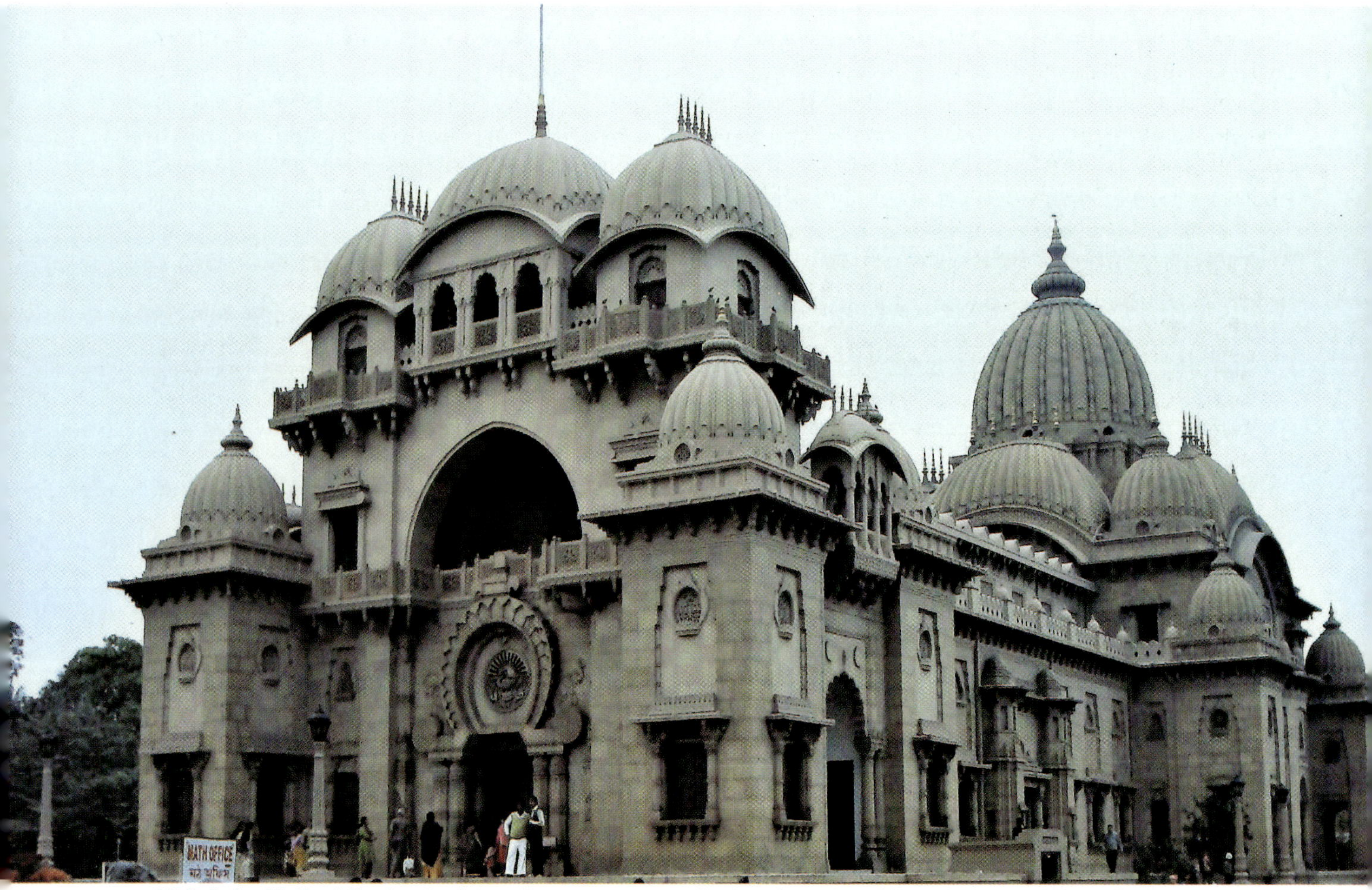

15.9: Belur Math at the bank of river Ganga, serves as the headquarter of the mission and its activities around the world — photograph by Madhukar K Bhagat

Universalism, **respect for other religions** and **harmony** with the other forms of worship and religious practices, were the other salient teachings of Ramakrishna. The mission and its followers were not merely tolerant of the Christian, Islamic and Buddhist thoughts but were respectful of them. They also synthesised the reverence to the Vedantic attributeless divine (*nirakara*) with the devotion of God with attributes (*sakar*), the rationalism with emotion and faith, *jnana* (knowledge) with *karma* (conduct, action). Even the highest of Vedantic ideals were harmonised with Puranic forms of worship of Kali, Shiva and other deities. Though they believe in the principle of Vedanta and Hindu philosophy as the guiding light for the movement, it was critical of the many practices associated with it, such as untouchability. It also relentlessly worked for education of women and their upliftment.

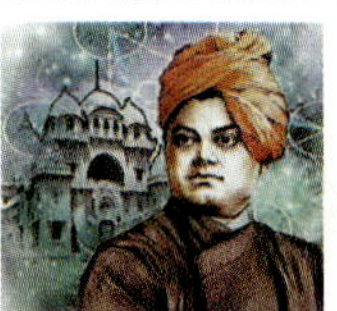

Ramakrishna: A Synthesis of Religious and Philosophical Diversity

—This catholicity of views may be regarded as another great contribution of Ramakrishna to the modern world which religion has divided into so many water-tight compartments. It had a special significance for the orthodox Hindus. The worship of images even of goddess Kali, which was the butt of ridicule by the Christian missionaries as well as Indian reformers, was demonstrated by Ramakrishna to be not only not incompatible with the highest spiritual development, but also as good a means of salvation as the worship of one God without any form.

"Many are the names of God and infinite the forms that lead us to Him. ***In whatsoever name or form you desire to call Him and in that very form and name you will see him.****" This teaching of Ramakrishnan supported by parables and tested by his own life, gave the Hindu revivalism a moral sanction of a philosophical basis, and a new spiritual significance of immense value.*

Dr. R.C. Majumdar, an eminent historian in 'British Paramountcy and Indian Renaissance' (pg 140); Volume X of series of 'History and Culture of the Indian People', by Bhartiya Vidya Bhavan

Over the period of years, the Ramakrishna mission has emerged not only as a pan-India organisation, but as a **world-wide spiritual and philanthropic movement**. Swami Vivekananda had founded the very first Vedanta Society of New York for the study and propagation of the philosophy of Vedanta. Now, many Vedanta societies are functioning all over the United States of America, representing the American arm of the mission. The movement, in later years, has also established a number of schools, colleges, hospitals, and other charitable institutions.

Vivekananda firmly believed that the rejuvenation of the individual as well as the nation has to be from within, and to this effect effort has to be from within. Accordingly, the mission continues to remain actively engaged in educational, medical and other philanthropic work, thus translating the ideals of Karmayoga in action. Thus, the message of Ramakrishna, the vision of Vivekananda and the work of the Mission has been instrumental not only in **practical application of the principles of Vedanta and synthesis of the varied philosophies and earlier reforms**, but also in the **reawakening of the Indian spirit and self belief** of its masses.

Address by Swami Vivekananda at the World's Parliament of Religions, Chicago, 11th September, 1893

The address of Swami Vivekananda at the World's Parliament of Religions, was indeed a watershed moment in the socio-cultural history of the country. It not only succinctly presented to the world the essence of Hinduism and Vedanta but also underlined the need for universality of perspective in religious and cultural thought. Plurality of Indian traditions and profoundness of its religious and cultural legacy, became apparent to the world, thus raising the self-belief of battered millions and infusing a sense of national consciousness. It was indeed the beginning of a movement.

Sisters and Brothers of America,

It fills my heart with joy unspeakable to rise in response to the warm and cordial welcome which you have given us. I thank you in the name of the most ancient order of monks in the world; I thank you in the name of the mother of religions; and I thank you in the name of the millions and millions of Hindu people of all classes and sects.

My thanks, also, to some of the speakers on this platform who, referring to the delegates from the Orient, have told you that these men from far-off nations may well claim the honour of bearing to different lands the idea of toleration. I am proud to belong to a religion which has taught the world both tolerance and universal acceptance. We believe not only in universal toleration, but we accept all religions as true. I am proud to belong to a nation which has sheltered the persecuted and the refugees of all religions and all nations of the earth. I am proud to tell you that we have gathered in our bosom the purest remnant of the Israelites, who came to southern India and took refuge with us in the very year in which their holy temple was shattered to pieces by Roman tyranny. I am proud to belong to the religion which has sheltered and is still fostering the remnant of the grand Zoroastrian nation. I will quote to you, brethren, a few lines from a hymn which I remember to have repeated from my earliest boyhood, which is every day repeated by millions of human beings: 'As the different streams having their sources in different places all mingle their water in the sea, so, O Lord, the different paths which men take through different tendencies, various though they appear, crooked or straight, all lead to Thee.'

2500 भारत INDIA

2018

स्वामी विवेकानंद

SWAMI VIVEKANANDA

15.10: Stamp of Swami Vivekananda with background of Belur Math released in 2018 — Courtesy, Department of Post

The present convention, which is one of the most august assemblies ever held, is in itself a vindication, a declaration to the world, of the wonderful doctrine preached in the Gita: 'Whosoever comes to Me, through whatsoever form, I reach him; all men are struggling through paths which in the end lead to Me.' Sectarianism, bigotry, and its horrible descendant, fanaticism, have long possessed this beautiful earth. They have filled the earth with violence, drenched it often and often with human blood, destroyed civilization, and sent whole nations to despair. Had it not been for these horrible demons, human society would be far more advanced than it is now. But their time is come; and I fervently hope that the bell that tolled this morning in honour of this convention may be the death-knell of all fanaticism, of all persecutions with the sword or with the pen, and of all uncharitable feelings between persons wending their way to the same goal.

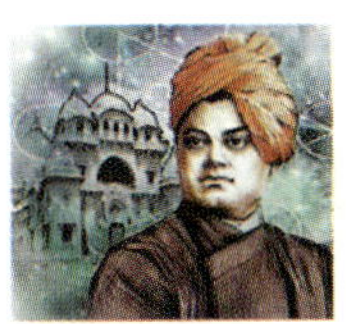

Theosophical Society

The **Theosphical Society** was founded by **Madam H.P. Blavatsky** (a Russian), and **Colonel Henry Olcott** (an American) in 1875 (in USA). Later, the society came into prominence under the leadership of **Mrs. Annie Besant,** with its headquarters moving to Adyar near Madras (now Chennai) in 1882.

The objective of the society was **attaining universal brotherhood** without the distinction of race, colour, creed, etc. It also aimed to promote studies in **comparative religions**, **science** and **philosophy**. Further, its stated objective also included investigation of the unexplained laws of nature and the powers latent in man. The Society had a split in 1895 and hence emerged the Theosphical Society Adyar, as a distinct entity, separate from its American arm.

Under Blavastky, the society believed in the existence of divine souls, termed as 'Mahatmas'. and in the theory of 'Intelligent evolution of all existence occurring on a cosmic scale'. Although such ideas came under criticism from certain rationalist thinkers, the emphasis on strengthening and reviving the glories of ancient India's religious and philosophical traditions did attract a number of followers in India. Under Annie Besant, the society continued to thrive for several decades and made contributions in the fields of philosophy, spiritualism, education and even philanthropy. Annie Besant herself was an eminent speaker, author of several books and as an educationist helped establish several educational institutions including the Benaras Hindu University of which she was one of the founders. As a member of the Indian National Congress and later as its president, she was also to emerge as an important leader in the Indian national movement in the early 20th century.

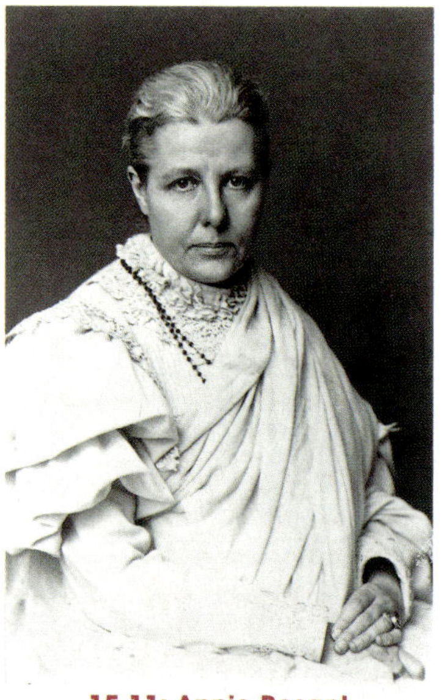

15.11: Annie Besant — Wikimedia Commons

Besides the above societies and associations, there were also some other religious organisations and sects of Hinduism which witnessed a revival in their activities. These included the **Vaishnava sect** of **Sri Vaishnavas**, hich formed an association in 1902; **the Chaitanya cult**, which saw a resurgence in Bengal and launched a literary movement to establish Sri Krishna as a full incarnation of the God and as an author of the Bhagavad Gita (an outstanding work of this genre being *Krishnacharita* of Bankim Chandra); **the Lingayats** which formed a Lingayat Association in 1884 and an all India Lingayat Conference in 1894; the followers of the **Tantra cult** who endeavoured to establish the esoteric meaning behind their rituals and practices; the **Smarta sect** who were the followers of Shankaracharya and started the Advaita Sabha in 1895 in Kumbakonam, the **Radha Soami Satsang** founded in 1861, which propagated **Surat Sabd Yoga** (union of the soul with the spirit current/ the Word) and **Deva Samaj** founded in 1887 and having similar ideals and activities as the Brahmo Samaj.

OTHER EMINENT REFORMISTS

Ishwar Chandra Vidyasagar (1820-1891) was an eminent **educator** and **reformist** who firmly believed in the education of the girl child and the emancipation of women, and started many schools for them. He opposed child marriage, and supported widow remarriage, which was legalised by the Widow Remarriage Act of 1856. His efforts were also instrumental in passing of the Age of Consent Act of 1891, fixing the minimum age of consummation of marriage at 12. He is also credited with rationalising and simplifying Bengali alphabets and making significant contribution to Bengali prose.

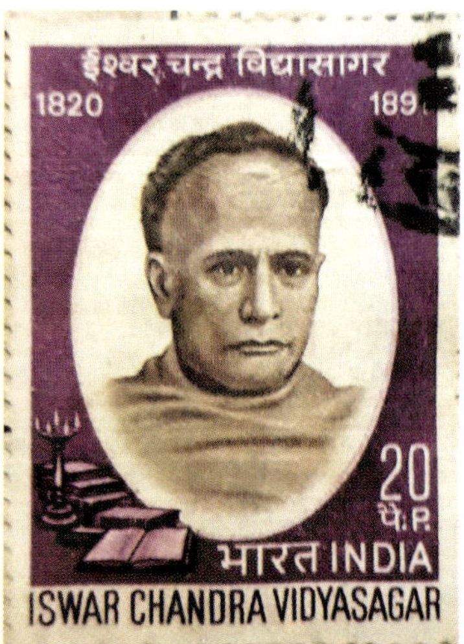

15.12: An Indian postage stamp of Ishwar Chandra Vidyasagar released in 1970 — photograph (personal collection) by Madhukar K Bhagat

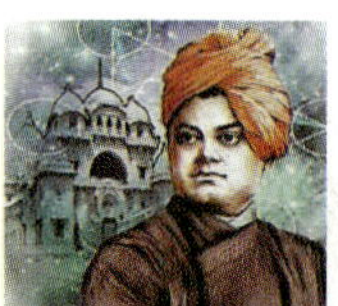

Jyoti Govind Rao Phule (1827-1890) also known as Jyotiba Phule, founded the **Satya Shodhak Samaj** in 1873 which opposed the untouchability, caste system and Brahmanical supremacy. He also worked for education of women and the oppressed caste of the region. He established the first girl's school in Pune in 1851 along with his wife Savitribai Phule and was in a way a pioneer of education of women in modern India. He also spearheaded the widow remarriage movement in Maharashtra.

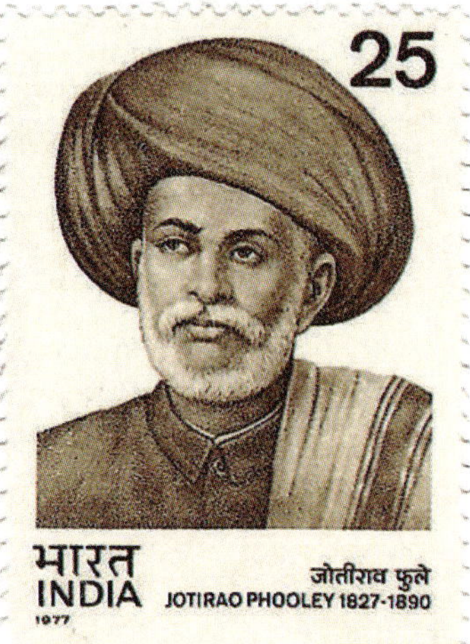

15.13: An Indian postage stamp of Jyotirao Phule released in 1977 — Courtesy, Department of Post

Kandukuri Veeresalingam (1848-1919) also referred as the Raja Rammohan Roy of Andhra, pioneered movement for **girls' education in Andhra** and also of widow remarriage. He founded the **Veda Samaj** in 1864 which opposed caste discrimination and supported widow remarriage. He also worked against child marriage and the dowry system. He was a litterateur whose novel *Rajashekhar Charitramu* is considered the first novel of Telugu literature.

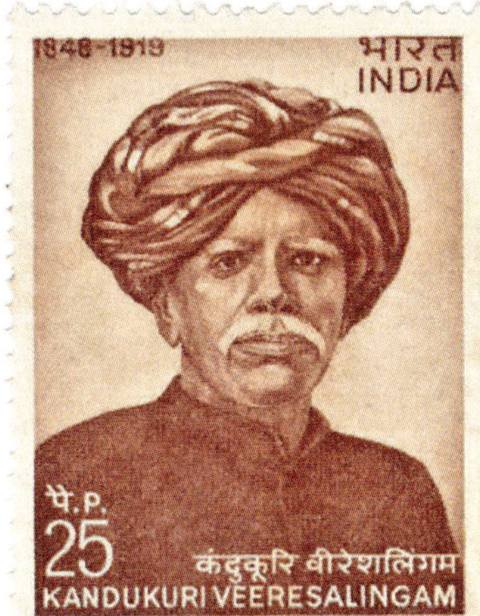

15.14: An Indian postage stamp of Kandukuri Veeresalingam released in 1974 — Courtesy, Department of Post

Dhondo Keshav Karve (1858-1962), also known as Maharishi Karve, was an eminent social reformer of the late 19th and early 20th century. He worked for women's education and remarriage of Hindu widows, and he himself had married a widow. He also established in 1883 the **Widow Remarriage Association** and the **Hindu Widows Home** in 1896. He also worked against the Devadasi system. He was another pioneer of women's education and started a Women's University in 1916 in Bombay in the name of SNDT university which continues to flourish even today as a prominent university of women. He was awarded **Bharat Ratna** in 1958 in the year of his 100th birth anniversary.

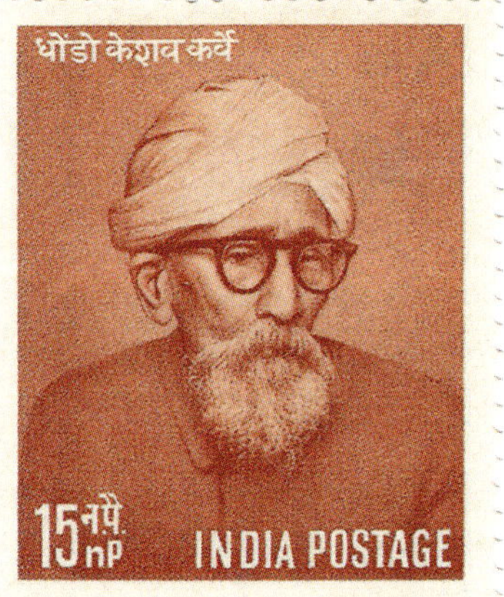

15.15: An Indian postage stamp of Dhondo Keshav Karve released in 1958 — Courtesy, Department of Post

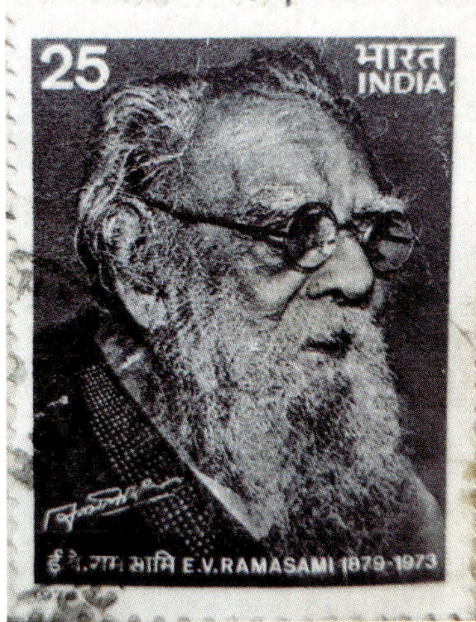

15.16: An Indian postage stamp of EV Ramasami 'Periyar' released in 1978 — photograph by Madhukar K Bhagat

E.V.Ramasami, revered as Periyar (1879-1973), was a prominent social activist of the early 20th century who started the **Self-Respect Movement** in the 1920s. He is also referred to as the father of the Dravidian movement, the objective of which was **upliftment of the Dravidians,** opposition to the caste system, and suppression by the Brahmins. He also opposed child marriage, supported widow remarriage and strived for attainment of women's rights.

REFORM MOVEMENT AMONGST OTHER RELIGIOUS COMMUNITIES

The Aligarh Movement

It was started by Sir Syed Ahmad Khan (1817-1898) and worked for **education and social upliftment of the Muslims**. Post First War of Independence of 1857, and the subsequent establishment of the British Rule in India, the Muslim society was in a state of decadence. It suffered social, cultural, educational and economic backwardness. Sir Syed Ahmed Khan, realising the above state of the Muslim society, wanted to bring its socio-cultural regeneration. He believed in imparting modern and scientific education to Muslims and asked them be broadminded and not to be secluded from modern ideas.

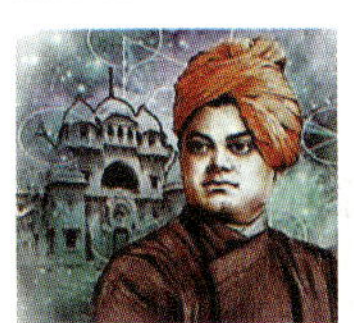

In 1866, he started the Muhammadan Educational Conference and in 1875 he founded the **Mohammedan Anglo-Oriental College at Aligarh** which became the centre of the reform activities and lent the name Aligarh Movement to the reforms initiated by him. This college was to become the Aligarh Muslim University in 1920. Sir Sayyid also founded in 1886 the *Muhammedan Educational Congress*, an organisation to reform and educate Indian Muslims which later came to be known as All India Muhammadan Educational Conference. He also worked for education of women and advocated removal of *purdah*. The reforms brought a sea change in the Muslim society and are at times considered to be a renaissance in the socio-cultural and educational realm of the Muslims of India.

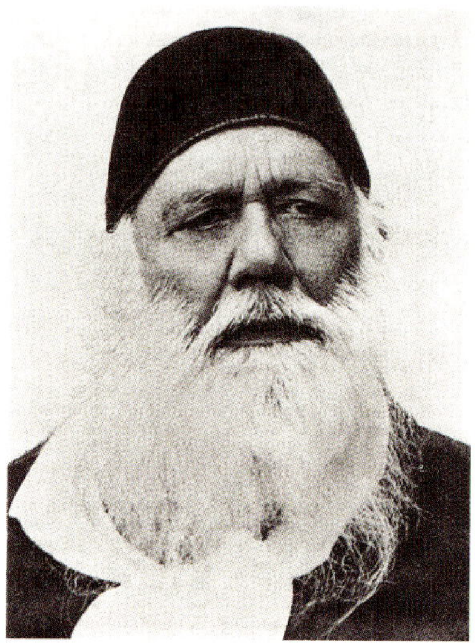

15.17: Sir Syed Ahmad Khan — Wikimedia Commons

The Ahmadiyya Movement

It was a revivalist Islamic and a messianic (based on a messiah) movement started in 1889 by **Mirza Ghulam Ahmad** (1835 -1908) who claimed to be a *Mahdi* (a guided messiah appearing at the end of times). The movement endeavoured to usher the true intent of Islam and bring Islam to its pristine form. It emphasised on universality of religion, principles of peace, brotherhood, justice and other salient principles of Islam, including the six articles of faith and five pillars of Islam. The movement became popular in northern India, particularly in the Punjab, Sind and United Provinces of the British India. It later had presence in other parts of the world. A number of schools and colleges, educational institutions were also opened by it; besides it also included missionary activities in its ambit.

Deoband Movement

Also referred as the Deoband School, this was a revivalist movement of Sunni Islam in the late 19th century. The movement was started by **Muhammad Qasim Nanautavi** (1832 – 1880) and **Rashid Ahmad Gangohi** (1828 – 1905) at the **Darul Uloom** (or Islamic academic centre) in Deoband (Saharanpur district-United Provinces) from where the name of the movement is derived. The movement emphasised on education in religious teaching and adhered to the Hanafi School of law. It also emphasised on the **teachings of Quran and the Hadith** (traditions of the Prophet) and other tenets of Islam. The movement also associated itself with the rising nationalism through its participation in the Khilafat movement and advocating the concept of composite nationalism for India. Although they remained a revivalist religious movement, they made contribution to Islamic education and its reforms.

Reform amongst Parsis

In 1851, **Naoroji Furdoonji**, **Dadabhai Nauroji,** and **S.S. Bengalee** founded the Religious Reforms Association of the Parsis (*Rehnumai Maz'dayasan Sabha*). The objective of the reforms was to establish the Zoroastrian religion to its pristine purity as well as to bring social reforms among the Parsis. They also started a journal *Rast Goftar* for socio-religious messages which remained the mouthpiece of the movement. The reforms strived to **remove orthodoxy** amongst Parsis and spread education, particularly amongst girls and also improve the social position of women.

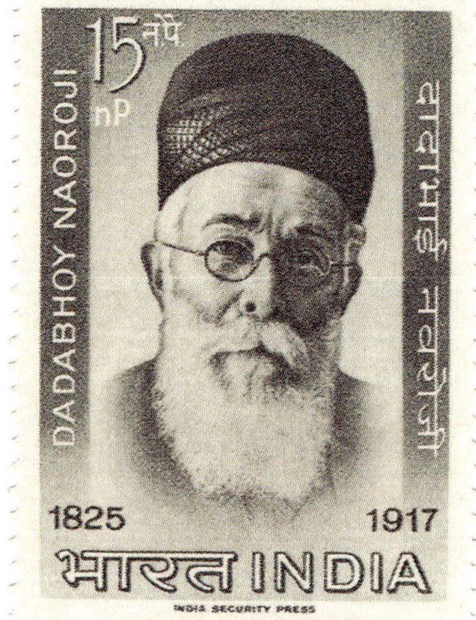

15.18: An Indian postage stamp of Dadabhai Naoroji released in 1963 — Courtesy, Department of Post

Reforms amongst Sikhs

The reform in Sikhs took place through several successive movements. The **Namdhari Movement** was founded by **Balak Singh** in 1812. It believed only in the practice of *Naam Simran* (taking the name of God) and eschewing other religious ritualistic practices, and hence acquired the name of Namdhari. It believed that the lineage of Gurus did not end with Guru Gobind Singh and considered Baba Balak Singh as the 11th Sikh Guru and his successor Baba Ram Singh as the 12th guru. The movement also emphasised on the Khalsa identity and the authority of the Guru Granth Sahib. Its followers were encouraged to give up eating meat and wear white clothes, and protection of the cow was taken up as one of the important tenets.

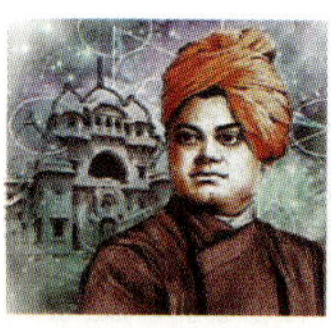

Nirankari Movement

It was started by **Baba Ram Dayal Das** in 1851. It aimed at worshipping the God as a *nirankar* (formless entity) and emphasised on Naam Simran. Thus, it strived to restore the practice of Sikhism prevalent during the days of Guru Nanak.

Another Sikh movement was the **Singh Sabha movement** which began in 1870s as a reaction to the proselytizing activities of the Christians, Muslims and Hindus in the Punjab region. The movement aimed in promoting the true Sikh religion and restoring it to its pristine glory. Besides reform in Sikhism, it also endeavoured to bring back in its fold of Sikhism those Sikhs who had converted to other religions.

Akali Movement

It was started in 1920s to improve the management of gurudwaras and Sikh shrines and is also referred to as the **Gurudwara Reform Movement**. It led to the introduction of the Sikh Gurudwara Act of 1925 bringing the Gurudwaras under the control of Shiromani Gurudwara Prabandhaak Committee. It was also associated with the Indian independence movement and actively participated in the Non-cooperation movement.

Women Social Reformers

The social reforms of the 19th and early 20th century incorporated several women-related issues, be it the banning of Sati, promoting widow remarriage, passing of the Age of Consent Act, (for consummation of marriage) and promotion of education of women etc. Although most of these reforms were led by men, the role of some of the women reformers too was significant, especially in the field of education of women. These women reformers led from the forefront despite the adverse social atmosphere and hardships faced and inspired a generation of women in turn.

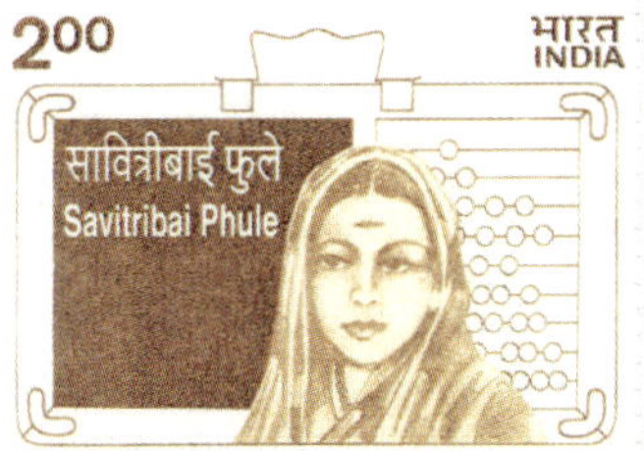

15.19: Savitribai Phule

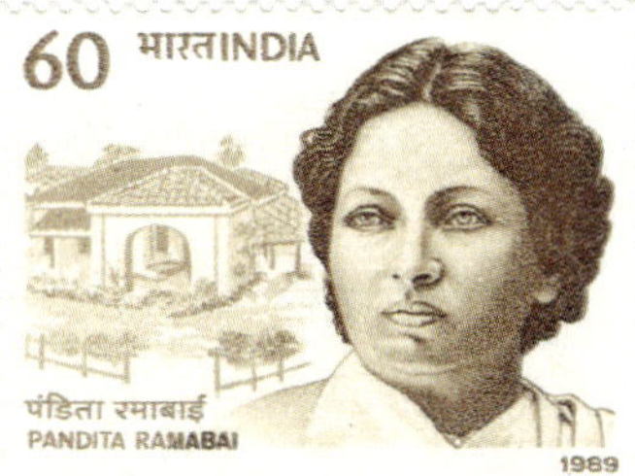

15.20: Pandita Ramabai

15.19 & 15.20: Savitribai Phule and Pandita Ramabai; among the earliest women social reformers of the 19th century — Courtesy, Department of Post

Considered to be a pioneer of women's reforms, **Savitribai Phule** (1831- 1897) made a stellar contribution to the education of girls and women. Along with her husband Jyoti Rao Phule an eminent social reformer and educationist, she started three schools for girls in Pune as early as 1851 and later founded around 18 schools. She also played a crucial role in the upliftment of backward classes. Another of her friends and associates, **Fatima Sheikh** (1831-1900), played a salient role in the educational endeavour and is considered to be the first female Muslim teacher. **Pandita Ramabai Saraswati** (1858- 1922) was another prominent reformer of this period who established Sharda Sadan, a school for child widows. Later she also established the Mukti Mission at Kedagaon Pune and Arya Mahila Samaj (1882). **Ramabai Ranade** (1862-1924) was another social reformer of this period who started schools for girls in Pune. After the death of her husband and another social reformer, Justice Ranade, she played a significant role in social activism to support the cause of women in the early 20th century. She also started Pune Seva Sadan, a home for women.

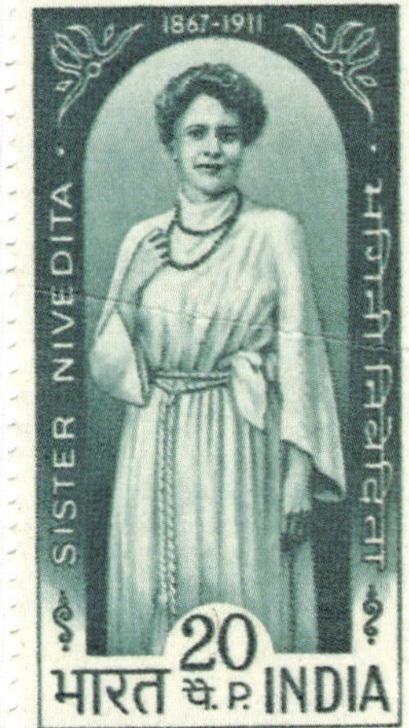

15.21: Sister Nivedita , a stamp from 1968; — Courtesy, Department of Post

Annie Besant (1847- 1933) and **Sister Nivedita** (1867- 1911), were among other pioneers of women's reforms of this period. Annie Besant was known for her work in the field of education and philanthropy and particularly for her leadership of the Theosophical Society which reached great heights under her stewardship. Sister Nivedita a disciple of Swami Vivekananda started a school for the girls at Calcutta. She is also remembered for her humanitarian work during the plague epidemic of 1899. Although born on foreign soil, both made India their home. They are remembered for their crucial contribution to the cause of Indian women in the late 19th and early 20th centuries besides for their contribution to political movements and Indian nationalism.

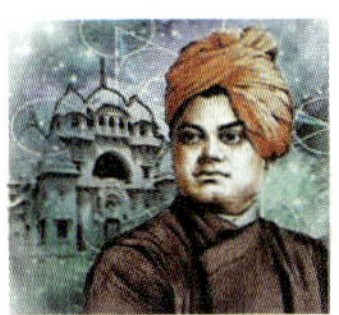

SOCIAL AND RELIGIOUS REFORMS AND THEIR IMPACT

The social and religious reforms had far-reaching effect on the Indian society and at times have been identified as a period of **Indian renaissance**. Some of these movements were **reformative.** They challenged the traditions and rejected some of the fundamental doctrines accepted since ages. Some others were **revivalistic**. They defended the old system, aligned with it, or endeavoured to regain the pristine glory of the past. The Brahmo Samaj, Prarthana Samaj, Aligarh movement, Ahmadiya movement Wahabi movement, the Parsi reform etc. are often considered in the former category. The Ramakrishna Mission, which did not completely reject idolatry and the ritualism, but synthesized it with the deeper Vedantic traditions and the Theosphical movement can be considered among the latter category. Many movements also incorporated the features of both. The Arya Samaj, which rejected idolatry, but aimed at reviving the Vedic traditions while considering the Vedas to be infallible, can be considered to combine the traits of both. But irrespective of the categorisation, they all left a significant mark on the socio-cultural milieu.

The influence of these movements ranged from education and emancipation of women to loosening of the vice-like grip of caste on the society; from the revival of the Vedic institutions to infusing rationalism and modernity in education and religious traditions. Education of women was started for the first time on an institutional basis. *Sati* was questioned and rejected. Widow marriages were accepted. Child marriages were discouraged. Untouchability was decried and several movements for temple entry of the down-trodden came to occur. Many of these reforms were later encapsulated as legislations passed by the British government. These provided a legal enforcement and hence proved a shot in the arm in the social upheaval. Among many of these prohibitory and enabling legislations were;

- The **Prohibition of *Sati* Act,** passed in 1829.
- **The Widow Remarriage Act of 1856** (legalising the widow remarriage)
- **Special Marriages Act of 1872** sanctioning the Inter-caste and inter-communal marriages
- The **Age of Consent Act of 1891** which raised the age of consent for consumption of marriage to 12, thus discouraged child marriages.
- The **Sharda Act of 1929**, which prohibited marriage of girls below 14 and of boys below 18.

The above socio-cultural reforms also had the effect of raising the consciousness of a national identity. With the rise of nationalism in the early 20th century, and in particular with the advent of Mahatma Gandhi on the national scene, the social reforms became an integral part of the Indian national movement itself. Abolition of untouchability, education and emancipation of women and communal harmony were specially emphasised upon by Mahatma Gandhi and were integral to the programmes of the Indian National Congress. With the rise of different forms of media such as press and cinema, social issues and reforms found a new form of expression through them. Finally, with the independence of India and framing of the new Constitution, issues like untouchability and protection of rights of women, besides others, became a part of the very constitutional and legal framework of the country.

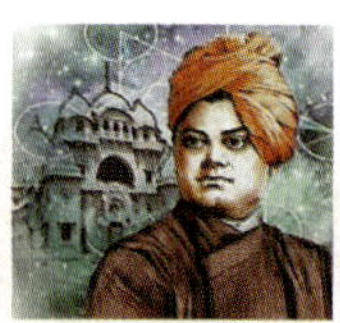

Paintings in Modern India

> *The artist is the lover of the nature; therefore he is her slave and her master.*
>
> — Rabindranath Tagore
>
> *I dream my painting and I paint my dream.*
>
> — Vincent Van Gogh

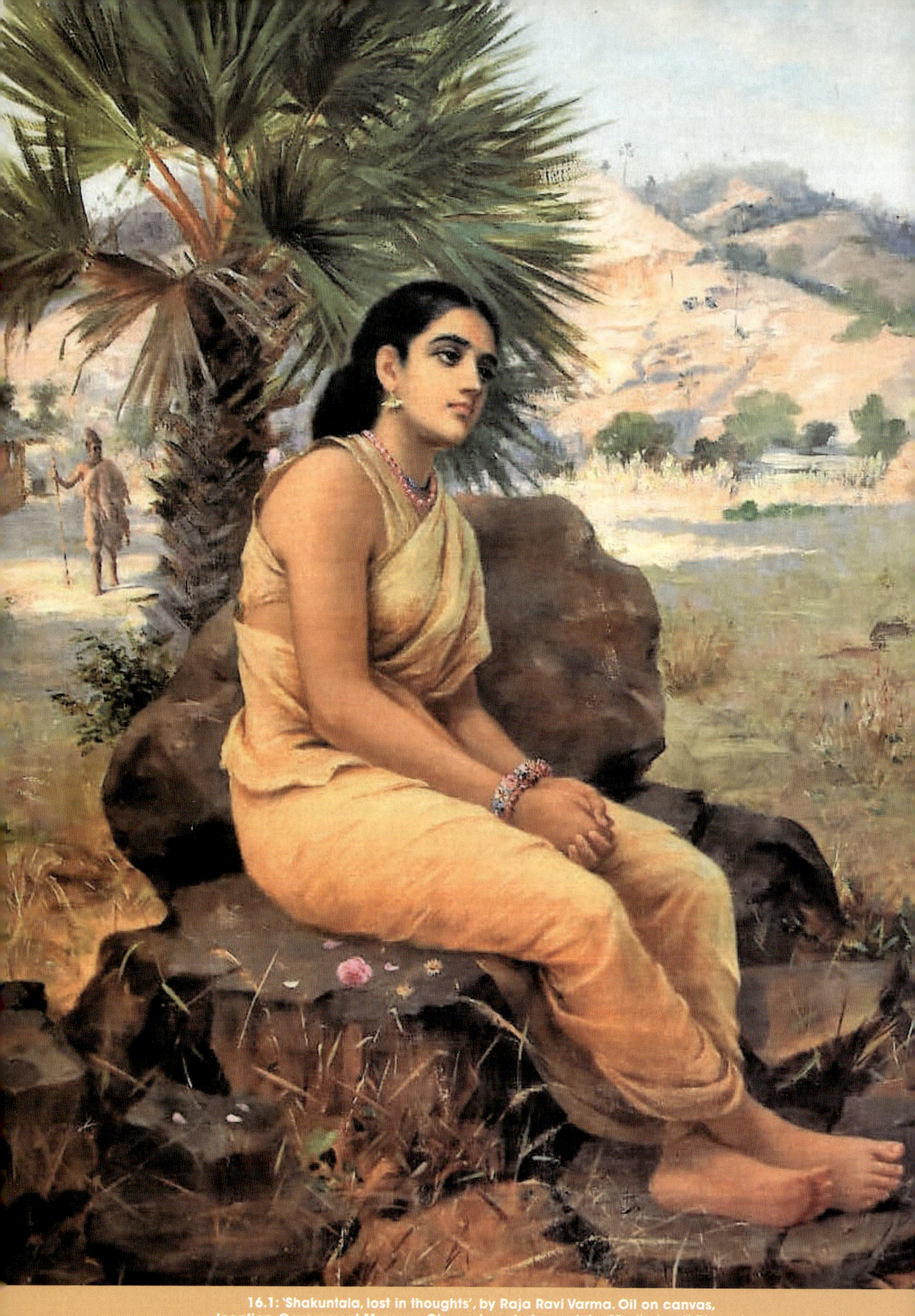

16.1: 'Shakuntala, lost in thoughts', by Raja Ravi Varma. Oil on canvas, location, Government Museum, Chennai — photograph by Madhukar K Bhagat

GROWTH OF MODERN INDIAN PAINTINGS

The term 'modern Indian paintings' refer to the styles of Indian paintings that began emerging since the mid- nineteenth century. By this period, the genre of miniature paintings as seen in the Mughal, Pahari, South Indian, and other schools of art had started to wane, and an increasing British influence was seen in the Indian paintings. These were commonly referred to as the **Company art**. However, scholars believe that the onset of the modern Indian paintings in a sense only happened with the advent of **Raja Ravi Varma,** whose subjects and ethos were uniquely Indian. This was followed by the **Bengal School of Art** which ushered a new era of **revivalist nationalism** in paintings and connected to the Indian roots in terms of style, as well as the subject. The famous post-independence **Progressive Artists' Group** (PAG) of Bombay was another important milestone which blended Indian art with more contemporary and abstract themes. Almost parallel to the growth of modern paintings has been the course of the folk paintings in India, which includes traditional art forms such as the **Madhubani painting**, **Warli painting, Kalamkari art**, **Kalighat painting** etc. These paintings included the subjects touching the everyday life of people and reflected the life and style of the Indian villages and the hinterland of India.

A number of art movements and artists have contributed to the growth of Indian paintings. A glimpse of the salient ones is brought out here.

THE BRITISH ART AND THE COMPANY PAINTINGS

The British/Western influence on the Indian paintings began with the advent of a number of prominent Western painters in India such as **Tilly Kettle, Johan Zoffany, George Chinnery, William Hodges Thomas Daniell** and **William Daniell** etc. Most of their paintings were in oil medium, and the perspective was western. Some of their paintings, particularly of Thomas Daniell and his nephew William Daniell, who had spent seven years in India, captured Indian landscapes and the images of some prominent monuments. These set of painters marked the advent of the **British Art School of India**.

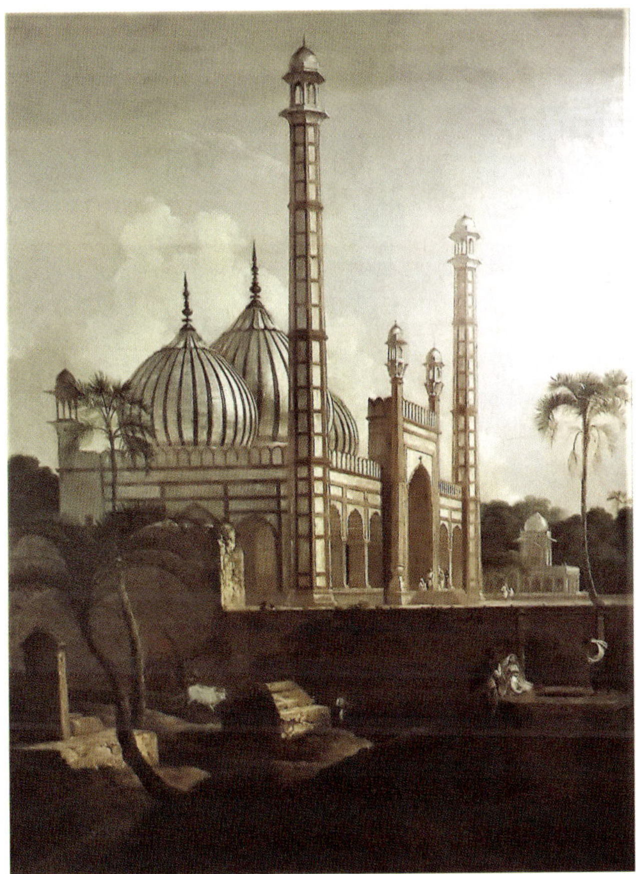

16.2: Mosque, by William Daniell, Oil on canvas; National Gallery of Modern Art, New Delhi — photograph by Madhukar K Bhagat

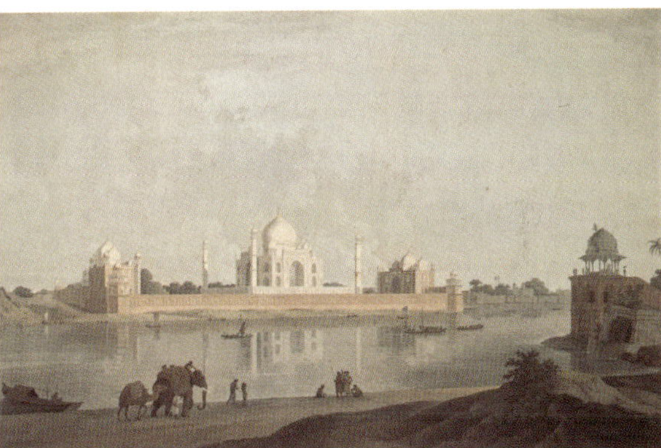

16.3: The Taj Mahal, an aquatint; drawn and engraved by Thomas and William Daniell (1801) — Wikimedia Commons

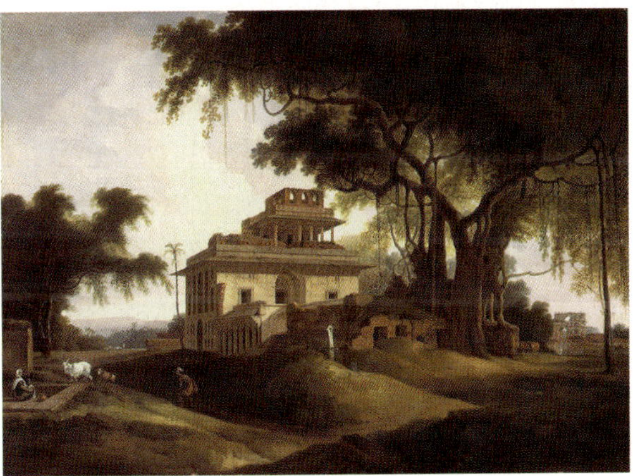

16.4: Ruins of the Naurattan, Sasaram, Bihar; by Thomas Daniell, 1811; oil on canvas — Wikimedia Commons

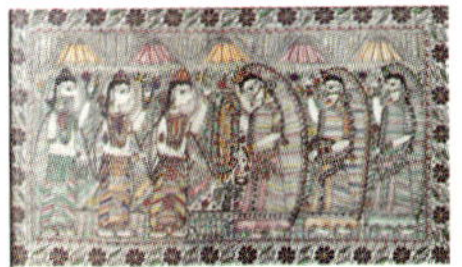

The Company Style

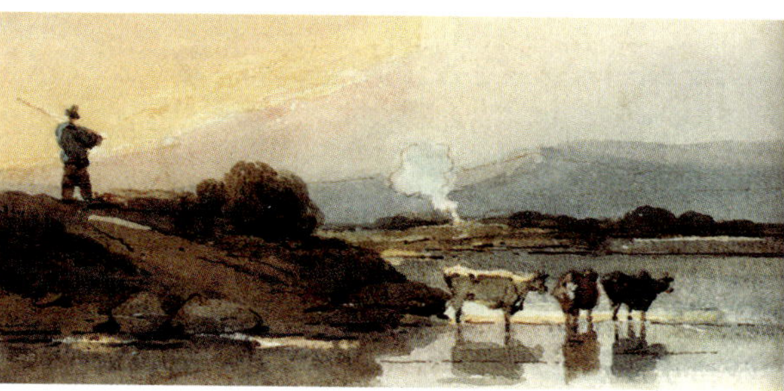

16.5: 'An Indian Herdsman on a Bank' by George Chinnery, 19th century, water colour — Wikimedia Commons

In the later years, the mingling of the Indian art style with the Western influence brought out what was referred to as the Company style of painting; as it emerged during the period of influence of British East India Company. It was a set of paintings done by Indian painters working under the British patrons, or hired by them temporarily, for capturing indigenous subjects/topics. Such paintings were popular with the British and other European travellers. They would come to India and wanted to have a glimpse a slice of the life of the people, the panorama and the diverse landscape and take those images back as their personal painting portfolios. The Indian painters had to adopt some of the techniques of European school, as this was the genre with which the European patrons and buyers were familiar with and valued. Thus, there emerged the Company style that was a blend of the European/British influence and also the extant Mughal, Rajput and other traditional styles of painting.

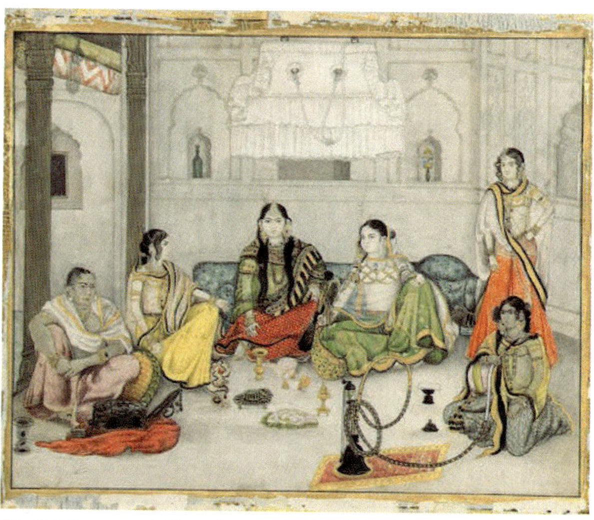

16.6: 'Group of Courtesans' (1800-1825), opaque water colour and gold on paper: a Company style painting — Wikimedia Commons

Many of these paintings were water colours, mostly done on paper. These were characterised by transparency and soft tones and would have a sense of vibrancy and visual appeal. Thus, they drew on the European water colour techniques, but also incorporated with them the indigenous style adopted from the Mughal and Rajput schools. The paintings typically had a mix of naturalistic representation and the features of the miniature Indian painting style with Indian subjects.

These Company style paintings became popular in the second half of the 18th century. These were first produced in the Madras Presidency, but spread to other centres in **Calcutta** (now Kolkata), **Murshidabad, Patna, Benares, Agra, Lucknow, Delhi**, and parts of western India, thus developing into regional and local Schools. However, this style which emerged as a need for documentation of the landscape, people, flora fauna etc., suffered a blow in the mid-19th century. With the advent of photography (around the 1840s), the demand for such paintings started to decline, as the new technology was much better suited for such documentation. In the second half of the 19th century, this art gradually withered and gave way to the Academic style of painting under the influence of the **European Academic Art movement**.

Patna Kalam: A Regional School Painting of the Commoners

The Patna School of Painting referred to as the Patna Kalam/Qalam, which flourished for nearly 200 years was perhaps amongst the very few independent schools of painting that captured the lifestyle of the common people. The School traces its origin to the Mughal school of painting which suffered a decline during the reign of Aurangzeb and subsequent rulers. Hence, its exponents migrated to other regions looking for royal patronage and support. One such group of artists is said to have migrated to the court of Nawab of Murshidabad, where the art of school of Murshidabad developed and flourished for some period. However, in the latter half of the 18th century, after the defeat of the nawab of Bengal at the hands of the British and the subsequent loss of patronage, the artists moved to the city of Patna in Bihar, which was the next bigger centre of the region. Here they received the support of the local aristocracy and the officials of the East India Company and the Patna School of Art evolved.

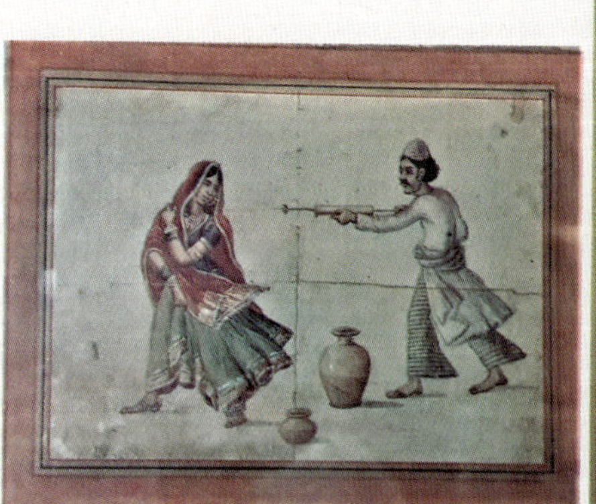

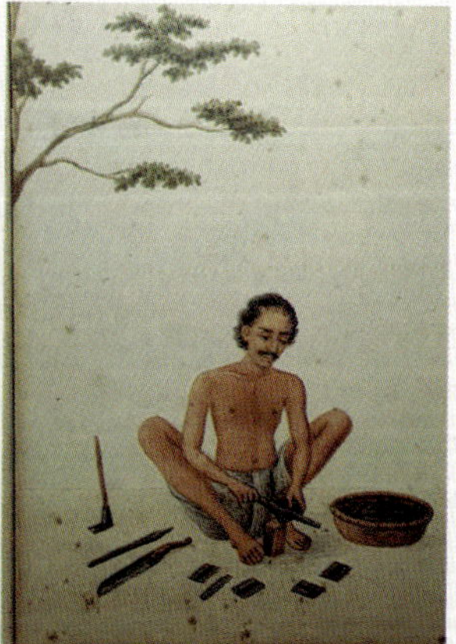

16.7 & 16.8: 'Holi', 'A Carpenter': Paintings of Patna Kalam, a unique school. Subjects painted on the white background without any decorative border depicting scenes from daily lives of common people, Patna Museum — photographs by Madhukar K Bhagat

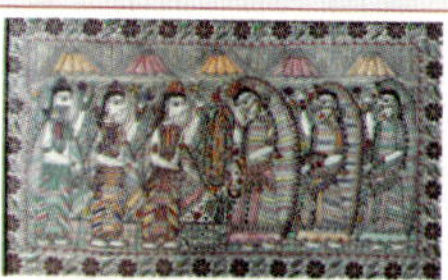

The School, while inheriting the characters of the Mughal art, also imbibed some of the water colour techniques of the European schools, thus combining the features of the indigenous tradition as well as the Company art. Like the Mughal School, this tradition involved use of varied and bright colours along with fine brush strokes. But the School dispensed with wide decorated borders while focusing on the main subject which itself was on a plain background. Further, unlike the royal arts, the subjects were exclusively drawn from the lives of the common people. These could be scenes of **local festivals and rituals, market place scenes, daily chores of ordinary people, monuments** etc.

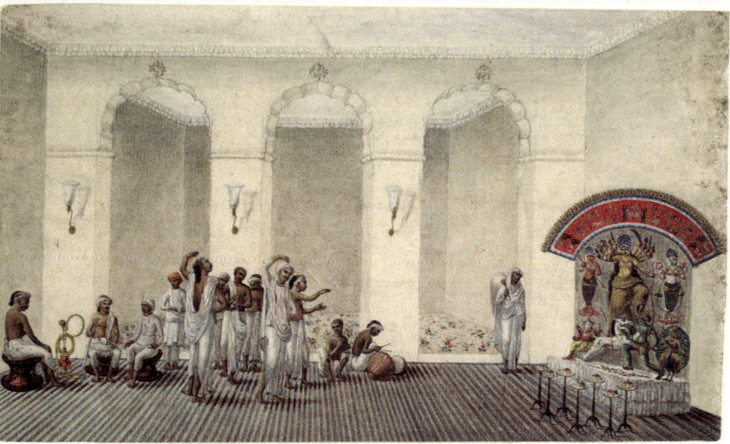

16.9: 'Durga Puja' by Sewak Ram; British library — Wikimedia Commons

Sewak Ram (late 18th century) and Shiv Dayal Lal (19th century), were among the celebrated painters of this School whose many works survive today. The School started declining after the advent of lithography and subsequently photography. Among the last of its established painters was Ishwari Prasad Verma, with whom this tradition survived as late as the 1950s.

PAINTINGS BY RAJA RAVI VARMA & THE GENRE OF ACADEMIC REALISM

Raja Ravi Varma

Raja Ravi Varma (1848 to 1906), can be described as among the **earliest of modern Indian painters,** and one of those painters who ushered Indian ethos and subjects to modern paintings. His art works were unique, as they combined the Western/European painting techniques with Indian sensibility and subjects and ushered a genre matching the western technique, and yet remaining quintessentially Indian.

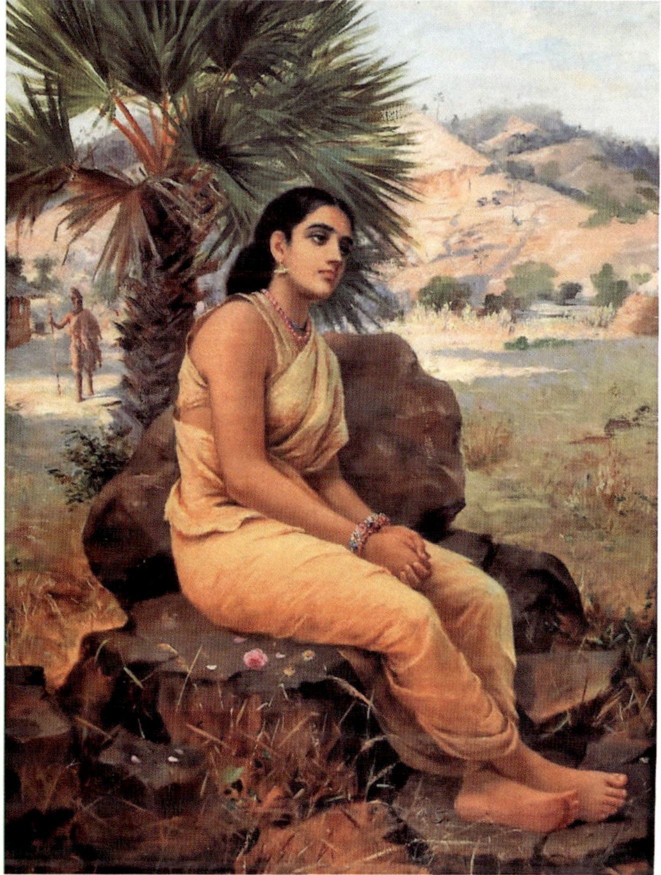

16.10: 'Shakuntala, lost in thoughts', considered amongst one of the masterpieces of Raja Ravi Varma. It is also referred to as 'Shakuntala under the shadow of an impending calamity'. Lost in the thoughts of Dushyanta, Shakuntala is oblivious of the visit of sage Vashistha (shown approaching in the background) and is cursed by him that her lover would lose all memory of her. However, he later relents on her pleading, and states that the curse would be reversed when he sees the signet ring given to Shakuntala. Oil on Canvas, 1901, location Government Museum, Chennai — photograph by Madhukar K Bhagat

The medium of his paintings included both oil and water colour. His paintings incorporated realism and perspective as in European art work. The use of light on skin and tonal effects added life-like quality to them. The **subjects** of his paintings were inspired from characters and scenes of Indian epics of *Ramayana* and *Mahabharata* and Indian mythologies. A unique contribution of his art was that the lithographs of these paintings were made available to people at relatively inexpensive prices. In later years, they served as the people's imagination of what gods and goddesses and other mythological characters would look like, and thus were an important source of popular calendar art. Besides the above, art scholars also identify the paintings of Raja Ravi Varma with representation of Indian women (particularly in sarees) from diverse backgrounds and different regions, their features, etc.

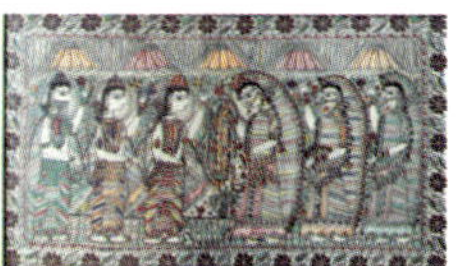

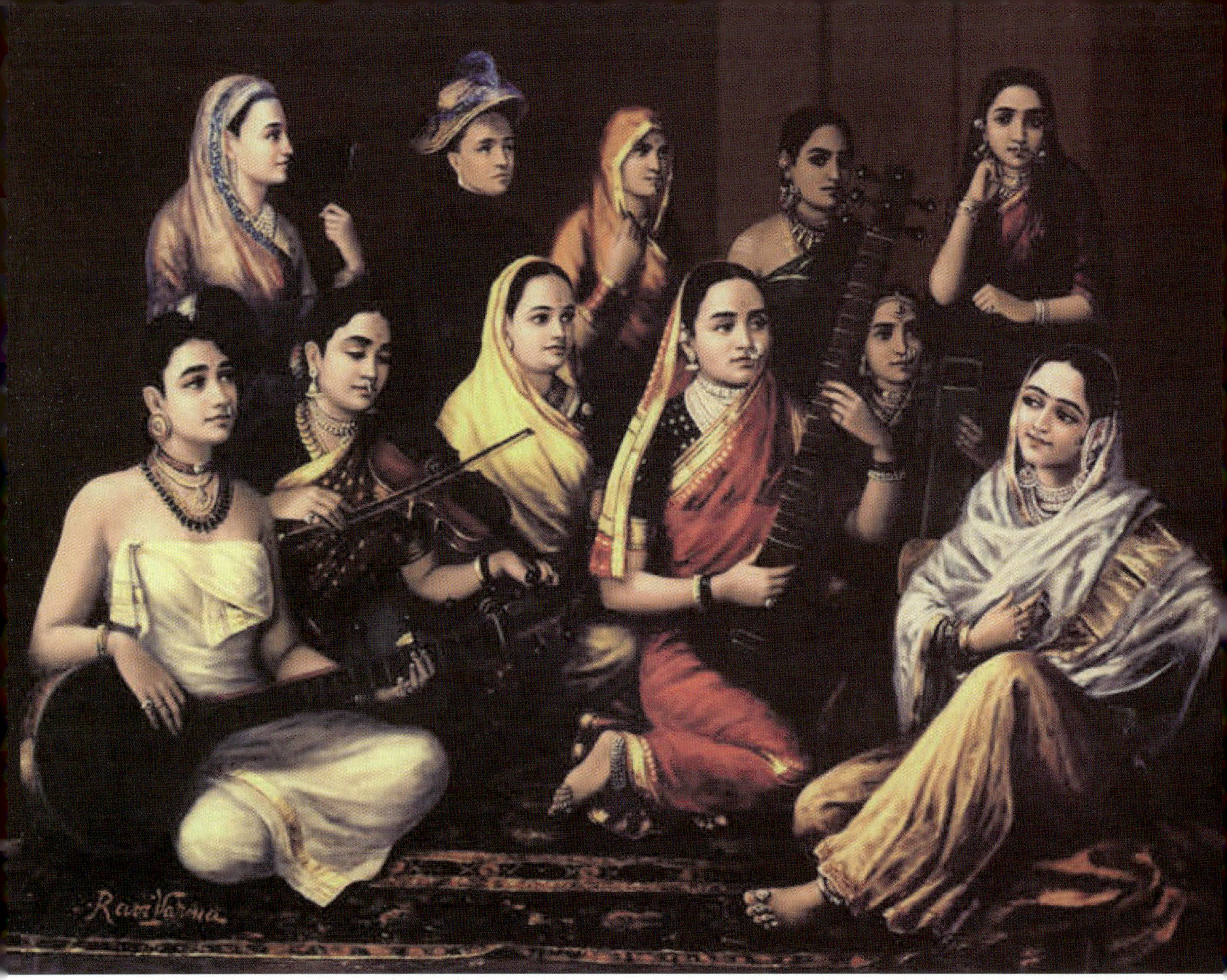

16.11: 'Galaxy of Musicians', oil on canvas, 1889, by Raja Ravi Varma. The painting depicts Indian women from different regions playing a variety of musical instruments, thus bringing out the diversity in regional customs, traditions, dresses, appearance etc. and yet their convergence in the art of music. The painting is also notable for its vibrancy of colours and effect of light on the characters — Wikimedia Commons

The most famous of his paintings are; *Shakuntala*, *Damayanti Hamsa Samvad, Arjuna and Subhadra, Rama Conquers Varuna,* (see chapter 3) *Jatayu Wars with Ravana* (see chapter 3, Ancient India book), *Lord Krishna as Envoy* (see chapter 3, **Ancient India** book of this series), *Victory of Indrajit, Ladies in Moon light,* and *Galaxy of Musicians* amongst many others. *Putrakamesthi-yagam*, is another masterpiece of a painting of Raja Ravi Varma, depicting a scene from Valmiki Ramayana depicting Dasharatha performing a *yagna* for seeking the boon of sons (see chapter 3 **Ancient India** book of this series).

Over a period of time, his paintings came under criticism. Some artists and scholars believed that his art was driven by popularity and was adrift from the soul of the folk and true Indian traditions. With the emergence of nationalism in India in the late 19th and early 20th centuries, which also

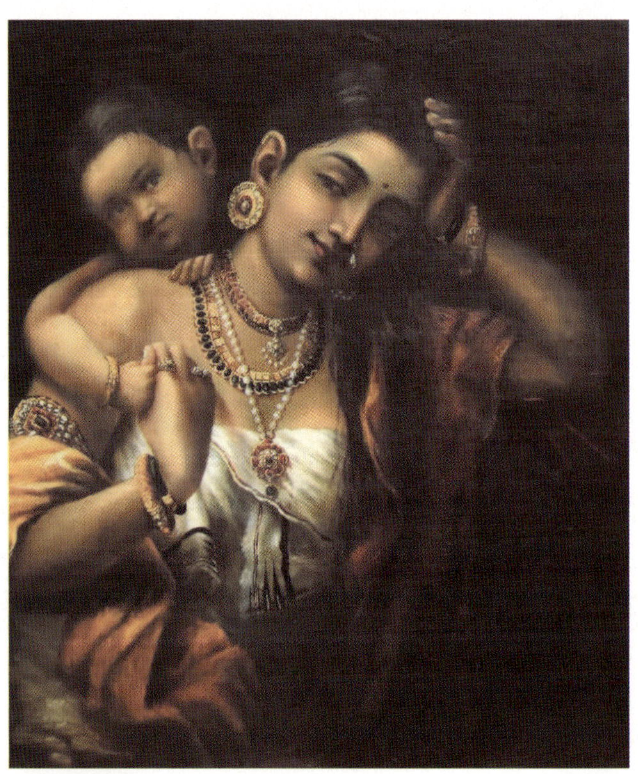

16.12: 'Krishna and Yashoda' by Raja Ravi Varma. The painting brings out the tonal effects and the effect of light. Oil on Canvas, size 94 cm by 90 cm; 1901, location Government Museum, Chennai — photograph by Madhukar K Bhagat

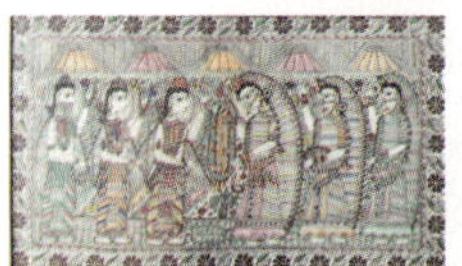

permeated the Indian art, the European Academic style was considered to be too alien to represent the Indian Gods and characters from Indian mythology.

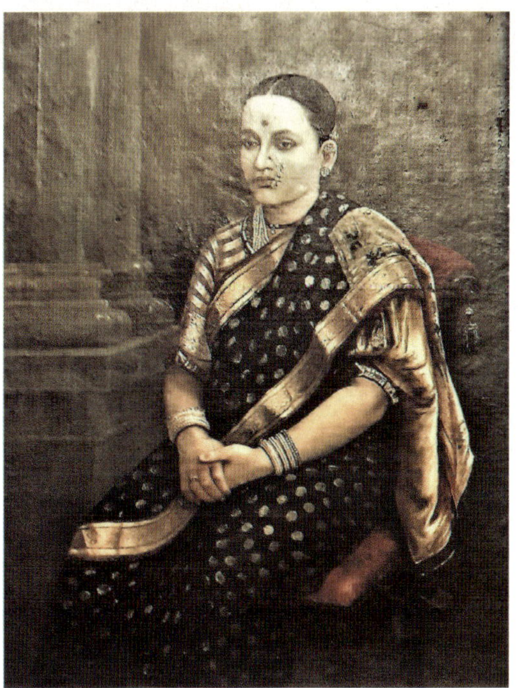

16.13: 'The Portrait of a Lady'; oil on canvas, by Raja Ravi Varma; National Gallery of Modern Art, New Delhi — photograph by Madhukar K Bhagat

Academic Realism

The period of mid to the late 19th century, was the genre of **Academic Realism of Indian paintings**. It saw a transition from the erstwhile Mughal, Rajput school styles and the Company style while adopting the European style of academic art (art style which was popular in European Academies). Thus, it incorporated the European technique of landscape and portraiture in the Indian paintings. With it, became popular the **easel and oil painting style** in India. **Naturalism**, or realism, was the quintessence of this style, which meant portraying the reality of subject with visual accuracy which was similar to photography. However, the subjects of these paintings would include Indian people, scenes of fairs and festivals, landscapes, Indian flora and fauna, dancers, trades, etc. With the establishment of the different schools of art by the British in places such as Madras (in 1850 referred to as **The Madras School of Art**), Calcutta (in 1854, referred to as the **Government College of Art**

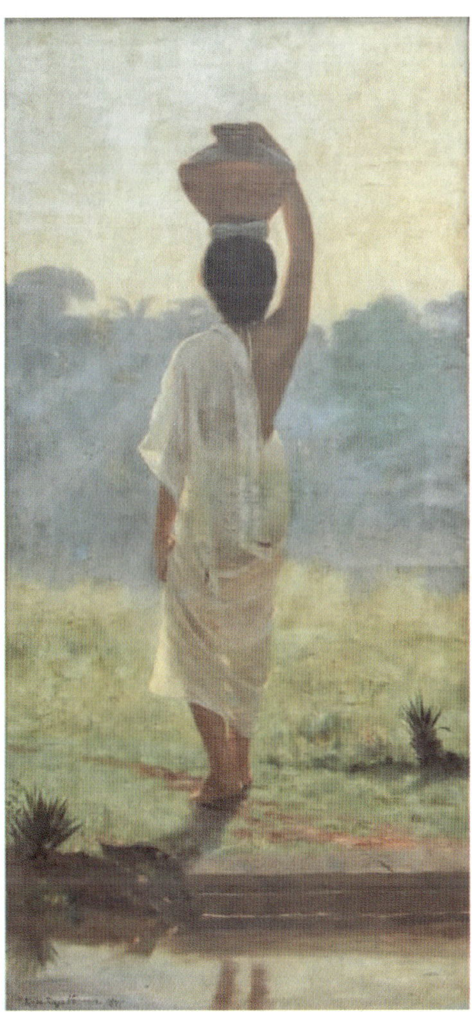

16.14: 'The Water Carrier', by Raja Raja Varma. The painting brings out the translucent effect of drapery. Oil on Canvas, 1894; location Government Museum, Chennai — photograph by Madhukar K Bhagat

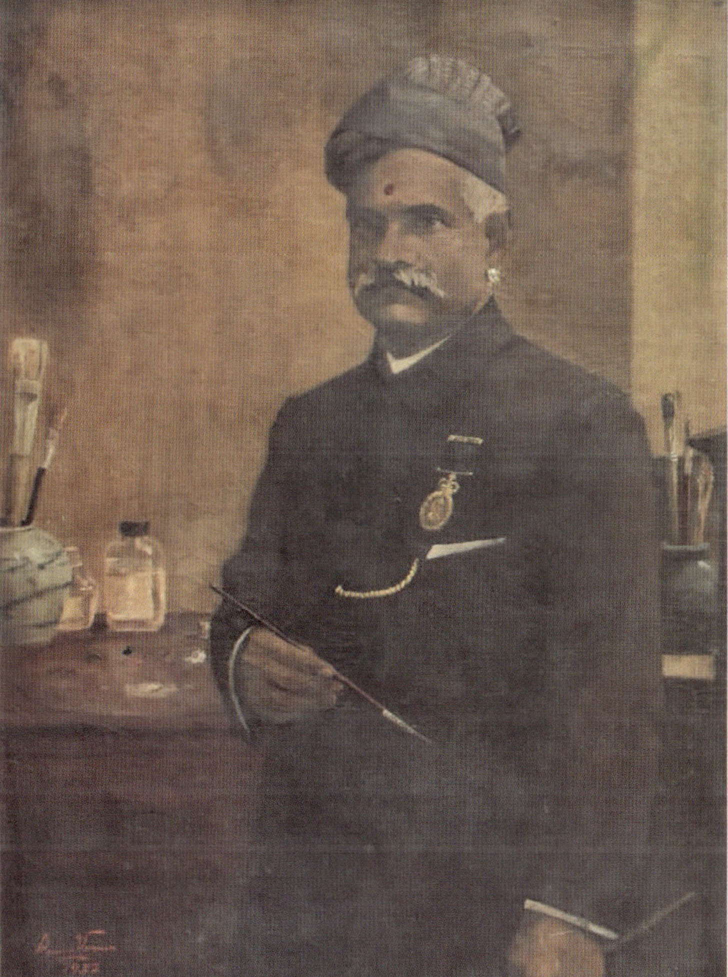

16.15: Portrait of Raja Ravi Varma by Raja Raja Varma. Oil on Canvas;1894; location Government Museum, Chennai — photograph by Madhukar K Bhagat

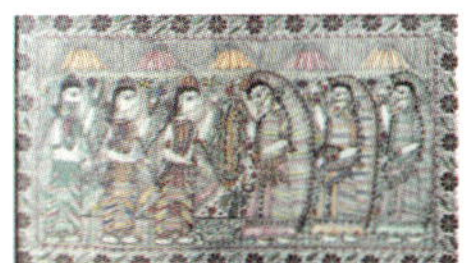

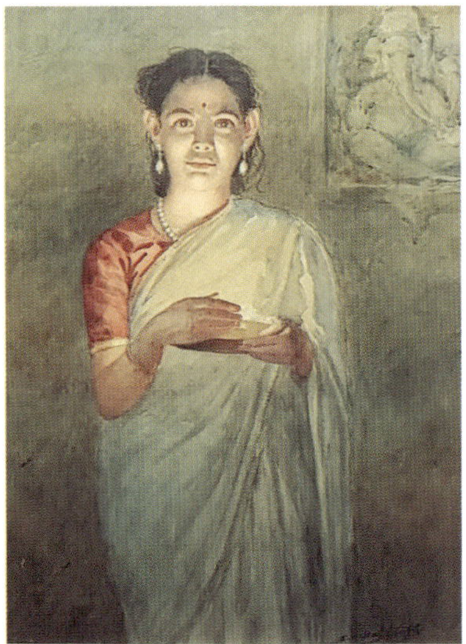

16.16: 'Niranjani'; water colour, bringing out the effect of light; by S.L. Haldankar, Central Museum, Nagpur — photograph by Madhukar K Bhagat

and Craft), Bombay (in 1857, referred to as the **JJ School of Art** or as the **Bombay School of Art**; founded by Jamshedjee Jeejabhoy) and **Lahore School** (in 1876, referred to as Mayo School of Industrial Arts), there emerged a generation of painters who were exponents of the Academic art and realism.

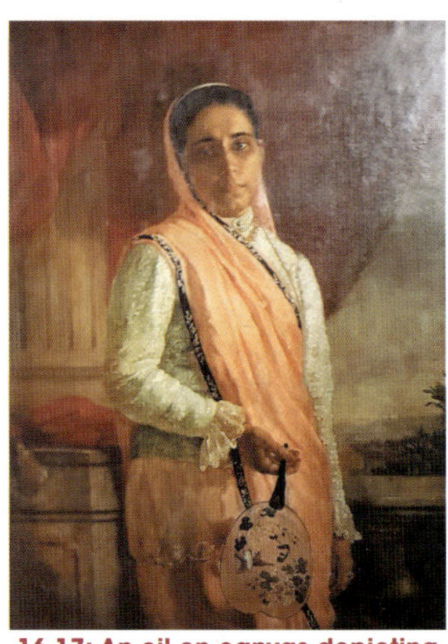

16.17: An oil on canvas depicting a woman by M.F. Pithawalla; National Gallery of Modern Art, New Delhi — photograph by Madhukar K Bhagat

Among the **prominent painters** of this genre in the late 19th and early 20th century were **Pestonjee Bomanjee** (1851-1938), **Mahadev Vishwanath Dhurandhar** (1867-1944), **A.X. Trindade** (1870-1935), **Laxmi Narayan Taskar** (1870-1937), **M.F. Pithawalla** (1872-1937), **Sawlaram Lakshman Haldankar** (1882-1968), **Gunwant H. Nagarkar** (1892-1956), **Hemen Majumdar** (1894-1948) etc. Further, **Raja Raja Varma** (1860-1905) (brother of Raja Ravi Varma) and **Raja Rama Varma** (son of Raja Ravi Varma) were also eminent painters of this period and of similar genre.

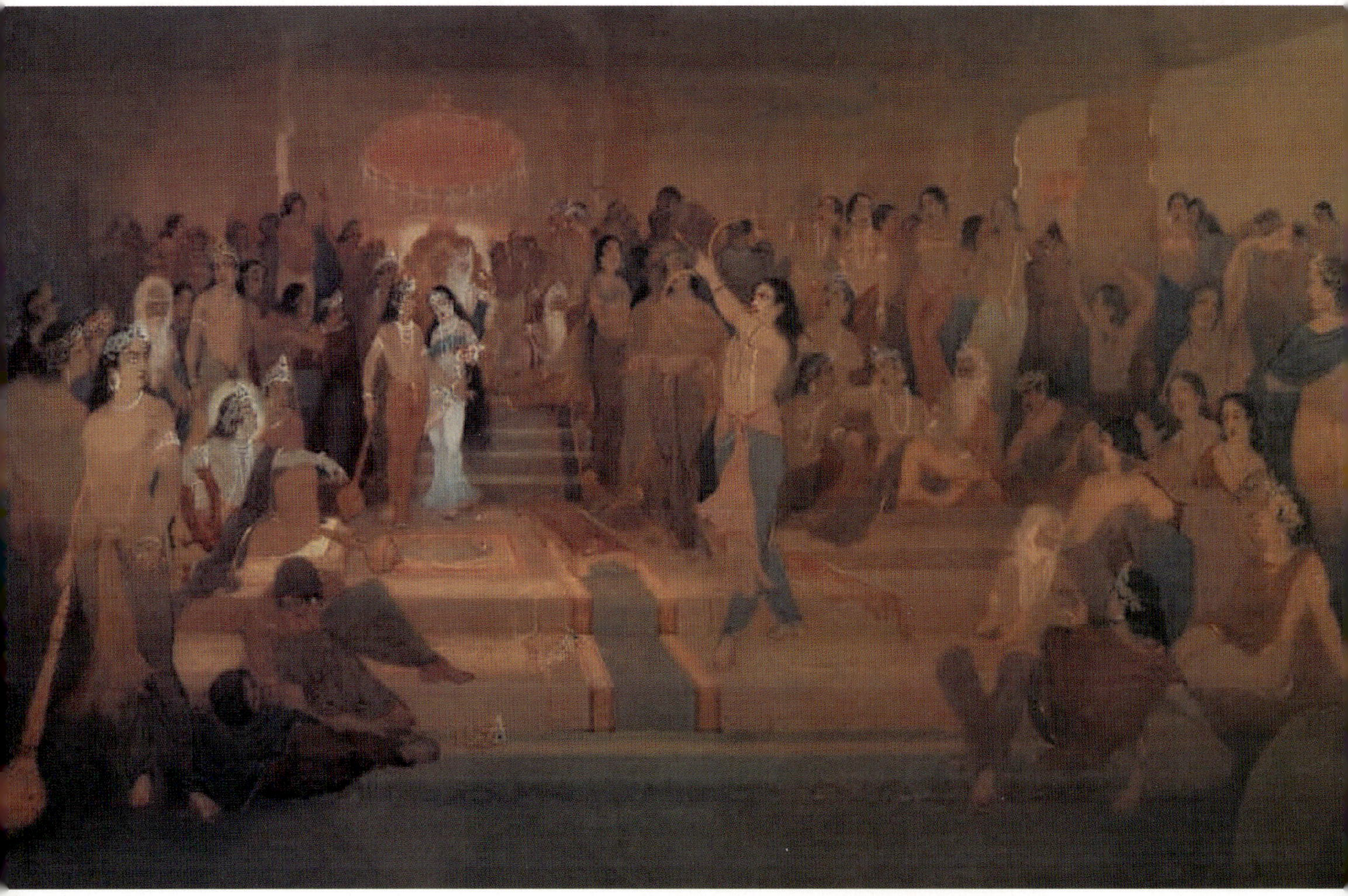

16.18: 'Draupadi Swayamvar', by Gunwant H. Nagarkar; water colour, reflecting wash technique of painting; Nagpur Central Museum — photograph by Madhukar K Bhagat

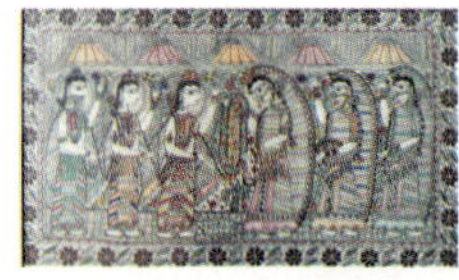

BENGAL SCHOOL OF ART

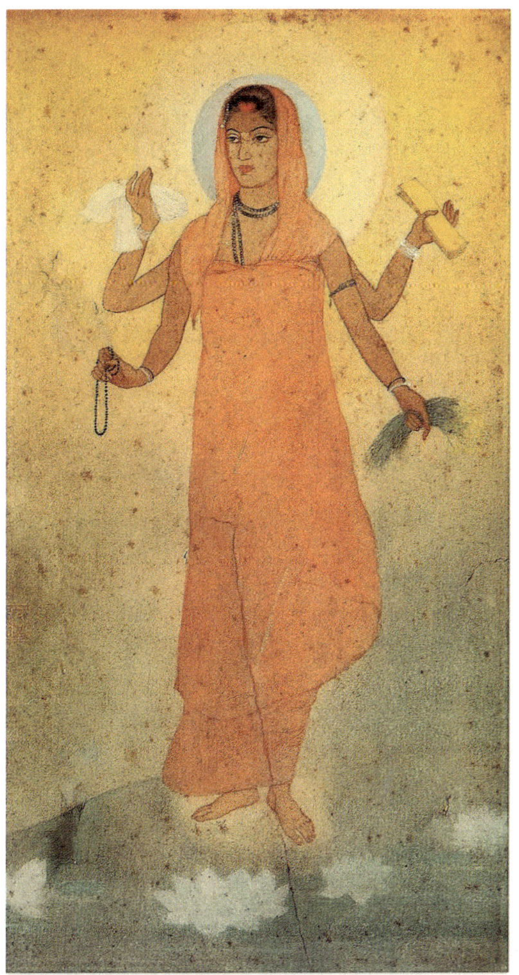

16.19: 'Bharat Mata' by Abanindranath Tagore — Wikimedia Commons

The Bengal School of Art

The nationalistic fervour which swept the country in the early 20th century, influenced Indian paintings too and led to the emergence of the **Bengal School of Art**; a movement of **revivalism** in Indian art. This art movement aimed to regenerate Indian art heritage by recognising and bringing alive its ancient and folk traditions of painting as well as connecting the art with people and their lives. It was against the Academic school and the Company style which were considered to be alien to the Indian ethos.

This art movement was started by **Abanindranath Tagore** (nephew of Rabindranath Tagore) along with **E.B. Havell** (Principal of Government Art School, Calcutta) and **Sister Nivedita** (an associate of Swami Vivekananda). It emphasised on an art which was Indian in all respects, including the ethos, the style, the subjects and even the material deployed. It drew inspiration from the murals of the ancient period and miniatures of the medieval period and developed a philosophy of pan-Indian Art.

Thus, the Bengal school was truly an **Indian school of art,** as its technique, character and subjects, were completely indigenous. In a way it was also an unorthodox school as it advocated against established 'Academic style' of painting as being promoted by the British and even against the established painters like Raja Ravi Varma and their art styles. It moved away from use of oil painting such as in western paintings, and popularised Indian paintings such as tempera, and incorporated painting techniques such as 'washes'. It was also influenced by the murals and the miniature style of paintings as was in the Ajanta paintings and the Mughal, Rajput and Pahari styles. The subjects of these paintings were completely indigenous and included the landscapes, portraits, historical scenes and anecdotes from daily life in the countryside, besides religious and mythological figures.

Abanindranath Tagore, the pioneer of this school, along with Havell, endeavoured to Indianise the art education in the Government Arts School, Calcutta. To promote and create wider awareness of the art movement, he even started the *Journal of the Indian Society of Oriental Art*. He himself was an eminent artist and his famous works include the *Bharat Mata, Krishna Leela series, Tales of Arabian Nights, Passing of Shah Jahan* etc. His endeavour led to the emergence of many new artists who developed their own unique styles and influenced the Indian art for the next half a century. Some of the other notable painters associated or inspired with this movement were **Rabindranath Tagore, Abanindranath Tagore, Gaganendranath Tagore, Nandalal Bose, Jamini Roy, Sunayani Devi, Ram Kinker Baij**, **M. R. Chugtai** and others.

However, some scholars do not consider the Bengal school to be a completely correct description of this movement. Although this revivalism in Indian art started from Calcutta, it was not just restricted to Bengal. Later, this trend was visible in other parts of the country and also inspired the eminent school of painters at Shantiniketan.

The Shantiniketan School

With the establishment of the Shantiniketan School by **Rabindranath Tagore,** and later with the founding of an art school (**Kala Bhavan**) in it, a new chapter emerged in modern Indian paintings. The Shantiniketan School further gave impetus to the movement of return of the art form to the **traditional Indian roots**. Nandalal Bose, one of the earliest students of Abanindranath Tagore, was a pioneer of this school, who was invited by Rabindranath Tagore to head the arts school or Kala Bhavan. He emphasised on a new language of art which was connected to the folk arts, common people and the Indian roots. He painted the famous **linocut of Dandi March of Mahatma Gandhi**. Later, in the 1937 session of the Indian National

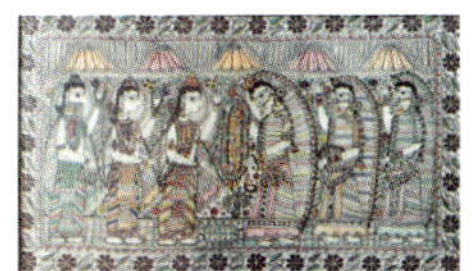

Congress at Haripura, he painted the famous **Haripura posters** which depicted the common rural folks engaged in daily chores such as a farmer tilling, a woman churning milk, a musician drumming etc., thus endeavouring to connect art with the masses.

The Shantiniketan School also helped in the emergence of a new generation of artists who spread the revivalism in Indian art in different parts of the country, like **K.Venkatappa** in South India. The school, and the new artists it nurtured, shaped Indian art for the next three to four decades. Some of the other eminent painters associated with Shantiniketan were **Benod Behari Mukherjee, Ram Kinker Baij, Asit Haldar, Kshitindranath Majumdar, Sarada Charan Ukil, Manishi Dey** and others.

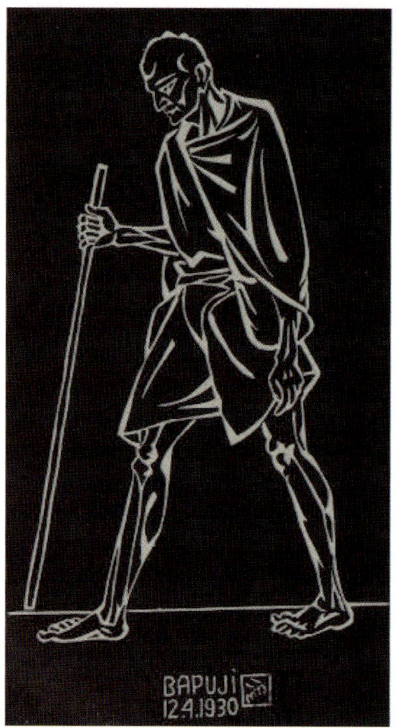

16.20: Dandi March and Mahatma Gandhi; 1930; Linocut by Nandalal Bose

This was also the period of early modernism and experimentation in the Indian art; a phase which also explored the different facets of art emerging elsewhere in the world. An important milestone in the Indian art evolution of this period was the visit of Japanese art nationalist **Kakuzo Okakura** to Shantiniketan and meeting with Rabindranath Tagore. The former believed in revivalism in Asian art and evolution of pan-Asian art as distinct from the western imperialistic art traditions. Later, his students were to showcase at Shantiniketan to Abanindranath Tagore and other students the **wash technique of water-colours** as an alternative to oil painting. The technique was adopted, modified and later evolved in the Indian art traditions.

Another significant influence in art was the **cubist style** of painting reflecting in the art work of Gaganendranath Tagore (brother of Abanindranath Tagore). This art form was inspired from the technique of German artists of **Paul Klee, Kandisky** and others, when in 1922, an important exhibition of their work travelled to Calcutta. **Gaganedranath** adopted the abstract cubist style in art to create building interiors using geometrical patterns.

Wash Technique & Cubism

The adoption of **wash technique** in water colours was a significant milestone in the Bengal art revivalism. The technique is said have Chinese and Japanese origin. It was adopted and further adapted to the Indian art context by **Abanindranath Tagore**, **Nandalal Bose** and other artists at Shantiniketan. The technique essentially involves application of diluted paints to create a semi-transparent effect, thus bringing out the reflection from the white surface of the paper. At times, a flat brush charged with water is applied to the painted and finished surface to have softer tonalities in the paintings. It is said that Abanindranath further innovated on this technique, wherein after a first semi-transparent and thin layer of paint, the painting would be literally dipped in water (a technique different from Japanese wash

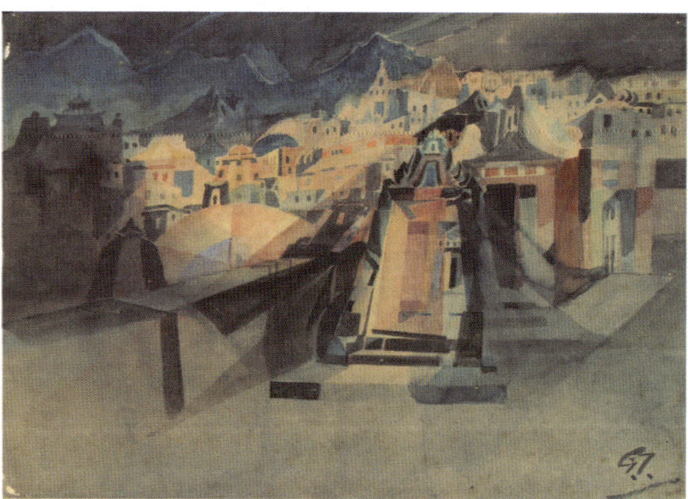

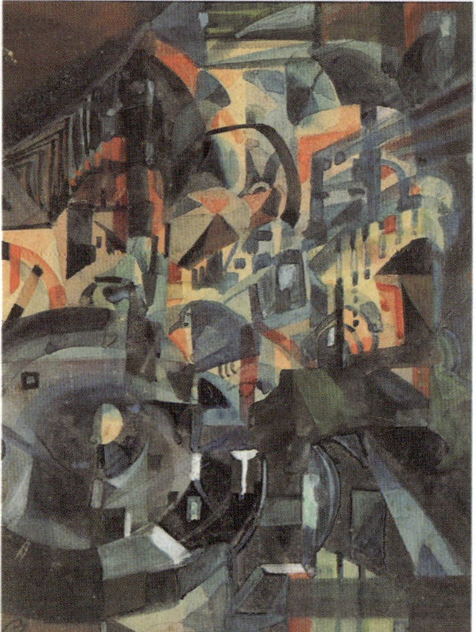

16.21 & 16.22: 'Dwarkapuri' and 'City by Night', cubist style paintings by Gaganendranath Tagore — Wikimedia Commons

technique). Thereafter, another transparent layer of paint would be applied and hence forth. The result would be a fusion of colours with softer tonalities,diminishing the harshness of the geometries of the figures in a dream like finish. (see *Bharat Mata* by Abanindranath Tagore) **Cubism** was a movement in the paintings and other art forms in the early 20th century in Europe which deeply influenced paintings, sculptures etc. It was also referred to as an *avant garde* (advanced and unorthodox) art movement. World famous artists like **Pablo Picasso, Georges Braque** and **Jean Metzinger,** amongst others, were considered to be its pioneers. The art involved analysis of the image, breaking it up in subcomponents and reassembling it in abstract geometrical shapes. Unlike realism, the art would involve representation of the subject from multiple perspectives. Thus, it endeavored to create a more abstract language of art.

In India, this movement took roots in the paintings of Gaganendranath Tagore who was among the few artists of early 20th century to adopt it with his own interpretation of the cubism style distinct from the European trend. **'A Bed of Arrows', 'City in the Night', 'Dwarkapuri'**, by Tagore are considered to be important paintings amongst others in this genre. In the post-independence period, Indian paintings were inspired by the world movement of modernism in paintings, particularly by the techniques of abstraction. Here, cubism too found a place in the works of painters like **Jehangir Sabavala** and others. At times, Indian cubism is considered to a precursor to the art movement, which later followed in the works of M.F. Hussain, Souza and other artists in the ensuing decades.

PROGRESSIVE ARTISTS' GROUP

Post-independence Indian art saw another significant leap with the formation of **Progressive Artists' Group of Bombay** with famous painters, **F.N. Souza, S.H. Raza, M.F. Hussain, K.H. Ara, H.A. Gade, and S.K. Bakre** (a sculptor) as its founders. Later, other eminent painters and artists such **as Tyeb Mehta, Gaitonde, Manishi Dey, and Akbar Padamsee** joined it. The group which came to existence post-independence in 1947 is said to have disbanded around 1956. But even in this short period of time, it made a significant mark on Indian art.

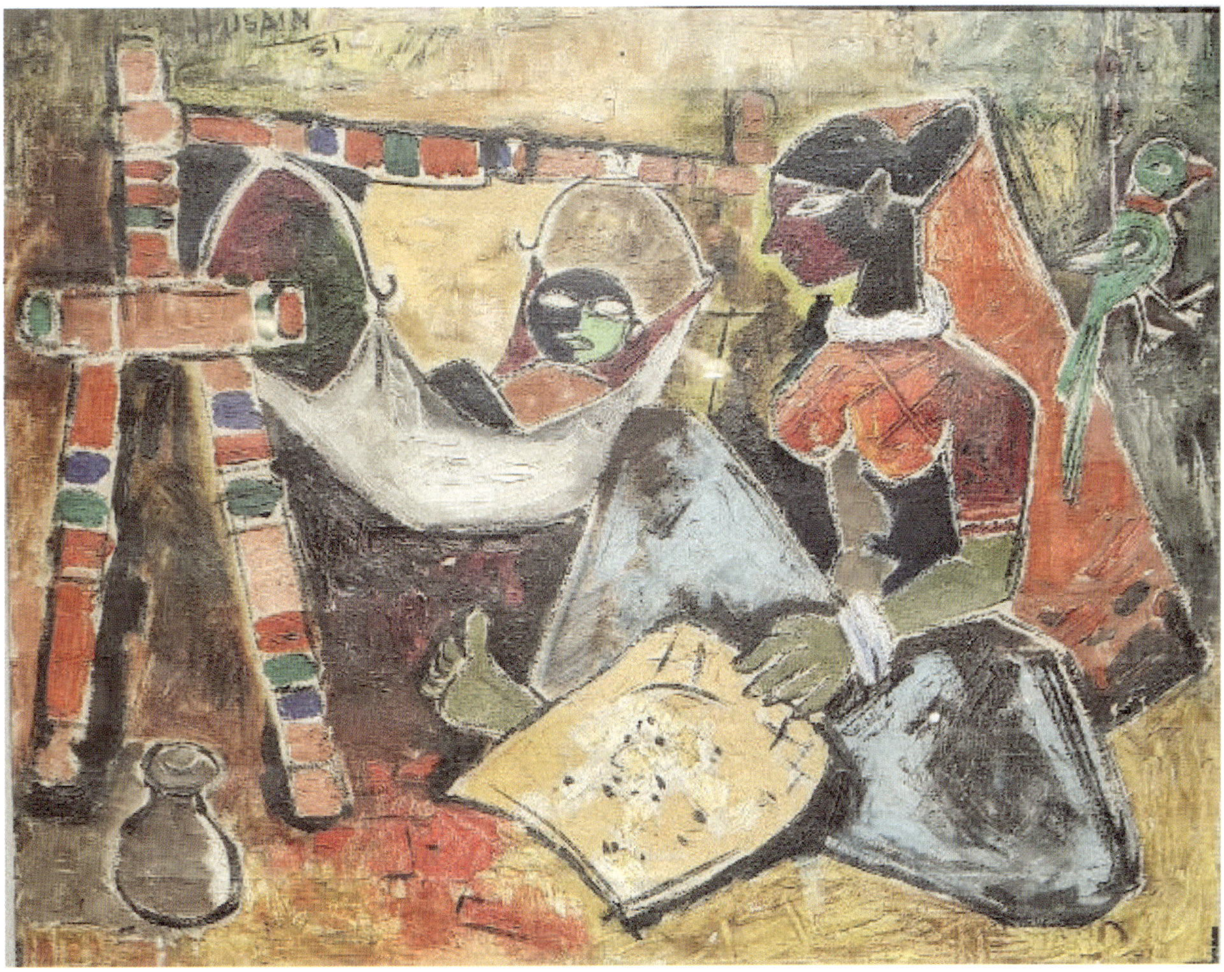

16.23: 'Mother and Child', an early work of M.F. Hussain, one of the founders of the Progressive Arts Movement; Chhatrapati Shivaji Maharaj Vastu Sangrahalaya, Mumbai; — photograph by Madhukar K Bhagat

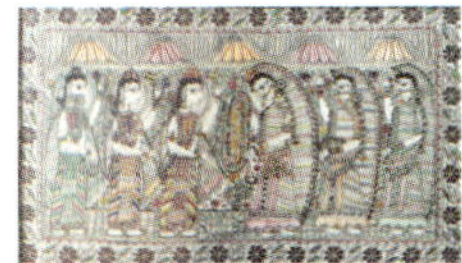

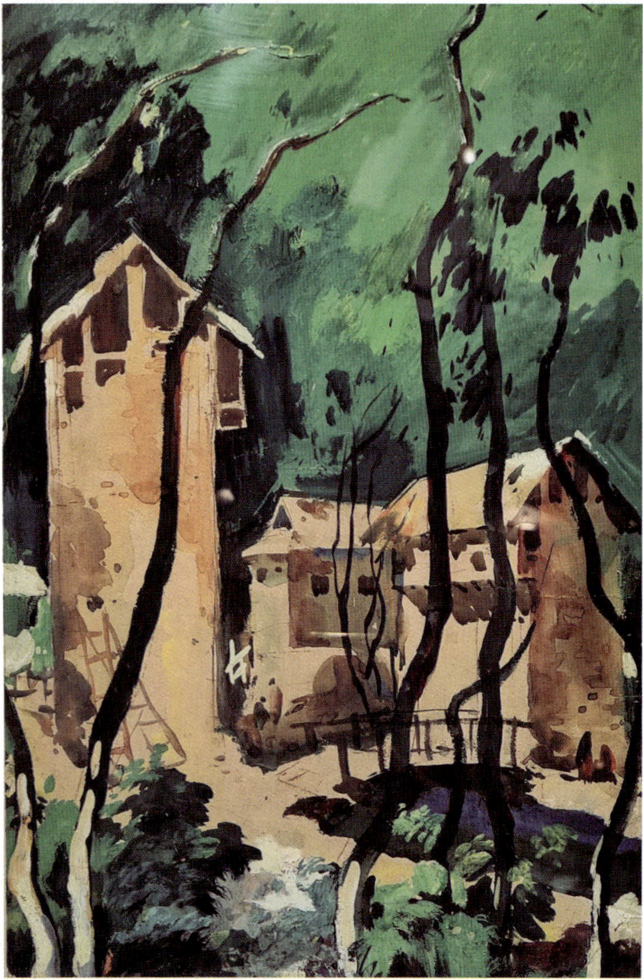

16.24: Landscape, watercolour on paper by S. H Raza, an early genre of his painting, Chhatrapati Shivaji Maharaj Vastu Sangrahalaya, Mumbai; — photograph by Madhukar K Bhagat

Each of these artists had a distinct style of its own. While Souza's paintings, particularly the nudes of women with exaggerated proportions, wanted to break from the conventions of beauty and the extant artistic traditions, that of Hussain endeavoured to explore modernism in the Indian context. It mixed the brush strokes and certain elements of cubism of the West with bright colours of the Indian art tradition. Raza, who began with landscapes, moved towards abstraction, while incorporating the use of *mandala* and *yantra* in his art. His later paintings incorporated a *bindu* (a point), representing spiritual unity of the Indian philosophy. Gaitonde was another artist pursuing abstraction through representation of translucent beams of light. Many other artists of this period like Tyeb Mehta, Akbar Padamsee, KK Hebbar and others worked between abstraction and figurativeness.

Thus these painters broke away from the revivalist nationalism of Bengal Art movement and set the path for modern and abstract art which synthesised Indian art tradition with 'European Modernism'. In the later years, new groups emerged, such as the 'Group 1890' led by J. Swaminathan. Many new artists also emerged with different genres such as new figurative art, new media art, digital art etc., while the older art forms of abstraction, folk art, washes, oil and easel art continuing to be practiced.

IMPORTANT MODERN INDIAN PAINTERS

Raja Ravi Varma (1848 –1906)

He is considered the first modern Indian painter whose art brought a fusion of western style and technique with the Indian ethos. The subjects included characters from the Ramayana, Mahabharata and Indian mythology. His paintings also provided an imagination of the appearance of the various gods

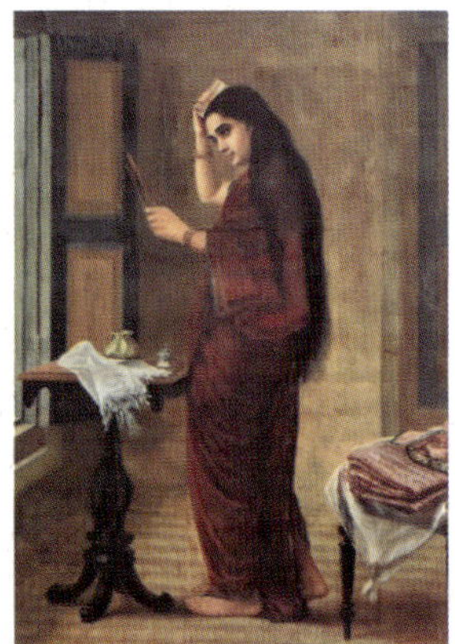

16.25: Lady With a Mirror

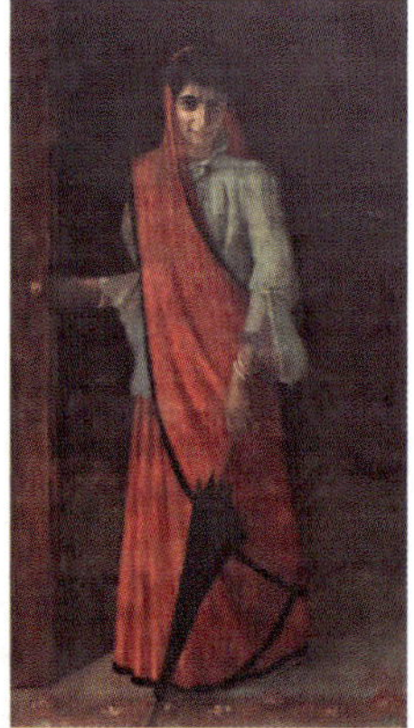

16.26: Going Out, a common lady

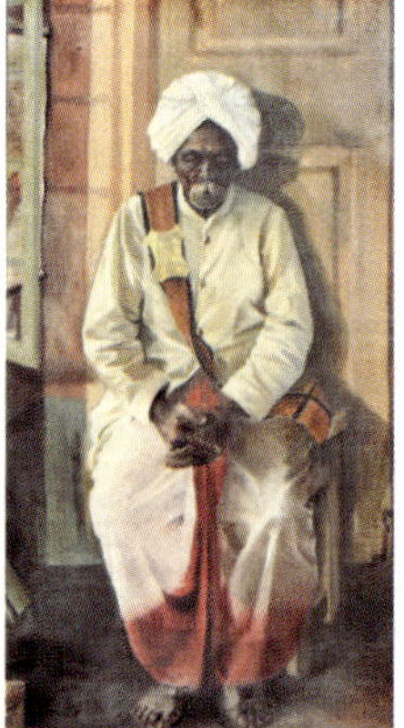

16.27: The Old Peon

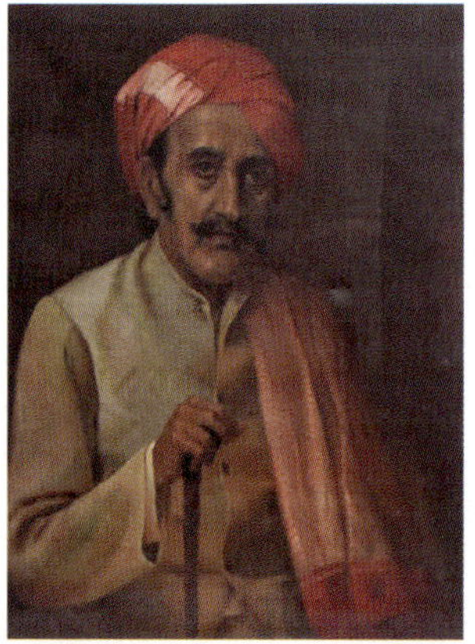

16.28: A Retired Sepoy

Paintings of Raja Ravi Varma of common people in day-to-day activities. Present location, Government Museum, Chennai — photographs by Madhukar K Bhagat

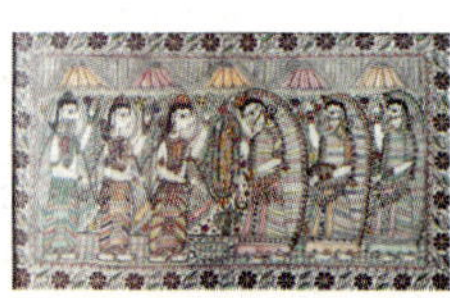

and goddesses. His work even included many characters from daily life. His oeuvre was indeed an inspiration for the next generation of Indian painters.

Abanindranath Tagore (1872-1951)

He heralded the nationalistic fervour in painting and the emergence of the Bengal School of Art movement which later culminated in a pan Indian art movement. He incorporated use of Indian techniques and material such as tempera, in the Indian paintings. He also adapted the wash technique and improvised it to the Indian context, thus ushering an innovative art form different from the 'European Academic art'. His famous paintings include *Bharat Mata, Tales of Arabian Nights, Krishna Leela series*, *The Passing of Shah Jahan, Journey's End, The Forest, Coming of Night, Mountain Traveller,* and *Queen of the Forest*, amongst many others.

16.29: The 'Passing of Shah Jahan' by Abanindranath Tagore — Wikimedia Commons

Nandalal Bose (1882-1966)

He was one of the most prominent artists of modern India and a protégé of Abanindranath Tagore and Havell. His uniqueness of paintings lay in his synthesis, particularly of the historic artistic tradition and contemporary Indian art. The subjects of his works included painting of scenes from daily Indian life, villages, mythologies, etc. His most famous paintings include the black and white **linocut of Dandi March** and Mahatma Gandhi. Under his supervision and guidance, the work of preparing nearly 400 painting posters depicting common people and their activities, was prepared for the Haripura Congress session of 1937. He was also entrusted with the work of illustrating the **original manuscript of the Constitution of India**.

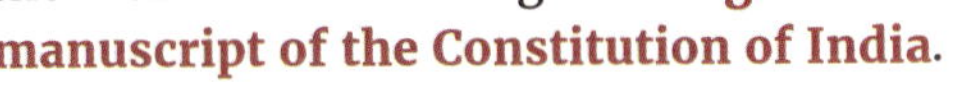

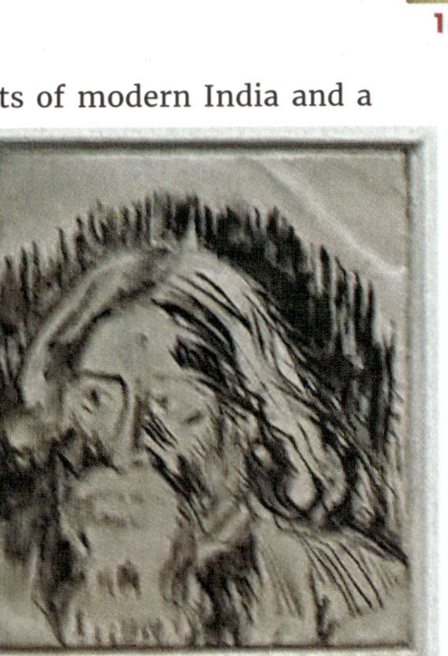

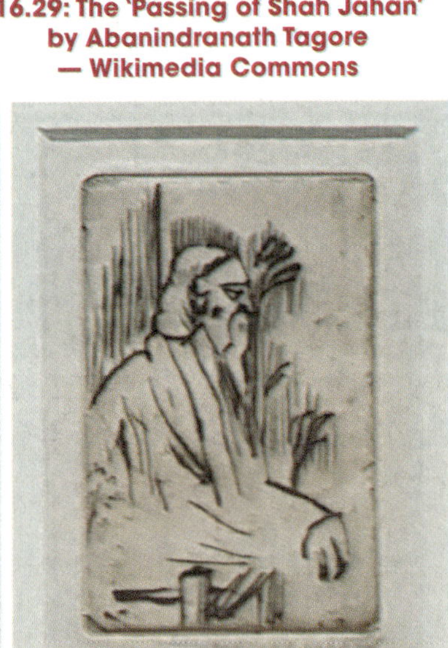

16.30 & 16.31: 'Rabindranath Tagore'; dry point on paper by Nandalal Bose, National Gallery of Modern Art, New Delhi — photographs by Madhukar K Bhagat

Rabindranath Tagore (1861–1994)

He made his foray in the world of paintings in his 60s. He had no formal training in this art. He had a highly imaginative and spontaneous style which would employ use of brush, rags, cotton, and even fingers. His subject/topics would include a wide range from mysterious human faces to bizarre beasts, mystic landscapes to birds and flowers, etc. His paintings had a limited pallet and were different from the more elegant Bengal school paintings. But it had imaginativeness, and drew inspiration from the Mughal and Pahari miniatures and from the Ajanta frescoes.

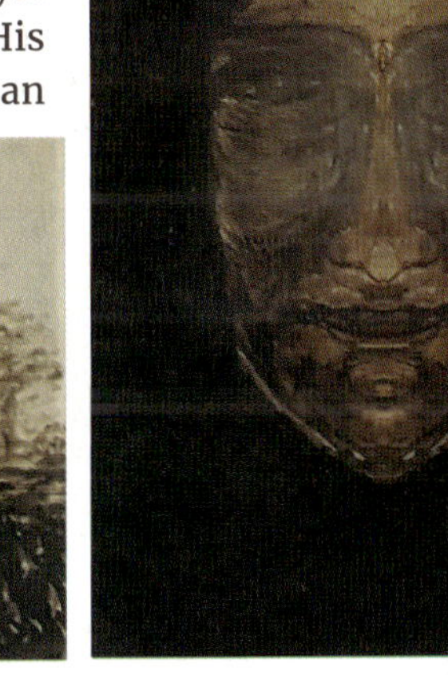

16.32 & 16.33: 'Landscape'; ink on paper, 'Head Study', paintings by Rabindranath Tagore; National Gallery of Modern Art, New Delhi — photographs by Madhukar K Bhagat

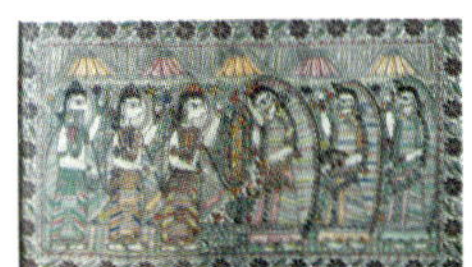

Jamini Roy (1887-1972)

He was one of the most famous pupils of Abanindranath, and himself a renowned painter, trained in the European Academic style. However, in the 1920s, he ushered a new style by incorporating the **Kalighat Style** and the style of village Patua artists of Bengal. His paintings involved use of inexpensive material by folk artists (rather than oil and canvas) and he painted ordinary men and women from the village. The use of colours was limited to seven earthy or mineral colours, and like village artists he even developed his own colours using vegetables and minerals. His famous paintings include the *Santhal Dance, Mother and Child, Gopini, Krishna and Gopiyan, Three Pujarins, The Last Supper, Mary and Christ* etc. In his lifetime, he is said to have produced a staggering 20000 paintings. He was awarded the **Padma Bhushan** in 1954.

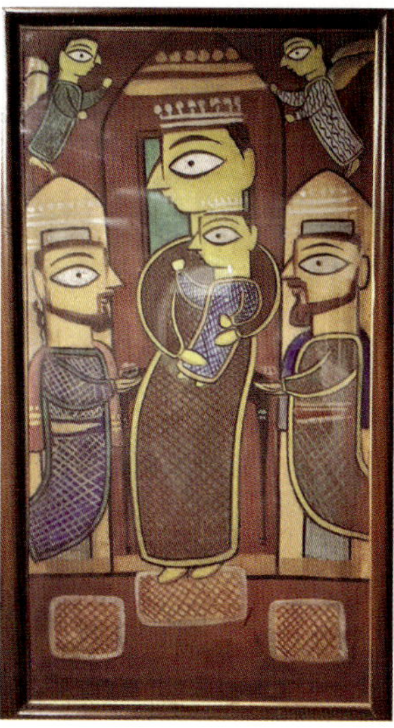

16.34 : 'Mary and Christ', tempera on cloth. Painting by Jamini Roy, National Gallery of Modern Art, New Delhi — photograph by Madhukar K Bhagat

Ramkinkar Baij (1906-1980)

He was another famous painter and a renowned sculpture of the Shantiniketan School. His works are often said to reflect the celebrations of nature and the everyday experiences. Scholars also regard his works to be a part of **contextual modernism**. Many of his works were inspired from the lifestyles of the *adivasi* (tribal) and marginalised communities living around Shantiniketan. Among his famous works are the sculptures of **Yaksha and Yakshi** (in the front gate of the Reserve Bank of India), **The Santhal Family** (1938 Shantiniketan) etc. He was also a Padma Bhushan awardee (1970).

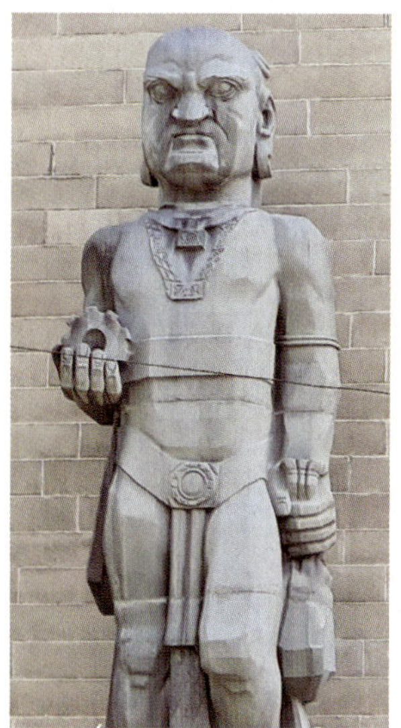

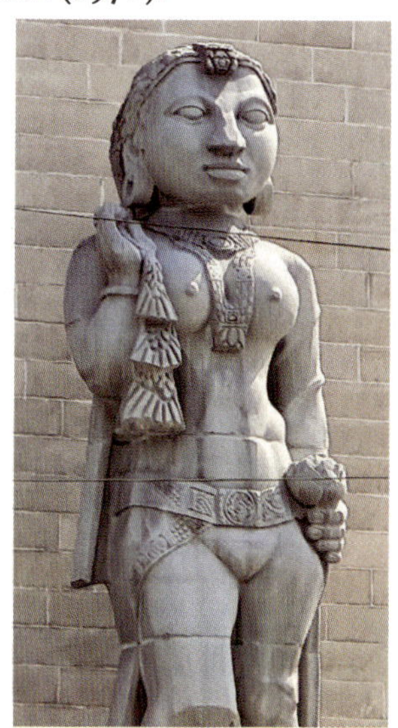

16.35: Sculptures of Yaksha and Yakshi by Ram Kinkar Baij (location Reserve Bank of India, New Delhi) — photographs by Madhukar K Bhagat

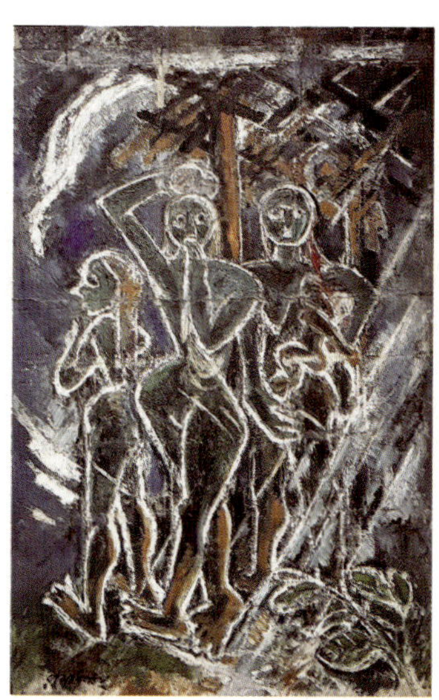

16.36: 'Shelter', oil on canvas; by Ramkinkar Baij, National Gallery of Modern Art, New Delhi — photograph by Madhukar K Bhagat

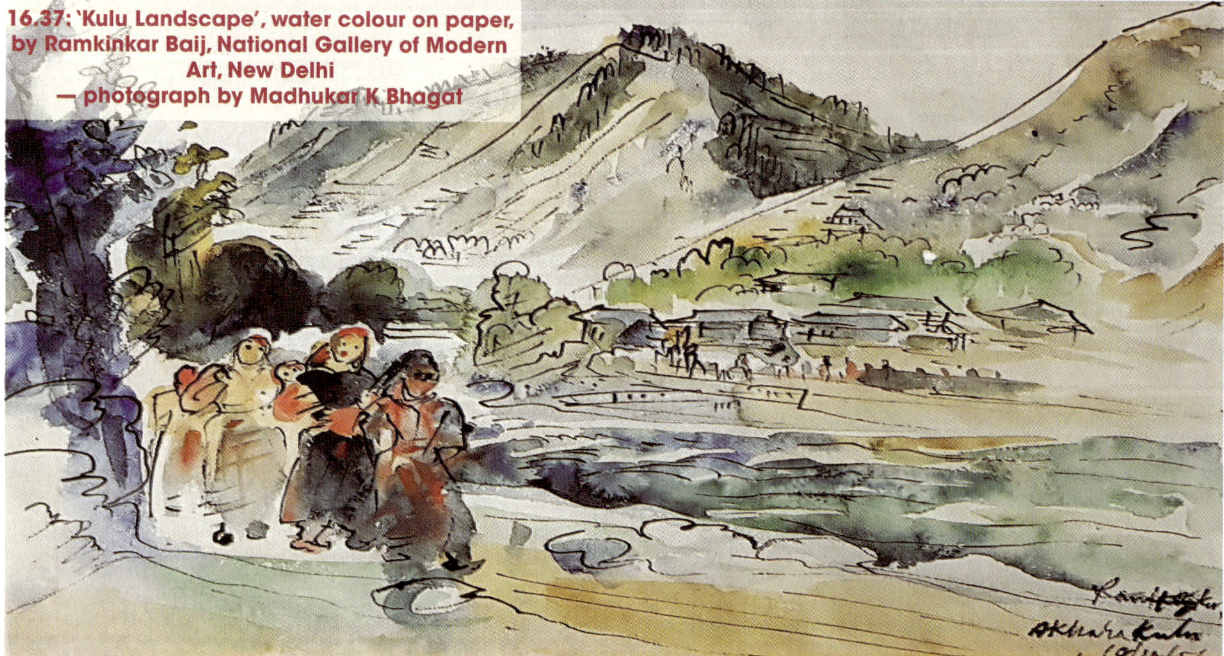

16.37: 'Kulu Landscape', water colour on paper, by Ramkinkar Baij, National Gallery of Modern Art, New Delhi — photograph by Madhukar K Bhagat

Contextual Modernism in Shantiniketan Art

Contextual Modernism refers to the **independent art movement of Shantiniketan** which focused on **humanism** and **cross culturalism** in art while incorporating the local and **regional elements** in it. It was a term coined in 1997 in a painting exhibition curated in National Gallery of Modern Art in Delhi, which covered the works of Nandalal Bose, Ramkinkar Baij, Rabindranath Tagore and Benod Bihari Mukherjee. In understanding the art of these masters of the Santiniketan school, they are not bracketed as one single genre or a monolith, but each with his own distinct style. Further, modernism in art was to be perceived not through the prism of any genre of style history etc., but in terms of the fundamental aspect of art and specifically in terms of the evolving historical and cultural perspective of the country/ region.

Amrita Shergil (1913 -1941)

She was an **early modernist painter**, who was half Indian and half Hungarian. She was educated in France and imbibed the experience of the modernism, impressionism and post-impressionism movements of Europe. Accordingly, her initial works were of Western style, particularly of the post-impressionism genre. However, her style and subjects underwent a change upon her return to India in the 1930s, and she incorporated the mural and miniature traditions of India in the European modernism styles. Her

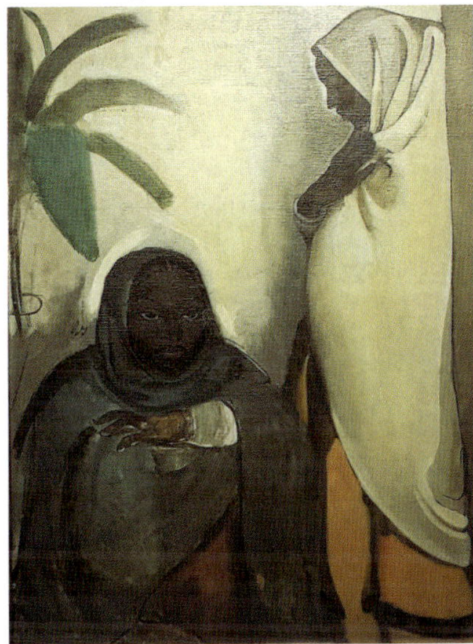

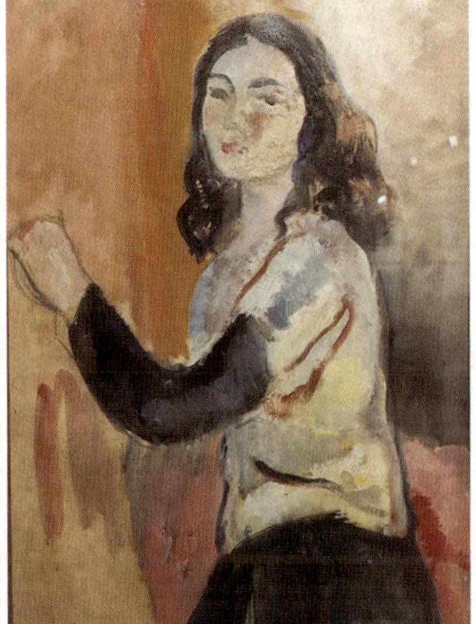

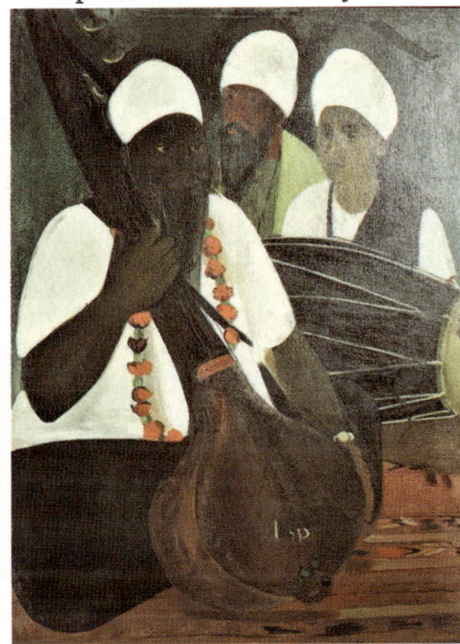

16.38, 16.39 & 16.40: 'Two Women'; oil on canvas, self-portrait, oil on canvas; musicians, oil on canvas. Paintings by Amrita Shergill; National Gallery of Modern Art, New Delhi — photographs by Madhukar K Bhagat

later works particularly reflected Indian ethos, the local people, their culture and lifestyles. She was also considered to be one of the foremost artists representing women and women related issues. The most famous of her paintings include, her self-portraits, the paintings of *Brahmacharis*, *Young Girls*, *Bride's Toilet, Three Girls, Musicians, Self-portrait, Two Women,* amongst others.

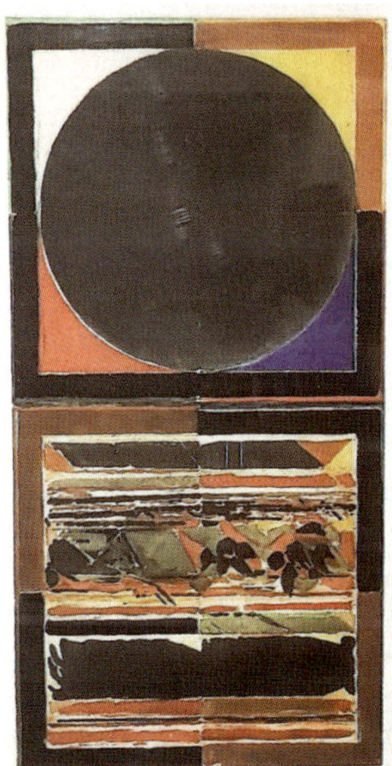

16.41: Untitled painting; oil on canvas by S.H. Raza, National Gallery of Modern Art, New Delhi — photograph by Madhukar K Bhagat

F.N. Souza (1924-2008)

He was another modern artist who was the founding member of Progressive Artists' Group (PAG), Bombay. His paintings were eclectic and are known for his inventive human forms. Many of his paintings also focus on women painted in nude with exaggerated proportions, so as to **break from the extant art traditions**. His well-known paintings include *The Mammon, Last Supper, Christ on Palm Sunday,* amongst others.

Syed Haider Raza (1922-2016)

He was another founding member of the Progressive Artists Group (PAG), Bombay. He was known for his abstract and expressionistic

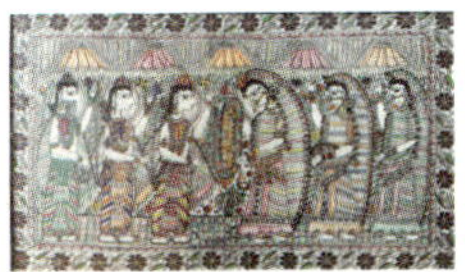

paintings which were done on acrylic and oil medium. Later in his career, inspired by Indian philosophy, his paintings started to revolve around the ***bindu*** (a dot) which to him symbolized the source of energy. His later paintings evolved to become **thematic** and **abstract,** as distinct from his earlier expressionistic themes. He was also a Padma Vibhushan awardee.

Maqbool Fida Hussain (1915-2011)

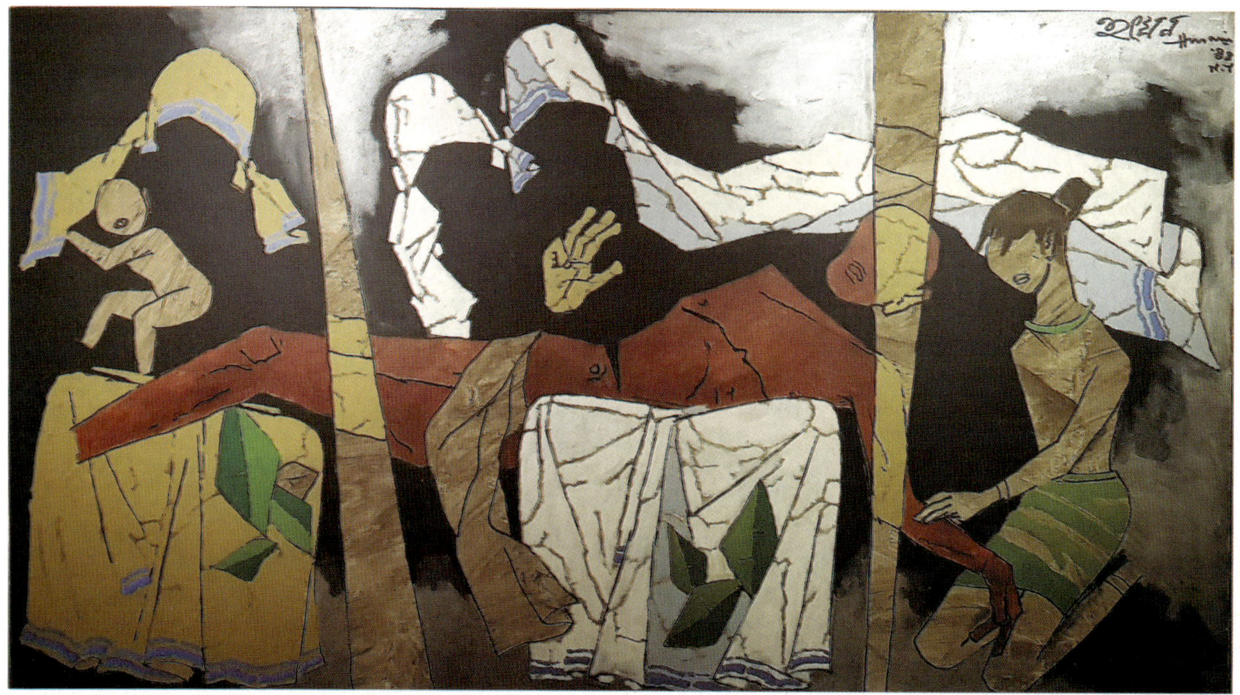

16.42: 'Mother Teresa', oil on canvas M F Hussain; National Gallery of Modern Art, New Delhi — photograph by Madhukar K Bhagat

He was another founding member of the Progressive Artists Group (PAG), Bombay. Hussain was a world acclaimed painter, often termed as the `Picasso of India'. His paintings were considered to be of **modified Cubist style** (an art movement of early 20th century, where art objects are analysed, broken up, and reassembled in an abstract form). His paintings were also famous for images of horses which represented free spirit and transition. Amongst his most prominent works were *Horses, Mother Teresa, Battle of Ganga Jamuna, Zameen,* etc. He was also a Padma Vibhushan awardee.

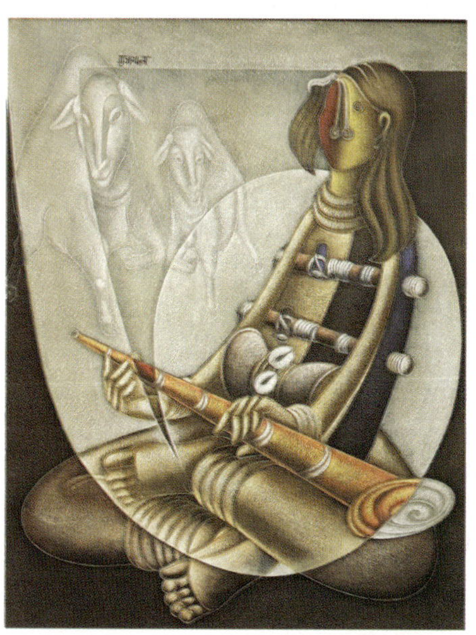

16.43: 'The Musician', oil on canvas, Satish Gujral, Bihar Museum, Patna — photograph by Madhukar K Bhagat

Satish Gujral (1925-2020)

He is a famous painter, muralist, sculpture, writer and also an architect. He was also a member of the Progressive Artists Group (PAG), Bombay. His style and technique involve **modernism,** but are rooted in **Indian ethos** and traditions.

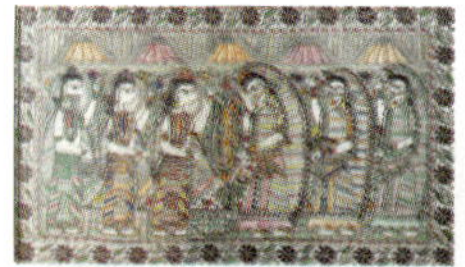

Tyeb Mehta (1929-2001)

He was a painter, sculptor and also a film maker. He was also a member of the Progressive Artists Group (PAG), Bombay. Mehta's works were characterised by **modernism** and **expressionistic styles**. His famous works include *Kali, Falling Bull, Mahishasura, the Triptych Celebration* etc. He was also a Padma Bhushan awardee.

Vasudeo S. Gaitonde (1924-2001)

He is amongst the foremost modern Indian **abstract** painters. A typical feature of his abstract paintings is **translucent beams of light** which are characterised by a meditative calm. However, he did not consider his paintings as abstract; rather he called them non-objective and a kind of personalized hieroglyphics and calligraphic invention. He is a Padma Shri awardee.

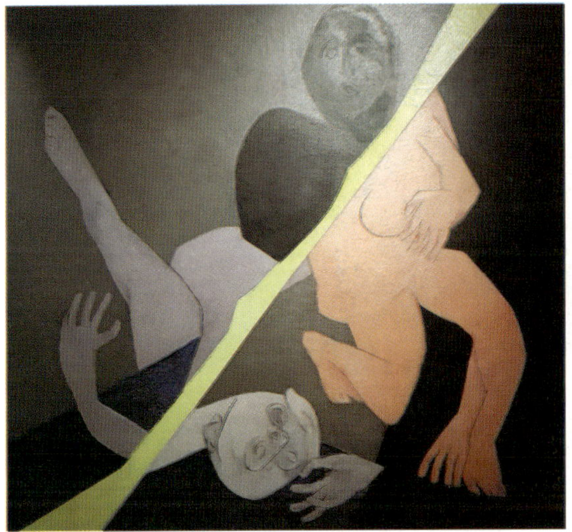

16.44: 'Diagonal', oil on canvas, Tyeb Mehta, National Gallery of Modern Art, New Delhi — photograph by Madhukar K Bhagat

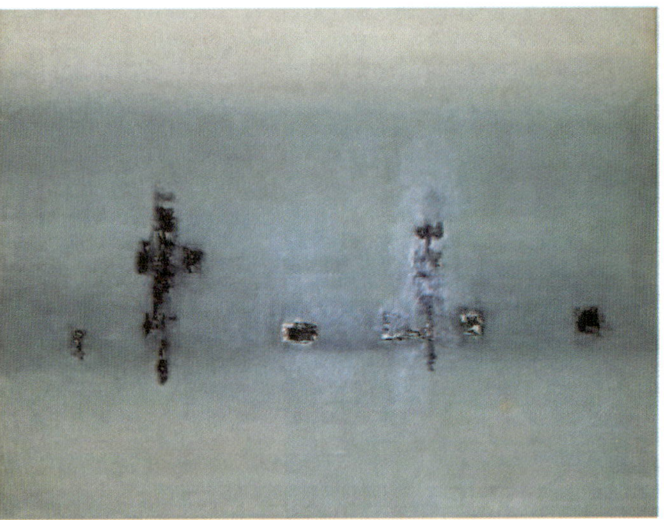

16.45: Translucent beams of light by Vasudeo Gaitonde; Central Museum, Nagpur — photograph by Madhukar K Bhagat

Ganesh Pyne (1937-2013)

He was a contemporary artist of the Bengal School of Art. His style is characterised by **surrealism** and dark imagery which revolve around subjects of Bengali folklore, mythology and fantasy. In his later career, he also drew from the *Mahabharata* focusing on the non-main stream characters like Ekalvya, Amba etc. His paintings included water colour, gouache, tempera and mixed media. Amongst his famous works are the 'Ape and the Flower', Mother and Child', besides other untitled works.

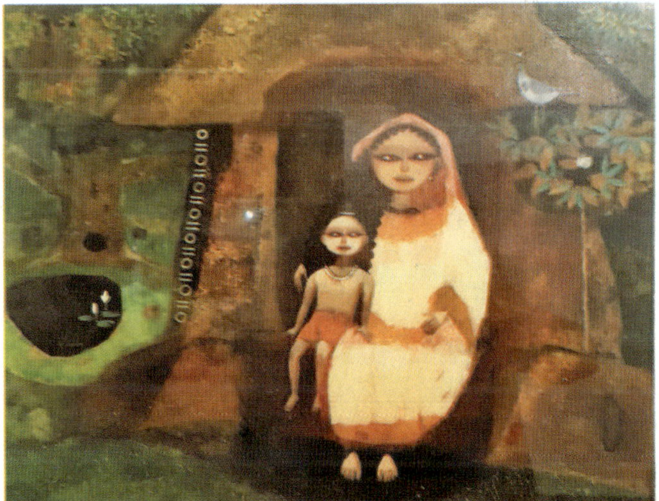

16.46: 'Mother and Child'; tempera on paper; Ganesh Pyne; National Gallery of Modern Art, New Delhi — photograph by Madhukar K Bhagat

Manjit Bawa (1941-2008)

The paintings of Manjit Bawa are noted for its **vibrant** colours, which are traditionally Indian, such as red, pink and violet. It thus drifted away from the existent tradition of colours like brown and grey. Further, the subjects were invariably drawn from Indian mythology, spirituality, and culture. Images of Indian Gods particularly of Shiva, Kali and Krishna are often a subject of his paintings. Amongst his famous paintings are *Krishna and the Bull, Govardhan, Heer*, *After 84, etc.*

SOME OTHER IMPORTANT ARTISTS

Other important artists of modern times include **Gaganendranath Tagore** (1867-1938), Jamini Prakash Ganguly (1876-1953) **Gopal Rao** (1880-1945), **D.P. Roy Chowdhury** (1899 -1975), **S.G. Thakur Singh** (1899 -1976), **Jehangir Sabavala**, (1922-2011) **Anjolie Ela Menon** (1940), **Dhiraj Choudhary** (1930), **Jatin Das**, **Jogen Chowdhury**, amongst others.

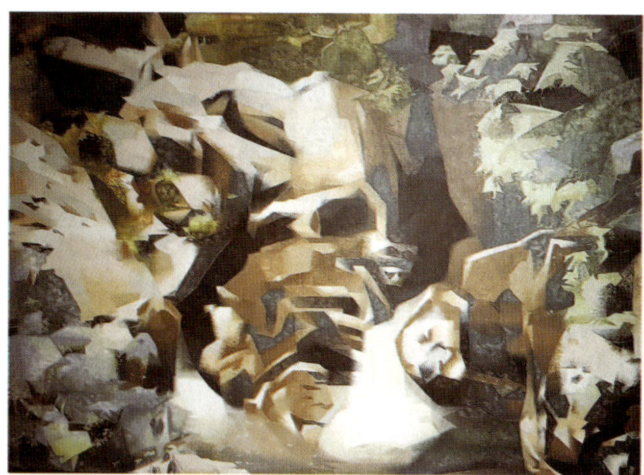

16.47: 'The Source'; oil on canvas; Jehangir Sabavala; National Gallery of Modern Art, New Delhi — photograph by Madhukar K Bhagat

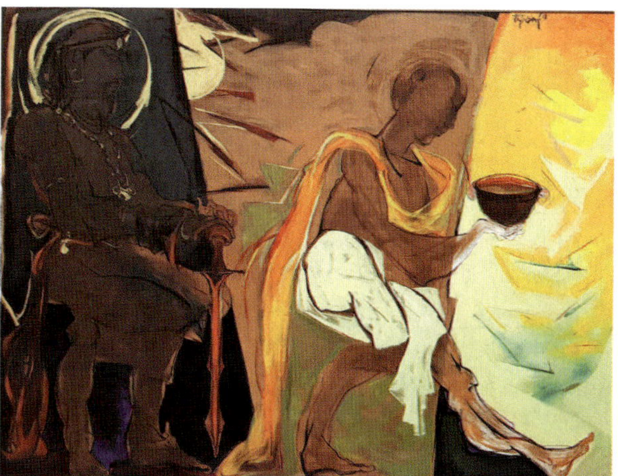

16.48: 'Emperor Ashoka'; oil on canvas; Jatin Das; Patna Museum — photograph by Madhukar K Bhagat

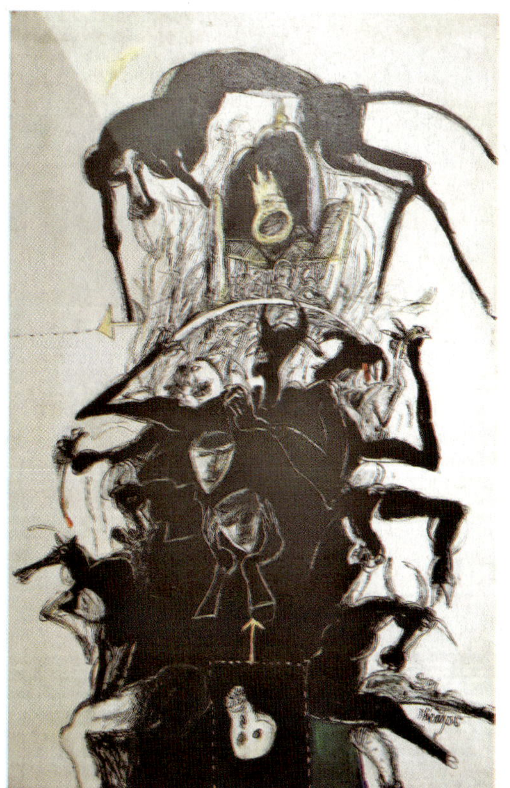

16.49 : An oil on canvas by Dheeraj Choudhary; Bihar Museum, Untitled — photograph by Madhukar K Bhagat

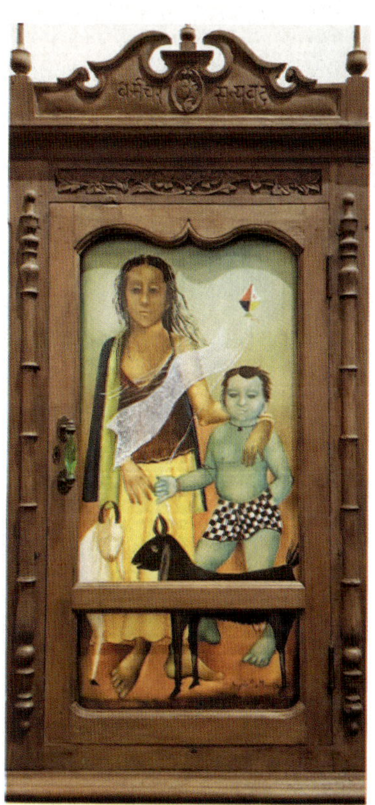

16.50 : Oil on canvas by Anjolie Ela Menon; Bihar Museum — photograph by Madhukar K Bhagat

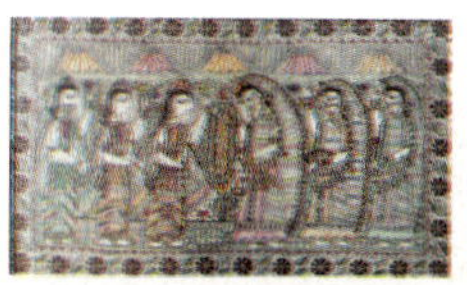

FOLK PAINTINGS

India has had a rich tradition of folk paintings since ancient times. These paintings, whose style, technique, and subjects are diverse have prospered in different regions of the country and are drawn on the local culture and tradition. The subjects of these paintings have also been varied. These may include the scenes, from community life as in **Warli** paintings, to subjects of *Ramayana*, *Mahabharata*, and Indian mythology as seen in the **Madhubani, Pattachitra,** and **Pichwai** paintings, from day-to-day happenings of rural life as seen in the **Kalighat** paintings, to rituals and ceremonies depicted in the **Paitkar** paintings.

These paintings are done on walls, floor of house, paper, scrolls, and even fabric. Events like birth, marriage ceremony, festivals, rituals, etc. are often the occasions for such art. Another feature of these traditional paintings is the use of natural and earthy colours available locally. Thus, these paintings have been in consonance with the local environment and reflect the indigenous ethos and culture. They are reposited in the folk knowledge and often have a tradition of several centuries. Some of the more prominent folk paintings and their features are highlighted in the next page.

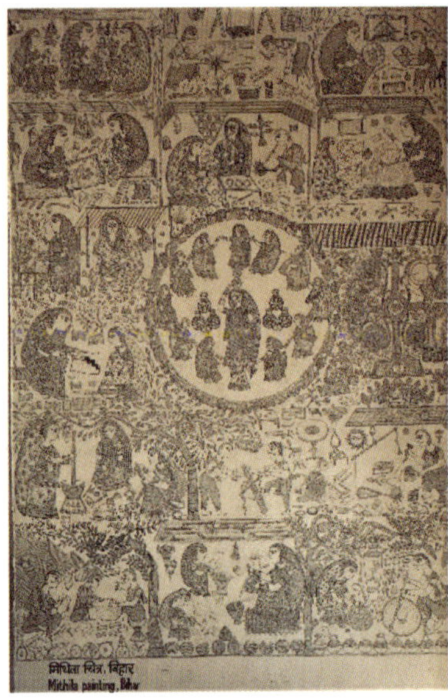

16.51: A Mithila painting on wall depicting activities from the daily lives, at National Crafts Museum, New Delhi — photograph by Madhukar K Bhagat

Madhubani Paintings

Popular in **Madhubani**, (Mithila region of **Bihar**), it is also referred as the **Mithila painting**. This style of painting is said to have originated when the king of Mithila, Janaka, asked the painters to draw the image of marital ceremony of Sita with Ram (the crown prince of Ayodhya).

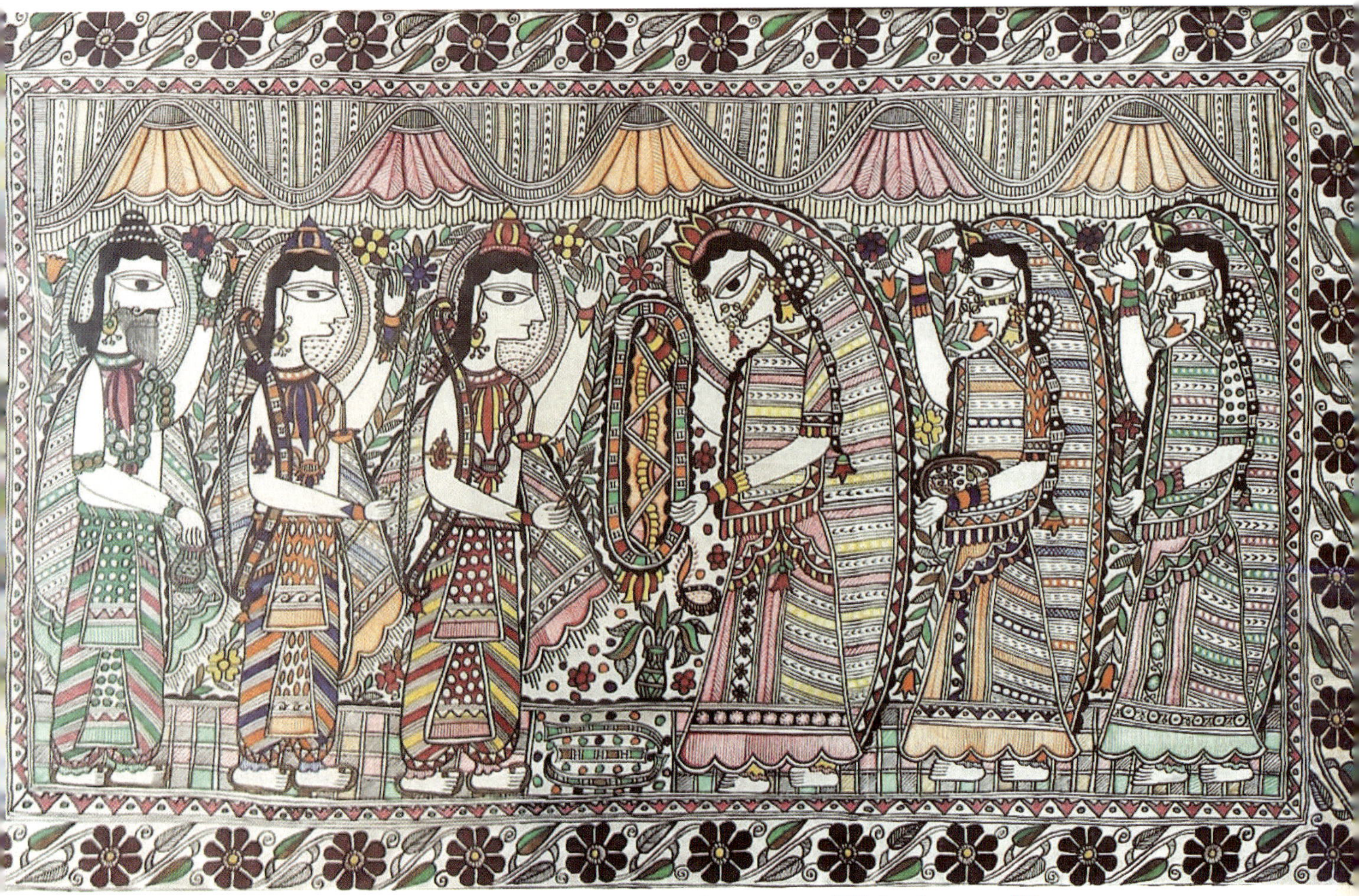

16.52: Madhubani painting on silk fabric, 'Swaymavar of Sita', unknown artist, — photograph (personal collection) by Madhukar K Bhagat

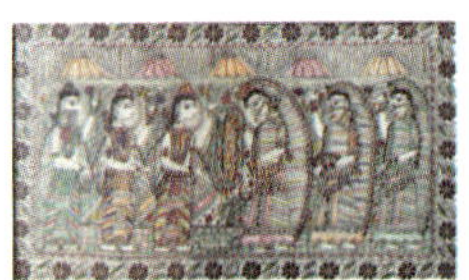

The paintings are traditionally done on the walls of houses, particularly in the central or outer courtyard, or the eastern part of the house which is the dwelling area of *Kuladevi*, and in the *devasthan* or *gosain ghar* (family shrine room). In recent times, these paintings are also done on a medium like canvas, cloth, or even pottery etc.

These paintings are done particularly on occasions like birth, marriage or festivals, or other ceremonial occasions etc. Scenes from the *Ramayana*; particularly the marriage of Rama and Sita, or return of Rama from exile, or Krishna playing with the *gopis*, or other events from mythologies/religious motifs, are often the subjects of these paintings. They also contain the images of fish (considered auspicious) and snakes (which are propitiated).

The features of subjects are usually exaggerated and are two-dimensional. The vacant spaces are decorated with designs and floral patterns. Rice paste, cow dung, and vegetable colours are the materials used.

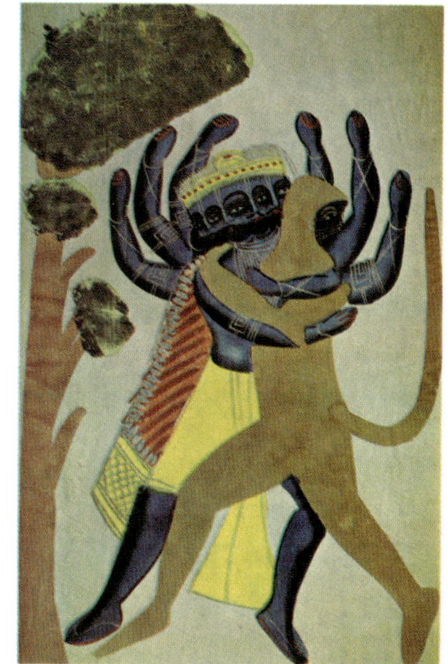

16.53: A fight of Ravana and Hanuman, a Kalighat painting from 1880 — Wikimedia Commons

Kalighat Paintings

Popular in West Bengal, this style of paintings originated in the 19th century around **Kalighat temple** in present day **Kolkata**, where rural artists would prepare these paintings. Originally, they contained images of Hindu gods and goddesses, mythological characters etc., but later diversified to scenes from rural life, daily activities, images of birds, animals, snakes and fishes etc.

These paintings are characterised by use of simplified figures and bold colours. They are made on cloth, or *patas*, or even on mill paper. These paintings also inspired the artists like Jamini Roy of the Bengal School of Art.

Pattachitra

This folk art from **Odisha**, refers to paintings which are done on **canvas** or **cloth** (*patta*-canvas/cloth; *chitra*-painting) and are like scroll paintings. These paintings have a centuries old tradition. Earlier, paintings were also done on palm leaf (referred as *tala pattachitra*). They were earlier made as offerings to Lord Jagannath in the temple of Puri and also in other temples of Odisha. Later, these paintings were also practised in West Bengal.

The subjects of the paintings were religious in nature, generally taken from an imagery of Lord Jagannatha. The daily or festival attires (*veshas*) of lord Jagannatha, Balabhadra and Subhadra are also the themes. *Jattipatra* (paintings for pilgrims to take away and place in personal temples), *Kanchi-kaveri pata* (episodes from the life of lord Jagannatha) and *Thia-badhia pata* (depicting aerial-lateral view of the temple) are some of the other forms of this art. Sometimes scenes from the *Gita Govinda* and other devotional poems are also taken.

The paintings use colours such as deep red, ochre, black and blue which are obtained from organic sources, lac, shells, and minerals. Colourful motifs and designs are some other features.

Bengal Pattachitra and Patua Art

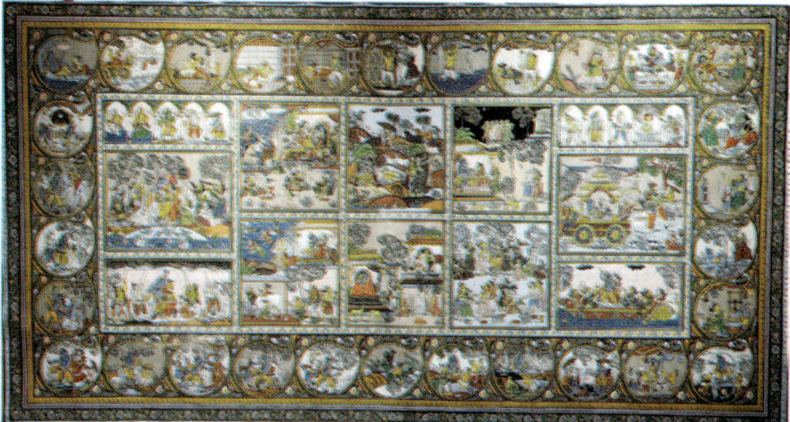

16.54: 'Story of Lord Krishna', a Pattachitra painting on paper depicting various anecdotes from the life of Sri Krishna, Chhatrapati Shivaji Maharaj Vastu Sangrahalaya, Mumbai; — photograph by Madhukar K Bhagat

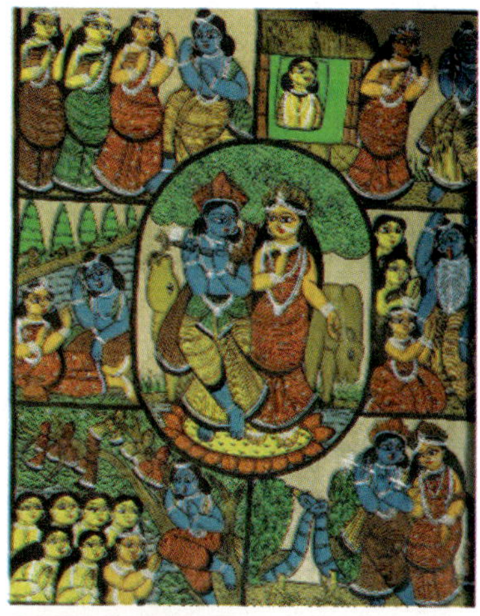

16.55: Pattachitra of Medinipur, West Bengal, depicting scenes of Sri Krishna and gopikas — photograph by Madhukar K Bhagat

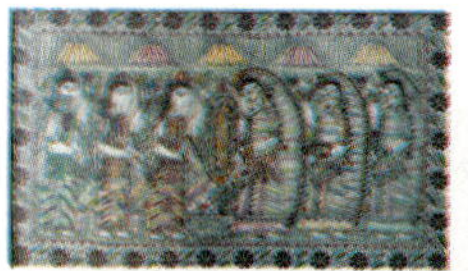

This is another centuries – old folk art which is popular in West Bengal. It captures a **series of paintings** on a long **vertical scroll** of paper. The subjects of the paintings generally are scenes from religious epics. The artists would earlier compose and sing songs from the epics and the relevant scene would be opened in the scroll before the audience. These are often referred to as the *mangal* stories of the gods and goddesses. The community of artists practising this art form are known as the **Patua**, which also lends the name to the art form.

The Bengal Pattachitra/Patua art is generally divided into several sub-genres. These include, *Durga Pat*, *Chalchitra*, *Tribal Pattachitra*, *Kalighat Pattachitra* and *Medinipur Pattachitra*.

Kalamkari Paintings

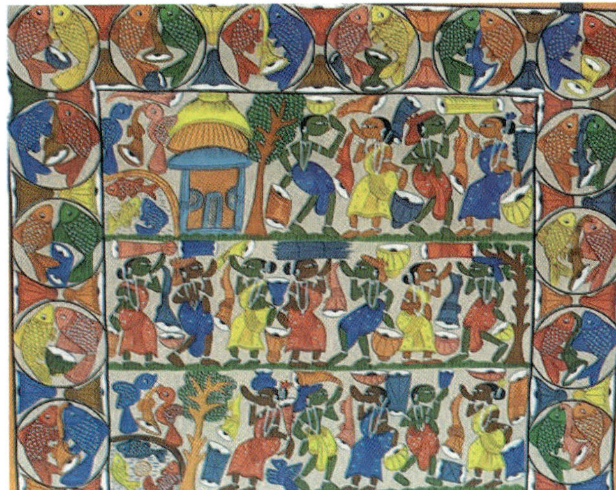

16.56: A tribal Pattachitra depicting scenes from the life of people and everyday activities — photograph by Madhukar K Bhagat

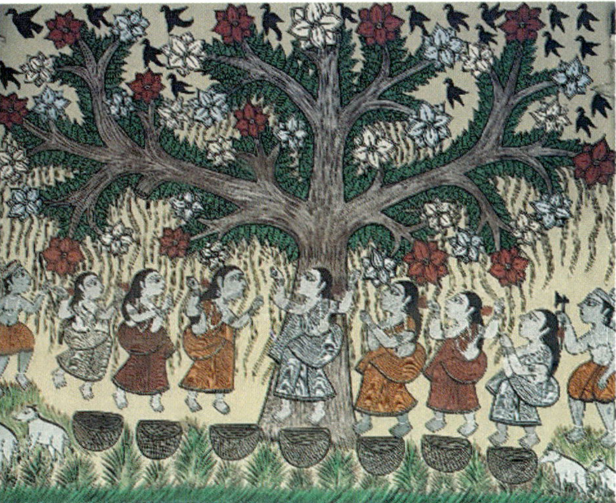

16.57: A Medinipur Pattachitra made on a wall; at National Crafts Museum, New Delhi — photograph by Madhukar K Bhagat

This form of painting is popular in the present-day **Andhra Pradesh** and **Telangana** region. Kalamkari or Vrathapani refers to paintings done on fabric by using ***kalam*** (pen) (*kalam*-pen; *kari*-craftsmanship). The subjects were usually religious in character taken from the epics *Ramayana and Mahabharata*. Two distinct styles: ***Srikalahasti*** style and ***Machilipatnam*** style are in vogue. Only natural dyes are used for the art. A series of steps are involved in the process of dyeing, colour-fixing and painting. The artists use sticks of bamboo or date palm with bundle of hair at one end as brush or pen. The art is centuries old and was popular during the medieval period, wherein it assimilated the Mughal and Persian influences. Later, it went into a decline before being revived in the modern period.

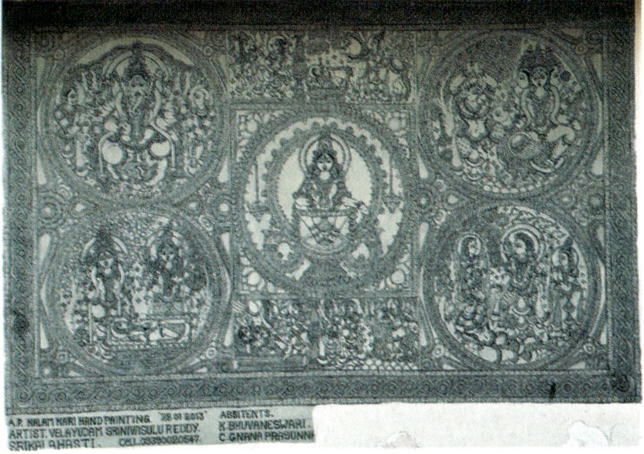

16.58: A Srikalahasti Kalamkari hand painting made on wall (painted on 28.01.2013) at the National Crafts Museum, New Delhi — photograph by Madhukar K Bhagat

Phad Paintings

This folk art popular in **Rajasthan** is done on **long scrolls of fabric/cloth** at the end of which bamboo shafts are tied for rolling the scrolls. The Phad paintings may range from 15 to 30 feet and are usually made of vegetable colours. The *Bhopas,* who are priest singers, carry the Phads and sing in praise of the deities. Thus, the Phads serve as moving temples of their folk deities such as Pabuji and Devnarayan. These folk deities are said to be often those brave men who sacrificed their lives in the protection of the cattle of the community from the robbers, and were hence deified as *bhomias.* Of late, the paintings may also carry images from epics such as *Ramayana* and *Mahabharata*, or scenes from treatises such as *Gita-Govinda*.

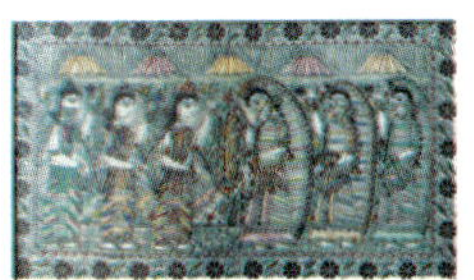

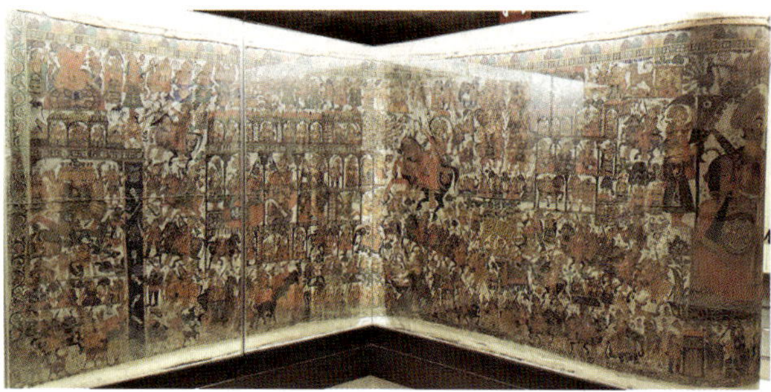
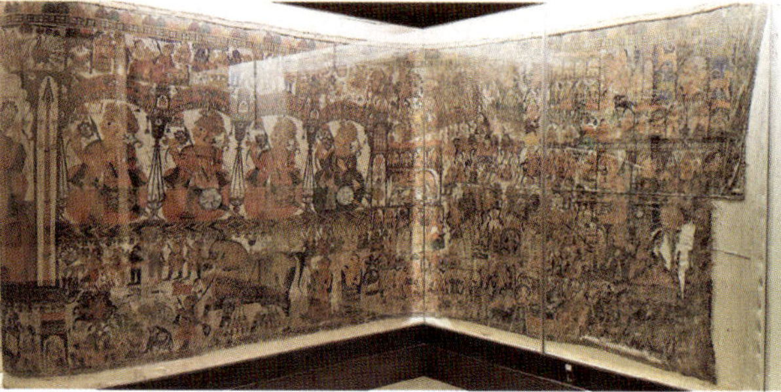

16.59 & 16.60: The two halves of a large scroll Phad painting of Pabuji, at National Crafts Museum, New Delhi — photographs by Madhukar K Bhagat

Pichwai Paintings

This is another set of folk paintings from **Rajasthan** which are done on **cloth** and are of **religious character**. The art is largely practised in the Nathdwara temple in Rajasthan and the subject of temple is Lord Srinathji, a form of Lord Krishna. The tradition is associated with the devotional Pushtimarga sect and the paintings depicting scenes from the legends of lord Krishna are hung behind the idol of the deity. The tradition is said to have originated in the 17th century and technically is similar to the genre of miniature paintings.

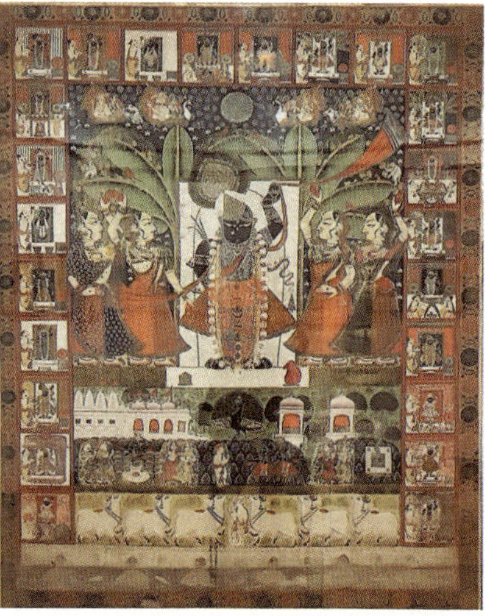

16.61: A Pichwai painting of Krishna as Srinath ji and the dancing gopis on the occasion of Sharad Purnima (Sept-Oct full moon); below a temple and on side panels are depicted 24 festivals associated with Srinath ji, Nathdwara, 1800, 115 by 117 cm cloth, National Museum, New Delhi — photograph by Madhukar K Bhagat

Thanjavur or Tanjore Paintings

This art is popular in **Thanjavur**, Tamil Nadu. It is essentially a combination of painting and craft which flourished in Thanjavur (Tamil Nadu) during the Maratha rule and thus it is centuries old. It is a **panel-based painting** done on wood, with figures encrusted with semi-precious stones, overlaid with gold foils, etc. Later, the paintings were done on glass. The subjects are generally religious figures, deities, etc.

Manjusha Art

Popular in **Bhagalpur** region of Bihar, it is also called **Angika art** as this region was a part of Ang Pradesh, a Mahajanapada. It is a centuries old folk art tradition. The current form of art is said to have originated and is based on the folklore of *Bihula-Bishari* and is associated with *Bishari puja* of the region. (*Bishari*: literal meaning `one who could reverse the effect of poison')

A unique feature of this art form is that it uses **only three colours**—pink, green, and yellow. It is often executed on boxes of jute, bamboo and paper (*Manjusha* in Sanskrit meaning `box') which are used to store the items for the *Bishari* puja. The boxes also depict scenes from the folklore, the flora and fauna of the region, and the images of Hindu gods and goddesses. Another salient feature of this art form is the use of different border styles. One of these borders depicts swirling snakes which are said to represent the love and sacrifice of Bihula the central character in the folklore.

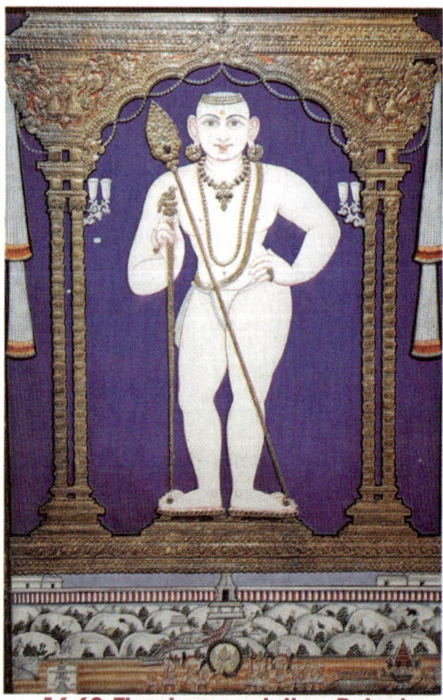

16.62: Thanjavur painting, Palani Dandayudhapani; Lord Murugan holding a spear, 20th century, Chhatrapati Shivaji Maharaj Vastu Sangrahalaya, Mumbai — photograph by Madhukar K Bhagat

Thangka Paintings

Originating in **Tibetan Buddhism**, the Thangka paintings also have an old tradition in India particularly in the established centres of Vajrayana-Tibetan Buddhism such as in Sikkim, Arunachal Pradesh, Ladakh and in Dharmashala regions of Himachal Pradesh. The Thangkas are in the nature of paintings which generally depict a ***mandala***, Buddha or other Buddhist deities like Boddhisatvas. The wheel of life (*bhavachakra*), a visual representation of the *Abhidharma* teachings is a popular theme of the *Thangkas*. These also serve as an aid in the teaching of Buddhist philosophies. Usually, these paintings are done on cloth fabric and are similar to scroll paintings, but in the modern period they may be even framed. Thangka- style/ Vajrayana school medieval cave paintings have also been found in Ladakh region, indicating their centuries old tradition in India (see chapter 11 on Medieval Paintings of **Medieval India** book).

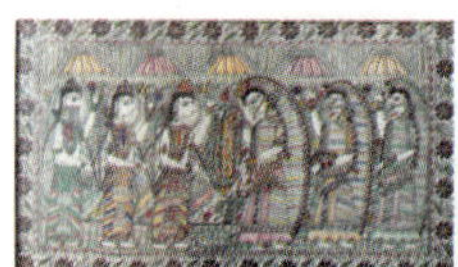

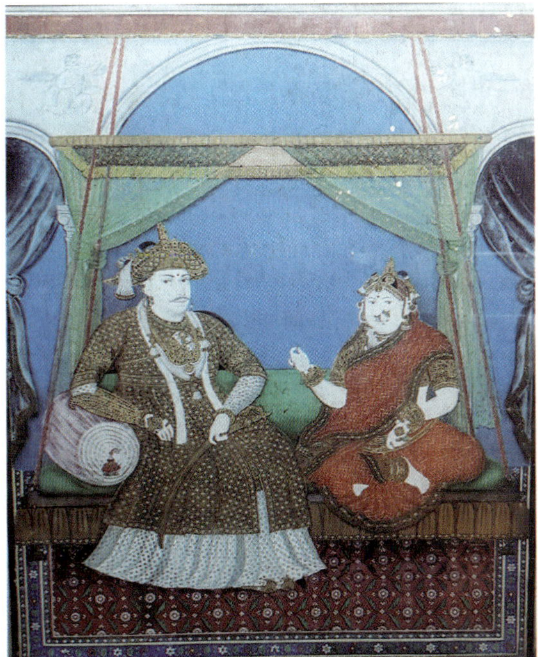

16.63: A Thanjavur painting of Sivaji and wife Saitamba Bai; 17th century; Government Museum, Chennai — photograph by Madhukar K Bhagat

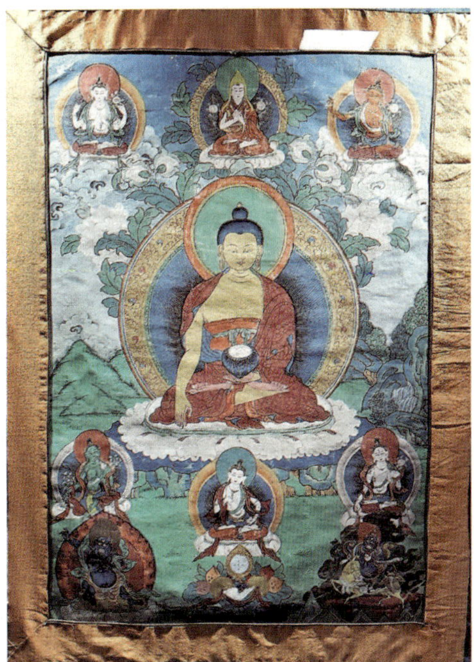

16.64: Gautam Buddha, Amoghapasha; a Thangka painting on silk fabric; Rahul Sankrityayan collection, Patna Museum — photograph by Madhukar K Bhagat

Cheriyal Scroll Paintings

They are a form of art which is limited to the **Telangana** region. It is a form of scroll painting in which panels of scenes are painted in a narrative form. The subjects could be stories/anecdotes from the epics, Puranas or other elements of Indian mythology. The paintings are often done on **cloth scroll** and prepared through an elaborate process. Usually these are in the vertical (portrait) orientation with the panels running in a horizontal frame. The art is now largely limited to the Cheriyal town and is also having a Geographical Indication tag (GI Tag).

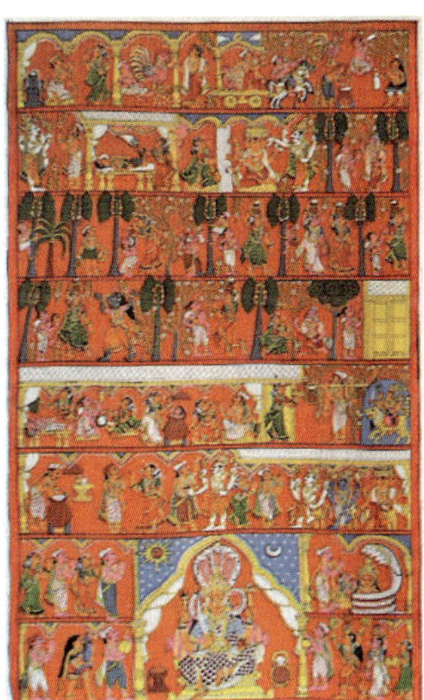

16.65: Cheriyal scroll paintings — Wikimedia Commons

Kalamezhuthu

It is a traditional ritual art of **Kerala** which is practiced specially in the Kalamezhuthu festival across the Bhagavathy (goddess) temples of the region. The art involves use of **coloured powder** to draw beautiful drawings on the floor of the temples, which are usually the image of the deity. The paintings generally use five colours. These are prepared using natural substances such as rice flour (for white), turmeric (for yellow), charcoal powder (for black), powdered green leaves (for green) and a mixture of turmeric powder and lime (for red). At the end of the festival and the rituals, the paintings are erased.

Alpana, Aipan, Rangoli, Kolam and other Floor-art Forms

Different regions of India have the tradition of **folk decorative art** made usually at the entrance of the houses. These may be ritualistic, plainly decorative, or made specifically on the occasions of festivals. Usually, natural substances such as rice flour, red ochre white stone powder, chalk and flower petals or other substances are used to create them. These are often depicted by varied geometrical patterns or other designs incorporating straight lines, curves, loops or a complex combination of such shapes. Shapes of flowers, petals or even images of deities may be drawn. Traditionally, this art has been practised by women-folk. *Rangoli* (Maharashtra, Karnataka), *Kolam* (Tamil Nadu), *Muggu* (Andhra Pradesh and Telangana), *Pookkalam* (Kerala), *Aripana* (Mithila-North Bihar), *Alpona* (West Bengal), *Aipan* (Uttarakhand–Kumaon), *Madana* (Rajasthan), *Chowk Pujan* (Uttar Pradesh), *Chowk-poorana* (Haryana, Punjab, Himachal Pradesh, Madhya Pradesh) etc. are some of its regional variations.

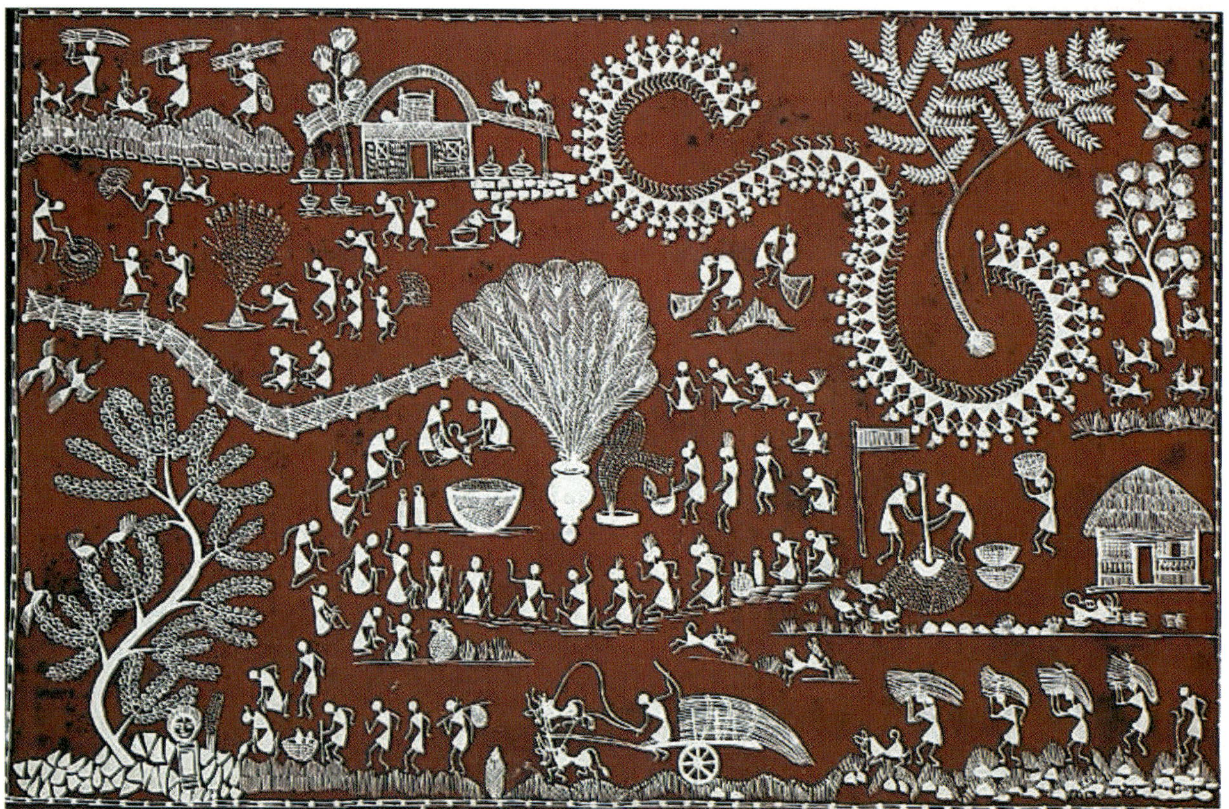

16.66: A Warli painting depicting the daily activities of people;
— photograph (personal collection) by Madhukar K Bhagat

TRIBAL ART

Different forms of art are integral to tribal culture and a variety of tribal art can be seen in different regions of the country. Amongst these, some of the most prominent ones are the **Warli paintings** (Maharashtra), **Gond paintings** (Madhya Pradesh); the **Santhal paintings** (West Bengal; Jharkhand) the **Bhil paintings** and the **Paitkar paintings. Saor** (Odisha), **Kurumba** (Tamil Nadu), **Godna** (tattoo of Chattisgarh tribals) **Jadu Patua** (Jharkhand), are some of the other tribal painting forms.

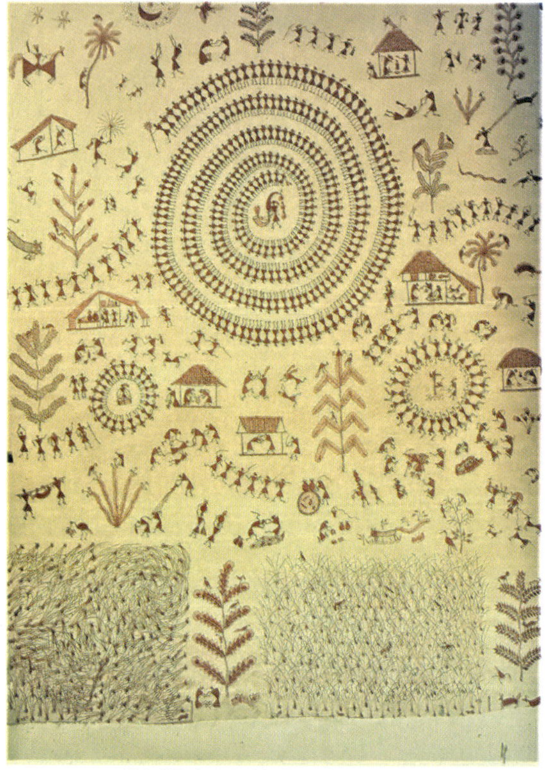

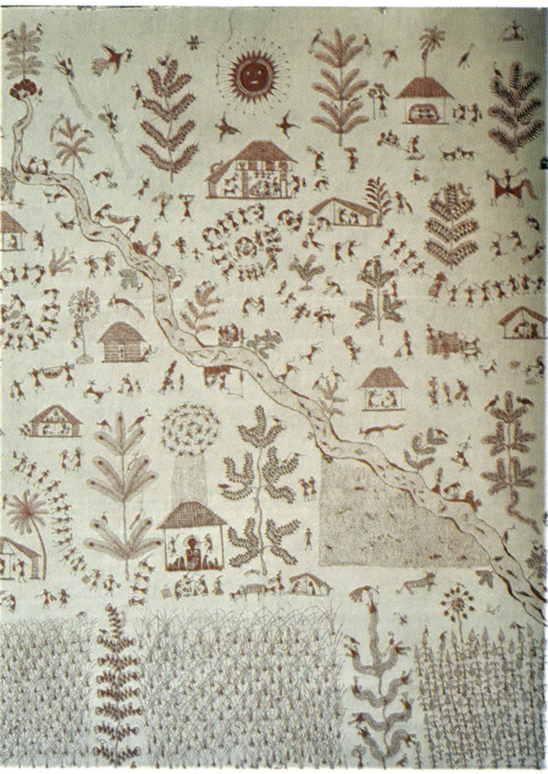

16.67 & 16.68: Two Warli paintings on wall, at National Crafts Museum, New Delhi
— photographs by Madhukar K Bhagat

Warli Paintings

This art form is practiced by **Warli tribes** in **Northern Maharashtra** and is considered amongst the finest example of tribal paintings. The paintings are usually done on clay hut walls of the tribals. Rice-paste with red ochre powder is used as a painting material with a bamboo stick chewed at one end and often used as a paint brush. The paintings are done specially on ceremonial occasions like marriages, births, sowing, harvesting etc. The tribal lifestyle is integrated with nature. Farming is an important form of livelihood, and along with nature and its elements influences the cultural life of the tribals, including their paintings.

The central portion of the painting is usually a square referred to as the *chauk* in which depicted is the image *Palaghat*, the mother goddesss symbolising fertility. Around this image are depicted the scenes of daily community life including dancing, planting saplings, hunting, fishing, festivals and rituals. Use of geometric figures like triangles, circles, rectangles etc. is a unique feature of these paintings. Each of the geometrical shapes are said to be symbolic. Human figures have a typical representation using triangles and straight lines, while white colour is predominant in a red ochre background.

Gond Paintings

They are done by the **Gond tribals** of **Madhya Pradesh** which are amongst the largest of tribes of Central India. Like the Warli paintings, Gond art is also usually done on the **walls of houses**. Of late, it has also been done on canvas and paper. The art is rooted in the different aspects of the tribal life. The paintings contain the images ranging from folk stories, local gods and goddesses, festivals, to flora and fauna, etc. Some of these paintings can also be votive art (done on fulfillment of certain vows) which are in the form of geometric drawings done on the walls of the houses.

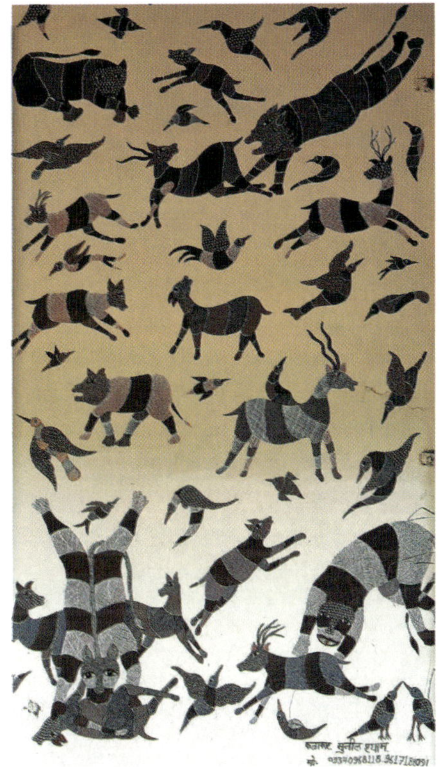

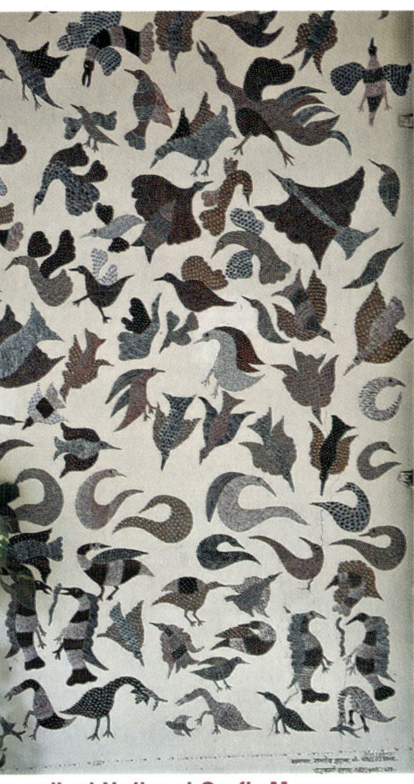

16.69 & 16.70: Two Gond paintings on wall, at National Crafts Museum, New Delhi; depicting hunting by animals (left) and different birds (right) — photographs by Madhukar K Bhagat

Santhal Paintings

They are popular among the **Santhal tribes of Jharkhand**, West Bengal and Bihar. The walls of the huts are the canvass of these paintings. The themes are taken from natural surroundings and objects of daily life which are integrated with leafy patterns. The images are simplistic, at times static, with almost a childlike diagrammatic representation. Images of people cutting wood, gathering firewood, fishing, scene of cultivation, dancing and singing, scene of going to market etc. are some of the subjects. The colours are bright and natural pigments are used. These are also said to be one of the oldest tribal paintings.

Paitkar Paintings

They are popular with the **tribals of Jharkhand**, with the village of Amadubi (in eastern part of Jharkhand) being an important centre of it. The tradition is centuries old and is also popular with the tribals in the adjoining states of West Bengal, Bihar etc. These paintings are essentially **scroll paintings** (similar to Patua art) and are made on palm leaves (or paper) referred to as *pata*. It uses soil, glue, and colours extracted from natural sources, stones, vegetables, etc. The subjects include scenes from daily life, stories of legends and mythologies, and even explore life after death. Mansa Devi, the deity of the tribals and even Hindu gods like Shiva, Durga and scenes from the epics are the subjects of this art.

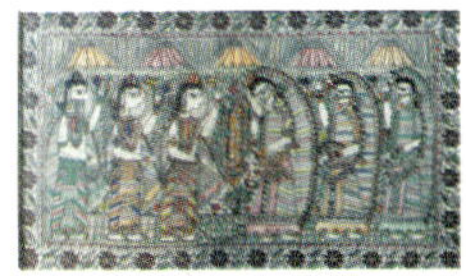

Bhil Paintings

This art form is popular in the **tribes of Bhils** who are largely present in central India, particularly in the states of Madhya Pradesh and Maharashtra. The paintings, like other tribal art, find expression on the walls of their huts. The painting materials are usually home-made, with colour pigments extracted from leaves and flowers of different plants. The brushes may be made of cotton swabs or rags which are fastened on wooden twigs. The subjects are usually taken from nature and the events of their daily lives. The sun, moon, animals, birds, tree, mountains and rivers and gods like *Bhilavat Deo Baramathya* (who has twelve heads) find expression in these paintings. Use of dots to fill the inner spaces of the paintings is a unique feature of their art work. Amongst Bhil art, the **Pithora paintings** has a special place as a ritual art. The Pithora horses are painted and offered to the gods. The images of these horses may also be painted on the walls of homes as a part of the ritual.

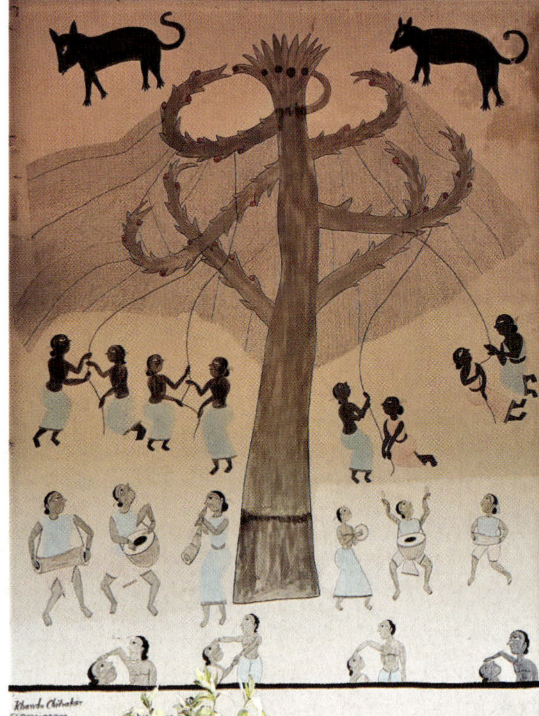

16.71: A Santhal painting on wall, at the National Crafts Museum, New Delhi; depicting celebration by people — photograph by Madhukar K Bhagat

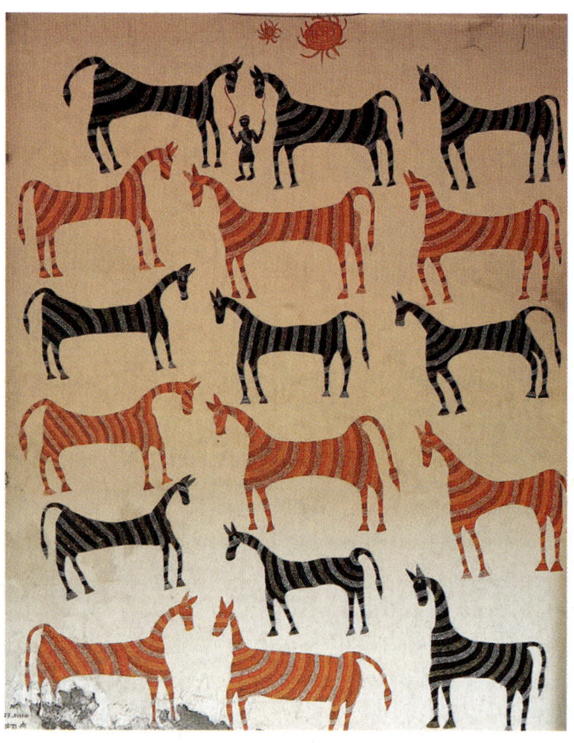

16.72: A Bhil painting depicting horses on wall, National Crafts Museum, New Delhi — photograph by Madhukar K Bhagat

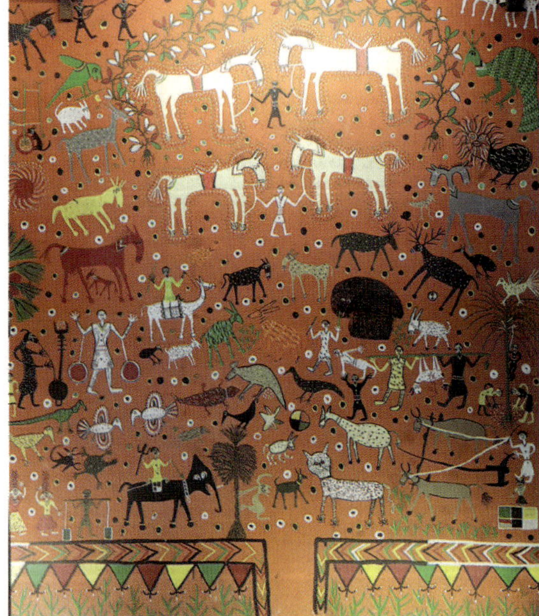

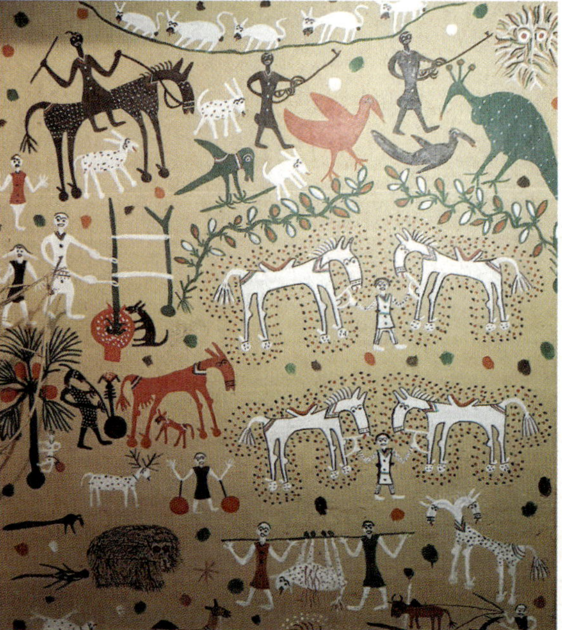

16.73 & 16.74: Pithora paintings of Bhils; a ritual with artistic expression. Manav Sangrahalaya, Bhopal — photographs by Madhukar K Bhagat

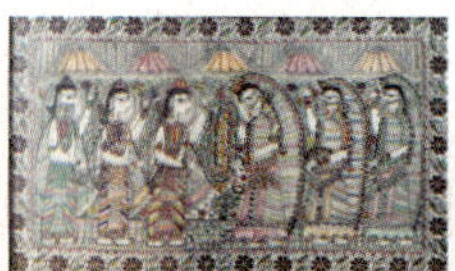

Music in Modern India

> *The touch of an infinite mystery passes over the trivial and the familiar, making it break out into ineffable music... The trees, the stars, and the blue hills ache with a meaning which can never be uttered in words.*
>
> — Rabindranath Tagore
>
> *"Music does not proceed from the throat alone. There is music of mind, of the senses and of the heart".*
>
> — Mahatma Gandhi

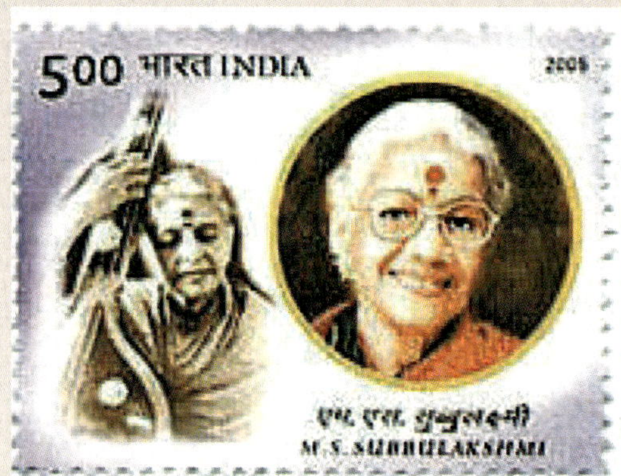

M S Subbulakshmi

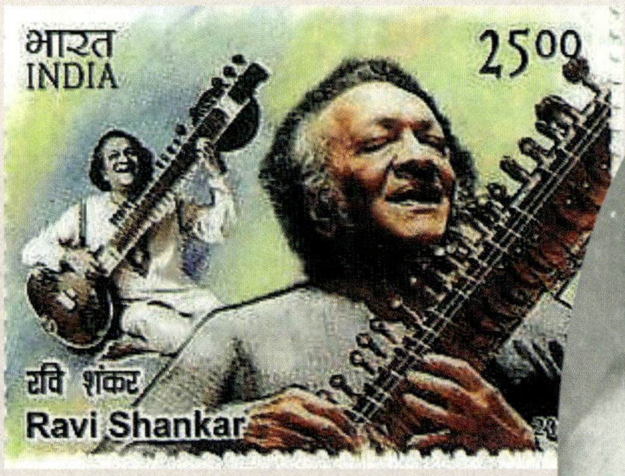

Ravi Shankar

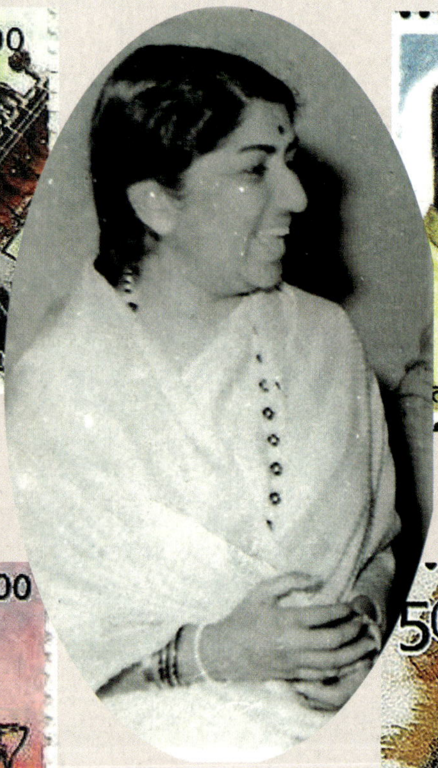

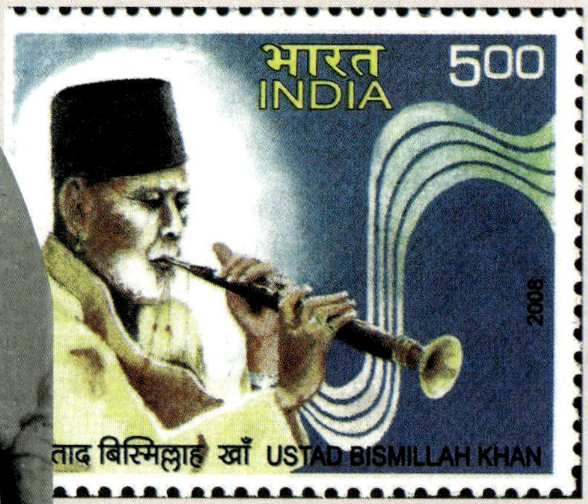

Bismillah khan

Lata Mangeshkar

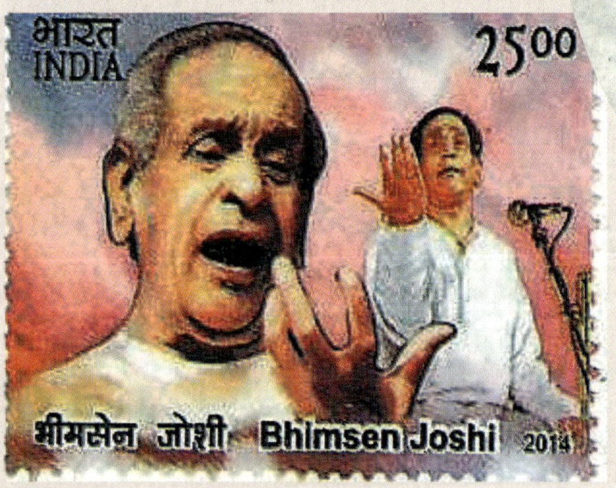

Bhimsen Joshi

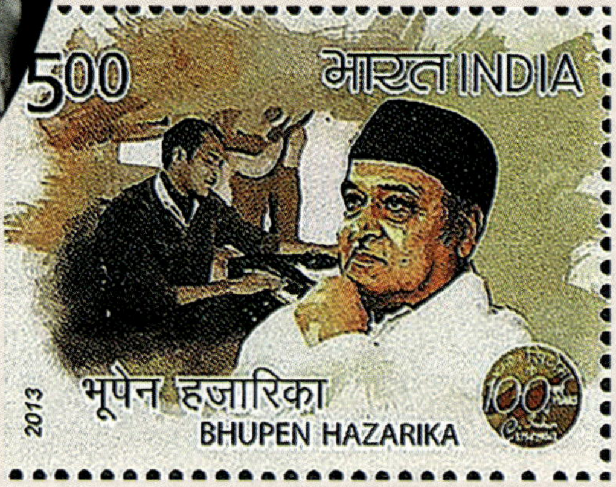

Bhupen Hazarika

17.1: Bharat Ratnas of Indian music; stamp images
— Courtesy, Department of Post

MUSIC CATEGORIES IN MODERN INDIA

Music in India has evolved through the ages. It was an intrinsic part of the Vedic traditions. Many elements of Indian music were compiled and structured in Bharata's *Natyashastra*. The medieval period saw a further evolution of Indian music. *Sangita Ratnakara* by Sarangadeva and *Sangeet Sudhakar* by Haripala are two milestones musical treatises of this period that document the medieval tradition of music. This period was also witness to the seeping in of the Persian and Arabic influences in the Indian music, and from which emerged new shapes and hues in this art. With the Bhakti movement, the tradition of devotional music was imbibed. Over the next few centuries, the growth of Hindustani and Carnatic musical traditions took place which remains the bulwark of the present day Classical musical system. Thus, modern Indian music has assimilated different features through centuries of evolution, and today it manifests in varied forms ranging from Classical to 'film music', from Carnatic to pop music and Western to folk music. The broad categories of music in vogue can be classified into the following:

- **Hindustani Classical music**
- **Carnatic music**
- **Light Classical music:** (a) Thumri, (b) Dadra, (c) Qawwali, (d) Kajri, (e) Tappa, (f) Ghazal, (g) Khayal, etc.
- **Devotional music:** (a) Bhajan, (b) Kirtan, (c) Shabad, etc.
- **Folk music**
- **Film and other popular music**
- **Western music**

The Hindustani Classical music, Carnatic music, different forms of light classical music and devotional music had a medieval origin and still retain their basic traits (discussed in Chapter 13—'Music & Dance in Medieval India'). In this chapter, the modern exponents of classical music, the folk music of India, the music of Indian films, and other forms of music in modern India are described in brief.

MODERN EXPONENTS OF INDIAN CLASSICAL MUSIC

The Indian classical system of music which includes the Hindustani classical and the Carnatic music has evolved over the centuries. Based on the fundamentals of *swara, raga* and *tala,* it has created a diverse and intricate framework of music, while imparting grounds of creativity to numerous generations of artists. Amongst these, there have been many doyens of classical music who have richly contributed to it and helped the music to evolve. While the medieval age brings forth the names of Sarangadeva, Haripala, Amir Khusrau, Haridas, Tansen, Baiju, Purandara Dasa, Thyagaraja, Muthuswami Dikshitar, Shyama Shastri amongst others, the modern classical music has its own shares of many greats. These exponents can be broadly categorised as the vocalists, and the instrumentalists. The system of music followed by them, viz. the Hindustani, or the Carnatic, and the genre of music (viz. *dhrupad, khayal, thumri, bhajan* etc.) are also some other bases of classification. The uniqueness of the Indian musical system is also in the *gharana* tradition (or lineage-family-style) with which these artists associate. While modern Indian music has produced many greats, a glimpse of some of the eminent exponents of classical music of the 20th century is what is endeavoured here. This also brings out as to how the Indian classical music has emerged and been recognised, at the world stage.

The Classical Vocalists

Among the great vocalists of India at the turn of the 20th century, the names which clearly stand out are that of **Alladiya Khan**, **Abdul Karim Khan** and **Vishnu Digambar Paluskar**. These can truly be said to be the pioneers of modern Indian classical music, who laid the foundation of new trends in music and inspired a generation of musicians.

Alladiya Khan *(1855-1946)*

A legendary Hindustani classical vocalist of the Jaipur-Atrauli gharana, he is widely recognised for revival and creation of many complex *ragas* such as *Sampoorna Malkauns, Bhoop Nat, Shuddha Nat, Nat Kamod*, *Basanti Kedar, Kaunsi Kanada*, *Dhavala Shree, Malavi*, *Savani Kalyan* and others.

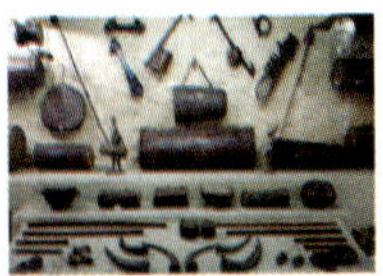

Abdul Karim Khan (1872-1937)

A classical singer who is also the founder of the famous **Kirana Gharana** of Hindustani classical music, Abdul Karim Khan was considered one of the most melodious classical singers of his time. His style is said to have brought innovation of the slow melodic development of the *raga* (*vilambit laya).* It also distinguished his style of *thumri* from that of the others, as it proceeded at a leisurely pace.

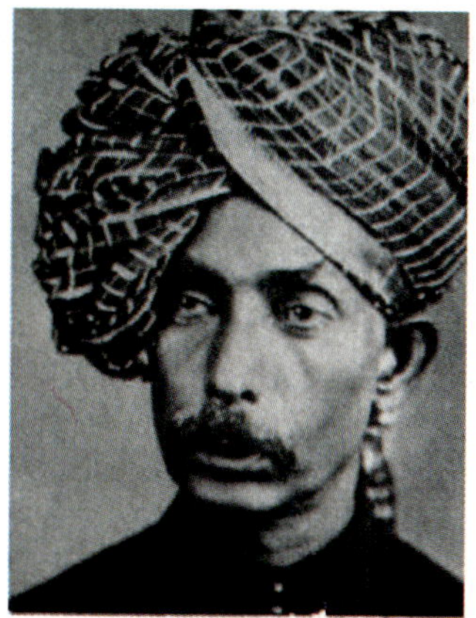

17.2: Abdul Karim Khan — Wikimedia Commons

Vishnu Digambar Paluskar (1872-1931)

Paluskar was an eminent Hindustani classical vocalist who is associated with the singing of the original version of the famous *bhajan* 'Raghupati Raghav Raja Ram'. He is also associated with the singing of one of the versions of the *Vande Mataram* in *raag* Kafi in a Congress session (in 1901). He was the founder of *Gandharva Mahavidyalaya* which began the formal education of music in a school environment, and thus opened the world of music to students outside the fold of the *gharanas*. He is also said to have started the concept of public concerts which were otherwise limited to temples, palaces and royal courts, thus earning greater repute and respect for the musicians amongst the masses. His composition on music titled *Sangeet Bal Prakash* (in three volumes) and his compilation of *ragas* in 18 volumes are considered milestone works.

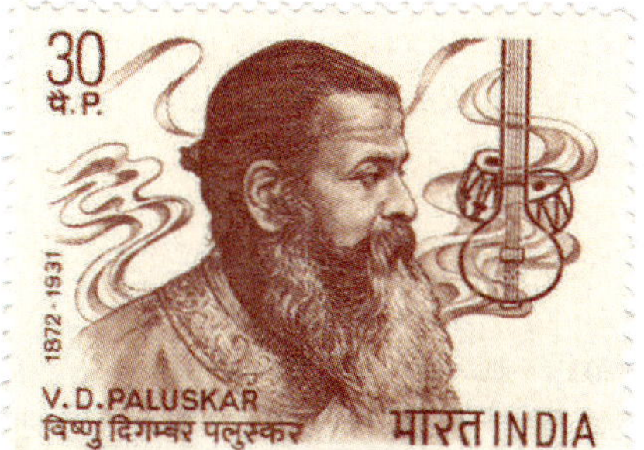

17.3: V.D. Paluskar, a stamp of 1973 — Courtesy, Department of Post

In the next generation of eminent vocalists, can be placed maestros like Bade Ghulam Ali, Siddheshwari Devi, Mallikarjun Mansur, Gangubai Hangal, Begum Akhtar, M.S. Subbulakshmi and D.K. Pattammal.

Bade Ghulam Ali (1902-1968)

A Hindustani classical vocalist of the Patiala Gharana, Bade Ghulam Ali excelled in different classical formats ranging from dhrupad to khayal. He was especially renowned for his rendition of ghazals. He also improvised on music, reducing the *alaps* of the *ragas* to suit the changing taste of the audience during public performances. (Sangeet Natak Akademi and Padma Bhushan awardee)

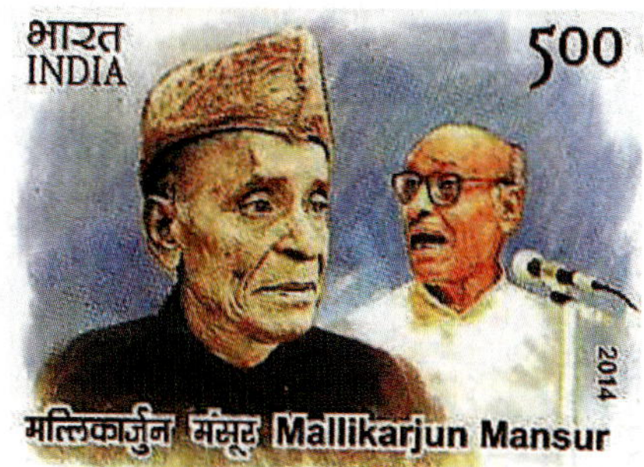

17.4: A stamp of Mallikarjun Mansur released in 2014 — Courtesy, Department of Post

Siddheshwari Devi (1908-1976)

She was a legendary vocalist, a master of diverse styles such as *khayal and thumri.* Although *thumri* is considered her forte, she was well versed with other classical forms such as *dadra, kajri, chaiti* etc. Another eminent classical Carnatic singer M.S. Subbulakshmi is said to have learnt *bhajan* from Siddheshwari Devi (Padma Shree awardee).

Mallikarjun Mansur (1911-1992)

An eminent vocalist hailing from Karnataka, Mallikarjun Masur was an exponent of the Hindustani classical styles of *khayal*. He belonged to the Jaipur-Atrauli Gharana and had a command over some rare and complex ragas. He was also known for bringing improvisation in the melody and the metre without comp-romising on the *bhava* and *rasa.* (Sangeet Natak Akademi and Padma Vibhushan awardee)

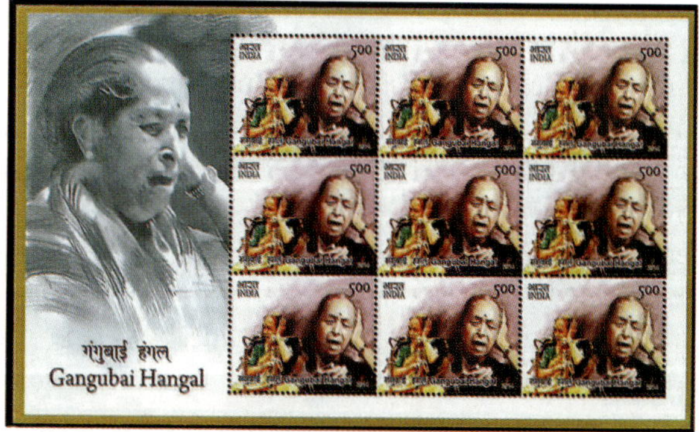

17.5: Gangubai Hangal, a stamp sheet released in 2014 — Courtesy, Department of Post

Gangubai Hangal (1913-2009)

She was another great artist who hailed from Karnataka and became an exponent of the Hindustani classical. She belonged to the Kirana Gharana and

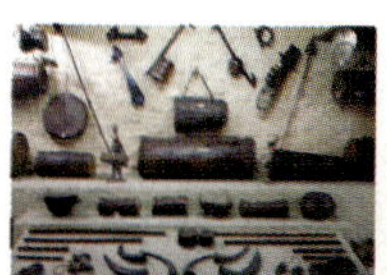

was known for her renditions in her deep and powerful voice. Although she initially performed *bhajan* and *thumri*, but later she was known for her renditions of *khayal*. (Sangeet Natak Akademi and Padma Vibhushan awardee).

Begum Akhtar (1914-1974)

A Hindustani Classical singer, Begum Akhtar is considered one of the greatest in the genre of *ghazals*, *dadra* and *thumri*. She was also an eminent playback singer and actor in the early days of Indian cinema. She was one of the earliest female artists to sing in public concerts and break away from the tradition of performance in the *mehfils* or private gatherings. (Sangeet Natak Akademi and a Padma Bhushan awardee).

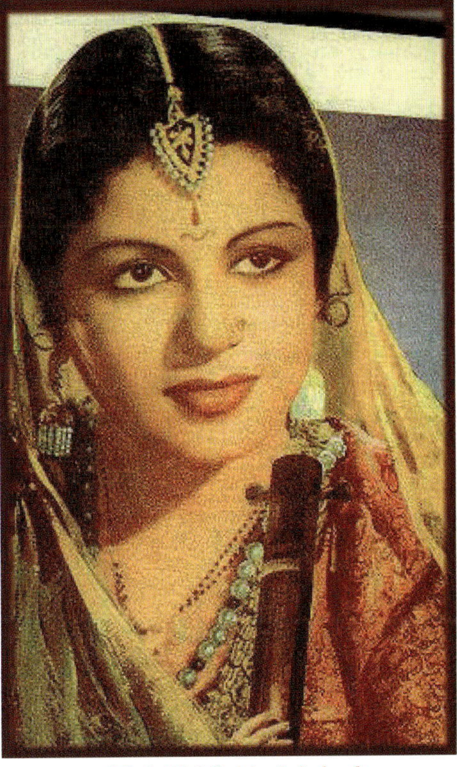

17.6: M S Subbulakshmi, a picture from the publicity material of movie Meera (1945) in which she acted — Wikimedia Commons

M.S. Subbulakshmi (1916-2004)

She was the first Indian artist to be awarded a **Bharat Ratna** (1998) and was indeed a doyen of Indian Classical. A vocalist of the Carnatic style, her singing was considered flawless, with perfect pronunciation of the Sanskrit hymns. She was the first Indian who performed in the U.N. General Assembly (1966) and the first Indian musician to receive the Ramon Magsaysay Award. Her many renditions include chanting of *Vishnu-sahasranama* and other *bhajans* such as *Bhaja-Govindam*, *Hari Tum Haro,* and the *Venkatesa Suprapbhatam* (early morning hymns) many of which are even now integrated with the life and rituals of the common masses.

D.K. Pattammal (1919-2009)

An eminent Carnatic singer, D.K. Pattamal is also known for her accomplishment as a playback singer in Tamil movies. Along with M.S. Subbulakshmi and M.L. Vasanthakumari, they form the trinity of Carnatic music of the 20th century. D.K. Pattammal was the first woman to perform a '*Ragam Thallam Pallavi*' in a concert, which was earlier considered an exclusive male domain owing to the complexities of the performance. She was also considered an authority on and rendered many of the compositions of Muthuswami Dikshitar. (Sangeet Natak Akademi and Padma Vibhushan awardee).

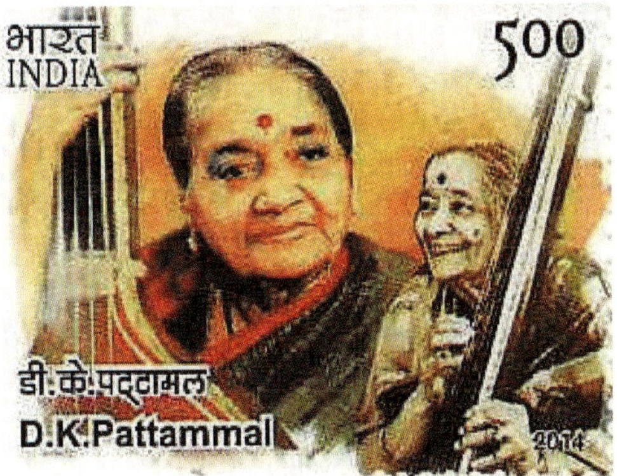

17.7: D.K. Pattammal, a stamp released in 2014 — Courtesy, Department of Post

Among the other greats of the vocal tradition are; Bhimsen Joshi, M.L. Vasanthakumari, Pandit Jasraj, Balamurali krishna and Dagar brothers, amongst others.

Bhimsen Joshi (1922-2011)

A Hindustani classical vocalist of the *Kirana gharana*, Bhimsen Joshi is considered one of the greatest experts of the *khyal* form of singing and also known for his renditions of *bhajans* and *abhangas*. He was especially renowned for the innovative and intuitive use of long *aakaar taans* in his renditions and sparing using of the *sargam taans*. Pandit Joshi also did playback singing for films. He was recognised as the face of the famous music video on national integration, *Mile Sur Mera Tumhara,* which was originally composed by him. He was bestowed the **Bharat Ratna** in 2009 and is among only a few of the artists to be conferred this highest award.

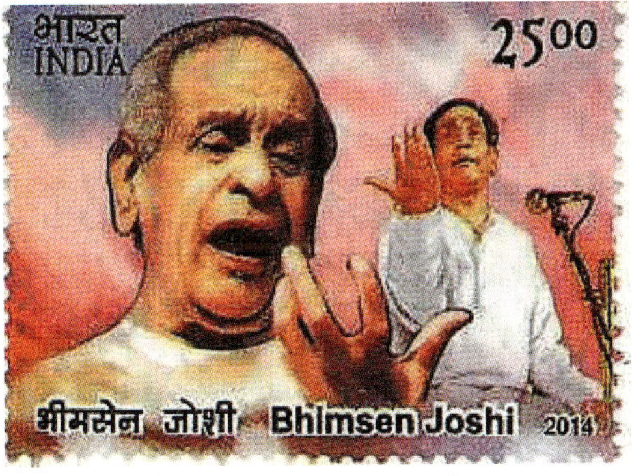

17.8: Bhimsen Joshi, a stamp released in 2014 — Courtesy, Department of Post

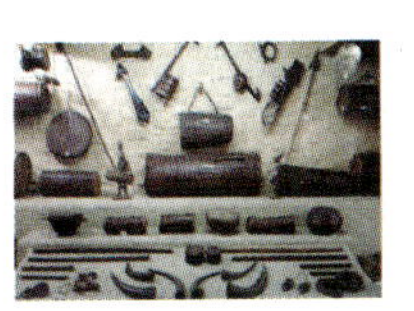

Kumar Gandharva (1824-1924)

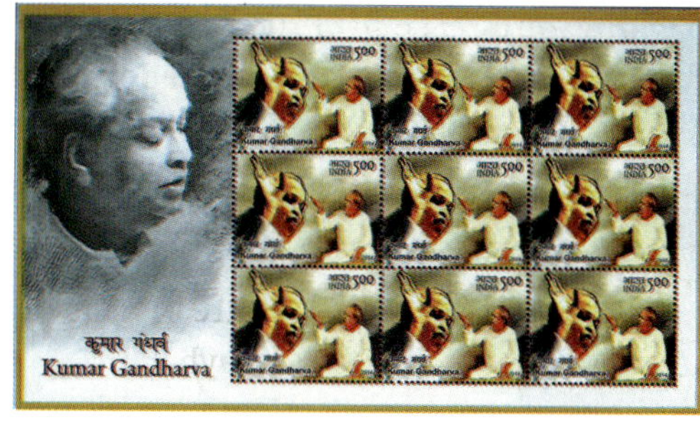

17.9: Kumar Gandharva, a stamp sheet released in 2014 — Courtesy, Department of Post

One of the most eminent Hindustani classical vocalists, Pandit Kumar Gandharva was considered a child prodigy. He is not only acclaimed for his musical finesse, but known for his courage in bringing innovation in music by overcoming traditions of gharana, creating new forms of singing, new *ragas* etc. He was also known for folk songs of Malwa and *nirguni bhajans* based on the teachings of Kabir. Debilitating tuberculosis in his youth restricted his singing, but he overcame it, made changes in the style of singing, and later also composed many *khayals* and *bandishes.* (Padma Vibhushan awardee).

M.L. Vasanthakumari *(1928-1990)*

She was a Carnatic vocalist and a playback singer for the movies. She was the youngest in the trinity of the Carnatic vocalists of M.S. Subbulaskhmi, D.K. Pattammal and herself. MLV (as she was popularly known) was renowned for her rendition of the *Ragam Thanam Pallavi*; besides she popularised a number of compositions of Haridas. Her leisurely and adventurous explorations of the *ragas* and bringing out the delineations of the rare *ragas* in her fluid voice are still considered as an unmatched artistry till date. (Sangeet Natak Akademi and Padma Bhushan awardee).

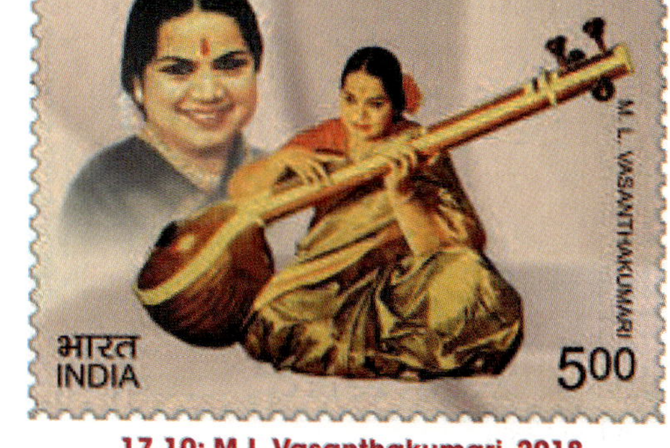

17.10: M.L. Vasanthakumari, 2018 commemorative stamp — Courtesy, Department of Post

Pandit Jasraj (1930-2020)

Pandit Jasraj was a Hindustani vocalist of the *Mewati Gharana.* His genre of singing included the classical, semi classical, devotional, filmi playback etc. Although considered an exponent of *khyal* style, he also incorporated the elements of *thumri* and other lighter styles. He is known for creating a *jugalbandi* based on ancient *moorchana* style where the male and female vocalists would be singing different *ragas* at the same time. Among his other innovations are an improvisation to *Haveli Sangeet,* which involves temple based semi-classical performances. He is also acclaimed for internationally popularising Indian classical music and starting schools of classical music in different cities of USA and Canada. (Sangeet Natak Akademi and Padma Vibhushan awardee).

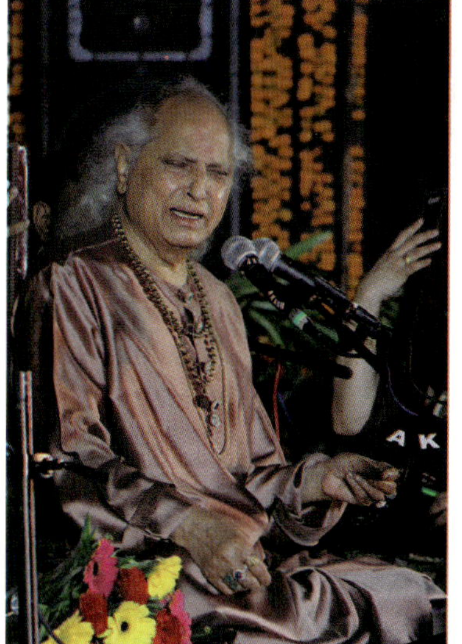

17.11: Pandit Jasraj, a 2015 picture — Wikimedia Commons

Balamuralikrishna (1930-2016)

An eminent Carnatic vocalist, Dr. Balamuralikrishna was also a music composer, playback singer and multi-instrumentalist. He is credited to have composed in all the 72 *malekarta ragas* and created new *ragas* such as *Lavangi, Mahati, Sumukham, and Sidhdhi* comprising four notes, while *Omkaari, Sarvashri,* and *Ganapathi* consist of only three notes. His myriad of compositions covers all the facets of Carnatic music and includes *varnas*, *krithis*, *thillanas* and *bhavageethas.* (Sangeet Natak Akademi and Padma Vibhushan awardee).

Dagar Brothers

A legendary lineage of Hindustani classical genre of ***dhrupad*** singing, the Dagars have been an unbroken family tradition of last 20 generations extending way back in the 15th century to Swami Haridas. The current generation comprised seven Dagar brothers. These included Nasir Moinuddin (1919-1966) and Aminuddin Dagar (1923-2000) (senior Dagar brothers), Nasir Zaheeruddin (1933-1994); Nasir Fayyazuddin Dagar (1934-1989) (junior Dagar brothers) and cousins Zia Mohiuddin Dagar (1929-1990) (Rudra veena exponent) and Zia Fariduddin Dagar (1932-2013), H. Sayeeduddin Dagar (1939-2017). The

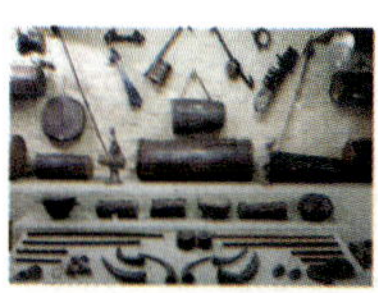

Dagar tradition is one of the four lineages of the dhrupad style of singing which is one of the oldest of the classical styles. It is characterised by sophisticated and serene rendition of the *alap* and the microtonal inflections which brings out the subtle variations in the various *ragas*.

Besides the above, the other great exponents of classical music are, **Krishnarao Ganesh Phulambrikar** (Hindustani vocalist), **Kesarbai Kelkar** (Hindustani vocalist, *khyal*), **Channulal Mishra** (Hindustani vocalist, khyal), **S. Srinivas Aiyyar** (Carnatic vocalist), **Girija Devi** (Hindustani vocalist, *thumri*), **Asgari Bai** (Hindustani vocalist, *dhrupad*), **C.R. Vyas** (Hindustani vocalist, *khyal*), **Shobha Gotru** (Hindustani vocalist, *thumri*), **Kishori Amonkar** (Hindustani vocalist, *khyal, thumri, bhajan*) **Ghulam Mustafa Khan** (Hindustani vocalist), **Prabha Atre** (Hindustani vocalist), **T.V.Sankanarayanan** (Carnatic vocalist), **Sudha Raghunathan** (Carnatic vocalist), amongst others.

Indian Musical Instruments

Musical instruments are the tangible and material facets of the art of music and integral to the performing art. Like all forms of music, India has had a long tradition of musical instruments of different kinds. In modern Indian music, a variety of musical instruments have thus been inherited through the ages, besides many added due to the cross-cultural influences. Be it the classical, the western the folk etc. each has its own tradition of musical instruments and accompaniment. Even the Hindustani classical and the Carnatic traditions have seen the evolution of musical instruments of different types. However, the musical instruments can be classified in the traditional systems into four broad types; (a) String instruments (b) Wind instruments (c) Percussion instruments (d) Non-drum percussion instruments.

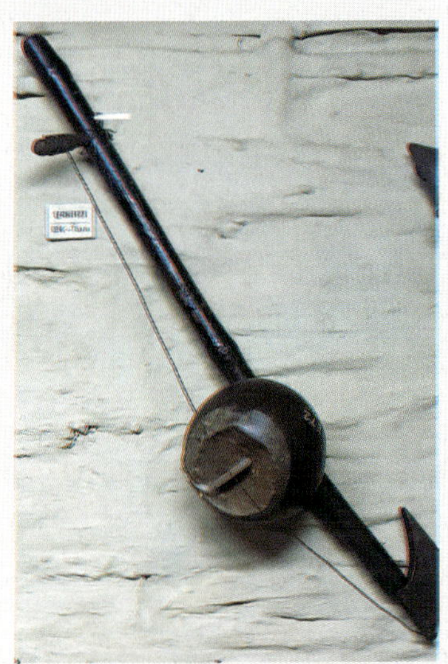

17.12: Traditional Ektara; a plucked single string instrument, Nagpur Central Museum — photograph by Madhukar K Bhagat

The **stringed instruments** (***tata vadya*** or **chordophones**) are those having a single or multiple strings attached and are played by plucking or bowing of the strings. The length of the string and the tautness usually determine the pitch of the note and even the duration of the sound. They can be further categorised as; the **plucked string instruments** and the **bowed stringed instruments**. The string instruments are also subdivided as the fretted and the non-fretted type, where frets present around the neck are used to identify/generate different microtones.

In the Indian classical system of music, the plucked stringed instruments include *sarod, sitar, tambura, rudra-veena, vichitra veena, ektara, gotuvadyam,* and *tumbi,* amongst others. The common Indian bowed string instruments include *dilruba, ektara, sarangi, esraj, chikara,* etc. Violin, a bowed instrument, off late has also gained acceptance in the classical music *Santoor* is a unique stringed instrument which does not fall in the above two categories as its strings are gently stuck with wooden mallets. It has a hundred strings usually arranged in 25 bridges of four strings each. It is also related to the broader category of instruments called *sat-tatntri veena* or the hundred stringed instruments.

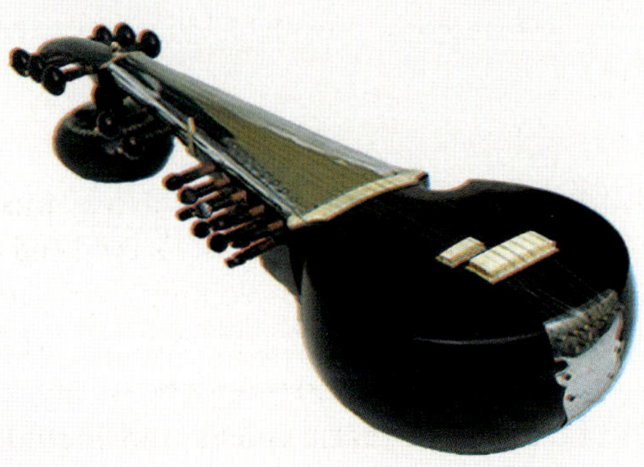

17.13: Sarod, a stringed instrument — Wikimedia Commons

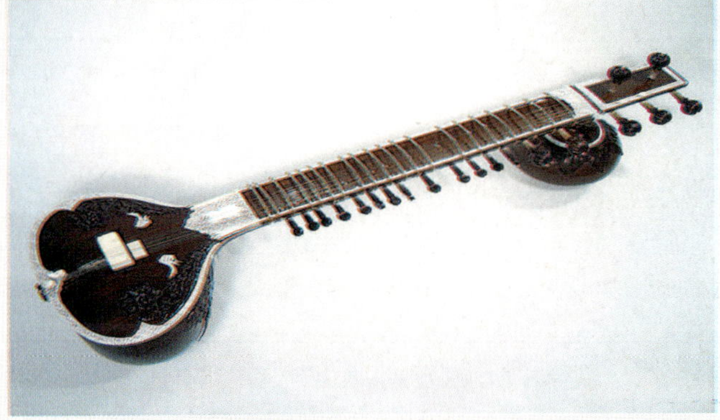

17.14: Indian sitar, a fretted string instrument — Wikimedia Commons

Wind instruments (***sushira vadya or* aerophones**) are played by blowing air into the hollow tubes of the instruments. By controlling the air movement by regulating the holes through fingers, different kinds of pitch of the note are generated. The wind instruments can be of the **flute type** or the **reed type**. The flute types have long hollow tubes with multiple holes to regulate the pitch. India has various types of flutes such as the *bansuri, alghoza* (double flute), *venu* (Carnatic flute), etc. The reed types have a reed inserted which vibrates when air is blown into the instrument. These instruments can be further categorized into the **single reed** types such as ***pungi, been*** or **double reed ones** such as ***shehnai*** and ***nadaswaram.*** Bagpipes are also a category of wind instruments. Indian bagpipes include *mashak*

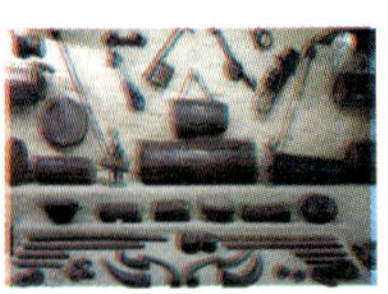

(North India) and *titti* (Andhra Pradesh). *Harmonium* is a kind of musical wind instrument where wind is not blown but pushed/pumped by hand.

The **membranous percussion instruments** (***avanaddha vadya*** or **membranophones**) comprise a hollow structure covered with a taut membrane which vibrates on beating/drumming and thus creates the desired sound. Traditionally, these would comprise animal skins spread over a frame. Pots and wooden barrels were some of the other structures of instruments in this category. These instruments can be classified as;

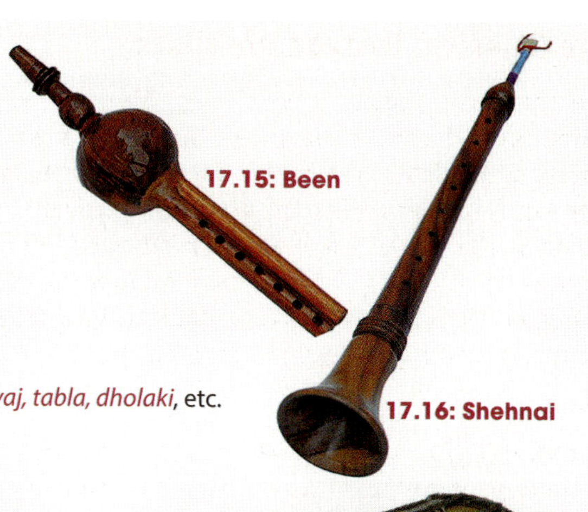

17.15: Been

17.16: Shehnai

- **Hand-drums** such as *damru, dholak, mridangam, pakhavaj, tabla, dholaki*, etc.
- **Hand-frame drums** such as *kanjira, daf*, etc.
- **Stick and hand drums** such as *dhol, idakka, chenda*, etc.
- **Stick drums** including *nagara, pambaichandi*, etc.

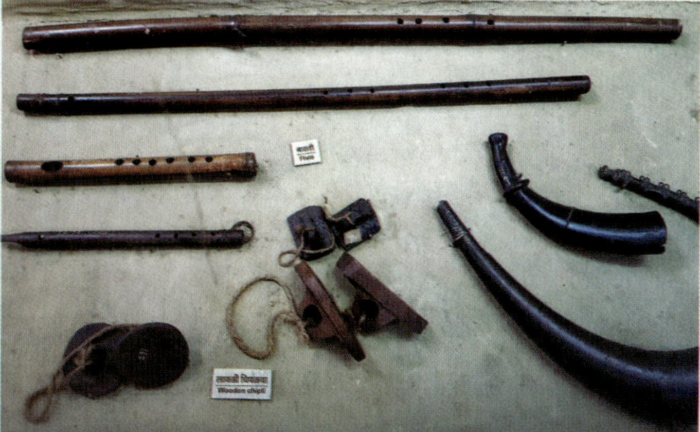

17.17: A collection of different kinds of bansuris (flutes) and horns, some traditional wind instruments, besides wooden chiplis used as percussion instrument. Nagpur Central Museum — photograph by Madhukar K Bhagat

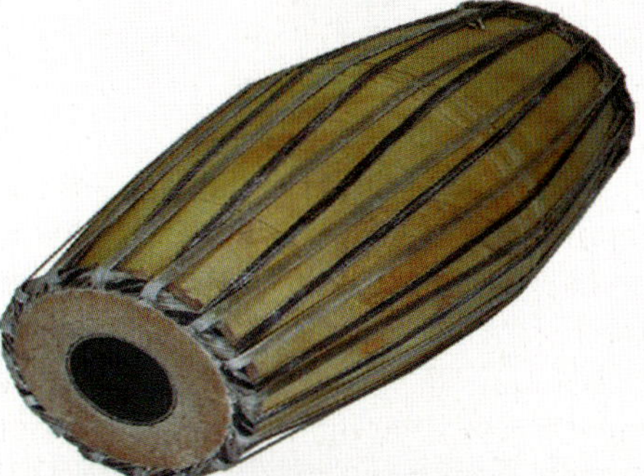

17.18: Mridangam, an *avanaddha vadya*

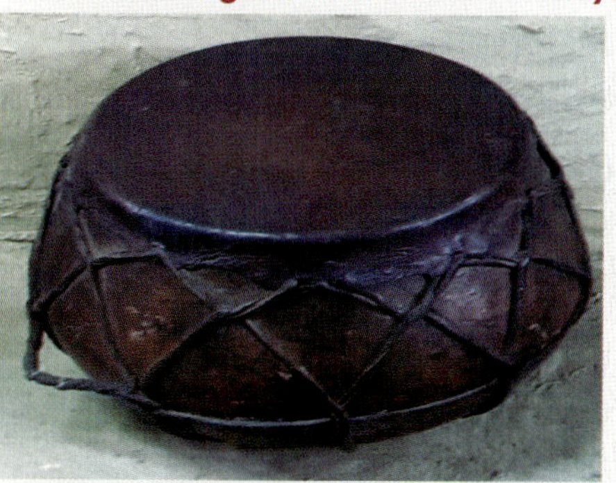

17.19: *Timaki*, a stick drum

The *avanaddha vadya* are also classified as ***oordhwaka*** drums that are placed vertically (eg. table, *chenda*), ***ankya*** drums which are placed horizontally (eg. *dholak, mridangam, pakhawaj* etc.) and ***alingya*** drums, which are held close to the body, such as *daf, dafli*. The fourth category is ***damaru***, which is a type of waisted percussion instrument (having a narrow waist in the middle). Traditional examples of it are *huddaka* (Himachal Pradesh) *timila* (southern states) etc.

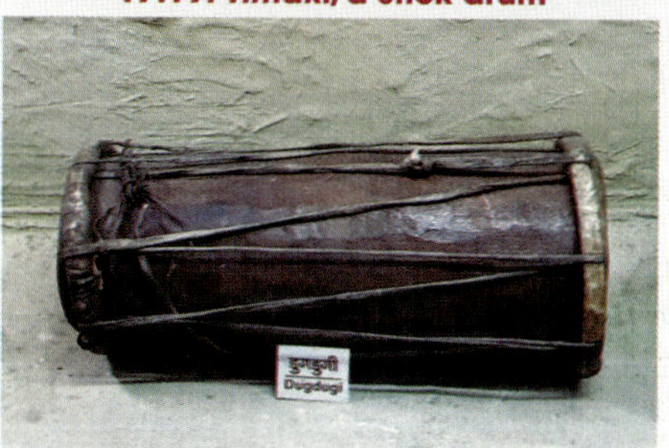

17.20: *Dugdugi*, a hand drum percussion instrument popular amongst tribals, Nagpur Central Museum — photographs by Madhukar K Bhagat

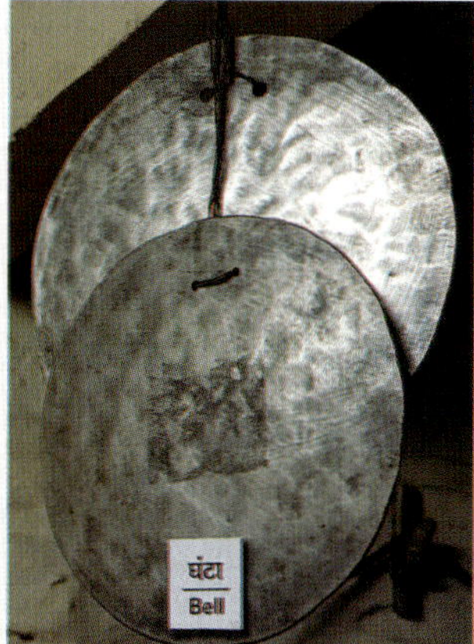

17.21: Ghanta, a traditional bell, a ghana vadya, Nagpur Central Museum — photograph by Madhukar K Bhagat

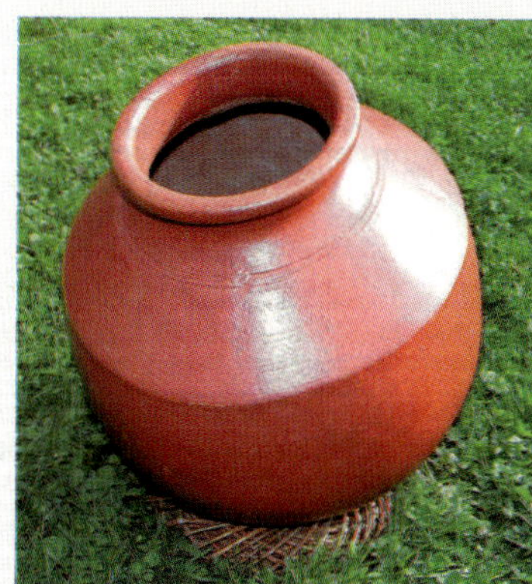

17.22: Ghatam, a *ghana vadya* — Wikipedia

Non-drum percussion instruments (***ghana vadya*** or **idiophones**) are those which produce sound when struck but do not have any membrane stretched on the body. These include instruments like *jaltarang, ghatam* (earthernware pot), *thali, manjeera, ghungroo, ghanta* etc. Essentially, these instruments do not require any tuning, are simple in nature and are largely used as musical accompaniment for the measure of rhythm.

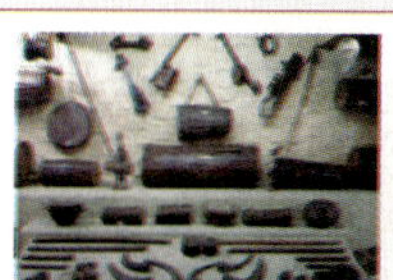

The Classical Instrumentalists

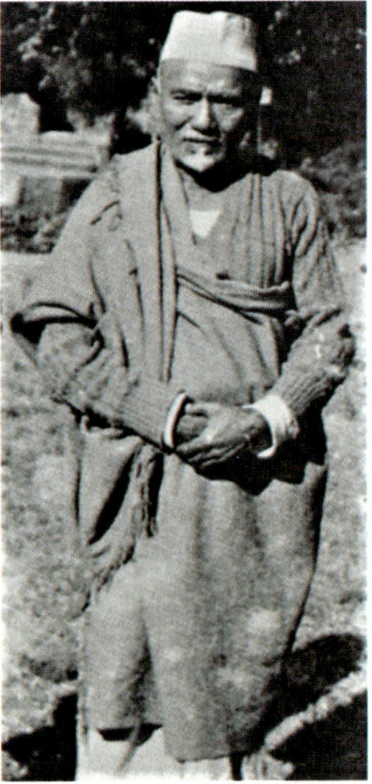

17.23: Baba Allauddin Khan, a photo from 1955 — Wikimedia Commons

The modern Indian music has been a witness to some eminent instrumentalists who have not only displayed exemplary mastery over a variety of musical instruments but enriched the musical tradition by creating new forms of ragas. Through their compositions, they have taken the Indian music to the world stage and carved out a niche for the instrumentalists even as solo artists. The likes of Allauddinn Khan, Bismillah Khan, Ravi Shankar, Allah Rakha, Ali Akbar Khan, V.G. Jog, Vilayat Khan are some of the many leading names from the early 20th century.

Allaudin Khan (1862-1972)

Allaudin Khan is the earliest and the foremost exponent among the eminent instrumentalists of the 20th century in the genre of classical music. Also referred as Baba Allauddin Khan, he was a virtuoso musician from Bengal and an expert sarod player. He was a composer and a multi-instrumentalist who had command over musical instruments like *sitar*, flute, *pakhavaj, mridangam*, tabla and even non-traditional instruments like mandolin, banjo etc. He laid the foundation of the Maihar gharana and created a number of *ragas.* He was one of the most notable teachers of music whose disciples included the who's who of Indian music and stalwarts like Ravi Shankar, Ali Akbar Khan, Annapurna Devi, V.G. Jog amongst others. (Sangeet Natak Akademi and Padma Vibhushan Awardee).

Bismillah Khan (1916-2006)

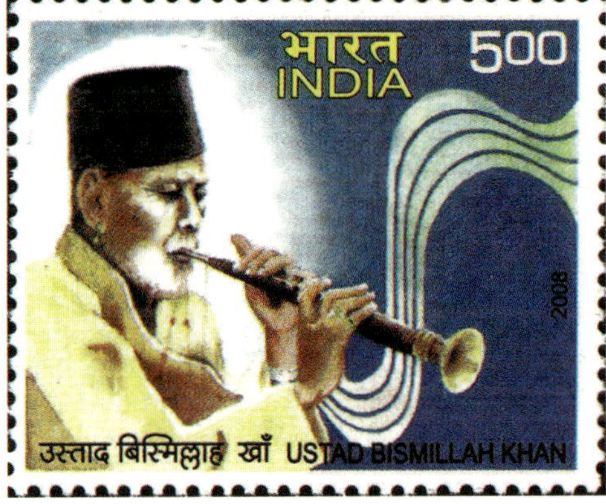

17.24: Bismillah Khan, a commemorative stamp released in 2008 — Courtesy, Department of Post

One of the greatest exponents of *shehnai*, Bismillah Khan and his music also popularised the instrument. His rendition of many complex *ragas* on *shehnai,* earlier considered impossible to perform on it, made it a part of the classical tradition from the earlier category of a ceremonial instrument. He was the musician who was asked to perform on the occasion of unfurling of the tricolour on the Red Fort on the eve of India's independence on 15th August 1947 and also performed repeatedly on All India Radio. Having played *shehnai* for years on the banks of Ganges and also for the Kashi Vishwanath temple, he was emblematic of the fusion of cultures as seen in the Indian music. He was a recipient of **Bharat Ratna** in 2001 and only the third musician to be conferred this award.

Allah Rakha (1919-2000)

Allah Rakha was a pre-eminent *tabla* player in the Hindustani classical genre of music. He has been known for his *jugalbandi* (accompaniment) with Pandit Ravi Shankar and bringing *tabla* before the international audience. Besides, he was an accompanist for many accomplished solo classical singers like Bade Ghulam Ali Khan, Allauddin Khan, Vasant Rai, Ali Akbar Khan. He was also famous as a solo performer, holding the audience enthralled with his wizardry as a percussionist, while bringing musical improvisation. He was a regular performer for All India Radio and was also associated with films giving music to many in the Bollywood and Punjabi movies. As an accompanist to many maestros in the Hindustani and Carnatic tradition, he is said to have brought the two traditions closer. (Sangeet Natak Akademi and Padma Shri Awardee)

Ravi Shankar *(1920-2012)*

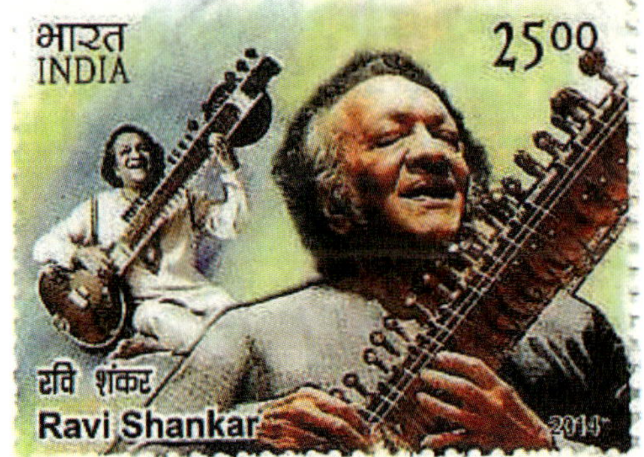

17.25: Ravi Shankar, 2014, commemorative stamp — Courtesy, Department of Post

One of the greatest exponents of sitar and Hindustani classical music, Pandit Ravi Shankar was also one of the best-known Indian musicians in the western world. His association with George Harrison (guitarist of the world-

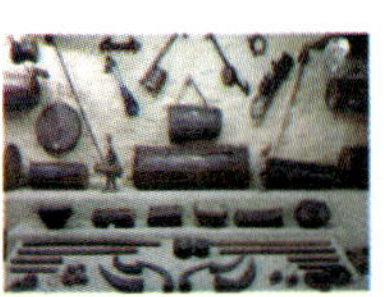

famous Beatles group), the influence of Indian music on the latter, along with his association with international acclaimed musicians like Yehudi Menuhin, put Indian music firmly on the world stage. A disciple of Allauddin Khan, Ravi Shankar was known for his distinctive performance, *jugalbandi* (duet) with *tabla* and introduction of many new *ragas*. He was widely acclaimed for his music score in the movies of *Apu Trilogy* of Satyajit Ray (in the 50s), music score of film *Gandhi* (1982) and many other movies. He was awarded the **Bharat Ratna** (1999) and many other national and international awards. (Sangeet Natak Akademi, Ramon Magsaysay, Knight Commander of the Order of the British Empire, Padma Vibhushan and Bharat Ratna Awardee).

Ali Akbar Khan (1922-2009)

Regarded as a virtuoso *sarod* player in the Hindustani classical genre, Ali Akbar Khan belonged to the *Maihar Gharana* and was the son and disciple of the legendary Allauddin Khan. He was known for creating many new ragas and also for his performance of *jugalbandi* with Pandit Ravi Shankar and Ustad Allah Rakha. He was a regular performer at All India Radio and widely acclaimed for his musical score in different films, particularly *Devi* (1960) of Satyajit Ray. He was also one of the key Indian musicians who performed, popularised and even taught Indian music in the USA. (Padma Vibhushan awardee and other international fellowships)

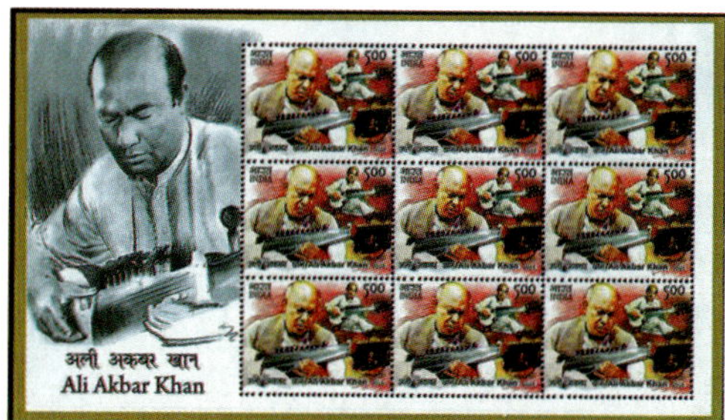

17.26: Ali Akbar Khan, a stamp sheet released in 2014 — Courtesy, Department of Post

> ***"Our sages developed music from time immemorial for the mind to take shelter in that pure being which stands apart as one's true self. Real music is not for wealth, not for honours, or not even for the joys of the mind – it is one kind of yoga, a path for realization and salvation to purify your mind and heart and give you longevity."***
>
> ***— Ali Akbar Khan***

V.G. Jog (1922-2004)

V.G. Jog belonged to the *Maihar Gharana* of Hindustani classical music and was a disciple of Allauddin Khan. He also received training from other eminent musicians. He was the leading exponent of violin in India and was singularly responsible for bringing this western instrument within the Hindustani musical traditions as well as conferring it the repute of a solo instrument. A frequent performer at All India Radio, he was acclaimed for his duet performance with Bismillah Khan and solo concerts. (Sangeet Natak Akademi and Padma Vibhushan Awardee)

Vilayat Khan (1928-2004)

Another eminent player of *sitar* in the Hindustani classical tradition, Vilayat Khan belonged to the Imdadkhani-Etawah Gharana. Considered a child prodigy for having cut a record at the age of six, he had a glorious career spanning nearly 70 years. He is credited with creating many *ragas* and reinterpreting some of the major ragas. He was an innovator of music and also developed a *sitar* style *gayaki ang*, where the instrument was so played to mimic the sound of human voice. A regular performer at the All India Radio, he gave the music in some films including *Jalsaghar* of Satyajit Ray and other Hindi movies. (He declined Padma Vibhushan and other Padma awards).

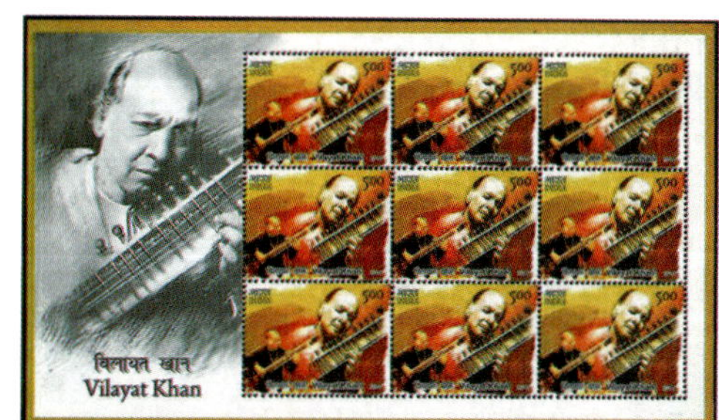

17.27: Vilayat Khan, a stamp sheet released in 2014 — Courtesy, Department of Post

Lalgudi Jayaraman (1930-2013)

An eminent violinist in the tradition of Carnatic music, Lalgudi Jayaraman is said to have reinvented the style of playing violin to suit the needs of classical music in the Carnatic tradition. His style is often referred as the *Lalgudi Bani* and he has composed several *kritis, tillanas, varnams* as well as dance compositions. His style and compositions also brought the Carnatic style of playing violin to the international stage. (Sangeet Natak Akademi and Padma Bhushan Awardee).

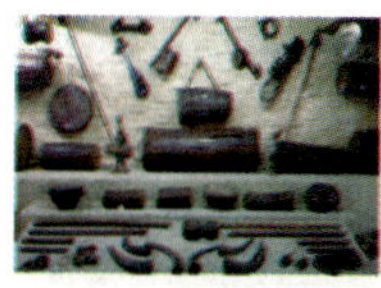

Hariprasad Chaurasia (1938)

He is an eminent flute player in the Hindustani classical tradition. A regular player at the All India Radio, he has also composed music along with Shiv Kumar Sharma for many of the popular films like *Silsila* (1980) *Faasle* (1985), *Chandni* (1989), *Lamhe* (1991) and *Darr* (1993) and others. Hariprasad Chaurasia has collaborated with several international musicians like John Mclaughlin and taken the Indian tradition of *bansuri* (traditional bamboo flute) to the international stage. He is known for his unique style whereby he has reinterpreted and adapted the *ragas* for play on the flute. (Sangeet Natak Akademi and Padma Vibhushan Awardee)

Shiv Kumar Sharma (1938-1922)

Shiv Kumar Sharma was an acclaimed exponent of santoor in the Hindustani classical tradition. Although santoor was a folk instrument of accompaniment in the traditional music of Jammu and Kashmir, it was due to the national and international accomplishments of Pandit Sharma that made santoor a part of the classical tradition and even a solo instrument. For this, he even brought changes in this 100 stringed instrument and in its style of playing to increase its melodic range, so as to suit to the flexibility of human voice required in the classical tradition. 'The Call of Valley', a music album along with Pandit Hari Prasad Chaurasia has been a highly acclaimed work besides many others. With the latter, he formed the successful duo of Shiv-Hari giving music in many hit Bollywood movies. (Sangeet Natak Akademi and Padma Vibhushan Awardee).

Amjad Ali Khan (1945)

A sarod player in the Hindustani classical tradition, Amjad Ali Khan is reckoned among the great exponents of classical music. He was born in a family of musicians who several generations ago are credited with the creation of the sarod by adapting it from the Afghani Rabab. Amjad Ali Khan is credited with creation of new ragas. He has been an experimentalist with music who is known for his fast and clear *taans* and who even made modification with the instrument to innovate. He has performed internationally in concerts such as at the Nobel Peace Prize Concert (2014), Hong Kong Philharmonic Orchestra etc. He has also been a visiting professor of music in international universities, thus promoting Indian music at the world stage, and has been much felicitated as an internationally acclaimed musician. (Sangeet Natak Akademi and Padma Vibhushan Awardee).

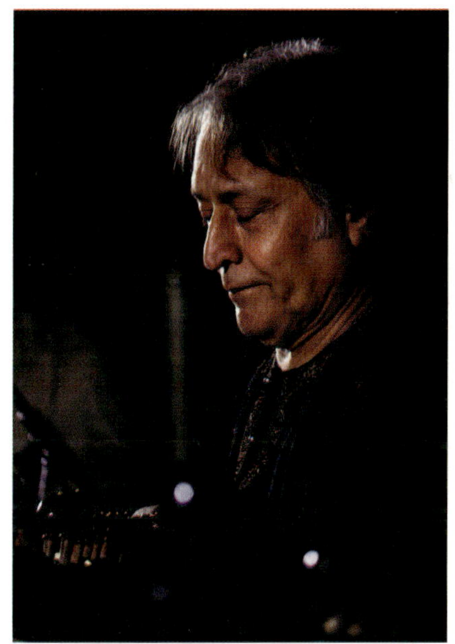

17.28: Amjad Ali Khan in a performance in 2020 — Wikimedia Commons

L. Subramaniam (1947)

He is an accomplished violin maestro in the Carnatic tradition as well as Western classical music traditions. He has performed/has collaborations with many international experts of music including Yehudi Menuhin, Stéphane Grappelli, Ruggiero Ricci and others. Besides, he has composed for Hollywood and other films, Carnatic pieces and western symphonies. He is renowned for his work in fusion music and also for his playing techniques (Sangeet Natak Akademi and Padma Bhushan Awardee).

Zakir Hussain (1951)

A tabla maestro in the Hindustani classical genre, Zakir Hussain is the son of Ustad Allah Rakha who has also been his teacher. A child prodigy, Zakir Hussain has performed as an accompanist to the leading classical exponents including the grand masters of music like Pandit Bhimsen Joshi, Pandit Ravi Shankar, Ustad Ali Akbar Khan, Pandit VG Jog, Ustad Vilayat Khan, Pandit Shiv Kumar Sharma, Pandit Hari Prasad Chaurasia, Pandit Jasraj. He has also been a much-acclaimed solo performer, who has given music score in several films and collaborated with international musicians like John McLaughlin and George Harrison. Along with ustad Allah Rakha, he has brought *tabla* as a Hindustani classical instrument on the international platform. (Sangeet Natak, Padma Bhushan awardee and Grammy winner)

Among some other eminent instrumentalists are **Hafiz Ali Khan** (1888-1972, *sarod*, Padma Bhushan), **Pandit Nikhil Ghosh** (1918-1995, *tabla*, Padma Bhushan), **Pandit Doreswamy Iyengar** (1920-1997, veena, Padma Bhushan) **Pandit Samta Prasad** (1921-1994, *tabla*, Padma Bhushan), **Pandit Ramnarayan** (1927, Sarangi, Padma Vibhushan), **Pandit Kishan Maharaj** (1923-2008; *tabla*; Padma Bhushan), **Kuzhur**

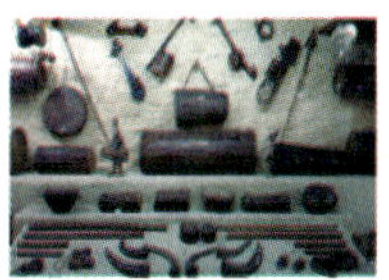

Narayana Marar (1925 –2011, *panchavadyam*, Padma Bhushan), **Ustad Abdul Halim Jaffar Khan** (1927-2017, *sitar*, Padma Bhushan), **Annapurna Devi** (1927-2018 *surbahar*, Padma Bhushan), **Sabri Khan** (1927-2015, *sarangi*, Padma Bhushan), **Arvind Parikh** (1927, *sitar* Padma Bhushan), **Pandit Ram Narayan** (1927, *sarangi*, Padma Vibhushan), **Pandit Buddhadeb Dasgupta** (1933-2018, *sarod*, Padma Bhushan) **Pandit Debu Chaudhary** (1935-2021, *sitar*, Padma Bhushan), **Ustad Asad Ali Khan** (1937-2011; *rudra veena*, Padma Bhushan), **N Rajam** (1938, violin, Padma Bhushan), **Sultan Khan** (1940-2011, *sarangi*, Padma Bhushan), **T.H. Vinayakram** (1942; Ghatam, Padma Shri), **Pandit Vishwa Mohan Bhatt** (1950; Mohan-veena; Padma Bhushan), **Pandit Budhatiya Mukherjee** (1955, *sitar*, Padma Bhushan), **U. Srinivas** (1969-2014; mandolin, Padma Shri).

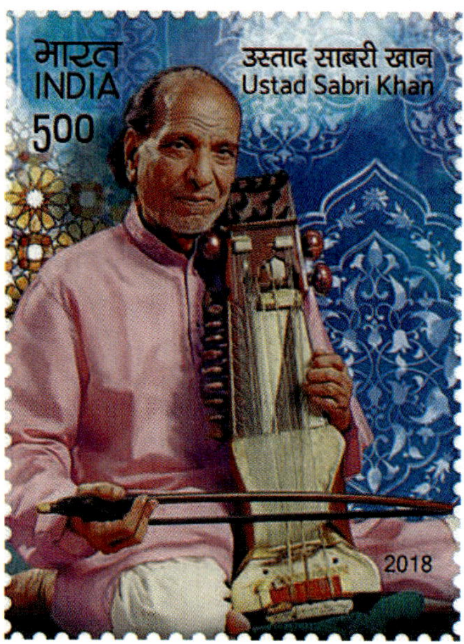

17.29: Sabri Khan, a stamp issued in 2018 — Courtesy, Department of Post

REGIONAL & FOLK MUSIC

India has a rich tradition of regional and folk music which has prospered over the ages in different parts of the country and local communities. It has flourished in the hinterland, in the villages, the tribes and communities and as traditional music infused in the very micro-culture of the population and preserved in the informal traditions. The ancient *Prabandha* music too was an informal music system. Unlike the formal music systems of Classical music, or even the light classical forms, the regional and folk music have not seen strict or definite structure of its musical arrangement, a formal set of rules or a pedagogical form of learning. It is ingrained in the culture and deeply influenced by the regional and local traditions, the language and dialect. The environment, the flora and fauna, and the occupation of the people, all are a determinant of this art.

Folk music is essentially a part of daily lives of the people. It is associated with their work such as agricultural activities and daily chores. Its objective may range from entertainment to devotion, to expression of joys and sorrows, to mark the festivities and lesser occasions. Be it child birth, betrothal, marriage or other events of life, it is an integral part of the tradition. Unlike other formal systems of music, folk music did not enjoy singular and life-long dedication of certain groups of artists, as the economics of life may not have permitted such an endeavour. Nor did it have royal patronage. The custodian of folk music has always been the common people and the local culture. Even the musical instruments associated with it are simple and at times local versions of *sarangi*, *ektara*, *dotar* or percussion instruments like *dholak*, *daf*, *nal* etc. The more formal ones like *tabla* and harmonium are late entrants in this art. Thus, regional and folk music has been emblematic of the very culture and ethos of the people. A diverse country like India is indeed blessed with a wide range of such musical tradition, some of which are described here.

What Constitutes Folk Music?

Though a formal definition of folk music may not exist, generally it is understood as the music of the common masses which is bereft of formal learning and reflective of the micro-culture. The issue as to what constitutes folk music has been deliberated by the International Folk Music Council (now known as the International Council for Traditional Music) and UNESCO International Music Council etc. Certain specific characteristics are now recognized and considered as essential characteristics of folk music.

Firstly, the music should be **easily distinguished from cultivated art music.** It should be an art form transferred from **generation to generation** through the **oral tradition**. The music should be **conceived and cultivated by the community** within itself. Further, it should be the **expression of the whole communit**y rather than an expression of an individual.

INDIAN STATES AND CULTURE OF FOLK SONGS

Jammu and Kashmir

The folk songs of Jammu and Kashmir are inspired by its spiritual culture of Sufism, Shaivism and Buddhism. The bounties of nature, the traditions of people, the stories of love and the toil of the peasants, all find a place in these songs.

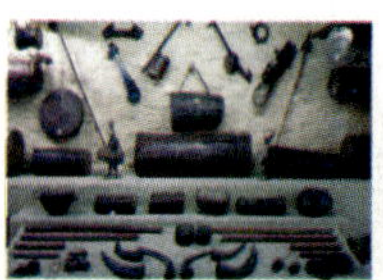

Chakri

Among the most popular of folk music of Jammu and Kashmir region is *Chakri*. It is a call and response/ responsorial form of folk singing. (Responsorial: choir singing where leader alternates with the choir in singing). This folk art is performed with instruments like *harmonium, rabab, sarangi, nout* (a clay pot like vessel), *geger* (brass or metal pot), *tumbaknari* (an earthen pot with high neck), *chimta* (tongs with jingles) etc. *Chakri* is also a medium for folk tale where stories of love, fairy tales or other folklores are performed. It is a part of the both Hindu and Muslim traditions in the state and specially performed during *henna* nights of wedding celebrations.

Sufiana Kalam

It is a classical form of music of Kashmir which is based on its own *ragas* referred to as *maqam*. The music is sung to the accompaniment of *santoor, Kashmiri saz, setar (Kashmiri sitar), wasool* (a percussion instrument smaller than *pakhawaj*) etc.

Hafiz Nagma

Hafiz Nagma is a folk form of music based on the classical form of Sufiana Kalam. The performance involves dance by a female (known as *hafiza*) to the accompaniment of music played by a number of male musicians. A popular instrument in these performances is *santoor* (a string instrument with hundred strings)

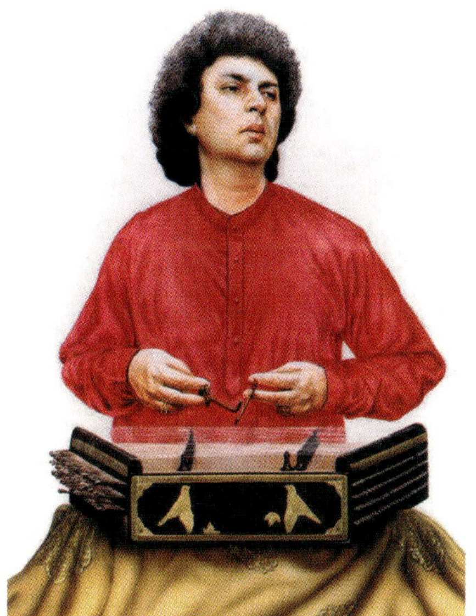

17.30: Pandit ShivKumar Sharma performing on santoor — Wikimedia Commons

Ladi Shah

It is a genre of folk music which involves story telling/narration generally in a humorous manner by a group of wandering musicians/performers. It also takes the form of satirical expression on the social and political conditions which are prevailing.

Wanawan

Also referred to as Wanwun, it is a traditional music and dance performed on the occasion of marriage in Kashmir. It is also called *Rouf.*

Bhakh/Bhakha

It is the traditional Dogri folk song which is popular in the Jammu region and is sung at the time of harvesting.

Surma

Surma is another folk song tradition in Dogri language where a young girl expresses her anguish on separation from her husband who has gone to serve in the army.

Punjab

The folk music of Punjab is associated with the agrarian traditions of the region, the rural life style and the celebration of events of the life cycle. It also encompasses different sub-regional traditions such as that of, Doaba, Malwa, Pothohar, Majha, and the hilly areas. Over the ages, the region having been a melting pot of different religions and cultures, it has assimilated a very diverse tradition of folk music. This is also manifested in its different forms such as the *Shabad*, *Gurmat Sangeet*, *bhakti sangeet*, *sufiana kalam, qawwali*, *kirtan, vaar* etc.

Tappa

Tappa is a semi classical form of vocal tradition of Punjab. Tappa is inspired by the folk songs of camel riders in the region. It is usually sung in Punjabi and Pashto language and is set in *ragas.* A feature of these songs is rhythmic and rapid notes and flashy tonal movements.

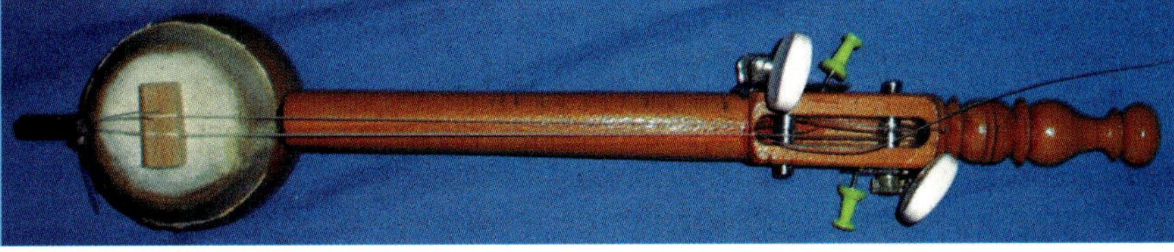

17.31: *Thumbi,* a stringed instrument popular in Punjab — Wikimedia Commons

Among the common **folk, songs** are those associated with events in life or **life cycle songs**. These include the songs at the time of birth and marriage etc. *Suhag* or *ghorian* are the

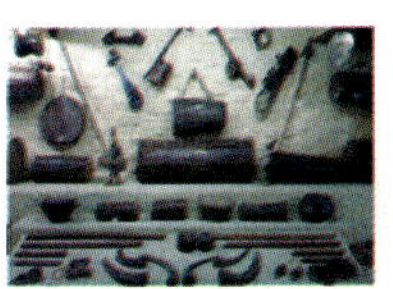

folk songs associated with the occasion of marriage. These are sung for the bride and groom respectively while praising the almighty and seeking his blessings for the couple. Similarly, ***milni, sohle, sehra, mahiya, lavan, kangana*** are some other folk songs associated with marriage and sung at the different points of the ceremony.

Punjabi folk songs also include the **seasonal melodies** such as *sawan ke geet* (rainy season), *jhulna pingan* (song sung on swings in monsoon), ***Lohri*** and ***Sankrant ke geet***. Another genre of folk songs is the love songs like ***dhola***, **ballads** such as those on Heer-Ranjha, ***vaar*** which are heroic songs, and ***kissa***, which are tales.

Himachal Pradesh

The folk songs of Himachal can be identified as per the various regions/valleys. These include the songs from Chamba, Kangra, Mandi, Bilaspur, Kullu and Shimla. The subjects vary from devotion to natural beauty, from day-to-day activities to festivals, from the seasons of the year to love. Ballads, narration of stories from Ramayana and Mahabharata, the challenges of hills, the nomadic and tribal culture, all are a part of this tradition.

Laman

Laman is a folk song of love popular in the Kullu valley. It is sung by group of young boys and girls where one groups sings a stanza and the other responds to it in form of song.

Jhuri Geet

This folk song is popular in the Sirmour region. These are essentially songs of separation which are imbued in *shringaar rasa.*

Haar

It is another folk song from Sirmour region which are narrative of the valour of the folk heroes.

Kunju-Chanchalo

Kunju-Chanchalo It is a genre of love songs famous in the Kullu and Kangda region. These are based on the love story of Kunju and Chanchalo and are as popular as the songs of Heer-Ranjha and Dhola-Maru elsewhere.

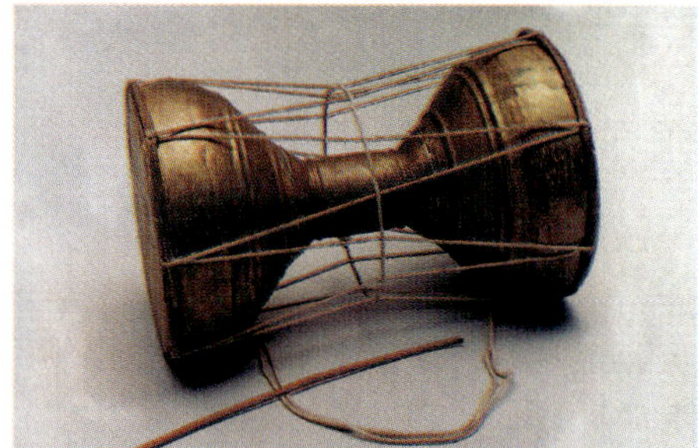

17.32: *Pohl,* a folk percussion instrument of Himachal Pradesh, hour glass shaped, made of brass with parchment at both ends, and tightened with cotton chord which is also tied at the centre to increase the tension. The instrument is suspended diagonally in the front and beaten by both hands — Courtesy, Sangeet Natak Akademi

Sukrat

It is a form of song which is sung on the occasion of night festival of *Sukrat* which falls in the month of *Chaitra*. The song is set to *raga Tilak Kamod* and its subject is the sorrow and gratitude of the subjects for their queen who laid her life for them.

Ainchaliyan

They are songs in the nature of religious ballads. These are sung at the bride's house after a wedding and by women at the home of an unmarried girl.

Uttarakhand

The folk songs of Uttarakhand are sung in the languages of Kumaoni and Garhwali. The songs reflect the beauty of the hills and are an integral part of different festivals, religious and other auspicious occasions. Their subjects often include folk stories, religious traditions, love ballads and even mundane issues of daily life. The folk instruments of the region include *dhol, damoun, daur, thali, turri, ransingha, dholki, masakbhaja, bhankora, hurka, been* etc. Nowadays, harmonium and tabla are also in use.

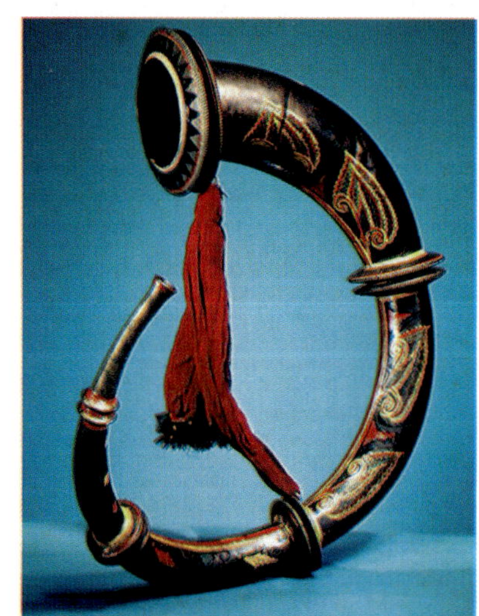

17.33: Ranasingha/Ranasringa; a vibrated horn aerophone, in the collection of Metropolitan Museum of Art — Wikimedia Commons

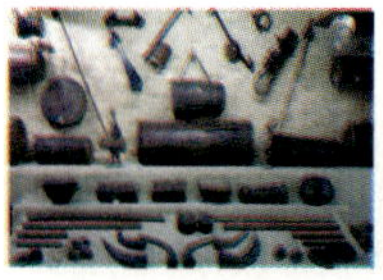

Mangal and Nyoli

They are two popular form of folk songs of Kumaon region. These are sung to the accomplishment of traditional musical instruments.

Shakunakhar–Mangalgeet

This folk tradition of Kumaon involves singing of different songs on different auspicious occasions viz. child birth, *chaathi* (sixth day of birth ritual) *namkaran sanskar* (naming ceremony) *janeyoo* (thread ceremony), marriage etc. These songs are sung by the ladies and generally without the accompaniment of musical instruments. The songs beseech the blessings of the divine deities.

Barhamasa

Barhamasa are folk songs popular in Kumaon region and describe the twelve months of the year. They bring out the specific qualities of the months and the environment. Besides, they also capture the human yearning and emotions of the common people.

A very famous song of Kumaon is *Bedu Pako Baro Mason*. The song is based on *raga Durga* and is melodious. It was composed in the 1950s by Mohan Upreti and B.M. Shah and is popular in the entire region.

Bajuband

It is a folk song of Garhwal, usually of love and sacrifice. This is sung by shepherds and also by women in the villages along with their daily work and chores.

Basanti

Basanti is a folk song of Garhwal region which welcomes the spring (*basant*). The onset of spring after the winters marks the blooming of flowers of different colours and the song is a celebration of the new life and colour which springs in the hills and valleys.

Ghasiyari Geet

It is another folk song of Garhwal region sung by young women in groups while proceeding to fetch grass (*ghans*) for the cattle from the forests. The song emphasizes on the significance of labour and also serves as a form of entertainment and brings togetherness in the otherwise mundane work. Sometimes it is also classified as *bajuband* form of song.

Chhopati

It is a folk song of love sung in Tehri and Garhwal region.

Besides, other common folk music forms include ***jagar*** (religious and ritualistic songs of invoking of gods and local deities), ***mandal*** (ceremonial song on occasion of marriage, thread ceremony etc.), ***panwara*** (songs in praise of warriors and record heroic deeds), ***khuder*** (songs of melancholy on separation from husband or from the maternal home), ***thadya*** (genre of court entertainment) and ***jhora*** (song of community dance).

Haryana

Traditionally, being an agrarian society, Haryana's folk art and culture see a profound influence of agricultural activities and rural lifestyle. The seasons of the year, events in the social life, such as rituals, ceremonies and festivities, devotional music and ballads are some other genres of folk music of the state. *dhol, dholak sarangi, been, pungi, daphli, chimta manjira, tumba* etc. are some of the of the traditional folk instruments to the accompaniment of which these folk songs are performed. Being in proximity of the states of Punjab and Rajasthan, cultural influences and similarity of folk traditions with these two states can also be seen in Haryana.

The traditional music of Haryana is categorized as those which are based on the *ragas* and the other usually called the *desi* (country) folk songs. The genre of *raga*-based songs includes *Alah*, *Jaimaphalla*, *Baramasa,* and *Phaga* amongst others.

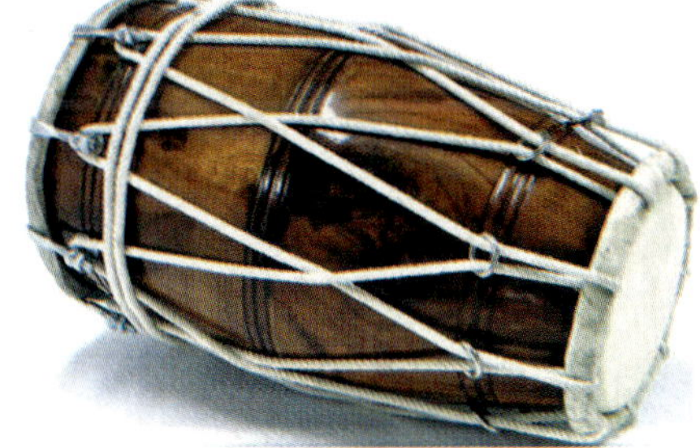

17.34: The traditional *dholak* — Wikimedia Commons

Alah

They are ballads which recount the bravery of Alah and Udal. *Jaimaphalla* are songs of bravery of Jaimal & Fatta, who were warriors in the army of Maharana Udai Singh II of Chittor, and lost their lives while defending with great bravery the Chittorgarh

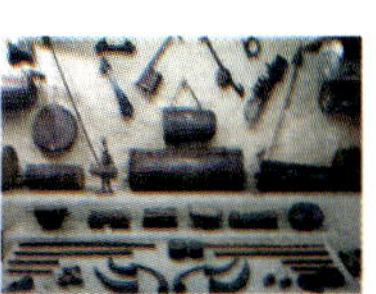

fort against forces of Akbar. ***Baramasa*** songs pertain to the twelve months of the year. ***Phaga*** songs welcome the month of *Phalgun*. Besides these, there are songs of *Holi* and *Teej* festivals.

The ***desi* song** category may include the genre of *Gharwa Gayan*, *Jhoolana*, *Patka*, *Rasia*, etc.

Ragas like *Bilawal, Bhairavi, Peelu, Kafi, Bhopali, Bhairavi, Chandrakauns* and *Desh* may also be a basis of their composition. Further, their beats may be based on *taals* such as *Teen-tal, Roopak, Dadra, Kehrwa* etc.

Ballads

Ballads are sung by a traditional group of people called *Jogis* and are another popular folk song category. These are called ***dohas*** and are songs of war and bravery and are like unwritten history of the community.

Bhajans

A category of religious songs, bhajans are performed in groups and are popular throughout the state.

Besides these, there are folk songs pertaining to birth, marriage, harvesting and also a category of songs which are sung with the folk dances.

Rajasthan

Rajasthan has a rich folk singing tradition popular amongst communities of *Langhas, Saperas, Manganiars, Bhopas,* and *Jogis*. Over centuries, their tradition has flourished with a distinct style of each of these. The desert, the life-giving monsoon, love and heroism, besides festivals and fairs are some common themes of the folk songs.

Maand

It is a folk singing style of Rajasthan which is also recognised in the classical circles. However, it is not recognised as a true or a full-fledged *raga*. Maand is considered similar to *thumri* and *ghazal*. It is said to be popular in the erstwhile royal courts of Rajasthan.

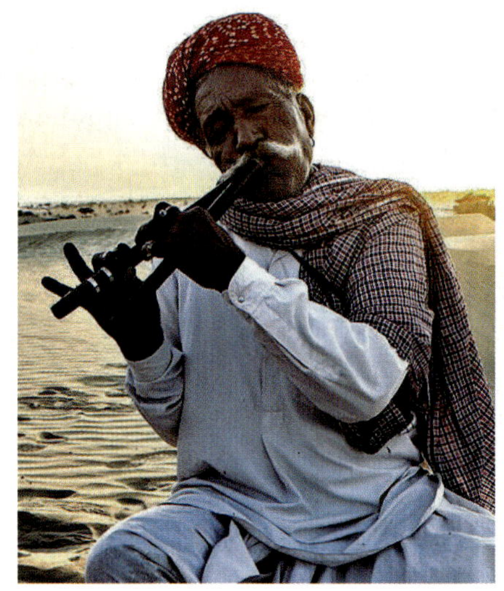

17.35: A folk musician playing Alghoza in the desert — Wikimedia Commons

Pankhida

Pankhida literally means lover. It is a folk song sung by peasants while doing work in fields. It is sung to the accompaniment of *alghoza** and *manzira* (a pair of clash symbols).

(*Alghoza ; a wind instrument with two pair of flutes, one for the notes and other for the drone)

Panihore/panihari

They are songs centered around water and wells. The lyrics describe chores which are connected with collection of water etc. In a water starved state, for centuries, women undertook the burden of fetching water from distant places in the scorching sun. The tradition of *panihari* (women who fetch water) songs developed as part of this routine and highlights the significance of water, wells etc. Besides, it also includes subjects of love, topics of daily life etc.

Lotia

It is another folk song associated with water and is sung during festivals, particularly in the *Chaitra* month by the womenfolk in Rajasthan. The *lotas* (vessels) containing water filled from ponds and wells are decorated with flowers.

Teej

Teej is an important festival of the region and an occasion for folk songs in Rajasthan. The festival, celebrated on the 3rd day of the new moon in the month of *Shravan*, is centered around the cosmic union of Shiva and Parvati, in the backdrop of the monsoon which brings life to the desert. Thus, the song also marks the celebration of the festivals and the monsoons.

Bhajans and Banis

They are a class of devotional songs of Rajasthan. These are played to the accompaniment of instruments like *dholak*, *sitar*, and *sarangi*. Besides the above, there are songs based on **epic ballads** recounting the tales of valour of folk heroes.

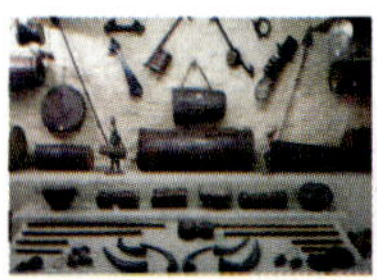

Uttar Pradesh

The large state of Uttar Pradesh located in the in the Gangetic plains has diverse geographical regions of Braj (western Uttar Pradesh), Poorvanchal (eastern Uttar Pradesh), Bundelkhand and Ruhelkhand. Each has a distinct culture and genre of folk songs. While *Rasiyageet, Hori, Phag, Languriya, Sohar* and *Jhoola* are popular in the Braj region, *Kajri, Sohar, Birha, Jhoola* and *Jhoomar* are the favourites of Poorvanchal. Among the folk songs of Uttar Pradesh are also those associated with devotion to Sri Krishna and is particularly popular in the Braj region. Festivals like Holi, and also the rainy season have also inspired many of the folk songs. Besides, the events of life like birth, marriages etc., have also been occasions for such songs.

Rasiyageet

They are folk songs of the **Braj region** of Uttar Pradesh which are sung in Braj Bhasha (a Hindi dialect). *Rasa* here refers to emotion and the songs have genesis to the singing in praise of lord Krishna describing his acts and antics.

Hori

They are songs sung on the occasion of festival of Holi in Braj. Its tradition is considered quite ancient and is based on the love pranks of Radha and Krishna.

Phag

Phag are the songs welcoming the month of *Phalgun* which marks the beginning of the spring season. These are the songs of joy and happiness and also set the tone for the coming festival of Holi which falls in this month.

Birha

It is a popular folk music of Poorvanchal region. Literally, the word *Biraha* means separation, and refers to the sorrow of separation from the beloved. In the last couple of hundred years, this music acquired greater popularity due to migration of workers from this region and traces of this folk music can be found even in the Caribbean and Mauritius etc. where these workers went. The song comprises verses where one side makes a point and the other replies to it in the same verse.

Languriya

It is a song considered a subgenre of *Rasiya* and is popular in Braj region, particularly during the *Navaratra* festivals. The *Languriyas* refer to the male devotees of Goddess Durga and also devotees of lord Hanuman.

Sohar

Sohar are sung on the occasion of child birth, particularly in the Prayagraj (erstwhile Allahabad) region and Poorvanchal (eastern Uttar Pradesh).

Kajri/Kajari

It is a folk song sung by the women during the rainy season. On the third day of the second half of the month of Bhadra, *kajri* is sung by women in night while dancing in semi circles.

Jhoola

Jhoola literally refers to a swing. This is a genre of songs which are sung in the rainy season when swings are built on the branches of tree and womenfolk gather around and sing while swinging.

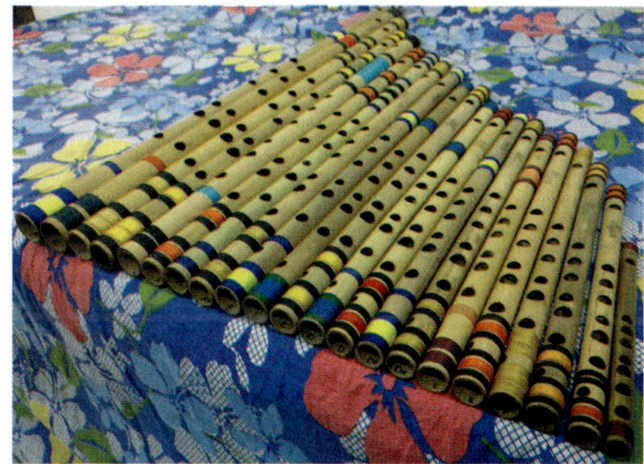

17.36: Different scales of bansuri (of bamboo) in a set; a common instrument in folk and classical music of Uttar Pradesh — Wikimedia Commons

Qawwali

It is a folk song and has origins in the Sufi traditions. It was sung in the praise of Allah, particularly on the mausoleums of the Sufi saints. This folk music is popular in most parts of Uttar Pradesh and northern India.

Community based songs

Apart from the above, there are folk songs which are based on certain communities, viz. *Kaharwa*, which is sung during weddings and *Dhobiya* which is popular in the washerman community.

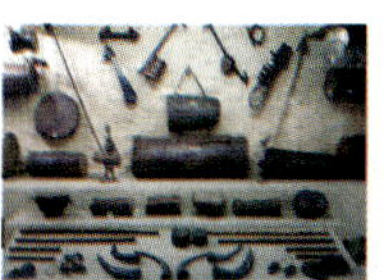

Besides the above, Bundelkhand is known for *Alaha* folk songs. Further, a class of folk music also pertains to folk theatres such as ***Ramleela, Raasleela*** and ***Nautanki*** which are popular in the state.

Bihar

Located in the Gangetic valley in the eastern part of the country, the state has a very ancient history and a rich heritage. Its folk traditions are intrinsically linked with socio economic activities of the common people and rituals associated with milestone events of life. Besides, ballads and devotional music are also a salient part of this culture. Bhojpuri, Magahi and Maithali are the three dialects in which the majority of these folk traditions are expressed. These folk songs are usually sung to the accompaniment of traditional instruments like *dholak, tambura, sarangi* and *manjira*.

Sohar

It is one of the most popular of folk songs which is associated with the birth of child. It is a Bhojpuri as well Maithili tradition, and sung by ladies, whereby well-being of the child is prayed for and the newborn is blessed. It is also popular in the neighbouring state of Jharkhand.

Sumangali

They are the folk songs which are sung on the occasion of marriage by womenfolk. It is an expression of blessings to the newly-weds. The tunes of the songs are handed over through ages and the singing incorporates only a few of instruments usually of the traditional kind.

Ropni-geet

They belong to the genre of songs associated with the agricultural activity of sowing of paddy. The ***Katni-geet*** are associated with its harvesting. These songs are sung in groups by the farmers working in the fields. It is a way of taking away the boredom of work while bonding in the process. Besides, it is a celebration of the process of agriculture and harvesting.

Chaiti and Kajri

They are other folk traditions popular in the Bhojpur region. These bear the classical influences and are considered semi-classical folk songs. *Chaiti* is sung to welcome the month of *Chaitra* which marks the beginning of new year and also in the month in which the birth of lord Rama is celebrated. *Kajri* often explores the longing of a maiden for her lover in the months of *Sawan* when monsoons arrive. *Kajri* literally means 'dark', and is allegorical to the dark clouds of the season of rains.

Hori

It is another genre of folk songs sung during the festival of Holi.

Besides the above, a category of devotional songs are also a part of the folk tradition. The folk songs associated with the festival of ***Chaath*** fall in the category of devotional songs. ***Hari kirtan*** and ***Astajama*** are some other devotional folk songs. The latter is associated with continuous chanting of *Hare Ram Hare Krishna* for 24 hours.

Amongst the other common **folk songs** are those associated with the tradition of **Bhikhari Thakur** (a prolific Bhojpuri poet, playwright and musician of early 20th century), and the **ballads associated with Kunwar Singh** (freedom fighter in the First War of Independence). The state, like the Purvanchal region of Uttar Pradesh, also has the tradition of *Biraha*. Songs of season such as *Barahmasa* and songs associated with numerous festivals including *Chaath*, are also a salient aspect of its folk tradition.

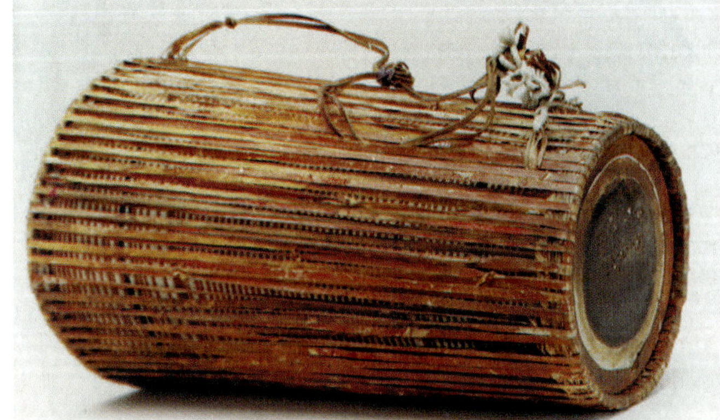

17.37: Mandar, a folk percussion instrument of Bihar, a bifacial drum covered with parchment and leather hoops at ends, slung around neck, placed horizontally, and played with both hands. — Courtesy, Sangeet Natak Akademi

Jharkhand

Located in the Chota Nagpur plateau, amidst forests and hills, this state has a traditional folk culture as well as tribal culture. The areas contiguous to the neighbouring states and particularly those bordering Bihar and Bengal also see the influence of the adjoining states regions in the folk music.

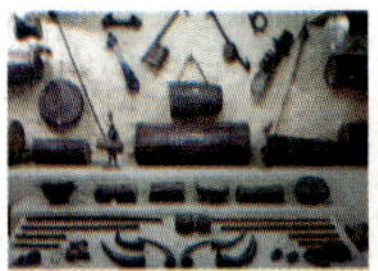

Jhumair (Jhumar)

It is one of the important folk music of the region which is performed in the harvest seasons and also at times of the festivals. The music is to the accompaniment of traditional instruments like *madal* (a form of hand drum) and *nagara* (drums played with stick). This folk tradition is also shared with adjoining regions in West Bengal (in Purulia and Bankura districts) besides with the bordering areas of Bihar. The *Jhumair* is further categorized as ***Janani Jhumar*** which is performed by the women, while the ***Mardani Jhumar*** is performed by the men who wear *ghungroo* (anklet bells), hold sword and shield and dance while holding their hands in a circle.

Domkach

It is another popular form of folk music which is performed on the occasions of weddings. Musical instruments like *dhak* (barrel shaped waist/neck drum played with sticks), *shehnai* and *nagara* are used in it.

Some folk songs are performed as per the time of the day. ***Pratkali*** is performed at the dawn, while ***Adhratiya*** is performed in the midnight.

Like in the state of Bihar, ***Phagua*** is another genre of folk song popular in Jharkhand which welcomes the month of *Phalgun* and sets the mood for the festival of Holi. Besides, there are folk music associated with different folk dances of the region.

West Bengal

The Bengali folk music has evolved through centuries long tradition of Bhakti and Sufism in the region. It is also influenced by; the classical music forms such as the dhrupad of Bishnupur *Gharana*, folk theatre like *Jatra*, folk dances like *Gombhira*, secular faith of saint poets like Lalon Fakir, philosophy of modern thinkers and musicians like Rabindranath Tagore. Besides, the inspiration of Bengal folk music encompasses the life and activity of the common people of the region.

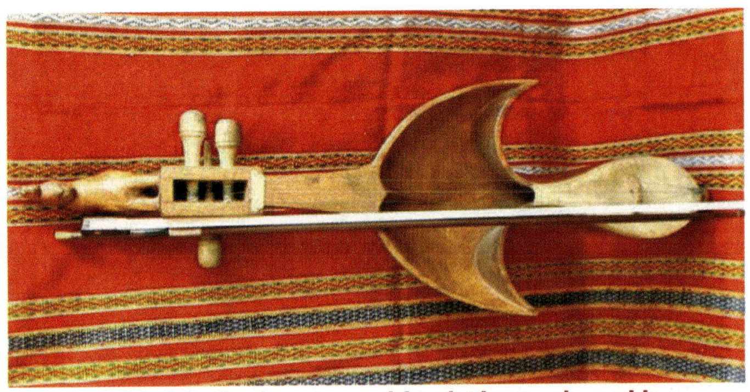

17.38: *Dhodro banam*, a string instrument used by the Santhal tribe in Jharkhand, West Bengal and Odisha — Wikimedia Commons

Baul

It is a folk music of West Bengal and adjoining regions with an age-old tradition. It is a kind of religious-spiritual music which harps on the love for divine and even transcends sectarian religious divide. Baul is also a kind of religious sect, following Vaishnava and Sufi traditions. As a musical tradition, it is centuries old and associated with mysticism. **Lalon Fakir**, a great philosopher and Sufi saint of late 18th century, is believed to have composed over 2000 Baul songs of which nearly 800 survive. His compositions are also referred to *Lalon Geeti* in the folk music traditions. These, and the Baul tradition, are said to have influenced Rabindra Sangeet, Nazrul Geta (song and philosophy of Nazrul Islam) and other thinkers.

Rabindra Sangeet

It refers to the musical tradition of **Rabindranath Tagore** and the repertoire of the music composed by him. The music and songs are particularly popular in West Bengal and adjoining regions. Over 2000 songs are said to have been composed by him that were influenced by Hindustani Classical, Carnatic, Baul, and other folk music of India. His songs and music explore numerous facets of human emotion.

Among other folk traditions based on the works of eminent musicians are; **Ramprasadi** which are **bhakti** songs in devotion to goddess Kali composed by Ramprasad Sen (early 18th century); **Nazrul Geeti**; based on the songs composed by poet and reformist Kazi Narul Islam (20th century) etc.

Shyama Sangeet

It is another devotional folk song in veneration of goddess Kali.

Patua or Poter Gan

It is folk music associated with *Pattachitra,* a form of folk theatre/mythological narrative of folk tales. Similarly, **Gombhira** is the song associated with the folk dance of Gombhira. **Jatra Pala** songs are associated with folk theatre of Jatra.

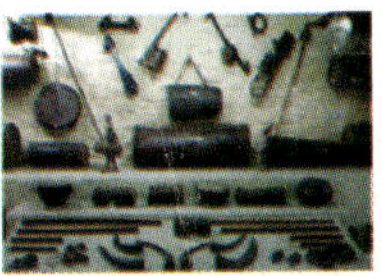

Bhatiali

It is the folk song of rivers sung by the boatmen and is popular in the Bengal delta region. The lyrics and subjects of these songs are often metaphorical, exploring human emotions and issues like the human body, the guru and the love of nature.

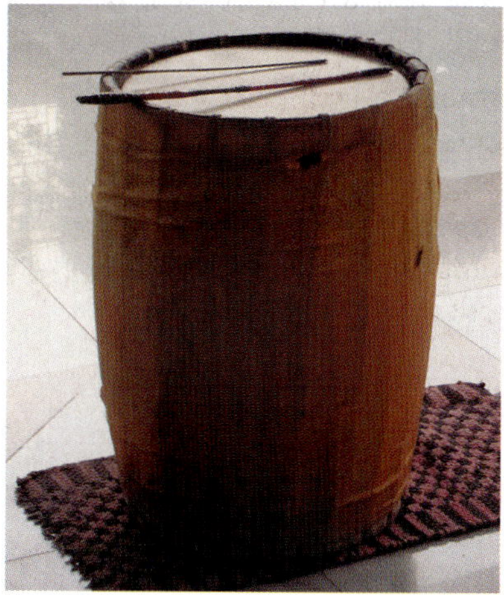

17.39: Dhak, a traditional stick drum of West Bengal — Wikimedia Commons

Bhawaiya

It is the folk song popular in Northern Bengal. It is considered the song of working class such as the buffalo herder (*mahishal*), the cart drivers (*gariyal*), elephant trainers (*mahouts*) etc. and explores subjects like loneliness and separation from their beloved/womenfolk.

Dhama/Dhamail

This is a folk song and dance and is performed by women during marriages and other auspicious occasion. It is popular in the Northeastern Bengal.

Dhenkir Gaan

It is another of the work-related folk songs of West Bengal, which refers to the genre of songs which are sung at the time of husking of paddy. It is also said to be similar to the songs of ceremony of marriage and thought to have a common point of origin.

Assam

The music of Assam is steeped in its age-old culture, the tradition of Bhakti ushered by Srimanta Sankaradeva and the culture of its numerous ethnic tribes. Amongst the most popular of the regional songs and music are the *Borgeets* and the *Bihu* songs. A uniqueness of Assamese folk songs is that their tunes are based on pentatonic scale (five notes per octave). The region also boasts of a variety of musical instruments some of which are only indigenous to the state. These include *pepa* (wind instrument) *toka/thorka* (bamboo slapstick for producing rhythmic clapping sound), *gogona* (jaw harp vibrating wind instrument), *xutuli/hutuli* (a bamboo/clay made instrument to produce whistle like sound), *bahi* (bamboo flute), *khram* (a long wind instrument), *madol*, *dhol* (drum) *bhortal* (cymbal like instrument), *bin* (wind instrument) etc.

Borgeets

It refers to the songs which were composed by Srimanta Sankaradeva in around 15th–16th centuries. These songs are set to specific *ragas* but may not have any *tala*. The prayer service in the monasteries (*satra*) was begun with these songs, hence these have devotional character. However, these songs are also sung out of the religious context and thus are truly a part of the folk tradition of Assam.

Amongst the **devotional songs** of the state are ***Dihanaam*** which is a type of prayer sung in praise of Sankardeva by the women. ***Bhatima*** (*Bhotima*) and ***Ghoxa*** are other folk songs in the devotional genre.

Bihu

It refers to the Bihu songs, Bihu dance, as well as the Bihu festival of Assam. Bihu is essentially a song of joyfulness, love and fertility. On the occasion of the Assamese new year, when the Bohag Bihu festival is celebrated, then these songs are sung. They are noteworthy for their music and literary content through which the blessings for the

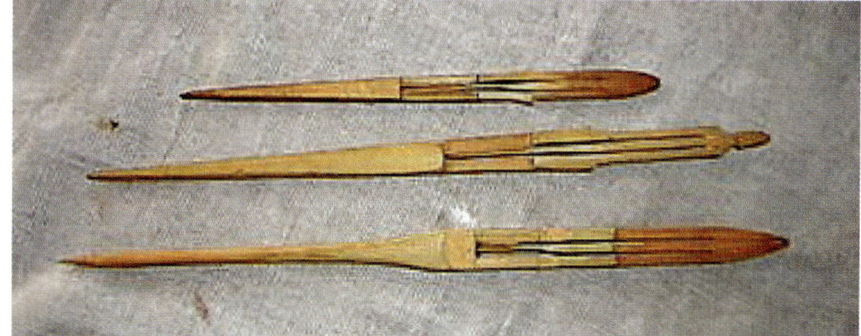

17.40: *Gogona*, a jaw-harp reed instrument of Assam — Wikimedia Commons

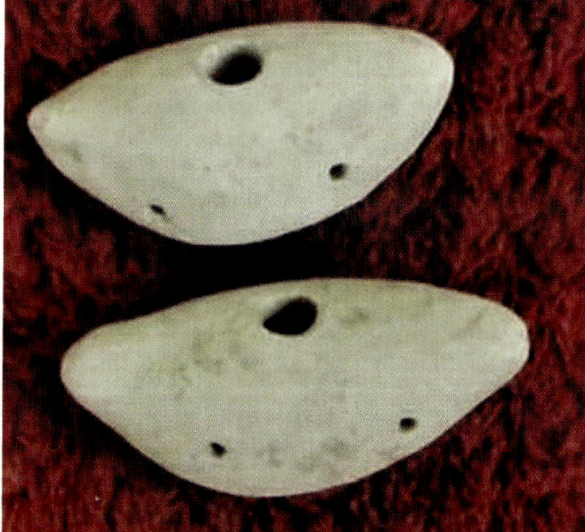

17.41: Xutuli, which produces bird like whistling sounds on playing by mouth — Wikimedia Commons

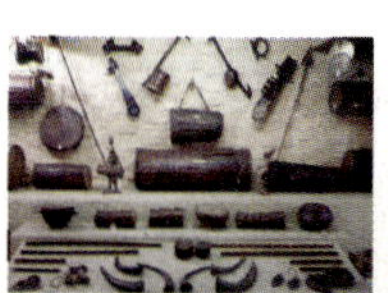

new year are expressed. Besides, marriageable young women and men may exchange their feeling of love. Thus, the song and dance also serves the purpose of courtship.

Among other folk songs of the state are the ***Ojapali*** (dance and song performance in group), ***Kamrupi*** (popular in Kamrup region) and ***Goalporiya Lokgeets*** (lyrical songs sung in Goalpara region in Goalparia language). Another folk song popular in parts of Assam (and in northern west Bengal) is ***Bhawaiya***, popular in the working class such as cattle herders, elephant trainers and cart drivers (see music of West Bengal). Besides the above, the folk songs of **Bodo, Karbi** and **Mising** tribes represent another genre of folk music of the state.

Manipur

The tradition of folk songs in Manipur is inspired by its Vaishnava religious culture as well as the lush green forests, mountains and plains. Its history and the culture of its tribes are also a determinant of its tradition of folk music.

Sankirtana

Sankirtana is a ritualistic singing, drumming and dancing of the Vaishnava people of Manipur. Through this art form, stories from the life of Sri Krishna are narrated. This folk tradition usually includes a group of singers and a few drummers and is usually performed in temple courtyards/halls or other such places. It is particularly notable for the fervour and energy. It is also popular in the neighbouring states of Assam and in Tripura in the Vaishnava community. It was recognised by **UNESCO** in 2013 as **'Intangible Cultural Heritage of Humanity'.**

Sankirtana: Ritual Singing, Drumming and Dancing of Manipur

Sankirtana is amongst a few folk dances/songs of India which are recognised by the UNESCO as an 'Intangible Cultural Heritage of Humanity'. While bringing out the significance of this art and recognising its enduring value, UNESCO has observed as below.

Sankirtana encompasses an array of arts performed to mark religious occasions and various stages in the life of the Vaishnava people of the Manipur plains. Sankirtana practices centre on the temple, where performers narrate the lives and deeds of Krishna through song and dance. In a typical performance, two drummers and about ten singer-dancers perform in a hall or domestic courtyard encircled by seated devotees. The dignity and flow of aesthetic and religious energy is unparalleled, moving audience members to tears and frequently to prostrate themselves before the performers. Sankirtana has two main social functions: it brings people together on festive occasions throughout the year, acting as a cohesive for within Manipur's Vaishnava community; and it establishes and reinforces relationships between the individual and the community through life-cycle ceremonies. It is thus regarded as the visible manifestation of God. The Sankirtana of Manipur is a vibrant practice promoting an organic relationship with people: the whole society is involved in its safeguarding, with the specific knowledge and skills traditionally transmitted from mentor to disciple. Sankirtana works in harmony with the natural world, whose presence is acknowledged through its many rituals.

Lai Haraoba songs

These are the genre of songs which are associated with the Manipuri festival of Lai Haraoba. The very meaning ofLai Haroba is, 'the festival of gods and goddesses', and is dedicated to Umang-Lai, the forest deity. Ougri Hagen, the song of creation, and Heijing Hirao, a ritualistic song, are sung on this occasion.

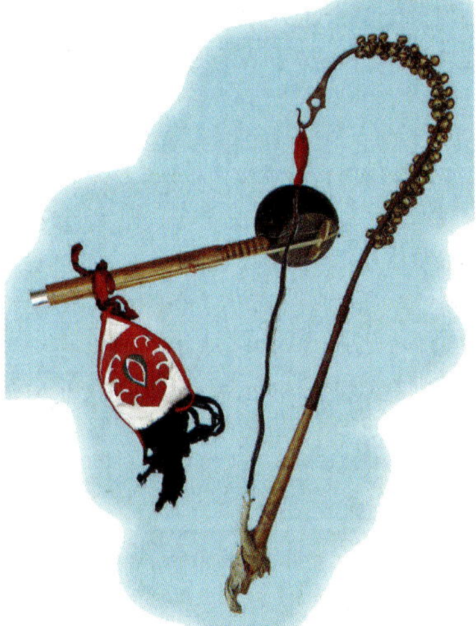

17.42: Pena, a folk musical instrument of Manipur, similar to a violin. An important musical accompaniment of the Lai Haraoba festival — Wikimedia Commons

Sana Lamok

It is a folk song which is sung traditionally at the time of the coronation ceremony of the *maaiba* (priest). In the past, it was also sung to welcome the king. It is sung to evoke the spirit of *Pakhangba*, the presiding deity.

Arunachal Pradesh

The music of the state is intricately linked to its rituals and ceremonies, its mythology and the folk history. A genre of its folk music pertains to its various dances which are a salient element of its culture. These dances may be ritualistic or celebratory and hence a wide variety of folk music has evolved. Among the most important of the folk music are; *Ja-Jin-Ja*, *Baryi*, and *Nyioga.*

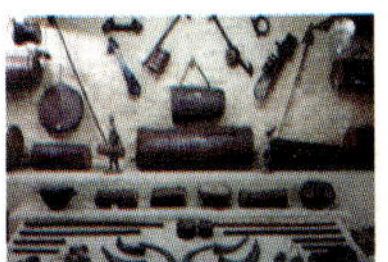

Ja-Jin-Ja

It is folk music which is sung in groups comprising both men and women. This can be on occasion of marriages, or other social functions, or as a part of feasts or general merriment.

Baryi

Baryi is sung during festivals and social/religious gatherings and narrates mythological stories and history of the people.

Nyioga

It is folk music sung during marriages, when the marriage ceremony has concluded and the bridal party has returned back. The bride is left at home and the joyous song includes subjects of advice to the bride for a happy married life.

Mizoram

The tribe of Mizos is known for the tradition of singing, and their folk songs are a salient heritage of the people. The repertoire of this tradition is so vast that they are said to have nearly a hundred different categories of folk songs. Their music uses traditional instruments like drum, gong and mouth organ, all made of bamboo and gourd.

Saikuti Zai

Also known as the songs of Saikuti, they are the genre of folk songs which are based on the poems/songs composed by Saikuti (a poetess). These songs are in praise of the brave warriors and hunters and inspire the young men to be so. **Lengzem zai** is another type which is in the category of love songs.

Chai hla

They are songs are performed to the accompaniment of dance during the *Chapchar Kut* festival. The dance is called Chai and the songs are known as Chai-hla. **Thiam hla** & **Dawi hla** are the category of folk songs which entail invocation and incantation. These are two verse forms and are chanted by the priests while performing ceremonies. **Bawh hla** chants are associated with successful return from a battle/raid after establishing superiority over the enemy. **Dar hla** are the genre of songs named after musical instruments. These songs are not sung in human voice, but solely meant for performance via musical instruments. Dar-hla literally means 'song for gong'. Besides, the above, several other categories of folk songs are popular in Mizoram.

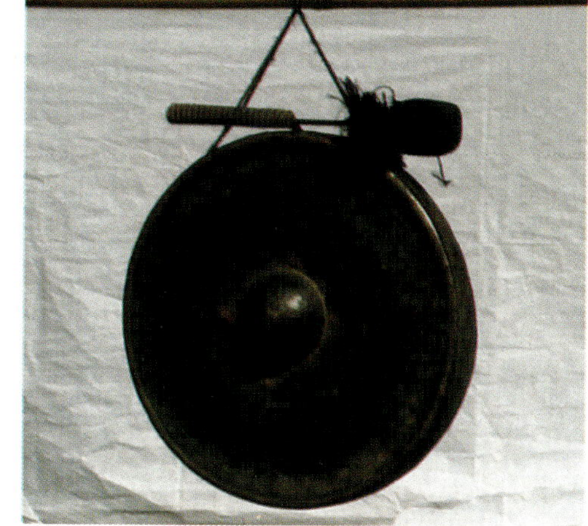

17.43: Darkhuang, a traditional musical drum made of brass — Wikimedia Commons

Sikkim

This state is home to various ethnic tribes including those of Lepchas, Bhutias and Nepalis. The culture of these tribes is also reflected in the folk culture and traditional music of the state. Besides, some influence of Western music is also seen. Dances are also an integral part of the communities with specific dances for different occasions. Hence the state also sees a tradition of folk music pertaining especially to these dances.

Tamang Selo

Tamang Selo is a musical genre which is popular among the Tamang people (Nepali speaking community of the state). The music conveys the feelings of love, sorrow, happiness. Its subjects also include day-to-day incidents and stories of folklore from the region. It is played to the accompaniment of music from Dhamphu (a *dafli*/tambourine like percussion instrument). The other instruments of accompaniment are *madal* (hand held Nepalese drum) and *tungna* (a plucked string instrument).

Gha To Kito

It is a traditional song and dance performance of the Bhutia tribe. It describes the natural beauty of the state such as that of the Kanchenjunga mountain, the rhodenderons, the caves and also the holy places.

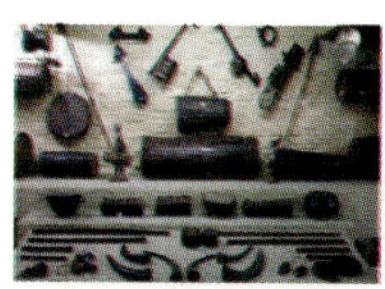

Meghalaya

Like other states of the Northeast, Meghalaya has a rich tradition of folk music which is influenced by the unique environment and the culture of the indigenous tribes. Literally meaning the abode of the clouds, the region sees very high rainfall and is covered with lush green forest in its hills and valleys. The folk music is an expression of the beauty of the nature and the life of the Khasi, Jaintia and Garo tribes of the state. Dances are an inseparable part of the culture of the people and the folk music also finds expression in the numerous dance forms as well as in the festivals of the region.

Khasi folk music

The traditional Khasi music is called ***phawar*** which is more of a chant. It is said to be composed impromptu as per the occasion. Besides, ballads are another genre of music which describes the deeds of legendary heroes and martyrs. Traditional musical instruments like *ksing shynrang*, *ksing kynthei* (Khasi drums considered as male and female), *tangmuri* (a double reed conical wind instrument), *shaw shaw* (cymbals), *nakra* (big drum) *ksing padiah* (small drum) and *besli* (flute) are the musical accompaniments.

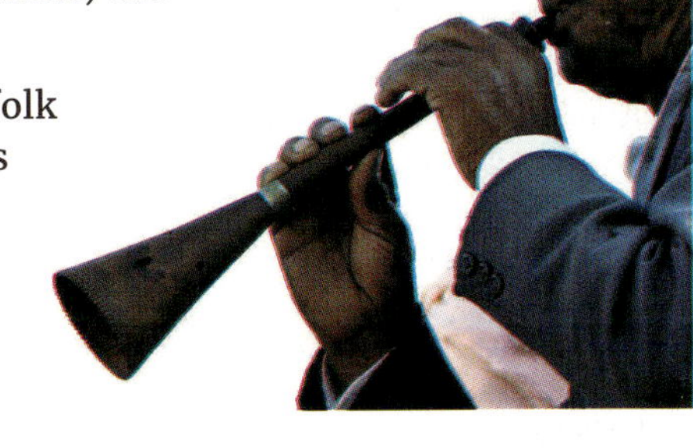

17.44: A tangmuri (double reed wind instrument) — Wikimedia Commons

The Khasi festivals are another occasion for the expression of its folk music. The five-day long **Nongkrem** dance festivals see continuous performance of the folk music. This festival is associated with good harvest. Unmarried women perform dances in the specially prepared fields, while men perform a dance of *Ka shid Mastieh* holding their swords and whisks in their hand. ***Ka Shad Shuk Mynsiem*** is another dance festival related to sowing period in which both men and women participate. Traditional musical instruments are played.

Garo folk music

The festival of the Garos include ***Wangala*** which is a harvest festival dedicated to Sun god for the fertility and also as a thanks giving for a good harvest. The three-day long festival is to accompaniment of folk music and dances like *Katta Dokka, Dani Dokka, Chambil Mesa* (Pomelo dance) and *Ajea*.

Jaintia folk music

Behdienkhlam is the most important festival of the Jaintia tribes which is to seek blessings for a good harvest as well as for good health. The three-day long festival sees young and old men dance to the tune of traditional music, while women are not a apart of these dances.

Besides the above, a variety of songs of the region are also related to the celebration of nature, the religious belief of the people, and rituals and agricultural activities.

Nagaland

The folk music of Nagaland is a reflection of the tribal culture of the state which is inhabited by nearly 14 tribes and sub-tribes. Music is an essential element of their tradition. The subjects range from songs of love and romance to historical songs of bravery and eulogy of ancestors, from songs of agricultural activities to songs of season. Some of the common folk instruments used in accompaniment are *libuh* (single string fiddle), *theku* (a string instrument), *asem* (drum), *jemji* (a blow horn), bamboo flute, *malen* (similar to flute), bamboo mouth organ, cup-violin etc. etc. Besides the traditional music, the Western music is also popular in the state.

Li

Li is a very popular folk music of Chokri tribe of Nagaland. It literally means 'song of the people' in the Chokri language. This category of songs is often sung to the accompaniment of the traditional instrument *libuh*. This is single stringed instrument (resembling the *ektara*). *Tati* is one such expression of *Li*.

Some other folk songs of the state include; **Heliamleu** which is a romantic song sung by the young and the old alike. **Hereileu** is a folk song which is a form of a narration by the elderly of the past battles or achievements. **Neuleu** is another song of the elderly, through which past achievements and legendary acts are conveyed and passed to the next generation. **Hekialeu** is a folk song which is sung by the old and young alike. When sung by the old, it is an expression of some interesting event of the past, particularly in their days of youth.

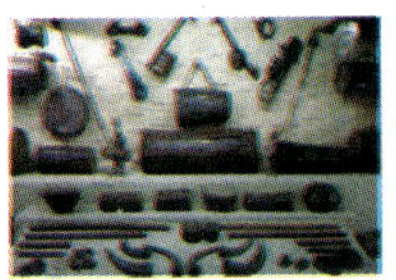

Besides, other forms of folk music pertains to different aspects of their lives and in particular to their festivals and dances.

Tripura

Like the other states of Northeast, Tripura has an abiding tradition of folk music which has deep interconnect with the people and the environment. The folk songs of Tripura are called Tipra Bharot. These are in the Tripuri language and are known as Rwchapmung. The beauty of nature, the festivals, rituals, emotions of love and activities of daily life are all its the subjects. They are sung to the accompaniment of instruments like *kham* (cylindrical drum like percussion instrument), *sumui* (flute), *sarinda* (bowed string instrument), *dangdu* (jaw harp), cymbals etc.

Jadukolija or Jaduni

They are among the popular songs of the region. These are songs based on love and romance.

Resekhagra

They are songs of demise sung to honour the sacrifice of the deceased, especially if it is for the country. Its music is sad and soulful.

Chamaritunmani

They fall in the genre of marriage songs. This kind of song is sung by the groom side towards the would-be in-law. *Hamjuk Rohomani* is another marriage song sung after the marriage, when the bride gets ready for departure for her husband's house.

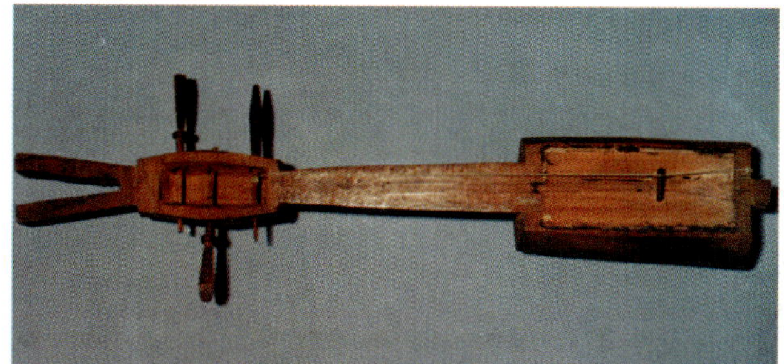

17.45: Chong Preng, a folk string instrument made of wood, wire and leather, similar to a rudimentary violin or fiddle, played with the help of a bow — Courtesy, Sangeet Natak Akademi

Mamita

It refers to the ceremony after the new harvest is kept in the granary and songs are sung in its celebration.

Among other common songs of the region are Waying Khilimani which is a lullaby, Hachwg Kamani, which are songs sung while travelling through the hills with load, and Garia Ruinani, which is a festival song pertaining to Garia Puja.

Gujarat

The tradition of folk songs in Gujarat has flourished for centuries and been preserved in communities such as *Barot* (geneaologists and traditional *vahi*-keepers), *Charan* (bards, genealogists and traders) and *Gadhvi* (bards, genealogists). The tradition of folk music includes the *sugam sangeet*, the devotional music, and narrative form of folk singing, besides music for the folk theatres.

Sugam Sangeet

It refers to the traditional folk music of the region practised for generations by the communities of *Barots, Charans* and *Gadhvis*. The music has melodious tune, is soulful, and has rich and meaningful verses. It is sung to the accompaniment of traditional instruments like *ektaro, ravanhattho*, (string instruments), *turi, bungal pava*, and *jantar*, (wind instruments) and *manjira and zanz* etc. (percussion instruments). The music of these communities is rendered in different poetic forms which include *doha, sortha*, and *chhand* (different form of verses).

Dayro and Lokvarta

They are narrative forms of folk music, through which religious and social messages are delivered. ***Marsiyas*** is another popular folk music, which is melancholic and similar to an elegy. Besides these, the common folk tradition includes ***lagna geets*** which are a genre of marriage related songs.

The devotional folk songs include ***bhajans***, which can be categorized as per the theme/lyrics into compositions such as *Prabhati, Katri, and Dhol* etc.

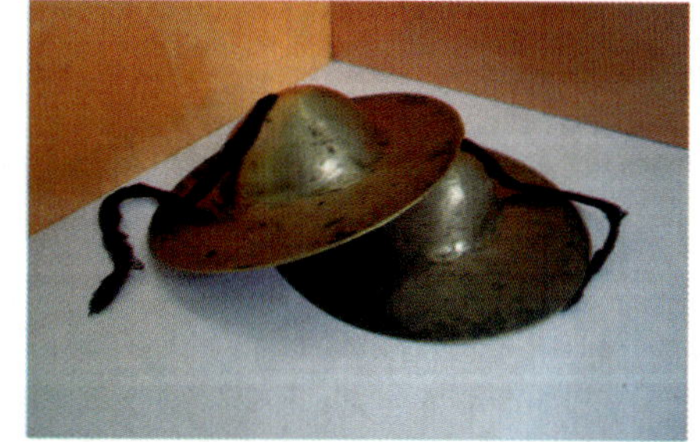

17.46: Manjira, a hand held cymbal which is used as a measure of rhythm — Wikimedia Commons

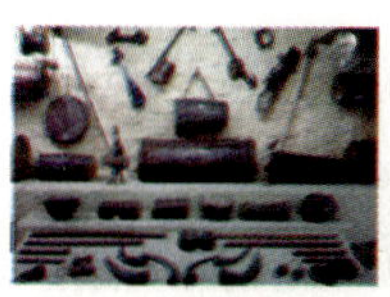

Another genre of folk music is that which is to the accompaniment of traditional dances like *Garba, Dandiya Raas, Padhar, Dangi and Tippani*. Besides, a class of folk music is also popular for folk theatre, such as *Bhavai* and *Akhyana*.

Maharashtra

The tradition of folk songs of Maharashtra, include songs sung in folk theatre and ballads, songs which are associated with working of farmers, songs associated with rituals and ceremonies, devotional songs, as well as semi-classical songs. These are truly reflective of the diverse culture and traditions of the state which has an old and rich history.

Lavani

It is the folk music of Maharashtra which is a combination of song and dance. The dance form associated with it is called *Tamasha.* It is performed on the beat of *dholaki,* a drum like instrument. *Lavani* is performed by female dancers and is a dance of entertainment. It is classified as *Nirguni Lavani* which is of the philosophical genre, while the other, *Sringari Lavani*, is a sensuous song and dance.

Powada

Powada is a kind of **ballad** describing a hero or a historical event, etc. The singer, who is the chief narrator of the story, is called *Shahirs*. Usually, a *duff* is played as accompaniment to keep the tempo. Earliest known *Powada* was *Afzal Khancha Vadh* (killing of Afzal Khan) written by Agnidas (in 1659).

Gondhal

It is a folk art which involves narration of mythological stories and folk legends as a song and dramatic performance. It is a part of the folk ritual for veneration of deities like Renuka and Bhavani and performed on auspicious occasions like marriages, thread ceremonies, religious festivals etc. The folk-art is practiced by members of the Gondhali community. The troupe usually comprises four to five members, with there being a main singer-narrator called *Naik*.

Koli Geet

It is amongst the more recognised folk songs of Maharashtra. It is popular in western Maharashtra and has a rich tradition of nearly three centuries.

Natya Sangeet

Natya Sangeet is another popular music from Maharashtra which is considered a semi-classical form of music. This tradition is said to be nearly 200 years old.

Bhaleri

It is a folk-song sung by the farmers working in the field. Besides these, the other folk songs include ***Owi***, which is sung by village women usually at dawn; ***Palane*** which is a lullaby, ***Artya*** is a song to protect from the wrath of diseases like small pox, plague etc. The genre of devotional folk songs includes ***bhajan, kirtans*** and ***abhangas.***

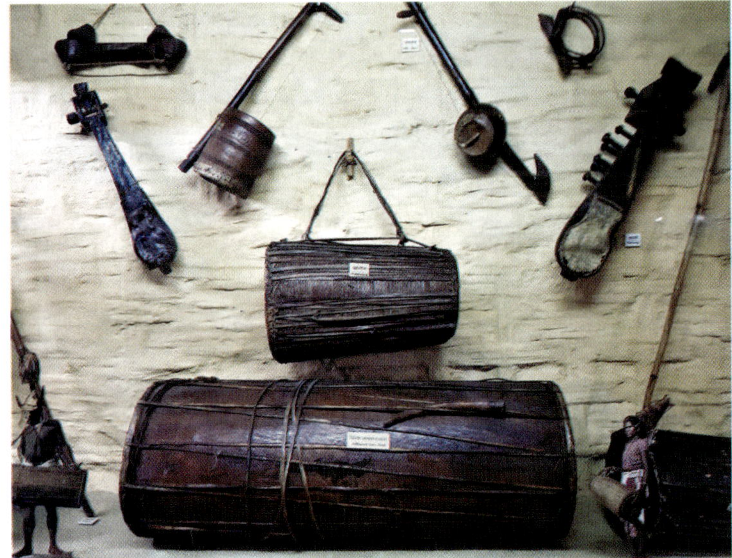

17.47: Dhol, pakhawaj, sarangi, ektara and other folk and tribal instruments of Maharashtra; Nagpur Central Museum — photograph by Madhukar K Bhagat

Goa

Goa has a unique folk tradition which is a fusion of two distinct cultures. Being in Portuguese occupation for nearly 450 years, the region has a profound influence of Portuguese culture and this is reflected in its folk arts. Thus, Goa has a tradition of Konkani and Portuguese folk songs, as well as a blend of these.

Among the more pristine of the Konkani folk songs is the ***Fugdi***, which is performed along with folk dance by women in religious festivals like Ganesh Chaturthi. It is also performed towards the end of the folk dance of ***Dhalo*** (ritual dance).

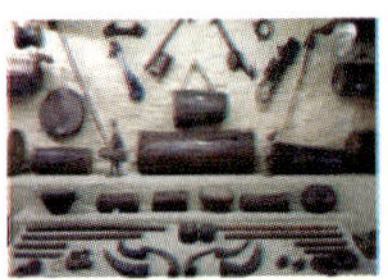

Dekkni

It is a typical Goan dance song which has Konkani lyrics and Hindu themes, but the music is a mix of Konkani and Western. It is sung to the accompaniment of *shehnai*, *tabla* and cymbals, and at times supplemented with violin.

Dulpod

Dulpod is another category of folk music which has a mix of Konkani and Western music, as well as a mix of lyrics, with words borrowed from Portuguese. This is also a Goan dance song. It is fast paced and its subjects include matters from daily lives of the common people.

Mando

Mando is amongst the most popular of Goan folk songs. Its music has elements of both Indian and Western (Portuguese) culture with a marked influence of the latter. The lyrics also incorporate words from both Konkani and Portuguese languages. Mando is a poetry as well as dance. Its music is melodious, full of passion and imbued with sweetness and sadness. Its theme is often romantic love and at times tragedy. Besides, issues like social justice and even the political resistance during the Portuguese rule, have also been its subjects.

Besides the above, a variety of other forms of Konkani music, such as the Portuguese Fado and Western classical art music, are also popular in the Goan folk culture.

17.48: *Ghumot*, a traditional membranophone folk instrument of Goa. Monitor lizard skin is mounted on an earthen pot. — Wikimedia Commons

Madhya Pradesh

The large state in the hinterland of the country is broadly divided into four geographical regions of Nimar, Malwa, Bundelkhand and Baghelkhand, each with a distinct repertoire of its folk music and songs. Festivals, devotion, arrival of spring and the rainy season, are often their subjects. Ballads and heroic deeds are also inspiration of some songs. Besides, a variety of folk songs also exist in the rich tribal culture of the state.

Alha

It is a form of ballad song popular in **Bundelkhand** region of Madhya Pradesh and also in the adjoining state of Uttar Pradesh. It narrates the heroic deeds and valour of Alha and Udal, the two warrior brothers in the medieval period, both of whom fought against Prithviraj Chauhan (in 1182). It is imbued with tales of chivalry, morality and other values.

Among other popular folk songs of this region are ***Faag (phaag)*** and ***Jaas***. *Faag* is a song associated with the festival of Holi, while the latter is associated with the worship of Devi (goddess). The rains are an inspiration for the ***Savani***, a folk song welcoming *sawan* (rainy season) which is sung by the women. ***Baraita*** is a narrative folk song of this region, wherein the stories and characters of Mahabharata or other historical stories are conveyed.

Nimar region is known for folk songs such as ***Nirguniya, Kalgi, Turra, Sant Singaji*** etc. The ***Nirguniya*** refers to the genre of songs incorporating the verses of *nirguni* medieval saint poets like Kabir, Raidas, and Dadudayal etc. ***Kalgi, Turra*** draw inspiration from Shaivism and Shaktism whose virtues they eulogies. The tradition comprises the genre of songs of Kalgi and that of Turra. It is a competitive form of folk singing where each style competes with the other. The *bhajans* of **Sant Singhaji** is another folk art popular in the Nimar region. ***Garba*** is a folk song of the region sung by the women on the occasion of *navaratra*, and venerates the Mother Goddess.

Birha, Bidesiya, Basdeva and ***Faag*** are some of the folk songs of **Baghelkhand** region. ***Birha*** is a traditional folksong which is sung while working in the fields and forests and tending to cattle. It has a predominance of *Shringaar* rasa and the subject is often separation from the beloved. It is sung as a question and response format between two groups (usually men and women folk). ***Bidesiya*** is a folk song popular in the entire Baghelkhand region and is sung typically during night in groups. ***Baasdeva*** is a singing community of this region which is known for songs pertaining to Shravan Kumar. ***Faag*** or the songs of Holi of this region, are different from that of others. These are sung on the beats of *nagara* and *dholak* (drums) by men.

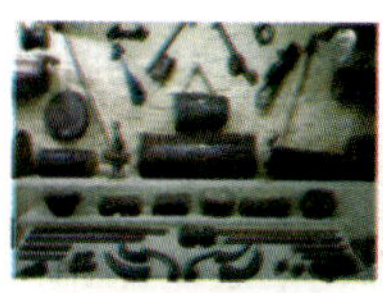

Malva

Malva is known for songs such as ***Ganesh*** which welcomes the saviour god (lord Ganesh) and is usually sung by women. ***Rasiya*** is another song popular in Malva as well as Nimar region, which is sung by women on the occasion of Holi. ***Bharthari*** is sung by the followers of *Nathpanth*a. It is usually sung in the morning hours to the accompaniment of a traditional instrument called Chinkara. ***Barsati*** is a folk song associated with the arrival of rains.

Besides, there are a variety of tribal folk songs associated with different tribes of the state. In Bastar, *Relo* is a folk song of the Muria and Singa (Sing Maria) tribes.

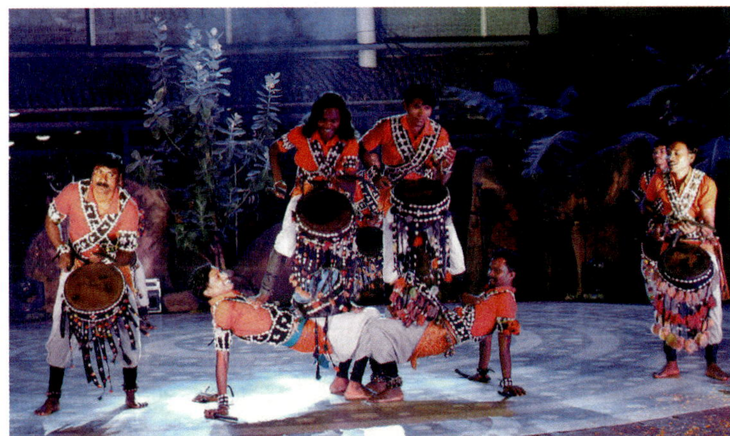

17.49: A musical performance with *gudum baja*, a membranophone percussion instrument popular with the tribals of Madhya Pradesh — Courtesy, Madhya Pradesh Tourism Board

Chhattisgarh

This is a state with a rich folk tradition which is well integrated in its tribal culture and the way of life of the people living in the forests, hills and plains. With a third of the state's population being of various tribes such as Gond, Kamar, Birhi, Kanver, Korva, Baiga, Halba, Pando, Uranv, Binjhwar etc., its folk music has a distinct flavour of this very tribal culture which is in itself thousands of years old. Broadly, the state's folk music can be categorized into those associated with; seasons of the year, festivals and rituals, significant events in the life of common people, children-oriented songs, general entertainment, dance accompaniment music and region-specific folk songs etc. Some of the traditional musical instruments of the state include; *gudum* (a membranophone percussion instrument) *daphra* (a percussion drum), *mohri* (bowed string instrument), *jhaanjh* (a sort of cymbal) and a *manjeera* (small, handheld cymbals), *sarangi*, *dhaf*, *dhafli* etc.

Pandavani

It is a form of folk music and folk theatre which involves narration of tales of Mahabharata. Bhima is said to be the hero in these narrations. It is also popular in the adjoining regions of Odisha, Madhya Pradesh, and Andhra Pradesh. Traditional musical instruments like *tambura* and *ektara* are used for accompaniment of the songs.

Among the **songs of season** are; ***Sawanahi***, which is the song of the month of *Sawan* and welcomes the rains, and ***Faag*** which is the song of celebration of the springs.

Songs of festivals include ***Sua*** songs, which are sung on the occasion of Deepawali/post Deepawali. This is primarily associated with agricultural harvest and is performed by women to the accompaniment of *Sua* dance, particularly in the districts of Dantewada and Bilaspur.

The songs associated with **life events** include; ***Sohar*** (songs on child birth), ***Bihav*** (songs for various days of long marriage festivities), ***Vivah*** (songs for ritual of marriage), ***Mrityu geet*** (song of demise) etc.

Goura

They are songs sung in the praise of various deities. Among other songs of the region are *Khuduwa, Pathoni, Chera-Chera, Dohe Bhojali, Dhankul, Loriya, Fugudi, Dewar, Danda etc.*

Odisha

Odisha has a very ancient tradition of music with king Kharavela (2nd century BCE) being a patron of art and music) Bharata's *Natyashastra* recognises *Odra Magadhi* (music of this region) as one of the four important forms of music. The current tradition of music in Odisha is traceable to the *Gita-Govinda* of Jayadeva (12th century). It is a tradition which is still alive in the Puri and other temples of Odisha which are at the heart of its culture. Thus, the **folk music** of Odisha is derived from its own **classical music** which is said to be different from the Hindustani classical and Carnatic music. Besides, it is also home to a variety of music traditions which includes **semi classical music**, **light music** and **tribal music**. Together, they comprise the five broad categories of music of Odisha.

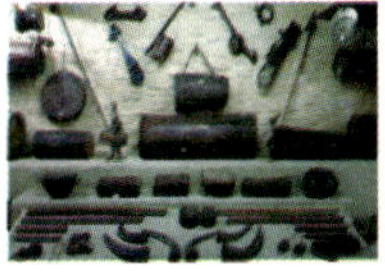

Some of the common forms of folk music are *Dalkhai, Jaiphula Rasarkeli* and *Mailajada*. These are musical accompaniments to dance forms which are performed by unmarried women/spinsters, while wearing a special costume.

Daskathia

Daskathia is a form of ballad singing. It is sung to the accompaniment of a unique musical instrument called *Kathi* or *Ram Tali*, which are wooden clappers and which lend name to the performance. The music is in the form of worship and offering made on behalf of the *das* (devotee).

Besides the above, *Ghumura-geet, Ghoda-naach, Danda-naach, Balipuja-geeta, Kendra-geet* are some other folk music forms.

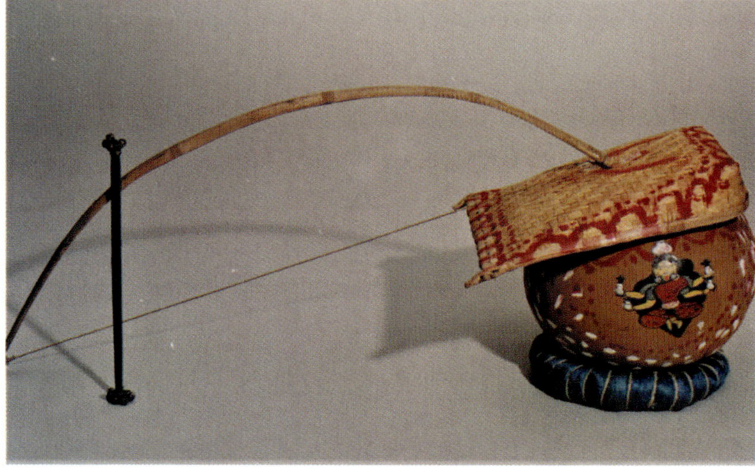

17.50: Dhana Koila, a unique folk instrument of Ganjam district of Odisha; a composite instrument made of wood, metal and earthenware comprising four parts, an earthen pot painted with folk motifs, a winnowing tray, a bow, and a wooden stick. The earthen pot acts as a resonator — Courtesy, Sangeet Natak Akademi

The folk instrument of the region include; *dhole* (a form of drum), *tamak* (single membrane drum), *mandal* (a drum shaped percussion instrument), *tasha* (drum instruments played with thin bamboo sticks), *muhuri* (a double reed wind instrument) amongst others.

Andhra Pradesh & Telangana

The states of Andhra Pradesh and the later formed state of Telangana are culturally rich. Their folk music comprises songs of different varieties which pertain to different aspects of an individual's life and social life. These include songs pertaining to harvest, social and religious rituals, working class songs, those pertaining to daily chores of women, songs on occasion of marriage, ballads devotional songs etc. Some of the common musical instruments used in the folk music are s*arada* (folk *veena*), *dappu* (flat faced drum), *dollu* (double headed drum) *damru*, *titti* (double reed wind instrument), *kombu* (a horn shaped long wind instrument), *thalam* (a type of cymbals), *ghungroo* (anklet bells) etc.

Burrakatha

Also referred as ***Jangamkatha***, it is a form of storytelling/ballad, which is popular in rural Andhra Pradesh. The troupe may comprise one lead singer along with one or two accompanying musicians. The ballad singers may wear make-up and costumes like stage actors and thus making it a dramatic form of ballad. A *tambura* (a string instrument with a hollow shell) is also played by the main narrator while reciting the story. The subjects are mythological, and at times contemporary social issues are also taken.

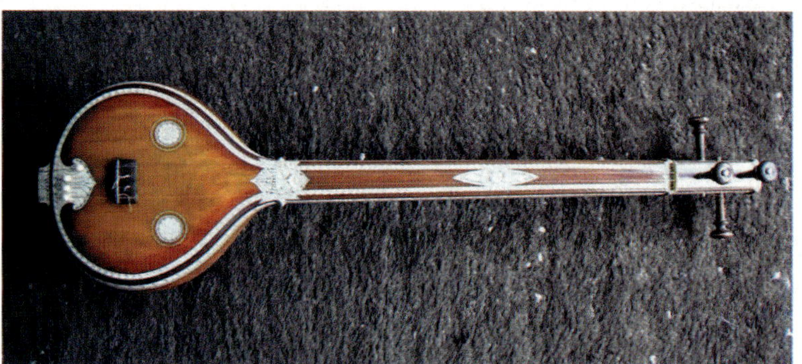

17.51: Carnatic Tambura — Wikimedia Commons

Among the **devotional** forms of folk music is *Oggu Katha* which is a narrative form of folk singing. Through the folk songs, the stories of gods and goddesses such as Mallana, Beerappa and Yellamma are described. *Oggu* are the traditional priests of the community who travel from place to place describing and singing in praise of the gods.

Harikatha

It is also a devotional folk music which involves, narration, song and music describing stories from an epic or the about the life of a saint. The narrators are referred to as *Haridasa*.

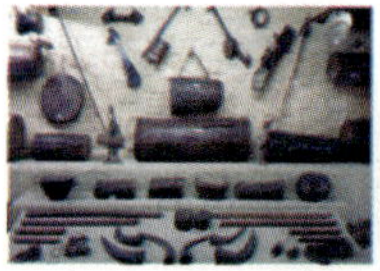

Sarada Kala

Sarada Kala another folk song of the devotional genre where the performers use a folk veena called *sarada. Tatvalu* is also in the category of devotional songs which are philosophical in lyrical content and dedicated to gods like Lord Shiva.

Sramika songs (Sramika Geyamulu)

They are the folk songs which pertain to the workers. These may be differentiated into men and women songs as well as those performed by different castes and communities.

Suvvi Paatalu

They are usually sung by the women folk in groups. The songs are in the form of questions and answers where one group responds to the other in verses.

Madiga Dappu

It is a folk form which is performed by an artisan group/community called *Madiga. Dappu* is a flat-faced drum which is played by them. This form of folk music is performed on numerous occasions. Besides the above, there are other categories of songs such as the love songs, children's songs, songs of the tribals.

Tamil Nadu

The folk tradition of Tamil Nadu is steeped deep in its history and dates to the Sangam age. The ancient texts like *Tolkappiyam, Ettuttokai* and *Sillappatikaram* (a bardic poetry titled the story of anklet) carry references to its music and dance. The tradition of Carnatic music and the trinity of Carnatic music, all have influenced its folk musical tradition. The repertoire of folk music of Tamil Nadu comprises devotional songs, occupational songs, those sung by women, songs of folk entertainment, besides those associated with its folk dances etc.

Villu Pattu

Also known as the 'bow song' it is a popular form of folk music of this region. It derives its name from the musical instrument which is bow shaped. The subjects of the song are usually theological which bring out the values of good over evil. The lead singer is also the main narrator/performer in this tradition.

Urumi Melam

It is a form of music associated with the playing of drum *urumi* (an hour glass shaped waist drum). The instrument is played with beating of sticks and the music is fast paced and repetitive. It was traditionally played to beckon the spirits, or to go in a trance, or as a devotional music during religious festivals and rites (eg. *Thaipusam*). As a form of folk music, it is often played to the accompaniment of another instrument *nadaswaram* (a double reed wind instrument) and *pambai* (traditional drum). It is also popular amongst Tamil communities outside India and particularly in Malaysia and Singapore.

Ammanaivari

They are songs which are sung in praise of the Chola monarch. These were the set of songs sung by women while playing the game of ball *Ammanai* (a wooden ball) and hence the name.

Kulavai Pathi (Kulavai song)

Kulavai Pathi is a form of occupational song which is sung before undertaking agricultural activities in the field. The song beckons the blessings of Lord Ganesh and other deities and is usually sung by the women. *Themmangu* and *Naatupura Paadalgal* are some other folk songs associated with the farming and harvest and related activities.

Nayandi Melam

It is a folk form of music which refers to a musical troupe of the villages. They would sing devotional songs, particularly before temples and festivals. However, they would also sing different categories of songs.

Lavani Pattu

Lavani Pattu is a recreational folk form. It is in the form of debate of two persons in a musical verse with each representing one side of the story of *Kamadahanam.*

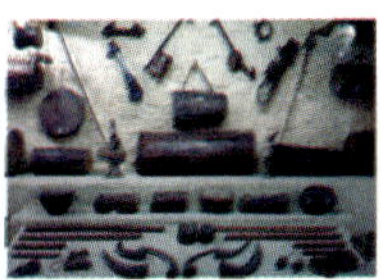

Women related songs include *Valai kappu* (songs pertaining to bangle-wearing ceremony), and *poochoottal* (songs pertaining to flower-decking ceremony) and other songs pertaining to period of pregnancy etc. Besides the above, a wide variety of folk music pertains to different **folk dances** such as *Karagattam*, *Poikkal Kudiraiaattam* (dummy horse dance), *Kummi Pattu* and folk theatre such as *Therukutthu* and puppet shows such as *Bommalattam*.

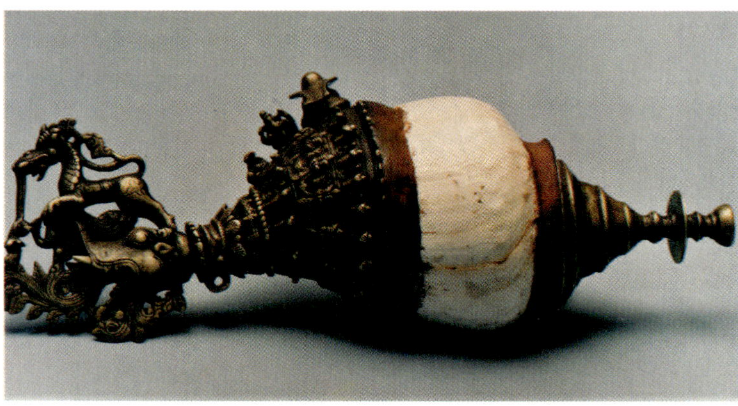

17.52: Devalai Sanghu; a conch shell wind instrument with funnel shaped mouthpiece of brass, used on religious/ ritualistic occasions in temples of Tamil Nadu, as a part of an ensemble of *panchavadya* (five instruments) — Courtesy, Sangeet Natak Akademi

Karnataka

Karnataka's musical tradition is considered unique. The Carnatic music has flourished in the state where legends like Purandara Dasa lived and systematized this musical genre. The dynasties of Vijayanagara, and later the Wodeyars, have been generous patrons of music and art. The northern regions of the state under the influence of Deccan Sultanate have seen the Hindustani Classical form flourishing. The Bhakti tradition of Nayanars, the Lingayat movement ushered by Basavanna and later the Dasa movement, were rooted in its musical tradition. This tradition was the vehicle of dissemination of the religious and philosophical messages to the masses. These have deeply influenced its folk music tradition which has been an integral part of its culture. The folk music embraces subjects ranging from devotion and philosophy to social occasions and daily lives. Besides, they are essential part of the numerous folk dances which are salient part of its folk culture.

Janapada Geethe

Janapada Geethe is the major folk musical tradition of the region. They are said to be the expression of joys and sorrows of the common folk. It essentially refers to a wide range of folk songs which touch different aspects of the lives of people. This can be of several categories which include;

Small – minor songs which are generally the occupational songs associated with agricultural activities, harvesting, marriages, festivals, daily chores or other songs for general entertainment.

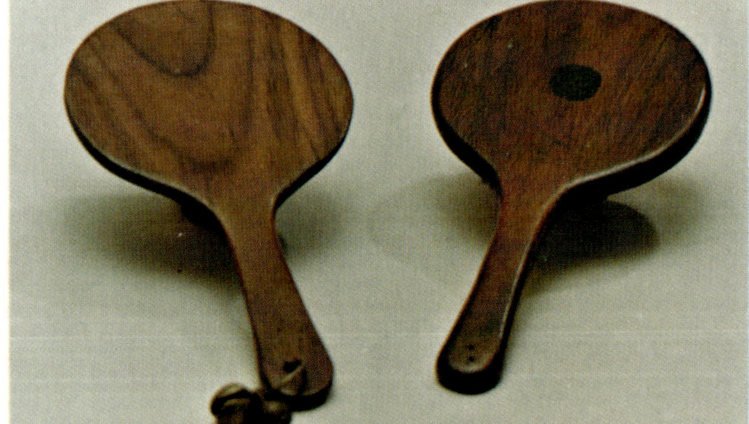

17.53: A chittika, a pair of wooden clappers (ideophones) traditionally used by devotional singers and mendicants of Karnataka — Courtesy, Sangeet Natak Akademi

Ballads are another genre of Janapad Geethe which incorporates tales of valour, narration of life of folk heroes, songs pertaining to deities and mythological figures etc. This can be further be divided into many sub categories.

Religious and philosophical songs such as those popularised by the *Dasa-Sahitya* are the next category. **Lullabies** and songs pertaining to children are another category of Janapada Geethe.

Bhavageete

It literally means 'emotion poetry' and **is** also considered a significant genre of folk songs. It is considered a mix of poetry and popular music of the region. It incorporates songs of diverse nature such as philosophy, nature and love.

Karadi Majalu

It is one of the folk music forms which is considered unique to the state. The musical performance incorporates a variety of instruments like *tala* (clash cymbals), *dollu* (double headed drum), *shehnai, surya-vadya, chandra-vadya* etc. The music is performed on festivals and auspicious occasions.

A large section of folk music of the region pertains to different forms of dances and folk theatre. These include the ritual dances *Kunitha*, folk theatre of *Yakshagana* and others.

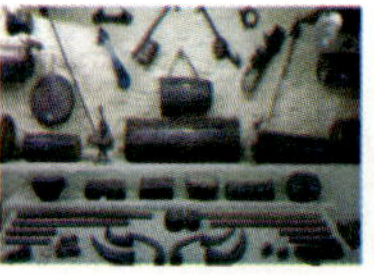

Kerala

The musical tradition of the state is rich, ancient and also an integral part of the ancient poetry-driven literature of Kerala. The tradition of music can be broadly divided into the *Margi* and *Desi* styles. While the *Margi* follows the classical traditions based on rules, the *Desi* traditions evolved out of the regional variations, with a lesser emphasis on the rules. This can truly be said to be the music evolving and permeating in the daily lives of the people. The music of Kerala is also unique for the deep influence of Carnatic music as well some influence of the Hindustani classical style (particularly in the regions in northern Kerala). The genre of devotional music, music related to festivals and rituals, music for different vocations, as well as that for the numerous and rich tradition of folk dances, all can be seen to exist and flourish. Some of the traditional musical instruments of the region include; *chenda* (cylindrical drum), *idakka* (hour glass shaped drum), *maddalam/madhalam* (heavy waist drum), *thimila* (hour glass shaped drum), *kombu* (long curved horn shaped wind instrument), *kuzhal* (double reed wind instrument) *elathalam/ilathalam* (small bronze cymbals), *kuzhithalam* (small metallic cymblas), *chengila* (hand held metallic gong), *nanthuni* (stringed instrument) etc.

Sopana Sangeetham

The classical tradition of Kerala is also called the *Sopana Sangeetham*. The music is of temple origin and developed as invocatory singing. The very term *sopana* implies, 'holy steps', and thus this music was sung from the steps of the shrine to its sanctum. The music is played with simple notes to the accompaniment of *idakka, chengila* etc.

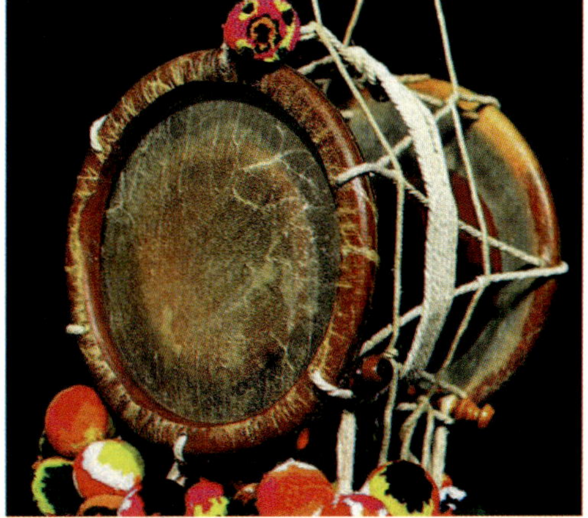

17.54: ***Idakka*, hour glass shaped drum — Wikimedia Commons**

The songs of **folk genre** (*paattu* in Malayalam) can be categorized into several types as per the region, community, occupational activity etc. Thus *Maapilla Paattu*, *Vanchi Paattu* etc. are regional folk songs, while *Bhadrakali Paattu, Ayyappan Paattu* are of the ritualistic genre. Similarly, there are separate categories of songs related to daily activities, pertaining to mythology, dances etc.

The **regional folk songs** include the **Mappila Paattu** which is the folk song of Malabar region (northern Kerala) which has a large Muslim population and reflects a fusion of different cultures. It has simple lyrics and its own traditional style which has influence of Hindustani music, with the lyrics having some traces of Arabic words. ***Vanchi Paattu*** is popular in central Travancore. The term *vanchi* means boat, and the songs represent the gentle rhythm of a rowing boat. ***Vadakkan Paattu*** is popular in Malabar region and is a genre of ballads. ***Thekkanpaattu*** is the folk song of erstwhile Travancore region (southern Kerala). It is sung to accompaniment of *villu* which is a bow shaped musical instrument and is also called ***Villu Paattu***.

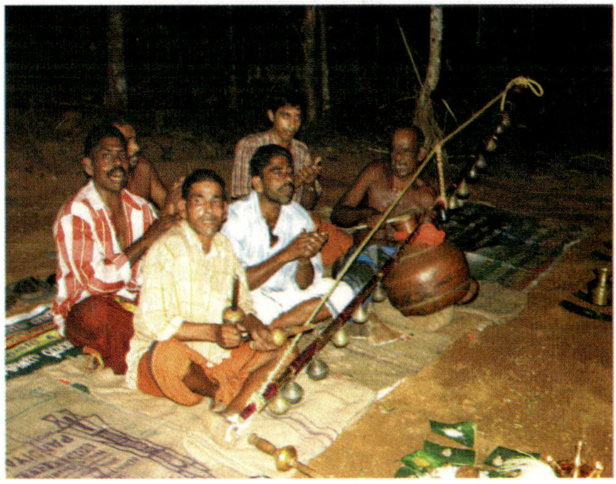

17.55: A performance on Villu Paatu by Kerala folk artists. A composite idiophone, the musical instrument comprises a long bow with bronze bells hung, a terracotta pot and stick with it. — Wikimedia Commons

Some of the **ritualistic folk songs** include the ***Bhadrakali Paattu*** (rituals before goddess Bhadrakali), ***Ayyappan Paattu*** (rituals before lord Ayyapa) and ***Kalamezhuthu Paattu*** (rituals before goddess Bhagvathi). Songs related to **work and occupation** are ***Vithukila Paattu*** (songs related to agriculture), ***Vandi Paattu*** (songs by minstrels and folk entertainers), ***Vanchi Paattu*** (boat song) etc. Further, there are mythological songs in art forms such as ***Thiruvathirakali*** (song and dance on the festival of *Thiruvathira*), etc., while songs of entertainment are called ***Vinodha Paattu.***

Besides, a genre of music also pertains to **dances** such as *Kathakali, Mohiniyattam* (considered classical dances) and other dances of folk genre such as *Koodiyattam, Theyyam, Thiruvathirakali, Chakyar Ottamthullal, Kolkalli, Krishnattam, Kummi etc.*

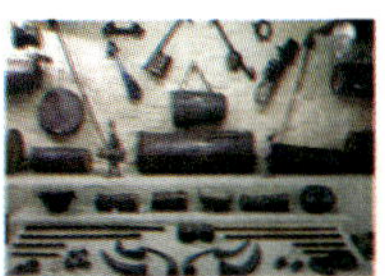

FILM MUSIC IN INDIA

Music is all about transporting people, speaking a language which languages fail to express.

— A. R. Rehman

Introduction

Film music is one of the most popular forms of music in India. As per estimates, it accounts for nearly 80% of sales revenue amongst all musical formats in the country. Churned out by the Bollywood (Hindi film industry), South Indian films and other regional film industries, this form of music has cut across the barriers of region and language and garnered immense popularity not only within the country but even a considerable international following. Thus, it would not be an exaggeration to deem it as the **most popular and visible** form of musical expression of the country. The film music can be said to be generic aggregation of music and songs produced by the Mumbai based film industry (the largest of all) besides those in West Bengal (Tollywood), Tamil Nadu, Kerala (Mollywood), Karnataka, Andhra Pradesh and some other states. Each has its own characteristics. While Hindi and Urdu are the languages in which the bulk of songs have been produced in Bollywood, the size of Bengali, Tamil, Telugu, Kannada, Punjabi, Marathi and even Bhojpuri film music is substantial. Besides, Odia, Gujarati, and languages of Northeastern states also have a reasonable presence in this industry.

A Brief History

The film music had its birth with the very first talkie film of India, ***Alam Ara (1931)***. The movie incorporated seven songs. The next movie *Shireen Farhad (1931)* was an out and out musical which was structured like an opera with nearly 42 song sequences. *Indra Sabha (1932)* which soon followed, had an incredible 69 song sequences (as per some accounts 71 songs sequences). Thus started the genre of Indian movies where songs were a crucial part of the movie and the template of as many as five to eight songs per movie was adopted as an unofficial norm for the next several decades. Integrated with dances, and with characters depicted as singing these songs (through lip-sync) rather than they being played in the background (like in some western movies), the songs were a complete musical experience which Indian cinema imparted. This made film songs an indispensable element of the movie experience where success of movies often hinged on the quality of songs and music. However, the popularity of songs was independent of the box office success of the movies. The centrality of songs to the films was all the more in the early years where the concept of playback singing had not arrived. Accordingly, many of the movie stars of the early years were accomplished singers like **Kundan Lal Saigal, Noor Jahan, Begum Akhtar, Suraiya, Ashok Kumar** and others.

The Popular Modes of Transmission

The films in themselves were not the only vehicles of transmission of its music. In the initial years, it was radio and the vinyl records which took this music to the masses. Magnetic tapes and television followed suit in the 70s and 80s. The 90s saw the music videos and CDs emerge as the platform for musical expression. In the new millennium, with new technology, the mode of capturing music again changed. Digital technology, internet, live streaming, FM radio and music-apps were the latest means through which music including the film music reached the people. But regardless of the technology and the means of its dissemination, film music has undoubtedly retained its popular appeal across all technology formats in nearly a century since its conception.

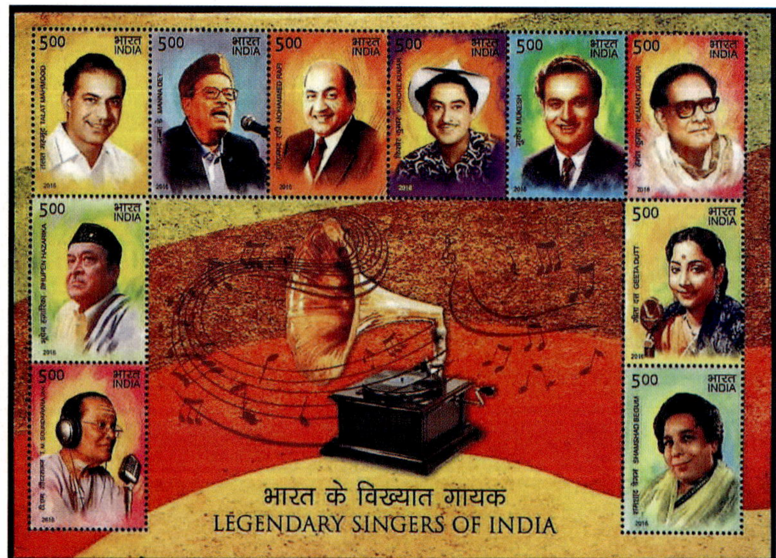

17.56: Legendary singers of India — Courtesy, Department of Post

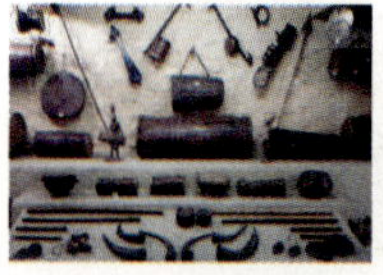

Indian Movies and Playback Singing

With the arrival of the technology of lip-syncing there emerged the concept of playback singing. Now the scene and the song need not be recorded together, rather it could be recorded in the comfort and controlled environment of the studio and be incorporated later in the film. This enabled the dissociation of the art of acting and singing, imparted a greater degree of freedom to the artists, thus bringing a quantum leap in the quality of production of music and songs. Hence emerged a highly specialized art of playback singing.

But the trade of production of film songs does not merely comprise the playback singers; rather it has brought highly skilled professionals of music composers/music directors, song writers/poets and instrumentalists, on the platform of musical production. The genre of music would be determined by the demand of the scene and the script. Invariably, choreographers and dancers would also be integrated in sync with the song. The vision of the director and the scale of production as determined by the producer all would come into play. Thus, playback singing needed the knitting together of multiple art forms and spawned several generations of skilled artists.

Playback singers in Bollywood

Playback singers have indeed been the backbone of this art. The 30s and early 40s saw the likes of **Kundan Lal Saigal, Suraiya, Begum Akhtar, Pankaj Mullick, Ashok Kumar, Devika Rani, Noor Jahan, and Shamsad Begum**, emerge as popular playback singers. While these were the early years of the industry, yet many greats of singing emerged, like Saigal, whose style not only inspired but was even emulated by the next generation of singers like Mukesh and Kishore Kumar to begin with.

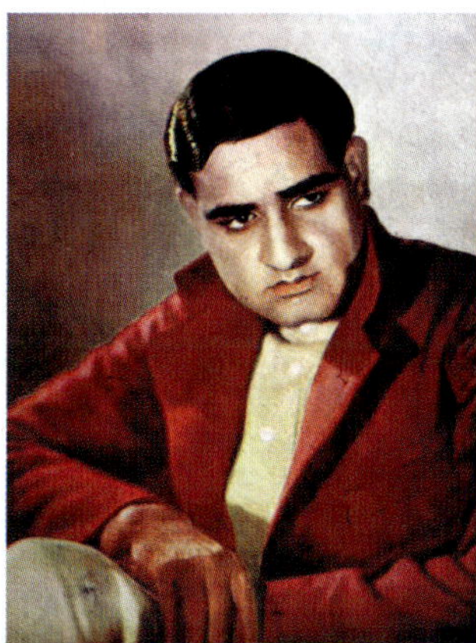

17.57: Portrait of Saigal from 1938 — Wikimedia Commons

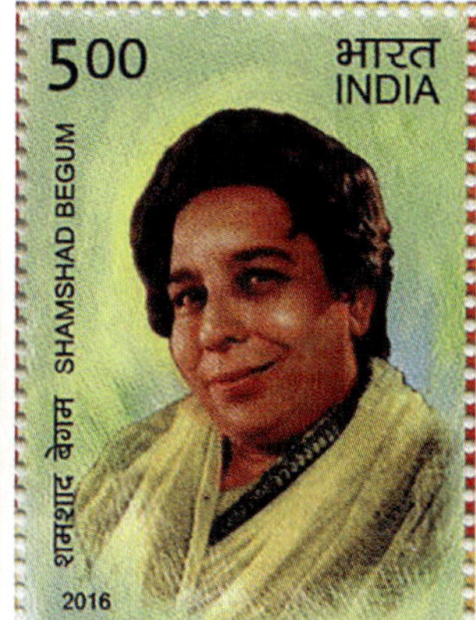

17.58 & 17.59: Shamshad Begum, Talat Mahmood stamps released in 2016 — Courtesy, Department of Post

The 50s, 60s and early 70s are said to be a golden phase in Indian film music. This period was the age of melodies. It saw the blooming of many stalwarts of playback singing like, **Talat Mahmood, Mohammed Rafi, Manna Dey, Mukesh, Lata Mangeshkar, Kishore Kumar, Geeta Dutt, Asha Bhosle, Hemant Kumar, Mahendra Kapoor, Sharda, S.D. Burman, Suman Kalyanpur** etc., who dominated the industry for the next few decades. Many of these developed their own quintessential style. While **Talat Mahmood** was known for his soft silky songs and dulcet ghazals, **Mukesh** was a master of melody and songs of somberness and melancholy. He was considered the onscreen voice of superstars of that generation including that of Dilip Kumar, Raj Kapoor, Sunil Dutt and Manoj Kumar. **Mohammed Rafi**, an extremely popular and talented singer of this period, was known for a wide range and different genres of song. **Kishore Kumar** was another versatile singer who mastered the fast paced, the melodious and the sad alike. With his unique vocal skills, he ushered yodeling in Hindi songs and even brought a touch of merriment and gaiety in them.

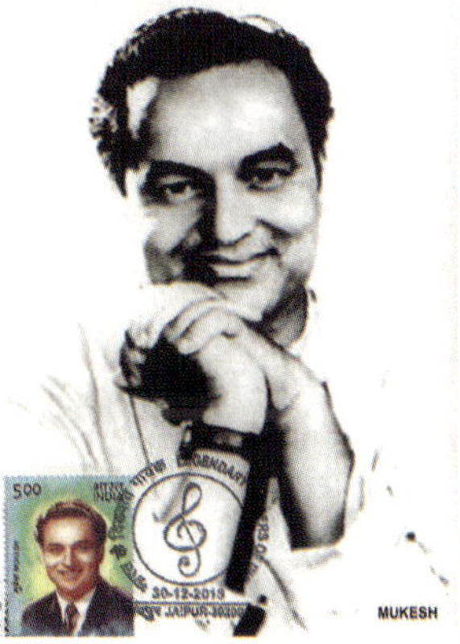

17.60: Mukesh, postal cover and a 2016 stamp — Courtesy, Department of Post

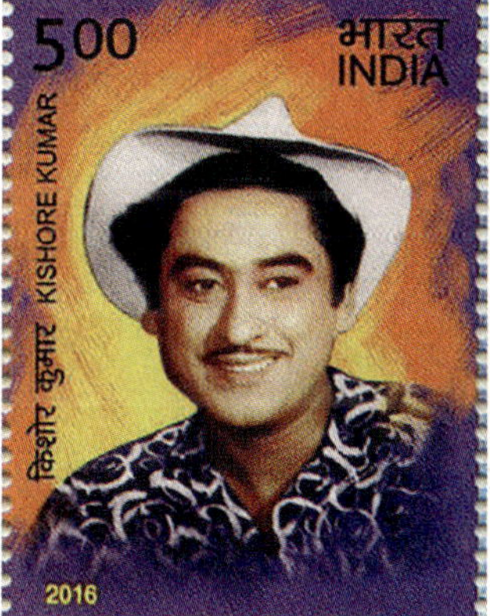

17.61: Kishore Kumar; a 2016 stamp — Courtesy, Department of Post

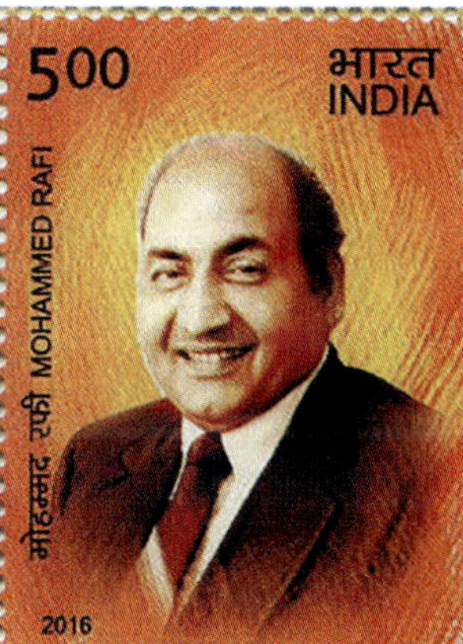

17.62: Mohammed Rafi; a 2016 stamp — Courtesy, Department of Post

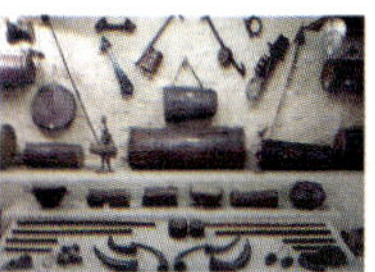

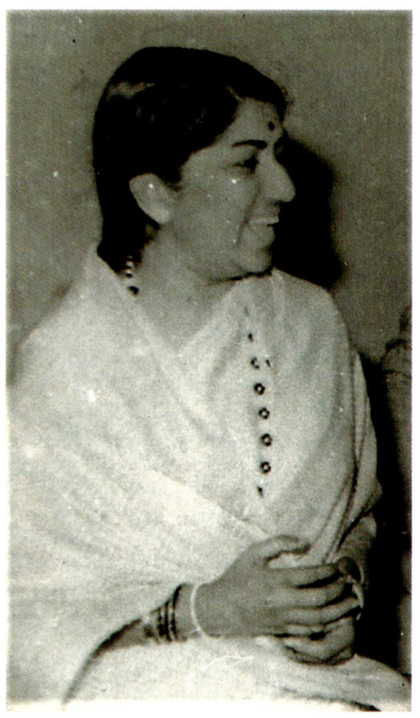

17.63: Lata Mangeshkar, a photo from 1953 — Wikimedia Commons

With a career spread over eight decades (1945 onwards), **Lata Mangeshkar** was the undisputed legend of Indian film and playback singing who delivered major hits in all the phases of the film history and worked with all generations of artists. Considered a soprano (one who can sing the highest of notes in all octaves), her oeuvre cannot be restricted to a specific genre of music or her fame to a specific song or a decade. Among her many great renditions, especially noteworthy is the patriotic song, '*ae mere watan ke logon*', sung on the 26th January 1963, in the backdrop of Indo-Chinese war. It is indeed a masterclass, which touches the very soul of the listener and instils the fervour of patriotism. She was awarded **Bharat Ratna** in 2001, the only playback singer then to be awarded so, and a true testimony to her art and contribution to the field of music. Among other greats of this generation was **Asha Bhosle**, (Padma Bhushan and winner of two National Film Awards) the younger sister of Lata Mangeshkar. She emerged from the latter's shadow to carve a niche for herself as a prolific singer who mastered the diverse genres, from racy to melodious, and from sensuous to sad.

The Bollywood in the late 70s and 80s saw a transition in the music genre. Melody of earlier years gave way to the fast-paced music and the disco beats of the 80s. Many new voices came in the industry including that of; **K.J. Yesudas, Usha Mangeshkar, S.P. Balasubramanyam, Preeti Sagar, Suresh Wadekar, Sulakshana Pandit, Poornima Srestha, Shailendra Singh, Shabbir Kumar, Hemlata, Vani Jairam, Mohammed Aziz, Aarti Mukherjee, Parveen Sultana, Vinod Rathod, Sapna Mukherjee, Sadhana Sargam** amongst others. This period also saw the debut of second generation of Bollywood singers in **Amit Kumar** (son of Kishore Kumar) and **Nitin Mukesh** (son of Mukesh). **Usha Uthup** (song of fame -*Rambha Ho*) was a new genre of singer specializing in rock and roll and fast paced music, while **Nazia Hasan** (song of fame - *aap jaisa koi*) literally ushered the genre of disco. **Salma Agha,** another singer brought the melody of ghazals back with her renditions and acting in the hit movie *Nikah*. **K.J. Yesudas** (eight National Film awards for best playback singer), **Balasubramanyam** (six National Film Awards), **Alka Yagnik** (two National Film Awards), **Anuradha Paudwal** (one National Film Award), **Udit Narayan** (three National Film Awards) **Kavita Krishnamurthy** and **Hariharan** (two National Film awards) were some of the great singers who debuted in the industry in this period and dominated it for the next couple of decades.

In the 90s, the popular music choice underwent a change and so did the music of Bollywood. The exposure to MTV and Channel V, the era of economic liberalisation and the global connect had changed the taste of audience and the demand of the films. A new crop of singers emerged including the likes of **Kumar Sanu, K.S. Chitra, Abhijit Bhattacharya, Sudesh Bhosale, Roop Kumar Rathod, Sonu Nigam, Sukhwinder Singh, Shankar Mahadevan** (three National Film Awards), **Sunidhi Chauhan, Sapna Awasthi,** and others. Many among these are big names of the industry even today. Some singers had their own distinct genre of playback. While **Alisha Chinai** was the queen of pop of this period (song of fame, *Made in India*), **Lucky Ali** was another prominent singer of this genre. **Ila Arun** (song of fame *choli ke peeche*) brought in the Rajasthani folk style. In **Jaspinder Narula** (song of fame, *pyaar to hona hi tha*), the genre of Sufi music found an expression. Among debutants of this generation, **Kumar Sanu** earned the sobriquet of the 'king of melody' and won five consecutive Filmfare Awards for best playback singer in the early 90s. Another celebrated singer of this generation is **Sonu Nigam**, a recipient of National Film award and two Filmfare awards, who is often likened to Mohammed Rafi.

In the new millennium, the genre of soulful Sufi music and ghazals made a comeback. The trend of Indian rock and pop was also on the rise. The shining singing stars which this generation has seen are **Shaan, Shreya Ghoshal, Arijit Singh, Rekha Bhardwaj, Krishnakumar Kunnath (KK), Himesh Reshamiya, Kailash Kher, Kumar Ganjawala, Monali Thakur, Ateef Aslam, Shilpa Rao, Rahat Fateh Ali Khan, Neha Bhasin, Kavita Seth, Shalmali Kholgade, Ankit Tiwari, and Kanika Kapoor** amongst others. Among the new generation of artists, **Shreya Ghoshal** (five National film Awards and seven Filmfare Awards) and **Arijit Singh** (one National Film Award and six Filmfare Awards) are undoubtedly the names to reckon with.

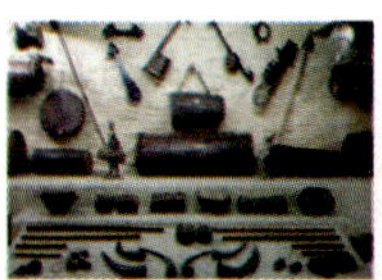

Playback Singers in Regional Films

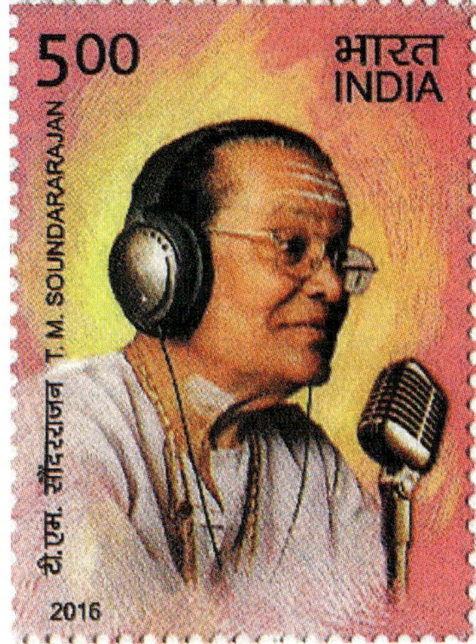

17.64: T M Iyengar Soundararajan, a stamp of 2016 — Courtesy, Department of Post

Among the playback singing in the **regional films**, some names which clearly stand out and can truly be considered as doyens of singing are;

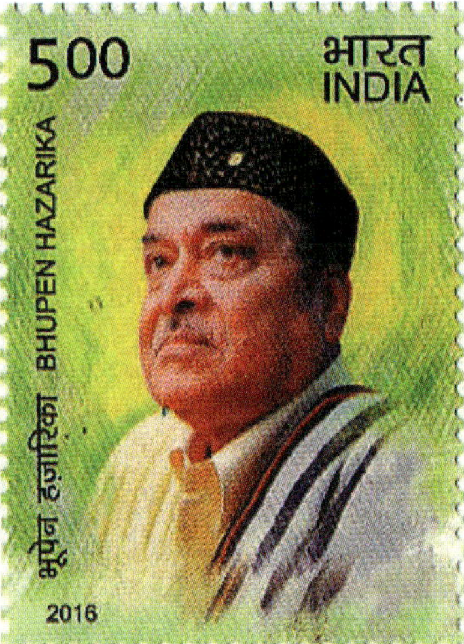

17.65: Bhupen Hazarika, postage stamps of 2013 and 2016 — Courtesy, Department of Post

T M Iyengar Soundararajan (1923-2013)

Popularly known as TMS, was a Carnatic musician and a playback singer of the Tamil films, who is believed to have sung in more than ten thousand songs in a career spanning over six decades.

Bhupen Hazarika (career 1939-2011)

He was an Assamese playback singer, poet, musician, filmmaker and lyricist who was known for his renditions in deep throated baritone voice. He incorporated the elements of folk music in his compositions and was a National award winner playback singer in many of the Bollywood movies. He was conferred the highest civilian award **Bharat Ratna** (in 2019) posthumously.

Hemant Kumar (career: 1935-1989) : Recipient of two National Film Awards, he has sung songs in Bengali, Hindi, Tamil, Marathi, Gujarati, Assamese and other regional languages.

Manna Dey (career: 1942-2013) : Recipient of two National Film Awards, sung songs in 14 languages including Bengali, Hindi, Tamil, Marathi, Gujarati, Bhojpuri, Assamese and other regional languages.

S. Janaki (career: mid 1950s till retirement in 2017: She was a Recipient of four National Film Awards, whose songs were recorded in Tamil, Kannada, Malayalam, Telugu and over 20 languages including international languages),

P. Susheela (career: mid 1950s till next six decades): She was a recipient of four National Film Awards, songs recorded in Tamil, Kannada and nearly 12 languages),

K.J. Yesudas (career: six decades since 1960s): Recipient of eight National Film Awards, sung songs in Malayalam, Tamil, Kannada, Telugu, Hindi, and nearly 12 languages, including Arabic and other international languages.

S.P. Balasubrahmanyam (career: mid 1960s till 2020): Recipient of six National Film Awards, recorded songs in Tamil, Kannada, Malayalam, Telugu and Hindi.

Vani Jairam (career: five decades since 1970s till 2022): A recipient of three National Film Awards, who sung in Tamil, Kannada, Hindi and nearly ten languages.

17.66: Manna Dey, a 2016 stamp — Courtesy, Department of Post

17.67: Hemant Kumar commemorative stamp 2003 — Courtesy, Department of Post

Hariharan (career: 1977 onwards): A recipient of two National Film Awards; he has songs in nearly 10 languages including, Tamil, Hindi, Malayalam, Kannada, Telugu and especially renowned for the genre of ghazals and fusion music.

M.G. Sreekumar (career: 1978 onwards): A recipient of two National Film Awards; he has sung is songs in more than 15 languages, including Malayalam, Tamil, Kannada, Telugu, Hindi, Sanskrit etc.

K.S. Chitra (career: 1980s and onwards): A recipient of six National Film Awards; she has songs in Tamil, Malayalam, Kannada, Telugu, Hindi and 15 other languages, including international languages.

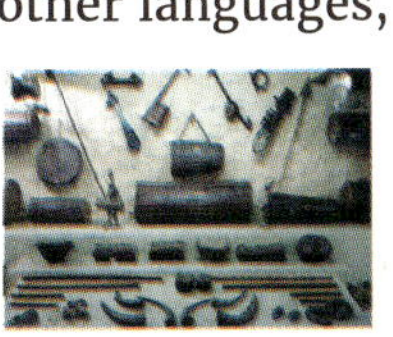

The Styles of Indian Film Music

The film music is a bouquet of diverse musical genres and cannot be strictly said to be a singular or exclusive musical style in itself. Rather, its beauty lies in it being a panorama of the numerous styles in vogue, with the films being a platform to corral and showcase this diversity. Although the song and music of the Indian films are said to fall under the category of Light classical music, however they are also based on, or draw inspiration, from various other forms, such as Hindustani Classical music, Carnatic music, folk songs, regional musical traditions, Western music and other emerging musical styles. Over the years, different genres of songs such as *dadra, thumri ghazal*, *bhajan*, *qawwali*, *disco*, *Indi-pop*, etc. all have found space in this bouquet and gained popularity at the Bollywood charts and in other regional film industries.

Thumri

The semi-classical styes of ***thumri*** and ***dadra*** were especially popular in the early years of Indian cinema. The music composers drew from the traditional music of the country and these, along with *ghazals, bhajans* and folk music, were the genres on which many film songs were based. One of the earliest forms of *thumri* in films was the song, *Piya Bina Nahi Aawat* (film- *Pativrata* 1935, singer-Saigal). Another *thumri* composed by Wajid Ali Shah, *Babul Mora Naihar*, has been a classic which has been sung through the ages. Its first appearance was in the movie, *Street Singer* in 1938, (music by R.C. Boral singer-Saigal). *Bajuband Khul Khul Jaye,* has been another popular *thumri* which was first sung by Lata Mangeshkar (1954). This was sung again in 2006 movie *Banaras* (music Himesh Reshamiya). In the new millennium, *thumri* was again seen in a few films and songs such as *Chhodo Na Mori Baiyan*, in film **Zubeida**, in 2001 (singer Richa Sharma, music A.R. Rahman) and *Aan Milo Sajana*, (film- **Gadar**, 2002 singer-Parveen Sultana & Ajoy Chakraborty, music- Uttam Singh), *Hamari Atariya Pe*, (film- **Dedh Ishqiya 2014**, Rekha Bhardwaj, Vishal Bhardwaj).

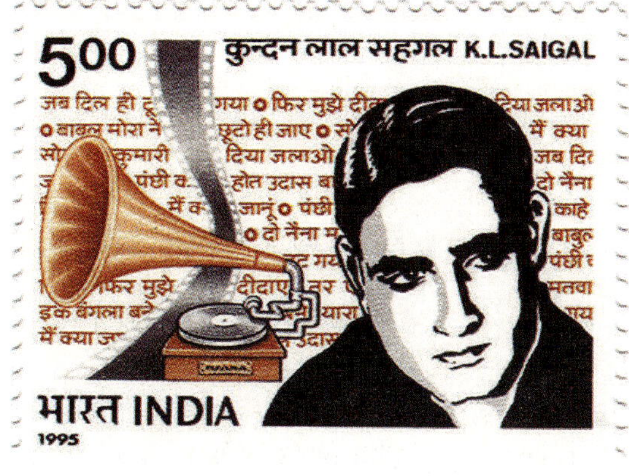

17.68: K L Saigal, one of the earliest playback, *thumri* and *ghazal* singer, stamp 1995 — Courtesy, Department of Post

Ghazals

The genre of ***ghazals*** has been popular in all times right from the very first talkie *Alam Ara.* They have featured in different films based on the requirement of the script and the mood expressed in the scene. A combination of Urdu poetry and musical melody, many ghazals have even drawn from the traditional *ragas.* The Indian film music has seen many versatile *ghazal* artists like **K. L. Saigal, Bade Ghulam Ali, Begum Akhtar, Talat Mehmood, Ghulam Ali, Jagjeet Singh, Chitra Singh, Pankaj Udhas, Talat Aziz, Bhupinder Singh, Penaz Masani, Hariharan** and others. Although the *ghazals* attributed to these maestros (and other *ghazal* singers) may be based on the lyrics of other poets, but often it is their singing and musical composition which has provided a popular identity to these ghazals. Traditionally, Ghazals have enjoyed substantial popularity on their own as musical albums, and also through public performances. However, films also imparted a wide platform for their dissemination. While films have at times drawn *ghazals* from popular albums, incorporating it in the script and thus gaining from its mass appeal, at many times, *ghazals* have also been composed exclusively for the movies. Thus, there exists a symbiotic relationship between the film music and the genre of *ghazals* and this association prospered over the decades.

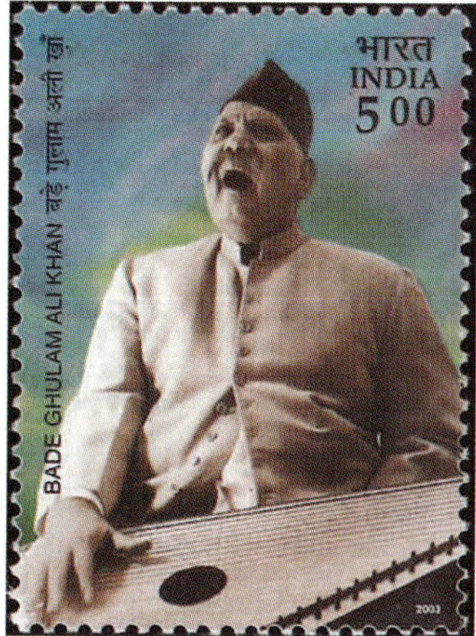

17.70: Bade Ghulam Ali; a commemorative stamp of 2003 — Courtesy, Department of Post

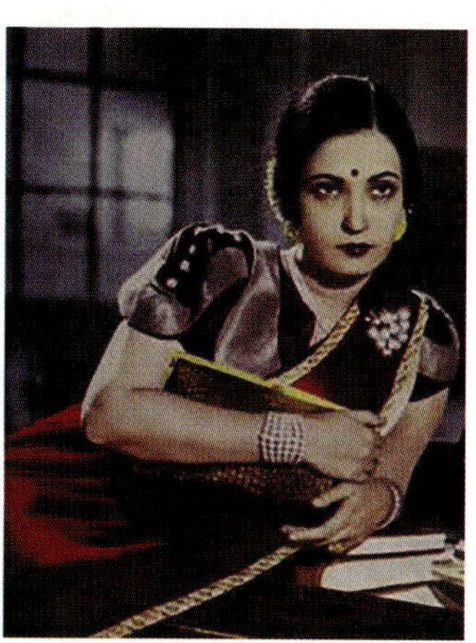
17.69: Begum Akhtar, screen shot from film *Roti* (1942), published in *Film India*, 1942 — Wikimedia Commons

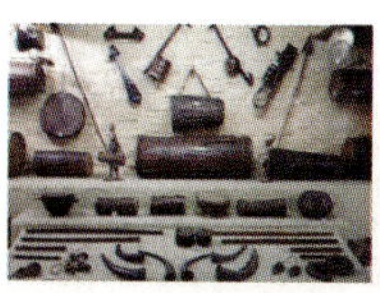

Uthaye Ja Unke Sitaam (film-*Andaaz,* 1949 singer Lata Mageshkar), *Dile Nadan Tujhe Hua Kya Hai* (film-Mirza Ghalib 1954, singer Talat Mehmood) are some popular ghazals of the early decades of Bollywood. Ghazals remained very popular in films in the decades of 60s-80s which is referred to as the golden period of *ghazals*. One such *ghazal* from this period is *Rang Aur Noor ki Baaraat Kise Pesh Karon* (film *Gazal*, 1964, singer-Mohammed Rafi, music-Madan Mohan). *Chupke Chupke Raat Din* (film-Nikah, 1982) sung by **Ghulam Ali**, *Jhuki Jhuki Si Nazar* (film-*Arth,* 1982) sung by **Jagjeet Singh** and *Chitthi Aayi Hai* (film-*Naam,*1986) sung by **Pankaj Udhaas**, are some of the other all-time popular filmi ghazals. Many melodious ghazals were composed till early 1980s, but a lull came soon thereafter. In the early 90s, some spurt in sub-type of romantic ghazals took place in movies such as *Aashiqui* (1990), *Dil* (1990), *Saajan* (1992) and others. But beyond the 90s, there has been a perceptible decline in their popularity, with ghazals only making sporadic appearance in movies and giving way to more racy music.

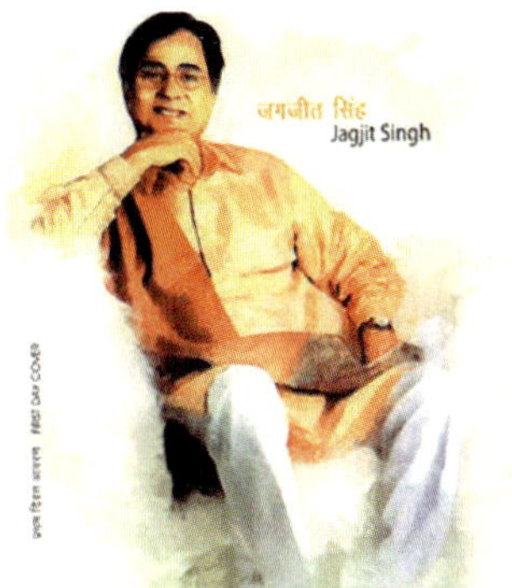

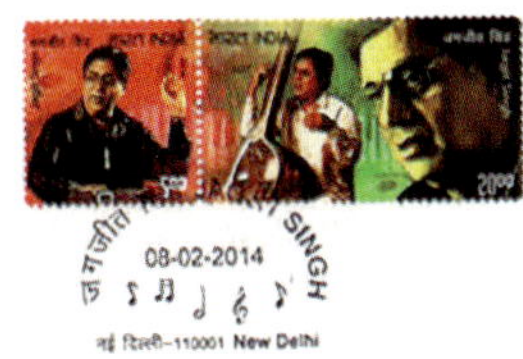

17.71: A first day cover and stamps of Jagjit Singh released in 2014 — Courtesy, Department of Post

Bhajans

It is another genre of music which has regularly found a place in film songs across the decades. These are essentially in nature of devotional songs which may be of the format of an individual prayer, a group song, or even of a responsorial format. With the initial movies drawing themes from Indian mythology and epics, this genre was a need of the film music. Over the years, many of these have ceased to remain songs from the movies and fully imbibed the character of songs of common prayer among the masses. The 50s and 60s were indeed a golden period of *bhajans* in movies. *Man Tadpat Hari Darshan Ko* (film-*Baiju Bawara*, 1952, singer- Naushad & Shakeel Badayuni), *Tu Pyaaar Ka Sagar Hai* (film-*Seema, 1955*, singer-Manna Day) and *Aye Malik Tere Bande Hum* (film- *Do Ankhe Barah Haath,* 1957, singer -Lata Mangeshkar) enjoy immense popularity as prayer songs even to these days.

Over the next few decades, many popular film bhajans were composed. These include, *Allah Tero Naam Ishwar Tero Naam* (*Hum Dono,* 1961, Lata Mangeshkar), *Tumhi Ho Mata, Pita Tumhi Ho* (film-*Main Chup Rahungi*, 1962), *Jyot Se Jyot Jagaate Chalo* (film-*Sant Gyaneshwar*, 1964), *Humko Man Ki Shakti Dena* (film- *Guddi*, 1971), *Yashomati Maiya Se Bole Nandlala (film- Satyam Shivam Sundaram,* 1978, singer *- Lata Mangeshkar & Manna Dey) Teri Hai Zameen Tera Aasman* (The Burning Train,1980) *Chalo Bulawa Aaya Hai* (film-*Avataar*, 1983, singer-Mahendra Kapoor), *Itni Shakti Hame Dena Data* (film *Ankush*, 1986) and others. The later years also saw a few of these melodious prayers in songs such as, *O' Palan Hare* (film-*Lagaan*, 2001, singers-Lata Mangeshkar, Udit Narayan). However, like *ghazals,* the trend of *bhajans* in the movie world has clearly waned.

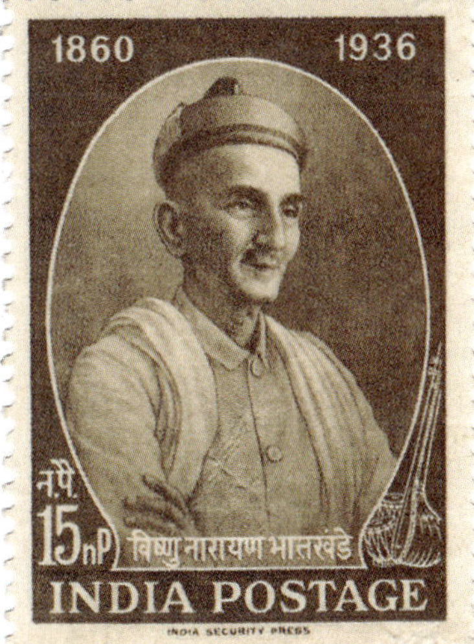

17.72: Vishnu Narayan Bhatkhande (1860-1936), a classical singer known for his *bhajans;* a commemorative stamp released in 1961 — Courtesy, Department of Post

Outside the films, *bhajans* have always enjoyed mass appeal with singers like **V.D. Paluskar, V.N. Bhatkhande, Pandit Kumar Gandharva**, (in the classical genre) and **Anoop Jalota, Anuradha Paudwal** amongst others, widely acclaimed for their renditions and body of works.

Qawwali

It has been another popular subgenre of film music which has seen reasonable presence on the silver screen, not only in Bollywood but in other regional film industries too. Filmi *qawwali*, however, cannot be considered the same as the traditional *Sufi-qawwali* which has devotion to *Allah*, or the spiritual love,

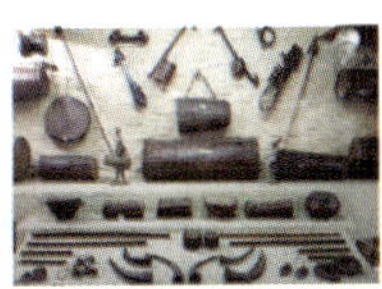

as its very soul. Besides, there exist differences in the structure of song. However, the *qawwali* of the films does emulate the music and the style of singing of the traditional *qawwali*, although their subjects may be devotion, love or even others. Amongst the earliest popular filmi *qawwalis* are; *Hamen To Loot Liya Mil Ke Husn Walon Ne* (*Al-Hilal*,1958, singer- Ismail Azad Qawwal), *Teri Mehfil Mein Kismet Aazma Ker Hum Bhi Dekhenge* (*Mughle-Azam*, 1960, Lata Mangeshkar & Shamsad Begum), *Na To Carvan ki Talash hai* (*Barasaat Ki Raat*, 1960; Manna Dey & Asha Bhonsle), *Ae Meri Zohra Jabeen* (*Waqt*,1965, Manna Dey), *Maula Salim Chisti* (Garam Hawa, 1973), *Jhoom Barabar Jhoom Sharabi* (*5 Rifles*, 1974), *Pardah Hai Pardah Hai* (*Amar Akbar Anthony*, 1977, Mohammed Rafi), *Shirdi Wale Sai Baba* (*Amar Akbar Anthony*, 1977) *Qurbani, Qurbani, Qurbani,* (Qurbani,1980).

In the next couple of decades, *qawwali* also took a back seat in Bollywood with the advent of the racy disco and other popular music formats. However, it had another *avatar* with the amalgamation of the Western music and techno-beats in what is called the *techno-qawwali*. Soon, dance routine also got incorporated as part of it on dance-oriented tracks, giving rise to another variation called *club-qawwali*. Songs such as *Kajrare Kajrare* (*Bunty Aur Babli*, 2005 Shankar Mahadevan and Alisha Chinai) could be put in this category. *Qawwali* again had resurgence in the films under the influence of the famous *qawwali* singers like Nusrat Fateh Ali Khan, Altaf Raja, Kailash Kher, Javed Ali and others. With soulful music of A. R. Rahman in songs such as *Khwaja Mere Khwaja* (*Jodha-Akbar*; 2008, singer AR Rahman), *Arzian-Moula, Moula, Mere Moula* (*Delhi-6*, 2009, singers Kailash Kher & Javed Ali), popularity of filmi *qawwali* has soared. Another touching *qawwali* song of this period is *Kun Faya Kun (Rockstar*, 2011 music A.R. Rahman, singer Javed Ali).

A popular and related genre of music is **Sufi music**, which is a devotional form of music of the Sufis and brings out the spiritual love for the Supreme. *Qawwali* is in itself a subtype of Sufi music and both the styles see nearly the same musical and singing exponents. Like *qawwali*, the traditional Sufi music is now finding increasing acceptance in the film industry.

Disco

Disco, unlike the other genres of music, did not emanate from the musical traditions of the Indian subcontinent but was a western influence. The music of disco is characterised by catchy tunes and rhythmic beats with repetitive vocals and up-tempo music. It invariably employs instruments like drums, bass guitars and synthesizers. As a form of music, it had its birth in the discos and night clubs in the 60s. The 70s were the golden period for disco in the Western world. However, it made an entry in the Indian films only in the 80s. While Western albums were already popular in India, experts reckon that the album of **Nazia Hassan**, (*Disco Deewane,* produced by Biddu) and her song *Aap Jaisa Koi* in the film *Qurbani* (1980) to have sparked the disco sensation in the Indian movies. There was a spate of disco music and dance songs in the films thereafter. Riding on this wave, the movie, *Disco Dancer* was produced in 1982 with several popular songs of the disco genre. The movie along with the songs was a huge success especially in overseas markets such as erstwhile U.S.S.R. and China.

Over the years, some of the noteworthy chart busters of disco are; *Aap Jaisa Koi* (*Qurbaani, 1980,* singer Nazia Hassan, music Biddu), *Hari Om Hari* (*Pyarra Dushman*, 1980 singer **Usha Uthup**, music Bappi Lahiri)) *Paisa O' Paisa* (*Karz*, 1980), *Jimmy Jimmy* (Disco Dancer 1982, singer Parvati Khan), *I am a Disco Dancer* (*Disco Dancer*, 1982, singer Bappi Lahiri), *Auva, Auva, Koi Yahan Nache* (Disco Dancer, 1982, singer Bappi Lahiri, Usha Uthup), *Disco-82* (*Khuddar*, 1982; singers – Kishore Kumar & Lata Mangeshkar), *Disco-station* (*Hathkadi*,1982, singer-Asha Bhonsle), *Jawaane Janeman* (*Namak Halal*, 1982, singer-Asha Bhonsle), *Boom Boom* (Star,1982 singer Nazia Hasan), *Jhoom Jhoom Jhoom Baba* (*Kasam Paida Karne Wale Ki*, 1984, singer Salma Agha) *Tamma Tamma Loge* (*Thanedar* 1990). The genre of disco in India was indeed a rage but a short lived one. Beyond early 90s, there were a few occasional bursts of disco music in the Indian films, but its heydays were already over.

Rock Music

It refers to the genre of western music which became popular in the 1950s and 1960s in America and was called **Rock and Roll**. The music is fast paced, often involves romantic songs (or other subjects) to the accompaniment of instruments like electric guitar, bass guitar, acoustics guitar, drums, keyboard,

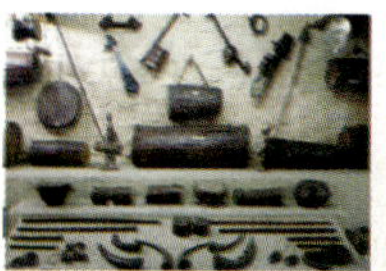

etc. A number of musical bands are associated with it. Its sub-genres include, **hard rock** (characterised by increased use of distorted electric guitar, bass guitar, drums and aggressive vocals), **psychedelic rock** (representative of psychedelic culture including subgenres of acid rock and others), **progressive rock** (classic rock or symphonic rock), **heavy-metal** (characterized by heavier drum and bass, long guitar solos, distorted guitar sounds etc.) and others. In India, this music has become popular as **Indian rock**, which is a music genre incorporating elements of mainstream rock music and Indian music. The genre became quite popular in the 60s and 70s in the movies as well outside the film world in the form of rock bands such as the Thunderbirds, Mystiks, Beat-X, and Flintstonem, and with singers like **Ashwani Bali** and **Usha Uthup** making waves.

The tryst of the India Rock with the movies is said to have taken place in this very period with notable songs like *Jaan Pehchan Ho* (*Gumnaam*, 1965 music-Shankar Jaikishan, singer-Mohd. Rafi), *Dum Maro Dum (Hare Krishna Hare Rama, 1971,* music-RD Burman, singer-Asha Bhonsle), *Yeh Mera Dil Pyar Ka Diwana* (*Don*, 1978, music-Kalyanji Anandji, singer-Asha Bhonsle). While the 80s were a period of romance of Bollywood with the disco beats, as the 90s arrived, there emerged a generation of youngsters fed on the music of MTV and Channel V with the opening of television broadcast. The coming decades of the new millennium also saw the coming of age of Indian Rock in its multitude of forms influenced by the Indian music and taste. These subgenres would include the likes of funk rock, pop rock, raga rock, and soft rock. Some scintillating songs of movies in this phase of Indian Rock were, *Bande* (Black Friday, 2004), *Alvida* (Life in a Metro, 2007) *Pichle Saat Dino Mein* (Rock On*, 2008*), Rock On (movie Rock On, 2008) *Nayan Tarse* (DevD, 2009) *Sadda Haq* (Rockstar 2011), *Nadaan Parindey* (Rockstar 2011) *Bhaag DK Bose* (Delhi Belly, 2011), *Sun Raha Hai Naa Tu* (*Aashiqui2* 2013), *Zinda* (*Bhaag Milkha Bhaag*, 2013) *Ae Dil Hai Mushkil* (movie *Ae Dil Hai Mushkil* 2016) amongst others.

Pop music and Indipop

Pop music also became popular in the western world in the 50s and 60s. As compared to Rock which gained ground in the same period, its musical attributes were softer, with an element of melody in it. Besides, it also borrows features from other musical styles such as *Latin County*, *Urban,* etc. In India, it is popular as **Indipop**, which is a fusion of western pop and Indian elements. Over the years, it has amalgamated in it, styles ranging from dance music to elements of classical, from features of folk to regional music.

This genre had a similar trend as disco and gained popularity in India in the 80s. With the opening of the broadcasting industry and the music channels like MTV, Channel V, FM radio gaining ground, its mass appeal in the 90s and 2000s substantially increased. As a music genre, it has enjoyed immense following outside the movie world, with several independent albums making waves; like *Disco-Deewane* (disco and pop genre; Nazia Hassan & Zoheb 1981), *Dhuan-Pari Hoon Main* (Suneeta Rao, 1991), *Thanda Thanda Pani* (pop and rap genre, Baba Sehgal 1992), *Johny Jokers* (Shweta Shetty 1993) *Made in India* (Alisha Chinai,1995), *Dole Dole* (Suchitra Krishnamoorthy, 1996), *Bolo Tara Rara* (genre-Bhangra-pop, Daler Mehndi, 1996), *Sunoh* (Lucky Ali, 1996), *Colonial Cousins* (Hariharan & Lesle Lewis, 1996), *O' Meri Munni* (Remo Fernandes 1998), *Boondein- Dooba Dooba* (band-Silk Route, 1998), *Breathless* (Shankar Mahadevan, 1998) *Yaad Piya Ki Aane Lagi* (Falguni Pathak 1999), *Deewana* (Sonu Nigam, 1999), *Tanha Dil* (Shaan, 2000), *Aapka Suroor* (Himesh Reshamiya, 2006) and others.

Pop music has followed a similar trajectory in the films also with many of the above artists being widely acclaimed playback singers of the movies. Some of their popular movie songs are, *Kate Nahin Kat te* (film-*Mr. India*, 1986; singer-Alisha Chinai), *Zooby Zooby* (film, *Dance Dance*, 1987, singer-Alisha Chinai), *Dekho Dekho Yeh Hai Jalwa* (film *Jalwa* 1987, singer-Remo Fernandes), *Humma Humma* (film-Bombay, 1995, singer-Remo Fernandes), *Ek Pal Ka Jeena* (film- *Kaho Naa Pyaar Hai*, 2000 singer Lucky Ali), *Aashiq Banaya Aapne* (film- *Aashiq Banaya Aapne*,2005 singer–Himesh Reshammiya), *Rang De Basanti* (genre Bhangra-pop, film-*Rang De Basanti,* 2006, singer Daler Mehandi, music-AR Rahman) amongst many others.

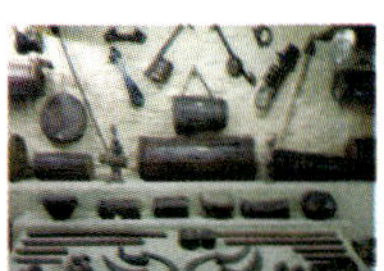

The Music Composers in Indian Films

While the playback singers have been the voice of the songs of Indian films and the movie stars the face of it, it's the music composers/music directors who impart the creative soul to it. The changing face of film music has ushered composers of different genre in its century old tradition. While the 30s and 40s were the fledgling years, many new innovations took place even in this period from playback recording to use of orchestra etc. The emphasis on the classical roots and folk traditions was more in this phase which saw the first generations of music composers. This included **Raichand Boral, Pankaj Mullick, Saraswati Devi, Anil Biswas, Khemchand Prakash, and Ghulam Haider** amongst others. Raichand Boral is often considered the pioneer of playback singing for introducing this concept in 1935 in the Hindi feature film *Dhoop-chaon*. He is also christened as the father of film music in India. Among other renowned film musicians of this age was Pankaj Mullick who introduced Rabindra Sangeet to film music. Saraswati Devi was the first female film music director and Anil Biswas introduced orchestral music and also incorporated folk elements like *Baul* and *Bhatiyali*.

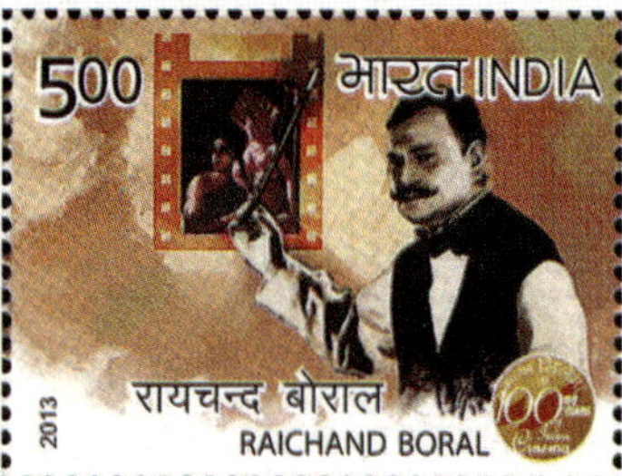

17.73: Raychand Boral, a commemorative stamp 2013 — Courtesy, Department of Post

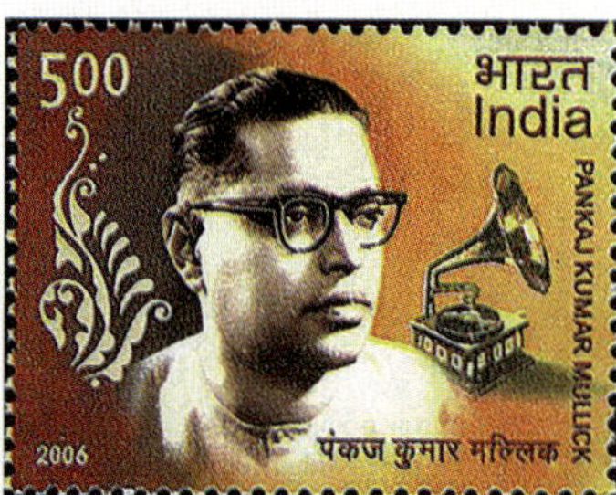

17.74: Pankaj Mullick, a commemorative stamp 2006 — Courtesy, Department of Post

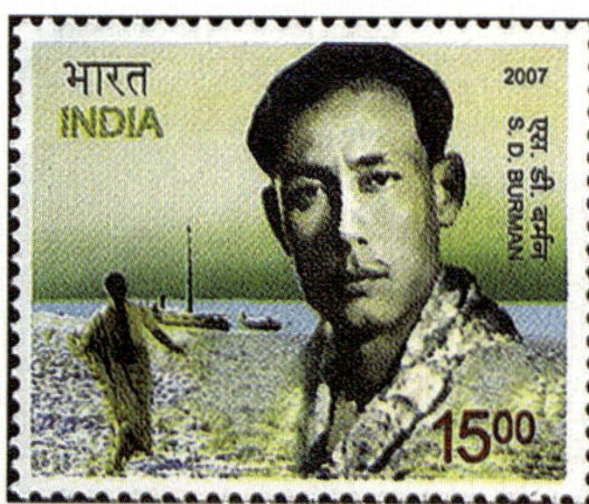

17.75: S.D. Burman, a commemorative stamp 2007 — Courtesy, Department of Post

The next phase of 50s and 60s, considered to be the golden age of film music, comprised many renowned names such as **Naushad Ali, S.D. Burman, Hemant Kumar, Madan Mohan, Shankar-Jaikishan (duo), O.P. Nayyar, C. Ramachandra, Salil Chowdhury, Hemant Kumar, Khayyam, Ravi, Roshan, Laxmikant-Pyarelal (duo), Kalyanji-Anandji (duo), Ravi, Usha Khanna, Jaidev, Roshan** and others. The music of this phase was based on the classical traditions, especially those of Naushad, Shankar-Jaikishan, Madan Mohan and Khayyam. In the music of Salil Chowdhury, a confluence of Indian and Western traditions emerged, based on the *ragas*, but the orchestration being Western. Khayyam's music had a touch of poetry and ghazal besides root in the *ragas*. S.D. Burman and Hemant Kumar are considered as among highly versatile composers and singers of this period. Madan Mohan's compositions had uniqueness of melody and he is particularly renowned for his ghazal music. A unique aspect of this phase of music was the emergence of many successful duos of music composers such as Shankar-Jaikishan, Laxminkant-Pyarelal and Kalyanji-Anandji. While Shankar Jaikishan won the Filmfare Award for best music composers nine times (with 20 nominations), Laxmikant-Pyarelal with 7 wins and 25 nominations hold the record for maximum number of nominations ever.

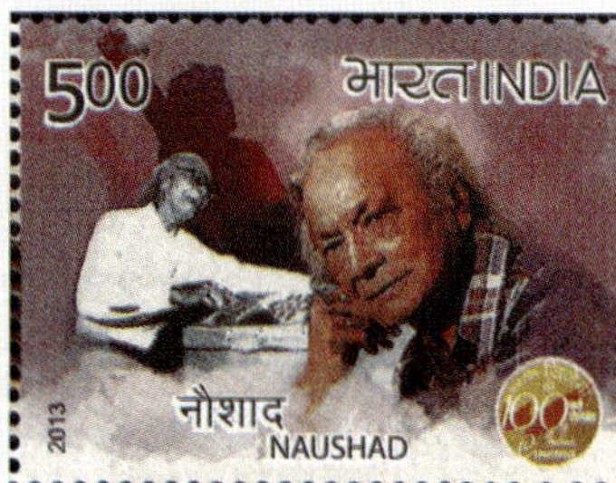

17.76: Naushad Ali, a commemorative stamp 2013 — Courtesy, Department of Post

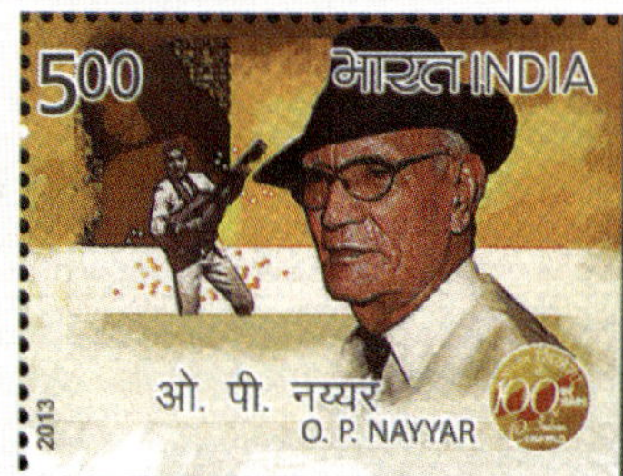

17.77: O.P. Nayyar, a commemorative stamp 2013 — Courtesy, Department of Post

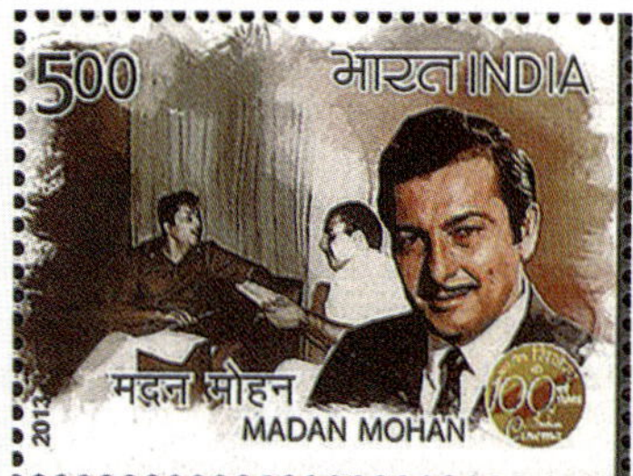

17.78: Madan Mohan, a commemorative stamp 2013 — Courtesy, Department of Post

The 70s saw the emergence of **R.D. Burman** (son of SD Burman) who in the coming decade would contribute immensely to the film music and be reckoned as among the all-time great music directors. **Rajesh Roshan** and **Ravindra Jain** are

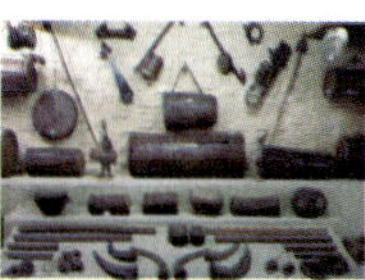

among the other celebrated composers of this decade. The music of 80s underwent a distinct change reflected in the fast paced and racy forms such as the disco. **Bappi Lahiri** was the undoubted king of this genre. **Anu Malik** and **Anand-Milind** (duo) are among the other successful composers of this period.

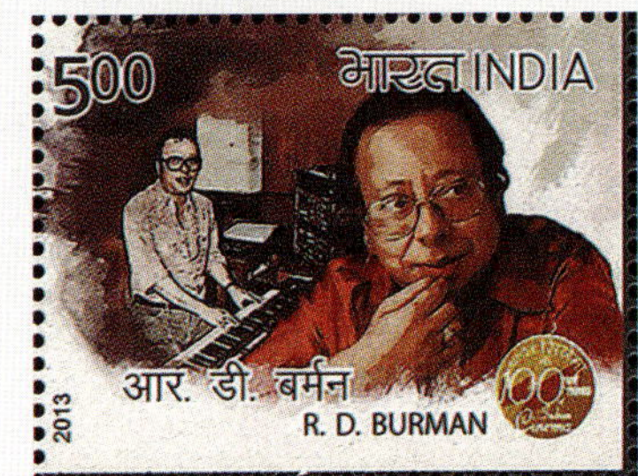

17.79: R D Burman, a stamp released in 2013 — Courtesy, Department of Post

With the advent of **A.R. Rahman** in the 90s, the music industry saw the emergence of one of its brightest stars. His music ushered the confluence of the melody of the Indian classical tradition and the Western music. With five National Film Awards, 15 Filmfare Awards and two Academy Awards (Oscars) amongst many others, he remains one of the most successful and acclaimed artists of the industry. The duos of **Nadeem- Shravan** and **Jatin-Lalit** and the trio of **Shankar-Ehsan-Loy** are among the other popular music composers of this period. **Himesh Reshamiya, Pritam, Vishal-Shekhar** (duo) **and Sneha Khanwalkar, Amit Trivedi** are among some of the successful composers in the new millennium.

Amongst the composers of **regional film music**, often considered the very best is **Ilaiyaraaja**, who has worked predominantly in the Tamil film industry and composed more than 7000 songs. His composition has been played even by the Royal Philharmonic Orchestra and he is acclaimed for integration of the western classical musical techniques with the Indian folk music and Indian traditional instrumentation. Amongst other great musicians in the regional film industry are **M.S. Viswanathan** (Tamil Films), **K.V. Mahadevan** (Tamil), **Vijaya Bhaskar** (Kannada, Tamil, Telugu, Malayalam, Marathi and other regional language films), **M.M. Keervani** (Telugu), **G Devarajan**, (Malayalam) besides others.

The Cultural Significance of Film Music

Beyond these notable genres which had longer run at the box office, Indian films have sporadically seen the styles of *bhangra*, folk, rock, reggae, punk and many others. Thus, films have offered space to all forms of music to flourish. Orthodoxy of style or purity of presentation have not been a determinant of what form prospers or what perishes. The only criteria of the selection of the genre have been the perception of the film artists as to the choice of the people. What succeeds eventually further prospers. Thus, the film music in itself has come to represent the genre of **popular music**. In doing so, it has cut across the sections of society, overcome, the barriers of language, the regional diversities, the divide of class and the vagaries of rural and urban choices. In a way, it is emblematic of those cultural elements with which the nation at a large identifies with. Thus, film music is truly our **collective cultural heritage**. Today, with a large Indian diaspora spread across the world from South Asia and Southeast Asia to the Americas, from Europe to South Africa, Indian film music has a global presence and is often seen as an unofficial brand ambassador of the Indian culture.

Indian Music and its Associated Institutions

Gandharva Mahavidyalaya

Established by V.D. Paluskar in early 20th century in Lahore, this institution is aimed at spreading and enrichment of Indian music. The current institution in New Delhi was established in 1939.

Sangeet Natak Akademi

As an institution of national eminence, it was established in 1952 by the Government of India. It is the apex institution of performing arts in India and aims to preserve and promote various arts including music, dance, and drama.

SPIC MACAY (Society for the Promotion of Indian Classical Music and Culture Amongst Youth)

It is a non-governmental organisation and a voluntary movement which aims to preserve and promote Indian classical music and culture amongst the younger generation. It has been successful in hosting a number of lecture-demonstrations and performances of eminent experts of music before lakhs of students in schools, colleges, and other educational institutions. It was established in 1977 by Dr. Kiran Seth.

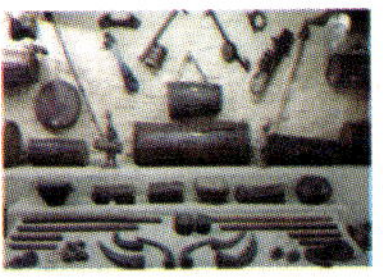

PICTURE GALLERY

Folk Musical Instruments of India

Idiophones

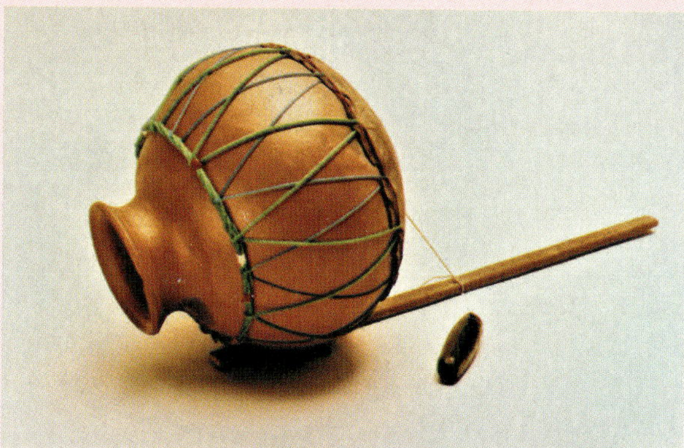

17.80: Pullava Kudam, a folk instrument of Kerala, made of earthen pot, attached strings and parched animal skin; popular in the performance of Pulluvan Paatu, a traditional folk song of the Pulluva community of Kerala.

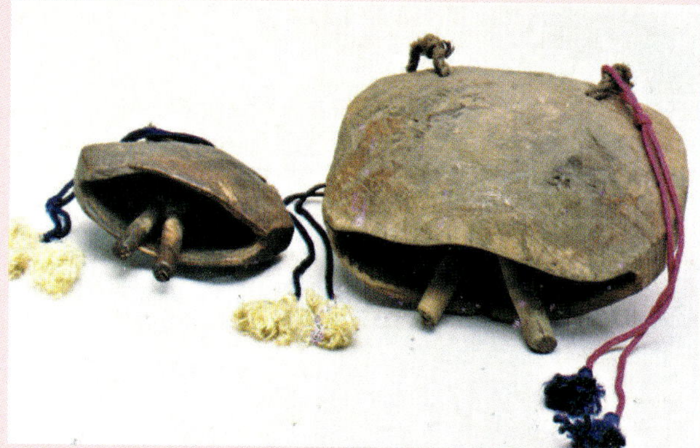

17.81: Tapri, a folk Idiophone used in Uttar Pradesh and other parts of North India

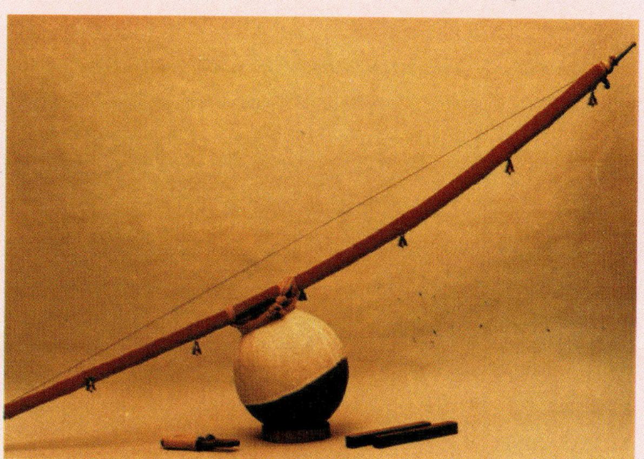

17.82: Villu Pattu, a composite idiophone with a long bow, small bells, terracotta pot and sticks, used in the performance of Villu Pattu (bow song-a form of musical storytelling) in Tamil Nadu

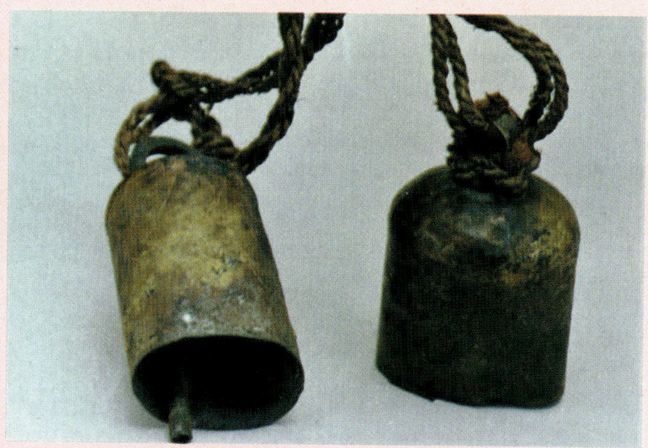

17.83: A double bell used as idiophone in traditional and tribal music

Photographs — Courtesy, Sangeet Natak Akademi

Stringed Instruments

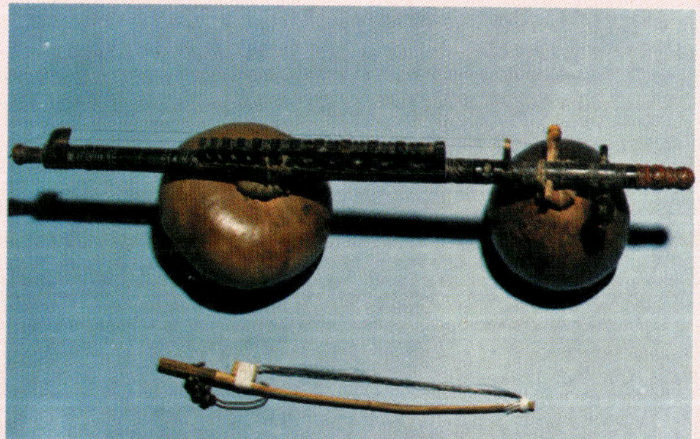

17.84: Jantar, a stringed instrument of Madhya Pradesh, having a wooden body with two attached gourds, two steel strings and played with a bow having strings of horsehair.

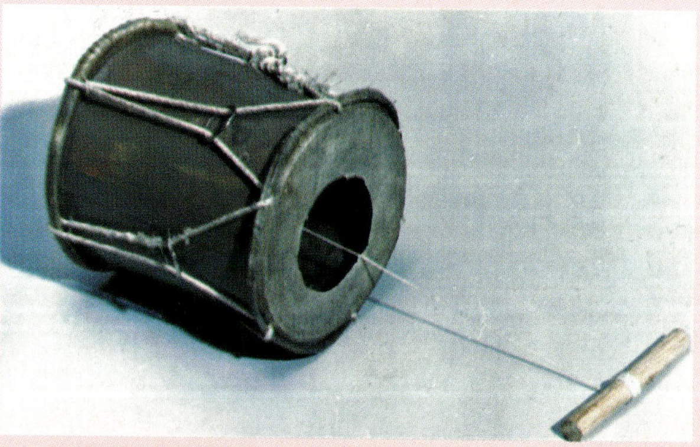

17.85: Gabgubi, a percussion stringed instrument, popular in West Bengal, having a wooden resonator made of a dried gourd with a string plucked with a plectrum

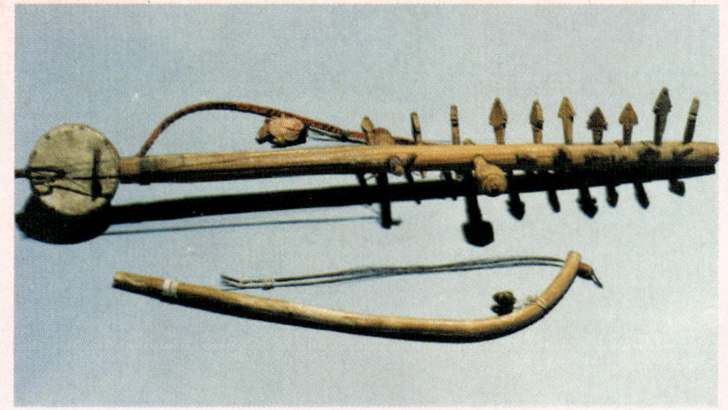

17.86: Ravan Hatta, an ancient bowed string instrument popular in Rajasthan

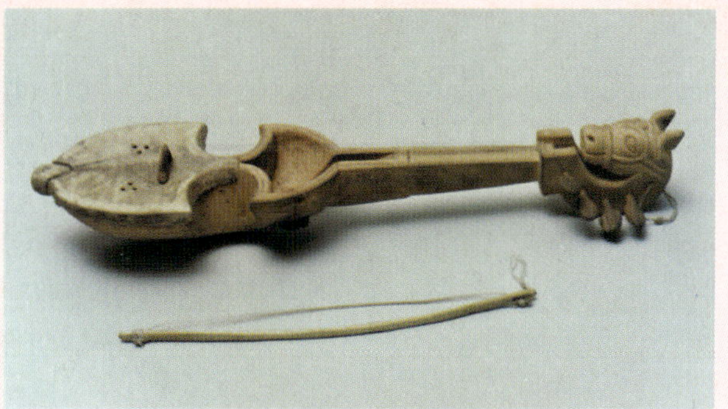

17.87: Kindari Davatara, another ancient bowed string instrument of Himachal Pradesh

Photographs — Courtesy, Sangeet Natak Akademi

Wind Instruments

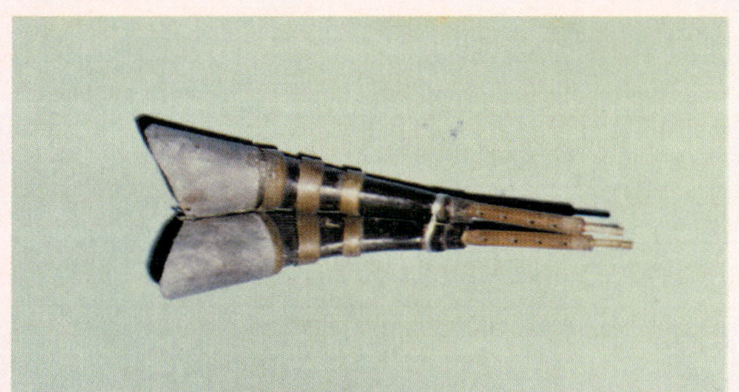

17.88: Pepa, a wind instrument of Assam made using animal horns, popular since ancient times, particularly in Bihu celebrations

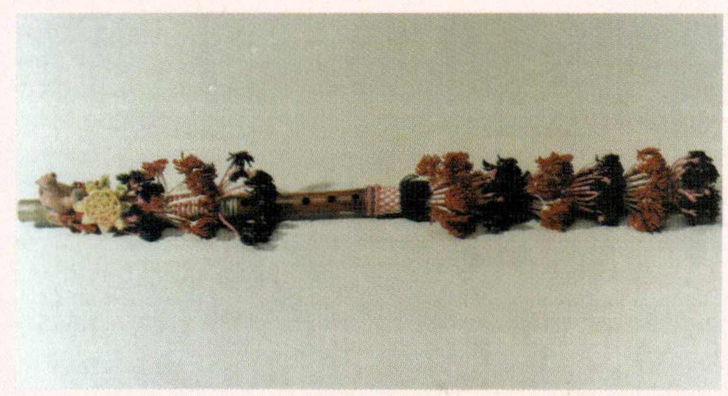

17.89: Bans, a wind instrument of Madhya Pradesh made of bamboo and nearly four feet long

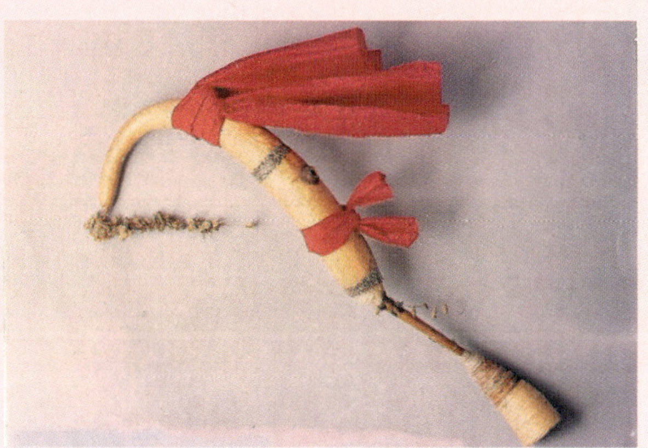

17.90: Tarpu, a single reed wind instrument of Gujarat, comprising a reservoir chamber with a hole for blowing air, bamboo pipe with holes and a horn/ horn-like resonant chamber

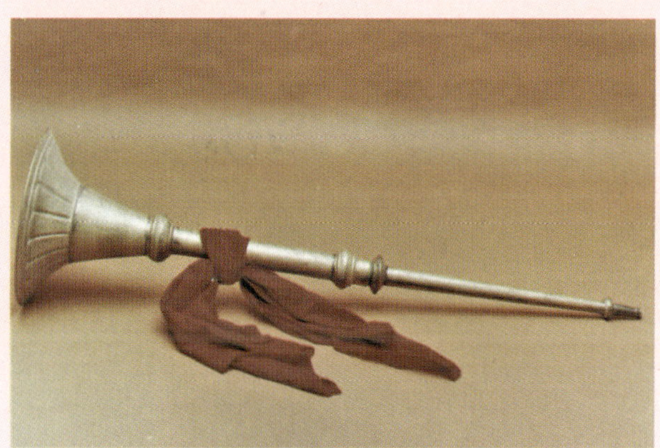

17.91: Karnal, a straight brass trumpet popular in Himachal Pradesh

Photographs — Courtesy, Sangeet Natak Akademi

Percussion Instruments

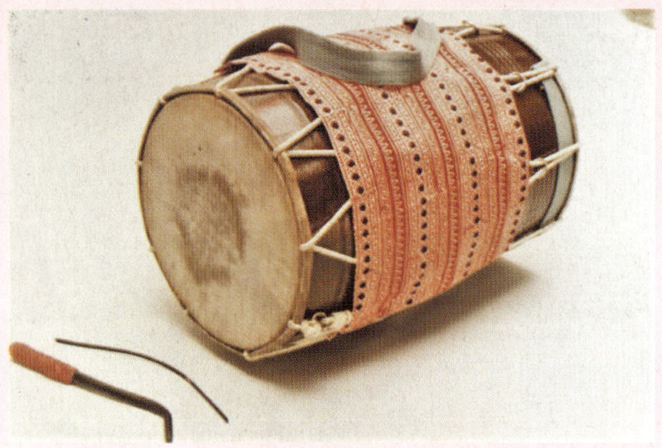

17.92: A traditional dhol of Punjab used in the performance of Bhangra, Gidda and other folk songs and dances

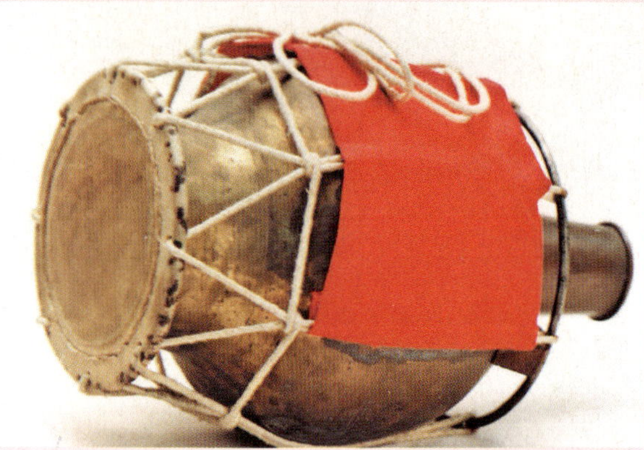

17.93: Burrakathi Dakki, a percussion folk instrument of Andhra Pradesh; comprises a pitcher-shaped brass vessel having a short neck and round belly with a wider end covered with animal skin; used in the performance of Burrakatha

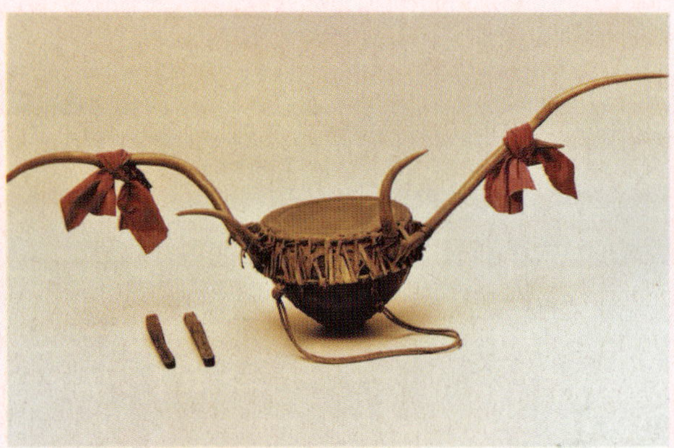

17.94: Nishan, a percussion instrument from Odisha, played with sticks called chimta. It is shaped like a vessel, made of rivetted iron sheet, covered with stretched animal skin and leather straps, with attached antelope horns

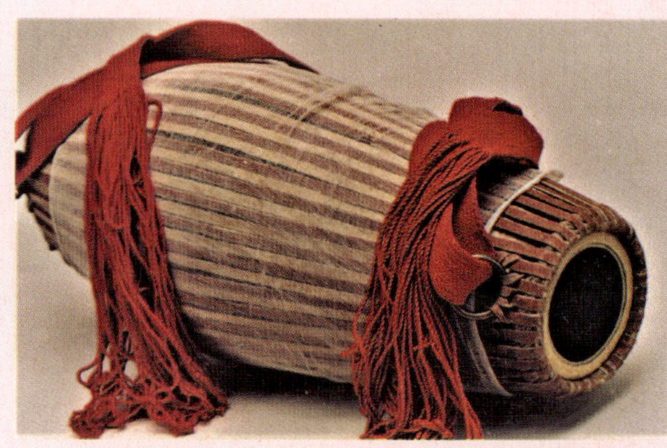

17.95: Pung, a traditional percussion instrument of Manipur used in Sankirtarna, Pung Cholam and other performances; made of softwood leather parchment and cotton

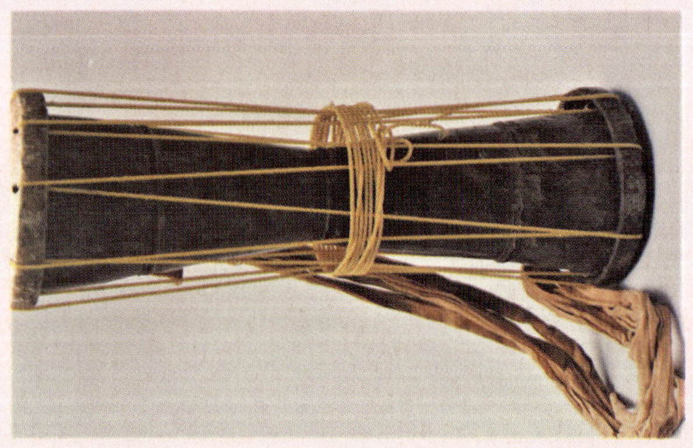

17.96: Thimla/Timla, an hourglass shaped percussion instrument of Kerala, often used in performances related to temple rites

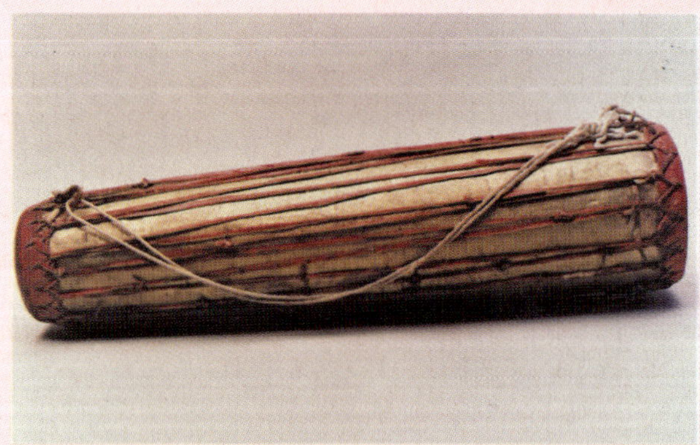

17.97: Dama of Meghalaya, a cylindrical bifacial percussion instrument with leather covered faces and red strap, popular in the tribal communities in hilly areas of Meghalaya and also in Tripura

Photographs — Courtesy, Sangeet Natak Akademi

18

Dances in Modern India

The yogi by controlling his breath and modifying his body, acquires the halo of sanctity. Even so the dancer, who dissolves her identity in rhythm and music, makes her body an instrument, at least for the duration of the dance, for the experience and expression of the spirit.

— Padma Vibhushan T. Balasaraswati, eminent Bharatanatyam dancer

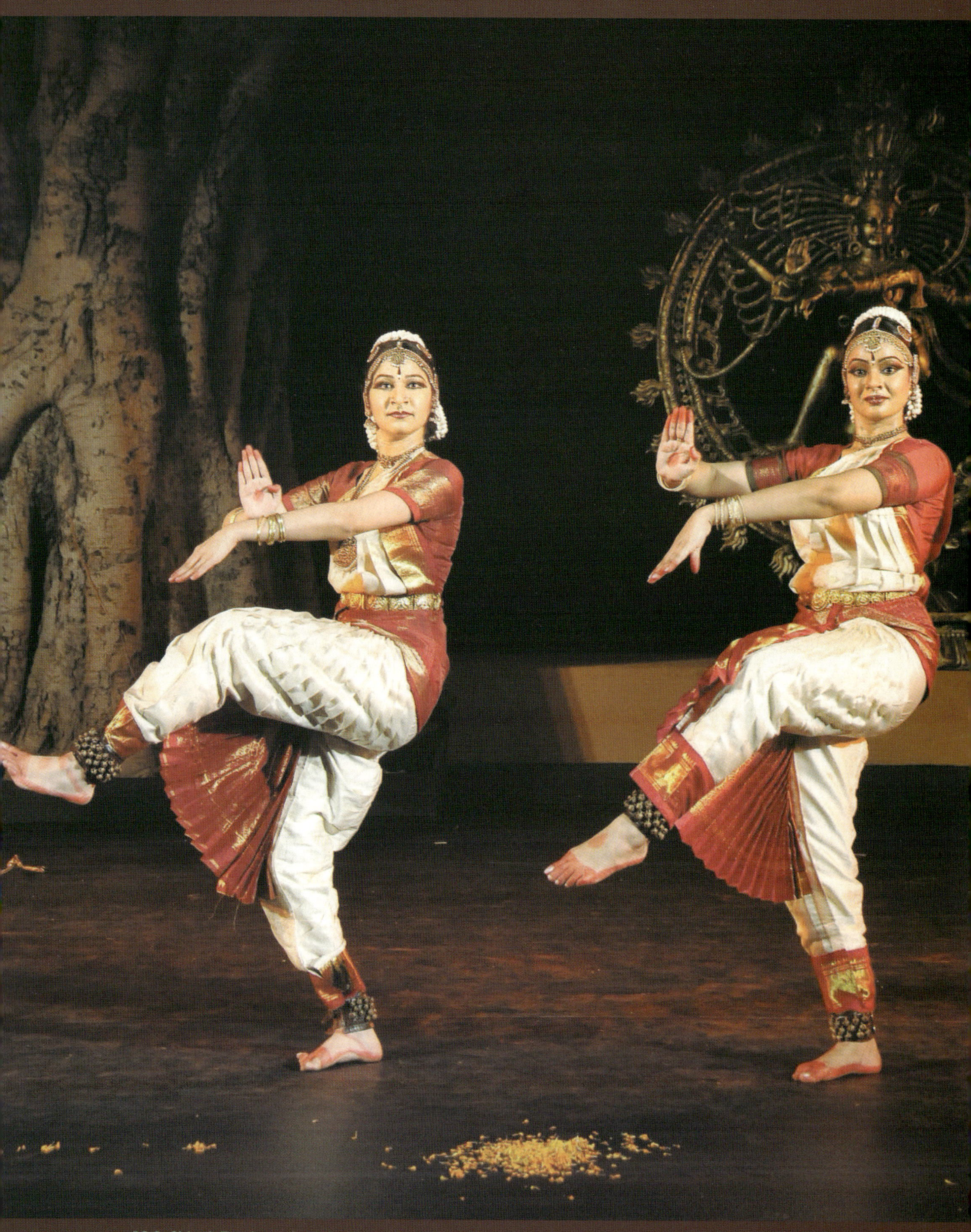

18.1: Shiva's Tandava depicted in a Bharatanatyam performance — Courtesy, Sangeet Natak Akademi

EVOLUTION AND CLASSIFICATION OF INDIAN DANCES

Dance in India, very much like music, is a rich and ancient tradition, tracing its origin to **Bharata's *Natyashastra*.** The ancient dances were classified in two broad categories, *Tandava* (masculine dances) and the *Lasya* (feminine dances). *Abhinaya Darpana* of **Nandikeshvara** identifies the three basic elements of dance; *Nritta, Nritya* and *Natya*. While *Nritta* refers to the **pure dance** implying the rhythmic and graceful body movements, *Nritya* refers to the **expressive part** of the performance which includes mudras, gestures, mime, etc., through which the emotions and sentiments are expressed. *Natya* refers to the **dance-drama** aspect of the performance through which the message or the story is conveyed. This includes the music, dialogue, costumes, symbolisms, stage effects, etc. *Sangita-Ratnakara* of **Sarangadeva** was another monumental work of the 13th century which documents the numerous dance forms. Thus, the Indian dances have inherited a wealth of ancient traditions. But over the years, they have also diversified, while absorbing the medieval influences and incorporating the regional culture. The dances of modern India can broadly be categorised into two types, (*a*) **Classical dances** and (*b*) **Folk and tribal dances.**

THE CLASSICAL DANCES

The term 'classical dances' are usually in reference to the dances which own their origin in theory or practice to the classical text of performing arts, the *Natyashastra*. Thus, the dances, their features, techniques, essential elements etc. were formalized and contained in the texts, or the *shastras*. These were distinct from the folk tradition of dances which was bereft of the pedagogical or formal learning and was more reflective of the microculture. Usually, eight forms of dances are recognised as the classical dances of India. These include, **Kathak, Odissi, Manipuri, Bharatanatyam, Kuchipudi, Kathakali, Mohiniattam** and **Sattriya**. As per some accounts, **Chhau** dance is also included in this category, however it is mostly considered as a folk-dance. While the ancient texts like *Natyashastra* and *Abhinaya Darpana* can be said to be the founding works of Indian dances, the medieval influences, the influence of the Islamic culture, the Bhakti movement, the temple practices and even the royal court influences, have had a significant bearing on their evolution. In the 18th and 19th centuries, many of these art forms withered. They were confined to the narrow domain of arts practiced by the courtesans and temple *devadasis* and were nearly lost, before being revived and brought in public domain in the modern times.

Kathak

The word 'Kathak' is derived from *Katha*, meaning a story. The dance originated as a narrative form of storytelling and is said to have developed as a form of narration of the epics and its tales by the ancient *kathakars* (story tellers and travelling bards). Mime and gestures are said to have later been incorporated in the art. It is recognised as one of the dance forms in *Sangita-Ratnakara* of Sarangadeva as early as the 13th century. Kathak became popular during the Vaishnavite wave of Bhakti movement as a narrative of Radha-Krishna love, particularly in the performance of the *Raas Leelas*. It was also a popular means of expression of the teachings in *padas* (verses) of the numerous Bhakti saints. Later, it flourished in the Mughal courts and emerged as an art of the royal milieu. Here, its character underwent a gradual shift to suit the taste of the courts and the changing need of the times. As it transited from a dance of the temple courtyards to that of the royal courts, it became a highly stylized art with the emphasis shifting to *nritya* (*bhava*), grace and sensuousness, from its earlier tradition of devotion. The themes of the *natya* gave way to pure dance of the *nritta* and the expressiveness of the *nritya*. In the nineteenth century, Jaipur, Raigarh and Lucknow emerged as its

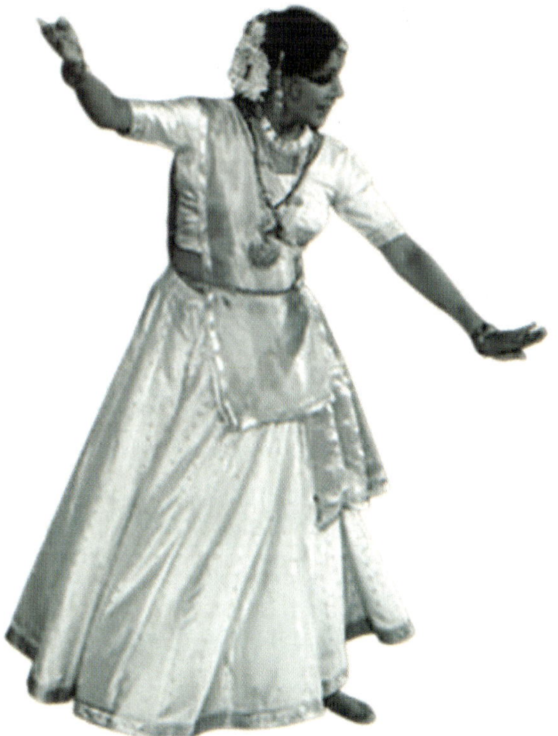

18.2: Shovana Narayan, an exponent of Kathak, in a performance — Wikimedia Commons

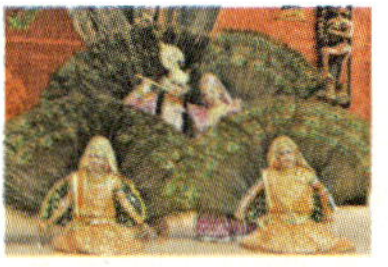

important centres. In the patronage of Kathak in the court of Wajid Ali Shah (last nawab of Oudh), the art saw the golden phase of its evolution. Thus, the art marks the **fusion of Indo-Islamic elements** of art and culture.

In the late 19th century, the association of this dance with *tawaifs* (courtesans) saw a misplaced opposition to the dance in the British rule, where the devotional character of the art was completely overlooked and it was mistakenly associated with eroticism and turpitude. However, in the 20th and 21st centuries, it has flourished through numerous public institutions, groups of dancers and even through the efforts of individual exponents like **Bindadin Maharaj** (1830-1918), **Kalka Prasad** (1850-1910), **Uday Shankar** (1900-1977) **Shambhu Maharaj** (1910-1970) and **Birju Maharaj** (1937-2022) amongst others. Today, it is widely popular in North India, particularly in the states of Uttar Pradesh, Delhi, Rajasthan, Madhya Pradesh, and some parts of western and eastern India. It has three distinct ***gharanas***; the **Lucknow**, the **Jaipur** and the **Benaras** *gharanas*. The Lucknow *gharana* which flourished under Wajid Ali Shah, and the Benaras *gharana,* are known for expressiveness of the moods and emotions (*bhava*), while the Jaipur gharana stresses on *laya* (rhythm).

Features of the dance

Kathak is a dance characterised by its circular pirouettes and dexterous footwork, which are often considered its distinguishing features. Use of *ghungroos* (ankle bells) by the dancers and rhythm-play, are some other significant elements of this art. It is based on a dance vocabulary which draws its expression from a variety of gestures and movements. These include the gestures of fingers and arms, upper body movement, facial and eye expressions, movements of neck and eyebrows and the stage movements, including bends and turns. Unlike some other classical dances, the legs and torso are generally straight. The dance is performed to the accompaniment of different Hindustani classical music and to the accompaniment of musical instruments like tabla, *pakhawaz, manjira, sarangi*, harmonium etc. *Thumri,* in particular, is a popular genre of accompanying music, the creative lyricism of which brings out the numerous hues of romantic love.

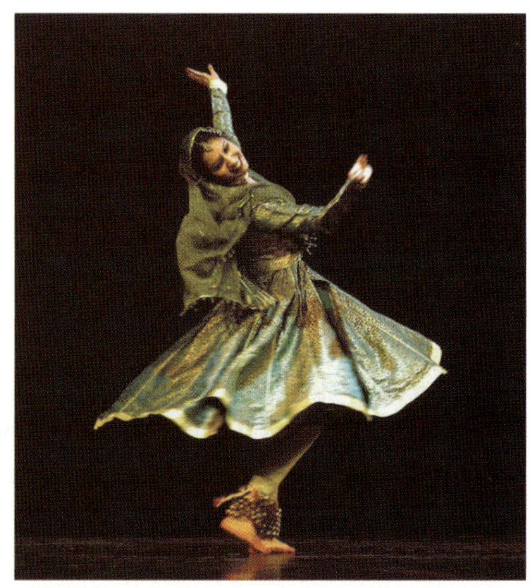

18.3: An artist performing circular pirouette of Kathak — Wikimedia Commons

The performance of Kathak consist of three main sections namely, ***vandana*** or (the invocation)/***salami*** (salutation), ***nritta*** or one pure (abstract) dance recital, and ***nritya*** or the expressive dance. The important elements of dance performance include ***amad*** (entry), ***salami*** (salutation), ***thaat*** (soft gliding movements), ***tukada, tora*** etc. or cadences which are fast rhythmic but small pieces of performance. The latter are usually a part of *nritta* or pure dance, which is performed on a *nagma* (a composition). Another sequence of performance is ***gata or gatabhava,*** which is *nritya* devoid of words. The performance is to a gentle rhythm to short narrative pieces such as episodes of Krishna Leela. *Nayakibheda* or representations of the eight types of *nayika*, is also a subject often related to the *gata* performance. The ***abhinaya*** performance of the *nritya* is done on various kinds of classical music. *Thumri*, *bhajan*, *dadra* and *ghazal* are some of the lyrical composition-based sequences in the *nritya* performance which may see a word to word or line to line synchronization of the dance.

Modern exponents

Some of the exponents of this dance in modern times include; **Uday Shankar** (1900-1977; Sangeet Natak Akademi and Padma Vibhushan awardee), **Shambhu Maharaj** (1910-1970; Sangeet Natak Akademi and Padma Shri awardee), **Sitara Devi** (1920- 2014, Sangeet Natak Akademi and Padma Shri awardee, Padma Bhushan declined), **Gopi Krishna (**1935-2014, Sangeet Natak Akademi and Padma Shri awardee), **Birju Maharaj** (1937–2022, Sangeet Natak Akademi and Padma Vibhushan awardee), **Puru Dadheech** (1939; Sangeet Natak Akademi and Padma Shri awardee), **Uma Sharma** (1942; Sangeet Natak Akademi and Padma Bhushan awardee), **Shovana Narayan** (1950, Sangeet Natak Akademi and Padma Shri awardee), **Prerana Shrimali** (1959; Sangeet Natak Akademi awardee) etc.

Odissi

This classical dance form originated in the region comprising the present day state of **Odisha.** It is a very ancient art form the origin of which can be traced to a period nearly 2000 years ago. Reference to it is

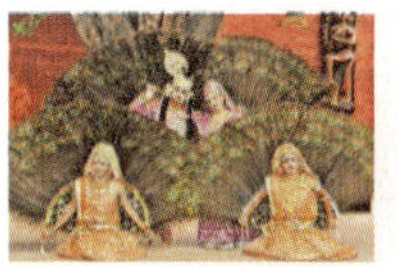

found in the Udayagiri and Khandagiri caves of 2nd century BCE in the ancient text *Natyashastra* as *Odhra-Magadhi,* a precursor to Odissi. Reference to Kathak is also seen in the hall of dance (*nata mandap*) at Sun temple at Konark built in the 13th century, besides in other temples of the region. In the medieval period, this dance was performed by the ***maharis*** or the ***devadasis*** (temple dancers) in the temples as a veneration of the deity. But later, these dancers got employed in the royal courts, leading to the degeneration of the art form. Subsequently, a class of boys called ***gotipuas*** was trained in this art, who performed in the temples and even outside it. In the British rule, the art was suppressed and suffered a decline. However, in the 20th century the art form has again been revived. It has also been remolded as a theatre art and integrated with the extant art of the region, the medieval sculptures of Odisha, its painting and literature etc. In this endeavour of revival, besides the institutional framework provided to the various classical dances, especially noteworthy are the individual efforts of **Pankaj Charan Das** (considered adiguru of Odissi in the 20th century), **Kavichandra Kalicharan Pattanayak** (an Oriya poet, dramatist and researcher who is said to have coined the term Odissi) and **Kelucharan Mahapatra** (Odissi performer and guru).

Odissi has evolved as a **temple dance** and the soul of the art continues to be the Vaishnava faith expressing the love and lore of **Radha and Krishna**. Lyrics of love from *Gita-Govinda* of **Jayadeva** and songs of medieval Oriya poets like **Upendra Bhanja** (17th century) and Banamali Dasa (18th century) find an expression in this art. It closely follows the tenets as brought out in the *Natyashastra*, *Abhinaya Darpana* and other texts and integrated them in its grammar of hand gestures, footwork and body movement. As a dance depicting love and passion, the *Nritta* and *Nritya* aspects are fully integrated in the performance. The facial expressions (*bhava*), the hand gestures and the body movements are together channelised by the performer to depict this and the other rasas.

Features of the dance

The primary units of Odissi are referred to as the ***bhanga***. These combine the units of body position *(belis)* and body movements in a variety of ways. Based on these, the primary postures of dance are ***chowk*** and ***tribhanga***. The *chowk* is a masculine stance which is imitating a square, where the weight is equally balanced on both the legs (also referred to as *sambhanga*). The *tribhanga* is a feminine and more graceful stance. Here, the body is bent/deflected at three positions; at the neck, torso, and knee (*tri-bhanga*: thrice-bent). The other basic elements of dance include, hand-gestures or *hastas*, footwork/foot gestures or *pada-bheda*, gaits and walks or *chalis*, and spins called *bhramaris*. The movements in the dance are soft and graceful and the performance is to the accompaniment of Odissi music on instruments like *pakhawaj*, flute, *manjira* and *sitar*.

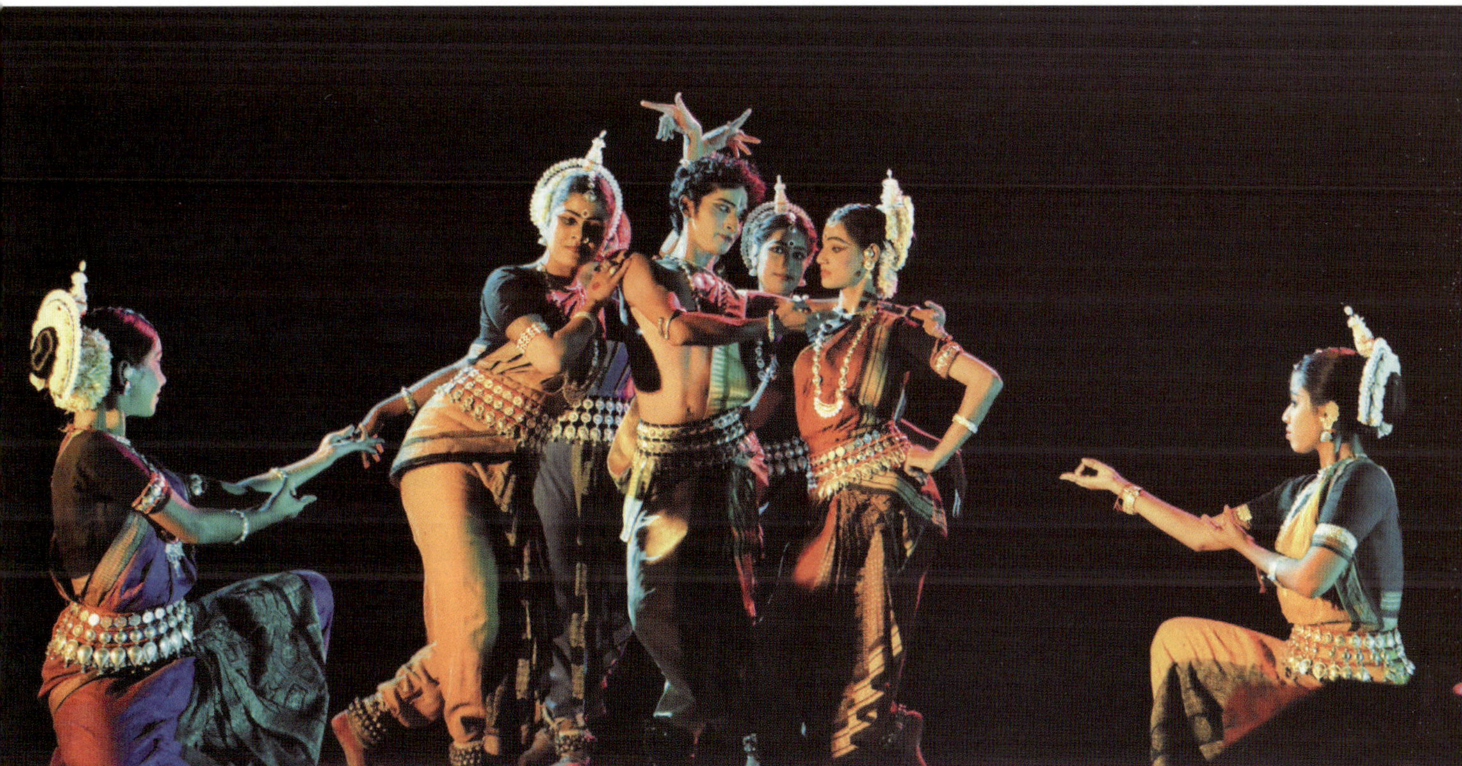

18.4: An Odissi dance performance depicting the *nritta* and *nritya* aspects — Courtesy, Department of Tourism, Odisha

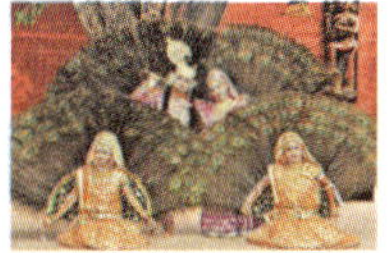

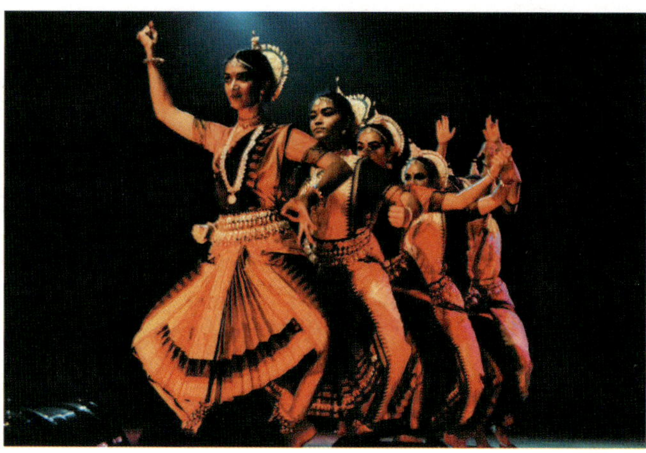

18.5: An Odissi performance bringing out the *chowk* posture — Courtesy, Department of Tourism, Odisha

An important constituent of an Odissi performance is the ***mangalacharan***, which marks the graceful entry of the dancer on stage, with flowers in her hands, making an offering (primarily to mother earth). This is followed by the invocation of the deity and ends with ***nritta*** (a pure dance sequence) involving salutation through ***trikhandi pranam*** (three-fold salutation) to *devas* (gods), guru and *lokas* and *rasikas* (fellow dancers and audience). The next step is called ***batu*** or the performance of basic steps of the *nritta* and highlighting the pure dance technique. This step of dance is in honour of lord Shiva and is to the accompaniment of fast paced music without any song or recitation. *Nritya*, which follows, incorporates *abhinaya* and marks the main feature of performance. It may be based on the compositions of *Gita-Govinda,* epics or other compositions of Odiya poets. ***Pallavi*** is the concluding item of the performance which is based on *abhinaya* and brings the element of *natya* or dance-drama. With more than one such item, it is called ***moksha,*** the climax of the performance, which signifies the objective of attaining salvation through the devotional performance. Thus, the art combines all the three elements of *Nritti, Nritya* and *Natya.*

Modern exponents

Its famous exponents include **Pankaj Charan Das** (1919-2003, Sangeet Natak Akademi and Padma Shri awardee), **Kelucharan Mohapatra** (1926-2004, Sangeet Natak Akademi and Padma Vibhushan awardee), **Deba Prasad Dasa** (1932-1986 Sangeet Natak Akademi awardee), **Sanjukta Panigrahi** (1944-1997 Sangeet Natak Akademi and Padma Shri awardee), **Sonal Mansingh** (1944; Sangeet Natak Akademi and Padma Vibhushan awardee), **Kumkum Mohanty** (1946; Sangeet Natak Akademi and Padma Shri awardee), **Gangadhar Pradhan** (1948, Sangeet Natak Akademi and Padma Shri awardee), **Geeta Mahalik** (1948; Sangeet Natak Akademi and Padma Shri awardee), **Kiran Segal** (Sangeet Natak Akademi and Padma Shri awardee), **Sharmila Biswas** (Sangeet Natak Akademi awardee), **Ratikant Mohapatra** (Sangeet Natak Akademi awardee), **Ranjana Gauhar** (Sangeet Natak Akademi and Padma Shri awardee), **Sharmila Mukherjee** amongst others.

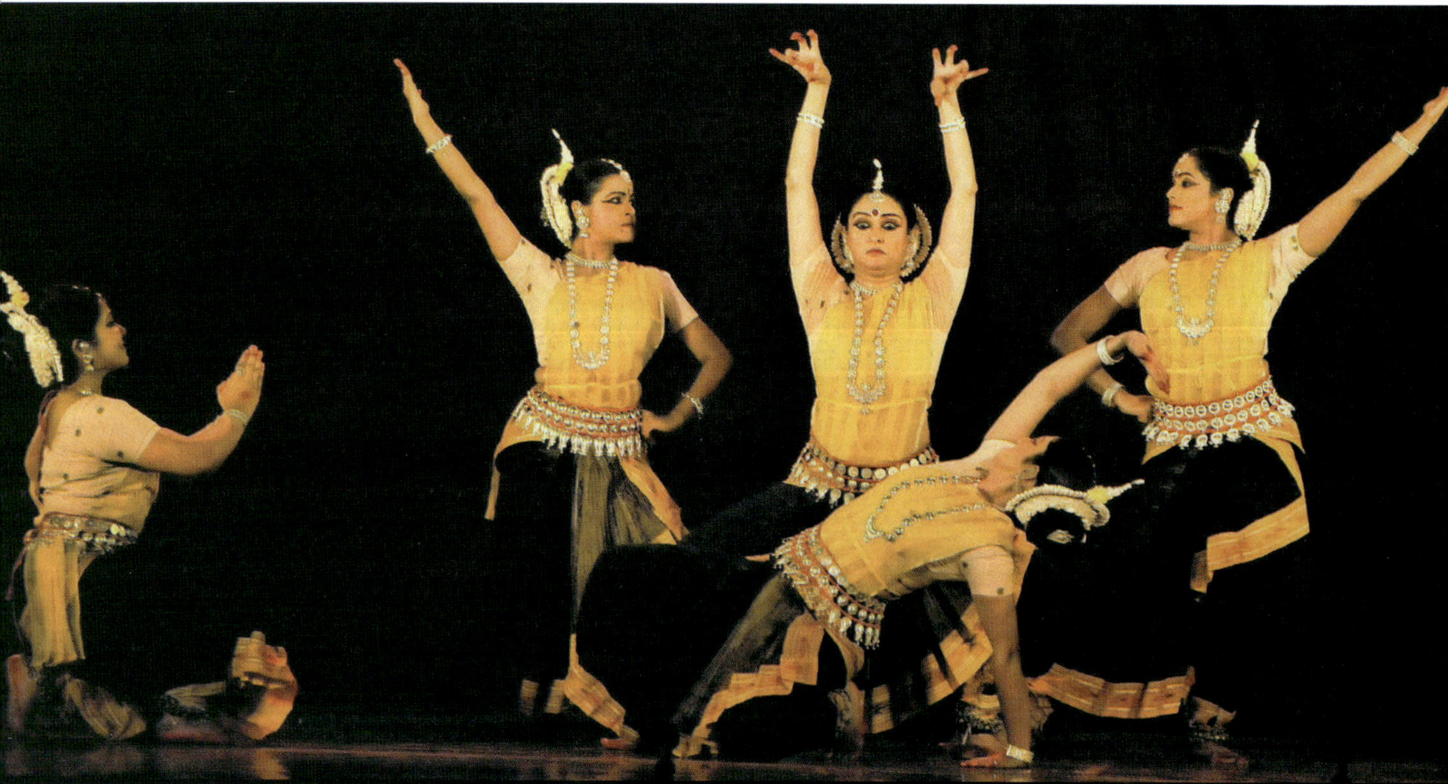

18.6: An Odissi dance performance by Sharmila Mukherjee — Courtesy, Sangeet Natak Akademi

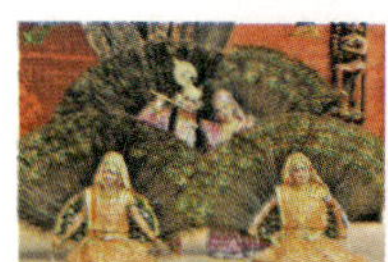

Sattriya

Sattriya is a **classical dance of Assam** which has its origin in Krishna Bhakti Vaishnavism. This dance is attributed to the 15th century Bhakti saint and reformer **Sri Sankardev**, and was a **means of propagation of the Vaishnava faith**.

The word *Sattriya* originated from *Sattara*, which were the monasteries or temples where the dance originated. The dances were performed by the Vaishnava monks, hence the dance form is **ritualistic** and has a **temple origin**. In the year 2000, it was recognized as a classical dance by the Sangeet Natak Akademi.

The dance and its elements trace its origin to the ancient text *Natya Shastra* and other texts. It borrows from the then extant dance traditions of the region which includes *Vyah Goa Oja-pali* (a Vaishnava dance tradition) as well as the *Devadasi* dance tradition of the region. Besides, elements of folk dances and other new features were also incorporated in it by Sankaradev.

18.7: Sattriya Dance, *Bishnu-Sayan* posture, depicting lord Vishnu resting on the Sheshnaag — Wikimedia Commons

In its repertoire, Sattriya includes all the three aspects of *nritta*, *nritya* and *natya*. It also incorporates one act plays which are called **Ankiya-Nat** which is a ballad form of dance-drama combining the religious as well as aesthetic elements. The themes are often related to Lord Krishna or other avatars of Lord Vishnu, besides stories from the epics of Ramayana and Mahabharata. The dance was traditionally performed by the male monks in groups. However, in its modern versions female dancers also perform.

Features of the dance

The fundamental unit of dance and the basic exercises of the dance grammar are called ***Mati-akhara/ Mati-akhora***. These are 64 in number and are similar to the classification as in *Natya Shastra*. They are further subdivided into pure exercises and basic dance units. Sattriya has principles strictly laid down with respect to *Aharyas* (attire), music, footwork, *hast mudras* (hand postures) and other aspects of dance. Like other classical dances, it also incorporates the *Lasya* (feminine) and *Tandava* (male) elements of dance. Over the period, it has evolved in two streams; the first is the ***Bhaona*** related repertoire which includes the ***Gayan-Bhayandar Nach*** and the ***Kharmanar Nach***. The second incorporates dances which are independent such as ***Chali, Jhumura, Nadu Bhangi*** and others. While *Chali* is considered to be more graceful and elegant, the *Jhumura* is the more energetic of the dances.

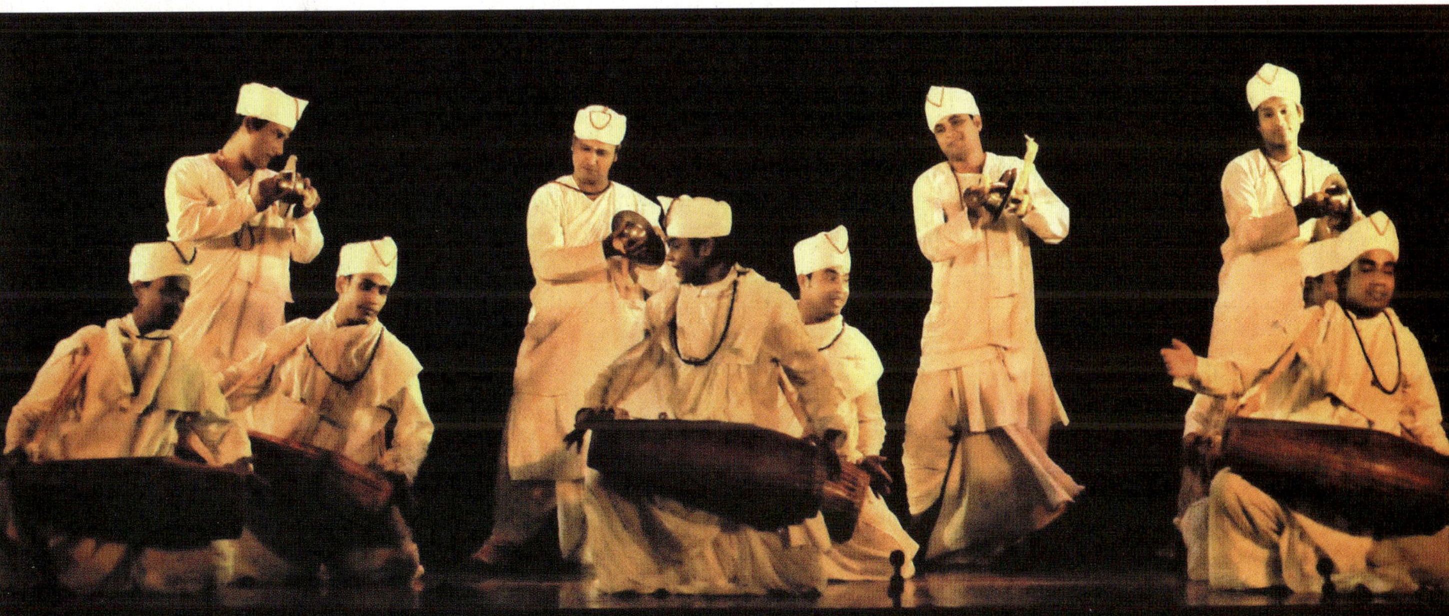

18.8: A Sattriya dance and Gayan Bhayandar nach — Courtesy, Sangeet Natak Akademi

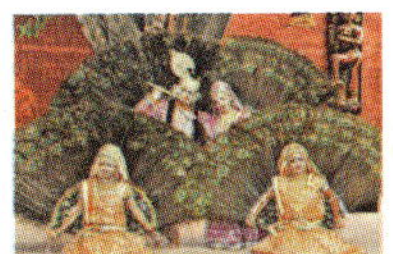

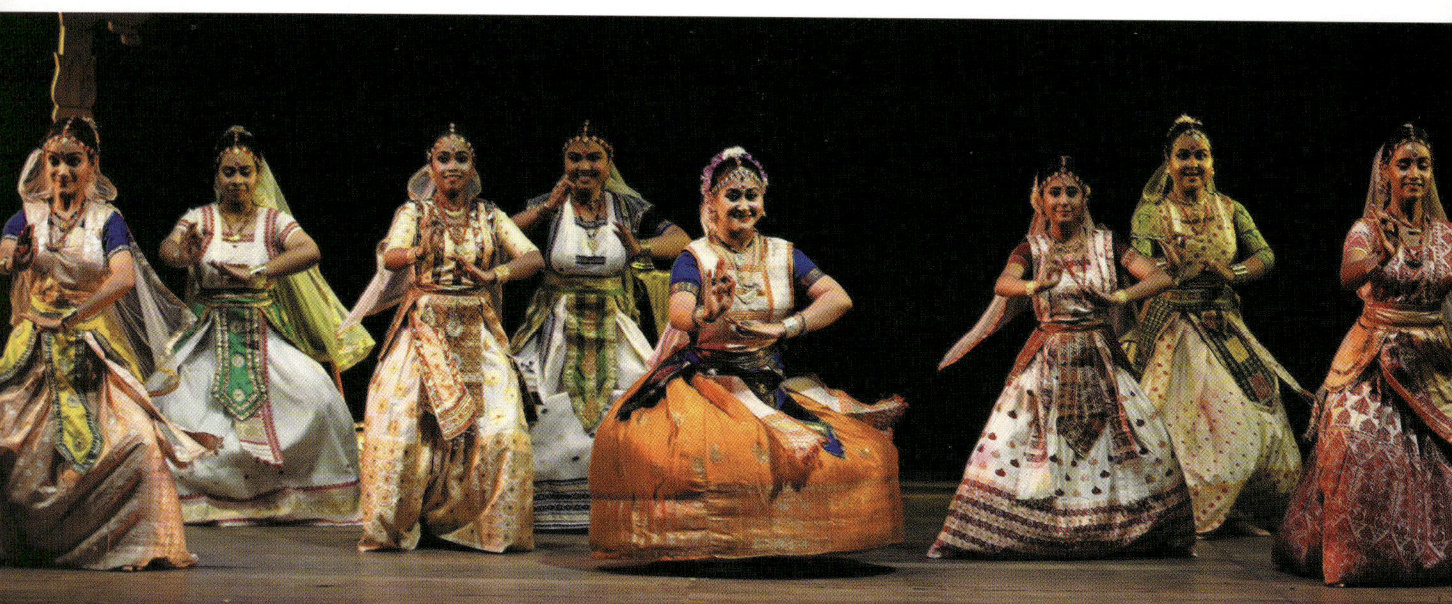

18.9: A Sattriya dance performance — Courtesy, Sangeet Natak Akademi

Sattriya dance is performed to the accompaniment of *Borgeets* which were composed by Sri Sankardev and other saints. *Khol* (two faced asymmetrical drums), *tala* instruments (cymbals) such as *bhortal, manjira* and *bihutal*, besides flute and other traditional instruments, are a part of the performance. Harmonium and violin are modern additions to the repertoire of accompanying instruments.

Modern exponents

Its exponents include **Jatin Goswami** (1933; Sangeet Natak Akademi and Padma Shri awardee), **Pradip Chaliha** (Sangeet Natak Akademi awardee), **Indira PP Bora** (1943; Sangeet Natak Akademi and Padma Shri awardee), **Ghanakanta Bora** (1950; Sangeet Natak Akademi and Padma Shri awardee), **Sharodi Saikia** (Sangeet Natak Akademi awardee), **Ramakrishna Talukdar** (1963; Sangeet Natak Akademi awardee), **Haricharan Bhuyan Borabayan** (Sangeet Natak Akademi awardee), **Anwesa Mahanta** amongst others.

Manipuri

This classical dance evolved in the state of Manipur (a state in Northeast India). The art is centuries old and traces its origin to *Natyashastra*. It is a **religious art** which is rooted in the **Vaishnava tradition** of the ethnic people of the Manipur valley (the *Meiteis*). As per scholars, the dance predates even the medieval Vaishnavite influence as it is associated and performed during the Manipuri festival of **Lai-Haraoba** which has an ancient tradition. During the festival, the priest (*maiba*) and priestess (*maibi*) enact creation of the universe. With the medieval Vaishnavite influence (15th century), compositions based on the lore of Radha and Krishna was introduced. In the 18th century, under the king Bhagyachandra, the concept of dance-drama (*natya*) in the format of Krishna Leela and Raas Leela, were introduced with elaborate costume and makeup. This is considered the golden period of the Manipuri *Raas Leela* dance. In the late 19th century, with the annexation of Manipur by the British, the dance suffered a decline. It was revived in the 20th century due to the efforts of Rabindranath Tagore. Other exponents and gurus of this art form including Naba Kumar, Senarik Singh Rajkumar, Nileshwar Mukherji and Atomba Singh, amongst others.

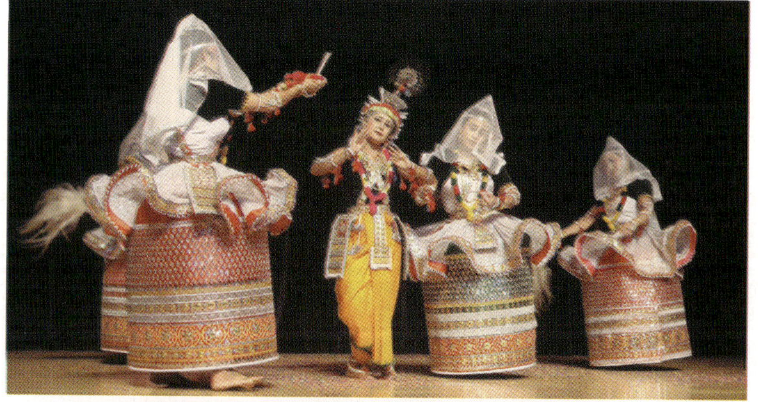

18.10: Manipuri *Raas Leela* performance in traditional costumes — Wikimedia Commons

Although the Raas-Leela is the mainstay of the classical Manipuri dance, it also includes dances pertaining to Shaivism (worship of Lord Shiva) and Shaktism. The Manipuri dance incorporates three dance forms, (*a*) **Rasa** or **Raasleela** which depicts the love of Radha and Krishna; (*b*) **Sankirtan** which is a devotional kirtan form of dance and (*c*) **Thang Ta** (also called Thang Pah) which

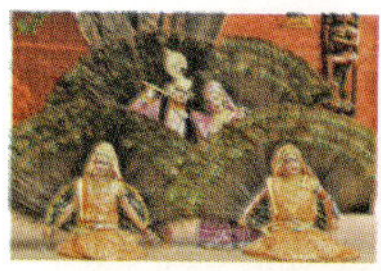

is a martial art form of dance. The **Rasa** dances are mainly of five types, four of which are performed in specific seasons, while the fifth can be performed in any season. The **Basant Raas** is performed on full moon in the spring time on arrival of the festival of Holi. **Maha Raas** is also performed on full moon in the period of November-December. The other three, **Nitya Raas**, **Kunj Raas** and **Diba Raas**, are performed during the day time. However, in all the rasas the predominant theme is that of the love of Radha and Krishna, with the separation of Krishna from other gopikas, their longing, desire and dejection also being depicted.

Features of the dance

In the Manipuri *Rasa* dances, the basic movement of dance is termed as *chali* or *chari*. The dancing technique involves depiction of the *rasa* using the **entire movement of the body**. There is no undue emphasis on facial expression or the *bhava* to express the *rasa*. Rather, the dancer may not even make an eye contact with the audience. Further, there is no use of ankle-bells (*ghungroo*), while the footwork is gentle. The stage movements also involve the movement of the whole body, thus distinguishing it from the other classical dance forms. Besides, the indigenous dance costume, particularly that of the women artists is unique and comprises the embroidered stiff skirt, light muslin garment on top, a white veil and Manipuri jewellery.

Pung Cholam and **Kartal Cholam** which are vigorous and acrobatic dances with the *pung* (drum) and *kartal* (cymbal) in hand, may serve as a prelude to the main performance of the *rasa*/*raas* dance. The **Raas Leela** is performed in three different styles and includes; the ***Tal Rasak***-which is accompanied with clapping; ***Danda Rasak***-which involves synchronous beats of the sticks; and the ***Mandal Rasak***-which involves *gopis* encircling Krishna. The **Manipuri Rasa** also incorporates the styles of *Tandava* (vigorous male dancer style) and *Lasya* (delicate style of females depicting Radha and other *gopis*). Overall, the dance incorporates a wavelike movement with one movement merging into other. Traditional instruments like *pung* (barrel drum), *kartals* (cymbals), harmonium, flute, etc. are used for the accompanying music.

Modern exponents

Besides the revivalists of this art in the early 20th century, the other exponents include, **Guru Bipin Singh** (1918-2000; Sangeet Natak Akademi awardee), **Elam Endira Devi** (1954; Padma Shri awardee), **Darshana Jhaveri** (1940; Sangeet Natak Akademi and Padma Shri awardee), **Yumlembam Gambhini Devi** (1945; Sangeet Natak Akademi and Padma Shri awardee) amidst others.

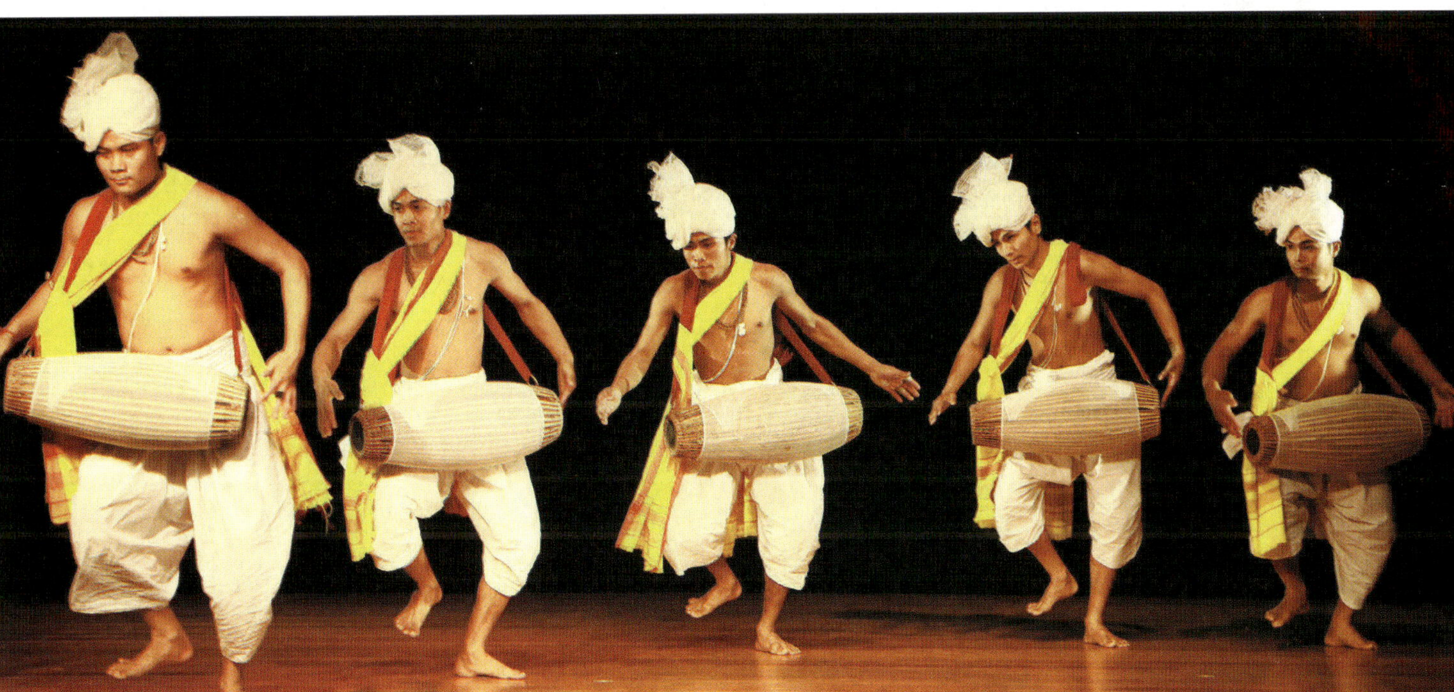

18.11: A Manipuri Pung Cholam performance — Courtesy, Sangeet Natak Akademi

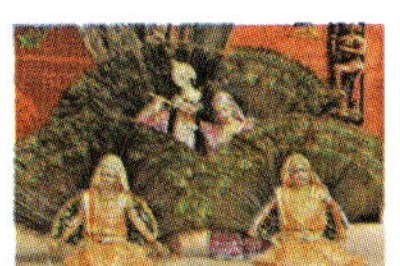

Bharatanatyam

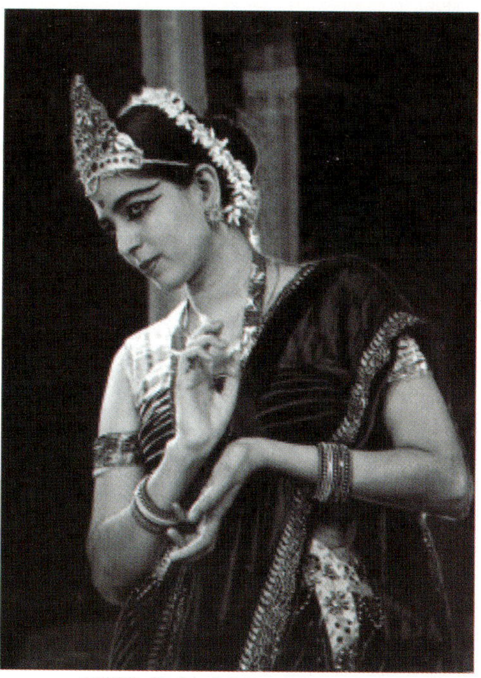

18.12: Rukmini Devi Arundale in a Bharatanatyam posture — Wikimedia Commons

Popular in **Tamil Nadu** and adjoining regions, Bharatanatyam is among the most ancient of Indian classical dance forms. Its origin can be traced to Bharata's *Natyashastra*. Reference to it is also found in Nandikeshvara's *Abhinaya Darpana*. The historical text *Silappadikaram* (2nd century CE) also has a direct reference to this dance thus making this dance form nearly two millenniums old. Besides, elements of this art are also seen in sculptures in the Chidambaram temple.

Bharatanatyam is essentially a **temple dance** art which was preserved through the ***Devadasi* system**. The *Devadasis* were women dedicated to the temple and married to the God and performed the art as a means of veneration of the deity. The dance was hence also known as *Dasi Attam*. But after the Devadasi system was banned by the British in around 1910, the art form declined. It was again revived in the 20th century and refashioned as a theatre art. The efforts of **Meenakshisundaram Pillai** (1869-1964) **E. Krishna Iyer** (1897-1968), **Rukmini Devi Arundale, T. Balasaraswati,** and **Yamini Krishnamurthy** are especially significant in preservation and popularisation of this art.

Bharatanatyam incorporates all the three elements of dance, viz. ***Nritta*** (pure dance), ***Nritya*** (solo and expressive dance), and ***Natya*** (dance-drama) and is set on the principles as prescribed in the Bharata's *Natyashashtra* and other classic texts. The dance is often descriptive and even interpretive of the mythological legends, anecdotes and even concepts and ideas form the Hindu texts. The dance themes may vary from devotion and divine love to *shringara* and romantic love. It is traditionally performed by women, where a dancer may undertake many roles and hence also known as *ekaharya*. The performance also involves emphasis on ***abhinaya*** (mime). This includes gestures, movement of hands, and expression of eyes and facial muscles. The ***Ardhamandala*** *(partial squat)* which involves the bending of knee with equal distribution of weight on both legs, is a typical posture. There is much emphasis on **rhythmic footwork.**

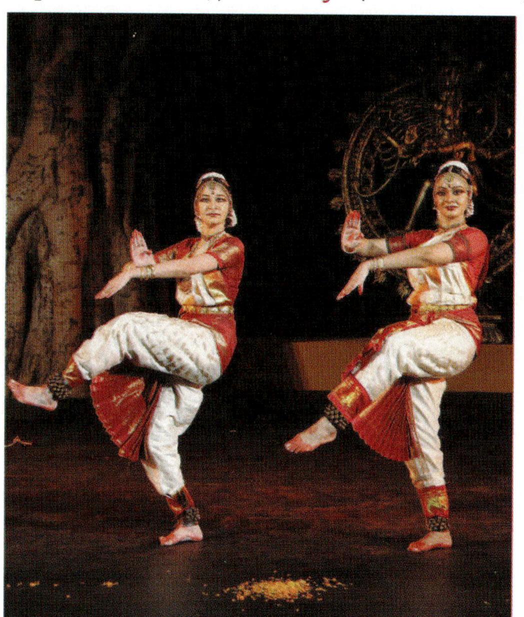

18.13: Display of Shiva's Tandava in a Bharatanatyam Performance — Courtesy, Sangeet Natak Akademi

Bharatanatyam is performed to the accompaniment of **Carnatic music** and has a rich repertoire of songs in Tamil, Telugu and Sanskrit. Many of the musical compositions of Bharatnatyam and its format of recital were composed in the 19th century by the famed quartet of Ponniah, Chinnaiah, Sivanandam and Vadivelu. The performance includes at least one vocalist, while the musical accompaniment is done on traditional instruments like **mridangam** (drum), **nadaswaram** (a long pipe), **nattuvangam** (cymbals), **veena**, flute, etc. Usually, the performance includes a dance conductor called **Nattuvanar** who recites the dance syllables and plays bronze cymbals.

Features of the dance

The performance of Bharatanatyam begins with ***Alarippu,*** an invocatory pure dance, which literally means, to adorn with flowers. Next in the sequence is ***Jatiswaram,*** a short pure dance (*nritta*) performed to the accompaniment of notes of a *raga* of Carnatic music which is bereft of any words (*sahitya*). This part of performance comprises *adavus* which are smaller pure dance sequences. ***Shabdam*** follows next, where the dancer expresses the *sahitya* (spoken words) through *abhinaya* (mime) aspect of the *nritya* (dance with expressions). This portion of the dance performance is in adoration of the Supreme. ***Varnam,*** the next part of Bharatanatyam, is the most significant composition signifying the very essence of this

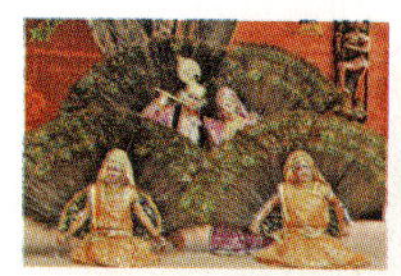

dance and exhibiting both the *nritta* and *nritya* aspects. The artist expresses the *sahitya* (the spoken words) by means of complicated and rhythmic patterns of dance in different speeds. Thus, the dexterity of *nritta* and expressiveness of *abhinaya* are fused in a creative

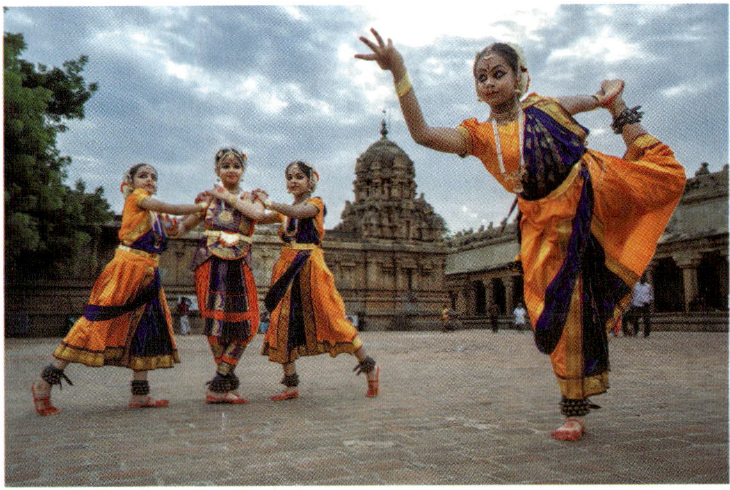

18.14: A Bharatanatyam dance performance by girls in a temple precinct — Courtesy, Tamil Nadu Tourism Development Corporation

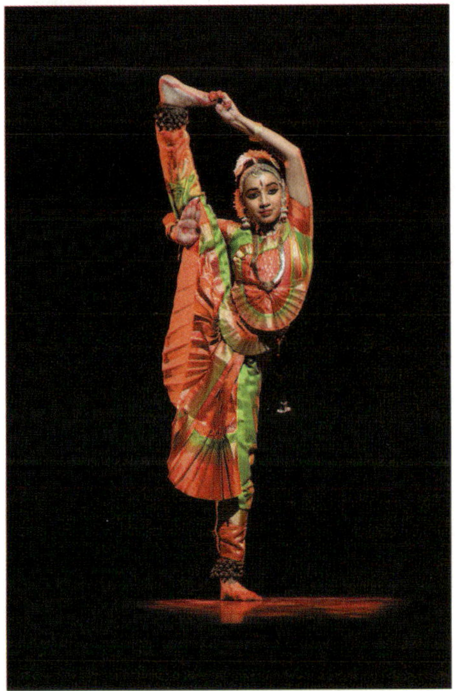

18.15: A Bharatanatyam performance — Courtesy, Tamil Nadu Tourism Development Corporation

choreography. Pursuant to it, the performance includes a number of *abhinaya* based items which explore different moods and *rasas* and include ***keertanam***, ***kritis***, ***padams*** and ***javalis.*** While in the ***keertanam*** the *sahitya* is of greater importance, in the composition of the ***kritis,*** the musical aspect assumes greater significance. These are of devotional characters based on mythological episodes connected with lord Vishnu, lord Shiva etc. ***Padam*** and ***Javalis*** are performed on the theme of love and often this love is of the divine. ***Tillana*** is the final part of the performance which incorporates a vibrant dance. It is to the accompaniment of music syllables with limited *sahitya*. *Mangalam (or Shlokam)* is the concluding portion which invokes the blessings of the Supreme.

Bharatanatyam: A Spiritual Journey

Bharatanatyam is an art which consecrates the body which in itself is considered to be of no value. The yogi by controlling his breath and modifying his body acquires the halo of sanctity. Even so the dancer, who dissolves her identity in rhythm and music, makes her body an instrument, at least for the duration of the dance, for the experience and expression of the spirit. The traditional order of Bharatanatyam recital viz. *alarippu*, *jatiswaram*, *varnam*, *padams*, *tillana* and the *shloka* is the correct sequence in the practice of this art, which is an artistic Yoga, for revealing the spiritual through the corporeal.

—T Balasaraswati, in her address in Tamil Isai Sangam in 1975

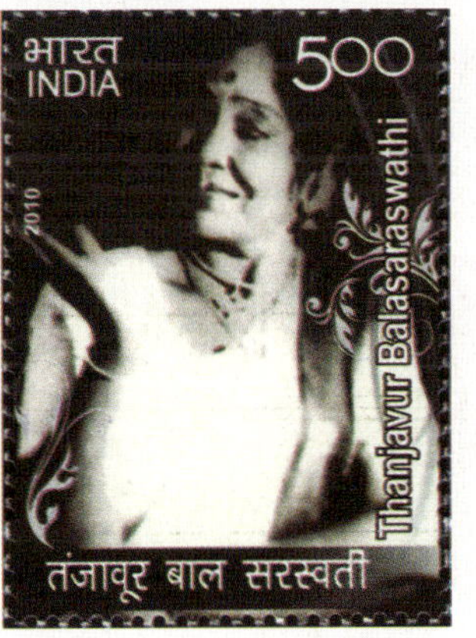

18.16: T. Balasaraswati, a stamp released in 2010 — Courtesy, Department of Post

Modern exponents

The exponents of this dance form are **Rukmini Devi Arundale** (1904-1986; Sangeet Natak Akademi and Padma Bhushan awardee) **T. Balasaraswati** (1918-1984, Sangeet Natak Akademi and Padma Vibhushan awardee), **Mrinalini Sarabhai** (1918-2016; Sangeet Natak Akademi and Padma Bhushan awardee) **Yamini Krishnamurthy** (1940; Sangeet Natak Akademi Padma Vibhushan awardee), **Sonal Mansingh** (1944; Sangeet Natak Akademi and Padma Vibhushan awardee), **Mallika Sarabhai** (1954; Sangeet Natak Akademi and Padma Bhushan awardee), and **S. Kanaka** (1947; Sangeet Natak Akademi and Padma Shri awardee) amongst others.

Kuchipudi

This classical dance form is popular in Andhra Pradesh, Telangana, and adjoining regions. It traces its roots to the ancient text *Natyashastra*. The modern version of the art is said to have originated in a village Kuchipudi in the Krishna district in the 17th century, under the aegis of a Vaishnava saint Siddhendra

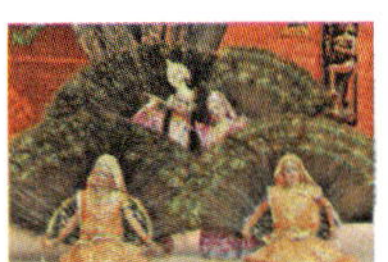

Yogi who formalized this art. One of his earliest works was the composition of a dance-drama called *Bhamaakalaapam*, based on the legend of Lord Krishna fetching the *parijata* flower for his beloved queen Satyabhama. Thus, this art form evolved as a dance-drama and themes from Krishna Leela and other Vaishnava traditions were performed. In the formative years the *Brahmin* boys were trained in this art, who also played the part of the female characters. Later, in the British rule, this dance suffered a decline like other temple dances which were banned. Subsequently, in the early 20th century, due to efforts of many reformers, chiefly **Vempati Venkatanarayan** (1871-1935), **Chinta Venkataramayya** (1860-1949) and **V. Lakshminarayan Shastry** (1886-1956), this art was revived. The latter also incorporated many new elements in it, including solo-dance and also trained female artists to perform this art.

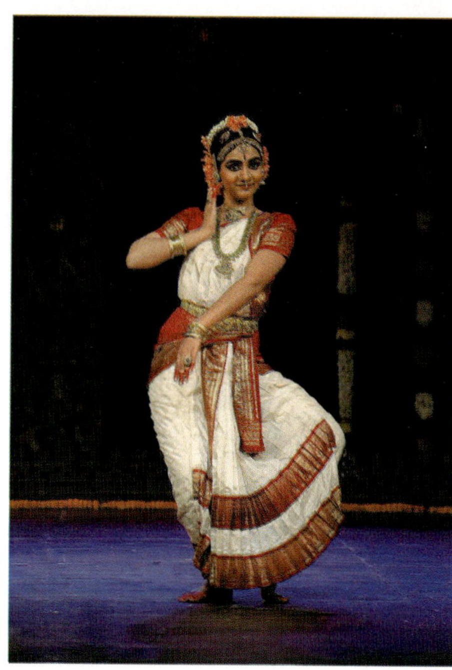

18.17: Kuchipudi performer in a *tribhanga* posture — Wikimedia Commons

Kuchipudi involves all the three elements of dance viz. ***Nritta***, ***Nritya***, and ***Natya***. It involves substantial stage movement and dexterous footwork. The style is quite expressive with use of gestures of hand, and expressions of eyes and face.

Some features of the dance form are similar to that of Bharatanatyam such as *ardhamandala* which is a partial squat with legs bent. However, while Bharatanatyam is a dance of temple tradition, where emphasis on geometric perfection and spiritual aspect is more, Kuchipudi is more sensuous with more supple body movements. Some performances exhibit dancing with several pots on their head or dancing on the rim of a brass plate.

Features of the dance

The performance of Kuchipudi begins with ***Ganesha Vandana*** or invocation. At this stage the performers in the drama are also introduced by stating their roles and who perform a short preliminary dance called *dharavu*. Next comes ***jatiswaram***, a *nritta* performance which is an abstract dance and is non-narrative. ***Shabdam*** which follows, is a narrative performance where rhythmic hand gestures are also employed to express the story. The subsequent part ***Tarangam*** of the performance comprises *Nrityaabhinaya* which is based on literary cum musical forms such as *padam, jaavli, shlokam* etc. The concluding portion of the dance is ***tarangam***. The dance is performed to the **accompaniment of Carnatic music** where the vocals are in Telugu language. Instruments like *mridangam*, *veena*, cymbal, flute, etc. are also used as accompaniment.

Modern exponents

The well-known exponents of Kuchipudi are **Vempati Chinna Satyam** (1929-2012; Sangeet Natak Akademi and Padma Bhushan awardee), **Indrani Rahman** (1930-1999; Sangeet Natak Akademi and Padma Shri awardee), **Yamini Krishnamurthy** (1940; Sangeet Natak Akademi and Padma Vibhushan awardee), **Raja Reddy** (1943) & **Radha Reddy** (1955) (duo are Sangeet Natak Akademi and Padma Bhushan awardees), **Veernala Jayarama Rao** (1951; Sangeet Natak Akademi Padma Bhushan awardee), **Sobha Naidu** (1956-2020; Sangeet Natak Akademi Padma Bhushan awardee), **Swapna Sundari** (Sangeet Natak Akademi Padma Bhushan awardee) amongst others.

Kathakali

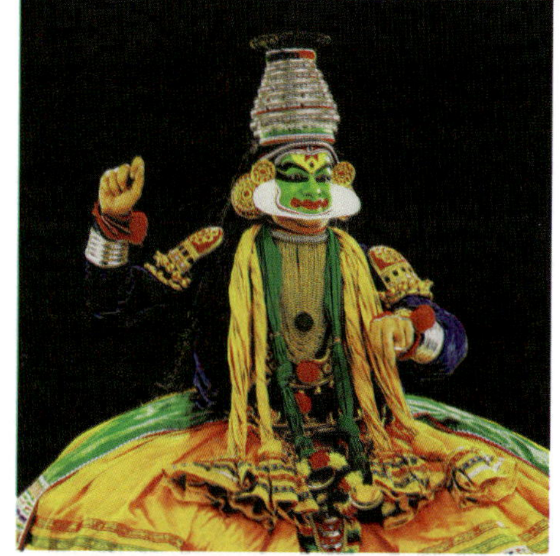

18.18: Sri Krishna depicted with green face and red lips in Kathakali — Wikimedia Commons

Kathakali is one of the major classical dance forms popular in **Kerala**. The word 'Kathakali' is derived from two words ***katha***— meaning 'story' in Sanskrit, and ***kali***— meaning 'performance or play' in Malayalam. Thus, it signifies the narration of a story through a play. Kathakali is said to have originated in around 17th century CE, but its roots are in the traditional temple arts which are centuries older. Hence the elements of Kathakali can also be traced to the Natya Shastra. The art draws from many

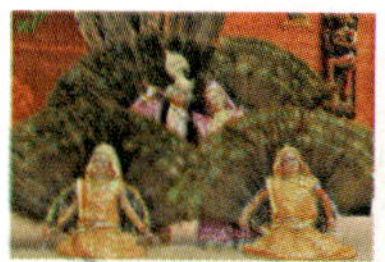

other regional dance forms of Kerala, viz. **Koodiyattam**, **Krishnanattam**, **Ramanattam**, and **Chakyar Koothu**, with **Krishnattam** being the immediate precursor to it. Some scholars suggest that even the martial art form of Kerala, Kalaripayattu has contributed to it. As a form of dance-drama as in vogue today, it was revived in the 1930s by the Malayali poet **Vallathol Narayana Menon**.

Kathakali, as a form of a dance-drama has a harmonious blend of dance, music, and acting. It dramatises the stories which have been adopted from the Indian epics like *Ramayana*, *Mahabharata*, *Krishna Leela*, etc. As a performance, it combines all the three elements of dance, viz. ***Nritta, Nritya,*** and ***Natya***. It also integrates different elements of ***Abhinaya*** (acting), which are (a) ***Angika*** – the physical aspect of acting brought out through gesturing and movement of the body and limbs, (b) ***Aharya-*** costume and makeup skills, (c) ***Vachika-*** the oral aspect of acting, and (d) ***Satvika*** – the emotional aspect of acting.

The **costume and makeup** of the artists in Kathakali is surely the most elaborate amongst all dance forms. The face makeup is quite detailed and deeply painted, appearing as if the performer is wearing a mask. Headgear, costumes and other makeup are done as per the characters in the dance drama. This includes seven basic makeups, viz. ***pacca/pacha*** (green), ***payuppu*** (ripe), ***katti/kathi***, ***kari***, ***tati***, ***minukku***, and ***teppu***. These are worn by different type of characters and depending on the attribute being represented by them. Further, the lips, eyebrows, eyelashes are all made to look prominent through makeup so as to bring out the specific attributes of the characters.

These characters are broadly categorized as per the *gunas* as the ***satvika*** (the heroes), the ***rajsika*** (kings and warriors), and the ***tamsika*** (devilish antiheroes). Different colours of the face represent different characters depending on the degree and combination of the *gunas* in the characters. Those with ***Pacha*** (green face) with bright red lips, represents ***satvika*** characters such as Rama, Krishna, Yudhisthira, Arjuna, etc. The *kathi* type characters are anti-heroes. They are also taken in the *rajasika* category as they may be great scholars, warriors etc. like Ravana, Kamsa etc. ***Thaadi*** (red) is the colour for the evil such as Dushasana or Hiranyakasyapu. In some cases, the green face has red dots or lines or even the cheeks or moustache or beard is coloured red, signifying an inherent vileness. The ***kari*** characters are those whose makeup has a black base and also wear a black costume. These include hunters, forest dwellers and even the demons etc. Yellow is the code for women, monks and mendicants. Bright radiant yellow represents noble and virtuous women characters like Sita, Mohini, Panchali etc. ***Vella Thaadi*** meaning white beard, indicates characters like Hanuman considered divine and enlightened, while ***Teppu*** is indicative of special characters like Garuda, Jatayu etc. which are messengers/carriers and do not fall in the other categories.

The makeup application is done in several stages. The basic makeup or *teppu*, which differs from character to character, is applied by the actors themselves. The second stage called *chuttikuthu* is applied by the makeup specialists, while the final stage involves wearing of the large billowing skirt and is called *uduthukettu.*

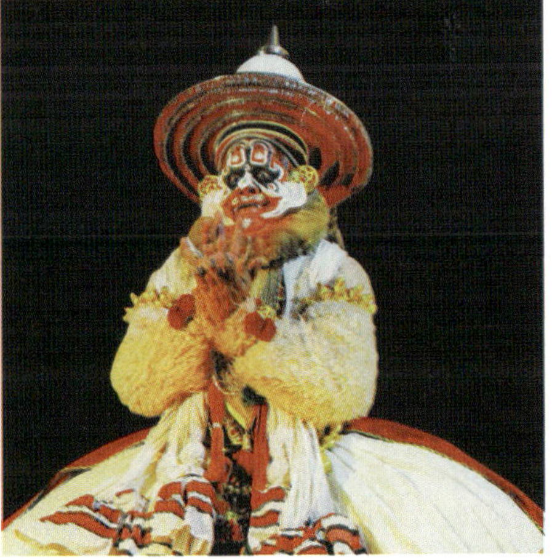

18.19: Hanuman depicted in Kathakali — Wikimedia Commons

The use of the entire body in the dance, including the hand (for hand symbols or *hasta mudra*), the facial muscles and eyes (for moods and expressions), is a unique feature of Kathakali performance. Even through movement of eyebrows and eyeballs, a wide range of emotions are depicted. These are to be in sync with the song, music and the narrative of the story. The dance incorporates all of the nine *rasas* and 24 major *mudras* in its repertoire. The performance also incorporates *kalasams,* which are pure dances where the actor has liberty to bring out his dancing skills and include rhythmic dance, quick turns, leaps and jumps etc.

Features of the dance

A Kathakali begins with ***Kelikottu*** which is calling attention of the audience and is done in the evening by playing drums and cymbals. A typical Kathakali performance may continue in stages till the whole night. After *Kelikottu, **Thodayama/Todayam*** comes next, which is a devotional invocatory performance involving one or two characters. ***Purappadu,*** a *nritta* (pure dance) performance follows in the sequence. At this stage, the role of the musicians assumes significance and is called ***Melappadam***, or performance by musicians. Next follows the ***Tiranokku***, which is the debut of characters on stage. This follows the main performance which is the ***natya*** or dance-drama. This depicts an episode or two or the whole of

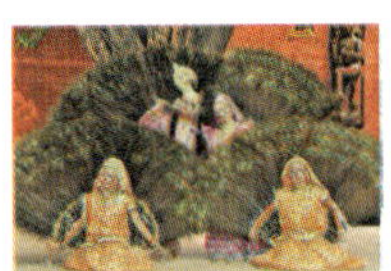

story from the epics etc. This may comprise *ilakiattam* where the actors freely bring out their skills in *abhinaya*. However, the larger part of the performance is based on *koodiyaatam* where the *abhinaya* is in complete conformity with the lyrics as sung by the accompanying musicians in the *padams*. The entire performance is to the accompaniment of ***Sopana Sangeet*** of Kerala, with musical instruments like *mandalam/maddalm* (barrel shaped drums), *centa/chenda* (cylindrical drums), *idakka* (hourglass shaped drums), *ilathalam* (bronze cymbals), *chengila* (a bell metal disc for percussion), *shankhu* (a conch shell) and other instruments for accompaniment.

Modern exponents

Exponents of this art form include, **Kunchu Kurup** (1881-1970, Sangeet Natak Akademi and Padma Bhushan), **Perumanoor Gopinathan Pillai** (1908-1987; Sangeet Natak Akademi awardee), **Kalamandalam Krishnan Nair** (1914- 1990; Sangeet Natak Akademi and Padma Shri awardee), **Chemancheri Kunhiraman Nair** (1916–2021; Padma Shri awardee), **Kavungal Chathunni Panicker** (1922-2007, Sangeet Natak Akademi and Padma Shri awardee), **Kalamandalam Ramankutty Nair** (1925-2013; Sangeet Natak Akademi and Padma Bhushan awardee), **Madavoor Vasudevan Nair** (1929-2018; Sangeet Natak Akademi and Padma Bhushan), **Kottakal Sivaraman** (1936-2010; Sangeet Natak Akademi awardee), **Kalamandalam Gopi** (1937; Sangeet Natak Akademi and Padma Shri awardee), **Kalamandalam Vasu Pisharody** (1943; Sangeet Natak Akademi awardee), amidst others.

Mohiniyattam

Mohiniattam/Mohiniyattam is another **classical dance form popular in Kerala**. The dance is said to have been structured by the Travancore kings and flourished particularly during the patronage of king Swathi Thirunal Rama Varma (reign 1813-1846). As per some accounts, in the 19th and the early 20th century, the art was associated with the temple Devadasis. In the early 20th century, owing to the negative British policy on the temple dances and later due to a ban on this dance, this art suffered a decline. Like Kathakali, it was revived by the Malayalam poet **Vallathol Narayana Menon** in the 1940s, along with other gurus of this dance. The institutional framework created by him and others in **Kerala Kalamandalam** (now deemed to be a university by the Government of India) has immensely helped in the revival and flourishing of the art.

The word 'Mohiniyattam' is derived from two words: Mohini, a mythological enchantress, and Attam (rhythmic motion or dance). Thus, the **dance of Mohini is the inspiration of this art**. Mohini is referred in Hindu mythology as an incarnation of Lord Vishnu, a celestial enchantress who emerges during the distribution of nectar between the *asuras* and *devas* after the churning of the ocean. She uses her beauty

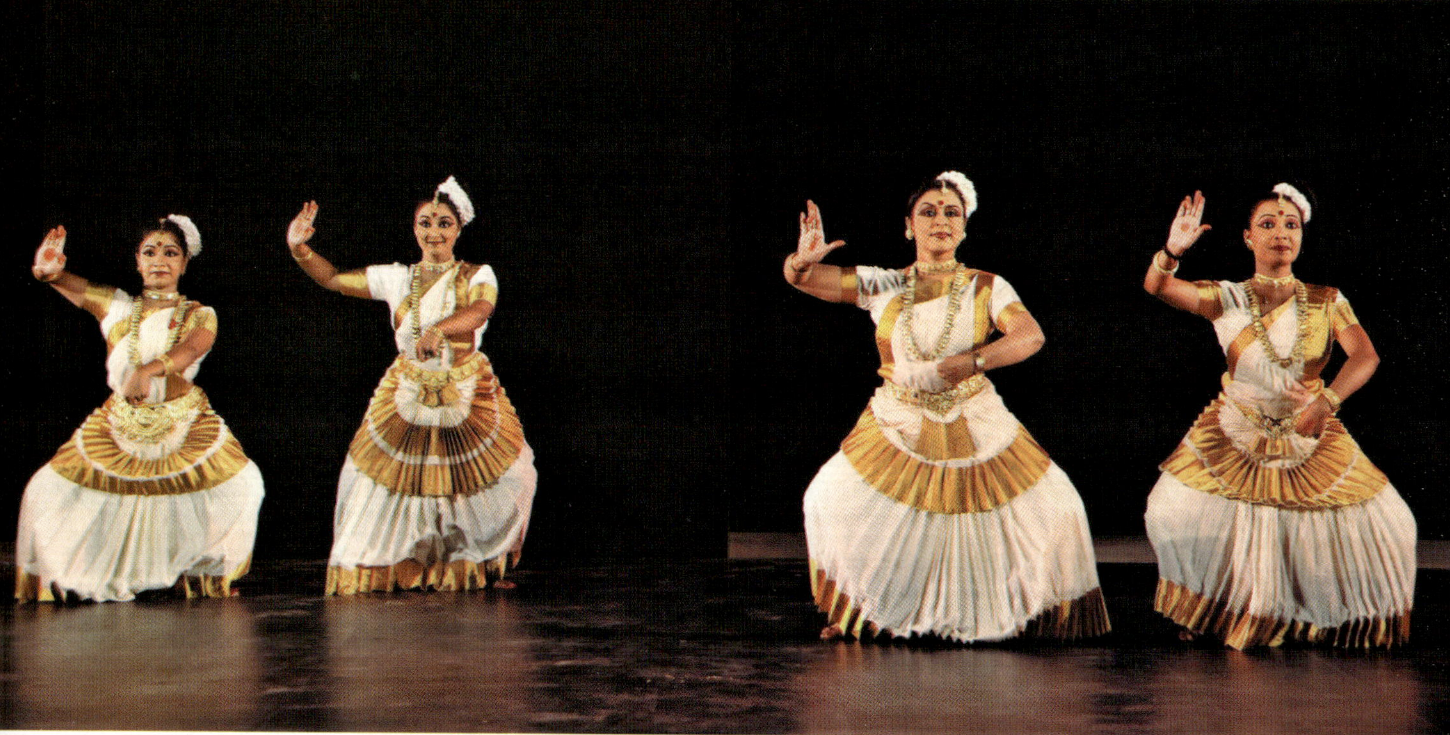

18.20: A Mohiniattam performance — Courtesy, Sangeet Natak Akademi

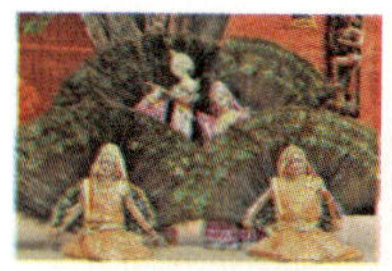

and exquisite charm to enamour the *asuras*, who place in her custody the nectar of immortality for equitable distribution amongst them. Mohini distributes it only to the good *devas,* and the evil *asuras* are thus prevented form attaining immortality. Also, the character Mohini is a central figure in the story of the defeat of *Bhasmasura*.

Features of the dance

Mohiniyattam, like other classical dances, traces its roots in the *Natyashastra*. As an art, it is a **feminine** and ***Lasya*** form of dance which incorporates graceful and swaying body movement akin to swinging palm leaves and gentle undulation of ocean waves. It does not involve abrupt body motion, sudden jerks, or even leaps. The footwork is soft and not terse, and the whole demeanour is graceful and sensuous. The dance lays emphasis on ***abhinaya*** and expression of the emotion of the character with which the performer identifies. The costume includes white/off-white, cream coloured *saris* with golden or coloured embroidery and borders.

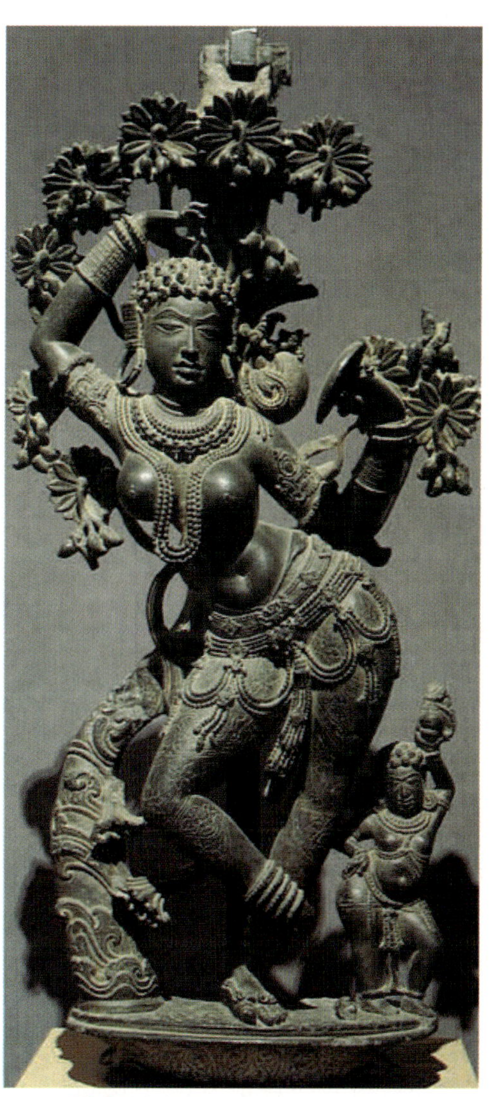
18.21: A bronze statue depicting lord Vishnu as Mohini striking a posture of Mohiniattam, location National Museum, New Delhi — Wikimedia Commons

The dance is usually performed solo in the *ekaharya abhinaya* tradition and is a combination of *nritta*, *nritya* and *natya*. It incorporates a repertoire of 24 hand gestures which are taken from ***Hastakala Deepika*** of Kathakali and other texts such as *Natyashastra*, *Abhinaya Darpana* etc. Special emphasis is laid in bringing out the subtlety of the facial expression in the art of *mukha-abhinaya. Ati bhanga* is considered a basic posture of Mohiniyatttam. It has knees bent towards outside with feet parted and an erect upper torso. The gentle swaying movement of the body and hips emulates the shape of figure of 8. The basic dance units are known as *ataavu/ atavukal*.

The traditional repertoire of Mohiniyattam includes includes; ***Cholkettu*** (invocation), ***Jatiswaram***, ***Padavarnam*** (a play with the underlying story or message), ***Padam*** (song), ***Tillana*** (dancers' response/interpretation of the musical melody) and ***Slokam***. A number of compositions are based on the works of Swati Tirunal which stress on the *sahitya bhava* (literary content). Besides, *Pandattam* and *Omanatinkal* (lullaby), which were introduced by Vallathol, are also at times incorporated. The entire performance is to the accompaniment of vocal song which is in a mix of Malayalam and Sanskrit. Music is in Carnatic style and traditional instruments like *mridangam* (barrel drum), *idakka* (hourglass drum), *veena*, *kuzhitalam* or *elathalam* (cymbals), etc. are played.

Modern exponents

Famous exponents of Mohinyattam include, **Kalamandalam Kalyanikutty Amma** (1915–1999, Sangeet Natak Akademi awardee), **Kalamandalam Satyabhama** (1937-2015; Sangeet Natak Akademi and Padma Shri awardee) **Kanak Rele** (1937; Sangeet Natak Akademi and Padma Bhushan awardee), **Bharati Shivaji** (1948, Sangeet Natak Akademi and Padma Shri awardee), **Kalamandalam Sugandhi** (1950; Sangeet Natak Akademi awardee), **V. K. Hymavathy** (1955; Sangeet Natak Akademi awardee), **Gopika Varma** (Sangeet Natak Akademi awardee), **Sunanda Nair**, **Jayaprabha Menon**, amongst others.

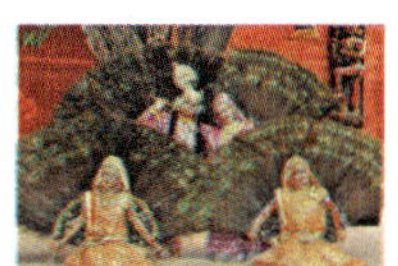

FOLK AND TRIBAL DANCES

India is a land of great diversity, which emanates from its natural endowments of geographical heterogeneity, varied weather and richness of flora and fauna. Over the period of several millennia, this has led to the culmination of varied culture, numerous languages, festivals and traditions. The pluralism this culture has inspired is also reflected in its numerous folk and tribal dances, which in themselves are rich and varied.

But **what are the folk dances**? A textual and a watertight definition may be elusive, but commonly folk dances are understood to be those set of dances, which are **vernacular and reflect the life of the people**. They are an **expression of the common culture of the people** and quite like folk music, follow the **oral tradition of learning and continuity**. They are bereft of a formal textual documentation like the classical dances, and seek reposition in the tradition of the community, while being fully integrated in their daily lives. The folk dances may be performed on a variety of occasions; be it the religious festivals, or the onset of a season, the celebration of the agricultural produce, or the occasions of birth, marriage, or other social events. They often serve as integral parts of rituals, or as an expression of the joy of the people, as a means of propagation of a story or a message, or simply as a form of community entertainment.

These dances are usually performed to the accompaniment of songs and some folk instruments, and hence integrated with the folk music. Traditional attire, or ones which may incorporate use of bright dresses, head gears, and even masks, as in some tribal dances, is quite common. Often, these dances are performed by common folks as a community dance, thus bringing a wider social participation. Easier steps and movements with less of rules and formal rigour as compared to the classical dance forms, are some of its other features. Though each state/region is endowed with a number of the folk and tribal dances, the features some of the popular dances are brought out here.

States/Regions and Important Folk & Tribal Dances

Jammu and Kashmir

With a confluence of different religions, cultures and communities, Jammu and Kashmir is indeed a melting pot of numerous folk arts and dances. Over centuries, diverse folk dances have evolved in the sylvan settings of its hills and valleys.

Kud

It is one of the popular dances of Jammu and Kashmir which is especially common in the hills around the Jammu region. The dance is in the **honour of the gods, particularly the regional and local deities** (*lok devata*/*gram devata*), as a thanks giving ritual for protection of the crops, cattle and people against natural calamities. The young and old, both participate in the dance, which is in the form of a village community dance. Kud is performed in nights with bonfires lit and may continue till the dawn. The dance movement is often spontaneous, while rhythm and fast beats dominate the music, which is from traditional instruments like *chhaina, narsingha* and local drums.

Dumhal

It is another very popular dance which is performed by the **men of Watal** tribe. Their attire comprising long colourful robes and conical caps, is a very noticeable feature. Dumhal is of the nature of a **ritual dance**, where men carry a banner in a procession which is dug in the ground, and men dance around it while singing in a chorus to the beats of drums.

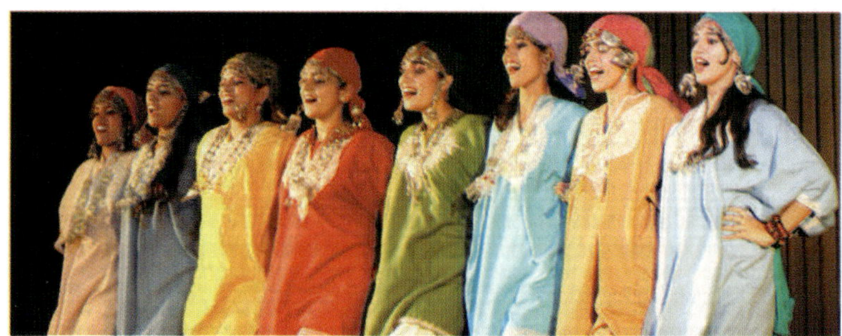

18.22: Rouf dance performed by women in synchonised steps — Courtesy, Jammu and Kashmir Tourism Development Corporation

Rouf

It is a dance performed by **women,** particularly on the festivals like Eid and Ramzan. The women stand face to face and perform the dance with synchronized and very notable footwork. The dance is also performed traditionally to mark the onset of spring.

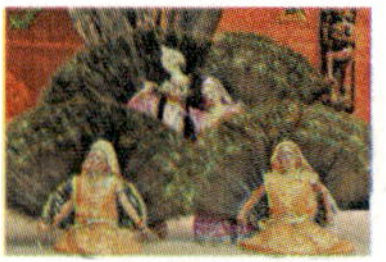

Among the other dances of the region are **Bhand Pather** - a theatre dance; **Bacha Nagma** - performed by boys on weddings and other functions; **Hafiza Nagma** - performed on weddings; **Bhand Jashan** - a soothing community dance in groups of 10 to 15, **Wuegi-Nachun** - performed by females in the Kashmiri Pandit marriages, **Dhambali dance** - performed by men in honour of sufi saints; amongst others.

Himachal Pradesh

Himachal Pradesh, which is a land of hills and valleys, is known for a number of folk dances. These are popular in the local and tribal communities. Some of the important folk dances of the region include; **Nati, Chham, Rakshasa, Dangi dance**, **Chhanak-cham etc.**

Nati

Amongst the various folk dances, **Nati** is the most popular and is also common in adjoining regions and states. It is usually performed to **celebrate new year as well as good agricultural harvest**. The dance is further categorised as **Kullu Nati, Kinnauri Nati, Shimla Nati, Gadi Nati**. Kullu Nati is the most popular amongst these and is performed on occasions of the festival of *Dussehra*. The dancers wear colourful tunic and the celebrations may last for hours. Nati may also be performed on occasion of marriages. The performance is to the music from traditional instruments like *dhol*, *nagara*, *narsingha*, *shehnai* etc. The performance of Kullu Nati by a record 9892 dancers mostly women, (on the 26th October 2015) during Dussehra festivities, has also earned a place in the **Guiness Book of World Record**s (in 2016) as the largest performance of a Nati dance.

Chham

It is a very colourful dance performed by **Buddhist monks** in monasteries. It is specially known for its elaborate costume which includes a decorated headgear and a finely crafted mask. The dance is performed on different occasions of festivities.

Rakshasa

It is popular dance in Kinnaur region and is performed with people wearing a **demon mask**. The demons represent the attack on the crops and the dance is believed to propitiate the good forces and ward off evil.

Dangi

It is another common dance/folk art which performed mostly by women who are holding hands form a semi-circle. The women wear their traditional dress and the performance is usually at the Nainadevi temple. It is based on traditional folklore of love of king and a common girl.

Chhanak cham

It is a dance performed in honour of lord Buddha. Especially noteworthy is the intricate costumes which are made from red and yellow glitters, with a large mask made of wood/paper-mâché and a headgear knowns as *chhanak.* The dance is performed by Buddhist monks and lamas while holding knives and swords.

Other folk dances of the state include; **Thoda** dance (war dance), **Mala dance** (garland dance, where dancers from a garland like pattern by crisscrossing arms), **Dalshone** and **Cholamba** dance of Ropa valley (performed earlier after killing of a tiger), **Shand** and **Shambu** (dances of Buddhist gompas), and a number of other tribal dances.

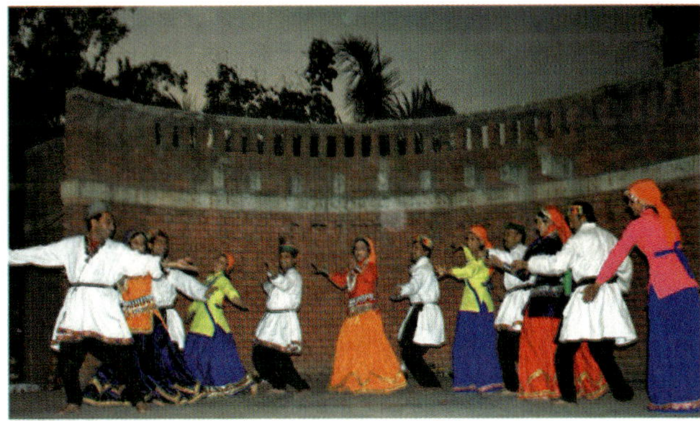

18.23: A Sirmauri Nati performance — Wikimedia Commons

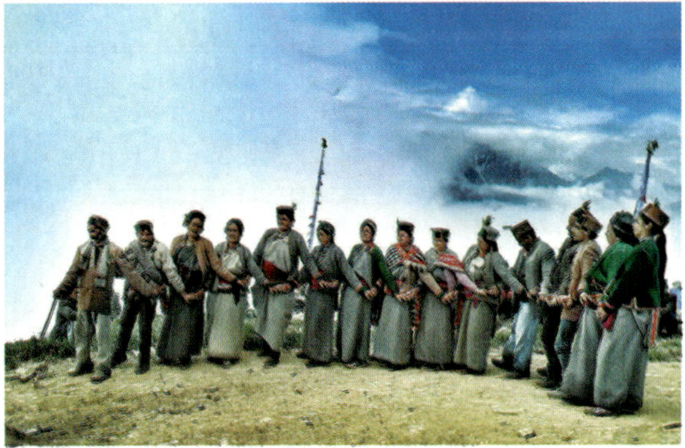

18.24: Mala dance of Kayang with performers crisscrossing their arms — Wikimedia Commons

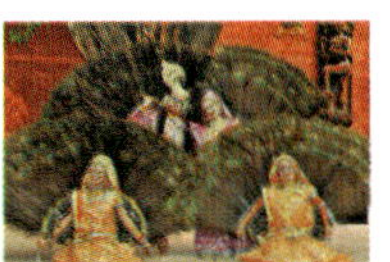

Punjab

Punjab, the land of five rivers, is known for its rural communities and agricultural lifestyle. Dances form an integral part of folk culture and these are imbued with the spirit of liveliness and energy of the people. **Bhangra** and **Gidda** are the most popular of the Punjabi folk dances.

Bhangra

It is performed by **men** to the fast beats of drums (*dhol*). It is an energetic dance performed usually with arms raised with kicks and leaps in a formation of a circle. The dance is to the accompaniment of *boliyan* (short songs) which are fast paced. Bhangra is essentially a celebratory community dance popular on the occasions of agricultural festivals like Vaisakhi etc.

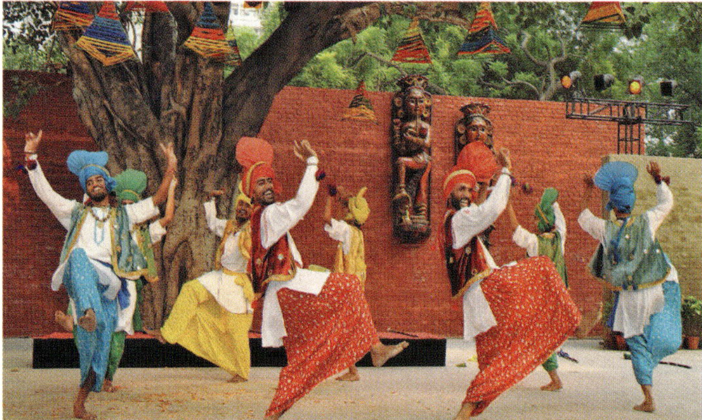

18.25: Bhangra dance of Punjab — Courtesy, Sangeet Natak Akademi

Giddha

It is a dance performed by **women** and is similar to Bhangra with an energetic up-tempo dance. However, it also incorporates feminine grace and elegance. The song is to the accompaniment of *boliyan* in a call and response form, where the leader recites the *boli* and the others repeat it. It is invariably accompanied with rhythmic clapping by the dancers. *Dhol*, a traditional instrument of folk dances of Punjab may be absent in Gidddha. Women wear clothes of a wide variety of colours and traditional ornaments. Festivals and other social functions are occasions for performance of Giddha.

Jhoomar/Jhumar

It is another popular dance form which is often performed by men at **wedding ceremonies**. The dance takes its name from the word *jhum*, which literally means 'to sway' and incorporates slow, rhythmic, swaying movements while dancing in circles. The dance is an essentially an expression of happiness, love and other emotions.

Jaago

It literally means to keep awake, is a dance performed usually a night before the occasion of marriage. The girls light candles and with earthen pots on their head, perform the Jaago folk dance celebrating the ensuing marriage.

The other folk dances of the region include, **Sammi** (dance of tribal communities in Sandalbar area), **Kikli** (performed by girls in pairs holding hands and moving in circles) **Malawi** (performed in the Malwa region by the bachelors), **Julli** (performed usually by Muslim *pirs*), **Dankara/Gatka** (performed usually with colourful staves resembling a marshal art), **Luddi** etc.

Rajasthan

The dances of Rajasthan are a true reflection of its communities, their culture and the life style of people. Among the most popular of the folk dances are **Ghoomar, Kalbelia, Bhavai, Kachhi Ghoda, Chakri** besides others.

Ghoomar

It is a traditional dance **performed by women** wearing coloured dresses with face covered with a veil. The dance involves pirouetting with a **swirl of *ghagras*** (long skirts), at the accompaniment of beats, with graceful movement of body. The very name of the dance is derived from the word *ghoomna* or to twirl around in circles. The dance is said to have been developed by the *bhil* tribe and later also adopted by other communities of Rajasthan. The dance is performed on weddings, religious festivals and other social occasions.

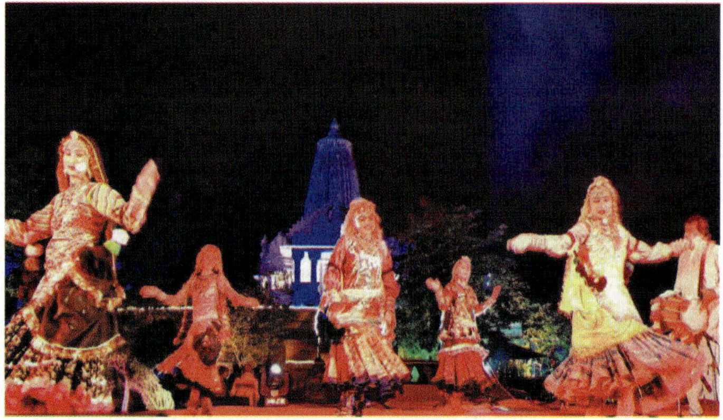

18.26: A traditional Ghoomar performance — Courtesy, Rajasthan Tourism

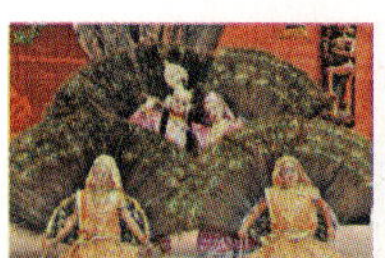

Kalbelia dance

It is performed by *Kalbelia* or *sapera* community (snake charmers). The dance is performed by **womenfolk** to the tune of *been* or *pungi* (a wood wind musical instrument used traditionally to capture the snakes) which is played by men. Besides, other folk instruments like *dufli, dholak and khanjari* are also played. The women are dressed usually in a black *lehenga* (long skirt) with *angrakhi* (upper garment) and *odhani* (head cloth). The dance resembles the movement of a serpent and incorporates sensuous gyrating and rhythmic movements. The dance was included in the list of **Intangible Cultural Heritage of UNESCO in 2010.**

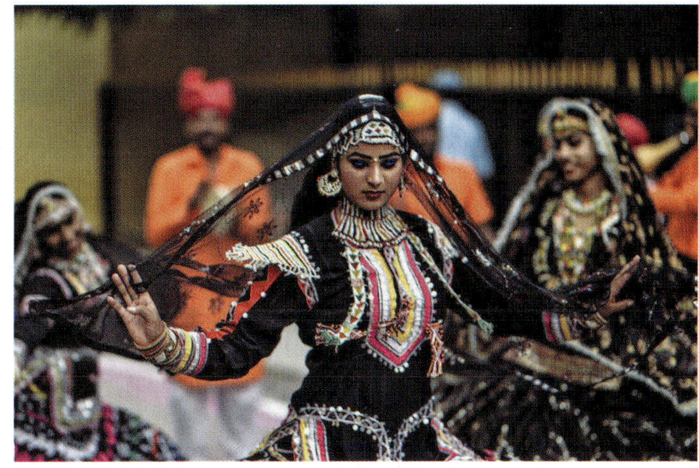

18.27: Kalbelia dance performance — Courtesy, Rajasthan Tourism

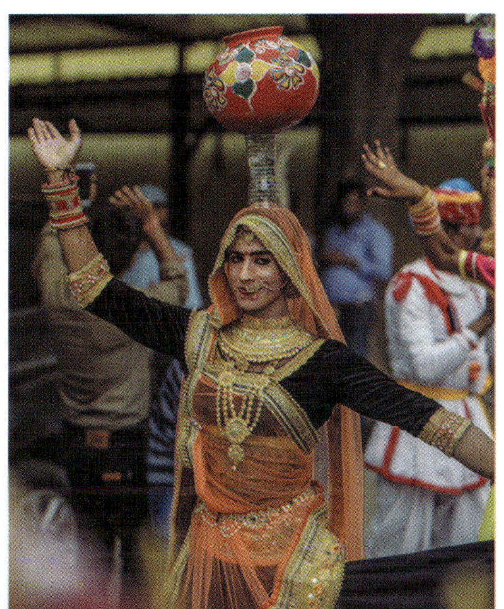

18.28: Bhavai dance performance — Courtesy, Rajasthan Tourism

Bhavai

It is another folk dance performed by **women**. The artists very skillfully balance a number of pitchers on their heads while performing the dance. At times, the highly skilled dancers also perch themselves on top of a glass or the edge of a brass *thali* (plate) while balancing the earthen or brass pitchers on their heads. This dance is often performed by the women of Jat, Bhil, Meeena, Kalbelia, Kumhar, Raigar and some other communities, who traditionally walked long distances while balancing the pitcher full of water on their heads in the dry deserts of Rajasthan.

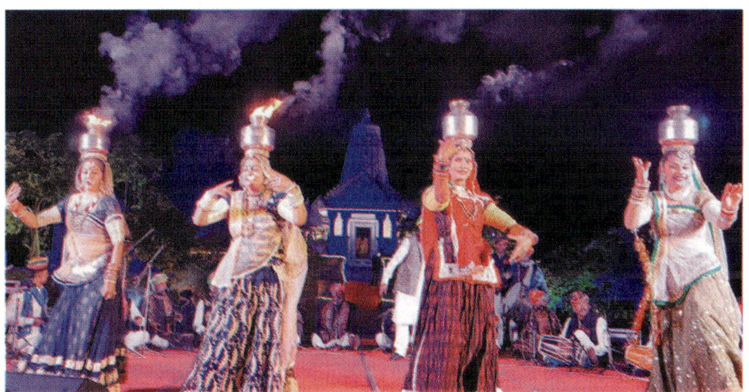

18.29: A Chari dance performance by womenfolk with brass pots and lamps lit over it — Courtesy, Rajasthan Tourism

Another similar dance is the **Chari dance** performed by the **women folk** particularly of the Gujjar community in Kishangarh. The dance is about the **art of collection of water** in the parched land. It depicts women balancing pots (*chari*) on their head and a lighted lamp atop it.

Kacchi Ghodi

It is one of the most popular folk dances of Rajasthan which is performed by men, especially on the occasion of a marriage/bridegroom's party. Wearing elaborate costumes of *dhoti* (lower garment) *kurta* (upper garment) and turban, the men perform this dance on **dummy horses** while holding naked swords. The dance is said to have

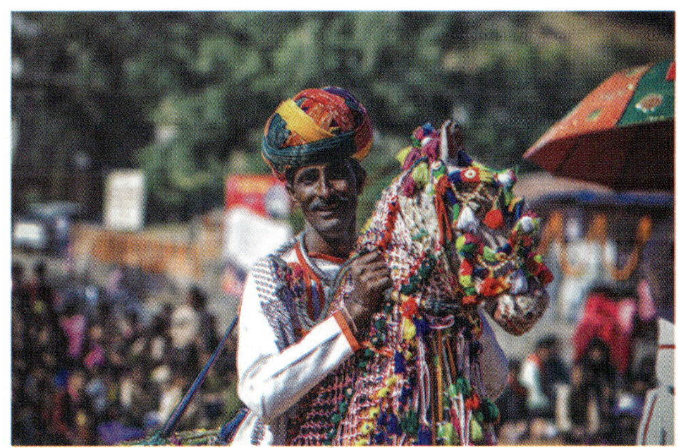

18.30: Kaccchi Ghodi dance performance — Courtesy, Rajasthan Tourism

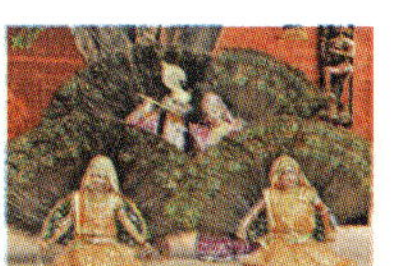

its origin in the community of bandits in the Shekhawti region, and through the accompanying songs, the exploits of these bandits is at times described.

Other popular folk dances of this region include the **Chakri dance** (women of Kanjar tribe perform *chakkars* or circular pirouttes), **drum dance** (performed by men in Jhalore region with large drums tied around their neck), **fire dance** (performed by the banjara community involving walking on fire, swallowing fire torches and blowing fire etc). Some other folk dances include **Gair dance, Gawari dance, Kathputli dance, Terah tali and Walar dance.**

Haryana

The state is known for a variety of folk dances, be it the **Raas Leela**, the **Phag dance**, the **Dhamal** dance, the **Loor**, the **Gugga** and the others. While some of these traditional arts have originated in the state, the others see some influence of the folk arts of the neighbouring states as well.

Raas Leela

It is inspired from the **stories of Lord Krishna and the love of the *gopikas*** towards him and has its origins in the Braj region, but is very popular in Haryana, particularly in the Faridabad district. Performed by the womenfolk who dance in ecstasy around the idols of Lord Krishna, there is unison between the sway of the body of the dancers and the tinkling of the anklets and bangles worn by them.

Phag

Phag, or the Phalgun dance, is a **harvest celebratory dance**, performed in the period of February-March. This period sees some respite in the agricultural activities and celebrates the agricultural produce. Besides, it also celebrates the onset of the month of *Phalgun*. The folk art is the form of a song and dance, which has separate songs for the men and the women folk.

Dhamaal

It is another dance which is traditionally performed in the month of *Phalgun*. The dance is especially popular in the district of Mahendragarh, Jhajjhar Gurugram etc. The dance reflects the deeper emotions of love, joy, sorrow and even the toils of labour of the rural folk. This dance too has a song and dance routine.

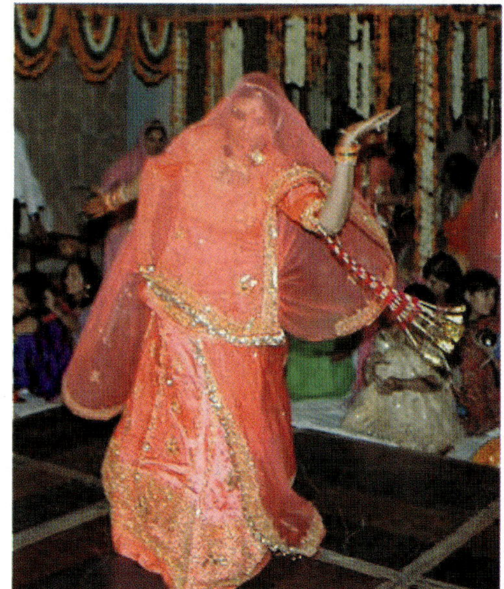

18.31: A Ghoomar dance performance — Wikimedia Commons

Ghoomar

It is another dance which though originated in neighbouring state of Rajasthan, is also popular in the Haryana particularly in the districts of Dadri, Hissar, Bhiwani etc. The dance is performed by the **womenfolk** on the occasion of Holi, Deepawali, Gangor Puja, where women devotees carry offerings for the temple on brass plates. Forming circles by joining hands and twirling in devotion, are some of the typical movements of this community dance.

Loor

It is another very popular dance which is performed around the festival of **Holi** in the regions of Bagar, Bangar and Dadri. The dance is performed involving two sets of girls/ women who stand facing each other. Through song and dance routine, they describe the experiences of courtship, marriage and post marriage life.

Among the other popular folk dances of the state are **Daph dance** (dance of spring season using *daph* a traditional instrument), **Khoria dance** (a variant of Jhumar performed exclusively by women), **Gugga dance** (performed in the month of Bhadon and dedicated to Gugga Pir) **Gangor Puja dance** etc.

Uttar Pradesh

Like the other aspects of culture, the art of folk dances is diverse and deep rooted in the folk traditions of Uttar Pradesh. These folk dances include the **Raas Leela, Charkula dance, Chapeli** dance, **Khyal, Kajri** and **Dadra,** besides different form of dances associated with folk theatres such as **Ramleela, Nautanki, Swang** etc.

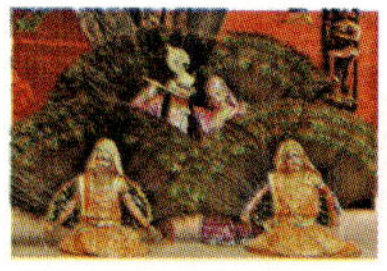

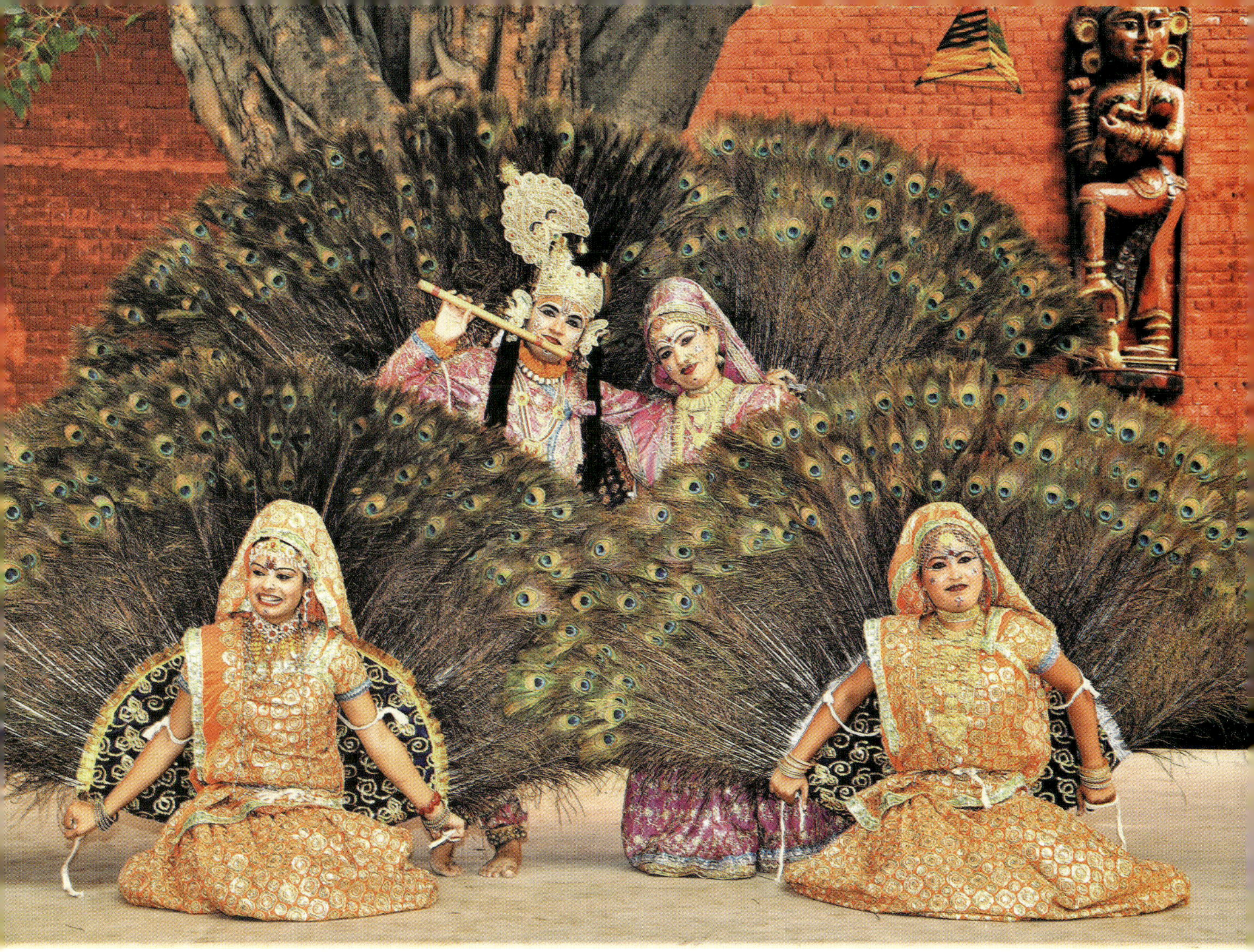

18.32: Raas Leela of Uttar Pradesh — Courtesy, Sangeet Natak Akademi

Raas Leela

Ras or Raas, popular in the Braj region, draws inspiration from the **legend of Sri Krishna** and the spiritual **love of the *gopikas*,** particularly of Radha for him. Thus, its roots can be traced to the Bhagavata Purana and the Gita Govinda. As a folk art, this centuries old tradition aims to emulate, the ecstatic dance of the *gopikas* on the banks of Yamuna in Vrindavan, to the tunes of the *murli* of Sri Krishna. Besides, other legends from the early life of Sri Krishna to his years of adolescence may also be enacted. The *Ras* is often performed by groups of people (*mandal*) who roam to different places, performing the dances to the accompaniment of the traditional instruments. It often takes the shape of a theatrical performance.

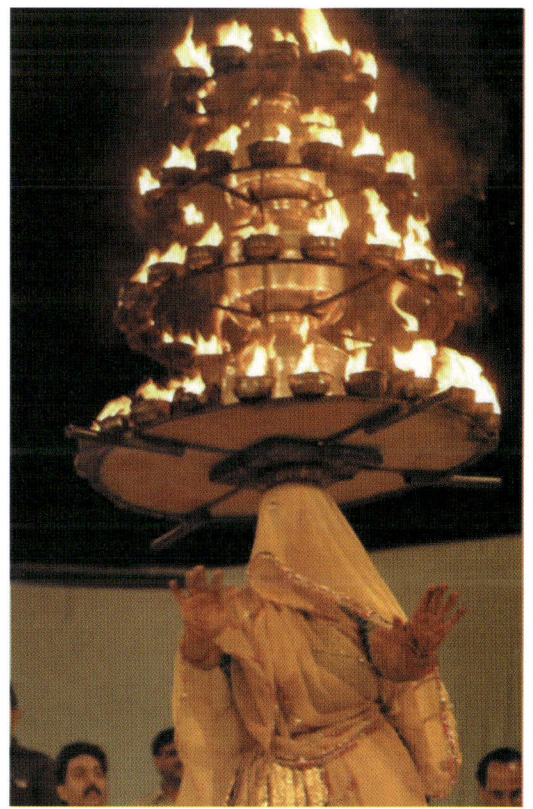

18.33: A Charkula dance performance — Courtesy, Wikimedia Commons

Charkula

It is another dance which is popular in the **Braj region** and is associated with devotion to Radha and Krishna. The dance is specially performed on the third day after the Holi festival when Radha is believed to have been born. As per legends, to announce the birth of Radha her grandmother ran out of the house with a *charkula* (a pyramid-shaped lighted lamp) on her head. This dance is performed by women who dance with a *charkula* on their heads which has as many as 108 lighted *diyas* on it.

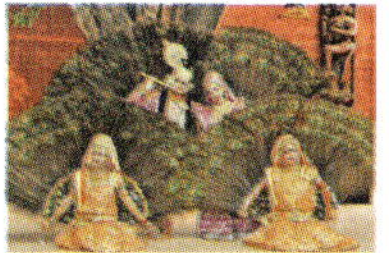

Amongst other folk dances, are a set of dances, which are also associated with the music of that kind. This includes dances of **Dadra**, **Khyal** and **Kajri** which are performed to accompaniment of Dadra, Khyal and Kajri forms of music. Another set of folk dances are those which specifically relate to the folk theatre and these include **Swang, Ramleela**, and **Nautanki**.

Uttarakhand

This pristine hill state is home to many folk dances, which also reflect the quintessential culture of the Kumaon and the Garhwal region. Among the most popular of the folk dances of the state are **Choliya, Pandav Lila, Chhapeli, Langvir, Jhoda, Chancheri** amongst many others.

Choliya

It is a dance popular in the Pithoragarh, Champawat Almora and Bageshwar districts of Kumaon region, the Choliya/Chaliya dance is a **war dance** which reflects the post-war celebrations. The dance is performed on the occasion of marriages and other auspicious occasions, with artists **dressed as soldiers** who are wielding swords and shields. The music is to the accompaniment of traditional instruments like *dhol, damru, ranassingha, nagphani, turi* etc. The dance is reflective of ancient martial arts tradition of the Kumaon region.

Pandav Lila or Pandav Nritya

It is essentially a re-enactment of the stories of the **Pandavas** from the epic Mahabharata and presented as a dance. Popular in the Garhwal region, the dance often continues for a few days to even a month. A common belief is that the energies (spirit) of the Pandavas enters the performing artists. The dance music is to the accompaniment of instruments like *dhol, damaru, bhankore* (trumpets) etc.

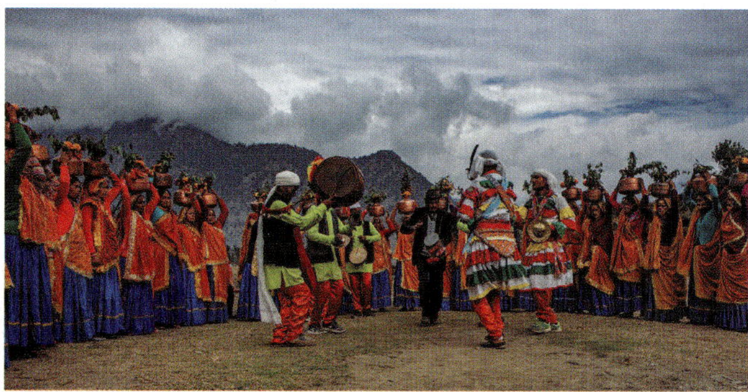

18.34: Choliya/Chaliya dance of Uttarakhand — Wikimedia Commons

Chhapeli

It is a dance of expression of **love of the young**. It is popular in the Kumaon region and is often performed in fairs and festivals. This folk art is also in vogue in some regions of Uttar Pradesh. The dance is performed by men and women in groups to the accompaniment of fast paced music. The men hold a *huddaka* around their shoulders and play it, while women hold a handkerchief, and at times, a mirror. Sometimes the role of females is performed by young boys in the dance. *Manjira*, flute and other traditional instruments provide the accompanying music.

Jhoda

It refers to the **dance by couples**. Here a group of several couples, while placing hands on shoulders of each other, form a circle and move forward and backward dancing to the tune of music. It is a spring time dance popular in the Kumaon region.

Chancheri

It is said to be an ancient form of Jhora dance and is popular in the Kumaon region. It is a collective dance where men and women form a semi-circle and dance to the music which is in slow tempo.

Langvir

It is an **acrobatic dance** popular in the Garhwal region. The dance involves a man going up a vertical pole and balancing his weight on belly, while at the same time spinning in this posture.

Ghasiyari

It is a folk dance of Garhwal region. This is a dance of the young women who venture out to collect grass and sing and dance in a group to bid time. Now it is largely limited to the social occasions.

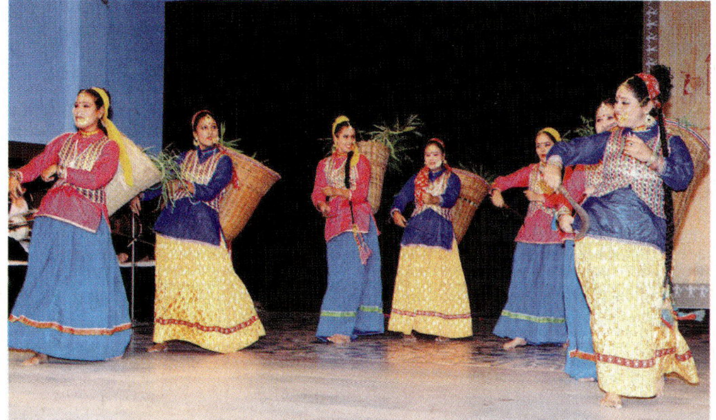

18.35: Women performing Ghasiyari dance — Courtesy, Sangeet Natak Akademi

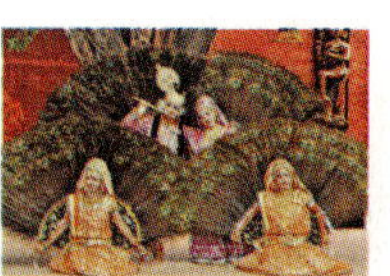

Besides, other folk dances of the region include; **Jhumelo** (literal meaning 'to sway'), **Tandi** (dancing in a series holding each other's hands), **Thadiya** (meaning courtyard; a dance organised on *Basant Panchami* in houselhold courtyards) **Chunfula** (a dance of joy and gaiety associated with goddess Parvati), **Bhotiya** (performed by the ancient Bhotiya tribe to liberate the soul of the deceased trapped as animals), **Mukhota** (a dance performed in the month of Baishakh wearing masks of various deities and demons), **Ramman** (a dance of Garhwal associated with Ramman festival held on Baisakhi in honour of local deity Bhumiyal Devta).

Gujarat

The dances of Gujarat are reflective of its rich tradition particularly its rituals and festivities, celebration of work and chores of the daily lives, besides the tradition of the tribals. These include **Garba Dandiya, Tippani, Hudo, Manirao** amidst others.

Garba

Garba is one of the most popular of folk dances of Gujarat. It is performed on the occasion of **festival of *Navaratri*,** traditionally by the **womenfolk**, as a form of worship of the mother Goddess Durga. The dance was said to be originally performed in the *garbhagriha* or sanctum of the temple of Goddess Durga in front of an earthen lamp; hence its name. Nowadays, it is performed before *aarti* as a worship ritual. Modern Garbas may also include men who along with women dressed in bright and traditional clothes and perform this dance as a community celebration.

Dandiya or Dandiya Raas

It is a dance performed traditionally by men using **sticks** and in leaping and twirling patterns (after *aarti*). It symbolises the battle of Durga and Mahisasura. Modern dandiya Raas is usually performed by both men and women who perform this dance in groups with a pair of partners facing each other. This dance is also performed on the occasion of **Navaratri** and has immense popularity in Gujarat and even abroad where Gujarati communities are residing.

Tippani

It is a dance popular in Chorwad region of Saurashtra which involves **women** standing in two rows facing each other while beating a *tippani* (a long wooden stick with iron block on end) while singing and dancing. The practice is said to have origins in the beating of lime with a *tippani* to work at the foundation of a house and the dance originated as a means to overcome the tedium.

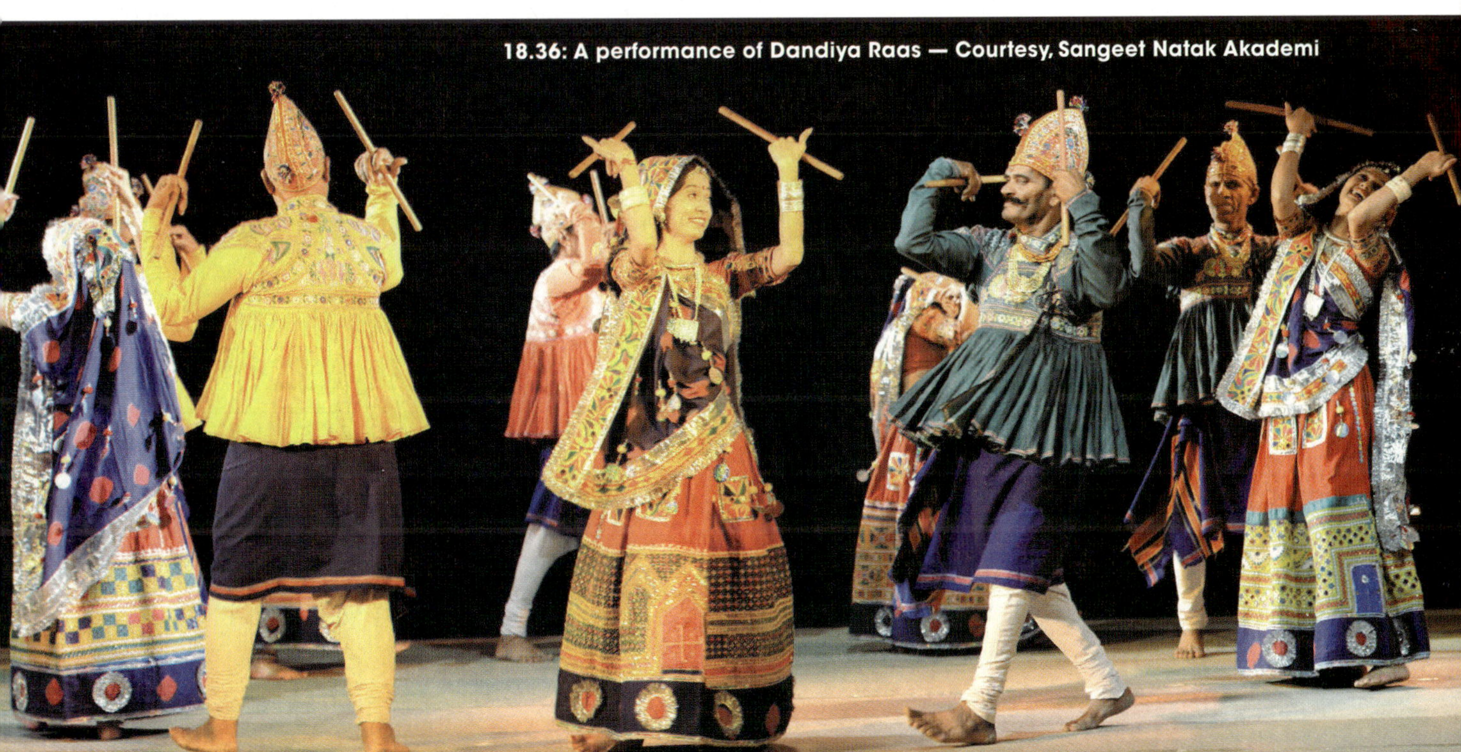

18.36: A performance of Dandiya Raas — Courtesy, Sangeet Natak Akademi

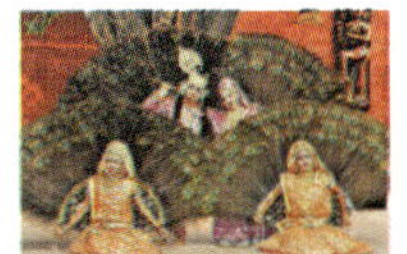

Hudo or Hoddoo

It is a dance performed by the Bharvad or shepherd community. The performers are in pairs and facing each other, they clap palms with each other while they shuffle on their feet back and forth, hence creating a dance rhythm.

Some of the other folk dances of the state are; **Maniaro Raas** (martial art dance form performed by men with sticks, popular in Saurashtra region), **Mer Raas** (performed by men of Mer or Meher community with sticks and popular in Surashtra region), **Gop Raas** (also called Dandiya Raas and performed in devotion to Sri Krishna and other Gopis), **Kanabi Raas** (performed by the farmers), **Kahalya** (performed by Dang tribals) state, while **Bhavai** is a form of folk theatre incorporating the traditions of folk dances.

Madhya Pradesh

The dances of Madhya Pradesh are reflective of the traditions of Central India and in particular the Bundelkhand region. It also reflects the culture of the tribals and of the local community and their connection with their roots.

Jawara

It is a dance popular in the Bundelkhand region and associated with **agricultural harvest** and hence celebrates prosperity. It is performed by both men and women. The women, balance a basket full of *jawar* (millet) on their head, while performing brisk dance movements.

Matki

It is a community dance of Malwa region of Madhya Pradesh and performed by **women** who dance, while balancing earthen pots or *matki,* on their heads. This dance is usually a solo performance where women are dressed in a colourful *saree* or *lehenga*. The music, played by men is to the beat of drums and other traditional instruments.

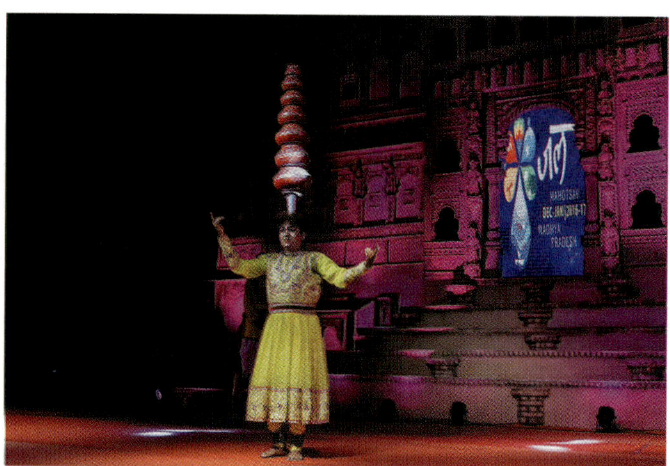

18.37: Matki Dance — Wikimedia Commons

Tertali

It is a **ritual dance** performed by **women of Kamar tribe**. It is performed usually by two or three women who start in a squatting position and have folk instrument *manjira* tied to different parts of the body. At times, they may even balance pots on their heads.

Some other dances of Madhya Pradesh include **Lehangi** (performed by the Banjara and Kanjar tribes), **Rai** (performed by the Bediya tribe of Bundelkhand), **Badhai** (performed in Bundelkhand on occasion of birth, marriage etc. to propitiate goddess Sitala for protection from natural calamities), **Grida** (associated with the harvest of Rabi crops) **Gangaur** (on festival of Gangaur for worship of Lord Shiva and Goddess Gauri) etc.

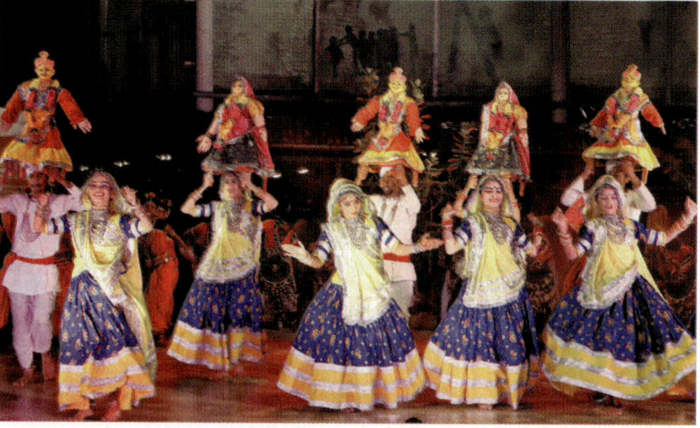

18.38 : Gangaur dance performance in the obeisance of Lord Shiva and goddess Gauri; dancers carrying overhead deity idols in the form of dolls
— Courtesy, Madhya Pradesh Tourism Board

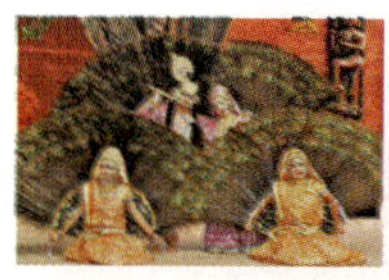

Chhattisgarh

A state endowed with rich tribal traditions, has a heritage of numerous folk dances, which include; **Saila, Raut Nacha, Gaur Maria, Karma, Pandavani, Panthi, Gendi etc.**

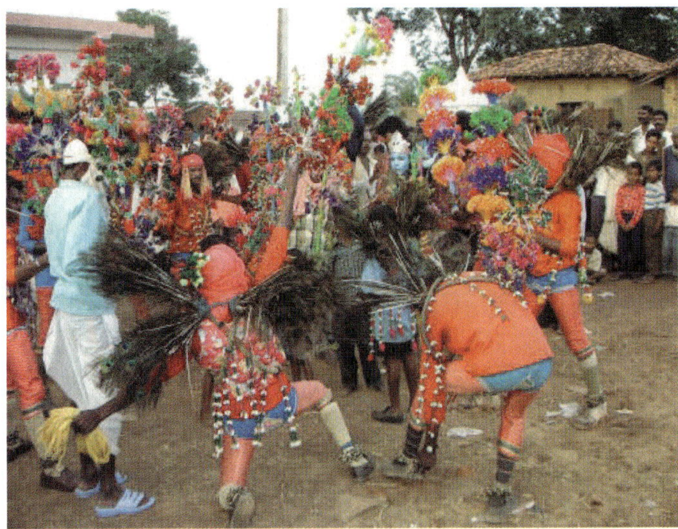

18.39: Raut Nacha of Chhattisgarh — Wikimedia Commons

Raut Nacha

It is a folk dance of the community of *Yadavas,* who consider themselves as descendants of Lord Krishna. It is performed on the occasion of the festival Dev-udni Ekadashi (for a week after Diwali). The dance incorporates **anecdotes of Krishna Leela,** specially the *rasa* aspect of it. The Rauts wear a special costume and dance in groups in the village pathways while holding a stick. Their songs include blessings to the householders and are to the accompaniment of traditional instruments like, *timki* (a percussion instrument made of earthenware and parchment), *mohri* (a double reed wind instrument), *dafda* (a percussion instrument like dafli)*, dholak, singabaja* (a horn wind instrument) etc. This dance is usually performed by men while children may also be included.

Gaur Maria

This dance form is performed by **Sing Maria tribes** (also called Bison horn Maria tribes) of Bastar district. It symbolizes the hunting spirit of the Gaur tribe (*gaur* literally means, bison). It is usually performed on the occasion of marriages, both by men and women who carry sticks in their hands dance in groups to the beats of drums. It is said to be a dance of joy and invocation.

Saila

It is a popular **tribal folk dance**, performed after the harvest season (in the month of *Agahan*) and also performed around Dashehra and Diwali festivals. It is a group dance in which the dancers holding sticks in their hands move around in circles while clapping them against each other's sticks. At the end of the performance, as a token of appreciation, the artists are given paddy by the villagers.

Pandavani

It literally means *Pandava vani,* and is a folk ballad form of dance drama which brings out the tales of the Pandavas.

Among other important dances of Chattisgarh are **Panthi** (of the Satnami community, the dance signifies the human life, spiritual values and teachings of Kabir, Ravidas, Dadu etc.); **Karma** (a dance of joy and gaiety performed by both women and men of Gonds, Oraons and Baigas tribes, at the end of rainy and beginning of the spring season); **Sua** (performed by Goura women keeping a parrot made usually of bamboo in centre and moving around while dancing and clapping); **Gendi** (a dance of the tribals in Bastar, where performers walk and dance on bamboo sticks to the beat of traditional drums).

Jharkhand

It is another state with rich tribal culture, where the folk dances reflect the closeness of the people with the elements of nature, their tradition of ancient wars and aspects of daily lives and chores. Its popular dances include; **Chhau, Paika, Santhal, Jhumar, Karma** and **Karsa** amidst others.

Jhumar/Jhumair

It is a **harvest dance** performed by the **tribal** people. This is also popular in Odisha. It is usually performed after the rains during the Karma festivals. A sub type of this dance, **Janani Jhumair** is performed by the women wearing colourful costumes. The performers dance in a group holding each other by their waist and synchronizing their movements to beats of *dholak*, *kartal* and *mandar* and music of other traditional instruments like *sarangi*. **Mardani Jhumair** is performed by men and is more popular in the tribes of Central India around Nagpur.

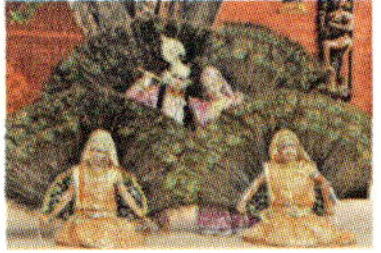

Chhau dance

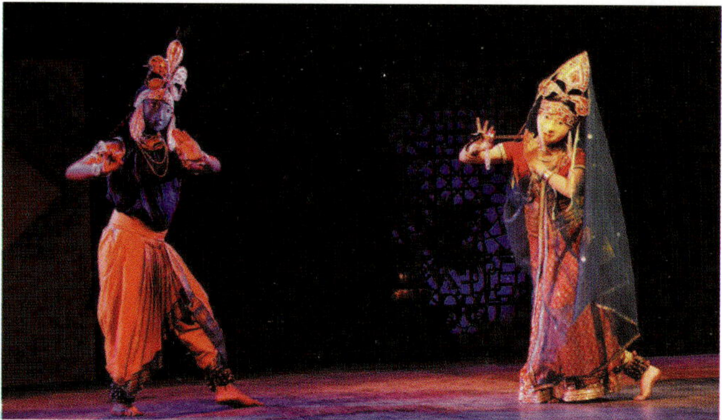

18.40: Radha and Krishna, a performance of Seraikela Chhau wearing the distinctive chhau mask — Courtesy, Sangeet Natak Akademi

It is popular in the tribal regions of Jharkhand, West Bengal, and Odisha. It has three different forms; **Seraikela Chhau** of Jharkhand, **Purulia Chhau** of West Bengal, and **Mayurbhanj Chhau** of Odisha. The **Seraikala school of Chhau** is influenced by the principles of the Bharatiya Natyashastra and the choreography is Odissi in composition and execution. Tales from mythology like the Mahabharata and Ramayana and others, are often the themes of this dance. The use of **masks** is a distinctive feature of Chhau (which literally means in Sanskrit, *chhaya* or shade). The music is to accompaniment of traditional instruments like *nagara, jhanj* (cymbal)*, mohuri* (double reed wind instrument made of wood and metal)*, turi* (a clarinet like instrument with a wooden body and brass bell)*, dhol, dhumsa* (a large cup shaped percussion instrument)*, bheri* (a drum kind of percussion instrument) and conch shells etc.

Paika

It is a martial arts form of dance popular in the Munda community. It is performed by men in a group while holding sword in one hand and a shield in the other. The performers wear bright coloured clothes and often adorn a turban. The dance represents the battle art of the community.

Santhal

It is a dance performed by the Santhal community (tribe), during the spring season, harvest season and other festive occasions. Essentially, it is a group dance where men and women adorn traditional costumes, which have decoration of flowers, leaves twigs etc., thus exemplifying their closeness to nature. The dance is performed to the beats of traditional instruments like *madal* and *nagara*.

Karsa

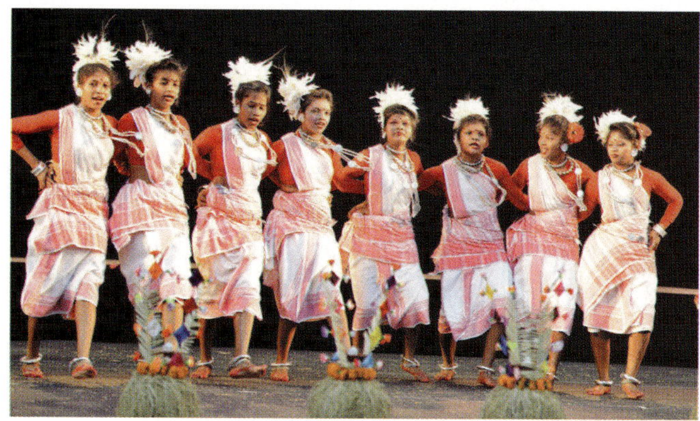

18.41: Karsa dance of Oraon tribals — Courtesy, Sangeet Natak Akademi

It is a dance of Oraon tribals performed by women, particularly on the occasion of marriages.

Among other popular dances of the state are **Karma** (performed in August in the Karma festival in dedication to the sacred Karma tree), **Hunta** (popular in Santhal Pargana as dance preparatory to hunting), **Barao** (community dance of Oraon men and women) **Sarhul/Baha** (festive dancing on occasion of Baha using *sal* and *mahua* flowers), **Sohrai** (on the occasion of harvest festival of Sohrai), **Domkach** (community dance performed particularly on marriages, where dancers hold hand and form a semicircle while dancing) **Mundari dance** (all community dance of Mundari tribals), **Ghora Naach** (horse dance performed during the weddings).

Bihar

The dances of Bihar are reflection of the rural life, the welcoming of the seasons, the celebration of the agriculture and the expression of the tribal culture. Amongst the most popular of the dances of the state are the **Kajri, Jhijhiya, Jhumar, Jat-Jatin, Karma and Jhumeri**, besides others.

Kajari

Kajari is a dance which is performed in the **season of rains,** that is the months of Shravan and Bhadra. It is a dance performed by the young girls who speak of their love and express their joy on the approach of this season. The dance is also symbolic of fertility and new life brought by the rains.

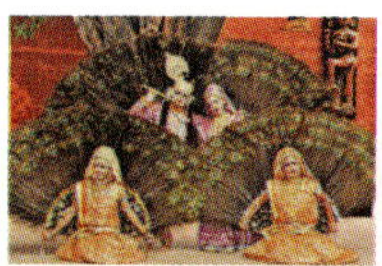

Jhijhiya

Jhijhiya is another dance which is associated with the rains. It is popular in the Koshi region and is performed by young girls during the season of drought, for **invoking the rain god Indra** to bless them with rains. The words of the accompanying song, *hali hali barsun Inder devata,* literally means, 'a prayer to the God of rains to send the showers quickly'.

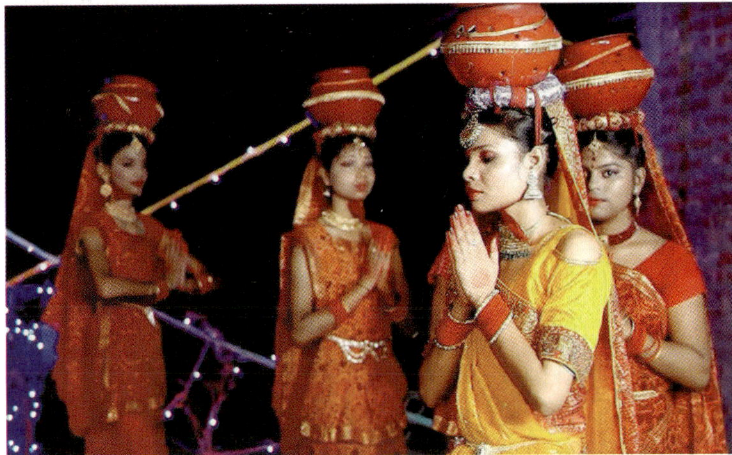

18.42: Women performing Jhijhiya dance — Wikimedia Commons

Jhumar

Jhumar is a dance of rural folk to **welcome the spring season** and an ode to the beauty of nature. The dance is performed by the women while men provide the musical accompaniment. The dance and the song may also be performed in the other seasons. Bhojpuri and Magahi Jhumars are the subtypes of this dance popular in the Bhojpur and Magadh regions.

Jhumeri

Jhumeri is a dance popular in the **Mithilanchal** region of North Bihar and celebrates the **turn of season** and arrival of the month of Kartik. It is performed on a clear moonlit night, particularly by the married women, and is said to have similarities to the Garba of Gujarat.

Jat-Jatin

Jat-Jatin is another popular folk dance of North Bihar of Mithila and Kosi region which is traditionally performed in monsoons and moonlit nights. The performers include a man and a woman who depict the **story of Jat and Jatin**, an emigrant husband and wife, their love, poverty and sorrow.

The other popular dances include **Karma dance** (a group dance around the karma tree in the tribal regions), **Sohar Khelwana** (a dance to celebrate the birth of a child), **Jharni dance** (performed by the Julaha community on the occasion of Muharram), **Dhamar Jogiya** (performed on the occasion of the festival of Holi) and **Krishi/Kishan Nritya** (performed by the farmer community on the sight of rains and good produce).

West Bengal

West Bengal, with its rich cultural tradition is home to numerous dance forms which draw from its religious social fervor, its centuries old bhakti tradition and the ethos of its tribes and communities. Some of the popular dances of the region are **Gambhira**, **Chhau**, **Alkap**, **Kirtan**, **amongst** others.

Gambhira

This dance is popular in the Malda district and other adjoining areas, the Gambhira/Gombhira is performed during the festival of **Chaitra Sankranti** and is related to the **agricultural harvest** as well as **religious mythology**. The word 'Gambhira' means *devalaya,* or the house of gods. It is also associated with lord Shiva (who is known as *gambhira*) and hence this festival and dance are associated with Shaivism, besides with other streams of worship including Shaktism and Vaishnavism. Gambhira dance is performed while wearing various types of **wooden masks** depicting Shiva, Chamunda, Kalika, Rama Hanumana etc. The dance is to the accompaniment of Gambhira song and music from instruments like *dhak* (drum) and *kanshi* (gong). It is also popular in the Muslim community of the region who have been the custodian of this dance, thus representing a blend of interfaith cultural tradition.

Chhau

This dance of Purulia district is another famous dance of West Bengal. A vigorous dance form which emanated from the **martial arts traditions** is particularly known for the use of **vibrant masks** and an **elaborate headgear**. The performance draws from the themes of Ramayana and Mahabharata and other mythological legends with the tale of *Mahishasura Mardini,* being a very popular theme. Dancers perform acrobatic movements to the tunes of accompanying music of *dhol* (drum), *dhamsa* (huge cup shaped drums) and *shehnai* (double reed wind instrument).

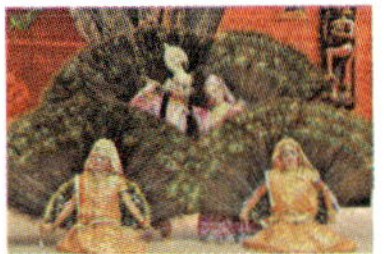

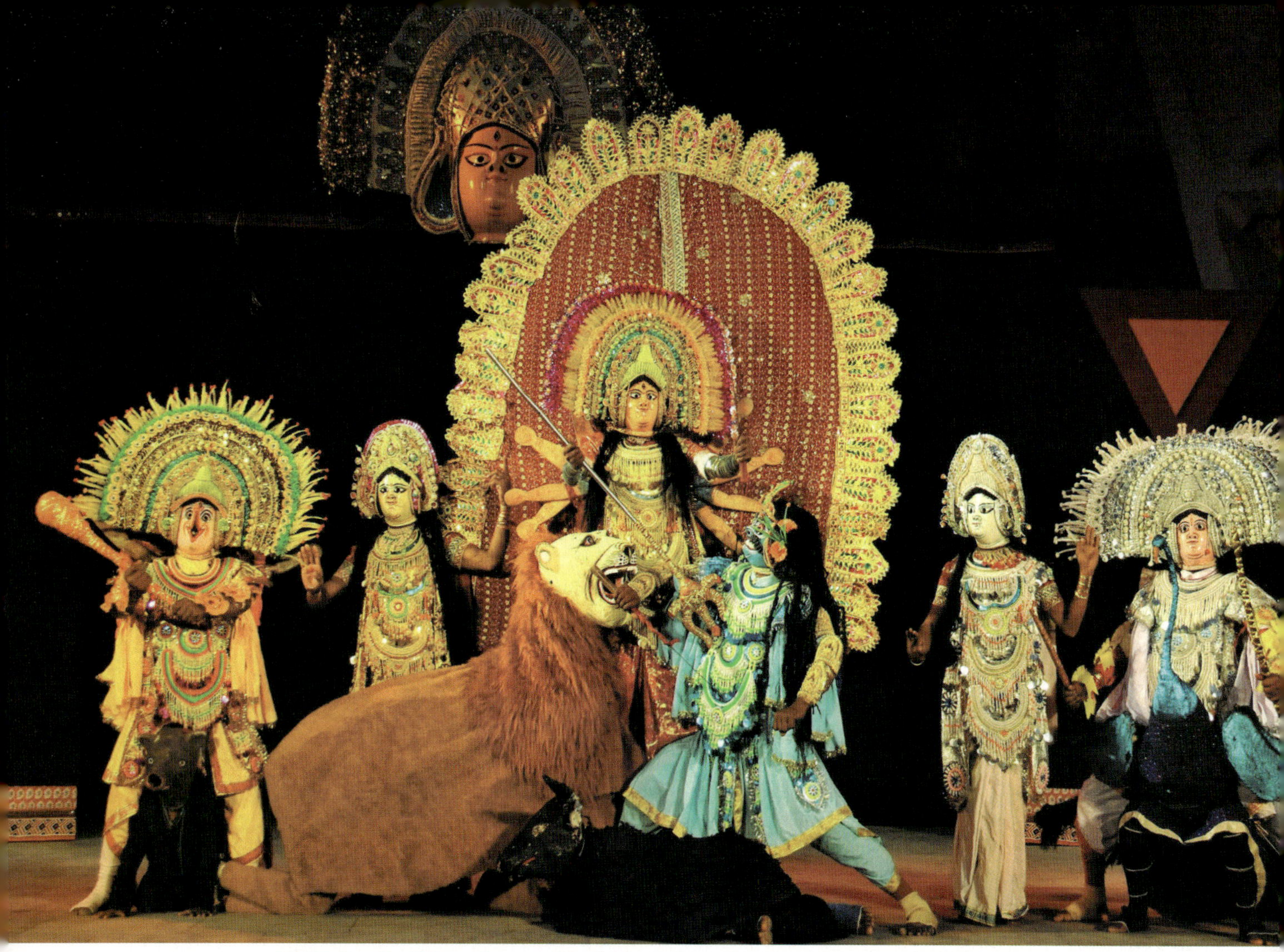

18.43: Purulia Chhau dance with vivid masks — Courtesy, Sangeet Natak Akademi

Alkap

It is a mix of dance with music and theatre and is performed by a group of artists. The subjects may dwell on various socio-economic issues of rural areas and thus serves as a medium of spread of social messages as well as rural entertainment.

Kirtan

It is a popular folk dance which is associated with the tradition of Bhakti (devotion). It is performed in the entire state and is said to trace its origin to ancient times, while becoming a popular tradition in the Bhakti movement spearheaded by **Sri Chaitanya**. The art involves song and dance in devotion to Lord Krishna. The accompanying instruments are *dhol* and *mridanga.*

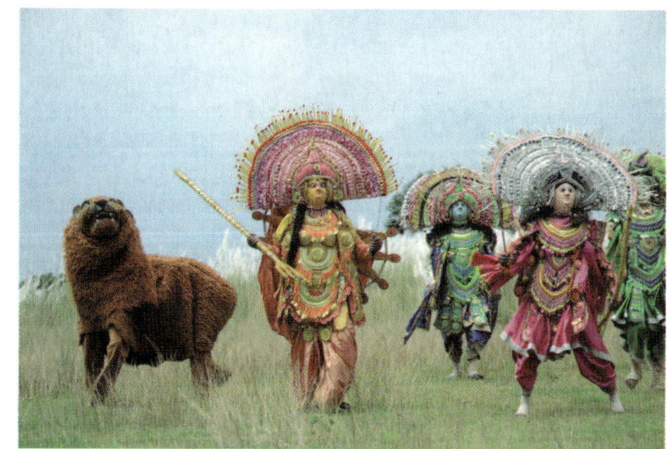

18.44: A Purulia Chhau performance in a natural open setting — Courtesy, Department of Tourism, West Bengal

Besides the kirtan dance, many other devotional dance forms are popular in the state which are performed on various religious festivals. These include, the **Gajan** (performed in Gajan festival in praise of Lord Shiva in month of Chitra) and **Durga Puja Dhak** (performed in the festivities of Navaratra).

Many dances of West Bengal are of **martial arts origin** or incorporate this tradition. This includes the **Bratachari Raibense**, a dance performed exclusively by the male dancers. The dance draws its source from the medieval age infantry traditions and includes vigorous dance movements, with mock fighting and acrobatics. **Laghur Nritya**, or stick dance, performed using long sticks, **Ranapa dance** where artists walk on stilts, **Dhali dance** (a dance with the shield) and **Paika dance**, are other war dances in this martial arts folk tradition.

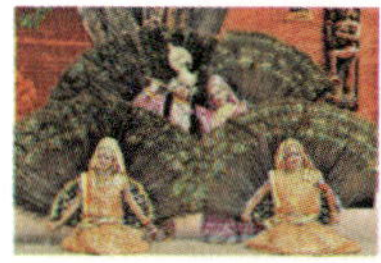

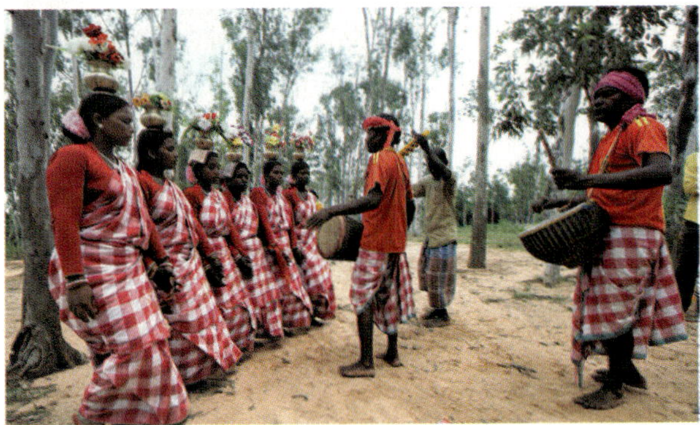
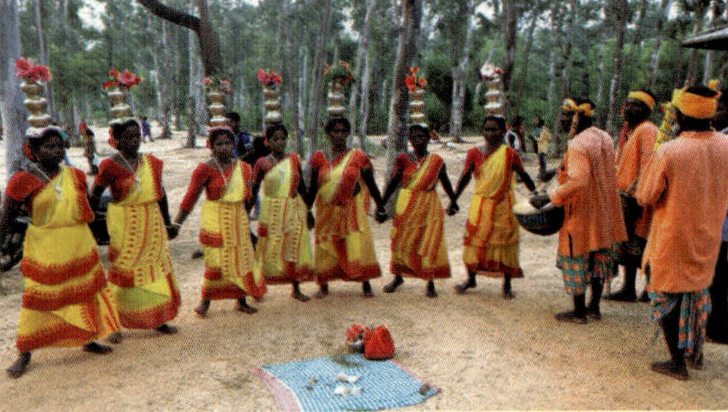

18.45 & 18.46: Santhali dance performances — Courtesy, Department of Tourism, West Bengal

A number of dances are associated with the **tribes** and the **communities** of the state and include **Santhali dance** (of the Santhali community in the Birbhum, Malda, Bankura and Burdhmann districts), **Mundari dance** (performed by the Mundari community on the occasion of the Karam Puja), **Natua and Rabha dance** (of the Rabha community), **Rajbanshi dance** (of Rajbanshi community of North Bengal in reverence to the Teesta river) and **Chaibari Nritya** (of the tea plantation workers of Northern Bengal).

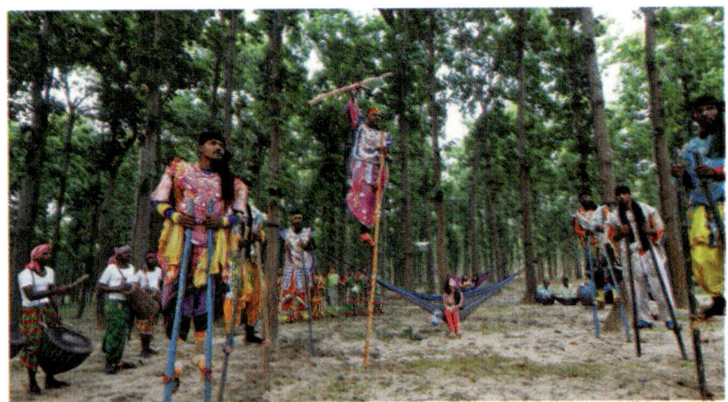

18.47: A Mundari dance performance amidst natural settings — Courtesy, Department of Tourism, West Bengal

Sikkim

It is a state endowed with natural beauty amidst the peaks of grand Himalayas and is known for a variety of folk dances. These are integrated with the life and activity of the people including their religion, agricultural practices and festivities. Among the most popular of the Sikkimese folk dances are **Tamang Selo**, **Yak Chham, Chu Faat, Chutkay** amidst others.

Tamang Selo

It is a traditional community dance of the **Tamang** people of the state. The dance is performed during the festival of Dasain (Dussehra). It is a dance of vigour and fun, reflective of the joy and colourful lifestyle of the people. The dance involves robust foot tapping and other moves to the music from the traditional instrument *damphu* (a large tambourine like percussion instrument).

Yak Chham

It is a dance of the **Bhutia** people and reflects the **movement of the yak**. It is popular with the herdsmen in the mountains who dress up as a yak (with a mask and other costumes). As a dance, it is reflective of the significance of the yaks in the life of the people, as they are dependent on it for transportation, food and even clothes. Essentially, it is a community dance, and performed to the music of traditional musical instruments. The Yak Chham dance performances in the monasteries of Rumtek, Pemayangtse and Enchey are especially popular. Another Chaam dance is the **Singhi Cham** which is a snow lion dance.

Chu Faat

It is a ritualistic dance of the Lepcha community performed in **veneration of Mount Khangchendzonga** which is the guardian deity of the Sikkimese people. *Chu* literally means 'the snowy range', while *faat* means 'to worship'. The dance is to the accompaniment of devotional songs with the dancers carrying butter lamps and green bamboo leaves.

Chutkay

It is a romantic group dance which is performed during the harvest season and other social occasions. The young male and female dancers gather to share their feeling of happiness and joy which is expressed in the dance.

Some other dances of the state include, **Sherpa dance** of the sherpa community which has special costumes and headgear; **Ghantu dance** performed by the young girls of the Gurung community; **Nyongri Nyot** which depicts the process of cultivation of maize; **Marooni** dance, which incorporates themes from the

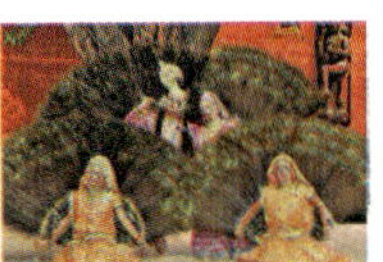

epics and mythology; **Chyap Brung**, a dance with this drum like traditional instrument; **Denong-Neh- Nah,** performed by young boys and girls in honour of Guru Rimpoche and other saints, besides other dances.

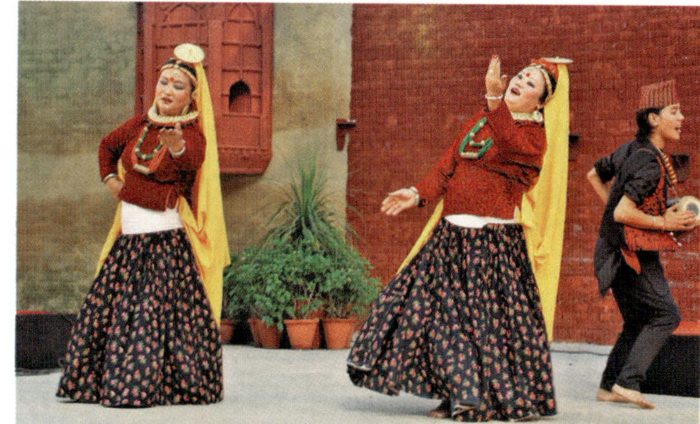

18.48: A Marooni dance performance, a dance of Sikkim incorporating themes from epics and mythdogy. — Courtesy, Sangeet Natak Akademi

Assam

It is the land endowed with nature's bounties and a rich ancient culture. It is replete with different dance forms, the most important and famous among them being the **Bihu**. The other dances include, **Jhumur**, **Bhortal** dance, **Bagurumba** amidst others.

Bihu

It comprises a set of colourful folk dances which are performed on the occasion of the different **Bihu festivals**. These festivals incorporate the celebration of agricultural harvest, welcome of the onset of different seasons as well as the rural socio-cultural milieu of the region. There are three different Bihus, and accordingly, different dances as per the festival and the occasion. Usually, Bihu is celebrated as a community dance where the dancers perform in a circle. The music, generally played by men, is to the accompaniment of traditional instruments like *dhol* (drum), *pepa* (flute) cymbals, bamboo clappers, hornpipes and others. The dance usually begins with a slow tempo and picks up pace with the music. Adorned in traditional and colourful clothing, both men and women perform the dance to the beat of drums. The women typically place their hands above the hips with their palms facing outwards. With brisk steps, flipping of hands and swaying of hips the dance progresses.

Bohag Bihu or the Rangoli Bihu: It is celebrated in spring and ushers the new year in Assam. The festival and the dance are also reflective of the agricultural tradition as it is the sowing time. Besides, this dance is an expression of the energy and exuberance of the youth, the romance of the young (as it is also the time of marriages) and therefore even a courtship dance. Thus, the dance and festival are also associated with fertility (both of the nature and humans) and joy.

The Magh or the Bhogali Bihu: It is associated with the collection of the harvest and religious rituals of offerings before Agni (god of fire). The celebrations and the dances are performed on the last of the month of *Pous* and the first day of *Magh*.

Kaati Bihu or the Kongali Bihu: It is the third of the Bihu festivals which falls on the last day of the month of *Ashwin*. As the new crop is not ready as yet and the levels of the previous harvest have gone down, this festival is relatively modest and the same is also reflected in the dance which may not be so exuberant. Prayers are also offered for a generous subsequent harvest.

Some of the other recognised Bihu dances are; **Moran Bihu** of the Moran tribe (centred around love and yearning of the youth), the **Deori Bihu** of the Deoris (a riverine tribe), **Mishing Bihu** of the Mishing tribe associated with Ali-Ai Ligang festival of seed sowing), **Jeng Bihu** of upper Assam region (performed only by women particularly on moonlit night) and **Mukholi Bihu** which is similar to rangoli Bihu (and is an expression of love and courtship amongst the youth).

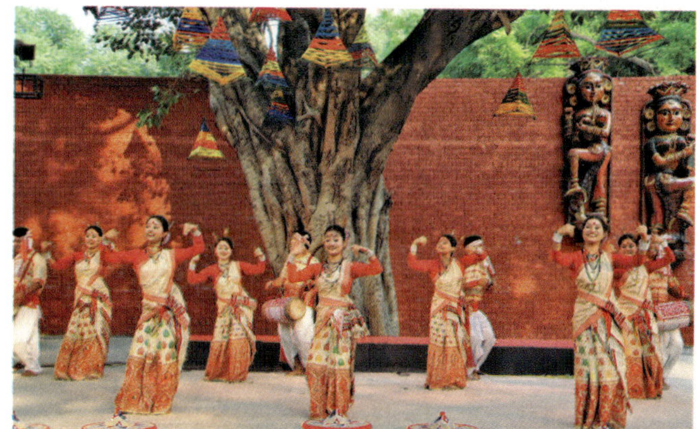

18.49: Bihu dance of Assam — Courtesy, Sangeet Natak Akademi

Jhumur: It is another dance of Assam which is especially popular with the workers of the **tea garden** (*kulis and adivasis)*. As a concept, it is secular performed by both young and old. The males usually play the music which is traditional instruments like *madal* (drum) *dhol*, *taal* (cymbals). The dance is largely performed by women who hold each other's waist and sway back and forth.

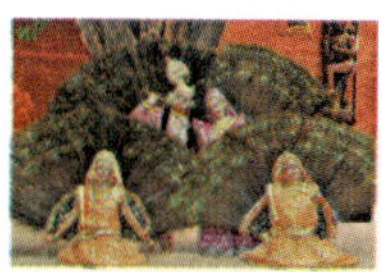

Bordoishikhla: It is a dance is performed by the **Bodo community**. The dance is also associated with harvest and welcomes a good monsoon. It's a colourful dance performed by young girls who hold bamboo clappers in their hand. The music is of the traditional instruments like *kham* (long drum), *siphung* (long flute of bamboo), *jotha* (cymbals), *charinda* (chordophone). The dance is also referred as the **Bagurumba** dance.

Bhortal dance: A unique dance of the Barpeta district, Bhortal dance is performed by a group of six to seven men who hold *bhortals* or cymbals in their hands. The dance is performed to a fast beat known as *Jhiya Nom.* The dance is said to be derived from the classical Sattriya dance and was developed by Narhari Burha Bhakat, a well-known Sattriya artist.

Among the other popular dances of the region are; **Domahi Kikang** of the Karbi tribe, **Mishing Gumrak** associated with Gumrak festival of the Mishing, **Bisuyo Jama** dance of the Deori tribe of Northeast Assam, **Rabha dance** of the Rabha community, the **Muchaglangnai** dance of the Bodo community.

18.50: Performance of Bhortal dance of Assam — Wikimedia Commons

Manipur

The dances of Manipur are an integral part of its social fabric and incorporate the religious fervour, the spiritual experience as well as the cultural milieu of the people, particularly of the diverse tribes of the state. Among the most important of its dance forms are the **Manipuri Rasa** which is considered a classical dance form. Classical Manipuri is also said to incorporate elements of traditional dances such as Manipuri Sankirtan and Thangata. Besides, its rich repertoire includes various other folk dances such as the **Lai Haraoba** dances and others.

The Lai Haraoba dances

Lai Haraoba is the festival of Gods of the **Meiti** people of the state and incorporates different ritualistic dances, through which the creation of the universe and reverence to the deities is depicted. This essentially represents the pre-Vaishnavite culture. The festivals begin towards the end of the year and continue in the new year (April-May). The dances are performed by the *maibas* (priests) and the *maibis* (priestess) in the temples of Umanglai, the ancestral god of the Meitis. The dance movements are smooth, rhythmic symbolic and ritualistic. The different segments of the festival incorporate different dance forms.

Meibi Laiching Jagoi

The first of these dances is the **Meibi Laiching Jagoi**, which is performed by two *maibis* and depicts the creation of the universe. The deities are invoked for an auspicious beginning and initiation of the celebrations. **Meibi Jagoi** dance, then enacts the creation and evolution of life. This dance is an offering to the guardian deities and beseeches their blessings for welfare of the entire community. **Thougal Jagoi Laisam Jagoi** is presented then by the men and women worshippers who pray for an auspicious beginning of the rituals.

Khamba Thoibi Jagoi

Another popular folk dance of the Lai Haroaba festival is **Khamba Thoibi Jagoi**, which brings out the story of Khamba a legendary hero and Thoibi a princess of Moirang who falls in love with Khamba. The dance itself is believed to have been performed by Khamba and Thoibi in the temple of lord Ebudhou Thangjing. Besides other dances are too enacted in the festival.

Thang-Ta

It is a traditional **martial arts** form of dance, which integrates the techniques of wielding weapons **Thang** (sword), and **Ta** (spear) and combat in an art. Thang-Ta is essentially a part of Manipur's martial arts technique called Huyen Langlon, with the latter incorporating armed combat or Thang-Ta and even unarmed combat. The Thang-Ta performance usually begins with *Khurumjaba*, where the performers seek the blessings of the lord and the gurus by while holding their weapons and instruments. The dance performed by men who are dressed like warriors, involves rhythmic movements which incorporate the basics of the marital art form and of wielding the weapons.

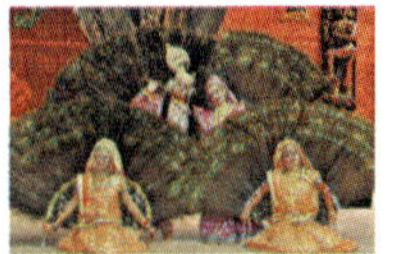

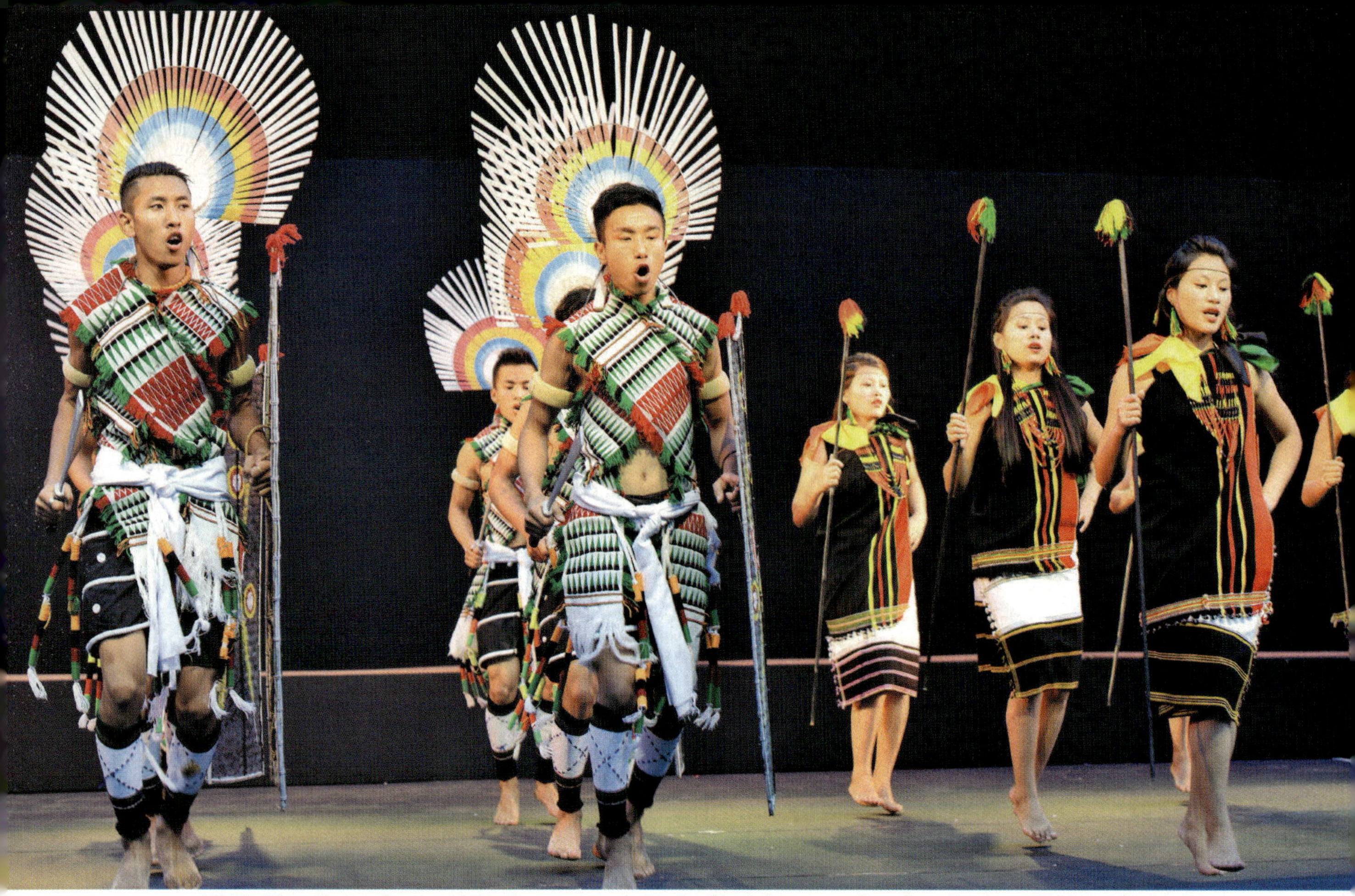

18.51: Mao Naga dance of Manipur, an agrarian festival dance — Courtesy, Sangeet Natak Akademi

Mao dance

It is popular in the Mao Naga community and performed by young girls and boys during the annual harvesting and seed sowing festivals. It is a colourful dance which incorporates graceful movements of the body and intricate footwork.

Among the other popular folk dances are, **Thabal Chongba**, performed in the festival of Yaoshang; **Luivat Pheizak**, dance of the Tangkhul Naga community; **Shim Laam** dance of the Rongmei community (also known as the fly dance); dances of the Kom tribe, Pung Cholom, Dhol Cholom, Pena Cholom, Dhol-dholak Cholom etc.

Tripura

A land endowed by the bounties of nature and inhabited by different tribes and communities, Tripura has some rich and unique dance forms. This includes the folk and tribal dances of **Hozagiri, Garia, Jhum, Lebang, Bomani** and others.

Garia/Goria

This dance is among the most important of folk dances of the region which is in dedication to the God Garia, praying for a good harvest. Jhum cultivation (clearing a selected land preparing and sowing it) is integral to the life of people and is done by the month of Baisakh. A week long Garia-puja ensues (middle of April) in which the farming community prays to the lord for a good harvest by means of song and this dance. The dance involves different hand movements and whirling. It is said to have over two dozen mudras. The dance is to accompaniment of singing, begins with a slow rhythm which increases in tempo as the dance progresses.

Hozagiri

It is a dance of the **Reang tribes** performed specially in the annual festival in the month of April. A ritual dance, it is dedicated to Goddess of wealth Maimuna. Thus, it is a part of community prayer for a good harvest. The dance performed by the Reang women is unique in its execution. The dancers **stand on an earthen pitcher while balancing a bottle on their head with a lighted diya (earthen lamp) on it**. The movement of the upper body is restricted in the dance to balance the bottle and diya while the lower body gyrates in wave like movements. The women adorn traditional dress with jewellery made of coin rings, covering the upper body substantially. The accompanying music is from traditional instrument, like kham (drum), bamboo flute and cymbals.

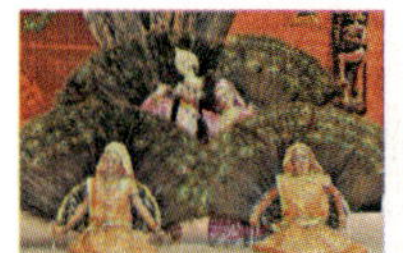

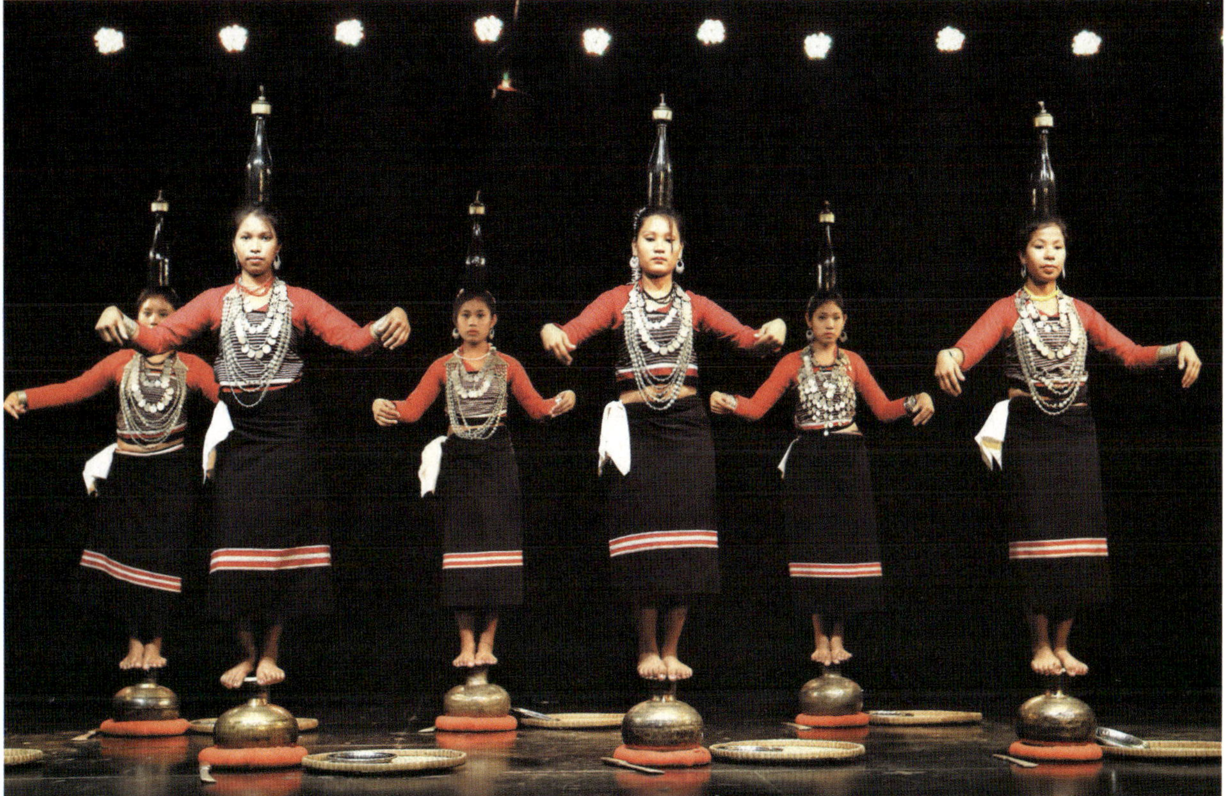

18.52: A Hozagiri dance performance of Reang tribes of Manipur; dancers balancing a bottle on their heads while standing on a pitcher — Courtesy, Sangeet Natak Akademi

Jhum

This is another folk dance which is associated with the practice of jhum cultivation. The farmers and labourers engaged in the practice of jhum cultivation sing and dance to take away the monotony of work and to work harder as a team. The dance is also performed on the occasion of the Sangrai festival.

Lebang Boomani

It is a dance performed by both men and women and is associated with **harvest**. Lebangs are colourful insects which visit the hill slopes in search of the sown seeds. The harvesters would catch these with the help of bamboo clappers and the amount of catch would signify as to how good the harvest would be. The dance involves men holding the wooden clappers, the clapping sound of which would attract the insects while women (who run to catch the insects) are dressed in bright clothes and holding colourful scarves. The dance proceeds with the performers forming a circle, with the musical accompaniment from Kham (drum), flute and cymbals, all made of bamboo.

Among other folk dances of the state are **Bizu/Bihju dance** of the Chakma community performed at the Chaitra Sankranti (marking the end and beginning of a new year); **Hai Hak** dance of the Halam community associated with Jhum cultivation; **Dailo Nritya** in celebration of the reaping of the harvest; **Wya** dance of the Mogh community in celebration of the Wya festival and for praying to lord Buddha; **Gajan** dance of the Bengali community in celebration of the Gajan festival and offering prayer to lord Shiva; **Cheraw** dance of the Darlong for well-being of the pregnant mothers and as a reposition of faith in afterlife.

Nagaland

Nagaland is a state known for its music and dance. Many of its dances are essentially in the nature of war dances. These are accompanied by enactment of war with gears suited for the mock-war like performance, accompanied by war cries and other colourful costumes.

Chang lo

Among the most popular of the dances of the state are **Chang lo** (performed by Chang Naga tribe) which is a war victory dance, **Modse** dance of Ao tribe, which is another of the war dances, **Zealing** dance (performed by the Zealing tribe) and is also a war enactment dance; **Udoho** dance (Angami war dance) which includes holding a spear and challenging/shouting at the opponents, and **Agurshikukula** (another war dance).

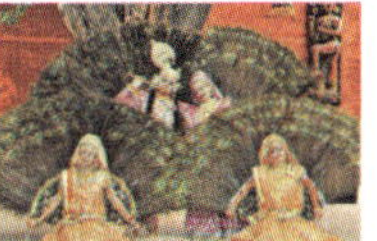

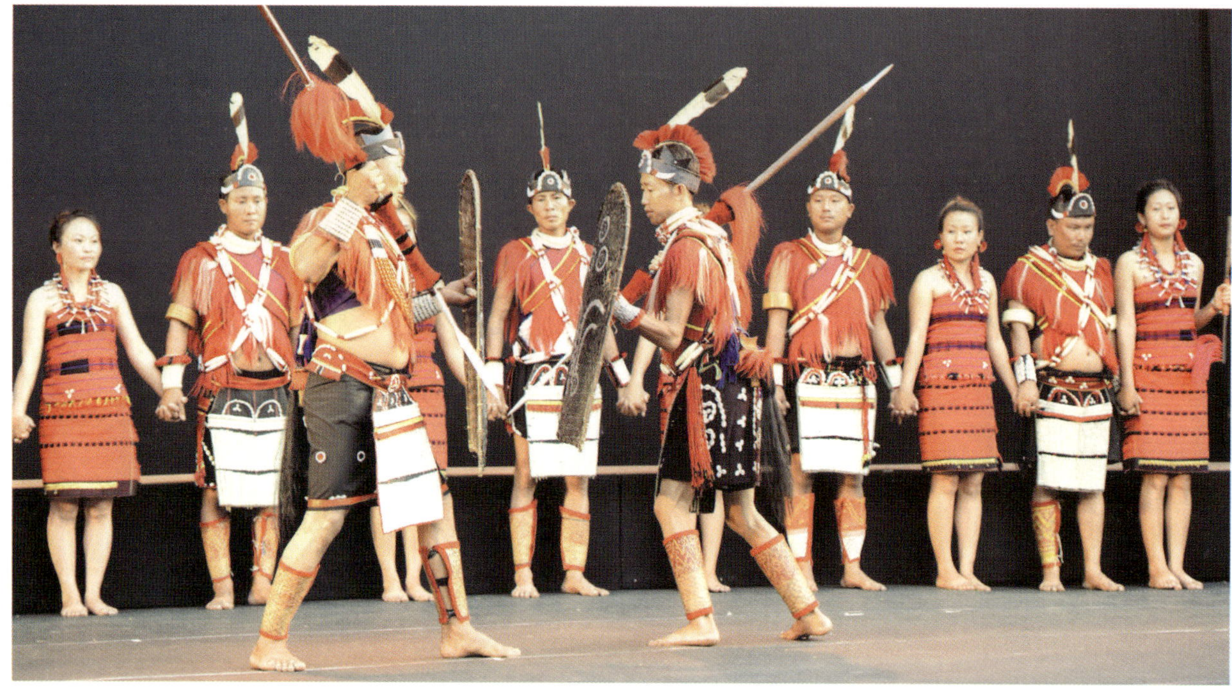

18.53: A warrior dance of Nagaland — Courtesy, Sangeet Natak Akademi

Other dances of the state include **Changai** dance (performed by the Chang tribe), **Butterfly** dance (Zealing tribe) **Kuki bamboo** dance, **Khamba Lim** (performed by men and women standing in two rows), **Leshalapatu** (dance by women) and **Mayur** dance, besides others.

Mizoram

The state is home to a variety of folk dances which include **Cheraw**, **Chailam**, **Khullam**, besides others. Amongst its dances, the **Cheraw** is considered to be the most popular which is performed by both the men and women together. The dance involves use of bamboo sticks which are placed horizontally on the ground with men clapping the sticks and women dancing in between them with intricate steps.

Chailam

This dance is performed on the occasion of the festival of 'Chapchar Kut'. Men and women both perform the dance and stand alternatively in circles. The women hold on to the waist of the man and the latter on the women's shoulder. In the middle of the circle are placed the musicians who play the drums and the horn.

Khullam

This is another popular dance which literally means 'dance with the guests'. It's a dance usually performed in a ceremony called *Khuangchawi*, which as per the customs and beliefs endows a special place in the society and eventually in the paradise or *Pialral*.

Other dances of the state include **Sarlamkai/Solakia Chawnglaizawn, Chheihlam, Tlanglam, Zangtalam.**

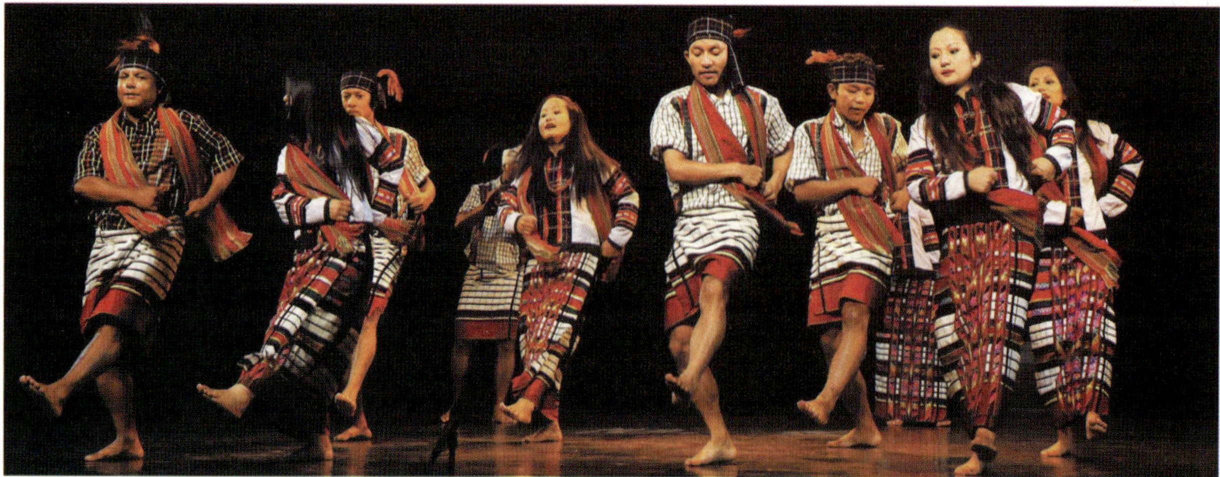

18.54: A folk-dance performance of Mizoram — Courtesy, Sangeet Natak Akademi

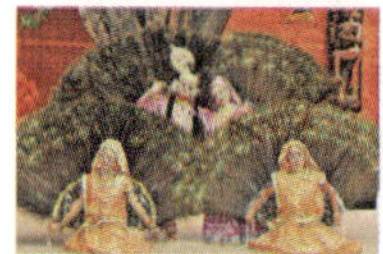

Odisha

Odisha is a land of rich ancient traditions. Among its popular folk dances are **Ghumura, Mayurbhanj Chhau, Gotipua, Jhumar, and Paika** besides others.

Ghumura

This dance is one of the most known and among the leading folk dances of Odisha. It is performed by the **Saora and other tribes** of the state. The dance is especially popular in the Kalahandi district, besides in Bolangir, Sambalpur and Cuttack. It draws its name from the **musical instrument Ghumura**, which is a pitcher shaped drum. It is tied around the neck of the dancer and played by the dancer during the performance. The steps of dance involve pirouettes, jumps and some intricate movements which are performed at a fast tempo. The movements give the impression of it being a heroic dance and suggest a possible early evolution as a war dance. However, in modern times, it integrates the culture of the people. The dance is also performed to the accompaniment of songs, the main theme of which ranges from issues of daily life, to hunting, to joys and sorrows of the people. The musical accompaniment is to instruments like *dhol*, *madal, taal* besides *ghumura*.

Mayurbhanj Chhau

This is another popular folk dance of the state. It is the third of the Chhau dances, the other two being the Seraikella Chhau of Jharkhand and Purulia Chhau of West Bengal. But unlike the other two Chhau dances**, it does not use any mask**. Mayurbhanj Chhau dance is said to have a **martial arts origin,** and initially, the artists were dressed as warriors, with a sword and shield in the hands. The dance in modern form mimics this tradition, however sans the sword or other weapons,

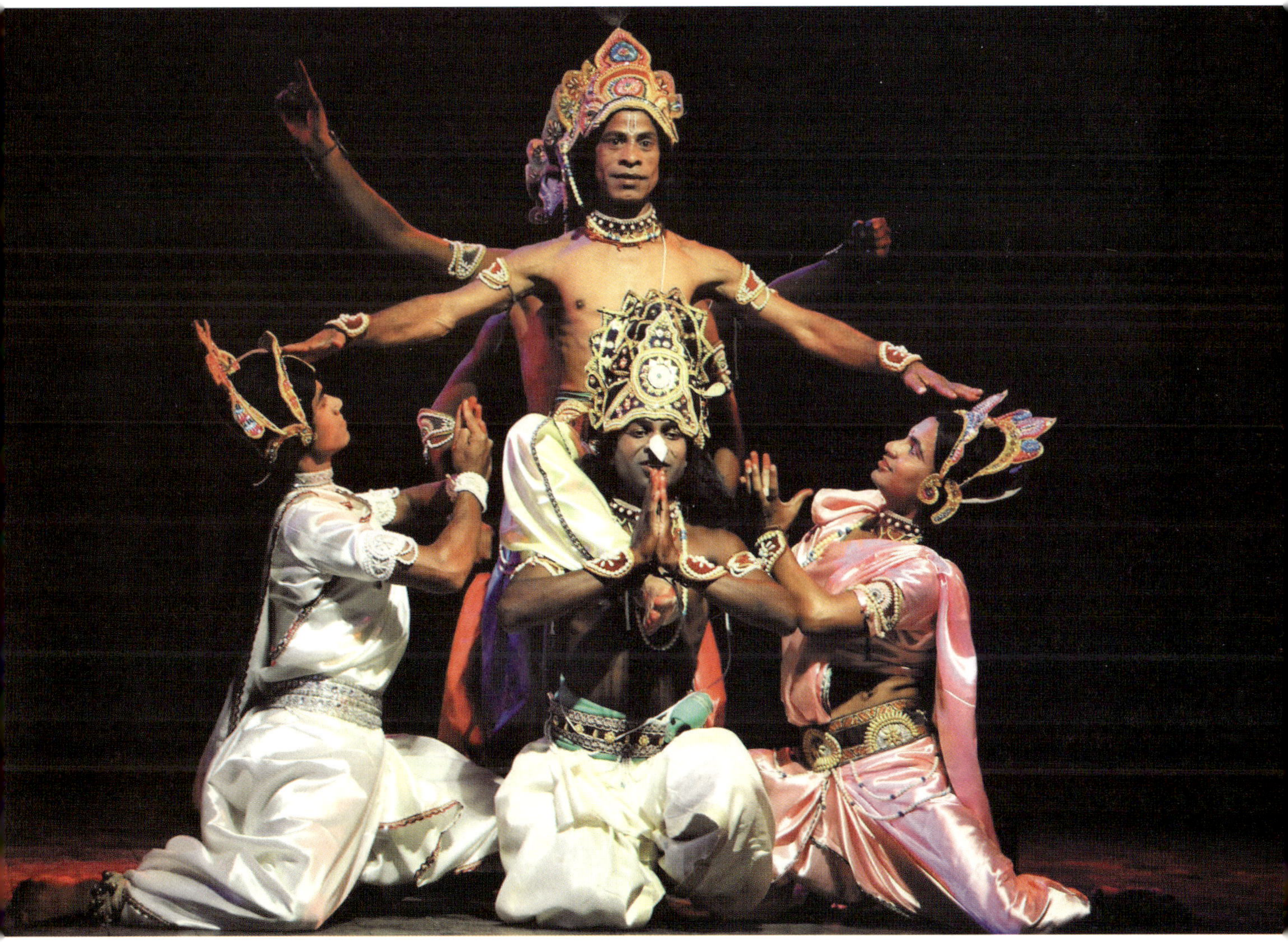

18.55: Garuda vahana, a Mayurbhanj Chhau performance — Courtesy, Sangeet Natak Akademi

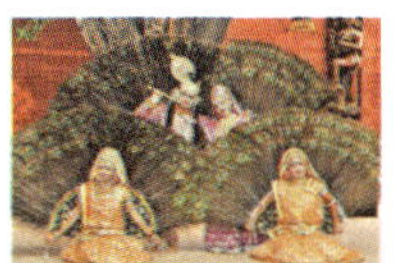

with only the body movement being representative of them. This dance is a form of dance drama, with the theme usually incorporating anecdotes of Mahabharata, Ramayana and those from the life of Sri Krishna.

Gotipua

This dance is a unique tradition of the state, for it involves **dance by young boys who dress-up as girls**. The art is said to have emerged from the *devadasi* system where women were dedicated as temple dancers. As there was objection to this tradition in many quarters, particularly during the British regime, the practice of training young boys in the dance who dress up as girls, emerged. Goti Pua literally means a single-boy. However, the dance usually involves a group of boys who are also usually associated with local *akhadas* (village clubs). The dance performance also incorporates acrobatic figures which draw

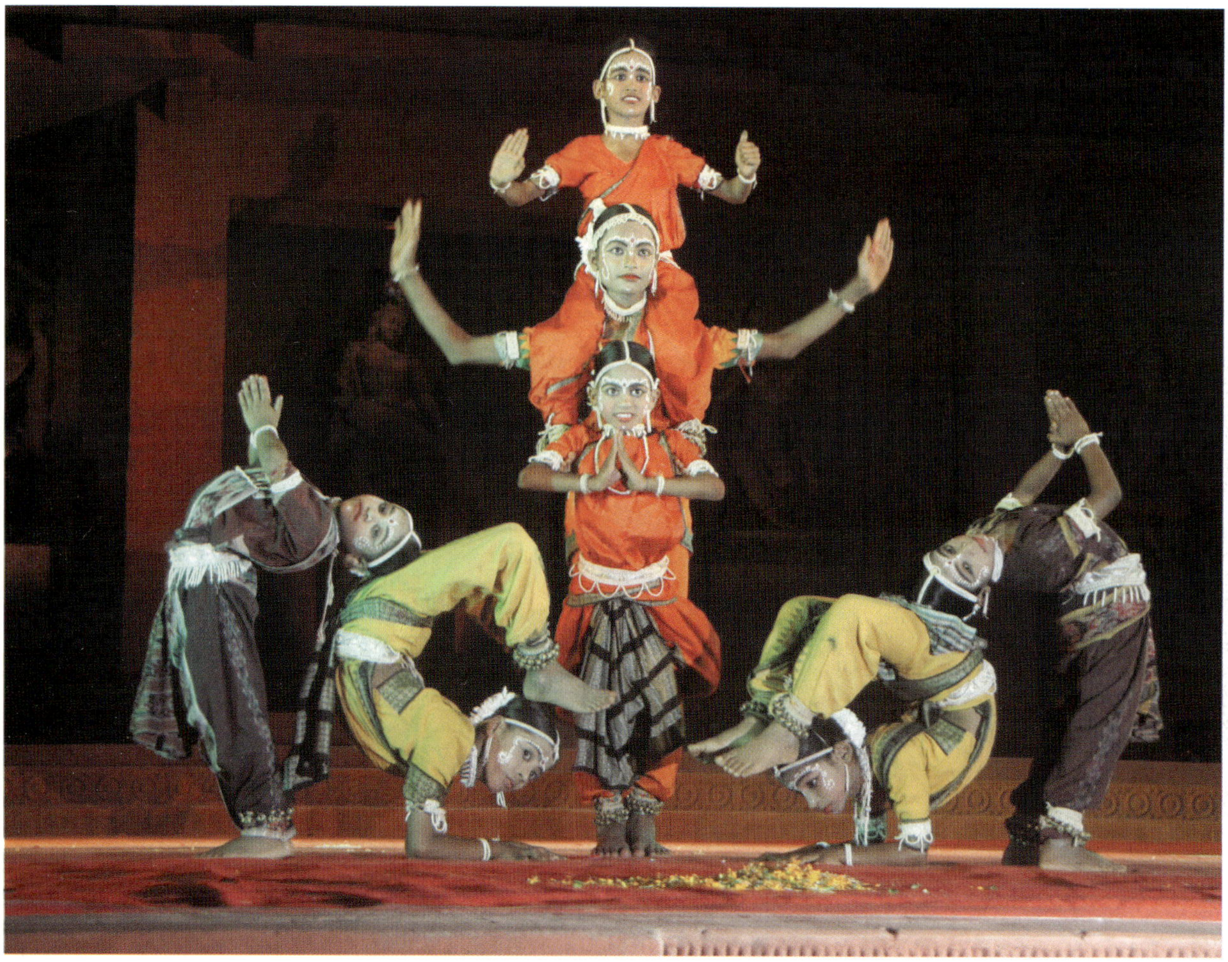

18.56: Gotipua dance — Courtesy, Department of Tourism, Odisha

inspiration from the life of Radha and Sri Krishna. Thus, the philosophy of this art is embedded in the *sakhibhava* culture where the devotees consider themselves to be consorts of Lord Krishna. Feminine grace and movements are its essential elements. *Vandana* (invocation), *sarigama* (celebratory dance piece), Oddisi dance, *abhinaya* (enactment of poetries like Gita-Govinda or others based on life of Sri Krishna) are some of its elements. The dance is performed at the various festivals and is also said to have influenced the classical Odissi dance.

Other folk dances of Odisha include **Jhoomar** (western Odisha folk dance performed on festivals) **Paika** and **Ruk Mar Nacha** (martial art form of dances), **Chaitighoda** (a dummy horse dance), **Dalkhai** (Sambal puri folk dance performed by unmarried girls on festive occasions, as prayers to goddess Dalkhai for well-being of their brothers) **Raserkeli** (folk dance of western Odisha performed by women), **Naga dance** (of Puri performed with different weapons), **Karma** (ritualistic tribal dances in obeisance to deity Karma-sani), **Baagha Naach** (tiger dance of Sambalpuri tribals), **Dhap dance** (of Kandha tribals of western Odisha) besides others.

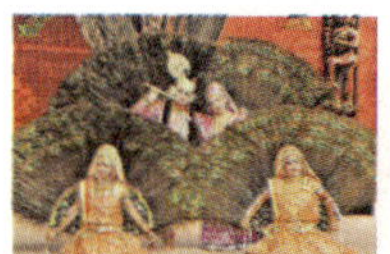

Maharashtra

The folk dances of Maharashtra have a long historical tradition, are rich as an art, and fulfill a vast range of socio-cultural purposes. While some folk dances like **Lavani** and **Koli** are popular as a means of entertainment, **Dindi** and **Kala** fall under the category of religious folk dances. While **Tamasha** is a folk theatre which integrates the art of folk dance, **Povada** brings out the achievements of the Maratha ruler Shivaji. **Dhangri Gaja** is unique as a community dance and pays obeisance to the deities.

Lavani

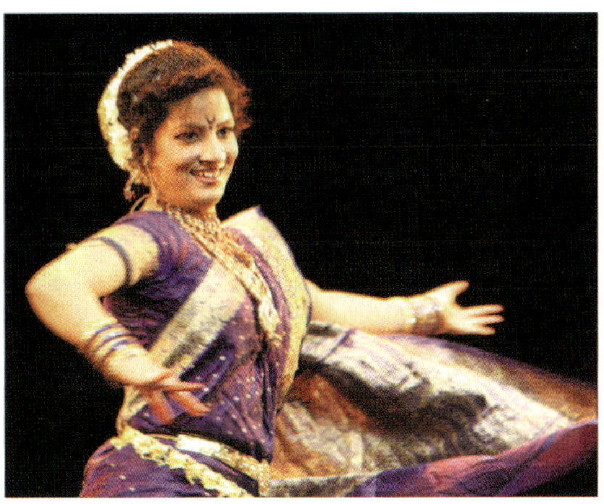

18.57: A Lavani dance performance — Wikimedia Commons

This is among the most popular of Marathi folk dances and also a prominent folk entertainment. The word Lavani is derived from Lavanya, which means **beauty**, and is traditionally performed by **women**. The dance is to accompaniment of Lavani song and to the rhythmic beats of the *dholaki*. As a dance, it is **sensuous and fast paced**. The accompanying words of the song may be naughty or even risqué with a vast range of subjects, socio-political satire or even the romantic experience of an individual falling under its ambit. The songs were earlier classified as *Niruguni Lavani* (philosophical) or *Shringari Lavani* (sensual). The dance performance is classified as *Phadachi Lavani*, involving a public performance over a larger set of audience; or *Baithakichi Lavani*, a seated performance before a select set of private audience (like a *mujara*). Lavani is also unique, for the female dancer performs in sarees which are nine yards long.

Dindi and Kala

They represent the genre of **religious folk dances** which are related to Lord Krishna and his playful antics. The dance is traditionally performed on the day of *Ekadashi* in the month of *Kartik*. In the Dindi dance, men and women gather in a circle with short sticks (*dindis*) in their hand and dance to the beats of mridangam (small drum) played by a musician who stands in a centre. The dance also incorporates a song led by a chorus leader. As the song proceeds, the music tempo picks up, and dancers form two rows or different geometric formations. In the Kala dance, the dancers, usually men, form a two-tiered circle with one set over the shoulder of the other. They attempt to break an overhanging pot which contains curd which then splashes over the dancers.

Koli

This is a dance of **fisherman community** of Maharashtra which is performed by both by the men and women who stand in different rows. While men stand holding the oars and emulate the rowing movement, the women stand on the opposite rows with their arms linked and taking to and fro dancing steps towards the men. The dancers may break the formation and again join together, thus symbolizing the waves and their movement.

Dhangri Gaja

It is a community dance performed by the Dhangars, a herding tribe of Sholapur district. Dressed in a typical Marathi dress of *dhoti*, *angarakha*, *pheta* and colourful handkerchiefs, the dance is performed to the tune of drums, played by a group of drum players.

The other important folk dance includes; **Pavri Nach** which is the dance of Kokna tribes of northwestern Maharasthra and **Povada** which is a form of ballad incorporating singing and dancing; **Lezim dance** in which dancers usually more than 20 perform to the tune of Lezims (cymbals).

Goa

Over centuries of political influence of different regimes, including the Portugeese, led Goa to emerge as a melting pot of different cultures. It's a state which is known for its vibrant music and dance which is integrated in the social fabric and cultural milieu of its people. Among the most popular of the Goan folk dances, are **Dekhni**, **Fugadi**, **Dhalo**, **Goff**, **Kunbi**, **Morulem** and **Dhangar** amidst others.

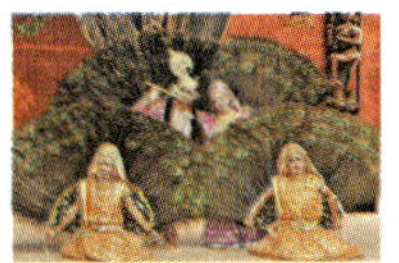

Dekhni

It is among the most popular of the Goan folk dances. Literally meaning **beauty** in Konkani language, the dance is performed by the **women** and represents the unique **cross-cultural influence** quintessential of Goa. Dekhni (or Dekni) is considered a semi-classical dance which is said to have origins in the *devadasi* system of temple dance girls, who were dedicated to the service of the lord. During the centuries of Portuguese rule, many of the Hindus converted to Christianity bringing an amalgamation of traditional folk arts and cultural practices. In modern times, Dekhani is performed often by Christian girls who are attired in traditional Indian costumes like sarees. The performance is usually by a group of women and is a combination of song and dance. The music is a mix of Indian and western styles while the dance steps may be taken from the classical dances like Bharatanatyam and Kathak. The dance is graceful with melodious song and music of folk drums *ghumat*. One popular performance enacts the life of a *devadasi* girl beseeching a boatman to ferry her across the river, which is known as *Hanv Saiba Poltodi Vetam* (first said to be published in 1895).

Dhalo

It is another popular folk dance which is performed by **rural women**. It is a dance of a special occasion to celebrate during week long festivities and performed on the moonlit night (Poornima) of the *Pausha* month (in winters). The womenfolk propitiate the deity Mother Earth and perform this dance post dinner at a pre-selected venue (called *mand*) in a courtyard of village house. The women arrange themselves in two groups of around 12 women each and link each other with their arms around their back. The women dance by moving forward and backward while singing in unison.

Fugadi

It is a category of group dance performed by **women** in the rural areas and the forests. Women dance either in a circle by joining their hands, or in parallel rows facing each other. The occasion of the dance is on festivals like Ganesh Chaturthi or other celebrations. The dance is usually to the accompaniment of a variety of Fugadi songs which are based on different community issues, Puranic tales or others. However, there is no musical instrument to accompany the performance. A type of this folk dance is Kalash Fugadi which is performed in reverence to goddess Mahalakshmi. Women carry a *kalash* (earthen pot) and blow into it while dancing rhythmically without there being any song.

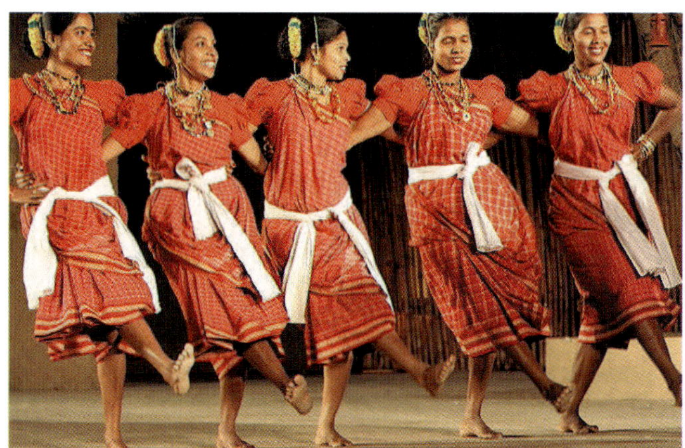

18.58: Fugadi dance performance, a folk dance of women in rural areas of Goa — Wikimedia Commons

Among other folk dances of the state are **Dhangar** dance by the Dhangar tribal community; **Kunbi** by the Kunbi tribal community (one of the earliest settlers of the region); **Ghode modni** which is a horse dance; **Goff**, performed while holding colourful cords; **Romta Mel**, thanks giving dance during the Shigmo festival in Northern and Central Goa; **Divlyan Nach** or **Lamp Dance**, a slow dance with lit lamps balanced on heads, **Tarangmel,** an energetic dance with colourful flags and streamers (*tarang*) performed during Holi and Dussehra.

Andhra Pradesh and Telangana

These regions have a tradition of dance which is a couple of millennia old and the classical dance form of Kuchipudi is an offshoot of this very tradition. Among the most prominent of folk dances of the region include **Andhranatyam, Veeranatyam, Burrakatha, Butta, Bommalu, Tapetta Gullu, Kolattam** and others.

Andhranatyam

This is among the **oldest of folk traditions** which is said to have a history of nearly 2000 years. It belongs to the Nattuva Mela tradition (dance by women), the other tradition being Natya Mela (dance by men) and is often considered an ancient classical dance. It was performed in the temples, royal courts and even in the Buddhist monasteries. Over the years it suffered a decline till it was revived in the 1970s. As a dance it involves graceful and delicate movements of the female artists and incorporates the *Agama*, *Asthana* and *Prabandha* styles.

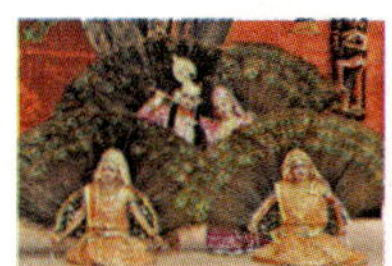

Veeranatyam

This is yet another very ancient art form which is also known as Veerangam or Veerabhadra Nrityam and literally meaning, **'the dance of the brave'**. The dance alludes to the emergence of Veerabhadra, a destructive form of lord Shiva, (on the occasion of death of Sati), who then unleashes destruction. Hence, it is vigorous and very expressive form of dance, portraying the anger of the deity and even performed with *Veer-khagam* (a sword). The music is to the accompaniment of traditional instruments like *dolu* (double headed drum), *tambura* (tanpura stringed instrument) etc. The dance emerged as a ritualistic art by the followers of the Shaivite Veerabhadra tradition, however now it is only a performing art.

Burrakatha

It is a form of a **ballad dance and singing**, in which a story or a message is conveyed by the dance to the audience. The earlier stories were from Hindu mythology/scriptures while contemporary and social issues are also now being taken up. Burra refers to the instrument of *tambura* which forms the main musical accompaniment. The narrator or the story teller plays the music while dancing to its tunes and also narrating the story. In modern times, this art form has been on steady decline.

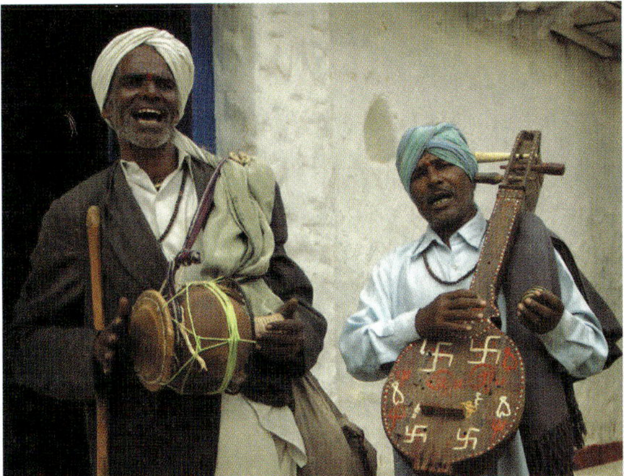

18.59: Burrakatha performance by musicians, a ballad singing and dance of Andhra Pradesh and Telangana — Wikimedia Commons

Other folk dances of this region are **Gobbi** (performed in *Sankranti* festival), **Bathukamma,** performed by women on the occasion of **Bathukama** (a floral dance festival); **Tapetta Gullu**, performed by earlier in northern coastal districts by shepherds (to appease the god of rains); **Butta Bommalu**, popular in West Godavari district (performed with masks over head and shoulders), **Kolattam** performed both by men and women in rural areas as a harvest dance (performed with sticks and similar to Dandia dance), **Vilasini Natyam**, female temple dance of *devadasi* tradition, **Bhamakalpam**, a theatrical dance drama, **Dhimsa** (tribal dance) and **Lambadi** (dance of semi nomadic tribes).

Karnataka

Karnataka has a rich tradition of dances which include the classical dance like Bharatanatyam, folk theatre like Yakshagana and different folk dances. These dances are integrated to the rituals and ceremonies, agriculture and harvest, festivals and activities of daily life. Among the folk dances is a class of dance termed as **Kunitha**, which are ritualistic folk dances. **Dollu Kunitha, Pata Kunitha** and **Goravara Kunitha** are among the most popular of these. Among the other folk dances of the state are, **Nagamandala, Garuda Gombe**, **Bhoot Aradhana** and others.

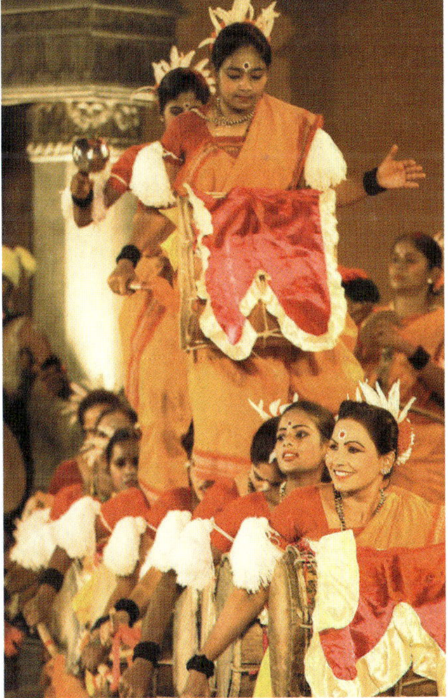

18.60: A Dollu Kunitha performance by women, a folk dance of Karnataka — Wikimedia Commons

Dollu Kunitha

It is performed by the Kuruba (shepherd) community of the *Beereshwara Sampradaya and* is among the most popular folk dances of the region. This Kunitha (ritual dance) derives its name from the prominent instrument used in the dance, **Dollu**, which is a large double headed drum. Each one of the dancers in the group of 16 performers wears it while dancing and singing. Essentially, it is a **ritualistic** dance performed by men. The leader of the dance holding the cymbals regulates the pace of the performance with its beats. As the dance progresses, the drum beats become vigorous, and the dance movements become quicken. Slow and fast rhythms alternate, thus weaving a pattern. In modern times, Dollu Kunitha is also performed by women.

Pata Kunitha

It is another of the ritualistic folk dances which is particularly popular in the Mysore region, especially in rural religious ceremonies. The dance is performed by around 10 to15 men who hold a *pata* which are

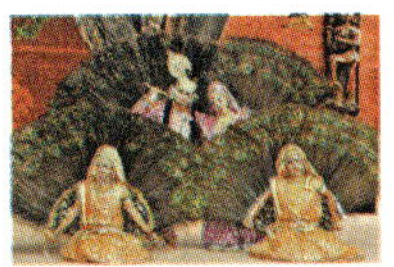

long bamboo poles with coloured decorative ribbons. The artists manipulate the pole while performing the dance steps to the rhythm of music which is largely from the traditional drums. In modern times the emphasis on the ritualistic narration is less, and greater emphasis is on the dancing skills while manipulating the long colourful poles.

Goravara Kunitha

It is popular in the Mysore and North Karnataka region and is a dance worshipping Lord Shiva. This is performed by around men (usually 10 to 12) who belong to the Gorava singing community.

Gaarudi Gombe

It literally means **'magical puppet'**, and is a folk art popular in the major festivals, particularly the Mysore Dusshera. The performers wear body suit puppets and character masks, which, put together, are 10 to 12 feet high. These are made of bamboo and paper-machie. The dancers are usually men, and the performance may even extend to several hours.

Nagamandala

It is a unique folk dance which is essentially a **ritualistic performance.** It is popular in southern Karnataka and is generally conducted in the period of April to December. The objective of the ritual is to quell/pacify the **serpent spirit**. The ceremonies involve performances by male dancers (known as *vaidyas*) which are done throughout the night. Music, ritual chanting and dance are a part of it.

Among the other folk dances are **Bhoot Aradhana** which is a dance personifying the holy spirit; **Veeragaase** a dance symbolic of heroism and valour of lord Veerabhadra; **Kombaat**, a religious dance performed in temples; **Suggi Kunitha**, a harvest dance; **Somana Kunitha**, dedicated to the mother goddess; **Jaggahalige Kunitha**, performed on Ugadi and Holi festivals, **Karadi Majalu**, a folk music and accompanying folk dance, and others.

Tamil Nadu

With a rich history of performing arts, the state is home to many dance forms like the classical **Bharatanatyam** and the folk forms of **Karakattam, Mayilattam, Oyilattam** and **Pampattam** amongst many others.

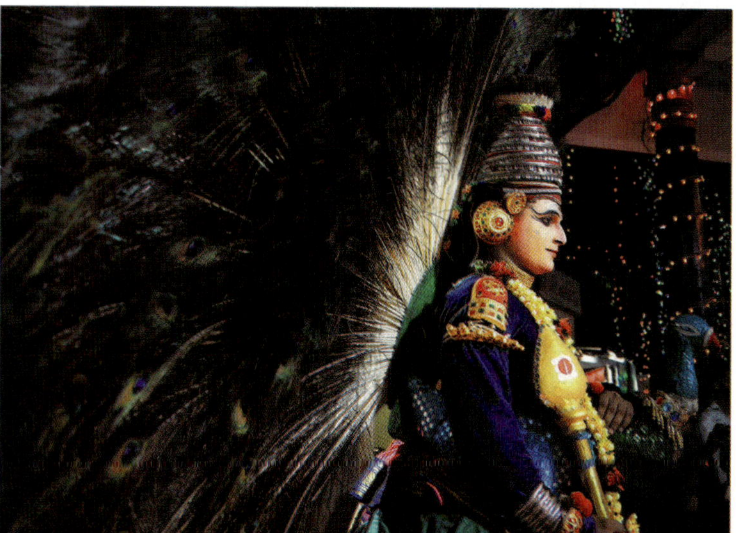

18.61: A Mayilattam performance — Courtesy, Tamil Nadu Tourism Development Corporation

Karakattam

It is a folk dance popular in the villages of Tamil Nadu, in which **dancers balance a water pot** on their head. It is performed in praise of and propitiation of the rain Goddess **Mariamman**. Usually, a part of different village festivals, it is a vibrant and energetic dance which also symbolizes happiness and merriment, with the dancers attired in colourful dress. The dance is divided into parts namely, *Atta Karagam* and *Sakthi Karagam,* and even incorporates certain form of acrobatics. The music is to the accompaniment of traditional instruments like *nadaswaram* (double reed wind instrument), *melam* (maddalam like drums) and *thavil* (drum; barrel shaped percussion instrument).

Mayilattam

It is performed by female dancers who are **dressed as a peacock**. It is usually performed in temples and shows respect to the peacock, the abode of lord Murugan (Kartikeya). Some other similar dances include, **Karadiattam** (dressed as bear), **Kaalaiattam** (dressed as bull) **Aaliattam** (dressed as demon), **Vedalaattam** (wearing masks depicting demons).

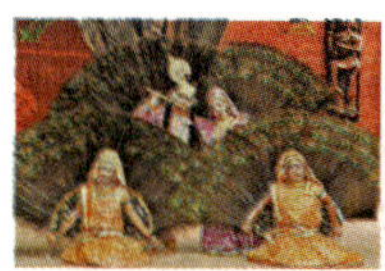

Oyilattam

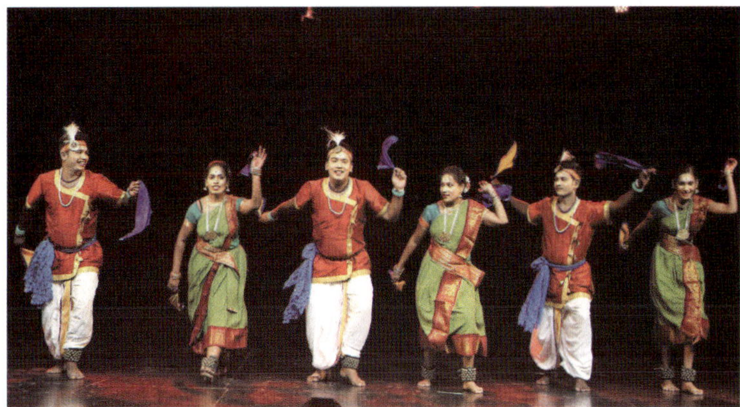

18.62: An Oyilattam performance; a folk dance of Tamil Nadu — Courtesy, Sangeet Natak Akademi

It literally means a **'dance of beauty'** (*oyil*-beauty; *attam* - dance). The dance is said to have originated in southern Tamil Nadu and is popular in Madurai, Tirunelveli, Tiruchirappalli and other adjoining regions. The dance is said to have been traditionally performed by men. However, in recent times, women also participate in it. Usually, the dance involved eight to ten men standing in a row wearing colourful clothes and holding flags/kerchief in their hands and performing to the rhythm of the music with specific hand and feet movements. More dancers, guests and onlookers could join them later. The dancers would also wear anklets and music would be to the accompaniment of traditional instrument like *thavil* etc. The occasions for this dance could be festivals, harvesting seasons and others. The dance could be performed in front of temples and other public places, particularly in the morning and evening hours.

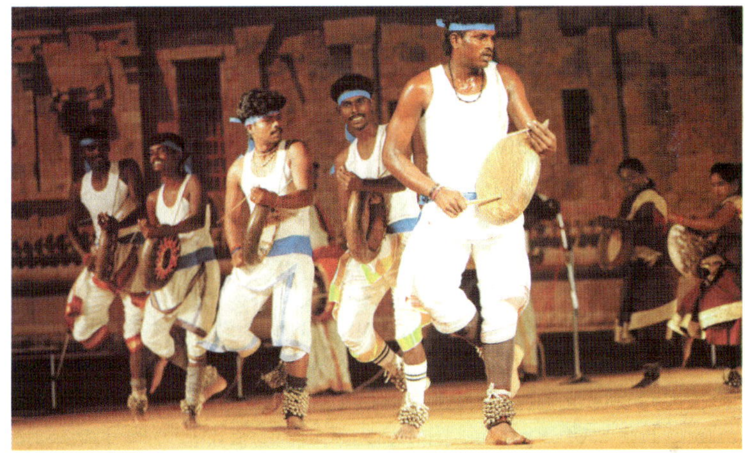

18.63: A Thapattam performance — Courtesy, Tamil Nadu Tourism Development Corporation

Puliattam

It is a dance performed by young men whose **bodies are painted as tigers** in bright yellow and black, with fangs, headgear, paws, claws tail etc. The dance is performed to the fast beats of drum emulating the energy and movements of tiger, like in its pounce and prance. It is usually performed in temple festivals and often draws large crowd of onlookers.

Among the other popular folk dances of this region include, **Kavadiattam** (religious ritualistic dance dedicated to lord Muruga); **Bagavatha Nadanam**, a temple dance performed in front of a lamp (in praise of lord Krishna), **Kai Silambu Attam**, a temple dance (performed in Navaratri or Amman festival; **Pampattam** (snake dance); **Silambattam**, a martial arts form of dance (involving fighting with sticks), **Poikal Kudirai Attam** (a form of horse dance); **Kolattam**, performed by rural women (with sticks in hand); **Thapattam** (dance to the beats of instrument *parai*); **Chakkaiattam,** dance by eight to ten in circle or parallel lines (while holding wooden pieces), amidst others.

Kerala

A state which boasts of being home to two classical dances (Kathakali and Mohiniattam), has a rich repertoire of several folk dances, with their sub-types numbering to nearly 50 (as per some accounts). Integrated with the life of people, religious and ceremonious occasions, the dances are specially known for their unique costumes and jewellery. Among the most popular of the folk dances are **Theyyam**, **Thiruvathirakali**, **Kolkalli**, **Chakyar koothu**, **Ottamthullal** and others.

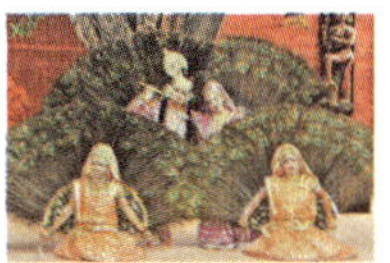

Theyyam

Having a history which is thousands of years old, and traceable to the Sangam period, Theyyam is a popular **ritual form of dance and worship**. Essentially a bouquet of ritual dances, Theyyam is said to **comprise nearly 400 to 450 sub-types** which include the more popular ones such as **Vishnumoorthy Theyyam** (a Vaishnav tradition), **Sree Muthappan Theyyam** (dedicated to Lord Vishnu and lord Shiva), **Padmadakki Bhagavathi Theyyam** (dedicated to Padmadakki Bhagavathi, a form of Devi), **Padikutti Amma Theyyam** (dedicated to the mother of god Muthappan), **Chamundi Theyyam** (dedicated to goddess Chamunda); amidst others. The dances are especially popular in the Northern Kerala region and are mostly performed by men, except **Devakothu Theyyam** which is performed by women. The Theyyams integrate a tradition which is ancient and tribal, as well as assimilates the aspects of mainstream Hindu religion. Some of its functional elements can also be traced in Islam and practitioner of other religions in the state. Besides, it also incorporates the elements of worship of village deity (*gram devta*), spirit worship, ancestor worship, hero worship, animal worship, serpent worship etc., thus imparting it a cross cultural connect.

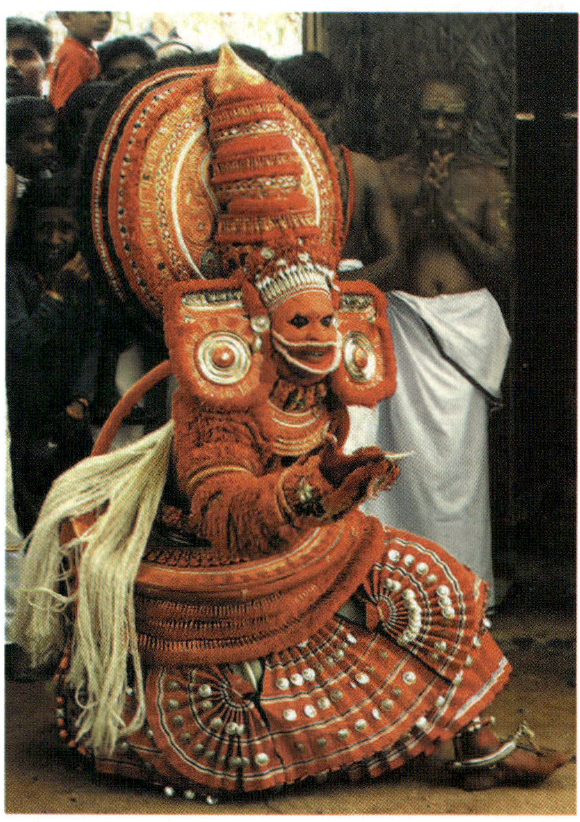

18.64: Bali Theyyam, a folk dance of Kerala; a form of Theyyam with noticeable special costume — Wikimedia Commons

Thiruvathirakali

It is a popular dance **performed by the women** to the tune of Thiruvathira songs. The dance was originally performed on the Thiruvathira day in the month of *Dhanu* (December -January) but now also performed on the other occasions and especially on Onam. Women gather in a circle around a *vilakku* (lamp), make floral offering, and dance to the tune of Thiruvathira songs, while clapping with their hands. Floral arrangement or dance on a floral carpet, is a special element of its performance.

Kolkali

Popular in the agrarian community, it is a rhythmic dance performed with wooden sticks. It's a group dance performed by nearly 24 persons, who move in a circle performing special steps, while beating the short sticks and keeping rhythm with the music, which rises in pitch. The circle expands and contracts as the dance progresses. It is performed both by men and women.

Chakyar Koothu

It is a performance art which depicts narration of anecdotes from the epics in the form of dances. The performance is usually done in temples on the occasion of festivals.

Ottam Thullal

It is a dance which was popularized in the 18th century by the Malayali poet KK Nambiar. While earlier the dance was performed by a single dancer, it was transformed to a group dance which conveys mythological stories. Colourful costumes of the performer is another salient feature of this dance form.

Other poular dance forms include **Padayani,** which is a martial art form of dance performed with masks; **Kakkarissi Kali,** a group dance popular in southern Kerala, particularly in the Kuravas; **Dapu Kali,** a group dance of Moplahs performed with the musical instrument Dappu (a form of drum); **Sarpam Thullal**, a folk dance performed in temples to appease the snake god; **Kaavadiyaattam,** a dance performed in the temples as an offering to lord Subramanyam.

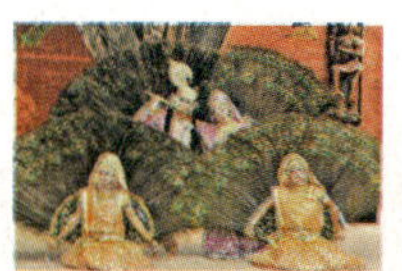

Indian Textiles and Handicrafts

> *The notion of education through handicrafts rises from the contemplation of truth and love permeating life's activities.*
>
> — Mahatma Gandhi

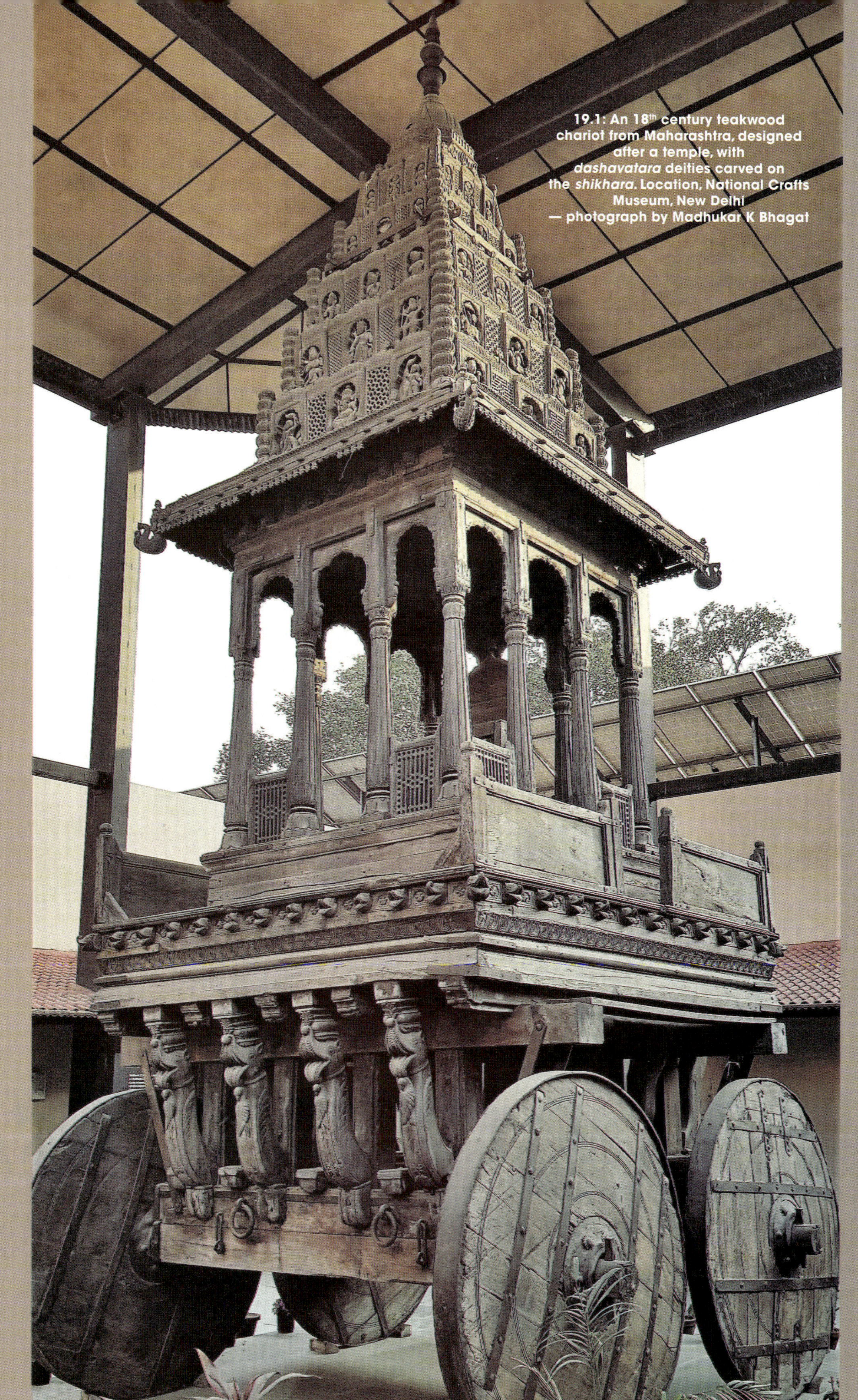

19.1: An 18th century teakwood chariot from Maharashtra, designed after a temple, with *dashavatara* deities carved on the *shikhara*. Location, National Crafts Museum, New Delhi — photograph by Madhukar K Bhagat

INDIAN TEXTILES AND RELATED HANDICRAFTS

A Brief History

The story of Indian textiles is thousands of years old. Fabrics and clothes have been an important means of fulfillment of human need, as well as a medium of expression of individual choices and was an art of the times. Indian textiles and handloom products have also been a part of world market since time immemorial. There were flourishing exports to ancient Egypt, Rome and Greece and they have been found even in the tombs of the pharaohs. The Indus Valley Civilisation and the Harappan culture reveal the cultivation of cotton and preparation of its fabric.

Coming to the later period and to the medieval ages, Indian handicraft expanded its repertoire to new materials, mixes, and artwork like *zardozi* under the Islamic influence. Thus, the story of Indian fabric grew from strength to strength. It reached new heights in terms of colour, design and fashion, particularly during the Mughal period. The 18th and 19th century CE saw the suppression of the Indian handloom by cheaper products of Manchester mills. This was an important economic and political ploy of the British regime, which successfully trounced India as an exporter of cloth to a producer of raw materials and a net importer of machine-made fabric.

Our freedom struggle has also been marked with revolts opposing the forced **indigo cultivation** and calls for supporting the Indian **khadi/handmade fabric**. Even Mahatma Gandhi's dream of a village republic envisaged production of yarn/hand spinning of khadi as a village/household industry.

TRADITION OF WEAVING AND WEAVERS

The tradition of weaving and weavers has been an ancient one. This has been passed on as a family tradition and also as a community tradition from generation to generation. As a result, it has grown over the centuries into a specialised art form which is replete in colour, design, embroidery, fabric, etc. Be it the **Kanjeevaram silk**, the **brocade work of Varanasi**, the ***zari* work of Surat**, the **embroidery of Kutch**, or the ***chikan* work of Lucknow**, they have essentially been a traditional craft for a long time in the weaving communities who have taken it to the level of an art form. A number of such weaving communities are known for their skills. These include *Vunkars* in Gujarat, *Mehers* in Orissa (now Odisha), *Ansaris* in Uttar Pradesh, *Devangas* and *Padmashalis* in South India, *Saliyas* in Kerala, and *Khatris* in Kutch among others.

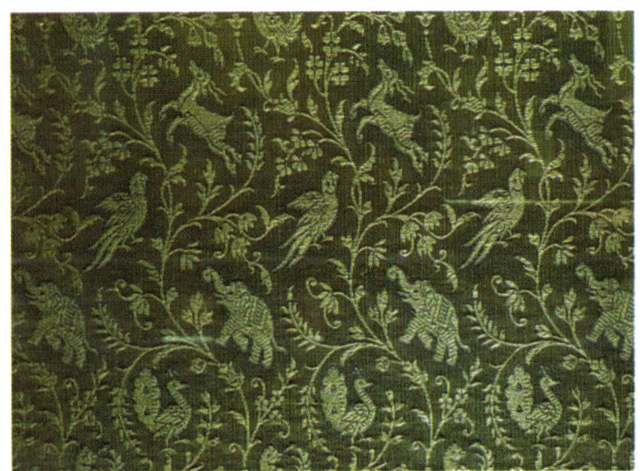

19.2: A section of Banarasi silk sari, intricate brocade work with zari, National Crafts Museum, New Delhi — photograph by Madhukar K Bhagat

Although the weavers were financially flourishing communities till the medieval period, today they are on the economic and social fringes. Traditional weaving may not be anymore more an economically remunerative craft. They have to compete with machine-made fabrics which are cheaper and mass produced at a much quicker pace, albeit not as intricate as the handloom products. Thus, the communities and artisans engaged in weaving, dyeing, embroidery, hand printing and applique work, are all now being pushed to the margins, although they are upholders of a **living craft tradition**.

The Geographical Indication (GI) Tag

The GI tag is an indication of a particular product corresponding to a specific geographical location or origin. For Indian products, the tag is granted by the Government of India (as a member of World Trade Organisation, permitted under Art 22(1) of Trade Related Aspects of Intellectual Property Rights (TRIPS)). India has enacted the Geographical Indication of Goods (Registration & Protection) Act 1999 which enables such identification of goods. The Act came into effect from September 15, 2003 and the Darjeeling tea was the first product to be GI tagged in India in 2004-05. This tag ensures that none other than those registered as the authorised user(s) or those falling under the geographical territory, are able to use the tag.

A geographical indication (GI) is a name or sign used on certain products which corresponds to a specific geographical location or origin (e.g., a town, region, or country). India, as a member of the World Trade Organization (WTO), enacted

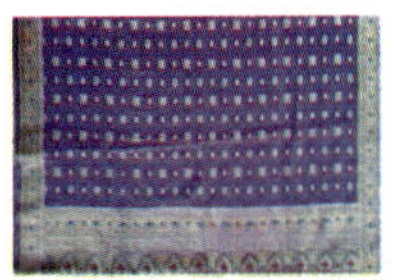

the Geographical Indications of Goods (Registration and Protection) Act, 1999 has come into force with effect from 15 September 2003. GIs have been defined under Article 22 (1) of the WTO Agreement on Trade-Related Aspects of Intellectual Property Rights (TRIPS) Agreement as: "Indications which identify a good as originating in the territory of a member, or a region or a locality in that territory, where a given quality, reputation or characteristic of the good is essentially attributable to its geographic origin."

Thus the GI tag ensures that none other than those registered as authorised users (or at least those residing inside the geographic territory) are allowed to use the popular product name. Since the the grant of the first GI tag in India in 2004-05 and till March 2024, nearly 643 products have been accorded GI tag in India under the categories of agricultural, food, handicraft and manufactured products.

POPULAR FABRICS IN TEXTILE WEAVING

Cotton, silk, wool, a mixture of these and even gold and silver have been traditionally used in India as fibre for weaving. The traditional products of these fabrics have dressed the kings and commoners for centuries and continue to do so.

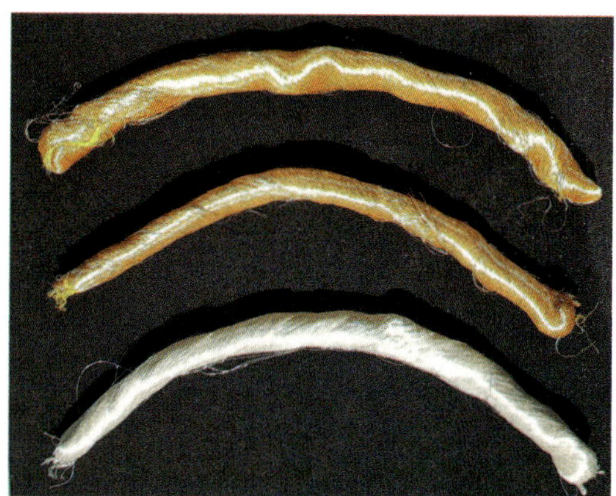

19.3: Zari fabric of gold and silver at National Crafts Museum, New Delhi — photograph by Madhukar K Bhagat

Cotton

Cotton is a natural fibre obtained from the fluffy balls growing on the cotton plants. Traditionally these were subjected to processes of ginning, bowing and spinning to obtain cotton threads of varying thickness, followed by weaving on a loom to obtain a fabric.

Cotton has been one of the most popular fabrics for thousands of years. **Indian muslin** (a fine cotton fabric) was used in the shrouds of the Egyptian kings and also in garments of the Mughal emperors. As a fabric which could absorb moisture and allow aeration (in summers) and yet retain heat in winters, it was ideally suited for the Indian conditions. The popular *khadi* industry is largely based on handspun cotton. The famous embroidery ***chikan*** work of Lucknow is done on cotton. The traditional ***Dhaniakhali*** saree of West Bengal which has been accorded **Geographical Indication (GI) tag** in 2012, is also made of cotton. Another traditional cotton product is the handwoven **Tangaliya shawl** of Saurashtra region of Gujarat. It has a history of nearly 700 years of handweaving of this product by the Dangasia community and is also accorded a **GI Tag**. The handwoven ***zari* cotton Venkatagiri saris** (Andhra Pradesh), **Balaramapuram saris and fine cotton fabrics** (Kerala), **Udupi handloom cotton saris** (Karnataka,) **Warangal *durries*** (Telangana) are amongst some of the other traditional cotton fabric products which have been accorded a GI tag.

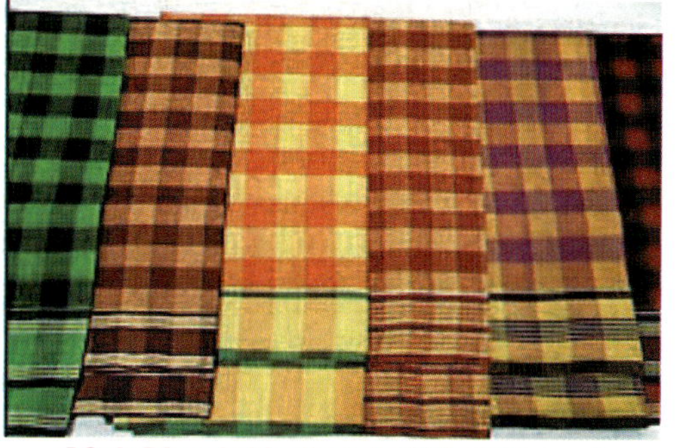

19.4: Dhaniakhali sari of West Bengal — Courtesy, Department of Tourism, West Bengal

Khadi

The word *khadi* is derived from *khaddar* and refers to a handspun coarse cotton fabric. This was obtained from the locally grown cotton which was then usually handspun by women on a spinning wheel and hand woven. Fabrics of silk or wool could also be so prepared by hand. Khadi came into national prominence on being promoted by Mahatma Gandhi during the *Swadeshi* movement of the early 20th century. The latter half of the 19th century had seen decimation of the Indian hand weaving with India becoming a mere exporter of cotton to the Manchester mills and a net importer of the cheaper fabric of its mills. Thus, weaving of its own cloth and boycotting the British goods and cloth got integrated in the *Swadeshi* or self-reliance movement of the Indian National Congress.

It is believed that Khadi as a 'movement' emerged around 1917-1918, when hand woven coarse cloth was produced through spinning by hand and weaving in the Sabarmati Ashram. Later, in 1922, Mahatma Gandhi founded a 'Khadi department' in the Indian National Congress and in 1924 an 'All India Khadi Board' was formed to promote the hand-woven *khadi*. Spinning of yarn by hand was promoted, and even the members of the Indian National Congress had to spin the yarn on traditional *charkha* (spinning wheel) and make payment of their fees by means of the yarn spun. Later,

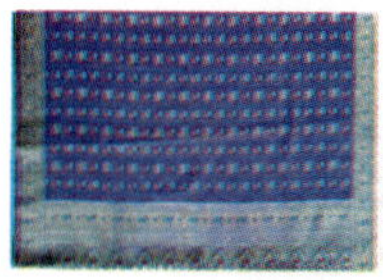

the Indian National, Congress also adopted the national flag with a *charkha* in its centre with the flag itself made of *khadi*. Thus, a fabric and an ancient tradition of weaving came to the centre-stage of the national movement, integrating with it the elements of economics and commerce of production, politics of the period, and also the people at the very grassroots of Indian society.

Over a period of time, *khadi* as a coarse cloth and as movement has evolved. As a fabric, the cotton may be mixed wool and even silk. It has improved its look and feel with a wide range of products such as *kurta, dhoti,* handloom *saris*, *chamba rumal* and even Tussar silk fabric and other products being included in its diverse range. Today, integrated with the village industries, *khadi* has become a brand of a hand-made fabric and diverse non-fabric products.

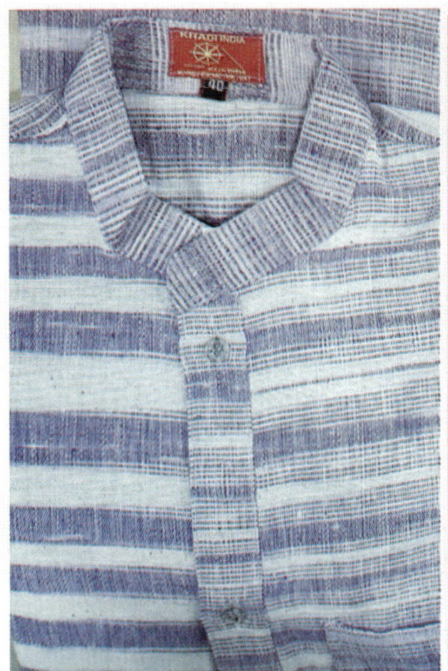

19.5: Kurta of coarse khadi

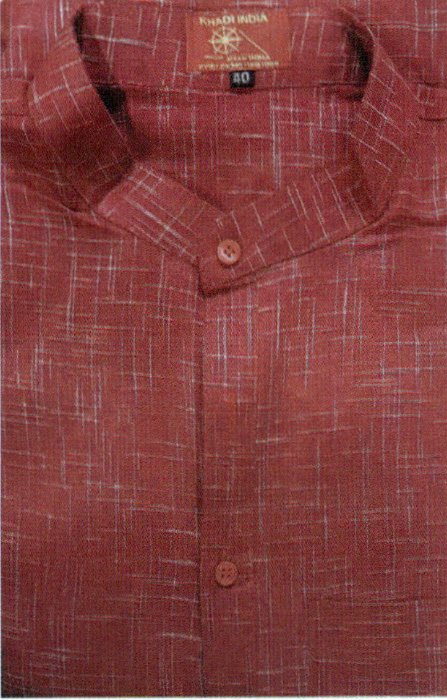

19.6: Kurta of fine khadi

— photographs by Madhukar K Bhagat

Silk

The art of silk-making came to India from China, although as per some historians, archaeological discoveries in Harappa and Chanhudaro suggest use of silk threads and possible existence of sericulture. Owing to its softness, lustre and tensile strength, silk is amongst the most prized of fabric materials.

Over the years, weaving of silk fabric, particularly silk sarees has become quite popular. The **Kanjeevaram silk sarees** (of Kancheepuram, Tamil Nadu) and the **Banarasi silk sarees** with brocade work (of Varanasi, Uttar Pradesh) are amongst the most famous. The latter are usually a part of bridal trousseau.

Assam is an important centre of silk production where different varieties of silk are produced which include, **Golden Muga**, **White Pat (Mulberry silk)** and **Eri silk**. Some other centres of silk production are also in the states of Jharkhand, Chhattisgarh, Bihar, Madhya Pradesh, etc. where **Tussar silk** is produced which has coarse and uneven texture. However, the bulk of Indian silk is of the variety **Mulberry silk,** which is produced in the states of Karnataka, Andhra Pradesh and Tamil Nadu.

Silk fabric has been used for creating a variety of specialised products, especially sarees, by using different weaving and dying techniques such as **tie and dye, resist dye** and others. These specialised works include the brocade work of **Banarasi sarees**, **Tanchois of Gujarat**, the resist dye technique of **Patola sarees of Gujarat** (Rajkot and Patan Patola), **Ikats of Odisha** (includes, Sambalpuri, Balangir, Sonepur, and other Ikats of Odisha), tie and dye technique of **Bandhej of Rajasthan** and **Gujarat**, and **Pochampally Ikats of Telangana**. The **Baluchari** silk sari of West Bengal depicting mythological scenes on *pallu*, is another traditional craft having **GI tag**.

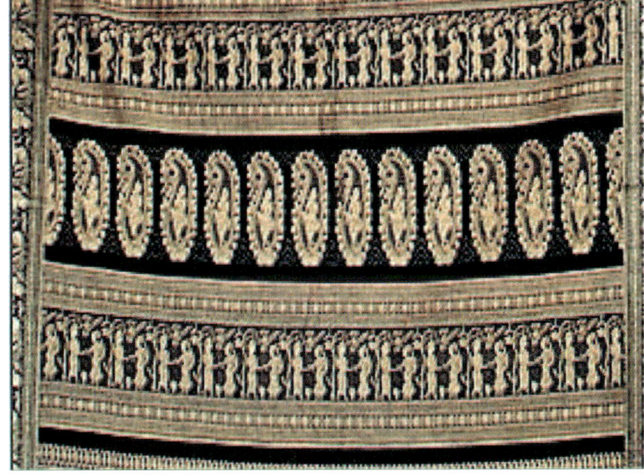

19.7: Baluchari sari of West Bengal
— Courtesy, Department of Tourism, West Bengal

The **Mysore silk (Karnataka), Kancheepuram silk, Salem silk, Arani silk** (Tamil Nadu) **Muga Silk of Assam, Bhagalpur silk (Bihar)** have been given the **Geographical Indication Tag (GI Tag).** Crafts and products such as **Banarasi** brocade sarees, **Ikats** of Odisha, **Patola** sarees of Gujarat, **Paithani** sarees of Aurangabad (Maharashtra), and **Baluchari** sarees of West Bengal have also acquired the **GI tag**. These products are usually made of rich silk fabric.

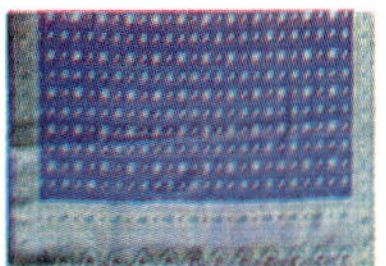

Types of Silk

There are four types of natural silk which are produced commercially. These include the **Mulberry silk** which is commercially the most important, the **Eri silk, Tussar silk (or Kosa silk),** and **Muga silk**. Silk is produced by silkworm which feeds on specific type of leaves. The caterpillar of the moth then spins a cocoon of the fine silk fibre. The cocoons are small and oval, generally the size of a pigeon's egg. The cocoons are boiled, and the silk is then extracted, reeled, twisted, dried, and polished. Depending on the type of worm employed and the type of leave it feeds on, different categories of silk is produced.

The **Mulberry silk** comprising nearly 90% of the entire silk production is produced by the Mulberry silkworm, which feeds only on the mulberry leaves. The **Tussar** silkworm feeds on a variety of plants such as *som, wali, arjun, jamun, oak, sakhua*, etc. This variety is coarser than the Mulberry silk.

Eri silk is produced by the castor silkworm which feeds on the leaves of the castor oil plant and produces white or brick red threads. The **Moga silk** is produced only in Assam in India and produces golden yellow silk threads. It feeds on Ashoka tree and castor leaves. The traditional costume of Assam, ***Mekhela Chadar*** is produced from it.

Banarasi Brocades and Sarees

Produced in the city of Varanasi (also known as Benares), the Banarasi brocade work on saris, is a traditional handloom work on silk fabric, incorporating *zari* (brocade work) in gold and silver. Known for their bright and rich look with intricate designs, these saris are relatively heavy and considered one of the finest silk sari works. The saris are brocaded with extra weft patterns and display designs of *buties* (small floral embroidery designs), *buttas* (a paisley design or an almond or pine cone shaped design with sharp and curved upper end), bells, creepers etc. in ground or border and the *anchal* portion of the dress. Some of the exclusive varieties of saris are *Jangla*, *Tanchoi*, *Vaskat*, *Cutwork*, *Tishu* and *Butidar*. Traditionally, these saris have been a part of the bridal trousseau and often worn by women on festivals, functions and other special occasions.

These saris have a history which dates back to the Mughal period in the 17th century, when the city of Varanasi was a flourishing centre of cotton and silk. The silk tradition continues to this day and the saris are even today made on the traditional handlooms. Each sari may take anywhere between 15 days to even six months for weaving.

As per estimates, around 6 lakhs weavers are associated with this traditional craft. In 2009 the 'Weavers Association of Uttar Pradesh' was granted **GI tag** for the '**Banarasi brocade and saris**'. A Banarasi brocade work can now only be referred to that originating from the districts of Varanasi, Chandauli, Mirzapur, Jaunpur, Bhadohi and Azamgarh.

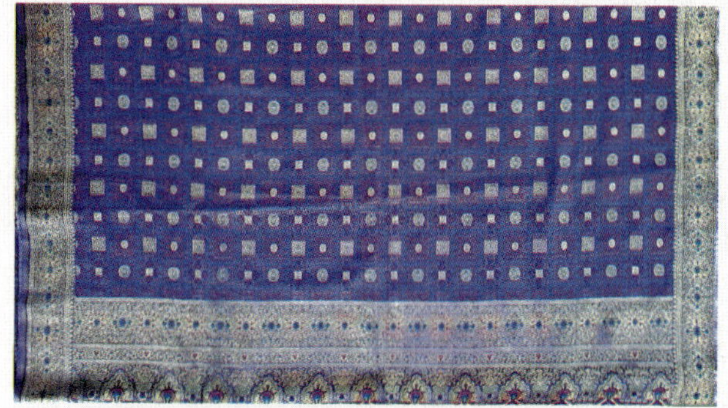

19.8: A silk Banarasi sari with brocade work and intricate designs; private collection — photograph by Madhukar K Bhagat

Silk and Cotton and other Mix

A mix of silk with other fibres is used to produce a variety of fabrics. ***Himroo*** is a mix of silk and cotton while ***Mashru* can use silk with cotton** (or wool). Generally, the warp of the cloth is of one type of fabric while weft is of another type. The ***Chanderi sarees*** (which has **GI tag)** manufactured in Chanderi, Madhya Pradesh are made of a mix of silk and cotton. They can also be of pure silk or pure cotton. They are known for the beautiful geometric patterns, images of flora, fauna, etc. woven into the fabric. **Kota**

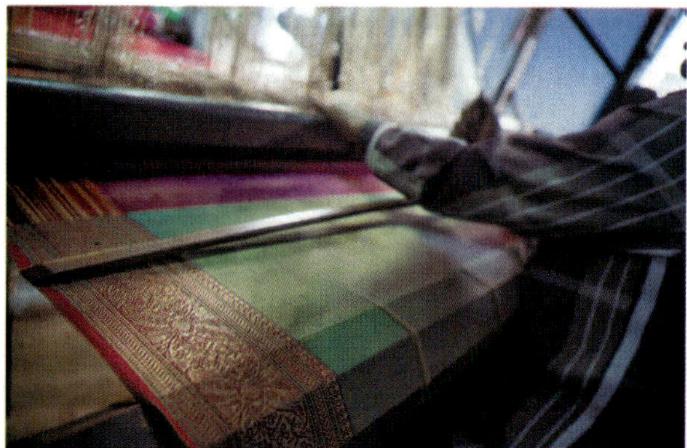

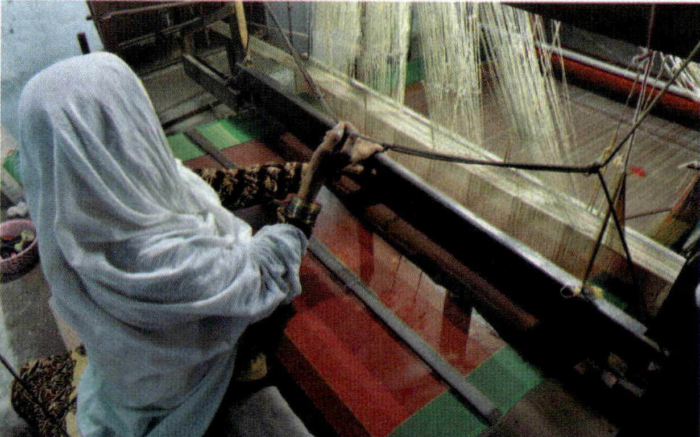

19.9 & 19.10: Chanderi saris being woven on handloom — Courtesy, Madhya Pradesh Tourism Board

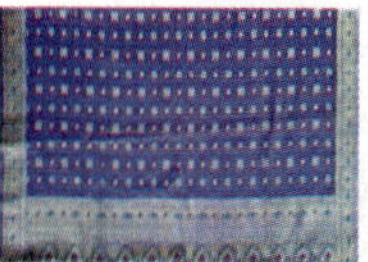

Doriya is another silk and cotton mix fabric, which is woven in pit looms in near Kota (Rajasthan). It is a light and very finely woven fabric with small square checkered texture and also accorded a **GI tag.**

Himroo and Mashru: Medieval Fabric Arts

The **Himroo** fabric, popular in Aurangabad is of medieval origin, a weaving art which developed during the 14th century CE with the shifting of the capital from Delhi to Aurangabad by Muhammad -Bin Tughlaq. Originating from the Persian word *hum-ruh* which means 'similar', the fabric is said to have emulated the Persian fabric of *Kinkhwab* which was woven with gold and silver threads. However, Himroo used a mix of silk and cotton with a very unique design of its own and thus and flourished as uniquely Indian/Deccan fabric. As per some scholars, wearing of pure silk was prohibited in Islam, but a mixed fabric wasn't, hence it gained popularity with the kings and nobles and became fabric of royalty. In the British reign the art declined. Although this weaving art gained some popularity post independence, today it is considered a declining tradition, with migration of artisans to other vocations, and competition from the powerlooms.

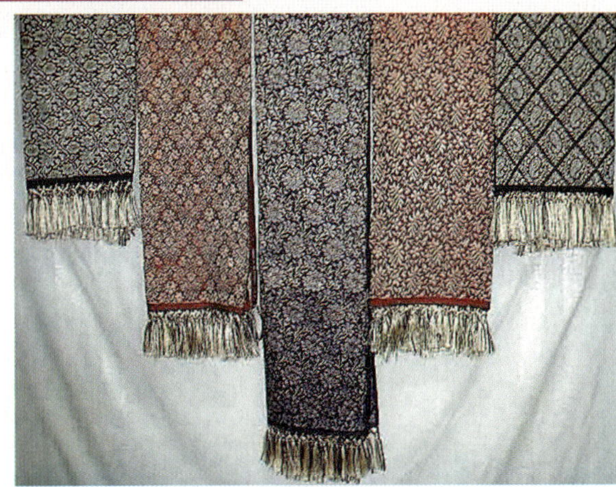

19.11: Himroo shawls exuding a silk fabric look — Wikimedia Commons

Mashru is another medieval fabric which is a mix of silk and cotton. The word 'Mashru' in Persian is said to mean, 'permitted' thus referring a dress which could be worn by the Muslims (as not being pure silk). As per Sanskrit etymology, the word is said to be derived from *Mishra* which means 'mix' referring to the mix of fabric. The blend of Mashru employs a bottom of cotton with the face of silk, thus retaining the touch and feel of cotton with the look and lustre of silk. As described in the 16th century CE treatise *Ain-i-Akbari*, it was the costume of the nobles and the courtiers. It remained a popular fabric in the Punjab and Gujarat region and other parts of western India.

Wool

Wool is a fabric prepared from the hair of animals. Generally, the hair of sheep is used for production of wool but that of goat and camel or other animals is also occasionally used. The hair of the Angora rabbit is used to produce **Angora wool** which is fine, soft, and silky. Similarly, ***shahtoosh*** is the fabric produced from the hair of the **Himalayan Ibex** which is so fine that an entire shawl is said to pass through a ring. Its production and sale is banned, as Ibex is an endangered species. **Kashmir Pashmina** is another famous fabric which is made of the wool of the local *Changthai* goat (of Kashmir) and has been accorded a **GI tag**. Pashmina shawls are specially known for its soft texture and warmth.

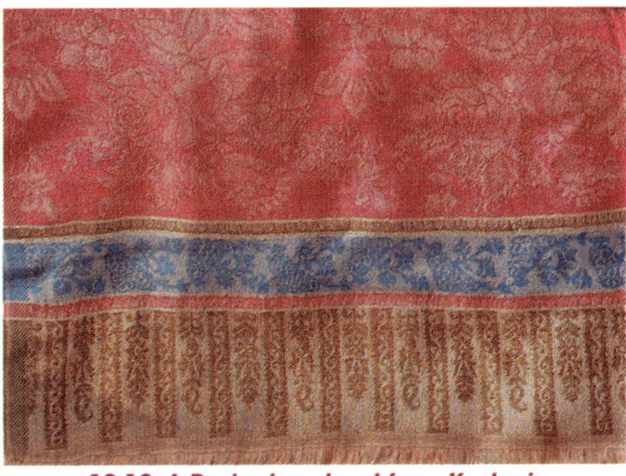

19.12: A Pashmina shawl from Kashmir — photograph by Madhukar K Bhagat

Wool has been used for thousands of years and thus this craft has developed many famous products. These include the *Jamawar* shawls of Kashmir (which could contain as many as 50 colours), the ***Dhabalas*** (of rough goat wool) of Kutch, ***Pheran*** (traditional Kashmiri dress), the **blankets and Pashmina shawls** of Nubra valley of Ladakh, **headgear of Kullu** (Himachal Pradesh) and a variety of woolen products of *Bhotias* and *Garhwals* of Uttarkhand. The **Kani shawl,** (of Kanimora, Kashmir) and **Tangaliya shawl, Kachch shawl** (of Saurashtra, Gujarat) the **Kullu shawl, Kinnauri shawl** (of Himachal Pradesh) are some other handicraft woolen products which have the **GI tag.** In certain products, wool may also be mixed with cotton or other fabrics.

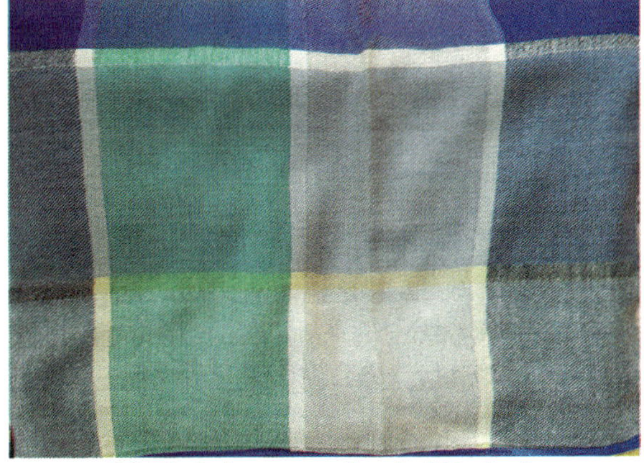

19.13: A Jamawar shawl of Kashmir — photograph by Madhukar K Bhagat

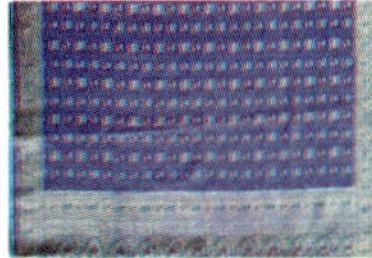

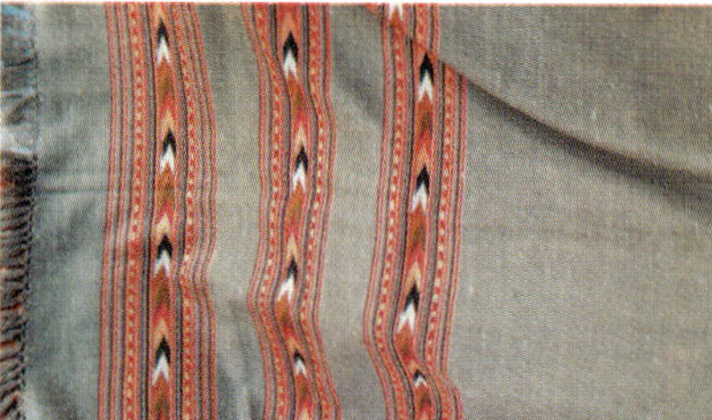
19.14: Kullu shawl of yak wool, coarse texture

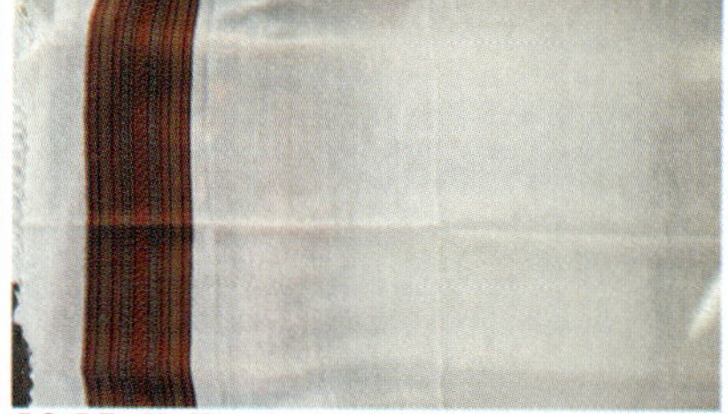
19.15: Kullu shawl of Angora (rabbit) wool, light and fine texture

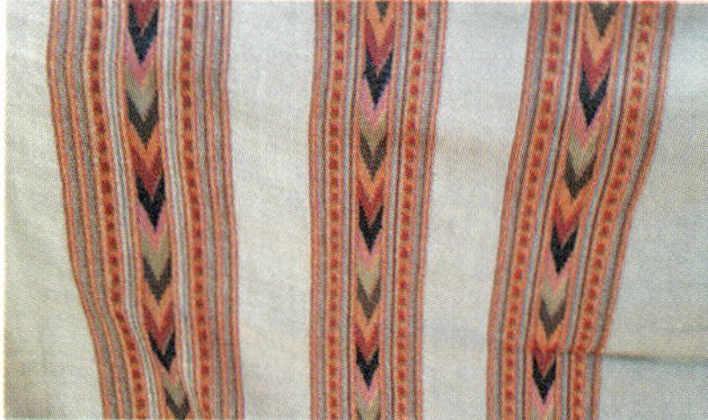
19.16: A Kullu shawl of sheep wool

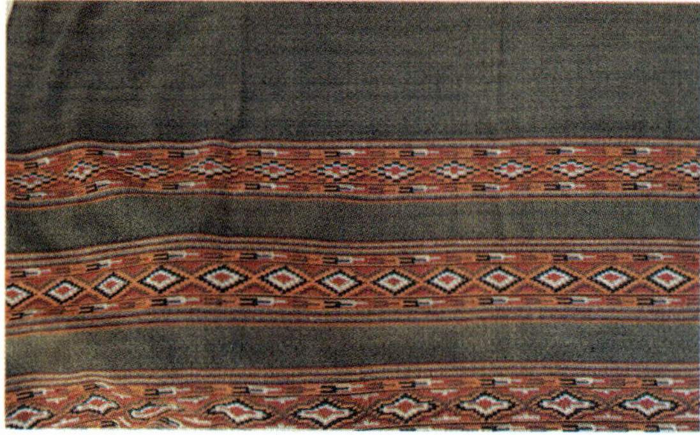
19.17: A woollen shawl with Kinnauri design

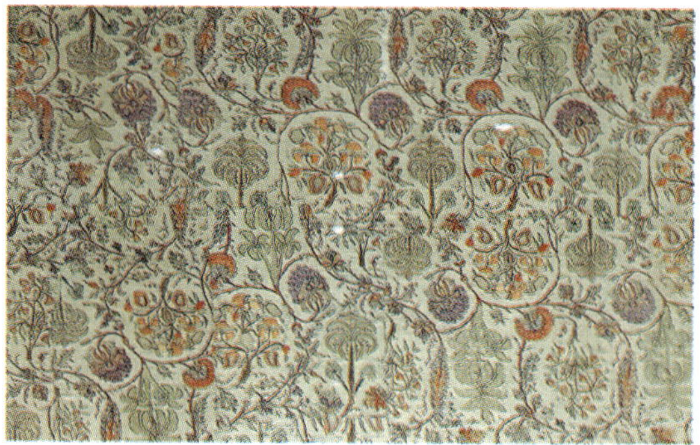
19.18: A Jamawar shawl from Kashmir (mid-20th century) with rich and intricate work

National Crafts Museum, New Delhi — photographs by Madhukar K Bhagat

Weft & Warp and Weaving of Fabric

Weft and warp are the basic thread components deployed on the loom to turn the yarn/thread into a woven fabric. While the wefts (referred also as woof) are the transverse threads, warps are the longitudinal/lengthwise threads which are strung vertically on the loom and are kept stationary. The weft threads move across them, usually once over the warp and then under the next warp and so on.

Warp We

19.19: Warp and weft — Wikimedia Commons

The looms, and in particular the traditional handlooms, inherently employ three basic movements; the shedding, the picking and the beating movements. With the help of a treadle, alternate warp threads are to be kept open. Thus, treadle is deployed to push the odd threads above and even threads below so that the weft thread can pass in between them.

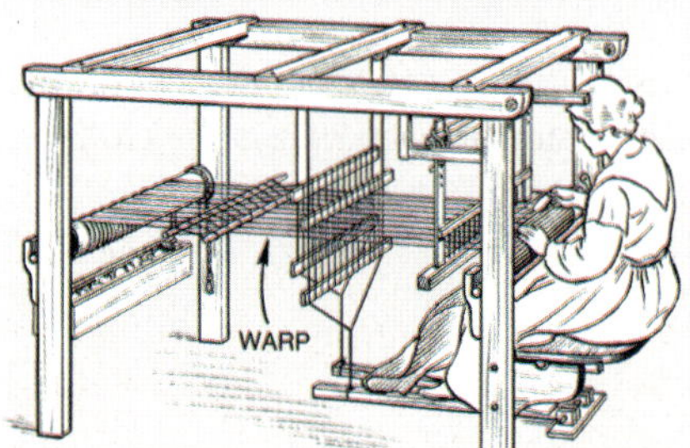

19.20: A warped loom, where the warp is wrapped onto the warp beam; as the cloth is made, the fell (woven part) is wrapped onto the breast beam next to the weaver — Wikimedia Commons

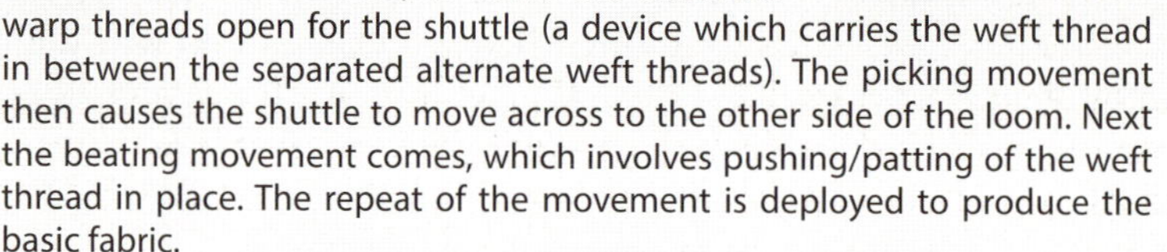
The first movement of shedding consists of moving the treadle with the feet, to make the alternate warp threads open for the shuttle (a device which carries the weft thread in between the separated alternate weft threads). The picking movement then causes the shuttle to move across to the other side of the loom. Next the beating movement comes, which involves pushing/patting of the weft thread in place. The repeat of the movement is deployed to produce the basic fabric.

Different regions of India have traditionally used different types of looms for weaving, some of which are; throw shuttle loom, fly loom, loin loom, pit loom, jacquard etc.

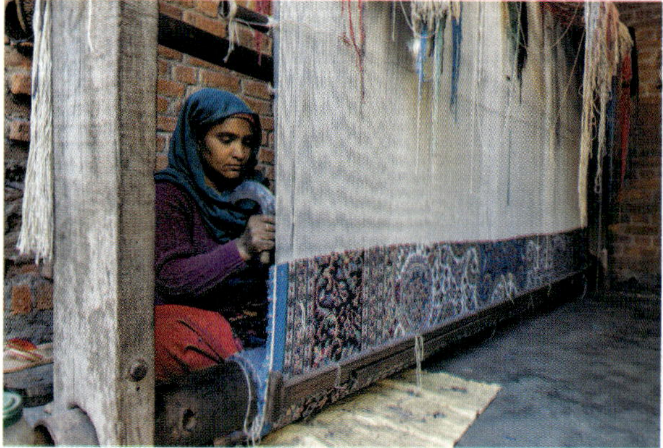
19.21: An artisan weaving a Gwalior carpet which has a mix of wool and cotton, a traditional handicraft of the city — Courtesy, Madhya Pradesh Tourism Board

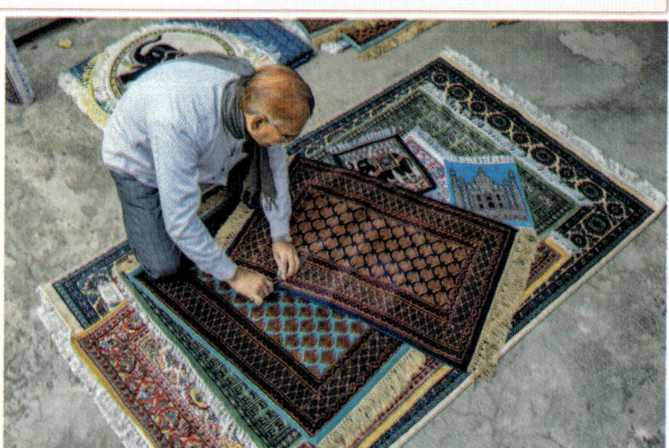
19.22: Clipping of loose fabric on carpet by a carpet weaving artisan at Gwalior to give it a final finish — Courtesy, Madhya Pradesh Tourism Board

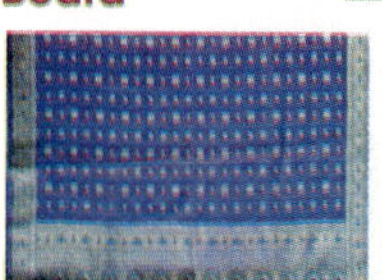

TEXTILE TECHNIQUES AND HANDICRAFTS

Textile techniques and handicraft have been used traditionally to bring out a variety of artistic products. Textile techniques refer to **loom decorated** and **post loom decorated** processes and techniques. Both these techniques are employed to add pattern, texture, and design to the fabric.

Loom Decorated Processes and Techniques

These techniques **impart artistic treatment** to the fabric while it is on the loom itself. In this technique, the texture is produced by varying the count of warp thread and by weaving them tightly or loosely. Further, by using different colours of warp and weft threads, different patterns are produced. Even the threads can be partially colured or uncoloured in places, as is in the process of Ikat where resist-dye technique is applied in the yarn itself to produce such partial colouration. Such yarn is then woven with great dexterity to produce a parttern/a design on the loom itself.

A popular example of the loom decorated technique is the weaving of cotton/wollen shawls specifically used in the Northeast states (such as in Nagaland). The women here use **narrow loin looms** which they attach to their waists. Different patterns such as birds and butterflies or shield and swords (as in warrior shawls) or others, are woven.

Post Loom Decorated Processes and Techniques

The post loom decorated fabrics involved several techniques such as;

- Dyeing and tie dyeing
- Hand printing, and hand painting
- Embroidery
- Applique and patchwork

Dyeing and tie dyeing

Dyeing refers to the process of colouring of fabric and that of fibre and yarn. Traditionally in India, yarn and fabric have been given a variety of colours, generally by using vegetable and mineral colours. Pomegranate, lac, and madder were used for pink, red and brown colours respectively. Yellow was generated from flower petals (particularly myrobalan) and black from iron castings. Similarly, pistachio shells produced green, onion skins produced reddish brown, and concentrated cow urine, a deep yellow. Dyeing a fabric fully (or partly) has been employed as a technique to add colours and designs to clothes.

In **tie dyeing**, the cloth/fabric is tied into small dots at several places using thread and then the dye is applied to create beautiful patterns wherever the fabric has been tied. **Resist dyeing** is another form of dyeing where a substance such as wax or mud is applied to certain portions of the cloth to prevent the portion from getting dyed, thus creating a pattern. *Bandhej* of Rajasthan (accorded GI tag) and *Bandhini* of Gujarat are examples of tie dyeing.

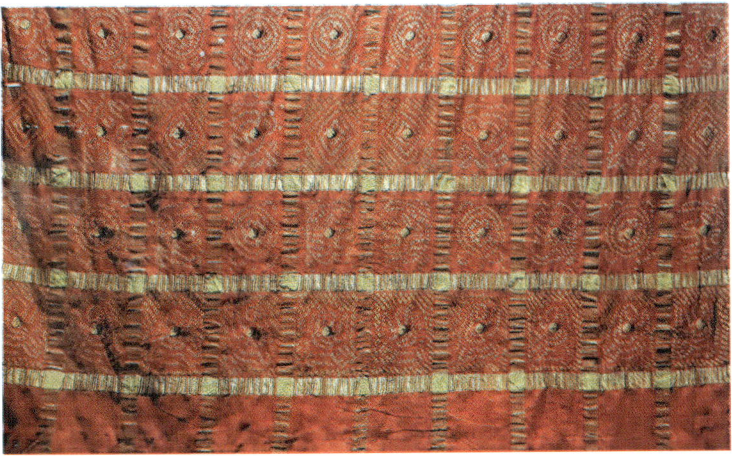

19.23: Ghar Chola silk sari from Gujarat with real gold work (usually for wedding occasion or gifting to bride post-marriage) National Crafts Museum, New Delhi — photograph by Madhukar K Bhagat

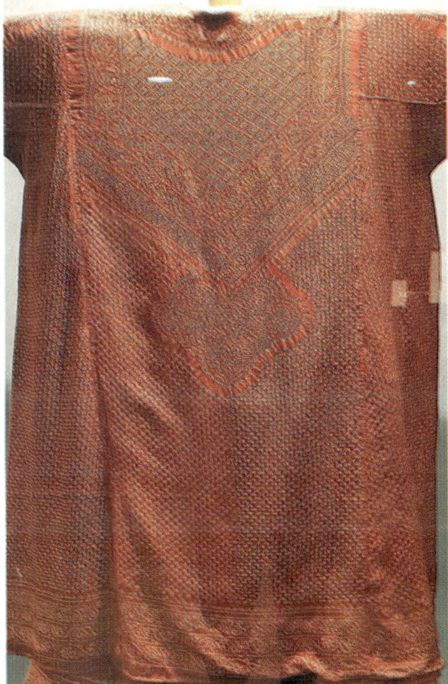

19.24: Bandhej from Anjar in Gujarat Examples of tie dyeing; National Crafts Museum, New Delhi — photograph by Madhukar K Bhagat

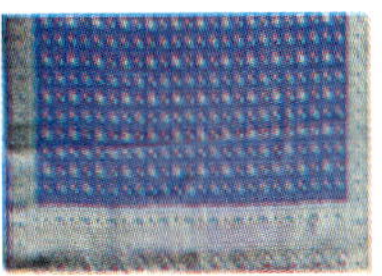

Ikat: A Tie and Dye on Yarn

Ikat is a technique of dyeing and weaving where resist dye/ tie and dye is applied to the yarn which is then used on the loom to produce pattern on clothes. In Ikat, individual yarns or bundles of yarn may be wrapped tightly, thus producing a sort of resist when the yarn is being dyed. This creates patterns of coloured and uncoloured portions on the yarn. It may be further subject to tie and dye with another colour and the process may be repeated several times to produce a variety of patterns on it. Thus, unlike the conventional tie and dye where the fabric is woven first and then patterns are imparted using the tie and dye process (making the latter a post-loom decoration process), Ikat is more of loom decorated process.

The dyed yarn of Ikat is then skillfully deployed in the weaving to produce a desired pattern on the fabric. As the production of pattern will depend as to how meticulously and accurately the dyed thread portions are getting positioned and weaved, Ikat fabric production is a very skillful art. This also results in a somewhat blurriness in the image as the exact positioning of the dyed and undyed portion of the threads may not happen. This blurriness thus remains a characteristic of Ikat.

Ikats are generally produced by using tie and dye on the warp threads. Since these threads are fixed on the loom, as such the pattern can be better controlled and be even seen on the loom before the weft threads are weaved. The weft thread may be normal threads of a single colour. Such weaving style is called single Ikat. The process of double Ikat involves weaving of warp and weft, both of which are tie-dyed, making the accurate determination of the pattern even more difficult. **Odisha Ikat** (Odisha), **Pochampalli Ikat** (Telangana) and **Patan Patola** (Gujarat) are some of the Ikat saris which are also accorded the **GI tag** and boast of the double Ikat making them very precious handloom fabric. The Odisha Ikat (also called *bandha* or *bandhakala*) particularly of Sambalpur, owing to its unique design, is referred to as poetry on loom. Both the Pochampalli Ikat and Patan Patola are known for their dexterity particularly on silk and are in vogue since medieval period.

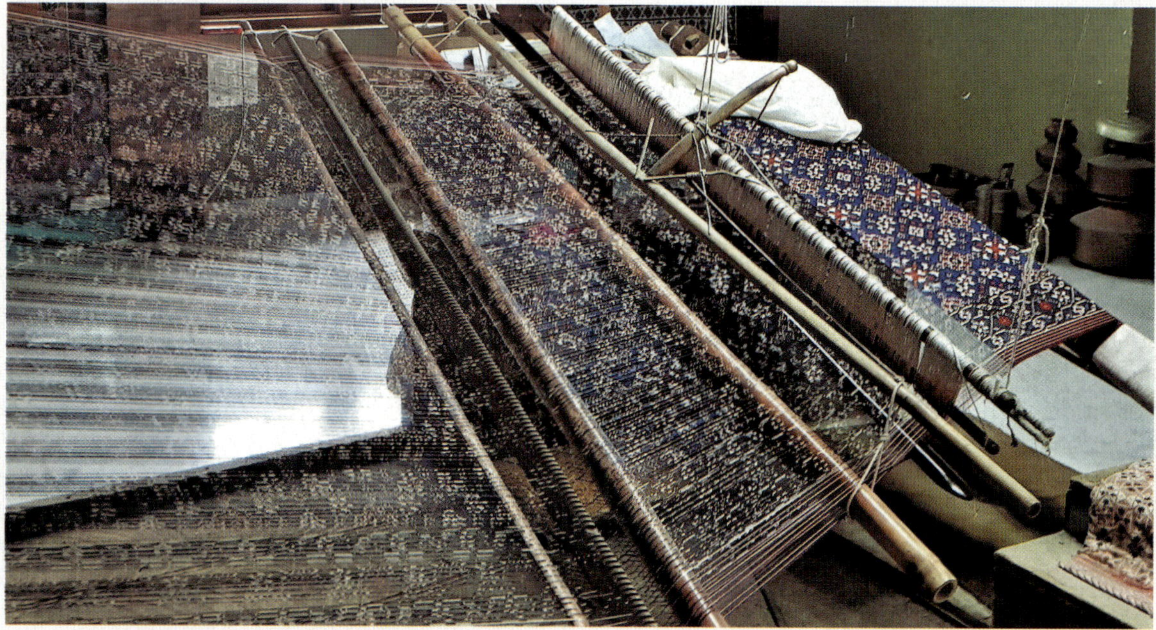

19.25: A double Ikat Patan Patola sari being woven (at Patan). On left, the arrangement of warp threads showing an emerging pattern, with the fabric nearing completion; on extreme right, showing a definitive pattern — photograph by Madhukar K Bhagat

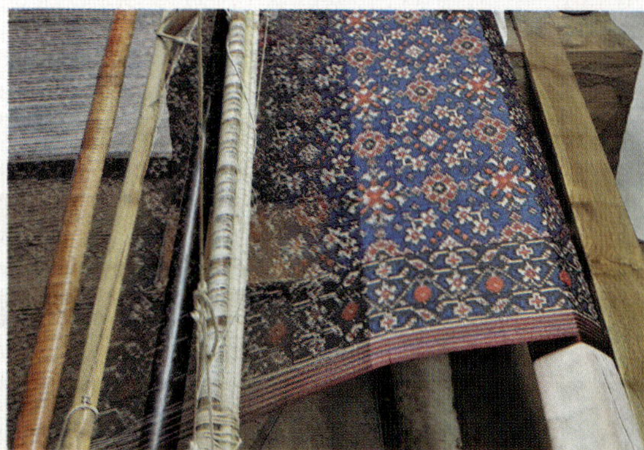

19.26: A closer look at the Patan Patola double Ikat fabric on the loom — photograph by Madhukar K Bhagat

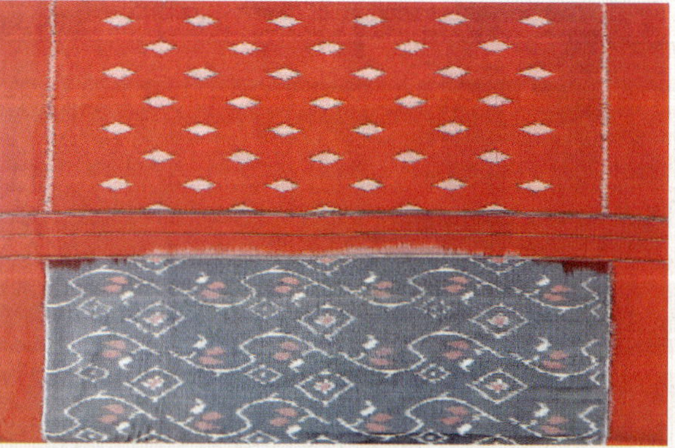

19.27: A Pochampalli Ikat sari of cotton fabric; — photograph by Madhukar K Bhagat

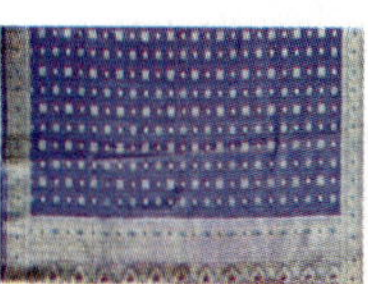

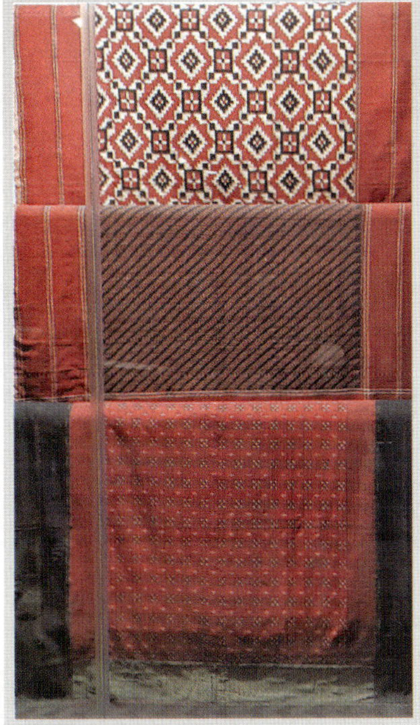

19.28: Pochampalli Ikat saris on silk

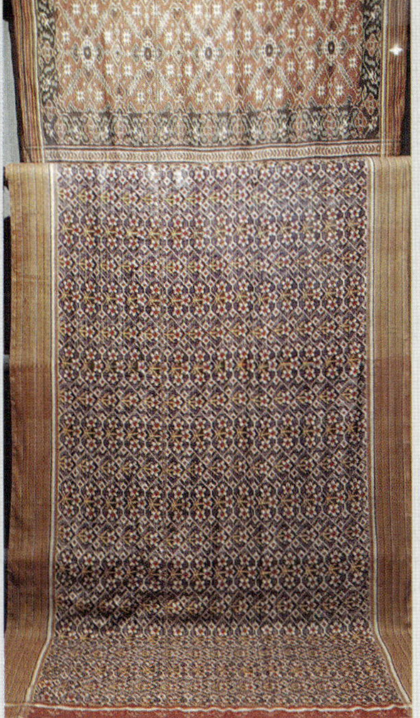

19.29: Double Ikat Patola saris of Patan, Gujarat

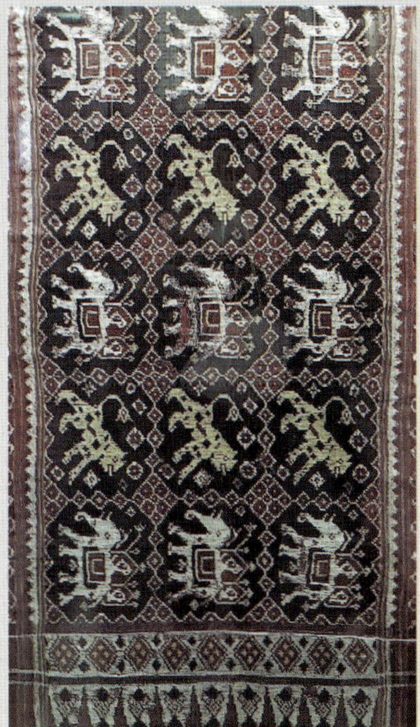

19.30: A Sambalpuri Ikat of Odisha

National Crafts Museum, New Delhi — photographs by Madhukar K Bhagat

Hand Printing and Hand Painting

Hand printing is done by means of blocks and is also referred as block or hand block printing. Usually, blocks made of wood or metal are prepared with intricate design. These are dipped in dyes/liquid colour prepared using vegetable colours. These are pressed on the fabric at desired places to create the required pattern. Different regions of country have their unique block printing style. Some of the famous block prints are **Bagh Prints of Madhya Pradesh** (from the tribal town of Bagh) which has **GI** tag, **Dhamadka of Kutch** (Gujarat), **floral butis design of Sanganer** (Rajasthan), **Bagru** (Rajasthan) **hand block print** (has **GI tag**), **Roghan painting and printing of Gujarat** and **paisley design** of Farrukhabad (Uttar Pradesh) (has **GI tag**).

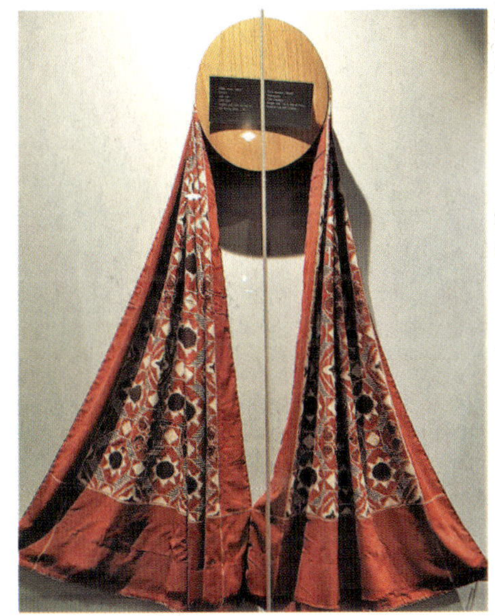

19.31: Telia *rumal* of 19th century, an Ikat tradition of Telangana of oil treatment of yarn, using natural vegetable dye; awarded GI Tag; National Crafts Museum, New Delhi — photograph by Madhukar K Bhagat

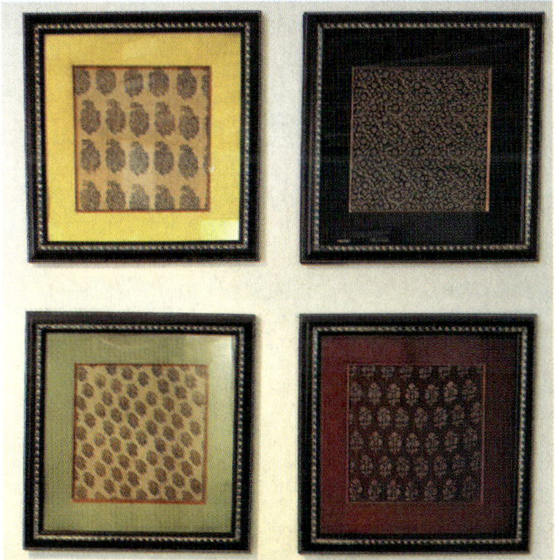

19.32: Traditional Bagh prints on fabric, at display in State Museum Bhopal — photograph by Madhukar K Bhagat

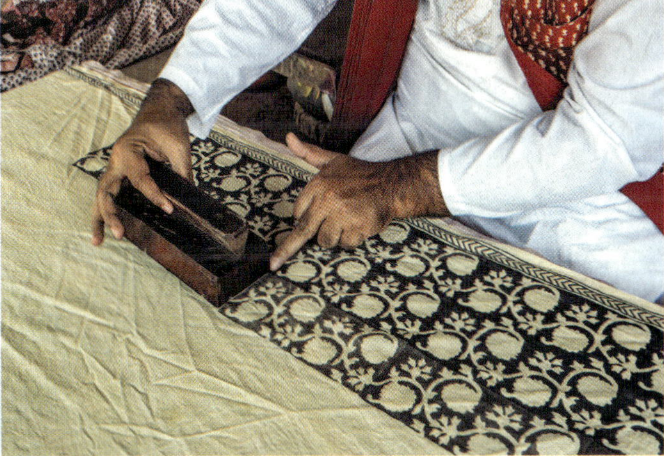

19.33: A hand block printing on fabric by an artisan of Bagh prints — Courtesy, Madhya Pradesh Tourism Board

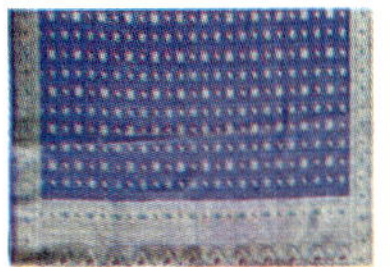

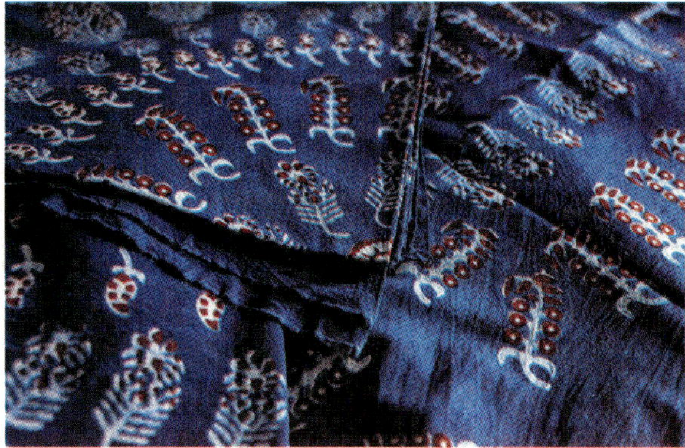

19.34: Nandana block printing with chilli and magnolia bud motifs, a printing technique of Bhil tribals — Courtesy, Madhya Pradesh Tourism Board

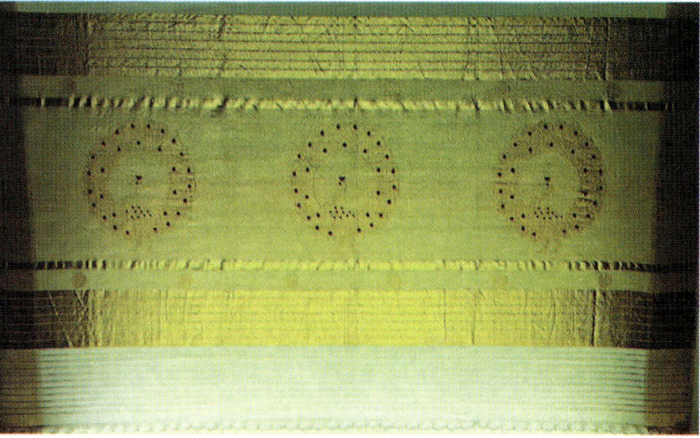

19.35: A saree with Roghan painting and printing, a unique art of Gujarat; National Crafts Museum, New Delhi — photograph by Madhukar K Bhagat

Hand painting

Fabric is also painted by hand to produce intricate and beautiful designs, particularly on sarees. One such craft is ***Kalamkari* of Andhra Pradesh**. This is of two types, the **Srikalahasti** and **Machilipatnam style,** both of which have a GI tag. In the former, a *kalam* (a pen) is used for drawing the pattern or the design on the cloth. Generally, religious motifs were earlier painted. Kalamkari can also be of block printing style. Machilipatnam Kalamkari falls in this category. In different regions nowadays, regional and folk art like **Madhubani paintings, Warli paintings,** etc. are also painted on silk and cotton fabric, particularly on sarees.

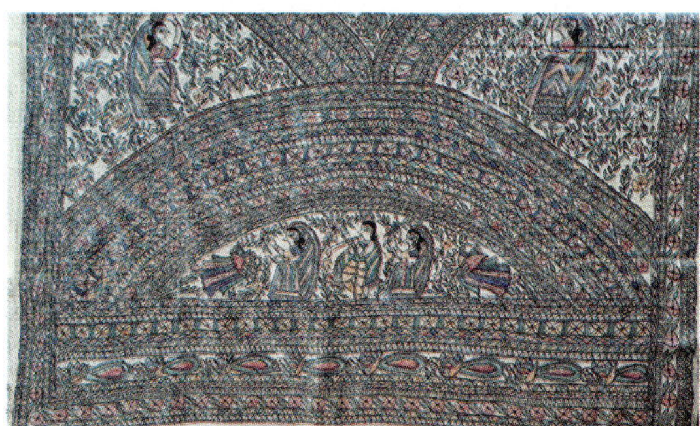

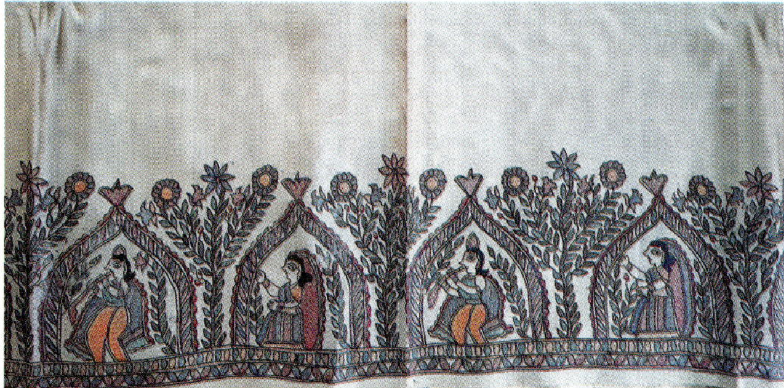

19.36 & 19.37: A sari of Bhagalpur silk (Tussar silk) with Madhubani painting — photographs by Madhukar K Bhagat

Embroidery

Embroidery refers to the art of creating patterns and designs on a fabric by means of needle and thread (or yarn). Thus, it can said to be decorating a fabric by stitching various designs. In India, embroidery has been popular for centuries. Marco Polo, the famous traveller in the 13th century CE, had referred to the Indian embroidery as one of the best in the world. Today, embroidery is a flourishing art popular in different parts of the country.

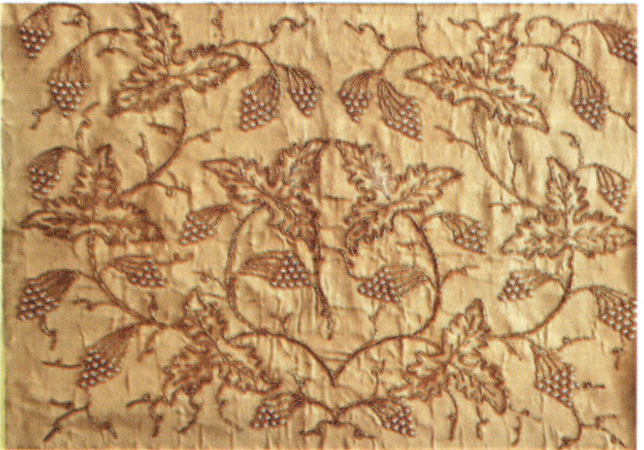

19.38: An exquisite embroidery on fabric at display at State Museum Bhopal — photograph by Madhukar K Bhagat

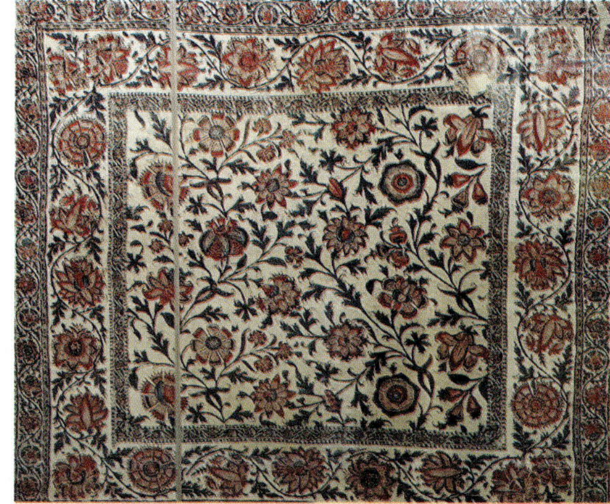

19.39: An exquisite Srikalahasti Kalamkari on fabric done using a *kalam*; National Crafts Museum, New Delhi — photograph by Madhukar K Bhagat

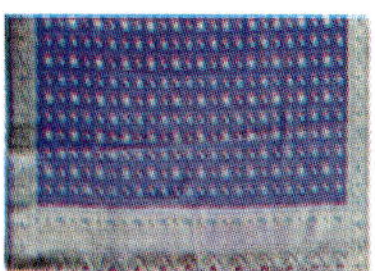

From the *Dorukha* shawl of Kashmir, to the mirror work embroidery of Kutch, from *Chikan* work on cotton of Lucknow, to *Kantha* work of West Bengal, India has a large gamut of embroidery work.

Embroidery of Different Regions

Aari : It is practised in **Kashmir and Kutch** (Gujarat) and employs the use of **beads with sharp edged needle** to create chain stitch type of designs on stretched fabric (chain stitch: a series of looped stitches forming a chain like pattern whether of curved or straight line). The needle with the hook at one end is known as Aari. This embroidery is known for delicate and fine thread work. The stitching may be done with silver or golden threads and is also embellished with beads and stones or other sequins.

Banjara Embroidery: It is popular with *banjaras* (gypsies) of **Andhra Pradesh** and **Madhya Pradesh.** It is a mix of **bead work, embroidery** and **applique work** and characterised by rich colours and geometric patterns and designs.

Chamba Ruma: It is embroidery done on ***rumals*** (handkerchiefs) **in Chamba region** in Himachal Pradesh. It is characterised by **intricate needle work** with designs of animal, birds, trees, geometrical patterns and articles of everyday use. Besides, images from Pahari paintings depicting the folklore of Sri Krishna or scenes of Ramayana etc. may also be an inspiration for the work. It is also awarded a **GI tag**.

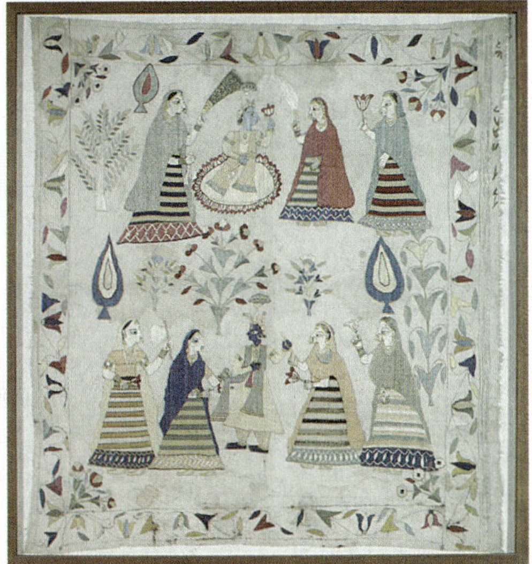

19.40: Chamba *rumal* depicting Sri Krishna with gopikas — Wikimedia Commons

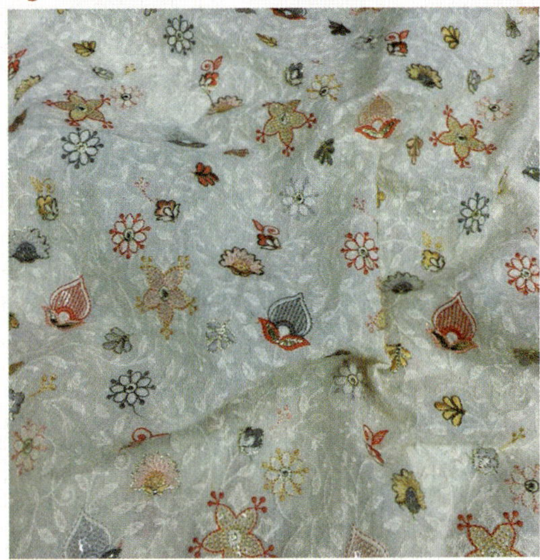

19.41: Chikan embroidery — Wikimedia Commons

Chikan: It is a famous work of **Lucknow** (Uttar Pradesh), which is recognized by a **GI tag**. This work is believed to have originated in the medieval period (apparently when empress Noorjahan was making a cap for her husband Jahangir). Essentially, in the nature of a thread embroidery where white or coloured thread is embroidered on a fabric. It involves **creation of intricate designs** of flower, paisleys, creepers, stars, etc. on cotton/muslin cloth or fine fabric which are usually white or of light colour. More than **32 different types of stitches** are practiced and the art is famous for beauty and dexterity.

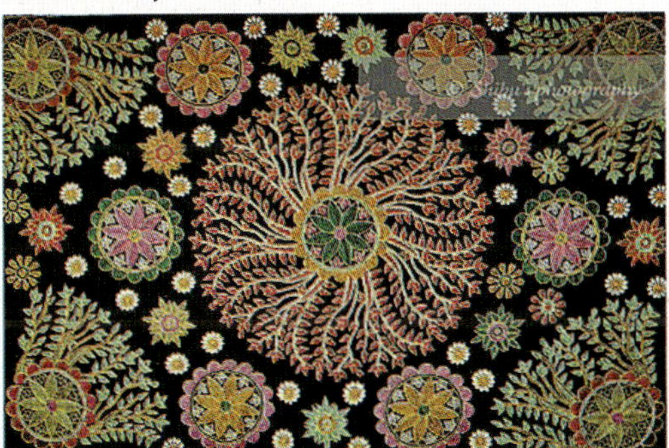

19.42: Modern Nakshi Kantha — Wikimedia Commons

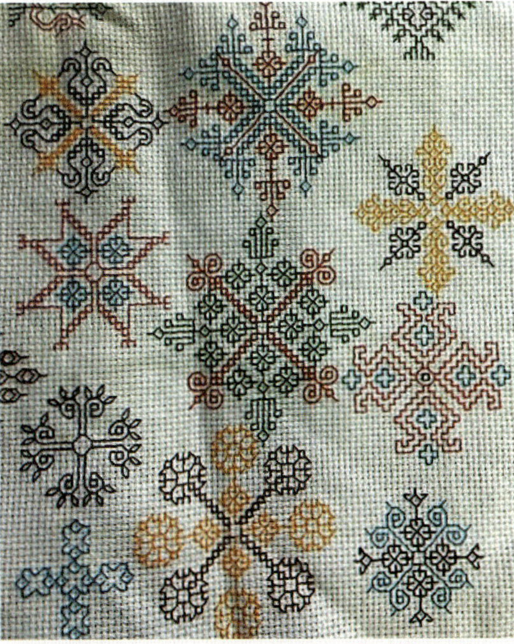

19.43: A Kasuti embroidery with different designs — Wikimedia Commons

Kantha: It is an embroidery technique popular in **West Bengal.** Traditionally, it was executed on old clothes, layers of which may be stitched together. The art involves giving thousands of stitches on the fabric, imparting it a puckered quilted look. Traditionally, it is done on quilts, *dhotis,* and *sarees*. Nowadays, it is even found on *dupattas,* shawls, pillow

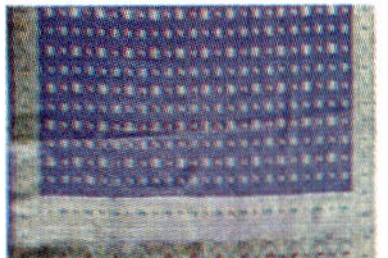

covers, etc. **Nakshi Kantha** is a type of traditional quilt made of old clothes. Motifs of flowers, birds and animals may be used. The art has been awarded **a GI tag**.

Kasuti: It is popular in **northern part of Karnataka** and has been awarded **a GI tag.** The work involves creation of designs which are pictorial in character, such as eight pointed stars, parrots, peacocks, Tulsi plant, temple chariots, etc. Religion flora, fauna articles of daily use etc., all can be the inspiration for the work. The stitching is done without knots such that both the sides look alike. Use of multicoloured cotton threads are employed. The tradtion is said very old and is said to be traceable to the Chalukya period of 6th to 8th century CE.

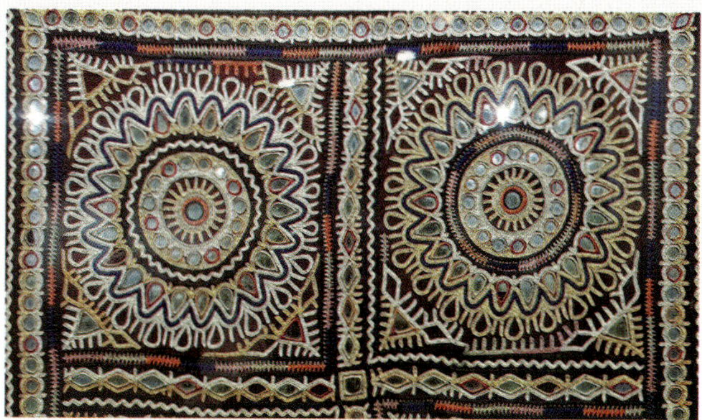

19.44: Intricate Kutchi Kadhai with mirror work, National Crafts Museum, New Delhi — photograph by Madhukar K Bhagat

Kashida or **Kashmiri embroidery:** It is an ancient art popular in **Kashmir.** This is done on a variety of products like woolen rugs and woolen *kurtas (phirans),* bed spreads, pillow covers, etc. The art involves intricate needle work with thick and colourful threads. The designs include natural motifs like trees, flowers, birds, trees, chinar leaves, etc. The art has a long tradition which is traceable to the Mughal period.

Kutchi embroidery: It is also called *Kutchi kadhai*, and is famous in the Kutch region of Gujarat. It is a tradition which is popular in the tribal community of the Kutch region. It is made on a variety of clothing, such as skirts, veils, cholis (blouse), quilts, etc. A variety of stitches such as square chain, double-buttonhole, running stitch, straight stitch etc. are deployed. A notable feature of the art is the bright and varied colour **mirror work** and designs of flowers, peacocks, parrots, elephants, etc. It has been recognized with a **GI** tag.

Mukaish or **Kamdani:** Also referred as **Mukeish**, this work is done in **Lucknow**. It involves **twisting of thin metallic threads** on fabric to create a variety of designs. Owing to there being only a few craftsmen of this work, it is said to be a declining art. In another variant of this art, the wire is attached to a small length of thread. This helps to make the work easier and is called **Kamdani.** Nowadays, both the art forms are used to enhance the work of Chikankari, with the pure Mukeish or Kamdani work becoming rarer.

Phulkari: This embroidery is popular in Punjab and is said to have originated in the 17th century CE. Phulkari literally implies **flower work** (*phul*-flower*; kari*-work*)*. It is also said to imply a headscarf with flower motifs designs on it. The base cloth used for this work is usually handspun *khadi*. Bright coloured threads are used and designs made on reverse/ wrong side of the coarse cotton fabric, using darn stitches. A whole *dupatta* with embroidery may appear like a decked with designs of flowers. The art also involves use of other designs and geometrical patterns. The art has been awarded a **GI tag.**

Sozani and Tilla: Sozani is the embroidery of **Kashmir** which is done using needles (sozni) on a variety of **shawls**. Designs involve motifs of flora and fauna and are created identically on both the sides. Sometimes these are also referred to as *dorukha* (two sided) works. It has been awarded a **GI tag**. The **Tilla** embroidery is done using **gold and silver thread** and may be on shawls *salwar kameez* etc.

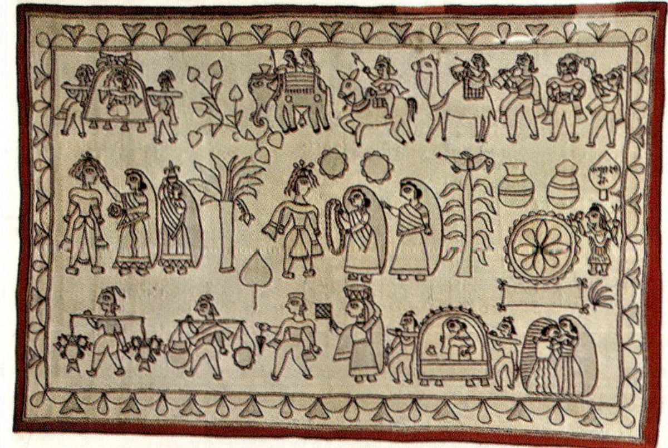

19.45: A Sujini Kantha work of Bihar, National Crafts Museum, New Delhi — photograph by Madhukar K Bhagat

Sujini: Popular in **Bihar,** it is a form of **embroidery** employed for making quilts and bed spreads Earlier, it was used to be done on **old clothes** with two layers of clothes with simple stitches. The designs include narrative themes and stories particularly from the daily life of the people. Many of the designs are also a form of narration of a story which may be religious or even social. The work has been awarded a **GI tag.**

Toda embroidery: It is practiced by the women of Toda community in the Nilgiri hills region of Tamil Nadu. The embroidery is done on the shawls which are called *poothkuli*. The red and black bands of the shawl are embroidered with designs like sun, moon, stars, eyes of peacock feathers and others. The art has been awarded a **GI tag**.

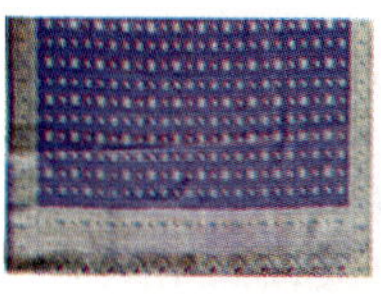

Zardozi: It is a form of embroidery work which traces its origin to the medieval period, particularly during the Mughal regime. It draws its name from Persian words *zar* (gold) and *dozi* (embroidery).This form of embroidery work is popular in **Uttar Pradesh**, particularly Lucknow. It involves metal embroidery on velvet, satin and silk fabric with use of gold, silver, and silk threads. However, nowadays metal wires with plastic core or silver/gold coated wires may be used. Besides, pearls, beads and stones may also be used. The designs are quite elaborate and the entire work is opulent. The Lucknow Zardozi has been awarded a **GI tag**.

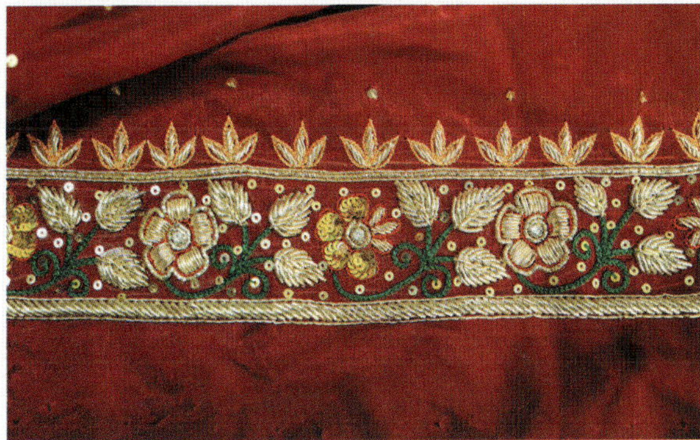

19.46: Zari zardozi work of Bhopal

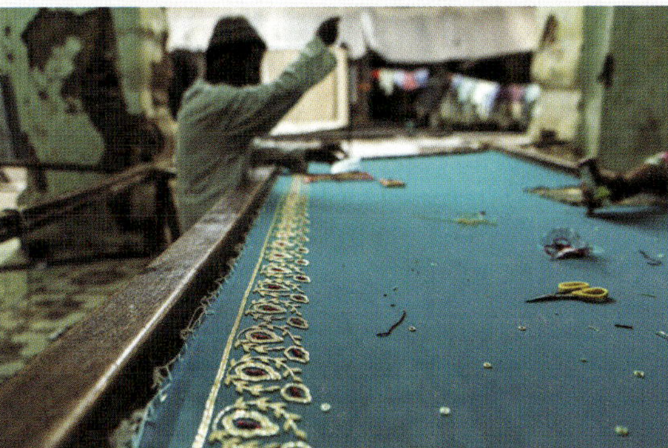

19.47: Craftsmen carrying zari-zardozi work at Bhopal

— Courtesy, Madhya Pradesh Tourism Board

Zari Work: It refers to intricate traditional work of **weaving threads made of gold and silver** into fabric. The work is primarily carried on silk and beautiful designs are created on the fabrics. Earlier, such work was associated with aristocracy. The **Surat Zari** is a famous work which has a **GI tag**.

Besides, some other forms of embroidery include; **Parsi embroidery** (practiced by Parsi community in Maharashtra), **Abhala Bharat** (mirror work embroidery of Gujarat), **Danka embroidery** (metal embroidery of Rajasthan), **Lambadi embroidery** (thread embroidery over a base with metal embellishment; Andhra Pradesh), **Kamal Kadai** (Andhra Pradesh), **Kaudi** (blanket or bed sheet embroidery of Karnataka), **Sandur Lambani embroidery** (stitch, mirror work and applique embroidery of Lambani tribals of Sandur, Karnataka; awarded GI tag), besides others.

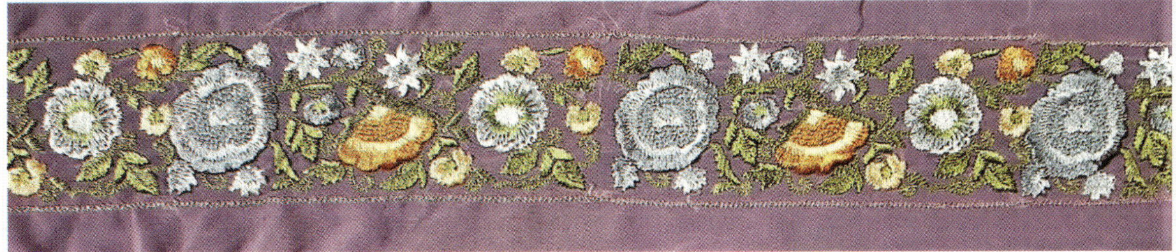

19.48: 'Parsi border on sari', a form of Parsi embroidery with exquisite floral motifs
— photograph by Madhukar K Bhagat

Applique and patchwork

Both of these art forms to the category of 'post loom decoration of fabric'. The word 'applique' is of French origin and means 'to put on'. **Applique** is created by stitching smaller pieces of fabric to a larger piece of fabric which is generally of contrasting colour and texture. **Patchwork,** on the other hand, involves sewing of smaller pieces of fabric together to create a large piece of fabric and thus, creating a design. India has a rich tradition of both the art forms. Some of the well-known crafts of applique/patchwork include:

Gota work of Rampur, Lucknow: Here, small pieces of *zari* ribbon are applied to the fabric to create intricate designs. Even strips of gold and silver ribbons (or other coloured ones) are used in bridal trousseau work. This work is also known as *phool patti ka kaam,* as variety of floral design are created on the fabric and has been accorded a GI tag.

Gota work is also famous in **Rajasthan** where it is referred as *Gota patti*. **Here the designs are first printed on the fabric.** Then the cloth stripes of cotton and metal, known as *Gota*, are woven separately and cut into small shapes. These are then stitched on the clothes, thus forming the required design.

Pipli: It is another famous applique work of Odisha which originated from the Pipili village near Puri (Odisha). Brightly coloured fabric pieces are sewn together to include images of human forms, animals, etc. This technique was practiced to prepare hangings for *rathyatra* processions. The work and has been awarded a **GI tag**.

Khatwa: It is the applique and patchwork of **Bihar** and is recognized with a **GI tag**. It is often seen in *shamianas* (decorative tents), wall hangings, and now even in table cloths, cushions covers, *saris,* and *dupattas*. This work is also done by **Rabari community in Gujarat** (Kutch) and in some other communities of Rajasthan.

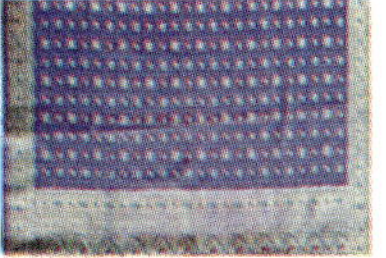

Kamala Devi Chattopadhyay: A Preserver of Indian handlooms, Handicrafts and Theatre

A freedom fighter and Gandhian, Kamala Devi Chattopadhyay was largely responsible for the revivalism of Indian handicrafts, handloom and theatre in post-independence-India. Through her diligent effort she established several institutions of eminence in this field which stand tall and continue to flourish. These include **Sangeet Natak Akademi, National School of Drama, Bhartiya Natya Sangha, Crafts Council of India, Central Crafts Council, World Crafts Council, and Delhi Crafts Council, besides Lady Irwin College**. Even today, all of these institutions are like the nucleus of cultural activities and beacons of light in their respective fields.

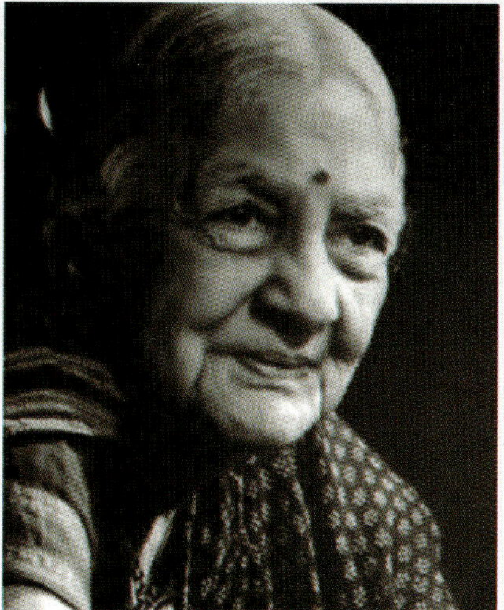

19.49: Kamala Devi Chattopadhyay — Wikimedia Commons

To her name lies the credit of many firsts; notably the first lady to stand in an election (from Madras constituency), besides, she was the pioneer of the cooperation movement and helped to revive the handicrafts and handlooms at the grass roots level. Through the cooperative efforts, she also helped around 50000 refugees post partition to settle in what is now known as **Faridabad**. A champion of the cause of women, she was also an eminent author having written nearly **18 books**. She was also a **Padma Vibhushan and Sangeet Natak Fellowship** awardee.

The preservation of the many of the handicrafts, handlooms, folk arts and thus the some of the quintessential Indian cultural heritage is truly because of her singular effort and vision.

HANDICRAFTS AND ITS TRADITION IN INDIA

Handicrafts refer to a wide variety of traditional products or works which are made by craftsmen by hand or by means of ordinary tools. They invariably involve skill and adroitness, usually acquired over generations, by practicing the work in local communities, tribes or regional pockets. The article produced may vary from relatively inexpensive objects of daily use to rich works of art and decoration, but all are valued for the dexterity of work and aesthetic appeal.

India has a rich and diverse tradition of handicrafts right from the Indus Valley Civilisation to the medieval period and further to the modern days. They constitute a salient facet of our country's cultural heritage signifying the richness of the culture reposited in crafts of the common folks. Even today, Indian handicrafts are a significant contributor to the economy, particularly of the rural sector, and also a contributor to the exports of the country. The domain of non-textile Indian handicrafts is quite diverse and includes **gems and jewellery, pottery, leather products, glassware, terracotta crafts, wooden products, brass, bronze, toys** and other **metal products,** to name a few.

GEMS AND JEWELLERY

Since time immemorial gems and jewellery have been an important means of expression of Indian art. Today, they are valuable items of export too. Jewellery handicraft includes many areas of specialisation such as antique jewellery, *Kundan* work, *Minakari*, silver jewellery, *Bidri*, *Filigree* work, etc.

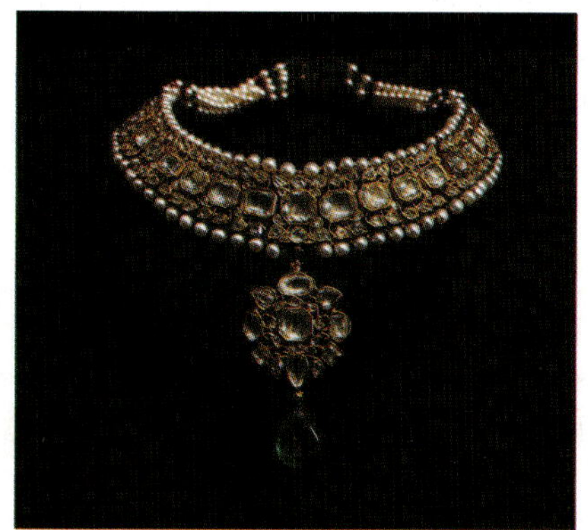

19.50: Kundan work of India; gold necklace with diamonds, pearls, rubies and emeralds; 19th to early 20th century, present location, British Museum — Wikimedia Commons

Traditional and Antique Jewellery

The work of manufacture of gold jewellery by the traditional artisans (*karigars*) is recognised by the Government of India (since July 2015) as a work of handicraft. These works involve making of traditional gold jewellery or antique gold jewellery (which has an old and ethnic appearance). The craft incorporates different techniques and traditional art forms such as Kundan work, Minakari, Filigree work, Bidri work etc.

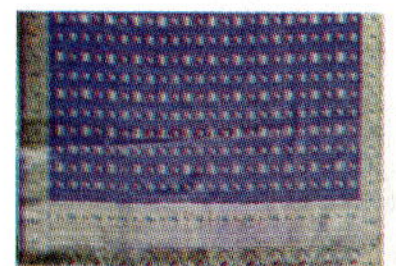

Kundan work: It includes making of traditional Indian gemstone jewellery with gems set in a gold/gold-silver mix base. The very word *kundan* literally means 'pure gold'. This form of traditional jewellery is often known for necklaces besides other jewellery.

Minakari

It is the art of enameling and decorating the surface of jewellery by attaching or fusing pieces of different mineral substances. This may be done by creating grooves or engravings on the surface and fusing it with the enamel. It usually involves creation of intricate designs with geometric figures and other shapes as surface decoration of ornaments and jewellery and may even extend to other objects like containers, vases or other art works. The tradition is said to have been introduced in India during the Mughal period and had Persian origins. Presently, the famous *minakari* works include that of Delhi, Jaipur, and Varanasi. The enamels used in this work may be of single colour (*ek rangi minakari*) or multi coloured (as in p*anch rangi* or five coloured *minakari*) thus determining the type of *minakari*. The **Gulabi** *Minakari* of Varanasi (which uses a pink rose like colour) is also accorded a **GI tag**.

Silver Jewellery Works

It is also known for many specialised handicraft techniques such as filigree and *Bidri* work, and has been a traditional craft of India for centuries.

Filigree work

It refers to making of jewellery involving delicate and intricate metal work. Usually silver and at times gold metals wires are used to form intricate jewellery designs which may be made of tiny beads, twisted metal threads or combination to create an artistic design. The well-known filigree works include that of **Cuttack** (Odisha) known as **Tarakasi** (accorded GI tag as Cuttack Rupa Tarakasi) and that of **Karimnagar** (Telangana).

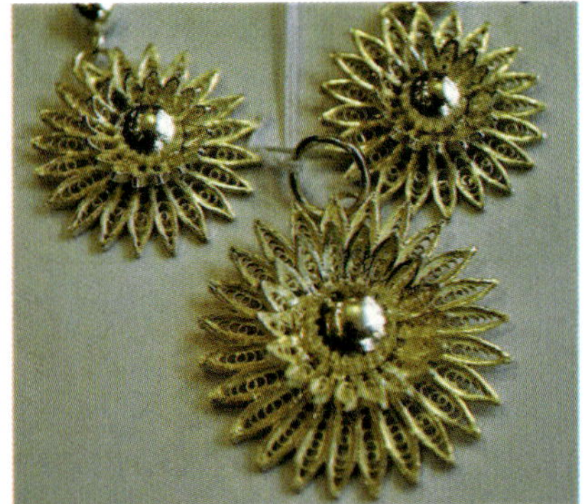

19.51: Tarakasi filigree pendant and earrings from Cuttack — Wikimedia Commons

The Tarakasi work

Common on the eastern coast of Odisha, it has a tradition of nearly 500 years, but now is mostly centred around the town of Cuttack. A variety of ornaments such as necklaces, arm-jewellery, anklets, toe-rings etc. are the specialty of Tarakasi works which incorporates designs of flowers, plants, birds and animals, besides that of the famous Konark *chakra*.

The silver filigree work of Karimnagar

It has a **GI tag** and is said to be an ancient art. Located in the northwestern region of Telangana, Karimnagar was an important town during the reign of the Nizams and acquired a rich tradition of this work with the Nizams as one of the chief patrons. Besides the jewellery and ornaments, the filigree work here boasts of articles of common use such as jewellery boxes, pill boxes, perfume containers, spoons, mementos of Charminar, ships boats etc.

Bidri work

This refers to the metal handicraft/metalware which is usually of silver with beautiful inlay work. It originated from the city of **Bidar** (in Karnataka) and hence the name of Bidriware to these products. The works is said to have medieval origin and became popular during the reign of the Bahmani sultans.

19.52: A traditional tribal silver jewellery with intricate work, mid-19th to early 20th century, National Crafts Museum, New Delhi — photograph by Madhukar K Bhagat

It involves working on white brass which is blackened through a chemical and mechanical process and also inlaid with silver. Thus, it creates a design of bright and white inlay of silver against a black background of brass. The Bidriware has also been conferred a **GI tag**.

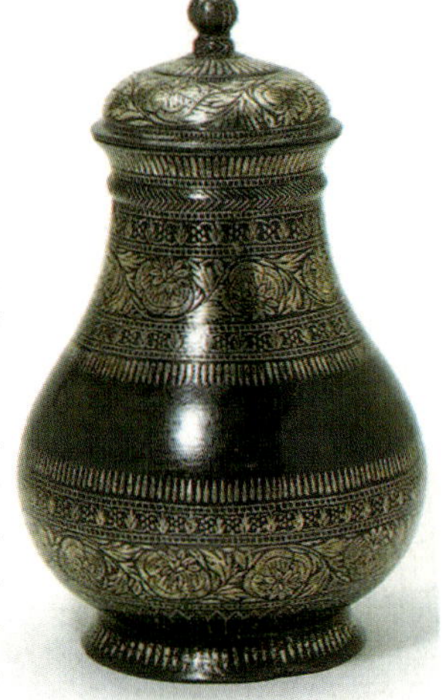

19.53: A cup and lid with Bidriwork from mid 19th century: current location Victoria and Albert Museum, London — Wikimedia Commons

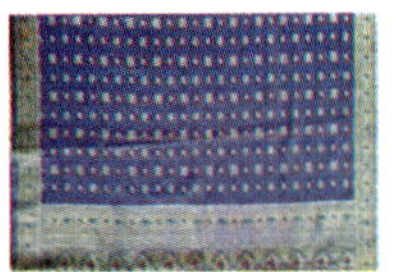

POTTERY WORK

Indian pottery has an ancient history which goes back thousands of years and predates even the Indus Valley civilisation. While earlier pottery making was limited to clay and terracotta potteries, in modern days, apart from the above categories, glazed and unglazed pottery are also commonly made. There are many important centres and styles of pottery making, some of which have even been accorded a GI tag. Potteries remain an ageless tradition and art reflective of an important tangible element of societal culture. A glimpse of this tradition is captured here.

Glazed pottery of Chunar (Uttar Pradesh)

It is a traditional craft popular in the region for centuries. Also awarded a **GI tag**, glazed and red clay terracotta of Chunar has been known for its decorative designs since the medieval period. However, with artisans migrating out of the region or shifting to other trades, this traditional handicraft is on its decline.

Khurja pottery

From the Bulandshahar region of Uttar Pradesh, it is another clay pottery which is popular since the medieval period. The craft has been awarded a **GI tag**. A variety of items of this glazed pottery ranging from artware to crockery, sanitary ware to electrical ware, are popular and even form items of export.

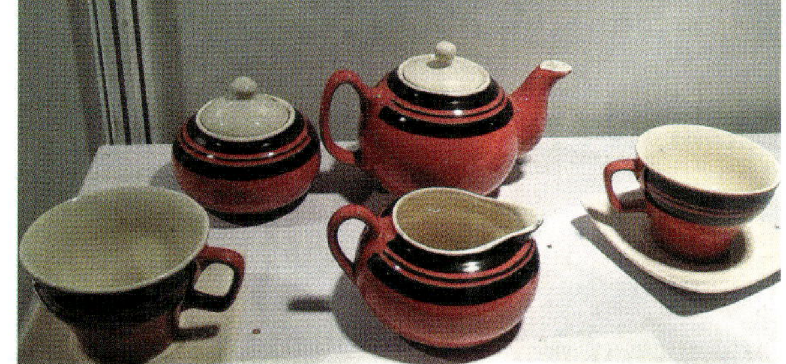

19.54: Khurja pottery — Wikimedia Commons

Blue pottery of Jaipur

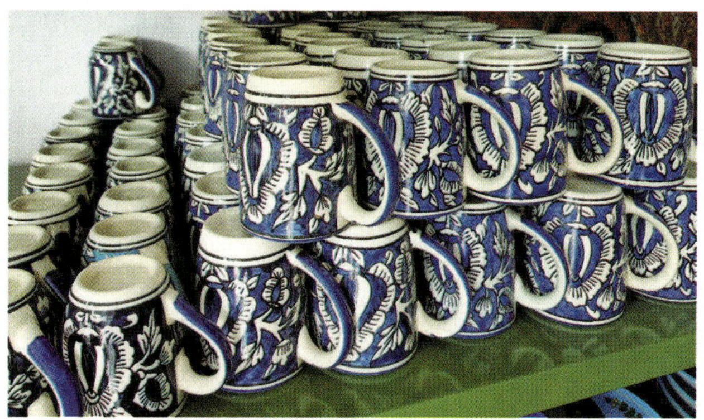

19.55: Mugs/cups of Jaipur blue pottery with traditional white and blue floral design features — Courtesy, Rajasthan Tourism Development Corporation

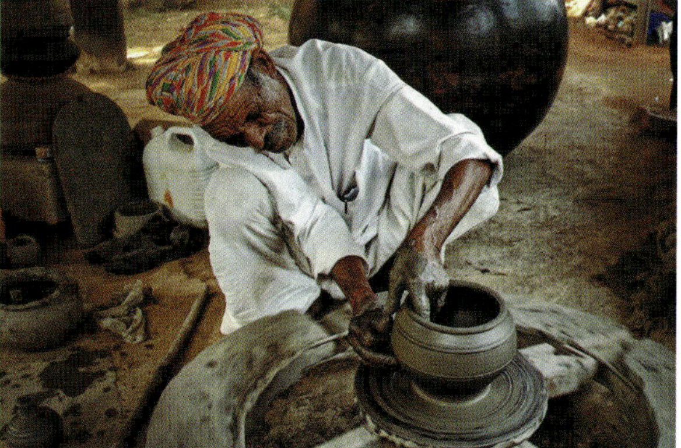

19.56: A potter in Jaipur shaping a pottery on a wheel — Courtesy, Rajasthan Tourism Development Coporation

This glazed pottery of Jaipur is known for its blue colour which is obtained by adding cobalt blue dye. This pottery tradition is centuries old, tracing its origin to the Mughal period and having Persian influence, with geometric designs and Arabesque patterns. Some of the pottery may bear the designs of animals, birds and others. A unique aspect of this pottery is that it is made of ceramic frit material (similar to Egyptian faience) and not the traditional clay. It may even have a semi-transparent effect. Generally, the pottery range comprises a variety of items of daily utility to decorative pieces. It has been accorded **GI tag**.

Black pottery of Azamgarh of Nizamabad (Uttar Pradesh)

It is known for its black, shiny appearance with silvery engraved designs. It is said to have resemblance to Northern Black Polished ware (Iron age pottery) and is known to be in vogue at least since the Mughal rule. The pottery is made of local clay which is rich in mica and kiln fired in an atmosphere of reduced oxygen (air) providing it a black colour. Subsequently, designs are engraved using sharp needles which are later filled with silvery powders of zinc and mercury or other amalgams of tin and lead, imparting its unique appearance. The

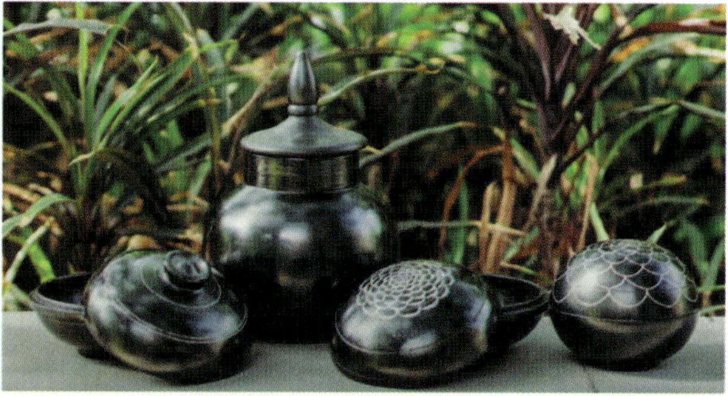

19.57: Black pottery of Nizamabad — Wikimedia Commons

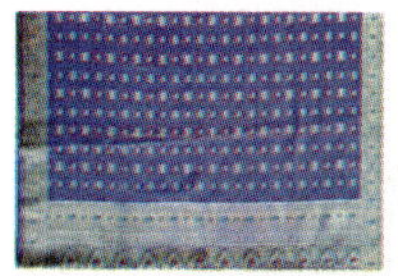

wares are polished at different stages using powdered vegetable matter, mustard oil etc., imparting it a characteristic shine. The pottery has been accorded a **GI tag.**

Black pottery of Manipur

It is a traditional craft called **Longpi,** popular with the Tangkhul tribe in Longpi (Nungbi village). It is said to be an ancient craft which is believed to trace its origin to the neolithic period. A unique feature of this pottery is that it is not made by using the potter's wheel. Further, it is produced using a mixture of local brown clay and a special variety of rock called serpentinite. The pottery is then fired and polished with a specific variety of tree leaves giving it a black metallic look. The pottery articles have been traditionally used as kitchenware and utensils and have market even outside the region.

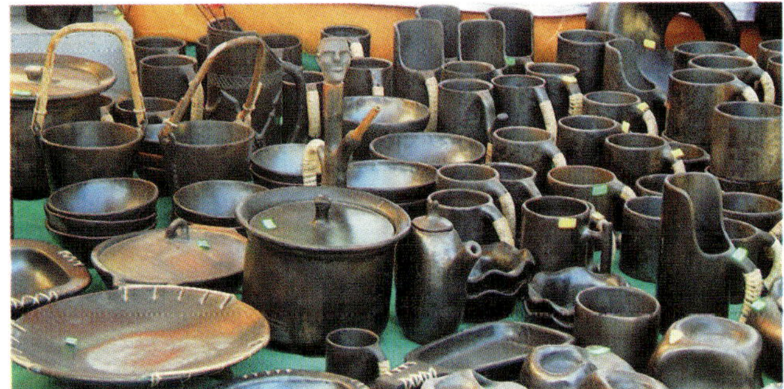

19.58: A variety of black Longpi pottery of Manipur prepared without using potter's wheel — Wikimedia Commons

Dal Gate pottery (glazed pottery of Kashmir)

It is popular in Srinagar and adjoining regions in Kashmir. This is a type of glazed pottery which is available in a variety of colours such as deep blue, green, brown, ochre, etc. Table wares and vases besides items of daily uses are some of the products made of glazed pottery. Owing to shrinking demand and migration of artisans to other vocations, the art of this glazed pottery has seen a declining trend.

Kagzi pottery of Alwar

This pottery popular in the Alwar region of Rajasthan. As the name suggests (*kagazi:* like paper) this pottery products are paper thin. This art is of medieval origin and products are made in a variety of shapes and colours.

Besides products like traditional and contemporary cooking wares and decorative flowerpots, modern items like delicate lamps and Tea-lights (small candle holders) are also popular in this art.

Khavada pottery of Gujarat

It is practised in the in the Kutch region. This pottery tradition is centuries old and is said to have similarity with the potteries found in Indus valley Civilization. The pottery items comprise utensils and decorative ware. The local clay (called Rann ki *mitti*) is fired in kiln and then a layer of *geru* (red-ochre paint) applied, giving it a characteristic warm appearance. This is followed by use of local organic paints (of red, black and white) and dyes, to impart a variety of designs which are often in form of dots and stripes. Like many other pottery traditions, this is also a declining art.

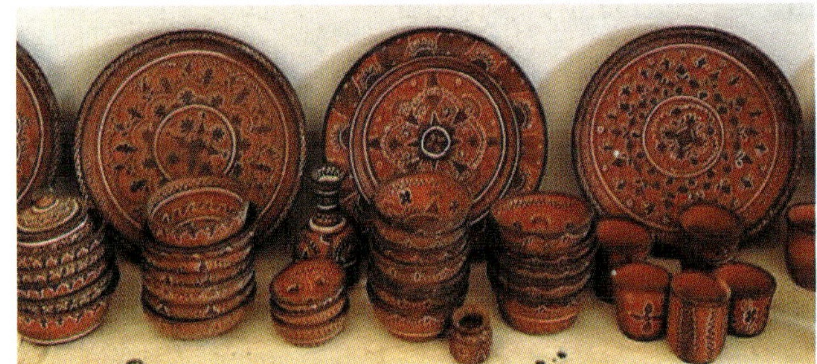

19.59: Khavada pottery — Wikimedia Commons

TERRACOTTA HANDICRAFTS

Terracotta refers to clay-based ceramic which has been prepared by firing of the earth (clay). The very word is derived from *terra cota,* which in Latin means 'cooked earth'. Usually, the terracotta crafts have a porous surface with brown, orange or deep ochre colours. The final products may be glazed or unglazed or coat of paints may be applied. The products are used for the purposes of art work, items of daily use, cooking ware or even for ritualistic purposes.

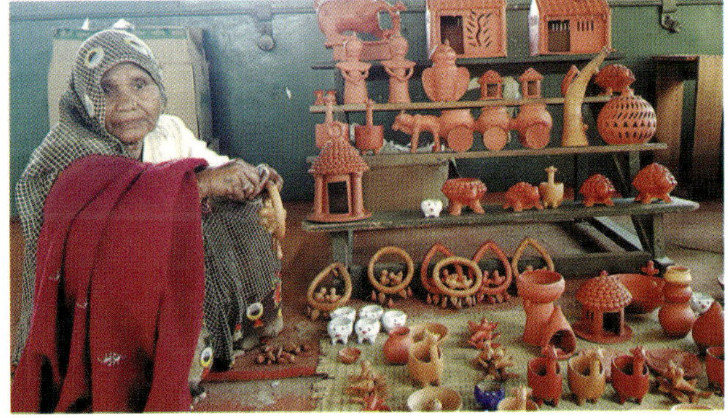

19.60: An artisan with different terracotta works from Dhamna in Chattarpur, Madhya Pradesh — photograph by Madhukar K Bhagat

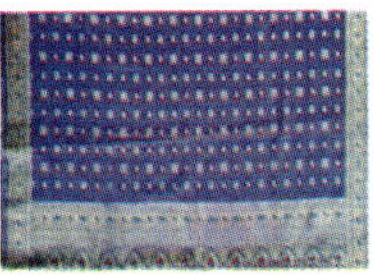

India has an ancient tradition of terracotta works which is seen even in the Indus Valley civilization. Today, it is a part of the folk as well as the tribal culture, with some famous terracotta works being **Bankura horse** (West Bengal), **Molela clay works** (Rajasthan), **Villianur terracotta works** (Puducherry) **Aiyanar terracotta** figures (Tamil Nadu), besides that of tribals of **Madhya Pradesh, Chattisgarh** (Bastar) and others. Terracotta crafts also flourishes in other states including, Jammu and Kashmir, Himachal Pradesh, Haryana, Bihar (terracotta horses of Darbhanga), Gujarat and Odisha.

Bankura horse

It is a tradition of West Bengal where the terracotta temples were once in vogue in the late medieval period. The terracotta tradition now continues in the arts and crafts of the region. The most famous of these is the **Bankura horse** or the **Panchmura horse** (Panchmura being a *gram panchayat* in Bankura district in West Bengal). This terracotta work here is displayed as an abstraction of the figure of the horse and was employed for ritualistic purposes. The region is also famous for its terracotta elephants. Besides Panchmura, other regions where this art flourishes are Sonamukhi, Rajagram and Hamirpur in West Bengal. This handicraft has been accorded **GI tag** as **Bankura Panchmura Terracotta craft.**

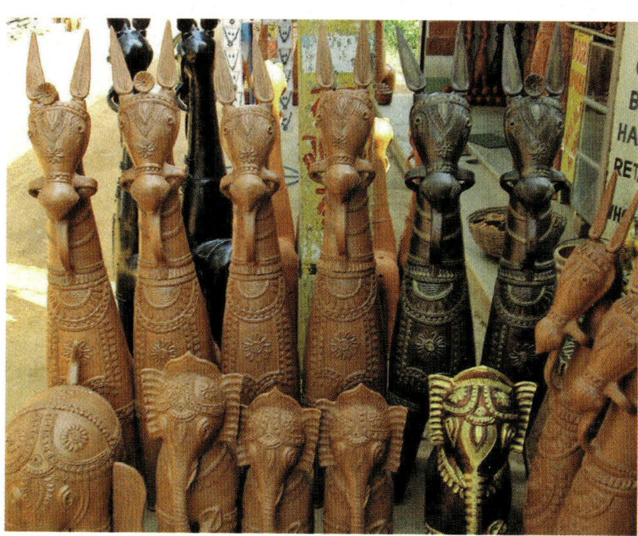

19.61: Bankura terracotta horses and elephants — Courtesy, Department of Tourism, West Bengal

Villianur terracotta works

It is another famous craft which is accorded a **GI tag**. The art has centuries old tradition in the village of **Villianur** in the Union territory of Pudducherry (erstwhile Pondicherry). The terracotta products are made of fine sand, green clay and other ingredients. Bamboo tools are often used for hand crafting the terracotta products. A unique feature of this art work is that terracotta works may range from a few inches (such as statues of lord Ganesha) to works several feet in height (such as 6 feet tall horses).

Molela clay work

It is another unique terracotta handicraft which is practised in Molela village of Rajsamand district of Rajasthan. This craft is essentially a hollow relief craft in the form of **votive plaques** (offered as consecration). The local artists of the village prepare terracotta plaques depicting the images of various deities such as Devanarayan and Nagaraj. Different deities are often depicted with different colours. These are prepared without the use of a mould.These plaques are bought by people from local communities and *bhil* tribals of Rajasthan, Gujarat and as far as Madhya Pradesh and are used by them for ritual purposes. This product too has been accorded a **GI tag**.

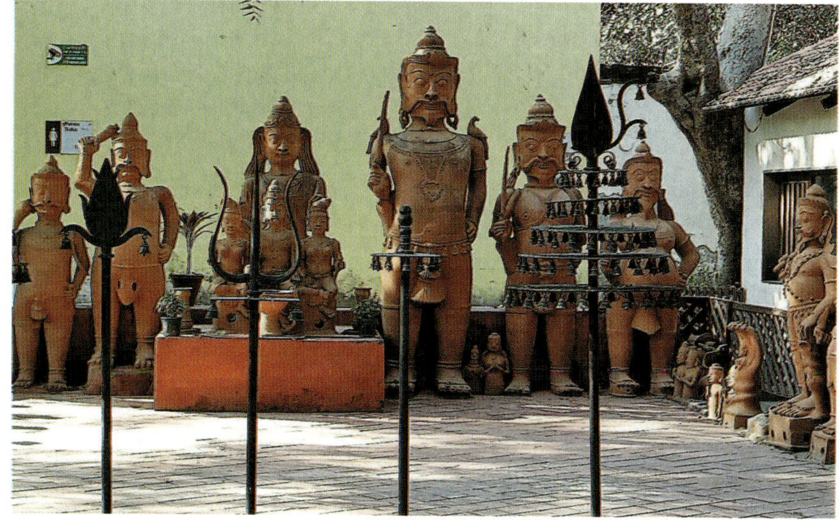

19.62: The image of Lord Ayyanar seated on a pedestal along with two consorts and other large terracotta figurines and votive offerings, at National Crafts Museum, New Delhi — photograph by Madhukar K Bhagat

Ayyannar terracotta horses and other works

It is another significant terracotta handicraft tradition which flourishes in Tamil Nadu, particularly in the Chettinad region and Pudukottai district. Lord Ayyannar, who is said to have originated from Lord Shiva and Lord Vishnu, is a powerful village deity, considered a protector of the village community. Large terracotta horses and other terracotta figurines are the votive offerings which are made to the lord by the farmers

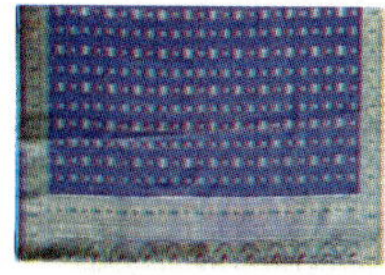

for good harvest. These are commissioned and made by the local potters (*velars*) and are a part of *puravi eduppu* (horse ritual) of the community. The image of lord Ayyanar seated along with his two consorts may often be in terracotta or stone alongside other votive terracotta offerings. The uniqueness of the works lies in the life-like and almost gigantic terracotta horses which form an army for the lord and his retinue, symbolically needed to move around (particularly in night) to protect the village community. These horses also form one of the **largest terracotta works**. Besides the above, the other significant works include **Gorakhpur Terracotta** of Uttar Pradesh, which has been accorded a GI tag.

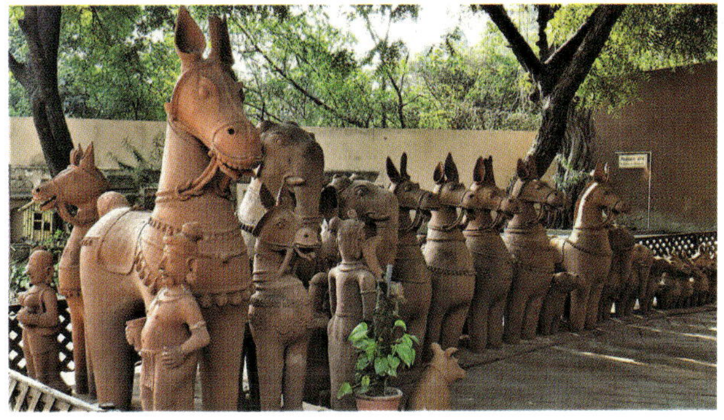

19.63: An army of terracotta horses of Lord Ayyanar, at National Crafts Museum, New Delhi — photograph by Madhukar K Bhagat

Clay Work of Sarguja, Chhattisgarh

Clay relief craft is a unique household tradition of the **woman** of the **Rajwar communi**ty in Sarguja district of Chhattisgarh. Different parts of the house hold are painted with a variety of motifs ranging from gods to human figures to flora and fauna. The clay relief work is done by hand and made out of unfired clay, straw and bamboo, and painted with natural/vegetable colours which are locally available. Walls, door panels, window screens (*jhinjhira*) and grain storage (*dodki*) are some of the house hold architectural elements so adorned.

A large grain storage jar is a salient and integral element of the household. This is often beautifully covered with clay work, colourful motifs and beautiful designs of humans, flowers, birds animals and plants. The storage structure is made of unfired clay over a framework of bamboo and wood. It is designed in two levels (tiers) with grain to be poured from a lid at the top level. A hole with a stopper in a lower level enables the grain to be drawn out.

The clay relief work of Surguja is indeed a unique community craft, imbued with a naivety of aesthetics, originality of thought and simplicity of execution.

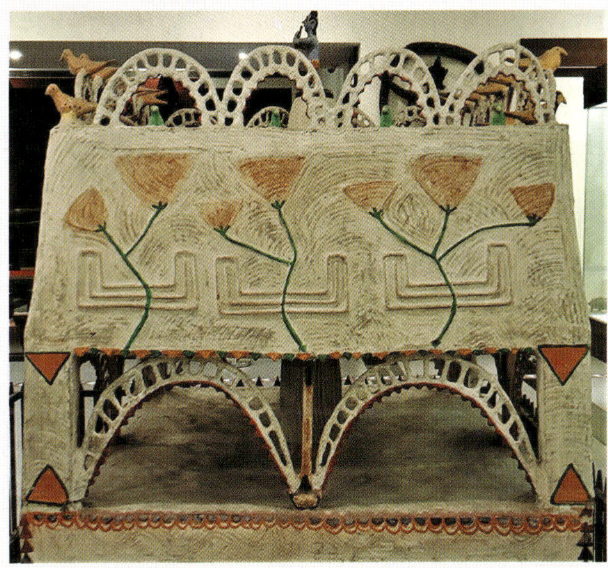

19.64: A clay grain storage jar (*dhodki*) of Sarguja, Chhattisgarh, carrying motifs of flower with clay figurine of parrots, other birds, and Krishna playing a flute atop; location National Crafts Museum, New Delhi — photograph by Madhukar K Bhagat

LEATHER PRODUCTS

Manufacture of leather products in India is a craft which is thousands of years old. Like other handicrafts, these have flourished in the local communities and regions, with the art skill being passed over the generations. Besides the articles of daily use such as shoes, bags, leather, apparels etc., leather products have also been an expression of art, with certain crafts being unique to leather works.

Be it the tradtional ***juttis*** popular in northern India or the **Kolhapuri chappal** of Maharastra, the handcrafted ***mojaris*** of Rahjasthan reminiscent of the medieval tradition, the stuffed **leather toys of Indore** (Madhya Pradesh), the **Usta** leather art of Rajasthan or the **Shantiniketan leather goods** of West Bengal, each has a uniqueness of its own which defines the craft of the region. Besides these, the states of Punjab, Haryana, Uttarakhand, Gujarat, Tamil Nadu, Karnataka and Union territory of Pudducherry have a long and distinct tradition of leather handicraft products. Today, leather products and items of leather handicraft are also an important item in India's basket of exports.

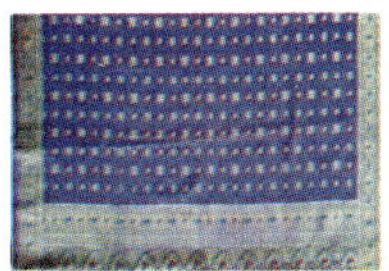

Juttis

These traditional shoes popular in the **Punjab** region and other parts of **northern India**, have a long history which dates to medieval period. Traditionally made of leather, embroidered with gold and silver threads, and bearing the hallmark of *kashidakari* art, these were once the footwear of choice of the Mughal and Rajput royalty. These shoes still remain in fashion, particularly as the footwear of festive occasions like marriages. The present *juttis* display extensive embroidery and beautiful designs (sans gold and silver work). They are usually foot-neutral (same for left and right foot) and end with a sharp upward bend like a moustache, giving them an identity of their own.

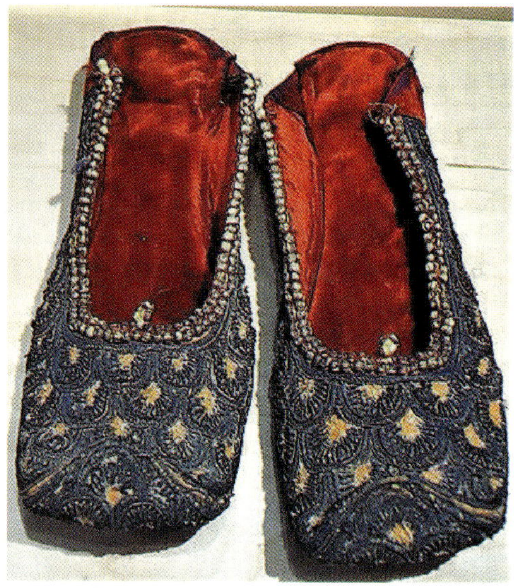

19.65: An Indian *mojari* from the 19th century with gold embroidery at Bata shoe museum — Wikimedia Commons

Mojaris

They are the traditional leather footwear is popular in Jaipur and Jodhpur regions of Rajasthan. They also have centuries old tradition in the region. Made of tanned camel leather, these are beautifully handcrafted, embroidered, embellished with mirrors, cowrie shells ceramic beads, sequins or other forms of decoration. As a slip-on leather foot wear they are similar to *juttis* of the Punjab region.

Kolhapuri Chappal

These are **leather slipper footwear** which traditionally is made in Kolhapur region of Maharashtra since the 13th century. The slippers are made of tanned leather, are beautifully handcrafted and are given a colour using vegetable dyes. These are open-toed with design of a T strap sandal. These are also accorded a **GI tag**.

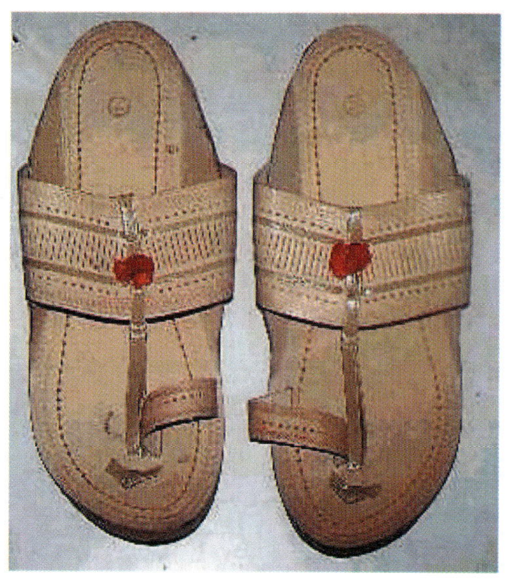

19.66: A Kolhapuri chappal — Wikimedia Commons

Usta art

Popular in Bikaner district of Rajasthan, this is essentially an art combination which is performed on camel leather and other surfaces such as walls, ceilings, glass, wood, etc.. Usta art in a way is a generic term referring to art of *naqqashi* and *manoti* performed by Usta artisans (literal meaning *ustad* or experts). This art involves embossing of various floral and other designs with gold foil on camel hide and other surfaces. A variety of colours with traditional dyes are added to the non-embossed surfaces. The art has a medieval tradition, when experts of this art from the court of emperor Akbar came to the court of Maharaja Rai Singh of Bikaner. Later, this art was seen in the Anup Mahal, Phool Mahal and Karan Mahal of the Junagadh palace. Today, this is a declining art due to paucity of experts and lack of support to the remaining artists. The art has recently been accorded a GI tag in 2023.

Stuffed leather toys of Indore

It is another famous handicrafts work in this category which has a tradition of decades. These toys are life-like miniature animal sculptures made of leather and other material. A skeletal framework is first made of wires which is then stuffed with waste paper and covered with cardboard pulp to bring out the anatomy of animals. This is then covered with leather which is painted and polished to give it a life-like quality. The toys have a substantial domestic as well as international demand. The handicraft has also been accorded a **GI tag**.

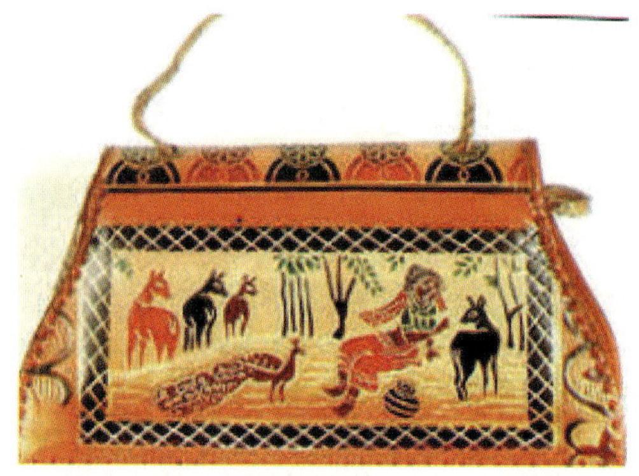

19.67: A Santiniketan leather bag with *batik* design — Courtesy, Department of Tourism, West Bengal

Santiniketan leather goods

It is a tradition which emanated from Santiniketan and Vishwa Bharti University in West Bengal around 80 to 90

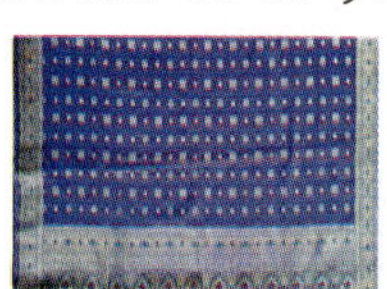

years ago. Today, it still continues to flourish here and in the surrounding villages. The leather goods are produced with vegetable tanned leather on which art work has been done such as *batik* print and techniques of touch dyeing are applied. A wide range of products are made today including handbags coin bags, ladies bags, pouches, footwear like *chappals* and sandals, cushion covers and others. The products have a good demand in the domestic as well as international markets. The craft has been accorded a **GI Tag**.

Among other famous items or crafts of leather would include saddles and ***kopis*** (bottles of camel hide) of Jaisalmer, **Kanpur saddlery** (accorded GI tag), **Agra leather footwear (accorded GI tag), Chamba Chappal** of Himachal Pradesh (accorded GI tag), **embroidered red leather items** of Madhya Pradesh, **leather puppets** (*Tholu Bomalatta*) and toys of Andhra Pradesh, Karnataka leather products painted with images from the mythologies and epics, *nagara* shoes (slip in traditional shoes similar to *mojaris* and *juttis*), besides other traditional products.

GLASS HANDICRAFTS

India has a long history of glass product manufacturing. Reference to glass products is said to be found in the epic *Mahabharata*. Over the entire course of history, evidence of glass craft has been found. However, this art received great impetus during the medieval period, especially during the Mughal rule, when glass engravings and foliated design on glass products came to be introduced. Glass works were also an important element of traditional craft such as Tanjore paintings, where it was integrated with the art of painting and decorated with gold and other precious stones. Today, a wide range of glass products and handicrafts are manufactured ranging from glass bangles and toys, to utility and decoration items like chandeliers, lamps crockery, bottles, even etched and stained glass.

Firozabad glass

Firozabad in Uttar Pradesh is one of the most important centres for manufacturing of a variety of glass products. This is a tradition which has flourished in the city from the medieval period, particularly during the Mughal rule. A large variety of products including glass bangles, glass toys, chandeliers, *Itra* bottles, utility bottles, flower vases, decorative lights, bulbs, candle stands, etc. are produced today. The uniqueness of this centre lies in the making of artistic glassware incorporating different colours and shades besides items of regular use. The Firozabad Glass has also been accorded a **GI tag**.

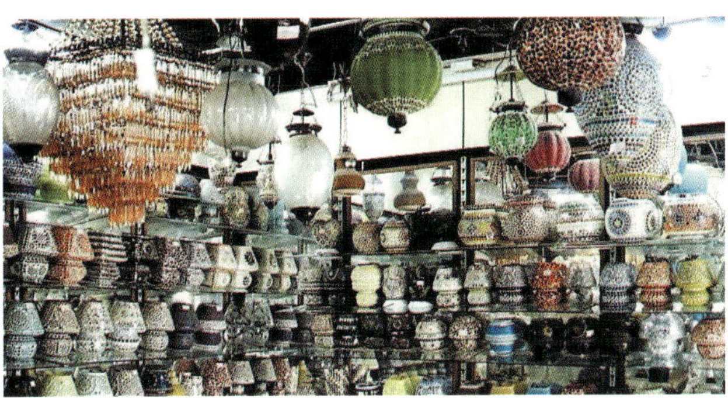

19.68: Firozabad glass work
— Courtesy, Directorate of Uttar Pradesh Tourism

Varanasi glass beads

Glass beads (*kanch ke moti*) are a speciality handicraft of Varanasi region of Uttar Pradesh, which has also emerged as one of the largest production centre and exporter of this tiny colourful item of decoration. Glass beads are an ornamental input in a variety of products such as clothing accessories, purses, jewelry etc. The beads of Varanasi are said to be unique, for, despite the close similarity, no two beads are identical. The product has been accorded a **GI Tag**.

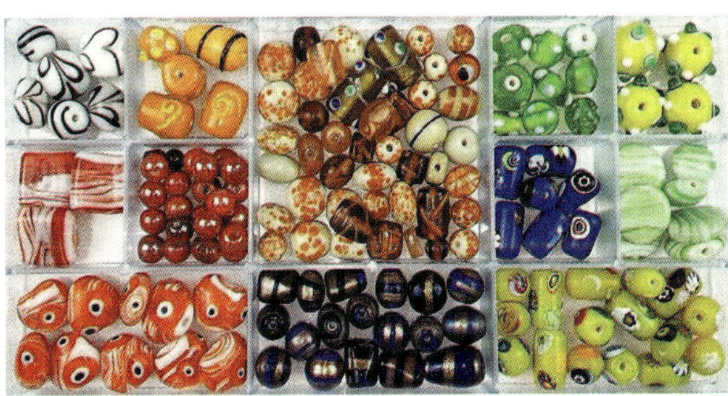

19.69: Glass beads of Varanasi
— Courtesy, Directorate of Uttar Pradesh Tourism

Glass bangles of Hyderabad

Among the famous glass bangle works, also figures the glass bangles of Hyderabad. This is a tradition extending to the medieval period to the reign of Sultan Quli Qutab Shah when a bridal market around the Charminar was established. Presently, a whole market known as *Laad baazar* flourishes here which deals in a variety of locally manufactured glass bangles. Besides, bangles made of lac are another speciality of this centre. The Hyderabad lac bangles have also been awarded GI tag (in March 2024).

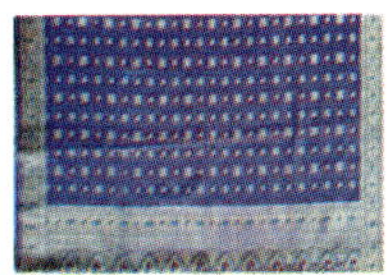

Tikuli art of Bihar

It is another important glass handicraft. The art involves making of small glass *bindis* called *tikuli* with gold and silver foil and other art work. The *tikulis* (or *tikali*) are tiny adornment, worn on the centre of the forehead, usually by the married women. The art is said to have nearly a 800-year-old tradition and was a flourishing craft and trade for centuries. Today, only a few of its practitioners survive, though effort of its revival are being made with the art and its technique diversifying to other products such as wall-hangings, coasters etc.

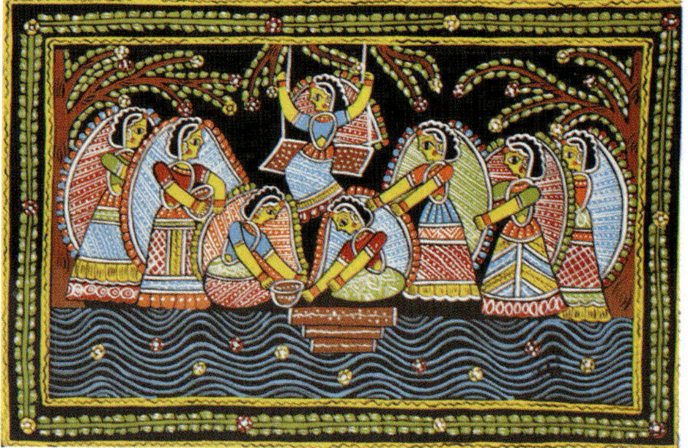

19.70: A Tikuli art now expressed as painting/ artwork in wall hangings — Courtesy, Bihar Tourism

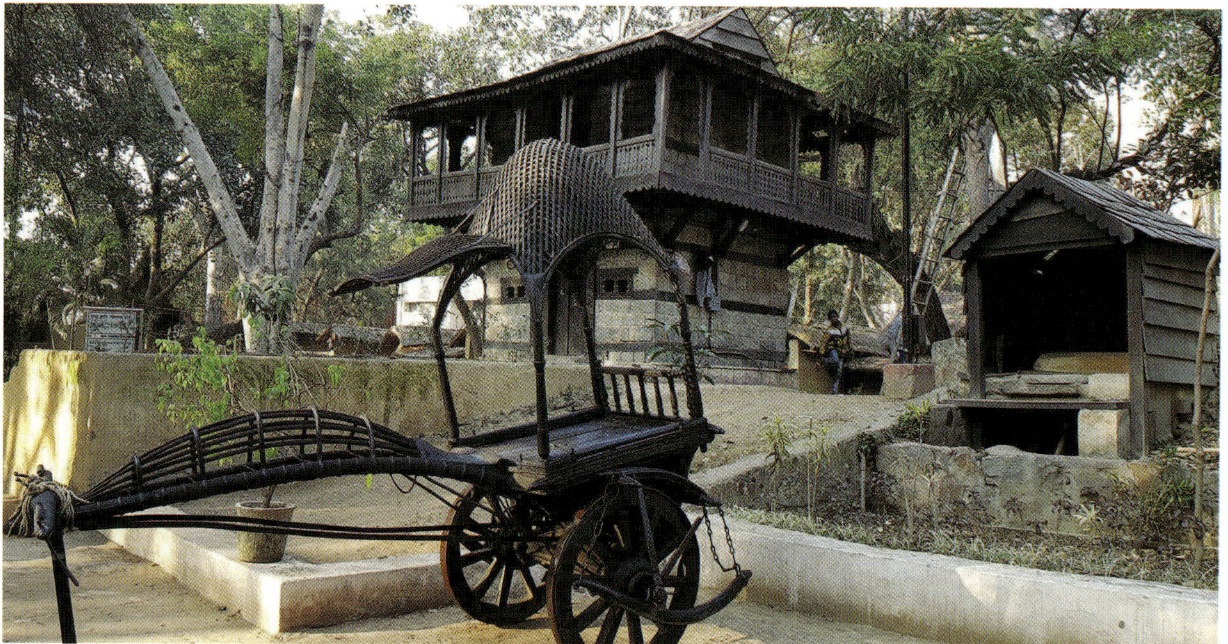

19.71: A traditional wooden chariot (*buggi*) and Kullu (Himachal Pradesh) wooden hut at National Crafts Museum, New Delhi — photograph by Madhukar K Bhagat

WOODEN HANDICRAFTS

Wood, a natural product, has been the material of choice in Indian tradition since time immemorial, for building a variety of structures and innumerable craft-work. India, being richly endowed with diverse vegetation; this art has prospered in each region of the country and different traditions of wood-work have evolved. From ancient temples to *havelis*, from ordinary huts to buggies, from crafted door panels to musical instruments, from items of daily use to luxurious furniture, from ordinary toys to exquisite crafted and semi-precious stone embedded art works, all have been a part and parcel of the story of wooden handicrafts.

While the Northeast region richly endowed with bamboo and cane has developed a range of handicrafts of this genre, Bastar is known for its tribal wooden crafts. Kashmir is famous for its walnut wood carving. Mysore rosewood inlay is another exquisite work and so is the sandalwood handicraft of the region. Screw pine which is in abundance in Kerala has seen a development of a variety of utility

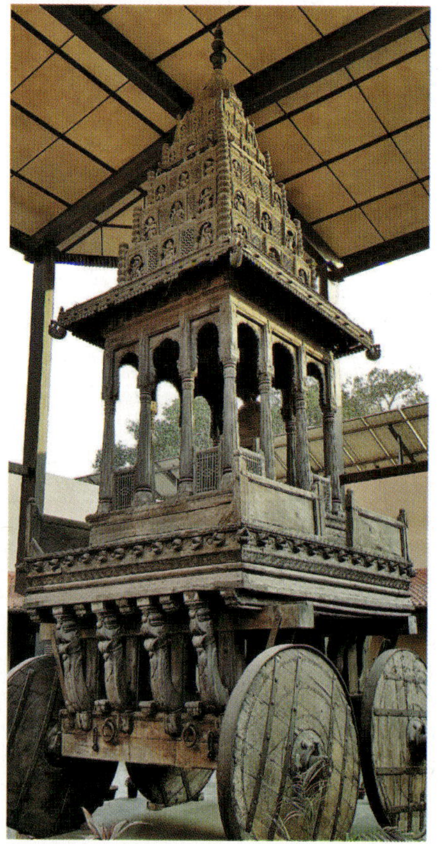

19.72: An 18th century teakwood chariot from Maharashtra, designed after a temple, with dashavatara deities carved on the shikhara (top). It is considered a Rama-ratha with image of Lord Rama and devotees carved on the front side under the canopy. Other sides depict other incarnations of lord Vishnu; location National Crafts Museum, New Delhi — photograph by Madhukar K Bhagat

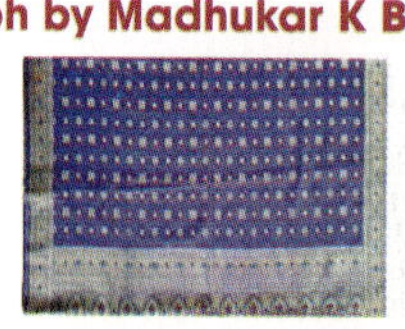

products. Besides these, almost all states have a tradition of wooden handicrafts. But today, many of the traditional handicrafts are waning owing to the migration of artisans to other crafts, competition from other cheaper material, or just on account of a fall in demand.

Kashmir walnut wood carving

One of the important crafts of Kashmir, this art is a centuries old tradition of the region and unique to it. Due to abundance of walnut trees and availability of skilled craftsmen, the art continues to flourish. The handicraft, which is essentially delicate and ornamental in nature, involves deep relief and intricate carving on walnut wood products. Tables, jewellery boxes, trays are some of the common products. Beautiful designs of rose, lotus, grape vines, chinar leaves and other foliate patterns adorn the surface. The craft has also been accorded a **GI tag**.

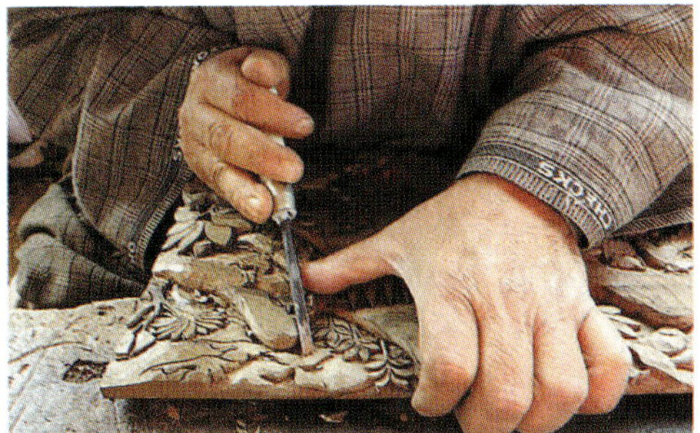

19.73: An artisan carving walnut wood — Wikimedia Commons

Sankheda furniture

Manufactured in the **Sankheda** village in Gujarat (near Vadodara), it is a famous teak wood furniture, which is made in a traditional design with lacquer maroon and gold polish. The furniture tradition is said to be at least a 500 hundred years old. Today, besides the traditional furniture, a wide variety of items including table tops, three-piece settees, rocking chairs, divans dressing tables and other products are made in a different colours. The craft has been accorded a **GI tag.**

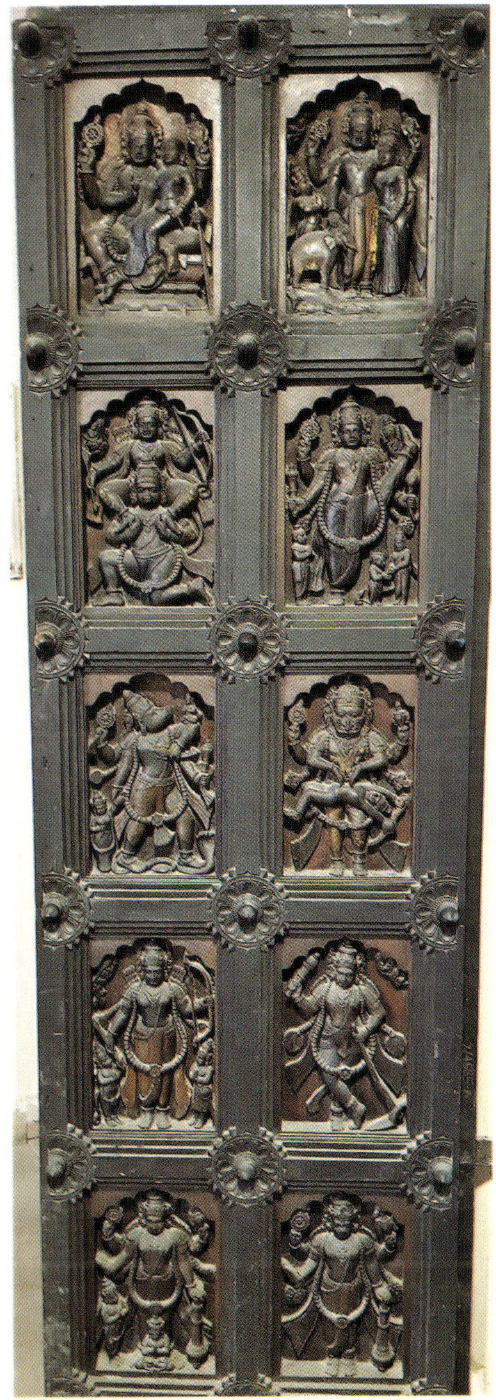

19.74: A large wooden crafted door panel, depicting *dashavatara* ; at National Crafts Museum, New Delhi — photograph by Madhukar K Bhagat

Bastar wooden craft

Popular in **Bastar** region of Chhattisgarh, this handicraft has also been recognized with a **GI tag**. The wood craft has been practiced since ages especially amongst **Muria** and other tribes, who produce a variety of traditional wooden craft besides items of daily and agricultural use. These include products such as wooden masks, musical instruments, decoration panels, items of daily use such as tobacco boxes, combs etc. Products are usually of teakwood, rosewood and whitewood. The craft is also associated with the custom of making pillars for the deceased (known as *Gudi*) which is prevalent in the Maria tribe.

Bamboo and cane handicrafts of the Northeastern states

They are an integral part of the lifestyle and economy of the state, particularly of the tribals. The region being rich in both bamboo and cane, the craft has flourished over centuries and has blended with the very fabric of life of the tribals. Today, an extremely diverse array of products related to art and fulfilling daily needs, are produced. These range from huts to bridges, from furniture to wares of daily use, from baskets to trays, from designer hand bags to decorative lamp shades, from a variety of musical instruments to dolls and toys etc.

The craft/products particularly important in the various states are; **Tripura** (famous products: *dulla* or fish basket, *pathee* or rain shield, trays, lamp shades, decorative fans, door screens, shopping bags), **Manipur** (famous products: bamboo houses, fencing furniture, fishing traps, flower vases), **Assam** (famous products: bamboo hut or *jhapi*

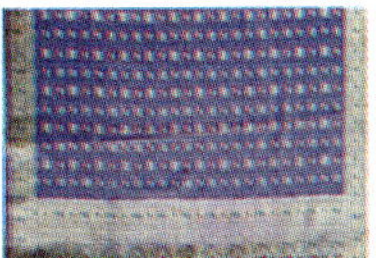

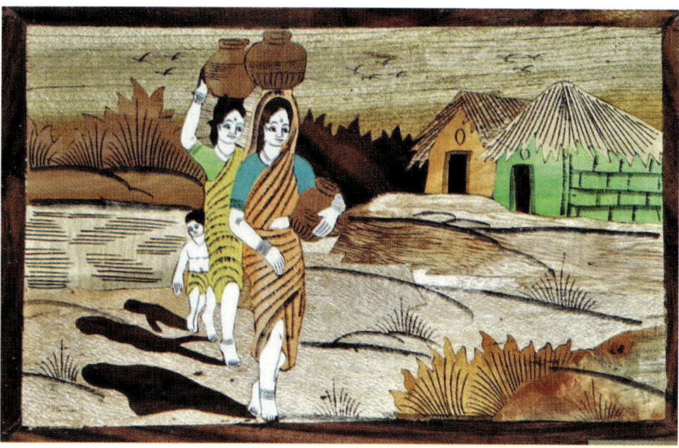

19.75: A wall hanging of Mysore rosewood inlay work depicting a rural scene — photograph by Madhukar K Bhagat

bamboo baskets), **Arunachal Pradesh** (famous products: houses, bridges, ornaments, baskets, barrels trays), **Meghalaya** (famous products: *khoks* or artistic baskets, *kurup* or special Khasi umbrella, mats, stools), **Mizoram** (bamboo/cane baskets, toys, pipes, umbrellas, weaving tools), **Nagaland** (famous products: bamboo furniture, cane baskets), **Sikkim** (furniture, mats baskets).

Mysore rosewood inlay

This famous work of Mysore region of Karnataka has a history dating to late 18th century, when it was a popular craft in the reign of Tipu Sultan. It involves making of various items of rosewood, in which decorative pieces of mother of pearl, sandalwood, ivory, etc. are fixed in excavated depressions carved out in the wood. Common items of this craft are table-tops, jewellery boxes, photograph by frames, door frames, furniture, decorative paintings, wall panels and other artefacts. The craft has been accorded a **GI tag**.

Sandalwood handicrafts

Another famous handicraft of Karnataka is the handcrafted sandalwood product. Popular in Mysore (Mysuru), Shivamogga and North Karnataka region, the craft is a centuries old tradition and even today it remains an important industry of the state. The intricately carved sandalwood figurines of this region are world famous. The handicraft also includes other products such as; deity idols, elephant statues, decoration pieces, miniature chariots, jewellery boxes, photograph by-frames, besides articles of common use such as combs, pen stands, trays, walking sticks etc.

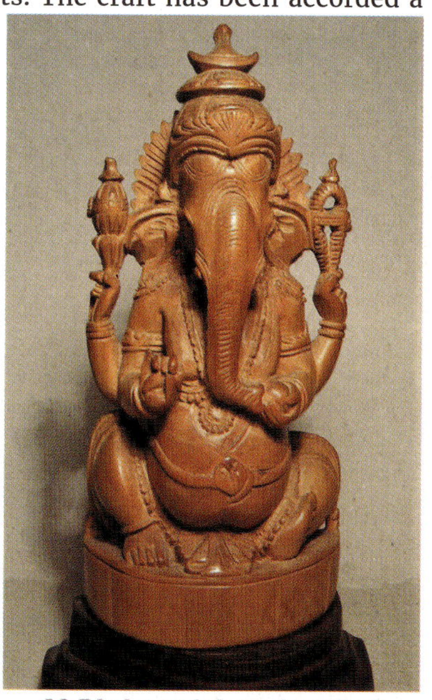

19.76: A sandalwood crafted statue of Lord Ganesh — Wikimedia Commons

Thammapatti wood carving

It is a signature artwork on wood practised by the skilled artisans of the Salem region of Tamil Nadu. Although the tradition has been inherited over generations, the artwork has been thriving in the Salem region, and in particular in and around Thammapatti town for at least 75 years. Records show that here, in 1948, Lakshmi Narasimha Swami's temple car was made by the artisan community. The artwork involves carving of idols of Hindu gods, idols denoting mythological events, temple cars, temple doors, images of other deities and *vahanas*. The carvings are imparted an antique finish. Their sizes may vary from two to six feet. A variety of wood from locally available trees is used. The craft has also been accorded a **GI tag.**

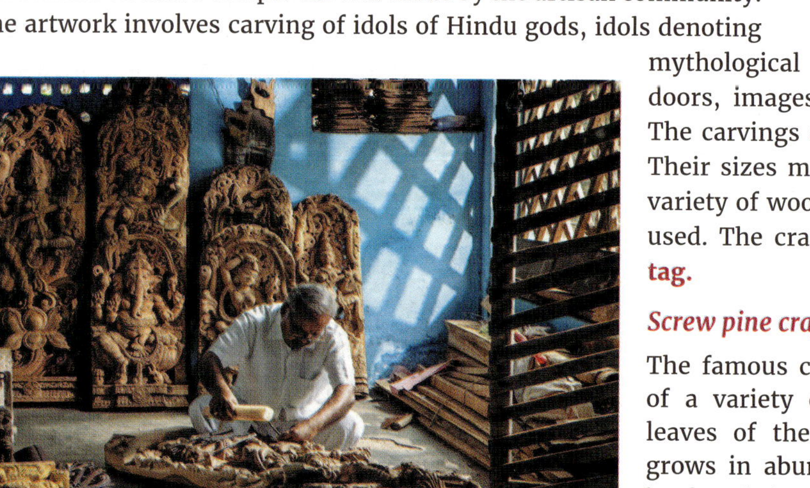

19.77: A Thammapatti craftsman carving out the idol of a deity, while several semi-finished works are seen on the far end — Courtesy, Tamil Nadu Tourism Development Corporation

Screw pine craft of Kerala

The famous craft of Kerala involves making of a variety of products by artisans using leaves of the screw pine plant. The plant grows in abundance, as it grows in wild in banks of rivers, ponds and backwaters. This craft is believed to be nearly 800 years old and has been a traditional cottage industry

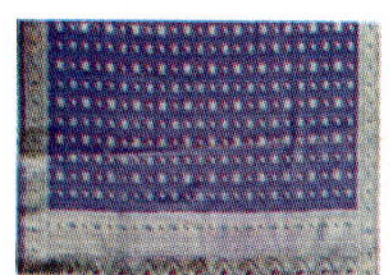

in the state. A unique aspect of the craft is that it mostly involves the women artisans. The most common of the screw pine products include mats, door mats, bed mats, wall hangings and prayer mats. Besides, items such as baskets, bags, pen holders, etc. are also made. The craft has also been accorded a **GI tag**.

Thanjavur veena

It is another wooden handicraft accorded GI tag is produced in Thanjavur by the local *Vishwakarma* community. The craft traces its history to the 17th century reign of the Nayaks of Thanjavur. The veena is unique, for it is manufactured from the local mature jackfruit tree wood. The veenas are of two types; the *Eknath veenas* made out of single piece of wood, and the three-piece veenas. The entire process of making may take 20 to 30 days. These veenas are engraved with delicate wood work and painted with motifs of gods, goddesses, birds and flowers.

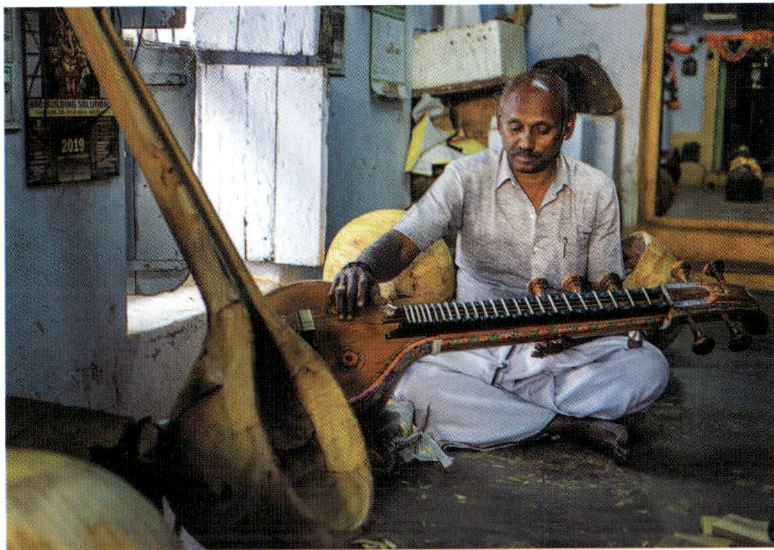

19.78: A craftsman with Thanjavur veena — Courtesy, Tamil Nadu Tourism Development Corporation

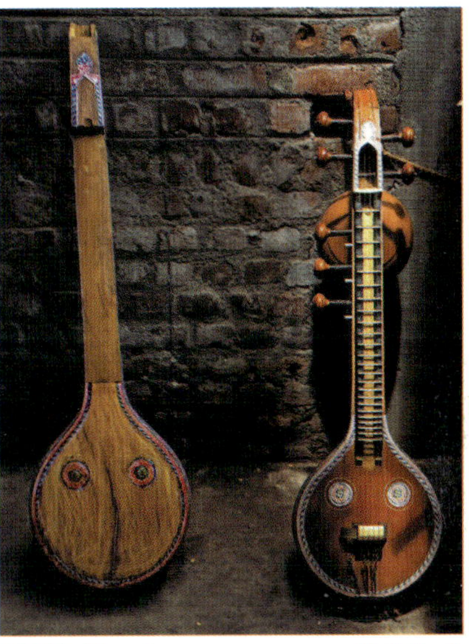

19.79: Thanjavur veena; semifinished and finished — Courtesy, Tamil Nadu Tourism Development Corporation

Besides the above, the other prominent wooden handicrafts include, **Banaras Wood carving, Saharanpur Wood craft** of Uttar Pradesh, **Bobbilli veena** of **Andhra Pradesh** (traditional Carnatic veena of jackfruit wood), **Madallam of Pallakad, Kerala** (traditional percussion drum made of jackfruit tree wood) **Udaigiri wooden cutlery** of Nellore district of Andhra Pradesh, **Arumbavur wood carvings** of Tamil Nadu, **Thanjavur Netti works** of Tamil Nadu (carving made of wood pith) **Sikki grass products** of Bihar (baskets and other products woven with grass), Moonj craft of Prayagraj, Uttar Pradesh (including Moonj grass products),Assam Pani Meteka craft (products of Pani Meteka grass), Miraj Tanpura and Miraj Sitar of Mahrashtra, Sawantwadi woodencrafts of Maharashtra (including wooden: toys, imitation fruits, household articles etc.), Chitrakoot wooden craft and toys of Uttar Pradesh, Bareily furniture of Uttar Pradesh (of cane , bamboo and wood), Wancho wooden craft of Arunachal Pradesh(including wood carvings of human faces, animals birds, smoking pipes and other items), all of which are also accorded **GI tag.**

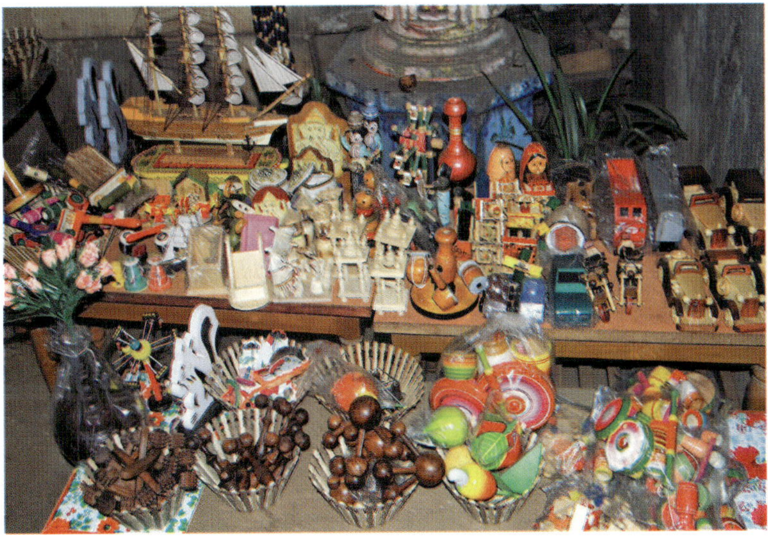

19.80: Sawantwadi wooden toys and handicrafs — Courtesy, Maharashtra Tourism Development Corporation

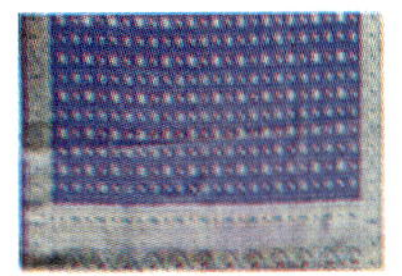

Bhoota Kola and the Wooden Bhoota Figures of Udupi

Among the Tulu community of South Karnataka (*Dakshina Kannada*) and Udupi district, exists a unique and centuries old tradition of the worship of *bhoota,* or spirits, around which has evolved a variety of rituals, community art and even wooden crafts. *Bhoota* or the ethereal spirit of deceased, particularly of the ancestors, powerful community leaders and those whose deeds were good and noble, are considered to be the protectors of the community. *Bhoota* worship involves veneration of these spirits through a variety of rituals and invoking them to seek their protection from any evil befalling upon them.

The tradition is associated with different legends, some of which are pre-Vedic, and some which are associated with, cult of Lord Shiva and the band of followers which comprised the *bhoota* or the spirts. The Bhoota-Kola tradition entails invoking of these spirits symbolized by masks and large wooden figurines, besides through ritual dances and other customs.

The woodcraft associated with this tradition is also unique and comprises large, imposing and at times awe inspiring figures emblematic of these spirits. These idols or figurines are usually made of jackfruit tree wood. These may vary in size from one to two feet, or to even as high as 16 feet. These are placed in *bhoota sthana (the place of the bhoota)* which can be on a stone platform or inside a thatched hut, or under a tree, where the village community can worship them. Some of the common idols are that of god Nandi (*vahana* of Lord shiva), the three headed *bhoota* (an incarnation of lord Shiva), the boar or *Varahaswamy* (a form of lord Vishnu).

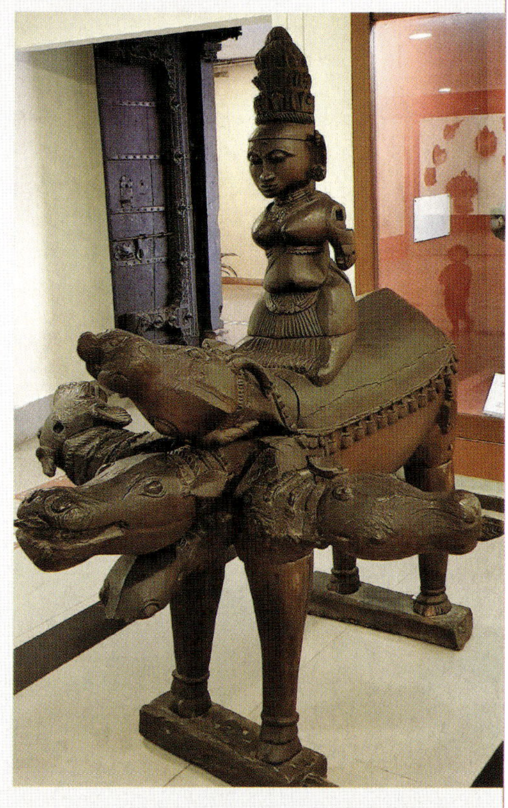

19.81: A Panchamukhi (five headed) Nandi of jackfruit wood made at Udupi; location National Crafts Museum, New Delhi — photograph by Madhukar K Bhagat

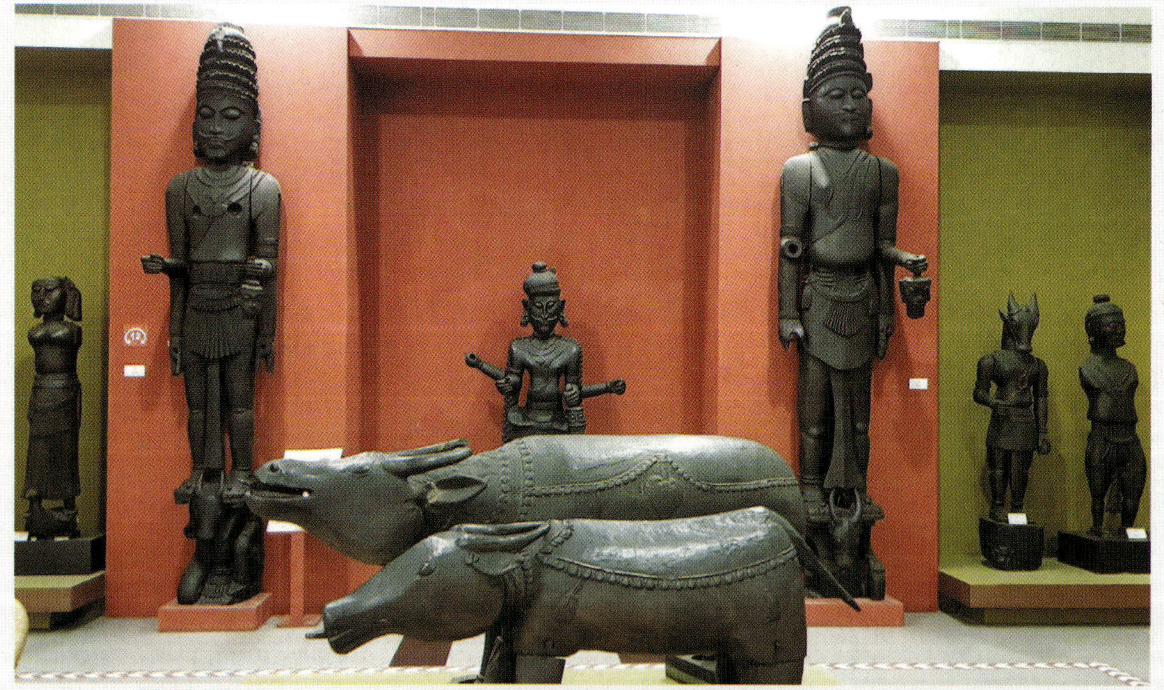

19.82: Lifesize and larger wooden ghost-idols at National Crafts Museum, New Delhi — photograph by Madhukar K Bhagat

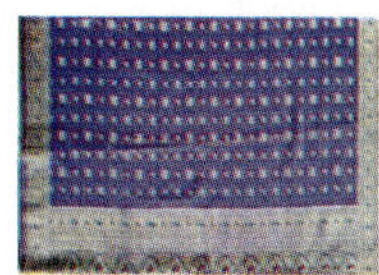

BRASS, BRONZE, WROUGHT IRON AND OTHER METAL HANDICRAFTS

Metal craft and metallurgy have been an ancient discipline In India. The bronze dancing girl statue of Mohenjodaro, the iron pillar of Mehrauli, the bronze statue of Nataraja of the Chola period and many bronze works of Pala period, are a testimony to the knowledge and practice of this craft in different parts of country and all phases of history. Over the centuries, this craft has been reposited in the communities which have engaged in metal work (such as *lohar* and *vishwakarma*). They were integral to the rural economy for manufacture and repair of a variety of agricultural and other equipments, besides articles of a daily use. This craft extended to iron, brass, bronze, copper, and later even to alloys such as bell metal, white metal (silver and gold work fell in the domain of jewellery making). Over a period of time, a variety of art forms got inscribed in the metal craft tradition viz. *nakkashi* (shallow engraving), deep engraving, *meenakari* (enamel work), inlay, damascening etc. These added to the aesthetics of the product and uplifted it to the domain of an art.

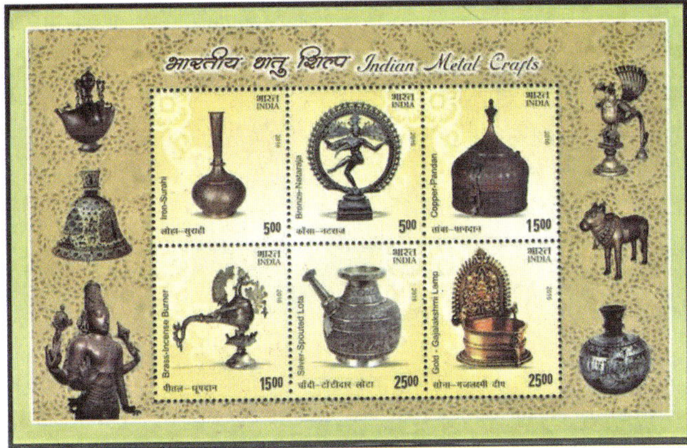

19.83: A stamp sheet (2016) depicting the metal craft of India — Courtesy, Department of Post

Today, the metal craft, like other forms of handicraft, is deep rooted in the folk traditions. These are a source of livelihood for the tribes and different communities who have imbibed the craft as a family or community tradition or as a vocation. Some of the more known, among the many metal crafts prevalent in the country are; **Moradabad metal craft**, **Bastar Dhokra art**, **bell metal work of Datia**, **Tarakashi of Mainpuri** (accorded GI tag), **Koftgiri of Jaipur** and **Swamimalai bronze works,** besides others.

Moradabad metal craft

The city of Moradabad in Uttar Pradesh is famous for **brassware,** a tradition which is nearly 200 years old and synthesizes the Islamic and Hindu art elements in the handicraft. (brass: an alloy of copper and zinc). *A* variety of brassware and other metal handicrafts with exquisite *naqqashi* (shallow engraving), deep engraving and *meenakari* (enamel work) are made here. These include flower vases, canters, *surahis*, bowls, decorative plates, *diya*-stands, candle-stands, *diyas,* brass idols, antique jewellery, tableware, besides other items of daily use. Different designs are engraved on them such as motifs of flowers, plants, birds, animals and others. The metal craft of Moradabad finds place in small household workshops to much larger units. It is a world-renowned flourishing trade of the city and a major item of export, which lends the city the epithet of *peetal nagari* (brass city). The Moradabad metal craft has also been accorded **a GI tag**.

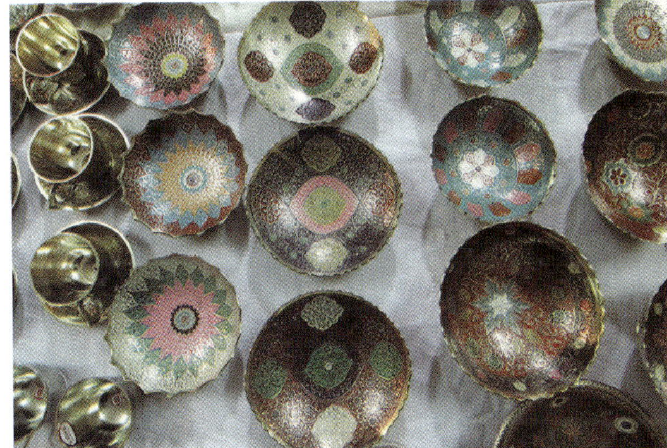

19.84: Moradabad brass bowls and glasses with a variety of decorative works — Courtesy, Directorate of Uttar Pradesh Tourism

Bastar Dhokra

The region of Bastar in Chhattisgarh is famous for **non-ferrous metal casting** (such as brass, bell metal) known as the Bastar Dhokra art. The craft has been in practice with the tribal communities (such as Ghawas) in the region for centuries. Dhokra art is essentially a metal casting technique using the lost wax process. This technique in itself has been in vogue since the Indus Valley Culture (as seen in the dancing girl figurine of Mohenjodaro). Human figurines, dancing figures, idols of gods and goddesses and other decorative works are the common Dhokra products. The Bastar Dhokra craft has been accorded a **GI tag**.

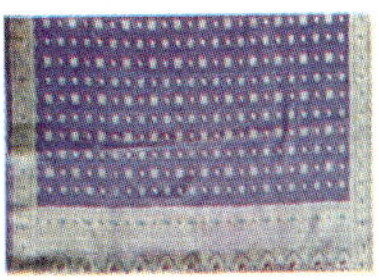

Adilabad Dokra of Woj community of Adilabad (Telangana)

It is another similar craft which is recognized by a **GI tag**. Both the Dhokra works are based on *cire purdue* (lost wax casting) where a clay core of the object to be cast is first prepared. This is coated, with bees and wax threads to give a fine shape to the cast. Then it is covered with another layer of clay which takes the shape of the bees wax, thus forming the outer layer of the mould. Molten metal is poured in this mould which melts the wax, causing it to drain out and allowing the molten metal to fill in.

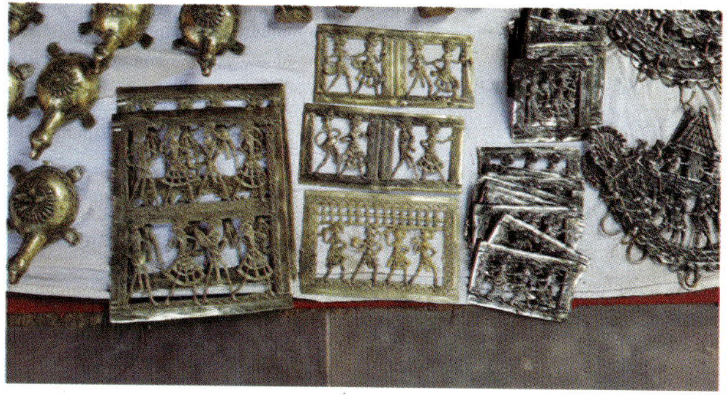

19.85: Different works of Dhokra craft

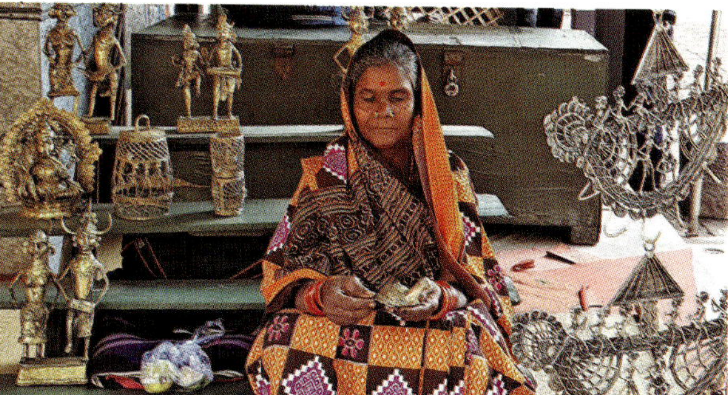

19.86: A Dhokra artisan with different craft items

— photographs by Madhukar K Bhagat

Bastar iron craft

Another famous metal craft of the Bastar region is the *loha shilpa* or the **wrought iron work** which has also acquired a **GI tag**. Dark metal figurines, images of deities, effigies of musicians, lamps, candle stands, toys etc. are some of the common products. A unique aspect of this craft is that the raw material used for it is mostly recycled scrap iron.

Bell metal of Datia/Tikamgarh

A variety of handcrafted articles are manufac-tur1ed at Datia and Tikamgarh (Madhya Pradesh) which are made of **bell metal** (a hard alloy). Essentially, this is also a tribal craft which has a tradition in the region of 250 to 300 years. While earlier the craft catered to the need of royalty, requirement of weaponry etc. and some items of jewellery of ordinary folks (such as anklets of women in Datia), today items of art and decorative works are produced. These include idols of gods, human and animal figurines, beside items of common use, toys etc. (at Tikamgarh) and lamp shades, mirror frames, temples, boxes with *jali* (at Datia). While a poignant aspect of the work of Datia is the ***jali* work** on the walls of the product, the Tikamgarh brass metal works are largely **plain** and **solid** in appearance, with some elements of decoration work. The craft has been accorded a **GI tag.**

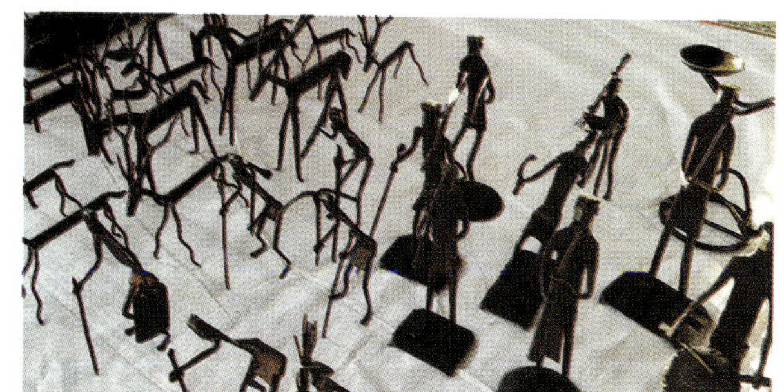

19.87: Different figurines of wrought iron of humans and animals

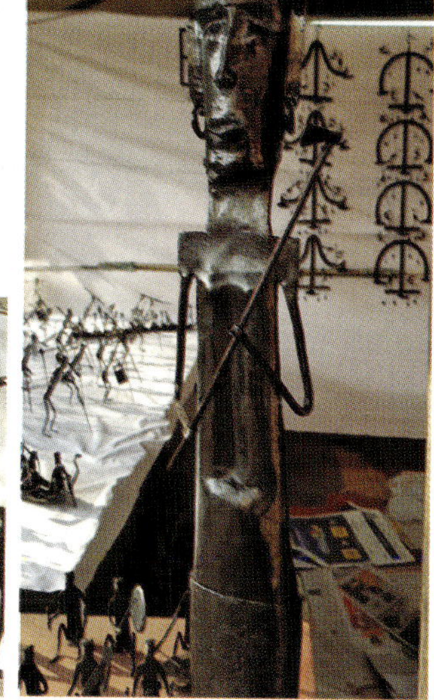

19.88: A large wrought iron figurine of a man with an axe

Wrought iron works, Jagdalpur, Bastar — photographs by Madhukar K Bhagat

Mainpuri Taarkashi

It is an art popular in Mainpuri district of Uttar pradesh since medieval period. It finds reference in the district gazetteer of 1910 as well as a reference by a British assistant collector in 1864. Tarkashi is **inlaying of brass in hardwood** such as *shisham* to form floral motifs and other beautiful patterns. This inlay is usually in the form of wires (or thin strips of metal) which are embedded in the design engraving chiseled out on the wood. Wooden boxes, idols of Radha-Krishna, centre tables, bangle boxes, wooden slippers (*khadaon*) etc., are some of the handicrafts bearing this art. It has been accorded a **GI tag**.

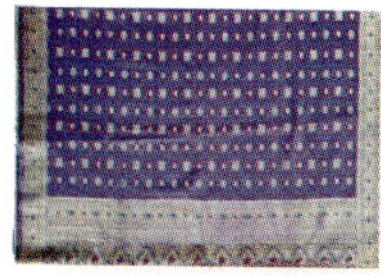

Koftagari and Tarkashi works of Jaipur

The ornamental metal work of **Koftagari** is popular in Jaipur and Mewar region of Rajasthan. It is an art which originated as a form of **decoration of weaponry** during the Mughal period. It entails inlaying of different metals into one another, typically of gold or silver into a contrasting and dark iron/steel metal. This is done in a form of **etching** or **damascening**. Handles of swords and daggers, shields, hunting knives, articles of utility such as boxes, cutlery etc. are some of the common items on which this work is carried out. The work of **Tarakashi** is also practised in the region. Apart from wooden boxes and idols, Tarakshi work on decorative wooden elephants is quite popular in the region.

Swamimalai bronze icons

The Swamimalai town located near Kumbakonam in Tamil Nadu is known for the craft of making of **bronze icons** and **statues**. It is a tradition which traces its history to the **Chola dynasty** and to the period of the construction of the great Chola temples, nearly 1000 years earlier. The bronze icons are usually of Hindu gods and goddesses and range from 6 feet to nearly 12 feet. They are made by the lost wax casting technique which can be of two types; solid or hollow cast. The hallmark of these bronze idols is the fine quality of the handicraft which is marked with precision and high crafting skills. The bronze icons have been accorded a **GI tag.**

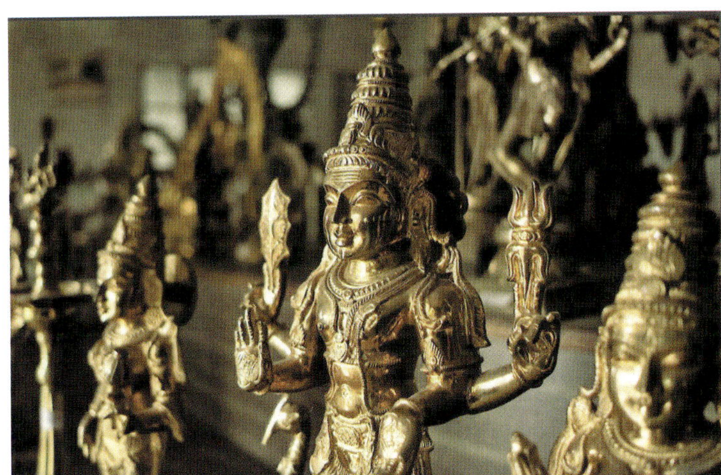

19.89: Bronze icons of Swamimalai (Thanjavur district), Tamil Nadu, a centuries-old tradition known for dexterity of work; accorded GI tag — Courtesy, Tamil Nadu Tourism Development Corporation

Besides the above, **Kamrupi Craft** of Assam (brass and bell metal works); **Budithi Bell and Brass craft** of Andhra Pradesh,**Thanjavur Art Plate** of Tamil Nadu (circular plate and a decorative artefact) **Pembarthi Metal craft** of Telangana (sheet metal work), **Benaras Metal Repouse craft** of Uttar Pradesh (metal design embossing), **Benaras Metal Casting craft** (including utensils for religious purposes and other decorative pieces), **Bengal Dokra**, **Karnataka bronzeware, Sarthebari Metal craft of Assam** are some other metal craft works which have been accorded a **GI tag**.

STONEWARE AND CRAFT

Stone craft is a very ancient tradition of India. The beautiful life-like sculpture of Yakshini of Didarganj (300 BCE) is a testimony to the evolution of this art. The Maurya, Gupta, Pala, Chola, Rashtrakuta, Chalukya, Hoysala and Chandela sculptures have added to the tradition of carving of stone as a medium of artistic expression. This stone craft continues even today and flourishes in some of the important traditional centres of this craft. In this tradition, some of the famous stoneware and craft products are, Makrana Marble works of Majasthan, Agra marble inlay works, the Konark stone carving of Odisha, the Mahabalipuram works of Tamil Nadu, besides others.

Makrana marble works

Makrana (Rajasthan) is famous not only for its marble, but also for marble work, carvings and inlays, sculptures, and a variety of handicraft items. These include the famous inlay work (pietra-dura) and the *jali* work in marble. Jaipur and other cities of Rajasthan are also known for marble works, while cities like Jaisalmer are known for works in red sand stone.

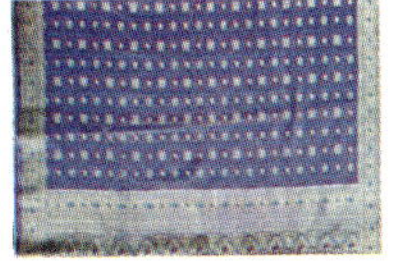

Agra and the region around it is also famous for works in marble. This is a medieval tradition which still continues. These works include the exquisite marble *jali* work, pietra dura or inlay work in marble, calligraphy and others.

Konark stone carving

It is an important handicraft of Odisha and an ancient tradition. Konark is an important centre for production of numerous statues and carvings in stones. The products are known for their skillful craftsmanship. These products are carved in different kinds of stone ranging from hard black granite to soft soapstone from makrana marble to sandstone. The stone craft products include idols of mythological figures, items of daily use like lamp-bases, paperweights, pen stands, stone-wares etc. The craft has been accorded a **GI tag**.

Mahabalipuram stone sculpture

It is another craft tradition which is flourishing for nearly 1300 years in the region and dates to the Pallava period. The sculptures are largely of Hindu deities, human and animal figures. These are known for intricate carving and very fine chisel work. The image of the deities and human figures are characterized by wide forehead, long eyes and an oval face. The figures are slender and curvaceous. The craft has been accorded a **GI tag.**

Among other stone craft works of India are, **Allagadda stone carvings** of Andhra Pradesh (accorded **GI tag**), **Durgi stone carvings** of Andhra Pradesh (accorded **GI tag**), **stone sculpture of Balaghat** of Madhya Pradesh, **sculpture on black soft stone of Gaya,** (of Pattharkati village) in Bihar (specializing in Buddhist sculptures, idols of Hindu gods, items of daily use) etc.

TOYS AND PUPPETS

Indian handicrafts are also known for a variety of toys and puppets. While these were meant as play items for children, or as a part of their entertainment through puppetry, now they are also known for their craftsmanship. Many of these are wooden products and have been accorded GI tag.

Kinhal wooden toys of Karnataka

The town of Kinhal in northern Karnataka is famous for its traditional wood craft, particularly for its toys and religious idols. The wooden toys comprise a variety of human and animal figurines which are exquisitely crafted and beautifully painted, giving them a lifelike appearance. These toys were carved out of wood, smoothened with tamarind paste and then painted with lacquered colours. The craft of wooden toys has also been accorded a **GI Tag.**

19.90: Wooden dolls of Kinhal, Karnataka, National Crafts Museum, New Delhi — photograph by Madhukar K Bhagat

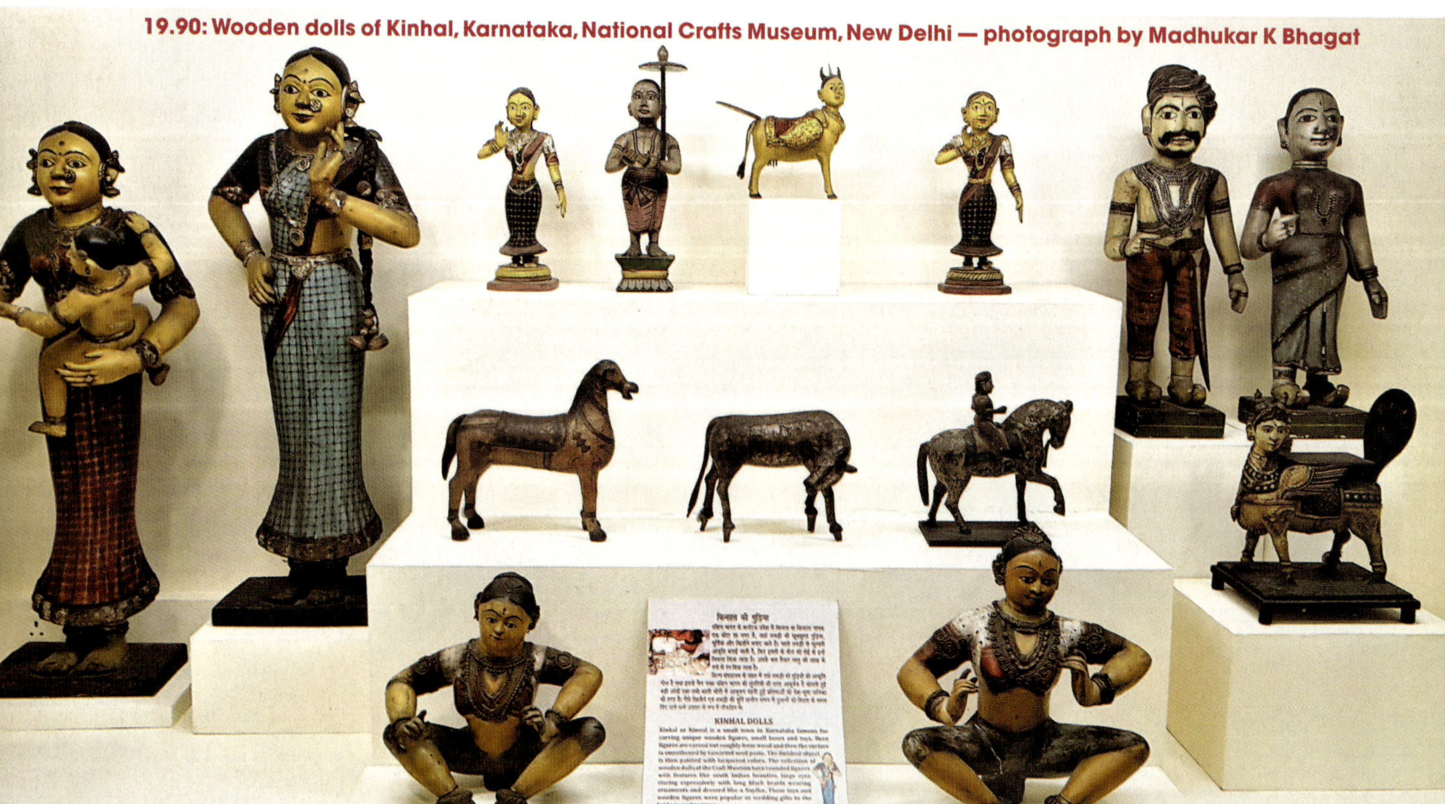

The Channapatna toys

They are wooden toys and dolls which are made in Channapatna town of rural Bengaluru. The toys are made from the wood of the tree locally called *Aale-mara* (ivory wood) with the lacquering of wood imparting the toys a bright shine and colour. The making of a diverse variety of toys has earned this place the name of *Gombegala Ooru* or the toy town. The craft has been accorded a **GI tag.**

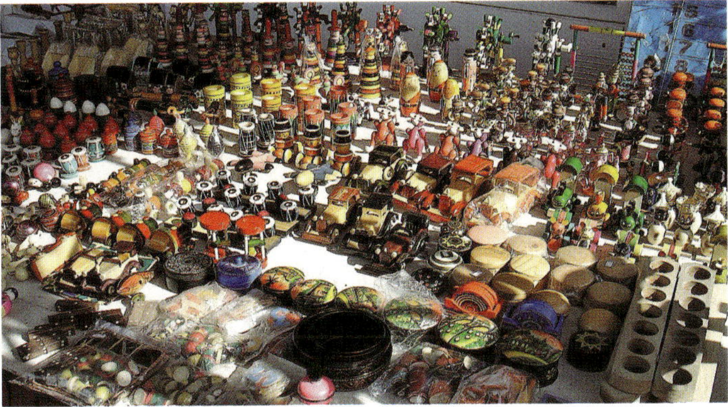

19.91: A bewildering variety of Chhanapatna toys and dolls — Wikimedia Commons

Nirmal toys

It is a nearly four centuries old tradition of Nirmal town of (Adilabad district) of Telangana. It is known for making a variety of life-like wooden toys made of a light weight *Poniki* wood. The most common of subjects of the toys include birds and animals, fruits and vegetables, besides gods and goddesses. The craft has been accorded a **GI tag.**

Kondapalli Bommallu

It is the traditional craft of doll making done by the women in Kondapalli village in NTR district of Andhra Pradesh. The dolls and puppets are usually made on the occasion of the festivals of Makar Sankranti and Dussehra. The tradition of making these toy dolls and puppets is said to be nearly 400 years old and is believed to have originated when some toy makers from Rajasthan migrated to this region. The toys include dolls/puppets of humans in rural setting, mythological figures, animals, birds, carts, chariots etc. These are crafted out of wood *Tella Poniki* (white sander) and are coloured using natural colour dyes, vegetable colours, and more recently even enamel colours. The craft has been recognised with a **GI tag.**

Varanasi wooden lacquerware and toys

It is a tradition of Varanasi city of Uttar Pradesh. This craft is said to have emerged from an earlier craft tradition of ivory crafting. However, post the banning of ivory trade, the artisans shifted to making of toys. These toys are crafted of eucalyptus wood, bright colours are applied to it and then lacquered (or even coloured lacquer is applied). These toys and dolls include a variety of subjects such as gods and mythological figures. Krishna playing the flute is one such popular toy. Besides, toys which are mobile, such as animals, birds etc. and figures which move their neck such as tortoise etc. is also a part of their diverse range. This craft has been accorded a **GI tag.**

19.92: Krishnanagar, (West Bengal) clay figurines (dolls) depicting rural life; each having a life-like quality and conveying dynamism of activity; National Crafts Museum, New Delhi — photograph by Madhukar K Bhagat

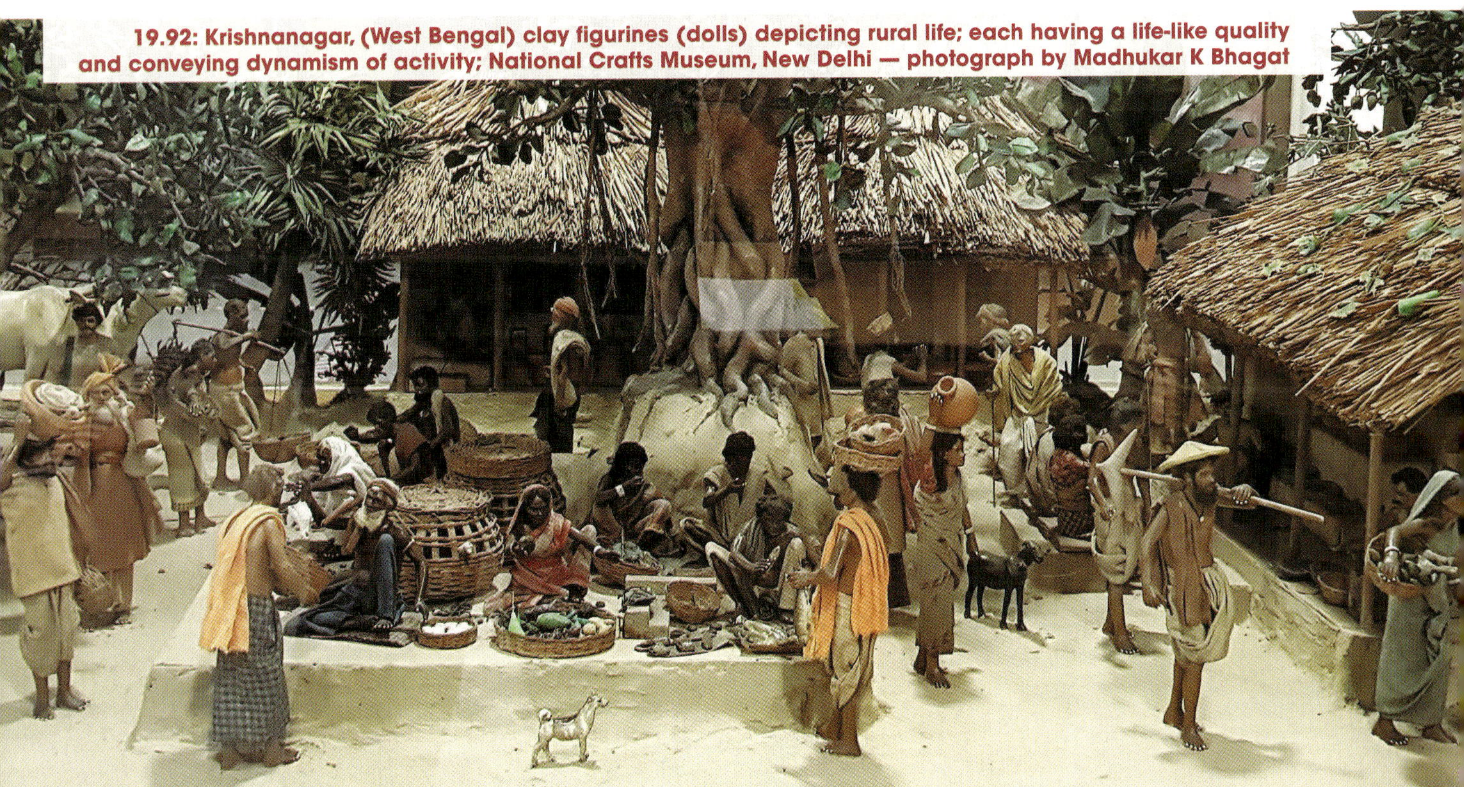

Andhra Pradesh leather puppetry

It is another traditional craft which has been accorded a **GI Tag**. The craft, called locally as *Tholu Bommalata* entails making of puppets out of goat leather. These are cut as per the shape of the character, then painted in the shadow puppetry to depict various characters from the epics of Ramayana and Mahabharata. This puppet craft is said to be more than 100 years old and is particularly popular in the Nimmalkunta township. Besides the puppets for show and for sale, leather lampshades, wall hangings wall partitions and curtain hangings are some of the other products which are spinoffs of this craft.

Clay dolls of Krishna Nagar

They are often considered by experts as one of the finest handcrafted toys. The art of making clay figurines/dolls in Krishnanagar district (Ghurni block) of West Bengal is traceable to the late 18th century. Dolls which usually are a few inches to less than a foot in size, are crafted on a variety of subjects ranging from common day folks, prominent personalities, rural activities etc. Animals, birds and plants all find space in this craft. The **realism** of the figurine and the **dynamism of activity** which these dolls reflect is simply bewildering. The dolls are made from clay dough by moulding and pressing technique. They are then baked in a furnace, followed by painting with brush with vibrant colours. The clay dolls have also won awards in several international exhibitions. (Application for GI tag under consideration)

Besides the above, the other important toy handicrafts are **Kathputli of Rajasthan** (puppets), **Thanjavur Doll** (a bobble headed doll of terracotta), **Ganjifa cards of Mysore**, **Karnataka** (a card game with cards having different artwork and images), **stuffed leather toys of Indore,** all of which are accorded **GI tag.**

PAPIER MACHE

Also referred to as chewed papier, paper-mache is an art of moulding of paper pulp and its consequent decoration. A mixture is made of paper/paper-pulp, glue and water which is moulded in a variety of shapes. Gradually, the mould becomes hard, thus retaining the shape it has been given. Subsequently, the product surface is decorated with a variety of colours and design. The traditional papier-mache crafts of India include, the Kashmir papier mache and Thirukannur papier mache.

Kashmir papier mache

This handicraft of Kashmir traces its history to 14th century and is believed to have been brought to the region by a Muslim saint. The art is charactersied by its beautiful design and use of vibrant and bright colours. Designs of a variety of flowers, vines, chinar leaves and birds are identifiable features of Kashmir papier mache. A variety of products such as different types of boxes, cups, bowls, vases, lamp bases, small toys etc. are made from papier mache. The craft has also been recognized with a **GI Tag.**

Thirukannur papier mache

This traditional art is popular in Puducherry. The specialty of this papier machie is that a variety of dolls and idols, including the images of deities are crafted. Besides, animals like elephant, cows, birds like peacock, dancing dolls and wall hangings are some other popular products. These are lacquered and polished in bright colours, with some even having metallic appearance. The craft has been recognized with a **GI Tag.**

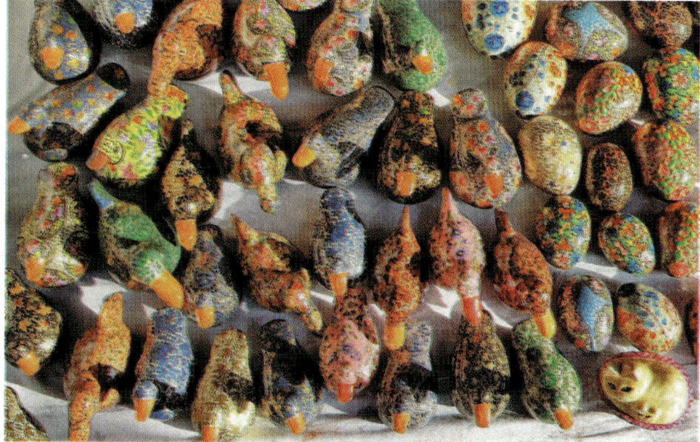

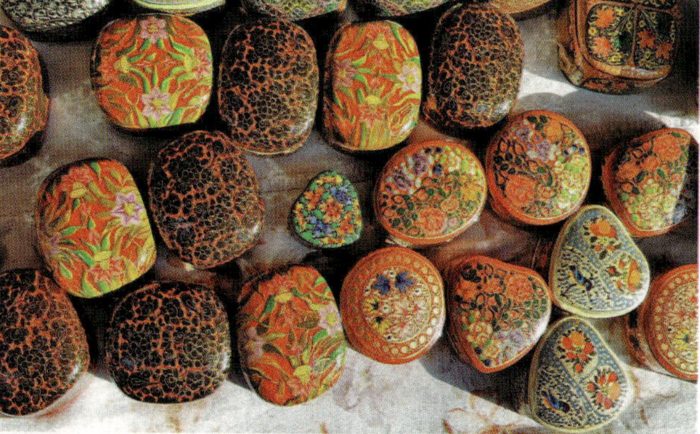

19.93 & 19.94: Kashmir papier mache boxes, birds and eggs with beautiful designs and eye-catching colours — photographs by Madhukar K Bhagat

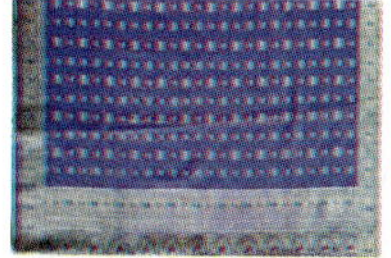

Masks: An Enduring Craft

The making of masks or *mukhoata*, is an ancient tradition and integral part of Indian culture. The craft has survived the journey of centuries and continues in the modern age reposited in the dances, folk theatres and customs. The masks were a means to portray the character being depicted in these folk theatres and dance-dramas. They would make the character come alive before the audience and imbue the performer with the spirit of the character.

The traditional masks are usually made of wood, papier-mache, saw dust, cloth and at times of metal and *shola* (wood pith). They are cut out as per the shape requirements of the character and decorated with a variety of colours. Those made of cloth and papier-mache could even be decorated with gold-silver threads or silk. The metal masks could be decorated with metal engraving and other metal works.

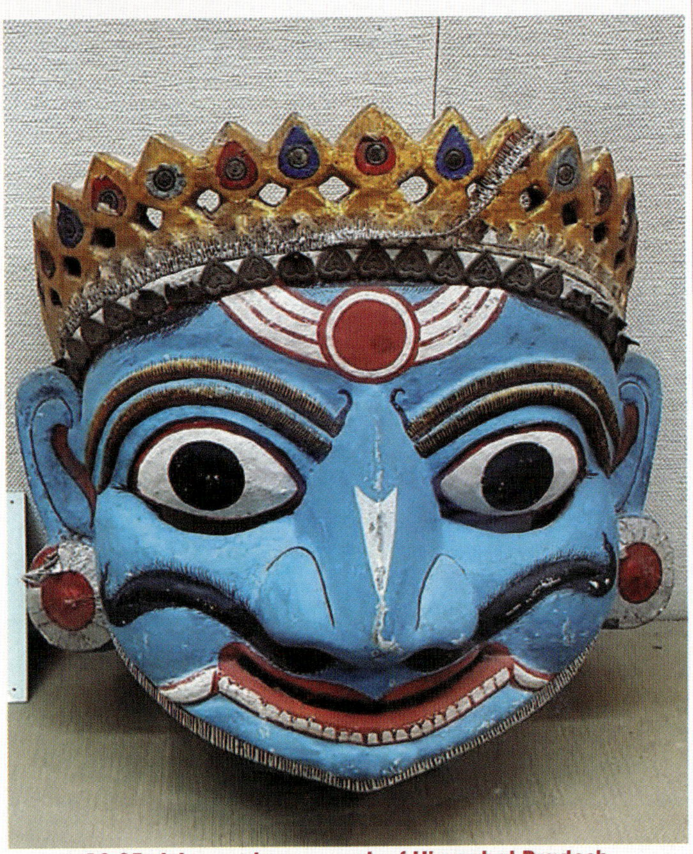

19.95: A Lama dance mask of Himachal Pradesh, a single piece wooden mask used in ritual Buddhist dances across monasteries from Ladakh, Himachal Pradesh to Arunachal Pradesh; location, Sangeet Natak Akademi — photograph by Madhukar Kumar Bhagat

Some of the important folk theatres and dances where masks have a special place are, Ramlila, where masks of a variety of characters ranging from Ravana (*rakshasa* mask), Hanuman, (monkey mask), Jatayu (bird-vulture mask) Jambvanta (bear mask) besides many others is adorned. The Chhau dance of Saraikela (in Jharkhand) and of Purulia (in West Bengal) the Shahi Jatra of Odisha, Bhand Pather of Kashmir, Dashaavatar Lila of Rajasthan are some of the other dances and folk theatres where masks are used. Besides, masks are also a part of **Gombhira** dance of West Bengal, **Yak Cham** and **Singhi Cham** of Sikkim, **Mukhaota dance** of Uttarakhand, **Cham, Rakshasa** and **Channak Cham** dances of Himachal Pradesh, **Garudi Gombe** of Karnataka, **Buttu Bommalu** of Andhra Pradesh, **Vedalattam** of Tamil Nadu and **Padayani** dance of Kerala.

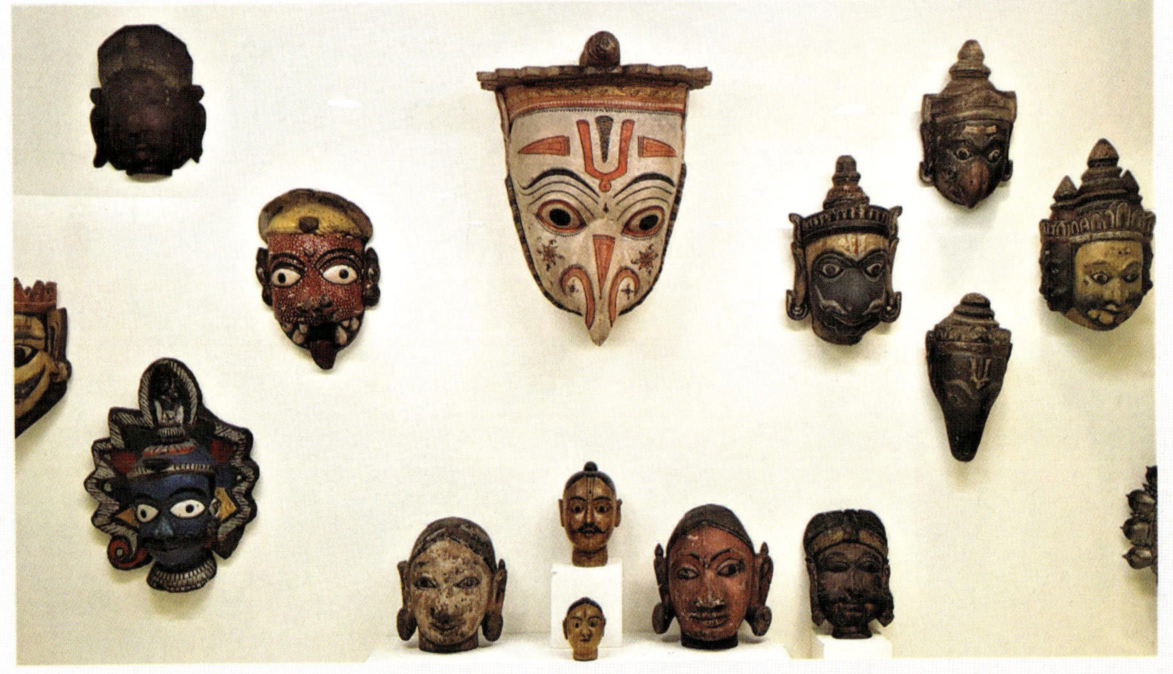

19.96: Chhau and other masks at National Crafts Museum, New Delhi — photograph by Madhukar K Bhagat

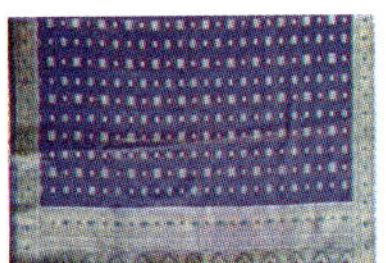

PICTURE GALLERY

The Making of Kanjeevaram Silk Sari

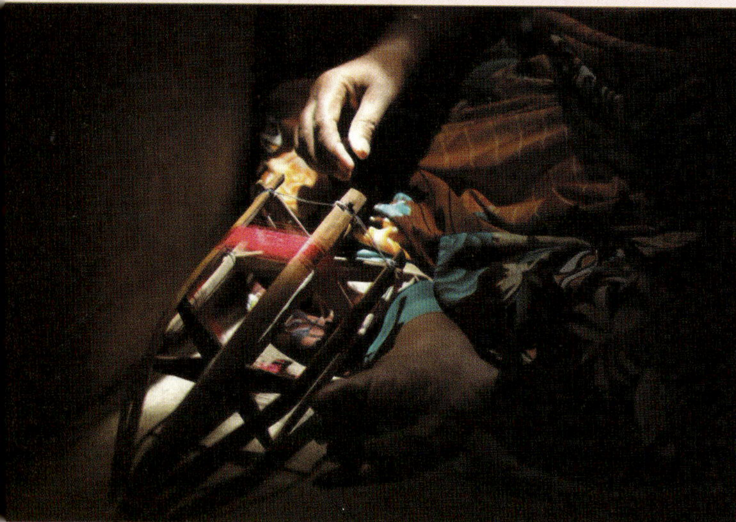

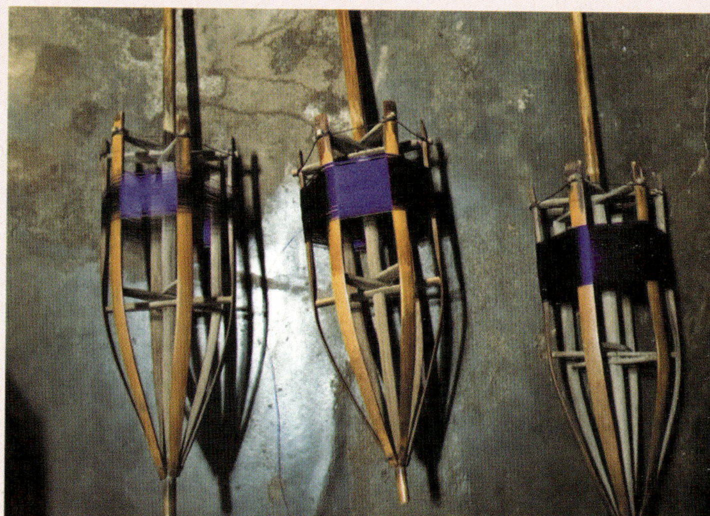

19.97 19.98

Silk thread spindles — Courtesy, Tamil Nadu Tourism Development Corporation

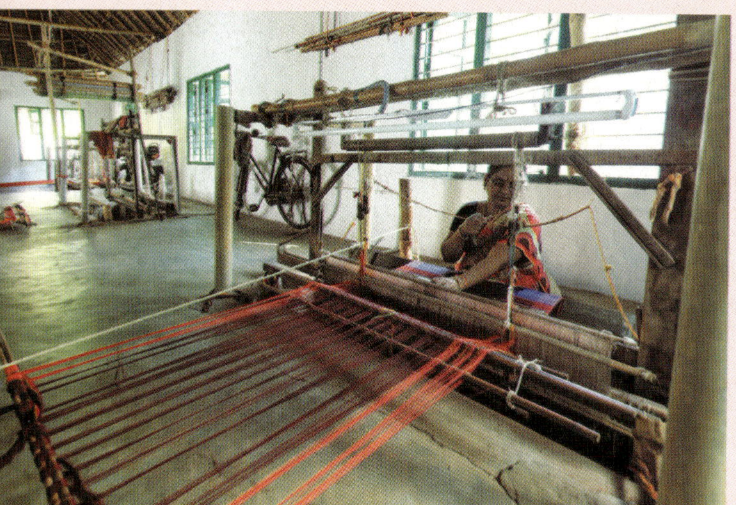

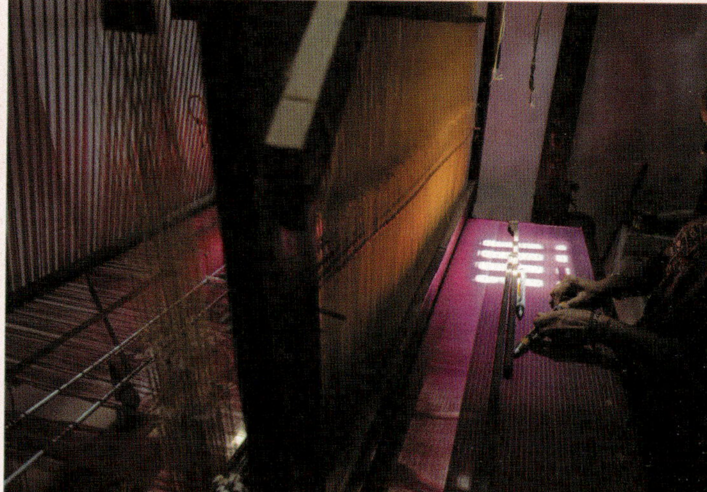

19.99: Weaving of silk sarees — Courtesy, Tamil Nadu Tourism Development Corporation

Block Printing

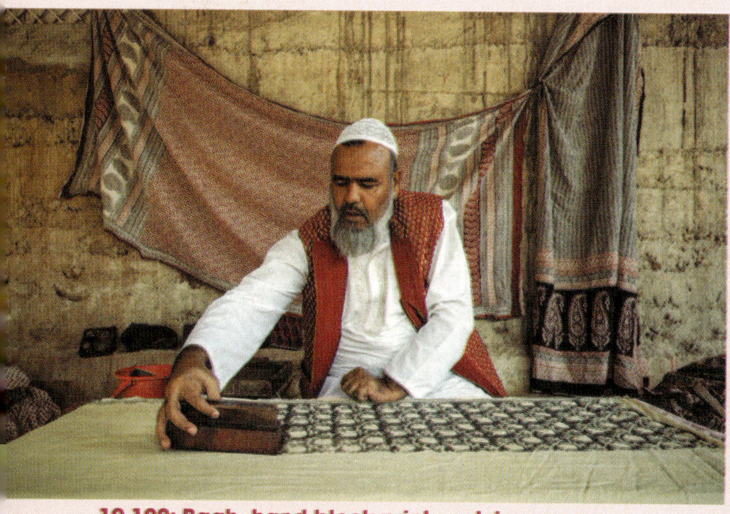

19.100: Bagh hand block print work in progress

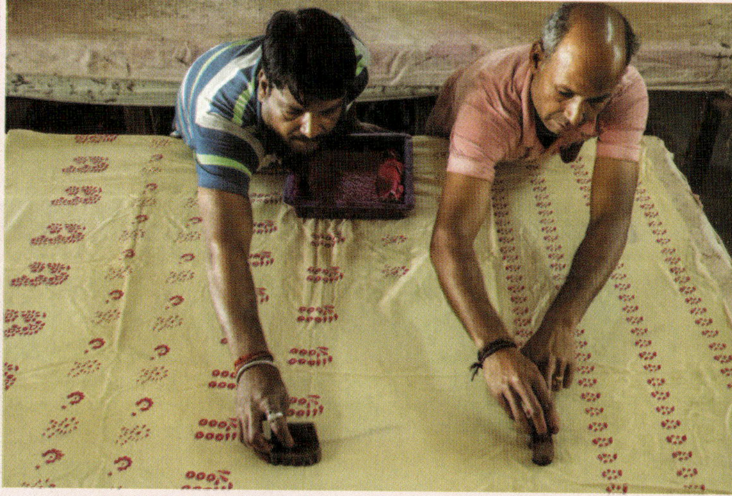

19.101: Nandana hand block print work in progress

Pictures — Courtesy, Madhya Pradesh Tourism Board

Different Stages of Crafting of Thanjavur Veena of Tamil Nadu

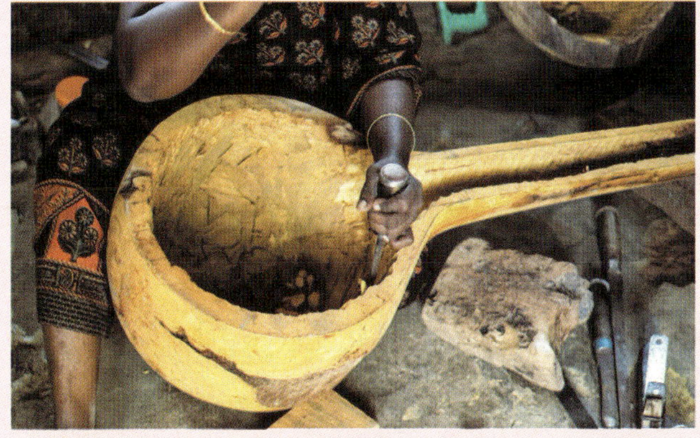

19.102

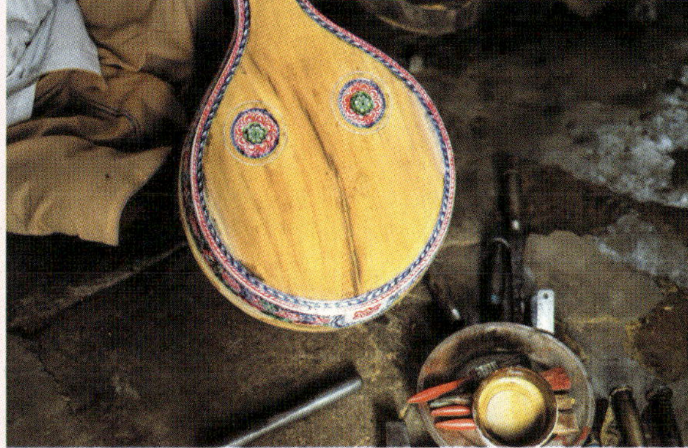

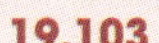

19.103

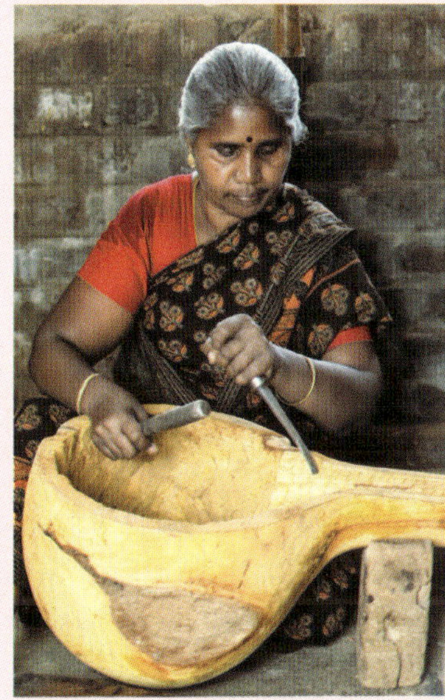

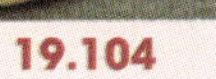

19.104

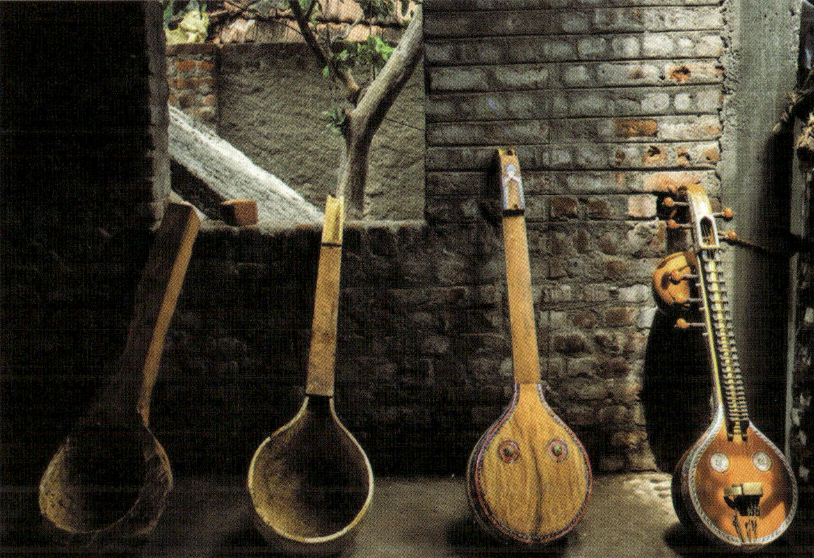

19.105

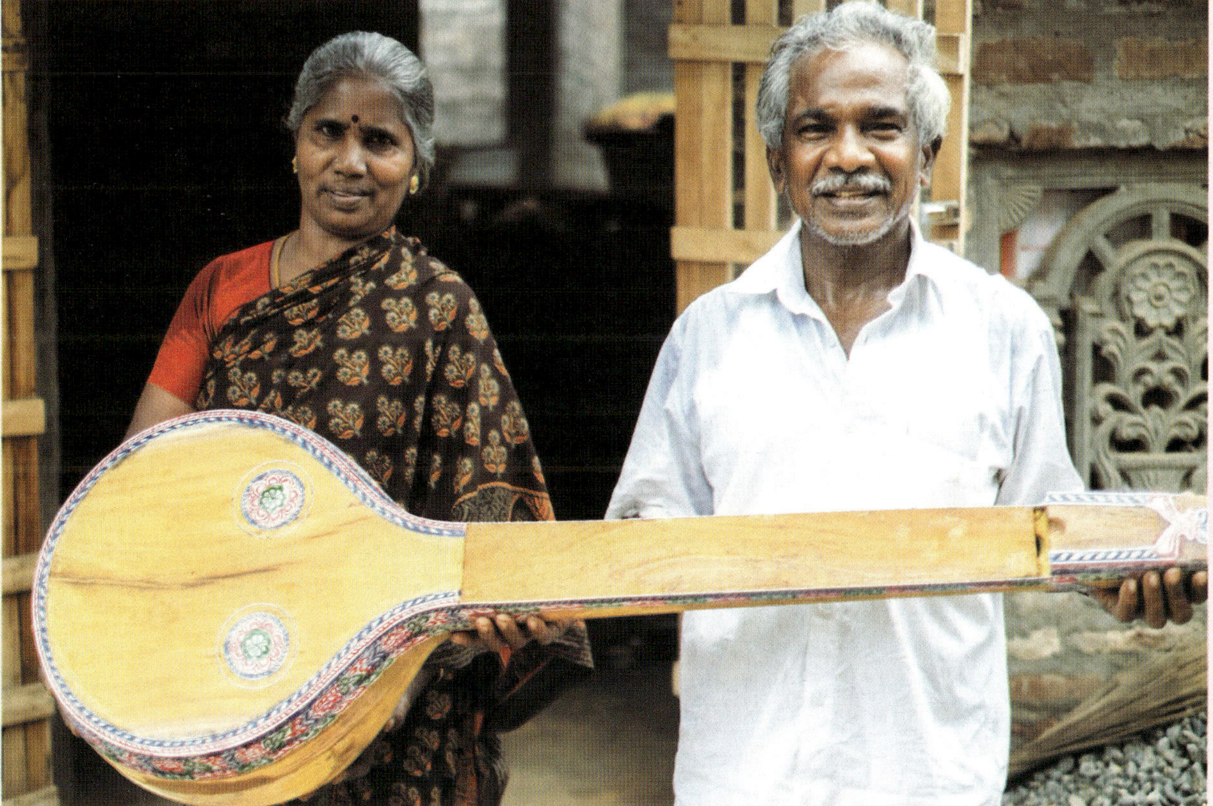

19.106

Pictures — Courtesy, Tamil Nadu Tourism Development Corporation

Metal Craft: Dhokra Art and Wrought Ironworks of Chhattisgarh

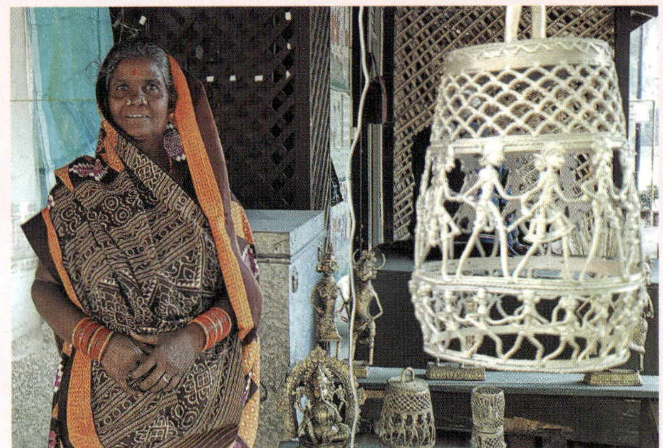

19.107: An artisan of Dhokra art of Bastar and various items of her craft

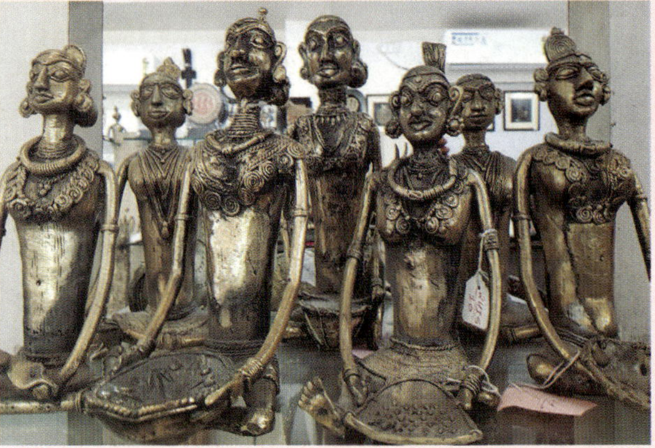

19.108: Human figurines of non-ferrous metal, a typical example of Dhokra art of Chhattisgarh

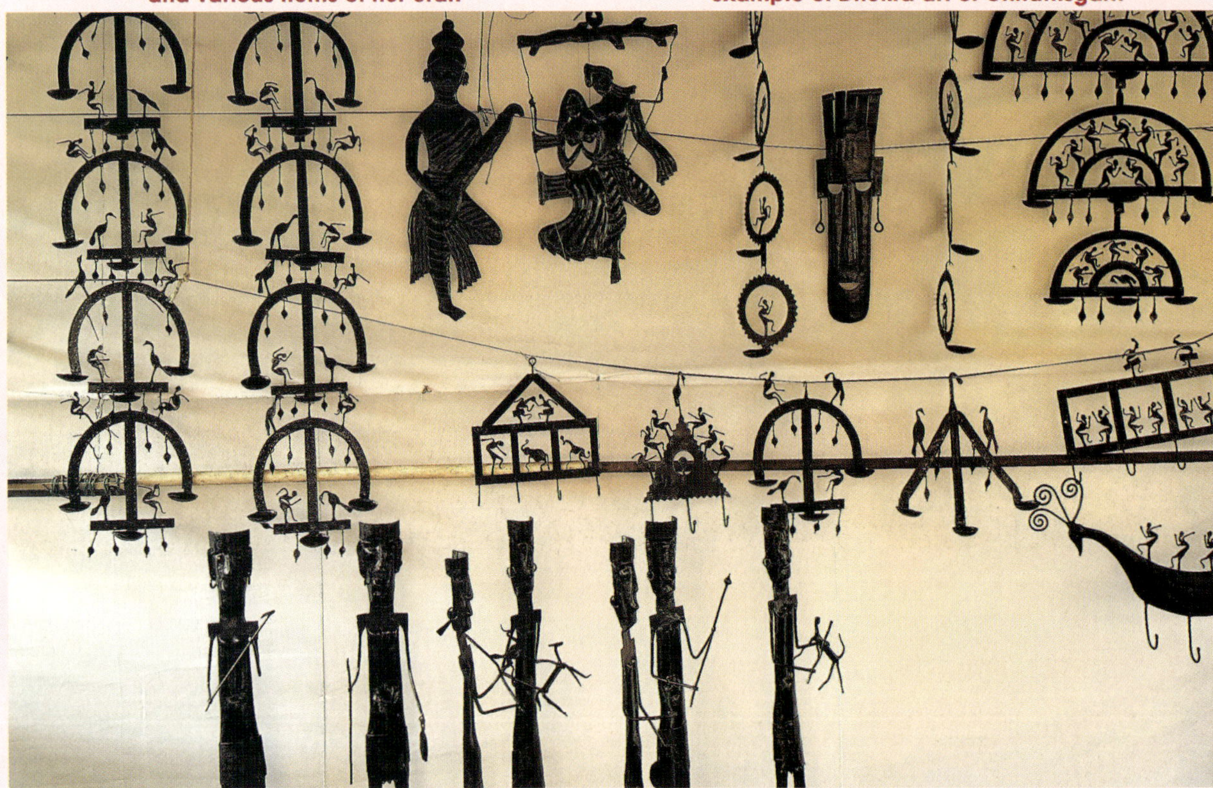

19.109: Wrought iron works, Jagdalpur, Bastar, Chhattisgarh; artistic wrought iron designs of different decorative items and human figures

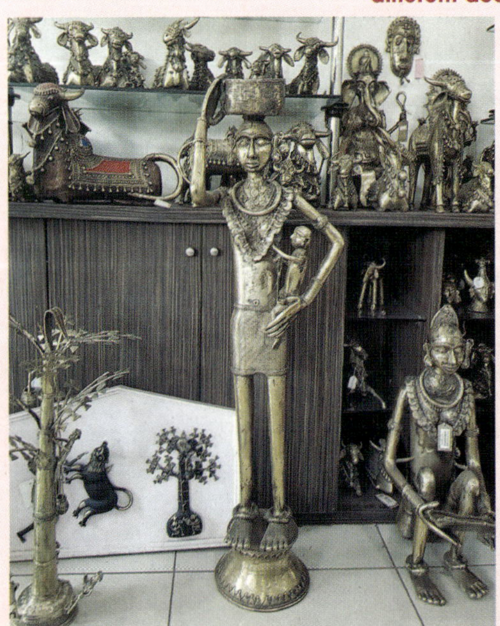

19.110: Large human figurines and more refined works of Dhokra art of brass and bell metal from Chattisgarh

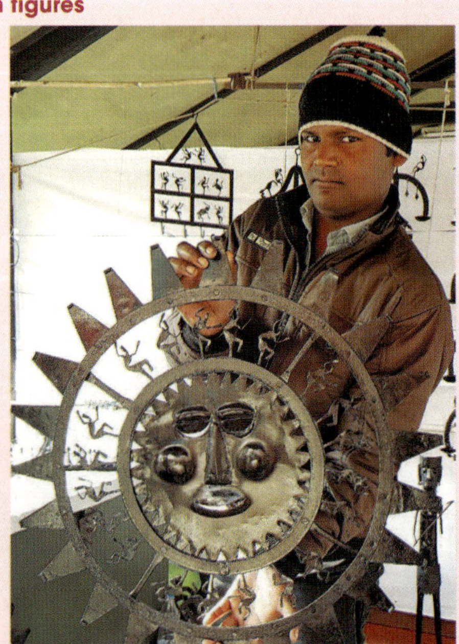

19.111: A wrought iron artisan with a design of a sun

— Photographs by Madhukar K. Bhagat

Terracotta Works and Pottery

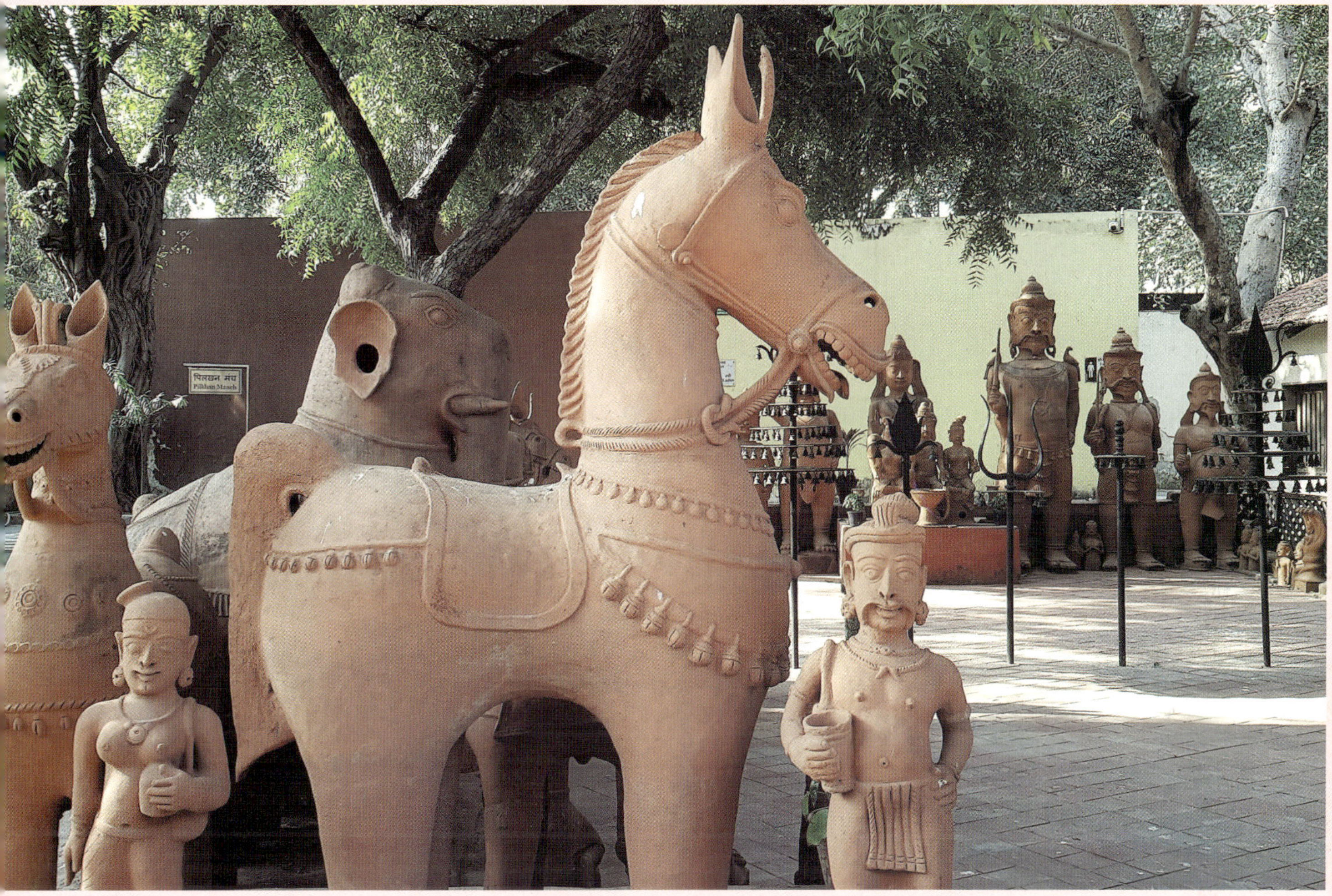

19.112: Terracotta horses of Lord Ayyanar and other figurines, popular in the Chettinad region of Tamil Nadu; at the National Crafts Museum, New Delhi — photograph by Madhukar K Bhagat

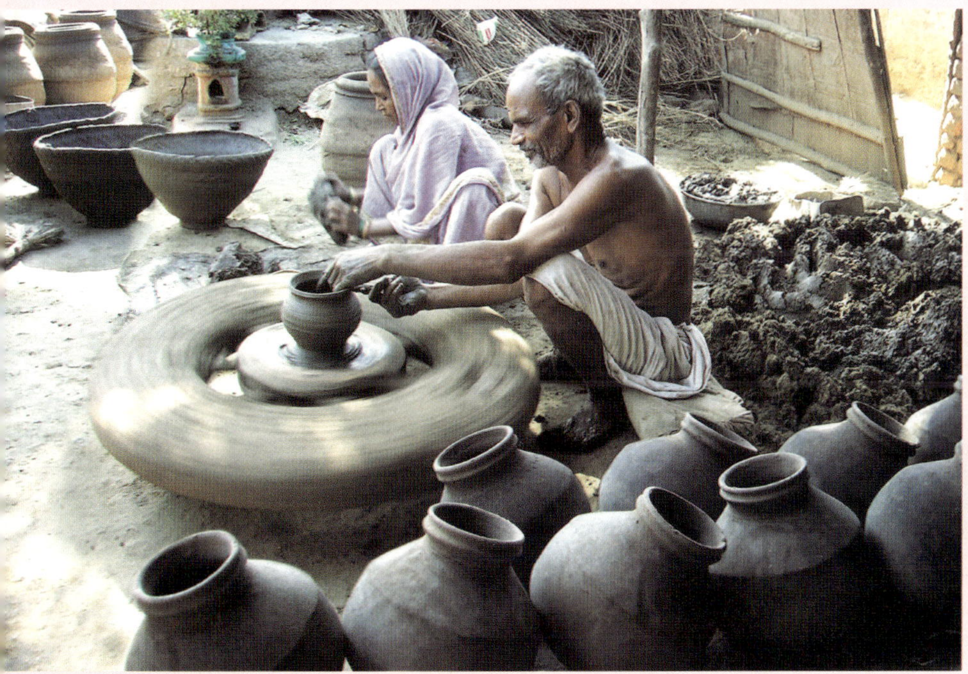

19.113: A potter spinning the wheel — Courtesy, Maharashtra Tourism Development Corporation

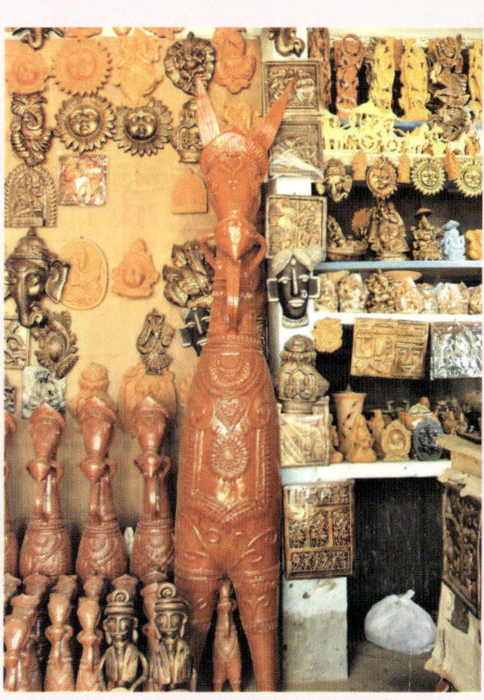

19.114: Bankura horse, other terracotta artefacts and wall hangings; from Bankura, West Bengal — Courtesy, Department of Tourism, West Bengal

Papier Mache Toys and Pattachitra Paintings, Raghurajpur, Odisha

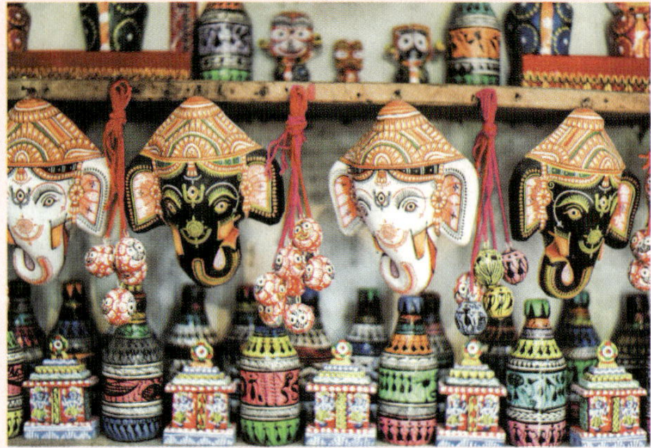

19.115: Papier Mache Ganesh masks and other articles

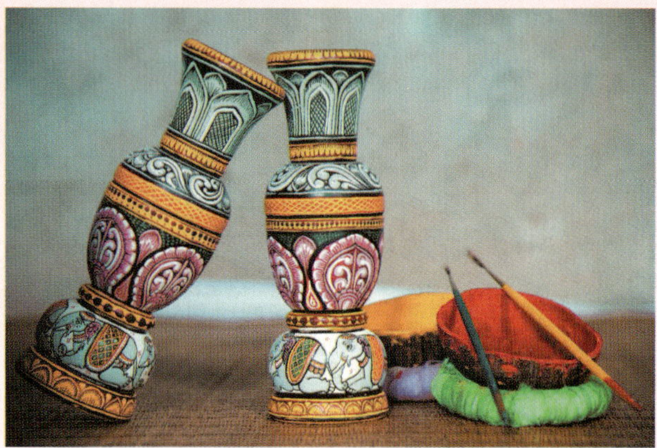

19.116: Papier Mache flower vases

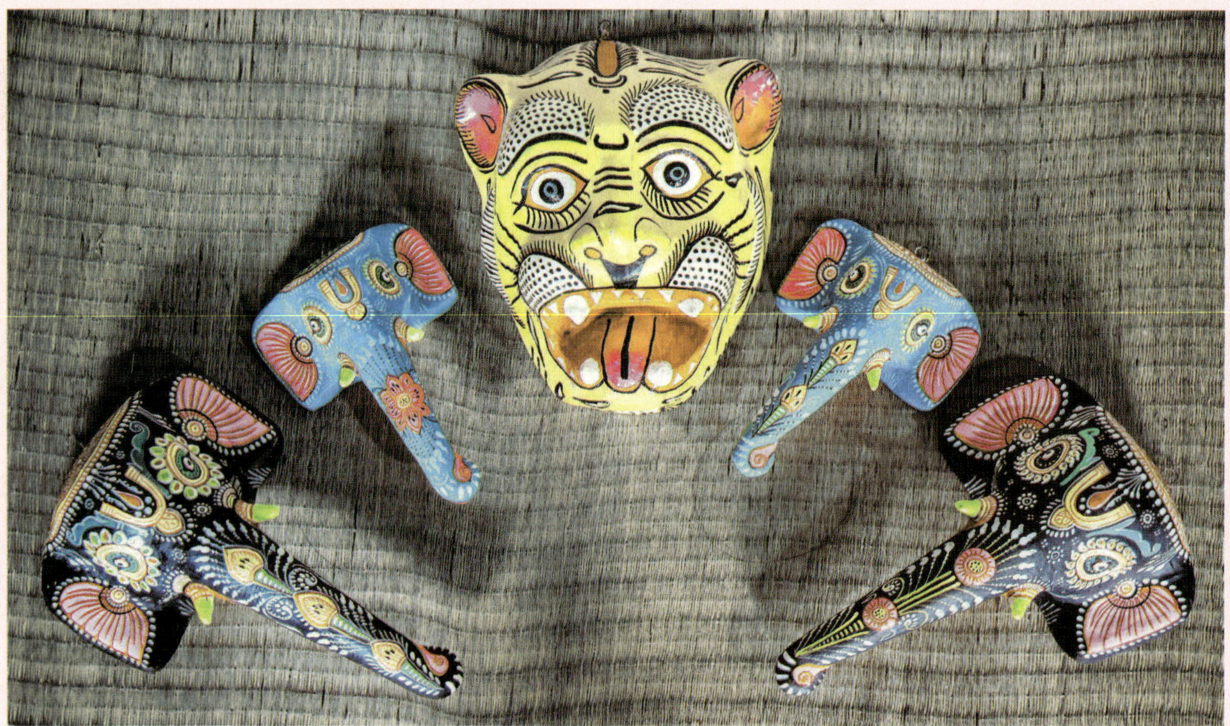

19.117: Papier Mache tiger and elephant masks

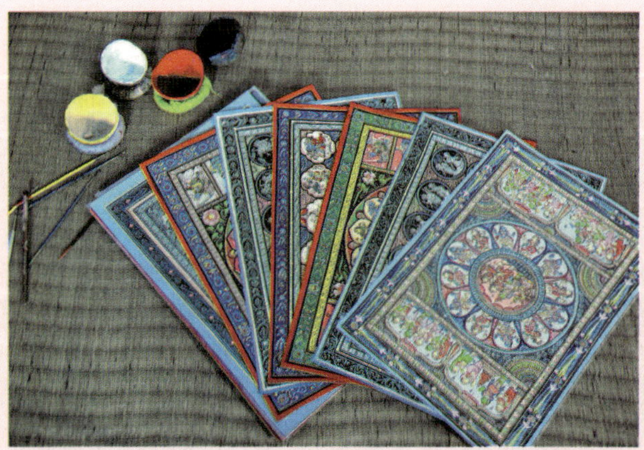

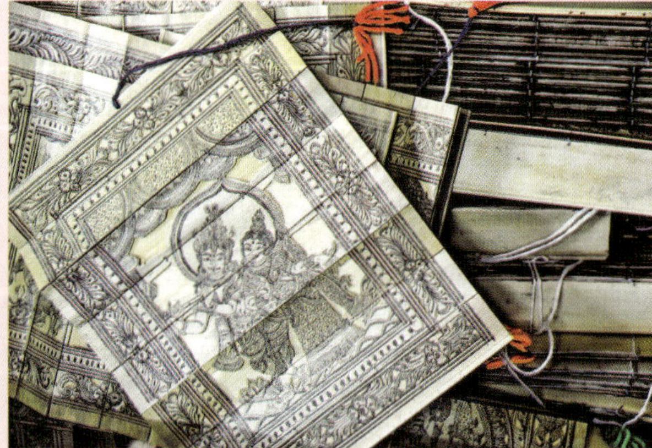

19.118: Pattachitra paintings using traditional colour and techniques

Papier-mache toys and masks with Pattachitra style painting from Raghurajpur village near Puri in Odisha. The village is home to artisans who have practised Pattachitra paintings and traditional crafts for several centuries
Pictures — Courtesy, Department of Tourism, Odisha

Firozabad Glass: A Product Having GI Tag

The making of glass bangles and other items in a factory at Firozabad, Uttar Pradesh

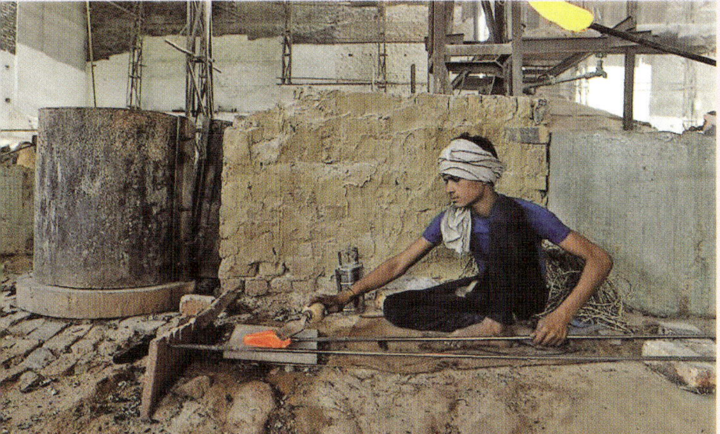

19.119: Melting of glass in a factory

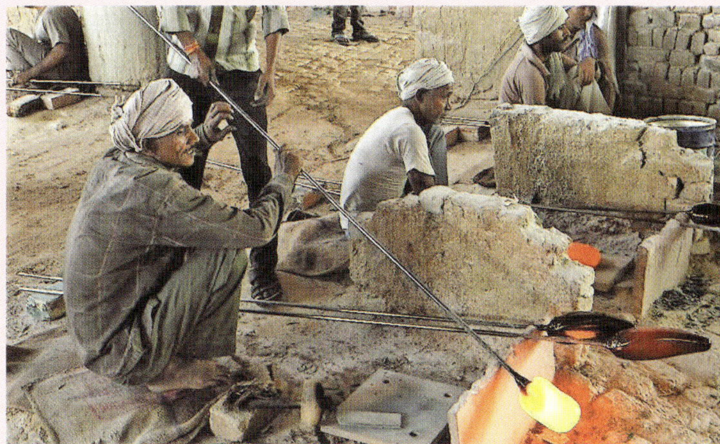

19.120: Glass making in progress

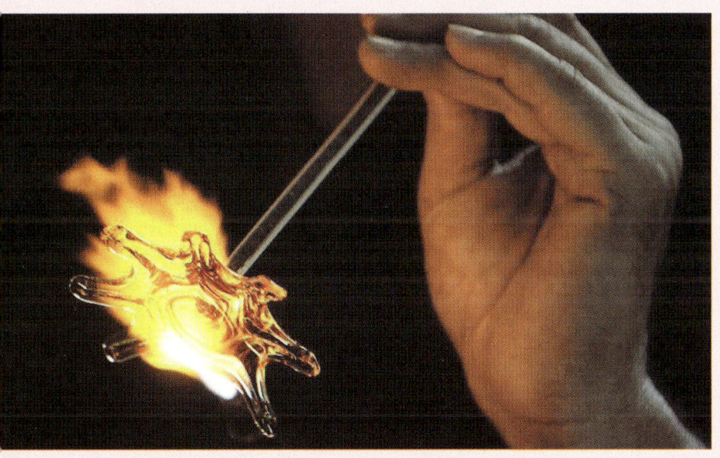

19.121: Blowing molten glass into shape

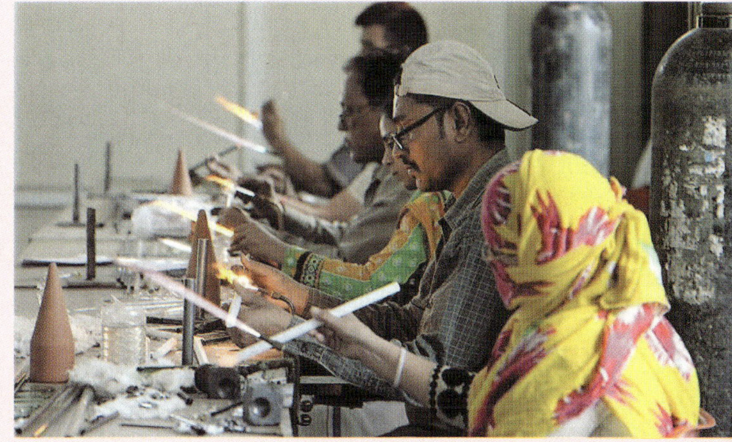

19.122: Glass items being made

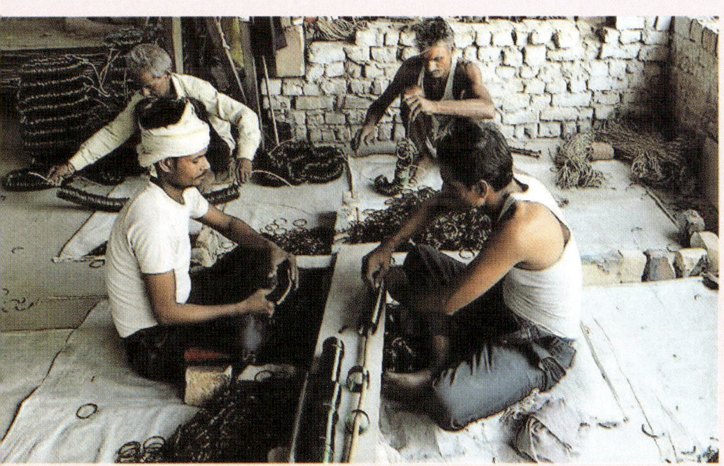

19.123: Bangles being made

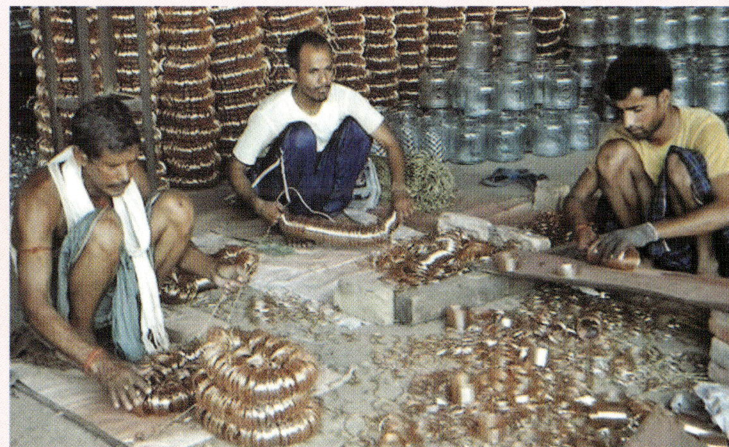

19.124: Bangles being segregated and bundled

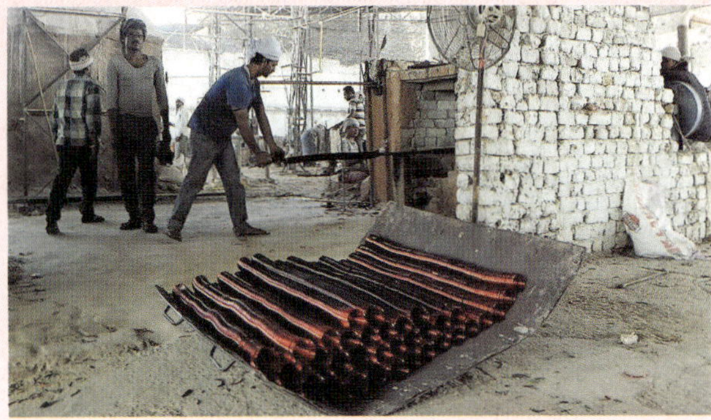

19.125: Raw bangles in factory

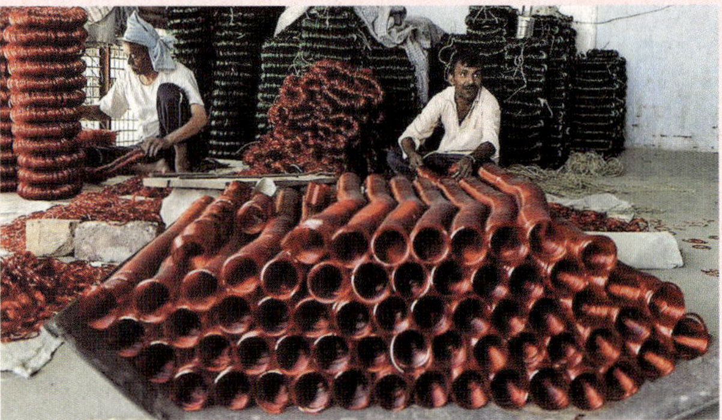

19.126: Bangles put into bundles

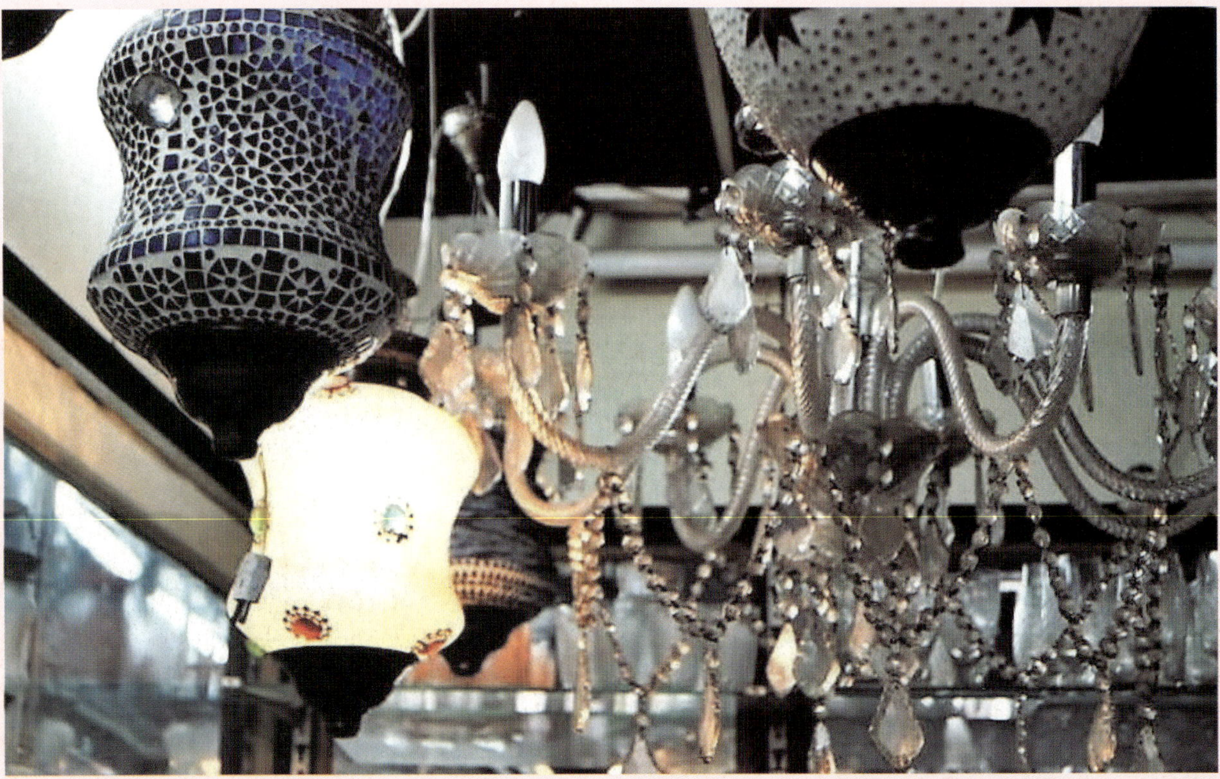

19.127: Glittering chandeliers ; an exquisite craft of Firozabad glassworks

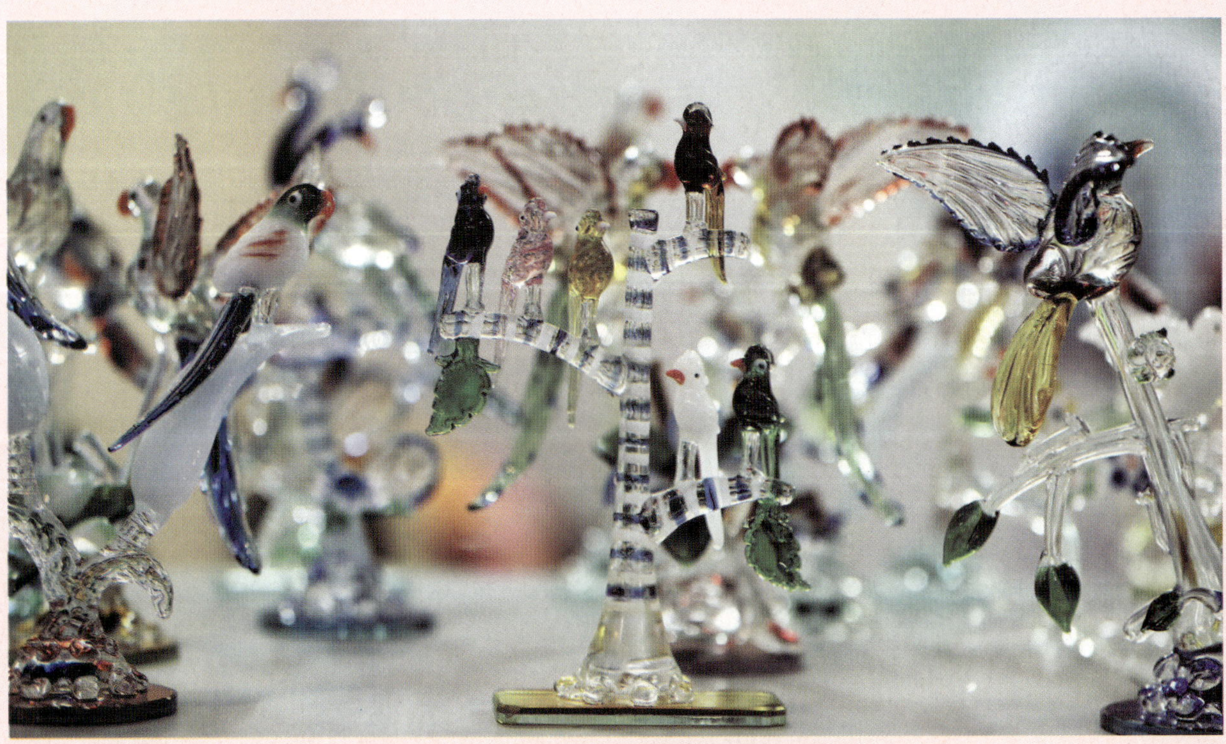

19.128: Colourful birds, another exquisite craft of Firozabad glassworks

All Pictures — Courtesy, Directorate of Uttar Pradesh Tourism

20

Language and Literature of Modern India

'निज भाषा उन्नति अहै, सब उन्नति को मूल'

— *भारतेन्दु हरिश्चन्द्र*

The progress of one's language is the basis of all progress.

— **Bharatendu Harishchandra**

A country that does not take pride in its language and literature can never progress.

— **Dr. Rajendra Prasad**

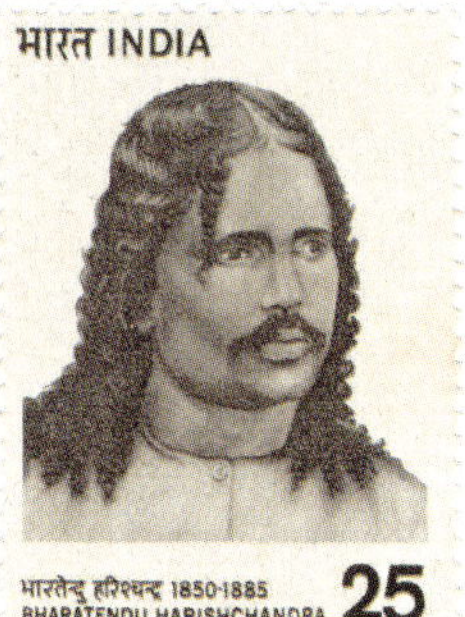

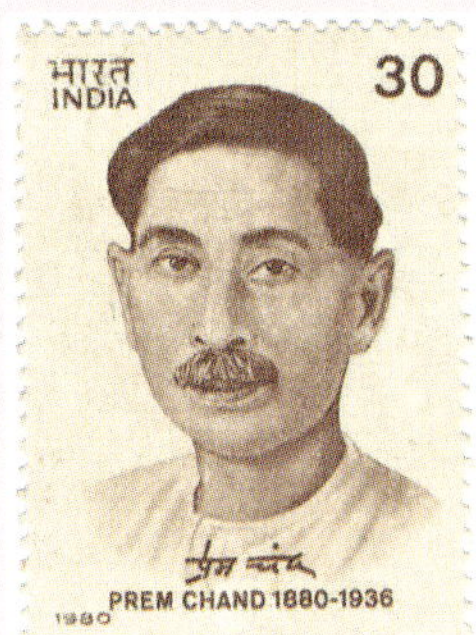

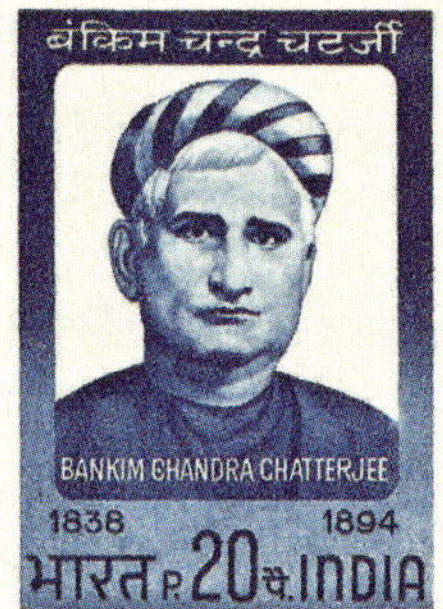

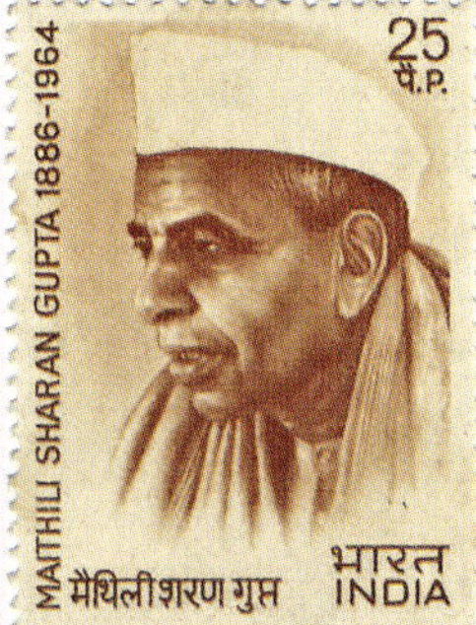

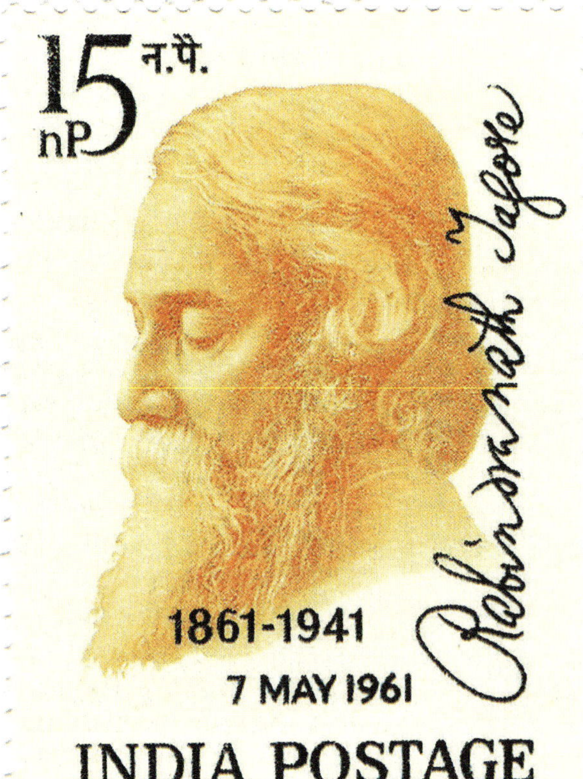

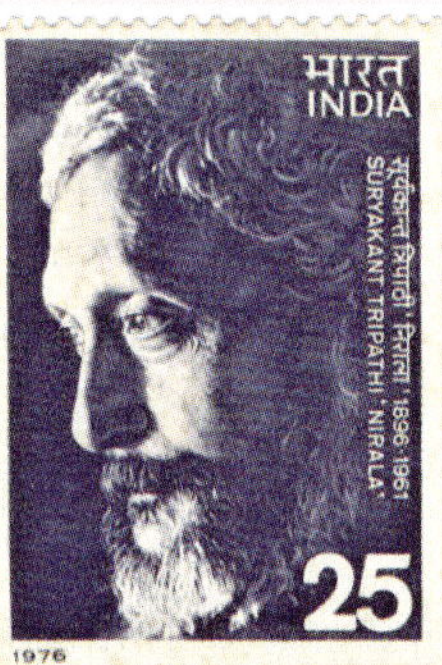

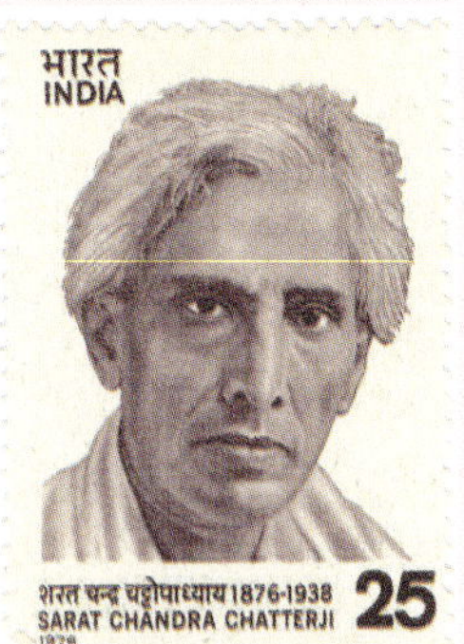

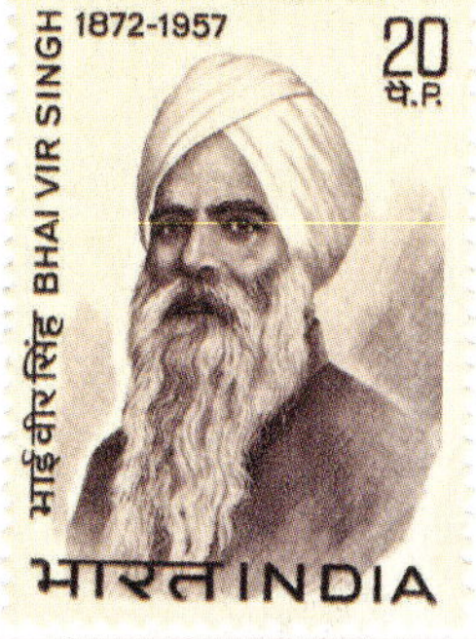

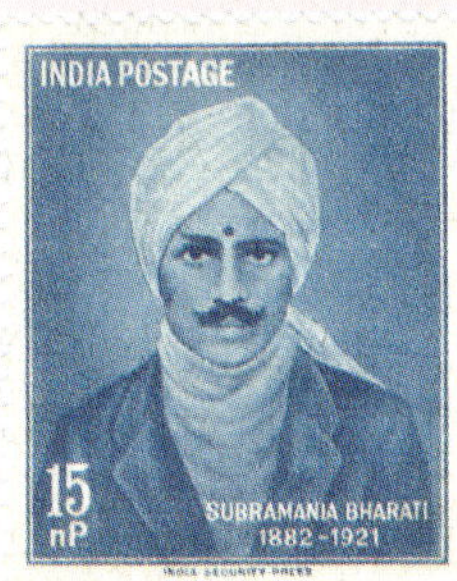

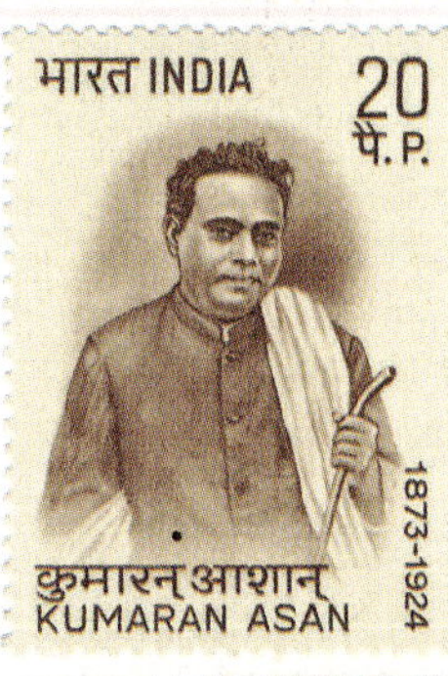

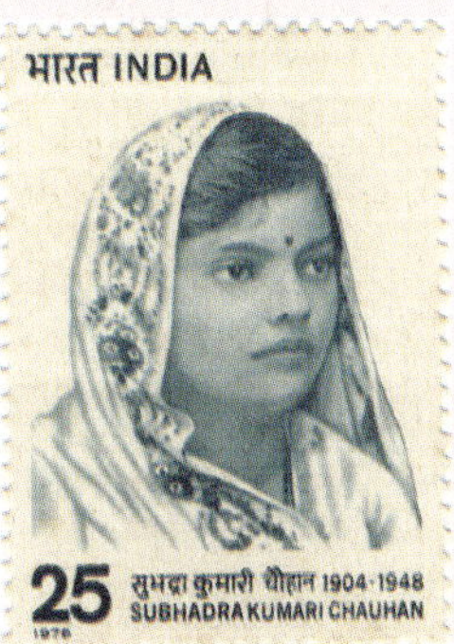

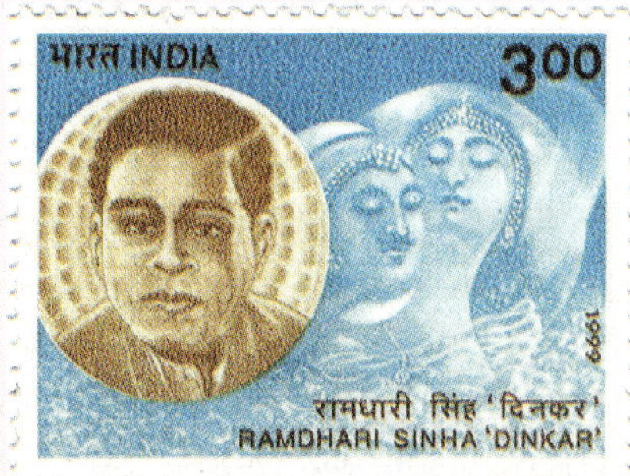

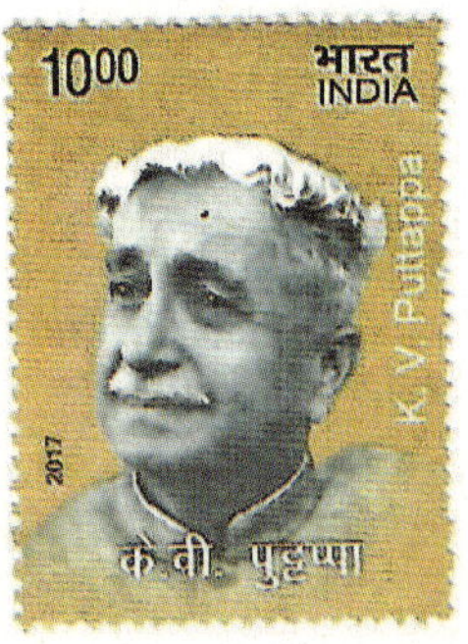

20.1 : Some stars in the firmament of Indian literature — Courtesy, Department of Post

EVOLUTION OF INDIAN LANGUAGES AND LITERATURE

Languages and literature are salient elements of the cultural mosaic of any society. The diversity of languages and the richness of their literature are truly a reflection of the extent of evolution of the culture of its people. The Indian languages and literature can rightly be said to be the most ancient in the world. The Vedas, and in particular the Rigveda, is said to be nearly 3500 (or more) years old. The Vedas, along with other ancient texts, such as the Puranas, the Dharmasutras, the Buddhist Pitakas and other Buddhist and Jain canonical texts, are a part of the great heritage of our ancient language and literature.

Over the period of several centuries, Indian languages and literature have evolved and diversified. They have assimilated the Buddhist and Jain influences of the ancient times, as well as the Arabic and Persian influences of the medieval period. The Bhakti movement added a new hue to the languages and literature, bringing them closer to the masses, and thus to the very roots of society.

With the passage of centuries, many ancient languages like Prakrit did not remain in vogue and Apabramsha (set of transition languages) emerged. From them, emanated languages like Hindi (*Khariboli*) and different other Indian languages. Further, from the intermingling of languages and cultures, also emerged a new language like Urdu. These new languages too have evolved with a distinct and a large literature of their own. As an official language, two non-native languages rose in prominence since the medieval period. While it was Persian that served as the court language and language of administration for centuries during the Mughal reign, the British rule saw English become the official language. These languages also served as languages of communication and connect and have left a legacy of their own. Thus, the story of Indian languages and their literature is indeed a saga of regional and temporal diversity, continuous evolution and literary enrichment.

The diversity of Indian languages is also reflected in the fact that **22 languages** are recognised in the **Eighth Schedule of the Indian Constitution**. Further, as per the 2011 census, there are nearly **121 major languages** and nearly **1369** minor languages (including dialects) in vogue in the country which are recognized as a mother tongue. Out of these, 30 languages are spoken by more than a million people, while 121 languages have a speaking population of greater than 10000. The 22 scheduled languages were spoken by nearly 96.72% of the population while the remaining non-scheduled languages are spoken by the rest 3.28% of the population. Many of these major languages also boast of their own literature, which in turn reflects the vastness of culture and the life of people of different regions.

What is Mother Tongue?

Colloquially considered to be the very first language with which a person is conversant with, or the language which a child acquired from her/his mother, mother tongue is often considered the primary language of expression of the very thought of an individual. It also imparts to the child a cultural and social identity; besides, it serves as the bridge for the acquisition of other languages. Although a watertight definition of a mother tongue may not be feasible, however, the census of 2011 has given a definitive description of what it considers as mother tongue.

It is the language spoken in childhood by the person's mother to the person. However, in case the mother died in infancy, the language mainly spoken in the person's home in childhood will be the mother tongue. In case of infants and deaf mutes the language usually spoken by the mother and in other cases or in case of any doubt, the language mainly spoken in the household. .... Census 2011

Mother tongue, or the native language, is often not just the medium of communication between the mother and child, but the language of conversation in the family and in many instances, even in the larger community. Understandably, this is the language the child is comfortable to begin with, and acquires proficiency through the practice of communication rather than though a formal learning. As per some researchers, it is believed that the level of language proficiency that is acquired by a speaker in a couple of years may require nearly seven years to the non-native speaker to attain. Considering the significance of the mother tongue, UNESCO has been advocating a child's mother tongue as the language of primary education.

INDIAN LANGUAGES AND THEIR CLASSIFICATION

Like other elements of Indian culture, the languages of India too have a bewildering diversity. Numerous races and sub-cultures in different regions have prospered over the millinnia. This has resulted in varied ethnolinguistic evolution. Several centuries of different foreign influences too have added to the potpourri of the Indian languages which trace their origin to different family groups. The modern Indian

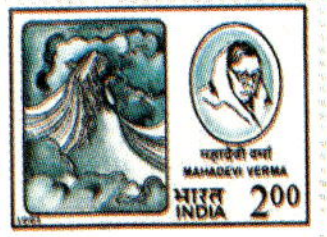

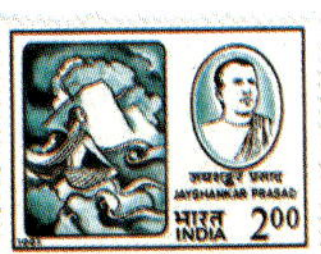

languages can broadly be classified into the following group of families.

(a) Indo-Aryan group
(b) Dravidian group
(c) Austric or Austroasiatic group
(d) Tibeto-Burman group
(e) Others

Indo-Aryan Group

The Indo-Aryan group of languages is a branch of the larger **Indo-Iranian group**, which in itself is a sub-family of **Indo-European** language group. This is the largest family of modern Indian languages in terms of the population speaking it. As per the 2011 census, the Indio-Aryan group comprises 23 languages of the 121 major Indian languages. Further, it includes all of the major languages of northern, western, and eastern parts of India. These include **Sanskrit, Hindi, Bengali, Oriya, Urdu, Punjabi, Marathi, Gujarati, Sindhi, Assamese, Dogri, Kashmiri, Konkani, Maithali, and Nepali**; amongst the languages in the Eighth Schedule of the Constitution. Besides, a number of other languages of these regions which are major or minor non-scheduled languages/dialects are also a part of this family. Some of these are **Bhili/Bhilodi, Bishnupriya, Halabi, Khandeshi, Shina** and **Lahnda.**

As per the 2011 Census of India, nearly **945 million speakers** (**78.07%** of the then population) **spoke languages of Indo-Aryan group** with Hindi being the language spoken by the maximum number of people and in the largest area of the country, in terms of the number of speakers (first language spoken).

Sanskrit, the oldest of Indo-Aryan languages

Amongst all of the Indo-Aryan languages, **Sanskrit is the oldest**. Its antiquity is traced to the Vedic texts which were composed in the earliest form of Sanskrit referred to as the **Vedic Sanskrit**. Considering that the period of composition of Rigveda is accepted to be around 2000–1500 BCE, the development of the language Sanskrit—which expressed the rich Vedic philosophy—would surely have taken place much earlier. Thus, Sanskrit as a language is in existence at least for the last five thousand years. The **Classical Sanskrit** was laid out in the grammar of **Panini** in the 5th century BCE. Over the centuries, Sanskrit served as the medium for composition of the Vedic, Buddhist, Jain, Puranic texts and later of the classical non-canonical literature. As a language, Sanskrit has had a profound influence on other Indian languages including some of the Dravidian languages.

Hindi, the language of the majority

A language spoken in central and northern India by nearly **528.3 million** people (as per 2011 census), Hindi is the Indian language with the largest geographical spread and maximum number of speakers. Out of the over 520 million of its speakers, 322 million people belonged to the category whose mother tongue was Hindi and the rest whose mother tongue is grouped under Hindi. Further, if the second and third spoken languages are considered, then Hindi is spoken by nearly **700 million** people which is approximately **57.1%** (of 2011) population. Thus, Hindi is the only language spoken and understood by the majority of Indian population. Over several decades, it has also spread and emerged as a link-language, or *lingua franca*, in different parts of the country.

Modern Hindi is said to have originated from *Khariboli* in the last 200 years. Today, it is recognised as one of the major Indian languages in the Eighth Schedule of the Constitution and it is also recognised as the **official language** of the country as per the Official Languages Act of 1963. (The Constitution or any legislation, however does not specify Hindi or any other language as the national language of the country). Hindi has the same script **Devanagari**, as that of Sanskrit, which is also the script of many other Indo-Aryan languages. Besides, it also shares a number of words with Urdu. Different variations and dialects of Hindi are popular in different parts of northern and central India.

After Hindi, **Bengali** followed by **Marathi**, is among the most spoken of Indo Aryan languages. As per 2011 census, Bengali has 97.23 million and Marathi 83.02 million of first language speakers. The other prominent languages of India are **Telugu** (81.1 million speakers), **Tamil** (69 million speakers), **Gujarati** (55.49 million speakers), **Urdu** (50.77 million speakers), **Odia** (37.52 million speakers), **Malayalam** (34.8 million speakers), **Punjabi** (33.12 million speakers), **Assamese** (15.31 million speakers) and **Kannada** (43.7 million speakers), **Maithili** (13.58 million speakers).

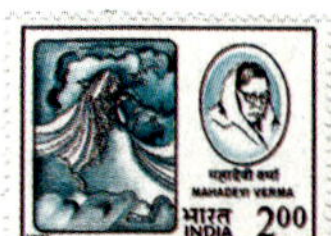

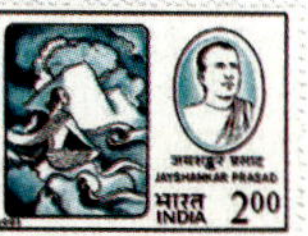

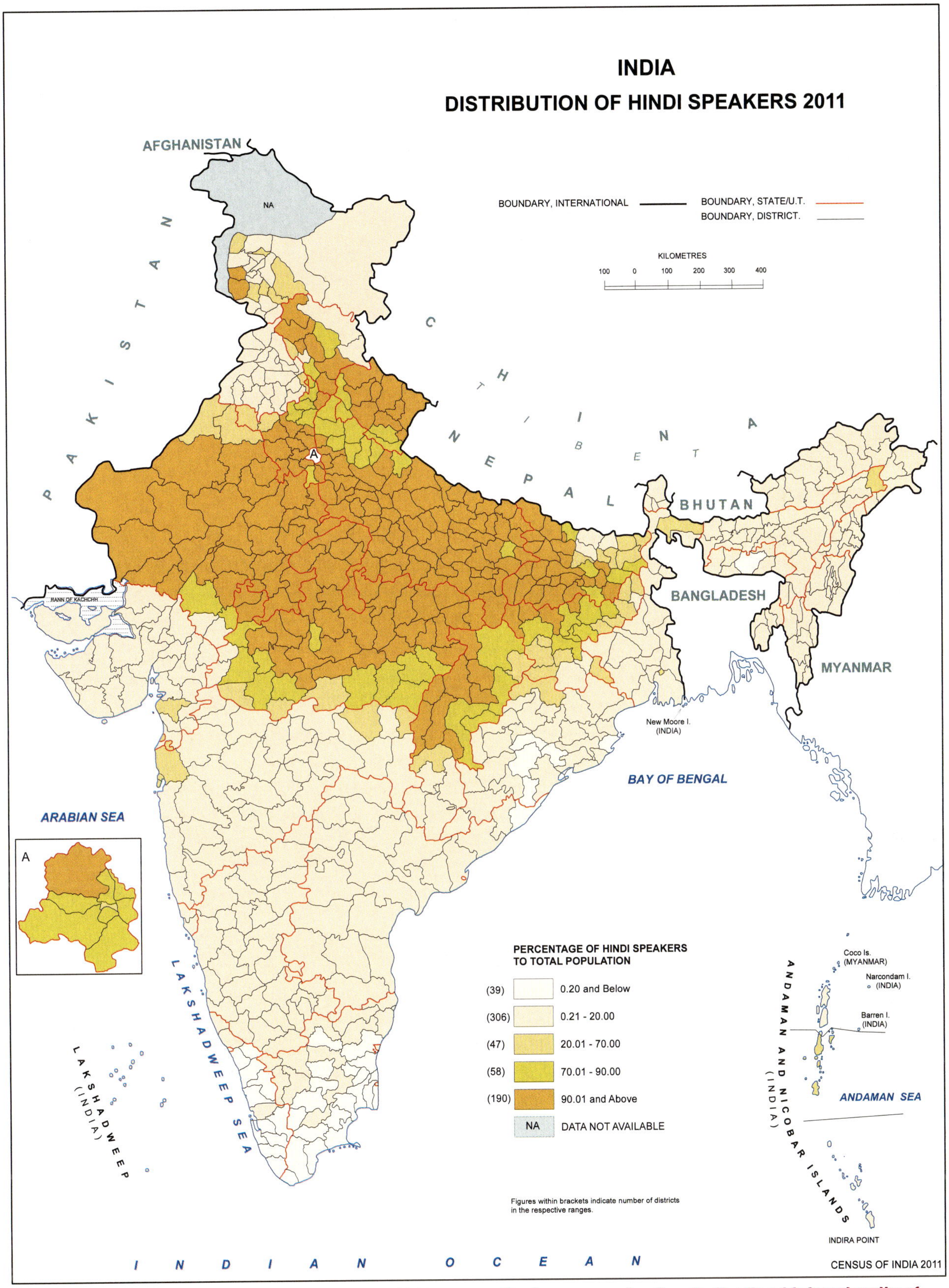

INDIA
DISTRIBUTION OF HINDI SPEAKERS 2011

BOUNDARY, INTERNATIONAL
BOUNDARY, STATE/U.T.
BOUNDARY, DISTRICT.

KILOMETRES
100 0 100 200 300 400

AFGHANISTAN
PAKISTAN
CHINA
TIBET
NEPAL
BHUTAN
BANGLADESH
MYANMAR
RANN OF KACHCHH
ARABIAN SEA
BAY OF BENGAL
LAKSHADWEEP SEA
LAKSHADWEEP (INDIA)
ANDAMAN AND NICOBAR ISLANDS (INDIA)
ANDAMAN SEA
New Moore I. (INDIA)
Coco Is. (MYANMAR)
Narcondam I. (INDIA)
Barren I. (INDIA)
INDIRA POINT
INDIAN OCEAN

PERCENTAGE OF HINDI SPEAKERS TO TOTAL POPULATION

Districts	Range
(39)	0.20 and Below
(306)	0.21 - 20.00
(47)	20.01 - 70.00
(58)	70.01 - 90.00
(190)	90.01 and Above
NA	DATA NOT AVAILABLE

Figures within brackets indicate number of districts in the respective ranges.

CENSUS OF INDIA 2011

20.2: Distribution of Hindi speakers as per 2011 census. Darker areas of yellow indicating higher density of Hindi speakers — Courtesy, Census Commissioner, Government of India

Dravidian Group

This is the second largest group of languages in India and comprises 17 languages. These languages are said to have **evolved indigenously** and not to have been influenced by Indo-Iranian/Indo-European languages. The Dravidian languages are spoken largely in the southern part of India and some parts

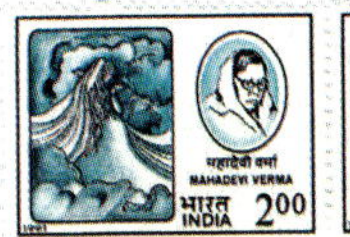
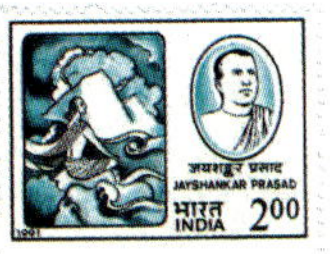

of central and eastern India. **Tamil, Telugu, Kannada** and **Malayalam** are the most important of the Dravidian languages and are included in the Eighth Schedule of the Constitution.

Amongst the Dravidian languages, **Tamil** is considered to be the oldest. Its antiquity is gathered from the fact that reference of it is also noted in the Tamil-Brahmi script in the cave walls near Madurai and in Tirunelveli in Tamil Nadu. The composition of the Sangam literature was also in the Tamil language. **Tolkappiyam,** the oldest surviving Tamil literary work, is an ancient work on Tamil grammar and also the oldest non-Sanskrit text. Experts believe this to be a work from 2nd to 1st century BCE, and hence would imply that the Tamil language would have originated several centuries prior to it.

As per the 2011 census, **Telugu** has the maximum number of first language speakers (81.12 million) followed by **Tamil** (69.02 million), **Kannada** (43.70 million), and **Malayalam** (34.83 million). In total, nearly **23.78 million** people or nearly **19.64%** of the Indian population speaks the Dravidian languages.

Besides the scheduled languages, some of the other non-scheduled languages of the group are **Tulu** which is popular in Dakshina Kannada, and **Kodava** (Coorgi) another language of South Kannada, both which are considered as literary languages. **Kurukh** in Eastern India, and **Gondi** in Central India, are also a part of this group. Two Dravidian languages are also spoken outside India and include **Brauhi** spoken in Baluchistan region (of Afghanistan and Pakistan) and **Kurukh**, spoken in parts of Nepal and Bhutan.

Other Language Groups

The other language groups include **Austric/Austro Asiatic, Tibeto-Burman** (a sub part of Sino-Tibetan langauages), besides **Negroid,** and **Tai-Kadai** languages and others. The **Tibeto-Burman** languages are spoken across the Himalayas, in Ladakh, Himachal Pradesh, Arunachal Pradesh, Meghalaya, Nagaland, Tripura, etc. These comprise 66 languages which is the maximum number of major languages (of the 121 major languages with 10000 or more of speakers) and covered 1.01% of the population (as per 2011 census). Among the scheduled languages of this group are **Manipuri** (also known as Meiti) and **Bodo**. Among prominent non-scheduled languages are **Karbi** and **Lepcha**, amongst others.

The **Austro-Asiatic** group (Austro meaning south), comprises 14 languages and covered nearly 1.11% of the population (as per 2011 census). These include languages spoken by the Mundas and Kols and some other tribes in central, eastern, and north-eastern parts of India. These include the **Khasi, Munda** (Mundari) , the **Santhali** and **Bhumij** languages, besides others. The **Tai-Kadai** language includes Kamrupi language (ancient language of Assam) and some other languages spoken in Arunachal Pradesh and Assam.

SCHEDULED LANGUAGES, OFFICIAL LANGUAGES & CLASSICAL LANGUAGES IN INDIA

Scheduled Languages

The Eighth Schedule of the Constitution includes 22 Indian languages. At the time of the enactment of Constitution, there were 14 scheduled languages including **Assamese, Bengali, Gujarati, Hindi, Kannada, Kashmiri, Malayalam, Marathi, Oriya, Punjabi, Sanskrit, Tamil, Telugu and Urdu**. Later, through constitutional amendments, eight languages were added. These include **Sindhi** (added by the 21st amendment of the Constitution), **Konkani, Manipuri, Nepali** (added by the 71st Amendment), **Bodo, Dogri, Maithili, and Santhali** (added by the by 92nd Amendment).

These Scheduled languages are entitled to representation in the Official Languages Commission. The government is also required to take measures for development of these languages.

Official Language

As per the Official Languages Act 1963, **Hindi, in Devanagri script,** has been accorded the status of the **Official language** of the Union, while English has been given the status of an additional language of the Union which may be used for the purposes of official work in addition to Hindi. Thus, Hindi and English continue to be used for official purpose in the Central Government and for communication between the Centre and the States. However, the states can conduct official business in a language as chosen by them and they may choose any of the scheduled languages for this purpose.

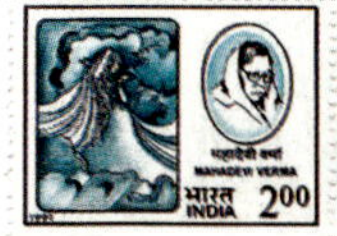

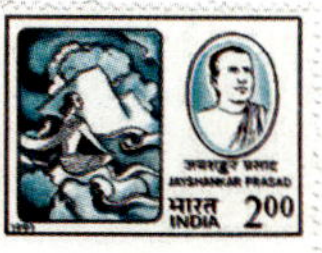

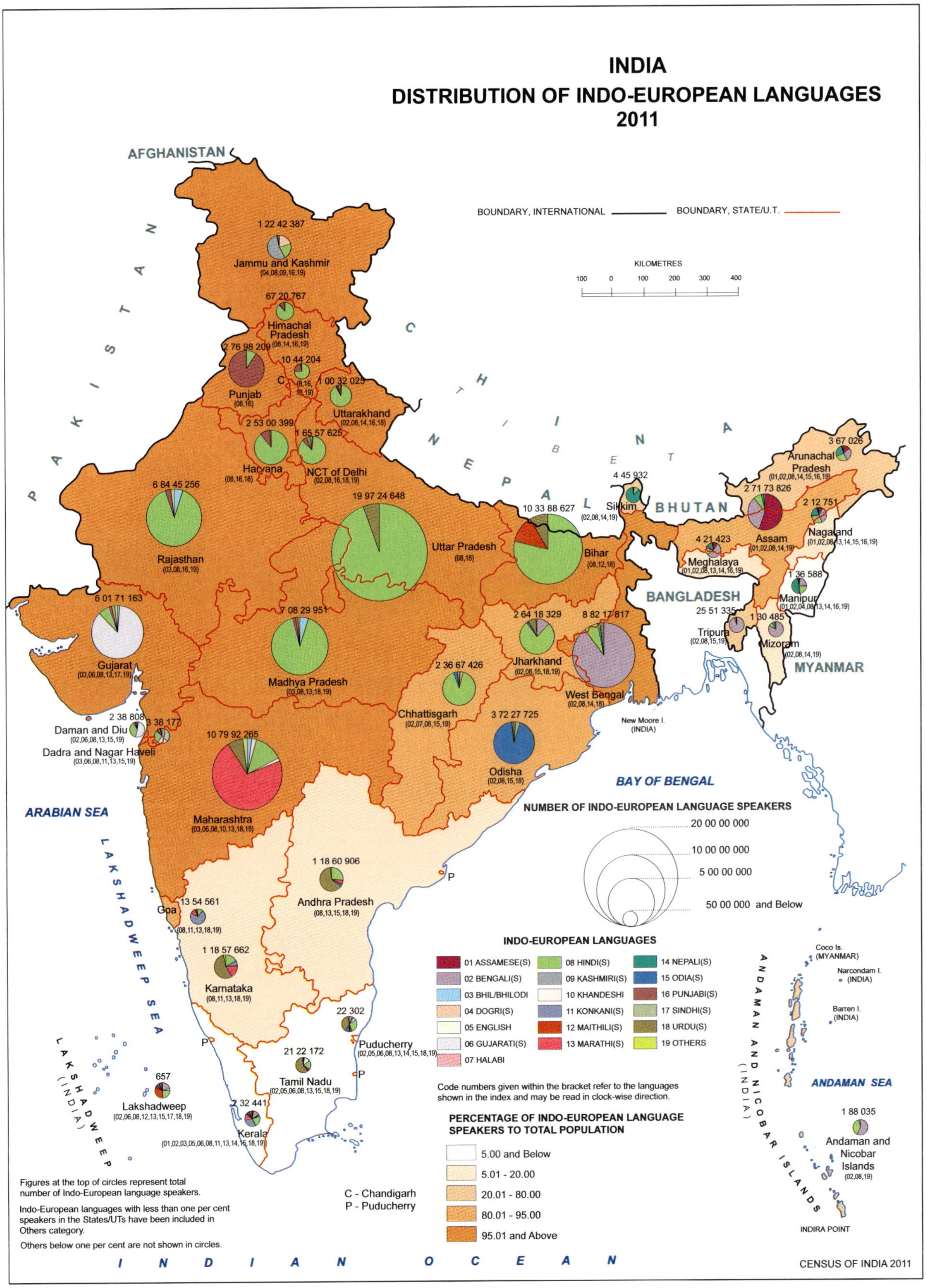

INDIA
DISTRIBUTION OF INDO-EUROPEAN LANGUAGES
2011

BOUNDARY, INTERNATIONAL ——— BOUNDARY, STATE/U.T. ———

NUMBER OF INDO-EUROPEAN LANGUAGE SPEAKERS: 20 00 00 000; 10 00 00 000; 5 00 00 000; 50 00 000 and Below

INDO-EUROPEAN LANGUAGES

01 ASSAMESE(S), 02 BENGALI(S), 03 BHIL/BHILODI, 04 DOGRI(S), 05 ENGLISH, 06 GUJARATI(S), 07 HALABI, 08 HINDI(S), 09 KASHMIRI(S), 10 KHANDESHI, 11 KONKANI(S), 12 MAITHILI(S), 13 MARATHI(S), 14 NEPALI(S), 15 ODIA(S), 16 PUNJABI(S), 17 SINDHI(S), 18 URDU(S), 19 OTHERS

Code numbers given within the bracket refer to the languages shown in the index and may be read in clock-wise direction.

PERCENTAGE OF INDO-EUROPEAN LANGUAGE SPEAKERS TO TOTAL POPULATION: 5.00 and Below; 5.01 - 20.00; 20.01 - 80.00; 80.01 - 95.00; 95.01 and Above

Figures at the top of circles represent total number of Indo-European language speakers.

Indo-European languages with less than one per cent speakers in the States/UTs have been included in Others category.

Others below one per cent are not shown in circles.

C - Chandigarh
P - Puducherry

CENSUS OF INDIA 2011

20.3: Courtesy, Census Commissioner, Government of India

Classical Languages

With a view to identify those languages which have a distinct and ancient literary tradition and richness of literary texts, the Government of India decided (in 2004) to select some languages as classical languages. Certain specific criteria were specified for determination of classical languages which include;

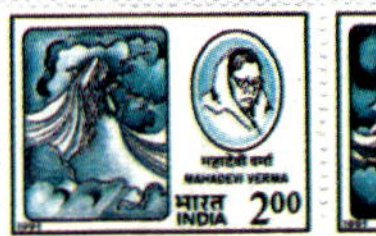

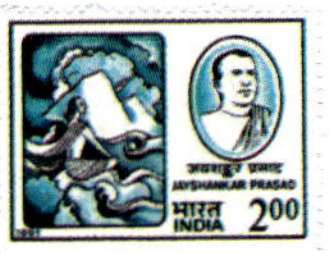

- Antiquity of texts
- Existence of a body of valuable ancient literature
- Originality of literary tradition
- Distinctness of the classical language and literature from its modern forms/offshoots

The objective was to preserve the literary heritage of such languages and to recognise and promote modern work in them. Till now, six Indian languages have been identified as classical languages.

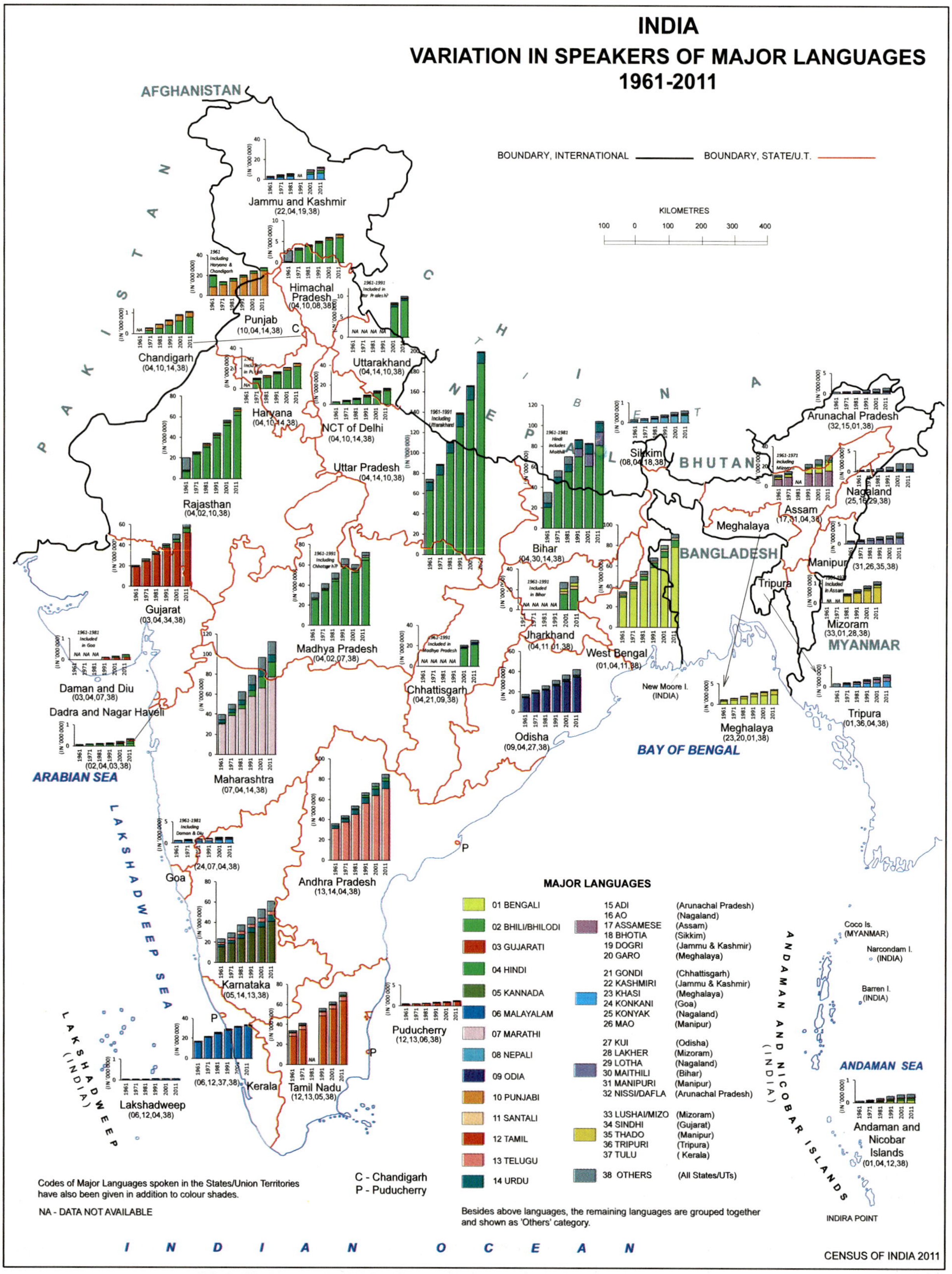

20.4: States and distribution of languages across various censuses — Courtesy, Census Commissioner, Government of India

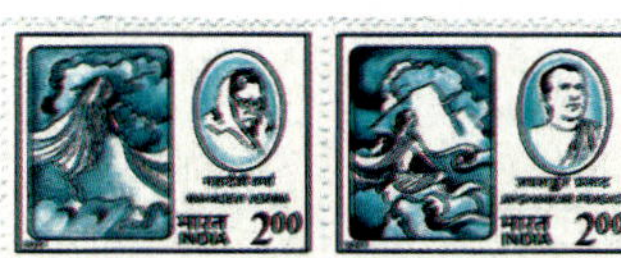

These are **Tamil** (recognised in 2004), **Sanskrit** (2005), **Telugu** (2008), **Kannada** (2008), **Malayalam** (2013) and **Odia** (2014), which is the last language to be accorded that status.

Further, as per Government of India's decision (vide resolution dated 01.11.2014) such languages are eligible for two major annual awards to scholars of eminence in these languages. There is also a establishment of a centre of excellence for studies in them. Besides, the University Grants Commission (UGC) is mandated to start a certain number of professional chairs in these languages at least in the central universities.

MODERN INDIAN LITERATURE AND ITS EVOLUTION

From the perspective of Indian literature, the phase of modern literature covers the period of **19th century** onwards, particularly the period of **1850** and later. This was a phase of change and turmoil in the Indian political and social setup and that reflected in the growth of Indian literature too.

By the 19th century, the British rule had become firmly established in India, and after 1858 it came directly under the British crown. At this juncture, a number of **socio-religious reforms** were also sweeping the Indian society. The Brahmo Samaj, Prarthana Sabha, the Deccan Education Society, the Arya Samaj and others opposed the centuries old decadent practices like *sati*, child marriage, and caste system. These worked for spread of education amongst the masses, particularly amongst the women. Thus, they had an important influence on the growth of literature in different regions.

Post the War of Independence of 1857, there was a gradual rise in the feeling of **Indian nationalism**. The formation of the Indian National Congress in 1885, which also brought the socio-economic issues and exploitation of the country to the fore, brought out the failure of British rule and further fueled Indian nationalism.

The **Bengal Renaissance** which culminated in the latter half of the 19th and early 20th century, along with similar regional movements, impacted different facets of the Indian arts and culture. Revivalism of the Indian traditions of art also reflected in the Indian literature.

In this phase there was also a growing exposure of Indians to the the **ideas of liberalism** and **individual** and **national freedom**. These found expression in many of the literary works. The growth of art and culture in Europe, America, Asia and elsewhere had its impact on the literary environment of India, particularly in the early 20th century.

Literature in the 19th Century: The Early Milestones

Various factors shaped Indian literature in the 19th and early 20th century. Given below are some of the important factors and milestones of this phase of evolution:

Printing press

The establishment of the first printing press in Serampore in Bengal (1800) by William Carey was a landmark event which enabled printing and distribution of newspapers and books in India. Although printing press had been established earlier in some parts of the country, it was only now that printing per-se came of age and also spread in the coming decades to most of the other regions of the country. With it, the era of handwritten manuscript gradually ended. Printing of books could become easier, quicker, cheaper. Most importantly, it now could have mass reach. This revolutionized Indian literature. It is said that between 1800 and 1832, nearly 2,12,000 books were published by the press of Serampore. The objective of the press was largely distribution of Christian publications like the *Bible* and other missionary tracts. However, the press is said to have also published a variety of newspapers, vernacular textbooks, magazines and books in almost 45 languages. This enabled a culture of reading of multifarious publications to gradually develop in Bengal and other parts of the country.

Growth of prose, particularly in the regional languages in the early 19th century, truly heralded the advent of modern literature. This could be possible with the development of press and the subsequent emergence of a variety of books and periodicals. With this new format of literature, came a marked departure from the centuries of the tradition of verses/poetry which had been a trait of the medieval period. Now the subject of literature too became more diverse, unlike that of the medieval literature, which was largely focused on spiritualism, socio-religious poetry (*Bhaktikal*), and later, the genre of love and romance (*Ritikal*).

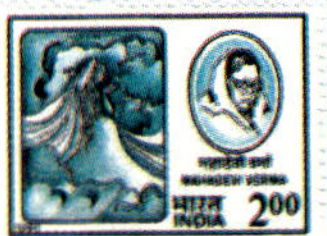

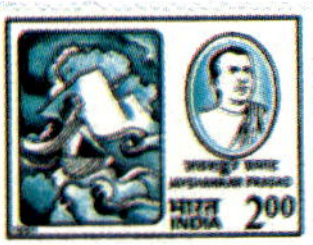

The works of prose, ***Durgesh Nandini*** written by **Bankim Chandra** (1865), ***Anand Math*** (by Bankim Chandra in 1882), ***Bharat Durdasha*** (1873), and the play ***Andher Nagari*** (1881) by **Bharatendu Harishchandra** were indeed milestone literary works. They not only covered diverse subjects but had a far-reaching impact. *Anand Math* written in the backdrop of the Sanyasi revolution (1770-1777), which erupted against the British (post the battle of Buxar), carried the song of *Vande Mataram* (now recognised as the national song of India). *Andher Nagari* was a satirical play on the misrule by a king; apparently symbolic of the British misrule. As per some accounts, it was written by Bharatendu in a single day for the 'Hindu National Theatre of Banaras'. Thus, the growth of literature also supported the growth of theatre and vice-versa, besides other aspects of Indian culture.

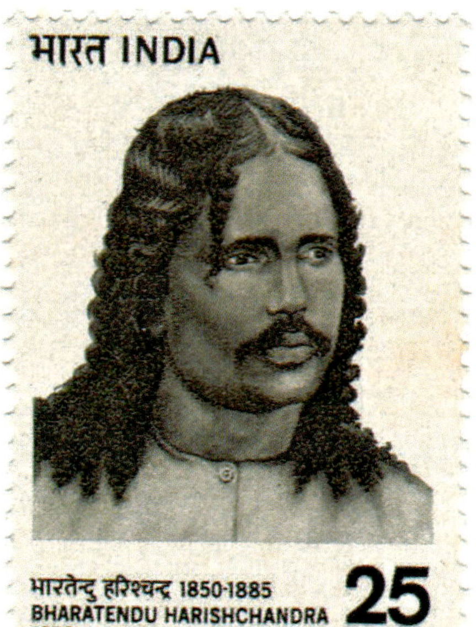

20.5: Bharatendu Harishchandra; considered the usherer of modern Hindi literature, a postage stamp released in 1976 — Courtesy, Department of Post

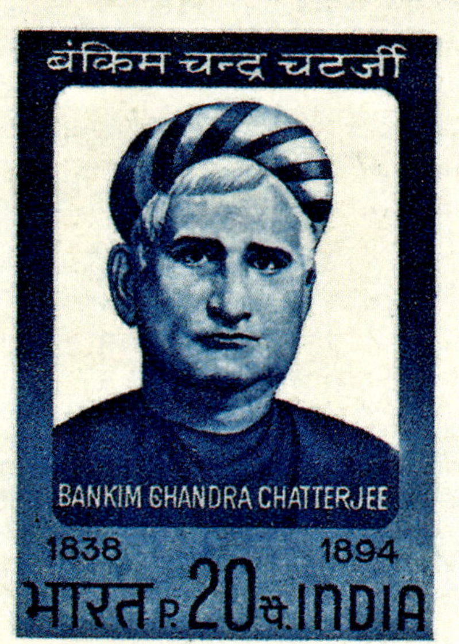

20.6: Bankim Chandra Chatterjee; christened as Sahitya Samrat, and one of the earliest Bangla litterateurs, a postage stamp released in 1969 — Courtesy, Department of Post

Bau-Thakurneer (1882) and *Rajarshi* (1885) were some of the early novels period written by **Rabindranath Tagore,** a monumental litterateur and poet of this period. **Peary Chand Mitra** (author of the first Bengali novel written in 1857), and **Michael Madhusudan Dutt** were some other prominent novelists of Bengali literature.

Apart from the above, Indian literature saw the emergence of novelists of many other Indian languages and prose. **Lala Srinivas Das** was the author of *Pariksha Guru* in 1882, which is considered the first novel in Hindi. Another popular fiction writer of the late 19th century was **Devaki Nandan Khatri** (1861-1913), whose historic fiction fantasy novel *Chandrakanta* (1888) was a runaway success and even popularised Hindi literature. This was followed by sequels of the same genre titled *Chandrakant Santati* which was a seven-part series. Nearly a century later, *Chandrakanta* was adapted into a mega television serial which enjoyed immense popularity in the 1990s.

Other prominent **writers of prose in the regional literature** included; **Lakshminath Bezbarua** (Assamese literature), **Fakir Mohan Senapati** (Odia literature), **Narmadashankar Lalshankar Dave** (author of *Narma Gadya* in 1865 & *Mari Hakikat*, the first autobiography in Gujarati), **Samuel Vedanayagam Pillai**, (Tamil literature, author of first Tamil novel, *Prathapa Mudaliar Charithram*), **Kandukuri Veeresalingam Pantulu** (author of first Telugu novel *Rajashekhara Charitamu*), **Oyyarathu Chandu Menon** (author of first major Malayalam novel, *Indulekha*), **Krishnamma Chetty** (author of the Telugu novel, *Sri Rangaraja Charitra* written in 1872) were some other eminent novelists of different regional languages of the late 19th century.

The growth of newspapers and **periodicals** was another significant milestone of the literary evolution. This had begun earlier with the establishment of the printing press. Some newspapers were also printed in the late 18th and the early 19th century in India such as **The Bengal Gazette**, (Calcultta, established 1780), **The Indian Gazette** (Calcultta, established 1780), **The Calcutta Gazette** (Calcutta, established 1782), **The Madras Gazette** (Madras, established 1795), **Samachar Darpan** (Calcutta, established 1818), **Bombay Samachar** (Bombay, established 1822). But the British looked at the press suspiciously. They frequently adopted the policy to muzzle it, despite protests and appeals from many quarters, including eminent Indians like Raja Ram Mohan Roy. It was only after the 'Press law' was passed in 1835 that the growth of press and newspapers started to take place at a reasonable pace.

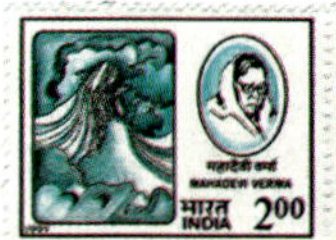
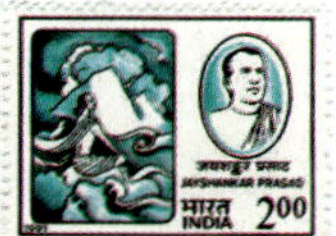

Indeed, their growth along with other factors, proved to be a watershed in the Indian literary and social landscape. The newspapers and periodicals were particularly instrumental in the development of prose. Journalism emerged as a whole new trend. Both the mediums also provided space to the literary as well as non-literary articles. An eminent author like Bankim Chandra considered as *Sahitya Samrat* (king of literature) of Bengal, had his earliest of publications in a weekly newspaper *Sangbad Prabhakar*. His much-acclaimed novel *Anand Math* had first appeared in public domain in a serial form in a literary magazine *Bangadarshan* founded by him (in 1872). Like him, as for many other authors, the newspapers and journals were the first medium of literary expression and stepping stones to a literary career.

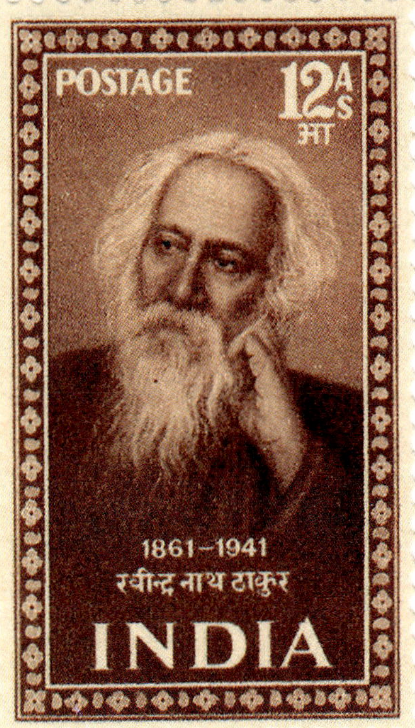

20.7: Rabindranath Tagore; a milestone in Indian literature (1861-1941); postage stamp released in 1952 — Courtesy, Department of Post

Further, while the books had their reach and specific market, newspapers and magazines could penetrate deeper in the Indian hinterland and could connect better even with the villages. Thus, they opened the world of literature to the common man. Both the platforms also enabled the expression of Indian thought and aided the growth of nationalistic fervour in the years to come.

The Growth of Indian Nationalism, post 1857, complemented the growth of literature and was as well aided by it. The second half of the 19th century was a period marked by a reformistic, revivalistic and nationalistic fervour. The social issues, particularly the plight of women, child marriages, education of women, and prohibition of widow remarriage, were often the main themes of many novels. ***Bishabriksha*** (1873), by Bankim Chandra, ***Indulekha*** (1889), the first novel in Malayalam by Chandu Menon, and later ***Chokher Bali*** (1901), ***Ghaire Baire*** (1915) by Rabindranath Tagore, were some of the novels of this genre.

The rise of nationalism and the critique of the British misrule were equally expressed in many of the literary works of this period. Bharatendu Harishchandra's ***Bharat Durdasha*** (Hindi, 1875) succinctly brings out the reasons for India's economic plight. Inter-alia, many social and internal factors, he highlights British misrule and consequential destruction of the rural economy and cottage industries to enrich its mills and economy, as the major cause. ***Andher Nagari*** (Hindi 1889) was another satirical play by Bharatendu on the perils of misrule. Bankim Chandra Chatterjee's ***Anand Math*** hails the motherland and the song ***Bande Mataram*** was an inspiration to the people during the partition of Bengal (1905) and continued to inspire several generations of nationalistic leaders. ***Devi Chaudharani*** (1884), another novel of Bankim Chandra which made a call for patriotic struggle against the British, specially inspiring the woman, was banned by the British. It was only post-independence of India that the ban was lifted. Subsequently the writings of **Dadabhai Naoroji**, **Gokhale** and **Tilak, Tagore, Aurobindo** and **Mahatma Gandhi**, were instrumental in the evolution of a pan-India conscious-ness and nationalistic fervour.

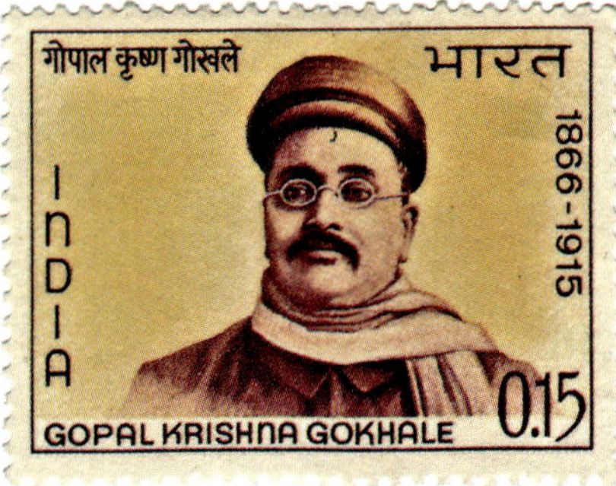

20.8: Gopal Krishna Gokhale, a stamp released in 1966 — Courtesy, Department of Post

English education too had its impact on the literary growth. The establishment of universities of Calcutta, Madras and Bombay in 1857 and new colleges like the Hindu College at Calcutta, acted as a catalyst to the English education. The adoption of English as a language of administration and consequential decline in the usage of Arabic and Persian, further added to the usage of English. Gradually, it led to the emergence of a new class of Indians who were educated in the British law and system and also exposed to western ideas and literature. It also led to the growth of English press and English literature in India. Some of the

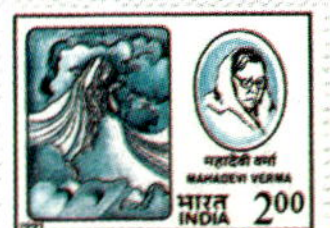
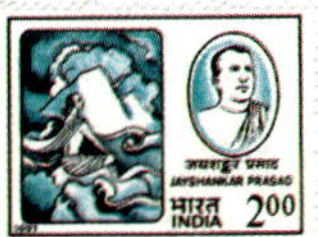

prominent English newspapers of this period were; **The Times of India** (Bombay; established 1838), **The Pioneeer** (Allahabad; established 1865) **The Madras Mail** (Madras; established 1868), **The Civil and Military Gazette** (Lahore; established 1872), and **The Statesman** (Bombay; established 1875). They continued to thrive even after independence.

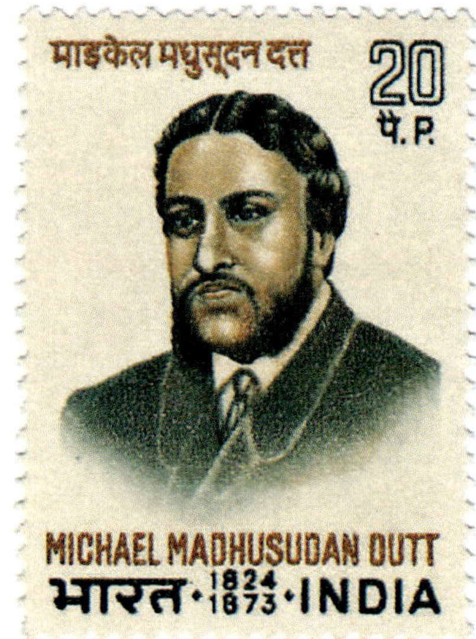

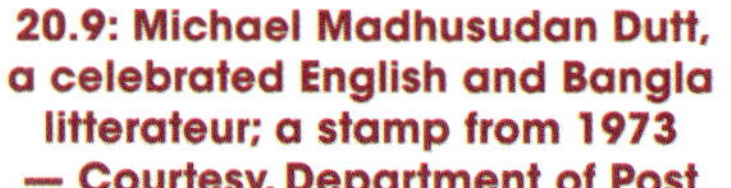

20.9: Michael Madhusudan Dutt, a celebrated English and Bangla litterateur; a stamp from 1973 — Courtesy, Department of Post

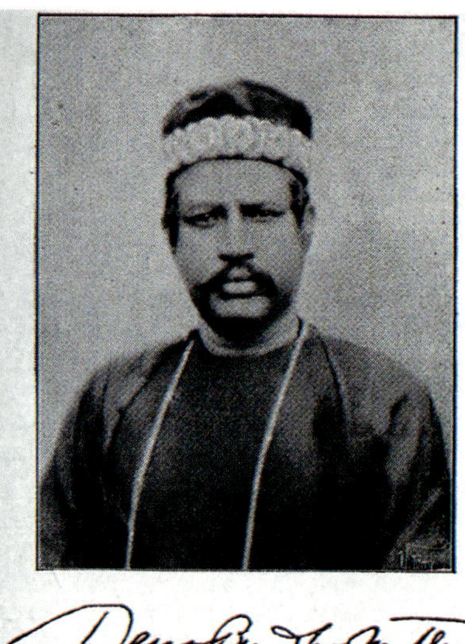

20.10: Dinobandhu Mitra who authored *Nil Darpan* (1860), brought the plight of indigo farmers — Wikimedia Commons

Raja Ram Mohun Roy, a reformist and an erudite scholar, was also a writer of English prose. **Henry Vivian Derozio**, a teacher, a thinker and an eminent English poet was an inspiration for his students. Though he died young, yet he left a reasonable body of verses, including the narrative poem 'The Fakeer of Jungheera'. **Michael Madhusudan Dutt**, a product of the Hindu College, and a bright star of the Bengal literary renaissance, began his career writing prose and poetry in English. **Aru Dutt** and **Taro Dutt** (sisters), and **Manmohan Ghosh** and **Aurobindo Ghosh** (brothers), and **Romesh Chandra Dutt** were some other Indian poets in this period. Besides, many of the popular literary works like that of Bankim Chandra were translated in English.

Drama as a separate genre also witnessed growth in the latter half of the 19th century. **Michael Madhusudan Dutt** (Krishna Kumari), **Girish Chandra Ghosh, Dinobandhu Mitra** (*Nil Darpan*; 1860), **Jyotirindranath Tagore**, (elder brother of Rabindranath Tagore) were some of the eminent Bengali dramatists. ***Nil Darpan*** brought out the plight of Indigo plantation workers in rural Bengal and is said to have inspired the Indigo revolt and was banned by the British. **Bharatendu Harsichandra** was indeed one of the most prominent dramatists of Hindi who wrote popular plays like *Satya Harischandra* (1875) *Andher Nagari* (1878), with the latter still being enacted at times.

The tradition of poetry also prospered in this phase of literature. **Mirza Ghalib** (1797-1869) was a celebrated name in Urdu poetry. Michael Madhusudan Dutt introduced numerous sonnets and other long verses in his momentous work *Meghnad Badh Kavya* (1861). **Rangalal Bandyopadhyay**, (poetic works; *Padmini Upakhyan*-1858, *Karmadevi*-1862, *Shurasundari*-1868 and *Kanchi Kaveri*-1879) was another illustrious poet of this period. **Hemchandra Bandyopadhyay, Nabinchandra Sen** and **Dwijendranath Tagore** (elder brother of Rabindranath Tagore) were some of the other eminent Bengali poets of this phase. **Lakshminath Bezbaruah** (Assamese), **Narmadashankar Lalshankar Dave** (Gujarati; *Jai Jai Garavi Gujarat* composed in 1873), **Keshavasuta** (Marathi), **Subramania Bharati** (Tamil), **Radhanath Ray** (Bengali and Odia), are counted among the renowned poets of the 19th century in other Indian langauages.

The advent of **Rabindranath Tagore** (1861-1941) was a milestone in Indian literature. In a literary career spanning nearly five decades, he wrote several momentous works of prose and poems, including novels, short stories, plays, essays, autobiography and travelogues. *Rajarshi* (1885), *Choker-Bali* (1902), *Nauka-dubi* (1905), *Gora* (1909), *Ghaire-Baire* (1916) were some of his well-known novels. For his compilation of poems ***Gitanjali***, which was also translated in English by him, he was awarded the **Nobel Prize for Literature** in 1913. His travelogues, letters and essays were compiled in volumes such as *Europe Jatrir Patro* (letters from Europe) and *Manusho Dhormo* (the religion of Man). Among his plays, ***Visarajan***, an adaption of the novel *Rajarshi*, *Dak Ghar* (The Post Office, 1912), *Chandalika* (Untouchable girl), *Achalyatan* (1912), *Muktadhara* (1920), *Rakta Karabi* (Blood Orleanders, 1926), are considered amongst his finer works of drama.

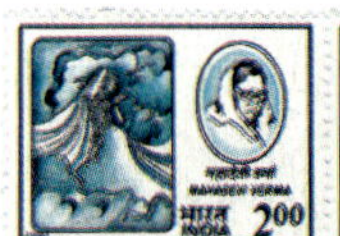

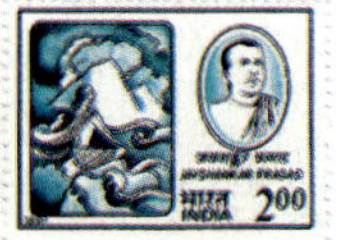

Where the Mind is Without Fear

Among the various beautiful verses in the collection of *Gitanjali* is the famous verse, '*Where the mind is without fear*'. The lines bring out the yearning of the poet and his prayer to the almighty, to endow the awakening of knowledge and reason to his country and to dispel fear, narrow-mindedness, dogma and divisiveness.

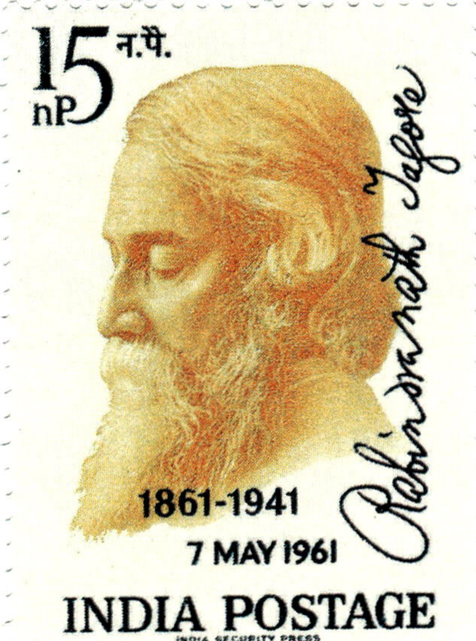

20.11: Rabindranath Tagore (1861-1941); postage stamp released in 1961on birth centenary — Courtesy, Department of Post

> GITANJALI
> (SONG OFFERINGS)
> BY
> RABINDRANATH TAGORE
> A COLLECTION OF PROSE TRANSLATIONS MADE BY THE AUTHOR FROM THE ORIGINAL BENGALI
> WITH AN INTRODUCTION BY
> W. B. YEATS
> MACMILLAN AND CO., LIMITED
> ST. MARTIN'S STREET, LONDON
> 1913

20.12: *Gitanjali*, an edition from 1913 — Wikimedia Commons

Where the mind is without fear and the head is held high;
Where knowledge is free;
Where the world has not been broken up into fragments;
By narrow domestic walls;
Where words come out from the depth of truth;
Where tireless striving stretches its arms towards perfection;
Where the clear stream of reason has not lost its way;
Into the dreary desert sand of dead habit;
Where the mind is led forward by thee;
Into ever-widening thought and action-
Into that heaven of freedom, my Father, let my country awake.

- 35th verse in the compilation *Gitanjali*

Human idealism, revivalism, transnationalism and bringing out the finer facets of human mind and emotions, were some of the traits of Tagore's writing. Although he excelled in all the formats, critics specially admire his **poems** and short stories, where he broke the barrier of literary styles and structure to take literature to newer heights. The experts often categorise his poetic journey into different literary phases each championing a different genre and style. Poems like *Manasi* (1890), *Sonar Tari* (1893), *Chitra* (1896) are considered to reflect his distinctive philosophy of life; romantic and mystical. The poems like *Naivedya* (1901), *Gitanjali* (1910) and *Gitamalya* and *Gitali* (1914), bring out the thirst for divine love and the yearning for divine communion. Indeed, Indian literature reached great heights with the advent of **Rabindranath Tagore** whose life was like a literary epoch.

Tagore and Nobel Prize

Gurudev Rabindranath Tagore was awarded the Nobel Prize for Literature in 1913 for his poetic work *Gitanjali* which was translated into English by him. Here are some excerpts from the webpage of the Nobel Prize committee elucidating as to reason for award and the quality of his works.

Prize motivation: *"because of his profoundly sensitive, fresh and beautiful verse, by which, with consummate skill, he has made his poetic thought, expressed in his own English words, a part of the literature of the West"*

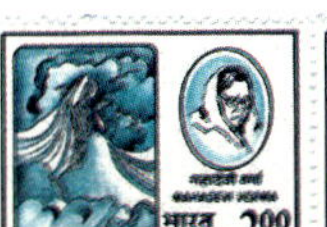
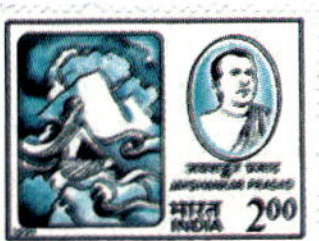

The work: *Rabindranath Tagore's writing is deeply rooted in both Indian and Western learning traditions. Apart from fiction in the form of poetry, songs, stories, and dramas, it also includes portrayals of common people's lives, literary criticism, philosophy, and social issues. Tagore originally wrote in Bengali, but later reached a broad audience in the West after recasting his poetry in English. In contrast to the frenzied life in the West, his poetry was felt to convey the peace of the soul in harmony with nature.*

Excerpts from https://www.nobelprize.org/prizes/literature/1913/tagore/facts/

Literature in the 20th Century

The literary landscape of the 20th century brought to the fore many stellar authors and poets, different genre of literary works as wells certain distinct phases of literary movements. Among the greatest of novelists of this period was **Munshi Premchand** (1880-1936) who wrote in Urdu and later in Hindi. Considered an *Upanyas Samrat* (or the emperor amongst novelists), he is said to have authored over 14 novels and nearly 300 short stories, besides essays and translations of literary works of other languages. *Seva Sadan* (1919), *Premashram* (1922), *Rangabhoomi* (1924), *Nirmala* (1925), *Gaban* (1931), *Karmabhoomi (1932)*, *Godaan* (1936), are amongst his most prominent novels. His last work *Godaan* is considered to be a masterly work which succinctly reflected the harsh socio-economic realities of rural India and exploitation of the poor. His collection of short stories is compiled in seven volumes of *Mansarovar*. Portraying the life of villages, bringing alive the common folks of our day to day lives and the tussle in their lives between idealism and realism, was a hall mark of his creative genius. In a way, he single handedly ushered the genre of realism in Indian literature.

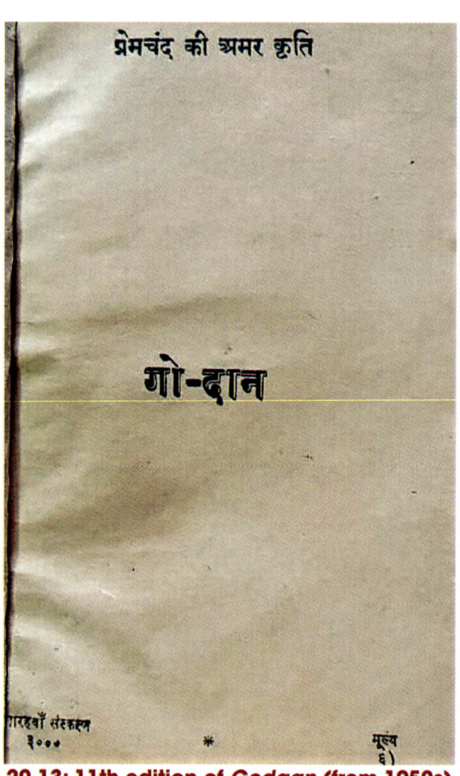

20.13: 11th edition of *Godaan* (from 1950s) private collection — photograph by Madhukar K Bhagat

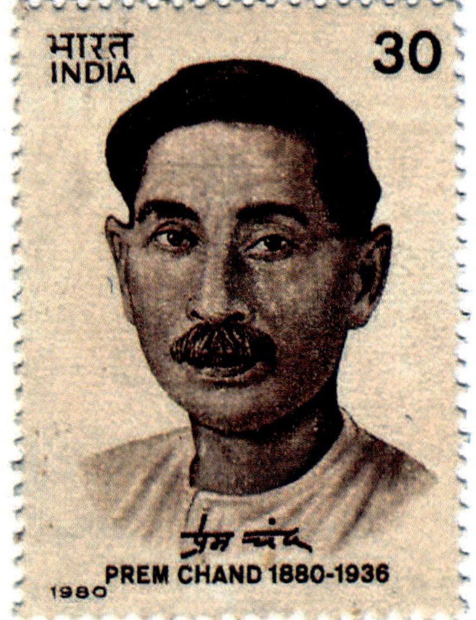

20.14: Munshi Prem Chand, a pre-emiment novelist and litterateur; postage stamp released in 1980 — Courtesy, Department of Post

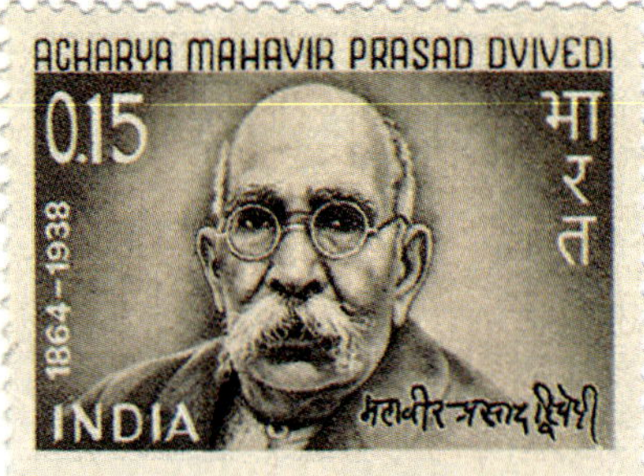

20.15: Acharya Mahavir Prasad Dwivedi, a stamp from 1966 — Courtesy, Department of Postt

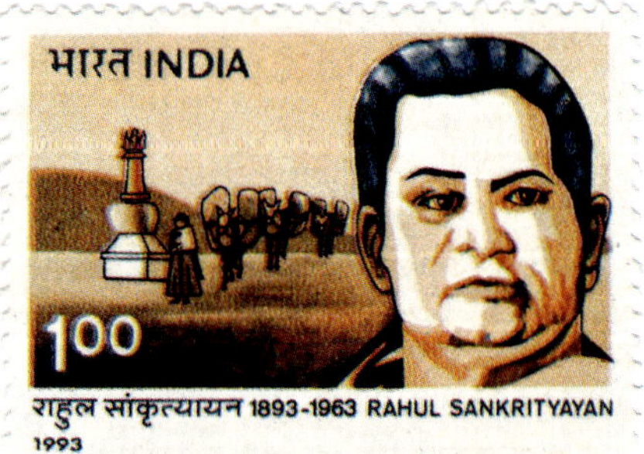

20.16: Rahul Sankrityayan, a great travel witer; a stamp from 1993 — Courtesy, Department of Post

Among other eminent **writers of Hindi prose** in the pre-independence period were; **Acharya Mahavir Prasad Dwivedi**, (1864-1938) editor of the esteemed *Saraswati* magazine, **Acharya Ramchandra Shukla** (1882–1942), critique, essayist and literary historian; **Vrindalal Verma** (1889-1969), a dramatist and novelist, **Rahul Sankrityayan** (1893-1962), among the greatest of travel writers, **Bhagwati Charan Verma** (1903-1981), novelist and author of *Chitralekha*, a novel adapted later into two movies, **Hazari Prasad Dwivedi** (1907-1978), a novelist and literary historian, **Yashpal** (1903-1976), novelist and short story writer, **Jainendra Kumar** (1905-1979), **Upendranath Ashq** (1910-1976), novelist, short story writer and playwright, **S.H. Vatsayayan Agyeya** (1911-1987), novelist, poet and literary critic, **Krishna Chander** (1914-77), author of over 20 novels and 30 short story collections, **Bhisham Sahni** (1915-2003), novelist and author of *Tamas* (made into a popular television serial later), **Amritlal Nagar** (1916-1990), novelist, playwright and short story writer, besides other litterateurs.

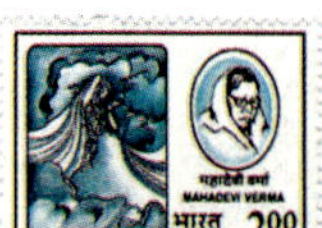

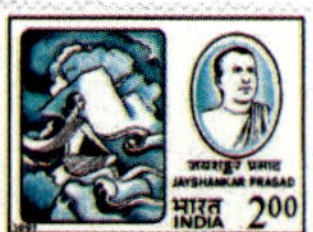

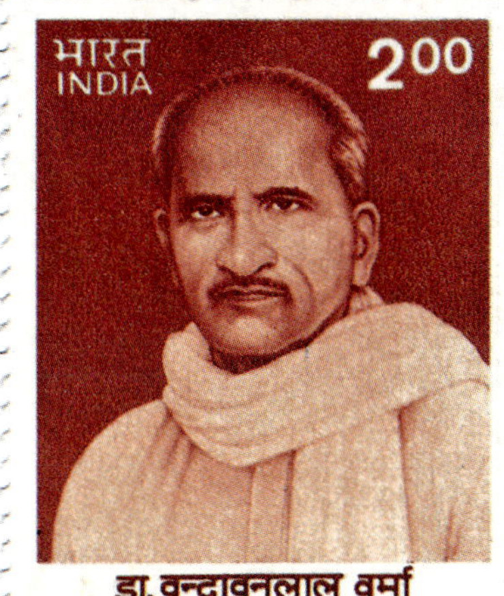

20.17: Vrindalal Verma, stamp from 1997 — Courtesy, Department of Post

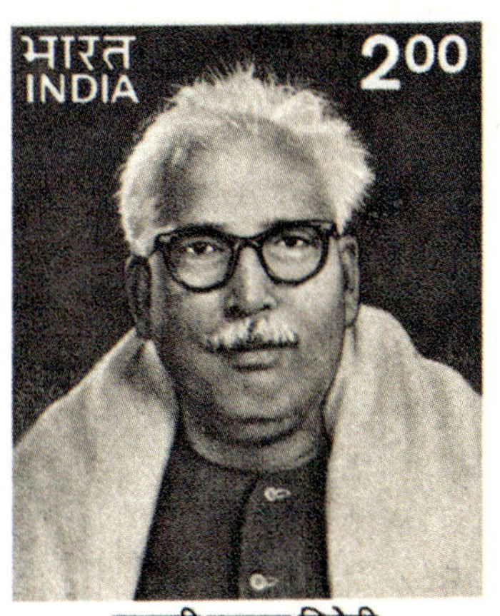

20.18: Hazari Prasad Dwivedi, stamp from 1997 — Courtesy, Department of Post

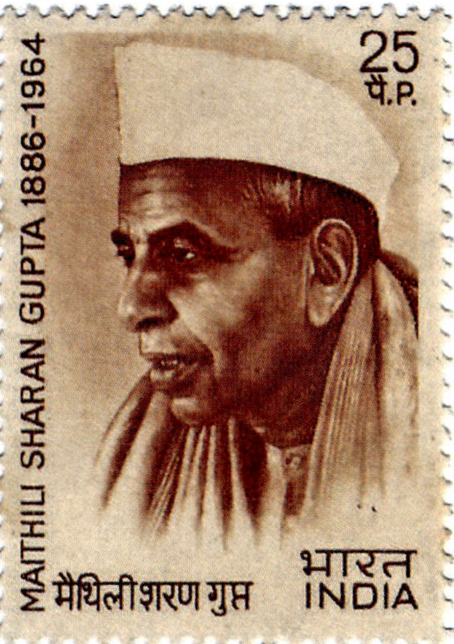

20.19: Maithili Sharan Gupta, 1974 postage stamp — Courtesy, Department of Post

The drama genre flourished too. *Skandagupta* (1928) *Chandragupta*, *Ajatashatru*, and *Dhruvswamini* (1933) were historical plays of **Jaishankar Prasad** (1889–1937) while *Janmejaya Ka Nag Yagya* was based on anecdotes of Mahabharata. **Bhisham Sahni**, **Mohan Rakesh** (1925–1972), **Naresh Mehta** (1922–2000) were some other eminent playwrights of this period.

Hindi poems witnessed a golden phase in the coming decades. *Chhayawaad,* a completely new genre of poems bloomed. **Maithili Sharan Gupta** (1886-1964; Padmabhushan awardee), the author of long narrative poems *Bharat Bharati, Yashodhara*, *Saket, Jayadrath Vadh* and *Panchavati*; **Jaishankar Prasad** (1889-1937;), author of *Kamayani*; **Suryakant Tripathi 'Nirala'** (1896-1961), author of *Ram Ki Shakti Puja, Parimal*; **Mahadevi Verma** (1907-1987, Jnanpith and Padma Vibhushan awardee), author of *Nihar*, *Neerja, Sandhya Geet, Sandhini* were considered the four pillars of the *chhayawaad* movement (the genre of romanticism).

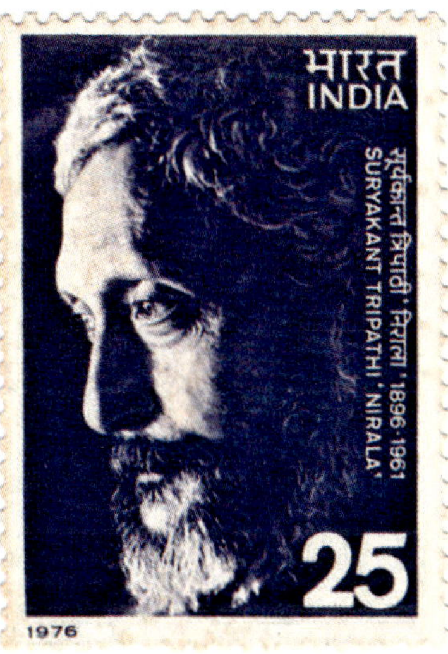

20.20: Suryakant Tripathi 'Nirala', a modernist and chhayawadi poet; 1976 postage stamp — Courtesy, Department of Post

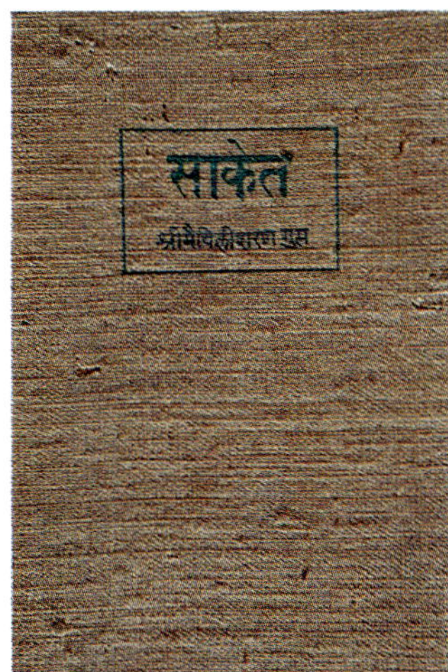

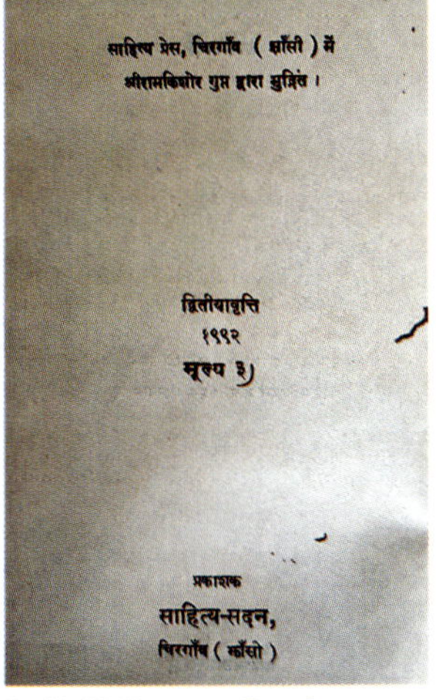

साहित्य प्रेस, चिरगाँव (झाँसी) में
श्रीरामकिशोर गुप्त द्वारा मुद्रित ।

द्वितीयावृत्ति
१९९२
मूल्य ३)

प्रकाशक
साहित्य-सदन,
चिरगाँव (झाँसी)

20.21 & 20.22: *Saket* by Maithili Sharan Gupta, 2nd edition from 1925 (*Vikram Samvat* 1992), private collection — photograph by Madhukar K Bhagat

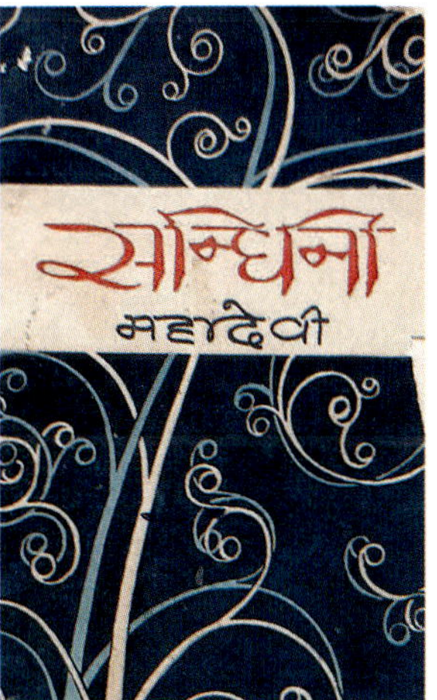

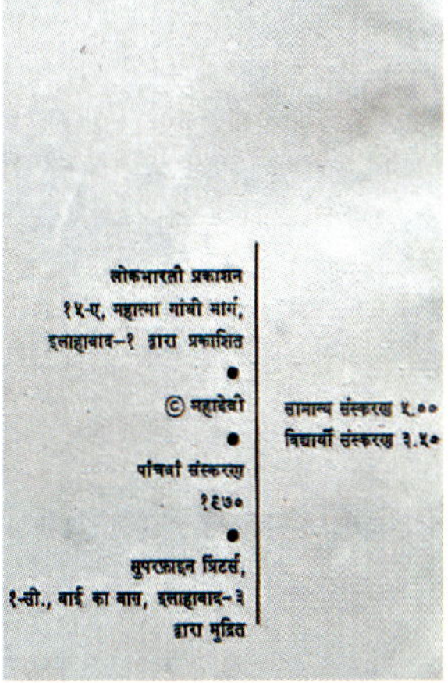

लोकभारती प्रकाशन
१५-ए, महात्मा गांधी मार्ग,
इलाहाबाद-१ द्वारा प्रकाशित

© महादेवी

पाँचवाँ संस्करण
१९७०

सुपरफाइन प्रिंटर्स,
१-सी., बाई का बाग, इलाहाबाद-३
द्वारा मुद्रित

सामान्य संस्करण ६.००
विद्यार्थी संस्करण ३.५०

20.23 & 20.24: *Sandhini*, a famous collection of poems by Mahadevi Verma, 5th edition from 1970; private collection — photograph by Madhukar K Bhagat

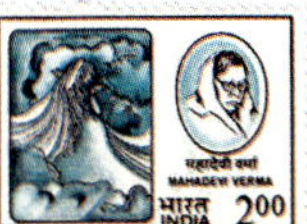

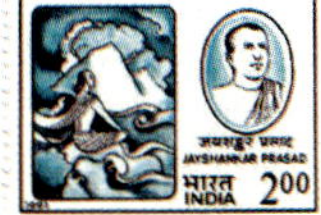

Iconic Lines of Mahadevi and Jaishankar Prasad

Amongst the various works of Mahadevi Verma and Jaishankar Prasad, *Yama* and *Kamayani* (respectively) are often quoted for their iconic lines.

मैं नीर भरी दु:ख की बदली! *(mai neer bhari dukh ki badli)* is the opening line of her poem from the compilation *Yama*, where the poetess recounts her sorrows. Last verse of the poem which expresses her solitude and melancholy are as below:

विस्तृत नभ का कोई कोना, मेरा न कभी अपना होना, परिचय इतना इतिहास यही उमड़ी कल थी मिट आज चली! मैं नीर भरी दुख की बदली	*Not any corner of the vast expanse of the sky, is ever going to be mine, This is my introduction and my history, I welled up yesterday and today I am gone. I am a tear-soaked cloud of sorrow.*

The opening verses of *Kamayani* by Jaishankar Prasad describe the concern of Manu who faces the torrent on the day of cataclysm.

हिमगिरि के उत्तुंग शिखर पर, बैठ शिला की शीतल छाँह एक पुरुष, भीगे नयनों से देख रहा था प्रलय प्रवाह।	*On the highest peak of Himgiri, Seated on the cool shelter of a big boulder, A person with drenched eyes, Was witnessing the flow of torrent on the day of cataclysm.*
नीचे जल था ऊपर हिम था, एक तरल था एक सघन, एक तत्व की ही प्रधानता कहो उसे जड़ या चेतन।	*There was water below and ice above, One fluid and one hard and solid, It was the expression of the same element, Be it called static (sterile and unyielding) or dynamic (flowing and life giving)*

(English translations by author)

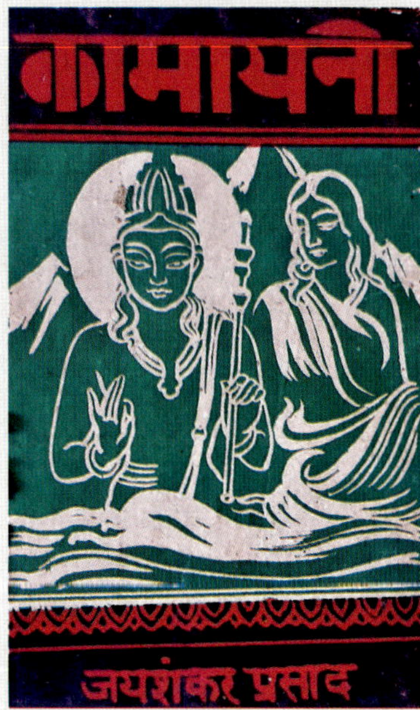

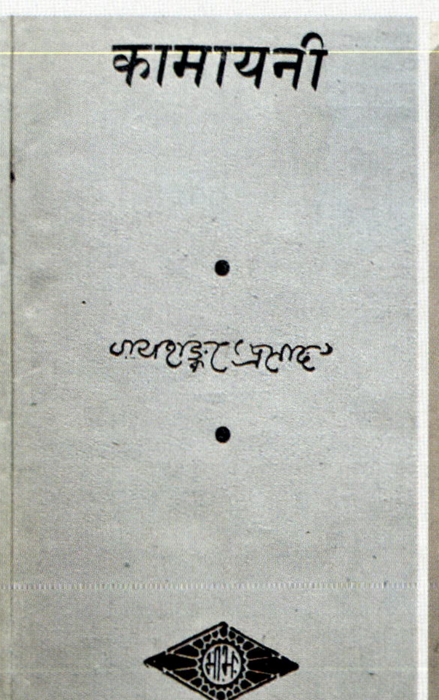

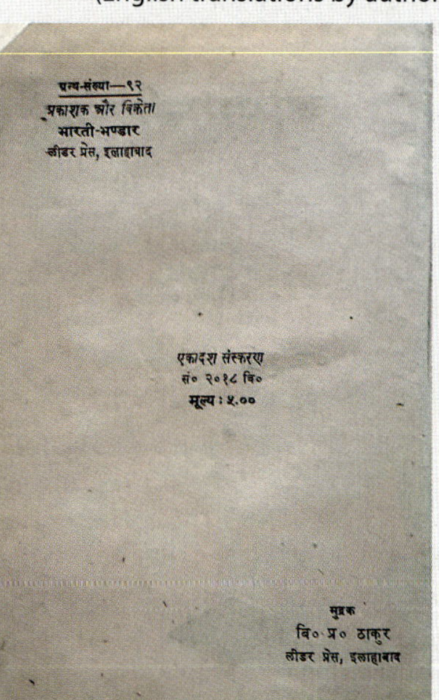

ग्रन्थ-संख्या—९२
प्रकाशक और विक्रेता
भारती-भण्डार
लीडर प्रेस, इलाहाबाद

एकादश संस्करण
सं० २०१८ वि०
मूल्य : ५.००

मुद्रक
वि० प्र० ठाकुर
लीडर प्रेस, इलाहाबाद

20.25, 20.26 & 20.27: *Kamayani* by Jaishankar Prasad, 11th edition from 1961 (*Vikram Samvat* 2018), private collection — photograph by Madhukar K Bhagat

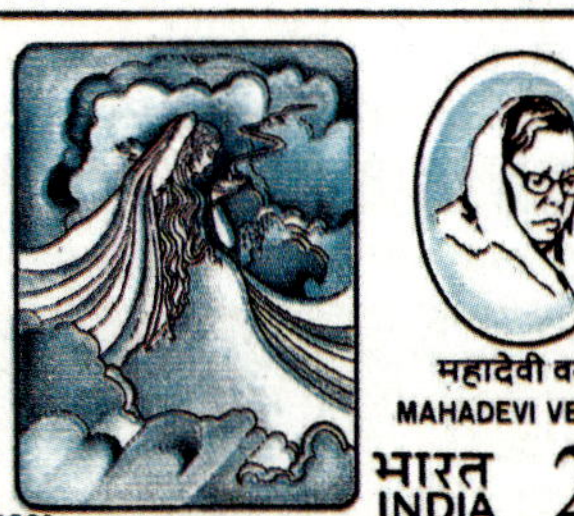

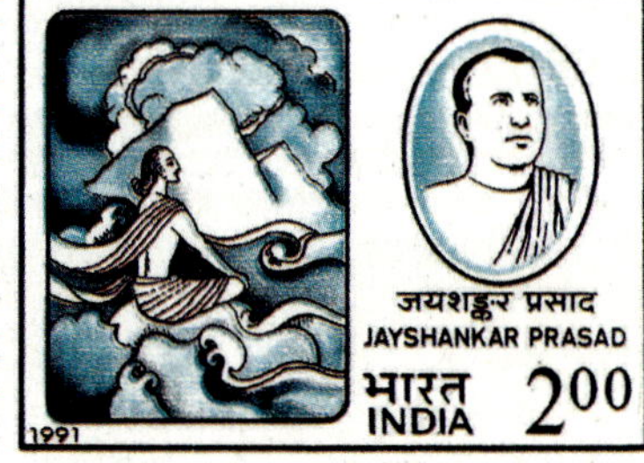

20.28: Mahadevi Verma and Jaishankar Prasad, pillars of chhayawad; postage stamps of 1991; symbolising the iconic lines from their poems — Courtesy, Department of Post

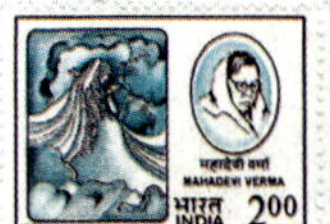

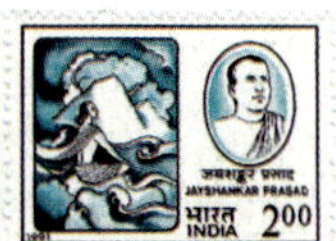

Nirala was also considered a modernist and literary innovator for unshackling poetry from the bonds of metre and fixed length of verses. Sumitranandan Pant, another great poet of this period, wrote on nature and was also considered an innovator. **Ayodhya Singh Upadhyaya 'Hariaudh'** (1865-1947) was one of the earliest eminent poets of modern Hindi whose work *Priyaprawas* (approximate publication period 1909-1913) is considered the first epic poem of *Khadi Boli*. His other prominent works include *Parijat* (1937), *Vaidehi Vanvas* (1940), *Rasa Kalash* (1940) and others. His literature helped modern Hindi inculcate the trend of Sanskrit derived Hindi words (*tatsam shabd*) as opposed to the then in vogue Persian and Urdu based words. **Makhanlal Chaturvedi** (1889-1968); Sahitya Akademi and Padma Bhushan awardee), author of *Him-Tarangini* and *Yug-Charan* is immortalized in his work *Pushp ki Abhilasha*. **Subadhra Kumari Chauhan** (1904-1948) inspired valour and nationalism with her poems like *Rani ki Jhansi* and *Veeron ka kaisa ho vasant*. Some of her other works like *Khilaone wala* and *Yeh kadamb ke ped* were contrastingly of the genre of children's poem.

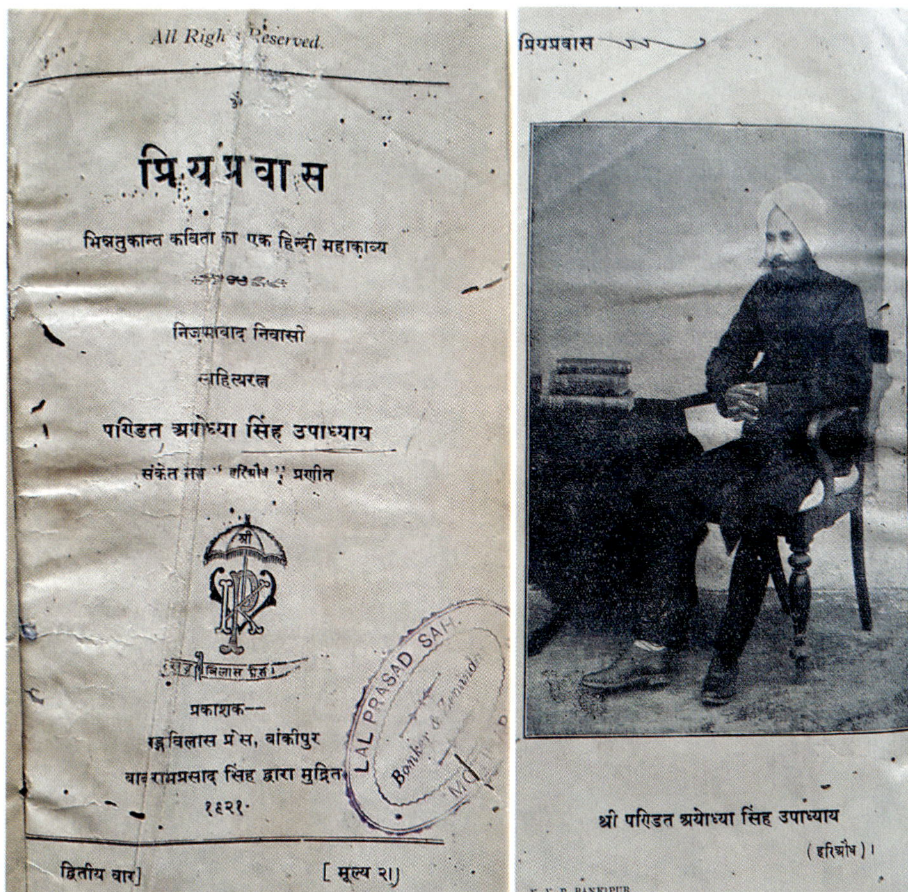
All Rights Reserved.

प्रियप्रवास

भिन्नतुकान्त कविता का एक हिन्दी महाकाव्य

निज़ामाबाद निवासी

साहित्यरत्न

पण्डित अयोध्या सिंह उपाध्याय

संकेत नाम "हरिऔध" प्रणीत

प्रकाशक—

खड्गविलास प्रेस, बांकीपुर

बाबू रामप्रसाद सिंह द्वारा मुद्रित

१९२१

द्वितीय बार] [मूल्य २)

20.29 & 20.30: *Priyaprawas*, an epic poem by Ayodhya Singh Upadhyaya 'Harioudh', and his photo published in the 2nd edition of the book in 1921, private collection — photograph by Madhukar K Bhagat

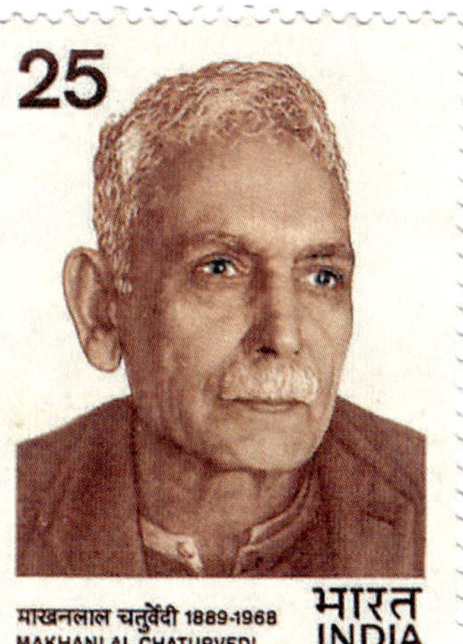

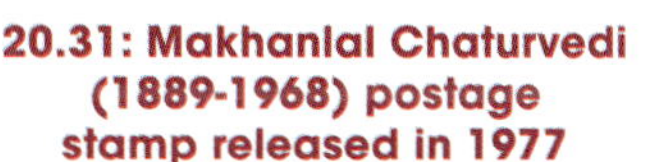

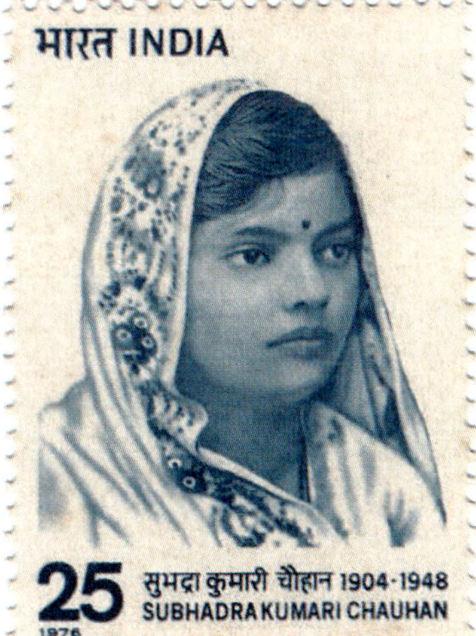

20.31: Makhanlal Chaturvedi (1889-1968) postage stamp released in 1977 — Courtesy, Department of Post

20.32: Subhadra Kumari Chauhan (1904-1948) postage stamp of 1976 — Courtesy, Department of Post

Ramdhari Singh Dinkar (1908-1974; Sahitya Akademi, Jnanpith and Padma Bhushan awardee) was the author of epic poems like *Kurukshetra*, and *Rashmi-Rathi* besides other seminal works like *Urvashi*, *Hunkar*, *Dilli*, *Parshuram ki Pratiksha* amongst many others. His poems, imbued with a sense of national consciousness and undertones of valour and action, served as an inspiration to the youth. **Harivansh Rai Bachchan** (1907-2003; Padma Bhushan, Sahitya Akademi awardee) was

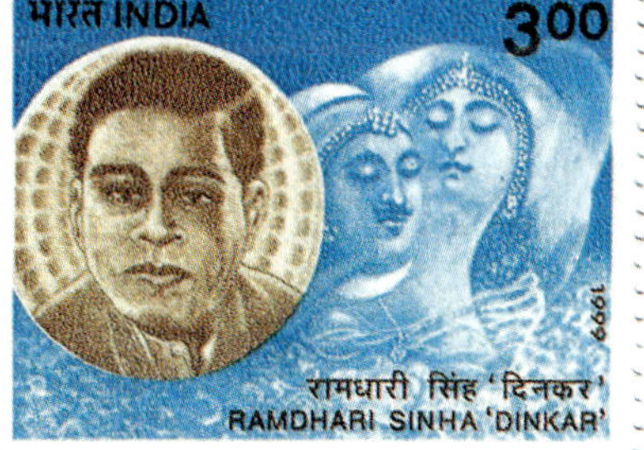

20.33: Ramdhari Singh Dinkar, an eminent poet who composed epic poems; postage stamp of 1999 — Courtesy, Department of Post

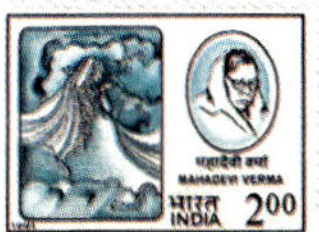

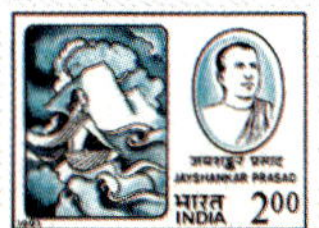

a part of the *Nayi Kavita* literary movement. His most famous work *Madhushala* (1935) is a work of the Chhayavaad genre reflecting shades of vedantic philosophy and Sufi traditions. **Nagarjun** (1911-1998; Sahitya Akademi awardee) was another eminent poet often referred to as the *Jankavi* (people's poet).

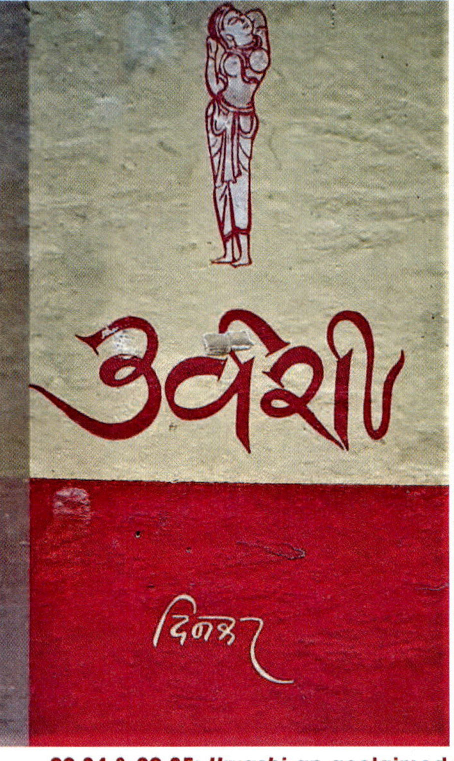

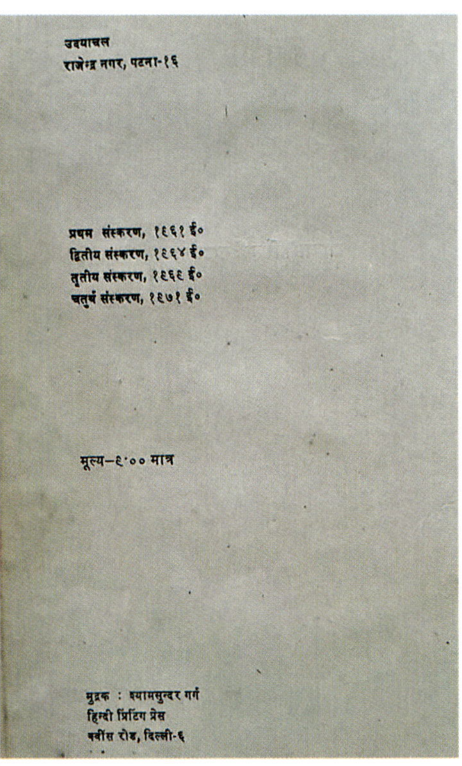
उदयाचल
राजेन्द्र नगर, पटना-१६

प्रथम संस्करण, १९६१ ई०
द्वितीय संस्करण, १९६४ ई०
तृतीय संस्करण, १९६९ ई०
चतुर्थ संस्करण, १९७१ ई०

मूल्य—९·०० मात्र

मुद्रक : श्यामसुन्दर गर्ग
हिन्दी प्रिंटिंग प्रेस
क्वींस रोड, दिल्ली-६

20.34 & 20.35: *Urvashi*, an acclaimed long poem by Ramdhari Singh Dinkar, 4th edition from 1971; private collection — photograph by Madhukar K Bhagat

The domain of above litterateurs was not limited to poems alone, though they were undoubtedly among the most respected poets of this literary phase. Many also excelled in prose, viz. Nirala authored eight major novels and many other short story collections as well as essay collections. Mahadevi Verma authored works such as *Smriti ki Rekhanyen*, *Ateet ke Chalchitra* and eight other major works. Jaishankar Prasad, besides composing poetry and epic plays, also authored several short story collections such as *Aandhi*, *Pratidhwani*, *Akashdeep*, *Indrajal* etc. ***Bhartiya Sanskriti ke Char Adhyaya***, a voluminous prose by Ramdhari Singh Dinkar, is considered a path breaking work in the field of Indian cultural history. Makhanlal Chaturvedi was also recognised as an essayist, playwright and a journalist. Nagarjun had authored over 15 novels and nearly seven short story collections.

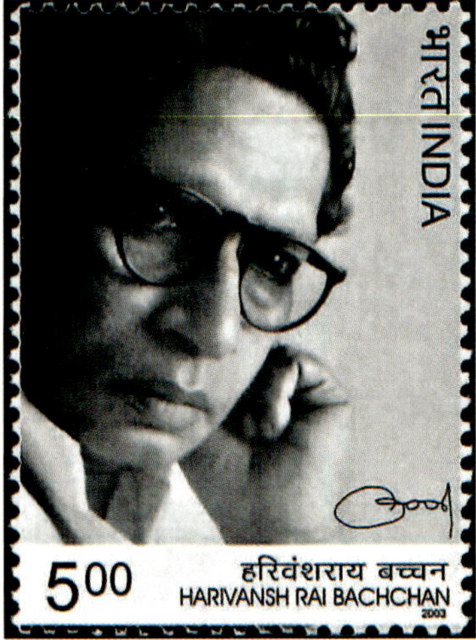

20.36: Harivansh Rai Bachchan, postage stamp of 2003 — Courtesy, Department of Post

Regional Literature of the 20th Century

The first half of the 20th century also saw the **regional literature** come of age. **Bangla literature** witnessed in this period the works of stalwarts such as **Rabindranath Tagore** and **Sarat Chandra Chattopadhyaya** (1876-1938), besides others. Rabindranath dominated the literary landscape with new hues emerging, particularly in his poetry. Sarat Chandra's works brought succinctly to light many of the social issues. His masterly novels have been adopted into nearly **50 movies** in different languages in the period of nearly a century and include landmark works such as *Bindur Chhele* (1914), *Parineeta (1916)*, *Devdas (1917)*, *Choritrahin (1917)*, *Bardidi*, *Shrikanta* and stories such as *Mej Didi*, *Swami*, amongst many others. **Kazi Nazrul Islam** *(1899-1976)* was one of the most eminent Bangla poets of the 20th century who was also known as the *virodhi kobi* (rebel poet). His large body of works includes several poems, novels, short stories, essays and nearly 2500 songs categorized as *Nazrul Giti.*

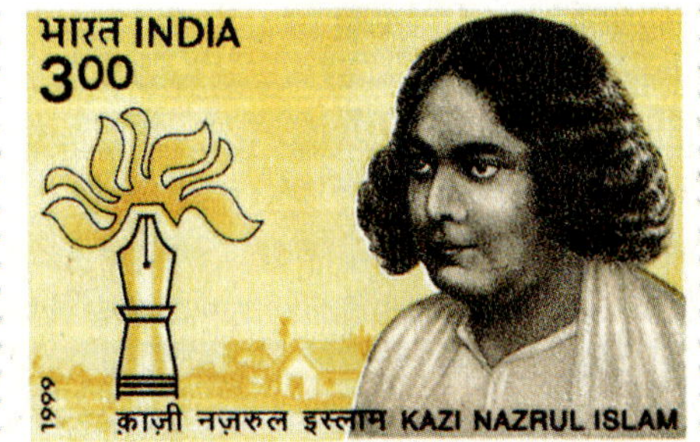

20.37: Kazi Nazrul Islam (1899-1976), postage stamp released in 1999 — Courtesy, Department of Post

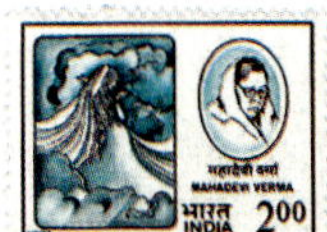

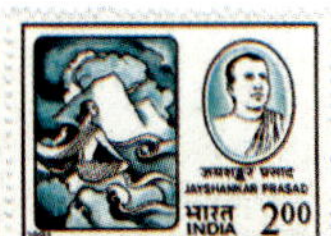

Tarashankar Bandyopadhyay (1898-1971, Padma Bhushan, Jnanpith and Sahitya Akademi Fellowship awardee, nominated twice for Nobel Prize for Literature) was a stalwart of Bengali literature who composed 65 novels, 53 story books and 12 plays besides other works. Among his prominent novels were; *Chaitali Ghurni* (1928), *Raj Kamal* (1935) *Dhatridebata* (1939), *Kalindi* (1940), *Kavi* (1944), *Ganadevata* (1943), *Panchagram* (1944), besides others. **Jibananda Das** (1899-1954; Sahitya Akademi awardee) was considered the most complete Bengali poet after Tagore, and popularly known as *Rupashi Banglar Kabi* (poet of beautiful Bengal). *Jhora Palak* (1927), *Dhushor Pandulipi* (1936) *Banalata Sen* (1942) *Mohaprithbi* (1944) were some of his early works. Besides many poems, he wrote 21 novels and 108 short stories, which were discovered only after his death. **Bibhutibhushan Bandyopadhyay** (1894-1950), author of *Pather Panchali*, *Aparajito* and others novels; **Manik Bandyopadhyay** author of *Putul Nachir Itikatha* and *Padma Nadir Majhi*, besides 38 novels and nearly 306 short stories, were other stalwarts of Bengali literature. **Bishnu Dey** (1909-1982 Sahitya Akademi and Jnanpith awardee) was a poet and academician who was associated with the new poetry movement of Bengal. His works were later a part of modernism and post modernism literary categories. Among his significant works are *Urvashi O Artemis* (1932), *Chora Bali* (1938), *Sandiper Char* (1947), *Smriti Satta Bhabishyat*.

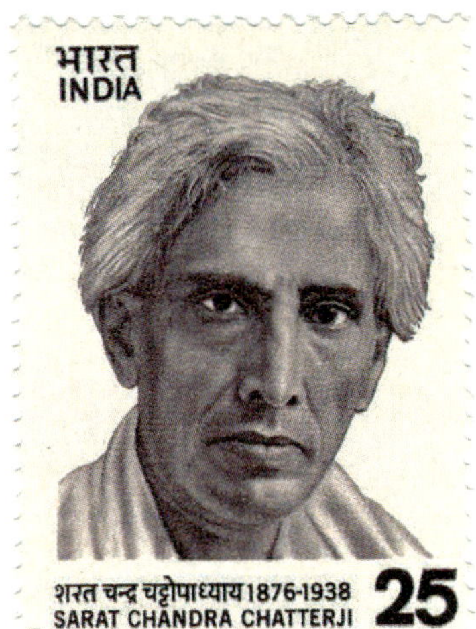

20.38: Sarat Chandra Chatterji, an eminent novelist whose works inspired many movies in different languages; (1876-1938), postage stamp released on birth centenary in 1976 — Courtesy, Department of Post

Shivram Mahadev Paranjape (1864-1929) was one of the early writers of modern **Marathi literature** who was also a journalist and freedom fighter. **Vishnu Sakharam Khandekar** (1898 to 1976) (Padma Bhushan, Sahitya Akademi Fellowship & Jnanapith awardee) is considered a doyen of Marathi literature. *Kraunchwadha, Ulka, Yayati* are some of his notable works, with the latter being considered a masterpiece of social realism, The Marathi literature also saw the emergence of *Ravikiran Mandal*, a group of eight poets engaged in socially relevant aesthetic oriented poetry, which brought the Marathi poetry to fame. **B. S. Mardhekar** (1909-1956), an eminent poet and novelist, and a part of the *Ravikiran Mandal* group is credited with bringing a substantial shift in the perception of Marathi poetry. His eminent works include; *Shishiragam*, *Kahi Kavita*, *Aankhin Kahi Kavita* (poems) and *Raatricha Divas*, *Tambdi Maati* and *Paani* (novels).

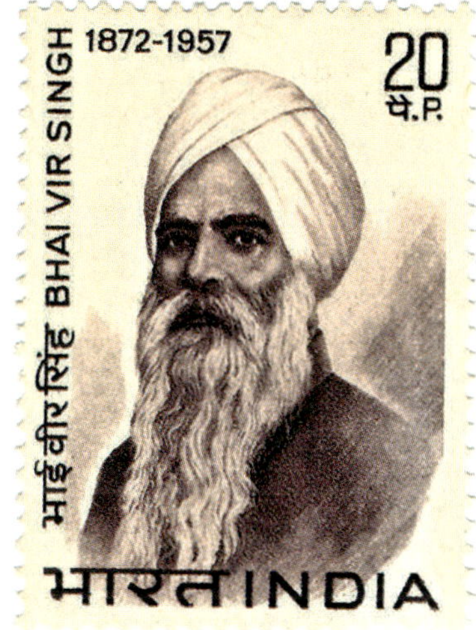

20.39: Bhai Veer Singh, eminent Punjabi poet, a stamp released in 1972 — Courtesy, Department of Post

Gujarati literature saw the emergence **of Uma Shankar Joshi** (1911-1981) (Sahitya Akademi & Jnapith awardee), a famous poet and novelist whose works saw a reflection of the Gandhian philosophy and the genre of realism. Some of his prominent works were *Nishith*, *Gangotri*, *Vishwashanti*, *Mahaprasthan*, besides others.

Punjabi literature flourished in the works of some eminent poets. **Bhai Vir Singh** (1872-1957 Padma Bhushan, Sahitya Akademi awardee) who is considered to have heralded modern Punjabi poetry composed *Rana Surat Singh* (1905), a long narrative poem in 13000 lines. His other significant works include *Sundari*, *Satwant Singh* (poem) and *Baba Naudh Singh* (a novel), besides other works. Other noteworthy Punjabi poets include, **Puran Singh** (1882-1932), who was also hailed as the Tagore of Punjab, **Kripa Singh** (1879-1939), who was known for his romantic poetries and **Mohan Singh** (1905-1978; Sahitya Akademi awardee), considered a pioneer in early Punjabi poetry. **Amrita Pritam** (1919-2005) was another budding poet and novelist of this phase of Punjabi literature.

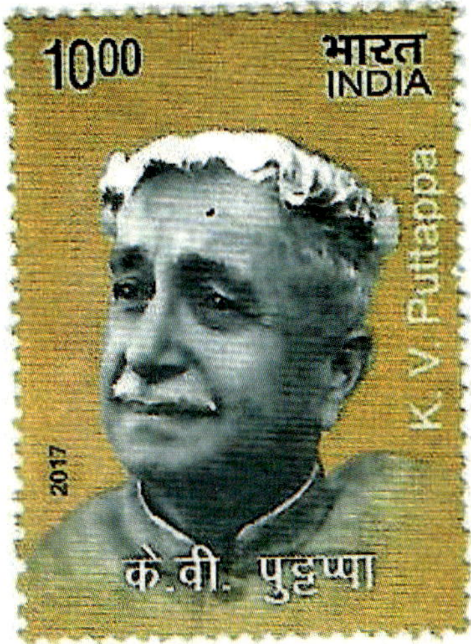

20.40: K.V. Puttappa, a renowned Kannada poet and novelist; a stamp from 1997 — Courtesy, Department of Post

In **Kannada** literature, **B.M. Srikanthaiah** (1884-1946) translated the *Kural* and *Silappattikaram*. **D.R. Bendre** (1896-1981) (Padma Shri and Jnanpith awardee), authored *Sakheegeeta*, *Kannada Meghadoota*, *Naaku Tanti*, besides many other works, and is considered one of the foremost

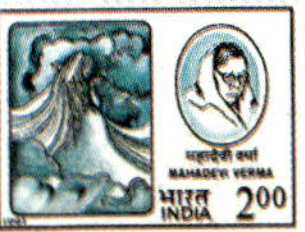

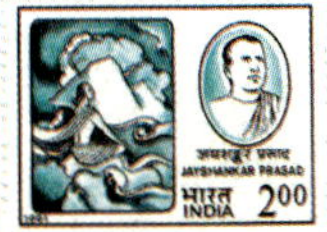

Kannada lyrical poet. **K.V. Puttappa** (1904-1994) (Padma Vibhushan and Jnanpith awardee), also known as **Kuvempu** was a renowned poet, novelist, and a playwright who authored *Sri Ramayana Darshanam* and *Chitrangada* which were epic poems. Recognised as the greatest of Kannada poets of the 20th century, he was a stalwart of the Navodaya movement of Kannada literature along with Bendre. **Gopalakrishna Adiga** (1918-1992) is credited with having pioneered a new style of Kannada poetry.

Subramania Bharati, considered the **father of modern Tamil literature** penned many poetic works including *Kannan Pattu* (1917; *Songs to Krishna*), *Panchali Sabatham* (1912; Panchali's Vow), and *Kuyil Pattu* (1912; *Kuyil's Song*).

Subramania Bharati: The Heralder of Modern Tamil Literature

Considered among the greats of Tamil literature, and even as the father of modern Tamil literature, Subramania Bharati and his works were instrumental in reviving modern Tamil literature and guiding it to greater heights. Below are excerpts written by Dr. K. R. Srinivasa Iyengar in ' Struggle from Freedom' (History and Culture of the Indian People , volume 11, published 1969)

Twentieth century Tamil literature could be described, not inaptly, the Age of Subramania Bharati. In ancient days Valmiki and Vyasa served human progress in Aryavarta; so too, says Rajaji (Rajagopalachari), "Bharati has served the Tamils in recent times by his writings". Bharati died in 1921, hardly forty years old, but already he had fulfilled his mission as incarnate Agastya, giving new life to the Tamil language and literature; although striving against tremendous odds, he had laid firmly the foundations of the Tamil renaissance that we have been witnessing during the last fifty years or more. Mother India and Mother Tamil were to him divine realities, not figurative abstractions; and in their service he found his joy and realisation as a poet.

His 'Collected Poems' make a volume of over 600 pages, and comprise patriotic songs, devotional lyrics, prose poems, and the three 'major works Panchali Sabatam *('Draupadi"s Vow),* Kannan Pattu *('Krishna Songs), and* Kuyil Pattu.

Bharati was both an intrepid and original singer, and his poems may be said to have set the pace of the cultural and political regeneration of the Tamils. In Panchali Sabatam, *Bharati made Draupadi's predicament in the Kaurava court the symbol of enslaved Mother India's plight in the comity of nations. And, at another level, Draupadi and Mother India became the Great Creatrix, the Parasakti, herself. The poem was, thus, not only a modern version of the Mahabharata story, but also a mantra of redemption for the Tamils or an enunciation of the religion of patriotism. In* Kannan Pattu, *Krishna mingles in the life-ways of the poet, and becomes now friend, now servant, now mistress, now father, now ruler. He is everybody, and everything, and is intimately involved in the poet's everyday life.* Kuyil Pattu *is a fable that fascinatingly explores the nature of Love, while* Oozhi-k-koothu *(Dance of Doom) is the most terrifyingly evocative of Bharati's lyrics. Although much is lost in translation, here is a rendering of the last stanza of* Oozhi-k-koothu:

When Time and the three Worlds Have been cast in a ruinous heap,
When the frenzy has ceased and a lone splendour has awakened,
Then auspicious Siva appears, to quench your terrible thirst.
Now thou smilest and treadst with him, the blissful Dance of Life!
Mother, Mother, You've drawn me, to see thee dance

– Excerpts from *Struggle from Freedom* (History and Culture of the Indian People volume 11)

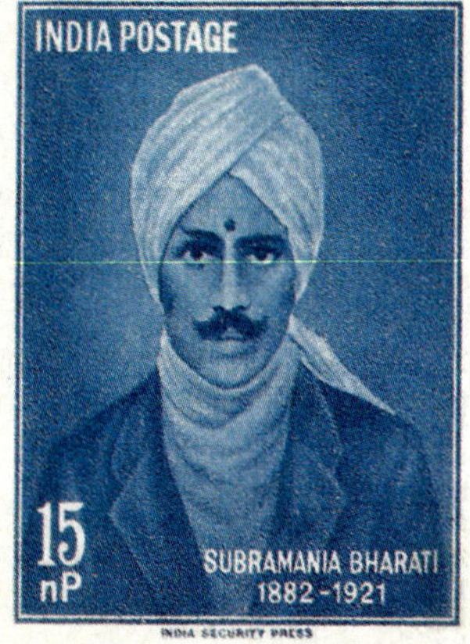

20.41: Subramania Bharati, considered as the father of modern Tamil literature; a stamp from 1960 — Courtesy, Department of Post

Malayalam literature witnessed the triumvirate of **Vallathol Narayana Menon** (1878-1958; Salient works: *Mahakavya Chitrayogam*, *Gangapati*, *Sahitya Manjari*), **Kumaran Asan** (1873-1924; salient works; *Veena Povu*, *Duravastha*, *Leela* and others) and **Ulloor S. Parameswara Iyer** (1877-1949; salient works; *Umakeralam*, *Karnabhushanam*, *Pingala*, *Kerala Sahitya Charitram*). **G. Sankara Kurup** (1901-1978; Padma Bhushan, Jnanpith and Sahitya Akademi awardee) was another great Malayalam poet, essayist and literary critique whose salient works include; *Sooryakanthi*, *Ithalukal*, *Odakkuzzhal* besides others. **S.K. Pottekkatt** (1913-1982; Sahitya Akademi and Jnanpith awardee) was a notable

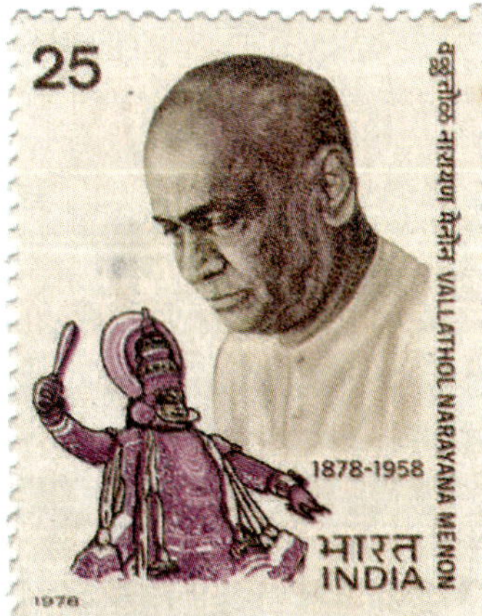

20.42: Vallathol Narayana Menon, one among the triumverate of greats of Malayalam literature;a stamp from 1978 — Courtesy, Department of Post

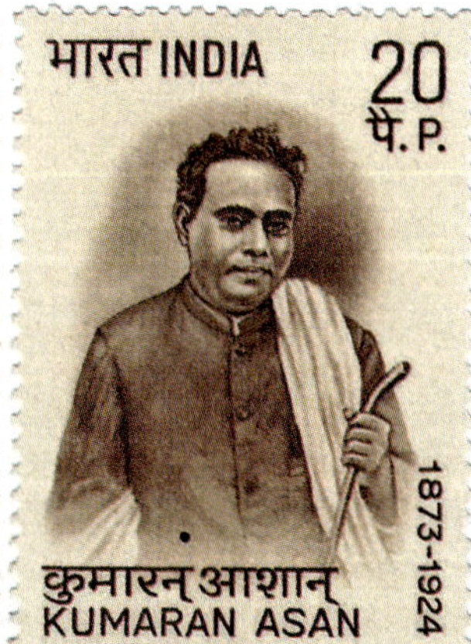

20.43: Kumaran Asan, another pillar of Malayalam literature; a stamp from 1973 — Courtesy, Department of Post

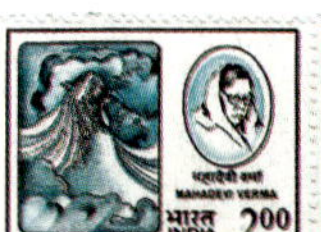

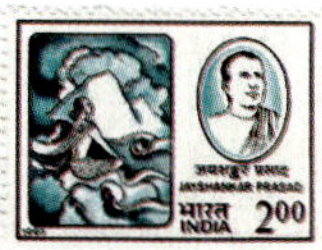

novelist, poet, short story and travelogue writer who authored nearly sixty books.

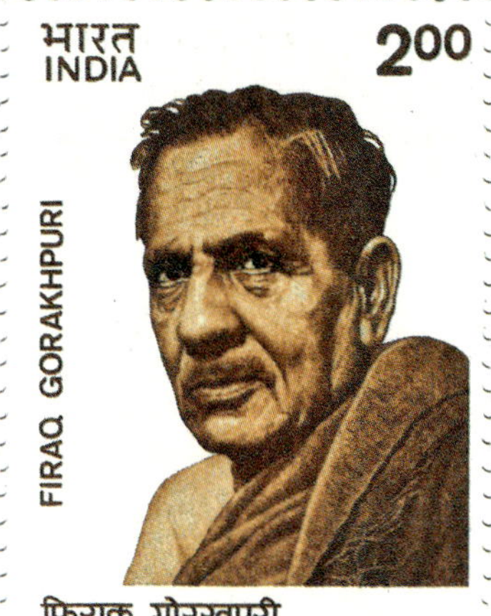

20.44: Firaq Gorakhpuri, an eminent Urdu poet, a stamp from 1977 — Courtesy, Department of Post

Urdu literature, especially poetry, flourished in this phase. Eminent poets like **Hasrat Mohani** (1875-1951), **Muhammad Iqbal**, (1877-1938) **Yagana Changezi** (1884-1956), **Jigar Moradabadi** (1890-1960), **Firaq Gorakhpuri** (1896-1982), **Josh Malihabadi** (1898-1992), **Faiz Ahmad Faiz** (1911-1984), **Sadaat Hasan Manto** (1912-1955) ushered a golden age of Urdu poetry. Besides, authors such as **Rashid Jahan** (1905-1952), **Ismat Chugtai** (1915-1991), and others, made notable contribution in novels, short stories and other forms of prose.

The genre of **English literature** saw the emergence of some renowned Indian authors who presented a completely different perspective with Indian background and milieu and brought international readership to Indian English literature. **Sarojini Naidu** (1879-1949) was an eminent English poet, besides being a nationalist, social reformist and an orator par excellence. Her first collection of poems was *The Golden Threshold* (1905) which was followed by the *Bird of Time* (1912), *The Broken Wing* (1917), besides several speeches and other writings.

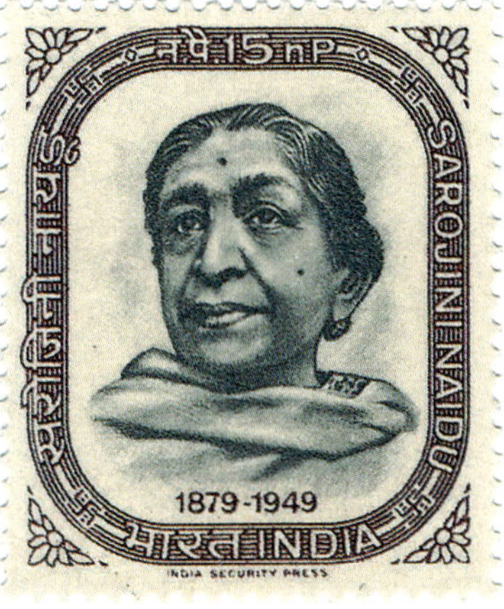

20.45: Sarojini Naidu, a stamp from1964 — Courtesy, Department of Post

Mulk Raj Anand (1905-2004, Padma Bhushan and Sahitya Akademi awardee) in his works *Untouchable* (1935), *Coolie* (1936) brought out challenges and suffering of those at the lower end of the caste hierarchy and economic echelons. The *Two Leaves and a Bud* (1937) *The Village* (1939), *Across the Black Waters* (1939), *The Sword and the Sickle* (1942) were some of his other seminal works.

R.K. Narayan (1906-2001 Padma Vibhushan, Sahitya Akademi Fellowship awardee) was another celebrated English author of this generation. In his book *Swami and Friends (1935),* Narayan creates a fictional town of Malgudi with ordinary characters and accounts of daily lives. In a career spanning over 60 years, he authored several significant works such as *the Bachelor of Arts (1937)*, *The Dark Room* (1938), *The Financial Expert (1952).* His most renowned acclaimed work is *The Guide* which was later made into a successful movie.

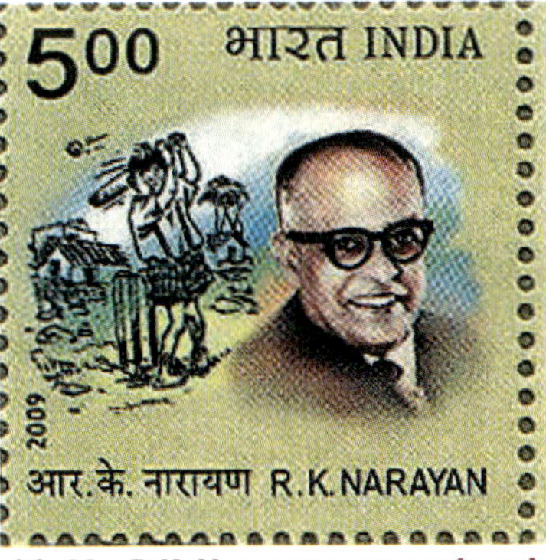

20.46: R.K. Narayan, an eminent English novelist; a stamp from 2009 — Courtesy, Department of Post

Raja Rao (1908-2006; Padma Vibhushan and Sahitya Akademi awardee) brought out the impact of Mahatma Gandhi's non-violent struggle against the British in his English novel *Kanthapura* (1938). Besides, his works had a deep influence of metaphysics. *Cow of the Barricades* (1947) was another of his other major works. **Ahmed Ali** (1910-1994), was another celebrated author of this period, who along with Raja Rao and Mulk Raj Anand, was a member of the *Progressive Writers Movement*. Though an author of Urdu, he also wrote in English with his major work being *Twilight in Delhi (1940).*

The Literary Movements and Genres in the 20th Century

The period of 20th century also ushered various literary movements and different genres. The socio-economic and political upheavals which the Indian society was undergoing, was truly reflected in Indian literature. In the next century of literary history, emerged different genres of writing ranging from reformistic to nationalistic, from spiritualism to *Chhayawad* from realism to progressive (*Pragativaad*) from post-independence experimentalism to post-modernism. While these changes were reflective of the evolving face of Indian literature and its response to the Indian society, they were not untouched by the movements in world literature and to an extent also assimilative of some of the trends of the latter. Given below are some of these literary movements.

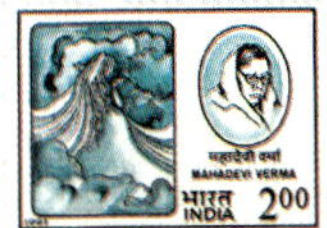

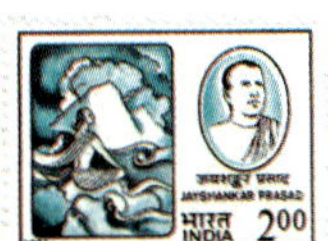

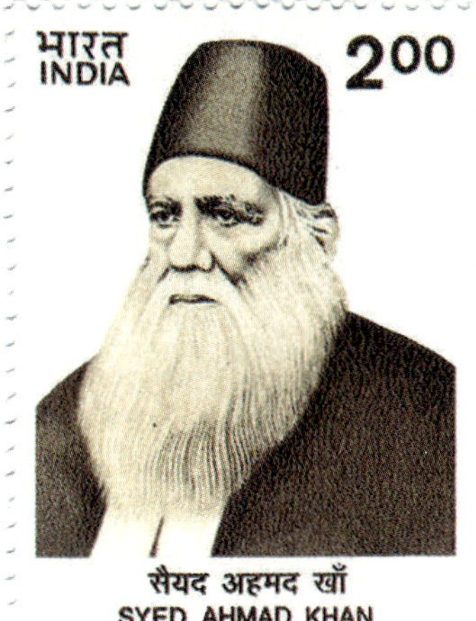

20.47: Syed Ahmad Khan, a reformer and educationst;postage stamp of 1998 — Courtesy, Department of Post

Reformism and Nationalism

Reform and revivalism was a social movement which India witnessed in the early 19th century and continued well into the 20th century. This also found a way in the literary expression of the society. **Raja Ram Mohun Roy**, one of the earliest reformist, was also an avid writer who expressed his views on Advaita, advocated a rationalist religion, and opposed evils like *sati* through his writings in the weekly newspaper *Samvad Kaumudi*. Similarly, publications and works such as *Rast Goftar* (founded 1854; Anglo-Gujarati paper) started by **Dadabhai Naoroji** for Parsi reforms, *Tehzeeb-ul- Akhlaq* (1871; Urdu), a journal published by **Sir Sayyid Ahmad Khan**, *Satyarth Prakash* (1875; Hindi) by **Swami Dayananda Saraswati**, *Shetkaryaha Asud* (1881 Marathi) by **Jyotirao Phule**, *Vivek Vardhini* (1881, Telugu; a journal for women's education), *Satihita Bodhini* (magazine on women's issues) by **Kandukuri Veeresalingam,** *High Caste Hindu Women* (1887) by **Pandita Ramabai** (a reformist) about the condition of Hindu women, were expressions of their thoughts in the realm of socio-religious reforms.

Besides these reformers who also made different publications an aid to their work, the social issues found a profound expression in the literary works of eminent authors of that time. These included, **Bankim Chandra Chatterjee** (*Bishabriksha*-novel, *Bangadarshan*-journal in Bengali), **Rabindranath Tagore** (*Chokher Bali*, *Ghaire Baire*; in Bengali) **Sarat Chandra** (*Shesh Prashno*-novel, *Narir Mulya*-essay; in Bengali) **Oyyarathu Chandu Menon** (*Indulekha* in Malayalam), **Hari Narayan Apte** (*Madhali Sthiti*, in Marathi), **Samuel Vedanayagam Pillai** (*Prathapa Mudaliar Charithram*, in Tamil), **Mulk Raj Anand** (*Untouchable, Coolie*; in English) and others.

Their writings were also instrumental in creating a **national consciousness**. Works like Bharatendu Harishchandra's *Bharat Durdasha* and *Andher Nagari* and *Durgesh Nandini* and *Anand Math* written by Bankim Chandra, were among the earliest of literary works of this category. *Poverty and Un-British rule in India* (1902) by **Dadabhai Naoroji,** which brings out the drain of Indian wealth by the British, *The Economic History of India* (Vol-1 in 1902; Vol-2 in 1904) by **Romesh Chunder Dutt**, which highlights the de-industrialization of the country in the British rule were the first works of its kind.

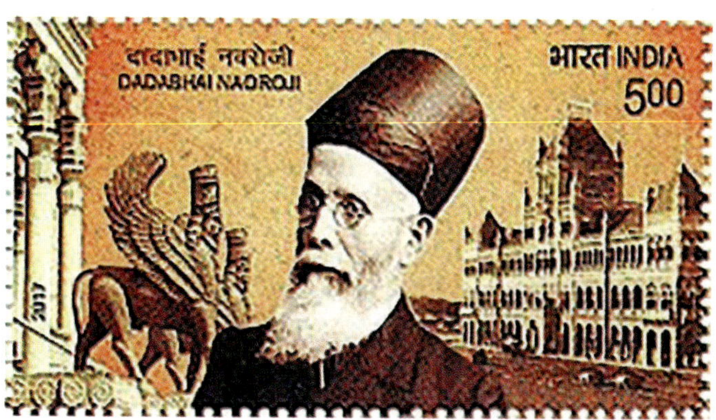

20.48: Dadabhai Naoroji, stamp from 2017 — Courtesy, Department of Post

Kesari (founded 1881, Marathi), *Mahratta* (founded 1881, English) by **Bal Gangadhar Tilak**, espousing the cause of Indian *swarajya* (self-rule), *Hitavada* (founded 1911, English) by **Gopal Krishna Gokhale,** were some important newspapers expressing the Indian nationalism. **Indian War of Independence** (1909, book)) by **V. D. Savarkar** christening the revolt of 1857 as a war of independence, was another significant work furthering Indian nationalism. *Sare Jahan se Accha*, a poem by **Iqbal** (part of *Taraneh Hindi* composed in Urdu in 1904) was like an anthem to people in opposition to the British Raj. His other patriotic works included *Tarane Milli*, *Himalaya* etc. *Pather Dabi* (1926), a novel by Sarat Chandra espoused the case of revolutionary radicalism and was even banned by the British.

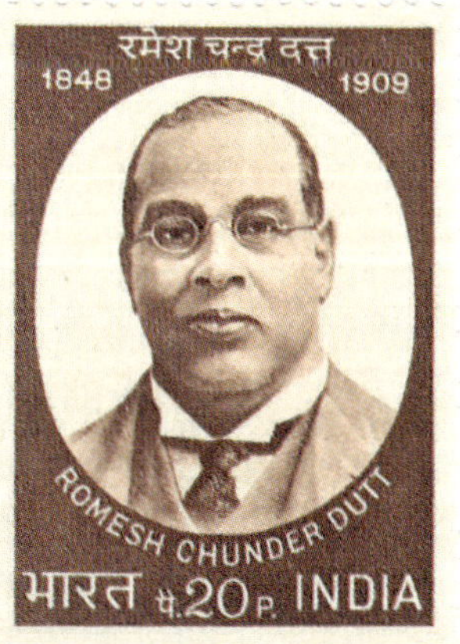

20.49: Romesh Chunder Dutt, a stamp from 1973 — Courtesy, Department of Post

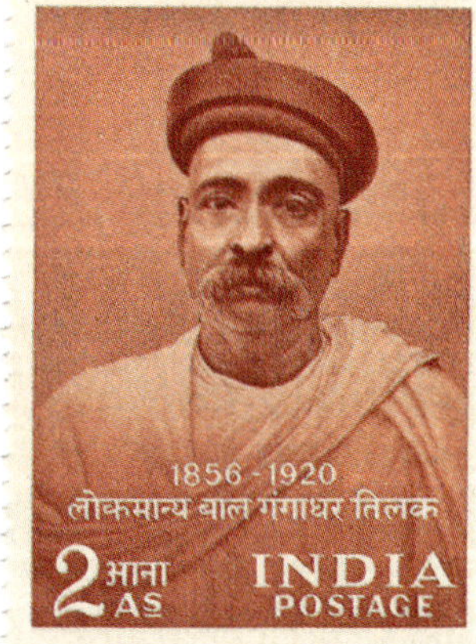

20.50: Bal Gangadhar Tilak, a stamp from 1956 — Courtesy, Department of Post

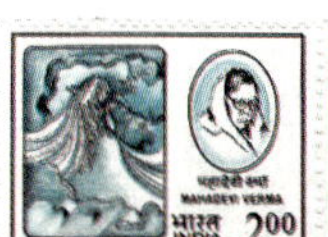

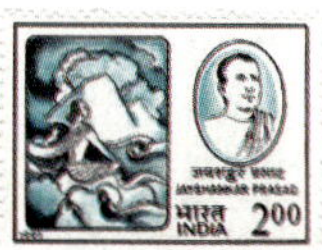

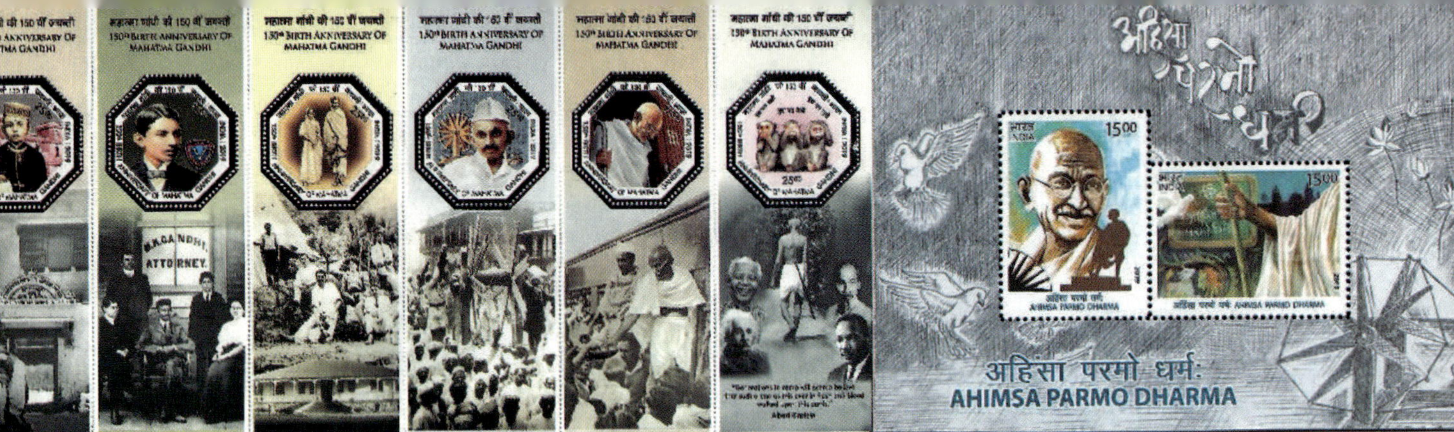

20.51 & 20.52: Commemorative stamp sheets issued on the occasion of the 150th birth anniversary of Mahatma Gandhi — Courtesy, Department of Post

In the voluminous works of **Mahatma Gandhi**, both the cause of social reforms and Indian nationalism were integrated, and found an enduring expression. He was a prolific writer, whose complete works ranged from autobiography and commentaries to books and articles and from essays to letters to the editors. These were compiled later by the Government of India in around 50000 pages. His works included his views on the social issues such as untouchability, status of women and education, as well as the unity of Hindus and Muslims. His book *Hind Swaraj*, or **Indian Home Rule** (first published 1909, banned by the British, revised by him later) is often considered a template for the Indian freedom struggle. He was also an editor of different newspapers and magazines, including the *Harijan* (in Gujarati, Hindi and English), *Young India* (in English), and *Navjeevan* (a Gujarati & Hindi monthly magazine). His last work, **India of My Dreams**, published on the day of India's independence, sets a blue-print for the socio-economic and political environment in an independent India. Besides, his ideals and deeds influenced a whole generation of Indian writers.

Besides the above, the works of **Lala Lajpat Rai** (*England's Debt to India*-1917), **Dr. Rajendra Prasad** (*Satyagraha in Champaran*-1922, *India Divided*-1946), **Jawaharlal Nehru** (*The Discovery of India*-1946 and other publications) and many other notable freedom fighters and writers were pertinent contributions in the genre of nationalism.

Spiritualism and philosophy

The literary evolution also encompassed spiritualism and philosophy. These were reflected in the works of Swami Vivekananda, Sri Aurobindo and Dr S. Radhakrishnan, besides others. Many of the works of **Tagore** even emphasised on humanism and universal values and touched upon the spiritual experience.

In **Vivekananda**, India found a reformist, a writer and an orator, who could converge the philosophies of the East with the rationalism of the West and integrate the social reforms with the spirit of nationalism. He ushered neo-Vedantism, unraveling the mysteries of the Vedas to the modern world. His works such as *Lectures from Colombo to Almora* (1897) reflect his views on the Vedantic philosophy and bring out as to how the principles of Vedanta can be applied in day-to-day life. His other works brought during his life time include; *Sangeet Kalpataru* (1887), *Karma Yoga* (1896), *Raja Yoga* (1896), *Vedanta Philosophy: An address before the Graduate Philosophical Society* (1896), *Bartaman Bharat* (in Bengali) (March 1899), *My Master* (1901). Besides, several others of his works were compiled after his life.

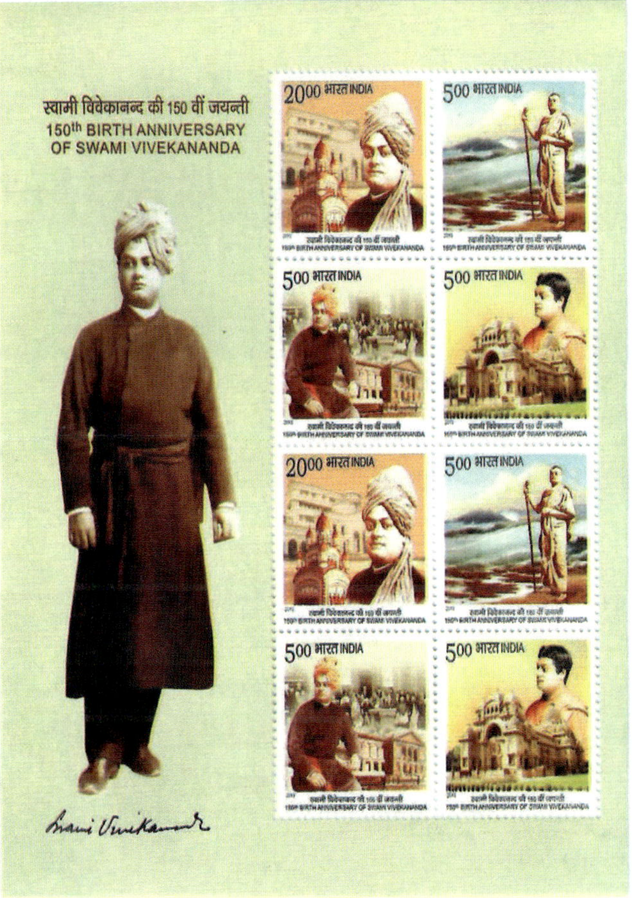

20.53: Stamps released on the occasion of the 150th birth anniversary of Swami Vivekananda — Courtesy, Department of Post

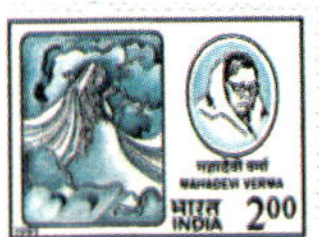

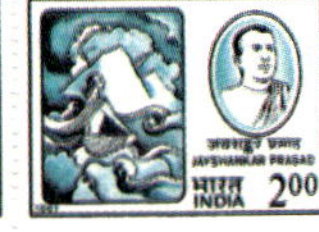

The works of **Aurobindo**, *Life Divine* (a collection of essays) and *Synthesis of Yoga*, reflect his conception of Yoga. Besides, the other significant works of this genre in his complete works (which were later compiled in a mammoth 36 volumes) include, *The Secrets of Veda*, *Vedic and Philological Studies*, *Essays on the Gita*, *The Renaissance of India with a Defence of Indian Culture*, amongst others.

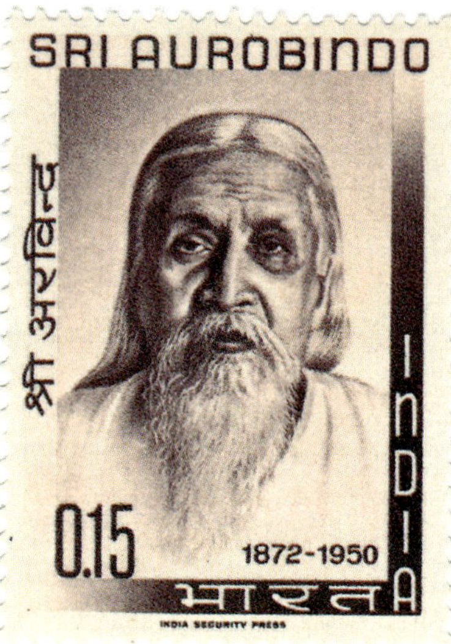

20.54: Sri Aurobindo, a stamp from 1964 — Courtesy, Department of Post

Dr S. Radhakrishnan was another prolific author of this genre, a great scholar of the comparative religion and philosophy, among the few who expounded neo-Vedantism (Vedanta in modern day context), besides being a great defender of the Hinduism and Indian philosophy. His publications, *Indian Philosophy* (two volumes 1923 and 1927) and *The Hindu View of Life* (1927) are momentous works of this field. Amongst his other prominent publications are; *The Philosophy of the Upanishads* (1924), *An Idealist View of Life* (1929), *Gautama-The Buddha* (1938), *Eastern Religions and Western Thoughts* (1939), *The Bhagavad Gita* (1948), *The Dhammapada* (1950), *The Principal Upanishads* (1953), *The East and West: Some Reflections* (1955), besides many others.

Among other works in the category of spiritualism, and philosophy were; *Srimad Bhagavad Gita Rahasya* (1915-Marathi), also known as *Gita Rahasya* or *Karmayog Shastra*, authored by **Bal Gangadhar Tilak** which expounds the theory of *nishkama karma; The Religion of Man* (1931), a compilation of lectures of **Rabindranath Tagore** and dealing with the themes of God, divine experience and humanity; *Gita-Mata* by **Mahatma Gandhi** which elucidated his interpretation of the Yoga philosophy; *Vedanta Philosophy* (1901) by **Abhedananda** (a direct disciple of Ramakrishna Paramhansa), *Talks on Gita* by **Vinoba Bhave;** *Five Hymns to Arunachala* (1914) and *Nan Yaar* (Who am I) (1923) by **Ramana Maharshi;** *Brahmacharya Sadhana* and *Yogi Guru*, by **Niranjananda Paramahamsa;** *Autobiography of a Yogi* (1946) by **Paramahamsa Yogananda,** *Bharat Shakti* by **Shuddhanand Bharati**, besides others.

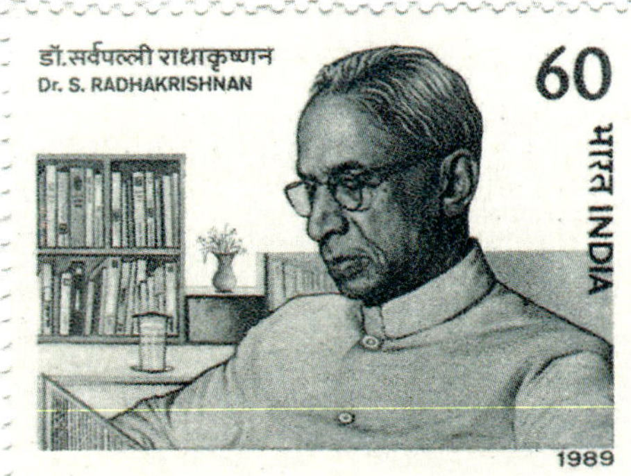

20.55: Dr S. Radhakrishnan, whose works contributed richly to the cause of Indian philosophy; a stamp from 1989 — Courtesy, Department of Post

Chhayavad literature

A new genre of Hindi poetry called *Chhayavad* emerged in the period between 1920s and 1930s with stalwarts like **Nirala, Jaishankar Prasad, Mahadevi Verma** and **Sumitranandan Pant,** besides others. It was characterised by humanism, love for nature and an expression of the innate feelings of the individual, and with the context of the words and expressions often being allegorical. Conformation to the *alankars*, viz. the stricter use of metre and rhyme was another of its traits. This was also considered to be neo-romanticsm genre of poetry. However, unlike the romanticism of the western poetry which tended to break free from the orthodoxy and the puritanical shackles of past, the *chhayawad* genre of poems were imbued in **romantic mysticism**.

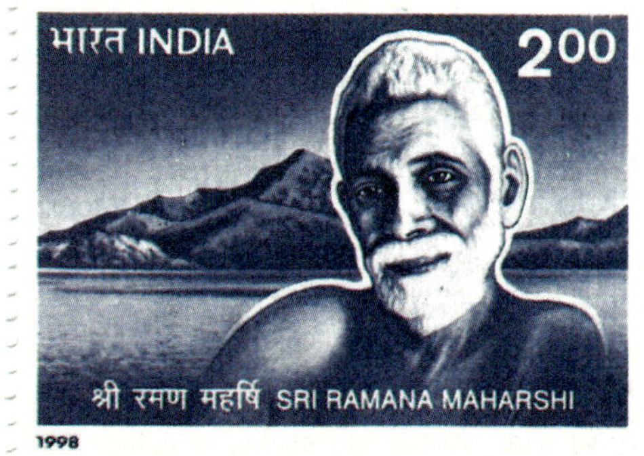

20.56: Sri Ramana Maharshi, a stamp from 1998 — Courtesy, Department of Post

Although primarily a genre in Hindi literature, some of the poetic movements of other regional languages also had similar features. These included *Navodaya* (new dawn/ rising sun) in **Kannada-** a form of renaissance poetry and literature; *Sabuj Juga* (the age of green) in **Odiya-**a style of romanticism, and *Ravikiran Mandal* - a group of eight poets in Marathi who emphasized on poetry for common masses.

Traits of this genre could also be seen in some of the works of; **Kumaran Asan** (*Veena Povu*: 1907; a philosophical and allegorical work in Malayalam) and **V.N Menon** (in Malayalam), **K.V. Puttappa** (also known as Kuvempu), **B.M. Srikanthaiah** and **D.R. Bendre** (in Kannada), **Vinayaka Krishna Gokak** (Kannada), **Viswanatha Satyanarayana** (in Telugu), **Kalindi Charan Panigrahi** (*Jadu Ghara*, *Puri Mandira*, *Mahadipa* in Oriya), and **Umashankar Joshi** (*Vishwashanti*, *Gangotri*, in Gujarati).

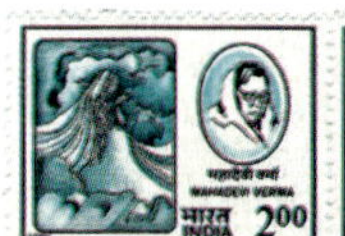
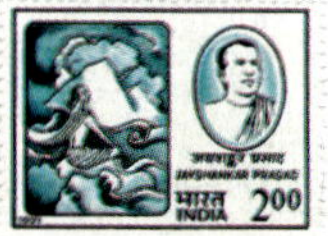

Realism in literature

Post *Chhayavad*, Indian literature acquired a new hue in the form of Realism. This meant depicting the life of the common people as opposed to the heroes and nobility, and bringing out the flaws and fallacies of their character rather than portraying them as ideal. The socio-economic environment and its hardships, the joys and sorrows of the commoners, and the turbulences and transitions occurring in the society, all were a part of it. The movement also brought out the social and moral issues plaguing the generation. Like the world literature which moved from the era of romanticism and idealism towards realism, Indian literature too witnessed this movement.

Although some elements of realism could also be seen in the 19th century in the works of Bharatendu Harishchandra, Bankim Chandra (*Anandmath*) and Tagore (*Ghare Baire*), it was in the 1920s and later, that this movement found strong moorings in the works of the likes of **Premchand** (Hindi), **Sarat Chandra Chatterjee** (Bengali) and others. ***Godaan*** (1936) by **Munshi Premchand** succinctly portrays the harsh realities of the then rural and social life. So do his other stories and novels such as; *Seva Sadan* (1919) - a story of a housewife turned courtesan who later manages an orphanage, *Ranga Bhoomi* (1924) - a story of a blind beggar, *Nirmala* (1925) highlighting the subject of dowry system, *Pratigya* (1927); dwelling on the subject of widow remarriage, *Gaban* (1931)-which brings out the middle-class compulsions and greed. All of these works make the ordinary characters of day-to-day life come alive. Similarly, the works of **Sarat Chandra** such as *Parineeta (1914), Debdas (1917)*, *Choritraheen (1917)*, are strong depiction of tales of common people and portrayal of man-woman relationships. His characters were realistic with their own imperfections and were caught in the shackles of social orthodoxy of the times.

Among other Indian authors of this genre were; **Vishnu S. Khandekar**, whose work *Yayati* is considered a master-class in social realism; **Bibutibhushan Bandyopadhyay** whose works (*Pather Panchali*-1929 & *Aparjito*) were later made into movies by Satyajit Ray. Other works of Bandyopadhyay include *Kanchan Mriga* (1931), *Ulka* (1934), and others. *Putul Nachir Itikatha* (1935, in Bengali) and *Padma Nadir Majhi* (1936, in Bengali) by **Manik Bandyopadhyay,** which were later translated into several languages and made into films, are also considered seminal works in realism.

Many Indian English authors in this period were writers of literary realism and included; **Mulk Raj Anand** (*Untouchable*-1935, *Coolie*-1936, *Two Leaves and a Bud*, 1937) **R.K. Narayan** (*The Guide*, *Swami and Friends*, *Bachelor of Arts*, *The Financial Expert*), **Raja Rao** (*Kanthapura*-1938), **Ahmed Ali** (*Twilight in Delhi*-1940) beside others.

Progressive literature

The next milestone of Indian literature was the growth of progressive literature in the pre-independence phase of the country. The influence of Marxism was felt in the society owing to the rise and success of the U.S.S.R. But more significantly, the influence of Gandhism was profound on Indian literature at this point of time. Mahatma Gandhi's opposition to imperialism which was based on non-violence and principles of truth and his emphasis on social reforms within the country, found an echo in the works of the litterateurs of the generation. The plight of people and the turbulence in Indian society of the mid 1930s caught the imagination of the writers to usher a phase of social realism.

In 1935, a handful of expatriate authors including Mulk Raj Anand, Sajjad Zaheer and others, formed *The Indian Progressive Writers Association* in London. Subsequently, 'The Progressive Writers' Association, (Calcutta; 1936) and *The All India Writers' Association* (Lucknow; 1936) were founded. The movement spread into many Indian languages, including Hindi, Urdu, Punjabi, Malayalam, and Telugu and influenced literature all over the country, thus formally heralding a phase of Progressive literature. This complimented the growth of ***Pragativad*** in Hindi literature which replaced the tradition of *Chhayavad*. Progressive literature movement was influenced by and dwelled on the themes of anti-imperialism, Gandhism, left orientation, socialism, Marxism, injustices suffered by common people, backwardness of the society and ills plaguing it. As a literary genre, it drew substantially from the realism style of writing, incorporating the influence of concurrent occurrences, social and political philosophies of the times.

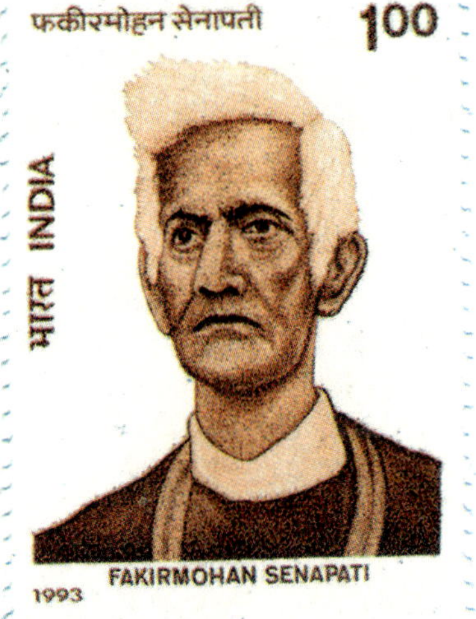

20.57: Fakir Mohan Senapati, an Odia poet, a stamp from 1993 — Courtesy, Department of Post

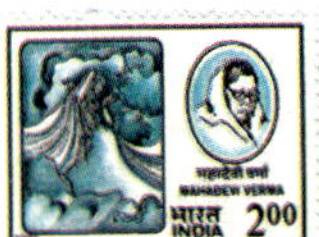

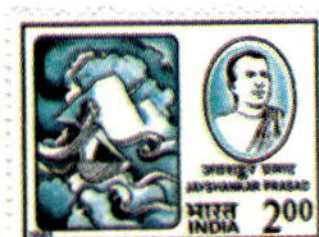

The later works of eminent authors like Premchand and Sarat Chandra reflected this trend. Another glorious example of this genre is found in the poems and novels of **Nagarjun** (Hindi) who earned the epithet of *Janakavi* (people's poet). This social realism was also seen in the works of regional literature like of **Samar Sen** (Bengali), **Fakir Mohan Senapati** (Oriya), **Vaikom Muhammad Basheer** (Malayalam), **T.S. Pillai** (Malayalam), **S.K. Pottekkatt** (Malayalam), **Shivaram Karanth** (Kannada), **Abdul Malik** (Assamese) and **Manik Mukhopadhyay** (Bengali), **Faiz Ahmed Faiz** (Urdu), **Ismat Chugtai** (Urdu) and **Amrita Pritam** (Punjabi). **Raja Rao, Ahmed Ali** and **Mulk Raj Anand** were some of the prominent English authors of this style.

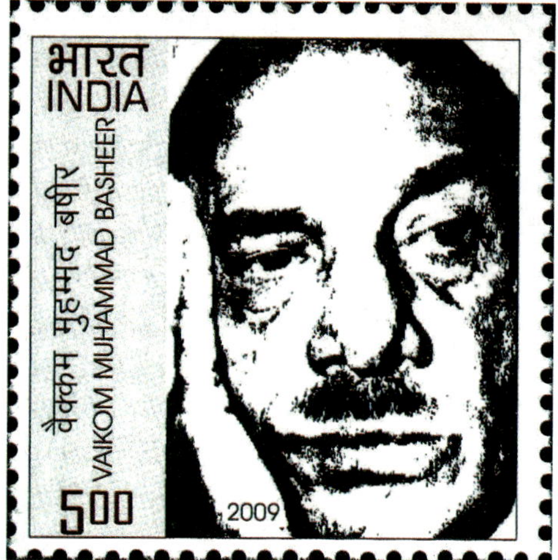

20.58: Vaikom Muhammad Basheer, an eminent Malayali litterateur; a stamp from 2009 — Courtesy, Department of Post

Literary Awards in India

In the post-independence India, a number of literary awards have been instituted with the objective of recognising and encouraging excellence in the field of literature. Some of these are awards bestowed by institutions of Central and State governments, while some are awarded by private foundations. A brief description of the prestigious literary awards of India is given here.

Sahitya Akademi award: Instituted in 1954, these awards are given annually by the **Sahitya Akademi of India** for the most outstanding books of literary merit published in any and each of the major Indian languages (during the last five years). The Sahitya Akademi confers these awards for 24 Indian languages including 22 of those in the Eighth Schedule of the Constitution as well as English and Rajasthani. The award consists of a cash award (Rs. 1 lakh and a citation plaque) and is the foremost literary honor in the respective Indian languages.

The Sahitya Akademi awards **Bhasha Samman** (since 1996) for significant literary contribution to languages and for the propagation, modernization or enrichment of the languages concerned (other than the 24 Indian languages). Besides, the Akademi also awards a prize for **translation** of critical and creative works in any of the 24 languages; a **Bal Sahitya Puraskar** (an award book for children), in the 24 languages since 2010, and also a **Yuva Puraskar** for the first book of young Indian authors (who are below the age of 35).

Sahitya Akademi has also instituted **Sahitya Akademi Fellowship** which is given to a select group of living writers (not more than 21 at any time) who are also considered as the immortals of Indian literature. **Dr. S. Radhakrishnan** was the first to be bestowed this award.

Some States have also instituted Sahitya Akademis and recognize the work in the regional languages by endowing annual awards which are referred to as the **State Sahitya Akademi Award**.

Jnanpith award: It is also considered among the most prestigious literary award which is conferred by Bharatiya Jnanpith since 1965. The award is given for most outstanding contribution towards literature for a work published by an author in the last 20 years (considered from the year of the award). Every year **only one** Jnanpith award (comprising cash prize of Rs. 11 lakh, a citation plaque, and a statue of Goddess Saraswati) is awarded to an Indian writer for writing in any of the Indian languages included in the Eighth Schedule to the Constitution and in English. **G Sankara Kurup** was the first to be awarded the prize for his work in Malayalam literature. The Bharatiya Jnanpith is a research and cultural institute founded in 1944 by Sahu Shanti Prasad Jain (an industrialist).

Moortidevi award: Instituted in 1983, this award is also granted by Bharatiya Jnanipth. It is awarded to Indian writers in any of the 22 scheduled languages, for a work which emphasises on **Indian culture** and **philosophy**.

Saraswati Samman: This is another prestigious award for contribution to **prose** or **poetry** in any of the 22 languages in the Eighth Schedule of the Constitution. Instituted in 1991 by the K.K. Birla foundation, it covers a cash award (of Rs. 15 lakhs), a citation, and a plaque. The first award was given to **Harivansh Rai Bachchan** for the four volumes of his autobiographical work.

Vyas Samman: It is another literary award instituted in 1991 by the K. K. Birla foundation given annually for a work in Hindi literature which has been published in the last 10 years. Ram Vilas Sharma was the first recipient of the award.

Post-Independence Literature: Different Genres & Phases of Literary Transition

Post-independence, Indian literature turned a new leaf. With the yoke of colonialism thrown off, the nationalism which was based on anti-imperialism was no more contextual. Thus, the earlier brand of nationalistic and progressive literature waned. This stage of Indian literature was deeply influenced by the new **hope of freedom**. But at the same time there remained the **pain of partition** and the anguish

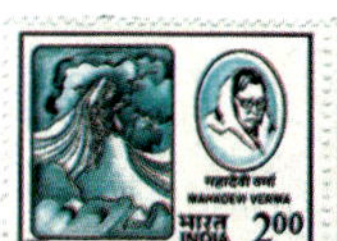

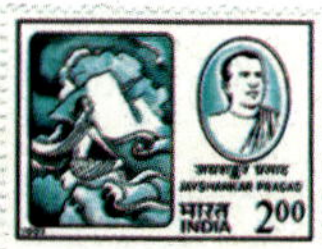

over the bloodbath preceding it and in its wake. Many works of eminent authors and poets reflect the joy of independence and the pangs of partition. The **martyrdom of Mahatma Gandhi** in 1948 deeply affected the society and the world of literature. As time passed, an element of despair pertaining to the unfulfilled-hopes after years of independence started to seep in. All this is reflected in Indian literature as well.

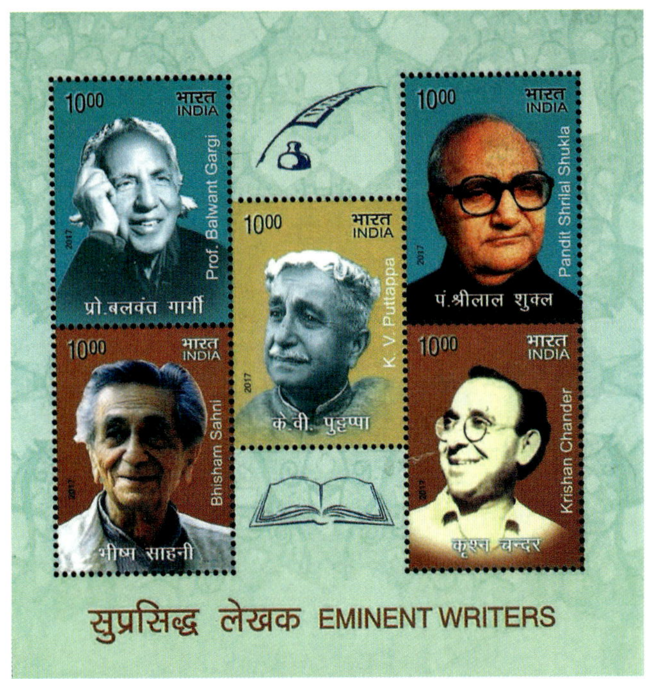

20.59: A stamp sheet of eminent writers — Courtesy, Department of Post

Some of the prominent authors and salient works of this period and those, who in the coming decades, captured these emotions of the society, were **Amrita Pritam** (*Ajj Aakhaan Waris Shah Nu*- poem, 1947; *Pinjar*- novel, 1950), **Khushwant Singh** (*Train to Pakistan*-novel, 1956 : English), **Faiz Ahmad Faiz** (Urdu), **Kartar Singh Duggal** (Punjabi, English Hindi), **Premendra Mitra** (Bengali), **Bhai Veer Singh**, **Bhisham Sahni** (*Tamas*- novel), **Yashpal** (Jhootha Sach), **Manohar Malgonkar** (*A Bend in the Ganges*, English novel) besides others. Amongst the Hindi poets, the angst of partition was expressed by **Nagarjun, Ramdhari Singh Dinkar, Sohan Lal Dwivedi** and **Bhavani Prasad Mishra** in their works. In 1947, **Agyeya** composed a series of poetry expressing the sorrow and sentiments on partition and the communal riots that followed. These were also brought in his book titled *Sharnarthee* (refugees).

Experimentalism in Post-independence Literature

The transition in the world and Indian society were palpable in the Indian literature, and more so were the transition in social outlook and values. As time passed, many new writers and poets emerged and new genres of writing such as **Modernism, Experimentalism** and **Post-modernism** started to take root. There were some writers and poets who believed in traditional Indian values. A new crop of Indian litterateurs also emerged who borrowed from the Western values of rationality and modernism. For some, the western literature and principles they enunciated provided the contextual ideal for the Indian society and literature, rather than the works of Tagore or the principles of Gandhi. This reflected in their quest for modernity as well as a search of identity. Some authors explored the inner reality in the context of modern outlook and changing paradigm. In this quest for new values and new literary expressions, emerged the genre of **experimentalism** in Indian literature, also referred to as the ***Prayogvaad*** in Hindi literature, which were analogous to the worldwide **Modernist** or the *avant-garde* movement.

S.H. Vatsyayan Agyeya (Sahitya Akademi, Jnanpith awardee) was one of the pioneers of ***Prayogvaad*** in Hindi poetry and is said to have ushered the ***Nayi Kavita*** (new poetry) Hindi literary movement. Among his prominent works are *Angan ke Paar Dwar* (poetry collection), ***Taar Saptak*** (compilation of poetry published in 1943), *Hari Ghaas Par Kshan-Bhar* (poem), *Baawra Aheri* (poem), *Trishanku* (essay collection) etc. Other prominent poets of the *Taar Saptak* compilation who ushered ***Nayi Kavita*** movement and had prominent influence on *Prayogvad* were**, Ram Vilas Sharma, Girija Kumar Mathur, Bharat Bhushan Agrawal, Nemi Chandra Jain, Prabhakar Machwe and Gajanan Madhav Muktibodh**. Among other notable poets of the **Nayi Kavita/ Modernist** movement **were Kunwar Narayan (Hindi), Dilip Chitre (Marathi), Arun Kolatkar (Marathi), Gopal Krishna Adiga (Kannada)**, besides others. Another genre of poetry around this time was the ***Pragateesheel*** Hindi poetry of which the prominent patrons were **Nagarjun**, **Dinkar** others. Both the genres were prevalent in the pre-independence period and continued to flourish even in the 50s.

Similarly, a ***Nayi Kahani*** movement based on *Prayogvad* was ushered with the works of **Nirmal Verma**. Poems like *Parinde* (1959), *Jalti Jhari* (1965) and novels like *Ve Din* and *Antim Aranya* were some of his celebrated works. Other eminent authors of this genre were; **Bhisham Sahni**, a writer, playwright and also an actor (salient works: *Tamas, Jharokhe, Kadian, Basanti*); **Mohan Rakesh**, a novelist and playwright (salient works: *Asadh Ka Ek Din, Laharon Ke Rajhans, Aadhe Adhure*); **Rajendra Yadav**, a novelist and editor of literary magazines (salient works: *Pret Bolte Hain, Saara Akaash* and others); **Amarkant**, short story writer and novelist (salient works: short stories such as *Deputy Collector*, *Dopahar ka Bhojan*); **Kamleshwar**,

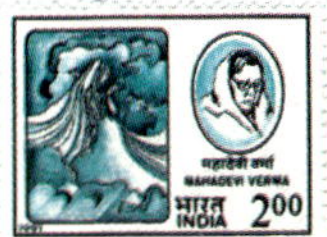

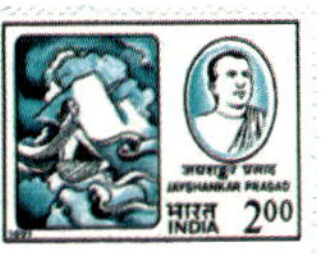

a novelist, short story and screen-play writer (salient works: *Agami Ateet, Amma, Hindustan Hamara, Kitne Pakistan*), and **Mannu Bhandari**, a novelist, short story writer (salient works: *Aap Ka Bunty Mahabhoj*, over 150 short stories).

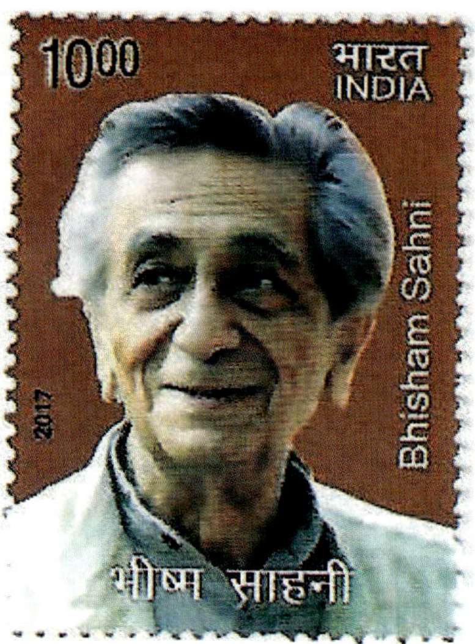

20.60: Bhisham Sahni, a Hindi novelist and story writer of eminence; a stamp from 2017 — Courtesy, Department of Post

In the coming age, the western ideals and principles of materialism could not provide all the solutions to the Indian challenges. Hence there started to emerge a genre of literary works which questioned these principles and their relevance in the Indian context. Thus came forth a section of Indian literature which was torn between the western ideal of materialism and Indian traditional values, eventually leading to a state of **crisis of identity** in Indian literature. The **period of late 50s and 60s** reflected this phase of Indian literature which is also referred by some scholars as a phase of **Dark Modernism**.

The phase of experimentation at times rooted itself as distinct from the western materialism, and yet it offered a quest for new values and also looked into the sources of those values. This offered a distinct voice and vision to the literature. Among such eminent authors and poets in the 60s and 70s were **V.K. Gokak** (Kannada), **Nabakanta Baruah** (Assamese), **Harbhajan Singh** (Punjabi poet), **B.S. Mardhekar** (Marathi) and **S.H. Vatsyayan Ajneya** (Hindi) and others.

Among other **sub-genres** in this phase were works supporting the cause of **marginalised** and **down trodden** sections (also referred to as the *dalit* and tribal literature). **Mahashweta Devi** (Padma Bhushan, Sahitya Akademi, Jnanpith, Ramon Magasaysay awardee) was one of the foremost Bengali authors and activist in this genre whose works such as *Aranyer Adhikar* (novel), *Chotti Mundi Ebong Tar Tir* (story) bring out the right of the forest dwellers and the plight of the tribals. Among her other much acclaimed general works are *Hazaar Chaurasi ki Maa* and *Rudali* (novels on which movies are based). Among the other prominent authors of this subgenre were **Namdev Dhasal**, **Narayan Surve** (Marathi poets), **Daya Pawar**, **Laxman Gaikwad** (Marathi novelist), **Joseph Macwan** (Gujarati novelist), **Devanur Mahadeva** (Kannada novelist).

Yet another subgenre explored the **depiction of mythology, folk legends** and **mythic thoughts** in modern day context. **C. Rajagopalachari** wrote the abridged retelling of Mahabharata (1951) and Ramayana (1957), English translation of Kamba Ramayanam and Thirukkural, besides works on Gita and Upanishads. **Vishnu S. Khandekar** (*Yayati*, Marathi novel), **U.R. Ananthamurthy** (*Samskara;* Kannada novel), and playwrights like **Girish Karnad** (Kannada author & playwright), **Badal Sircar** (*Evam Indrajit*; Bengali play), **Mohan Rakesh** (Hindi) **Ramakanta Rath** (Oriya) and **Sitakant Mahapatra** (Oriya), were some others who explored this category of literature.

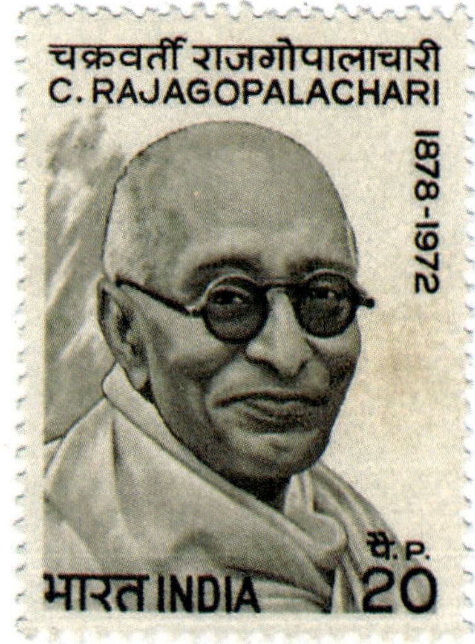

20.61: C. Rajagopalachari, a stamp from 1973 — Courtesy, Department of Post

Satire was another sub-genre which attained readership popularity as well as literary acclaim. **Sharad Joshi** (Sahitya Akademi awardee) and author of famous satirical plays *Ek tha Gadha* and *Andhon ka Haathi*, is among the notable writers of this category. He was also an author and poet, besides a famous script writer, whose works include scripts of famous movies such as *Choti si Baat* (1975), *Utsav* (1984), *Dil Hai Ki Manta Nahin* (1991), and popular television serial like *Yeh Jo Hai Jindagi* (1984-85) *Vikram aur Betal.* **Harishankar Parsai** (Sahitya Akademi awardee, short story writer, humorist and satirist), **Kaka Hathrasi** (Padmashri awardee, poet, humorist and satirist), **Ashok Chakradhar** (Padmashri awardee, poet, humorist and satirist), **Shail Chaturvedi** (poet, humorist and satirist) and **Pradeep Chaube** (poet, humorist and satirist) were others who attained fame in the category of satire. *Hasya Kavita* (poems of wit and humour) which was also laced with satire was another complementary genre, with eminent poets like **Gopal Prasad Vyas** (Padma Shri), **Surender Sharma** (Padma Shri), **Hullar Muradabadi** and others.

Some of the works of this period also explored issues pertaining to women and their rights. **Ashapurna Devi** (Bengali novelist; Padma Shri, Jnanpith & Sahitya Akademi Fellowship awardee), penned her

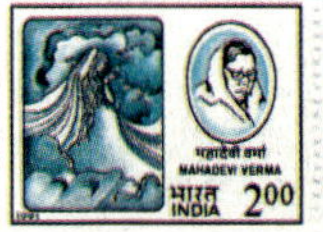
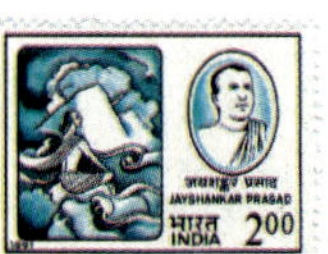

famous trilogy *Pratishruti* (1964), *Subarnolata* (1967) and *Bakul Katha* (1974) which explored the **restrictive socio-economic conditions of women,** gave a voice to the struggle of women and highlighted the abject need for equal rights. **Krishna Sobti** and **Mridula Garg** were some other authors of this category.

Besides, there are many authors and poets whose works are not classified into any of the above genres. Some of these eminent litterateurs include **Bhawani Prasad Mishra** (Hindi poet & Sahitya Akademi awardee), **Vishnu Prabhakar** (Hindi novelist, short story and travelogue writer; Padma Bhushan & Sahitya Akademi awardee) **Krishna Sobti** (Hindi novelist; Jnanapith and Sahitya Akademi awardee), **O.N.V. Kurup** (Malayalam poet and novelist; Padma Vibhushan, Jnanpith and Sahitya Akademi awardee).

Contemporary Literature and Post Modernism

In the period of the 80s and beyond, Indian literature has further evolved. It continued to reflect the transition of the society and the aspirations and feelings of the common man. The predominantly rural culture of pre-independence, and to a large extent of the 50s and 60s, gradually waned. The economic liberalization of the 90s and the opportunities it heralded changed the society and the rural-urban composition in India. Coming to the new millennium, increasing material prosperity and the booming city-culture which ensued, caught the fancy even of the world of art and literature. The changing commerce of literature also had a significant impact on literary creativity. But what perhaps has had the most monumental influence on the society is the advent of information and communication technology. All these changes have influenced the contemporary literature.

Quite like the trends in world literature, Indian literature also evolved into a new genre. While Modernism was a literary movement in the post-independence period in India, including in its ambit phases of Experimentalism and Dark-modernism, the literature since the 80s and beyond is said to reflect the new genre of **Post-modernism**. This phase of literature is characterised by its proximity to the life of a common man. Unlike the past phases, it may not be the harbinger of a social message or a philosophical ideology. But what is witnessed in the society is reflected in modern literature. The truth and reality which the writer perceives and which the reader can identify with, often form the substance of the work. Language too may be bereft of the ornamentation of the past and be marked with pointedness and simplicity and yet exude a beauty. This phase is also referred to as the *Uttara Adhunik* in the Hindi literature.

Post Independence: Eminent Litterateurs and Their Salient Works

Hindi literature

The post-independence era inherited a rich tradition of Hindi literature which had witnessed different phases of literary growth and movements. The Hindi poetry had seen its golden age and moved from *Chhayavad* (romanticism) to *Pragativaad* (progressive movement). On the eve of independence, it was evolving into *Prayogvaad* (experimentalism) and witnessing a *Nayi Kavita* movement. In its wide sweep, the Hindi literature included the nationalistic (*rashtravadi*) as well as regional (*anchalic*) works. Many doyens of Indian literature like Premchand, Jaishankar Prasad, Maithili Sharan Gupta, Surya Kant Tripathi 'Nirala', Mahadevi Verma and Dinkar had enriched it with their immortal works. Thus, Hindi literature of the post-independence period was an inheritor of a glorious past and represented an evolving and vibrant body of works, responsive to the changing society and in tandem with the growing world literature.

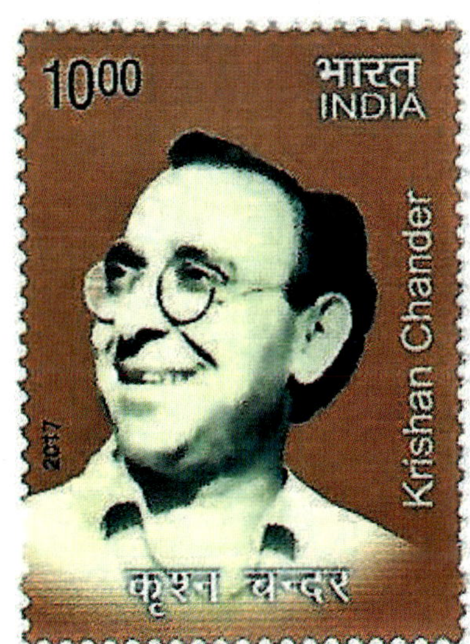

20.62: Krishan Chander, a prolific and popular Hindi and Urdu novelist, short story and film script writer; a stamp from 2017 — Courtesy, Department of Post

The immediate **post-independence literature** was witness to a glitterati of authors and poets who were already well established and were names to reckon with. These included some eminent litterateurs like **Yashpal, Krishan Chander, Agyeya, Shivmangal Singh Suman, Nagarjun, Bhawani Prasad Mishra, Amritlal Nagar, Bhisham Sahni, Jainendra Kumar, Upendranath Ashq, Krishna Sobti,** and others. In the subsequent decades, several notable works of critical acclaim emanated from their pens.

Amongst the poets, S.H. Vatsyayan Agyeya (Sahitya Akademi, Jnanpith awardee) along with others of the *Tar Saptak* group were associated with the *Prayogvaad* and the *Nai Kavita* movement. Counted in his salient works are *Shekhar Ek Jivani, Trishanku, Tar Saptak*, besides others.

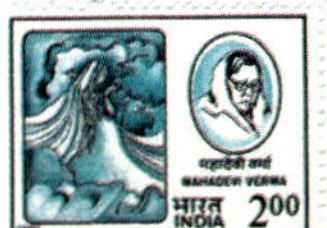

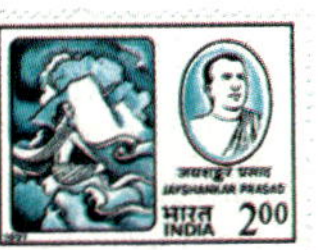

Nagarjun (Sahitya Akademi Fellowship awardee), a part of the Nai Kavita movement as a *Pragativaadi Kavi*, was also reckoned as a *Jankavi*, or people's poet, whose breadth of poetry attracted audience from the very elite to the ordinary villagers. Also, a travelogue writer of eminence, his salient works include poems like *Badal ko Ghirte Dekha Hai* (also a travelogue), *Ao Rani Hum Dhoenge Palki* (a sarcastic criticism of extravagant welcome of British queen), besides many other works.

Shivmangal Singh Suman (Padma Bhushan & Sahitya Akademi awardee) was another outstanding poet of this period whose salient works includes *Hillol* (1939), *Jeevan Ke Gaan* (1942), *Pralay Srijan* (1950), *Vindhya Himalaya* (1960), and *Mitti Ki Baarat* (1972), besides others.

Among the writers, **Yashpal** (Padma Bhushan & Sahitya Akademi awardee) had a wide canvas of works which include novels, short stories, essays, travelogues and plays. His two volumes of *Jhootha Sach* (1958 & 1960) which dwell on the events around partition are often compared to world classics such as *War and Peace*. Among his other salient works were, *Pinjre ki Uran* (1939), *Meri Teri Uski Baat* (1976), besides others.

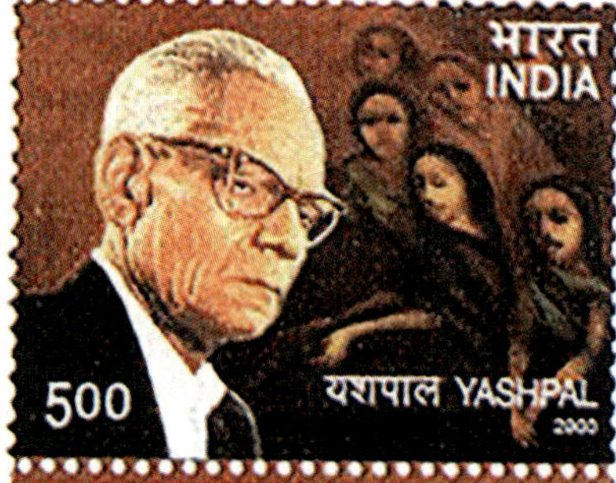

20.63: Yashpal, a stamp from 2000 — Courtesy, Department of Post

Bhisham Sahni (Padma Bhushan & Sahitya Akademi Fellowship awardee) was another towering literary figure of this age whose magnum opus *Tamas* (1974) is a compelling account of the horrors of partition and the ensuing bloodshed. Among his other significant works are; *Bhagya Rekha* (1953), *Pahla Patha* (1956), *Bhatakti* and *Raakh* (1966) which are short stories, and *Jharokhe* (1967), *Basanti* (1979), *Mayyadas Ki Madi* (1987), *Kunto* (1993) and *Neeloo*, *Nilima*, *Nilofar* (2000) which are novels, besides plays and children short stories for children.

Amritlal Nagar (Padma Bhushan & Sahitya Akademi awardee) considered a creative literary genius, was known for his works entailing complex storylines and diverse range of characters and at times deemed a literary successor of Premchand. Among his notable works are *Vatika* (1935), *Aadmi, Nahin! Nahin!* (1947), *Ek Dil Hazaar Dastaan* (1955), *Meri Priya Kahaniyan* (1970)-short stories and *Boond Aur Samudra* (1956), *Amrit Aur Vish* (1966), *Agni Garbha* (1983), *Peedhiyaan* (1990)-novels, besides others.

Krishna Sobti (Jnanpith & Sahitya Akademi Fellowship awardee), a novelist and a short story writer, also referred to as the grand dame of Hindi literature, was a part of *Nai Kahani* movement. A uniqueness of her style was incorporating the idioms of Punjabi, Urdu and at times Rajasthani, with her Hindi writing. Her much-acclaimed work *Mitron Marjani* (1966) candidly brings out the issues of women's sexuality. Among her other notable works are *Lama, Nafisa* (1944), *Sikka Badal Gaya* (1948-a story about partition), *Suraj Mukhi Andhere ke* (1972), *Zindaginama Zinda Rukh* (1979), besides others.

The decade of the 50s saw the emergence of many new novelists and poets whose works are still considered as landmarks of Hindi literature. Some of these celebrated authors are **Phanishwar Nath Renu, Kamleshwar, Nirmal Verma, Mannu Bhandari, Naresh Mehta, Rajendra Yadav Vishnu Prabhakar, Gajanan Muktibodh, Mohan Rakesh, Rangey Raghava** and **Dharamveer Bharati,** besides others.

Phanishwar Nath Renu's landmark work *Maila Anchal* was an epitome of *Anchalik Sahitya* (regional literature) where he succinctly captures the rural life and the societal challenges therein. Another of his novels *Mare Gaye Gulfam*, was made into a successful movie (*Teesri Kasam*). Yet another of his stories, *Panchlight* (meaning petromax) was made into a short tele-film and later into a Bollywood movie (*Panchlait*-2017).

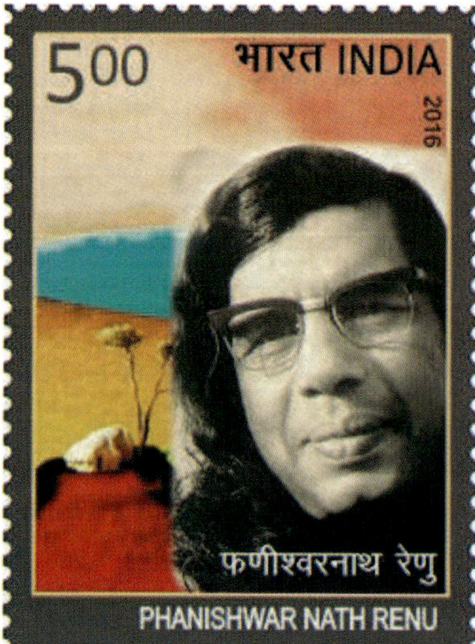

20.64: Phanishwar Nath Renu, a master of regional literature; a stamp from 2016 — Courtesy, Department of Post

Vishnu Prabhakar (Padma Bhushan & Sahitya Akademi awardee) was an eminent short story writer and novelist who also wrote plays and travelogues. His works were marked with the sense of patriotism and social message. Some of his novels are *Dhalti Raat* (1951), *Nishikant* (1955), *Parchhai* (1968) *Ardhnarishwar* (1992). Some of his noteworthy short stories include; *Rehman Ka Beta* (1947), *Zindagi Ke Thapede* (1952), *Dharti Ab Bhi Ghoom Rahi Hai* (1959), *Safar Ke Saathi* (1960) etc.

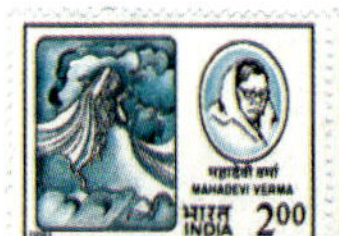

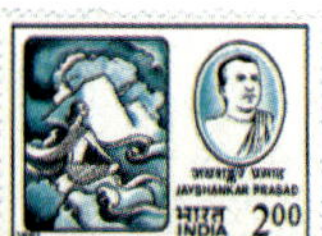

Nirmal Verma (Padma Bhushan, Jnanpith & Sahitya Akademi Fellowship awardee) was a stalwart of the *Nayi Kahani* movement whose works like *Parinde* (1959), *Jalti Jhari* (1965), *Pichli Garmiyon Mein* (1968) – short stories-and others, set new yardsticks for experimental literature. His other pertinent works include *Ve Din* (1964), *Lal Teen Ka Chaat* (1974), *Raat Ka Reporter* (1989) which were novels.

Mannu Bhandari (Vyas Samman & Sahitya Akademi Fellowship awardee) another pioneer of the *Nayi Kahani* movement is known for authoring over 150 short stories and some acclaimed novels (*Aap Ki Bunty* and *Mahabhoj*). She has also been a screenplay writer and a playwright.

In the **decade of 60s and 70s,** Hindi literature continued to flourish in the works of several emerging authors and established litterateurs. Among the debutants and emerging authors of this phase were several whose works received critical acclaim in the coming years and include **Srilal Shukla, Amarkant, Narendra Kohli, Govind Mishra, Mridula Garg, Ashok Vajpayee, Ramdarsh Mishra, Kailash Vajpayee, Usha Priyamvada, Raghuvir Sahay, Gopal Das Neeraj** besides others.

Srilal Shukla (Padma Bhushan, Jnanpith, Vyas Samman & Sahitya Akademi awardee) is most remembered for his acclaimed work *Raag Darbai* (1968-novel). His other salient works include, *Sooni Ghaati Ka Sooraj* (1957), *Makaan* (1976), *Pehla Padaav* (1987), *Bisrampur Ka Sant* (1998), besides others. His works were often satirical and brought out the falling moral and social values in the changing towns and villages.

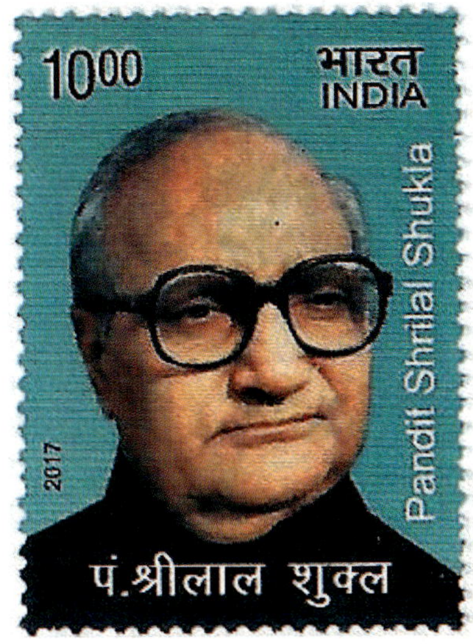

20.65: Srilal Shukla, a Hindi novelist and satirist; a stamp from 2017 — Courtesy, Department of Post

Amarkant Shukla (Jnanpith, Vyas Samman & Sahitya Akademi awardee) was another thespian of the post-independence literature whose works reflected social realism and were similar to Premchand in style and tenor. His notable works (short stories) include *Deputy Collector, Dopahar ka Bhojan, Zindagi aur Jonk* and *Hatyaare*. Besides, he also authored six novels.

Govind Mishra (Saraswati Samman, Vyas Samman & Sahitya Akademi awardee) is an author of more than 50 books including 11 novels, several short story collections, travelogues and essays. His eminent works include *Dhool Paudho Par, Paanch Anangano Wala Ghar, Kohre Mein Kaid Rang*, besides others.

Mridula Garg (Sahitya Akademi awardee), a novelist, short story and essay writer, has publications in Hindi as well as English, with over 30 books to her credit. She has written on a variety of topics including areas such as women's sexuality which otherwise is an area of unease and discomfiture in literary works. Through her columns she has also expressed her views on topics like environment, women and children besides others. Some of her salient works include, *Uske Hisse Ki Dhoop* (novel, 1975), *Tukra-Tukra Aadmi* (short stories, 1976), *Daffodil Jal Rahein Hain* (short stories, 1978), *Main Aur Main* (novel, 1984) , *Jadoo Ka Kaleen* (play, 1993), *Miljul Mann* (novel 2010).

In the period of **80s -90s** and in the new millenium, Hindi literature has witnessed a gradual waning of the publications as compared to the previous decades. Loss of readership on account of the onslaught of digital media, drop in the readership habit, shifting of reader base more towards English, more promising authors taking up English as a language of preferred choice, lesser commercial viability of Hindi publications or others, could be some of the reasons for this shift. Nevertheless, some eminent authors and notable works have come up. Some of these include, **Kedarnath Singh, (**Jnanpith and Sahitya Akademi awardee, *Akaal Mein Saras,* poem), **Manohar Joshi** (Sahitya Akademi awardee; script writer of tele-serials like *Hum Log Buniyaad* and others), **Amritlal Vegad** (Sahitya Akademi awardee; *Saundaryini Nadi Narmada, Narmada ki Parikrama*), **Atal Bihari Vajpayee** (poetry: *Meri Ikyavan Kavitayen, Kya Khoya Kya Paya,* prose: *Kucha Lekha, Kucha Bhashana*), **Daya Prakash Sinha** (Padma Shri, Sahitya Akademi awardee; plays *Samrat Ashok , Rakt Abhishek),* **Uday Prakash (**Sahitya Akademi awardee; *Mohandas,* a novella) **Chitra Mudgal (**Sahitya Akademi awardee; *Post Box No. 203, Naalasopara,* a novel), **Ramesh Chandra Shah** (Padma Shri, Sahitya Akademi awardee; *Gobar Ganesh, Vinayak,* novels), **Anamika** (Sahitya Akademi awardee; *Tokri Mein Digant 'Theri Gatha,* poem), **Nasira Sharma** (Vyas Samman & Sahitya Akademi awardee, *Parijaat, Kagaz ki Naav*, novels), **Mamta Kalia**, (Vyas Samman, *Dukham Sukham*, novel), **Geetanjali Shree** (International Booker prize, *Ret Samadhi*, novel), besides others.

As the 21st century progresses, though the conventional Hindi literature has not/may not be as prolific as the 20th century, yet creative expression in Hindi is likely to grow. What is likely to change is the medium of expression. In the new millennium, newer forms of literary and creative expressions have emerged apart from the paper-based pages of the conventional novels and story books. Be it the electronic

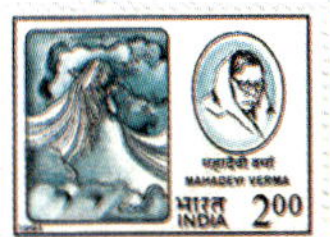
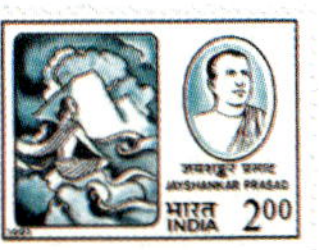

media such as television or the digital world, or the newly emerging web-based content, demand for literary and creative writers for areas such as scripts for tele-serials, web-series, advertisement etc. is bound to rise. Besides, areas such as electronic journalism and digital world are bringing opportunities which are also transforming the literary and creative expression. Thus, the market and demand has not diminished, rather it is likely to grow. Over the years, the pace of modern life has diminished the appetite for the encompassing and time sapping voluminous literature and hence the creative expression is changing in its nature to more concise works, be it shorter poems, stories or novels. Thus, Hindi literature and creative writing would continue to flourish, however its nature and form of expression is likely to undergo a change, as it has over the centuries.

Post-Independence Regional Literature

Regional literature in post-independence India has flourished. The rise of newspapers, television and films, besides books, have helped regional literature find new forms of expression. State, national and international recognition too has attracted fresh writers and more talent in literature. Some of the notable authors and poets of this period who have contributed immensely to the regional literature include the following.

Birendra Kumar Bhattacharya (Jnanpith & Sahitya Akademi awardee) was an **Assamese** novelist, journalist and academician whose notable works include *Mrityunjay, Iyaruingam* and *Aai.*

Abdur Rehman Rahi (Padma Shri, Jnanpith & Sahitya Akademi awardee), an eminent **Kashmiri** poet, translator and critique is known for his works such as *Nawroz-i-Saba* and *Siyah Rood Jaeren Manz*, (poetry collection).

Qurratulain Haider (Padma Bhushan, Sahitya Akademi and Jnanpith awardee), was an **Urdu** novelist, short story writer and a journalist. Her salient works include; *Aag ka Darya, Patjhar ki Awaz, Raushni ki Raftar* and others.

Shankha Ghosh, (Padma Bhushan, Sahitya Akademi and Jnanpith awardee) was a **Bengali** poet and literary critic. His salient works include; *Dinguli Rataguli, Babure Prarthana.*

Satya Vrat Shastri (Sahitya Akademi and Jnanpith awardee), a Sanskrit scholar, poet and grammarian, is amongst only a few literary exponents of the language who has wirtten three *Mahakavyas*, besides many other works which include; *Ramakirtimahakavyam*, *Brahattaram Bharatam*, *Sribodhisattvacharitam*, *Vaidika Vyakarana* etc.

M.T Vasudevan Nair (Padma Bhushan, Sahitya Akademi and Jnanpith awardee), **Malayalam** author screenplay, writer and film director; whose salient works include *Naalukettu, Manju, Kaalam and Asuravithu.*

Ravuri Bharadwaja (Sahitya Akademi and Jnanpith awardee) was a **Telugu novelist**, short story writer, who also wrote children's literature. His salient works include *Paakudu Raallu, Jeevana Samaram.*

Bhalchandra Nemade (Padma Shri, Sahitya Akademi, Jnanpith awardee), a **Marathi** novelist and poet; whose salient works include *Kosala, Bidhar*, *Hool*, *Jareela*, *Jhool*, and *Hindu: Jagnyachi Samruddha Adgal,* besides others.

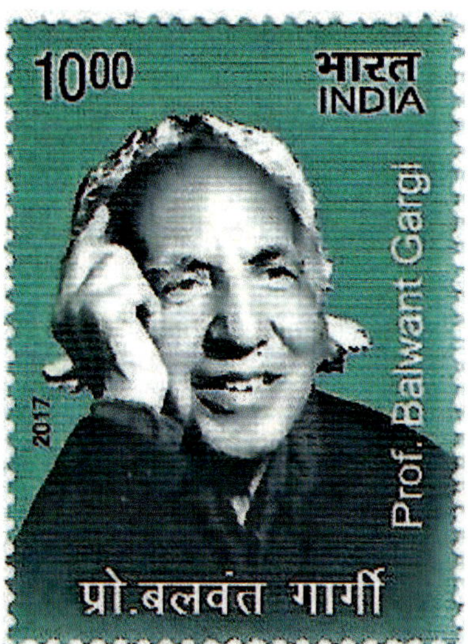

20.66: Balwant Gargi, Punjabi litterateur of eminence, theatre director and an academic; a stamp from 2017 — Courtesy, Department of Post

Gurdial Sangh Rahi (Padma Shri and Jnanpith awardee), a **Punjabi** novelist whose salient works include, *Marhi Da Deeva, Addh Chanani Raat.*

Raghuveer Chaudhari, (Sahitya Akademi and Jnanpith awardee), a **Gujarati** novelist, poet and newspaper columnist whose salient works include, *Amrita* and the *trilogy Uparvas*, *Sahwas* and *Antarvas.*

Pratibha Ray, (Padma Bhushan and Jnanpith awardee; salient works: *Yajnaseni*, *Shilapadma*) an **Odia novelist**.

Maimoni Raisom Goswami, (Jnanpith & Sahitya Akademi awardee) **Assamese** writer, poet and scholar. Among her salient works are: *Chinavar Srota*, *Datal Hatir, Une Khowa Howda.*

Damodar Mauzo, (Jnanpith & Sahitya Akademi awardee), a **Konkani** novelist, short story script writer, and critique whose salient works are; *Karmelin, Tsunami Simon*, *Teresa's Man and (Other Stories from Goa).*

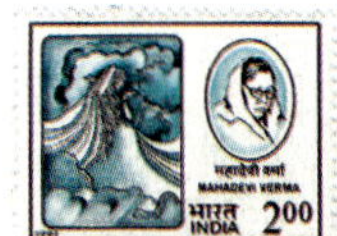

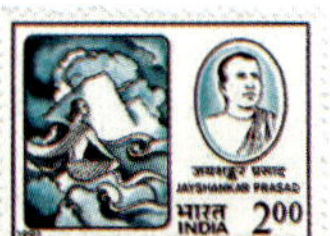

Among some other eminent authors and poets of regional literature in this period are; **Viswantha Satyanarayana** (Telugu), **Gopinath Mohanty** (Odia), **Akilan** (Tamil), **K. Shivaram Karanth** (Kannada), **Jaswant Singh Rahi** (Punjabi), **Pannalal Patel** (Gujarati), **Masti Venkatesha Iyengar** (Kannada), **Jayakanthan** (Tamil), **Sachidananda Routray** (Odia), **Vishnu Vaman Shirwadkar Kusumagraj** (Marathi), **Subhash Mukhopadhyaya** (Bengali), **Rajendra Shah** (Gujarati), **Rehman Rahi** (Kashmiri), **Balwant Gargi** (Punjabi) **Ravindra Kelkar** (Konkani), **Nilamani Phookan** (Assamese), **Ravuri Bharadhwaja** (Telugu).

Post Independence Urdu Literature

Urdu as a language has found patronage in different parts of the country, particularly in north and north western India, transcending state and regional boundaries. Its literature too flourished in the post-independence period. This was a phase where Bollywood films, and in particular Hindi film music, gained mass popularity. Largely based on the Hindustani tongue, film scripts and song lyrics incorporated Urdu words and poetry, thus providing a platform to the Urdu literature, besides invigorating the readers, interest in Urdu poetry. Thus, a generation of Urdu poets who received critical literary acclaim, also came to be associated with the film world. These included some renowned Urdu poets such as Sahir Ludhiyanvi, Ali Sardar Jafri, Kaifi Aazmi, Akhlaq Muhammad Khan and Javed Akhtar, besides others.

Ali Sardar Jafri (1913-2000; Padma Shri and Jnanpith awardee) was a distinguished Urdu writer, poet, critique and film lyricist who was earlier associated with the Progressive Writers Movement and Progressive Urdu Writers Movement. His notable works include *Dharti Ke lal*, *Pardesi*, *Mera Safar* and *Sarhad*. The last anthology was gifted by Indian Prime Minister Sri Atal Bihari Vajpayee to his counterpart during the Lahore summit in 1999.

Kaifi Azmi (1919-2002; Padma Shri and Sahitya Akademi Fellowship Awardee) was a distinguished poet, lyricist and songwriter for the Indian films who was also a part of the Progressive Writers Movement. He is credited for his contribution to over 65 Indian films, either as a lyricist or a song writer, some of the popular ones of which are *Kagaz ke Phool* (1959), *Haqeeqat* (1964), *Heer Ranjha* (1970), *Arth* (1982), *Razia Sultan* (1983).

Enduring Lines of Kaifi Azmi

Amongst the most memorable and inspiring poetry of Kaifi Azmi is '*kar chale hum fida*', which was picturised as a song in film *Haqeeqat* (1964). Penned in the backdrop of the Indo-Chinese war of 1962, the poetry and song immortalize the emotions, valour and sacrifice of the ordinary soldiers. The opening verses are;

Kar chale hum fida jan-o-tan sathion,
ab tumhare hawale watan sathion.

Having sacrificed my body and life,
O'friends I part with the custody of this nation and place it in your hands.

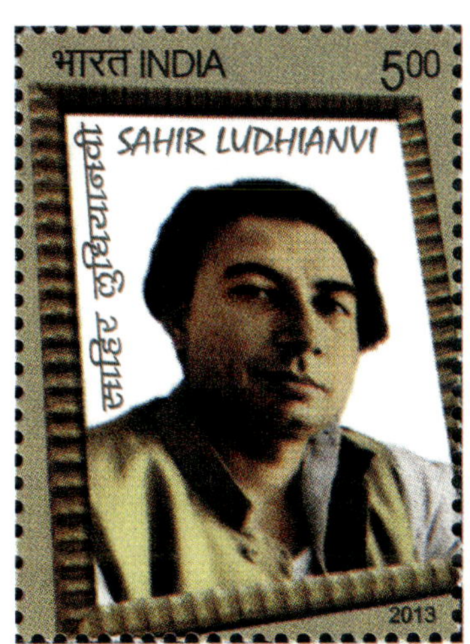

20.67: Sahir Ludhianvi, a stamp released in 2013 — Courtesy, Department of Post

Sahir Ludhianvi (1921-1980; Padma Sri awardee), a film song lyricist, who was also associated with the Progressive Writers Movement, is often remembered for the lyrics of film *Kabhi-Kabhi* (1976) titled *Main pal do pal ka shayar hoon.*

Shakeel Badayuni (1916-1970) was another famous Urdu poet, lyricist and song writer, who wrote many memorable songs for Bollywood movies, including hit movies like *Baiju Bawra*, *Mughal-e-Azam*, *Chaudawi Ka Chand* etc.

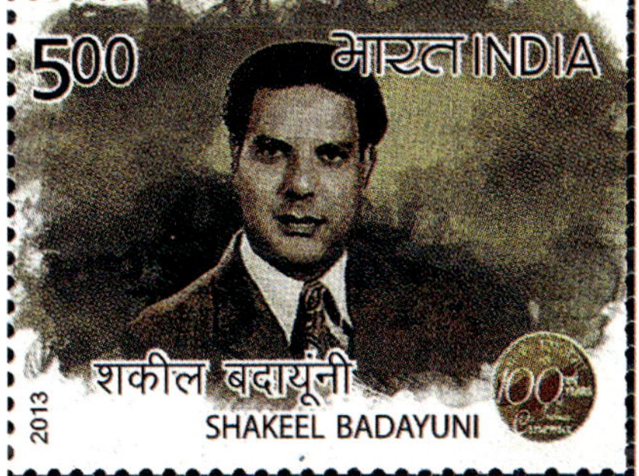

20.68: Shakeel Badayuni, a stamp released in 2013 — Courtesy, Department of Post

Akhlaq Muhammad Khan (1936 -2012; Sahitya Akademi & Jnanpith Awardee) was a poet, lyricist and an academician. Among his most famous poetic works are *Ism-e-Azam* (1965), *Hizr ke Mausam* (1978) and *Khwab ke Dar Band Hain*. He is also remembered for his lyrics in movies such as *Gaman* (1978) and *Umrao Jaan* (1981).

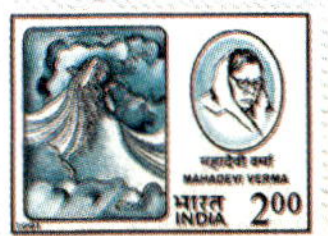

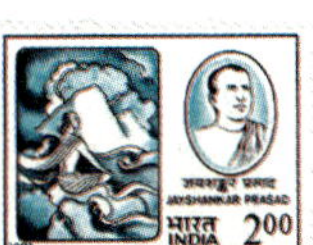

Javed Akhtar (1945; Padma Bhushan & Sahitya Akademi Awardee) is a famous poet, lyricist and screen play writer. His poetic works include *Tarkash* (1995) and *Lava* (2012). He along with Salim Khan penned the script of many successful Bollywood movies in the 70s and 80s. Javed Akhtar has been associated (as a pair, or individually) with the script/ lyrics nearly 40 commercial movies.

Besides the above, the works of the earlier generation of Urdu poets like **Firak Gorakhpuri**, **Qurratulain Haider**, and **Ismat Chugtai** (novelist, short story writer and film maker), **Qazi Abdul Sattar** (novelist), were also very popular and received critical acclaim.

Post Independence English Literature

The growth of English literature is indeed a crucial part of the story of India's literature and its evolution. While the pre-independence period saw many notable 'Progressive writers', the post-independence English literature too grew from strength to strength. As the decades passed, there was a perceptible increase in the popularity of English as a language of academic instruction and an inter-regional connect. The greater integration of the Indian economy to the world economy, post-liberalisation of the 90s, and increasing trade and commerce, have further added to the significance of English as an academic language and a language of international opportunities. The increasing exposure to the world of literature helped in augmenting the popularity of Indian English literature. At the same time the growing number of Indian emigrants has also created a demand for Indian English literature in the international market.

In the new millennium, with information technology making Indian and world literature easily and economically accessible, there is a spurt in its popularity in the domestic market. Perhaps what has aided the most in Indian English literature's substantial commercial success is the emergence of a generation of Indian writers who have gained national as well as international acclaim. This in turn has attracted wider readership and brought a spurt in the growth of domestic English publications as well. Thus, in this period, Indian English literature achieved popularity and success, which is surely an envy of the Indian languages.

Over the years, Indian English authors have rooted their works largely in the Indian social substratum whose characters, subject, as well as language is quintessentially Indian. The generations of authors who have grown up in independent India have discarded the baggage of English as a foreign language or the colonial hangover associated with it. Today, with a growing urban population feeding on the international digital media and varied web contents emanating in English, the disconnection with the language and culture it endeavours to portray, has gradually waned. A snapshot of the evolution of the English literature in this post-independence era is given below.

The decades of 50s and 60s saw several celebrated works of the renowned triad of previous generation. In these years these came up some of the acclaimed works of **Mulk Raj Anand** (*The Private life of an Indian Prince*-1953; *The Road*-1961; *Morning Face*-1968), **Raja Rao** (*The Serpent and the Rope*-1960; *The Cat and Shakespeare: A Tale of India*-1965) and **R.K. Narayan** (*The Financial Expert*-1952; *Waiting for the Mahatma*-1955; *The Guide*-1958, *The Maneater of Malgudi*-1962, *The Vendor of Sweets*-1967).

In the 50s, came a series of books by **Khushwant Singh** (1915-2014, Padma Vibhushan and Sahitya Akademi Fellowship awardee) whose *Train to Pakistan* (1956-novel) written in the back drop of partition and the ensuing riots, has remained an all-time bestseller. His other eminent works in a literary career of nearly sixty years include, *The Mark of Vishnu and Other Stories* (1950), *I Shall Not Hear the Nightingale*, (novel 1959), *Black Jasmine*, (short story-1971), *Delhi: A Novel*,(1990), *The Company of Women* (1999) besides others and works of non-fiction such as, *The History of Sikhs*, (1953, 1963, 2004) etc. In this very period, **Nirad C. Chaudhari** (1897-1992) authored his masterpieces, *An Autobiography of an Unknown Indian* (1951) and *A Passage to England* (1959) which are considered among the great works of Indian English literature.

In the 50s, were also published the very first works of **Ruskin Bond** (born 1934; Padma Bhushan and Sahitya Akademi awardee). *Room and the Roof* (1955) and *The Vagrants in the Valley* (1956) were works authored when Ruskin Bond was still in his teens. In a long and illustrious career stretching in the new millennium, he has authored more than 500 short stories and some of the most memorable children's literature. Some of his acclaimed works are; *Our Trees Still Grow in Dehra (1991)*, *Flight of Pigeons* (the Hindi movie *Junoon* was based on it), *Blue Umbrella* (also made into a Hindi movie) besides others.

Nissim Ezkiel (1924-2004; Padma Shri & Sahitya Akademi awardee), considered a foundational figure in post-colonial Indian poetry) came up with a series of works which reflect his modernist innovation in style, subject and technique. *Time To Change* (1952), *Sixty Poems* (1953), *The Discovery of India* (1956) were some of his early poetic works. Of special significance was his poems; *The Night of Scorpion* which appeared in the collection, *The Exact Name* (1965) and the *Latter Day Psalms* (1982) which was awarded the Sahitya Akademi prize.

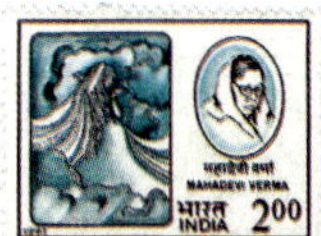

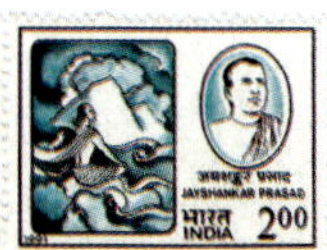

Nayantara Sehgal (Sahitya Akademi awardee) penned several of her memoirs in the 50s and 60s including *Prison and Chocoloate Cake* (1954) which recounts the turbulent childhood and the socio-political environment in the pre-independence growing up years. *From Fear Set Free* (1963), *Storm in Chandigarh*, *Rich Like Us* (1985) are some of her other notable works. **Mohan Malgonkar** was another notable writer of and the 60s who authored several works in fiction and non-fiction. This includes his acclaimed work *A Bend in the Ganges* (1964), besides others such as *A Combat of the Shadows* (1962) and the *Distant Drum* (1960). **Anita Desai** (born 1937, Sahitya Akademi awardee), a distinguished author short listed for the prestigious Booker Prize thrice, penned her first novels in the 60s. *Cry; The Peacock* (1963), *Voices in the City* (1965) were some of her early works, while *Fire on the Mountain* (1977) won her critical acclaim.

In the 70s, came the first of the many English novels of **Manoj Das** (Padma Bhushan, Sahitya Akademi Fellowship awardee) who by then was already an established author of Odia literature. Some of his salient works were *The Crocodile's Lady: A Collection of Stories* (1975), *Cyclones* (1981), *A Tiger at Twilight* (1991), *The Escapist*, (2001), besides others.

The 80s and 90s saw a flurry of Indian authors whose works made a mark in the world of English literature. **Vikram Seth** (Padma Shri and Sahitya Akdemi awardee), a prominent novelist and poet, came up with his celebrated works, *Mappings* (1980 – poem), *Golden Gate* (1986 – a novel in verse), *A Suitable Boy* (1993) and *An Equal Music* (1999), besides others.

Amitav Ghosh (Padma Shri, Sahitya Akademi and Jnanpith awardee) is another celebrated author of this generation whose popular and critically acclaimed works include, *The Circle of Reason* (1986-debut novel), *Shadow Lines* (1988), *The Calcutta Chromosomes* (1995), *The Glass Palace* (2000), *Sea of Poppies* (2008) and *River of Smoke (2011)* (last two being a part of Ibis trilogy).

In 1989, **Shashi Tharoor** (Sahitya Akademi awardee) made his debut with *The Great Indian Novel*. *The Show Business* (1992), *The Riot* (2001) are among his other works of fiction. His most notable non-fiction work amongst many is, *The Inglorious Empire: What The British Did to India* (2017), which succinctly brings out the systematic siphoning of the Indian wealth during the British misrule.

In the **decade of 90s** came the commercially successful and critically acclaimed novel, *The God of Small Things* (1997; winner of Booker Prize) by **Arundhati Roy**. Her second novel *The Ministry of Utmost Happiness*, came two decades later in 2017. Besides, she has also authored several essays which were compiled and published in the *Algebra of Infinite Justice.*

The **new millennium** has also seen several new authors making debut and enriching Indian English literature. They explore new subjects and new horizons, though no specific or common genre per-se. Some of the most notable of these are **Arvind Adiga** (*White Tiger*-Booker Prize awardee novel); **David Davidar** (*The House of Blue Mangoes*-2002, *Solitude of Emperors*-2007); **Jahnavi Barua** (*Next Door*-2008, *Rebirth* 2010), **Chetan Bhagat** (genre popular fiction, salient works; *Five Point Someone*-2004, *Two States*-2009) besides others.

Indian Born Expatriate Authors of English Literature

A number of Indian born expatriate authors have richly contributed to the world of English literature. **Nirad C Chaudhari** was among the earliest. **Kamala Markandaya** (1924-2004) was another eminent Indian author who migrated to Britain. Her notable works included *Nectar in the Sieve* (1954), *A Silence of Desire* (1960), *Possession* (1963), *Two Virgins* (1973), besides many others which often delved on the issue of the clash of cultures. **Lakshmi Holmstrom** (1935-2016) was another Indian expatriate in Britain who translated many of the Tamil works in English, besides penning short stories and novels; particularly in the 90s and 2000s. (*Sangati, Sillpaddikaram*-translation, *In A Forest, A Deer*-short stories).

Perhaps the most celebrated author in this category is **Salman Rushdie** (1947 born), an Indian-born British-American author, best known for his works like *Midnight's Children* (1981) and *Satanic Verses* (1988). While the former was feted with the Booker Prize in 1981 and accorded the title of best novel of all Booker winners in the 25th and 40th anniversary of the prize, the latter incited death threats and even attempted assassination against him. A writer of genre of magic realism and historical fiction, his other popular works include the *The Moor's Last Sigh* (1995) and *The Ground Beneath Her Feet* (1999), besides others.

Anita Desai (1971 born and daughter of Kiran Desai) whose very second book, *The Inheritance of Loss,* won the Booker Prize (2006) is another prominent author in this category. In 1987, **Rohinton Mistry** (Indian born Canadian author) made his debut with the novel, *Tales from Firozsha Baag*. His other works include *Such a Long Journey* (1991), *A Fine Balance* (1995) besides others. **Vikram Chandra** is an Indian American popular novelist of the 90s who is known for his bestsellers, such as *Red Earth and Pouring Rain: a Novel* (1995), *Love and Longing in Bombay: Stories* (1995) and *Sacred Games* (2006) (a popular web series).

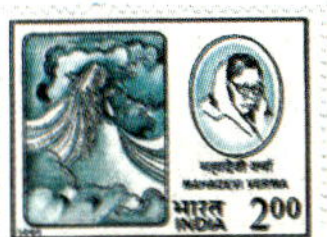

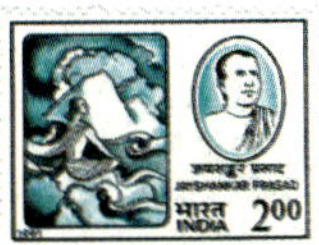

Hindi Literaure and The Phases of Evolution

Hindi language and literature has evolved through several centuries and has witnessesd and assimilated several socio-cultural, philosophical and political influences. The history of Hindi literature is broadly divided into four phases: the **Adikal**, the **Bhaktikal**, the **Ritikal,** and the **Adhunik Kal.**

The Adikal: The **Adikal** or the early/foremost period of Hindi literature spans a period of nearly four hundred years, from the middle of 10th century till the end of the 14th century. The literary works which were usually in the form of poems, eulogised the heroic deeds of Rajput kings and warriors. These included some grand works such as *Prithviraj Raso* by **Chand Bardai** and **Narpati Nalha's** *Visaldev Raso*. Hence, it is also referred as the ***Veergatha-kal*** (age of valour) in Hindi literature. Besides, this period also saw works of *Siddhas* and *Nathpanthis* which brought out the religious ideologies (such as works of Gorakhnath).

Bhaktikal: The next phase of Hindi literature, **Bhaktikal** (15th to 17th century) saw saint poets such as **Surdas, Kabirdas, Tulsidas, Nanak, Meerabai, Rahim**, and others, whose works were inspired by *bhakti* or the spirit of devotion to God. These compositions were mostly in **Avadhi** or **Braj Bhasha,** which were precursors of the Khadi boli or modern Hindi. These were in the form of verses which were largely composed in *Dohas* (two liners), *Chaupais* (four liners), etc. The poets and literary works of this period are also classified into ***Nirguna***—or believers of a formless and attributeless God such as those of **Kabir, Nanak**, etc. and ***Saguna***—or believers of God with attribute/form which include the works of **Surdas, Tulsidas, Mirabai**, etc.

Ritikal: The next phase, **Ritikal**, comprised poets whose works were largely in *Sringara-rasa,* as opposed to *Bhakti-rasa* of Bhaktikal or *Veer-rasa* of Adikal. The emphasis in this phase shifted to the description of the physical beauty of Lord Krishna and his consort Radha. Later on, the element of devotion and spiritual values gradually waned from the poem. Thus, sensuousness, physical beauty, and romance became the primary attributes of the works. Poets like **Biharidas** and **Keshavdas** were the leading poets of this genre.

Adhunik Kal: The next phase in this journey of evolution was **Adhunik Kal** and modern Hindi literature. The *Adhunik kal* is said to begin in the middle of the 19th century with the phase **Bharatendu Yug** (1869–1893). This was followed by **Dwivedi Yug** (1813–1937). The period post 1937 has been referred as **Adhunik Yug,** or the contemporary period.

The advent of **Bharatendu Harishchandra** in the literary scene in the mid 19th century heralded the modern period of Hindi literature, and thus it is quiet appropriate that he is referred as the father of modern Hindi literature. His works included prose, poetry, collection of plays, and translations. *Bharat Durdasha* and *Andher Nagari* were acclaimed plays which aroused the national consciousness. *Prem Madhuri* and *Raag Sangraah* were amongst many of his collection of poems while *Bharatendu Granthavali* is the collection of essays written by him.

Mahavir Prasad Dwivedi whose works ushered the **Dwivedi Yug** played a very significant role in establishing the modern Hindi literature, particularly the style of writing prose. His critical works include *Sahitya Sandarbh* and *Vichar Vimarsh*. He was also the editor of the prestigious *Saraswati* magazine whose editor he was from 1903-1920 and helped in evolution of Hindi prose.

Another stalwart of this age was **Maithili Sharan Gupta** who was the author of poems of the epic tradition like *Saket, Jayadrath-Vadh,* and *Yashodhara*. He popularised the use of Khariboli in Hindi literature. For his famous book *Bharat Bharati*, he was given the title of 'Rashtrakavi' by Mahatma Gandhi.

The next phase of Hindi literature saw the emergence of a number of poets of the ***Chhayavad*** genre; a style of poetry built on romanticism which had deeper and symbolic meaning other than the literal meaning of the verses. This phase included many eminent poets who were considered the pillars of *Chhayvaad* and included **Jaiashankar Prasad,** (works include *Kamayani, Chandragupta, Skandagupta, Dhruvswamini, Janmejayka Yagya, etc.*); **Suryakant Tripathi Nirala** (*Ram Ki Shaakti Puja, Parimal, etc.*); **Sumitranandan Pant** (*Chidambara*); **Mahadevi Verma** (*Mere Bachpan Ke Din, Neerja, Sandhya Geet, etc.*)

This phase also saw another stalwart of Hindi poetry, **Ramdhari Singh Dinkar** who is also considered a Rashtrakavi, whose works contained elements of *Chhayavad* as well as of next genre of progressive literature (*Kurukshetra, Rashmirathi, Urvashi, Parshuram ki Prateeksha, Sanskriti ke Chaar Adhyay, etc.*).

The period after *Chhayavad* called *Adhunik Yug* or contemporary literature saw emergence of new genres of literature. The first was the ***Pragativada*** or the **progressive movement**. This movement, which also was seen in the regional literature focused on the social realism. It emphasised on rootedness to the soil, brought out the plight and misery of the underprivileged, and explored the life of ordinary people. It was also inspired and influenced by the Gandhian and the Marxist philosophies. Eminent litterateurs of progressivism were **Premchand** (*Godan, Nirmala, Seva-Sadan,* etc.), **Nagarjun** (*Patarheen Nagna Gach* and *Kal Aur Aaj*) (Sahitya Akademi awardee), **Dinkar**, **Bhagwati Charan Verma** (*Chitralekha* and *Bhoole Bisre Chitra*) (Sahitya Akademi and Padma Bhushan awardee).

Pragativad was followed by ***Prayogavad***, or experimentalism, which could also be said to be a reaction to the earlier genres of *Chhayavad* and *Pragativad*. Thus, the poems of this phase experimented with new themes and unexplored areas of literature. **S.H. Vatsyayan**, **Ajneya**, **Shivmangal Singh Suman**, **Nirmal Verma,** and **Dharamveer Bharati** were prominent litterateurs of this phase.

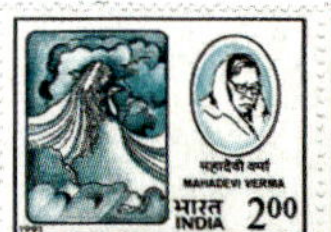

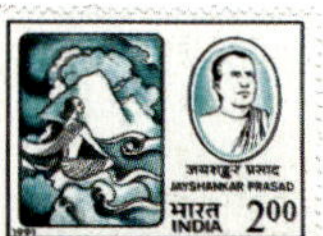

Apart from the growth of poetry in the above phases, prose writing in Hindi literature also evolved substantially. This comprised the writing of novels, plays, short stories, essays etc. **Pt. Devaki Nandan Khatri** was the earliest writers of novels (*Chandrakanta, Chandrakanta Santati*), while the greatest litterateur of Hindi prose was **Munshi Premchand.**

The post-independence literature was characterised by the occurrences which marked the Indian socio-political scene, viz. independence, partition, etc. It reflected the hopes and despair of people who were caught between the Indian ideals and Western values. This phase is referred to as the phase of realism in Hindi literature.

Like other regional literature, the next phase of Hindi literature is called **post-modernism**. It deals with issues of the common man and life as it is without the prejudices and ideologies of the previous literary genres.

REGIONAL LITERATURE & ITS EVOLUTION THROUGH THE AGES

The regional literature of India is quite diverse and vast. There are 22 scheduled languages and many other major languages each of which has a rich literature with a history ranging from hundreds to thousands of years. Here, a snapshot and salient elements of the prominent regional litterateurs and salient works are highlighted.

Assamese Literature

The earliest literary works of Assamese literature include the *Charyapadas* (Buddhist songs) of 8th to 12th century CE; the *Prahlada Charita* of **Hema Saraswati** (14th century CE). The **medieval literature** of the post Vaishnavite period includes works of **Sankardeva** such as *Kirtana-Ghosha*, *Harishchandra-Upakhyana*, etc. Other important litterateurs of this period include **Madhavdev**, **Damodardev**, etc.

The **modern literature** of Assam incorporates the works of **Hemchandra Barua, Lakshminath Bezbaruah,** and **Hemchandra Goswami.** Other prominent litterateurs of the 20th century are **Rajnikanta Bordoloi** (novelist and journalist), **Birendra Kumar Bhattacharya, Syed Abdul Malik** (Sahitya Akademi and Padma Bhushan awardee), **Navakanta Barua** (Sahitya Akademi and Padma Bhushan awardee), amongst others.

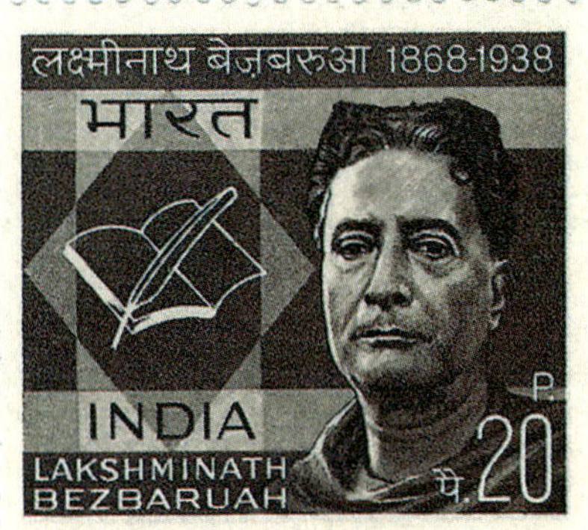

20.69: Lakshminath Bezbaruah, an Assamese poet, novelist and playwright; a stamp from 1968 — Courtesy, Department of Post

Bengali Literature

The earliest Bengali literature can be traced to the *Charyapads* and *Charyageet* of the 8th century CE, which were the songs in the Vajrayana and Tantric Buddhist tradition. Later, the *Panchali* and *Mangal-kavya* of the 12th and 13th century were composed in the region. *Panchali* was a genre of folk songs incorporating folklore and regional tales. *Manas Mangala* were hymns in praise of Manasa Devi which were composed by Kana Haridatta (13th century) and Bijay Gupta (15th century). *Geet Govinda* by **Jayadeva** (12th century) was another great literary work of this region. The Vaishnava texts of **Chaitanya** are examples of Bhakti literature composed in the medieval period.

In modern times, the greatest literary figure was **Rabindranath Tagore** who received the Nobel Prize for Literature (1913) for his collection of poems *Geetanjali*. His oeuvre which extends to poems, novels, plays and short stories, besides other works has dominated the literature of the region for nearly half a century. He also composed the poems adopted as national anthems of India and of Bangladesh.

Amongst other great litterateurs are **Bankim Chandra** (composed novels *Durgesh Nandini* and *Anand Math*), **Michael Madhusudan**

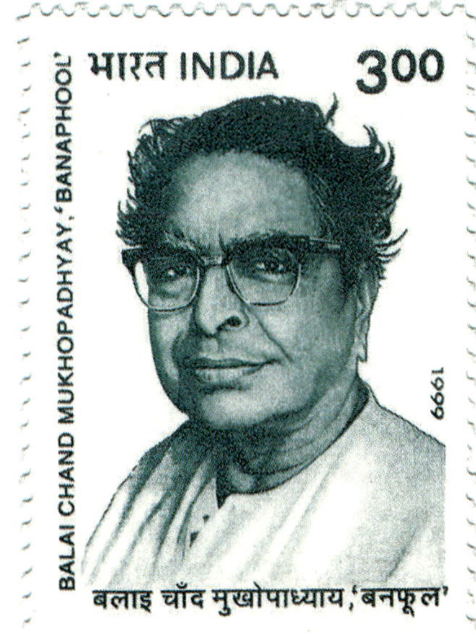

20.70: Balai Chand Mukhopadyaya a prolific Bangla writer; Banphool, a stamp from 1999 — Courtesy, Department of Post

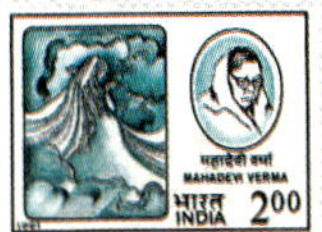

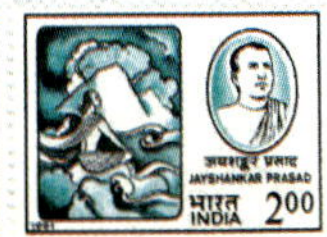

Dutta (composed literary epics like *Tilottama Sambhav Kavya*), **Kazi Nazrul Islam, Sunil Gangopadhyay,** and **Subhash Mukhopadhyay** (poet) (Sahitya Akademi and Jnanpith awardee), **Balai Chand Mukhopadyaya Banphool** amongst others.

Gujarati Literature

Gujarati literature is divided into three parts—the *Pracheen Sahitya* (early literature), *Madhyakalin Sahitya* (medieval literature, and *Arvachhin Sahitya* (modern literature). The **early literature** (up to 1450) comprised Gujarati writing by Jain authors which were in the form of *Rasas*, *Phagus*, and *Vilasas*. *Bharteshvara Bahubali-rasa* by **Salibhadra Suri** and **Vijaysena's** *Revanagiri-rasa* were important works of this time.

The Medieval literature comprised the Bhakti literature of saint poets like **Narsinh Mehta** who wrote *Surata Sangrama*, *Sringar Mala*, *Sudama Charit*, and *Govind Gaman*. **Akshaydas** (or Akh.), **Syamaldasa Bhatt,** and **Premananda Bhatta** were other great poets of the 17th and 18th century.

20.71: K.M. Munshi, a freedom fighter and prominent contributor to Gujarati, Hindi and English literature; a stamp from 1988 — Courtesy, Department of Post

Among the modern Gujarati litterateurs, the most important are **Dalpatram**, **Narmadashankar** (composed *Rajrang*, Gujarati dictionary), **K.M. Munshi**, **Mahatma Gandhi** {wrote *Satyana Prayogoor* (My Experiments with Truth) and *Satyagraha* in South Africa}, and **Umashankar Joshi** (Sahitya Akademi and Jnanpith awardee).

Kannada Literature

The Kannada literature can be divided into three phases, **old** (450 CE –1200), **middle** (1200 to 1700), and **modern** (1700 onwards). The Early and Middle phase literature were largely of religious origin which were of Jaina, Virashaiva, or Vaishnava tradition. *Kavirajamarga* (850 CE) written by Rashtrakuta king **Amoghavarsha** is the earliest known Kannada text. **Pampa** (9th century) and **Ponna** (10th century) were great poets of this phase.

In the **medieval period**, an important Kannada text was *Kumaravyasa Bharata* written by **Kumar Vyasa.** This contained the first ten *parvas* of Mahabharata. **Nijaguna Sivayogi** (15th century), a poet saint of Virashaiva tradition compiled *Viveka Chintamani,* an encyclopedic treatise on astronomy, medicine, poetry, musicology, dance-drama, etc.

Among the important **modern litterateurs** are **Kempu Narayana** of the 19th century (composed *Mudramanjusa*) and L. Lakshminarayanappa (composed *Rama Pattabhishekam*).

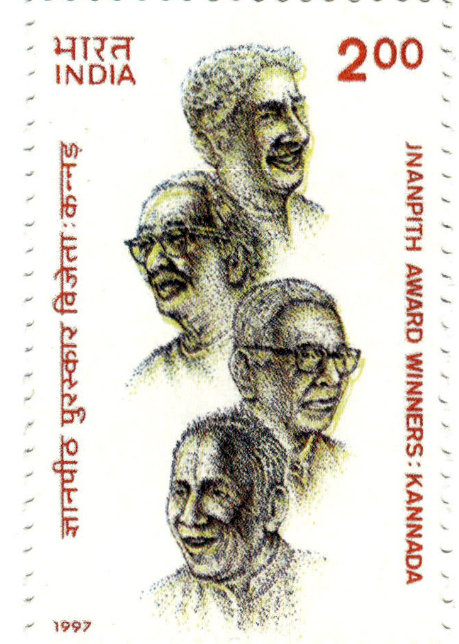

20.72: Kuvempu, Gokak, Bendre, Iyengar: Jnanpith awardees of Kannada literature, a stamp from 1997 — Courtesy, Department of Post

Among the post modern Kannada writers of acclaim are **Vinayaka Krishna Gokak** (Jnanpith and Padma Shri awardee), **U.R. Anantamurthy** (Sahitya Akademi, Jnanpith, and Padma Bhushan awardee), **D.R. Bendre** (Sahitya Akademi, Jnanpith and Padma Shri awardee), **K.V.Puttappa Kuvempu (**Sahitya Akademi and Padma Vibhushan awardee), and **M.V. Iyengar** (Jnanpith awardee).

Kashmiri Literature

Kashmiri is among the oldest languages of India tracing its origin to as early as the 5th to 6th century. In the course of evolution, it has been influenced by a variety of languages such as Sanskrit, Tibetan, Hindi, Persian, Dogri, etc.

Kalhana's *Rajatarangini* is the oldest Kashmiri literature (12th century). *Mahanaya-Prakasha* of **Rajanaka Shiti Kantha** is another important composition of the 14th century. In the medieval period, **Habba Khatoon** (poet and ascetic) composed *Lol* (poems on love and romance). She is also called the Nightingale of Kashmir. Further, in the medieval period, a Kashmiri adaptation of Ramayana was also brought out by Prakash Ram Bhatt.

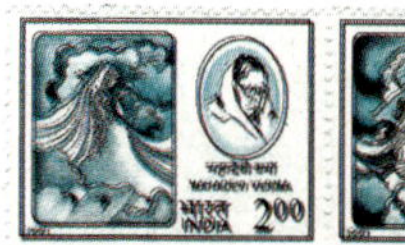
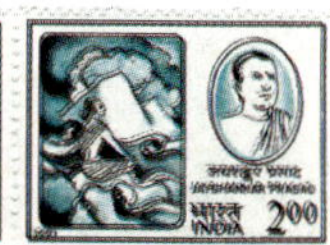

Important modern Kashmiri poets and litterateurs include **Rahman Rahi** (poet), (Sahitya Akademi, Jnanpith, and Padma Shri awardee), **Dinanath Nadim** (poet), and **Motilal Kemmu** (dramatist).

Malayalam Literature

Malayalam as a language traces its origin to the 9th century. As per scholars, the earlier forms of Malayalam literature could be an admixture of Malayalam and Tamil, Malayalam and Sanskrit, or pure Malayalam. *Ramacharitam* by **Cheeramakavi** (8th century) is among the oldest, Malayalam literature. Another milestone work in ancient Malyalam literature is *Bhasa Kautilya* (12th century), a commentary on *Arthashastra*.

In the **medieval period, C. Namboothri's** *Krishnagatha* is an important treatise, while **T. Ramanujan Ezhuthachan** (17th century) is considered as father of modern Malayalam language. His works include *Adhyatma Ramayanam*, *Sri Mahabharatam*, *Bhagwatam*, *Uttara Ramayanam*, etc.

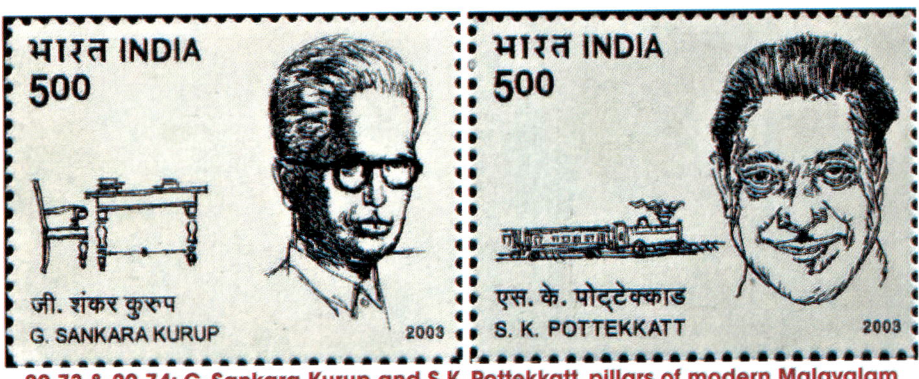

20.73 & 20.74: G. Sankara Kurup and S.K. Pottekkatt, pillars of modern Malayalam literature; stamps from 2003 — Courtesy, Department of Post

Written in 1887, *Kundalata* by T. M. Appu Nedungadi is considered the first Malayalam novel. The important modern Malayali litterateurs include **O. Chandu Menon** (novel writer), **P. Kesavadev**, **T.S. Pillai**, **Vaikom Mohammed Basheer** (Sahitya Akademi and Padma Shri awardee), **G. Sankara Kurup** (Sahitya Akademi, Jnanpith, and Padma Bhushan awardee), **S.K. Pottekkatt** (Sahitya Akademi and Jnanpith awardee), and **M.T. Vasudevan Nair** (Sahitya Akademi, Jnanpith, and Padma Bhushan awardee), amongst others.

Marathi Literature

The literature in Marathi is around a thousand years old and is divided into **old/ancient literature** (1000 to 1800) and **modern literature** (1800 onwards). The first major work in Marathi is considered to be *Viveka Sindhu* by Mukund Raj (12th century).

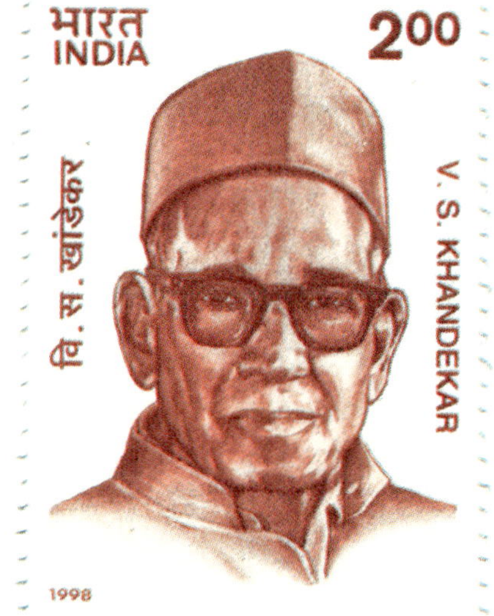

20.75: V. S Khandekar, eminent Marathi novelist, a stamp released in 1998 — Courtesy, Department of Post

In the medieval period the *bhakti* saints too made immense contribution to Marathi literature. This includes **Dyaneshwar's** (13th century) *Dnyaneshwari* and *Amrutanubhav*, **Namdev's** (14th century) *bhakti* poetry, *Eknath's* (16th century) *Eknathi Bhagwat*, **Tukaram's** (17th century) over 3000 *Abhanga* poetry, and **Samarth Ramdas's** (17th century) *Dasabodha.*

Keshavsuta (19th century) can be said to be the first **modern Marathi poet**. **Madhav Julian** was another prominent poet who formed the *Ravikiran Mandal* which comprised poets who wrote romantic and Victorian poetry. **Hari Narayan Apte's** *Madhali Sthiti* is considered the first Marathi novel.

With the beginning of journalism in the 19th century, a number of personalities associated with social reforms and freedom movement contributed to the national cause through Marathi journalism and literature. This includes **Jyotiba Phule** (*Deenbandhu*; a journal), **Bal Gangadhar Tilak** (newspaper; *Kesari*), and **Gopal Krishna Gokhale** (newspaper; *Sudharak*)

Post-independence, prominent Marathi litterateurs include **Vijay Tendulkar** (playwright; Padma Bhushan awardee and Saraswati Samman), **Vishnu S. Khandekar** (Sahitya Akademi, Jnanpith, and Padma Bhushan awardee) (novelist), **Vishnu Vaman Shirwadkar** (poet, playwright, and novelist; Jnanpith and Padma Bhushan awardee), **Vinda Karandikar** (poet, writer, and critic; Jnanpith awardee), **Bhalchandra Nemade** (novelist and critic; Jnanpith and Padma Shri awardee).

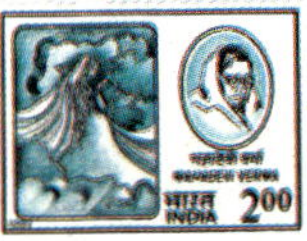

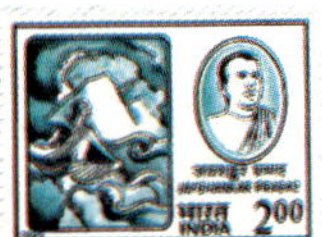

Mizo Literature

This literature is composed in the **Mizo tawng** language which is the main language of Mizo people. It has undergone major evolution in the 19th and 20th century, with Mizo alphabets being created in 1894 and the first Mizo language book published in 1896 which is *Mizo Zir Tir Bu*: (A Mizo primer).

The early Mizo literature was brought out by Christian missionaries. Prominent writers of the 20th century include **Liangkhaia** who published a number of articles in the monthly *Kristian Tlangau* and also authored *Mizo chanchin*.

Other prominent litterateurs were **Awithangpa** (poet) and **Pu Rokunga** (poet). **Nuchhungi Renthlei** and **Laithangfala Sailo** (prose and short stories), were also recipients of Padma Shri award.

Oriya Literature

The Oriya literature can be traced to the *Charyapadas* written in the 8th century CE. The earliest important Oriya literary work can be said to be *Chandi Purana*, *Vilanka Ramayana*, and *Mahabharata* written by **Sarala Das** in the 14th century. *Rama-Bibah*, written by **Arjuna Dasa**, was another important literary work in the nature of an epic poem.

The medieval Oriya literature was inspired by Bhakti movement, particularly Chaitanya's Vaishnavism.

Ramchandra Patnayak's *Harvali* was a novel of the 17th century. The 19th century saw three great Oriya poets in **Rai Bahadur Radhanatha Ray, Madhusudan Rao,** and **Phakiramohana Senapati.** Phakiramohana Senapati was a novelist and poet who contributed significantly to Odia literature in the 19th century.

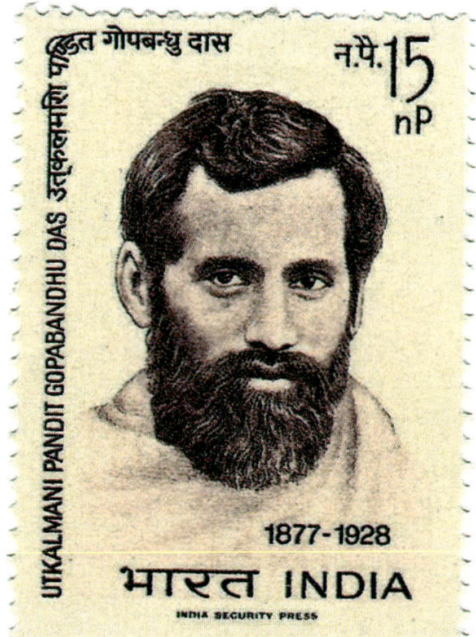

20.76: Gopabandhu Das, a journalist, reformer, poet, political activist and an Odia novelist, a stamp released in 1968 — Courtesy, Department of Post

Important Oriya litterateurs of the 20th century include **Gopa Bandhu Das Gopal Chandra Praharaj** (compiled *Purnachandra Odia Bhashakosha)*, **Annada Shankar Ray** (poet and essayist; Sahitya Akademi and Padma awardee), **Kalindi Charan Panigrahi** (poet and novelist), **Ramakanta Rath** (poet; Sahitya Akademi, Saraswati Samman, and Padma Bhushan awardee), **Sitakant Mahapatra** (poet and critic; Sahitya Akademi, Jnanpith, and Padma Vibhushan awardee) besides others.

Punjabi Literature

The tradition of Punjabi literature can be traced to the Sufi saint Fariduddin Ganjshakar (Sufi saint and poet) (12th and 13th century). Further, the teachings and composition of the 10 Sikh gurus and other related religious literature form the bulk of the Punjabi literature of the medieval period. This includes the *Janam-sakhis* (biographies of gurus), *Bachnas* (sayings), *Paramarthas* (commentary on scriptures), *Gurbani,* etc.

Heer-Ranjha by **Waris Shah**, and *Sohni-Mahiwal* by **Fazal Shah**, were romantic, non-religious stories of this period. The medieval Punjabi literature also incorporates heroic poetry, *Vaar* which are Punjabi ballads. Guru Gobind Singh's *Chandi di Vaar* (depicting battles of Goddess Durga with demons, is also an example of epic heroic poetry.

Litterateurs of modern period include **Amrita Pritam** (writer and poet; Sahitya Akademi, Jnanpith, and Padma Vibhushan awardee), **Jaswant Singh Rahi** (poet; designated as Rashtrakavi by Government of India), **Pash, Kulwant Singh Virk** (Sahitya Akademi awardee), **Balwant Gargi** (playwright, novelist; Sahitya Akademi, and Padma Shri awardee), **Harbhajan Singh** (poet; Sahitya Akademi and Saraswati Samman) among others.

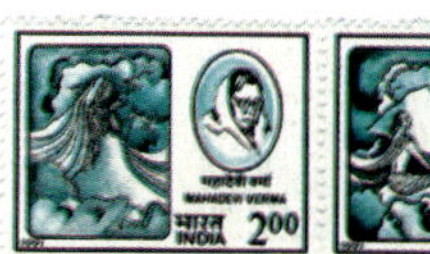
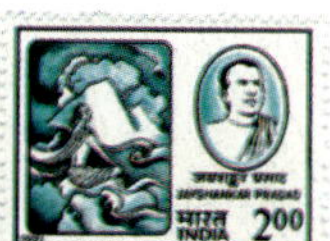

Sindhi Literature

Sindhi literature is centuries old. The earliest reference to Sindhi literature is found in references of Arab historians. Records of Sindhi literature are also noted in the heroic ballads of **Shah Abdul Karim** of the 16th century. The most important contribution to Sindhi literature in the medieval period is the poetic compendium *Shah-Jo- Risalo* by **Shah Abdul Latif** who was a Sufi poet.

In the modern Sindhi literature, the important contributors are **Kishanchand Bevas** (poet), **Dayaram Gidumal** (poet), **Hyder Bakhsh Jatoi** (poet), and **Kauromal Chandanmal Khilnani** (prose). In the post-independence period, renowned contributors to Sindhi literature are **Ram Panjwani** (Padma Shri awardee), **Sundri Uttamchandani** and **Prof M.U. Malkani** (Sahitya Akademi awardees) besides others.

Tamil Literature

Tamil literature is one of the oldest literatures of India after the Sanskrit literature. Its history is traced to the Sangam period of the 3rd century BCE to 4th century CE. The *Tolkappiyam- a* commentary on grammar and phonetics, and *Thirukkural* or *Kural*, by **Thiruvalluvar** are great masterpieces of this period.

The subsequent centuries saw a mass of religious literature of the Alvars, Nayanars, and Virashaivas. The period of Cholas saw great literary works such as *Kamba Ramayana* (adaptation of Valmiki Ramayana, also called Ramavataram) by Kamban.

In modern period, **Samuel Vedanayagam Pillai** was the first Tamil novelist. **Subramania Bharati** was a renowned litterateur who wrote inspirational and patriotic poems and songs. **U.V. Swaminatha Iyer** (poet) worked for revival of interest in Sangam literature.

Other prominent Tamil litterateurs of the modern period are **Akilan** (novelist and short story writer; Jnanpith awardee) and **Jayakanthan** (writer and journalist; Sahitya Akademi, Jnanpith, and Padma Bhushan awardee) amongst others.

Telugu Literature

The history of Telugu literature is nearly a thousand years old with the earliest account of Telugu literature being noted in the translation of Mahabharata in Telugu from Sanskrit by **Nannaya Bhattaraka** who composed the *Andhra Mahabharatam*. Telugu literature was subsequently influenced by Lingayat movement or the Virashaivism.

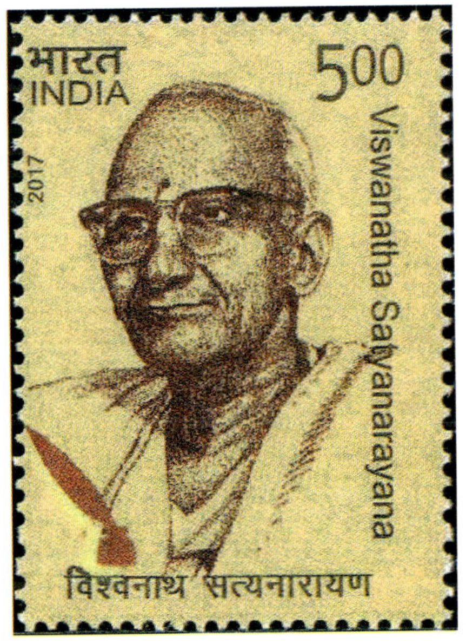

20.77: Viswanatha Satyanarayana, an eminent modern Telugu litterateur; a stamp released in 2017 — Courtesy, Department of Post

The medieval period of Telugu literature (14th and 15th century) is referred as the age of **Srinatha**. During this period, evolution of the **Prabandha style** composition took place. Srinatha was a court poet and composed *Salivahana Saptshati, Shivaratri Mahatyam, Harivilasa,* etc.

The Vijayanagara empire period (14th to 17th century) was the golden period of Telugu literature and it is said that eight Telugu luminaries called the *Ashtadiggajas* were a part of king Krishnadevaraya's court.

In the modern period, **K. Veeresalingam Pantulu** is considered as the father of modern Telugu literature and is credited to have written over a 100 books. He also played a prominent role in the development of Telugu journalism.

Other important litterateurs of modern Telugu are **R. Subba Rao** (poet), **G. Appa Rao** (poet), **K. Venkateswara Rao**, **Viswanatha Satyanarayana** (Sahitya Akademi, Jnanpith, and Padma Bhushan awardee), C. Narayan Reddy (Jnanpith and Padma Bhushan awardee), and **Ravuri Bharadhwaja** (Sahitya Akademi and Jnanpith awardee).

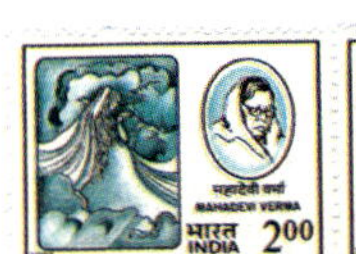
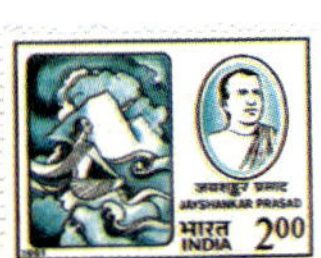

Urdu Literature

Urdu as a language developed around the 14th century as a result of the confluence of the Hindu and Islamic cultures. The language derived its vocabulary from Arabic and Persian and also from the Sanskrit based Prakrit.

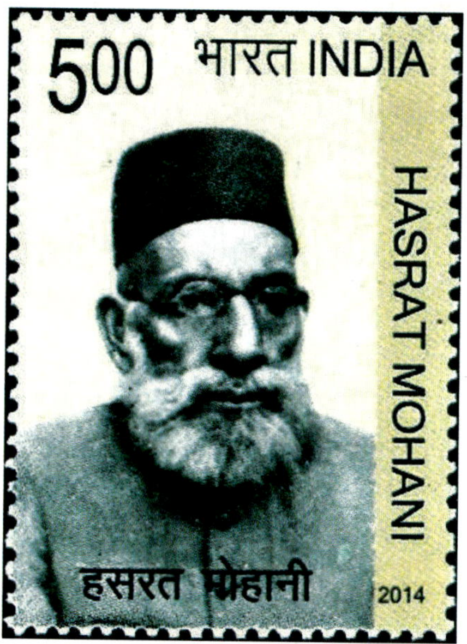

20.78: Hasrat Mohani, a poet and freedom fighter who coined the slogan *inquilab zindabad* (long live the revolution); a stamp from 2014 — Courtesy, Department of Post

Amir Khusro was one of the earliest and the greatest influence on the growth of its literature. It also gained from the teachings and compositions of Sufi saints such as **Khwaja Banda Nawaz Gesu Daraz**. **Muhammad Quli Qutb Shah**, ruler of Golconda, and a distinguished poet, brought secular context to Urdu literature. **Ibrahim Adil Shah**, a ruler of Deccan (17th century) was another royal Urdu poet of medieval period. Wali Mohammad Wali (17th century) is considered by scholars as the father of Urdu poetry.

In the 19th century, **Bahadur Shah Zafar** the last Mughal emperor, was a prominent Urdu poet; while **Mirza Asadullah Khan Ghalib** (19th century) is considered to be the greatest of Urdu poets. Among the other renowned Udu poets of this period were were **Mir Taqi Mir** (in 18th- 19th century) and **Mohammad Ibrahim Zauq** (19th century). The Aligarh movement by **Syed Ahmad Khan** (19th century) was a prominent influence on Urdu literature too. **Hasrat Mohani** (poet), **Muhammad Iqbal** (poet), **Munshi Premchand** (novelist), **Krishan Chander** (novelist), **Rajinder Singh Bedi** (writer, screen writer), **Saadat Hasan Manto** (short stories), and **Faiz Ahmed Faiz** (poet) are prominent Urdu writers of pre-Independence India. The partition of India had its impact on Urdu literature too.

During the post independence period, the prominent Urdu litterateurs were **Ismat Chugtai, Qurratulain Hyder** (Jnanpith, Sahitya Akademi and Padma Bhushan awardee), **Rashid Jahan** (short stories and plays), **Firaq Gorakhpuri** (Jnanpith, Sahitya Akademi, and Padma Bhushan awardee), and **Qazi Abdul Sattar** (novelist). In the new millennium, like other literatures, Urdu literature also experiences the upheavals of modern times. The challenge to tradtional literature, demand of commerce, diminshing readership base, influence of English on the tradtional market, emerging electronic and digital contents besides other factors, are the headwinds faced by Urdu literature. Evolving as per the times, remaining relevant in the modern context and thus contributing to the common culture of India, remains the challenge to Urdu as well as other languages and literature of today.

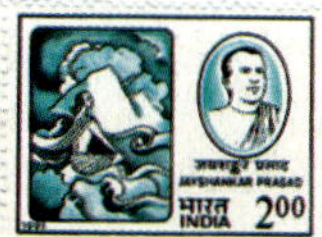

Folk and Modern Theatre of India

यथो हस्त तथौ दृष्टि,
यथो दृष्टि तथौ मनः ,
यथो मनः तथो भाव,
यथो भाव तथौ रस !
-नाट्यशास्त्र

Wherever the hand goes, the eyes follow,
Wherever the eyes go, the mind follows,
Wherever the mind goes, there is an expression of inner feelings,
Wherever there is an expression of inner feeling, emotions are evoked.

— *Natyashastra*

"All the world's a stage.

And all the men and women merely players;

They have their exits and their entrances,

And one man in his time plays many parts."

— William Shakespeare, English poet, playwright

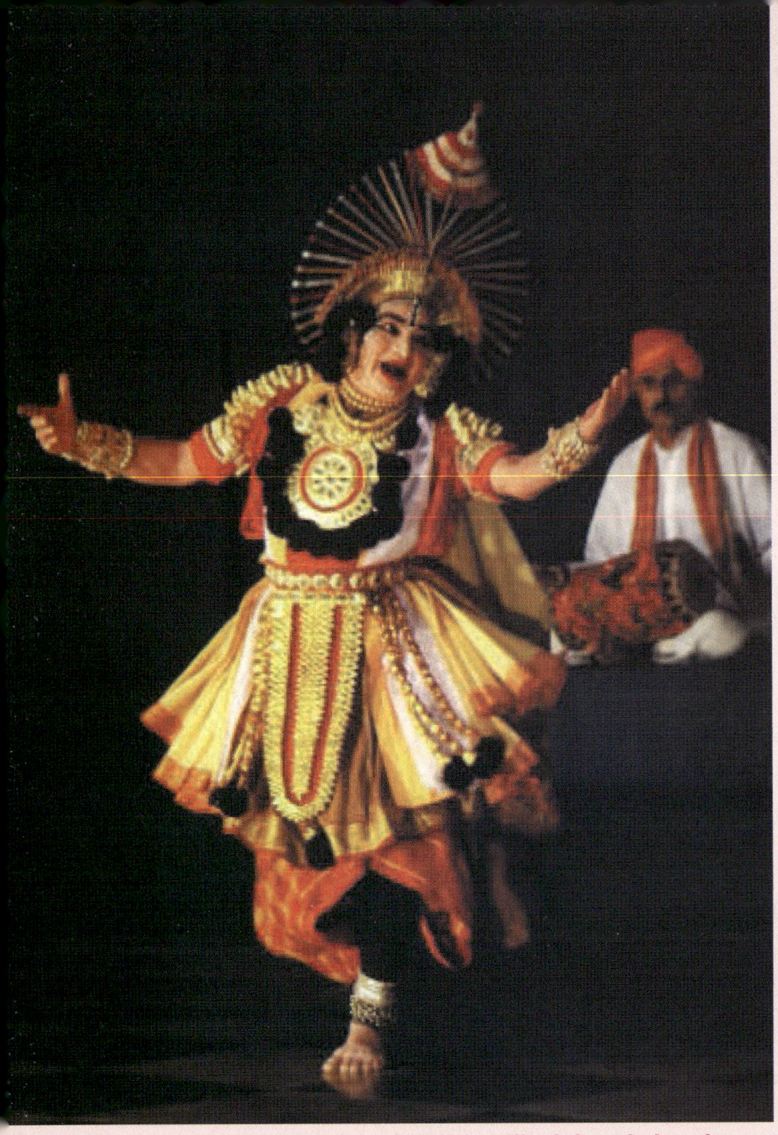

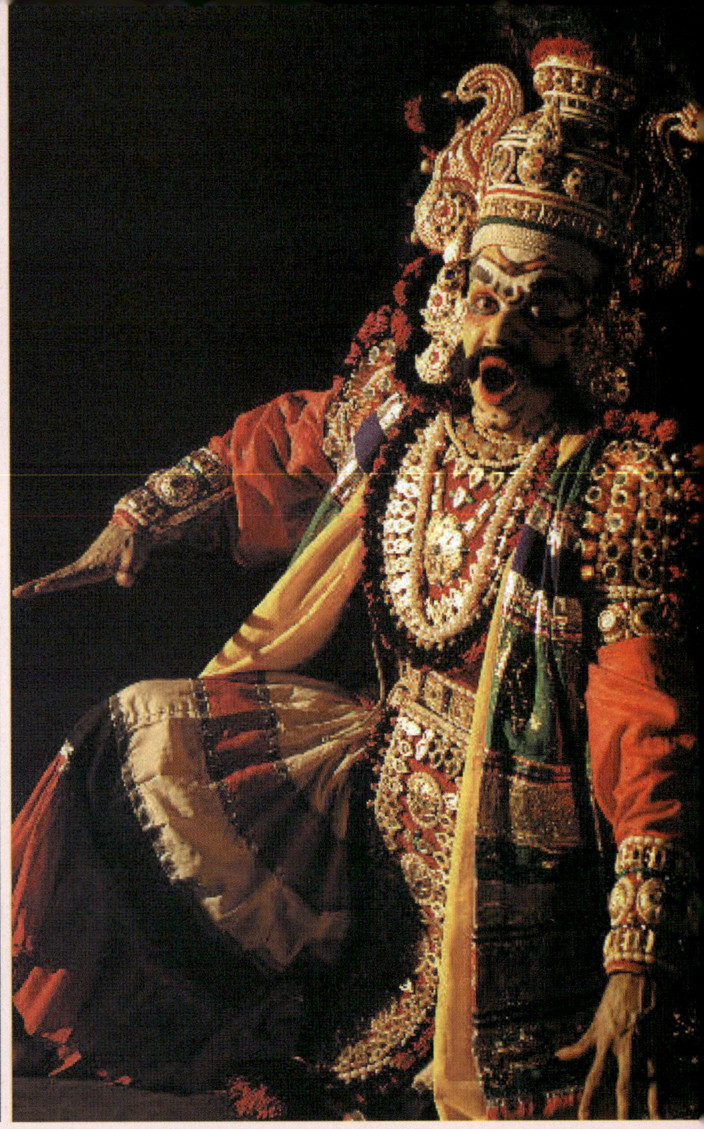

21.1 & 21.2: Artists with elaborate headgear, makeup and costume performing Yakshagana — Courtesy, Karnataka Tourism Development Corporation

21.3: A Koodiyattam performance — Courtesy, Sangeet Natak Akademi

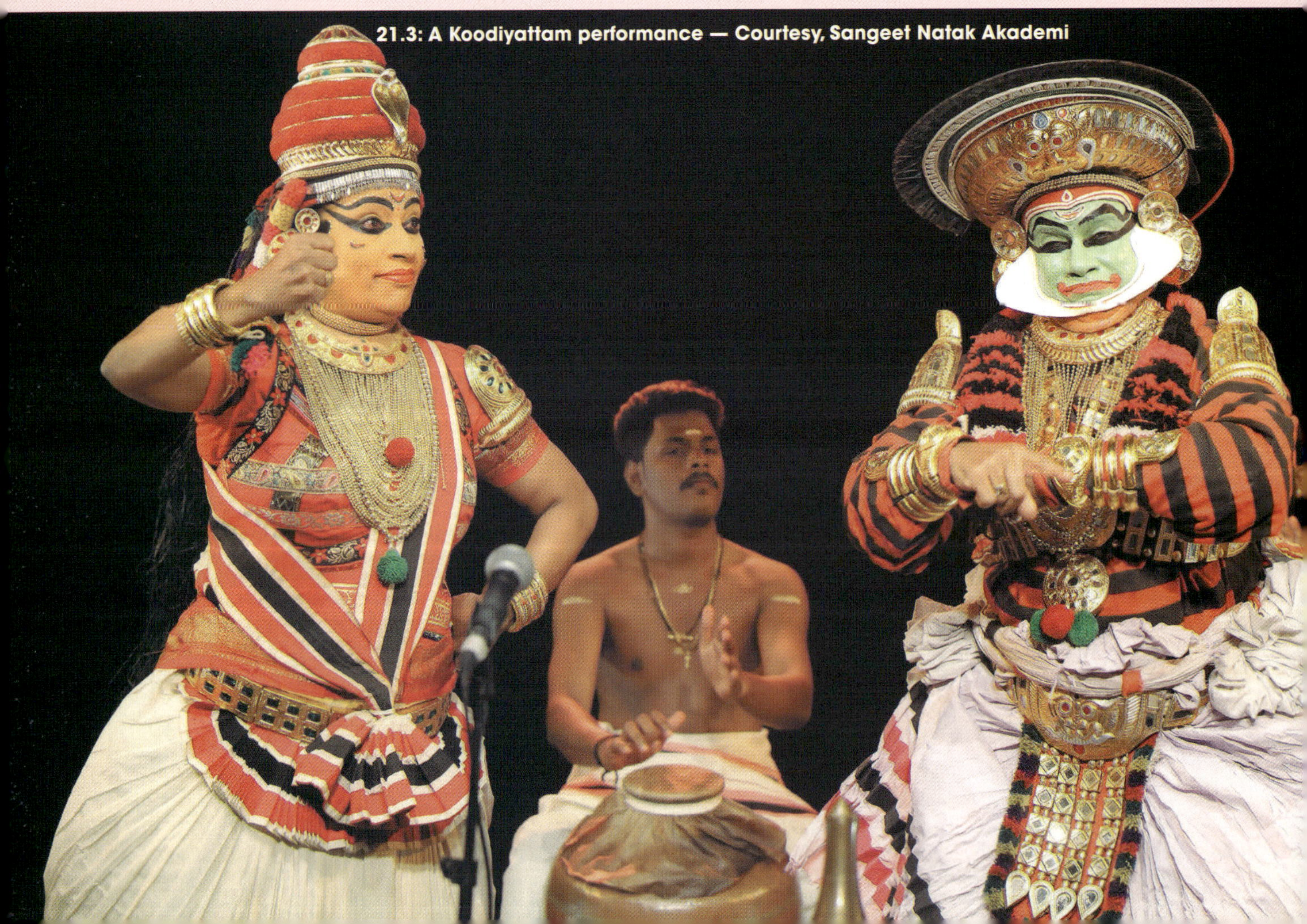

INDIAN THEATRE AND ITS ORIGIN

Theatre is a performing art which is a personified expression of a human narratives, stories, anecdotes, events and activities. Like other art forms, it is a vital means to express the human emotions, sentiments and ideas of the people and society. The art is often presented in a collaborative manner over a stage or a specified area of performance, before a group of people. Over the centuries, theatre has been one of the important tools of social communication as well entertainment of the masses. As a performing art, it is integrative of the various elements of art and literature and thus reflective of the culture of the people.

Theatre and Drama

Theatre and drama are two terms which are used with respect to the performing art, albeit used interchangeably. The word 'drama' is of Greek origin, derived from the word deed (or act) and thus signifies action. Drama is a generic word which represents many forms of fiction which may be performed in a form of a ballet, mime, opera or play. Thus, mime, where the story is conveyed through the action of the body and some expressions, is a form of drama. Ballet brings out the story in form of a dance, while opera combines it with song and music and at times with dance movements. Plays afford a larger freedom of expression through spoken words as well as bodily movement and action. Thus, drama is essentially an abstract work which is brought to live by the performers.

On the other hand, theatre as a performing art can be said to be the personification of the drama on a stage or in front of people. This is a collaborative process which requires the playwright, a play or an act, an actor/a set of actors, technicians, and also a stage or the physical set up for staging the play. The term 'theatre' also refers to the physical infrastructure which is essential for staging a play, which in the modern context may include the building, the space, the staging area, the audience area, the curtains, the sound and light systems, besides other paraphernalia. While theatre is one of the ways in which drama is brought before the public or performed, other platforms or means of expression of drama can be radio, television, movies and of late, web-based series.

The tradition of theatre in India has a history of several thousands of years. Over centuries, this ancient heritage has seen periods of great bloom as well as phases of gradual waning. The earliest reference to Sanskrit drama is found in the works of **Panini** in the 4th–5th century BCE, and later in *Mahabhashya* of **Patanjali** in the 2nd-1st century BCE. Theatre and its various forms are documented in the ***Natyashastra*** by **Bharata** (200 BCE to 200 CE), one of the leading treatises of dramaturgy, and an encyclopaedic work of ancient Indian theatre. A work which integrates dance, music and acting with theatre, also brings out the origin of drama, the description of the various types of theatre (playhouse), the preliminaries of a play, besides other salient elements of acting (*abhinaya*), dance, music, dramatic construction, costumes, makeup, props, etc. Nandikeshvara's *Abhinaya Darpana* was another ancient text which elucidated the elements of Indian drama. *Abhinavabharati*, by Abhinavagupta, composed in the 10th-11th century CE is yet another important treatise, which is in nature of a commentary on *Natyashastra.*

Over the period of centuries, there was evolution of the classical Sanskrit theatre. This comprised a wide variety of Sanskrit plays written by eminent dramatists of the ancient world such as **Ashvaghosha**, **Kalidasa**, **Bhasa**, **Sudraka**, **Bhavabhuti** and others. The classical Sanskrit theatre reached a golden phase by the 5th century CE. This theatre was traditionally performed on sacred grounds such as in temples and its courtyards, and later on, in palaces. Its objective was to educate as well as entertain the people. As a form of art, it was bound by certain rules and traditions. For example, a *sutradhar* (holder of strings) who was like a stage manager/director, was considered integral to the play. Invocation of God and pre-play rituals (*purvaranga,* comprising music and dance) at the beginning of the theatrical performance was another salient element. The theatre itself could employ male as well as female actors, or both. But certain types of sentiments and characters were considered better suited for either male or female and hence there was a typecasting of roles to a certain degree.

Natyashastra and Different Genre of Plays

Bharata's *Natyashastra* identifies 10 types of dramas or *Rupakas* which are *Nataka, Prakarana, Samavakara, Iharmriga, Dima, Vyayoga, Anka, Prahasana, Bhana,* and *Vithi*. Amongst these, the *Nataka* and *Prakarana* were two types of plays which were emphasised upon in the *Natyashastra.* The *Natakas* were often based on epics and Puranas. As per Bharata, the central character in the *Nataka* was to be virtuous, of striking abilities, glorious, and preserver of the *dharma* and the Vedas. Thus, it was a heroic form of play often based on the lofty themes of Gods and virtuous kings. *Shakuntala* by Kalidasa and *Uttararamacharita* by Bhavabhuti are some glorious works of this genre.

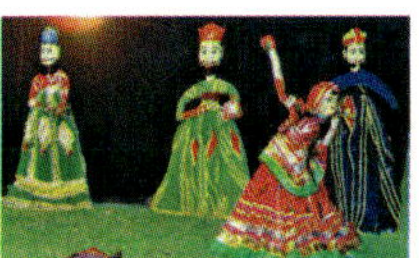

The other popular format, *Prakarana,* was to be the author's own creation and not based on an inspiration from an epic or retelling of its parts. The characters could have different sorts of *vrittis* (viz. attributes). It could be a work dwelling on ordinary human beings from daily social lives. *Mrichchhakatika* (the Little Clay Cart) of Sudraka is a notable work of this category. *Prakarana* could also not have less than five acts and not more than 10. In general, the plays would have anything between one to 10 acts. There could be one act plays as well, which could further be of different category such as *bhana* – a single character-based mono-acting, or in which the actor carries a dialogue with an invisible character. *Prahasana* was another one act play which literally means farce, and could deal with characters such as courtesans and crooks. Thus, a variety of plays were specified with very well-defined rules.

Though the Sanskrit theatre was quite popular in the 1st millennia, it suffered a decline thereafter. The lack of royal patronage, diminishing significance of Sanskrit as a mass language, and emerging languages like *Prakrit* which were becoming popular, were some of the factors responsible for this decline. Further, the orthodoxy of the Sanskrit theatre also restricted the creative manoeuvrability of the playwrights. With the advent of the Islamic regime, Sanskrit theatre suffered a further decline and remained alive only in a few pockets of the country. However, its elements did remain preserved in the form of folk and rural theatres even in the periods of 15th to 19th centuries. Thus, the ancient art form has survived through the ages and influenced the arts of drama, particularly in the folk form even through the modern age.

Different forms of theatrical expression: With the changing times, evolving culture and new technology coming up, theatre in the modern times has taken different forms of expression. These broadly can be said to be the **folk theatre**, the **modern theatre**, and the **cinema**. Also, web serials and movies streaming exclusively through other electronic and digital platforms (OTT) is the new entrant. While the traditional **folk theatre** continues, reposited in the lore and traditions of the people and connected to their roots, **modern theatre** drawing from the European and traditional cultural influences has also evolved. However, the art of communication through drama took a new form in the 20th century with the advent of the talkies and growth of **Indian cinema**. In the later years, technology has given birth to different forms of platforms for the artistic expression including radio, television, web-series and internet based digital content.

Though the culture and time has changed and so has the platform for this artistic expression, its essence remains the same. A dynamic artistic communication of human ideas, feelings and emotions in the context of the changing society and its values, has emerged in the modern times.

FOLK THEATRE

Folk theatre is indeed a salient element of our cultural heritage and a centuries old enduring, abiding and **living tradition**. It is a fusion of different elements of performing arts including **dances, singing** and **music**, besides literary arts like **poetry**/writing of **verses**. Arts of **pantomime**, **ballad recitation** are some of its other elements. Further, it even **integrates numerous traditional crafts** like puppetry and those arts which find an expression in costume making and other accessories to the theatre. The different elements of *Nritta*, *Nritya* and *Natya* are at times seen encapsulated. As traditional theatre based on the language of the local communities, it has not been bound by the classical rules and expresses the creativity and spontaneity of the common people. Over the centuries, it has served as a medium for dissemination of religious messages and a means of social communication. At the same time, it has also helped in integration of communities, besides serving as a salient form of folk entertainment.

The Indian theatre tradition is several thousands of years old as seen in its reposition in the Natyashastra. However, the tradition of folk theatres can be traced to the early phase of the 2nd millennium CE when the classical Sanskrit theatre started to decline. While the former was more established and urban oriented, the folk theatre had its roots in the rural society, was simpler in form, and had a deeper connect with the common people. However, it was the Bhakti movement, and in particular the period of 15th to 16th century, which provided a fillip to the folk theatre and disseminated the art form, far and wide.

While the early character of this theatre was religious, over a period of centuries, even secular folk theatre evolved. In modern times, folk theatre may broadly be classified as those which are **religious or secular**. Thus, today the folk theatre is either **ritual based** or **entertainment oriented**.

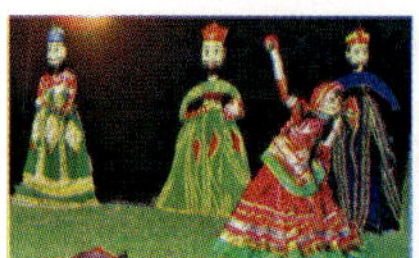

Folk theatre continues to remain integral to the local culture and is popular in different parts of India. Some prominent forms of folk theatre include **Ramlila, Krishnalila, Nautanki, Jatra, Tamasha, Bhavai, Yakshagana, Bhand Pather,** and **Swang**. These have been in vogue for centuries and all of these have been an important means of spreading religious and social messages, as well as entertainment.

Ramlila

This folk theatre is an enactment of the story of the life of **Lord Rama**. Ramlila literally means, **'Rama's play'** (*lila*). This terminology is believed to implys a playful drama, which is a recounting of Lord Rama's life. As per some accounts, it also signifies a joyful or playful engagement in the affairs of this material world by Lord Rama, who is an incarnation of Lord Vishnu. Ramlila is truly one of the most significant of folk theatres of the country and is especially popular in Uttar Pradesh, Bihar, Madhya Pradesh, and other parts of India. Many forms of this folk theatre are prevalent even in Southeast Asia and East Asia particularly in Bali, Indonesia, Malaysia and Thailand. Besides, in various other countries, this tradition has taken roots; like in Fiji, Mauritius, South Africa, Trinidad and Tobago, Caribbean islands and others where the indentured labours and other Indians migrated.

The tradition of Ramlila is centuries old. Scholars believe that the written account of the great epic would have been compiled around 1st century CE, while the actual creation of this epic could have taken place much earlier. Over a period of several thousand years, the legacy continued to survive due to the oral tradition of lore, tradition of bards and also due to the tradition of the Ramilias. While the earlier Ramlilas may have been based on the **Valmiki Ramayana**, most of the modern Ramlilas in the country incorporate the episodes from the **Ramcharitamanas** of Tulsidas which brought the Sanskrit epic close to the common masses. The Ramlila is usually performed during the festivals of **Navaratri and Dussehra**. The performances of different episodes often stretch over a period of 10 days. The burning of the effigies of Ravana, Meghanad and Kumbhakarana, marks the conclusion of the Ramlila, which takes place on the 10th day. Some Ramlilas may even last for an entire month as is the case of those of Ramnagar.

Among the most significant and representative of the Ramlilas, are those of; **Ayodhya, Ramnagar, Vrindavan, Varanasi, Almora, Satna** and **Madhubani**. The conduct of the Ramlilas has mostly taken place through people's participation. Often, voluntary Ramlila committees (*samiti*) have provided the organisational support, and community funding has been the source of finance. Over the centuries, Ramlilas have served as a **living cultural tradition**. It has emerged as an institution in itself, which has transcended the cultural, ethnic and religious diversity and provided a stable anchor amidst the changing cultural phases and turbulent times.

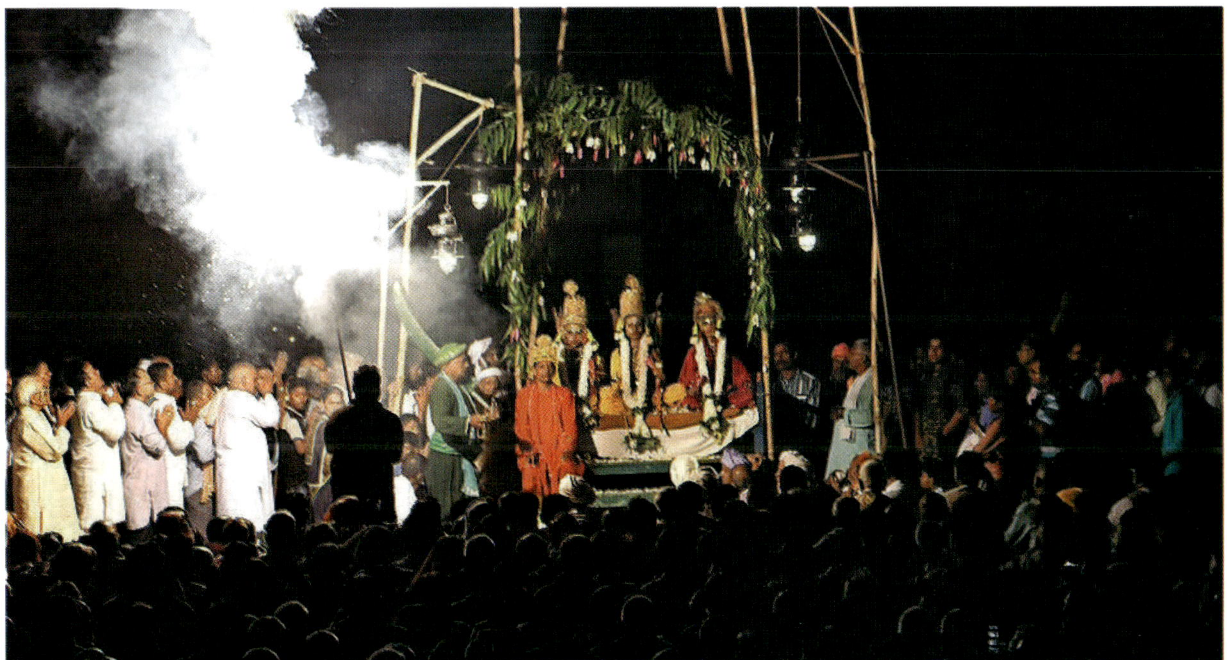

21.4: Ramnagar Ramlila, an intangible cultural heritage — Wikimedia Commons

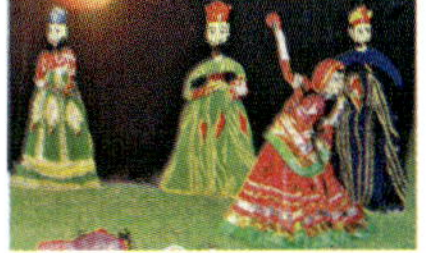

Ramlila: An Intangible Cultural Heritage of Humanity

The UNESCO, in 2008 has recognized, 'Ramlila; The Traditional Performance of Ramayana', as a masterpiece of oral and intangible cultural heritage of humanity. Some of the significant observations from the citation of UNESCO are as below.

Ramlila, literally "Rama's play", is a performance of the Ramayana epic in a series of scenes that include song, narration, recital and dialogue.

......The majority of the Ramlilas recount episodes from the Ramacharitmanas through a series of performances lasting ten to twelve days, but some, such as Ramnagar's, may last an entire month. Festivals are organized in hundreds of settlements, towns and villages during the Dussehra festival season celebrating Rama's return from exile. Ramlila recalls the battle between Rama and Ravana and consists of a series of dialogues between gods, sages and the faithful. Ramlila's dramatic force stems from the succession of icons representing the climax of each scene. The audience is invited to sing and take part in the narration. ***The Ramlila brings the whole population together, without distinction of caste, religion or age.*** *All the villagers participate spontaneously, playing roles or taking part in a variety of related activities, such as mask-and costume making, and preparing make-up, effigies and lights. However, the development of mass media, particularly television soap operas, is leading to a reduction in the audience of the Ramlila plays, which are therefore losing their principal role of bringing people and communities together.*

Krishna Lila and Rasalila

Krishna Lila, which literally means 'the play of Krishna', is analogous to Ramlila and recounts the story of **Lord Krishna** or anecdotes which are associated with his life. Like Ramlila, the tradition of this folk theatre is centuries old and can be traced to the Puranic period. The theatre itself draws from the Bhagvata Purana, Vishnu Purana and other classical works such as Gita-Govinda (the 12th century poetic work of Jayadeva). This folk theatre is performed in different parts of the country and is especially popular in the Braj region of western Uttar Pradesh. Childhood pranks of lord Krishna, his love for the Gopikas, and subjugating Kalia serpent and other demons, could be some of the common themes, besides many others.

Rasalila draws from the tale of divine love of the Gopikas for the lord Krishna. *Rasa* literally means a 'quality' or 'aesthetics' It even applies to 'sentiments'. Rasalila refers to that play (anecdote) from the life of Sri Krishna, where the ***gopikas* dance with Krishna**. This dance is referred to as the dance of divine love. The anecdote refers to a night in Vrindavan, when the *gopikas*, on listening to the melodious music from the flute of Sri Krishna, sneak out from their households to the forest of Vrindavan. Lord Krishna, through *maya*, appears to be dancing with each of the *gopikas*. The dance which lasts through the night appears to be of one *kalpa* to the *gopikas*. The dance in itself symbolizes the **yearning of the human soul (represented by the *gopikas*) for the love of the Divine (Sri Krishna)** and is an example of *shuddha bhakti* (pure devotion).

Rasalilas are represented through a sequence of dances in a dance-drama style. It has been the inspiration for many classical dance forms including Kathak, Manipuri, Odissi, Kuchipudi and Bharatanatyam. The folk art is popular in the Braj region in Western Uttar Pradesh, Nathdwara region of Rajasthan (amidst the followers of the Pushtimarg), in West Bengal in the followers of the Gaudiya Vaishnavism, besides in the other parts of the country.

Nautanki

It is one of the most popular forms of folk theatre, especially in Northern India in the Hindi speaking states of Uttar Pradesh, Bihar Rajasthan, Madhya Pradesh, Haryana etc. It is a **secular** form of folk theatre which is entertainment oriented. Considered to have originated from other folk traditions like Bhagat and Swang, Nautanki is **an opera form of theatre** where the performance is based on acting through singing. The verses which form the dialogue are in different metres. The themes are often based on mythologies, romantic tales, stories of local heroes, etc. Anecdotes from the *Mahabharata*, *Ramayana*, the tale of Raja Harishchandra, story of valour, like of Amar Singh Rathod, love lores like Laila Majnu, or local legends like Daku Sultana are some popular Nautanki performances.

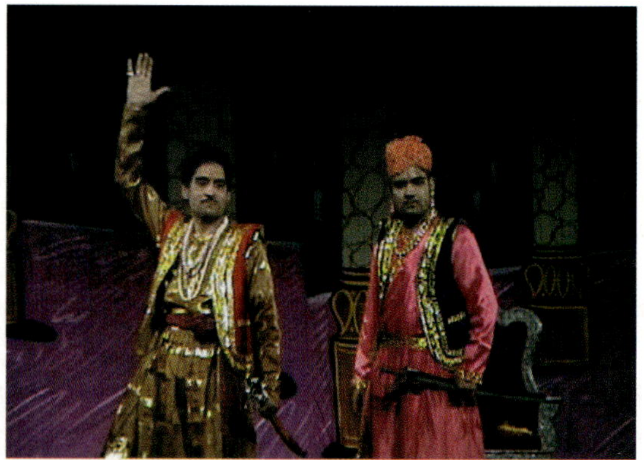

21.5: A nautanki performance of Amar Singh Rathore by Sangeet Natak awardee Nautanki artist Pt. Ram Dayal Sharma and Dr. Devendra Sharma — Wikimedia Commons

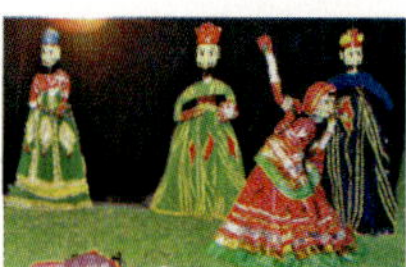

As a folk theatre, it is centuries old and was the main stay of rural entertainment, particularly in the period prior to the rise of the Hindi film industry. The performance is held usually on a raised platform constructed temporarily in a central location in a village. The beats of traditional instrument of Nakkara/ Nagara (a percussion instrument) mark the beginning of the performance which begins in the late evening and may last through the night. With the advent of movies, television and other forms of digital entertainment, Nautanki, like many other forms of folk theatre, is on a decline.

Jatra

This form of folk theatre is popular in **West Bengal and Odisha**, besides in some parts of Bihar, Assam and Tripura. Jatra literally means, 'a **procession** or a journey'. It is said to have originated in the medieval period in the form of fairs and processions in honour of the gods. It is also incorporated as a part of the rituals, certain form of musical plays as eulogy of the gods or the story of their legends. **Krishna Jatra** was a common theme popularized in the region with the Bhakti movement of Chaitanya and *Rukmini Haran* was one of the earliest Jatras in which Sri Chaitanya is said to have performed.

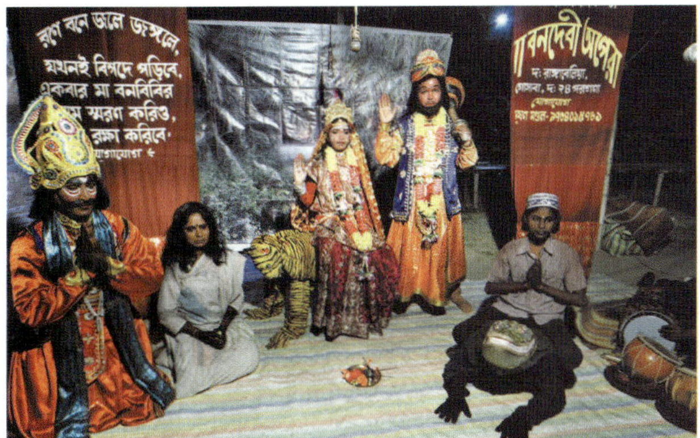

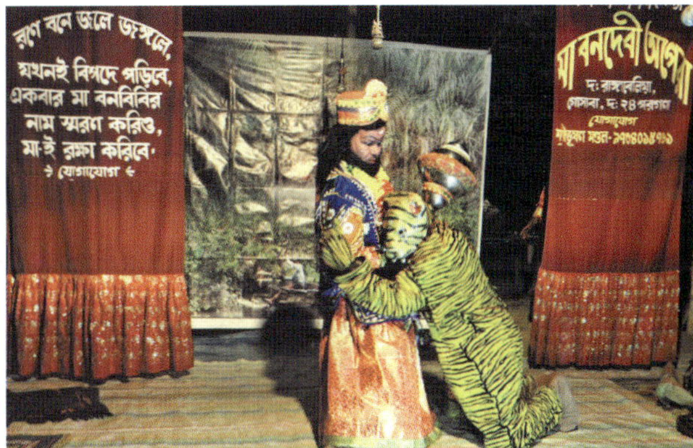

21.6 & 21.7: Jatra peformances — Courtesy, Department of Tourism, West Bengal

Today, Jatra is a **musical form of a theatre** in which anecdotes from epics, mythologies, historical stories, and even topical, social and political issues are depicted. Thus, while it originated as a ritualistic theatre, over a period of time it transcended into a secular folk theatre. Later, it even became a part of the 'Bengal Renaissance'. It also played an important role during freedom struggle in spreading of messages of non-violence and those against untouchability.

Traditionally, Jatras, very much like Nautanki and other folk theatres, were performed by an exclusive male cast. Over the years, women have also become a part of the cast and troupe. Jatras were performed often in an open-air theatre and with all sides open. The performances were usually of four-hour long plays, which were preceded by an hour long musical concert. The performance invariably includes dramatic monologues, songs, dances and other musical routines. The overall performances are melodramatic, with delivery of dialogues being very stylized.

Bhand Pather

This is a popular folk theatre of **Kashmir** region and has been in vogue for several centuries. The word *bhand* literally refers to a **jester,** while *pather* refers to a drama. Thus, this art forms draws its name from the community of *bhands* who were folk theatre actors. Nearly 12 types of Bhand Pathers are recognized to be performed by this community.

The performance in a Bhand Pather revolves around a **key issue** and is expressed in form of dances, music, and acting. The Pather is invariably characterised by the use of **satire** and **wit** to evoke laughter, particularly by the *maskhara* or a jester, who is a key element of the performance. Mimcry, lampooning, satire and wit are important elements of their performance, which is meant to evoke humour as well as to drive home the key issue endeavoured to be conveyed. Through these performances, a variety of social and even political issues are taken up, be it anti-social practices, issues

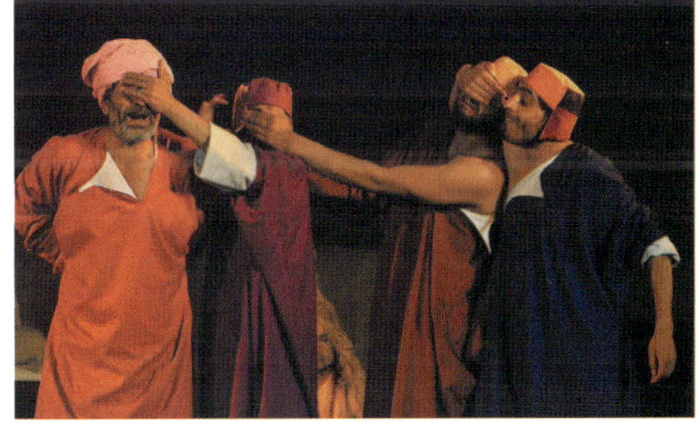

21.8: A Bhand Pather performance at IGNCA — Wikimedia Commons

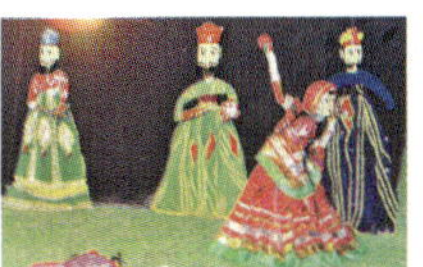

of corruption in the government bodies, religious issues or problems of the common people. Thus, this folk art is not only secular, but provides a medium of expression to highlight the salient issues of the society in an entertaining and humorous manner.

Swang

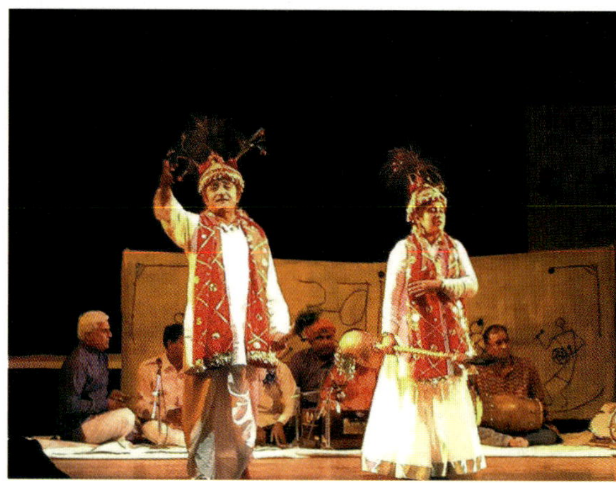

21.9: A Swang performance of Raja Vikramaditya at Mandi House, New Delhi — Wikimedia Commons

This folk theatre is popular in Haryana, Rajasthan, western Uttar Pradesh and also in the Malwa region of Madhya Pradesh. Also referred as Saang, the word Swang literally means to 'imitate or to disguise'. Thus, the folk art refers to the pretension of being the character in the performance. The origin of this folk theatre can be traced to the 16th century and is said to also have influenced other forms of folk theatre. It was originally a verse and music-based theatre but evolved to include prose also. Today, it is more of a **dialogue-based theatre** and involves theatrics and mimicry along with song. The performance is done in an open air set up with a comparatively small makeshift stage, with minimal of props. The themes of Swang are varied, drawing from the epics and mythology to the tales of morality, from the local legends to the stories of valour, and in modern times, from health and hygiene to women's education and empowerment.

Maach

It is a traditional theatre of Madhya Pradesh which has a history of nearly three hundred years. This form of theatre is said to have originated from the Khyal theatre form of Rajasthan. The word 'Maach' is derived from the word manch, which means 'a stage'. Thus, it refers to the stage-based performance. Maach as a theatre form is characterised by **prominence of songs** between dialogues. The acting part is comparatively subdued with greater emphasis on singing. Many of its performers are noted for their singing. Music being a key element, the performance draws substantially from the Hindustani classical ragas. The musical accompaniment is from traditional instruments like *dhol, sarangi,* harmonium etc. Like other folk theatres, its themes are drawn from the epics and the Puranas, from the local legends and the Malwan heroes. Contemporary social issues and problems of the region like dacoity, landless labour etc. also reflect in these performances.

Bhaona

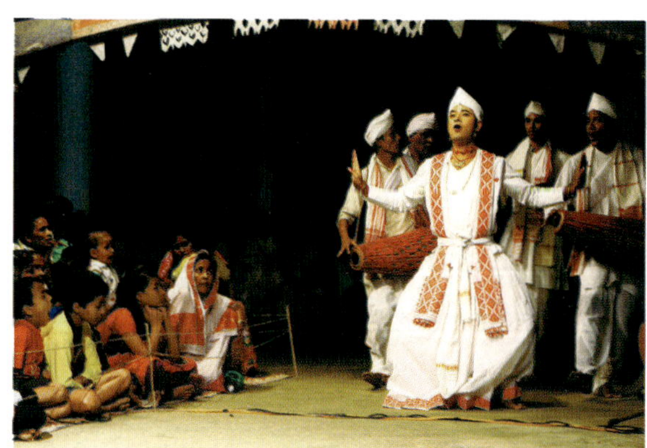

21.10: A sutradhar in a Bhaona performance — Wikimedia Commons

It is a folk theatre popular in **Assam, Bengal and Odisha**. A form of it is also seen in Uttar Pradesh (Vrindavan in Mathura). Bhaona originated as a religious and ritualistic theatre and has a tradition which is more than 500 years old. It was started by **Srimanta Sankardeva** who himself created the first Bhaona, 'Chinha Yatra' and also performed in it. The word Bhaona implies staging of plays, while the play itself is referred to as the 'Ankia Nat' which means one-act plays. The performance is in a make-up stage (Namghar) open in all sides with audience seated in the three sides, while the fourth, representing the presence of gods.

The Ankia Nat begins with the story being first narrated by a *sutradhar* followed by the performance. The Sutradhar, who explains the play at different stages, is an integral part of Bhaona and a very significant element of it. The other performers include the actors, the *gayans* (singers) and the *bayans* (instrumentalists), with the latter two categories being part of the orchestra. The dialogues are delivered in Brajavali or in present times in Assamese. The themes of the plays are generally religious. It may draw from the puranas, the epics, mythology, local legends, but generally ends with the message of triumph of good over evil.

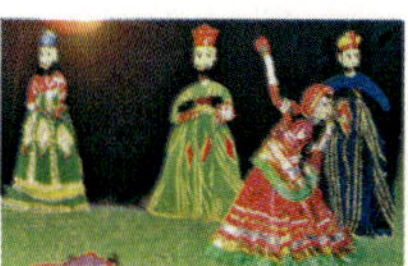

Bhavai

It is the folk theatre form of **Gujarat** and is particularly popular in the Kutch and Kathiawar region. The word 'Bhavai' is said to have originated from the word *bhava* of Sanskrit, which means 'expression' or 'emotion', thus implying to express through the medium of this folk performance. As per some scholars, the word Bhavai is a compound word constructed from *bhav,* which is the world and Aai which means the mother, thus alluding to the worship of mother goddess Amba. Bhavai is also known as **Vesha** (get up) or **Swang** (to pretend to be somebody else).

This folk theatre is centuries old and is said to have originated in the 14th century. Poet Asaita Thakar (in 14th century) is believed to be the first composer of Bhavai and is credited to have composed nearly 360 Bhavai plays. Through the ages, this tradition has been practiced by a community of people known as Bhavaiyas. It is a ritualistic as well as an entertainment theatre, which is performed in front of temples, especially during the **Navaratri festivals**. The performance usually starts in the evening and continues till midnight.

The performance begins with the lighting of a lamp, and invocation of the goddess Amba, lord Ganesh and Goddess Kali by the *Nayak* who is the chief of the performers. The *Vesha* performance follows suit, with the entire performance being subdivided into several acts and each act called a *Vesha*. The role of women is invariably played by men. The music draws from the Hindustani classical style modified to suit Bhavai performance. It is to the accompaniment of traditional instruments like *bhungal* (wind instrument), tabla, flute, *pakhawaj*, *rabaab*, *sarangi*, *manjeera*, etc.

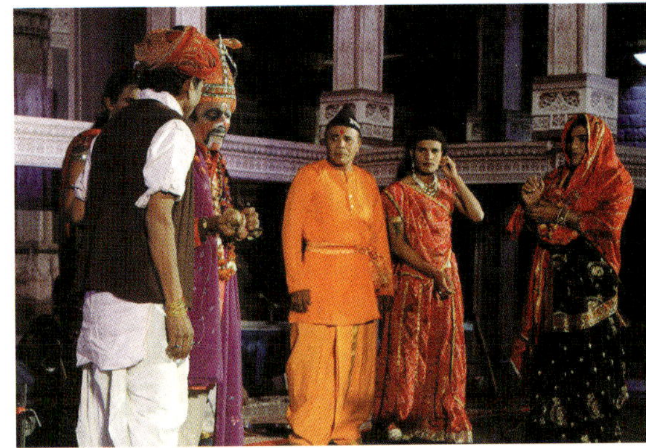

21.11: Bhavai performance at Bharat Bhavan, Bhopal — Wikimedia Commons

The theme can be varied from mythological to social, from valour to love stories. Singing and dancing are integral elements along with narration of lyrics and drama. Besides, **humour and satire** play a significant role. The caste system, social rigidities and hollow social practices of upper class, are at times at the receiving end of these performances. Thus, we can see in Bhavai a rare synthesis of devotional and romantic sentiments with social issues and satire, making it a unique folk art.

Akhyana

It was another medieval folk theatre of the region which was popular in Gujarat and parts of Rajasthan. Literally meaning in Sanskrit, 'to narrate', Akhyana was a musical theatre in which **stories from religious texts** would be narrated by the professional story tellers (*granthika*). It would incorporate a Sanskrit poetry accompanied by music, singing and acting to convey the tale. However, this theatre suffered a decline beyond the 17th century and almost became extinct by the 19th century. Over the years, some efforts have been made for its revival.

Tamasha

It is the traditional folk theatre of **Maharashtra** and has evolved from other folk arts such as Gondhal, Jagran and Kirtan. The word 'Tamasha' is an import in Marathi from the Urdu vocabulary and literally implies 'a show or a spectacle which is filed with activities and excitement'. Thus, the word implies an open show of theatrical entertainment. As a form of folk theatre, it became especially popular in the 18th and 19th century in the late Peshwa period, where it also served as a form of entertainment for the troops.

In its modern form, Tamasha incorporates and relies heavily on the song and dance as a medium of expression. While earlier, dancing boys known as *Nachya* would play the roles of women, now the female actresses have become the chief exponent of the dances in the plays and are known as *murki*. Through the music, adept and brisk footwork and gestures, the emotion in the act is expressed vividly. Besides, the traditional Tamasha also incorporates a role of a *sutradhar*, or a jester, known as *songadaya*, and a *sahir* who is a poet-composer.

Tamasha is often categorised as two main types; the *Dholaki Fadcha* Tamasha which includes song dance and theatre and is considered a more comprehensive form of art. The second is the *Sangeet Baricha* Tamasha. The performance of a typical Tamasha comprises two parts; the *Gan Gavalan*, where the *Gan* is invocation of lord Ganesha, while the *Gavalan* describes the story of *gopikas* and Sri Krishna. The other

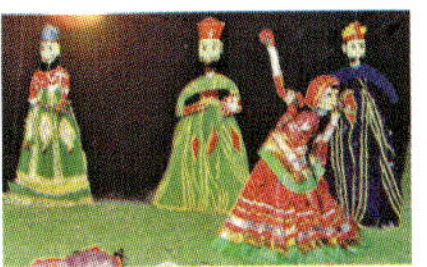

part is *Vag*, which is a folk tale performed to the tunes of songs such as Lavani and expressed through the medium of dance by the female actress. Besides this form, (incorporating Gan Gavalan and Vag), various other forms of Tamasha are also popular.

Dashavatara

It is the folk theatre of the **Konkan and Goa** regions. The name of the theatre is derived from *dashavatara* or the ten incarnations of Lord Vishnu. This is also the main theme of the performance. The theatre is said to have originated around 800 years ago, and is still popular, particularly in rural areas of Goa, Sindhudurg and other Konkan regions of Maharasthra. It is performed during the annual festival of the village deity. The performance begins around midnight and may continue till dawn. It is generally without any props and is divided into two parts; the *Poorva-rang* and the *Uttara-rang*. The ***Poorva-rang*** (initial session) is the preliminary presentation and precedes the proper act. The *Uttara-ranga* (latter session) also called the *Akhyan*, brings forth the **story of one of the 10 *avataras* of lord Vishnu**. These avataras being; *Matsya* (fish), *Kurma* (tortoise), *Varaha* (boar), *Narasimha* (lion-man), *Vamana* (dwarf), Parashurama, Rama, Krishna, Buddha and Kalki. Bright makeup and costumes are used to depict the characters. The music is to the accompaniment of three instruments; a paddle harmonium, the tabla and the *zanj* (cymbals). Today, Dashavatara is a popular form of drama and is often looked upon as an art of the classes.

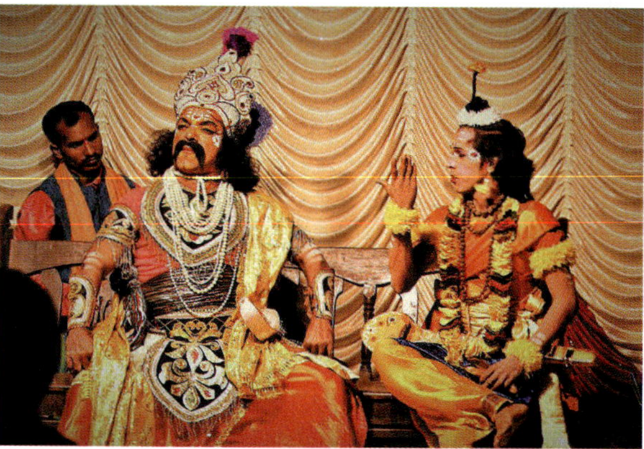

21.12: Dashavatara folk theatre in Konkan region of Maharashtra State in India — Wikimedia Commons

Yakshagana

It is the traditional theatre of **Karnataka** which is also popular in some parts of Kerala. Udupi district in Karnataka and Kasargod in Kerala are some important centres of this art. Yakshagana is often considered a versatile form of theatre as it combines the arts of music, dance, dialogue, stage techniques, costume and makeup with a unique style of its own. The word Yakshagana is made of the words *yaksha* (celestial beings) and *gaana* (the song and music). Thus, this art form alludes to the music and dance performance of ***yakshas*** who were celestial being and considered very adept in the fine arts.

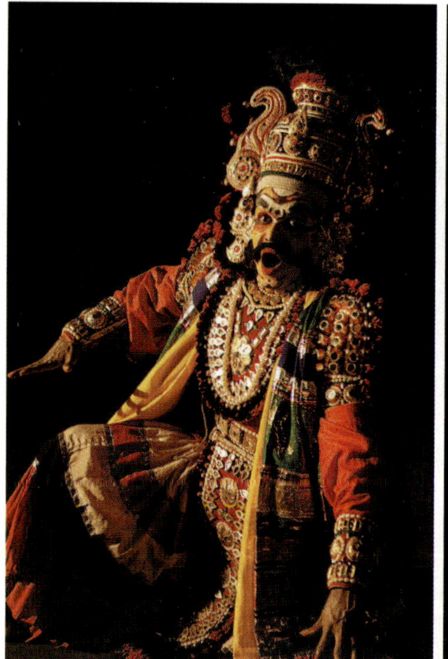

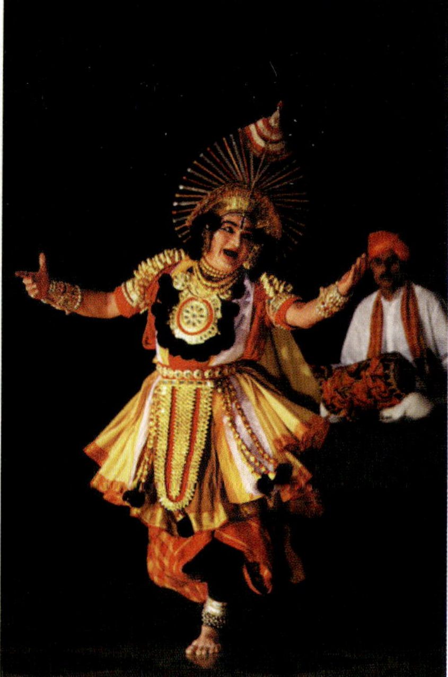

21.13 & 21.14: Artists with elaborate headgear, makeup and costume performing Yakshagana — Courtesy, Karnataka Tourism Development Corporation

The performance begins usually at the dusk and may last up to the dawn. Each of these performance usually focus on a anecdote or a substory called *prasanga* which is often taken from the Ramayana and Mahabharata. Some of the popular episodes/*prasangas* from Mahabharata are; *Abhimanyu vadh, Draupadi swayamvar, Karna-Arjuna Yuddh, Subhadra vivah* and from Ramayana; *Raajyaabhishek, Lav-kush Yuddh, Baali-Sugreeva yuddh* etc.

The music of Yakshagana is also considered to be separate from Carnatic and Hindustani classical though they may have had common roots. Traditional instruments employed in the performance are *chande*

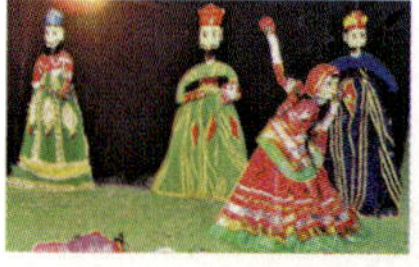

(drums), *maddal* (double faced barrel drums), *taala* (metal mini clappers), flute, harmonium etc. One of the most unique aspects of Yakshagana is the costume of the performers, which comprises a large sized and elaborate headgear, coloured faces, costumes covering the entire body and *gejje* (musical beads) on the legs.

Therukoothu

It is the popular folk drama of **Tamil Nadu**. It is believed to be very ancient and has been traditionally performed in temples of Tamil Nadu. The wider term for this art form is Koothu, which is referred to an informal dance structure representing scenes from epics and mythologies. It is divided into Therukoothu, which is a performance done by a travelling procession, and Kattaikoothu, which refers to the stationery overnight performances. However, in present day the terms are often used interchangeably.

Therukoothu is considered to be originally a ritualistic performance and was associated with the cult of worship of the mother goddess who is propitiated as **Draupadi Amman**. It is also said to be associated with harvest and performed after the agriculture harvesting is done as a part of 20 days festival.

The folk theatre usually incorporates a set of eight plays based on the life of Draupadi, the wife of the Pandavas. A *sutradhara*, at the beginning of the plays, narrates the story in brief to give its gist. The plays also incorporate a jester, referred to as *komali* who entertains the audience with his buffoonery. The artists representing different characters have bright and heavy makeup with headgear, sparkling shoulder plates and wide skirts. The actors also double as singers and perform the songs in high pitched voice to reach the audience. Traditionally, it has been a theatre where only men have performed. However, in the modern form, women are also a part of the theatre.

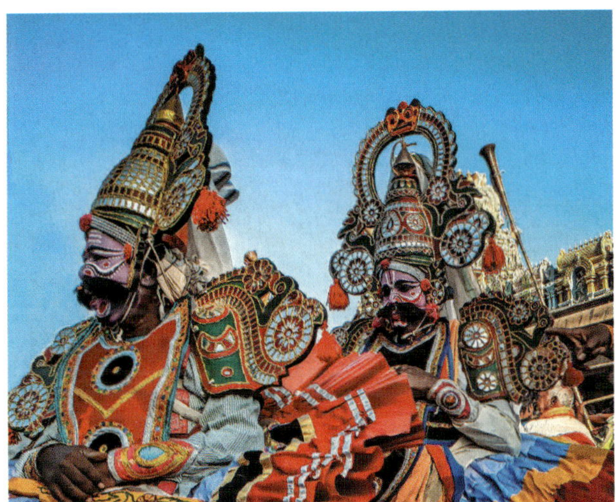

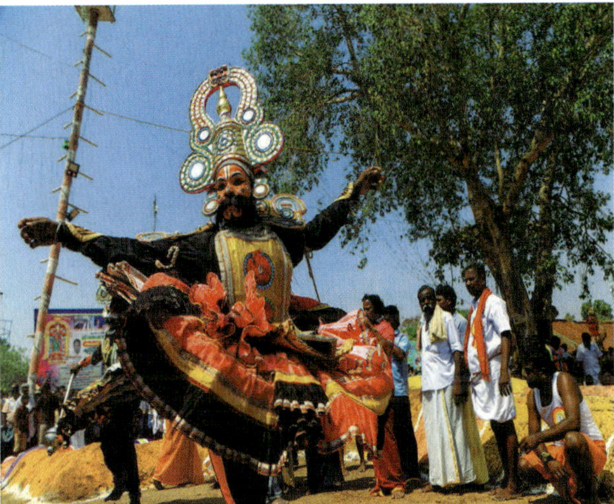

21.15 & 21.16: Therukoothu performances — Courtesy, Tamil Nadu Tourism Development Corporation

Koodiyattam

It is one of the folk theatres popular in Kerala and is the **oldest surviving theatrical tradition**. Tracing its origin to nearly 2000 years ago and based on **classical Sanskrit theatre** traditions, it is indeed a unique art form and a living ancient heritage. The word Koodiyattam/Kutiyattam in Malayalam literally means 'combined acting' and is a confluence of the traditional Koothu performance with the Sanskrit theatre tradition.

The heritage of Koodiyattam has been preserved over the centuries by the Chakyar community of Kerala who have been the traditional performers of the art. The performances have been held inside the temple precinct in theatres called *Koothambalams*. Thus, this art emanates from the **ritualistic** tradition and till very recently any performance of the art outside the temple precincts was forbidden. The skills of the art have been passed through the centuries as a family tradition in this community, with the training itself said to be taking as many as 10 to 15 years. The performance fully integrates all the four elements of acting as identified in Bharata's *Natyashastra* and includes *aangikam* (involving expression through different parts of the body), *vaachikam* (expression through speech), *sathvikam* (expression of physical reactions to emotions) and *aahaaryam* (expression through costume, ornaments and props). *Neta abhinaya* (eye expressions) and *hasta abhinaya* (expression through gestures) are highly evolved in this art.

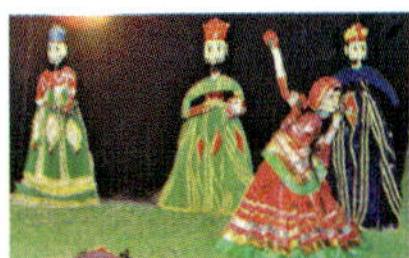

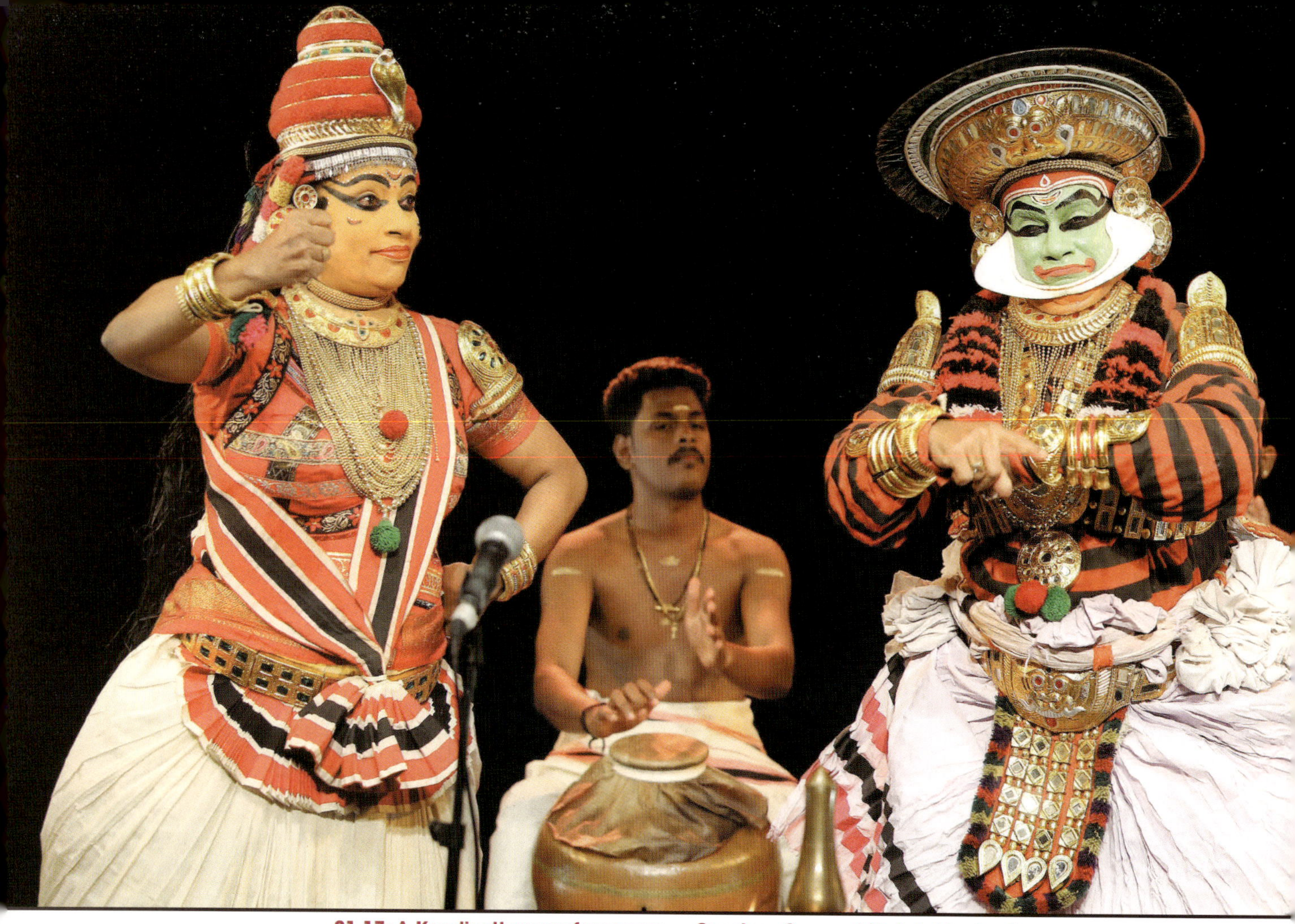

21.17: A Koodiyattam performance — Courtesy, Sangeet Natak Akademi

The performance is based on specific anecdotes of the epics or other mythological tales (eg. *Subhadra Dhananjayam*, *Prathimaabhishekam, Naagaanandam etc.)* These are referred to as the *ankams*. These may be divided into several acts which, together, may spread to a period of over 100 hours over several nights. While in earlier times, the performance would last nearly 40 nights, in the modern period it stretches to around eight nights. The performance is divided into three main parts. The first is *purapaddu*, where the first actor makes an entry and performs a verse along with *nritta* (pure dance). This is succeeded by expressions of the mood and the sentiments of the main character of the play as brought out through *abhinaya*. The second part is *nirvaham*, which may be like a retrospective and extends to the point of beginning of the actual performance. Other characters are also brought to the fore. These two are solo acts. The final part is Koodiyattam, which is the play itself. This part deploys as many performers as the demand of the play. The *sutradhar* or the narrator, and the *vidushak*, are the main protagonists. Use of heavy makeup facial colours, costume and headgear are some of its other features. The music in the performance is from traditional instruments. The *mizhavu* (a drum made of leather stretched over a copper vessel) being the main accompaniment, while the others include *idakka* (hour glass drum), *shankhu* (conch shell), *kurumkuzhalm* (double reed wind instrument) and *kuzhithaalam* (cymbals).

While having survived through the centuries, owing to the temple patronage and support from the feudal class, today this art is rapidly shrinking, owing to the years of training required and lack of adequate financial support to the practitioners. Only a handful of artists survive today, although efforts for preservation and sustenance of this art are being made.

Koodiyattam: An Intangible Cultural Heritage of Humanity

The UNESCO, in 2008 has recognized, 'Koodiyattam, the Sanskrit Theatre,' as a masterpiece of oral and intangible cultural heritage of humanity. Some of the significant observations from the citation of UNESCO are as below.

Koodiyattam, Sanskrit theatre, which is practised in the province of Kerala, is one of India's oldest living theatrical traditions. Originating more than 2,000 years ago, Koodiyattam represents a synthesis of Sanskrit classicism and reflects the local traditions of Kerala. In its stylized and codified theatrical language, neta abhinaya (eye expression) and hasta abhinaya (the language of gestures) are prominent. They focus on the thoughts and feelings of the main character.

.....The actor's art lies in elaborating a situation or episode in all its detail. Therefore, a single act may take days to perform and a complete performance may last up to 40 days.

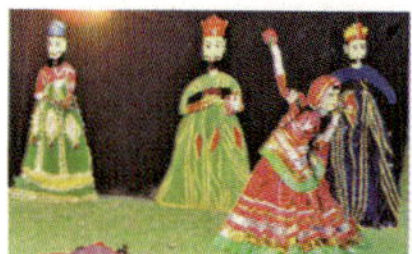

Krishnattam

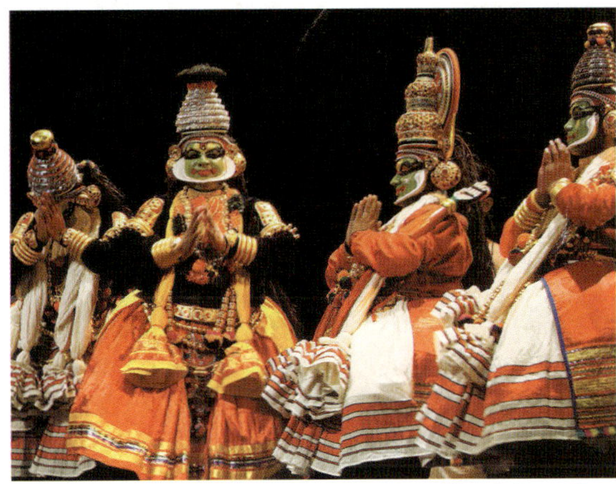
21.18: Krishnattam performance with elaborate makeup of the artist — Wikimedia Commons

This is another traditional theatre of Kerala which originated in the mid-17th century CE, under the patronage of king Manaveda of the then Calicut province. Krishnattam is a synthesis of two words; Krishna (referring to lord Krishna) and *attam* (eight). Thus, this folk form of dance-drama **incorporates eight plays** which are connected to the **theme of lord Krishna** and drawn from various anecdotes associated with his legend. These plays are performed in eight consecutive days and include; *Avataram* (incarnation/birth of Sri Krishna), *Kaliyamardanam* (the subjugation of Kalia), *Rasakrida* (sport of dance/ dance of Krishna with gopis), *Kamsavadham* (slaying of Kamsa), *Swayamvaram* (swayamvara/marriage of Sri Krishna to Rukmini, Jambhavati and Satyabhama), *Banayuddham* (battle with Banasura), *Vividavadham* (slaying of Vividha) and *Swargarohanam* (ascent to swarga/heaven).

Like the traditional art of Koodiyattam, the artists of Krishnattam too require several years of practice before they can perform. The dance-drama itself incorporates all the four elements of acting as brought out in Bharata's Natyashastra viz., *angikam*, *vachikam*, *aharyam* and *satvikam*. The presentation of the artists involves elaborate makeup with facial colours, head gear, shoulder plates, chest and other ornaments, wide skirts, ankle bells etc. Out of this, the headgear is considered the most sacred of the costumes. The Guruvayoor temple of Lord Sri Krishna (in Guruvayoor, Kerala) is presently the main centre of performance of this art.

Mudiyettu

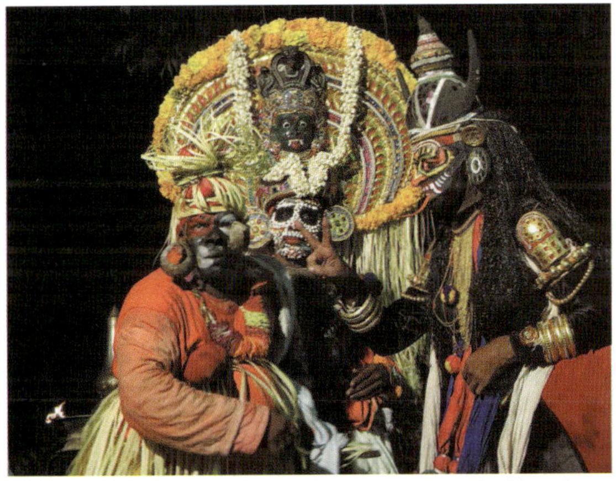
21.19: Mudiyettu at Kezhur Kavu temple, Kerala — Wikimedia Commons

It is another important folk theatre popular in Kerala. This is usually performed in the post-harvest season and is **dedicated to Goddess Kali**. It is **ritualstic theatre** which offers oblation to the goddess Bhadrakali and depicts her triumph over asura Darika. The characters in the play are Shiva, Narada, Darika, Danavendra, Bhadrakali, Kooli and Koimbidar (Nandikeshvara). Elaborate costumes and heavy makeup are employed for the artists along with paint face, headgear and other accessories (as is a practice in other traditional arts of Kerala). Mudiyettu however has flourished as a village community art where different sections/castes of the village community contribute variedly in its performance. **In 2010, Mudiyettu was included in the UNESCO's list of Intangible Cultural Heritage of Humanity.** This is the second folk art from the state of Kerala so to be recognized.

Mudiyettu: An Intangible Cultural Heritage of Humanity

The UNESCO, in 2010 has recognized, 'Mudiyettu, the ritual theatre and dance drama of Kerala,' as a masterpiece of oral and intangible cultural heritage of humanity. Some of the significant observations from the citation of UNESCO are as below.

Mudiyettu is a ritual dance drama from Kerala based on the mythological tale of a battle between the goddess Kali and the demon Darika. It is a community ritual in which the entire village participates. After the summer crops have been harvested, the villagers reach the temple in the early morning on an appointed day. Mudiyettu performers purify themselves through fasting and prayer, then draw a huge image of goddess Kali, called as kalam*, on the temple floor with coloured powders, wherein the spirit of the goddess is invoked. This prepares the ground for the lively enactment to follow, in which the divine sage Narada importunes Shiva to contain the demon Darika, who is immune to defeat by mortals. Shiva instead commands that Darika will die at the hand of the goddess Kali. Mudiyettu is performed annually in 'Bhagavati Kavus', the temples of the goddess, in different villages along the rivers Chalakkudy Puzha, Periyar and Moovattupuzha.*

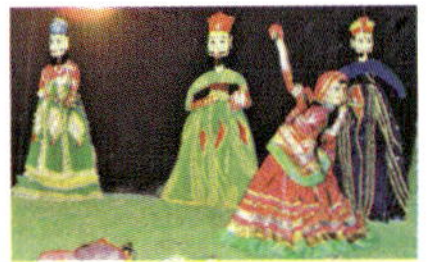

Mutual cooperation and collective participation of each caste in the ritual instils and strengthens common identity and mutual bonding in the community. Responsibility for its transmission lies with the elders and senior performers, who engage the younger generation as apprentices during the course of the performance. Mudiyettu serves as an important cultural site for transmission of traditional values, ethics, moral codes and aesthetic norms of the community to the next generation, thereby ensuring its continuity and relevance in present times.

PUPPET THEATRE

Puppet theatre is a form of folk theatre, which involves performance by means of manipulation of certain inanimate figures referred to as puppets, using human skill and craft. The figures may be those of humans, animals or other animate and inanimate objects. These are prepared by craftsmen and manipulated by skilled artist called puppeteers. Quite like the conventional theatre, puppet theatre too has story or a theme which is too be conveyed to its audience. The puppets are the representatives of various characters of the story which are controlled by, imparted movement, and lend voice, by the puppeteer. A variety of techniques may be used by the puppeteer to control the limbs of the puppet and to impart it the desired movement. These may be ranging from rods and strings, to direct manipulation using the fingers and hands, thus creating different types of puppet theatres.

In India, like in many parts of world, puppetry has been a prominent form of entertainment theatre for centuries. As per some accounts, there is evidence of discovery of a terracotta doll in the Indus Valley Civilisation (dating 2500 BCE), which had a detachable head and could be manipulated with a string. One of the earliest references to puppets is found in the Tamil classic ***Silappadikaram*** which is considered to have been written in around the 1st century CE-2nd century CE and as per some accounts in the 5th - 6th century CE. In *Natyashastra,* which is a treatise on conventional theatre, the conductor cum director of the theatre is referred to as the *sutradhaar* which literally means 'the holder of the strings', a term derived from the marionette theatre. Thus, puppets in India have a history of nearly 2000 years.

In the past, puppetry has been based mostly on stories in epics, mythology and legend. Later, it also diversified to local folklore. Modern puppetry is evolving more themes which may be based on social issues. Puppetry has different traditions and forms in different parts of the country. This is based on styles of puppetry, painting, sculpture and presentation craft. Broadly, puppets in India are categorised into four types which are, **string puppets, glove puppets, rod puppets** and **shadow puppets**. The salient features of these art forms and their regional characteristics are briefly brought out here.

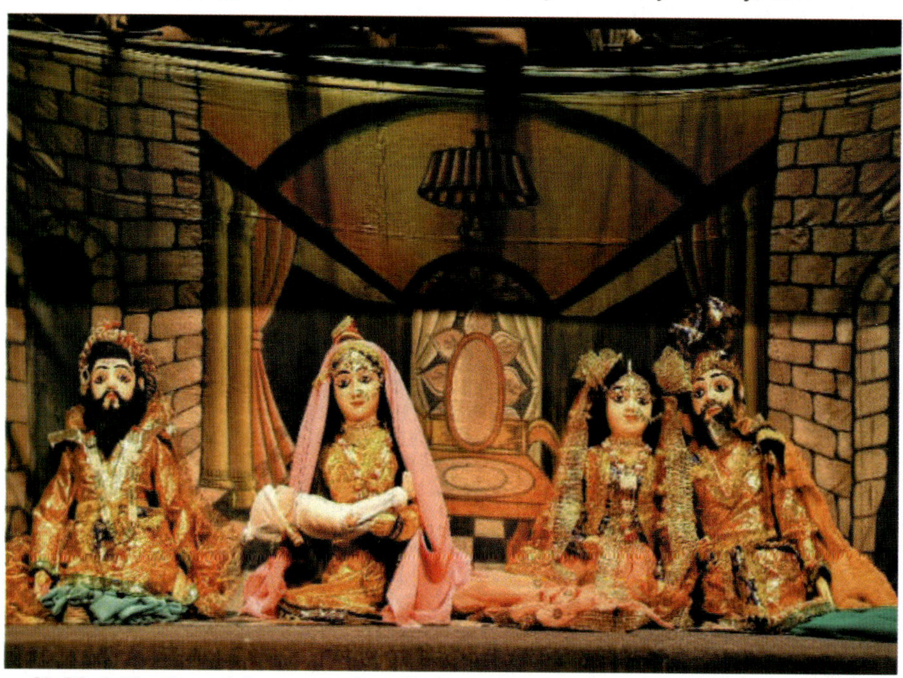

21.20: A Manipur string puppet performance. Artists manipulating the puppets with the strings suspended from the top — Courtesy, Sangeet Natak Akademi

String Puppets

Also referred as marionettes, these are usually of the size of a doll. The puppets have jointed limbs which are controlled by strings which allow greater flexibility of movement. The string puppets are considered the most versatile of all puppet forms and also are one of the most ancient of different puppet forms. Rajasthan, Odisha, Karnataka and Tamil Nadu are some of the states where this puppet is popular. Besides, traditional string puppet art is also practied in the North-eastern states of Assam, Tripura and Manipur.

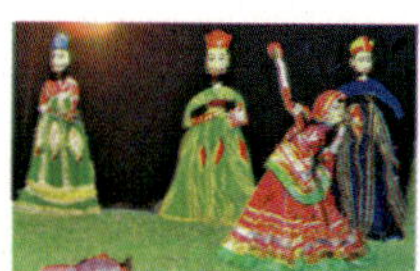

Kathputli is the string puppet of **Rajasthan**. These stringed puppets are carved from a single piece of wood and are of the size of dolls. They are covered in colourful Rajasthani costumes with exaggerated features such as large eyes, oval faces, arched eyebrows, and large lips. Another feature of this puppet is that they do not have legs and wear the traditional long skirt on the lower body. With two to five strings, the puppeteers control the puppets which are tied to the fingers. The performance is done to the accompaniment of regional music. The performance may cover ballads such as the deeds of Amar Singh Rathore or other folk tales or even entertaining stories. The puppet stages are usually a makeshift one, with a black backdrop behind which the puppeteer controls the strings.

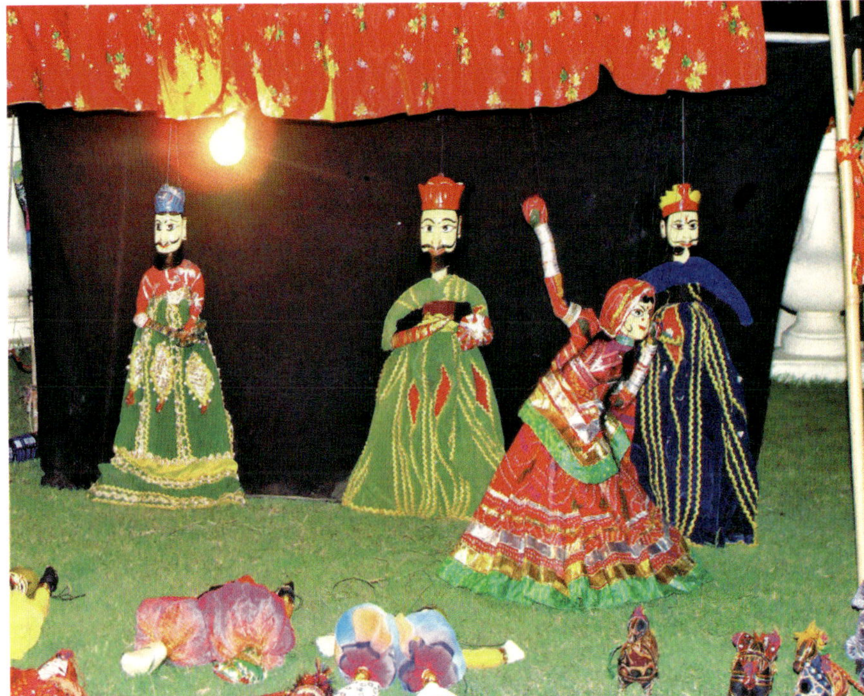

21.21: A Kathputli puppet show in Udaipur, Rajasthan in a small make shift bamboo stage with black backdrop. Large marionettes in action, and a number of smaller puppets on the foreground — photograph by Madhukar K Bhagat

Kandhei Nacha of Odisha is another form of the stringed puppet. Like the Rajasthani *Kathputli,* they too are made of light wood, have no legs and the lower part of the figure are covered in long flowing skirts. However they have more joints, enabling greater manipulation and versatility of movement. The costumes have resemblance to those of the *Jatra* procession. Puppeteers also use a triangular wooden prop to which the strings are attached which enables the manipulation of puppets. The performance is to the accompaniment of the traditional music which is at times also influenced by the Odissi dance. A specific form of *Kundhei* is the *Gopalila Kundhei* which brings out anecdotes from the life of Lord Krishna.

Sutrada Gombeyata is the string puppets of Karnataka. These are designed like characters from *Yakshagana*. Different *prasangas* (anecdotes) of *Yakshaganas* are enacted in them. The puppets are usually of one to one and a half feet in length, are made of soft wood and sometimes rags are stuffed inside. The puppets have joints in shoulders, elbows, legs, hips and knees which enable better manipulation of the marionettes. Some may even have movable jaws and multiple heads. Another feature of these puppets is the use of five to seven strings to manipulate the puppets which may be done by two to three puppeteers at a time. The technique is more complicated but allows greater dexterity of movements. There is an accompanying musician and the music of *Gombeyata* is a combination of the folk and classical forms. The *Gombeyata* stage is like a box which is closed on three sides and with a front opening of 15 to 20 feet. The traditional shows were carried out in the light of a lamp (now electric bulb) and may last a whole night.

The **Bommalattam** of Tamil Nadu is the heaviest and largest of puppets and is as high as 4.5 feet and may weigh up to 10 kilograms. These are also among most articulate of the puppet forms and combine the techniques of string as well as rod puppets. Like other marionettes, they are made of wood, but the strings which are used for manipulation are tied to an iron ring. The puppeteer wears this ring on his head like a crown which allows for control of the puppet movements by the movement of his head. Some of the Bommalattam puppets also have jointed arms and legs which are manipulated by rods. The performance of Bommalattam is associated with temple festivals, marriages and other social occasions. Another feature of it is the initial rituals and elaborate preliminaries which include *Vinayaka Puja, Komali, Amanattam* and *Pusenkanattam.*

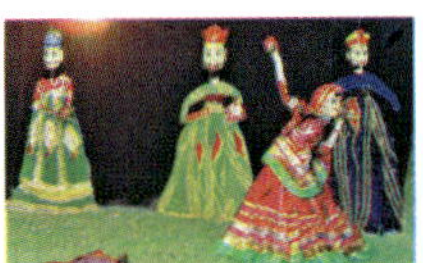

Rod Puppets

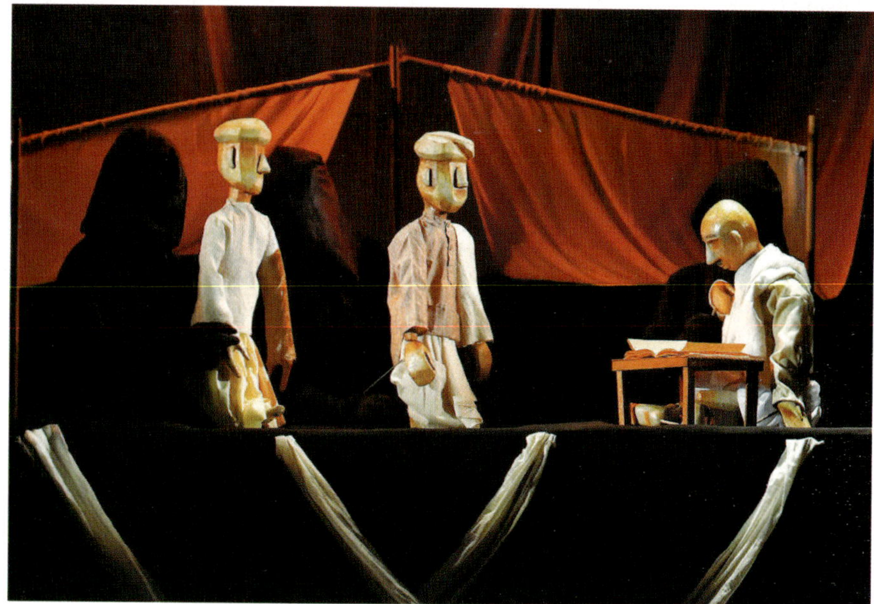

21.22: A rod puppet performance with large wooden puppets — Courtesy, Sangeet Natak Akademi

Popular mostly in West Bengal, Bihar and Odisha, rod puppets are much larger than the other puppet forms. These are characterised by the frame of the puppet being supported by a rod, the manipulation of which enables to control the movement of the puppet.

Putul Nach is the tradition of the rod puppets in **West Bengal** and also in parts of Assam and Tripura. (*Putul* literally means 'the puppet' and *Naach* refers to dance). This theatre is also referred to as *Danger Putul Naach* in West Bengal. The puppets are carved out of wood. Earlier, these rod puppets could be of human size, however nowadays they are usually of 3–4 feet. The design of these puppets involves a rod supporting the frame of the puppet, with the neck, shoulders and both hands of the puppet joined to the rod. This rod is placed in a bamboo made hub, which in turn is tied to the waist of the puppeteer. Thus, the puppeteer by dancing and by moving his body imparts movement to the puppets. The puppets can be held by the puppeteer behind the screen, with the body of the puppet rising above the screen and visible to the spectators. The puppets are adorned with costumes similar to the *Jatra* artists and are performed to accompaniment of music of drum, *shehnai*, cymbals, harmonium similar to that in *Jatra* procession. The *Putul Natch* is often performed in rural fairs and festivals and begins with a typical Jatra-style declamatory announcement which is meant to attract the viewers.

Kathi Kundhei is the rod puppet theatre of Odisha. These rod puppets are smaller in size than the West Bengal *Putul* and are typically one to one and a half feet in length. They usually have three joints. But unlike the conventional rod puppets, their hands are joined by strings. Thus, the elements of rod and string puppets both arecombined to provide greater dexterity of movement. The puppeteer usually sits behind a screen, while the puppet is propped above it to be visible to the audience. The performance is to the tune of folk and Odissi music which usually begins with the veneration of the deity through a ritual performance called *stuti*. This is followed by the enactment of the episodes from the epics, *Puranas,* and mythology, following the typical Odisha *Jatra* tradition.

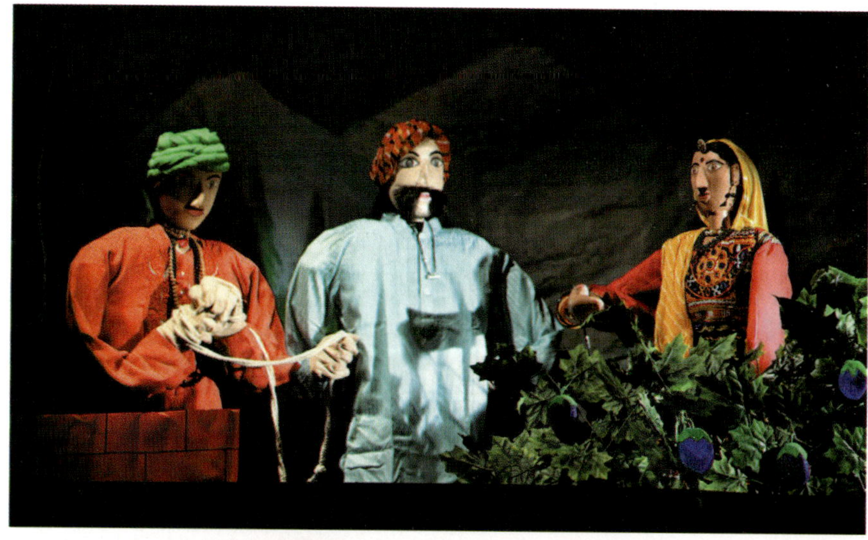

21.23: A rod puppet performance depicting Dalo-Talwadi, a humorous Gujarati folk story — Courtesy, Sangeet Natak Akademi

Yampuri is the rod puppet of Bihar. These rod puppets are made of a single piece of wood with no joints, making the manipulation more complicated. These puppets are also made of wood. The performance is held on wheeled stage to the accompaniment of traditional regional music. The name Yampuri means the abode of *Yama,* the lord of death. The performance opens with the scene of the

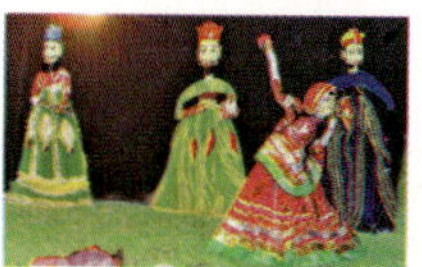

Yampuri, and Yama making an entry followed by his messenger Chitragupta who keeps the record of the deeds of the humans. The different characters which are deceased make their entry before Yama. Their deeds are readout by the Chitragupta based on which Yama pronounces his judgement of awarding heaven or banishing to the hell.

Glove Puppets

In this form of puppetry, the puppets are small and are worn on the hand. These are also called hand, palm, or sleeve puppets. The puppet heads are usually made of light materials such as papier-mâché cloth or even light wood. Two hands emerge from the neck region, and the remaining portion of the puppet is simply covered with a long flowing skirt. The index finger of the puppeteer's hand is usually inserted in the head of the puppet while the middle finger and thumb are placed in the two arms. Thus, with the movement of fingers and palm, the manipulation of the puppets is done.

Pavakoothu is the glove puppet of Kerala. This form of glove puppet came into origin as a result of influence of *Kathakali* dance in the 18th century. The puppets are of size 1–2 feet. The heads and arms are carved out of wood, but joined together with cloth. This is cut and stitched into the shape of a small bag. The puppets are decorated with colourful costumes, face paint, head gear, etc. which are similar to that of a Kathakali performer. They are worn on the hand by the puppeteer and manipulated to produce the movement. The performance is to the accompaniment of traditional music from folk instruments such as *chenda*, *chengila*, *elathalam,* conch shell etc. Usually, the play involves episodes from the epics and mythology.

Sakhi Kundhei is the glove puppet of Odisha which is based on anecdotes/stories revolving around love of Radha and Krishna. The theatre is on decline and limited mainly to the Cuttack region. Unlike other puppet forms, this is a performance by a solo puppet operator. The puppeteer manipulates the puppets with his right hand, while with his left hand playing the *dhol* which is attached to the hip. The puppeteer also sings from medieval Odiya compositions which recount the anecdotes associated with Lord Krishna, Radha and the *gopikas.*

Benir Putul which literally means the 'merchant's puppet' is the traditional glove puppet of West Bengal. The word *benir* also refers to the braiding of hair and thus alludes to twisting and turning movements of the puppet akin to the braided hair. The puppets are typically 10 inches to a foot in height. A unique aspect of the puppet is that its head is made of baked clay while arms are made of wood. These are dressed in long skirts made of cotton. The puppeteer wears one puppet in each of his hands while skilfully enacting movement, dance and conversation between the two puppets. The puppeteers perform usually in pairs with one controlling the puppet while other playing music on a drum or a *damru* (hour glass small drum). Both the performers may sing and the twirling of the puppets may produce accompaniment of music by the bracelets tied around the waists of the puppets. Among the common *Benir Putul* performances are the anecdotes of the life of Radha and Krishna. Another popular and entertaining performance is based around a couple *Madan* and *Puti* who are constantly fighting amongst themselves.

Gulabo-Sitabo are glove puppets popular in **Uttar Pradesh**. *Gulabo-Sitabo* are the names of the two female characters of the performance. The characters may represent the two sister-in-laws, or the wife and the mistress, or the two co-wives of the same person. While Gulabo is the dominating of the two, and the scintillating mistress, Sitabo is the milder one and the worn out and overworked spouse. The theatre incorporates the exchanges between the two protagonists which is

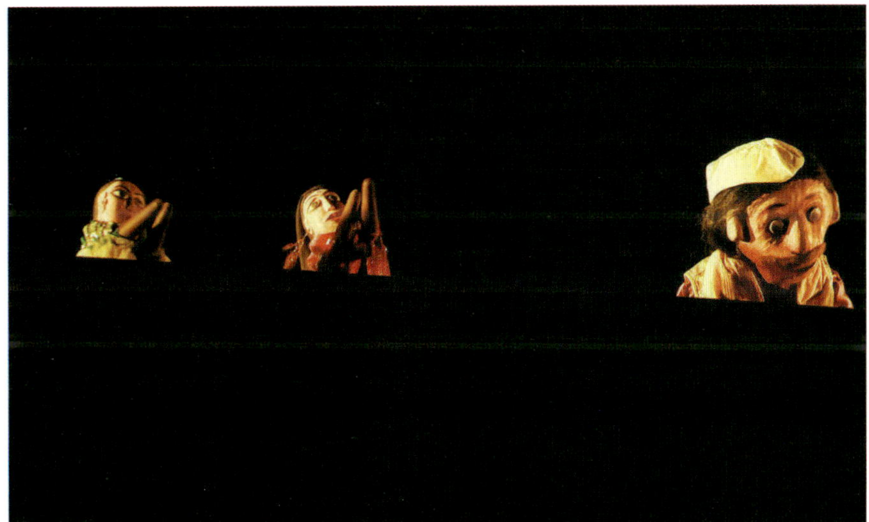

21.24: A performance of Gulabo Sitabo glove puppet of Uttar Pradesh — Courtesy, Sangeet Natak Akademi.

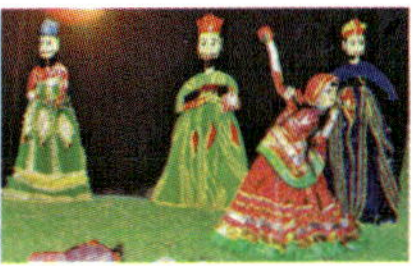

laced with local humour and at times bawdy jokes. The puppets which are nearly of two feet height are made of papier-mâché and are dressed in colourful costumes with facial-features painted over them. The performance is to the accompaniment of music from *dholak* and *manjira* with local songs sung by the puppeteer. Once a popular folk theatre, particularly in Lucknow in the post-independence period, it is now a dying art.

Shadow Puppets

Shadow puppetry involves casting of shadow of cut-out figures (of puppets) on screens and conveying the story or the message through the movement of these shadows. The puppets are flat figures which are cut out of leather. These are treated to make it translucent. These puppets are pressed against a screen with a strong light source behind enabling the formation of colourful shadows. The movement of the cut out and their manipulation between the light source and the screen helps in creation of colourful moving images which can be seen by the audience on the other side of the screen. Different type of leathers such as antelope, deer, goat sheet and buffalo has been traditionally used in different regions. The cut-outs of different characters viz. gods and heroes are made of different types of leather while those of demons etc made of other kind of leather. A wooden or bamboo rod runs vertically through the cut out which helps the puppeteer to hold and move the image. Some of these puppets may have joints in limbs or in body parts, while some may jointless. The depiction of moving images on a screen is particularly fascinating and captures the imagination of the viewers. Shadow puppets are particularly popular in Karnataka, Andhra Pradesh, Odisha, as well as in Tamil Nadu, Kerala and Maharashtra.

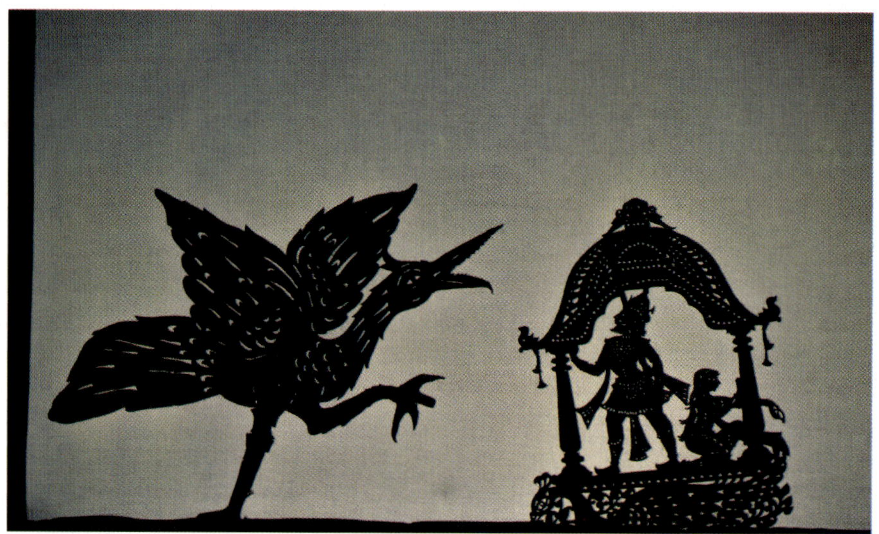

21.25: A traditional shadow puppet performance depicting the scene from Ramayana of the abduction of Sita by Ravana and his fight with Jatayu — Courtesy, Sangeet Natak Akademi

Togalu Gombeyata is the shadow puppet of Karnataka. The word *togalu* refers to leather while Gombeyata refers to dance performance by a figure or a doll. This theatre is broadly of two types; the *Chikka* theatre uses small figures (8 to 12 inches high) while the *dodda* theatre uses larger figures which may be from a foot to even four feet high. The length of the figures also signifies their social status; viz. kings are depicted with large size puppets. The puppets usually travel from place to place and are set up in temple precincts or outside the villages. A white cotton fabric sheet stretched between the bamboo poles serves as the screen. While earlier, oil lamps and later, hurricane lamps were the light source, in recent times neon lights are used. The performance begins with the invocation of Lord Ganesha and goddess Saraswati and episodes from Ramayana, Mahabharata, other puranas or even folk tales are the subject of the play. This is to the accompaniment of regional music and song. It is a demanding art which is losing practitioners and popularity by the day and stares at a bleak future.

Tholu Bommalata is the shadow puppet theatre of **Andhra Pradesh**. The term literally means 'the dance of the leather puppets' (Tholu: leather; Bomma: puppet: Atta: dance). The art has a very ancient history and were popular in ancient India and was performed by travelling bards. The art was practised as early as in the Satavahana period in the 4th century CE and also spread to different parts of Southeast Asia. Over the years, they flourished with the royal patronage. These puppets are usually large in size and may even be up to 3 to 4 feet in height. Their elbow, wrists, shoulders and waists and knees, all are fixed with joints, providing greater dexterity of movement. As many as three puppeteers may be required for their manipulation. A special aspect of these puppets is that the character's cut-outs are coloured on both the sides and cast a colourful shadow on the screens, making the character come alive. The performance begins with the invocation of the deity and episodes from the epics and the puranas are usually depicted. The accompanying music is drawn from the classical music of the region. A typical performance may last six to eight hours.

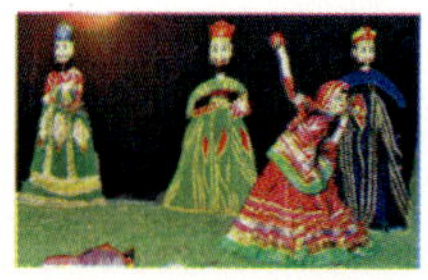

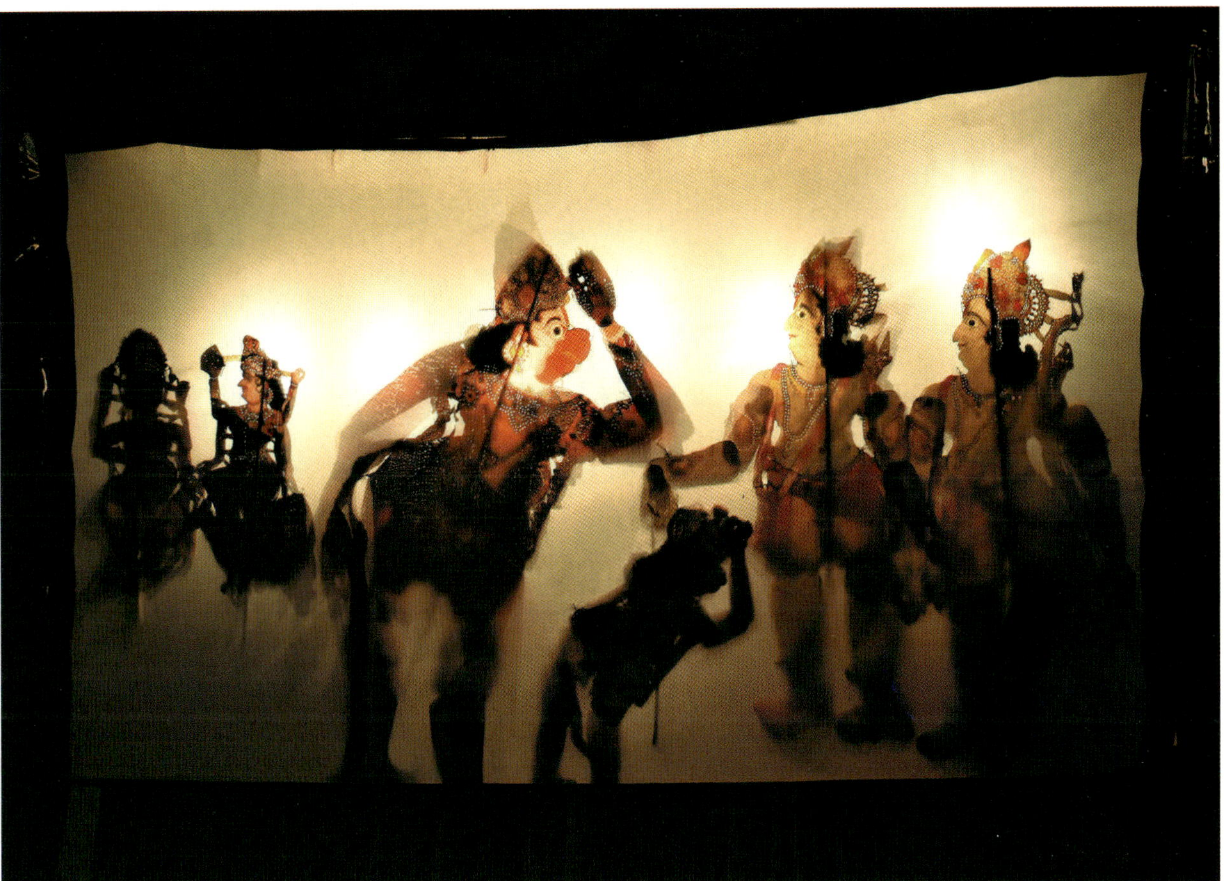

21.26: Performance of the *Sunder Kand* episode from Ramayana in Tholu Bommalata, a colourful shadow puppetry of Andhra Pradesh — Courtesy, Sangeet Natak Akademi.

Ravana-chhaya, which is the shadow puppetry form of **Odisha,** is considered as one of the most theatrical forms of shadow puppetry. The puppets are of one piece and have no joints, making their manipulation more complex. They are not coloured, and throw opaque shadows on screens and thus have no articulation besides the shapes. The puppets are usually of small size, with the largest of figures not being more than a couple of feet in length. Besides, the human and animal characters of the play, the cut-out of different props such as trees, hills etc. are also prepared. The performance is usually done during religious festivals. The troupe erects a stage in the village field. These stages are usually of size 5 metre by 3 metre, with a cotton screen of size 5 metre by 1 metre attached to a straw frame, receiving the projection of the shadows. The puppet troupe comprises eight people, four of which are puppeteers while the other four provide the accompanying music and sing in Odiya. Literally, this art form means the shadow of Ravana who fought against Rama. It is believed that the latter, an incarnate god, had such a powerful aura that he did not cast a shadow, while Ravana did cast a shadow, which brings out the contrast between the two. It depicts the story of Ramayana based on *Vichitra Ramayana* composed by the Oriya poet Bishwanath Khuntia in the 18th century.

Chamadyacha Bahulya is the shadow puppet of Maharashtra. The word *chamadyacha* implies leather while *bahulya* means figure, thus signifying the leather-figures or puppets. The puppet theatre is especially popular in the Pinguli village region, which is bordering Maharashtra, Goa and Karnataka, where a specific Thakur/Thakar community has practiced this art for several generations. The puppets of Maharashtra may range from 5-6 inches to marginally more than a foot. These are made of buffalo leather and do not have any perforations, articulations or joints. Sometimes, one of the arms may be made mobile, with a single pin attached to the arm allowing for its movement. A typical feature of this puppet is that the characters of kings, gods etc. bear Mughal type feature with moustache beards and also wearing baggy pants. The troupe comprises a puppeteer who is also a story teller, a helper and two accompanying musicians. The performance which is based on epics local legends and folk tales is to accompaniment of music from instruments such as *dholak* and *pakhawaj*.

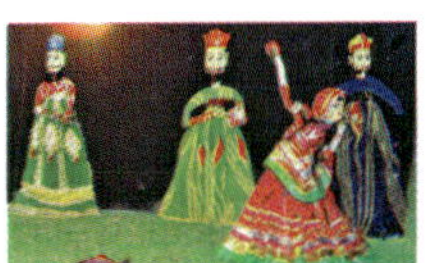

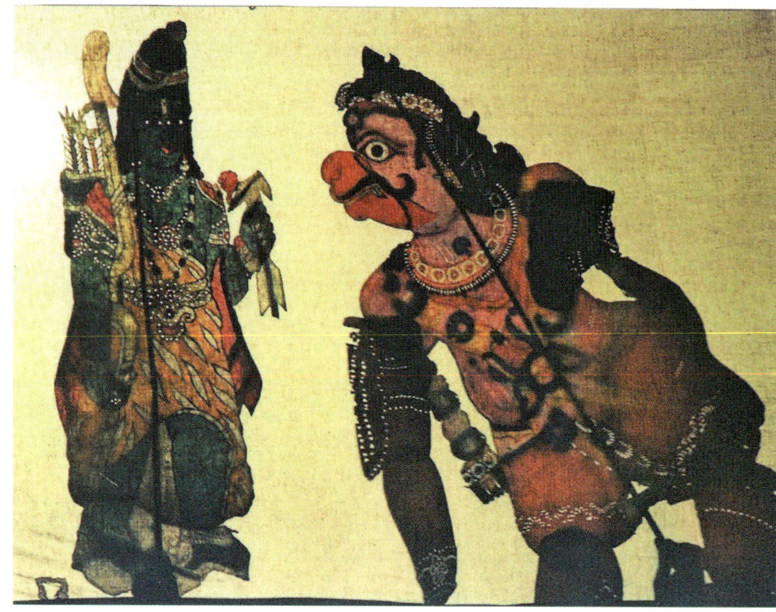

21.27: Tolu Bommalattam, the colourful shadow puppet of Tamil Nadu — Courtesy, Sangeet Natak Akademi

Tolu Bommalattam is the shadow puppet theatre of Tamil Nadu. The very term *Tolu* (leather) *Bommalattam* (puppet) signifies leather puppet. The theatre is performed as a family folk art with a troupe comprising of three to nine people of the family. Traditionally, this puppet theatre was performed by the Nandikar community who had migrated from Maharashtra region a couple of centuries ago. The puppets are made of perforated leather are thick and opaque and hence cast dark shadows. The play showcases the stories from the Ramayana, the story of Nallathangal, or the wedding of God Murugan with goddess Valli. A unique feature of the puppet performance is that the main puppeteer's wife or some other lady from the family sits in front of the screen on the side of the audience and plays the harmonium. She repeats the different significant phrases sung by the puppeteer, jokes, comments and the dramatic turn of events, to emphasise upon them and also to invoke the audience's interest.

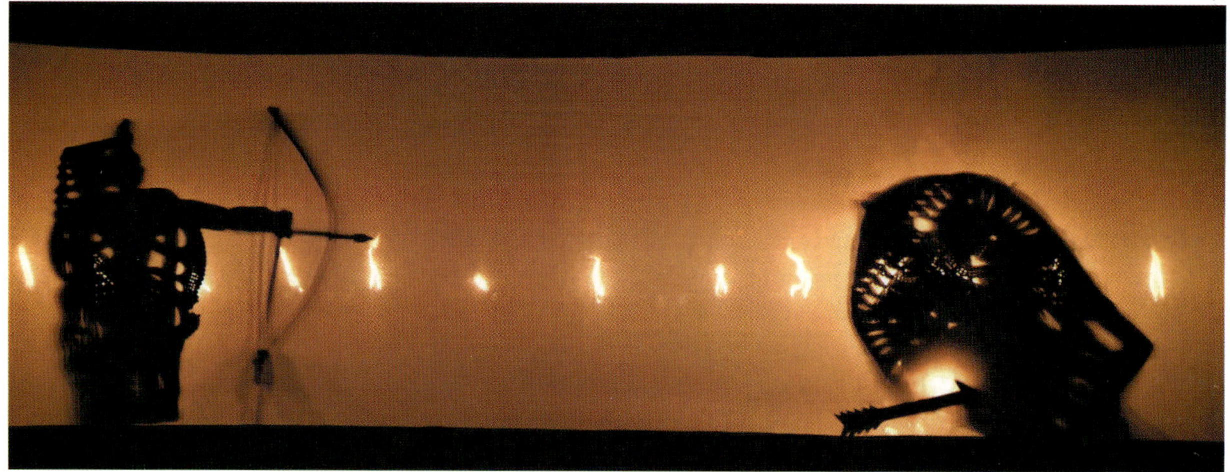

21.28: Tholpavakoothu performance depicting Lord Rama slaying Ravana — Courtesy, Sangeet Natak Akademi

Tholpavakoothu is the shadow puppet theatre of Kerala. This is also popular in parts of Tamil Nadu. The term *Tholpavakoothu* is derived from three words, *Tholu* – leather; *Pavai* - doll; *Koothu* - drama or play, thus signifying the performance of the play of the leather puppet. This folk theatre has been in existence for at least five centuries. The reference to *Pavai Koothu* is also seen in the *Kurals* which were composed more than 2000 years ago.

The performance of *Tholpavakoothu* is unique; for this is the only form of shadow puppet which is performed in a fixed theatre in temple precincts. As per the legends, when the Rama and the Ravana war were being waged, goddess Bhadrakali was battling the demon Darika and as such she could not witness the battle of Rama and Ravana and the slaying of the latter. As such as per her desire, the performance of the *Kamba Ramayana* (a Tamil version of Ramayan) is done in the temple precincts of Bhadrakali. A permanent stage *koothumadam,* a three-sided enclosure which is nearly 42 feet wide is erected, on which a white fabric screen is used for projection of the shadows. The source of light is from 21 lamps, made in coconut halves or in earthen lamps. The height of the leather puppets ranges from 8 inches to 16 inches and nearly 130 such puppet figures are prepared. As per some accounts, some performances may need up to 180 to 200 puppets. The performance may last whole nights, and the entire play of the Kamba Ramayana (*Ramavataram*) may take nearly 21 nights. However, some performances can be shorter of 7 to 14 days or

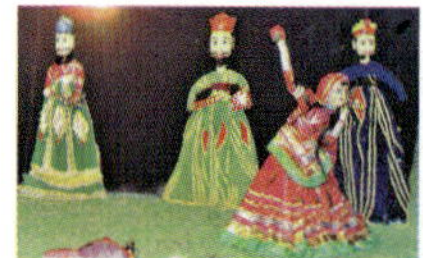

even longer of 41 or 71 days. The Ramayana performance is the only repertory of this theatre. Another noteworthy aspect of Tholpavakoothu is that the performance is based on the recitation of Tamil verses of the Ramayana, while their explanations are given in Malayalam. The troupe generally has nearly 40 members and is the biggest for any puppet theatre. The performance is to the accompaniment of music from instruments such as *chenda*, *maddalam*, *ilathalam*, conch, *ezhupara* and others.

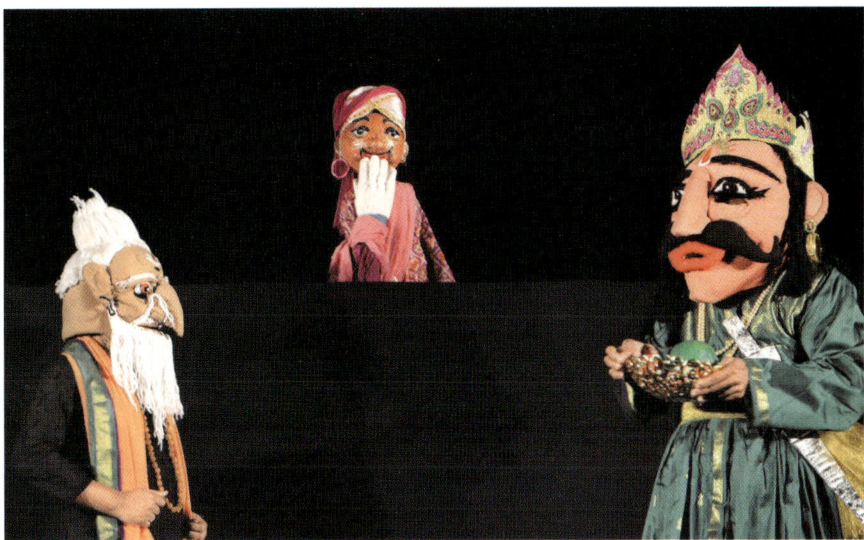

21.29: A modern puppet performance depicting the story of Vikram and Betaal — Courtesy, Sangeet Natak Akademi

Like other forms of puppet theatre, Tholpavakoothu and its patrons are dwindling owing to other form of mass entertainment emerging. The artists are now experimenting with shorter duration performance and other themes. With newer generations moving to the other and more paying vocations, the base of the performing artists is also shrinking and most of these folk-art forms are experiencing a declining trend.

MODERN INDIAN THEATRE

The emergence of modern Indian theatre can be traced back to the colonial period. It draws its roots from different sources and in particular to its folk tradition as well as the Western Proscenium theatre. **The Calcutta Theatre** built in 1779 with Warren Hastings as its patron marked the establishment of the modern theatres in India. One of the earliest theatrical performances in India was the staging of a play in 1971, titled, *Chhadmabeshi* (*The Disguise*), a comedy. This was translated in Bengali by Russian musician and linguistic translator, **Gerasim Stepanovich Lebedev** with the help of a local linguist **Goloknath Das**. The play included Bengali actors and actresses and marked the beginning of the Proscenium theatre in India.

Proscenium Theatre

This was a form of theatre which had an arched frame stage where the stage/acting area was separated from the audience seated in the auditorium. The concept of Proscenium theatre was itself of Greek origin and later came in prominence in Italy in the mid-17th century. The audience could view the play as if it was through a frame carved out. This acting area could also be separated from the auditorium through the stage curtains which could create a sense of spectacle and aid scene changes. This concept was different from the other closer formats of theatre, such as 'open staged theatre' and the 'theatre in the round' where audience could be closer to the stage.

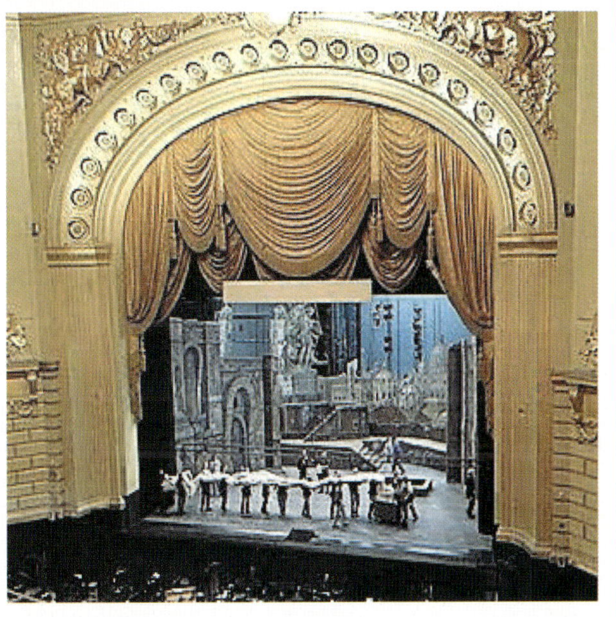

21.30: A proscenium theatre at the War Memorial Opera House in San Francisco. The golden Proscenium arch and the stage curtains which hang from it, form a sort of vertical frame which separates the staging and the audience areas — Wikimedia Commons

In the 1830s, under the patronage of some rich Bengali families emerged some Bengali theatres which were outside the domain of the traditional folk forms. In 1843, *Sita Swayamvar* written by **Vishnu Das**

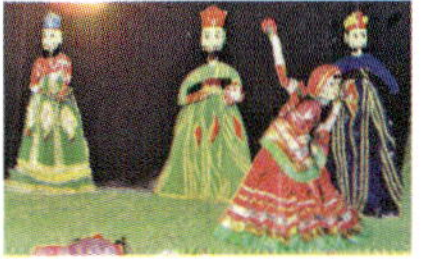

Bhave was staged before the ruler of the princely state of Sangli, marking the emergence of Marathi theatre. It drew inspiration from the Yakshagana tradition of Karnataka. **Dalpatram**, a Gujarati poet wrote the first modern Gujarati play, *Laxmi Natak* in 1850, which was inspired by the ancient Greek comedy play *Plutus* by Aristophanes. Later, the British also established a professional theatre in Calcutta, and in 1848 an Indian actor for the first time played Othello in it. *Inder Sabha* written by **Agha Hasan Amanat** and staged in 1853 is the first Urdu play and an opera. This was said to be produced at the behest of Nawab Wajid Ali Shah. By the 1850s, a number of private theatre enterprises had developed in Calcutta as well as Bombay and elsewhere. This marked the beginning of the modern theatres in India.

In the colonial period, and particularly from the mid-19th century, Indian theatre underwent a revival. Henceforth it also remained an important form of entertainment as well as for the spread of socio-cultural messages. The modern theatre which emerged in the latter half of the 19th century was not to the detriment of the folk theatre; rather it coexisted with it and was influenced by it. While the format of the modern theatre was Proscenium in appearance, its aesthetics in particular, drew from the folk theatre roots. Many of the conventions of the folk theatre such as the opening prayer song, duets, stylised speech, and tableaux were combined with the western theatrical form. Over a period of decades, theatres also took the shape of commercial ventures which moved out of the private houses and mansions and were accessible to public as ticket-based productions. Theatre flourished in different parts of the country and particularly the Bengali, Hindi, Marathi, Gujarati, Parsi, Tamil and Telugu theatres which were in the forefront of this movement.

The Early Productions

Buro Shaliker Ghare Ro by (1860) **Michael Madhusudan Dutt**, *Nil Darpan* written by **Dinabandhu Mitra** (1858-1859) and its commercial production (1872) by **Girish Chandra Ghosh**, *Satya Harishchandra* (1876), *Bharata Durdasha* (1875) and *Andher Nagari* (1881) by **Bharatendu Harishchandra** (poet, writer playwright and theatre manager), *Jhansichya Raniche Naatak* (1870), *Afzal Khan Chaye Mrutyuche Naatak* (1871) by **Vishnu Das Bhave**, were some of the eminent plays of this period which were commercially produced. In 1872, Girish Chandra Ghosh founded the National Theatre, a first Bengali professional theatre company, which took the *Nil Darpan* performance to different parts of the country and bringing out the tyranny of the British indigo planters over the peasants and farm labour. This eventually led to a ban on it by the British. *Chakar Darpan* (Mirror of Tea-Planters, 1875) by **Dakshina Charan Chattopadhyay** brought out the oppression of the tea planters criticising their inhumane treatment. The play was banned by the British government. Subsequently, the Playwrights Dramatic Performance Act 1976, was passed, which empowered the government to prohibit public dramatic performances that it found seditious, obscene or defamatory. Henceforth the playwrights adopted historical figures and mythological contexts to depict concurrent issues and thus creating a genre of plays such as *Andher Nagari,* where the British misrule was conveyed in a veiled manner.

In the late 19th and early 20th century, *Shakuntala* (1880) in Marathi by **Annasheb Kirloskar**, *Kinchit Jalajog* (1873), *Purubikram* (1874), *Hothath Nabab* (1884) in Bengali by **Jyotirindranath Tagore** (elder brother of Rabindranath Tagore), *Manonmaniyam* (1891) in Tamil by **P. Sundaram Pillai**, *Kanyasulkam* (1892) in Telugu by **Gurajada Apparao** were written. Works of **Rabindranath Tagore** such as *Chitrangada* (1892), *Raja* (1910), *Dakghar* (1913) and *Raktakarbi* (1924) in Bengali were some of the masterpieces which were staged. The element of nationalism albeit in the historical context, was also brought out in plays like *Mir Qasim* (1906), *Chhatrapati* (1907), and *Sirajuddaulah* (1909) by **Girish Chandra Ghosh** and *Mebar Patan* (The Fall of Mewar), *Shahjahan* (1910), and *Chandragupta* (1911) by **Dwijendralal Ray** in the Bengali theatre.

The Nature & Themes of Plays

In this phase of the evolution of theatre, its content evolved in a manner quite distinct from the ethos of the ancient Indian theatre. The narrative was not restricted to the epic tales of the gods and the celestial figures or the heroic deeds of the great kings, but centred on the common man, the social lives and its problems. *Bharat Durdasha* by **Bharatendu Harishchandra,** which succinctly brings out the reasons for deprivation of India in the colonial rule, and *Andher Nagari* were very categorical in their nationalistic theme and touched on the lives of the common folks. So were the plays like *Nil Darpan* which brought out the plight of the indigo cultivators under the British regime and *Chakar Darpan* which criticised the inhumane treatment of the tea plantation workers. *Naba Natak* and *Kulin Kulsarbasva* (1854), by **Ramnarayan Tarkaratna** opposed polygamy. The historic plays like *Mir Qasim* and *Sirajuddaulah*

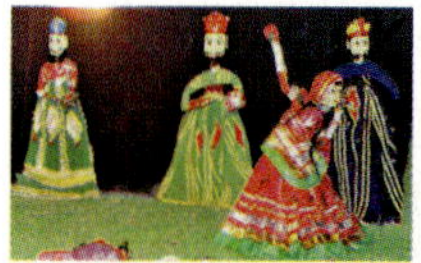

elucidated the fall of dynasties on account of betrayals. Others like *Chandragupta* and *Mebarpatan* explored the elements of nationalism in these historic dramas.

Kanyasulkam by **Gurajada Apparao,** succinctly portrayed the evil practice of marrying of young girls to much older brides for a fee. *Raktakarabi* by **Tagore** is centred on the theme of the demeaning influence of our greed in human lives whereby it reduces the beautiful life into a machine-like state which is nothing more than an instrument of production. Tagore brings out as to how the greed of those in power is likely to result in a human protest against such a state. **Dwijendralal Ray**, besides the historic plays (like *Chandragupta*, *Mebarpatan*) also wrote social plays like *Parapare* and *Babganari* which portay the evils of caste system. Thus, the plays of this period infused an element of **social-realism** in the drama. This element of realism became starker in the works of Sisir Kumar Bhaduri (plays: *Chanakya*) Naresh Mitra, Ahindra Choudhury and Durga Das Bannerji (in the 1920s) in the Bengali theatre.

Coming to the 20th century, and particularly around and after the First World War, Indian theatre again experienced the winds of change. This was influenced by the socio-political environment, rising nationalism and parallel movements in the world of art and literature. In the 1920s and 30s, experimental and amateur theatre movement emerged. This was evident in the works of Gujarati playwrights like **Chandravardan Chimanlal Mehta** whose themes were based on the social context. His work *Aag Garhi* (Fire engine) about an ailing fireman is said to have heralded amateur Gujarati theatre. *Sarjanhar* inspired by Gandhian ideology and based on the theme of untouchability was another important play of a social genre.

Another domain which experienced a radical change was the themes of the plays and structure of the theatre. The theatre by now had become largely a **commercial production**. Though it had moved out of the palaces and mansions and was accessible to the general people, but it was still limited mostly to the **urban auditoriums**. The creativity element of drama was gradually tempered with the commerce of the enterprise. Theatre, barring a few exceptions, had less of any political leanings or political messages and themes. This was one element which the theatre had largely become bereft of.

The rise of nationalism, the emergence of the Bengal revivalist school, the emergence of the Progressive Writers Movement in 1936 and the growth of the communist movement, eventually led to the birth of **Indian People's Theatre Association (IPTA).** With it, the theatre started to become people centric, with a view to bring cultural awakening and infuse a sense of nationalism in the masses. Theatre now had to also move closer to the people. In its new form, theatre had to become **portable** and **mobile** to reach out to the masses and bring forth the social and political change it endeavoured. There was the birth of experiments such as **street theatre** which had minimum of props. This brought theatre to the doorsteps of people, to the small *mohallas* of cities and to the rural landscape. And all this brought a change in the character in at least a segment of Indian Proscenium theatre. This was to have an impact even in the coming decades. Though the Proscenium theatre continued and grew, the decadent theatre of the rich a century earlier, which flourished in private mansions as a means of entertainment of the nobility and elite, had no place. Theatre now had a mission.

Indian People's Theatre Association: The Emergence of a New Movement

IPTA was founded in 1943 as a socio-cultural off-shoot of the Communist movement with a view to spread the message of India's freedom struggle and to bring a cultural awakening in the masses through the medium of plays. The movement drew its roots in *Progressive Writers Conference* in 1936, the establishment of the *Youth Cultural Institute at Calcutta* in 1940, and the setting up of the *People's Theatre* in Bangalore in 1941. The name Indian People's Theatre Association was suggested by renowned scientist Dr Homi Jahangir Bhabha who was inspired by a book of Romain Rolland (Nobel Prize awardee French novelist and dramatist) on the concept of people's theatre.

The organisation and its units in different parts of the country were referred to with different names. Its units in North India and in the Hindi speaking region were called the *Bharatiya Jan Natya Sangh*, while in Assam and Bengal it was *Bharatiya Gana Natya Sangh,* and in Andhra Pradesh as *Praja Natya Mandali*.

Scholars at times consider the emergence of IPTA to be a consequence of the Bengal famine. *Bhookha Hai Bengal* (Bengal is hungry) was a choir and a slogan of many plays which highlighted the man-made Bengal famine of 1943. Many eminent leaders, freedom fighters, litterateurs, theatre personalities and people from other walks of life came to be associated with it. This included the likes of **Anna Bhau** (social reformer and poet), **N.M. Joshi** (trade union leader), **EMS Namboodiripad** (communist leader and later first chief minister of Kerala), **Khwaja Ahmed Abbas** (notable film director, screen writer and novelist), **Vallathol Narayana Menon** (preeminent Malayalam poet), **Raja Rao** (notable English author), **Amritlal Nagar** (acclaimed Hindi novelist, playwright and short story writer), **Nemi Chandra Jain** (poet, critic and theatre personality), **Balraj Sahni** (renowned stage and film actor), **Bimal Roy** (popular and critically acclaimed film director), **Dina Pathak** (notable theatre personality and film actress), **Salil Chowdhury** (acclaimed music

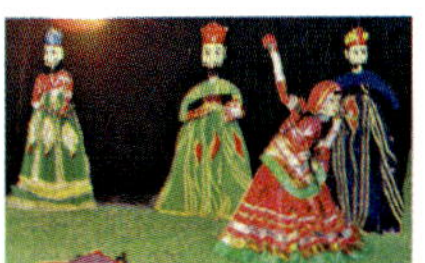

director, lyricist and poet). Besides, its conferences were also attended/presided by mainstream leaders. Its eighth national conference organised in 1958, was inaugurated by Dr. S. Radhakrishnan (the then Vice president of India).

In its inceptive days, ***Nabanaa*** (*New Crop*) by **Bijon Bhattacharya** proved to be a path-breaking play as it highlighted the great tragedy of famine and touched a raw nerve of the people. Besides, it was also a movement to collect famine relief. *Dharti Ke Lal* was a film produced under the aegis of IPTA in 1946. In the decade of 50s, IPTA staged several plays all over the country. However, in the 60s and 70s, the movement survived only through its state units such as that of Bombay, Bihar, Uttar Pradesh, Kerala, and Andhra Pradesh which continued to remain active. In the 1980s, the movement had a resurgence at the national level and continues to flourish, having completed nearly eight decades of its existence.

IPTA ushered certain fundamental changes in the very nature of theatre. In the initial decade of its formation, the plays staged were not entertainment based, commercial ventures, folk themed or even apolitical. Rather they were imbued with the nationalistic fervour and a social purpose. Anti colonialism and anti-fascism were the hues and undertones of many plays, particularly those staged by IPTA in the pre-independence period, while in the post-independence period it brought out the new social and political issues. This also influenced the mainstream theatre and art world. Besides creating awareness about the emerging challenges of the commoners and endeavouring to usher socio-political change by inducing a grass root movement in theatre, it also portrayed the contemporary reality through the medium of theatre. Over the years, it has also inspired several theatre groups which have experimented with street and other forms of contemporary theatre.

आई पी टी ए
IPTA
भारत INDIA 200
1994

21.31: A stamp issued in 1994 to commemorate 50 years of IPTA. It carries the logo of IPTA, a drummer, which symbolises one of the earliest forms of communication — Courtesy, Department of Post.

THE REGIONAL THEATRES OF THE 19th AND EARLY 20th CENTURIES

Regional theatres have flourished in different parts of the country, each with its own folk roots and local cultural influences. Most of the regional theatres witnessed a move towards modern forms which were based on the proscenium theatre, while also drawing upon their regional traditions. Over the years the different regional theatres have also seen certain common traits, be it the colonial influence, emergence of theatre as a means of entertainment, and later its evolution as a powerful social platform. From old Sanskrit classics to drawing inspiration from European plays, from historical and mythological plays to original regional works, were some other common characteristics of all. With the emergence of the films as the mainstream means of social entertainment, all regional theatres experienced varying degree of decline. They continue to face the existential challenge in the new millennium as well, with some theatres springing back with vigour and finding a new meaning for themselves. An attempt is made here to bring out the modern evolution of some of the more prominent regional theatres.

Bengali Theatre

Bengali theatre was one of the leading regional theatres of the country. The very first modern play was staged in Calcutta in 1795 by Lebedev and Goloknath Das, where the actors were also Bengalis. In 1831, *Hindu Rangamancha* was established by **Prasanna Kumar Tagore** in Calcutta which staged the English translation of Bhavabhuti's Sanskrit drama *Uttara Ramacharitam*. In 1835, **Nabin Chandra Basu** staged a famous play *Bidyasundar* in his mansion. Later, many other private theatres also flourished, including *Jorasanko Natyashala* (1854), private theatres of Ashutosh Deb (1857), besides theatres such as *Vidyotsahini Mancha* (1857) by **Kaliprasanna Singha**, *Belgachia Natyashala* (1858), *Metropolitan Theatre* (1859), *Shobhabazar Private Theatrical Society* (1865), *Bahubazar Natyashala* (1866) and *Bagbazar Amateur Theatre* (1868). *National Theatre* founded in 1872 by **Girish Chandra Ghosh** was the first Bengali professional theatre company which toured in large parts of the country, staging historical and social plays, as well as adaptation of classics from the Indian and Western theatre.

Among the great playwrights of this period were **Michael Madhusudan Dutt** (plays: *Sermista*-1859, *Padmavati* - 1859, *Ekei Ki Boley Sabyata*-1860, *Krishna Kumari*-1860 and *Buro Shaliker Ghare Ron*-1860) and **Dinabandhu Mitra** (*Nil Darpan*-1860, *Nabin Tapasvini*-1863, *Biye Pagla Budo*-1866, *Sadhabar Ekadashi*-1866, *Lilavati*-1867, *Jamai Barik*-1873 and *Kamale Kamini*-1873). **Dwijendralal Ray** was another eminent playwright of this period known for penning historical plays like *Tarabai* (1903), *Rana Pratapsingh* (1905),

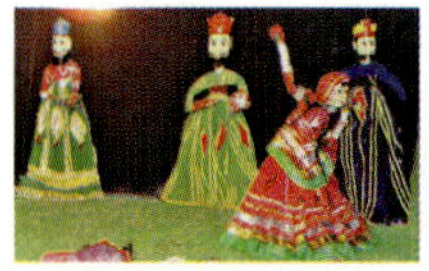

Mebar Patan (1908), *Nurjahan* (1908), *Shahjahan* (1909) and *Chandragupta* (1911). Besides, he composed mythical and social plays as well, the latter were known for their critique of the feudal structure and caste system.

Rabindranath Tagore, a prolific playwright, who wrote many plays of different genres in literary career of over five decades, was an institution in himself. His works included, *Valmiki Pratibha* (1881), *Kal Mrigya* (1882), *Mayar Khela* (1888), *Visarjan* (1890), *Chitrangada* (1892), *Raja* (1910), *Dakghar* (1912), *Achalyatan* (1912) *Muktadhara* (1922), *Raktakarbi* (1926) and *Chandalika* (1932). He evolved a genre of plays albeit different from the contemporaries. Hindu classics, folk elements, music and dance were all integrated in the experimental theatre which was at times staged in an opera like format in Santiniketan. *Visarjan,* which was an adaptation of his novel *Rajarshi,* is often regarded by critics as his finest drama. *Dak Ghar* (The Post Office) received rave reviews even in Europe. The appeal of its subject, of a child's monotonous existence who ultimately falls asleep signifying death and spiritual freedom, transcended the borders. The issue of untouchability is brought to the fore in *Chandalika* in the backdrop of the anecdote of Ananda a disciple of Lord Buddha, asking for water from Chandalika, an untouchable girl. *Raktakarabi* (Blood Oleanders) explores the struggles of the subjects against a kleptocratic ruler.

Other notable personalities associated with the Bengal theatre included **Sisir Kumar Bhaduri**, a stage actor and theatre founder. He is also referred to as the pioneer of modern Bengali theatre for having introduced realism and naturalism in it. **Utpal Dutt** (theatre and film actor), and the founder of *Little Theatre Group* (1949), was another eminent theatre personality who was also associated with IPTA movement. **Sombhu Mitra** (Indian theatre personality, playwright, producer, director stage and film actor) was the founder of the famous *Bohurupee Theatre* group in Calcutta (1948). This theatre staged many of Rabindranath Tagore's play including *Raktakarabi, Bisarjan Raja* and others. **Bijon Bhattacharya** (Jnanpith awardee) was a notable playwright theatre and film actor who also was associated with the IPTA movement. Some of his acclaimed plays include *Nabanna* (Fresh Harvest-1944), *Jabanbandi* (Confession), *Mara Chand* (Dead Moon-1951), *Gotranatar* (Change of the lineage-1959), *Garbhabati Janani* (Pregnant Mother - 1969). *Nabanna*, a drama about the Bengal famine and its intensity, was staged in various parts of the country by IPTA and later by the *Bohurupee Theatre* of Sombhu Mitra. It received critical and commercial success, the proceeds of which were used for famine relief.

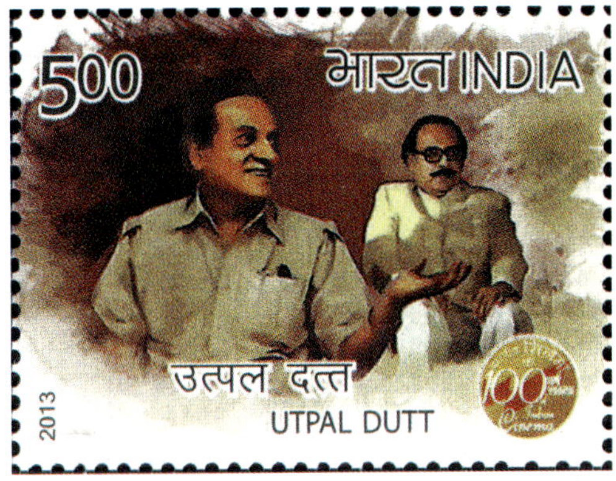

21.32: A stamp on Utpal Dutt, an eminent theatre and film actor, released in 2013 — Courtesy, Department of Post

The post-independence period saw the emergence of another eminent theatre personality in **Badal Sarkar** (Padma Shri & Sangeet Natak Fellowship awardee) who authored more than 50 plays. His celebrated works include, *Evam Indrajit* (Also Indrajit-1963), *Baki Itihas* (Remaining History-1965), *Pagla Ghoda* (Mad Horse-1967), *Baasi Khabar* (Stale News), *Prastava* (Proposal), *Juloos* (Procession) and *Saari Raat* (Whole night). His plays reflected the anti-establishmentarian mood, particularly during the height of the Naxalite Movement in the West Bengal of 70s. He took the Proscenium theatre completely in the public arena by launching the street theatre movement. The **Third Theatre** movement or *Teesra Manch,* hence emerged, bringing a change in the very expression of theatre. Other distinguished playwrights of this period were **Mohit Chatterjee** and **Arun Mukherjee**.

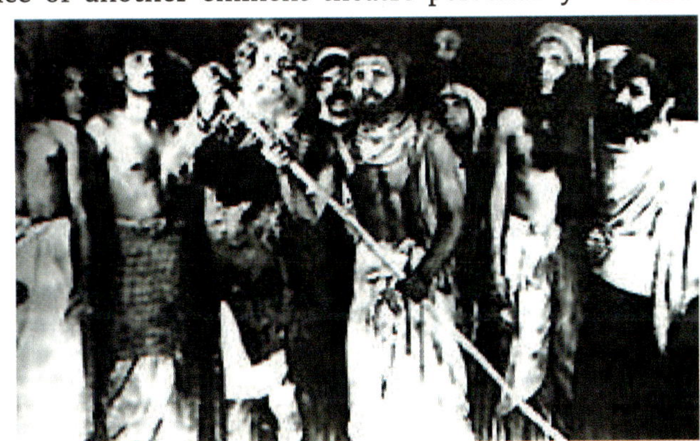

21.33: A scene from Nabanna — Wikimedia Commons

Bengal was one of the leaders of the theatre movement and still has a rich theatre culture. While in the 60s and 70s, theatre groups such as *Bohurupee* and *Nandikar* flourished, later groups such as *Alternate Living Theatre*, Rangroop and others have emerged strong. Many new directors, actors and playwrights have come up which hold a strong promise of the modern Bengali theatre.

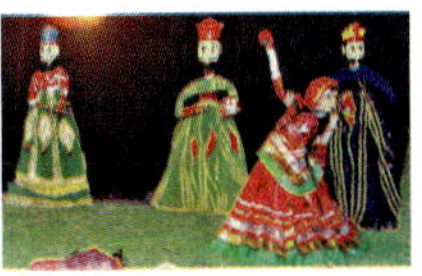

Assamese Theatre

The Assamese theatre has a history of several centuries which is traceable to the socio-religious reforms carried out by Sri Sankardeva in the 15th century and to the traditions of *Ankiya Naat* and *Bhaona*. The modern theatre in Assam developed like in the other regional theatres in the middle of the 19th century. The influence of the Bengal renaissance as well as the theatre movement in Bengal, was a prominent factor in spurring the growth of modern playwrights and theatre in Assam.

Among the modern playwrights of Assam, the earliest reference is received of **Gunabhiram Barua** (1837-1898), an eminent historian and dramatist who wrote *Ramnabami Natak* in 1857, which was published as a book in 1870. The play is a tragic-drama of the love of a young widow Nabami and his lover Ram. Another eminent playwright of this period was **Hemachandra Barua** (1835-1897) a litterateur and a social reformer, who wrote *Kaniar Kir* (1861), a comical play which decried the consumption of opium.

Lakshminath Bezbarua (1864-1938) was one of greatest modern literary figures of Assam who wrote several novels, plays and poems. He authored several of Assamese dramas which include comical plays like *Litikai* (1890), *Nomal* (1913), *Pachoni* (1913), *Chikarpati-Nikarpati* (1913), besides others such as *Joymati Kunwari* (1915), *Belimaar* (1915) & *Chakradhwaj Singh*a (1915). Among other playwrights of this period was **Ratneshwar Mahanta** (1864-1893) who wrote character plays like *Harishchandra Nataka.* The plays of **Jyoti Prasad Agarwala** (1903-1951) incorporated music and dance such as in *Sonit Kunwari* (1925), *Karengar Ligri* (1930), *Rupalem* (1938), *Nimate Konya* (1964) besides others.

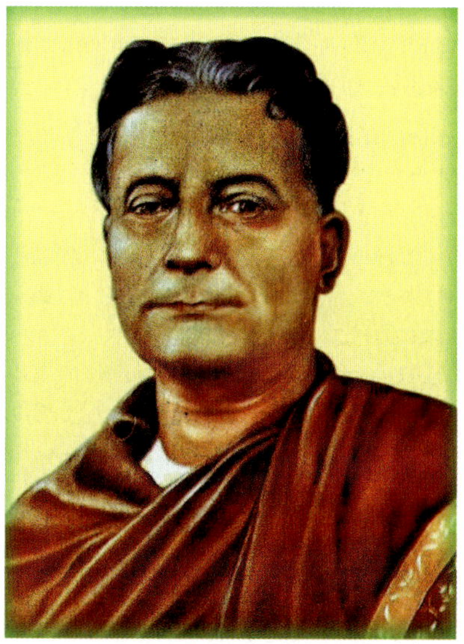

21.34: Lakshminath Bezbarua, an eminent Assamese novelist, poet and playwright — Wikimedia Commons

Benudhar Rajkhowa (1872-1955) was a prolific playwright of late 19th & early 20th century, who authored nearly 14 works of drama. Some of his works include *Deka Gabhoru* (1889), *Dorbaar* (1902), *Kalyug* (1904) besides others. **Atul Chandra Hazarika** (1903-1986; Padma Shri, Sahitya Akademi awardee) also authored several plays which were based on mythology and historical characters such as *Narakasur* (1930), *Kurukshetra* (1936), *Shakuntala* (1940) *Chatrapati Shivaji* (1947) and *Rukmaniharan* (1949).

The **format of theatre** in Assam gradually transitioned from its traditional *Bhaona* and other folk forms. There was development of non-Proscenium, **commercial mobile theatres** in Assam which were the centres of dramatic activities, besides there were local dramatic clubs. The Proscenium and western format theatre came up later, particularly in the post-independence period.

Among the earliest of the **mobile theatres** was formed by **Brajnath Sharma** (1894-1960), a notable playwright and actor who in 1930 formed the historic *Kohinoor Opera Party*. The group travelled from place to place performing on makeshift stages, thus laying the foundation of *Bhryamyman* mobile theatres in Assam. Another popular mobile theatre was the *Sila Kalika Opera Party*. In 1963, **Achyut Lahkar**, also known as the father of mobile theatre in Assam, formed the *Natraj Cine Theatre* group which performed as a mobile theatre. It took Assamese drama to different parts of other states such as West Bengal, Bihar and Uttar Pradesh. In 1976, **Ratan Lahkar** founded the *Kohinoor Theatre* (a mobile theatre) which has been performing since then in the last five decades. Its plays are based on Indian and Assamese culture, besides the works of Shakespeare. Among some of its eminent stage performances are *Rumal* (2010), *Path* (2015), *Devdas* (2013). It even performed the famous Hollywood movie *Titanic* as a stage performance.

Odia Theatre

The modern theatre in Odisha is said to have emerged in the latter half of the 19th century. Although the evidence of a drama *Padmabati Haran*, written in 1934, is noted in the accounts of some scholars, the play *Babaji* written and enacted by **Jagan Mohan Lala** in 1877 is considered the first modern Odia play. This drama of the social genre, created awareness regarding the issue of unethical practices of those considered holy men and distinguishes them from genuine spiritual preachers.

At this stage, the Bengali theatre also influenced and inspired the Odia playwrights. **Ramashankar Ray** who was a prolific Odia playwright, had earlier seen a Bengali play being staged in Cuttack (in 1878)

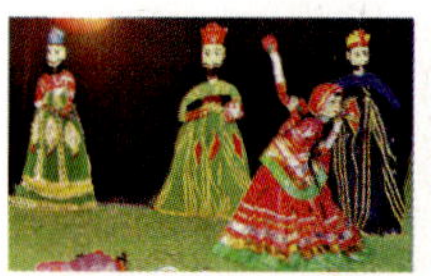

and was inspired to create Odia plays. He wrote *Kanchi-kaveri* (1881), besides 14 plays of historical and mythological genre. Among other noteworthy playwrights of this period were **Padmanabha Narayana Deb, Kampal Mishra, Bhikhari Charan Patnaik,** besides others.

In the 20th century, the prominent playwrights include **Godabarish Misra** (1886-1956, Sahitya Akademi awardee), a poet and dramatist who is known for eminent works of drama such as *Purushottama Deba*, *Mukunda Deba* besides others. **Aswini Kumar Ghose** (1892–1962) was another dramatist of this phase, who was known for historical dramas such as *Kala-Pahad* and *Tipu Sultan.* Many of the plays of the above two playwrights were staged by the *Radha Krishna Theatre Party* of Puri, which remained a prominent theatre group of Odisha. Subsequent to the death of its founder **Banamali Pati**, it came to be known as the *Banamali Art Theatre* and remained active till the late 1929-1930. Besides it and a few permanent theatres which came up in the 1940s, the Odia theatre in the first half of the 20th century was largely propagated through the touring theatre groups.

Kalicharan Pattnaik (1898-1978 Sahitya Akademi awardee) was one of the most notable playwrights of the pre-independence period who heralded the genre of socially relevant Odia plays as well as dance-dramas. *Pratisodha* (1937) was the first of his plays amidst more than 20 social, historical and dance dramas. He also founded the theatre group the *New Odisha Theatre* (1939) which remained active in the 1940s.

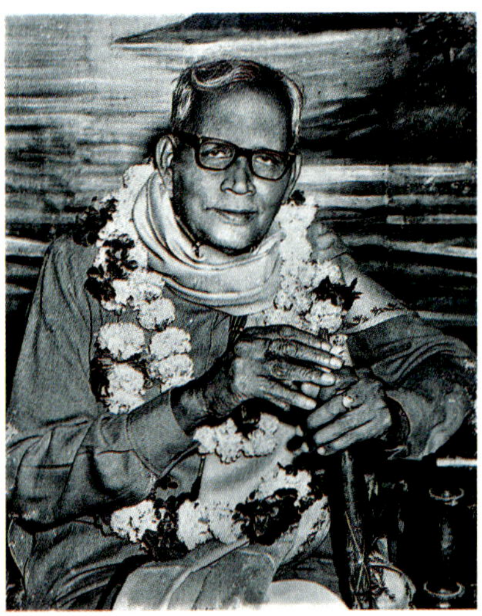

21.35: Kalicharan Pattnaik, an eminent playwright, literary and artisitic figure — Wikimedia Commons

In the post-independence period, the prominent playwrights were **Ramchandra Misra**, a humorist and satirist; **Bhanja Kishore Patnaik** whose plays were based on national integration, communal harmony and other socio-political issues and **Gopal Chhotray** who wrote more than 15 original plays and eight adaptations. In 1940s and 50s, many professional theatre groups also came up, which included *Annapurna Theatre* having branches in Puri and Cuttack, *Bharati Theatre* in Cuttack. *Rupashri* and *Janata Kalasri* were some other theatres of this period. However, beyond the 1970s, the commercial theatres in Odisha suffered a decline. In the 80s and beyond, the mantle of theatre in Odisha is largely on organisations like Odisha Sangeet Natak Akademi and other smaller amateur theatre groups.

Marathi Theatre

Marathi theatre was one of the most prominent regional theatres, which flourished in the middle of the 19th century. It had its birth with the performance of *Sita Swayamvar* in 1843 which was composed by **Vishnudas Bhave**. The play which marks the beginning of the modern Marathi theatre, was staged before the ruler of the princely state of Sangli. With the success of *Sita Swayamvar,* other episodes from Ramayana were enacted in the coming years. Later, he produced other plays as a part of his moving troupe, including *Jhansichya Raniche Naatak* (The Drama of Queen of Jhansi-1870), *Sawai Madhavrao Yancha Mrityu* (The Death of Sawai Madhavrao 1871) *Afzal Khan Chya Mrutyuche Natak* (The Play of the Death of Afzal Khan-1871), *Malhar Rao Maharaj* (King Malhar Rao-1875). Bhave included some of the techniques of the western theatre such as changeable scenery, but tried to keep the characters close to what was encountered in everyday life, thus engendering a modern theatre with western and Indian elements.

The commercial theatre in Maharashtra emerged after the foundation of *Kirloskar Natya Mandali* by **Annasaheb Kirloskar**. *Shakuntala* (1880), a Marathi adaptation of the classical Sanskrit play *Abhigyana Shankuntalam*, was a commercial success. This paved the way for other commercial theatres to develop. A number of eminent playwrights emerged thereafter, including Kolhatkar, Govinda Ballal Deval (1855-1916), Krishnaji Prabhakar Khadilkar (1872-1948), Ram Ganesh Gadkari (1885-1919) amongst others. **Govind Ballal Deval** wrote many of the adaptations of Sanskrit classics in Marathi. This included different adaptations of the Sanskrit classics such as *Mrichchhakatika*, *Vikramorvashiyam*, *Shap Sambhram* (an adaption of Kadambari) besides others.

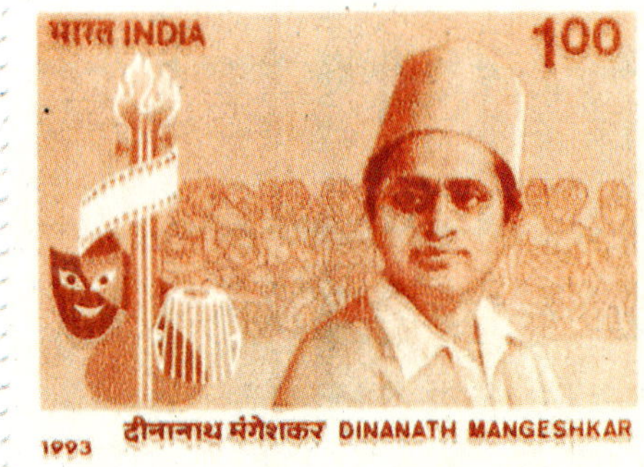

21.36: Dinanath Mangeshkar, stage actor singer and producer of plays, father of legendary singer Lata Mangeshkar, a 1993 stamp — Courtesy, Department of Post

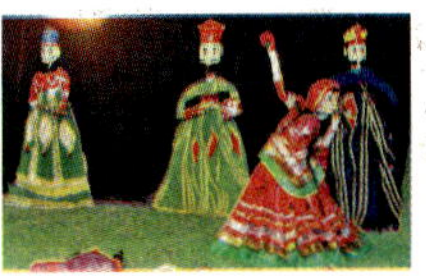

Keechak Vadh (the Killing of Keechak–1906), by **Krushnaji Prabhakar Khadilkar** was symbolic of the British exploitation of India and was eventually banned in 1910. **Ram Ganesh Gadkari** wrote four plays which were considered as masterpieces by the critics. These included *Ekach Pyala*, *Prema Sanyas*, *Punyaprabhav*, *Bhava Bandhan*.

A uniqueness of many plays of this period was that these were often musicals and were known as *Sangeet Natak.* It was a genre which continued for nearly next five decades and till the early 20th century in the Marathi theatre. This also led to the emergence of many popular theatre singer-actors such as Bhaurao Kolhatkar (1863-1901), Bal Gandharva (1888-1967), Keshavrao Bhole (1896-1967) and Dinanath Mangeshkar (1900-1942). **Bal Gandharva** (Padma Bhushan awardee) was specially known for playing roles of female characters when women were not allowed to participate in plays. **Keshavrao Bhole** was also the founder of a theatrical company *Natya-Manvantara.* **Dinanath Mangeshkar,** besides being an actor and singer, also produced several commercially successful and acclaimed plays which were known for their songs and their patriotic content.

In the **post-independence** period, the tradition of Marathi theatre was carried forward by some eminent playwrights which included Chintamani Tryambak Khanolkar (1930-1976), Vishnu Vaman Shirwadkar (1912-1999), Jayavant Dalvi (1925-94), Vijay Tendulkar (1928-2018), Govind Purushottam Deshpande (1938-2013) and Satish Vasant Alekar (1949).

Khanolkar (Sahitya Akademi and Sangeet Natak Akademi awardee) was known for his experimental plays such as *Ek Shunya Bajirao* and *Ajab Nyaywartulacha.* **Shirwadkar** (Padma Bhushan, Sahitya Akademi and Jnanpith awardee) authored over 20 plays. His adaptation of Shakespeare's *Macbeth* (as *Rajmukut*) and *Othello*, were staged with prominent actors of the time playing the characters. **Alekar** (Padma Shri & Sangeet Natak Akademi awardee) is a founder of Theatre Akademi of Pune and is among the progressive playwrights of Marathi theatre. He is known for plays like *Mahanirvan* (1974), *Mahapoor* (1975), *Atirekee* (1990) besides others.

Vijay Tendulkar (Padma Bhushan, Sangeet Natak Akademi Fellowship awardee) is considered among the preeminent Marathi playwrights and theatre personality of this period. He was also a movie and television writer and a political journalist. His plays, which were often of unconventional themes, reflect social realism. He is best known for critically and commercially successful plays such as *Shantata! Court Chalu Ahet* (Silence! Court is in progress-1967), *Ghashiram Kotwal* (1972), *Sakharam Binder* (1972). Among his over 30 plays, some of his other well-known ones were; *Gruhastha* (Householder-1947), *Shrimant* (The Rich-1956), *Manoos Nawache Bet* (An Island Named 'Man'-1958), *Gidhade* (The Vultures-1961), *Kamla (1981)* and *Kanyadaan* (Giving away of a daughter in marriage-1983). *Mitrachi Goshta* (1981), which was centred on a love triangle and the taboo subject of same-sex attraction, is described by critics as much ahead of its time.

Gujarati Theatre

Gujarati theatre had its advent in 1850 when the first play *Laxmi Natak* written by **Dalpatram** (an esteemed Gujarati poet) was staged. This was a play inspired by Greek comedy *Plutus* of Aristophanes. In its early days, Gujarati theatre was influenced by the European theatre as well as the Parsi theatre movement. In 1852, a Shakespearean play was performed in Surat by a Parsi theatre group. Subsequently in 1853, there was the formation of *Parsee Natak Mandali* which was founded by **Faramjee Gustajee Dalal**. In Bombay the group performed the play *Rustam Sohrab* based on the tales of Rustam and Sohrab from the 10th century Persian epic *Shahnameh* of Firdausi. Another play *Dhanji Gharak* (a farce) was also performed by the group.

The early days of Gujarati theatre saw entertainment based Parsi theatre which used a mix of Gujarati with Urdu and English. These also incorporated some elements of the Bhavai folk theatre. But unlike Bhavai, which did not have a stage-based performance, raised platforms as stage and Proscenium theatre format were added to Gujarati theatre. Another theatre group was also formed by Dalpatram, which staged Gujarati plays. This helped in reforming the use of Gujarati language used in the theatre and eliminate the crude elements of Bhavai. Gradually the number of Gujarati plays increased, which led to the Gujarati theatre forming an identity distinct from the Parsi theatre and the Bhavai tradition.

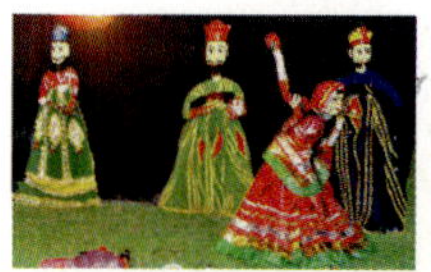

Arya Subodh Natak Mandali formed in 1878 staged its first production *Bharthari* in Saurashtra region and continued to do so for many years. Among other theatre companies formed in this period were *Deshi Natak Samaj* by Dahyabhai Dholashaji, *Natak Uttejak Mandali* (1875–94) and *Gujarati Natak Mandali* (1878-1889) besides others. While the latter lasted for a period of nearly 10 years, its successor theatre group, *Mumbai Gujarati Natak Mandali* flourished for nearly 60 years (1889–1948). It is credited with production of more than 100 plays in this period; besides introducing many actors and directors and other artistes, thus truly enriching the tradition of Gujarati theatre.

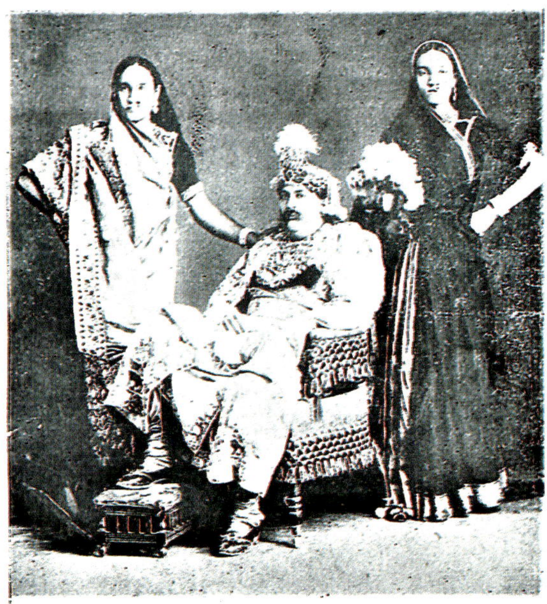

21.37: A performance of the play *Vikramcharit* (written by Mulani) in 1900, at *Mumbai Gujarati Natak Mandali.* Actors: Jethalal Nayak, Dayashankar Vasanji and Jayshankar Lakhwadwala. Female cast played by male actors — Wikimedia Commons

In the 19th century, a part of Gujarati theatre continued with its repertoire of religious and mythological plays while another section of commercial theatre adopted the route of entertainment-based theatre. A major shift in the Gujarati theatre took place with the effort and works of Ranchhodbhi Udayram Dave (1837-1923), a playwright and producer, who is considered as the father of the modern Gujarati theatre, and Chandravardan Chimanlal Mehta (1901-1991) who pioneered the movement of realism in Gujarati theatre.

Ranchhodbhai Dave wrote 10 original and four adapted plays from the Sanskrit theatre. He developed a drama troupe which helped Gujarati plays to come on their own and as distinct from the Parsi theatre. His work *Lalitha Dukh Darsak* (1866) about an educated girl marrying an illiterate boy, was an offbeat yet successful play of its time. His production on *Raja Harishchandra* (1871) is said to have inspired a young Mahatma Gandhi. His other notable plays include *Taramatiswayamvar* (1871), *Premrai Ane Charumati* (1876), *Bhanasur mad-mardan* (1878), *Madalasa ane Hritudhwaj* (1878), *Nala-Damatanti* (1893), *Nindya Shringarnishedhak Roopak* (1920) besides others. **Chandravardan Mehta's** work *Aag Garhi* (*Fire engine*) about the life of an ailing fireman, marked the beginning of amateur theatre in Gujarat. This was later translated into *Iron Road* by him. In a career spanning several decades, Mehta wrote over 25 plays.

Besides the above, *Sarjanhar* was another iconic play of the 20th century which dealt on the issues of untouchability and was based on Gandhian value. In the 1920s and 1930s, **Bapulal Nayak** and **Jaishankar Bhojak Sundari** (played female characters) became extremely popular with many successful plays. Also, in this period, a prominent theatre *Ranbhoomi Parishad,* formed in 1937 in Ahmedabad, helped to take the Gujarati theatre forward. **Indian National Theatre,** formed in 1943 in Bombay, was another organisation in this period which staged many Gujarati plays.

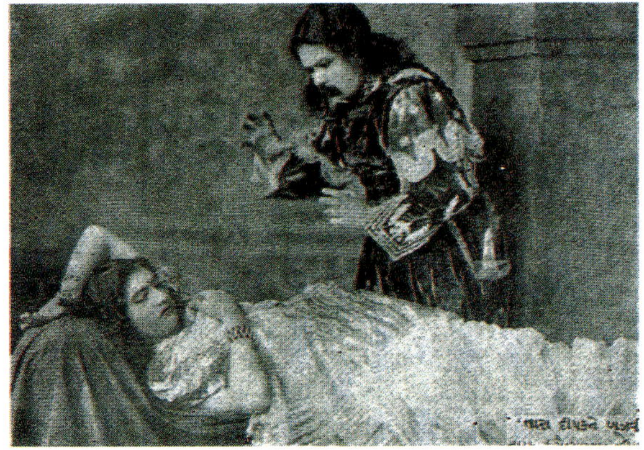

21.38: Saubhagya Sundari, a popular play by Mulani, staged in 1901 at *Mumbai Gujarati Natak Mandali.* Actors: Bapulal Nayak and Jaishankar Sundari — Wikimedia Commons

In the post-independence period, *Nat Mandal* and *Rang Mandal* provided impetus to the movement, while *Rangabhumi* emerged as a successful commercial theatre. The centre of theatric creativity spread to cities of Ahmedabad and Baroda, besides Bombay. Celebrated playwrights like **K.M. Munshi**, **Pragji Dosa**, directors like **Shanta Gandhi** (directed famous play *Jasma Odan*-1968) and actors like **Dina Pathak** (who acted in famous play *Mena Gujari* performed before the President of India in 1957), besides other theatre personalities, have enriched the Gujarati theatre. Though the growth of Gujarati theatre thereafter slowed in the late 20th century, in the new millennium it has seen a new promise.

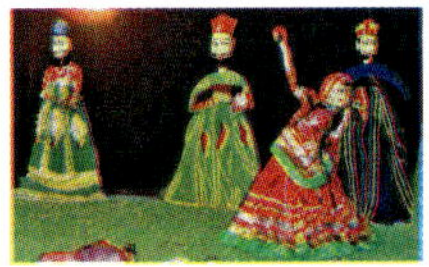

Parsi Theatre

Parsi theatre was another important theatrical movement which flourished in parallel to the Gujarati and Marathi theatres in Bombay and Gujarat. Eminent theatre personality **Framjee Gustajee Dalal**, who launched the *Parsi Natak Mandali*, was the pioneer whose effort helped the launch of Parsi theatre in the 1850s. By the 1860s, as many as 20 Parsi theatres were operating in Mumbai.

Parsi theatre of the 19th century were initially producing Indianised versions of the Shakespearean plays and other classics. Later, the plays were a blend of fantasy and realism and was incorporated in classical forms and folk dramas. Indian musicals along with the western techniques were added. This theatre excelled in dramatic production and structure. It would also include a combination of songs and dances, comic scenes etc. These were incorporated in a structure of five acts, accentuated with their declamatory acting. (*declamatory acting*: an acting style expressing emotion through grand movement and oratory projection). Their theatre troupes toured different parts of the country, particularly northern and western India, as well as parts of southern India. It enjoyed substantial popularity as an entertainment-based theatre, particularly from the 1850s to the 1930s. The design, scale and structure of Parsi theatre was instrumental in further influencing the regional theatres where the Parsi theatre would tour in the coming decades. Many of the regional theatres would emulate the template of the Parsi theatre, specially in the beginning phase of the regional theatres in the late 19th and early 20th century.

Later, with the growth of regional theatres in different parts of the country, the influence of the Parsi theatre tended to wane, with local support being more pronounced for the regional theatre. Also, with the arrival of the talkies and with the increasing popularity of Hindi cinema, the appeal of the Parsi theatre diminished, as films became the mainstay of public entertainment. However, the effect of entertainment-based masala with a mix of Hindi and Urdu (Hindustani) was definitely a legacy of this theatre in the film industry and Bollywood movies in later years.

Post-independence Parsi theatre saw the emergence of **Adi Pherozeshah Marzban** (1914–1987; Padma Shri and Sangeet Natak Akademi awardee) an eminent theatre personality, who is credited with having introduced the element of realism in Parsi theatre. Among his successful plays are; *Katariyun Gap* (The Head Is Lost), *Ardhi Rate Ahat* (Knock at Midnight), *Kaka Thaya Vanka* (Uncle Behaves Funny), *Behram ni Sasu* (Behram's Mother-in-law). Some of his English plays were also commercially very successful and include *Ah! Norman* (an adapted play). Another famous theatre personality of this theatre was **Nadira Babbar** whose group *Ekjute* (1981) came up with the production *Yahudi Ki Ladki* (The daughter of a Jew) which marked a revival in the Parsi theatre style.

Tamil Theatre

Madras (now Chennai) was another important regional centre where theatre flourished in the late 19th century along with centres such as Calcutta (Kolkata) and Bombay (Mumbai).While the traditional folk theatre had existed and flourished for centuries, the emergence of modern Tamil theatre took place only in the second half of the 19th century with the British influence of the Proscenium theatre. The initial years of Tamil theatre also witnessed the Parsi theatrical influence which were entertainment based, and which made tours in the larger towns of the region. Thus was born the modern Tamil theatre, which retained elements of its folk theatre in the form of the subjects of the play and the singing and dancing traditions, but also incorporated the stage structure and scenic arrangement of the western Proscenium with the entertainment driven grandness of the Parsi theatre.

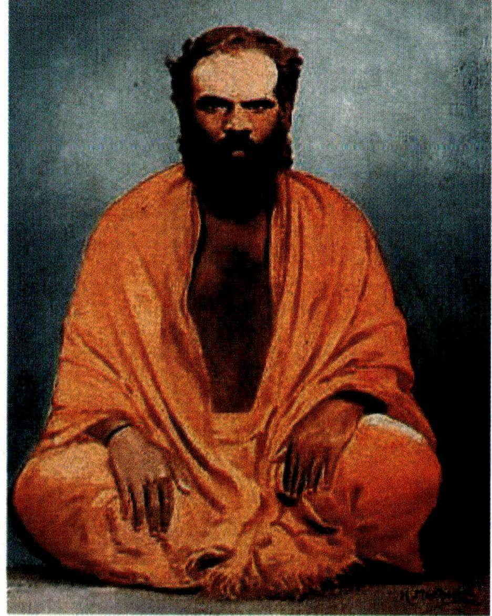

21.39: Sankardas Swamigal, the father of modern Tamil theatre, a picture from a journal in 1967 — Wikimedia Commons

Among the earliest of modern Tamil dramas is the work *Manonmaniyam* written in 1891 by **P Sundaram Pillai** (1855-1897). Around this time, many Tamil commercial companies emerged and flourished in the region. These were known for their song and dance extravaganza as well as for their grand settings. Among the earliest of the Tamil theatre companies were those of the **Iyer Brothers**, Ramudu Iyer and Kalyanarama Iyer in the late 19th century and another was the drama company of **Samy Naidu**. It was in these two companies that

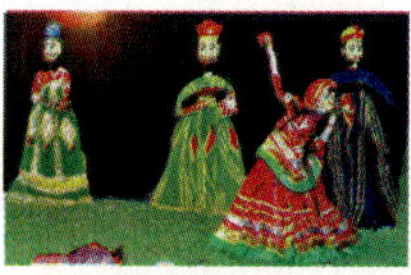

the initial years of **Sankardas Swamigal** (1867-1922) was spent, who is hailed as the father of modern Tamil theatre. Sankardas wrote the script of more than 50 plays. Later, his *Boys Company,* which trained young boys in *gurukula* system of theatre, emerged as the next generation of legends of the Tamil theatre. This included the likes of Nawab Rajamanickam, T.K. Shanmugam, M.R. Radha, K. Sarangapani and S.G. Kittappa.

P.V.S. Mudaliar (1873-1964, Padma Bhushan awardee) was another legend of Tamil theatre in the late 19th century and early 20th century. He is reputed to have written nearly hundred plays in his lifetime and formed the *Saguna Vilasa Sabha* (1891) which helped to revive the Tamil theatre.

T.S. Rajamanickam (1906-1974) colloquially called Nawab Rajamanickam, for his essaying the role of a *nawab* in the play *Bhakta Ramadas,* was another notable theatre personality of the 20th century. His theatrical journey began early at the age of 8 in the *Boys Company* of Sankardas. In 1933, he formed his own troupe *Devi Bala Vinoda Sangita Sabha*, which staged various plays like *Complete Ramayana, Yesunatar* (Lord Jesus), *Inbaskaran* (Ocean of Joy) and other mythological plays, which ran for hundreds of shows.

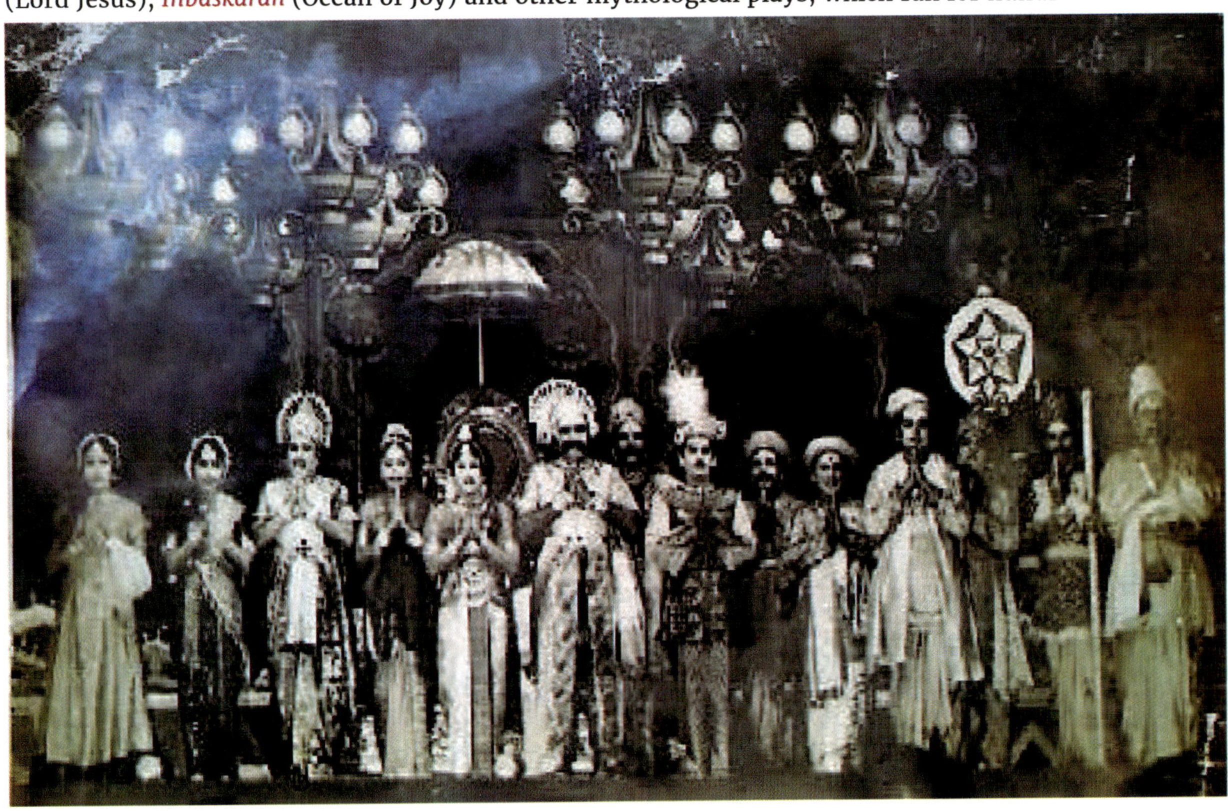

21.40: A scene from one of the performances of one of the dramas of TKS Brothers, a prominent Tamil theatre company of the 1930s-1940s — Wikimedia Commons

T.K. Shanmugam (1912-1973) another protégé of Sankardas, formed *TKS Brothers,* a very popular theatre which was known for the grand settings. In the late 1930s and 40s, *TKS Brothers* staged many social dramas which also espoused the emerging social causes and divergent views. Even in the post-independence period they staged several popular productions under the banner *T.K.S. Natak Sabha*.

In the post-independence period, *T.K.S. Natak Sabha* played a significant role in furthering the cause of Tamil theatre and nurturing in their early years, many eminent personalities of Tamil theatre and films. These include veterans like **N. S. Krishnan** (an eminent actor and comedian of Tamil theatre), **S.V. Sahasranamam** (Sangeet Natak Akademi awardee, theatre and film actor), **K. R. Ramasamy** (theatre and film actor), **S. V. Subbiah** (theatre and film actor), **A. P. Nagarajan** (theatre personality actor director and film producer), **S. S. Rajendran** (actor and director of theatre and films) and **M. S. Draupadi** (theatre and film actress) and **Kamalahasan** (Padma Bhushan awardee theatre and film actor).

S.D. Sundaram (1921-1979) was another stalwart of the Tamil theatre of this period who was a playwright, lyricist and dialogue writer who formed the *Sakthi Naadaga Sabha* (Sakthi Drama Society). The play *Kaviyin Kanavu* (Poet's Dream) which was in the nature of his dream/vision for an independent and better India, was so popular that it is said to have been staged nearly 1500 times.

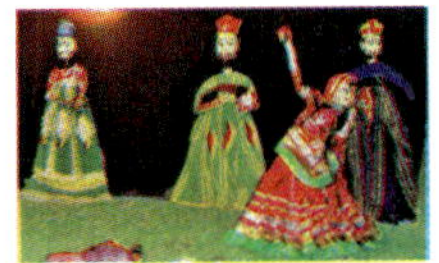

Another popular form of theatre in post-independence India was ***Sangita Natakam*** or the musical drama. Among the great exponents of this form of theatre was **S. G. Kittappa** (notable stage actor and singer), **K. B. Sundarambal** (a theatre and film actress singer, also referred as the queen of Indian stage) and **M. K. Thyagaraja Bhagavathar** (theatre and film actor, singer and producer, considered as among the most successful Tamil film actors). However, the drama company culture which was popular in the pre-independence phase, came to an end with the *National Theatre* of **R.S Manohar** being the last.

A theatrical movement which emerged in the 40s and continued post-independence was the *Sabha* culture, and this later filled the void of the drama companies to an extent. These were small theatrical groups with paid membership. They were largely a closed group which had a ready audience in the form of its members but were largely non-professional/amateur in nature. Over 100s of such groups had come up and were in a way unique to Tamil Nadu. The leftist theatre movement like IPTA could not become popular in Tamil Nadu as it witnessed the grassroot Dravidian movement, which also took the shape of a political theatre and saw some works such as that of Annadurai. In one of these works, *Sivaji Kanda Hindu Rajyam* Chinnaiah Pillai Ganesan played the lead, and later was played by **Sivaji Ganesan**, a veteran stage and film actor.

K. Balachander, **Cho Ramaswamy** and **Komal Swaminathan** were some eminent playwrights of the 60s and 70s. In the 80s and 90s and the later period, *Nija Nataka Iyakkam* (1978-Madurai) founded by **M. Ramaswamy**, the *Pariksha* theatre led by **Gnani Sankaran** and the group *Koothu-P-Pattarai* played an important role in Tamil theatre. Besides, a number of smaller groups and other playwrights and artistes have come up. The growth of *Doordarshan* (Government of India's autonomous television broadcast) in the 80s and early 90s, different cultural festivals, governmental and autonomous institutions have also helped in the growth of Tamil theatre.

Telugu Theatre

The Andhra Pradesh region has a long tradition of folk theatre, but like other regional theatre movements, the modern Telugu theatre too emerged in the late 19th century with the colonial influence. **Korada Ramachandra Sastry** (1815-1900) is believed to have composed the first original work of Telugu drama with his work *Manjarimadhukariamu* (1860). However, for lack of confirmatory evidence, some experts consider *Narakasura Vijaya Vyayogamu* (1871) by **Varanasi Dharmasuri** to be the first such original work.

In the subsequent decades, several works of translation from the Sanskrit classics and English followed. **Vavilala Vasudev Sastri** who translated works like *Caeser's Story* (*Sizaru Charitramu*-1875), is also said to have composed the first Telugu social drama *Nandaka Rajyamau* (*Nandaka's kingdom*) in 1880. However, these were plays written with the perspective of literary publication and were not staged. In 1880, the veteran social reformer **Kandukuri Veeresalingam** staged in the Proscenium theatre format *Vyavahara Dharama Bodhini*, written by him. This ushered the beginning of Telugu theatre.

Kanyasulkam (1891) written by **Gurajada Apparao** (1862-1915) was one of the early milestones of Telugu drama. The play which literally means the *bride price*, highlighted the derogatory social practice of marriage of young brides to elderly bridegrooms in the Telugu Brahmin community where the practice was prevalent at that time. Besides, it also highlighted the poor social condition of the widows. The play which was in the genre of a comedy, was acclaimed and staged several times over the years and Apparao wrote the second version of it in 1909.

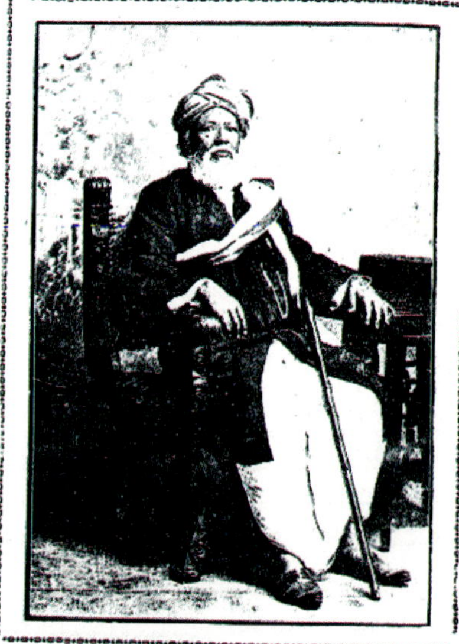

21.41: Vedam Venkataraya Sastry, a portrait from his drama *Bobbili Yudham* (1920s - 1930s) — Wikimedia Commons

Vedam Venkataraya Sastry (1853–1929) was another eminent playwright who composed original Telugu drama as well as translated Sanskrit drama in Telugu. Among his original works were *Prataparudriya natakam* (Prataparudra's Play-1897) in the genre of historical drama, and *Usha-natakam* (Usha's Play-1901). He also formed a drama group *Andhra Bhashabhimani Nataka Samajam* (1899).

In the late 19th and early 20th century, the twin poets **Divakarla Tirupati Sastry** (1872–1919) and **Chellapilla Venkata Sastry** (1870–1950), who are also considered as harbingers of modern Telugu poetry, played a significant role in dramatising several of the epics in Telugu in singable verses. They also composed several works of

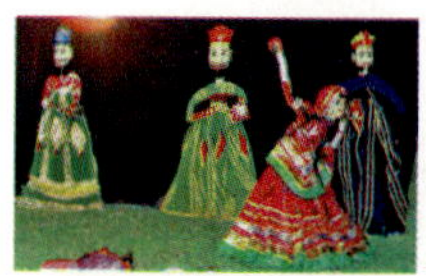

original Telugu drama. Referred together as **Tirupati Venkata Kavulu** (literal meaning, poets Tirupati & Venkata), they were the authors of several acclaimed plays such as *Pandavodyogavijayalu,* which remained popular with many drama clubs and theatres. Other notable works include *Panditarajamu*, *Gajanana Vijayamu*, *Prabhavatee-Pradyumnamu*, besides others. In the early 20th century, another eminent Telugu writer was **P. Lakshminarasimha Rao** (1865-1940), who was an essayist and a dramatist. He is often referred as the Telugu Shakespeare for his notable contribution as a playwright.

In the late 19th century, several **Telugu theatre groups** were also formed. In 1881, a drama troupe called *Dharwada Nataka Samajam* had toured northern coastal towns of Andhra Pradesh with a series of Hindi plays. These inspired the local community to form theatre groups called *nataka samaj*. The Parsi theatre groups which used to tour with their grandiose set up also influenced the culture of theatre in the region. In 1881, a Telugu theatre group, *Hindu Nataka Samajam* was founded. It staged nearly 30 plays in Guntur and adjoining areas. Another prominent theatre group was *National Theatrical Society* founded in 1885. Besides, some other troupes of this time included *Jagan Mitra Samajam* (1882) in Visakhapatnam. In the next couple of decades, several theatre groups were formed in different towns of Andhra Pradesh. However, the first commercial theatre was started in Rajahmundry in 1906.

In this period, the various theatre groups besides staging the prose-based plays (*gadya natakam*), also staged *sangeet natakam* or verse based plays, which were quite popular. The early 20th century was a golden period of Telugu theatre. Several *natak samajams* and commercial companies were formed and flourished. Some of the more prominent of them are; the *Surabhi Theatres*, the *Mylavaram Bala Bharathi Nataka Samajam* in Mylavaram (1913-1928), the *Seetharamanjaneya Nataka Samajam* in 1921 at Eluru, (known as *Mote Vari Company* after the founder) besides others.

Surabhi Theatre Group: An Enduring Theatrical Tradition

Among the various Telugu theatre groups of this period, the most illustrious is indeed the **Surabhi theatre group.** It was formed around the last decade of the 19th century by **Vanarasa Govind Rao**. Their family was then engaged in shadow puppetry (*Tholu Bommalata*) but took up theatre and formed a family group in the Surabhi village of Kadapa district. The first play performed by them was *Keechak Vadham,* which earlier used to be performed by them as a shadow puppetry. Later, other plays from epics and mythology were performed. A uniqueness of its performances was that female characters were played by the women, a practice still not in vogue in other theatres.

With the passing of years, different members of the family joined the theatre group and in the coming decades the family members also established their own theatre groups. The group has travelled to different places and performed in especially erected tents and later halls. The Surabhi theatre group has continued till date. Over the years, several generations of members have entered the stage with many being feted with awards (such as **R. Nageswara Rao** awarded Padma Shri in 2013). With nearly 125 years of theatrical experience, it is a witness to the history and grand tradition of Telugu theatres.

In the 20th century, T. Raghavacharya also known as **Bellary Raghava** (1880-1946) emerged as a preeminent playwright and actor of the Telugu theatre and later of Telugu cinema. Among his notable works were *Harishchandra*, *Padukapattabhishekamu*, *Savitri*, *Brihannala*, *Ramarajucharitra*, *Ramadasu*, *Tappevaridi*, *Saripadani sangatulu*, etc. He also founded the *Amateur Dramatic Association of Bangalore* (1909). His production of *Tappevaridi* (1930) in Madras received critical acclaim and heralded a new chapter of Telugu theatre.

21.42: Bellary Raghava, a pre-eminent playwright and actor of Telugu theatre and cinema — Courtesy, Department of Post

C. Pullayya (1898-1967) was another notable figure of Telugu theatre who later made several silent and talkie films. **Vemuri Gaggaya** (1895-1955) was a pioneer of Telugu theatre in this period. He was an eminent stage actor and founded *Mylavaram Bala Bharathi Nataka Samajam* in Krishna district in the early 20th century. Later, he joined Pullayya in films and acted in acclaimed movies such as *Sati Savitri* (1933) and *Sri Krishna Leelalu* (1935).

Among the **actors of Telugu theatre** of this phase the most notable was indeed **Kalyanam Raghuramaiah** (1901-1975, Padma Shri and Sangeet Natak Akademi awardee). Popularly known as Eelapata Raghuramaiah, he played the role of mythological figures such as Krishna, Dushyanta, Narada etc. for nearly 60 years. He is said to have given more than 20000 stage performances and is considered a thespian of Telugu

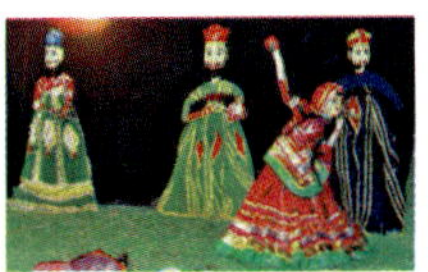

theatre and films. He was also an eminent stage singer who was called the nightingale of the stage by Rabindranath Tagore.

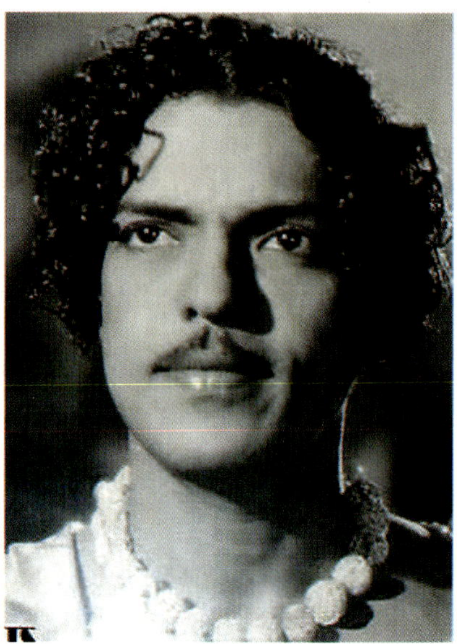

21.43: Kalyanam Raghuramaiah, a thespian of Telugu theatre and films — Wikimedia Commons

Sthanam Narasimha Rao (1902-71) was another prominent theatre and film actor who specialised in portraying the female characters. Said to have made more than 1500 stage appearances, Sthanam was remembered for his roles of Satyabhama in *Srikrishna Tulabharam* and as the character Madhuravani in Gurajada Appa Rao's drama *Kanyasulkam.* **V. Naggaya** (1904-1978, Padma Shri awardee) was a theatre and film actor, besides a director singer and a music composer. Though in later career he remained a part of the Telugu film world, he was also associated with *Ram Vilas Sabha*, a Telugu theatre association. In the genre of Telugu theatre and film actors, another significant name is that of **Banda Kanaklingeswara Rao** (1907-1968, Sangeet Natak Akademi awardee) who was also a member of Kendriya and Andhra Pradesh Sangeet Natak Akademi. He also broadcasted many plays through the All India Radio. **Peesapati Narasimha Murty** (1920-28 to 2007, Sangeet Natak Akademi awardee) was another eminent theatre and film actor of this period.

While the Telugu commercial theatre flourished in 20th century, with its extravagance and with the coming of the talkies, it could not sustain and gradually faded. At this stage, there was the birth of amateur theatre groups. With the wave of nationalism gripping the country in 30s and 40s, many plays with a nationalistic fervour were played by them. At this point, there was also the growth of realism in Telugu theatre. While issues pertaining to women had been showcased earlier also, social issues like, economic inequality, class conflict, exploitation of the labour-class etc., brought in realism as well as an element of activism in theatre.

In the **post-independence phase** of Telugu theatre, **Gollapudi Maruti Rao** is a name which stands out. A theatre and film actor, dramatist, screenwriter, playwright and litterateur, Rao is known for plays such as *Kallu* (1975-made into a film later), *Oka Chettu-Rende Puvvulu* (which was purchased by Ministry of Information and Broadcasting for popular exhibition), besides others. His *Vandemaataram,* was among the first in Telugu on the subject of the Sino-Indian war. He also wrote a volume of essays on Telugu theatre (prescribed as a text book by Andhra Pradesh government) and two research articles on Telugu play writing and amateur theatre. **Acharya Aatreya** (1921-1989) was a poet, playwright and screenwriter known for his works in Telugu theatre and cinema. **S. K. Misro** (born 1945-) is a veteran actor of Telugu theatre, television and films of this period.

Among the actors and theatre personalities of the new millennium is **Rathna Shekar Reddy**, a theatre and film actor, who is also the co-founder of *Samahaara,* a Hyderabad-based prominent theatre group. Like other regional theatres, Telugu theatre in the 21st century survives and has a following of its own, but its heydays as the predominant means of public entertainment a century ago, or as a mainstream public platform, is far behind.

Kannada Theatre

Although having a rich culture of folk theatre such as *Yakshagana*, modern theatre developed in the Karnataka region with the influence of the British rule and permeation of the Parsi and Marathi theatre in the Karnataka region, particularly in its larger towns. In the 2nd half of the 19th century, some theatre troupes also emerged in Karnataka such as the *Halsagi/Halasi Company* and others. However, these early theatres of the 19th century are often considered by the critics as semi-professional theatre. But in the early 1900s, the *Gubbi Company* theatre founded by **Gubbi Verana** brought professionalism in Kannada theatre. Inspired by the glamour of Parsi theatre, Gubbi Verana took theatre to a new scale, with plays drawn from the epics being staged with grand sets. He is also credited with being among the early theatre stalwarts to cast women in female roles.

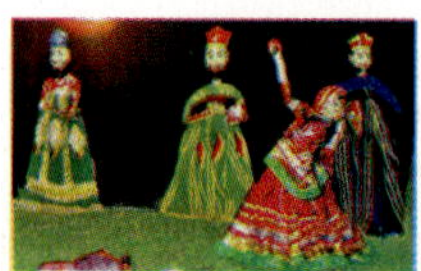

The periods of 1930s and later, were a stage of great literary growth in Kannada wherein eminent litterateurs such as Bendre, Kuvempu and others ushered *Navodaya* literary movement and modern literature in Karnataka. This period also brought evolution of the Kannada theatre and invoked the interest of youth, particularly in the urban areas. The period saw the emergence of **T.P. Kailasam** (1884-1946) considered among the great playwrights of modern Kannada theatre. Kailasm authored nearly 20 plays and steered away from the epic dramas while bringing realism in theatre. He was also known as *Prahasana Prapithamaha* (father of humour) for introducing wit and humour in his Kannada plays. With lesser number of characters, little requirement of sets, a mix of Kannada with English, laced with humour and depicting the modern life, his plays resonated with the youth and inspired the subsequent generations of playwrights.

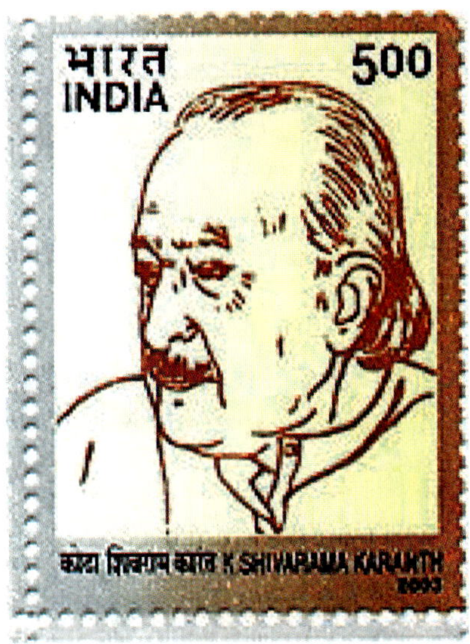

21.44: K. Shivarama Karanth, a commemorative stamp of 2003 — Courtesy, Department of Post

K. Shivarama Karanth (1902-1997 Padma Bhushan, Sangeet Natak Akademi Fellowship and Sahitya Akademi Fellowship awardee) was another eminent playwright of the 20th century. He wrote nearly 31 plays; besides he was also an author of several novels, and an environmentalist. **Sri Ranga** (1904-1988 Padma Bhushan, Sangeet Natak Akademi and Sahitya Akademi awardee) who wrote on Sanskrit drama, and **A.N. Krishna Rao**, were some other notable playwrights of this period.

In the **post-independence period** too, the Kannada theatre flourished. Several eminent playwrights, directors and theatre personalities have shaped the Kannada drama in this period. The most notable of these are B.V. Karanth, Palaya Lankesh, Chandrashekhara Kambara and Girish Karnad, M.S. Sathyu, besides others.

B.V. Karanth (1929-2002 Padma Shri Sangeet Natak Akademi awardee, winner of six National Film Awards) was an eminent playwright and director of plays and films. A graduate from the National School of Drama and later its director, Karanth directed more than 100 plays in Kannada and different languages. The theatre group *Benaka* (1974) launched by him staged several plays across Karnataka, besides directing several plays with children.

M.S. Sathyu (1930 born, Padma Shri, Sangeet Natak Akademi Fellowship awardee, winner of National Film Awards) is an eminent film director and a theatre designer as well as director. He has directed several critically acclaimed and successful plays like *Dara Shikoh*, *Bakri*, *Amrita*, *Kuri*, *Akhri Shama Mudra Rakshas*, besides others. He also represented in the World Theatre Olympics in 2018 (held in India) and is also a patron of the IPTA.

Girish Karnad (1938-2019; Padma Bhushan and Jnanpith awardee) is considered among the preeminent modern playwrights, besides being a notable theatre and film director as well as an actor. Amongst his earliest works is the play *Yayati* (1961) which draws a parallel between the lust of a king and the modern materialistic greed. His next work *Tughlaq* critiques the impractical idealism of the medieval emperor and also drawing modern parallels. The work was staged in the National School of Drama by Ebrahim Alkazi besides elsewhere, nationally and internationally. *Hayavandana* (1971), *Anjumallige* (Angulimal-1977) *Naga Mandala* (1988) were some amongst his other acclaimed plays.

Palaya Lankesh (1935-2000, Sahitya Akademi awardee) was a writer, playwright and filmmaker, who authored nearly 10 plays. Some of these such as *Nanna Thangigondu Gandu Kodi* (Need a Groom for my Sister-1963) focused on issues of women, while *Kranti Bantu, Karanti* (Here comes Revolution-1965) was centred on the themes of law and order and naxalism.

Like other regional theatres, Kannada theatre too witnessed a diminishing popularity in the 80s and 90s and beyond. Firstly, films proved to be a rival of theatre, and later the television and now the web-based series and films pose a stiff competition. However, acting and theatre continue to survive and feed the electronic and digital world.

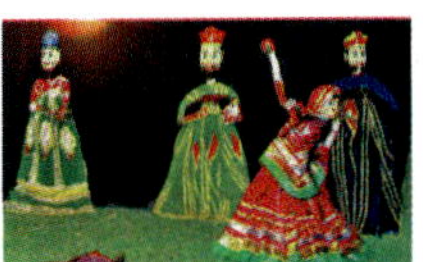

Malayalam Theatre

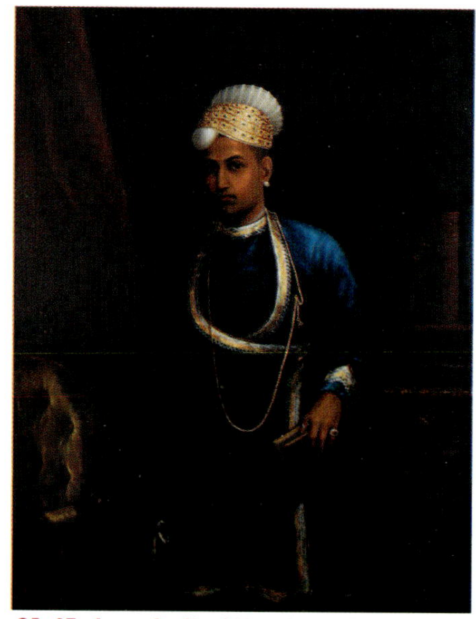

21.45: A portrait of Kerala Varma Valiya Koil Thampuran, the usherer of modern Malayalam drama; by eminent painter Raja Ravi Varma; location Changanassery Lakshmipuram Palace — Wikimedia Commons

Drama in Malayalam is a centuries old tradition, with performing folk arts such as Kathakali and Therukootu being popular in the masses. However, the advent of modern drama in Kerala can be said to have begun with the publication *Manipravala Shakunthalam*, a translation of Kalidasa's classic *Abhijnana Shakuntalam*. This work was composed by **Kerala Varma Valiya Koil Thampuran** in 1882. It also ushered a tradition of translation of other Sanskrit classics such as *Janaki Parinayam* (1889), *Malavikagnimitram* (1890), *Vikramorvasiyam*, *Uttararamacarita* (1892), *Svapnavasavadattam*. These and other translations were carried out by some of the eminent Malayalam litterateurs of that time such as **Kerala Varma Valiya Koil Thampuran, A. R. Raja Raja Varma, Attoor Krishna Pisharody and Vallathol Narayana Menon**. In the 19th century, Malayalam dramas also witnessed the influence of the western plays, and many of the English classics of Shakespeare and other works were translated in Malayalam. In 1884, influenced by western drama traditions, **C.V. Raman Pillai** composed a farce named *Chandramukhi Vilasam*. Subsequently, more such farces such as *Kuruppillakkalari, Doctarkku Kittiya Micham* were written by him.

Original works of Malayalam literature also started being composed in the late 19th century. The earliest of such works was composed by *Chandramukhi Vilasam* (1884) by **C.V. Raman Pillai.** *Kalyani Natakam* (1889) by **Kodungallur Kochunni Thampuran** was also among the early dramas of Malayalm. In the coming years, a number of original Malayalam works were written. *Lakshanaasangam* (1891), *Gangavatharanam* (1892), *Chandrika* (1892), and *Uma Vivaham* (1893) written by **Kunhikuttan Thampuran** were some other original works of this period. **Changanasseri Ravivarma** was another notable playwright, who wrote *Kavisabharanjanam* (1892), while *Bhagavad Doothu* (1892) was composed by **Naduvath Achan Namboothiri**. *Chakki Chankaram* (1893), by **Munshi Rama Kurup**, and *Dusparsha Natakam* by **Seevolli Narayanan**, were among other significant Malayalam works of drama of this period.

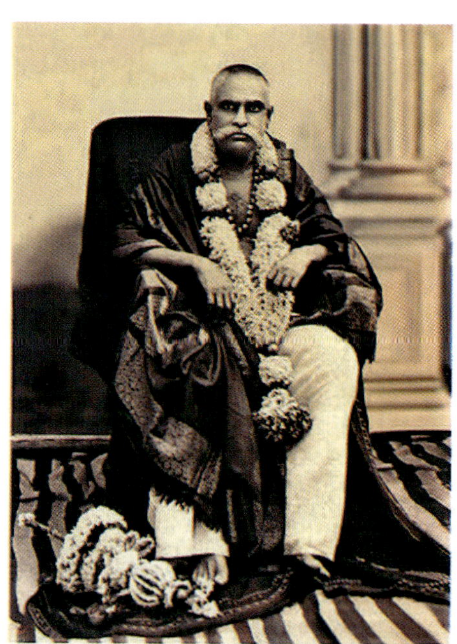

21.46: C.V. Raman Pillai, the composer of the first original Malayalam drama — Wikimedia Commons

The late 19th century Malayalam drama was influenced by the travelling Tamil drama troupes and the **influence of the Tamil musical dramas** could be seen on these early Malayalam works. In this genre of Malayalam drama, some prominent compositions were *Sangeeta Naishidham* by **T. C. Achutha Menon**, *Sadarama* by **K. C. Kesava Pillai,** and *Balagopalan* by **Kuttamath**. However, the Tamil musical dramas comprised long drawn-out songs, which offered little space to the prose and in a way restricted the drama and its creativity itself. This trend of imitating the Tamil musicals and producing low quality works was mocked by **Munshi Rama Kurup** in his play *Chakki Chankaram* (1893) and also by **Seevolli Narayanan Nampoothiri** in *Dusparsha Natakam* (1900). The Malayalam theatre soon overgrew this type of dramas, although an element of it did survive in some later theatrical productions.

Among the great Malayalam playwrights of the late 19th and early 20th century was **C.V. Raman Pillai** (1858-1922), an eminent novelist and playwright, who is often compared to Bankim Chandra Chatterjee (Bengali literature) and Hari Narayan Apte (Marathi literature). In a career spanning several decades, he wrote many novels and nearly 11 plays. Many of these were farces/satires and include acclaimed works such as, *Chandramukheevilasam* (1884), *Kurupillakalari* (1909), *Docṭarku Kiṭṭiya Micham* (1916) besides others. In the genre of farce and comedies which were popular at that time, some other playwrights who contributed were; **E. V. Krishna Pillai** (1894-1938) who wrote nearly 20 works of farce and comedy; **N. P. Chellappan**

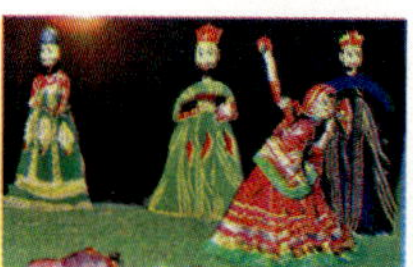

Nair (1903-1972), a playwright and short story writer who wrote more than 20 plays in the genre of social comedies and **T. N. Gopinathan Nair** (24 April 1918 – 24 May 1999), one of the most prolific Malayalam playwrights who wrote nearly 29 plays including several one act plays.

Among the other prominent playwrights of the **20th century** were, **K. Padmanabha** (1898–1976) who was known for dramas based on patriotism, sacrifice and justice, with the central characters displaying valour and heroism. **K. Kumara Pillai** (1900-1988) who was the younger brother of K. Padmanabha Pillai was another noteworthy author of this period, whose works include *Harishchandra*, *Mathruka Manushyan* besides others. **V.T. Bhattathiripad** (1908–1998) composed the acclaimed drama *Adukkalayilninnu Arangathekku* which brought out the plight of the Nambudiri community women and heralded a new genre of social plays. *Thotilla* written by **T. Sivasankara Pillai** (1912-1999; Padma Bhushan, Jnanpith and Sahitya Akademi Fellowship awardee), *Kootu Krishi* (co-operative farming -1950) by **E. Govindan Nair** (1906-1977; Sahitya Akademi awardee) and *Pradhanmantri* (Prime Minister-1940) by **P. Kesavadeva Pillai** (1904-1983, Sahitya Akademi Fellowship awardee) were some other plays in the category of social-political dramas.

Around the late 19th century, *Manomohanam*, the **first professional theatre company** was formed in southern Kerala, while in central Kerala, *Rasikaranjini Natana Sabha* was founded. Commercial theatres, many of which were based on *Sangeet Natak* also flourished. A major shift in the organisation of theatre in Kerala was observed in the 1930s and later in 40s. The progressive writer movement active in the other parts of the country was also prevalent in Kerala. The growth of nationalism had permeated in the Kerala theatre culture. With the advent of IPTA, theatre associated itself with the communist movement which was already strong in Kerala. Hence a leftist theatrical movement emerged in Kerala which was also associated with social theatre.

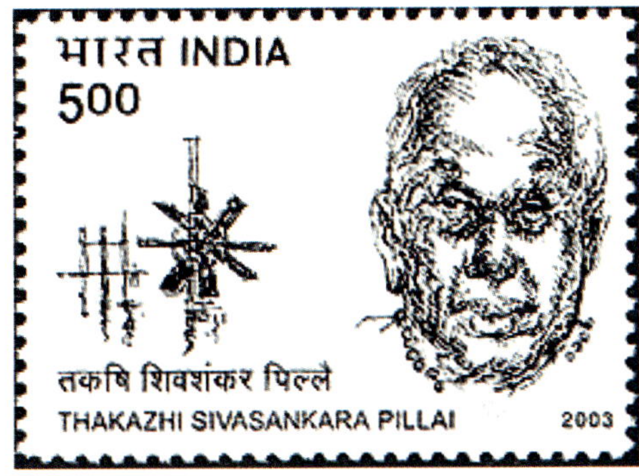

21.47: T Sivasankaran Pillai, a doyen of Malayalam literature; postage stamp issued in 2003 — Courtesy, Department of Post

In 1948, *Malabar Kala Samiti* was formed to promote amateur drama. This later grew into *Kendra Kala Samithi*. Some eminent playwrights were associated with this movement including **M. Govindan** (writer and cultural activist), **E. Govindan Nair** (poet and playwright), **V. T. Bhattathiripad** (dramatist and activist). Later, under the influence of the IPTA and growing leftist movement, the Kerala Progressive Writers group founded the **Kerala People's Art Club** with which many veteran writers and playwrights of the period were associated. This group had the most significant influence on theatre in Kerala. It staged its first play *Ente Makanaanu Sheri* (My Son is Right) in 1951. In 1952, its second production *Ningalenne Communistakki* (You Made Me a Communist), turned out to be a trailblazing play. It heralded a generation of people's theatre movement and street plays which were connected with the social issues and the leftist ideologies.

Among the other prominent theatre groups which came up in Kerala were, *Navasamskara Samithi* (Trivandrum; 1950) which aimed at bringing reforms in Malayalam theatre; *Kalavedi* (1956) with which many notable playwrights and theatre personalists of the time were associated; *Nataka Kalari*, another theatre group of this time helped in the growth of indigenous theatre. *Kalidasa Kalakendra* (1963), was formed as a professional theatre group. Besides, many other groups also came up in later years.

The **post-independence** period saw the emergence of playwrights such as **C.J. Thomas** (1918-1960) and **C. N. Sreekantan Nair** who infused modernity in Malayalam drama. The work of Thomas pioneered experimental theatre. His work *Avan Veendum Varunnu* (Behold! He Comes Again-1949), is often considered the first modern Malayalam play. Many of his plays criticised the religious ills. *Ishsvruksham,* (The Poisonous Tree) another of his popular plays, staged in 1958, even mobilised protests against the state government. Sreekantan Nair received acclaim for his Ramayana trilogy *Kanchana Sita*, *Saketham* and *Lankalakshmi.* He also launched in Kollam the *Nataka Kalari*, a forum for the promotion of theatre and was instrumental in introducing surrealism in theatre.

The Malayalam theatre also witnessed the emergence of **one act plays** and **radio plays**. The trend of these emerged in the 1940s, and remained popular in the post-independence period. While K. Ramakrishna Pillai and N. N. Pillai were the stalwarts of the one act plays, P. Bhaskaran, Sreekanatan Nair, R.S. Kurup, besides others, were known for the radio plays. This phase of experimentalism also witnessed the translation of Greek classical plays into Malayalam.

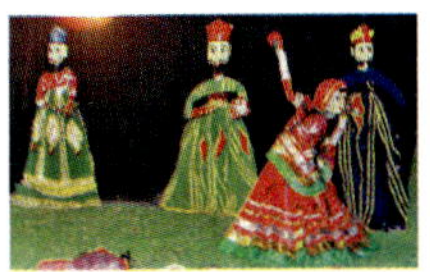

The post-independence Malayalam theatre, particularly from the late 1940s and later, witnessed a golden phase. While in the 50s, the political-social theatre spread due to the influence of IPTA and leftist ideology, in the 60s there was a growth of the indigenous theatre which was called *Thanathu Nataka Vedi.* This endeavoured to explore the cultural roots of the Malayalam theatre and to develop its folk forms. The 70s witnessed the growth of experimental theatre. Even in the later decades the academic experimentation in theatre has continued. However, in the 80s and 90s and beyond, the Malayalam theatre, like other regional theatres, has not sustained its growth. As an art form which feeds to the electronic and digital arts, sustenance of theatre itself becomes a necessity, but the popularity and access of films, television and other forms of electronic media also limits the growth of theatre.

Hindi Theatre

In its modern form, Hindi theatre had its inception in the 2nd half of the 19th century like other regional theatre movements. Popular in the North and Central India, besides in parts of Western India such as Rajasthan, the theatre movement was influenced by the centuries old folk traditions of Ramlila, Rasalila and Nautanki, besides the classical Sanskrit drama tradition. But it emerged in its modern avatar due to the singular efforts of **Bharatendu Harishchandra**, who is also reckoned as the father of modern Hindi literature. Bharatendu was a playwright; theatre-actor, stage manager and producer who single handedly heralded the movement of Hindi theatre in Kashi (Varanasi). He wrote as many as 18 plays and translated many of the Sanskrit classics, the influence of which is seen in his works. He was also influenced by the Bengal renaissance and the growth of nationalism in the country. Some of his acclaimed dramatic works include *Vaidika Himsa*, *Himsa Na Bhavati* (1873), *Satya Harishchandra* (1876), *Bharat Durdasha* (1875), *Nila Devi* (1881) and *Andher Nagari* (1881). In *Bharat Durdasha*, Bharatendu symbolically brings out the reason for the deplorable state of India, while highlighting British misrule and mutual discord as the primary factors for it. *Andher Nagari* (City of Darkness-1881) is a political satire, which succinctly highlights the perils of misgovernance and which is metaphorically alluding to the British misrule and exploitation. Bharatendu was also the director of the *Hindu Natak Samaj* which staged his plays in the city of Varanasi.

The period of 20th century saw the emergence of some prominent playwrights in the Hindi literature. These included eminent litterateurs like **Jaishankar Prasad** who authored several plays of historical genre such as *Skandagupta*, *Chandragupta, Dhruvaswamini* and *Ajatashatru*. **Maithili Sharan Gupt** wrote plays like *Tilottama* (1916), *Chandrahaas* (1921) and *Anagha* (1925). Among other notable playwrights of this period were, **Upendranath Ashq** (notable plays: *Jai Parajay*-1937, *Swarga Ki Jhalak*-1938, *Lakshmi ka Swagat*-1941-43, *Qaid*-1943), **Laxmi Narayan Misra** who was known for realism in plays such as *Sansyasi* (1931), *Rakshas Ka Mandir* (1931), *Mukti ka Rahasya* (1932), *Rajyoga* (1934); **Ramkumar Verma** who authored several successful one act plays, such as *Prithviraj ki Ankhen* (1936) and *Reshmi Tai* (1941), *Charumitra* (1941 or 1942), besides others. Critics often consider *Charumitra,* a historical one act play, to be a masterpiece.

Bhikhari Thakur and the Theatre of the Oppressed

In the early 19th century, drawing inspiration from the folk theatre traditions, **Bhikhari Thakur** (1887-1971; Padma Shri awardee) a poet, actor folk-singer and folk dancer, launched a Bhojpuri theatre troupe in North Bihar region. Thakur wrote more than a dozen plays, including monologues and musicals, and was christened as the Shakespeare of Bhojpuri (a dialect of Hindi in parts of Bihar and Uttar Pradesh). His theatre brought out the various social issues particularly those of women and caste and had a profound role in launching a folk-theatre based social activism, awareness and reforms. He himself belonged to a marginalised community and understood the plight of the so-called lower castes as well the rural women who lacked rights and social identity of their own. His famous play *Bidesiya* (1917), brought out the issues of poverty and migration and the consequent pain of a married women who waited for years for her husband to return home, only to find him to have remarried. *Gabar-ghichor* is often likened to the famous playwright Bertolt Brecht's play the *Caucasian Chalk Circle*. It is centred around the dispute before a village *panchayat* (village court) over the custody of a 15-year-old boy, being claimed by the mother, the women's husband who returns from migration after 15 years and the biological father of the boy with whom the women had illicit relationship.

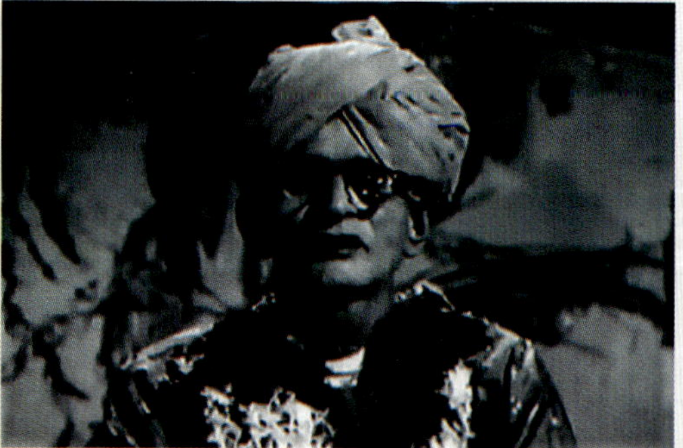

21.48: Bhikhari Thakur, a still from the 1963 movie *Bidesiya* in which he recites a few lines of his own poem — Wikimedia Commons

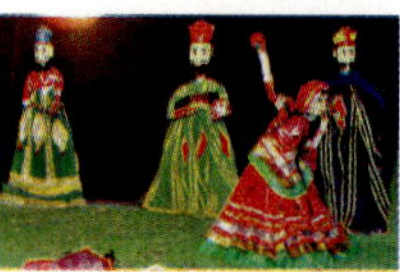

In a career spanning nearly five decades he wrote and staged several plays. These included, *Biraha Bahar* (his first play and a musical in *Biraha* singing tradition), *Beti Bechawa* (highlights the issue of marriage of young girls to older men by their fathers for money) *Bidhwa Bilap* (depicts the plight of a widow), *Bhai Birodh*, *Kaljug Prem* etc. The play *Beti Bechawa* is said to have so deeply touched and inspired many a people that during its performances they avowed never to commit this atrocity.

His travelling troupe staged his plays in different parts of Bihar, Uttar Pradesh, West Bengal Odisha and even in Assam. Bhikhari Thakur also ushered the *Naach* style (also referred as Bidesiya style) of theatre which entailed male actors impersonating as female characters. Based on his famous play *Bidesiya,* a Bhojpuri movie *Bidesiya* was also made in 1963. Bhikhari Thakur remains as one of the greats of regional and folk theatre in modern times.

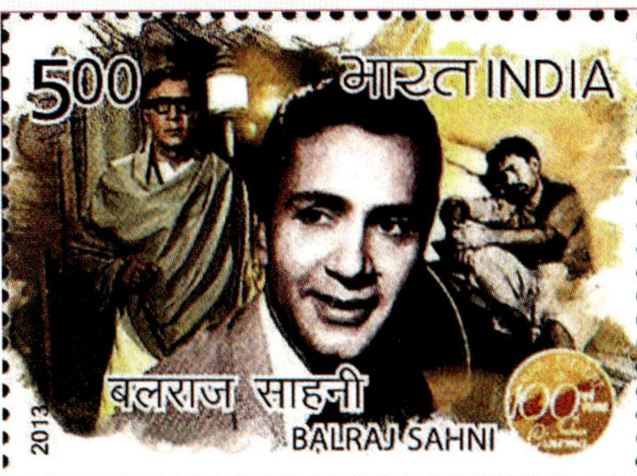

21.49: Balraj Sahni, a stage and film actor of eminence, a commemorative stamp of 2013 — Courtesy, Department of post

In the early 20th century, despite the composition of some acclaimed plays by very eminent playwrights, the mainstream Hindi theatre per-se did not enjoy substantial popularity in public. Later, with the dawn of the era of talkies and Hindi cinema, the patrons of Hindi theatre further dwindled. But with the emergence of the **IPTA** movement in the 1940s, Hindi theatre received a shot in the arm. In this period, there rose a whole new generations of theatre personalities and playwrights amidst the growing theatre movements elsewhere in the country. This included the stalwarts like **Balraj Sahni** (playwright stage and film actor; 1913-1973; Padma Shri awardee), **Durga Khote** (stage and film actor; 1905-1991; Padma Shri & Dada Saheb Phalke awardee), **Zohra Sehgal** (stage and film actor, 1912-2014; Padma Vibhushan & Sangeet Natak fellowship awardee), **Uzra Butt** (stage actor, 1917-2010), **Dina Pathak** (stage and film actor; 1922-2002), and **Prithviraj Kapoor** (stage and film actor, theatre personality and film producer; Padma Bhushan & Dada Saheb Phalke awardee). The latter also ran successfully for many years, Prithvi Ttheatre, a travelling theatre troupe.

Prithvi Theatres: A Journey of Several Decades

Started by Prithviraj Kapoor in 1944-45, Prithvi theatre was a travelling theatre troupe which toured different parts of the country. In its 16 years of existence, it staged more than 2600 performances and in every of which Prithviraj Kapoor performed. The theatre was instrumental in invoking a feeling of nationalism in the youth and even encouraging them to participate in the freedom struggle and the Quit India movement. One of the most successful plays of this theatre was *Pathan*, a story of friendship between a Muslim and a Hindu. The play which was first staged in 1947 is said to have had nearly 600 performances in Bombay (Mumbai).

Despite the successful run of this theatre, its audience gradually waned and drifted to the increasingly rising popular Bollywood movies. The diminishing revenue, the costs and logistics of a large travelling theatre troupe, eventually forced Prithvi Theatres to shut it down as did other such travelling theatre troupes. However, in 1978, Shashi Kapoor (son of Prithviraj Kapoor) merged another existing theatre (the **Shakespeare Theatre group**) and formed **Prithvi Theatre** in Bombay (in memory of Prithviraj Kapoor). Thus, this theatre evolved from a travelling troupe moving around the country to a theatre of reckoning located in the present-day Mumbai. With more than 500 performances every year, the show in this theatre goes on.

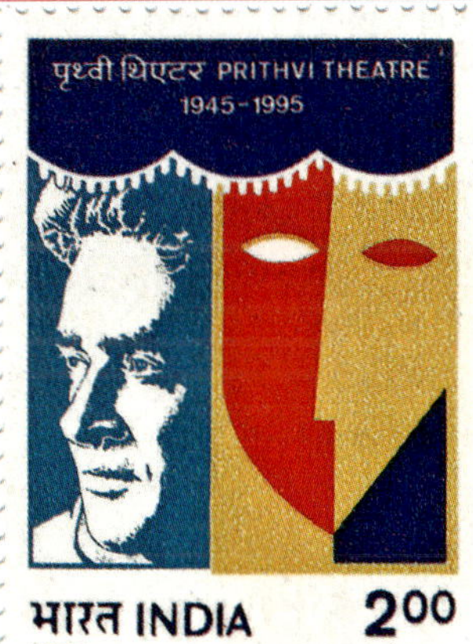

21.50: Image of Prithviraj Kapoor and emblem of Prithvi Theatre on a commemorative stamp on 50 years of the theatre in 1995 — Courtesy, Department of Post

POST INDEPENDENCE PLAYWRIGHTS

In the **post-independence** India, Hindi theatre and the theatre movement in general, received a fillip with the formation of the **Sangeet Natak Academy** (1952) by the Government of India, which also served as the national academy for music and dance. Later, with the formation of the **National School of Drama** (NSD) in 1959 (which had *Bharatiya Natya Sangh* as its precursor), Hindi theatre moved to a higher trajectory. The inceptive stages of the School saw it being led by eminent theatre personalities such as **Ebrahim Alkaji** (1962-1977, Padma Vibhushan and Sangeet Natak Akademi Fellowship awardee), **B.V. Karanth** (1977-1982; Padma Shri and Sangeet Natak Akademi awardee) amidst others. Ibrahim Alkazi was himself was an outstanding drama teacher and theatre director who was known for his disciplinarian

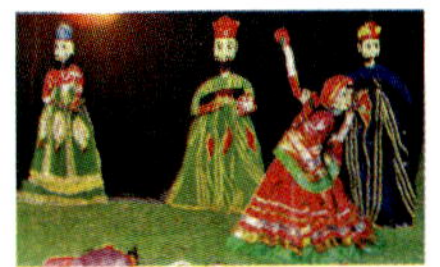

approach to learning of the creative art and helped stage more than 50 plays in his life time. Some of these included the best known and critically acclaimed plays of modern Hindi theatre including, *Asadh Ka Ek Din* by Mohan Rakesh, *Andha Yug* by Dharmaveer Bharti and *Tughlaq* by Girish Karnad. The years of Ebrahim Alkazi at NSD shaped the Indian theatre movement and helped the Proscenium as well as the traditional open air format theatre flourish.

National School of Drama: A Monumental Institution of Indian Theatre

The National School of Drama (NSD) has emerged over the years as the preeminent institution of Indian theatre. Formed in 1959, it started as one of the constituent units under the *Sangeeet Natak Akademi*. At this stage, the *Asian Theatre Institute* which had been formed by *Bharatiya Natya Sangh* with the assistance of UNESCO was merged with NSD. Thus, it had its inception and evolution in the initial years as an institution functioning within the domain of the Government of India. But later in 1975 it was granted a status of autonomous organisation within the Ministry of Culture. Thereafter, it also moved to a new location in Bhawalpur house (also known as Mandi house) in Central Delhi where it is currently located.

A national centre of pedagogical training in dramaturgy, including acting, direction and other stage crafts, the school has a well-defined curriculum with a comprehensive syllabus incorporating all aspects of theatre, in a three-year training programme. Theory is merged with practice, where plays are produced by students and staged before public. The School has also two performance wings. The first is a **Repertory Company of NSD** formed in 1964. This is a professional theatre group which as well carries experimental theatrical productions. It has staged hundreds of productions in Delhi as well as different parts of the country, besides international staging of its productions. Its second wing, the **Theatre in Education** (formed in 1989) is an important theatre resource centre of the country which also incorporates actor-teacher groups engaged with children and conducting curriculum-based workshops, plays and theatre education in schools.

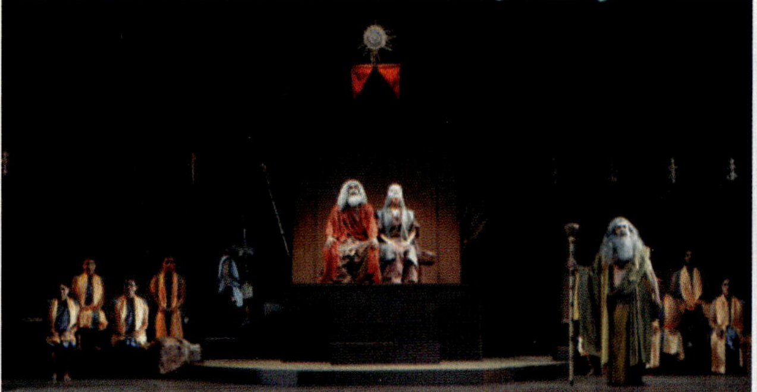

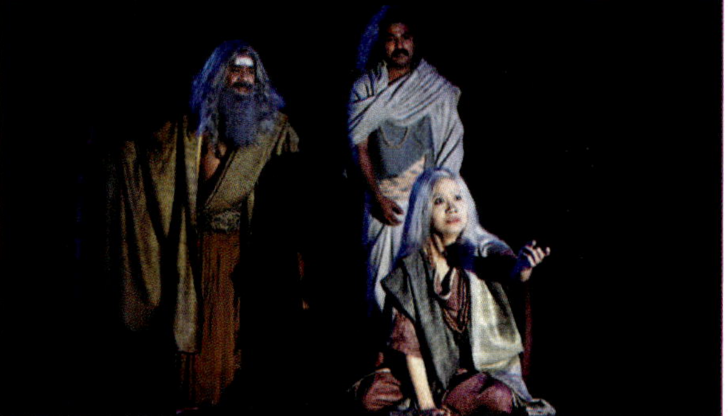

21.51 & 21.52: Performance of *Andha Yug* at National School of Drama — Courtesy, National School of Drama

Over the years, besides staging innumerable memorable productions, NSD has also engendered several generations of who's who of the theatre world and film acting community. Out of the several veterans graduating from the institutes who have enriched the world of art, some of the eminent NSD graduates are highlighted here.

B.V. Karanth (graduated -1962; Padma Shri awardee): A playwright film director, pioneer of parallel cinema, director of NSD, Kannada theatre personality and Kannada film director.

Om Shivpuri (graduated 1963): An eminent theatre and character film actor who was also among the first NSD Repertory Company actors, and later also its first chief.

Sai Paranjpye (graduated 1963; Padma Bhushan awardee): A film director and screen writer of several award-winning movies, besides playwright and director of many plays.

Nadira Zaheer Babbar (graduated 1971; Sangeet Natak Akademi awardee): Theatre and film actress specially known for founding Mumbai based theatre group *Ekjute* in 1981.

Om Puri (graduated 1973; Padma Shri, officer of the Order of the British Empire awardee): A veteran film actor of Hindi, regional and international films with two National Film Awards.

Naseeruddin Shah (graduated 1973, Padma Bhushan awardee): An eminent stage and film actor of international repute, prominent in parallel cinema movement and winner of three National Film awards.

Rohini Hattangadi (graduated 1974): A notable film actress known for her character roles and acting in Hindi, several regional cinemas and international projects like Gandhi for which she won BAFTA award.

Pankaj Kapoor (graduated 1976): A versatile, stage, film and television actor who is also a story, screen writer and a director, a winner of three National Film Awards.

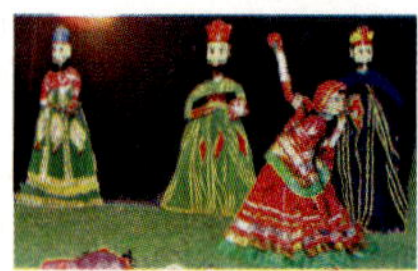

Anupam Kher (graduated 1978 Padma Bhushan awardee): A film actor director and producer, who has given stellar performances in many character roles in national and some international movies, has won two National Film awards.

Some other notable graduates who earned critical acclaim in the theatre and film world are, **Raj Babbar** (graduated 1975), **Virendra Razdan** (graduated 1977), **Raghubir Yadav** (graduated 1977), **Satish Kaushik** (graduated 1978), **Alok Nath** (graduated 1980), **Neena Gupta** (graduated 1980), **Ratna Pathak** (graduated 1981), **Deepa Sahi** (graduated 1981), **Mita Vashisht** (graduated 1987), **Ashish Vidyarthi** (graduated 1990), **Ashutosh Rana** (graduated 1994).

THEATRE GROUPS IN POST-INDEPENDENCE PERIOD

The post-independence period witnessed the emergence of several theatre groups in different parts of the country. While some have been instituted by the central and state governments, many were the endeavours of individuals or a motely group of people. But these have made a mark of their own in regional as well as national theatre and contributed to the legacy of modern Drama. Besides the IPTA theatre movement and the National School of Drama, which have had an enduring impact on the modern theatre, some of the other prominent theatre groups and their founders are highlighted here.

Sombhu Mitra and Bohurupee Theatre

An eminent stage and film actor, playwright and director, Shambhu Mitra (1915-1997; Padma Bhushan, Sahitya Akademi Fellowship and Ramon Magsaysay awardee) was associated with the IPTA movement from its very inception. He had co-directed *Nabanna* along with Bijon Bhattacharya which spearheaded the IPTA movement. He founded the *Bohurupee* Theatre Group in 1948 which staged several of Tagore's plays such as *Raktakarabi*, *Bisarjan* etc., besides other plays of prominent playwrights. Films like *Dharti Ke Lal* and several others were also directed by him. *Bohurupee* theatre played an important role in Bengali theatre in the late 40s and 50s.

Habib Tanveer and Naya Theatre

A popular Urdu and Hindi playwright, theatre actor and director Habib Tanveer (1923-2009; Padma Bhushan, Sangeet Natak Akademi Fellowship awardee) was associated with the *Progressive Writers* movement as well as with IPTA. Hailed as among the pioneering actor-managers of Indian theatre, Tanveer successfully produced several acclaimed plays such as *Charandas Chor* (1975), *Gaon ka Naam Sasural Mor naam Damad*, *Kamdeo ka Apna Basant, Ritu ka Sapna,* which are considered to be modern classics. Besides, he wrote the famous play *Agra Bazar* (1954). He founded the *Naya Theatre* group in 1959 in Bhopal. Here he worked with the tribals for years, exploring their folk traditions in drama and music and creating an indigenous performance *Nach,* which was akin to a new theatrical language, where a chorus provided a commentary through song. His new theatre techniques took drama to the very folk roots and were marked with simplicity and yet elegance, and with powerful communication.

Safdar Hashmi and Jan Natya Manch

A fire brand theatre activist, who took street theatre to the masses, Safdar Hashmi (1954-1989) was one of the modern pioneers of people's theatre, who transformed it as a medium to fight for civil liberties. He founded the theatre group *Jan Natya Manch* (People's Theatre Front; JANAM, for short) in 1973. This theatre developed in a way from his experiences out of IPTA, of which he was member. The theatre group is reputed to have given nearly 4000 performances of 24 street plays. Some of these include; *Gao Se Sahar Tak* (on challenges and distress of small farmers), *Hatyare aur Apharan Bhaichare Ka*, *Teen Crore* (on unemployment), *Aurat* (on crime and violence against women), *DTC Ki Dhandhli* (on inflation), *Kursi, Kursi Kursi* (on the accusation of rigging of elections in early 70s).The street play, *Machine,* was performed in a trade union meeting in 1978 purportedly before a 2, 00,000 strong gathering of workers. In 1989, Safdar Hashmi was killed while performing a street play *Halla Bol* which espoused the rights of trade union workers. SAHMAT (Safdar Hashmi Memorial Trust) continues to organise street theatre as a means of taking up civil and socio-political issues besides organising other cultural and literary activities.

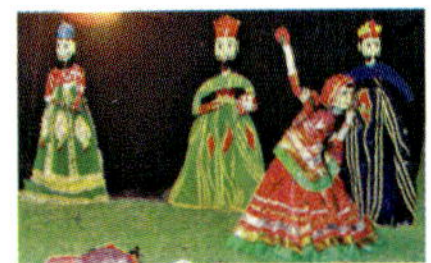

Other Theatre Groups

Little Theatre Group, founded 1949 in Kolkata by Utpal Dutt was an active group of the 50s and 60s. It enacted plays with leftist ideology such as *Kallol* (1965), *Manusher Adhikar*, *Louha Manob* (1964), *Tiner Toloar* and *Maha-Bidroha,* besides English plays of Shakespeare and Brecht.

Shri Ram Centre of Performing Arts (New Delhi), which was established under the aegis of Indian National Theatre Trust in 1958 runs a certified two-year acting course, besides staging a number of plays of eminent playwrights under the SRCPA repertory company (established 1980). It continues to flourish as a centre of various theatrical activities including theatre festivals, workshops, puppet shows besides commercial shows.

Nandikar Theatre group founded in 1960 is among the oldest of the prominent theatre groups which continues to remain active. The group was associated with many theatre personalities and film and theatre actors in 60s and 70s including, Asit Bandyopadhyay, Ajitesh Banerjee, Asit Banerjee, Ajay Ganguly Satyen Mitra and Satyajit Ray who designed the group logo. Over the last six decades the group has staged several acclaimed plays nationally as well as internationally.

Shatabdi theatre group which was established in 1967 in Kolkata by eminent playwright and film personality **Badal Sirkar**. It performed critically acclaimed plays like *Ebong Indrajit*, *Basi Khabar*, and *Saari Raat* etc. and helped to take the drama out of proscenium theatre to public arena.

The Madras Theatre group is among the oldest of the active theatre groups which stages the English plays. In the last five to six decades, it has staged more than 240 productions. Eminent actors and theatres personalities have been associated with it including included Thambi Kadambavanam, Ammu Mathew, Girish Karnad and others.

Akshara Theatre was founded in 1972 by **Gopal Sharman**, a playwright and a poet, along with his actress wife **Jalabala Vaidya**. The much-acclaimed work of Gopal Sharman, *Ramayana* in English has been staged over 2000 times. It is unique as it is a one-woman modern presentation of the classic, which is performed by Jalabala Vaidya and has been staged even on Broadway. Besides, the theatre group has also staged several other socio-political dramas, many of which are written by Gopal Sharman.

Kohinoor Theatre group of Assam, founded in 1976 by **Ratan Lahkar**, is unique as it is a mobile theatre group. It performs plays which are based on Indian and Assamese culture besides those of Shakespeare and others.

Rangamandala Repertory company at **Bharat Bhavan**, Bhopal, which since 1980s, has staged more than 1000 shows of over 50 plays, many of which are in Chattisgarhi, Bundeli and Malavi dialects of Hindi and thus integrating theatre with local cultural roots.

Lokadharmi Naadakaveedu is a theatre group based in Kochi established in 1991 by Chandradasan, a famous actor, Director and writer from Kerala. It continues to flourish since then, staging plays at state and national level.

Koothu-P-Pattarai is a prominent Chennai based theatre group which is active for more than three decades. Besides staging public performances, the group is also engaged in conduct of workshops and training. A unique aspect of this theatre is incorporation of elements of folk theatre, dances, choreography and bringing improvisation using elements of mime and martial arts, thus developing an alternate theatre movement.

The Pierrot's Troupe founded in 1989 in Delhi by **M. Salim Alam** has staged in the last three decades over 2000 performances touring across India as well as many international performances. The plays in Hindi, Urdu and English have received critical acclaim as well as good popular reception.

Ansh, founded in Mumbai in 1993 by **Makarand Deshpande** and **Kay Kay Menon** (theatre personalities, film and theatre actors) is known to produce original and thought provoking plays.

Post-independence Evolution of Hindi Theatre

In the post-independence period, Hindi theatre has flourished in various regional centres which include Delhi, Bhopal and Indore in Madhya Pradesh, Patna in Bihar, Kanpur and Lucknow in Uttar Pradesh, Mumbai and Pune in Maharashtra, besides in other states. The state cultural centres and

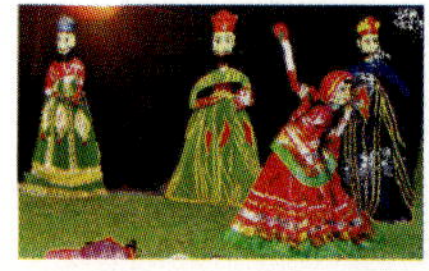

academies for art in Jaipur, Shimla, Lucknow, Bhopal and Chandigarh have also helped in the growth of theatre in these regions. Besides, non-state theatre groups founded and run by some eminent theatre personalities have also helped Hindi theatre to evolve. Besides the National School of Drama, the prominent theatre groups in Delhi include, *Shri Ram Kala Kendra*, *Three Arts Club* (founded 1943), *Yatrik* Theatre group (founded 1964) *Theatre Action group* (1973) founded by **Barry John**, *Dishantar* founded by **Om Shivpuri**, and *Asmita* Theatre group founded by **Arvind Gaur**. At Bhopal the leading groups were *Bharat Bhavan Rangamandal repertory* and *Prayog* Theatre Group of Prof Satish Mehta. *Kala Sangam* group led by Satish Anand at Patna, *Anamika* and later *Padtaik* theatre groups in Kolkata led by Shayamanada Jalan, *Rang Karmee* founded by Usha Ganguly in Kolkata, *Swantantra Theatre* of Abhijeet Choudhary in Pune and and *Sehar* of Mritunjay Prabhakar in Patna and Delhi are some other noteworthy groups.

New forms of theatre, besides proscenium and street theatre have also come up which also tend to connect to the folk roots and experiment with newer forms of theatrical expression. While Hindi theatre came into its own in the 60s and 70s in the different regional centres, in the 80s and 90s with the onslaught of movies, and later with the popularity of television, its mainstream appeal dwindled. At times, Hindi theatre came to be perceived as a preparatory ground for film and television artists and a career therein. However, Hindi theatre continues to grow in the new millennium with private theatre groups, along with governmental and autonomous institutions like the National School of Drama.

Ancient Sanskrit Classical Plays and Playwrights

The tradition of drama in Indian literature and culture is a very ancient one where the rules and structure besides the elements of theatre are all encapsulated in a treatise in Natyashastra. The ancient age, and in particular the Classical age (the period of 4th to 8th century CE), witnessed the composition of many great works of Sanskrit drama, or classics, as they are referred to. These works set the standard for the drama, besides being an inspiration to several centuries of playwrights. Even in the modern period when Proscenium theatre became the mainstay of the theatre movement, the old classics did not lose their appeal. Rather, they have been translated in different languages by modern playwrights, re-interpreted and even staged several times over the last one and a half centuries. To say that these classics continue to inspire and influence modern theatre would be no exaggeration at all. Here are recounted some of the ancient classics and their playwrights.

Asvaghosha (80 CE to 150 CE) is considered one of the earliest of Sanskrit dramatists. Although better known for his work *Buddhacharita* (an epic poem on Lord Buddha) he also composed ***Sariputra-Prakarana*** in nine acts. However, the said treatise has only been available in fragments.

Bhasa (2nd century BCE to 2nd century CE) is credited with having written 13 plays. These were lost for centuries and only discovered in 1913 by T. Ganapati Sastri as a part of repertoire of plays being used in *Koodiyattam* performances. Prior to it, Bhasa was known from the references in the works of Kalidasa (5th century CE) who in his work *Malavikagnimitram* refers to Bhasa as a celebrated dramatist and so does **Rajashekhara,** the famous poet of 9th century CE. The best known of the compositions of Bhasha is ***Swapna-Vasavadatta*** (the dream of *Vasavadatta*), a romantic drama of Vatsa king *Udayana* and *Vasavadatta,* the daughter of the ruler of Avanti. His other plays include *Pratijnayaugandharayana, Pancharatra, Charudatta, Dootaghatotkacha, Avimaraka, Balacharita, Madhyamavyayoga, Karnabhara Urubhanga, Abhisheka* and *Pratimanataka.*

Sudraka (2nd century BCE to 5th century CE): a great dramatist of the classical age composed the famous play ***Mricchakatika*** (The Little Clay Cart). It's a story of *Charudatta,* an impoverished Brahmin who falls in love with a courtesan *Vasantasena* who is being pursued by somebody else. The play explores various emotions of love, humour, villainy, deceit, and intrigue. *Vinavasavadatta* and *Padmaprabhritaka* (a *bhana* -short one-act monologue) were the other compositions of Sudraka.

Kalidasa (4th -5th century CE) was one of the most famous playwrights and litterateurs whose works ***Abhijnana-Shakuntalam, Malvikagnimitram***, and ***Vikramorvasiyam*** are considered to be masterpieces and the best examples of Sanskrit plays. His *Meghdutam* (poem), *Raghuvamsa* (epic poem), and *Kumarasambhava* (epic poem) are some of his other exemplary works. While *Malavikagnimitram* is the story of King *Agnimitra's* love with exiled servant *Malavika*, *Vikramorvasiyam* is another love story of mortal king *Pururva* with celestial nymph *Urvashi*. *Abhijnana-Shakuntalam* is

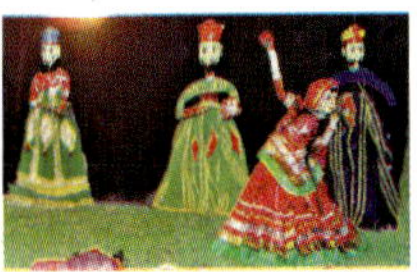

a story of King *Dushyanta's* marriage to *Shakuntala*, daughter of a sage, their separation, and later the king forgetting about her and how he eventually recalls her and accepts her as his wife. It is a work which has been translated into many languages, including English, and staged repeatedly over the decades.

Bhavabhuti (8th century CE) composed *Mahavira-charita* (early life of Rama) and *Uttar-Ramacharita* (later life of Rama). Another of his famous plays is *Malati-Madhava* (based on the romance of *Malati* and *Madhava).*

Vishakhadatta (4th century CE to 8th century CE) was a famous poet and playwright who composed the acclaimed plays *Mudrarakshasa* (which is about ascent of Chandragupta Maurya) and *Devi Chandraguptam,* (the story of defeat of King Ramagupta by a Saka king and its avenging by Chandragupta II).

Harshavardhana (590 to 647 CE) the great Indian emperor, is also credited with having written the plays *Ratnavali* (about beautiful princess Ratnavali), the Buddhist drama *Nagananda* (a story about the self-sacrifice of Vidyadhara King Jimutavahana to save the *Nagas*) and *Priyadarsika*.

Rajashekhara (9th to 10th century) was an eminent poet and playwright who was also a court poet of Gurjara Pratiharas. He wrote the famous play *Karpuramanjari.*

Important Awards for Indian Theatre

Sangeet Natak Akademi Puraskar : This award is conferred by the Sangeet Natak Akademi of India for significant contribution in the fields of **music, dance, theatre and other traditional arts and puppetry**. It is the highest award given to practising artists in these fields of art, and comprises a citation, a brass plaque, and a cash award. The award has been given since 1952 for various crafts associated with theatre, viz. acting, direction, play writing, etc. The award for acting is conferred for different regional theatres, viz. Assamese, Bengali, Hindi, etc.

Kalidas Samman : This award is instituted and given by the Madhya Pradesh Government (since 1980). It is conferred for contribution in the fields of **classical dance, classical music, theatre, and plastic arts**.

Nandi Awards : This award given by the government of Andhra Pradesh for excellence in the field of Telugu cinema, Telugu theatre and Telugu television.

Kalaimamani Awards are given by government of Tamil Nadu for excellence in the fields of literature, music and theatre.

Besides the above, some other awards instituted by private organisations and foundations have also come in prominence, including the **Mahindra Excellence in Theatre Awards** (META) which considers theatre entries from different languages and awards, the best productions and theatre practitioners.

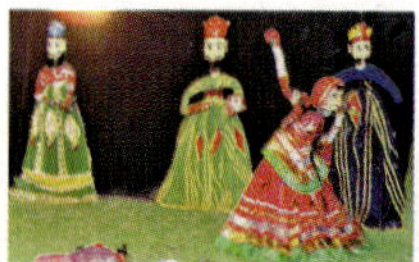

Indian Cinema

> *Cinema's characteristic forte is its ability to capture and communicate the intimacies of human mind.*
>
> — Satyajit Ray

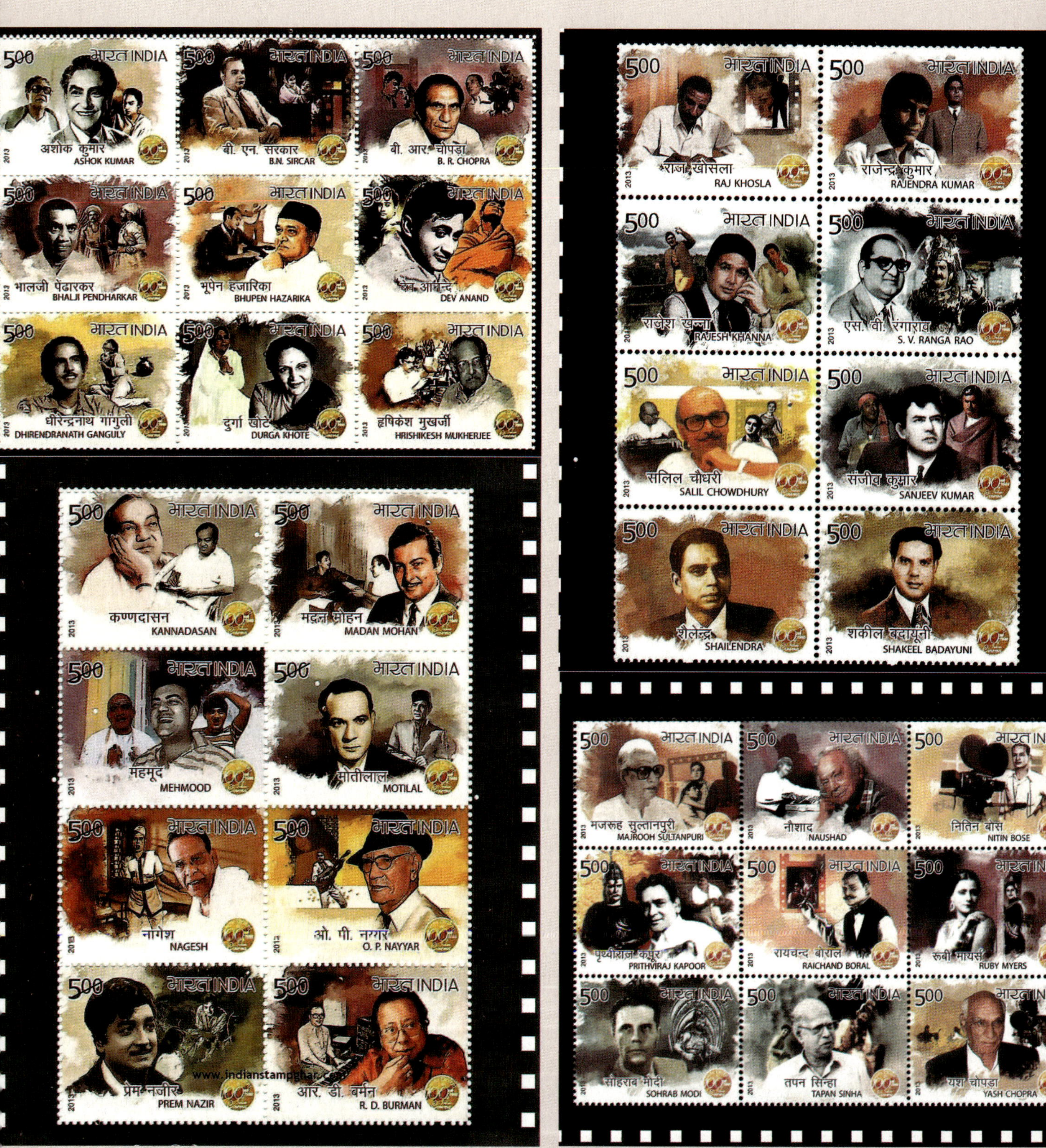

22.1: Stamp Sheets released on the occasion of hundred years of Indian cinema in 2013, depicting the icons who left a deep impression in this multidisciplinary domain; images — Courtesy, Department of Post

INDIAN CINEMA : A MEDIUM OF CULTURAL AND ARTISTIC EXPRESSION

The history of world cinema is nearly 125 years old and that of Indian cinema marginally less. Despite the relative recent evolution of cinema, today, it is one of the most popular and profound social mediums of artistic expression. As an art it shares many skills and attributes essential to theatre, viz. acting, direction, script writing, etc., and therefore, in a way, theatre was a precursor to cinema. But over a period of time, it has emerged as a distinct art form, substantially overtaking theatre in popularity, reach and versatility of artistic expression.

In a century and a decade of its existence, Indian cinema has emerged as the largest film industry of the world (in terms of the sheer volume of movies produced) with over 2886 feature films (in 2021-22) produced in different languages. It generated revenues of nearly Rs. 15,000 crore (approximately $2 billion) in 2022 (as per the CII report of 2022). While the Mumbai-based Hindi film industry, (colloquially referred to as Bollywood) is the biggest in terms of the number of movies produced, many regional film industries, such as Tamil, Malayalam, Kannada and Telugu (referred to as the South Indian Film Industry), Bengali, Marathi and Bhojpuri are also large and quite popular. In the 2020s, the South Indian film industry has come up in a big way both in terms of the volume of production, film revenue, as well as the quality of the movies. With this, the Indian movie industry has truly become a multilingual one.

Indian cinema emerged as a mass media in the early part of the 20th century. In the initial decades of the 20th century, it occupied a similar social space as theatre, whereby it served as a means of entertainment for the masses and a tool for social communication. Over a period of time, owing to its versatility of pictographic depiction, ability to capture diverse subjects, depth of social and geographical reach, and a comparative lower entertainment cost to the masses, it gained in popularity tremendously. It also made a significant impact not only as a popular means of entertainment, but even as a platform for spreading awareness on a host of social issues. In the tumultuous years of the pre-independence and in the struggles of the post-independence years, Indian cinema provided succour to a distressed country. In its myriad tales, our masses have been transported, albeit temporarily, to fairylands and realms of idyllic existence. The glitz and glamour of a few hours of the silver screen has alleviated the anguish and harshness of their daily lives and imparted a moment of exhilaration in an otherwise mundane existence. Over the years, cinema has emerged as the most popular as well as the most dominant form of entertainment, eroding the social space of the folk theatre and modern theatre as well. As a means of mass-communication too, it has brought to the fore numerous issues ranging from social evils, plight of women, challenges of rural life and other diverse national issues. In modern times, as challenges keep changing, so did the themes of modern cinema. Modern cinema continues to experiment and is endeavouring to keep abreast of the times.

As Indian cinema has grown from strength to strength, it has also contributed richly to the socio-economic and cultural landscape of the country. As an economic sector, it has contributed significantly and generated employment opportunities in thousands, in different crafts and trades and earned valuable foreign exchange as well. As a medium of expression, cinema has mirrored the occurrences in the society. At times, what is depicted there is reinforced in the society as well. The very nature of movies have been the reflection of the changing socio-economic demography. Fashion, as a trend, has borrowed widely from the film world and vice-versa. Over the years, Indian films have also got intertwined with art forms like music, singing, dancing, acting, script writing and composition of lyrics, cinematography and other art forms. Many of these trades have evolved through the platform of the movies, and thus the latter has become an **important medium for cultural and artistic expression.**

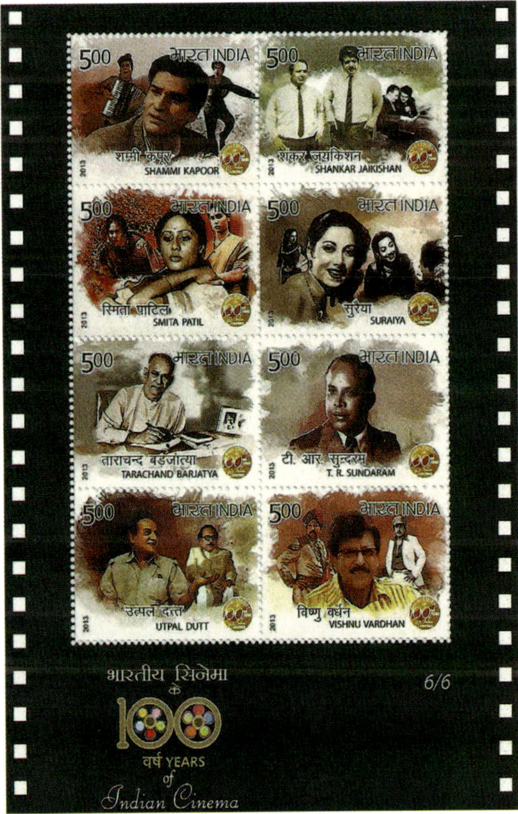

22.2: A stamp sheet released in 2013 on the occasion of 100 years of Indian cinema — Courtesy, Department of Post

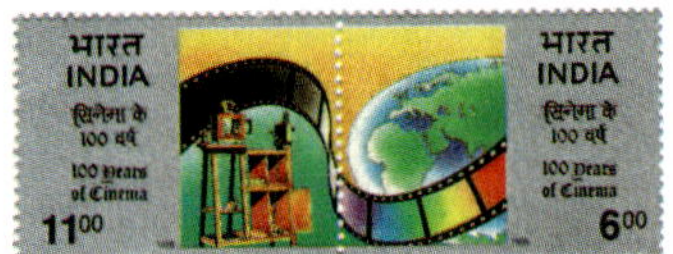

As an industry, its reach has been wide, covering large parts of South and South East Asia, Russia, China, North America, parts of Europe and Africa, besides other parts of the world where the Indian diaspora is in sizeable numbers. In many of these countries, Indian films are the primary means to offer a glimpse of Indian culture and ethos, and have thus become its unofficial ambassadors. In these far-flung countries, the local population has often witnessed Indianness from the prism of Indian cinema and thus to those unacquainted with Indian culture, India and its culture tend to become what the movies portray.

HISTORY OF INDIAN CINEMA

The First Exhibition

The world witnessed the first public screening of cinema on 28th December, 1895, in Paris. Ten short films made by **Lumiere Brothers** (the inventors of the cinematograph) was witnessed by an amazed humanity. The first exhibition of a motion picture in India took place the very next year on the 7th of July 1896, at Watson Hotel in Bombay (now Mumbai). On this day, the commercial screening of six short films, for the ticket price of rupee one, was done by the Lumiere Brothers. These short films included; *Entry of Cinematographe*, *The Sea Bath*, *Arrival of a Train*, *A Demolition*, *Ladies and Soldiers on Wheels* and *Leaving the Factory*. Subsequently, in 1899, **Harishchandra Sakharam Bhatwadekar**, who was one of the witnesses to the 'Lumiere brothers' show, made different short films on various day-to-day activities. The first of these was *The Wrestlers*, which was shot during a wrestling match in Bombay (now Mumbai). Thus began the dawn of the age of movies in India.

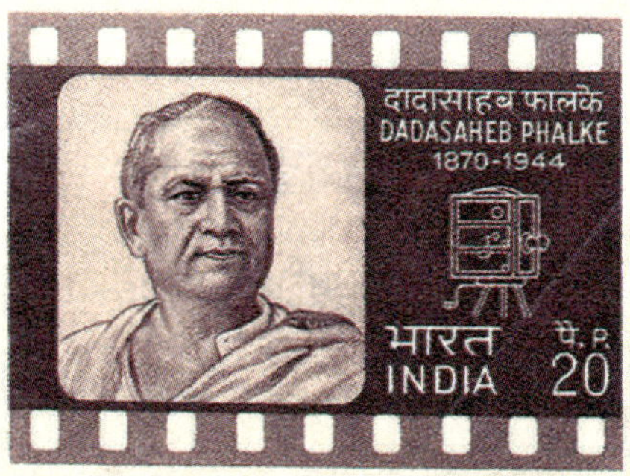

22.3: Dadasaheb Phalke, considered as the father of Indian cinema; a 1971 stamp of India — Courtesy, Department of Post

The Era of Silent Films

Within a couple of decades of the first screening, India witnessed the arrival of the era of full-length silent films. In 1912, **R.G. Torney** and **N.G. Chitre** made the first silent feature film *Shree Pundalik*. However, this was a recording of a play, *Shree Pundalik*, and also, it was a not a complete Indian effort. Accordingly, the Government of India as well as film scholars do not consider it as the first Indian silent film. The eminent filmmaker **Dadasaheb Phalke** produced *Raja Harishchandra* in 1913, the first Indian feature film of the silent era. Interestingly, the female roles in this film were played by male actors, as no women were available at that time to play the female roles. Some of the other early films of Dadasaheb Phalke were *Mohini-Bhasmasur* (1913), *Satyavan Savitri* (1914) and *Lanka Dahan* (1917). The last was a commercial success and perhaps the first box office hit of those days.

In 1918, two film companies were formed, the *Kohinoor Film Company* and *Hindustan Film Company*, the latter by Dadasaheb Phalke. In 1919, *Madan Theatre Limited* (a company) was formed by **Jamshedji Framji Madan** which owned a set of theatres and also oversaw the production and distribution of the movies of the chain. By the 1920s, film making was firmly being established as a commercial

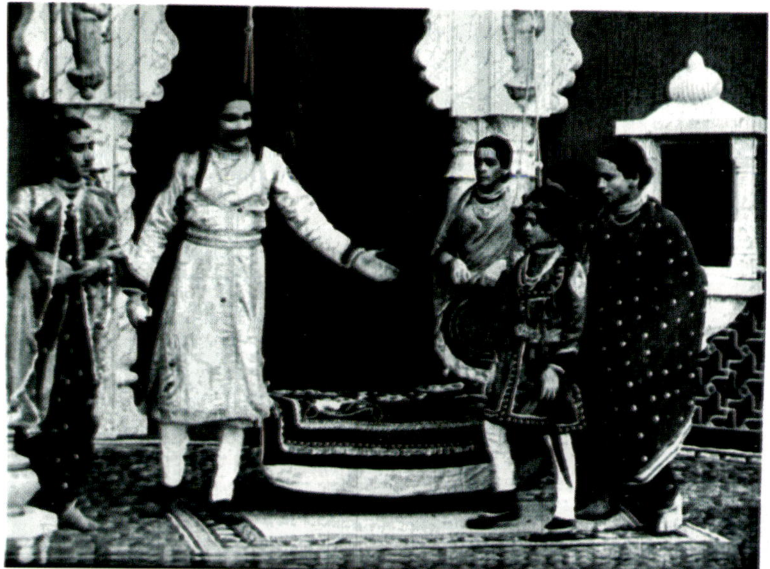

22.4: A scene from the movie *Raja Harishchandra* (1913), the first Indian feature film of the silent era — Courtesy, NFDC-National Film Archives of India, (Pune)

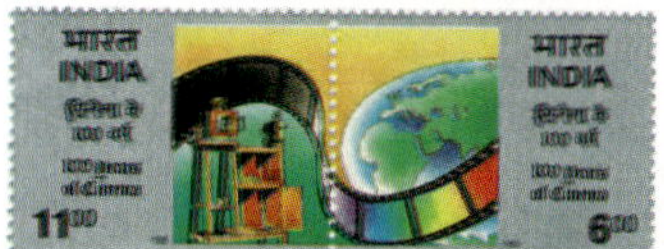

venture, and by early 1930s more than 200 films were being produced every year. Some of the other noteworthy films of the silent era were *Keechaka Vadham* (1917-1918) by **R. Nataraja Mudaliar**, *Nala Damayanti* (1921), *Noor Jehan* (1923) by **Madan;** *Maya Bazaar* (1923) by **Baburao Painter**, *Anarkali* (1928) by **Ardeshir Irani** and *Gopal Krishna* (1929) by **V.Shantaram**.

By the early 30s the era of silent movies had reached a crescendo. With only three movies in 1911 (the first year of silent movies), it reached 200 movies in just a couple of decades by 1931. But this year also marked the beginning of the end of the silent era as the first talkie was also made in the year 1931. By 1934, the production of silent movies declined to just seven, also making it the very last year of the silent movies.

22.5: Ardeshir Irani on the sets of *Alam Ara*, the first talkie — Wikimedia Commons

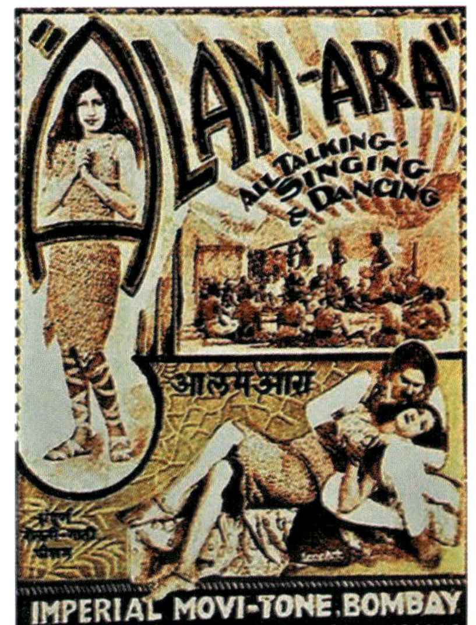

22.6: The publicity poster of the first talkie *Alam Ara*. No film or gramophone record of it survives now except for the publicity material — Wikimedia Commons

The First Talkie Film

Alam Ara (literal meaning: *The Jewel of the World*) was the first Indian talkie film. It was directed and produced by **Ardeshir Irani** and was released on 14th March, 1931. The film was a major breakthrough for the upcoming industry as it ushered a new generation of talkie films. Produced in Hindustani language (mix of Hindi and Urdu), it was a movie in the genre of a fantasy. As a film, it was a commercial success as well as appreciated for its songs and its overall production. *Kalidas* (1931) was the first talkie film of South India. It was released around seven months after *Alam Ara*. The film was produced in Tamil-Telugu languages (substantially in Tamil and partly in Telugu) and was directed by **H.M. Reddy** and produced by Ardeshir-Irani. The two films are indeed landmark productions of the Indian film industry. By the time of India's independence, the Indian film industry was fully entrenched in the production of diverse movies. 280 movies in 15 different languages were produced, which included 183 in Hindi, 33 in Bengali, 29 in Tamil, six in Telugu, besides others.

PRE-INDEPENDENCE CINEMA

Acclaimed Films and Eminent Filmmakers

Although movie making was in nascent stages during this period, yet it saw the emergence of many eminent filmmakers and productions. *Amar Jyoti* by **V. Shantaram** was the first Indian film to be screened at the Venice Film Festival (1936). *Sant Tukaram* in Marathi (1936) directed by **Vishnu Govind Damale** was also screened at the Venice Film Festival (in 1937) and was even adjudged one among the best three films. **Himanshu Rai** (1892-1940) was one of the pioneers of Indian cinema; he was a successful producer, writer and actor known for works such as *Achhut Kanya* (1936). **V. Shantaram** (1901-1990, recipient of Padma Vibhushan and Dadasaheb Phalke Award) directed many acclaimed movies of this period. These include movies such as *Duniya Na Mane* (1937), *Manoos* (1939), and *Dr. Kotnis Ki Amar Kahani* (1946). These movies were also acclaimed for the various social issues they brought to the fore.

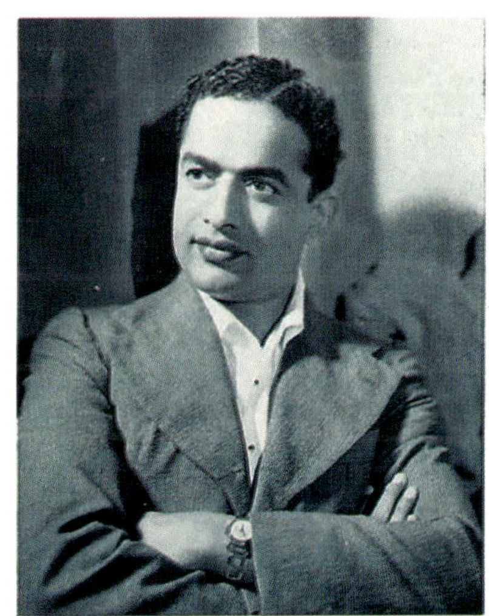

22.7: V. Shantaram; eminent actor, film director and a partner in the Prabhat Film Company — Wikimedia Commons

Sohrab Modi (1897-1984, recipient of the Dadasaheb Phalke Award) was another highly distinguished actor, director and producer. Some of his noteworthy films of the pre-independence period include *Khoon*

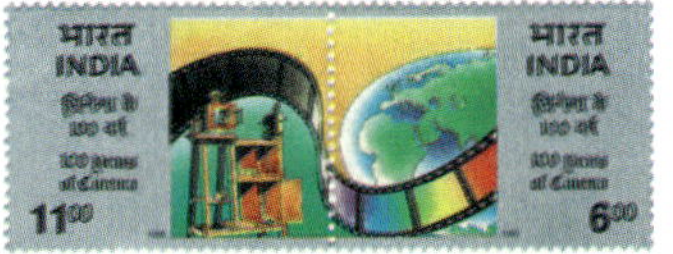

Ka Khoon (1935), *Jailor* (1938), *Taj Mahal* (1941), *Sikander* (1941) and *Prithvi Vallabh* (1943), besides others. **P.C. Barua** (1903-1951) was another eminent filmmaker, who made many successful movies in different languages. Some of his noteworthy films include; *Devdas* in Bengali (1935), *Devdas* in Hindi (1936), *Maya* (1936), *Mukti* (1937), *Devdas* in Assamese (1937), *Jawab* (1942), *and Pehchan* (1946). Some of the other filmmakers of great repute and their movies in this period include; **Mehboob Khan** (1907-1964; *Aurat* and *Ek Hi Raasta* and others); **Baburao Painter** (1890-1954, *Sairandhari* in 1920, *Surekha Haran* in 1921, *Sati-Padmini* in 1924), **Dwarka Das Sampat** (1884-1958), who established Kohinoor Film Company and made films such as *Vikram Urvashi* in 1920, *Bhakta Vidur* in 1921, *Kulin Kanta* in 1925, and **Bimal Roy** (1909-1966) who made films such as *Udayer Pathey* in 1944 and *Anjangarh* in 1948.

The Genre of Movies

The films in the early phase of the silent era were often based on **religious** and **mythological characters** or **devotional themes**. These included movies such as *Raja Harischandra* (1913), *Mohini Bhasmasur* (1913), *Lanka Dahan* (1917), *Nala Damayanti, Sri Krishna Janam* (1918), *Keechaka Vadham* in Tamil (1918), *Kaliya Mardan* (1919), *Buddha Dev* (1923), *Bhakta Prahalad* (Malayalam) *Sant Tukaram* etc. Some movies were also based on **historical characters**, such as *Kalidas, Sati-Padmini, Noor Jahan, Anarkali,* etc.. These early movies were essentially in the nature of cinematic retelling of stories of the epics and the Puranas, or those whose characters were drawn from the pages of history. The trend was quite similar to the early regional theatre movement of the second half of the 19th century, wherein the playwrights took inspiration from mythology, history and old Sanskrit classics.

However, the movies of the late 1920s, 1930s and 1940s diversified substantially, subject-wise. They dwelled on a variety of **social issues;** besides many were of the genre of **popular entertainment**. Some of the movies brought out women related issues and included some acclaimed works such as *Achhut Kanya, Manoos* and *Duniya Na Mane*. *Achhut Kanya* (literal meaning: untouchable woman) was a Hindi movie of 1936 and had a cast of acclaimed actors like Ashok Kumar and Devika Rani. It dealt with the subject of a *dalit* women and her position in the then society. For the period of 1930s, it was truly a reformist movie with a message. *Manoos* (1939), by V. Shantaram, was also a reformist social drama. It boldly depicted a touchy issue of the time; the status of prostitutes, the love of a policeman for such a woman, and his effort to reform her. *Joymoti* in Assamese (1935) was another woman-oriented movie with a female protagonist.

Some movies also broached also on the subject of **nationalism** and **India's freedom struggle**, but were banned by the British government. *Bhakt Vidur* (1921), *Wrath* (1930) and *Raithu Bidda* (1938-Telugu) were some such productions. *Raithu Bidda*, in particular, was a movie which spoke about the evils of the zamindari system and displayed peasants uprising against the zamindars. The song in the movie *Kismet* (1942), *door hato ae duniya walon Hindustan Hamara haye* (*O' people of this world, get away*, *Hindustan is ours*) became a song of inspiration and protest during the Quit India movement. With the birth of the Indian People's Theatre Association (IPTA), the Bengal famine, and plays such as *Nabanna* (1944) gaining substantial traction with the masses, came a genre of movies like *Dharti Ke Lal* (*Children of the Earth* in 1946). Produced by **Khwaja Ahmad Abbas** and directed by him and **Bijon Bhattacharya**, the film received critical acclaim for its bold and realistic portrayal of the disastrous Bengal famine (1943). It also depicted the sweeping socio-political changes taking place in the period of World War-II. *Neecha Nagar* (1946) directed by **Chetan Anand** (an Indian adaptation of Maxim Gorky's *Lower Depths*) starkly portrayed the gulf between the lives of the rich and poor and won the **Palme d'Or** at **Cannes film festival** (1946). Thus, the genre of **social realism** which had already swept Indian literature and embraced the modern theatre also, permeated in the Indian movies. This was a precursor to what was to emerge later as a 'parallel cinema'.

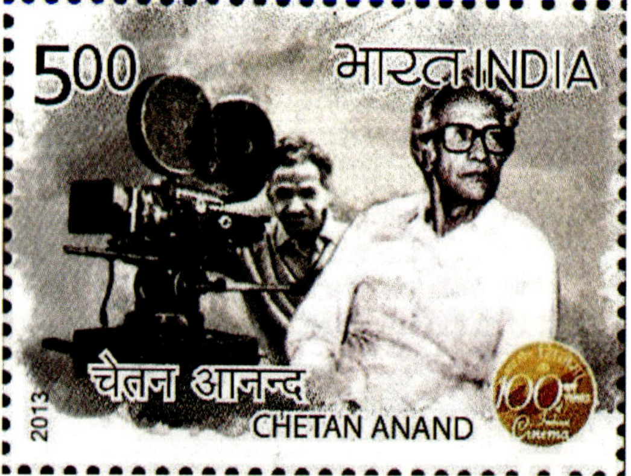

22.8: Chetan Anand, the director of *Neecha Nagar*, an iconic movie of the 1940s; stamp image — Courtesy, Department of Post

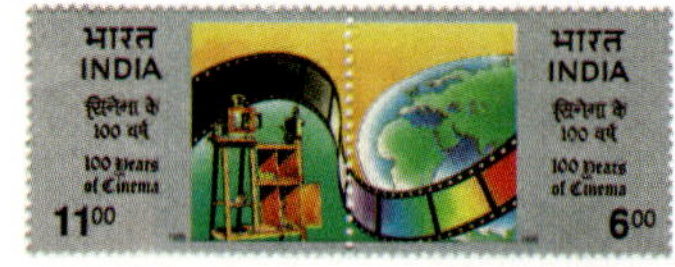

Movies of the **entertainment genre** were also quite popular in this period. *Shirin Farhad*, produced as early as 1931, was structured like an opera with nearly 42 song sequences. *Inder Sabha*, produced in 1932, had a whopping 69 songs (and as per some accounts 71 songs), the most in any film ever. The movie which was based on the 1853 play *Inder Sabha* (an Urdu play of Agha Hasan Amanat), was an out and out entertainer and ushered the culture of songs as a means of popular entertainment in Indian movies. Social dramas were also quite popular in this period. Among the various movies of the entertainment genre, a special mention must be made of the productions by **Wadia & Wadia,** such as *Hunterwali, Toofan Mail, Punjab Mail, Flying Rani,* etc. which were centred around a female protagonist. These were quite popular and commercial hits of the period. These films featured the Australian-Indian actress **Mary Evans** (1908-1996), nicknamed '**Fearless Nadia**' who acquired cult popularity as an actress and stunt woman and emerged as one of the earliest female leads in the Indian film industry.

The Film Production Companies

The film production companies played a crucial role in entrenching the popularity of movies in the pre-independence period. While in post-Independent India, movies were often known by the actors therein, it was the production houses which were more associated with the identity of the films. Some of the important production houses of this phase were **Bombay Talkies**, **Prabhat Films**, **New Theatres** and **Filmistan. A.V.M.** (**A.V. Meiyappan**) **Film Company** and **Gemini Pictures** were some important production houses of South India. Bombay emerged as the most important centre of production, while Pune also enjoyed some popularity as a production centre, particularly in the pre-independence period.

Black and White *vs* Colour Movies

Although the talkies era began in the early 30s, the movies in India were produced largely in white and black, unlike some parts of world where in the decades of the 20s and early 30s, colour films were gaining in popularity. The first Indian colour film is said to be *Sairandhri* (1933) directed by V. Shantaram and produced by the Prabhat Film Company. The colour films were processed and produced in Germany. However, the genre did not catch up in India till the 1950s, and in the pre-independence phase, movies remained in black and white.

Actors and Actresses

Among the very first of actors of Indian cinema were **Dattatraya Dabke** and **Anna Salunke** who acted in *Raja Harischandra* (1911). Dabke played the male lead in the movie and went on to play the role of the leading character in some more movies. Salunke, who had played the female lead in *Raja Harischandra,* continued to be cast in female roles in other movies of Dadasaheb Phalke. In *Lanka Dahan,* he even played both the roles of Rama and Sita, thus essaying the **first ever double role in Indian cinema.**

Some of the most prominent male actors of the era of talkies were:

Sohrab Modi (1897–1984) a veteran actor, director and filmmaker, who acted in movies such as *Khoon Ka Khoon* (1935) and *Sikander* (1941) and others.

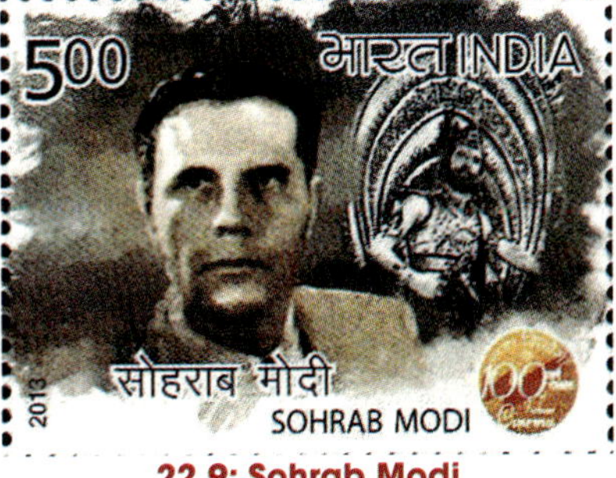

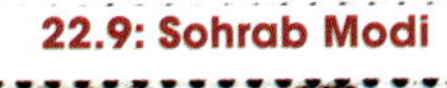
22.9: Sohrab Modi

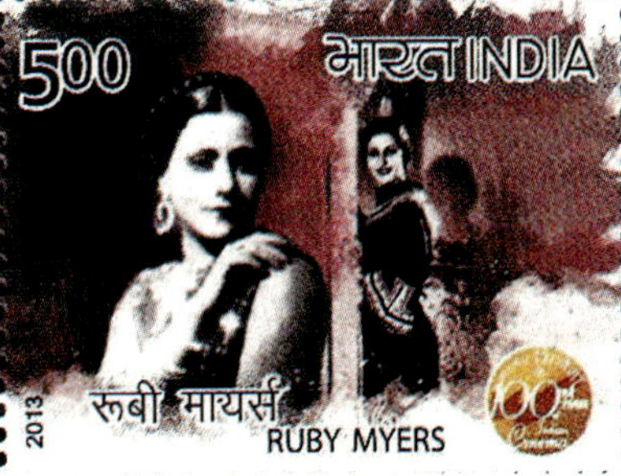

22.10: Ruby Myers

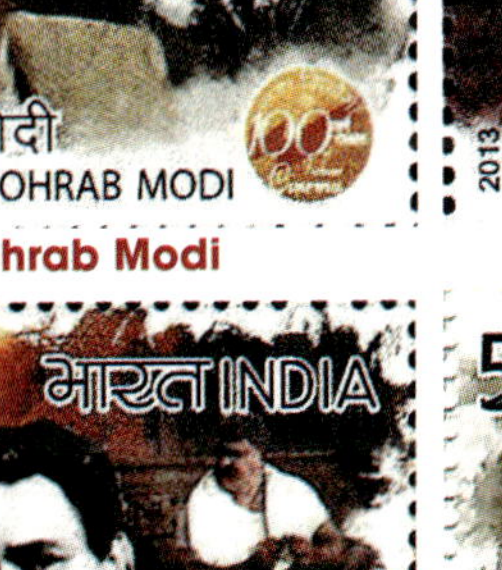
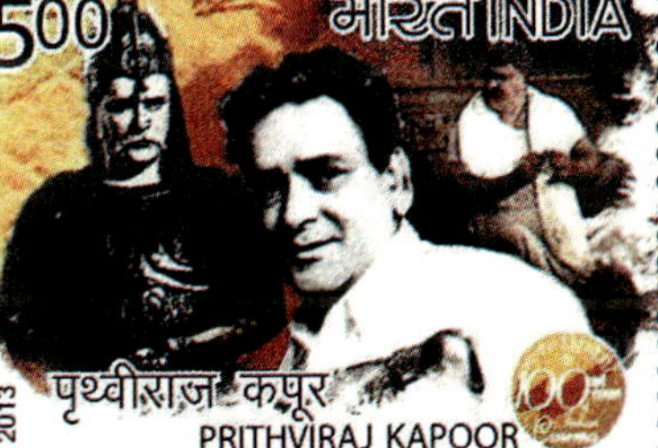

22.11: Prithviraj Kapoor

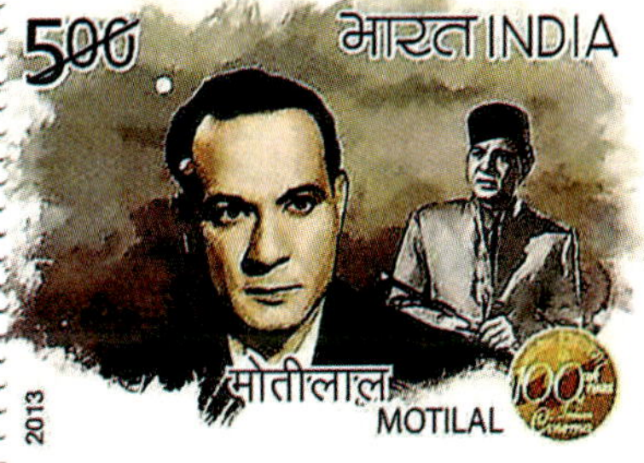

22.12: Motilal

Eminent actors of the pre-independance period; commemorative stamps issued in 2013 — Courtesy, Department of Post

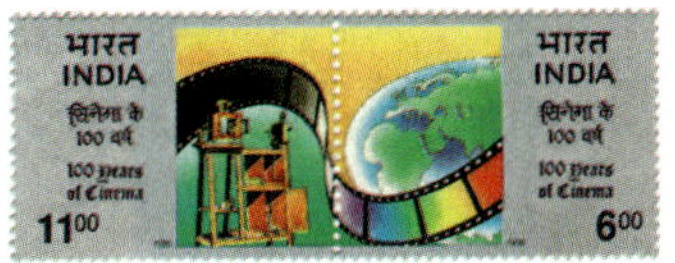

V. Shantaram (1901-1990), a recipient of Padma Bhushan and Dadasaheb Phalke awards, was an eminent actor and filmmaker (of silent as well as talkie era), whose work is epitomised by highly acclaimed movies such as *Dr Kotnis Ki Amar Kahani*.

Kundal Lal Saigal (1904-1947), an eminent singer and actor, is considered the first of the 'stars' of Indian cinema.

Dinshaw Billmoria (1904-1942), was a popular romantic hero of the 1930s who acted in many of the silent era as well as talkie movies.

Prithviraj Kapoor (1906-1972), recipient of Padma Bhushan and Dadasaheb Phalke awards, was an actor and filmmaker, known for his foundational contribution in the nascent stages of the film industry.

Ashok Kumar (1911-2001), recipient of Padma Bhushan, Sangeet Natak Akademi and Dadasaheb Phalke awards, was a stalwart of Indian cinema who acted in acclaimed movies such as *Achhut Kanya* (1936) and many other hit movies in the pre-independence and post-independence period, in a career spanning over five decades.

Motilal Rajvansh (1910-1965), was among the earliest of natural actors who acted in nearly 60 movies from the 40s to the 60s, including some critically acclaimed movies such as *Mr Sampat* (1952) and *Devdas* (1955).

The actresses in the very early days of cinema were far and few, so much so that Dadasaheb Phalke could not find a single woman to act in the movie *Raja Harishchandra*. Eventually, he had to cast a man (Anna Salunke). But despite the social inhibitions and backlash that acting in films brought in at that period, some brave women emerged as successful stars in the coming decades. Some of them are:

Kamlabai Gokhale, who was among the first actresses of Indian cinema acted in films like *Mohini Bhasmasur* (1912), *Devi Devayani Sharmistha* (1931), *Chandrahasa* (1933).

Durga Khote (1905-1991), was a recipient of Padma Shri and Dadasaheb Phalke awards and acted in early movies such as *Ayodheche Raja* (1932), *Amar Jyoti* (1936), and *Bharat Milap* (1942). She was the foremost amongst the leading ladies, a veteran actress of Indian cinema, with an acting career of 200 movies spanning over five decades.

Ruby Myers (1907-1983), was a recipient of Dadasaheb Phalke Award and also known as Sulochana. She acted in films such as *Telephone Ni Taruni* (1926), *Typist Girl* (1926), and *Wild Cat of Bombay* (1934). She was among the highest paid actresses of her time.

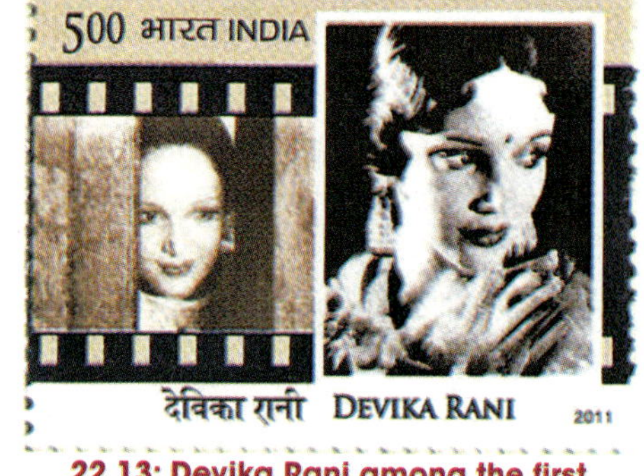

22.13: Devika Rani among the first of leading ladies — Courtesy, Department of Post

Devika Rani (1908-1994), was a recipient of Padma Shri and Dadasaheb Phalke awards, and an actress who was highly acclaimed for her work in movies such as *Achhut Kanya* (1936) and many others. She is often considered as the 'first lady' of Indian cinema.

Mary Evans (1908-1996), enjoyed great popularity as 'Fearless Nadia' in movies such *Hunter Wali* (1935), *Toofan Mail* and others.

Zubeida Begum Dhanrajgir (1911-1988), who acted as the main lead in *Alam Ara* (1931), the first talkie, and other hits such as *Devdas* (1937).

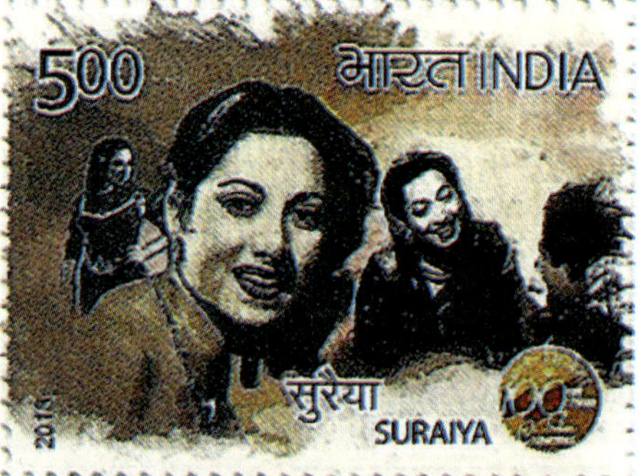

22.14: Suraiya, a renowned singer and eminent actress of the pre-independence era — Courtesy, Department of Post

Esther Victoria Abraham (1916-2006), an actress and a model popularly known as Pramila, acted in movies such as *Mahamaya* (1936), *Hamari Betiya* (1936), *Ulti Ganga* (1942) and others.

Shanta Apte (1916-1964), a Marathi and Hindi actress as well as a singer, was known for her roles in movies such as *Amar Jyoti* (1936), *Duniya Na Mane* (1938).

Naseem Banu (1916-2002), was known for her beauty. She acted in acclaimed movies like *Khoon Ka Khoon* (1935), *Pukar* (1939) and several other hit movies, acquiring a star status.

Leela Chitnis, Suraiya, Kamini Kaushal, Shobhana Samarth, were some other well-known actresses of the movies of the pre-independence era.

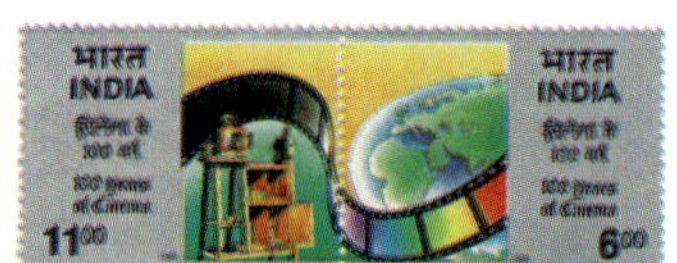

Multifaceted actors of early Indian cinema

A noteworthy feature of the actors and actresses of this period was their multifaceted abilities and dabbling with different domains of film production. As the art of playback singing had not yet developed, many popular actors of this period were also acclaimed singers and this included the likes of **Kundan Lal Saigal**, **Noor Jahan**, **Begum Akhtar**, **Suraiya**, **Ashok Kumar**, **Kanan Devi** and **Savithri Ganesan**. Many of the early actors like **Sohrab Modi**, **Paidi Jairaj**, **L.V. Prasad** and **V. Shantaram** were successful directors and producers. **Esther Victoria Abraham,** besides being a successful actress, was the first woman film producer. **Shobhana Samarth**, a film actress of the talkie period, later, also directed and produced movies. Another genre of actors, were those who excelled as film as well as theatre actors. These included the acting veterans such as **Prithviraj Kapoor**, **Balraj Sahni** and **Utpal Dutt**. Prithviraj Kapoor had also started a travelling group called *Prithvi Theatres*, while Balraj Sahni was also associated with the IPTA. Utpal Dutt later launched the *Little Theatre Group*.

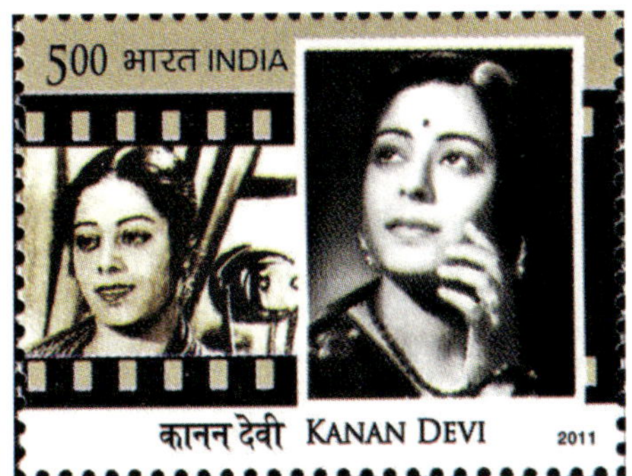

22.15: Kanan Devi

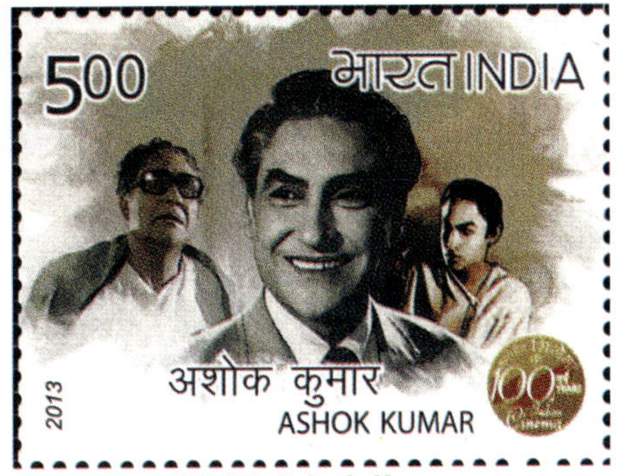

22.16: Ashok Kumar

Early actors and singers and Dadasaheb Phalke awardees — Courtesy, Department of Post

CINEMA IN POST-INDEPENDENT INDIA

In the post-independence period, and particularly in the **1950s** and **1960s**, Indian cinema made notable advances. This period ushered in what is also referred to as the **golden age of Indian cinema**. In 1951, the Government set up the Central Board of Film Certification (CBFC) to regulate the content of the movies. In 1953, the **first technicolour movie** *Jhansi Ki Rani* was produced by Sohrab Modi. This literally brought colour to the Indian movies and was truly the beginning of a new age for Indian cinema. With the growth of commercial cinema in the 50s, India leaped ahead in the production of movies and is said to have become the second biggest film industry of the world, a position it continued to enjoy even in the coming decades. Many critically acclaimed movies were produced in this decade including, *Do Bigha Zameen* (1953) by Bimal Roy, the *Apu Trilogy* (1955-59) by Satyajit Ray, besides many others, all of which ushered a genre of cinematic neo-realism.

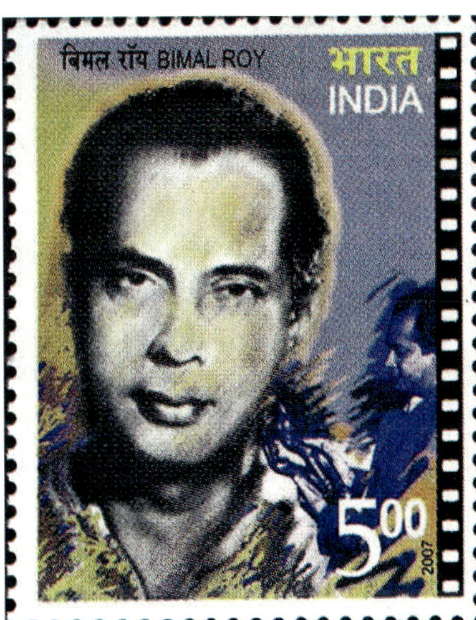

22.17: Bimal Roy, one of the eminent and acclaimed directors of early cinema; a stamp from 2007 — Courtesy, Department of Post

Several Indian movies in the 1950s received **international recognition**. *Do Bigha Zameen* (1953) by **Bimal Roy** was yet another Indian movie after *Neecha Nagar* (1946) to win an award at the **Cannes Film Festival.** Inspired by Tagore's poem *Dui Bigha Zomi,* the movie succinctly reflects the harsh socio-economic reality and the struggle for survival for the rural landless poor who migrate to cities to eke out a living and in hope for a better life. The decade witnessed the works of a cinematic genius **Satyajit Ray** (recipient of Bharat Ratna), who is considered among the all-time greats in Indian and world cinema. Satyajit Ray was awarded at the Cannes Film Festival in 1956 for the film *Pather Panchali* which is another landmark movie. Ray's two other films of the Apu trilogy, *Aparajito* and *Apur Sansar,*

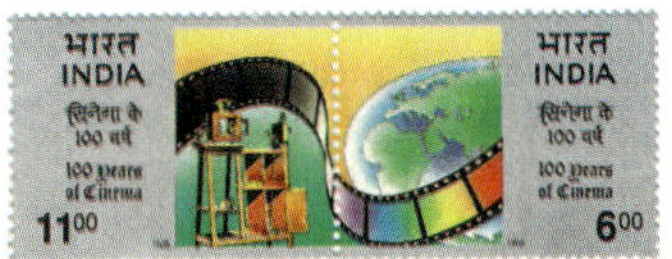

were highly acclaimed and are considered to be the harbingers of social realism. Another landmark movie of this genre was *Mother India* which was directed by **Mehboob Khan**. It also won an Oscar nomination in 1958 in the category of 'Best Foreign Language Film', the first Indian movie to get such a nomination. **Sivaji Ganesan**, a versatile Tamil actor, was awarded as the best actor at the Afro-Asian Film festival in 1960.

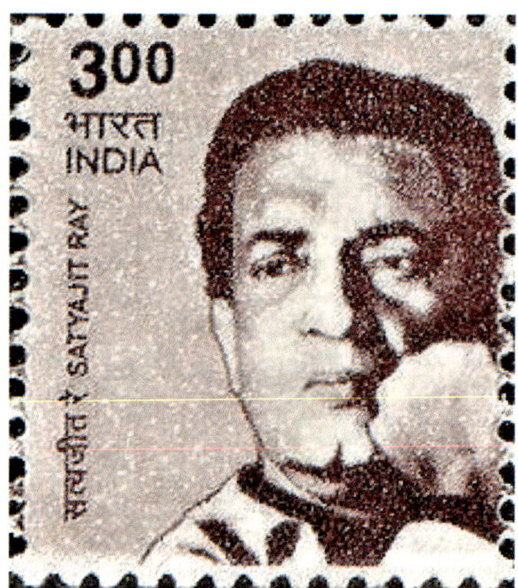

22.18: Satyajit Ray, Bharat Ratna and Dadasaheb Phalke awardee, a leading film personality of Indian and world cinema — Courtesy, Department of Post

Popular movies in the post-independence period too saw a huge surge. This **entertainment** genre was marked by social drama, romantic stories and melody of Indian music. Some memorable movies of this category include; *Barsaat* (1949), *Awaara* (1951), *Shree 420* (1955) and *Jagte Raho* (1956) of **Raj Kapoor**; *Baazi* (1951), *Pyaasa* (1957), *Kagaz Ke Phool* (1959) and *Chaudavi Ka Chaand* (1960) of **Guru Dutt**. Some movies of other film makers which received critical acclaim as well as commercial success, include; *Baiju Bawra* (1952) by **Vijay Bhatt**, *Aan* (1952), *Mother India* (1957) of **Mehboob Khan**, *Parineeta* (1953), *Devdas* (1955) and *Sujata* (1959) of **Bimal Roy**, *Boot Polish* (1954) of **Prakash Arora**, *Mirza Ghalib* (1954) by **Sohrab Modi**, *Jhanak Jhanak Payal Baje* (1955) and *Do Aankhen Barah Haath* (1957) of **V. Shantaram**, *Naya Daur* (1957) of **B.R. Chopra,** besides many others. These popular movies, besides being of the genre of romance (*Barsaat*, *Kagaz Ke Phool, Chaudvi Ka Chaand*), social drama (*Pyaasa*), romantic tragedies (*Devdas*) musical-romantic drama (*Baiju Bawra, Jhanak Jhanak Payal Baje*), crime-drama (*Awaara*), comedy-drama (*Shree 420*), were also imbued with social realism as in *Jagte Raho* and *Pyaasa*.

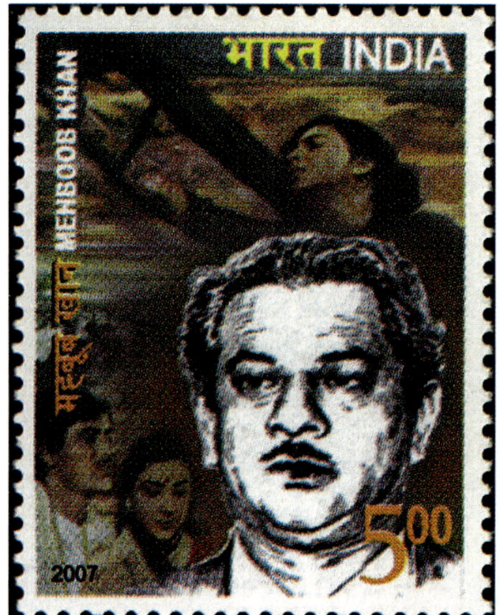

22.19: Mehboob Khan, an eminent director-producer of post independence cinema who directed acclaimed movies such as *Mother India* (1957); stamp from 2007 — Courtesy, Department of Post

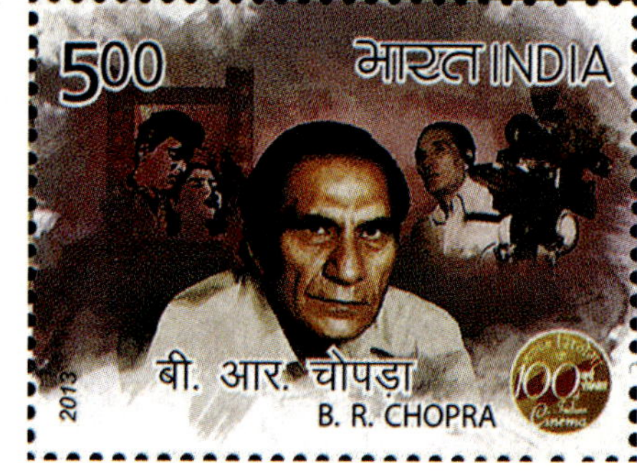

22.20: B.R. Chopra, a Padma Bhushan & Dadasaheb Phalke awardee, director and producer of several popular movies from 50s to 80s, including *Naya Daur* (1957), *Humraaz* (1967), *Nikaah* (1982) and his magnum opus, the *Mahabharata* television serial (1988); stamp from 2013 — Courtesy, Department of Post

National Film Awards

The National Film Awards are the most prestigious awards in the domain of Indian films. Instituted by the Government of India in 1954, the award aims at recognising and encouraging the aesthetic and technical excellence in Indian cinema, and is viewed as a medium of appreciation of cultures of different regions of the country. The annual awards are decided by a panel constituted by the government under the Directorate of Film Festivals and bestowed annually by the President of India on the eve of the `International Film Festival of India'.

The award initially recognised the best regional movies. However, since 1967, separate awards for the categories of artists and technicians were also instituted. The awards are given in three broad sections; 'Feature Films', 'Non-Feature Films', and 'Best Writing on Cinema'. Besides, a 'life time achievement award' referred to as the *Dadasaheb Phalke* award is also given. The feature film awards include the *Swarna Kamal* for; 'best feature film', 'best director',' best popular film, and others. The *Rajat Kamal* award is given for the 'best actor', 'best actress', 'best supporting actor' and 'best supporting actress', besides others.

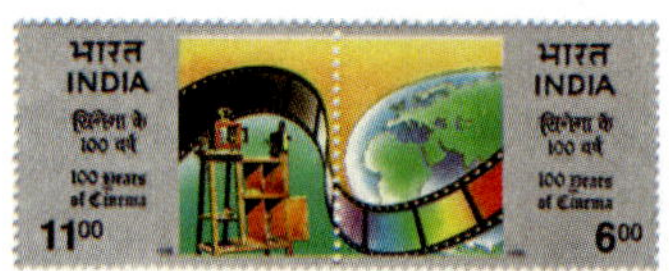

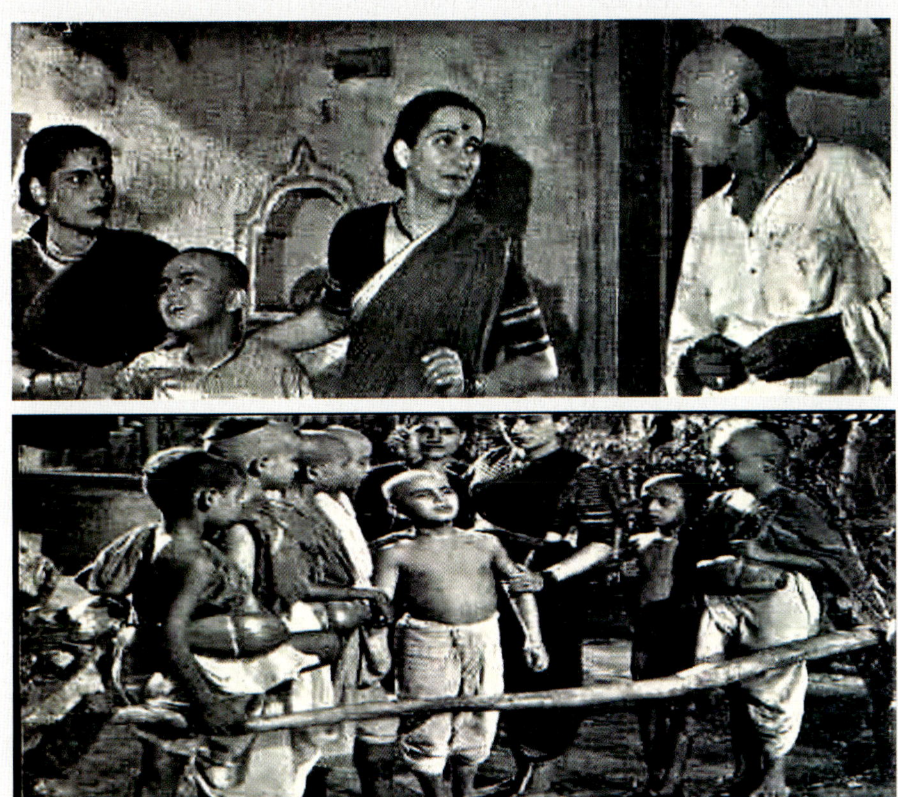

22.21 & 22.22: Stills of the film *Shyamachi Aai* which won the first National Film Award for the best feature film. Pictures as published in the catalogue of the first National Film Awards in 1954 — Courtesy, Directorate of Film Festivals, National Film Development Council

In the first edition of the awards, the President's Gold Medal for 'all India best feature film' was given to *Shyamachi Aai*, a Marathi film produced and directed by P.K. Atre, while *Do Bigha Zameen* (Hindi), produced and directed by Bimal Roy, won the 'certificate of merit'. In the nearly 70 years history of the awards, the feature film which has won the maximum number of awards in different categories is *Lagaan* which won eight awards in the year 2001. The award of best actor instituted in 1967 was first won by Uttam Kumar; while Amitabh Bachchan has won it for the maximum number of times (four). Nargis Dutt was the first recipient of the award for the best actress, while Shabana Azmi has won it five times, which is the highest for any cine artist (as best actor/actress).

The Decade of the 60s

The decade of the 60s, a part of the glorious golden age of Indian cinema, saw a fresh breath of entertainment-based movies. There was a transition from the concept of social realism and rural fixation. The urban settings, plush lifestyles and foreign locales were the new in thing. A diverse variety of films came up, which included the then in vogue romantic and drama films, and comedy, which was becoming increasing popular. Mysteries, thrillers and suspense movies also started to find a place. Song and dance routine had become firmly entrenched and became bigger and better in the 60s. While the melody of Indian music continued to thrive, there was also the introduction of western music in Indian film songs (*Jaan Pehchan Ho* from *Gumnaam*, 1965).

Among the iconic movies of the 60s was ***Mughal-e-Azam*** (1960), an epic historical drama. This was the costliest movie of its time and a huge commercial success which received as much critical adulation for all the aspects of movie making. Among other celebrated movies of this decade were, *Sahib, Biwi Aur Gulam* (1962), *Bandhini* (1963), *Sangam* (1964), *Dosti* (1964), *Waqt* (1965), *Guide* (1965), *Jab Jab Phool Khilen* (1965), *Anupama* (1966), *Love in Tokyo* (1966) *Ram Aur Shyam* (1967), *Jewel Thief* (1967), *An Evening in Paris* (1967), *Padosan* (1968), *Brahmachari* (1968), *Bhuvan Shome* (1969) and *Aradhana* (1969).

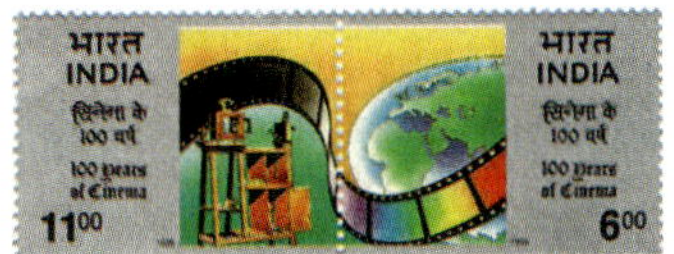

This decade also witnessed a genre of very successful **mystery thriller** movies such as *Bees Saal Baad* (1962), *Woh Kaun Thi* (1964), *Gumnaam* (1965), *Teesri Manzil* (1966), *Mera Saaya* (1966), *Anita* (1967) and *Hamraaz* (1967). Some **patriotic movies,** such as *Haqeeqat* (1964; based on the Sino-Indian war of 1962) and *Upkaar* (1967), were also very well received. The 60s also saw some **dacoit/bandit** movies such as *Jis Desh Mei Ganga Bahti Hai* (1960) and *Ganga Jamuna* (1961), a trend which continued in the subsequent decades, and later was replaced by the category of 'smuggler' movies.

The actors of post-independence were often cast in specific acting genres, as character actors, heroes, heroines, villains, comedians and others. At times, the success of the movie and their exemplary individual performances in a specific role, typecasted them in a typical acting mould. Nevertheless, this period did see the emergence of some doyens of Indian cinema and acting who transcended the acting genres. Among the successful and acclaimed character actors in the decade of 50s were; **Balraj Sahni** who acted in movies such as *Dharti Ke Lal* (1946), *Do Bigha Zameen* (1954), *Chhoti Bahen* (1959), *Kabuliwala* (1961); **Pran** (1920-2013), a recipient of Padma Bhushan and Dadasaheb Phalke awards, whose acting career spanned over six decades. Some of his noteworthy movies include *Ziddi* (1948), *Sheesh Mahal* (1950), *Azaad* (1955), *Devdas* (1955) *Adalat* (1958), *Aadmi* (1968); **Utpal Dutt** (1929-1993), recipient of Sangeet Natak Akademi Fellowship, who acted in several Bengali movies in the 50s, including those of Satyajit Ray, and in acclaimed movies such as *Bhuvan Shome* (1969) of Mrinal Sen. Some other character actors of this period include **A.K. Hangal** (1914-2012), an eminent theatre and film actor, who in a career of over 40 years, acted in nearly 225 movies; **Om Prakash** (1919-1998), who played leading roles in the 40s and 50s before transitioning to the character roles and went on till the 90s; **Iftekhar** (1920-1995), who acted in over 400 films from mid-40s to early 90s, and **Om Shivpuri** (1938-1990), a notable theatre and film actor.

Among the **mainstream heroes** of this period were thespians like **Dilip Kumar, Raj Kapoor** and **Dev Anand**, christened as the trinity of the then commercial cinema. **Dilip Kumar** (1922-2021), recipient of Padma Vibhushan, Dadasaheb Phalke awards, was a 'method actor' who was amongst the most commercially successful as well as critically acclaimed actors of this generation. Considered a tragedy king, with roles in movies such as *Devdas* (1955), he was equally adept in playing roles in social dramas (*Daag* in 1952) and romantic roles (*Naya Daur* in 1957) and historical dramas (*Mughal-e Azam* in 1960). **Raj Kapoor** (1924-1988), recipient of Padma Bhushan and Dadasaheb Phalke awards, personified in his roles in *Awaara* (1952), *Shree 420* (1955) the tramp and the naivety of villagers and the emerging suburban city life. His movies, particularly *Awaara*, received immense international popularity in overseas markets of Asia, Africa, Caribbean and erstwhile Soviet-bloc, with the song *'Awaara-Hoon'*, acquiring a cult status. **Dev Anand** (1923-2011), recipient of Padma Bhushan, Dadasaheb Phalke awards, emerged as the evergreen romantic hero of the 50s and 60s. Some of his noteworthy movies were *Baazi* (1951), *Jaal* (1952), *CID* (1956), *Kala Pani* (1958), *Guide* (1965), *Johnny Mera Naam* (1970), and some others. Among the other eminent actors of the period were **Guru Dutt, Rehman, Pradeep Kumar, Sunil Dutt,** (recipient of Padma Shri and National Film Award, **Rajendra Kumar** (recipient of Padma Shri), **Raaj Kumar, Premnath** and others.

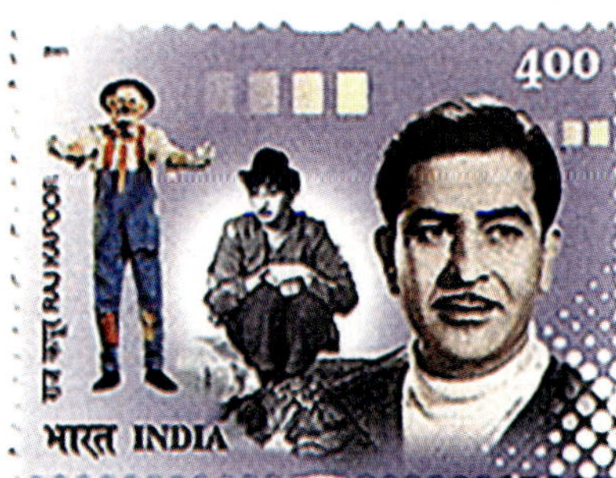

22.23: Raj Kapoor, the showman of Indian movies

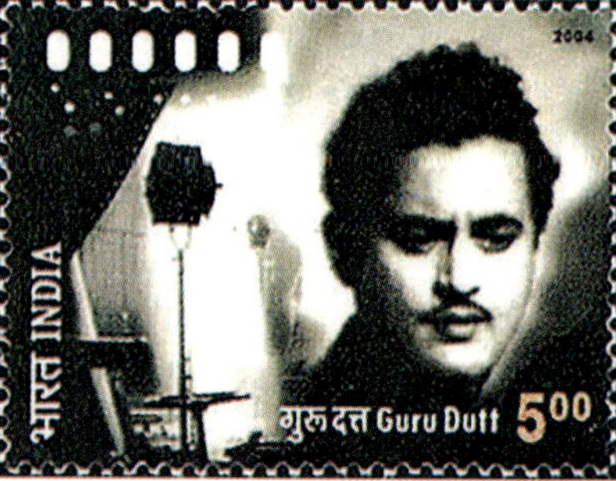

22.24: Guru Dutt, a veteran actor and director, whose movies struck a balance between the art and entertainment world

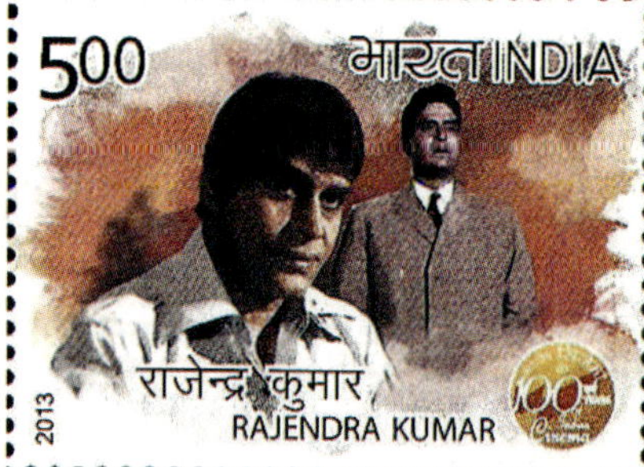

22.25: Rajendra Kumar, popularly known as Jubilee Kumar for his several successful films that completed silver jubilee

Stamp images — Courtesy, Department of Post

Among the successful **actresses of Bollywood** in this phase were **Madhubala, Meena Kumari, and Nargis Dutt,** who were as much as the queens of glamour and beauty as much as they were acclaimed for their acting skills. **Nutan, Waheeda Rehman, Vyjayanthimala, Padmini, Nirupama Roy, Mala Sinha** were some other successful and celebrated actresses of the 50s and 60s. **Nargis** (1929-1981), recipient of the Padma Shri award was one of the most acclaimed and successful actresses of Indian cinema,

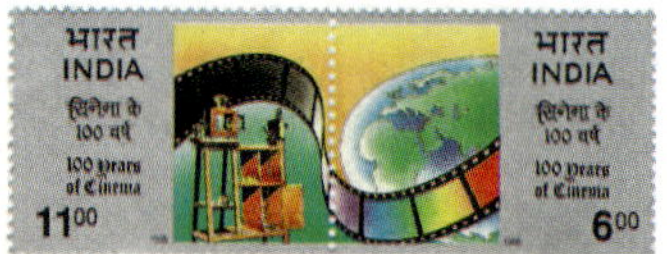

who performed diverse roles ranging from romantic to tragedy and from drama to comedy with equal ease. She is known for her acting in movies like *Barsaat* (1949), *Awaara* (1951), *Shree 420* (1955) and *Mother India* (1957). *Mother India* was also nominated for the Oscar awards from India and for which her performance was highly appreciated.

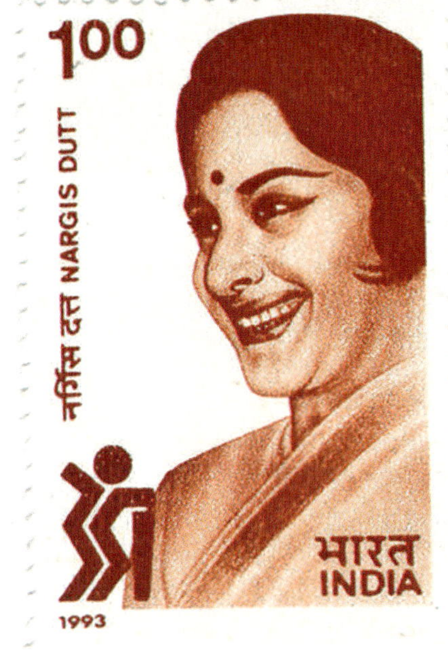

22.26: Nargis Dutt, an acclaimed actress of post independence, a stamp from 1993 — Courtesy, Department of Post

Madhubala (1933-1969), considered as one of the most beautiful of actresses of the Indian screen ever, acted in nearly 60 films in a short career spanning two decades. Among the movies where her performance was appreciated were; *Neel Kamal* (1947), *Mr. and Mrs. 55* (1955), *Chalti Ka Naam Gaadi* (1958), *Mughal-e Azam* (1960), *Half Ticket* (1962) besides others. Considered as one of the finest actresses of her time, **Meena Kumari** (1933-1972) was later christened as the tragedy-queen of Indian cinema. Her acting was highly acclaimed by critics as well as by the public at large, especially in movies like *Baiju-Bawra* (1954), *Parineeta* (1955), *Bhabhi Ki Chudiyan* (1961) and *Sahib Bibi Aur Gulam* (1962). **Waheeda Rehman,** recipient of Padma Bhushan, Dadasaheb Phalke award & National Film Award, was acclaimed for her acting skills and had a string of hits in the late 50s and 60s, which include *Pyaasa* (1957), *Chaudvi Ka Chaand* (1960), *Guide* (1965), *Neel Kamal* (1968), and *Reshma Aur Shera* (1971).

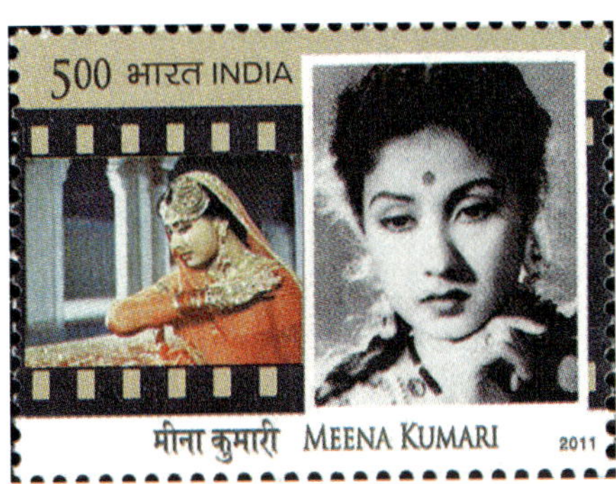

22.27: Meena Kumari

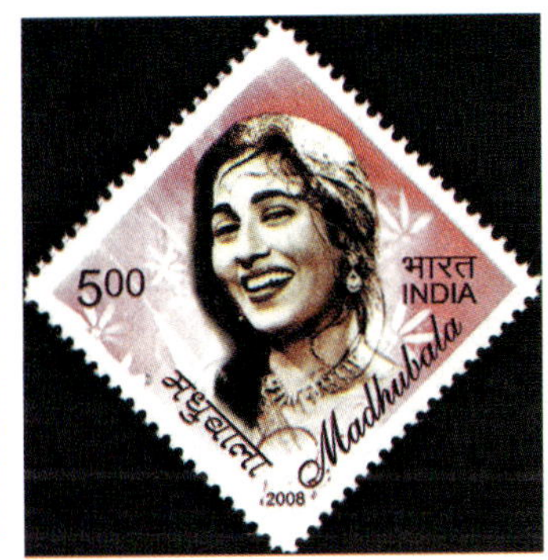

22.28: Madhubala

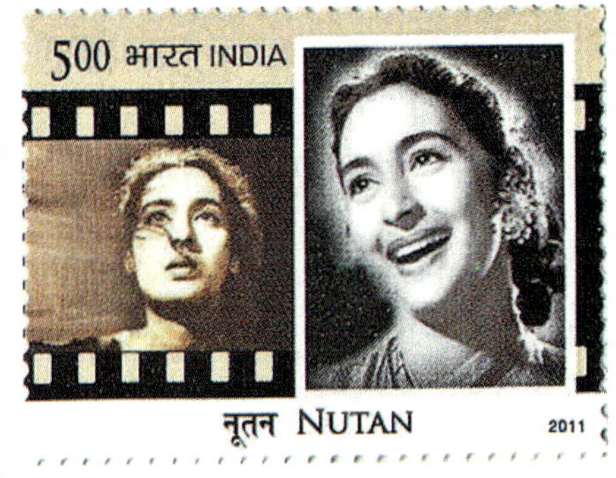

22.29: Nutan

Leading actresses of the 50s & 60s; stamp images — Courtesy, Department of Post

The period of the 60s saw the emergence of new stars who dominated Bollywood in the coming decades. Among the actors of reckoning were **Manoj Kumar, Shammi Kapoor, Shashi Kapoor, Dharmendra** and **Rajesh Khanna;** with the latter billed as the first superstar of the Bollywood in the late 60s and early 70s. **Manoj Kumar** (recipient of Padma Shri & Dadasaheb Phalke Award), acted and directed several patriotic movies like *Shaheed* (1965) and *Upkaar* (1967). **Shammi Kapoor** played the romantic lead in mainstream movies, comedies and thrillers like *Junglee* (1961), *Professor* (1962), *Kashmir ki Kali* (1964) and *Teesri Manzil* (1966). He was especially renowned for his dancing skills. **Shashi Kapoor** (recipient of Padma Bhushan & Dadasaheb Phalke Award) too starred in several romantic movies like *Jab Jab Phool Khilen* (1965). **Dharmendra** (recipient of Padma Bhushan award) debuted in the early 60s and had a successful career spanning six decades. He played a variety of roles in this decade in movies such as *Bandini* (1963), *Pooja Ke Phool* (1964), *Aakashdeep* (1965), *Aankhen* (1968), before being typecast in the macho hero mould in his later movies.

New actresses of this period included **Sharmila Tagore, Saira Banu, Asha Parekh, Leela Naidu, Sadhana, Helen, Mumtaz, Nanda, Aruna Irani, Tanuja and Hema Malini** besides others. **Sharmila Tagore** (recipient of Padma Bhushan & two National Film Awards) started her acting career as a child artist in the movies of Satyajit Ray. Among the successful movies which established her Bollywood credentials were *Kashmir Ki Kali* (1964), *Anupama* (1966), and *Aradhana* (1969), besides others. Her appearance in a bikini in *Evening in Paris* (1967), the first for an Indian actress, was considered a very bold move and marks a transition in Indian movies. **Saira Banu** was known for her beauty, style and glamour and had a successful run in the 60s with many hit movies such as *Junglee* (1961), *Ayee Milan Ki Bela* (1963), *Padosan* (1967) and *Purab aur*

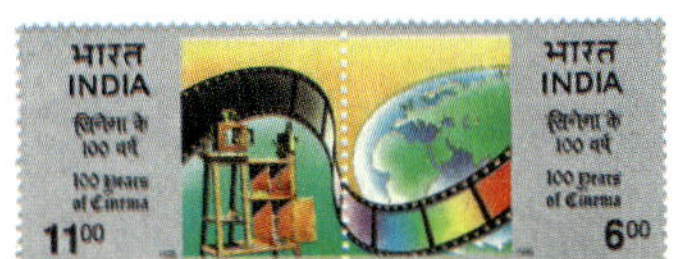

Paschim (1970). **Asha Parekh** (recipient of Padma Shri & Dadasaheb Phalke Award) was another eminent actress of this decade with successful movies such as *Jab Pyaar Kissi Se Hota Hai* (1961), *Teesri Manzil* (1966) and *Kati Patang* (1970).While other actresses were largely cast in the lead roles, **Helen** (recipient of Padma Shri) acquired a distinction of playing supporting and character roles that often revolved around her unique dancing talent. In a career of several decades and nearly 1000 movies, she literally danced her way to success with many song and dance routines, which, many decades later, were to be christened as 'item numbers'.

The genre of comedies became increasingly popular in the decade of the 1950s and early 1960s. This was a category of movies which was less in vogue in the previous decades. Several comedies were produced in post-independence period and they received as much of commercial success and acceptability as the category of romance, social drama and social realism. Some of the noteworthy comedies of this period included *Mr and Mrs 55* (1955), *Baap Re Baap* (1955), *Chalti Ka Naam Gaadi* (1957), *Anari* (1959), *Jhumroo* (1961), *Half Ticket* (1962), *Man Mauji* (1962), *Padosan* (1968) besides others. Many of these movies had the actor–singer virtuoso **Kishore Kumar** in the lead role, who came to personify this genre of films.

In many Indian films of this phase there also emerged a distinct place for **comedian actors**. They were often cast as the friend of the hero (main lead character) or in other supporting roles. Soon certain actors started specialising in it and earned the epithet of comedians. Many of the comic actors who made their debut in this period include some of the stalwarts of this genre such as **Asit Sen, Johnnie Walker, I.S. Johar, Rajendra Nath, Deven Verma, Mukri** and **Mehmood**. The latter was so popular in the 60s and 70s, that he commanded as much respect and price in the movies as many of the mainstream heroes of the time. Mehmood was known for his stellar comic performances such as that in *Padosan* (1968). Thus, a distinct role for comedians emerged, which was a uniqueness of Indian movies of the 50s and 60s. It remained a trend even in the next few decades, till the character actors and even the mainstream heroes and villains starting fulfilling this demand of the script.

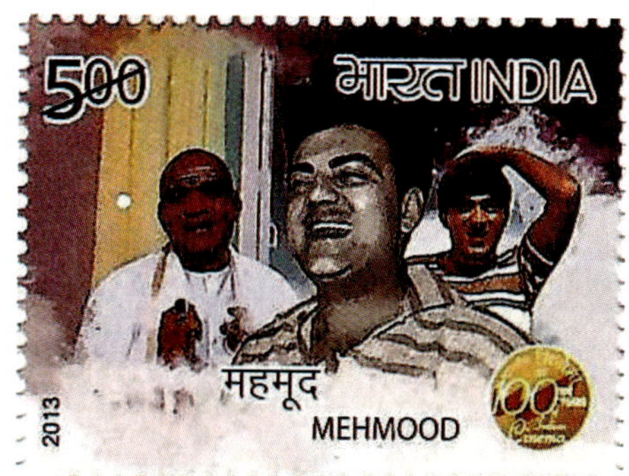

22.30: Mehmood, a character actor and comedian, a stamp from 2013 — Courtesy, Department of Post

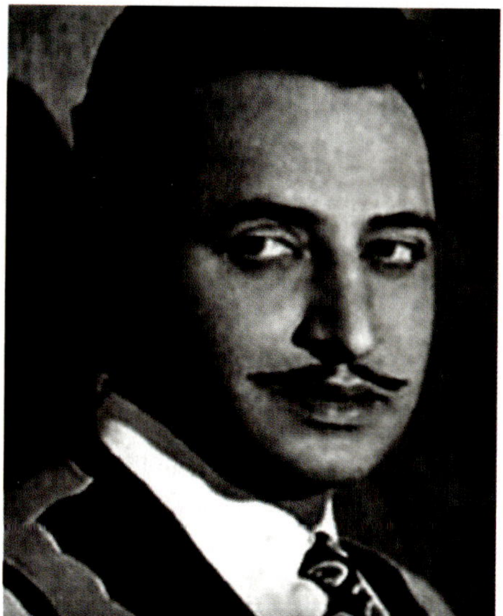

22.31: Pran, an iconic villain and character actor of Bollywood from 1940s to 2000s — Wikimedia Commons

Villains, a distinct category, also emerged in this chapter of Indian cinema, with certain actors specialising and also getting typecasted in it. Amongst the most glorious of villains of Indian cinema was **Pran** (recipient of Padma Bhushan & Dadasaheb Phalke award) who portrayed the negative character in hundreds of movies, especially in the decades of the 40s to 60s. Some of his memorable performances were in movies such as *Jis Desh Mein Ganga Behti Hai* (1960), *Purab Aur Paschim* (1967), *Ram Aur Shyam* (1967) besides others. **K. N. Singh** (1908-2000) was another iconic villain of this period and was appreciated in movies like *Jwaar Bhata* (1944), *Awaara* (1951), *Jaal* (1952), *CID* (1956), *Howrah Bridge* (1958), *Chalti Ka Naam Gaadi* (1958) and *An Evening in Paris* (1967). Among the other notable villains of this period were, **Ajit** (1922-1988), **Jeevan** (1915-1987), **Madan Puri** (1915-1985), **Sujeet Kumar** (1934-2010) and **Prem Chopra** (born 1935). Prem Chopra acquired a cult status as a mean villain of the 1960s and 1970s. Thus, with the typecasting of villains, the Bollywood commercial movies themselves got typecasted with straight jacketed roles of heroes, heroines, comedians and villains. To this formula was added a liberal sprinkle of song and dance routine. Thus, a mould of a commercial movie was cast, which proved difficult to break even in the subsequent decades.

The movies of the 50s and 60s clearly reflect the **evolution of Indian cinema.** A variety of subjects were taken up by movie makers, ranging from landlordism and exploitation of the peasantry (as in *Do Bigha Zameen*) to the disenchantment and unfulfilled hopes of the millions (as in *Awaara*), from a grand historical tale (as in *Mughal-e Azam*) to the subject of materialistic aspiration and spiritualism (as in *Guide*), from the issue of untouchability and casteism (as in *Sujata*), to honour and sacrifice (as in *Mother*

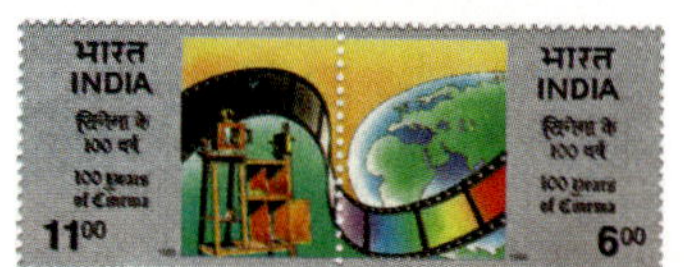

India). The genre of movies also depicted the widest of spectrum including romance, drama, comedy, tragedy, suspense and thrillers. The film music was characterised by melodies like never witnessed before nor attained later. All the crafts of movie making matured. In the movies of Bimal Roy, V. Shantaram, Satyajit Ray, Mehboob Khan and others, Indian movies received international recognition. The popular genre of movies of Raj Kapoor (such as *Awaara*) attracted wide international popular appreciation and appeal. The Indian film industry had already become the second largest commercial film industry of the world and was vying for the numero-uno position. Truly, this was the **golden age of Indian movies**.

The Film and Television Institute of India

The establishment of the **Film Institute of India** in 1960 in Pune was an important development in the history of movies in post-independent India. The institute was established in Pune in the land of the erstwhile Prabhat Studios (which was established here in 1933). It offered a diverse range of courses in the art of film making. In just a decade of its formation, the institute was entrusted the work of training of television artists and different crafts of television production. Thus evolved the **Film and Television Institute of India**, an autonomous body under the Ministry of Information and Broadcasting. Various in-service courses for the artists and technicians of the public broadcaster Doordarshan were added to it, in addition to the various courses on film making. Over a period of time, the institute has established itself as a centre of excellence and eminence for training technicians, actors and directors for film and television industry. Different diploma and post graduate courses of one to three years duration in film direction, editing, cinematography, audiography, acting, art direction, computer graphics & animation are offered.

While eminent faculties like **Satyajit Ray** and **Ritwik Ghatak** have been associated with the FTII, its notable alumni includes the who's and who of film industry including the stalwarts like **Adoor Gopalakrishnan** (renowned film director), **Jaya Bachchan** (film actress), **Shatrughan Sinha** (film actor), **Raza Murad** (film actor), **Sanjay Leela Bhansali** (film director), **Danny Denzongpa** (character actor in films), **Mani Kaul** (film director), **Satish Kaushik** (character actor in films), **Rakesh Bedi** (character actor in films and television), **Mithun Chakraborty** (film actor), **Naseeruddin Shah** (film actor), **Mukesh Khanna** (film and television actor), besides others.

Cinema in the 70s and 80s

The cinema of the early 70s was characterised by the rise of two superstars namely, **Rajesh Khanna**, a 'romantic hero', and later **Amitabh Bachchan** as 'an angry young man. Rajesh Khanna (recipient of Padma Bhushan) is credited with acting in a solo lead role in a record 15 hit films from 1969 to 1971. Among his celebrated movies are *Aradhana* (1968), *Kati Patang* (1970), *Khamoshi* (1970), *Anand* (1971), *Haathi Mere Saathi* (1971), *Amar Prem* (1971), *Bawarchi* (1972), *Namak Haram* (1973), besides others. Many of these early 70s movies were based on a similar formula of success; romance with shades of other genres.

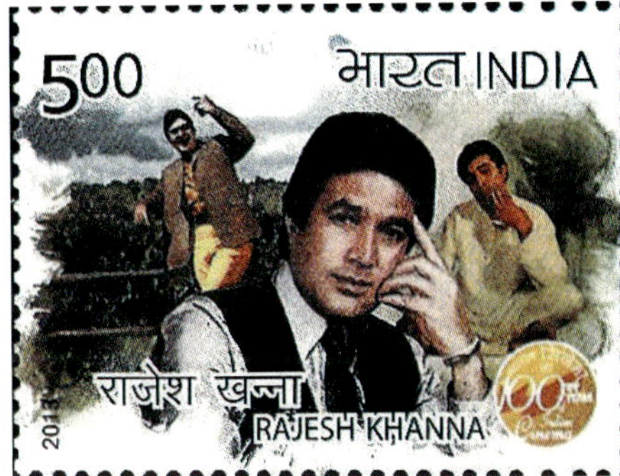

22.32: Rajesh Khanna, the superstar of early 70s, a commemorative stamp of 2013 — Courtesy, Department of Post

However, the very nature of the commercial movies underwent a change from the musical romances of the late 60s to the genre of crime and violence with the success of movies such as such as *Zanjeer (1973), Deewar (1975)* and *Sholay (1975)*.This heralded another superstar of the movie world and a one like never witnessed before. **Amitabh Bachchan** (recipient of Padma Vibhushan and Dadasaheb Phalke award) who had a rather tepid debut in the late 60s became a one-man industry in the movie world with a string of successes in the mid-70s. His initial movies depicted the simmering discontent and disillusionment of the masses, particularly of the urban youth. The slums, the squalor and the anti-establishmentarian sentiment were aptly depicted by the films and very effectively channelised by Bachchan in characters which were ready to take on the high and mighty. These were at times considered the contextual reinterpretation of the bandit/ dacoit movies of the 60s, but in a more diverse setting and with the theme of fight against the corrupt and inefficient system. Bachchan acted in movies of different genres

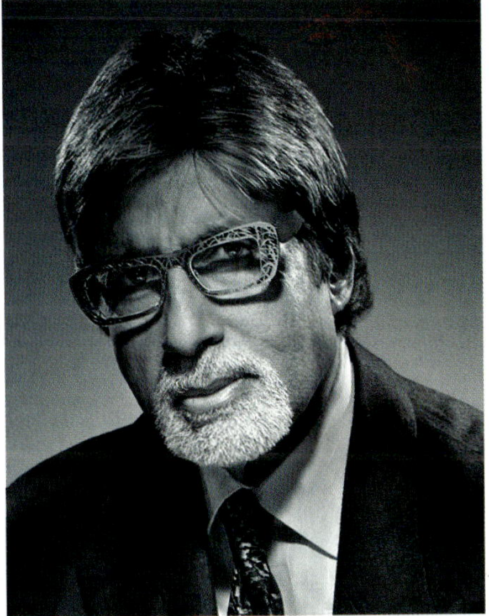
22.33: Amitabh Bachchan (recipient of Padma Vibhushan and Dadasaheb Phalke Award), superstar of Bollywood — Wikimedia Commons

such as romantic movies; *Mili* (1975), *Kabhi Kabhi* (1975), dramas like *Namak Haram* (1973) and *Abhimaan* (1973), thrillers like *Parwana* (1971), and comedy like *Chupke Chupke* (1975). However, the masala-movies based on the 'angry young man' image of his, became the biggest box office grossers. Among the other highly successful films of Bachchan of the 70s and 80s were *Amar Akbar Anthony* (1976), *Trishul* (1978), *Don* (1978), *Muqaddar Ka Sikandar* (1978), *Mr Natwarlal* (1979), *Dostana* (1980), *Yaraana* (1980), *Lawaaris* (1981), *Namak Halal* (1982), *Shakti* (1982), *Coolie* (1983), *Sharabi* (1984), *Aakhri Raasta* (1986), *Shahenshah* (1988), besides others. Among other successful lead actors of the 70s were **Vinod Khanna,** (recipient of Dadasaheb Phalke award), **Jitendra, Rishi Kapoor** (recipients of National Film Awards), **Shatrughan Sinha, Mithun Chakraborty** (recipient of three National Film Awards).

Among the most versatile actors of this phase of Indian movies was **Sanjeev Kumar** (recipient of two National Film Awards) who made his debut in the 60s. He played lead roles as well as characters of different shades, including drama, tragedy and comedy in some highly acclaimed and successful movies such as *Dastak* (1970), *Khilona* (1970), *Koshish* (1972), *Parichay* (1972), *Sholay* (1975), *Mausam* (1975), *Trishul* (1978), *Pati Patni Aur Woh* (1978), *Angoor* (1982). This period also witnessed some other lead and character actors such as **Amol Palekar, Feroze Khan, Naveen Nischol, Sachin, Rakesh Rohan, Vinod Mehra** and others. The 70s also saw the emergence of **Amjad Khan** as a legendary villain with the iconic role of the dacoit Gabbar Singh in the film *Sholay*. **Danny Denzongpa** and **Ranjeet** were some other actors popular in villainous roles in this period.

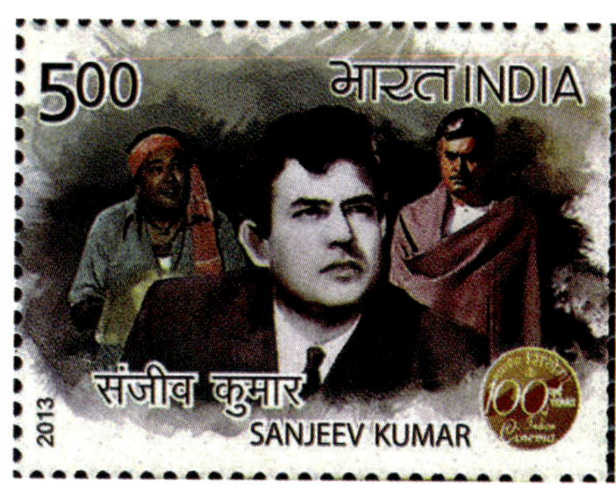

22.34: Sanjeev Kumar, a versatile character actor of Indian cinema, a commemorative stamp of 2013 — Courtesy, Department of Post

The successful actresses of this decade include, **Hema Malini, Rakhee, Jaya Bhaduri** (later Jaya Bachchan), **Zeenat Aman, Dimple Kapadia, Parveen Babi, Rekha, Jaya Prada, Tina Munim** (later Tina Ambani), besides others. Amongst the most successful mainstream actresses and christened as a 'dream girl', **Hema Malini** (recipient of Padma Shri award) has acted in movies over five decades. Starting with *Sapno ko Saudagar* (1968) in the late 60s, she has been part of many successful and acclaimed movies which include *Seeta Aur Geeta* (1972), *Sholay* (1975) in the 70s, to *Razia Sultan* (1983), *Andha Kanoon* (1983) in the 80s, to *Baghbaan* (2003), *Aarakshan* (2011) in the new millennium. **Rekha** (recipient of Padma Shri and National Film Award) was another celebrated actress known for her acting skills. She is seen as an actress who transformed herself in terms of appearance as well as acting skills (from the run of the mill to the very best) in the industry. In a career spanning over five decades, she has been a part of several successful movies such as *Sawan Bhado* (1970), *Namak Haram* (1973), *Muqaddar Ka Sikander* (1978), *Mr. Natwarlal* (1978), *Umrao Jaan* (1981), *Utsav* (1984), *Khoon Bhari Maang* (1988), *Khiladiyon Ka Khiladi* (1996), besides others. **Smita Patil** and **Shabana Azmi** were the most acclaimed actresses of this period who were successful in the parallel movies as well as in the mainstream cinema. In a similar film trajectory starting in the mid-70s, both acted in movies of similar genre and are regarded as among the finest actresses of the movies and the theatres.

The **movies of the 70s** marked a clear departure from the genre of 60s and earlier. The romantic musicals were replaced by the darker and violent crime thrillers. Anti-establishment sentiment espousing the growing disenchantment from the system started to take the centre stage. This was the changing realism within the movies and was reflective of the change and restlessness within the society. However, this genre was punctuated with musical romantic dramas such as *Pakeezah* (1973); comedies such as *Chupke Chupke* (1975), *Golmaal* (1979) and teenage romance dramas such as *Bobby* (1973), *Julie* (1975) besides others. A new genre of ***masala* movies** emerged which combined the flavours of drama-melodrama, romance, comedy and action besides being a musical. This trend is said to have started with *Yaadon Ki Baraat* (1973) and was followed by many others in the 70s and later decades. Parallel cinema continued to flourish with movies such as *Uski Roti* (1971), *Ankur* (1974), *Nishant* (1975) and others. But perhaps the movies of 70s are best remembered for the emergence of superstars, Rajesh Khanna and Amitabh Bachchan who completely dominated the industry in their heydays. In a way, their crazy public appeal was largely reflective of the stupendous growth of Indian cinema and its massive popularity among the masses as witnessed never ever before and perhaps never later.

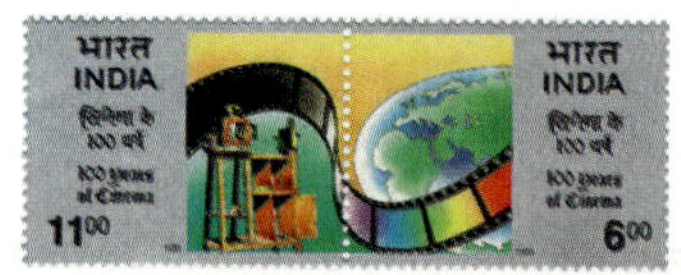

Parallel Cinema: A Movement Within the Movies

The term `parallel cinema' refers to the genre of the movies depicting social realism. These were colloquially called `art movies' as opposed to the mainstream entertainment oriented commercial cinema. In the decade of 40s and 50s, movies were influenced by a wave of cinematographic realism and naturalism. It endeavoured to depict the social reality through the camera's lens, especially the elements which were a critique of the society and seemingly bitter and harsh. The intent of these movies was to go beyond popular entertainment and to bring the focus on the theme and the social message it strived to convey.

Many reasons are attributed to the emergence of parallel cinema in India. These include the influence of social realism as also reflected in other art forms such as theatre and literature. Further, the decade of the 40s and the period of post-independence was a phase of great transition which was marked by the hope of a new India amid the despair over the partition, the bloodshed and the unrealised dreams. The parallel movies endeavoured to capture these very emotions of the people. Recognition of such movies in international and national award functions, particularly in the 50s, came as a shot in the arm for this category of production.

Parallel cinema movement in India in its different phases was also influenced by similar movements elsewhere in world cinema. This included the *Italian neo-realism* of post-World War-II period (1945-1952), *French New Wave* (late 1950s) and the *Japanese New Wave* (1950s to 1970s) in cinema. The movements within the country in the field of literature such as the *Progressive Writers Movement* and the sweeping socio-economic-political changes in the coming decades also had profound influence on this brand of movies.

Film scholars trace the earliest of this category of movies to *Savkari Pash* (1925) of **Baburao Painter** in the silent era. It depicted the hardships of a poor peasant losing his land to the machinations of a greedy village moneylender and eventually being compelled to migrate as a mill worker. Several other movies of this genre were produced in the 1930s and 40s. These include *Achhut Kanya* (1936) directed by **Franz Osten** depicting the issue of untouchability; *Neecha Nagar d*irected by **Chetan Anand** and written by **K. A. Abbas** highlighting the rich-poor divide; *Duniya Na Mane* (1937), a social classic on women's empowerment and *Manoos* (1939), a reformist social drama by **V. Shantaram**.

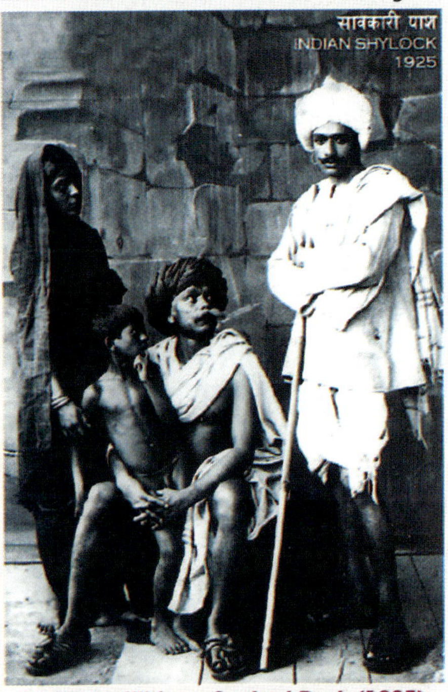

22.35: A still from *Savkari Pash* (1925) earliest of the genre of parallel cinema, a movie by Baburao Painter — Wikimedia Commons

In the post-independence period, many of the pioneers of social realism and parallel cinema were filmmakers from West Bengal. These included stalwarts like **Satyajit Ray** (Bharat Ratna) who directed the acclaimed *Apu* trilogy of *Pather Panchali* (1955), *Aparajito* (1956), *Apur Sansar (*1959). **Ritwik Ghatak** (recipient of Padma Shri, & National Film Awards) was known for movies like *Meghe Dhaka Tara (1960) and Jukti Takko Aar Gappo (*1974). **Tapan Sinha** (recipient of Padma Shri, Dadasaheb Phalke & ten National Film Awards) was known for movies like *Kabuliwala (*1957), *Sagina Mahto (*1970). **Mrinal Sen (**recipient of Padma Bhushan, Dadasaheb Phalke award and 18 National Film Awards) was known for movies like *Bhuvan Shome* (1969), *Mrigayaa* (1976). Their movies created what was known as the *new wave of Eastern India*. Some movies of 1950s such as *Do Bigha Zameen* of Bimal Roy, *Mother India* of Mehboob Khan, and *Do Aankhen Barah Haath* of **V. Shantaram** also belong to the similar genre, albeit they were also a commercial success like the other mainstream movies.

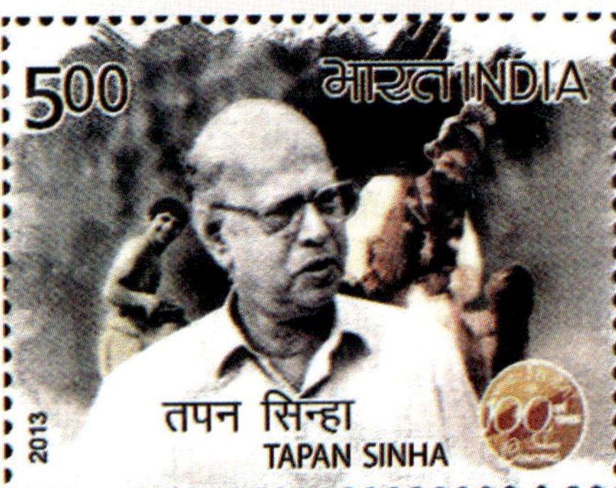

22.36: Tapan Sinha, a veteran film director of the art movies, a commemorative stamp of 2013 — Courtesy, Department of Post

Coming to the 1970s, the parallel cinema continued to flourish with movies such as *Pratidwandi* (1970), *Shatranj Ke Khiladi* (1978) by **Satyajit Ray**, *Ankur* (1974), *Nishant* (1975), *Manthan* (1976) *Bhumika* (1977) and *Junoon* (1978) by **Shyam Benegal** (Padma Bhushan, Dadasaheb Phalke & eighteen National Film Award recipient) and *Bhuvan Shome* (1969) and *Mrigayaa* (1976) by **Mrinal Sen** (Padma Bhushan, Dadasaheb Phalke & eighteen National Film Awards recipient). **Mani Kaul** (recipient of National Film Awards) was another master of this genre whose movies *Uski Roti* (1971), *Ashadh Ka Ek Din* (1972), *Duvidha* (1974) were widely acclaimed. **Adoor Gopalakrishnan** (recipient of Padma Vibhushan, Dadasaheb Phalke & seventeen National Film Awards) engendered a wave of realism in Malayalam cinema with *Swayamvaram* (1972).

In Marathi cinema, acclaimed works like *Samna* (1974), *Jait Re Jait* (1978), *Sinhasan* (1979), were directed by **Jabbar Patel**. Kannada movie *Samskara* (1970), based on the novel of U.R. Ananthamurty and directed by **Pattabhirama Reddy** was another masterpiece. *Pasi* (1979), a Tamil language drama directed by **Durai** was another acclaimed work. *Maya Darpan* (1972), by **Kumar Sahni** (recipient of National Film Award), *Dastak* (1972), by **Rajender Singh Bedi** (recipient of Padma Shri & National Film Award), *Vamsh Vriksh* (1971), by **Girish Karnard** (recipient of Padma Bhushan), *Koshish* (1972), by **Gulzar** (recipient of Padma Bhushan, Dadasaheb Phalke, five National Film Awards & Sahitya Akademi award), *Garam Hawa* (1974) by **M.S. Sathyu**, *Ghatashraddha* (1977) in Kannada by **Girish Kasaravalli,** *Godhuli* (1977), by **B.V. Karanth**, were some other parallel films of the 70s.

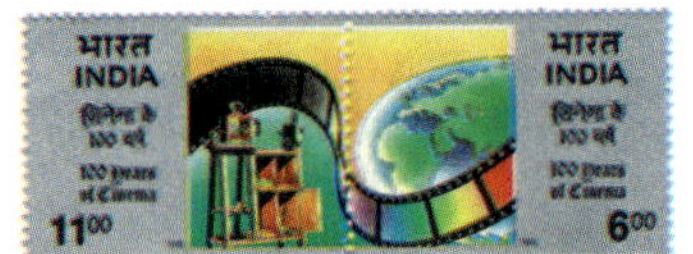

By this period, another genre of movies had emanated which tended to strike a balance between the art and the entertainment world. The critics christened them as the **'Middle Cinema'**. **Rishikesh Mukherjee** (recipient of Padma Bhushan, Dadasaheb Phalke & eight National Film Awards) is said to be a pioneer of this genre. His movies like *Anari* (1959), *Anupama* (1964), *Majhli Didi* (1967), *Aashirwaad* (1968), *Anand* (1971), *Bawarchi* (1972), *Abhimaan* (1973), *Namak Haraam* (1973), *Chupke Chupke* (1975), *Gol Maal* (1979), *Khubsoorat* (1980) besides others, were not only successful commercially but succinctly bring out the changing ethos of the Indian middle class. They also endeavoured to reflect the societal value systems while incorporating the flavours of humour, emotions and drama. *Pyaasa* (1957), by **Guru Dutt** is another acclaimed movie of this category, which blurred the delineation between the art and entertainment cinema. **Basu Chatterjee** was another master of this school. His movies *Rajnigandha* (1974), *Chhoti Si Baat* (1975), *Chitchor* (1976), *Khatta Meetha* (1977), *Baton Baton Mein* (1979), *Chameli ki Shaadi* (1986), were light hearted takes on the middle-class issues and values.

Coming to the 80s, many other eminent filmmakers have also directed notable films of this genre. This includes directors like **Adoor Gopalakrishnan** (*Elippathyam* in 1982; Malayalam), **M.S. Sathyu, Girish Karnard, P. Lankesh** (*Ellindalo Bandavaru* in 1980, Kannada) **Govind Nihalani** (*Aakrosh* in 1980, *Ardha-satya* in 1983, *Party* in 1984, *Tamas in* 1988), **Sai Paranjpayee** (*Sparsh* in 1980), **Aparna Sen** (*36 Chowringhee Lane* in 1981), **Kundan Shah** (*Jaane Bhi Do Yaron* in 1983), **Shyam Benegal** (*Mandi* in1983), **Shekhar Kapoor** (*Masoom* in 1983), **Mahesh Bhatt** (*Arth* in 1982, *Saaransh* in1984), **Basu Chatterjee** (*Ek Ruka Hua Faisla* in 1986), **Gautam Ghosh** (*Paar* in 1984), **G. Aravindan** (*Chidambaram* in 1985, Malayalam), **Ketan Mehta** (*Bhavani Bhavai* in 1980 in Gujarati; *Mirch Masala* in 1987), **Vijaya Mehta** (*Pestonjee* in1988), **Mira Nair** (*Salaam Bombay* in 1988), **Buddhadeb Dasgupta** (*Bagh Bahadur* in1989), **Saeed Akhtar Mirza** (*Albert Pinto Ko Gussa Kyon Aata Hai* in 1980, *Mohan Joshi Hazir Ho* in 1984, *Saleem Langde Par Maat Ro*, *Naseem* in 1995).

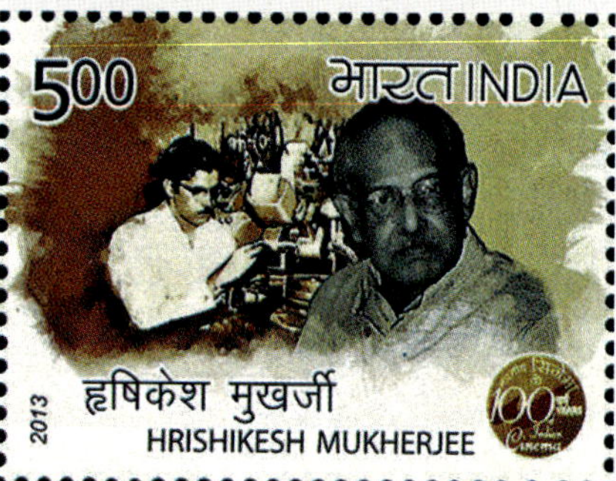

22.37: Hrishikesh Mukherjee, a master of the 'Middle Cinema'; a commemorative stamp of 2013 — Courtesy, Department of Post

However, by the 80s the divide between the parallel and the popular cinema became sharper. Not many parallel movies of this period could be called a large commercial success or became as popular as the mainstream movies, although they would win critical acclaim. By the end of the 1980s, the decline in parallel cinema had also begun.

In the 1990s, the focus was on popular entertainment and by the mid-90s there was a perceptible decline in parallel cinema. One of the primary reasons for this was the rising cost of film making and the lesser returns on the so-called art movies, which did not have the same market value as the popular films. Although the formation of the National Film Development Council (NFDC) by the Government of India in 1975 had helped this category of films to secure the necessary finance for their production, the sustenance of this movement also required returns on the production. However, the channels of distribution and theatrical display of movies did not have any separate arrangement for the movies of the art-world. This was particularly true for the India of 90s, beset with the growing economy and changing values. The opening of the economy and the shifting of social focus and taste of the masses in 1990s and 2000s brought a shift to the movies of popular entertainment. The commerce of parallel cinema started becoming unviable, resulting in amalgamation of the social themes with entertainment, and heralding the decline of this distinct genre of movies. Although the 90s did witness some art movies like *Ek Doctor Ki Maut* (1990) by **Tapan Sinha**, *Mathilukal* (1990) by **Adoor Gopalakrishnan**, *Sooraj Ka Satwa Ghoda* (1992) and *Mammo* by **Shyam Benegal**, *Rudaali* (1993) by **Kalpana Lajmi,** but their heydays were clearly behind.

The new millennium did witness a spurt in some of the movies which had greater substance and were not merely of the pulp entertainment category. These were not exactly the art movies of the 60s and 70s and were dubbed as the **offbeat cinema**. They included the elements of social realism as well as entertainment. Thus, social realism or parallel cinema as a distinct stream of movies did not flourish in this period either, but its clone as an offbeat movie can be said to have found a place in the cinematographic landscape of the country. Among the reputed directors of this genre in the period can be recounted **Rituparno Ghosh** (*Utsab* in 2000), **Aparna Sen** (*Mr and Mrs. Aiyer* in 2002), **Deepa Mehta** (*Water* in 2004), **Mani Ratnam** (*Yuva* in 2004), **Sudhir Mishra** (*Hazaar Khwahishen Aisi* in 2005), **Jahnu Barua** (*Maine Gandhi ko Nahin Mara* in 2005) **Anurag Kashyap** (*Black Friday* in 2004, *Dev D* in 2009), **Revathi** (*Mitr My Friend* in 2002, *Phir Milenge* in 2004), **Amol Palekar** (*Anahat* in 2003), **Manish Jha** (*Mathruboomi* in 2003), **Nagesh Kuknoor** (*Iqbaal* in 2006), **Bhavan Talwar** (*Dharm* in 2007), **Kiran Rao** (*Dhobi Ghat* in 2010), besides others.

With the increasing exposure to the world cinema in the 2020s, the taste of the audience is again witnessing a change and the demand of movies with greater substance is surely on the up. With OTT and Web providing a newer platform for the movies, cinema has a space even for the niche audience and the experimental director. Irrespective of the terminology to describe them, a greater hope lies for the productions dabbling with social realism.

The decade of the 80s witnessed the emergence of India as the largest film production centre, and earning its major centre, Bombay (now Mumbai) the epithet of 'Bollywood'. The decade made a beginning with commercially hit movies unleashing the new **wave of disco**. *Qurbani* (1980), which featured songs of the pop sensation Nazia Hasan and music by Biddu, and *Disco Dancer* (1982), with songs of Bappi Lahiri became big hits. The songs of *Disco Dancer* garnered immense international popularity in the Soviet Union, Middle East, Turkey and Africa. Even in China, its songs enjoyed great appeal. Many later movies tended to emulate this successful formula of masala and disco beats. But the genre which dominated the commercial films in the entire decade was that of **action and romance**. This was the recipe of some of the biggest hit movies and their success meant that more would toe the line.

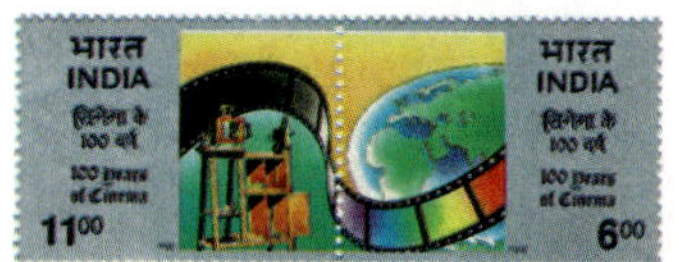

While many commercially successful movies like *Shaan* (1980), *Dostana* (1980), *Laawaris* (1981), *Naseeb* (1981), *Rocky* (1981), *Vidhata* (1982), *Shakti* (1982), *Meri Zung* (1985), *Karma*, (1986), *Aakhri Raasta* (1986), *Tezaab* (1988) and *Shahenshah* (1988), were action oriented, the love-romance and musical category also saw some noteworthy movies in *Ek Duje Ke Liye* (1981), *Chashme Baddoor* (1981), *Love Story* (1981), *Qayamat Se Qayamat Tak* (1988), *Chandni* (1989) and *Maine Pyaar Kiya* (1989). There were occasional mixes of action, romance and comedy such as *Namak Halal* (1982), *Mr India* (1987) and others. But by and large, the commercial cinema of the 80s lacked the variety and innovativeness which the other decades came up with.

Critics have often lamented at the decade of 80s for its stereotyped movies and falling standard of music. This was typical of the late 80s which was also besieged with the rise in home video viewership, video piracy and a relentless decline in the theatre footfall, a trend which continued in the early 90s. However, the early 80s did come up with new genre of movies and some memorable middle cinemas such as *Sparsh* (1980), *Khubsoorat* (1980), *Chashme Baddoor* (1981), *Katha* (1982) *Masoom* (1983) *Saath Saath* (1982), *Jaane Bhi Do Yaaron* (1983), *Kissi Se Na Kahna* (1983) *Jhoothi* (1985). Besides, several acclaimed art movies were also produced like *Aakrosh* (1980), *Albert Pinto Ko Gussa Kyon Aata Hai* (1980), *36 Chowringhe Lane*(1981), *Ardh Satya* (1983), *Mandi* (1983), *Paar* (1984), *Mohan Joshi Hazir Ho* (1984), besides some others.

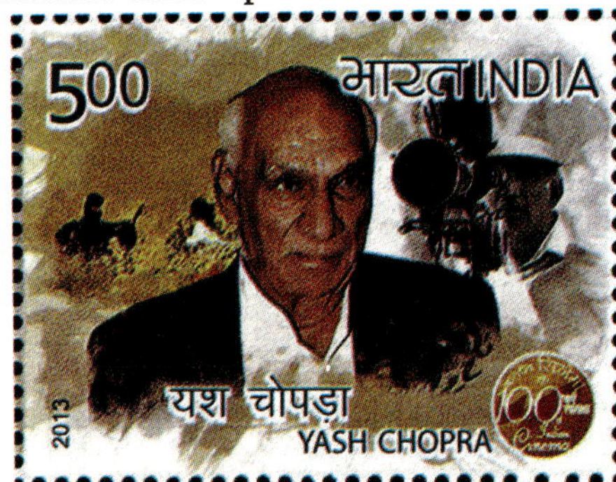

22.38: Yash Chopra, (recipient of Padma Bhushan, Dadasaheb Phalke and National award). One of the most successful directors of popular movies of the 60s, 70s & 80s with mega hits such as *Waqt, Deewar, Trishul, Kabhie Kabhie, Chandni* etc — Courtesy, Department of Post

Like every decade, a new set of actors sprung on the silver screen, while the older generation continued to hold its own. Among the newbies of the 80s were **Raj Babbar** (*Insaaf Ka Tarazu* 1980, *Umrao Jaan* in 1981, *Nikaah* in 1982), **Kamal Haasan** (*Ek Duje Ke Liye* in 1981), **Jackie Shroff** (*Hero* in 1983, *Karma* in 1986, *Ram Lakhan* in 1989), **Sunny Deol** (*Betab* in 1982, *Sultanat* in 1986, *Chaalbaaz* in 1989), **Sanjay Dutt** (*Rocky* in 1981, *Naam* in 1986), **Kumar Gaurav** (*Love Story* in 1981), **Anil Kapoor** (*Mashaal* in 1984, *Karma* in 1986, *Mr India* in 1987, *Tezaab* in 1988, *Ram Lakhan* in 1989) and **Aamir Khan** (*Qayamat Se Qayamat Tak* in 1988, *Raakh* in 1989) besides some others.

Among the most successful actresses of this decade were **Sridevi** (*Solva Sawan* in 1979, *Himmatwala* in 1983, *Tohfa* in 1984, *Aakhri Raasta* in 1986, *Mr India* in 1987 & *Chandni* in 1989) and **Jaya Prada** (*Sargam* in 1979, *Mawalli* in 1982, *Tohfa* in 1984, *Sharaabi* in 1984, *Aakhri Raasta* in 1986). Sridevi (recipient of Padma Shri) was hailed as the **first female superstar** of Bollywood and whose acting skills and presence in a movie itself could woo the crowds. Jaya Prada has been considered as one of the most beautiful faces of Indian cinema and was also acclaimed for her acting talent. **Madhuri Dikshit** (recipient of Padma Shri) and **Juhi Chawla** were two new actresses who debuted in the latter half of 1980s and were highly successful in the coming decade as well. Madhuri, with blockbusters such as *Tezaab* (1988), *Ram Lakhan* (1988), *Tridev* (1989), *Dil* (1990), *Beta* (1992), *Hum Apke Hain Kaun* (1994), *Dil to Pagal Hai* (1997) was another commercially bankable female superstar of the late 80s and 90s. She was also acclaimed for her acting in movies like *Parinda* (1989), *Dil* (1990), *Anjaam* (1994), *Pukar* (2000), *Lajja* (2001) and *Devdas* (2002). Among other stars of this period were Meenaskhi Sheshadri, Mandakini and others.

Owing to the wave of the parallel cinema which was strong in the 70s and early 80s, a number of versatile **character actors** emerged in the movie world. Many of these eminent actors were also the product of the **National School of Drama (NSD)** and the **Film and Television Institute (FTTI),** formed in the earlier decades. Among this school of actors and actresses were the likes of **Naseeruddin Shah** (recipient of Padma Bhushan & three National Film Awards), **Om Puri** (recipient of Padma Shri & two National Film Awards), **Saeed Jaffrey** (Padma Shri awardee), **Farookh Sheikh** (recipient of National Film Award), **Anupam Kher** (recipient of Padma Bhushan, two National Film Awards), **Pankaj Kapoor** (recipient of National Film Award), **Kulbhushan Kharbanda, Satish Kaushik, Satish Shah, Nana Patekar** (recipient of Padma Shri & three National Film Awards), **Smita Patil** (recipient of Padma Shri & two National Film Awards), **Shabana Azmi** (Padma Bhushan & recipient of five National Film Awards for best actress), **Deepti Naval**, **Neena Gupta** (recipient of National Film Award), besides others. Many of these artists were also a part of mainstream cinema, a trend which became further accentuated as the art movies gradually withered in the late 80s and early 90s.

Naseeruddin Shah is an acclaimed character actor of this period who has made a mark in the parallel as well as the mainstream film genres with movies such as *Nishant* (1975), *Aakrosh* (1980), *Sparsh* (1980), *Albert Pinto ko Gussa Kyon Aata Hai* (1980), *Mandi* (1983), *Ardh Satya* (1983), *Jaane Bhi Do Yaaron* (1983), *Masoom* (1983) *Jalwa* (1987), *Mirch Masala* (1987), *Tridev* (1989), besides others. **Anupam Kher** is another versatile actor known for his performance in films like *Saaransh* (1984), *Karma* (1986), *Pestonjee* (1988), *Ram Lakhan* (1989), and *Daddy* (1989), besides others. **Smita Patil** and **Shabana**

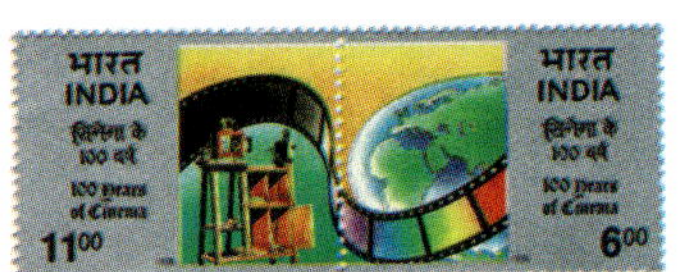

Azmi were both versatile stage and film actresses. They have acted in movies of similar genre in the same period, and at times, in the same movies; *Arth* (1982) and *Mandi* (1983). Highly accomplished and critically acclaimed, they were also successful in the mainstream movies, viz. *Shakti* (1982), *Namak Halal* (1982), *Amrit* (1986) of Smita Patil and *Amar Akbar Anthony* (1977), *Parvarish* (1977), and *Avatar* (1984) of Shabana Azmi.

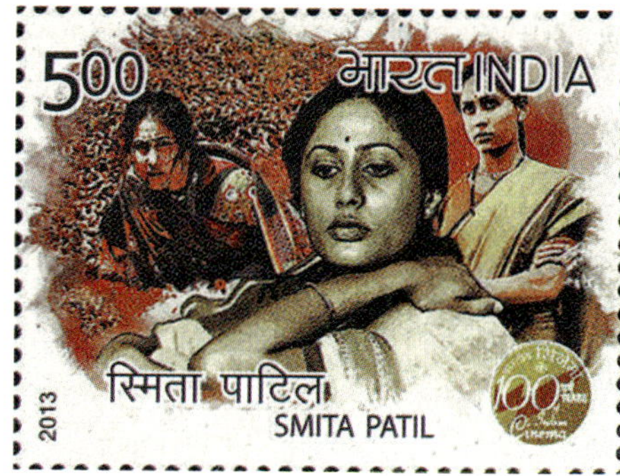

22.39: Smita Patil, a versatile actress of the parallel and commercial movies, stamp 1983 — Courtesy, Department of Post

In the late 70s and early 80s, another legendary actor and iconic villain burst into the film world. **Amrish Puri** made a rather late entry in movies (he was in his 40s) with films such as *Ankur* (1974) and *Manthan* (1976). But it was only in his 50s that he got the major roles as a villain in movies such as *Hum Paanch* (1980), *Vidhata* (1982), *Shakti* (1982), and *Hero* (1983). In his oeuvre of nearly 400 movies, his most famous role as a villain was that as *Mogambo* in *Mr. India* (1987). Among other acclaimed villains and character actors of this decade and early 90s were **Kader Khan** and **Shakti Kapoor** who also enthralled the audience with their comic roles. Besides, Gulshan Grover and Sadashiv Amrapurkar also made their mark as character actors and in villainous roles.

The Decade of the 90s

The **early 90s** did not change the theme of Bollywood movies or its fortunes substantially. Rather, the audience which was moving away from theatres due to the onslaught of home videos, got another means of entertainment in the form of satellite TV, which further accentuated the falling revenue of movie theatres. With economic liberalisation and greater connect with the world, the Indian audience was perhaps looking for new genres and themes. However, Bollywood continued to routinely churn out those which were based on action and romance. Some romantic musicals like *Dil* (1990), *Dil Hai ki Manta Nahin* (1991) and *Saajan* (1991), however did commercially well, along with a few action genres such as *Agneepath* (1990), *Ghayal* (1990) and *Hum* (1991). Anti-hero movies such as *Baazigaar* (1993) and *Darr* (1993), a novelty for Bollywood then, followed suit and brought some succour to the struggling industry. However, it was the success of *Hum Apke Hain Kaun* (1994), a family entertainment drama cum musical, seeped in the Indian value system, which attracted the family audience back to the theatres and in a way marked a turning point for the fortunes of Bollywood.

Another change witnessed in the 90s was in the background of the movies which had substantially changed to an urban setting from the rural landscape of the 60s and 70s. Perhaps, with greater economic prosperity and a burgeoning urban-middle class, there was a change in the aspirations and celluloid tastes of the people. This was also a reflection of the changing socio-economic demographic profile of the country. But the era of 90s is perhaps best remembered for the romantic musicals which followed in the latter half of the decade. It included mega hits like *Dilwale Dulhaniya Le Jayenge* (1995), *Dil To Pagal Hai* (1997), *Pardes* (1997), *Kuch Kuch Hota Hai* (1998) and *Hum Dil De Chuke Sanam* (1999). In the late 90s, came a completely different genre of movies which was dark and eclectic. Referred to as the **Mumbai Noir/ Bombay Noir**, it portrayed the city's dangerous underworld. *Satya* (1998), a harbinger of this trend was followed in the coming decades with movies such as *Company* (2002), *Black Friday* (2004) and others.

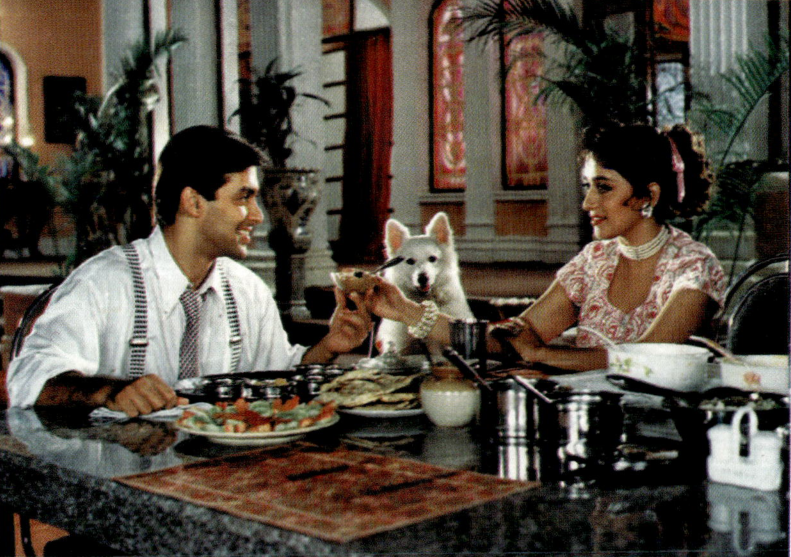

22.40: *Hum Apke Hain Kaun* (1994), a family entertainment drama which brought the waning family audience back to the theatres in the 1990s — Courtesy, NFDC-National Film Archives of India, (Pune)

From the perspective of the successful actors of the decade, the films of the 90s were largely dominated by the **Khans.** This included the troika of **Aamir Khan**, **Salman Khan**, and **Shahrukh Khan** whose popularity and dominance

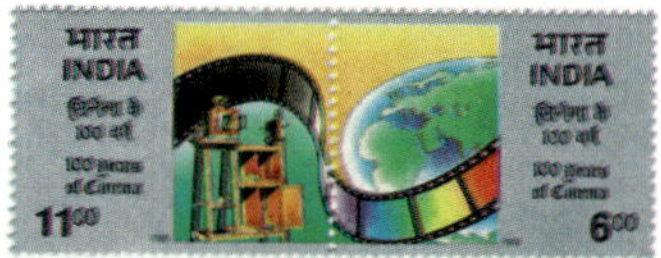

continued even in the next two decades. **Govinda** was another successful star of this phase with a series of action-comedy movies such as *Raja Babu* (1994), *Coolie no.*1 (1995), *Hero no.1* (1997), *Dulhe Raja* (1998). **Akshay Kumar** (recipient of National Film Award) with his series of *Khiladi* movies which included *Khiladi* (1992), *Main Khiladi Tu Anari* (1994), *Sabse Bada Khiladi* (1995), and *Khiladiyon ka Khiladi* (1996) was also a successful star. But his best was to follow in the subsequent decades with a diverse array of hit movies under his belt. **Ajay Devgan (**recipient of Padma Shri & four National Film Awards) was another successful and acclaimed actor, who drew appreciation for popular as well as critical works. **Saif Ali Khan** (recipient of Padma Shri & National Film Award), Sunil Shetty, Bobby Deol, Akshay Khanna, were some other male leads of this period. Among the popular and acclaimed character actors and villains of this decade was **Paresh Rawal** (recipient of Padma Shri & two National Film Awards) who also dabbled with comedy and different shades of characters in the coming years. **Manoj Bajpayee** (recipient of Padma Shri & three National Film Awards) was another acclaimed actor who debuted in this period and made a mark as a male lead and a character actor in the movies of subsequent decades.

Among the successful actresses of this decade were Madhuri Dixit (recipient of Padma Shri), Juhi Chawla, Manisha Koirala Pooja Bhatt, Shilpa Shetty, Tabu, Sonali Bendre, Karishma Kapoor, Raveena Tandon, Urmila Matondkar, Kajol, Rani Mukherjee, Aishwarya Rai (recipient of Padma Shri award), and Mahima Chaudhary. **Tabu** (recipient of Padma Shri & two National Film Awards), **Raveena Tandon** (recipient of Padma Shri & National Film Award), **Kajol** (recipient of Padma Shri), **Karishma Kapoor** (recipient of National Film Award) and **Rani Mukherjee,** are among the actresses of this period acclaimed for their acting skills.

The New Millennium Movies

In the new millennium, Indian movies moved from strength to strength, be it in terms of the volume of production or the quality of movies. A salient feature of Indian cinema in this period was its burgeoning **international appeal**. With their commercial distribution reaching as many as 90 countries, and the popularity of Indian films and stars soaring in the foreign markets, Indian movies had their best international presence. The large Indian diaspora abroad also fuelled the international demand. Further, with the films getting the status of industry in 2001, enabling better finance and other incentives, the export of Indian films picked up substantially. Another feature of the Y2K (2000s) industry was the wide popularity of the **multiplex theatres** as compared to the larger single screen ones which had been in vogue in the previous century. The better ambience, a variety of movie options in the same multiplex, coupled with the adjoining market and entertainment options of these complexes, was a huge draw for the new millennial generation. Now the experience of watching a movie was not merely limited to the film screened, but in the offing was a larger social entertainment which was associated with the malls and multiplexes screening them. This altered the very nature of the audience; the nature of the movies being demanded and in turn ushering a change in the Indian movie culture.

The **nature of movies** during this phase also witnessed a palpable change. These were marked with better story lines, improved special effects, technological and cinematographic innovation etc. which were in consonance with the changing taste of the Indian audiences as well as the international demand. The genre of Indian movies too showed significant diversification and evolution. *Lagaan* (2001), a musical drama based on the colonial history and the game of cricket, was off the beaten path, but proved to be a huge commercial success. It earned critical acclaim and international awards, including a nomination at the Academy Awards (Oscars). *Iqbal* (2005), the story of a deaf and mute boy's zeal to become a cricketer and play for India; *Chakde* (2007) (which was based on the Indian women's hockey team success), *Bhaag Milkha Bhaag* (2013), the story of the Olympic sprinter Milkha Singh; *Dangal* (2016), a story about the success of the wrestler Geeta Phogat and *Gold* (2018), which traces the story of the independent India's first hockey team's success in the 1948 Olympics, were some other hit movies of the **sports genre**. The newer movies also experimented with newer themes such as the **Shakespearean trilogy** by Vishal Bhardwaj of *Maqbool* (2003), *Omkara* (2006) and *Haider* (2014). *Black* (2005), a story of a deaf, mute and blind girl, *Taare Zameen Par* (2007) a story of a dyslexic child, and *Paa* (2009), a story of a child suffering from progeria, (a rare disease), were some commercially successful movies centred on the theme of **medical ailments** of its protagonist.

A Wedenesday (2008), *Peepli Live* (2010), *Ship of Theseus* (2012), *Lunchbox* (2013), *Queen* (2013), *PK* (2014), *Piku* (2015) were some other movies which did not tread the run of the mill route of action and romance and yet were acclaimed by the audience as well as by the critiques. Some other notable successful movies of this category which carved a niche of their own were *Swades* (2004) which dwelled on the conflict between the love for the country and allure of promising foreign career; *Rang De Basanti* (2006), which centred on the patriotic fervour of a young generation of friends and their fight against government corruption, *Khosla Ka Ghosla* (2008), a comedy drama which highlighted the illegal usurpation of property by land mafia; *Rock On* (2008), a musical drama about the life of the friends of a rock band; *Three Idiots*

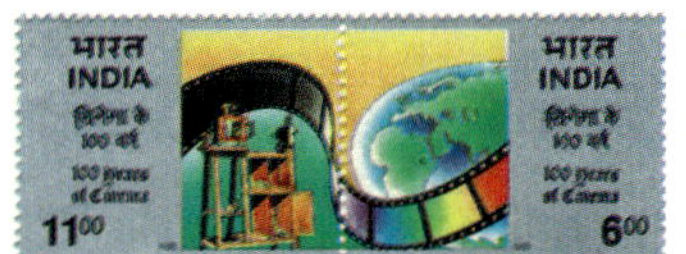

(2009) which was based on the theme of pursuance of excellence rather than the conventional success; *Zindagi Na Milegi Dobara* (2011) a comedy drama tracing the adventures of three childhood friends who reunite over a three-week road trip; *Paan Singh Tomar* (2012), the story of an armyman turned sportsman who turned a rebel dacoit; *Barfi* (2012) a romantic comedy of a deaf and mute boy and his relationship with two young girls; *OMG* (2012), a comedy drama which is satirical of the religious ritualism and dogma; *Jolly LLB* (2013), the story of fight of an advocate to seek justice for victims of an accident, *Gully Boy* (2019), a musical drama which narrated the success story of a street rapper, amongnst others. All came up with novel themes and narratives.

Another notable category of mainstream movies which emerged commercially successful was those which drew inspiration from **historical characters and backdrop.** These included *Ashoka* (2001), *Jodhaa Akbar* (2008), *Bajirao Mastani* (2015), *Padmavaat* (2018), *Manikarnika: The Queen of Jhansi* (2019), *Tanhaji: The Unsung Warrior* (2020) besides some others. The **love and romance** genre too were quite popular and included blockbusters such as *Kaho Na Pyaar Hai* (2000), *Dil Chahta Hai* (2001), *Tere Naam* (2003), *Veer Zara* (2004), *Fanaa* (2006), *Tanu Weds Manu* (2011), *Rockstar* (2011) and others. **Action and crime thrillers,** a legacy of the previous decades, continued to enjoy popularity with productions such as *Kaante* (2002), *Kaminey* (2009), *Gangs of Wasseypur* (2012), *Drishyam* (2015) and *Andhadhun* (2018). Besides, **thriller dramas** were also produced, which included some successful and acclaimed works such as *Black Friday* (2004), *Kahaani* (2012), *Highway* (2014) and others.

Many **comedies** were also in vogue in these decades including *Hera Pheri* (2000), *Munna Bhai* MBBS (2003), *Golmaal; Fun Unlimited* (2006), *Malaamal Weekly* (2006), *Phir Hera Pheri* (2006), *Dhamaal* (2007), *Bheja Fry* (2007), *Housefull* (2010), *Delhi Belly* (2011), *Badhaai Ho* (2018), *Total Dhamaal* (2019), *Doctor G* (2022) besides others. Drama, action cum romance, political thrillers, horror and masala were some other categories of movies churned out in this period. But unlike the earlier decades, the trend of conventional art or parallel cinema as a separate genre with a distinct set of directors and actors specialising in it, had largely waned. Movies with offbeat themes, or those depicting social realism, were largely integrated with the mainstream commercial cinema, with actors straddling across them.

Among the emerging mainstream actors of this generation were; Hrithik Roshan, Abhishek Bachchan, John Abraham (recipient of National Film Award), Arjun Rampal (recipient of National Film Award), Shahid Kapoor, Ranbir Kapoor, Abhay Deol, Farhan Akhtar (recipient of National Film Award), Ranveer Singh, Arjun Kapoor, Siddharth Malhotra, Vicky Kaushal (recipient of National Film Award), Varun Dhawan, Sushant Singh Rajput, Tiger Shroff, besides others. The eminent actresses of the new millennium include Kareena Kapoor, Priyanka Chopra (recipient of Padma Shri and National Film Award), Katrina Kaif, Vidya Balan (recipient of Padma Shri and National Film Award), Deepika Padukone, Kangana Ranaut (recipient of Padma Shri & four National Film Awards), Anushka Sharma, Sonam Kapoor and Sonakshi Sinha. Among the newer generation, some of the popular actresses are Parineeta Chopra (recipient of National Film Award), Alia Bhatt, Shraddha Kapoor, Taapsee Pannu, Disha Patani and Bhoomi Pednekar.

The diverse genre of movies also encouraged the growth of a bountiful crop of character actors. Some acclaimed character actors of this period were, Boman Irani, Rajat Kapoor, Arshad Warsi, Kay Kay Menon, **Irrfan Khan** (recipient of Padma Shri and National Film Award), Konkona Sen Sharma (recipient of National Film Award), Radhika Apte, Kalki Kochelin (recipient of National Film Award), Ayushman Khurana (recipient of National Film Award), Nawazuddin Siddiqui (recipient of National Film Award), besides others. A notable feature and a marked departure from the previous several decades, was the absence of any new actor who specialised exclusively in the villainous roles. Many a time, it was the character actors who undertook the negative roles, while occasionally it was the mainstream heroes who donned this mantle. Some of the offbeat films were even altogether bereft of villainous roles.

With the Indian movies coming of age, it also opened the gates for many successful actors of previous generations who were now cast as character actors in several movies. Many roles were specially written for them and even centred on them, a trend starkly different from the 80s and 90s, where the younger generation actors ruled the roost in the action-romance or masala movies. With diverse and more mature storylines, many actors of the earlier generations rediscovered their magic touch and some even made a comeback in the industry. This trend also tapped many facets of the acting talents of these actors which were hitherto limited to stereotype roles.

Amitabh Bachchan scripted a new innings of his career with critically acclaimed acting in movies such as *Mohabbatein* (2000), *Aankhen* (2002), *Kaante* (2002), *Baghbaan* (2003), *Sarkar* (2005), *Black* (2005), *Cheeni Kum* (2007), *Paa* (2009), *Rann* (2010), *Aarakshan* (2011), *Piku* (2015), *Pink* (2016), *102 Not Out* (2018), *Gulabo Sitabo* (2020) and others. Another actor who did a makeover of his acting repertoire was **Rishi Kapoor** with movies such as *Namastey London* (2007), *Do Dooni Chaar* (2010), *Agneepath* (2012), *D-Day* (2013), *Kapoor and Sons* (2016), *Mulk* (2018), *102 Not Out* (2018), *Sharma Ji Namkeen* (2022) etc. Some other actors

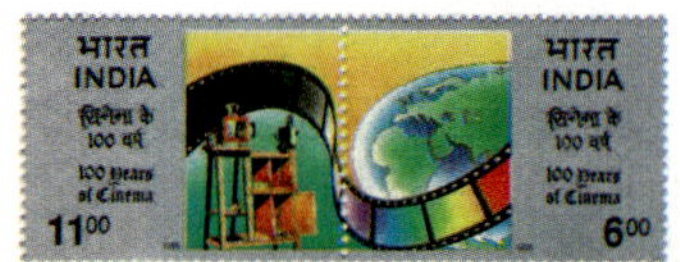

in this category were, **Hema Malini** in *Baghbaan* (2003), *Baabul* (2006), *Buddha Hoga Tera Baap* (2011), *Ek Thi Rani Aisi Bhi* (2017), **Jaya Bachchan** in *Fiza* (2000), *Kabhi Khushi Kabhi Gham* (2001), *Kal Ho Na Ho* (2003), *Laaga Chunari Mein Daag* (2007), **Dimple Kapadia** in *Leela* (2002), *Pyaar Mein Twist* (2005), *Being Cyrus* (2005),Cocktail (2012), *Finding Fanny* (2014), **Rekha** in *Lajja* (2001), *Krish* (2006), *Yatra* (2007), *Super Nani* (2014), **Sridevi** in *English Vinglish* (2012), *Mom* (2017), **Madhuri Dikshit** in *Gaja Gamini* (2000), *Lajja* (2001), *Devdas* (2002), *Aaja Nachle* (2007), *Dedh Ishqiya* (2014), *Kalank* (2019), besides others.

With newer platforms of cinematographic expression emerging in the second decade of the 21st century which included the web-based services and 'over the top' (OTT) platform, Indian movies witnessed a definite generational shift in the nature of movies being demanded and the quality of cinema being produced. International movies came closer to the Indian audience even in the smaller towns and villages. For viewers, spoilt for choice from a bevy of world movies, substandard Bollywood productions, or even those with passable standard, would cut no ice. Further, Indian regional cinema not only emerged strong, but also proved to be a tough competitor for Bollywood. Newer content, innovative themes, strong storylines and cinematographic quality were not only desirable, but also essential for the mainstream movies to survive. Thus, the new millennium witnessed Indian movies evolving and reaching higher peaks of cinematographic expression.

THE REGIONAL CINEMA

With as many as 22 constitutionally recognised languages, nearly 1369 dialects, rich literary and diverse folk traditions, India is a *potpourri* of different regional cultures. This is truly reflected in the Indian regional film industry which has evolved alongside the mainstream Hindi movies (Bollywood) over the past 100 years. Today, it is a flourishing industry with films in as many as **25 regional languages** (besides Hindi and English) and nearly 1500 films produced in it (as of 2019).

Among the regional film industries, the most prolific in terms of the number of movies produced and the revenue generated are the South Indian films which include Telugu, Tamil, Kannada and Malyalam films. These are followed by the Bengali, Marathi, Bhojpuri and Gujarati films. With the dubbing of movies, multi-language productions and OTT, the regional movies now have a reach to national as well as international audience, particularly to Southeast Asia, Middle East and other parts of the world where there is presence of the Indian diaspora.

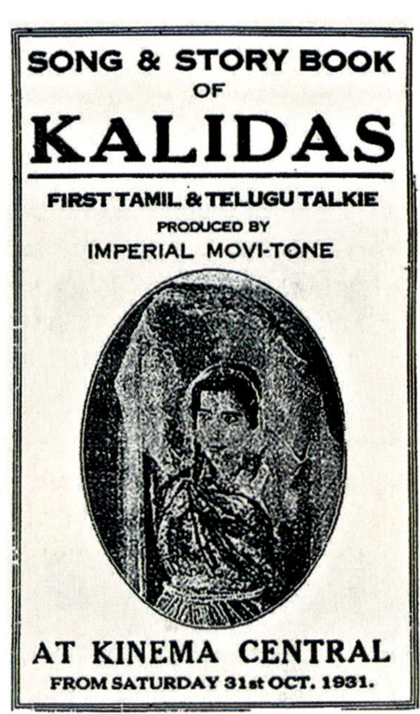

22.41: The song and story book of *Kalidasa*, the first regional Tamil-Telugu talkie film — Wikimedia Commons

In the last few decades, the four southern film industries have shown tremendous growth. These have extended their distributorship and viewership not only in the neighbouring states where they were earlier centred, but also pan India. In the 2020s, the southern film industry grew by leaps and bounds. As per a CII report published in 2023, while the Indian film revenue from all sources was pegged at Rs. 15,000 crore in the year 2022, it comprised Rs. 7,836 crore from the southern film industries itself. Clearly the regional cinema, and in particular the Southern movies, have given mainstream Bollywood a run for its money. With national and international acclaim and awards to many of the regional movies, particularly the south, it can be said unequivocally that regional Indian cinema has well and truly arrived.

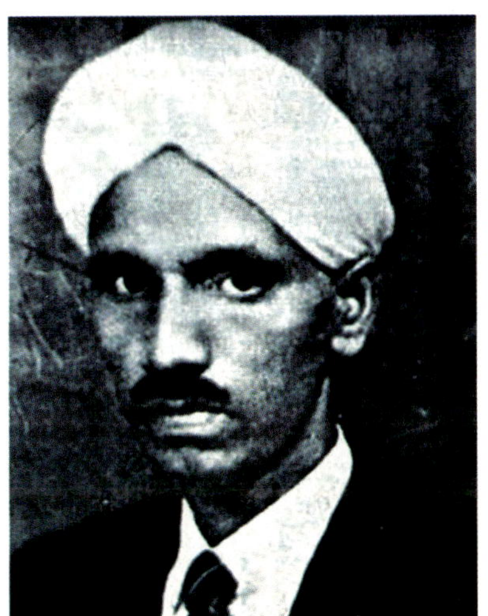

22.42: R. Nataraja Mudaliar, earliest pioneer of Tamil cinema and maker of the first regional movie *Keechaka Vadham* (1917-1918) — Wikimedia Commons

The Early Regional Language Films: *Shree Pundalik*, a Marathi film of the silent era made in 1912 was the earliest of the regional movies. Made by **R.G. Torney** and **N.G. Chitre**, *Shree Pundalik*, however, was in the nature of a recording of a play. Besides, it was a not a complete Indian effort either as it was recorded by a British cameraman and the film processed in London. As such, *Keechaka Vadham* produced in 1917-1918 by **R. Nataraja Mudaliar** in Tamil is considered the

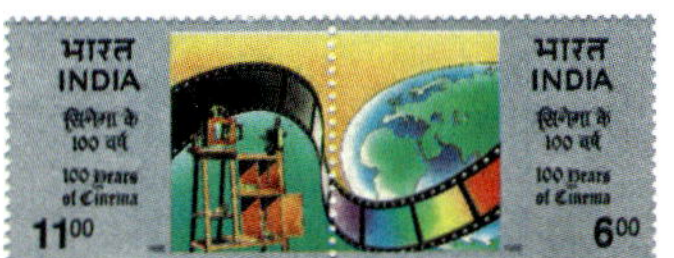

first regional language cinema of India. *Bhishma Pratigyna* (1921) produced by **Raghupati Venkaiah Naidu** was the first Telugu film, while *Vigathakumaran* (1928) **by J.C. Daniel** was the first Malayalam movie of the silent era.

In the era of the talkies after *Alam Ara* was produced in 1931, Ardeshar Irani also produced *Kalidas*, a bilingual Tamil-Telugu movie in 1931. Closely following it was the Marathi movie *Ayodhyecha Raja* (1932) produced by **Shantaram Rajaram Vankudre** (V. Shantaram), which was based on the story of Raja Harishchandra. Another regional talkie of this period was *Sati Savitri*, a Telugu film produced by **C. Pullayya** in 1933. *Joymoti* produced in 1935 by **Jyotiprasad Agarwalla,** was among the earliest of Assamese movies.

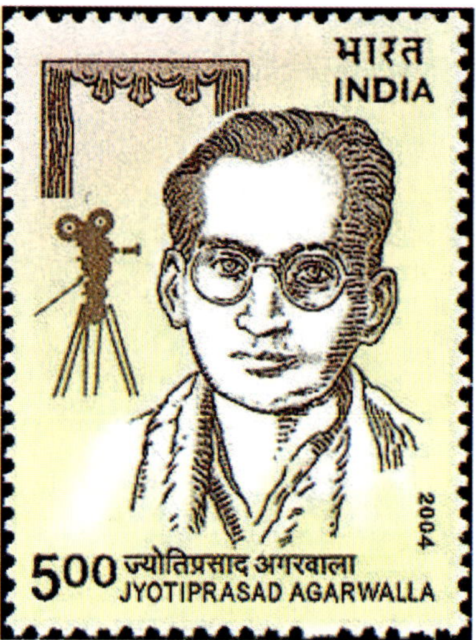

22.43: Jyotiprasad Agarwalla, playwright, songwriter and one of the earliest Assamese and regional movie filmakers; stamp image — Courtesy, Department of Post

Over a period of time, each centre of production has developed and displayed a certain characteristic of its own with which the industry has been identifiable, particularly in certain phases of its evolution. The Bengali movies displayed an unmatched mastery of the craft with some of the greatest of directors like Satyajit Ray, Mrinal Sen, Tapan Sinha, Ritwik Ghatak, Debaki Bose, Gautam Ghosh, Buddhadev Dasgupta, Aparna Sen, Rituparno Ghosh and others. In the decades of 50s to 90s, they engendered and sustained the beautiful world of parallel cinema. Malayalam and Kannada cinema followed suit in the 70s to 90s and crafted masterpieces with eminent directors like Adoor Gopalakrishnan (Malayalam), M.T. Vasudevan Nair (Malayalam), G. Aravindan (Malayalam), Shaji N. Karun (Malayalam), Pattabhirama Reddy, B.V. Karanth (Kannada), Girish Kasaravalli (Kannada) besides others. In the new millennium, the Telugu and Tamil industry has been identified with some grand tales and some masterly movies in the works of directors such as Mani Ratnam (Tamil), Kamal Haasan (Tamil), S.S. Rajamouli (Telugu) and Sukumar (Telugu). Other regional movies too have seen some acclaimed filmmakers/directors such as Prahlad Keshav Atre (Marathi), Jahnu Barua (Assamese) beside others.

Although the regional industries have crafted an identity of their own, yet there have been many interchanges and crossovers with the mainstream Hindi cinema. Tapan Sinha, Mrinal Sen and Rituparno Ghosh were some of the masters who successfully ventured in the Hindi film world as well. Many stars of Bollywood had their career debut in the regional film industries or continued to act in them even after attaining stardom in the Hindi movies. The list includes the likes of Vyjayanthimala, Sharmila Tagore, Hema Malini, Rekha, Jaya Prada, Sri devi. Some stars like Rajnikanth, Kamal Haasan, Chiranjeevi, Venkatesh and others have also made successful forays in the world of Hindi movies. Many other mainstream Bollywood actors/ actresses have also acted in the regional movies, particularly in the Southern movies. Remake of successful Hindi movies into regional ones and vice-versa has also occurred many a times. Of late, a trend of releasing of movies with subtitles/dubbing into different languages and with multi language sound track has also become popular. Thus, these different industries which largely existed in silos are now showing increasing interconnect and influence on each other while also competing with each other.

Bengali Cinema

Among the earliest of the regional film industry, and at one time the very hub of Indian film production, Bengali cinema is a vibrant centre of Indian movies, which has been churning out critically acclaimed and popular films over the period of last century. With many eminent directors like **Satyajit Ray, Tapan Sinha, Mrinal Sen, Debaki Bose, Ritwik Ghatak, Aparna Sen, Gautam Ghoshe, Buddhadev Dasgupta, Rituparno Ghosh** and others producing masterly works, Bengali cinema has led from the forefront in the world of art and parallel cinema. In the process, it has earned national acclaim and international fame for the Indian films.

As a production centre of movies, Bengali cinema has led from the front and has truly been an industry pioneer, bringing to Indian Cinema the earliest of the filmmkers like Hiralal Sen, and film companies like Madan Theatres. The development of a flourishing cinema in the Tollygunge area of Calcutta inspired the colloquial name of Tollywood which was given by an American cinematographer-writer (Wilfred E Deming) in 1932. The name remained etched in the annals of film making, and in subsequent decades it further led to christening of similar names like Kollywood (Tamil), Mollywood (Malayalam), Tollywood (Telugu), Sandalwood (Kannada) etc.

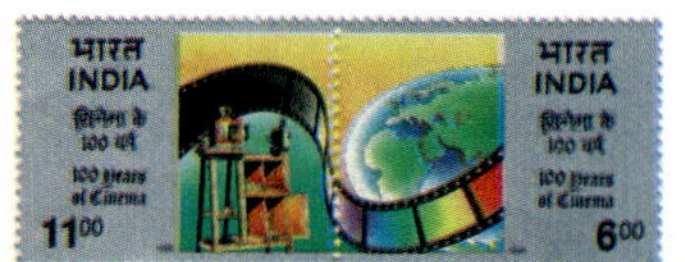

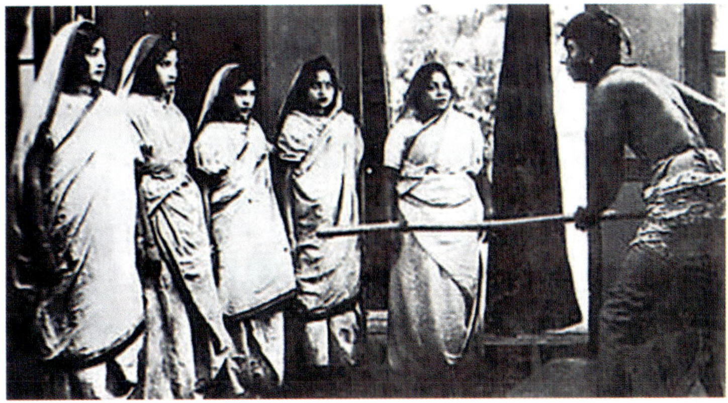

22.44: A scene from *Dena Paona* (1931), the first Bengali talkie — Wikimedia Commons

Bengali cinema, which in later decades became an epicentre of realism in cinema, has singularly bagged **20 National Film Awards for the best Indian film** in the 68 years of the awards (till 2020 National Film Awards). This is the maximum by any regional industry and exceeds even that of the Hindi films (12 awards of best national film). It also garnered several international awards for movies such as *Pather Panchali* of Satyajit Ray (award at Cannes, Berlin and Venice Film Festivals in 1956) and *Parashuram* and *Khariji* of Mrinal Sen (awards at Berlin Film festival in 1979 and Cannes Film festival in 1983 respectively), besides others. Bengali cinema has carved a niche of excellence in the world of movies.

The early phase of Bengali cinema

The **first Bengali movie** was a silent film called *Bilwamangal* (1919). Directed by **Rustomji Dhotiwala,** the film was produced under the banner of *Madan Theatres*. By this period several prominent film companies had come up in Calcutta (now Kolkata), which included the famous *The Royal Bioscope Company* of Hiralal Sen which was founded in 1898 for display of bioscopes in theatres. Besides, there were the *Indo British Film Company* (1918) which was a Bengali owned company, and the *Madan Theatre Productions*. Even before the era of full-length silent films, Bengal had seen several short length films made by **Hiralal Sen**. This included the likes of a recording of the theatrical performance of the play *Alibaba and the Forty Thieves*, a documentation of the 'Bengal anti partition demonstration' (which took place in the town hall in Kolkata on 22nd September 1905). Besides, he is also credited with making two advertising short films, the very first of such films in India.

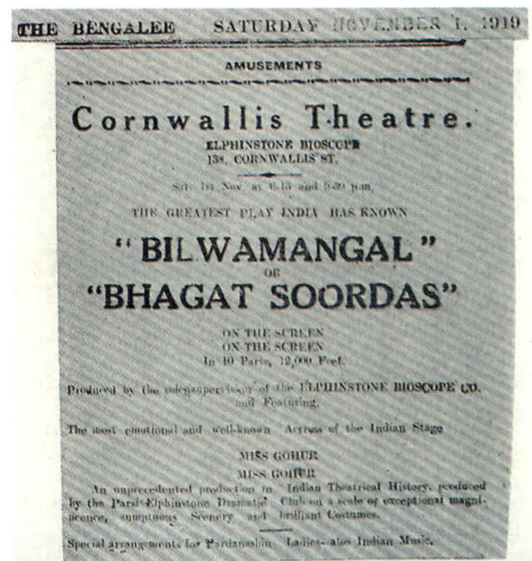

THE BENGALEE SATURDAY NOVEMBER 1, 1919

AMUSEMENTS

Cornwallis Theatre.

ELPHINSTONE BIOSCOPE
138, CORNWALLIS ST.

THE GREATEST PLAY INDIA HAS KNOWN

"BILWAMANGAL"
OR
"BHAGAT SOORDAS"

ON THE SCREEN
ON THE SCREEN

MISS GOHUR
MISS GOHUR

22.45: A paper cutting of *Bilwamangal*, the first silent Bengali cinema of 1919 — Wikimedia Commons

In the **era of the talkies,** *Jamai Shashthi* was the first Bengali venture (a short length film). It was produced under *Madan Theatre Productions* in 1931. This was in the same year as the release of *Alam Ara*. Another Bengali talkie *Dena Paona* (full length film), was released later in December 1931. This movie was produced by *New Theatre Calcutta* which was founded in 1931 by **Birendranath Sircar** (recipient of Padma Bhushan & Dadasaheb Phalke award). Sircar was among the most eminent of the film producers of this period and produced successful movies like *Natir Puja* (1932), *Chandidas* (1932), *Devdas* (1935), besides others. A number of talkies followed in the 30s and 40s with actors like Dhirendranath Ganguly, Pramathesh Barua and Debaki Bose. They were also among the most prominent of film personalities in the early Bengali cinema who later directed many acclaimed movies. Other noteworthy actors of this period include Bhanu Bandhopadhyay (sr.), Amar Chowdhury, Ahindra Chowdhury, besides others.

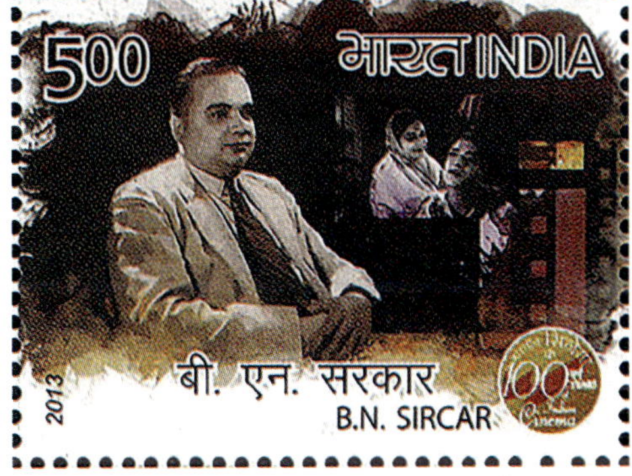

22.46: Birendranath Sircar, one of the early film producers of Bengali cinema; stamp image — Courtesy, Department of Post

Dhirendranath Ganguly (recipient of Padma Bhushan & Dadasaheb Phalke Award) was an eminent actor, director and producer who also established several film companies. He is also considered as the founder of the Bengali cinema. **Pramathesh Barua** directed the iconic movie *Devdas* (1935) which was based on the novel by Sarat Chandra. In this movie, he himself played the central role. His other successful films include *Maya* (I & II) in 1936, *Devdas* in Hindi (1936), *Devdas* in Assamese (1937), *Mukti* (1937), *Adhikar* (1938) and others. **Debaki Bose** (recipient of Padma Shri) directed some celebrated movies of the time as well, which

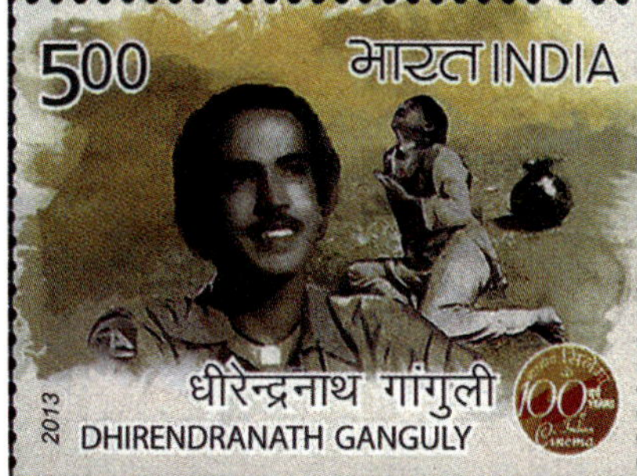

22.47: Dhirendranath Ganguly considered as the founder of Bengali cinema; stamp image — Couresy, Department of Post

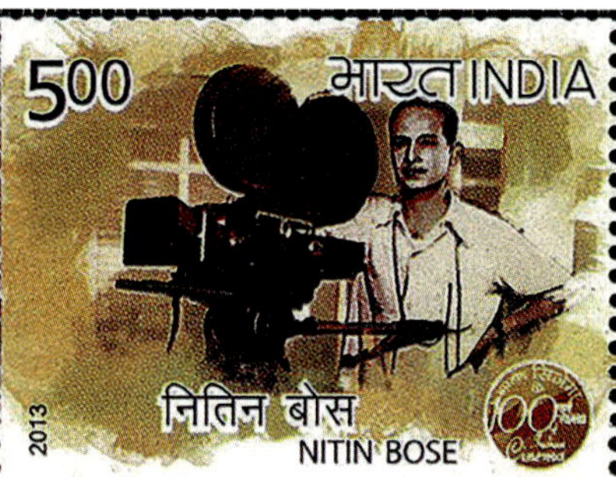

22.48: Nitin Bose, among the early directors of Bengali cinema; stamp image — Courtesy, Department of Post

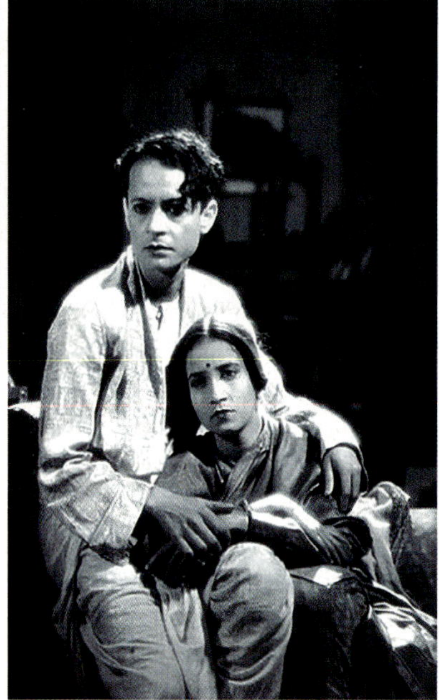

22.49: Pramathesh Barua and Jamuna Barua, early stars of Bengali cinema; a scene from *Devdas* (1935: Bengali) — Wikimedia Commons

include *Geeta* (1934), and others. *Sagar Sangamey* (1959), directed by him won the National Film Award for the best Indian film. **Nitin Bose** (recipient of Dadasaheb Phalke award) was another notable film director of this period whose movie *Bhagya Chakra* (1935) was the first to introduce **playback singing** in the Bengali film industry. Among the leading ladies of this phase were **Kanan Devi** (recipient of Dadasaheb Phalke award), a singer and actor, considered the first lady of Bengali cinema; **Chandrabati Devi,** who acted in the cult movie *Devdas* (1935); **Sumitra Devi,** considered among the most popular actresses of 1940s; **Sandhya Rani** who acted in nearly 250 Bengali movies; besides **Sadhana Bose**, **Umasashi**, **Padmadevi**, **Chhaya Devi**, **Jamuna Barua** and others.

The golden phase of Bengali cinema

The period of 1950 and extending till mid 70s is often considered as a golden phase of Bengali cinema. It ushered a wave of realism and modernist cinema also referred as the 'New Wave Cinema of Eastern India'. *Pather Panchali* in 1955 (winner of National Film Award for best Indian film) of **Satyajit Ray** (recipient of Bharat Ratna & Dadasaheb Phalke award) was a landmark film of this age for Bengali as well as Indian cinema. This was followed by his other two films of 'Apu Trilogy' viz. *Aparajito* (1956) and *The World of Apu* (1959). The films won three National Film Awards, besides seven awards at the Cannes, Berlin and Venice film festivals. **Tapan Sinha** (Padma Shri) was another veteran film maker, who was known for his diverse genre of movies in a career straddling six decades. He also won two National film awards for the best Indian film, for the movies *Kabuliwala* (1956) and *Hatey Bazarey* (1967). His other noteworthy movies include *Louha Kapat* (1957), *Kshudita Pashan* (1960), *Apanjan* (1968) and popular Hindi movies like *Sagina Mahato* (1970), children's movie *Safed Haathi* (1978) and *Ek Doctor ki Maut* (1990).

Mrinal Sen (recipient of Padma Bhushan & Dadasaheb Phalke Award) was another pre-eminent film maker of the legendary quartet comprising Satyajit Ray, Tapan Sinha, Ritwik Ghatak and himself. His movies were awarded a staggering eighteen National Film Awards in different categories including the best Indian films for *Bhuvan Shome* in Hindi (1969), *Chorus* in Bengali (1974), *Mrigayaa* in Hindi (1976), *Akaler Shandhaney* in Bengali (1980). *Bhuvan Shome* is also considered a landmark movie for ushering a 'New Wave' cinema movement in India. Sen also received international critical acclaim with awards at the three prestigious international film festivals of Cannes, Venice and Berlin.

Ritwik Ghatak (recipient of Padma Shri), the fourth of these eminent filmmakers, was known for his films depicting social realism. Besides, he also took up the issue of feminism in his movies. His acclaimed movie *Meghe Dhaka Tara* (1960), succinctly depicted the issue of partition of Bengal post the partition of India, and its aftermath. *Jukti Tako Aar Gapo* (1974), another of his films, won the National Film Awards for the best story. In recent times, many of his movies have evoked interest for their resemblance to popular international movies. This includes *Ajantrik* (1958), having likeness to the Herbie films (1967-2005) and *Bari Theke Paliye* (1958), having resemblance to François Truffaut's *The 400 Blows* (1959).

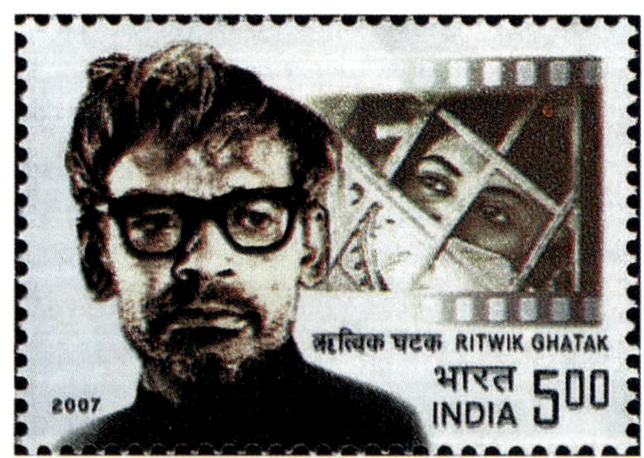

22.50: Ritwik Ghatak, one of the stalwarts of the golden phase of Bengali cinema, a stamp from 2007 — Courtesy, Department of Post

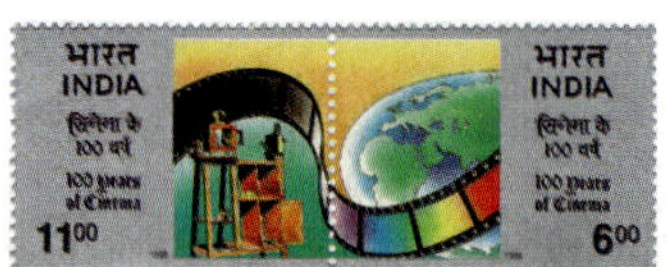

Some other acclaimed movies of this phase include *Jalsaghar* (1958) and *Devi* (1960) by **Satyajit Ray**; *Neel Akasher Neeche* (1958), *Punascha* (1961), *Aakash Kusum* (1965) by **Mrinal Sen**; *Jatu Griha* (1963), *Aarohi* (1964) by **Tapan Sinha**; *Komal Gandhar* (1961) and *Subarnarekha* (1962) by **Ritwik Ghatak**, *Harano Sur* (1958), *Saptapadi* (1961), *Saat Paake Bandha* (1963), by **Ajoy Kar**; *Sagar Sangamey* (1958) by **Debaki Bose**; *Dada Thakur* (1962) by **Sudhir Mukherjee** and *Uttara Falguni* (1963) by **Asit Sen**, besides others.

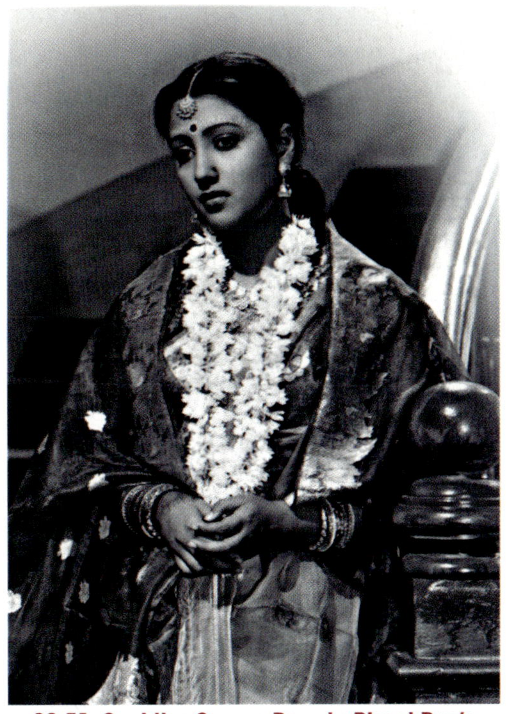

22.51: Suchitra Sen as Paro in Bimal Roy's *Devdas* (1955) — Wikimedia Commons

In the decade of the 50s and 60s, beyond the world of art movies, the popular Bengali movies also flourished. However, they witnessed a definite departure from the social conformist movies of the previous decade. The 50s brought in a 'new popular modern', wave of movies. A predominant genre of this wave was the romances, apart from drama, comedy and thrillers. Depicting this romantic genre were the lead couple and stalwarts of Bengali cinema, **Uttam Kumar** and **Suchitra Sen** (recipient of Padma Shri). Among their popular movies were *Sharey Chuattor* (1953), *Agni Pariksha* (1954), *Sabar Uparey*(1955), *Shap Mochan* (1955), *Sagarika* (1956), *Harano Sur* (1957), *Indrani* (1958), *Chaowa Pawa* (1959), *Bipasha* (1962), *Uttar Falguni* (1963) besides others. Both Uttam Kumar and Suchitra Sen were highly acclaimed actors, won many awards, and were among the most popular Bengali actors ever.

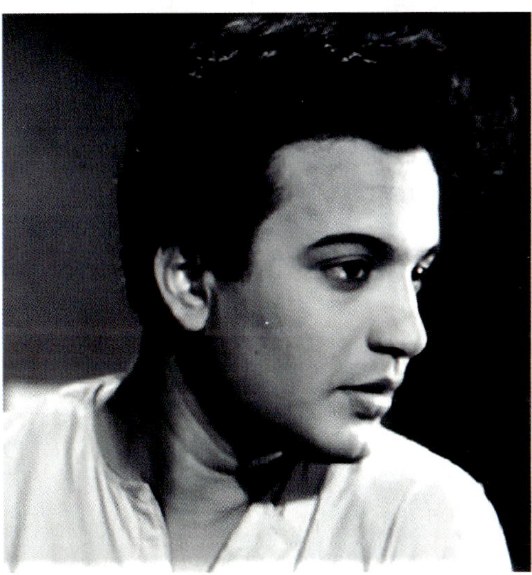

22.52: Uttam Kumar, a celebrated actor of popular Bengali cinema; a still from the movie *Indrani* (1958) — Wikimedia Commons

Soumitra Chatterjee (recipient of Padma Bhushan & Dadasaheb Phalke award) was another veteran of Bengali movies who is also acclaimed as among the greatest of Indian cine-actors. Starting with *Apur Sansar,* he acted in as many as 14 movies of Satyajit Ray. Besides, he also worked with all the leading directors of the Bengali films of that period. He was also conferred '*Commandeur' of Ordre des Arts et des Lettres* (1999), the highest award of artists in France; besides the Highest Civilian award of France, *Commandeur de la Légion d' Honneur (2017)*. **Utpal Dutt** (recipient of National Film Award for best actor), an eminent character actor who acted in nearly 100 movies in four decades was another versatile actor of Bengali cinema. He was equally popular in Hindi movies as well. **Bhanu Bandopadhyay**, **Anup Kumar** and **Rabi Ghosh,** were some other notable cine-artists who made their mark as comic actors.

Among the actresses of Bengali cinema, **Sabitri Chatterjee** (recipient of Padma Shri) was one of the leading ladies of the 50s. In a career spanning six decades, she acted with the prominent actors and in the movies of the celebrated directors of the industry. **Aparna Sen** (recipient of Padma Shri), was a popular star of the 60s, who later also made her mark as an eminent director. In a career of several decades, she received as many as nine National Film Awards in different categories. **Sharmila Tagore** (Padma Bhushan & recipient of National Film Award for best actor award) was a prominent actress who acted in many of Satyajit Ray movies (*The World of Apu* (1959), *Devi* (1960), *Nayak* (1966), *Seema Baddha* (1967) and *Aranyer Dinratri* (1970). She was also the leading star of Bollywood in the 60s and early 70s. Some other notable actresses of this period include **Madhavi Mukherjee,** a recipient of National Film Award for best actress, who also acted in many of Ray's movies, **Sabitri Chatterjee** (recipient of Padma Shri), **Karuna Banerjee**, **Sandhya Roy, Supriya Devi, Debashree Roy** (recipients of National Film Award) and others. Besides, many other actresses like **Jaya Bhaduri**, **Moushumi Chatterjee** and **Rakhee**, who worked initially in Bengali movies, went to become prominent Bollywood cine-stars.

The **period of 70s**, specially the first half of the decade, continued with the momentum of the 50s and 60s. *Seemabaddha* (1971) by Satyajit Ray and *Chorus* (1974) by Mrinal Sen were the winners of the

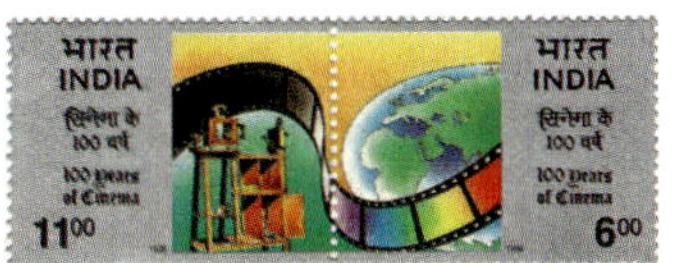

National Film Award for the best Indian feature film. Mrinal Sen displayed his magical touch again with *Mrigayaa* (1976) in Hindi and *Akaler Shandhaney* (1980) which was bestowed the best film award once more. Among other acclaimed movies in this period were *Malyadan* (1971) by Ajoy Kar, *Ek Je Chillo Desh* (1974) by Tapan Sinha, *Nimantran* (1972) by **Tarun Majumdar** (recipient of Padma Shri) all of which won the National Film Award for best feature film in Bengali in their respective years. *Sonar Kella* (1974) by Satyajit Ray, another movie which won the National award was based on Ray's eponymous novel which brings to life Ray's creation, the famous detective Feluda.

Satyajit Ray: A Wizard of Cinematographic Expression

A colossal of Indian cinema and reckoned as among the greats of world film makers, Satyajit Ray was indeed an institution of cinematographic expression. With his very first directorial venture *Pather Panchali* winning him national and international acclaim, including the inaugural Best Human Document Award at the Cannes Film Festival (1955), Ray etched his name in the annals of film making for ages to come. His movies explored social realism and presented them in a manner as never before. His cinematography and nuanced presentation, imbued in subtle yet deep rooted messages, which were the soul of his creativity, transformed his movies from a mass media to a sculpted work of art.

Ray, who started in the advertising industry, took to film making, inspired by the works of masters of neo-realism in world cinema. His first venture *Pather Panchali* (an adaptation of an eponymous work of the Bengali writer Bibhutibhushan Bandopadhyay) was made on a shoestring budget with a non-professional crew. The movie had to be completed in several stints due to paucity of funds. He himself did the scripting, editing, casting and scoring, besides designing his own credit lines and publicity material. And yet he came up with a work which finds mention in the list of all-time great movies.

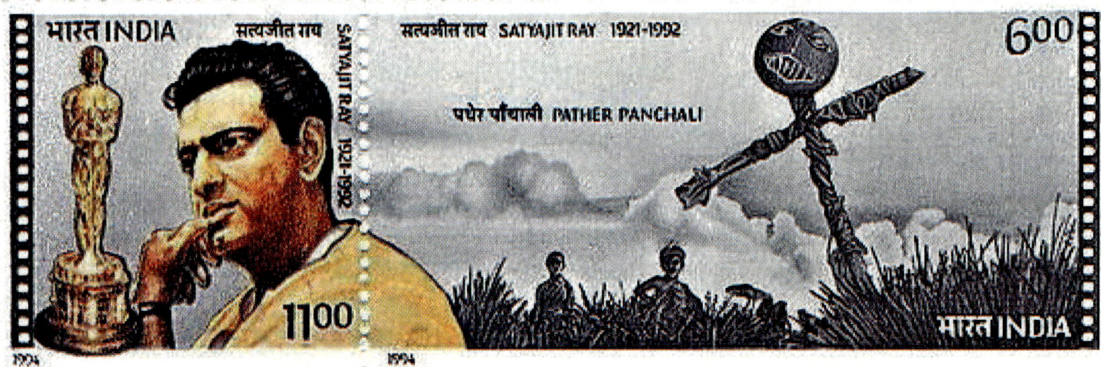

22.53: Satyajit Ray, on a stamp set from 1994, with a scene from his first movie *Pather Panchali* depicted on the stamp on the right; stamp images — Courtesy, Department of Post

The **Apu Trilogy** (*Pather Panchali* in1955; *Aparajito* in 1956 and *Apur Sansar* in 1959) captures the life of a boy in a poor family of rural Bengal; his transition to adulthood and migration to the bustling city of Calcutta. Indeed, it is a story of millions across societies, of their hopes and aspirations. It is also the story of the transition in the social demography and of the villages being lost to the cities. Among his next set of movies were *Jalsaghar* (1958), which depicts the hardships of a landlord who has fallen on bad times in a decaying zamindari system and his endeavour to maintain a façade of well-being. *Teen Kanya* (1960), based upon short stories of Tagore has three women as central characters in three different stories, and *Devi* (1961), brings out the fallout when faith decays to superstition. The latter also decries the limited space available to women in a patriarchal society.

Charulata (1964), one of the favourites of Ray, is another woman-oriented movie, which explores the feelings of Charulata caught in a monotonous conjugal life. The work is based on a novel by Tagore titled *Nastanirh*. Another set of movies of Ray, called the Calcutta Trilogy comprises *Pratidwandi* (1970), *Seemabadha* (1971) and *Jana Aranya* (1975). Based on different novels, these were social dramas, and bring out the influences of modern city life, the rat-race, the culture of greed, the economic challenges of middle class, besides other social issues. Thus, Ray's works bring out the issues of society in a setting of realism. He also attempts to create a social consciousness, but in a highly nuanced manner. His works also transcended different genres as seen from the comedy and light hearted ones such as *Gopee Gyne Bagha Byne* (1969) and *Hirak Rajar Deshe* (1980) which are musical fantasies involving the characters *Gopee* and *Bagha*. Ray, as an author, created the famous detective Feluda. Two of his movies *Sonar Kella* (1974) and *Jai Baba Felunath* (1979) were based on his *Feluda* novels. Another of his literary creation was *Professor Shanku,* a scientist. However, these works were largely in the genre of children's and young adult literature but which also fascinated the larger audience.

Among his other acclaimed movies were; *Ashani Sanket* (1973), his first movie, in colour, *Shatranj Ke Khiladi* (1978), the only full-length Hindi movie of Ray, *Ghaire Baire* (1984), a romantic drama, *Ganashatru* (1990), a social drama highlighting corruption in society and *Agantuk* (1992), the last of Ray's films.

In his cinematic career of nearly 40 years, Ray made 36 movies, including feature films, documentaries and other shorter films. He received 36 National Film Awards, the Dadasaheb Phalke Award, several international awards including those at Cannes, Berlin, Venice film and Moscow film festivals. In 1992, he was also bestowed an Academy Honorary Award. He has also received an honorary doctorate from Oxford university. The Lifetime Achievement Award at the International Film Festival of India is instituted in the name of Ray. He was honoured in 1987 with 'The Commander of the Legion of Honour', the highest order of merit of France, and in 1992 he was conferred the **'Bharat Ratna'**, the highest civilian honour of India.

The **period of the 80s** is generally reckoned by critics to have experienced a dip in the quality of Bengali films. The genre of realism and the class of movies which had once won international acclaim for Bengali cinema had witnessed a decline. Even the popular cinema was facing a crisis, with changing industrial and social demography and the challenges posed by the increasing popularity of television and the home videos. However, there were some new filmmakers like Buddhadeb Das Gupta, Gautam Ghosh and Aparna Sen, besides the masters of the earlier decades, who kept the flag of Bengali cinema flying high.

Buddhadeb Dasgupta, an emerging film maker of the late 70s and 80s, came up with movies which were much appreciated critically. Some of his renowned works of this phase include *Dooratwa* (1978), which won the National Film Award for the best Bengali feature film, *Grihajuddha* (1982), *Andhi Gali* (1984) in Hindi and *Phera* (1988). *Bagh Bahadur* (1989), in Bengali & Hindi, another of his masterly works, brings out the hardships of rural life of Bengal and was adjudged best Indian feature film at the National Film Awards.

Another eminent filmmaker of this generation was **Goutam Ghose** whose very first movie, *Dakhal* (1981) won the National Film Award for the best Indian feature film. *Paar* (1984), in Hindi, and *Antarjali Yatra* (1987), were some of his other acclaimed movies of the decade. **Aparna Sen's** directorial debut, *36 Chowringhee Lane* was awarded the National Film Award for best direction as well as best Indian feature film in English. Her next movie *Paroma* (1984), claimed honours as the best Bengali feature film at the National Film Awards. *Sati* (1989), was another noteworthy film of hers, which explores the gender bias of society, particularly of the 19th century rural Bengal. *Ghaire Baire* (1984), and *Ganashatru* (1989), by Satyajit Ray were some other outstanding films of the decade.

The **decade of 1990s** and beyond witnessed a **revival in Bengali cinema**. One of the architects of this makeover was **Rituparno Ghosh** (1963-2013) whose very second directorial venture *Unishe April* (1994) won the National Film Award for best Indian feature film. The movie which was acclaimed critically and successful commercially, ended the drought of the niche art films amidst the flood of action and masala films in the Bengali cine industry. The movie explored the relationship of a mother and a daughter and the psyche of a woman. His later movies also delved into women-related issues as well. Among his other acclaimed films are *Dahan* (1997), based on a story of molestation of a woman; *Asukh* (1998) which explores human relationship from the perspective of a protagonist woman; *Shubho Mahurot* (2003), a thriller based on Agatha Christie's novel (*The Mirror Crack'd from Side to Side); Chokher Bali* (2003), based on a novel of the same name by Rabindranath Tagore and again centred on women; *Sab Charitro Kalpanik* (2008), takes one through the journey of a woman's self-discovery where she is caught in conjugal life with an insensitive spouse. *Abohomaan* (2009), explores the relationship of an elderly man falling in love with a young woman. All of these won the **National Film Awards for the best Bengali feature film**.

Some other of his noteworthy movies include *Bariwali* (2000), *Utsab* (2000) which won the National Film Award for best direction; *Raincoat* (2000), the winner of the **National Film Award for best feature film in Hindi**, *Antar Mahal* (2005); *The Last Lear (2007)*, which won the **National Film Award for best feature film in English**, *Noukadubi* (2011) which is inspired by Tagore's novel *Noukadubi*. The movies of Ghosh explored different facets of human relationships and very sensitively portrayed them, particularly the issues of women. His creative genius transcended the barrier of language and excelled in varied genres of movies, making him one of the most acclaimed filmmakers of the new millennium.

This period also witnessed Buddhadeb Dasgupta coming up with some commendable movies. *Charachar* (1993), *Lal Darja* (1996), *Mondo Meyer Upakhyan* (2002), *Kaalpurush* (2005), were some of his acclaimed works, all of which were adjudged the best Indian feature film winner at the National Film Awards. *Uttara* (2000), a thriller drama exploring human vices and violence in an otherwise peaceful rural Bengal, was another highly acclaimed movie of Buddhadeb Dasgupta, bringing him several international awards as well as the National Film Award for best director. *Antaheen* (2008) by **Aniruddha Roy Chowdhury** was another winner of the best Indian feature film at the National Film Awards. Aparna Sen came up with some of her best directions in this period, including *Paromitar Ek Din* (2000), *Mr and Mrs Iyer* (2002) in English, *15 Park Avenue* (2005) which won the National Film Award for Best feature Film in English, and *The Japanese Wife* (2010) in Bengali, English, Japanese, and *Goynar Baksho* (2013).

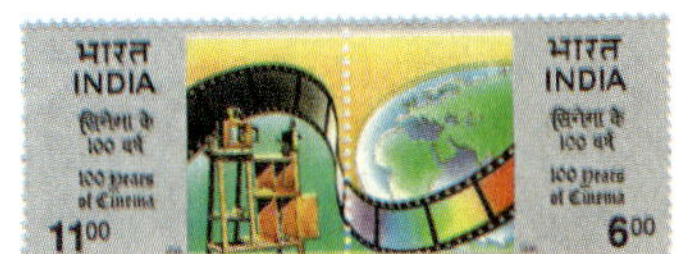

The new millennium has also seen the emergence of new Bengali directors of repute which include **Suman Ghosh** and **Subrata Sen**. Further, the work of the directors of newer generation such as **Aniruddha Roy Chowdhury**, **Shoojit Sircar**, **Srijit Mukherjee** and **Sujoy Ghosh** has also brought the world of art and commercial cinema closer. Some of the notable Bengali actors of this phase of Bengali cinema include; **Dipanker De**, **Mamta Shankar**, **Prosenjit Chatterjee**, **Anjan Dutta**, **Rupa Ganguly**, **Satabdi Roy**, **Indrani Haldar**, **Rituparna Sengupta**, **Debolina Dutta**, **Churni Ganguli**, **Jissu Sengupta**. Among the promising actors of the new millennium are Konkona Sen Sharma, Sudipta Chakraborty, Raima Sen, Paoli Dam, Anirban Bhattacharya, Ananya Chatterjee, Rahasaan Noor, Ritwick Chakraborty, Abir Chatterjee, besides others.

The Bengali cinema enjoys a unique position in the Indian film industry as the earliest of the centres where Indian cinema was nurtured and also as a harbinger of the art cinema. Its movies are steeped in realism and explore the different facets of human society and relationships. The moorings of Bengali cinema's penchant for class, perhaps lies in the cultural renaissance of Bengal, which nurtured the great masters like Tagore and Sharat Chandra and others. Their works in turn have inspired the cinema of many of the masters like Satyajit Ray and Rituparno Ghosh. With the new millennium and changing facet of the Indian movies, the cinema of Bengal too is witnessing a transition. It is regaining its sublime touch. It is witnessing the coming closer of the popular and art movies. The future of cinema of Bengal is definitely bright.

Telugu Cinema

Telugu cinema, colloquially christened as Tollywood, has been one of the most popular and flourishing regional film industries of the country. For nearly a century, its central region of influence has been the Andhra Pradesh and Telangana region and other parts of South India. However, the new millennium added another chapter to its story of growth, and it gained substantial popularity in other parts of India as well. In the 2020s, it emerged as one of the fastest growing movie industries of the country. In the year 2022, the industry saw the sales of nearly 233 million tickets, making it the **largest film industry of India in terms of the box office**. The Ramoji Film City in Hyderabad (established in 1996) with nearly 1666 acres of land and a diverse set of film production is also the **largest film studio complex in the world** and has earned a place in the **Guinness Book** of World Records. With it, the Telugu movie production has also reached new heights, especially in terms of visual effects, cinematography and other film crafts.

Although Telugu cinema has been known for some grand movies for the mass audience, many art movies like *Daasi* (1988), *Thilaadanam* (2000) and *Vanaja* (2006) have been critically acclaimed and earned international awards too. Among the most notable of Telugu films in recent times have been *Bahubali: The Beginning* (2015); *Bahubali: The Conclusion* (2017) and *RRR* (2022), epic action-drama films of **S.S. Rajamouli.** All the three movies were among the biggest of the box office grossers in India. The second of the Bahubali movie also won the **Saturn Award** (instituted by Academy of Science Fiction, Fantasy and Horror Films, USA) as the best international movie. *RRR*, another blockbuster Telugu movie won a string of awards including **Academy Award** (Oscar award) and **Golden Globe Award** (awarded for best original song) for its song *Naatu Naatu*. The latter also won the **Critics' Choice Award** (given by American-Canadian Critics Choice Association) in the category of the Best Foreign Langauge Film.

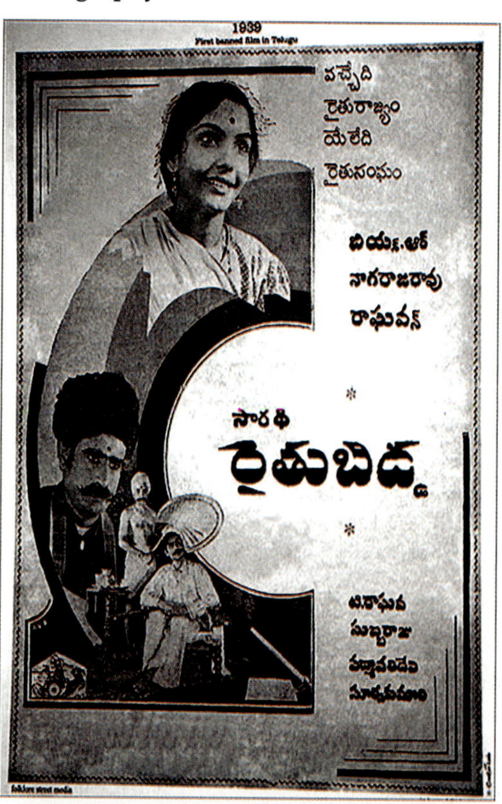

22.54: Film poster of *Raithu Bidda* (1939), an iconic social reformist Telugu movie, which was banned by the British — Wikimedia Commons

The Telugu cinema had its origin through the endeavour of the notable film maker **Raghupati Venkaiah Naidu** who was involved in making of short movies as early as 1909. Through his efforts, came the first full length Telugu silent film *Bhishma Pratigna* (in 1921) and for his pioneering contribution, he is also reckoned as the father of Telugu cinema. *Bhakta Prahlada* (1932) by **H. M Reddy** and *Sati Savitri* by **C. Pullayya** (1933) were some of the early talkie

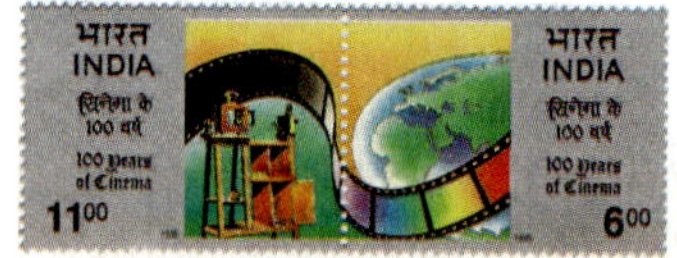

movies. In the early phase of Telugu cinema, when the industry was caught in the genre of mythological and religious themes, **Gudavalli Ramabrahmam** directed *Raithu Bidda* (1939), a much-acclaimed social reformist drama and one of the earliest of this genre.

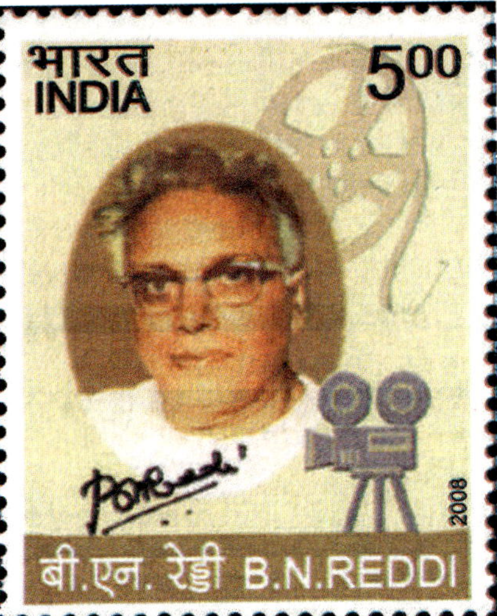

22.55: B. N. Reddi, a veteran director of Telugu films and the first film personality from southern India to be bestowed with the Dadasaheb Phalke Award; stamp image — Courtesy, Department of Post

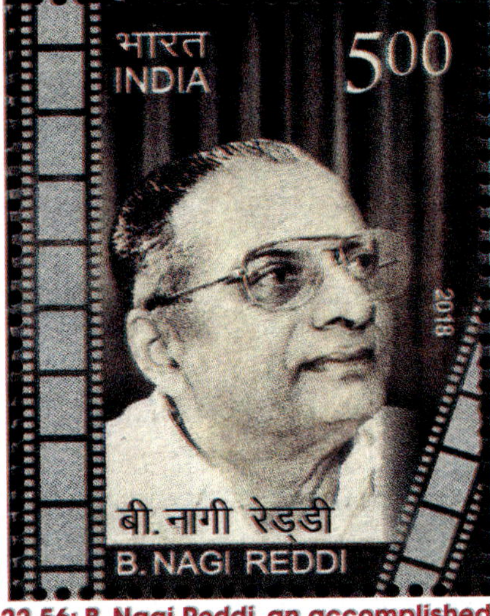

22.56: B. Nagi Reddi, an accomplished director and producer and the younger brother of B. N. Reddi, also a recipient of Dadasaheb Phalke Award; stamp image — Courtesy, Department of Post

Among the most notable of directors of this industry in the pre-independence period were **H.M. Reddy**, **B.N. Reddy** (the first recipient of Dadasaheb Phalke Award in the southern film industry) and **Gudavalli Ramabrahmam** (the director of the critically acclaimed movie *Raithu Bidda*). Among the eminent directors of the post-independence period include **K.V. Reddy** whose repertoire included films of the folk, social and fantasy genre. **L.V. Prasad** was another notable director of this generation and was the recipient of the Dadasaheb Phalke Award. Also a formidable actor, he had the unique distinction of acting in the first talkie films in three languages; *Alam Ara* (Hindi), *Kalidas* (Tamil) and *Bhakta Prahlada* (Telugu) all released in the year 1931.

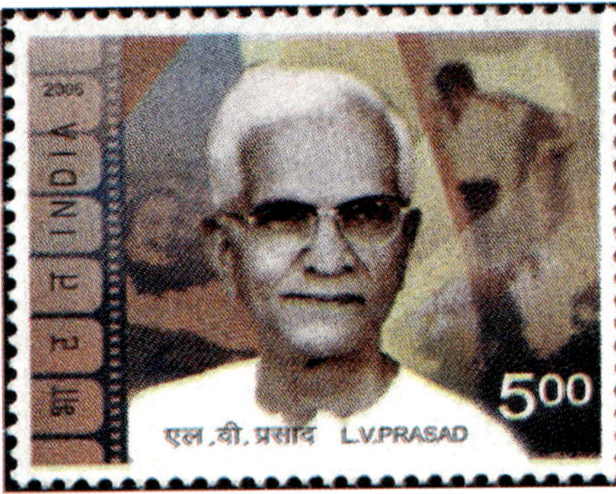

22.57: L.V. Prasad, eminent director and actor, who acted in the first talkie films of three different languages; stamp image — Courtesy, Department of Post

Some other distinguished directors active in the decade of 50s to 90s include **Ghantasala Balaramayya, B. Nagi Reddi** (recipient of the Dadasaheb Phalke Award and also producer and director), **B.A. Subbarao**; **Adurthi Subba Rao** (recipient of seven National Film Awards); **V Madhusudan Rao** (winner of National Film Award for best feature Film in Telugu in 1967); **K.Vishwanath** (recipient of Padma Shri and Dadasaheb Phalke Award); **Dasari Narayana Rao** (recipient of two National Film Awards, who directed over 150 films and a Limca Book of records holder for maximum number of movies directed), **Singeetham Srinivasa Rao**, (recipient of two National Film Awards); **Jandhyala,** (recipient of Padma Shri and National Film Awards, especially known for movies of the comedy genre); **Vamsy (**recipient of National Film Awards); **Chandraharam**, **Kamalakara Kameshwara Rao**, **(**recipient of National Film Awards) besides others.

Among the recent directors of acclaim is **S.S. Rajamouli** (director of *Bahubali* in 2015, *Bahubali-II* in 2017, *RRR* in 2022) a recipient of Padma Shri, National Film Awards and several international awards. **Sukumar** (director of *Pushpa: The Rise* in 2021, one of the Telugu blockbusters) is another distinguished director of recent times, besides others.

Telugu cinema has seen some eminent actors and stalwarts, the most noteworthy being **N.T. Rama Rao** (recipient of Padma Shri & National Film Award) popularly known as NTR. He was truly a doyen of Indian cinema and acted in over 300 movies. **Akkineni Nageswara Rao** (recipient of Padma Vibhushan and Dadasaheb Phalke Award) was another acclaimed actor of the decade of 50s and 60s. **P. Bhanumathi** (recipient of Padma Bhushan) was considered the first female superstar of Telugu cinema. **V. Nagayya** (recipient of Padma Shri), **Allu Ramalingaiah** (recipient of Padma Shri), **S.V. Ranga Rao**, **Savitri Ganesan**, **Sharada** (recipient of three National Film Awards), **Lakshmi** (recipient of National Film Award), **Chiranjeevi** (recipient of Padma Bhushan), were some of the other eminent actors/actresses of Telugu cinema in the post independence period.

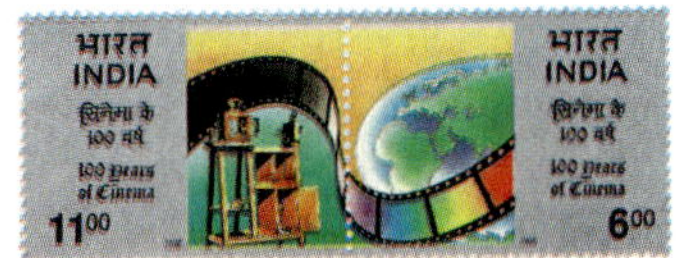

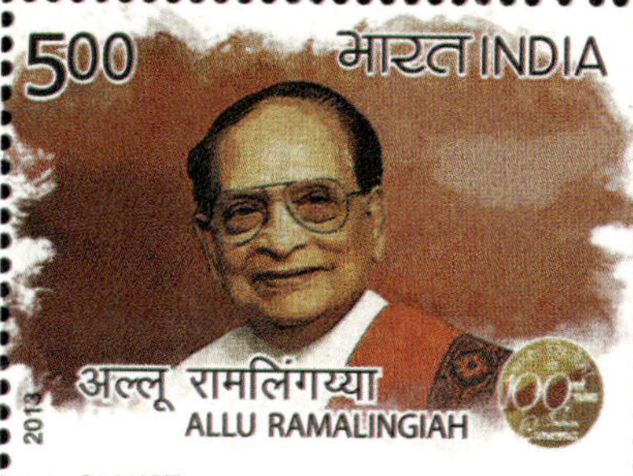

22.58: Allu Ramalingiah, a character actor, comedian and film producer of Telugu cinema — Courtesy, Department of Post

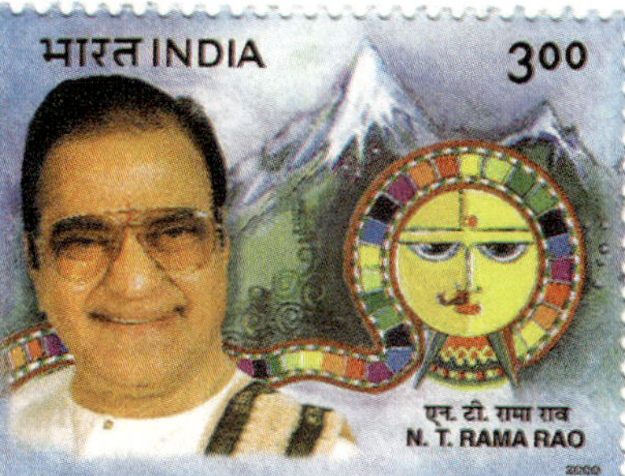

22.59: N.T. Rama Rao, a veteran Telugu actor and former Chief minister of Andhra Pradesh — Courtesy, Department of Post

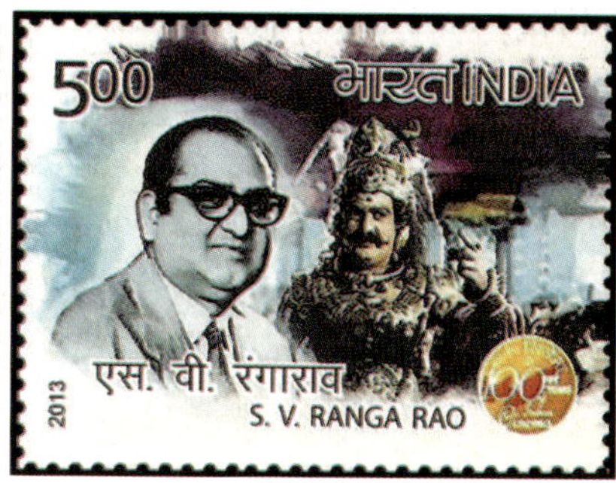

22.60: S.V. Ranga Rao, an acclaimed actor of Telugu cinema — Courtesy, Department of Post

Jaya Prada and **Sridevi** were outstanding actresses of Telugu and Tamil cinema who also gained immense popularity in Bollywood. Among the notable recent actors and actresses include **Mohan Babu** (recipient of Padma Shri) **Chiranjeevi**, **Soundarya**, **Venkatesh**, **Rambha**, **Nagarjuna**, **Mahesh Babu**, **Prabhas**, Jr. NTR, Rana Daggubati, Shruti Hassan, Samantha Ruth Prabhu, Kajal Aggarwal, Tamannah Bhatia, Anushka Shetty, besides others.

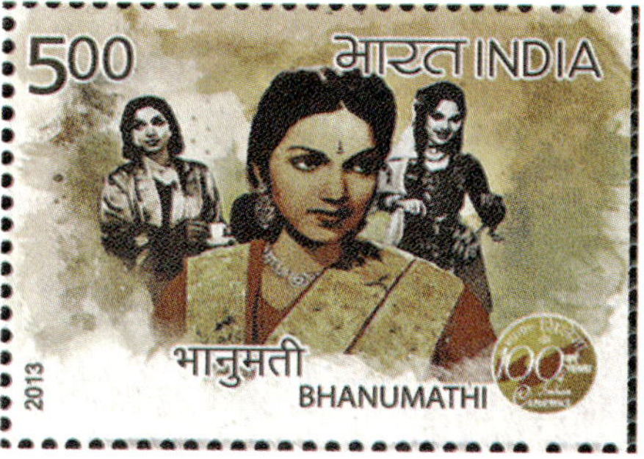

22.61: Bhanumathi, an acclaimed and popular actress of Telugu cinema; stamp image — Courtesy, Department of Post

Tamil Cinema

Tamil cinema has been one of the most important and vibrant regional film industries of the country. In the year 2022, with a revenue of around 2950 crore (followed by 2500 crore by Kannada films), it emerged as the leading regional industry of the country. Tamil movies, which earlier had their presence limited in the state of Tamil Nadu and in the adjoining states, have now a national as well as international presence. While in the past they have been known for the grand movies which catered to a mass audience, of late, Tamil cinema is also earning critical acclaim.

In the era of the silent movies, *Keechaka Vadham* (1918), directed by **R. Nataraja Mudaliar** was the first silent full-length Tamil movie to be produced. *Kalidas* (1931), directed by **H.M. Reddy** was the first Tamil-Telugu movie which came in the same year as *Alam Ara* (the first Indian talkie). By the end of the 30s itself, the movie industry centred in Kodambakkam area of Madras (now Chennai) had become a major centre of movie production. Besides Tamil cinema, it also catered to the other southern movie industries, Hindi cinema and even the Sri Lankan industry, thus becoming a de-facto capital of the southern movie industries.

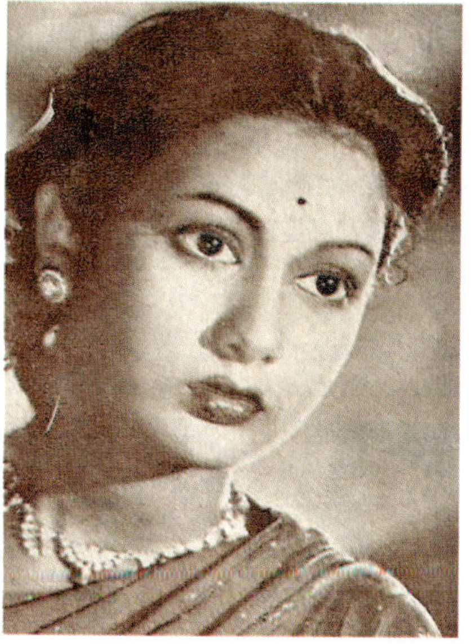

22.62: Savitri, a veteran actress and singer of early Telugu-Tamil cinema — Wikimedia Commons

Among the pioneers of Tamil film industry was **A. V Meiyyappan**, a notable director and film producer, and **S.S. Vasan** a journalist writer, film director and producer. Among the other greats of Tamil movie direction was **K. Balachander** (recipient of Padma Shri, nine National Film Awards & Dadasaheb Phalke Award), who, with his masterly movies, brought out the intricacies of human relationship and set aside the stereotype of Tamil cinema. Many stalwarts of Tamil movies like Rajnikanth, Kamal Haasan, Jaya Prada, Sridevi, Srividya and Jayasudha, amongst others, were either launched by him or are considered his protégés. **J. Alexander** (recipient of three National Film Awards) who is also known as Mahendran, was another maestro who directed acclaimed movies such as *Mullum Malarum* (1978), *Uthitripookkal* (1979), and *Nenjathai Killathe* (1980). Among the other masters of direction in the Tamil industry in the post-independence period were **Bharathiraja** (recipient of Padma Shri and six National Film Awards), who was known for a realistic and sensitive portrayal of village life, and **C.V.Sridhar**, a screen writer, director and producer of eminence.

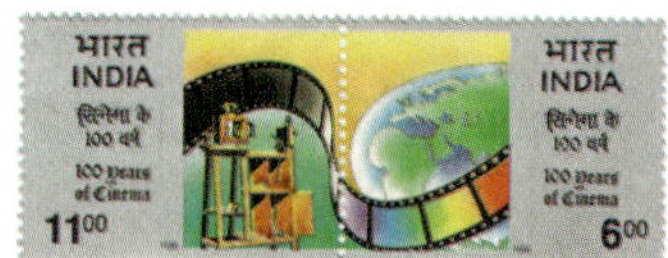

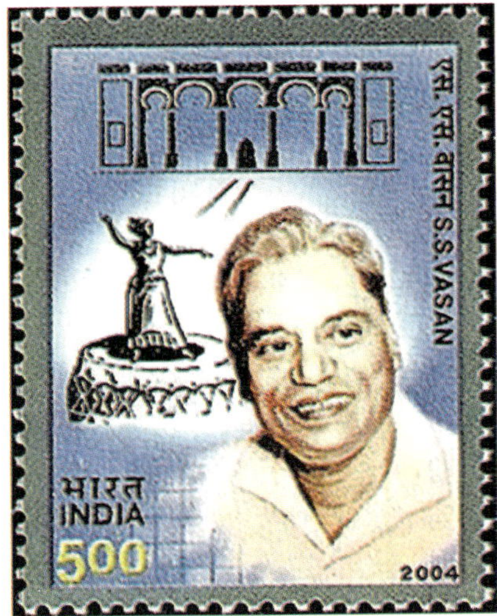

22.63: S.S. Vasan, journalist, writer, director and producer, an eminent film personality of Tamil cinema, stamp of 2004 — Courtesy, Department of Post

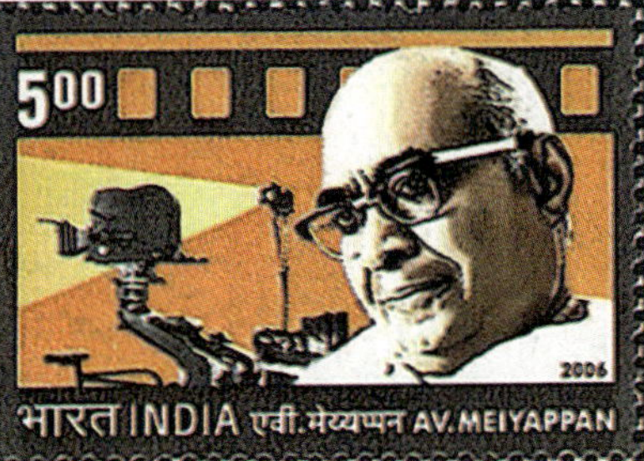

22.64: A.V. Meiyyapan, an early film director and producer of Tamil cinema; stamp of 2006 — Courtesy, Department of Post

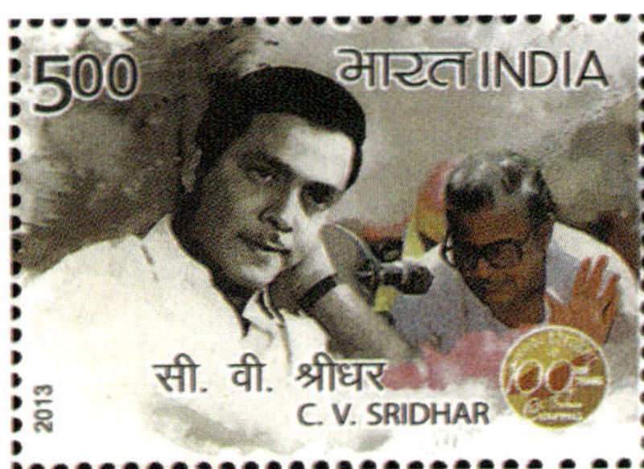

22.65: C.V. Sridhar, an eminent Tamil film maker, recipient of Certificate of Merit and President's silver medal for best feature film in Tamil in 1959 and 1962 respectively. Stamp of 2013 — Courtesy, Department of Post

In the decade of 80s and 90s, Tamil movies witnessed the magic of **Mani Ratnam** (recipient of Padma Shri & six National Film Awards) who is credited to have revolutionised Tamil cinema. Each of his movies had a uniqueness of their own. He is renowned for films such as *Nayakan* (1987), *Anjali* (1988), and *Ponniyin Selvan* (2022), and for his trilogy on the subject of terrorism (*Roja* in 1992, *Bombay* in 1995, *Dil Se* in 1998) and the romantic trilogy (*Mouna Ragam* in 1986, *O-Kadhal Kanmani* in 2015, *Alaipayuthey* in 2000). He has also directed movies in Hindi, Kannada, Telugu and Malayalam. Among other notable directors of Tamil cinema are; **Balu Mahendra** (recipient of six National Film Awards), **K. Bhagyaraj**, **Kamal Haasan**, **Selvaraghavan**, **Gautham Vasudev Menon**, **Bala**, besides others.

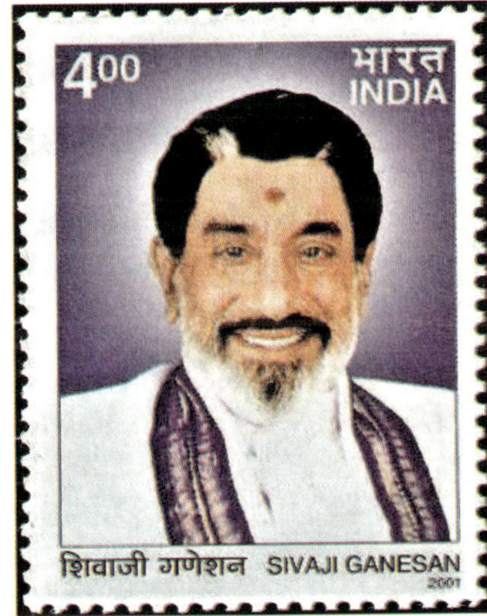

22.66: Sivaji Ganesan, a doyen of Tamil cinema, stamp image — Courtesy, Department of Post

Among the thespians of Tamil cinema is **Sivaji Ganesan** (recipient of Padma Bhushan and Dadasaheb Phalke Award) who acted in more than 250 films and is considered among the greatest of Indian actors of all times. **Ramasamy Ganesan** (a.k.a. Gemini Ganesan) was another veteran in the post-independence Tamil films and was specially known for his romantic movies. Another popular actor of this period was **M.G. Ramachandran** who also received the National Film Awards (1971) for the best actor. **Rajnikanth** (recipient of Padma Vibhushan and Dadasaheb Phalke award), a superstar of Tamil films, is undoubtedly among the most successful and popular actors of Tamil movies as well as Indian cinema. His repertoire of more than 160 films in a career spanning five decades, extends to Hindi, Kannada, Telugu and Malayalam, besides Tamil movies. Another acclaimed Tamil actor and film maker is **Kamal Haasan** (recipient of Padma Bhushan & three National Film Awards) who is also known for his stellar performances in mainstream Bollywood and other regional films. Among the other and recent actors of reckoning in Tamil films are **Prakash Raj** (actor, director & producer and recipient of five National Film Awards), **R. Madhavan**, **Dhanush** (actor & producer, and recipient of four National Film Awards), **Ajith Kumar**, **Suriya** (recipient of two National Film Awards), **Joseph Vijay**, besides others.

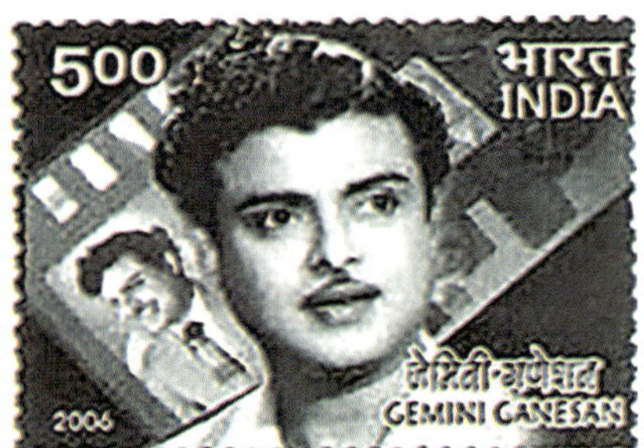

22.67: Gemini Ganesan, a popular Tamil star of romantic movies; stamp image — Courtesy, Department of Post

P. Bhanumathi was among the earliest of the acclaimed Tamil actresses who was also extremely popular in the Telugu films. **Padmini Ramachandran** (popularly known as Padmini) was another famous actress of the post-independence period who worked with the early stalwarts of the Tamil industry and also in Hindi and other regional films. **N. Savitri** (a.k.a. Savitri Ganesan), a renowned actress of Telugu was also very popular in Tamil movies. **Sowcar Janaki**

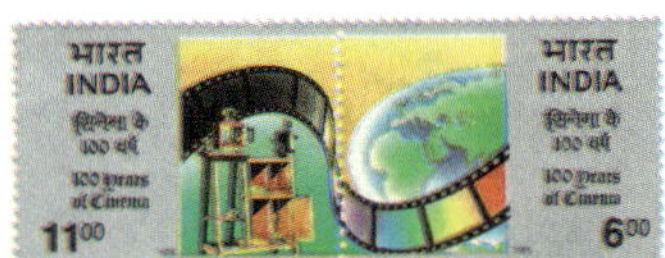

(recipient of Padma Shri award) is another prominent actress of the post-independence period who has acted in nearly 300 movies of Tamil, Telugu and Kannada. Among the female superstars of Tamil cinema was **J. Jayalalthia,** who debuted in the mid-60s and acted along with the greats of Tamil cinema such as Sivaji Ganesan and M.G. Ramachandran. In a career of nearly two decades, she acted in nearly 140 movies in different languages. **Vijayashanthi** (recipient of National Film Award for best actress) is another acclaimed actress of Tamil films who is hailed as a superstar and has acted in nearly 187 movies in a career of four decades. Among other popular actresses are **K.R. Vijaya**, **Radhika Sarathkumar**, **Suhasini Mani Ratnam** (recipient of National Film Award for best actress), **Silk Smitha**, **Nayanthara**, **Aishwarya Rajesh**, **Varalaxmi Sharathkumar**, besides others. Of special mention are the names of Jaya Prada and Sridevi who were popular in Bollywood and also acted in many Tamil movies and other regional cinema.

22.68: Dr. M.G. Ramachandran (Bharat Ratna), a popular film personality, and later the chief minister of Tamil Nadu; a stamp from 1990 — Courtesy, Department of Post

Tamil movies have always had immense popularity in the region with many superstars like M.G. Ramachandran, J. Jayalalitha and Rajnikanth evoking a demigod like status among the masses. The tryst of the Tamil film world and politics has also resulted in M.G. Ramachandra (Bharat Ratna) and J. Jayalalitha, successfully transitioning to politics and becoming the chief ministers of the state, while many other actors/actresses have played an active political role.

Kannada Cinema

Considered to be the fourth largest film industry of the country after Bollywood, Tamil and Telugu cinema, Kannada films have seen increasing popularity in the 2020s. In the year 2022, its revenue from the 207 films that were produced, reached over Rs. 1,500 crores (as per CII report). Kannada cinema (also known as Sandalwood) has been popular in the state of Karnataka as well as the adjoining states. Owing to OTT platforms, dubbing and multi-language releases, its popularity in other states as well as international appeal has gradually risen.

Sati Sulochana (1934), directed by **Y.V. Rao** was the **first movie** in the era of the talkies. This was produced by *South India Movietone* which was founded by **Chamanlal Doongaji** in 1932 in Bangalore, which thus laid the foundations of the Kannada cinema. *Bhakta Dhruv* (also produced in 1934) was the second Kannada talkie film. *Bhagat Kumbara* (1949) and *Mahakavi Kalidasa* (1954) were some other early Kannada films which were based on mythological/historical characters. This trend also continued in the coming decades with movies such as *Bhakta Kanakadasa* (1960), *Ranadheera Kanteerava* (1960), *Satya Harischandra* (1965) and others.

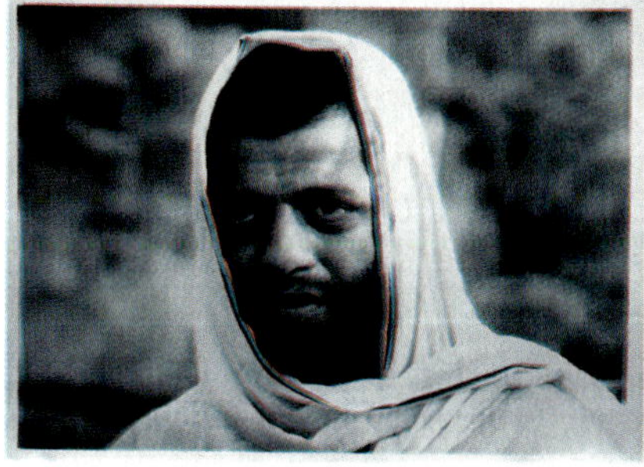

22.69: A still from the Kannada movie *Samskara* (1970-literal meaning 'funeral rites') which features acclaimed actor Girish Karnad. A winner of the National Film Awards for Best Feature Film, it is said to have ushered the parallel film movement in Kannada cinema — Courtesy, NFDC-National Film Archives of India, (Pune)

Over the years, Kannada cinema has been known for works which have repeatedly earned it critical acclaim, particularly in the decades of 70s and beyond. With a rich Kannada literary tradition, many movies have been inspired or based on acclaimed literary works. Falling in this category are movies such as *Samskara* (won the National Film Award in 1970 for best Indian film), directed by **Pattabhirama Reddy** and based on *Samskara* by U.R. Ananthamurthy, *Kaadu* by **Girish Karnad** based on *Kaadu* written by Srikrishna Allanhalli, and *Chomana Dudi* (won the National Film Award in 1975 for best Indian film) directed by **B.V. Karanth** which was based on *Chomana Dudi* written by Shivarama Karanth.

Among other acclaimed works are *Ghatashraddha* (1977), *Tabarana Kathe* (1986), *Thaayi Saheba* (1997) and *Dweepa* (2001) directed by

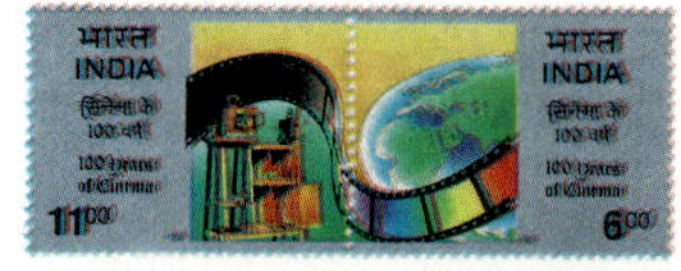

Girish Kasaravalli, all of which have won the National Film Award for the best Indian film in the respective years. Kannada cinema has also been known for offbeat and experimental works. *Mysore Mallige* (1992), a film by **T.S. Nagabharana** was based on a poetic work (of 1942) of the same name by K.S Narasimhaswamy and won the National Film Award for best Kannada film as well as for the best lyrics. *Pushpaka Vimana,* a silent film by **Singeetam Srinivasa Rao** was unique and much appreciated by the audience and critics alike. Among the recent popular Kannada cinema are *Lucia* (2013), *Ulidavaru Kandanthe* (2014), *Rangi Taranga* (2015), *Raajakumara* (2017), *KGF Chapter-1* (2018), *Kantara* (2022) *KGF chapter-2* (2022), besides others.

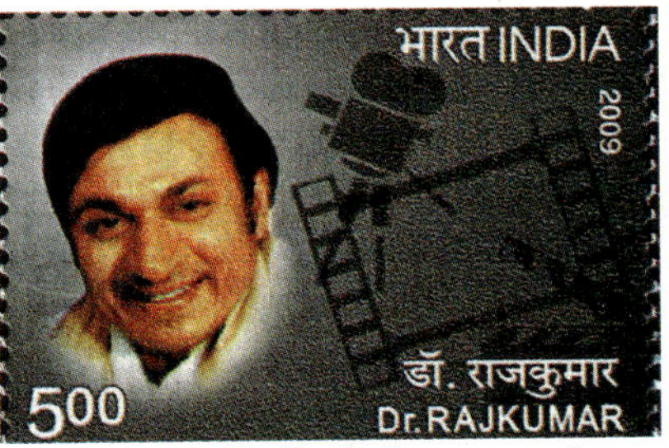

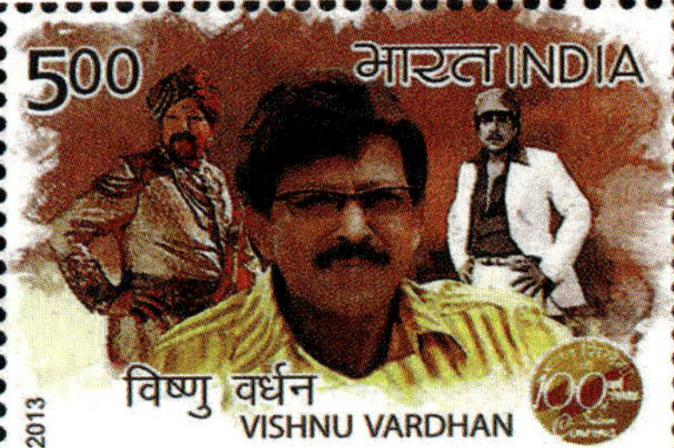

22.70 & 22.71: Dr. Rajkumar, a doyen of Kannada movies; Vishnu Vardhan, a Kannada matinee idol stamp images — Courtesy, Department of Post

Among the doyens of Kannada movies are **Honnappa Bhagavathar**, an actor, director and singer who played a significant role in Kannada cinema in the pre-independence as well as the post-independence period. Among the greatest of actors of Kannada and Indian cinema is **Dr. Rajkumar** (recipient of Padma Bhushan & Dadasaheb Phalke Award) who has the unique distinction of also winning National Film Award for singing. His repertoire includes nearly 208 movies, many of which won the National Film Awards for the best Kannada film. Among the other eminent actors of Kannada cinema are **Shiva Rajkumar** (actor and producer), **Anant Nag**, **Vishnu Vardhan**, **Shankar Nag** (actor, director and filmmaker, recipient of two National Film Awards for best films), **Puneeth Rajkumar**, **Ramesh Aravind**, **Ambareesh**, **Sudeepa**, **Ganesh**, besides others.

Among the successful Kannada actresses are **B. Saroja Devi** (recipient of Padma Bhushan), a veteran having acted in 200 movies with a lead role in 161, in a career spanning three decades. **Kamala Kumari** (also known as Jayanthi, was a veteran of Kannada and Tamil cinema having worked in nearly 500 movies. **Kalpana** was another popular actress of the 60s and 70s. **Manjula**, who acted in more than 100 films, was among the most successful Kannada actresses of the 70s and 80s. **Aarathi** was another notable actress of this period. Among the other successful actresses of the later decades are **Suhasini**, **Saritha**, **Malashri**, **Sudha Rani**, **Soundarya**, **Ramya**, **Radhika Pandit**, **Prema**, **Rakshita**, besides others.

Malayalam Cinema

One of the most acclaimed of Indian cine-industries, Malayalam cinema is known for its storylines, cinematography, technical excellence and overall quality of production. Over the period of last several decades, and in particular from the 70s, the industry has won several international and national awards including 12 National Film Awards for the best feature film (as of 2020 National Film Awards). Besides, it has also received several other National Film Awards, viz. best actor, best actress and best director.

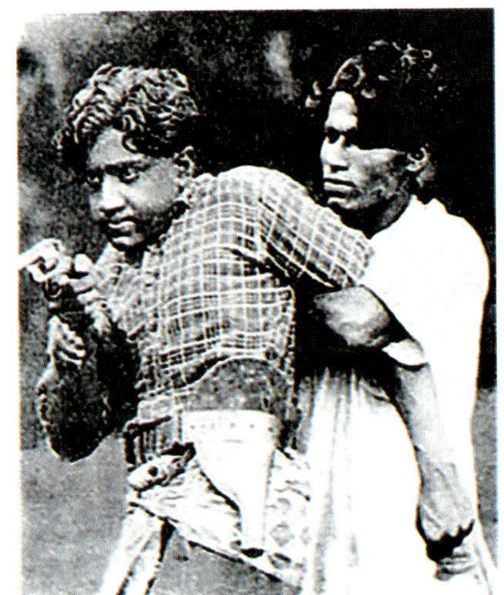

22.72: A scene from *Vigathakumaran*, the first Malayalam silent movie — Wikipedia

The Malayalam film had its birth with the silent film *Vigathakumaran* (1928) directed and produced by **J.C. Daniel**. *Balan* (1938) by **S. Nottani** was the first Malayalam talkie film. This movie was produced by **T.R Sundaram** (an actor, director and producer) under the banner of *The Modern Theatres Ltd*, one of the earliest Malayalam film companies. In the 1920s, the film industry of the region had its presence in Thiruvananthapuram. However, by the 1940s, the film industry had shifted its base to Madras (now Chennai) adversely affecting the production of Malayalam movies. Thus, in the pre-independence period, there were only a few Malayalam movies, and as per some accounts, these were just two silent movies and three talkies. In the post-independence period, the production of movies increased to

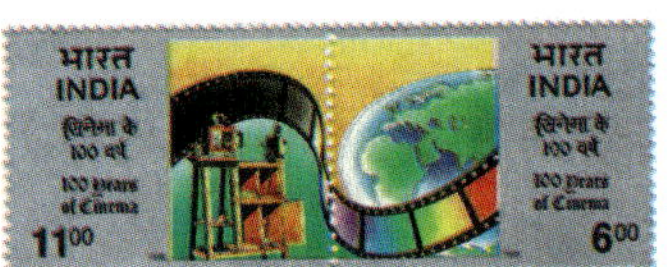

30 movies in a year in the 1950s, and then to 40 movies in the 1960s. In the 1980s, Malayalam film industry became based in Kochi. Thereafter, the productions zoomed to nearly 125-130 movies per year and reaching to as high as 175 to 180 per year in the 2020s. Over the years, Malayalam films have made a mark as niche films with appreciable artistic sensibilities. However, in terms of the box office turnover or movies of mass-market consumption, Malayalam productions have had lesser success than their Tamil, Telugu or Kannada counterparts.

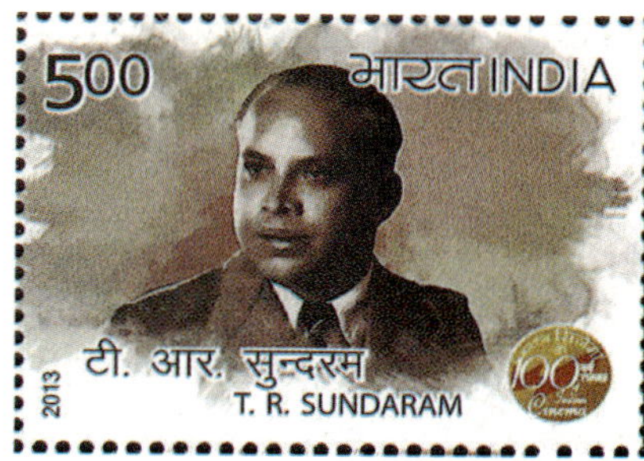

22.73: T.R. Sundaram, an early Malayalam actor, director and producer stamp image — courtesy, Department of Post

Among the critically acclaimed and award-winning Malayalam movies, the earliest was *Chemmeen* (1965) by **Ramu Kariat** which won the National Film Award for the best feature film of India. It also became a blockbuster. In the 70s, *Swayamvaram* (1972) by **Adoor Gopalakrishnan** and *Nirmalayam* by **M.T.Vasudevan Nair** (1973) won this honour back-to-back. Around a decade later, *Chidambaram* (1985) by **G. Aravindan**, *Piravi* (1988) by **Shaji N. Karun,** again won this award in the 80s. In the 90s, Adoor Gopalakrishnan and Shaji N. Karun were bestowed this honour for the films *Kathapurushan* (1995) and *Vanaprastham* (1999) respectively. In the new millennium, the feat was repeated by the movies *Shantham* (2000) by **Jayaraj**, *Pulijananmam* by **Priyanandanan** and *Kutty Srank* (2009) by Shaji N. Kurun. *Adaminte Makan Abu* (2010) by **Salim Ahmed** and *Marakkar: Lion of the Arabian Sea*, by **Priyadarshan** were the two other Malayalam movies honoured with this apex national award.

Among the other acclaimed movies are *Ellipathayam* (1982), written and directed by Adoor Gopalakrishnan, *Swaham* by Shaji N. Kurun, which also won international awards. Some other noteworthy films were *Guru* (1997), a fantasy drama by **Rajiv Anchal**, *Jallikattu* (2019) by **Lijo Jose Pellissery** which was India's official entry to the Academy Awards (Oscars).

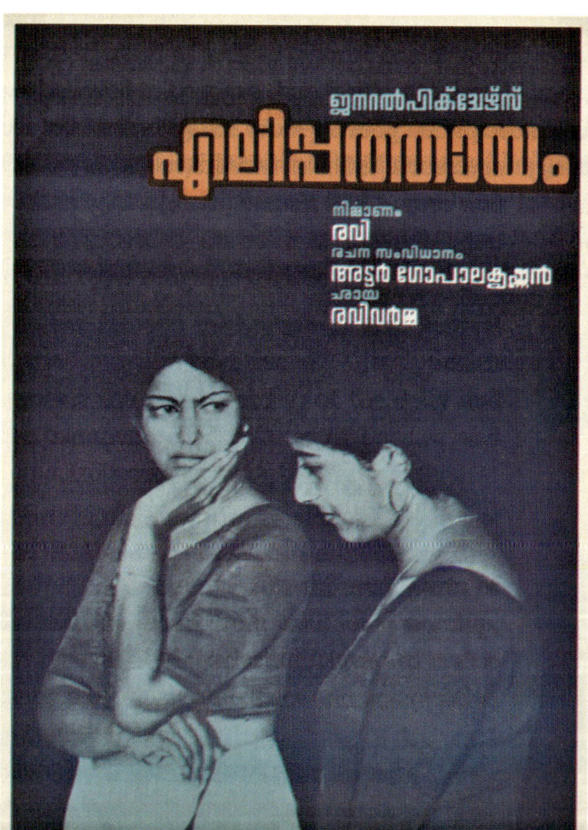

22.74: *Ellipathayam* (1982), one of the acclaimed Malayalam movies, written and directed by Adoor Gopalakrishnan, a master filmmaker in the golden age of Malayalam cinema

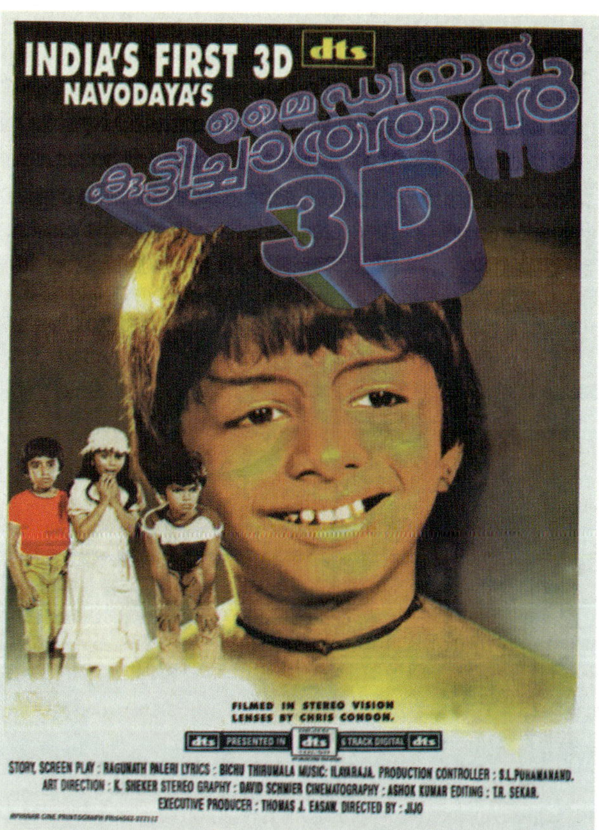

22.75: *My Dear Kuttichathan* (1984), the first Indian movie in the 3D format, a children's fantasy genre of Malayalam movie

Movie poster images — Courtesy, NFDC-National Film Archives of India, (Pune)

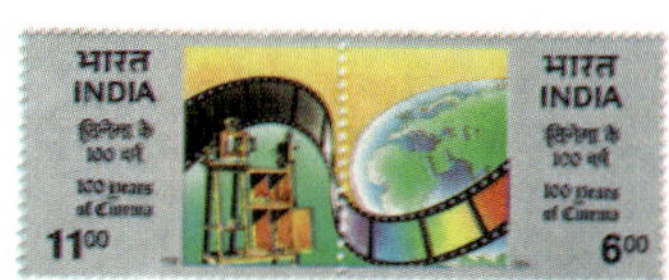

Malayalam cinema is also known for its experimentative work. *My Dear Kuttichathan* (1984), a Malayalam film, was the first Indian movie in the 3D (three dimensional) format, while *Thacholi Ambu* was the first cinema scope (wide aspect ratio format) movie to be produced. Among the popular genre of Malayalam movies, some noteworthy inclusions are *Thaniyavarthanam* (1987), a drama film dealing with Kerala's rural orthodoxy and superstitions, *Vidheyan* (1994), a drama exploring the psyche in a master-slave relationship, *Thanmathra* (2005), a drama film portraying the effect of Alzheimer's disease, *Pranchiyettan & the Saint* (2010), a satirical comedy, *Drishyam* (2013), a crime thriller, *Munnariyippu* (2014), a psychological thriller.

The Malayalam cinema has evolved through the decades. The 1970s ushered a new genre of movies which were nuanced and marked by depth and excellence, with filmmakers such as **Adoor Gopalakrishnan**, **G. Aravindan**, **M. T. Vasudevan Nair** and **K. G. George** bringing laurels. The period of 1980s to 1990s is often considered a **golden age of Malayalam cinema**, with other directors like **Shaji N. Karun**, **Padmarajan**, **Bharathan**, **Priyadarshan**, **Rajiv Anchal** and others joining the coterie of the veterans of the previous decades. Cinema of this period also endeavoured to bridge the gap of the art and commercial worlds and earned acclaim as well as revenue for the industry. In the decade of 2010 and beyond, the movies entered a new phase referred to as the **new generation films** or the **new wave films**. This was led by a fresh band of directors such as **Aashiq Abu**, **Anwar Rasheed**, **Amal Neerad** and **Sameer Thahir**. The new wave films were not the star-studded dramas of the previous decade. They were made on a smaller budget but brought in new talents of acting, script writing, music, cinematography etc. Some of the successful movies which ushered this new wave were *Traffic* (2011), *City of God* (2011), *Salt N' Pepper* (2011) and *Chaappa Kurishu* (2011). Thus began a new chapter in Malayalam cinema.

Among the actors of reckoning of Malayalam movies, the foremost name is that of **Prem Nazir** (recipient of Padma Bhushan), an iconic actor of the period 1950s to 1980s. He held the **Guinness Book of World Records, of being a lead actor** in 720 films. He holds the world record of playing a role with the same heroine in 130 films, of acting opposite eighty heroines and of release of 30 films in a year in which he plays lead role. **Thikkurissy Sukumaran Nair** (recipient of Padma Shri) was an actor, director, playwright, scriptwriter and a stalwart of Malayalam movies, acted in over 700 films. **Sathyan,** a master of realistic acting, **Thilakan** (recipient of Padma Shri & National Film Award), **Bharat Gopi** (Padma Shri & National Film Award recipient), **Jayan**, a cultural icon (actor, stunt performer and also a naval officer), **Mammootty** (recipient of Padma Shri & three National Film Awards), **Muraleedharan Pillai** (recipient of National Film Award for best actor), **Mohanlal** (recipient of Padma Bhushan and five National Film Awards), were some other stalwarts of the Malayalam cinema. **Suresh Gopi**, **Rahman**, **Siddique**, **Fahad Faasil**, **Prithivraj Sukumaran** are some other noteworthy actors of Malayalam cinema of the decade of 90s and onwards.

P.K. Rosy, who acted in the *Vigathakumaran*, was the first actress of Malayalam movies. **Philomina**, a veteran of Malayalam cinema acted in nearly 750 movies with her role in *Godfather* (1991) being considered a very powerful portrayal. **Sukumari** (recipient of Padma Shri & National Film Award) made an appearance in a staggering 2500 movies in a career spanning five decades. **K.P.A.C. Laitha** (recipient of two National Film Awards) is another renowned actress acclaimed for her acting. **Urvashi** (recipient of National Film Award), **Manju Warrier** considered the first female superstar of Malayalam cinema, **Shobhana** (recipient of two National Film Awards for best actress), **Srividya**, who acted in nearly 800 movies, **Meera Jasmine** (recipient of National Film Award) and **Seema**, are some other acclaimed actresses of this industry.

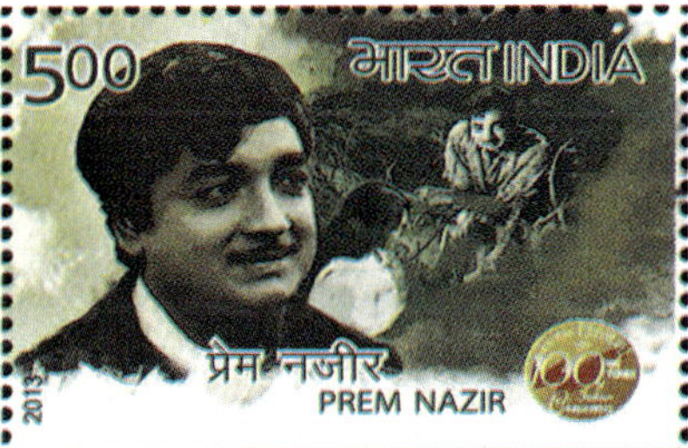

22.76: Prem Nazir, one of the finest actors of Indian movies and a doyen of Malayalam cinema — Stamp image, Courtesy, Department of Post

Other Regional Film Industries — Marathi, Bhojpuri, Odia, Assamese, Gujarati & Punjabi

Among the other vibrant **regional film industries** are the Marathi and Bhojpuri cinema, each with more than 100 movies produced every year (as per the number of films certified by Central Board of Film Certification in 2019). Among these the **Marathi film industry** has the richest legacy. Marathi cinema is also considered the fountainhead of Indian cinema with *Sri Pundalik* (1912-Marathi) being considered as the first film

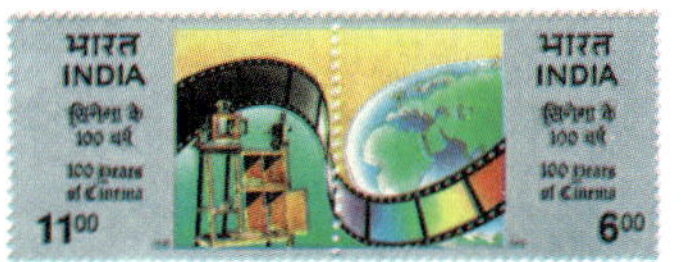

by some scholars. The later years also saw the works of some eminent filmmakers like **Dadasaheb Phalke** whose production *Raja Harischandra* (1913-first silent movie) had subtitles in Hindi, English as well as Marathi. **Baburao Painter** was another acclaimed Marathi filmmaker of this period. The first Marathi talkie movie was *Ayodhyecha Raja* (1932). In the post-independence period, *Shyamachi Aai* by **Acharya P.K. Atre** received the honour to be the first Indian film to receive the President's Gold Medal for the All India Best Feature Film, which is now better known as National Film Award for Best Feature Film.

Marathi industry witnessed a golden age in the 50s and 60s, with eminent directors like **V. Shantaram**, **Bhalji Pendharkar**, **Master Vinayak**, **Acharya Atre** and others. However, in the later years, it suffered a decline, owing perhaps to the Hindi film industry strengthening its roots in Mumbai and the Marathi industry experiencing difficulty in competing with it. However, the industry is seeing an upswing in the production and quality of movies in the new millenium which augurs well and promises a brighter future.

Bhojpuri cinema, with a nearly Rs. 2,000 crore turnover (as in 2017) is also a significant regional film industry. Adding to its burgeoning box office figures and the increasing number of viewers, it is the geographical distribution of Bhojpuri cinema which also makes this once fledgling centre of movies, now an important national player. The industry and its production is largely based in Lucknow and Patna, with Bhojpuri being spoken by a large population in Eastern Uttar Pradesh, Western Bihar and adjoining *terai* region of Nepal. *Ganga Maiyya Tohre Piyari Chadhaibo* (1963) by **Vishwanath Shahabadi** was the first Bhojpuri cinema. With a large migrant population in different states of India, Bhojpuri cinema has distribution in cities like Mumbai, Delhi, Kolkata and other metros as well. As Bhojpuri is still being spoken in countries like Guyana, Trinidad and Tobago, Fiji, Surinam, Mauritius, South Africa etc. where the workers/indentured labour had migrated a century or several decades ago, Bhojpuri cinema enjoys international demand as well as overseas popularity. With popular stars like **Ravi Kishen** and **Manoj Tewari** enjoying great appeal and occasional appearance of megastars like **Amitabh Bachchan** in *Ganga* (2006), *Gangotri* (2007), and *Ganga Devi* (2012) and **Mithun Chakraborty** *Bhole Shankar* (2008) besides others, in Bhojpuri cinema, this regional industry is gaining in esteem and is future is definitely looking up.

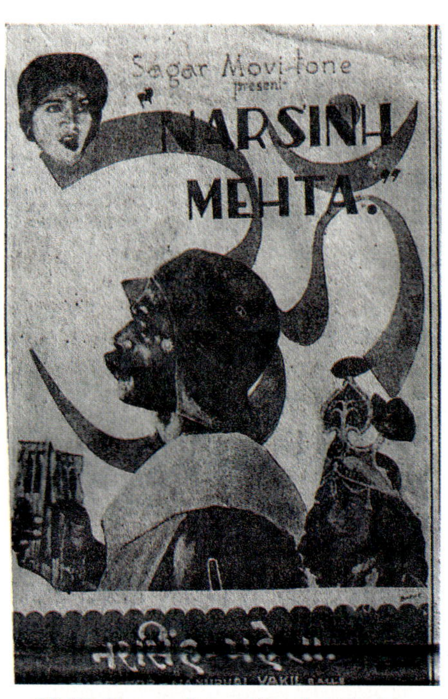

22.77: The poster of *Narsinh Mehta*, the first Gujarati talkie of 1932 — Wikimedia Commons

Among other important regional film industries are **Gujarati**, **Punjabi**, **Odia and Assamese**. The regional cinema has passed through different phases of growth, with rise in their production post-independence, subsequent decline and an ascent in the recent times. The demand for regional movies, availability of finance, channels of distribution, theatres for display, availability of regional artists and technical human resources, besides the dominance of the Hindi cinema, have all been the constraints for most of these industries. Of late, the support from State governments in the form of policy and finance, besides granting of tax free status to regional cinema in some states and other measures, have helped. The development of regional television channels aided the demand of the regional films. Further, with OTT platform breaking the shackles of distribution and display, cinema is looking up for most of the regional film industries.

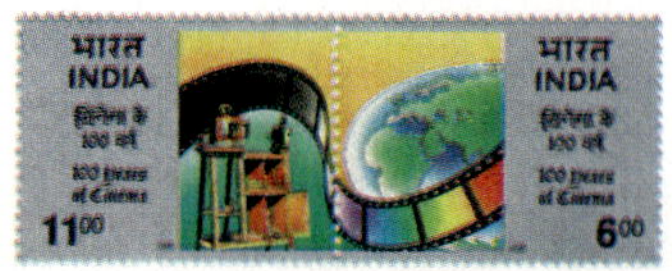

PICTURE GALLERY

Indian Cinema : Some Early Masterpieces

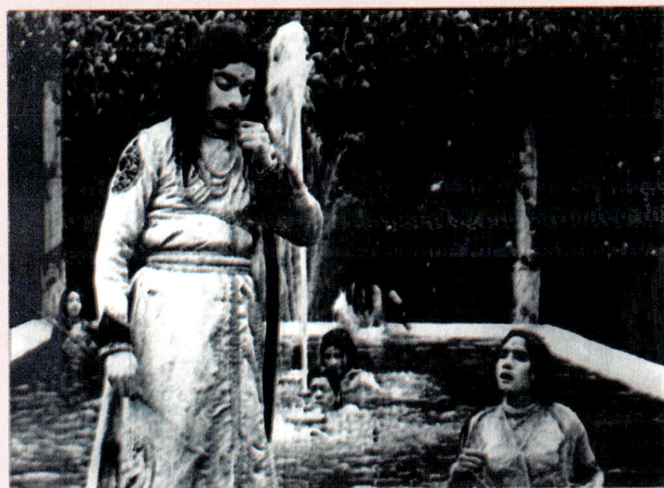

22.78: A scene from the movie *Raja Harishchandra* (1913), the first Indian feature film of the silent era.

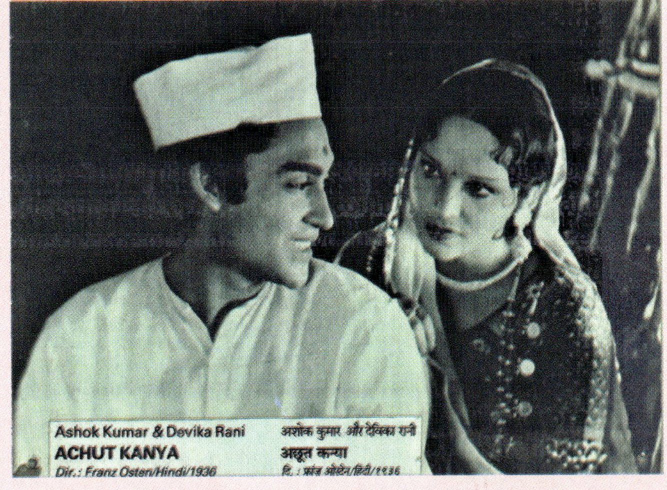

22.79: A scene from the movie *Achhut Kanya* (1936) starring acclaimed actors Ashok Kumar and Devika Rani; the movie directed by Franz Osten is considered among the earliest reformist films with a strong social message.

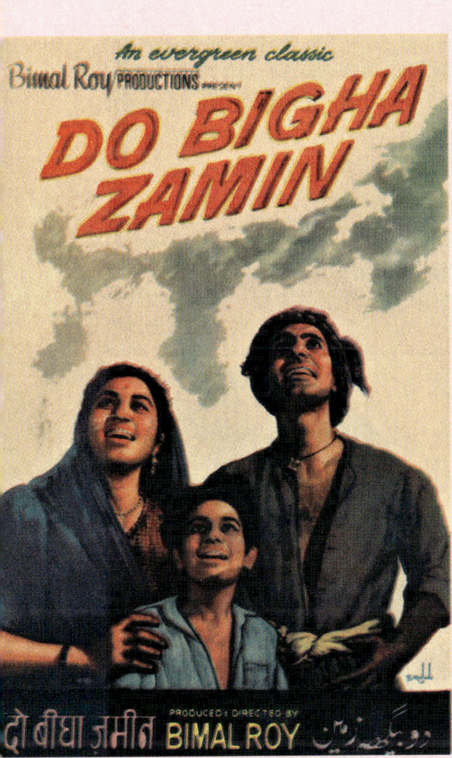

22.80: *Do Bigha Zameen* (1953), by Bimal Roy, an iconic movie that won an award at the Cannes Film Festival (1956), depicted the utter despondency of the rural landless poor migrating to large cities in the hope of survival.

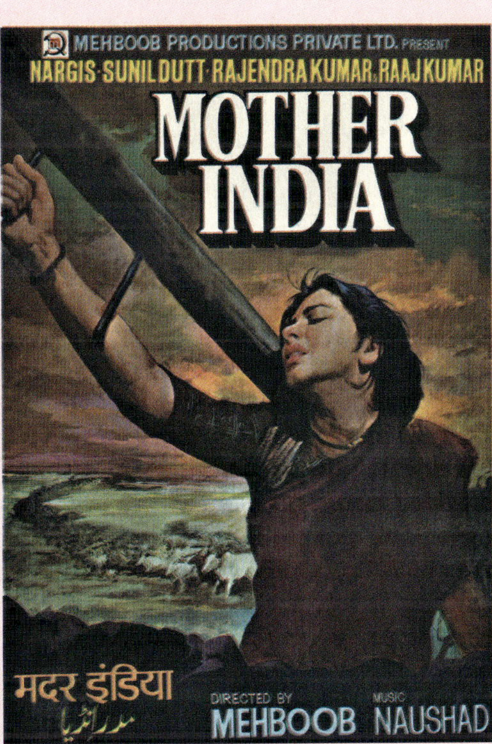

22.81: *Mother India* (1957), another landmark movie which was directed by Mehboob Khan, won an Oscar nomination (1958) in the category of 'Best Foreign Language Film', the first such Indian movie.

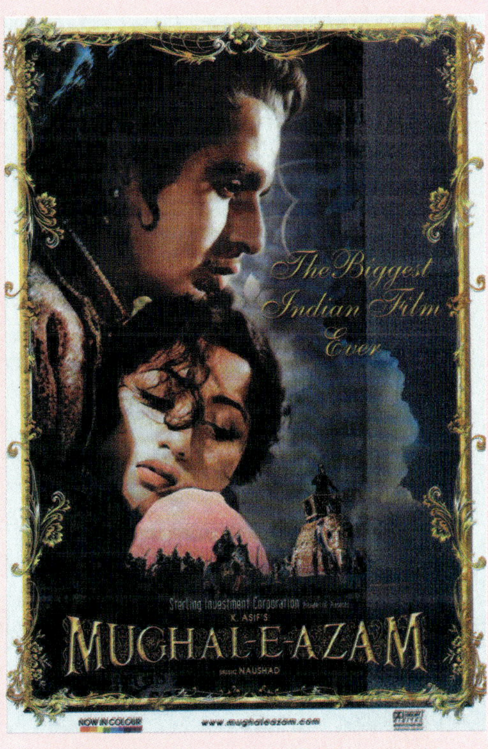

22.82: *Mughal-e-Azam* (1960), an epic historical drama directed by K Asif was the costliest movie of its time and a huge commercial success that also received critical acclaim.

All pictures — Courtesy, NFDC-National Film Archives of India, (Pune)

Parallel Cinema : The Confluence of Art and Movie Making

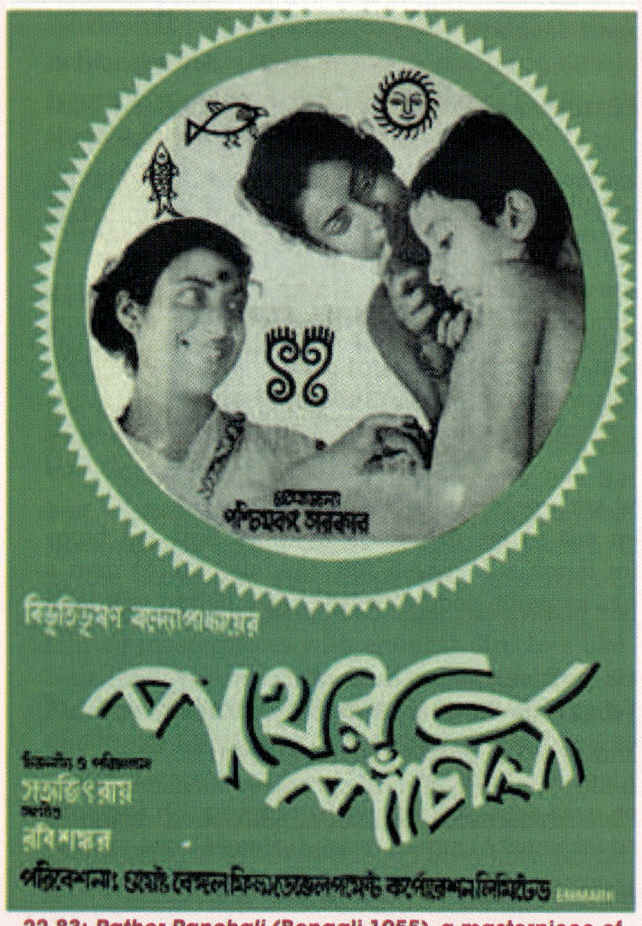

22.83: ***Pather Panchali*** **(Bengali-1955), a masterpiece of Satyajit Ray and the first of the films of the 'Apu Trilogy' that won the inaugural 'Best Human Document Award' at the Cannes Film Festival (1955).**

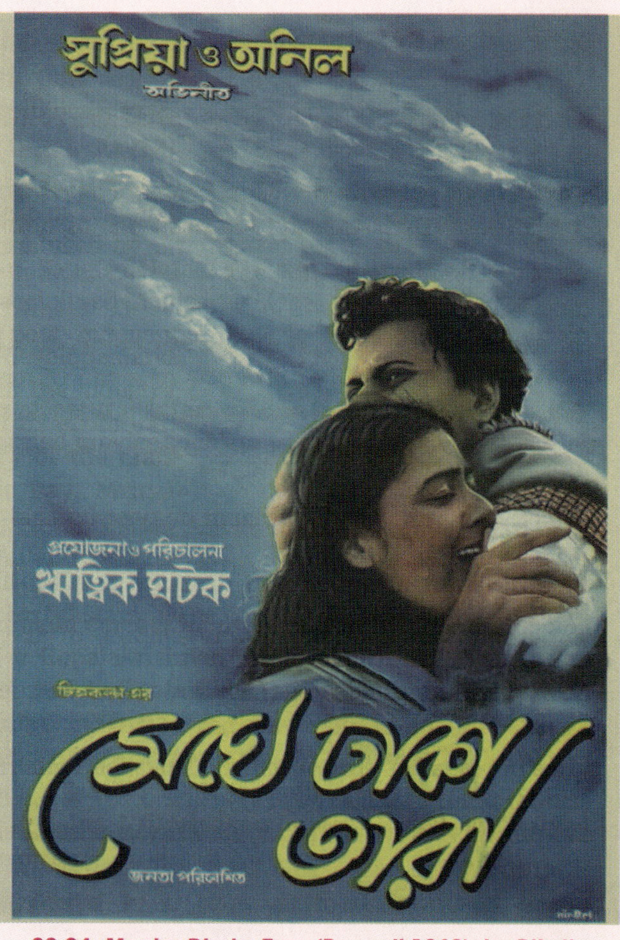

22.84: ***Meghe Dhaka Tara*** **(Bengali-1960), by Ritwik Ghatak, another master movie maker, was a part of a trilogy depicting the issue of the partition of Bengal post the partition of India and its human fallout.**

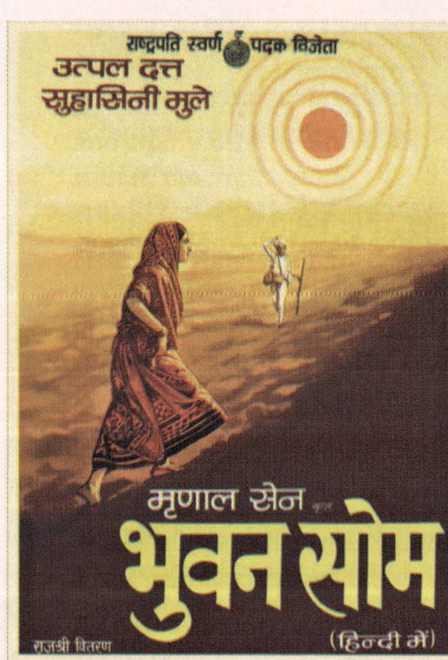

22.85: ***Bhuvan Shome*** **(Hindi -1969), a landmark movie of Mrinal Sen, a maestro who dabbled in Bengali as well as Hindi cinema and was a contemporary of Ray and other masters of the golden age of parallel cinema.** ***Bhuvan Shome*** **is also believed to have ushered a 'New Wave' cinema movement in India.**

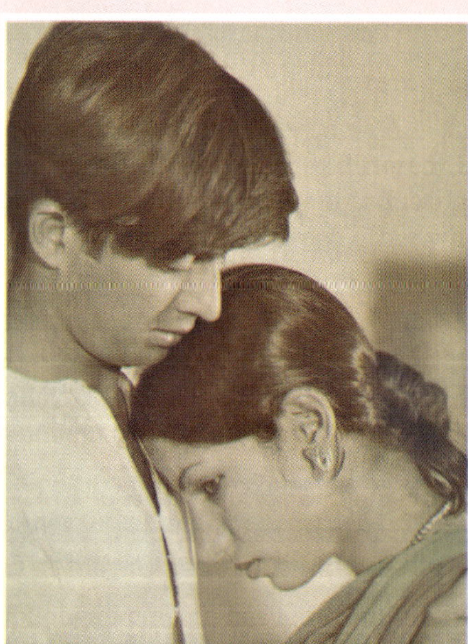

22.86: ***Ankur*** **(Hindi- 1974), another gem of parallel cinema by Shyam Benegal, won three National Film Awards, besides international recognition. It also marked the debut of acclaimed actors Anant Nag and Shabana Azmi.**

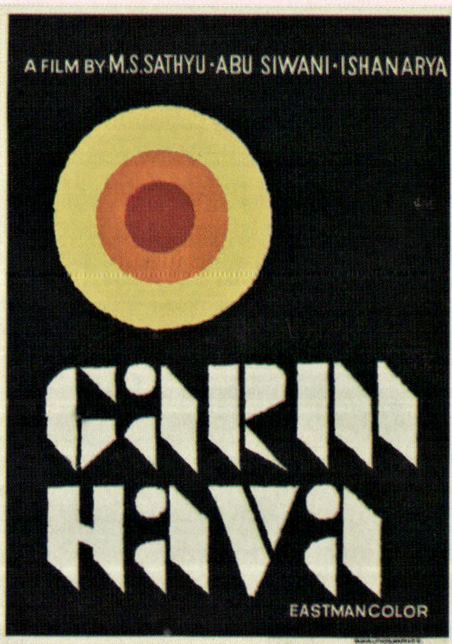

22.87: ***Garam Hawa*** **(Hindi-1974) by M.S. Sathyu, a film that brings out the pangs of partition as experienced by a Muslim middle-class family; a winner of National Film Awards, besides international accolades.** ***Garam Hawa,*** **along with** ***Bhuvan Shome*** **and** ***Ankur,*** **marked the New Wave cinema movement in India.**

All pictures — Courtesy, NFDC-National Film Archives of India, (Pune)

Several Shades of the 70s

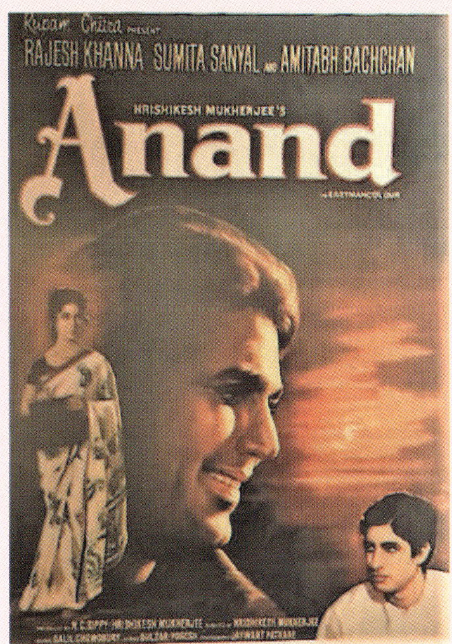

22.88: ***Anand*** **(1971), a commercially successful and critically acclaimed musical drama directed by Hrishikesh Mukherjee, starring Rajesh Khanna in the lead and Amitabh Bachchan in a supporting role.**

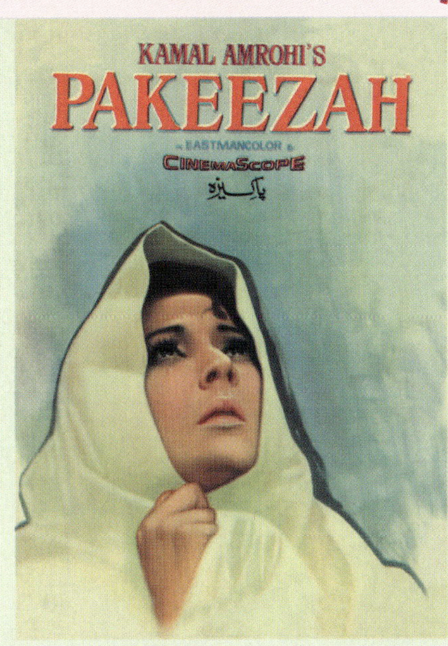

22.89: ***Pakeezah*** **(1972), a musical romantic drama, by Kamal Amrohi, and the last of the movies of Meena Kumari, is said to have been in production for nearly 15 years. A blockbuster of the year, it is also reckoned for its Muslim social genre — Courtesy, NFDC-National Film Archives of India, (Pune)**

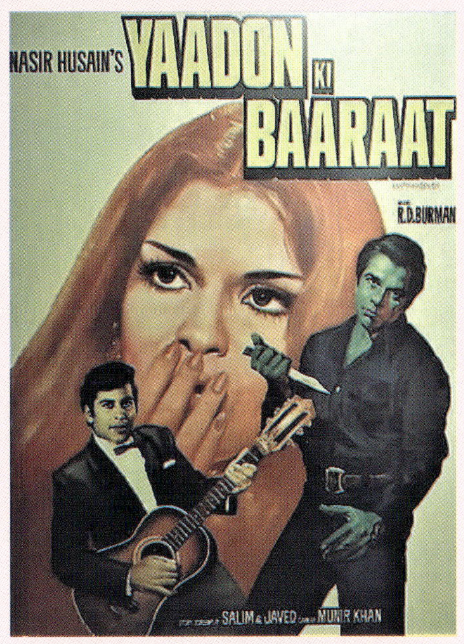

22.90: ***Yaadon Ki Baaraat*** **(1973), Dharmendra, Zeenat Aman and other lead multi-starrer, a thriller, action, romance, comedy, musical and drama, all mixed to engender a new genre of** ***masala*** **movies in Bollywood.**

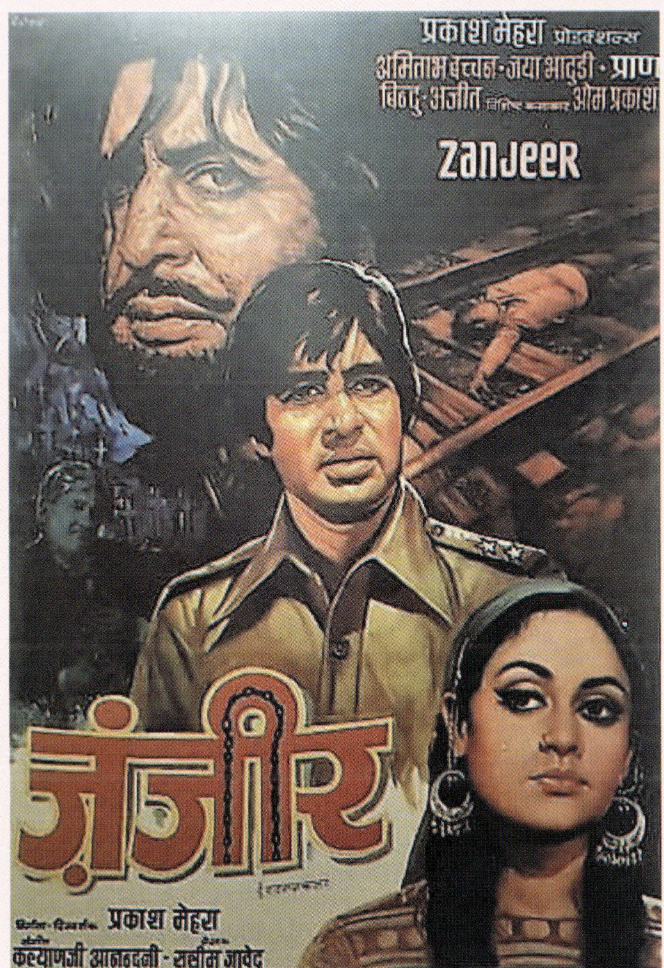

22.91: ***Zanjeer*** **(1973), an Amitabh Bachchan, Jaya Bhaduri starrer, an action-crime thriller which draws upon the then anti-establishmentarian sentiment in society and heralds the angry young man image of Amitabh Bachchan.**

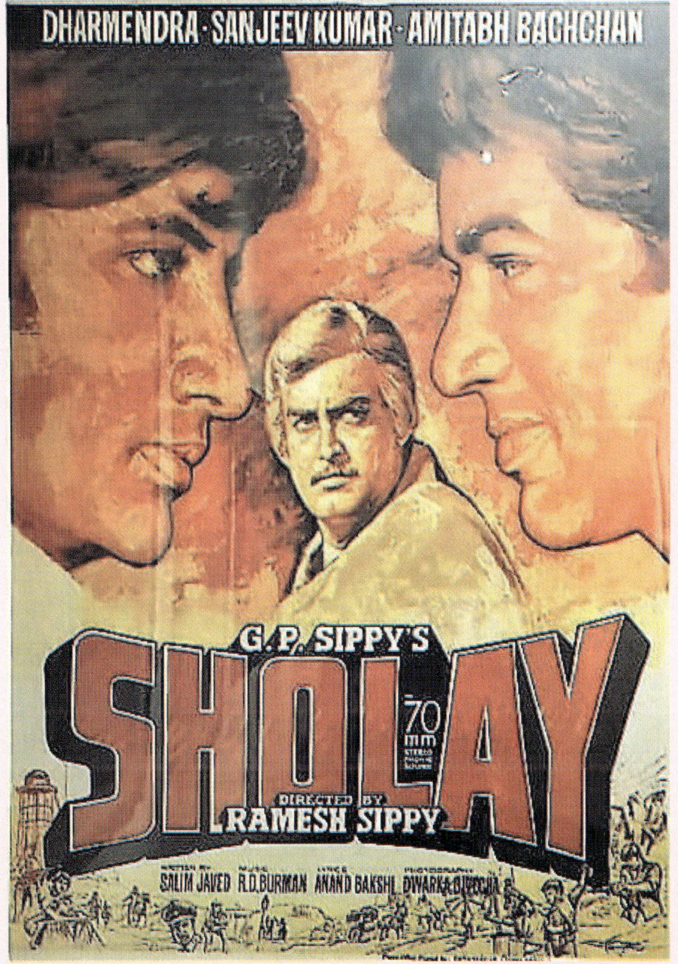

22.92: ***Sholay*** **(1975), an action-crime-thriller with shades of comedy and musicals, a multi-starrer with Dharmendra and Amitabh Bachchan, along with Hema Malini and Jaya Bhaduri in lead roles and supported by Sanjeev Kumar. Amjad Khan plays the iconic villain, Gabbar Singh. A super-duper hit, one of the highest-grossers ever and one of the most influential Indian films.**

Posters of Anand, Yadon ki Baraat, Zanjeer and Sholay, location India Habitat Centre, New Delhi — photographs by Madhukar K Bhagat

The Romantic Musical Dramas: A Recipe for Blockbusters of the 80s and early 90s

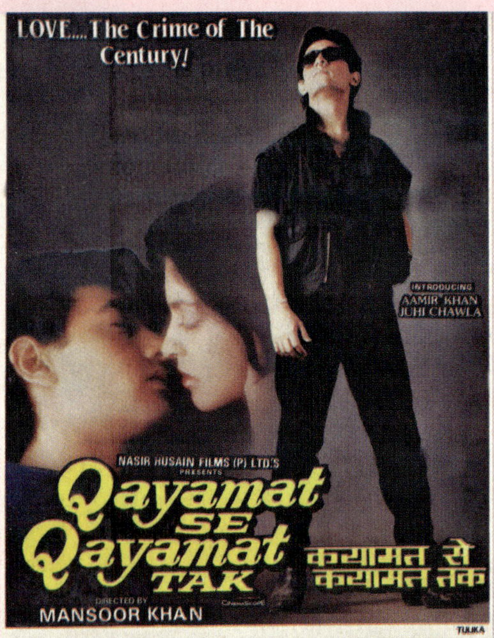

22.93: ***Qayamat Se Qayamat Tak*** **(1988), a Mansoor Khan (director) Nasir Hussain (writer) production, a milestone movie known for its tragic romance. The movie, made Aamir Khan and Juhi Chawla stars of the gen-next, was also known for its song 'Papa Kehte Hain' which was to become a teenage sensation.**

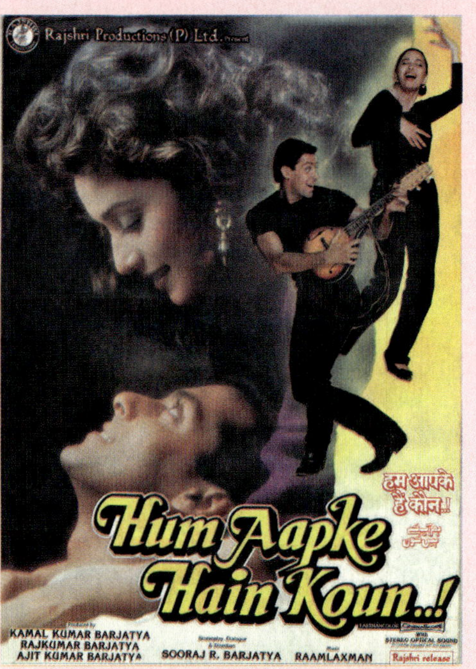

22.94: ***Hum Apke Hain Kaun*** **(1994), another romantic musical and family entertainment drama that had Salman Khan and Madhuri Dixit as the lead pair and which wooed the hitherto waning family audience back to the theatres.**

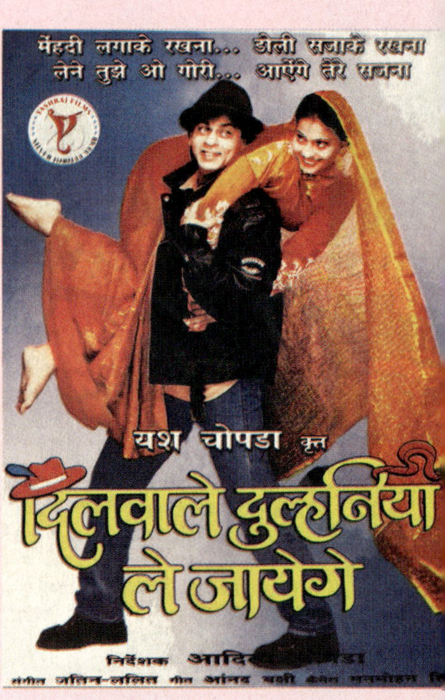

22.95: ***Dilwale Dulhaniya Le Jayenge*** **(1995), a Shahrukh Khan and Kajol starrer, was another musical romantic super-duper hit of the 1990s.**

Games & Sports Amongst Other New Genres in the New Millennium

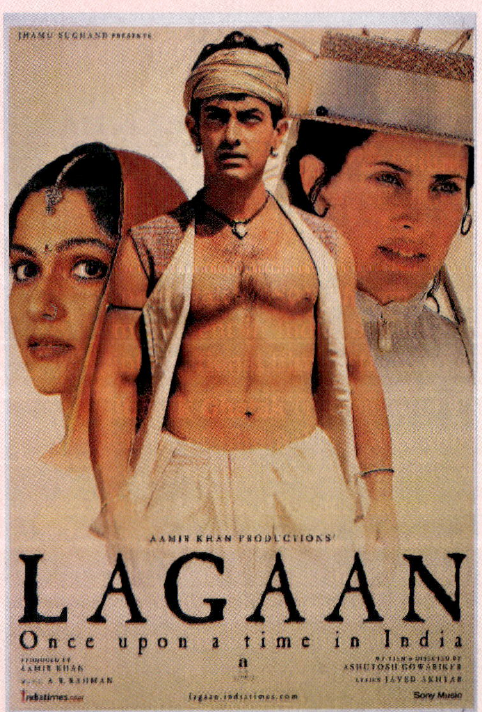

22.96: ***Lagaan*** **(2001), a musical drama based on the colonial history and the game of cricket, earned critical acclaim and international awards, including a nomination at the Academy Awards (Oscars), besides huge commercial success.**

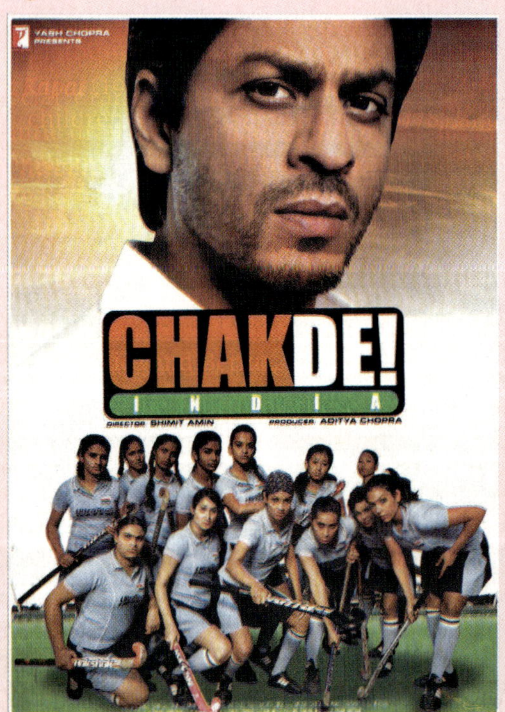

22.97: ***Chakde*** **(2007), a movie based on the Indian women's hockey team's success, earned a National Film Award for Best Popular Film providing Wholesome Entertainment.**

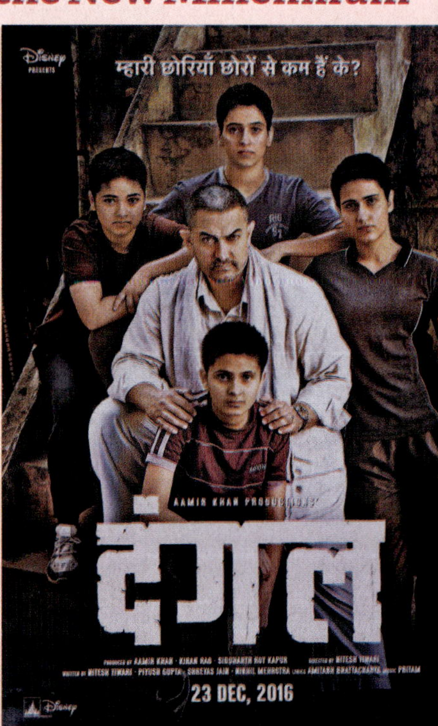

22.98: ***Dangal*** **(2016), showcased the story of the struggle and success of the wrestler Geeta Phogat which further inspired a generation of women wrestlers It won critical acclaim as well as huge commercial success.**

All pictures — Courtesy, NFDC-National Film Archives of India, (Pune)

The New Cinema of the New Millennium

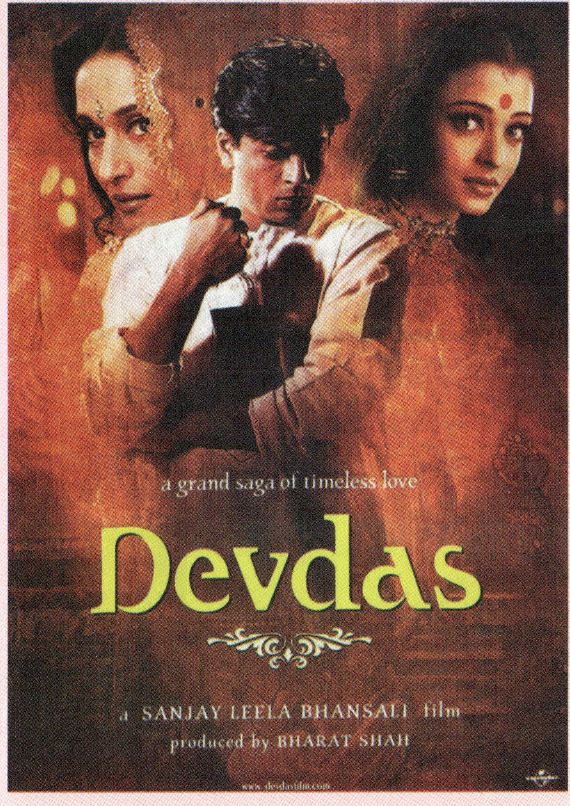

22.99: ***Devdas*** **(2002), an oft-repeated tragedy in Indian movies, based on the eponymous novel of Sarat Chandra Chattopadhyay, confluences with the mega-production style of Sanjay Leela Bhansali to engender commercial success and critical accolades.**

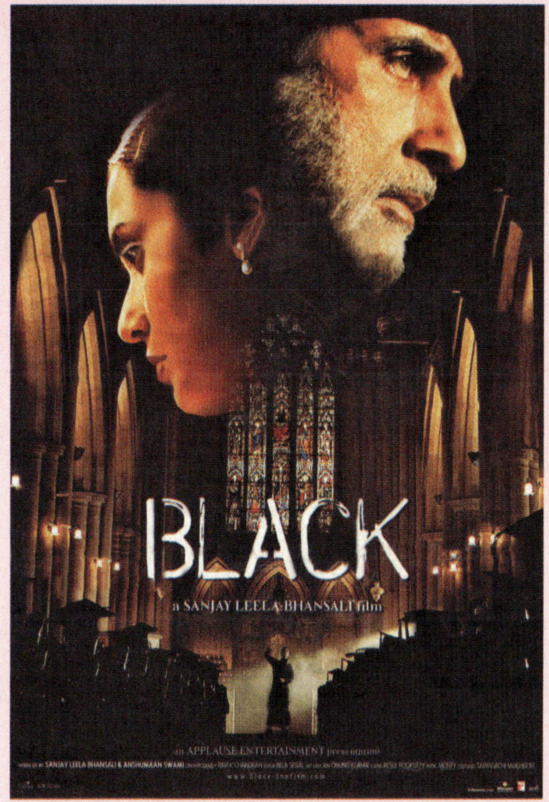

22.100: ***Black*** **(2005), a story of a deaf, mute and blind girl, an experimental film that casts mainstream actors Amitabh Bachchan and Rani Mukherjee in unconventional challenging roles, earning all round accolades, several National Film Awards and commercial success.**

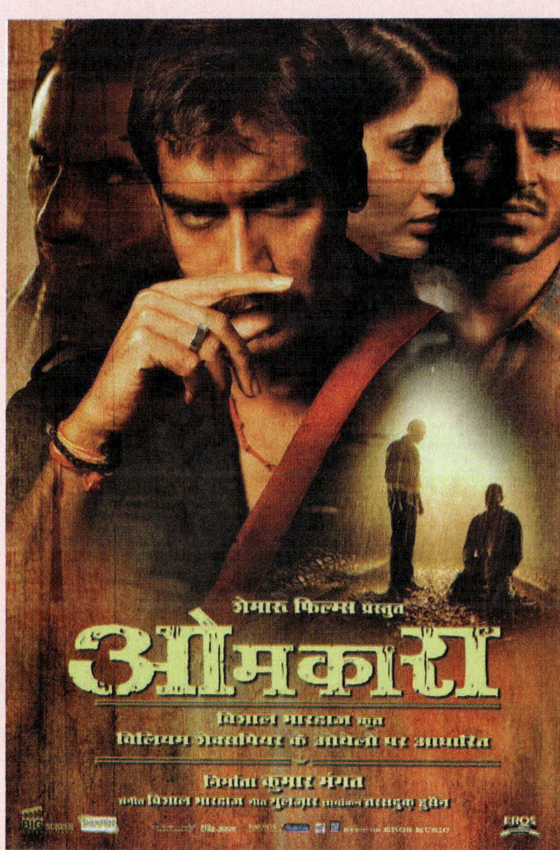

22.101: ***Omkara*** **(2006), the second movie in the Shakespearean trilogy by Vishal Bhardwaj, a crime drama genre, drew box-office success as well as critical acclaim and three National Film Awards.**

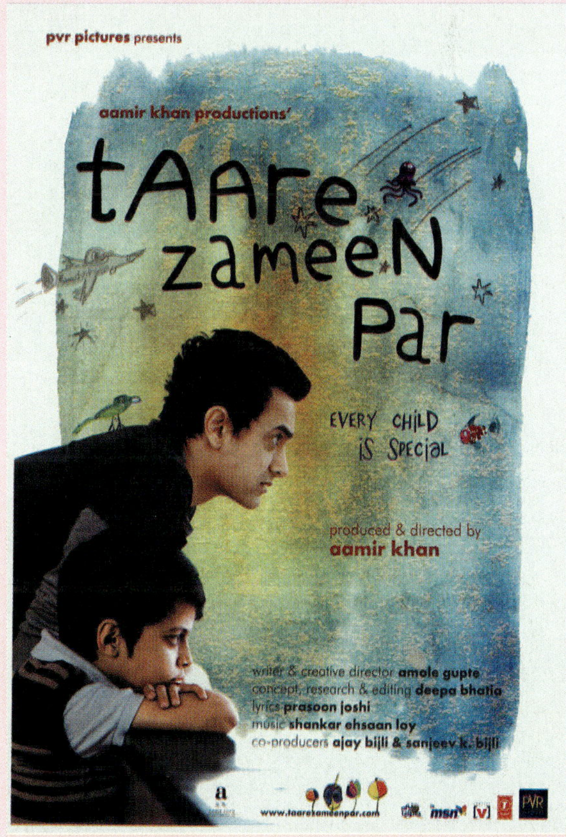

22.102: ***Taare Zameen Par*** **(2007), a psychological drama making a sensitive portrayal of the struggles of a dyslexic child and his teacher-mentor, a commercial success and winner of three National Film Awards.**

All pictures — Courtesy, NFDC-National Film Archives of India, (Pune)

The Age of Southern Mega Movies

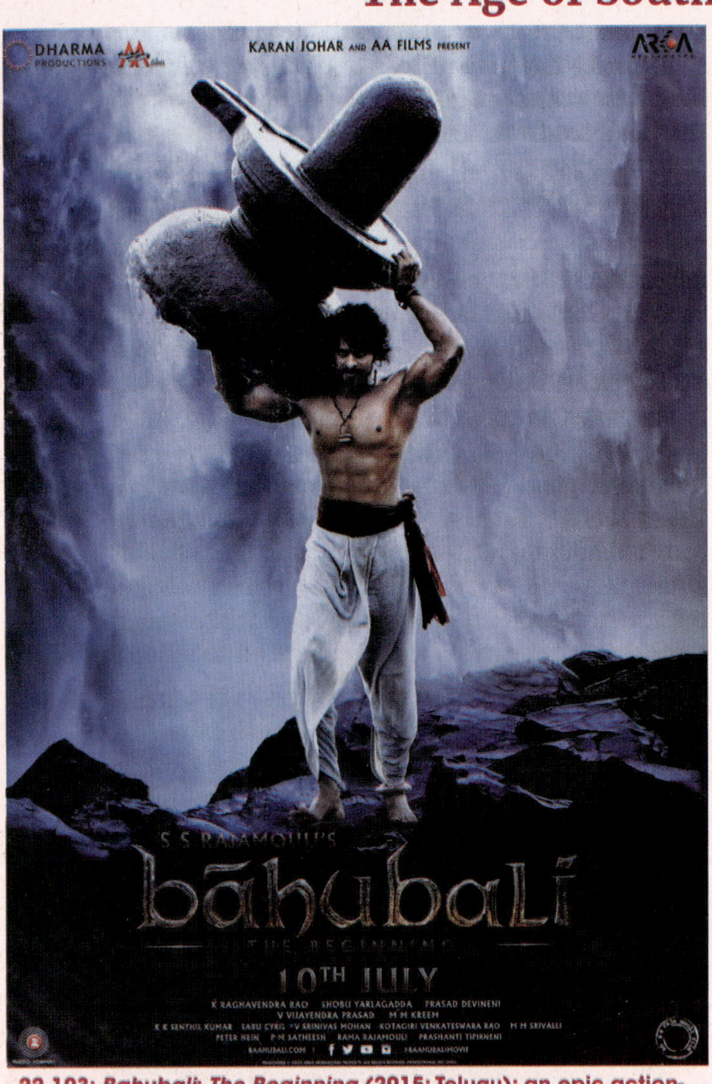

22.103: ***Bahubali*: *The Beginning*** **(2015: Telugu); an epic action-drama movie, the first of the two-part Bahubali series by S.S. Rajamouli, the costliest movie and biggest box office grosser till the year of its release.**

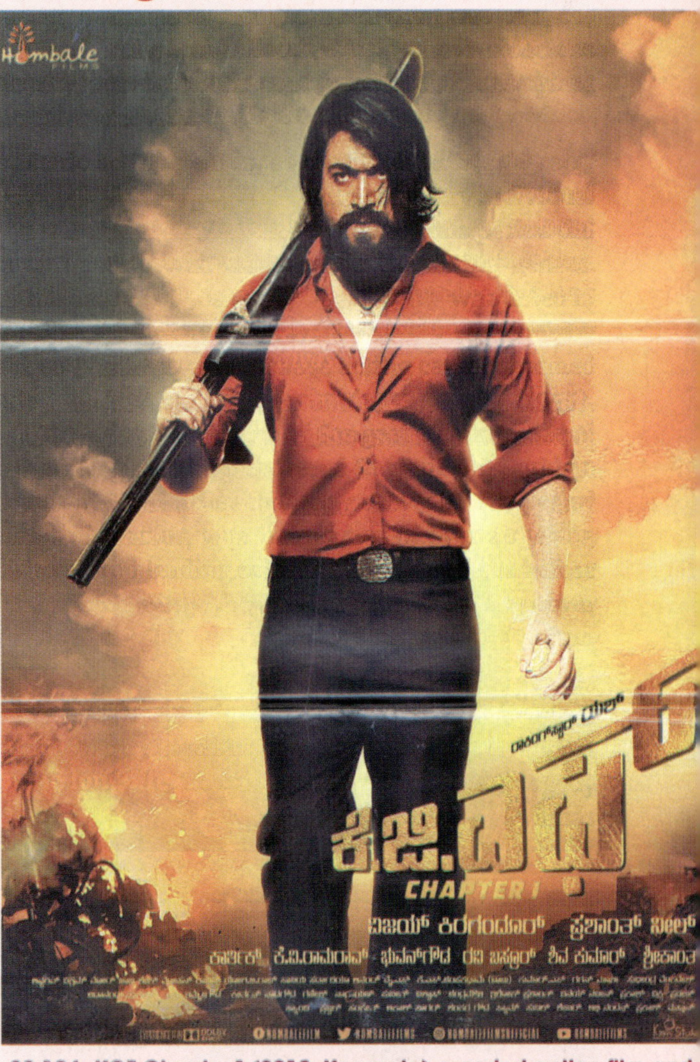

22.104: *KGF Chapter-1* (2018: Kannada) a period action film and the first of the two-part KGF series, was the costliest Kannada film ever, a huge commercial success in different parts of the country and international markets, besides winning critical acclaim.

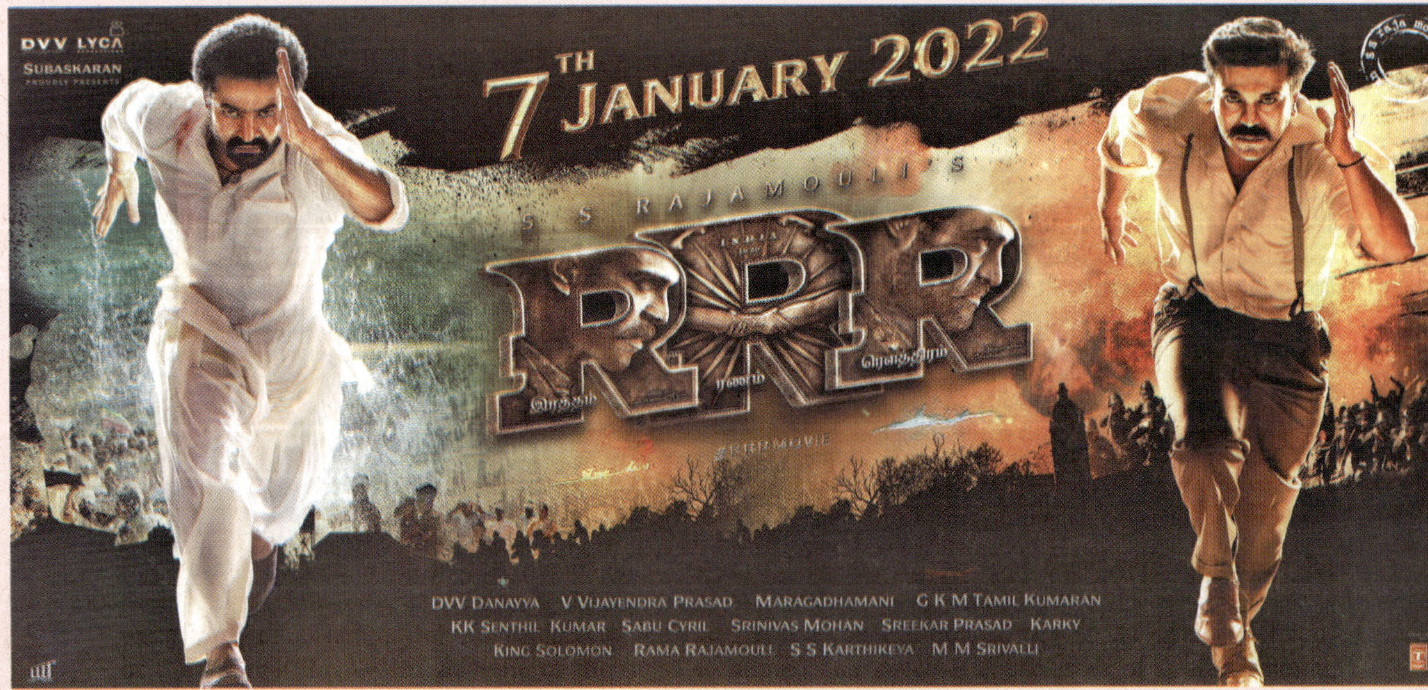

22.105: *RRR* (2022-Telugu), another blockbuster historical-fiction and action-drama Telugu movie by S.S. Rajamouli that won an Academy Award (Oscar award) and Golden Globe Award for its song *Naatu-Naatu*, besides other awards; also broke all previous records of commercial success.

All pictures — Courtesy, NFDC-National Film Archives of India, (Pune)

Festivals & Fairs in Modern India

If India is not secular then India is not India at all.

— Atal Bihari Vajpayee

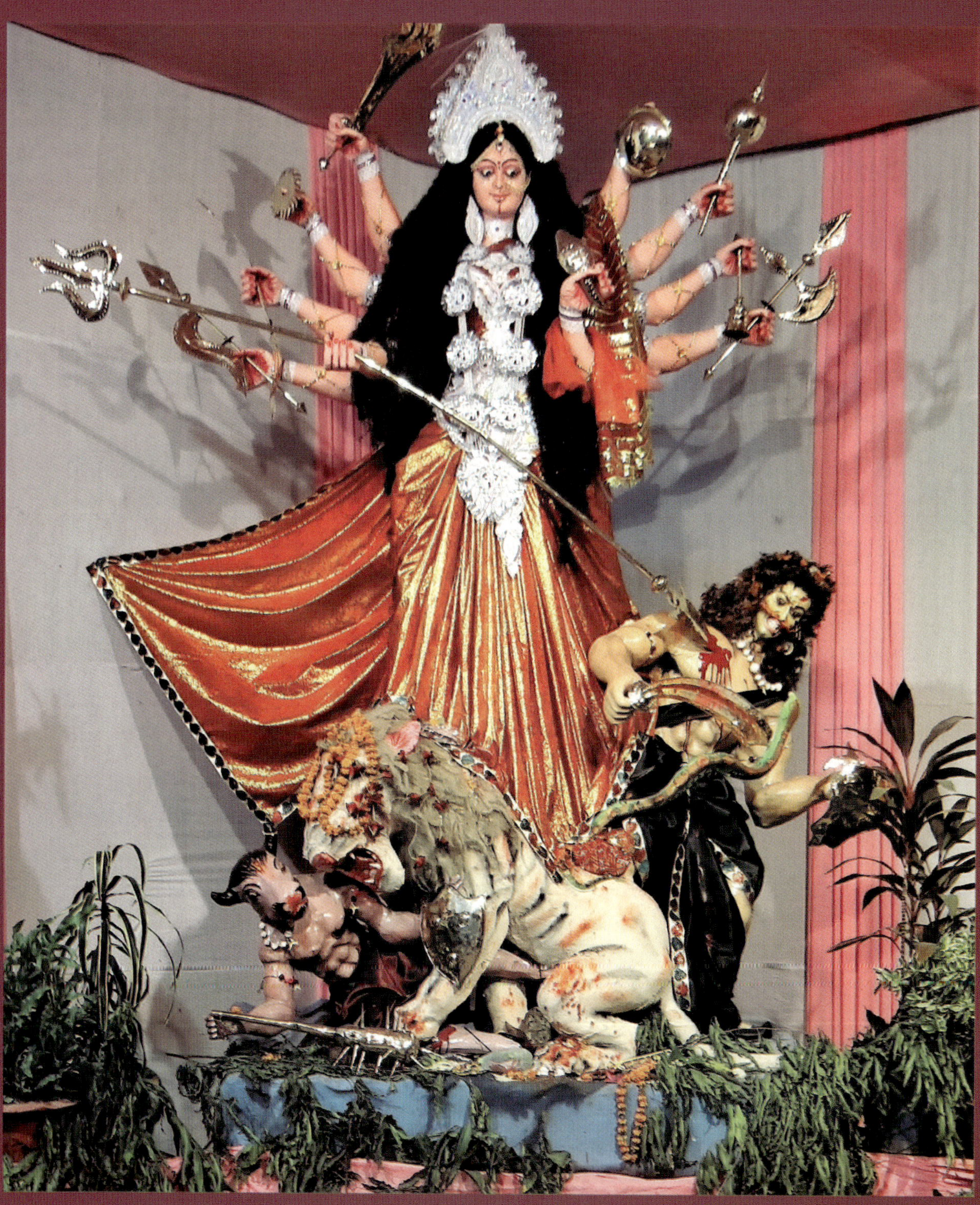

23.1: Goddess Durga mounted on her vehicle/mount lion, slaying demon Mahishasura, depicted by the idols on the occasion of the Durga Puja festival — photograph by Madhukar K Bhagat

FESTIVALS IN MODERN INDIA

Festivals are an expression of human joy. They are cultural manifestations of the institutions of religion and customs. Besides, they are also a reflection of the enduring traditions of a society and its socio-economic activities. They have been an integral part of Indian society since time immemorial. With an unmatched diversity ushered by seven prominent religions of the world, over 1300 spoken languages and dialects, inhabitants of several races and ethnicities, a multitude of geographical and climatic zones and a myriad of social practices and customs, India has become a home to a fascinating variety of festivals. These festivals are reposited in the traditions of people, amongst different communities, celebrated in different parts of the country and for varied reasons.

While many festivals have a religious character, some are related to socio-economic activities such as agriculture and harvest. Many are even related to practices associated with occasions like birth, marriage, death etc. Some are celebrated to mark the arrival of the new year, of new seasons or even a new phase of the moon. While festivals like Deepawali, Dussehra, Holi, etc. are celebrated in large parts of the country, others like Pongal, Baisakhi, Onam and Bihu, are common within a specific community or a region. All have significance and reasons for celebration and add colour and gaiety to the social life.

India, a pluralistic society since ages, has evolved a tradition of inter-community celebration of festivals. Though festivals like Deepawali, Holi, Vijayadashmi, Eid, and Christmas are festivals preserved within the religious and customary traditions of a particular community, they invariably witness participation across the country and of the members of other religious communities as well. Over the years, festivals have become a bridge of interconnect and dialogue between the communities, thereby aiding in social cohesion and the creation of bond amongst the masses. Festivals of India can truly be said to be synonymous with its **culture of pluralism and inclusivity**.

Major Festivals of Hinduism

Deepawali

Also known as Diwali or the **festival of lights**, this major Hindu festival is celebrated across communities throughout India, and now in many parts of the world as well. Deepawali falls on the day of the new moon (*Amavasya*) in the month of *Kartik* (October–November). It marks the return of Lord Rama to Ayodhya after vanquishing Ravana and completing his exile. Lighting of lamps, bursting of crackers, exchange of gifts, worship of Goddess Lakshmi (as an endower of good fortune and wealth) and of lord Ganesha, (the god of wisdom), are the common forms of its celebration. In eastern India, worship of goddess Kali on this day is also quite common. As a festival of lights, **Deepawali signifies the eternal light, that vanquishes the darkness from our lives**. This, in turn, is symbolic of the knowledge which banishes ignorance.

Besides being a major festival of Hindus, Deepawali holds special significance in other communities as well. In **Jainism**, Deepawali marks the day of the liberation (attainment of *moksha*) of the 24th Tirthankara, Mahavira. *Harivamsa Purana*, a Jain treatise composed in the 8th century CE, is considered as amongst the oldest of the treatises which carries the account and significance of Deepawali in Jainism. In one of its *shlokas,* it also mentions the celebration of Deepawali on the day of enlightenment of Mahavira.

In **Sikhism**, the day of Deepawali is celebrated as the *Bandi Chor Diwas*, (literal meaning: the day of release of the prisoners). On this day, the sixth Sikh Guru Hargobind was released from the prison of Mughal emperor Jahangir. But owing to his insistence and out of reverence to the Guru, 54 kings were also released from the prison by the emperor. As per some accounts, this festival is also celebrated since the days of the third Guru Amardas, who, after building a holy well, ordained bathing in it, and as a measure of community bonding called for celebrations on the occasions of Baisakhi and Deepawali. The **Newar Buddhists** of Nepal, followers of Vajrayana Buddhism, also celebrate Deepawali similar to Hindu tradition, by offering prayers to the goddess Lakshmi, the deity of prosperity.

Deepawali is also celebrated by the Hindu communities in different parts of the world including Nepal, Malaysia, Singapore, Sri Lanka, Pakistan, Bangladesh, Mauritius, Fiji, Guyana, Trinidad and Tobago, and Suriname. In recent years, with the expatriate Indian population having its presence in many of the European countries, America and other parts of the world, Deepawali is one festival of India that has gained international visibility and recognition.

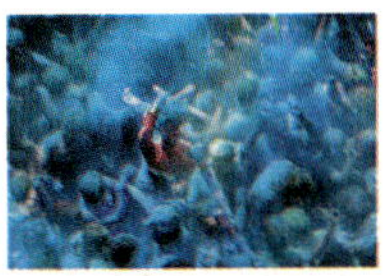

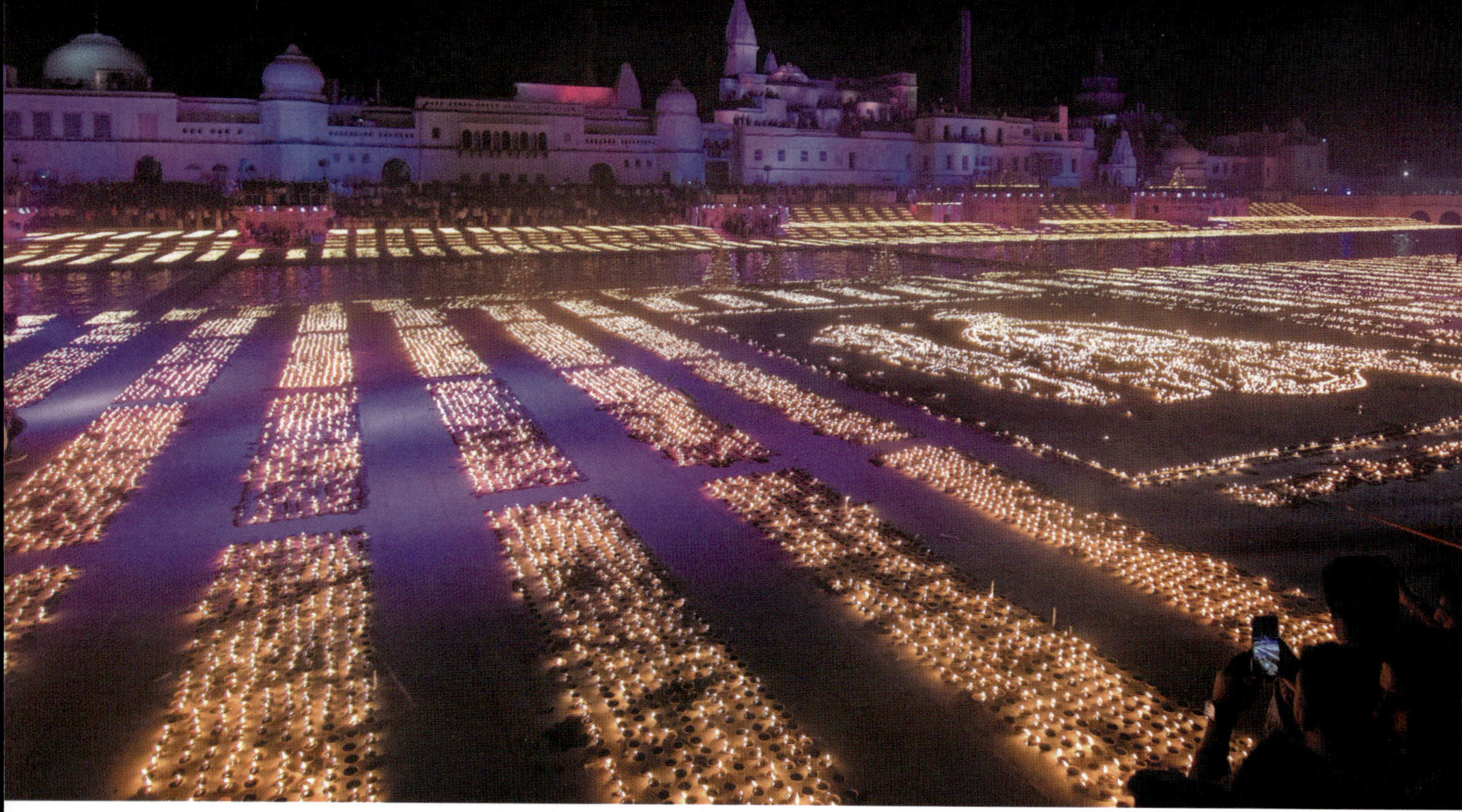

23.2: A view of the celebration of Deepotsav on the banks of the river Sarayu in Ayodhya on the occasion of Choti Deepawali (a day prior to Deepawali). The event of Deepotsav 2022 entered the Guinness Book of World Records with the lighting of 15.76 lakh *diyas* by 19000 volunteers — Courtesy, Directorate of Uttar Pradesh Tourism

Holi

Holi is a **festival of colours** that is celebrated on the last full moon day (*Purnima*) in the lunar month of *Phalgun* (March-April). The festival is unique for its tradition of people smearing and spraying colours on each other. In an atmosphere imbued with a riot of colours, songs and dance, the celebrations are marked with gaiety and unmatched revelry. It is one festival that cuts across communities and transcends the social hierarchy, and distinctions of caste, class, gender and age, thus engendering social interconnect and syncretism. It is also a day to forget the bygones and discords and to cleanse and renew our relationships.

A day prior to Holi is celebrated in many parts as the day of *Holika-Dahan*. As per the mythological anecdote associated with it, Holika the sister of *asura* Hiranaykashyapu, who wanted to kill his son Prahlada (a staunch devotee of lord Vishnu), was burnt in a pyre in which she entered with Prahlada, while the latter survived. This is despite Holika being endowed with a boon of not being harmed by the fire, while Prahlada was bereft of any such boon. As per some accounts, it also signifies the slaying of Hiranayakashyapu by Lord Vishnu, incarnated as Narasimha (man-lion), thus, symbolizing the victory of good over evil.

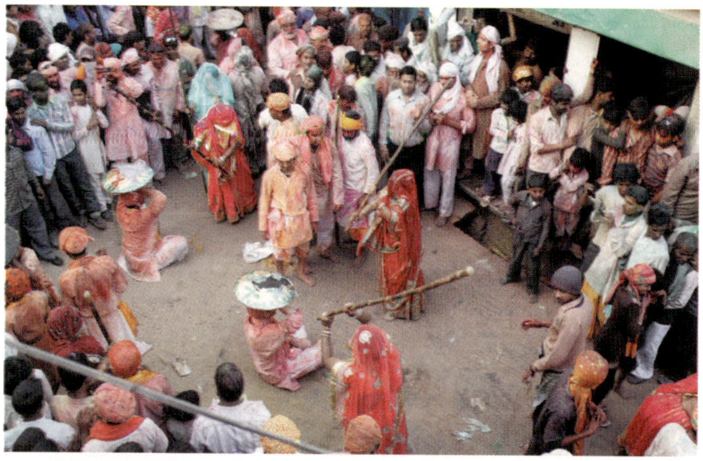

23.3: Lath Maar Holi at Barasane village, a centuries-old tradition — Courtesy, Directorate of Uttar Pradesh Tourism

Holi also marks the **arrival of spring**, a season that is associated with love and invocation for a good harvest. The festival is associated with the legends of the love of Radha and Lord Krishna and his frolic with the *gopikas*. The **Holi of Braj region** in Uttar Pradesh is renowned for depicting this love. Another version of Holi in the Braj region is the *Lath Mar* Holi, where women hit the men gently with sticks (lathi) who protect themselves with shields. As per legends, the tradition owes its origin to

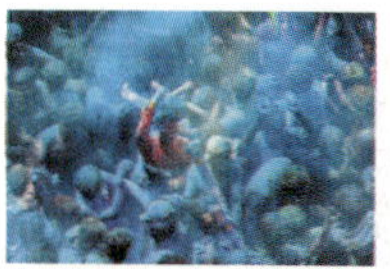

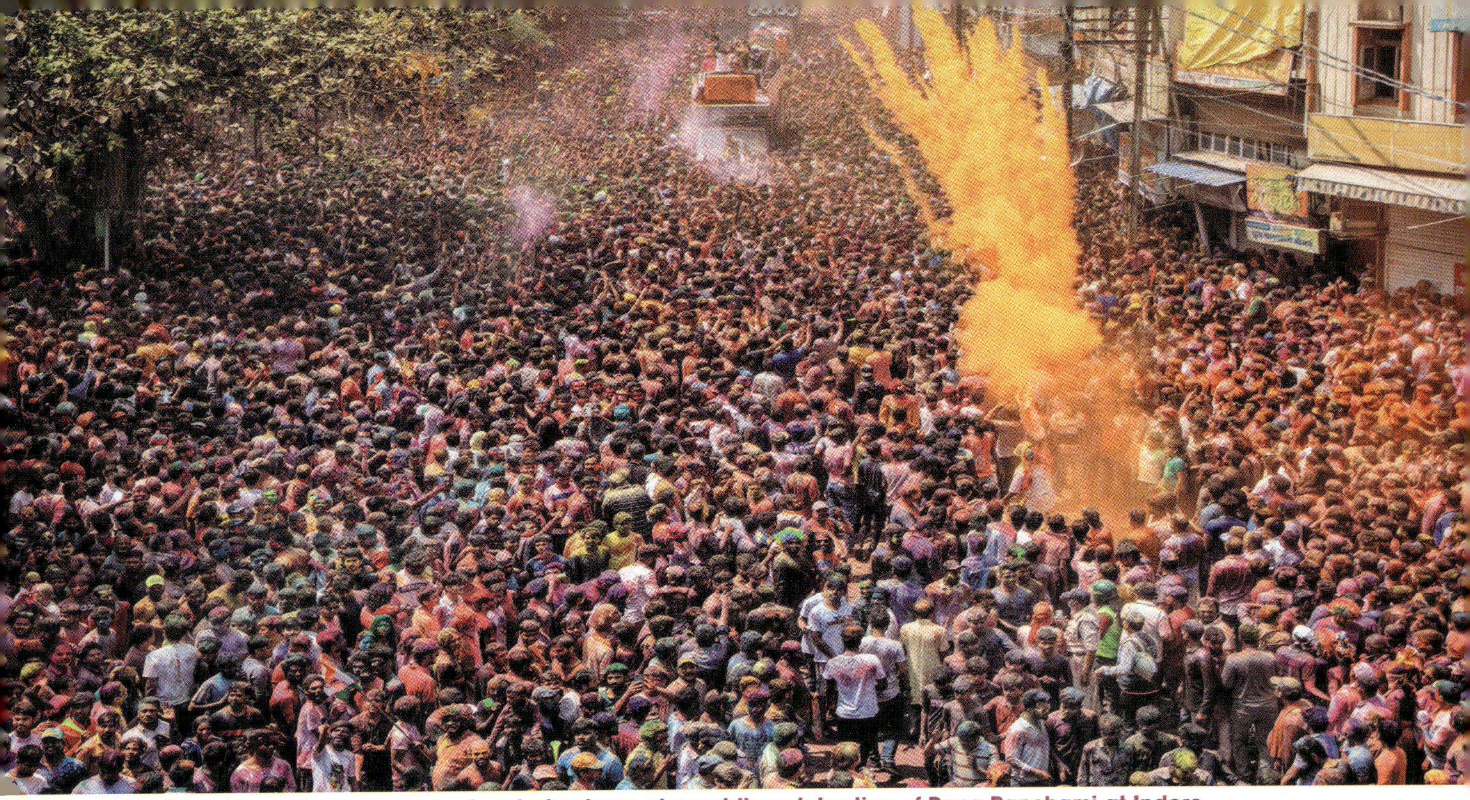

23.4: A sea of people and a burst of colours at a public celebration of Rang Panchami at Indore — Courtesy, Madhya Pradesh Tourism Board

the times of Lord Krishna, who, along with his friends, came to Barsana from Nandgaon to play Holi with Radha and other *gopis*. But instead, they were welcomed with sticks. This is also symbolic of the fun and frolic of the festival which cuts across all the social barriers.

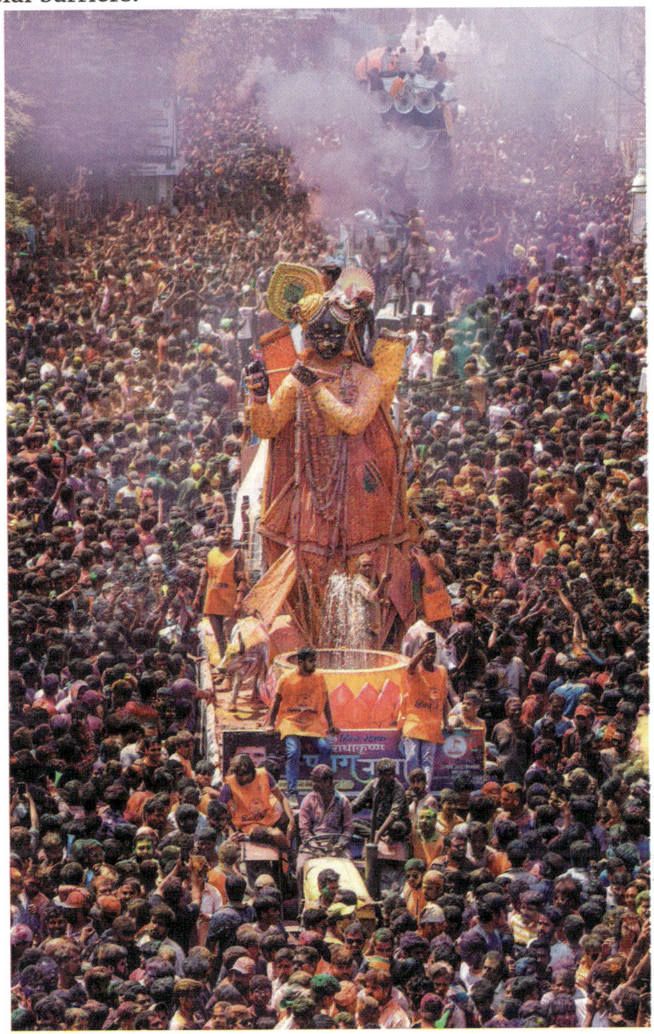

23.5: A large idol of Sri Krishna and a crowd of revellers, celebration of Rang Panchami at Indore — Courtesy, Madhya Pradesh Tourism Board

Holi is celebrated in different parts of India. In East Uttar Pradesh, Bihar and Jharkhand, it is referred to as the *Phagua*. Similar customs are followed which comprises *Holika Dahan*, followed by playing with colours the next day and greeting each other and distribution of sweets later in the evening of the day of Holi. In West Bengal, it is celebrated as *Dol Jatra* (swing festival) where the idols of Krishna and Radha are placed on a decorated swing and worshipped. Besides, people also play with *gulal* (colours). A similar tradition also exists in Odisha, where it is referred to as *Dola* or *Pushp Dola,* and in Assam where it is referred to as *Dol Jatra.*

From Jammu-Kashmir to Himachal to Uttarakhand and in other states of North India, there exist similar Holi traditions. In Uttarakhand, *Baithaki Holi, Khari Holi, and Mahila Holi* are also celebrated. The two former versions incorporate the singing of melodious songs that are fun or may even have a spiritual connotation. In Punjab, different local traditions are added to the festival which includes celebrations from eight days prior to Holi. Decoration of the walls of the houses with art such as *rangoli* and holding of wrestling matches in some parts of the state are also traditions associated with this festival.

In Maharashtra, the day of Holi Purnima is celebrated as *Shimga* where traditional dishes

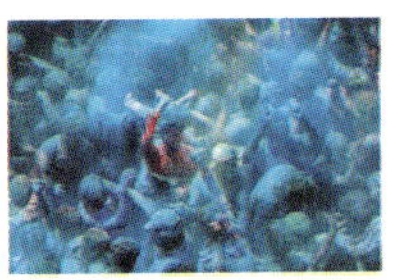

are prepared followed by the lighting of the bonfire in the evening. On its fifth day, *Rang Panchami* is celebrated with colours. This tradition is also popular in parts of Madhya Pradesh and Chhattisgarh. In Karnataka, this day is celebrated as *Kamana Habba* (the day of *Kama*) or the *Kama-dahana* (the day of the burning of the *Kama*). As per legend, on this day, lord Shiva, distracted by Kamadeva in his penance, opened his third eye, thus reducing him to ashes. The **day is symbolic of extinguishing of our desires through wisdom and knowledge.** A similar tradition also exists in Tamil Nadu, but in addition, the day is also celebrated as *Panguni Uthiram* where the rituals of marriage of Shiva and Parvati and that of other deities are performed. It is believed that on this day when Lord Shiva, distracted by Kama, opens his eyes, he also witnesses the penance of Parvati and grants her the boon of marrying her. He later restores Kamadeva who reunites with his beloved Rati. Thus, the festival also signifies love.

Holi also has a large international community celebrating it. Our neighbouring countries such as Nepal, Pakistan and Bangladesh which have some Hindu communities; and countries such as Fiji, Mauritius, Surinam, Trinidad and Tobago and Guyana, where indentured labour went a century or more ago, also celebrate this festival. In Indonesia, Balinese Hindus also celebrate Holi. Besides, many other countries with expatriate Indian population, also celebrate this festival of colours.

Vijayadashami/Dussehra

Another major Hindu festival that has pan-India celebrations, Vijayadashmi/Dussehra, signifies the **victory of good over evil.** The festival falls on the 10th day of *Shukla Paksha* of *Ashvin* month (September–October) and in different parts of the country, it has different significance and traditions. In northern and western India, the festival marks the victory of Lord Rama (an incarnation of Lord Vishnu) over Ravana. In the southern and eastern parts of India, the festival is preceded by nine days of worship of Goddess *Durga* who vanquished the demon *Mahishasura* and many other *asuras*. The nine days are also referred to as *Navaratra*. In many parts of the country, both traditions are followed. Yet another significance of the festival is that on the 20th day after Dussehra, arrives the festival of Deepawali which marks the return of lord Rama to Ayodhya. Thus, the arrival of Dussehra begins a period of festivities which culminate in Deepawali.

Ramlila, the enactment of the story of lord Rama is one of the most important traditions which is associated with Dussehra. Inspired by the *Ramcharitmanas* of Tulsidas, (the retelling of the epic Ramayana), Ramlila involves the enactment of the tales of the epic over a period of nine days in a folk theatre format. The 10th day culminates in the burning of the effigies of Ravana, Kumbhakarna and Meghnad, thus symbolizing the triumph of good over evil. The **traditional performance of Ramlila** enacted during the Dussehra festival has been **inscribed by UNESCO in 2008 in the list of the Intangible Cultural Heritage of Humanity.** The most famous among the various Ramlilas are considered those of Ayodhya, Ramnagar and Varanasi, Vrindavan, Almora, Satana and Madhubani.

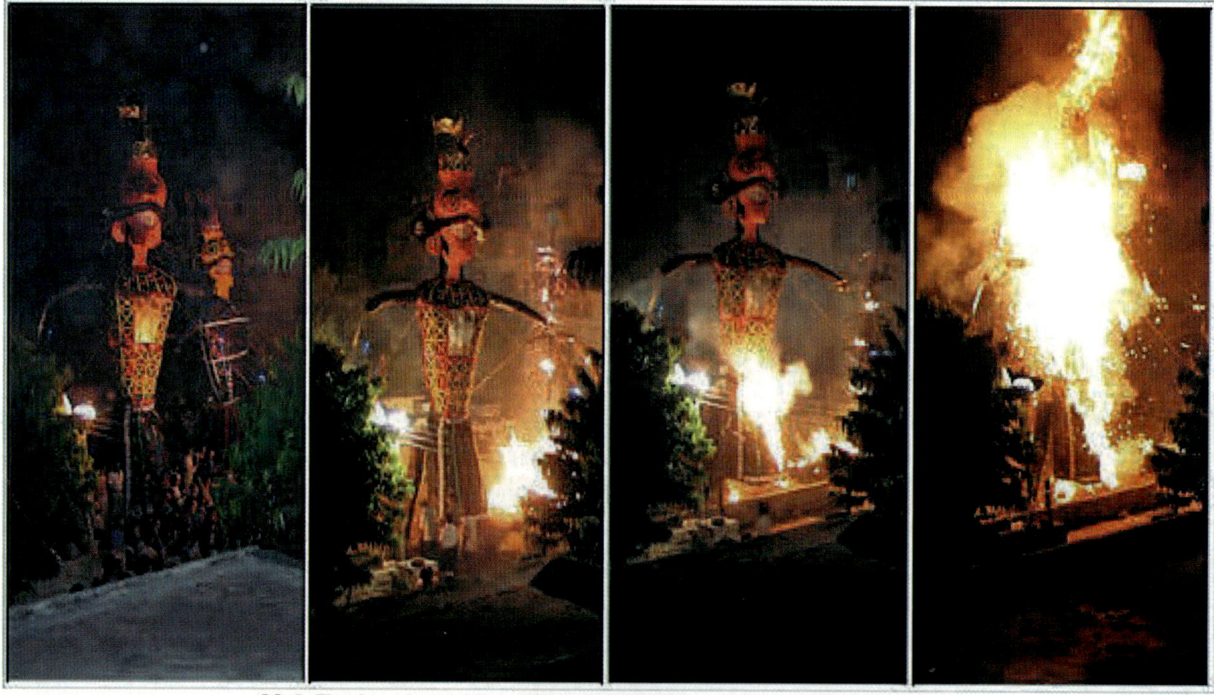

23.6: The burning of the effigy of Ravana — Wikimedia Commons

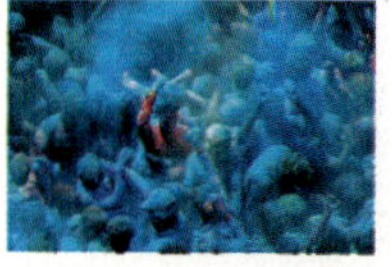

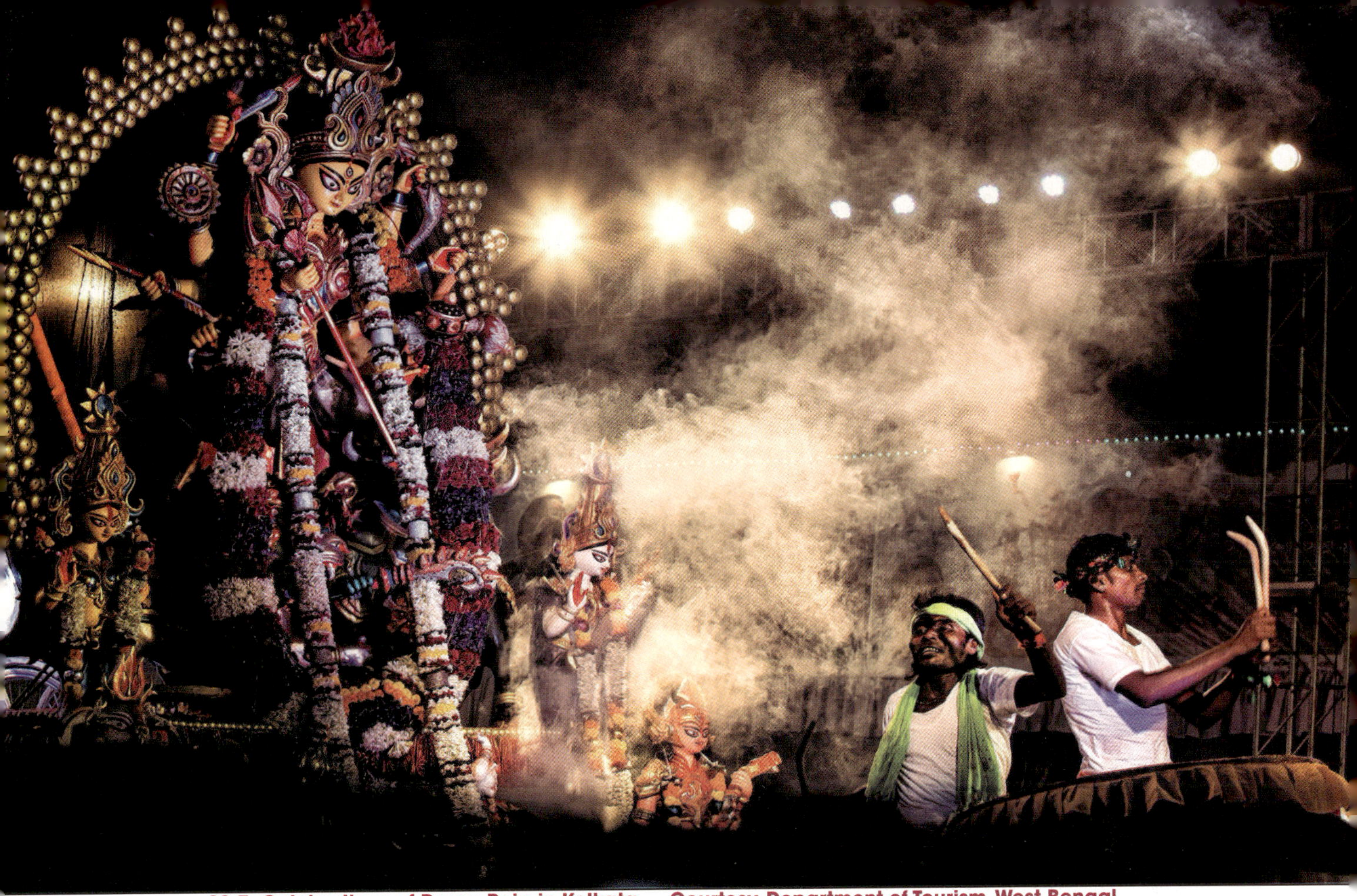

23.7: Celebrations of Durga Puja in Kolkata — Courtesy, Department of Tourism, West Bengal

Another socio-religious tradition associated with the festival and popular in East and South India is the **worship of Goddess Durga**. As per legend, the Goddess vanquished the mighty and invincible *asura* Mahishasura (the shape-shifting demon who took the form of a buffalo). As homage to the Goddess, nine days of worship over the period of Navaratra are held which involve the scriptural recitations and performance of the rituals associated with the worship. Makeshift structures called *pandals* are specially erected in public spaces to house the deities. The entire set of ceremonies and associated festivities is organised largely through voluntary efforts by groups of individuals, societies and other religious as well as non-religious organisations. On the 10th day, the clay idols of the Goddess and other deities are immersed in water bodies, symbolising their return to their abodes and thus marking an end to the festivities.

The Durga Puja of the West Bengal region is especially renowned for the religious fervour and grandeur with which they are celebrated. The **Durga Puja of Kolkata** is also inscribed since 2021 in the **'UNESCO list of Intangible Cultural Heritage of Humanity'**.

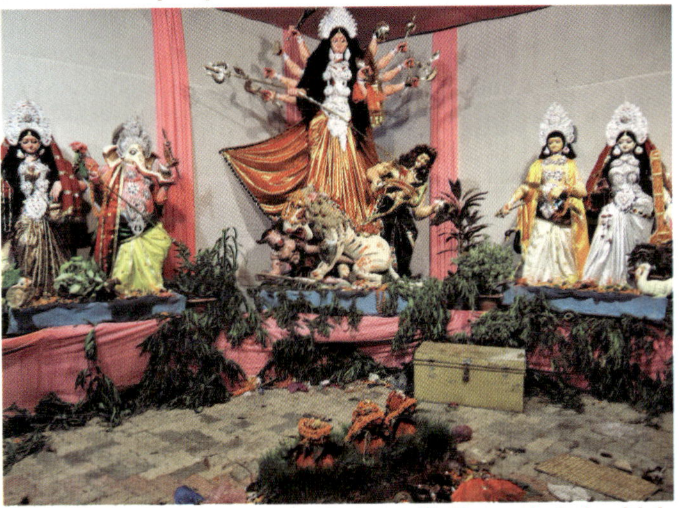

23.8: A Navaratra pandal at Patna, with decorated clay idol of Goddess Durga, other deities and the demon Mahishasura. A ritualistic *kalash* which is established can be seen in the foreground — photograph by Madhukar K Bhagat

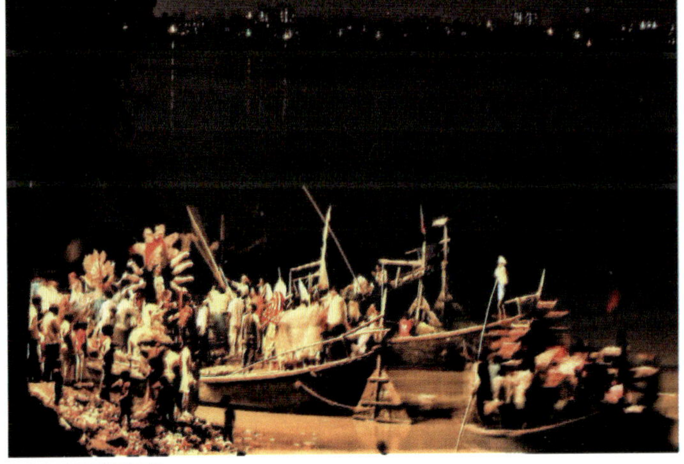

23.9: The immersion of the idols of Goddess Durga in the evening on the 10th day (Vijayadashmi), on the banks of river Ganga at Patna — photograph by Madhukar K Bhagat

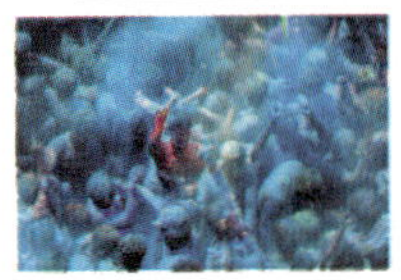

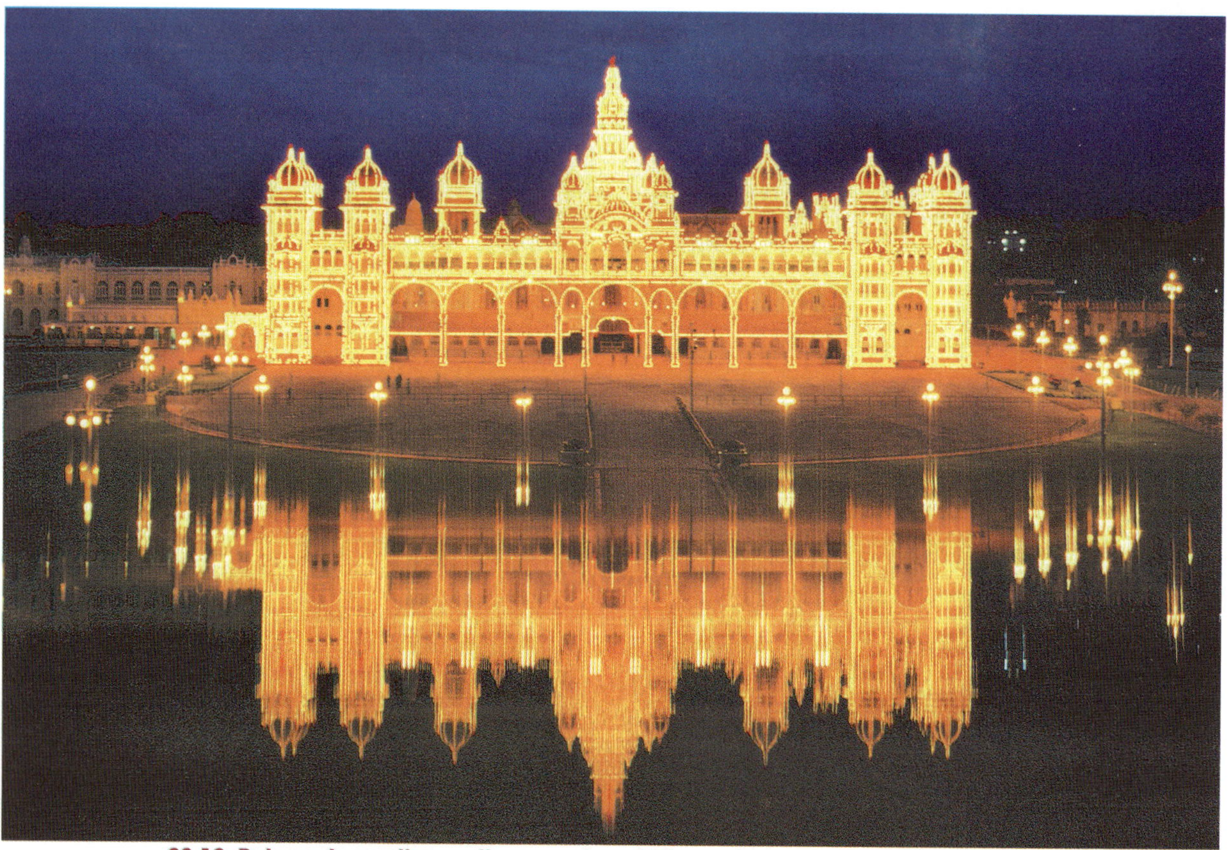

23.10: Palace decoration on the occasion of Mysuru Dasara, at Mysore, Karnataka — Courtesy, Karnataka State Tourism Development Corporation

Another grand as well as historic tradition of **Dasara** (Dussehra) is that of **Mysuru**. The celebrations which are believed to be more than four centuries old and started during the period of the Vijayanagar empire, are still continued by the Wodeyar kings of Mysuru. Worship of Devi Chamundeshwari (Durga), celebrations in the royal palace, special martial procession including elephants, camels and horses and grand festivities, are some of the highlights of this royal religious tradition.

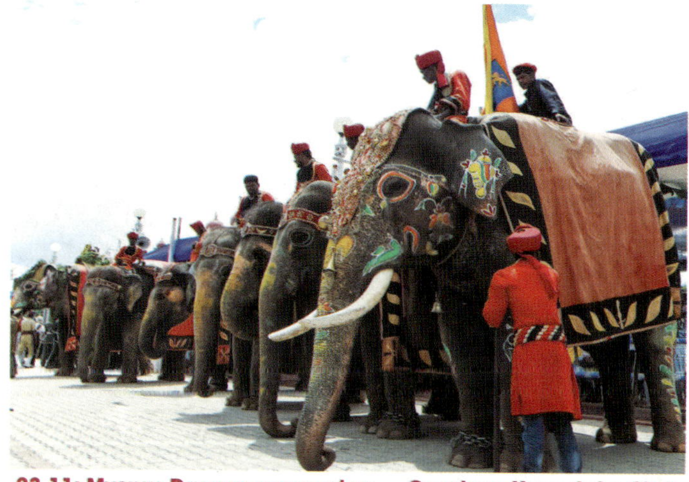

23.11: Mysuru Dasara procession — Courtesy, Karnataka State Tourism Development Corporation

Another famous celebration of this festival is the **Navaratri** tradition of **Gujarat**, which involves the ritual worship of the deity and the community folk dances of *Dandiya* and *Garba*. In December 2023, the **Garba of Gujarat has also been inscribed on the UNESCO representative list of the Intangible Cultural Heritage of Humanity**. In different parts of the country, apart from traditional worship, the festival of Vijayadashmi/Navaratri is also marked by music and dance and organisation of traditional fairs.

Festivals Associated with Birth of Deities, Prophets and Religious Leaders

India is a land where several religions have found space and bloomed. It is also the upholder of the tradition of the celebration of the birth of the deities, prophets and other religious leaders. This genre of festivals is also an occasion to remember the ideals and values associated with the lives of the venerated deities and hallowed prophets. Besides, they are also a reflection of the religious rituals and traditions. The cultural celebrations which ensue, are an occasion for social connect and festivity. Over the period of centuries, these festivals have ushered inter-faith respect and strengthened India's culture of pluralism and inclusivity.

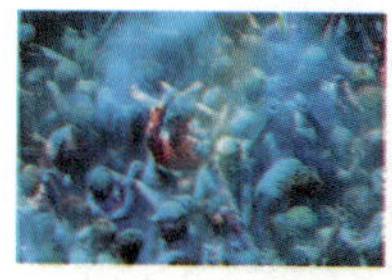

Ram Navami, a major Hindu festival, celebrates the **birth of Lord Rama** who is considered the seventh incarnation of Lord Vishnu. It falls on the ninth day of *Shukla Paksha* (the phase of the ascending moon or bright fortnight) of the *Chaitra* month (March–April). The festival is also preceded in many parts of India with the observation of the *Chaitra Navaratri,* which incorporates the worship of Goddess Durga for nine days. The day of Ram Navami is considered very auspicious by the Hindus as Lord Ram, a human incarnate, is considered to be an epitome of virtues and the one who set **ideals for emulation** for mankind. The devotees often observe a fast on this day and *bhajans* and *kirtans* in praise of the Lord are performed in Rama temples. Discourse from the holy *Ramayana* or the *Ramcharitamanas* which are termed as *Rama Katha*, is another significant event of the day. *Ratha yatras* of Sri Rama, Lakshmana and Sita are also organised in many places. The celebrations in Ayodhya, the birthplace of Lord Rama, are specially marked with great fervour and devotion. On this day, taking a dip in the Saryu River at Ayodhya is considered very auspicious.

Krishna Janmashtami or Janmashtami is the festival of celebration of the **birth of Lord Krishna** who is considered the eighth incarnation of lord Vishnu and is also regarded by the devotees as the Supreme God. This festival falls on the eighth day of *Krishna-paksha* (dark fortnight) of the month of *Shravana* (August–September). Lord Krishna is believed to have been born in Mathura. Accordingly, the celebrations of the Braj region, the place of his birth, are particularly famous. Like the festival of Rama Navami, devotees observe fast on this day with *bhajans*, *kirtans*, other rituals, songs and dances to celebrate the birth of the Lord. *Katha* recitals from the *Bhagavata Purana* or other recitals from the life of Lord Krishna are particularly common. As Lord Krishna was born at the stroke of midnight, the festivities continue to this hour.

As per the legends associated with his birth, Lord Krishna was born at a time when his parents Devaki and Vasudev were in captivity and as his birth happened, they were miraculously freed from the shackles. Vasudev then took the child to be raised with Yashoda and Nanda in Gokul. The legends associated with his birth and stories often form a part of the special tableaus which are made on this occasion. Enactment of *Krishna-Leela* is also done to celebrate his birth. The Lord is worshipped as a child and his childhood antiques are also showcased. The incidents of his breaking the pots and stealing butter from the other village households, is the essence of the tradition of *Dahi-Handi* which is popular in celebrations in Maharashtra. Different teams vie to form a human pyramid and break the earthen pots which are hung at a considerable height, symbolizing the butter pots broken by the child Krishna.

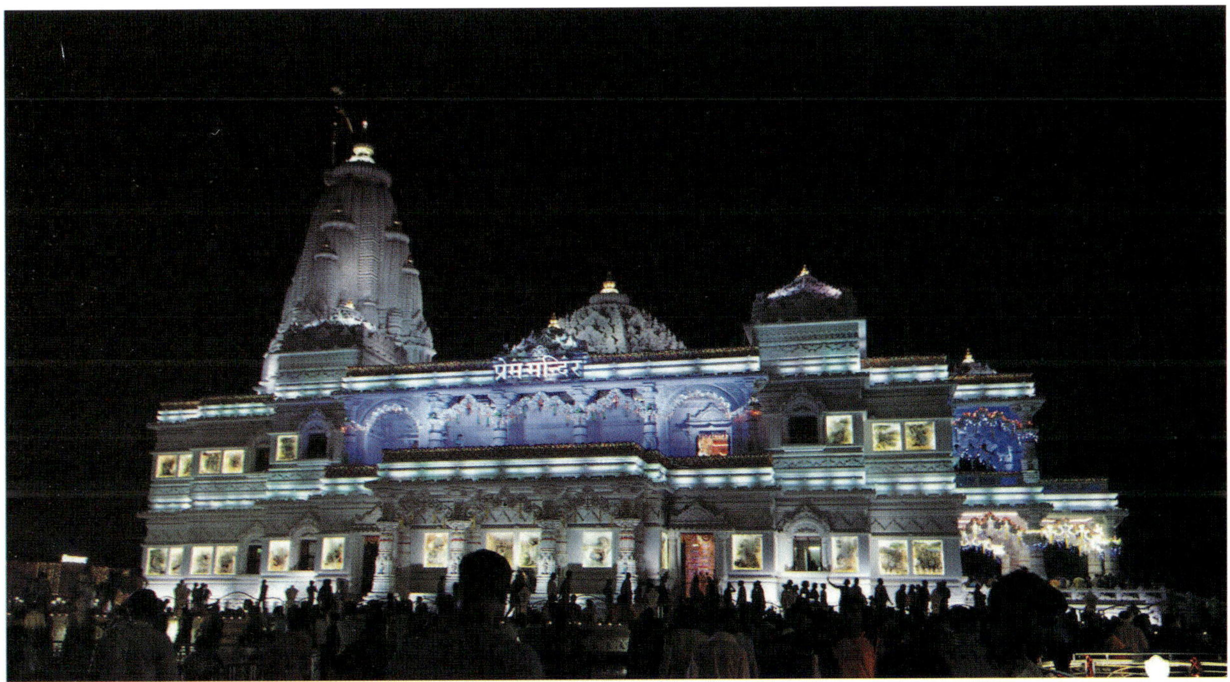

23.12: The famous Prem Mandir at Vrindavan, decorated on the occasion of Janmashtami — Courtesy, Directorate of Uttar Pradesh Tourism

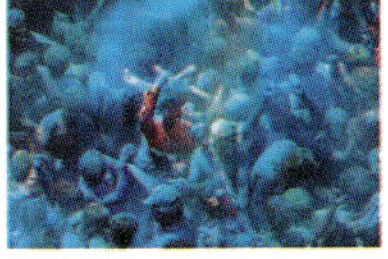

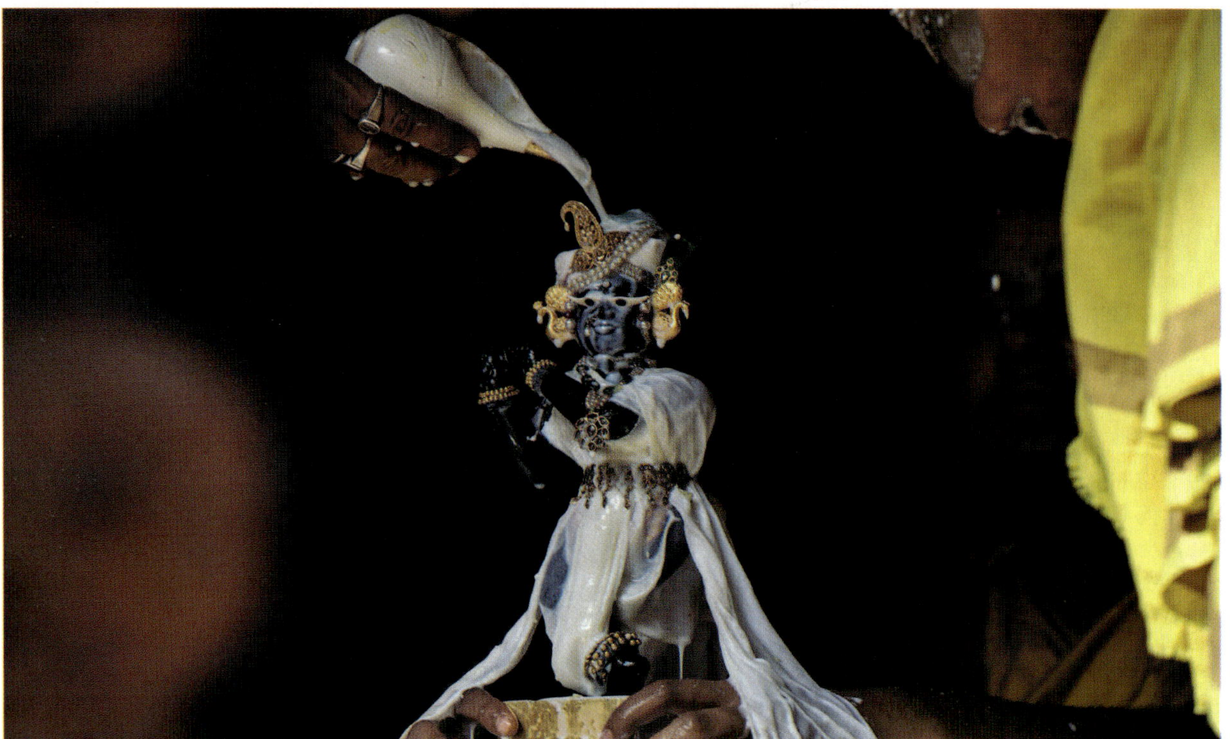

23.13: A small idol of lord Krishna venerated through rituals on Janmashtami — Courtesy, Directorate of Uttar Pradesh Tourism

While Lord Rama symbolizes the ideal, **Lord Krishna symbolizes eternal love**. His life signifies the different aspects of this love whether as a child to Yashoda, as a consort to Radha or a friend and guide to Arjuna. Thus, **love and compassion for fellow human beings and love for the divine** is the key message of this festival.

Maha Shivratri, literally meaning 'the great night of Shiva', is a Hindu festival observed on the 14th day of *Krishna Paksha* (dark/waning moon fortnight) the month of *Magha* (February–March). The festival is an occasion to venerate Lord Shiva, one of the principal deities of Hinduism and a part of the trinity of Brahma, Vishnu and Mahesh (the creator, the preserver and the destroyer). As per the legends associated with the festival, on this day. Lord Shiva consumed the poison that emanated from the churning of the ocean by the *devas* and the *asuras* and thus he saved the world from annihilation. As per another belief, on this day, Parvati was married to Shiva, an event which symbolizes the union of the *Jivaatma* (the enduring individual self) with the *Parmatma* (the Supreme Being). As per some beliefs, on this day, Lord Shiva manifested himself to Brahma and Vishnu, as the fiery *lingam,* which had no origin or end. (When the two gods were caught in an argument as to who was the greatest of gods). Thus, unlike other festivals of this genre, Maha-Shivaratri is not associated with the birth of the deity, who is otherwise considered an eternal and Supreme God. As per some scholars, the tradition of this festival is considered to be nearly **2500 years old** and can be traced to the Puranic age.

The festival is associated with the worship of lord Shiva in the temples and homes. Chanting of mantras and other rituals, offering of milk, honey, fruit and *bael-patra* to the deity (leaves of wood-apple tree) performance of yoga, meditation and devotees keeping fast, are some traditions associated with the festival. The celebrations and worship of lord Shiva often continue throughout the night which is considered very auspicious as a night of spiritual awakening. Devotees also throng the *jyotirlinga* temples in different parts of the country. Unlike other festivals where cultural revelry and gaiety are integral parts of the celebrations, Maha Shivaratri is marked with solemnness, fasting, praying, introspection and social harmony. Devotees also take vows of *daya* (kindness), *kshama* (forgiveness), *satya* (telling truth) and *ahimsa* (non-injury).

Lord Shiva is considered the *adiyogi* (primeval yogi). He is also venerated as the Mahadeva or the god amongst the gods. As an *adiguru* he is also considered the greatest teacher. Thus, the festival **signifies overcoming darkness and ignorance** through the blessings of the divine lord and **symbolizes the knowledge and discipline essential for the spiritual salvation** of the devotee.

Ganesh-Chaturthi, also known as Vinayaka Chaturthi, is another major festival of Hindus which is celebrated in different parts of the country as well in other countries with followers of Hinduism. It is especially popular in Maharashtra, Gujarat, Madhya Pradesh, Karnataka, Goa and Telangana where it is celebrated for 10 days. The festival marks the birth of **Lord Ganesha** and falls on the fourth day of the 2nd fortnight (*Shukla-paksha*) in the month of *Bhadrapada* (August–September).

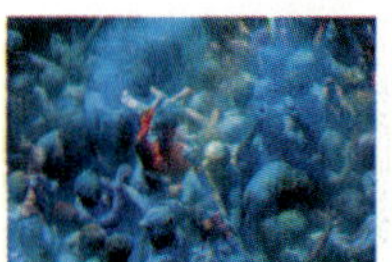

Lord Ganesha is the son of Goddess Parvati and Lord Shiva. As per legends associated with his birth in the Puranas, he was created by Parvati out of turmeric mud of her body and infused life. Given the task to guard when Parvati was bathing, Ganesha didn't recognize Shiva and prohibited him from entering while the latter also did not know it was him. In the argument and events which followed, an enraged Shiva severed the boy's head with his *trishul.* However, seeing the sorrow and anger of Parvati which threatened to end the world, Shiva promised to bring him back to life. He instructed the *devas* to go in the northwards direction and bring the head of the first living creature they encountered. This happened to an elephant that Shiva implanted on the body of the boy. Thus, was born a god with the head of an elephant and the body of a man. Shiva also blessed him to be the first to be worshipped by the devotees and so he was christened Ganesha (the god of the followers/devotees). Although different anecdotes of his creation are in vogue, Lord Ganesha is unanimously accepted as the first worshipped among the gods. He is the God who is the endower of knowledge and wisdom and the remover of the obstacles.

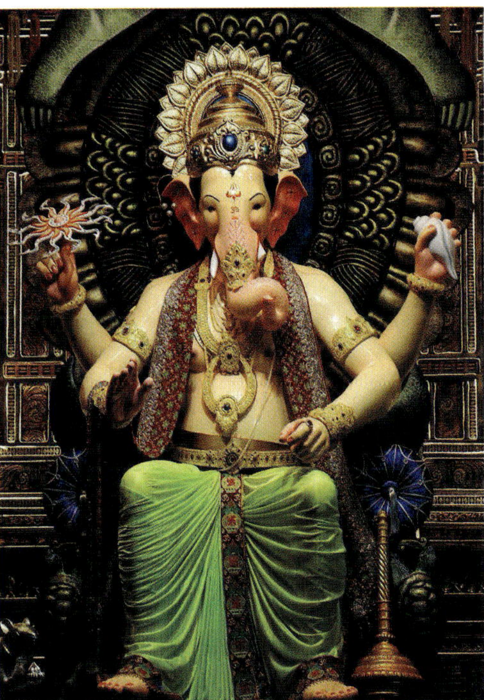

23.14: The idol of Lord Ganesha placed on the occasion of Ganesh Chaturthi at Lal Baug in Mumbai, one of the most popular public places for the festival, popularly known as Lalbaugcha Raja — Wikimedia Commons

The festival of Ganesh Chaturthi begins with the installation of the clay idol of the deity in homes and public places and *pandals* (make-shift tents). Rituals of *pran-pratistha* or invocation of the deity in the idol and other forms of ritual worship follow. Fasting, praying, *bhajan* and *kirtan* are traditions associated with the festival. Distribution of *modaka* or *ladoo,* sweets considered the favourite of the deity, is a salient feature of the festival. On the 10th day of Anant-Chaturdashi, the clay idol is taken for immersion in a procession marked with gaiety and enthusiasm. The immersion and dissolving of the idol in water, symbolise the departure of the deity to his heavenly abode. **Lord Ganesha epitomizes the quest for true knowledge that vanquishes the obstacles in spiritual pursuits** and hence he is the **god of learning and wisdom** who is invoked before every ritual and religious tradition.

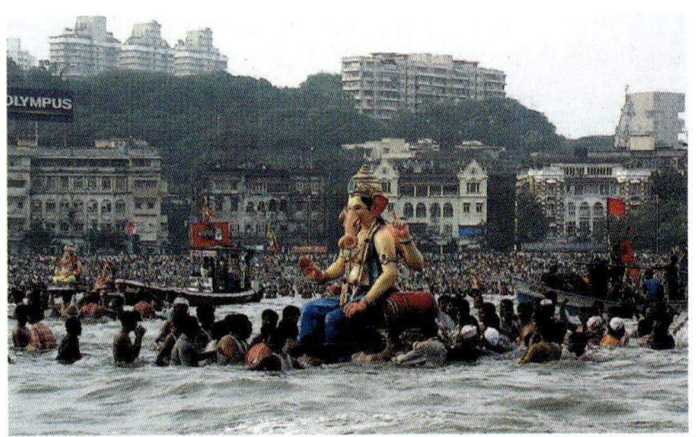

23.15: Ganesh Visarjan or the immersion of the idols of Lord Ganesha in the sea at Mumbai on the occasion of Anant Chaturdashi — Wikimedia Commons

Buddha-Purnima is a celebration of birth of **Lord Buddha.** This festival is observed on the full moon day (*purnima*) of the month of *Vaisakha* (April–May). It is celebrated by the Buddhist community in South, South-East and East Asia, besides other parts of the world. Lord Buddha is also venerated in Hinduism and is considered as the ninth incarnation of lord Vishnu. As such, the festival is also celebrated by the Hindu community. Although scholars do not have unanimity as to the exact date of his birth, Lord Buddha is believed to have been born around 563 BCE to 468 BCE in Lumbini in present-day Nepal. Intrigued by the four sights of a sick man, an old man, a dead man and a monk, the prince Gautama abandoned his royal comforts in search of the eternal truth as to the cause of human sorrow.

On this day of Buddha Purnima, Gautama is believed to have discovered the eternal knowledge under a *pipal* tree in Bodh Gaya and thus became the Buddha. It is also believed that on this very day, he shed his mortal body attaining *nirvana* (*nibanna*) at Kushinagar. Thus, the three great events of lord Buddha's life which are his birth, enlightenment and *nirvana* all happened on this auspicious day.

The festival is also known as ***Vesak*** (derived from the word Vaisakh) in the Buddhist community of South and Southeast Asia. The day is marked, by the veneration of lord Buddha in various temples, observance of different rituals as per the local traditions, reaffirming one's faith in the teachings of

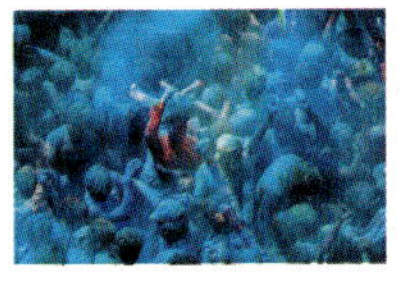

Buddhism and renewing once vows to follow the eightfold path of Buddhism. Singing of hymns in praise of the *Triratna* (the Buddha, the *Dhamma*, the *Sangha*) and other mantras, offering of flowers, burning of candles and incense sticks in the temples, recital from Buddhist scriptures of the *Pitakas* and meditations are the other activities associated with this festival. In India, the festival is particularly noteworthy in the Buddhist centres of Bodhgaya, Sarnath and Kushinagar, besides others.

Lord Buddha's life embodied the quest for **eternal knowledge** and the **path of salvation**. Buddha Purnima is a reminder to the world of his teachings of the **'four noble truths'** and the '**eight-fold path'** and in particular, of the '**middle path'**; away from extremes of asceticism and indulgence, as the right course for human salvation.

Mahavir Jayanti or **Mahavir Janma Kalyanak**, is the major festival of the Jain community. It marks the day of the **birth of Lord Mahavira**, the 24th and the last Tirthankara of the Jains. The festival is observed on the thirteenth day of *Shukla paksha* (bright phase) of the month of *Chaitra* (March–April). Lord Mahavira was born to King Siddhartha and Queen Trishala in 599 BCE in Kundagram village of *Vajji ganrajya* (present-day Vaishali). He relinquished his worldly life of comfort in search of truth. After years of asceticism, he attained *keval gyan* (true knowledge), thus becoming the *Jina* (or the conqueror), or *Mahavira* (the great one).

The day of Mahavir Jayanti is observed with the veneration of lord Mahavira and vows of observation of the principles and practices of Jainism. The idol of lord Mahavira is carried out in a procession. Ritual worship is carried out with the *abhisheka* of the idols of the deity (anointment) and chanting of verses from the Jain scriptures. Discourses on Jainism, prayers in temples and meditations are some other practices observed.

The teachings of Jainism emphasize on **Ahimsa,** and accordingly this festival also **signifies the principle of ahimsa, piety on all living creatures and universal tolerance**.

Milad un-Nabi or **Eid-e-Milad** is the celebration of the day of birth of **Prophet Muhammad**, whose teachings have laid the foundation of Islam. It is also referred to as **Mawlid** or **Maulid-Nabi**. Prophet Muhammad is believed to have been born in 570 CE in Mecca. While the followers of the Sunni faith of Islam consider this day to have occurred on the 12th day of **Rabi-al-Awwal** (the third month of the Islamic lunar calendar) the Shia faith observes the birth on the 17th day of the **Rabi-al-Awwal**. The day is also significant, for it is believed by some to be also the death anniversary of the Prophet.

Milad-un-Nabi is an important festival for the nearly 172 million observers of the Islamic faith in India (as per the 2011 census) and is observed throughout the country. The celebrations include decorations of houses, taking out of processions with green banners and flags (green symbolising heaven), recitals from the holy Quran, offering of community prayers, discourses about the life of the holy prophet etc. Donation to the poor is also a salient element of this festival and **signifies compassion for fellow beings, a key element of the teachings of Islam**.

Christmas is the celebration of the birth of **Jesus Christ** whose teachings have laid the foundation of Christianity. It is observed the world over on the 25th of December. Although Christians are a minority community in India, there are 26 million Christians (as per the 2011 census) who are distributed in different parts of the country, making Christmas an important festival in India. The celebration of Christmas is particularly marked with long festivity and great enthusiasm in the states of Goa, Kerala, Meghalaya, Nagaland, Mizoram, and Arunachal Pradesh where there is a substantial Christian population besides in the union territory of Puducherry and the city of Mumbai.

The celebration begins with a midnight mass held in churches on the night of 24th December. At midnight, singing of Christmas carols and other festivities are organised. The lighting of candles in the churches as a mark of reverence to Jesus, greeting each other with merry Christmas (or other forms of greeting), exchanging of gifts and a feast thereafter follows. Some other traditions associated with this festival are the decoration of the Christmas tree and the decorations of the houses with large star-shaped paper lanterns. A feast or roast turkey is popular in the West and has some following in India too. However, different local delicacies as per the regional traditions and cuisines of India may replace this custom. Santa Claus, a man in a red dress with a white flowing beard, bringing gifts to children, is another custom that is popular in the festival and is particularly looked forward to by children even of other faiths.

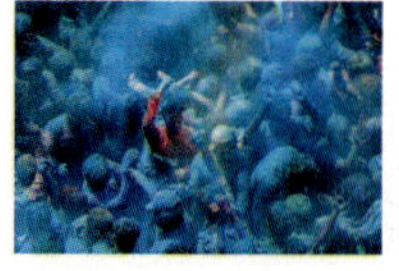

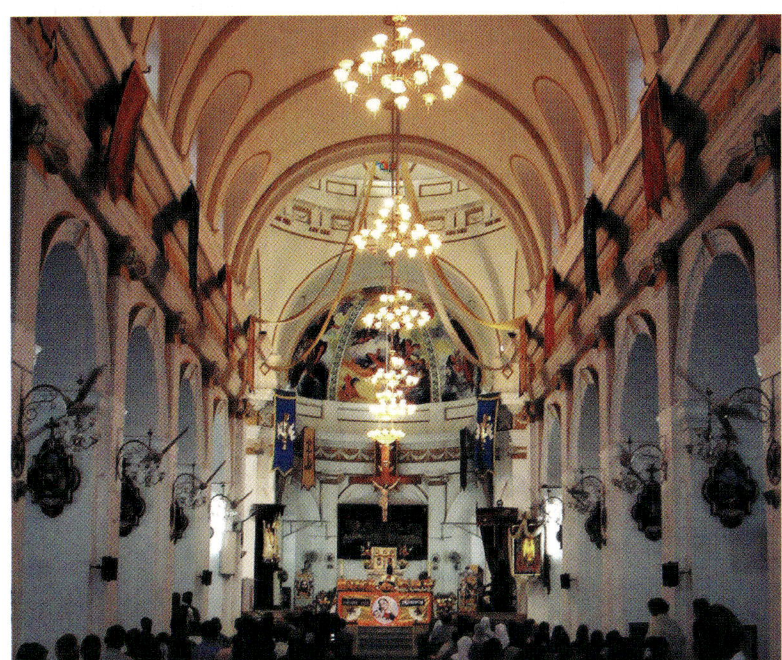

23.16: Christmas mass and celebrations at the Immaculate Conception Cathedral at Puducherry — photograph by Madhukar K Bhagat

Although a festival of a minority community in India, there is enthusiastic and festive participation as well of other communities. This truly **signifies the message of Christ as one of love and brotherhood which Christmas epitomises**.

Gurupurab or Gurupurb, refers to the celebration of the **anniversary of the Sikh Gurus**. Also referred to as *Prakash Utsav*, the most important Guruparabs are the birth anniversary of, **Guru Nanak**, the first guru and **Guru Gobind Singh**, the tenth and the last guru. The martyrdom of Guru Arjan Dev and Guru Teg Bahadur, the installation of Guru Granth Sahib in Harmandir Sahib at Amritsar and the formation of **Khalsa Panth** on the day of Baisakhi, are other important occasions of Gurupurab. These festivals are celebrated throughout the Sikh community in India and other parts of the world.

The Guru Purab of the birth of Guru Nanak usually falls in the month of November. However, this may vary from year to year as per the lunar calendar. The festivities usually involve a three-day celebration with the gurudwaras being its focal point. The first day of celebrations begins with an *akhand path* (a continuous prayer service) which is held two days prior to the day of the birth of the Guru. The second day is marked by taking out a *nagar kirtan*, a procession of the Guru Granth Sahib by the *Panj Piare* (the five beloved of the Guru) on a palanquin. Martial art performances or *Gatka* involving fighting with swords and other forms may follow suit. The day of Guru's birth begins with an early morning recitation of *Asa-di-var* (morning hymns) and later recitals from the Sikh scriptures, singing of hymns and *katha* recitals. After the *Ardas* (set of prayers in three parts) distribution of *Kada*/*Karah prasad* takes place. This is followed by a special *langar* (congregational feast). Here, people of all faiths are welcome to have the food prepared in the community kitchen of the Gurudwaras as the blessings of God and the Gurus.

The Gurupurab associated with the birth of Guru Gobind Singh usually falls in the month of December or January. The tradition is similar to that followed on the birth anniversary of Guru Nanak which includes *akhand path*, procession, *kirtan*, *katha* and *langar*. The celebrations at Patna Sahib Gurudwara the birthplace of the last Guru, is especially noteworthy on this occasion. The Gurupurab of the martyrdom of Guru Arjan Dev (the fifth Guru) falls in April-May. The traditions are similar. However, owing to the summer heat at this time of year, the practice of distributing cold sweetened drinks to all is a noteworthy custom incorporated over the years. Guru Teg Bahadur's martyrdom is said to have taken place on 11th November 1675 at Chandni Chowk in Delhi. The celebrations in Gurudwara Sis Ganj at Chandi Chowk

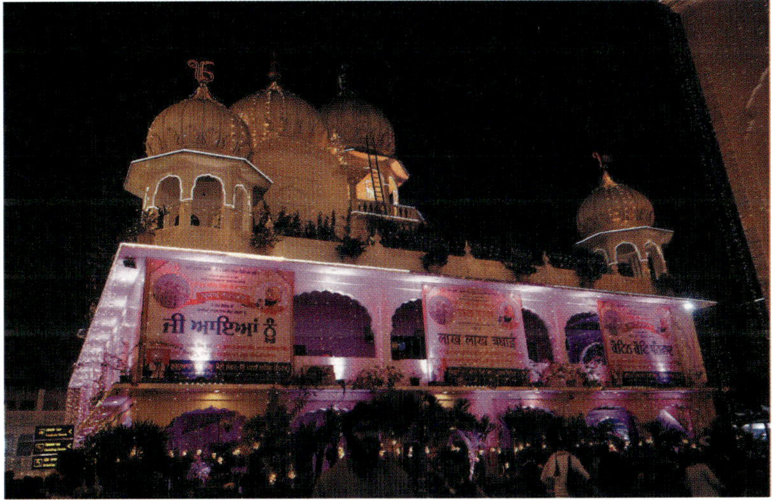

23.17: Celebration of the Prakash Utsav of Guru Gobind Singh ji at Patna Sahib Gurudwara — Courtesy, Bihar Tourism

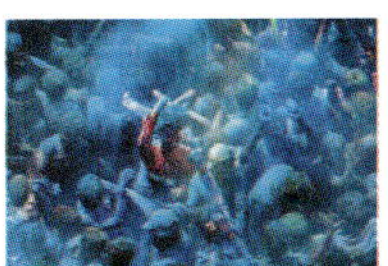

in Delhi are particularly poignant. The last Guruparab is dedicated to the Guru Granth Sahib, the holy scripture of Sikhism. It is believed that on the 3rd of October 1708, Guru Gobind Singh, just a few days before his passing away, declared the Guru Granth Sahib as the subsequent Guru of the community. Thus, this day (besides other Gurupurabs) **signifies the dedication of Sikhs to the teachings of the Guru Granth Sahib**.

Fundamental Beliefs in Sikhism: A Brief Perspective

Amongst the major religions of the world, Sikhism is the youngest and is only 500 years old. It originated in the Punjab region in the teachings of Guru Nanak (in the 15th century) and in that of the subsequent nine Gurus. Today, it has nearly 28–30 million followers the world over with nearly 21 million Sikhs in India (constituting nearly 1.72 % of India's population as per the 2011 census).

Faith and Fundamental Beliefs: Sikhism is a monotheistic religion that believes in one God, who is considered to be *Saguna* (with attributes) as well as *Nirguna* (without attributes). It is also a monistic religion where the world is considered to be a reflection of the creator and hence, not an entity separate from it. It considers God to be *Sat* (or truth), *Sat Guru* (true guru), *Kartar* (creator), *Nirankar* (without form), *Akal Purakh* (timeless being), and *Wahe Guru* (praise to Guru). God is omnipresent (*Sarv Vyapak*), infinite, and is signified by *Ik-Omkar* which represents the divine melody of the one Supreme Being.

Sikhism emphasises on **realisation of truth as the highest ideal**. But it does not prescribe the path of asceticism and self-mortification for this; rather the Sikh Gurus also led a life of a householder. It professes one to be *Gurmukh* (or God-conscious) and to follow the path of *Japa* (recitation of the name of God), *Kirtana* (devotional prayer), and *Naam-Simran* (reciting and singing the names of God). It emphasises that humans should be wary of the five thieves in the path of salvation, which are **ego**, **anger**, **greed**, **attachment**, and **lust**. It also underscores the significance of leading an active life which is imbued in **truthfulness**, **fidelity self-control** and **purity** to attain the highest ideal of salvation. Selfless **service** to others, striving for **justice** and belief in the **prosperity of all** are some of the other ideals of Sikhism.

Scriptures in Sikhism: Sri Guru Granth Sahib or the Adi Granth is the Holy Book of the Sikhs which comprises 1430 pages and is divided into 33 sections. It comprises 5894 verses or *Shabads* composed largely by the Sikh gurus and some by other saints of the Bhakti period such as Kabir, Namdev, Ramanand, Pipa, Ravidas, Sheikh Farid, and others. Guru Nanak (the first guru) contributed 974 hymns while guru Arjan Dev contributed 2218 hymns. After the tenth and last guru Guru Gobind Singh, the Guru Granth Sahib has been declared as the eternal Guru and the guiding light of Sikhism. The holy scripture begins with the *Mul Mantar* (or *Mool Mantar*) which is a prayer of *Ik Omkara* or that One Supreme God and encapsulates the essence of the religious doctrine of Sikhism. Translated from Gurumukhi, it broadly states as below;

There is one supreme being/Creator,
the eternal reality (true name),
the creator,
without fear, devoid of enmity/hatred,
immortal,
never born, self-existent,
(known by) the grace of the Guru.

The Khalsa: Although the initial development of Sikhism was influenced by the devotion to God and the *Bhakti* movement, the persecution of Guru Arjan Dev and Guru Teg Bahadur at the hands of Mughal Emperors (Jahangir and Aurangzeb respectively) is said to have led to the birth of a military order within Sikhism. The Khalsa, literally meaning *the pure*, was introduced by Guru Gobind Singh (the tenth and the last Guru) as the *Sant-Sipahi* (a saint-soldier) to protect the freedom of conscience and religion. It sought to bring purity and strength in its followers through knowledge of *shaastras* (scriptures) and the power of *shastra* (weapons) through *gnana* and *Kriya Shakti*. It exhorted its followers to wear the five symbols of *kesh, kangha* (comb), *kada* (steel bracelet), *kaccha* (short drawers), and *kirpan* (sword) which today also remain and signify the physical identity of the Sikhs.

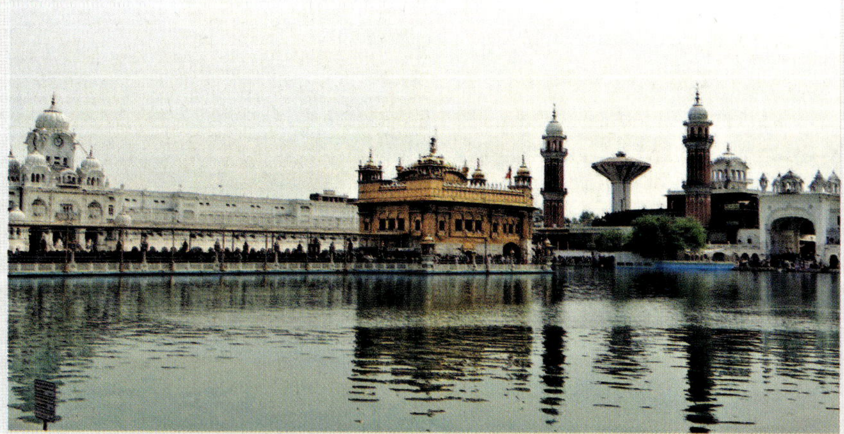

23.18: The Golden Temple/Suvarn Mandir or Sri Harmandir Sahib at Amritsar, among the holiest of Sikh shrines — photograph by Madhukar K Bhagat

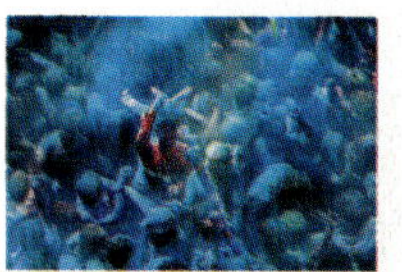

Khordad Sal is the celebration of the **birth** anniversary of **Prophet Zoroaster** or Zarathustra and is one of the important festivals of the **Parsi community** of India that follow Zoroastrianism. It is celebrated on the sixth day of the Parsi month of *Farvardin* which falls in the August-September period. The day is marked with an offering of special prayers and the organisation of grand feasts called *jashan*. Homes are also cleaned and decorated with *rangoli*, and new garments are worn with children wearing vermillion spots on their foreheads and also adorning beautiful flowers. The festival is also considered an occasion for the people to reflect on their lives and actions and to plan for their future.

Other Important Religious Festivals

Religious festivals associated with Hinduism

Basant Panchami is celebrated on the fifth day of *Shukla Paksha* (bright half/rising phase of the moon) of *Magha* (February-March). It marks the onset of the spring season and the arrival of Holi which is forty days hence. This festival venerates **Goddess Saraswati**, the deity of learning, music and other arts. It is celebrated with fervour in most parts of the country and is particularly popular in the East. Here it is referred to as the **'Saraswati Puja'** or the day of worship of Goddess Saraswati, a major festival, which is enthusiastically celebrated in schools and colleges. Idols of the deity are placed in *pandals* and ritually invoked. Following a similar tradition as in Durga Puja, ritual worship is performed of the deity, followed by the immersion of the idol the next day.

In the southern States of Karnataka and Andhra Pradesh, it is known as **Sri Panchami** (*Sri*: a name of the Goddess). In Punjab and other Northern states, the festival has seasonal significance where the arrival of spring and the agricultural harvest is celebrated by different communities. The tradition of Basant Panchami is also popular in the Sikh community since the times of Maharana Ranjit Singh (18th century CE) and is celebrated with events such as the flying of kites.

Yellow is a colour that is also associated with the festival. It is considered the colour of the deity. Women in particular, wear yellow clothes and prepare yellow rice and sweet dishes which are yellow in colour too. Basant Panchami symbolises **knowledge** and learning, and at the same time celebrates the arrival of **spring** the season of love and bountiful agricultural produce.

Raksha Bandhan or Rakhi another important festival celebrated throughout the country is unique, for it celebrates the love and sibling relationship of a **brother** and a **sister.** The festival falls on the *Poornima* (full moon day of the month) of *Sravana* (August–September). The sister ties a sacred thread on the wrist of her brother and she prays for the latter's well-being, while the brother avows to protect her. The festival is especially important in the Brahmin community and is associated with the ritual of change of *Janaeyu,* or the sacred thread worn by men.

The festival traces its origin to ancient times with references of the festival being found in *Bhavishya Purana*. The legend of Draupadi tying a piece of cloth on the finger of Krishna when it gets cut and Krishna vowing to protect Draupadi, is also at times associated with this festival. As per some historical accounts, a reference to this festival is also seen in the medieval period where Rani Karnavati, who is unable to defend Chittor against the attack of Bahadur Shah, the Sultan of Gujarat, sends *rakhi* to the Mughal emperor Humayun and asks for her protection.

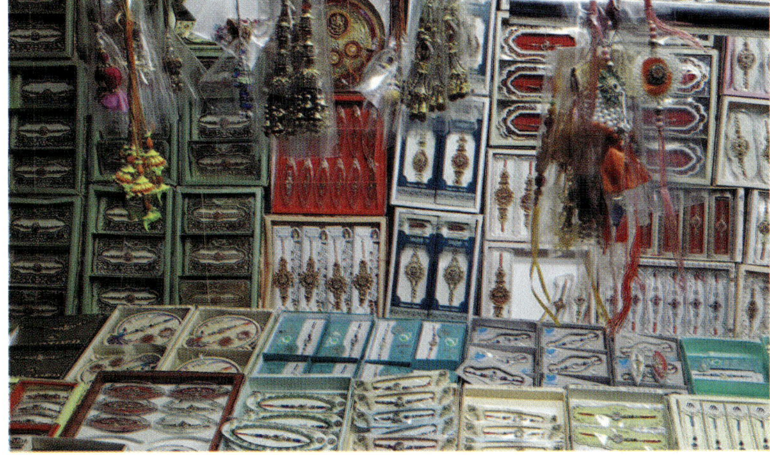

23.19: Various designs of *rakhi*, from simple threads to ornate ones — photograph by Madhukar K Bhagat

The festival is not restricted to just siblings but to even those who accept each other as brother and sister. Thus, it transcends the divide of communities and religious barriers. The rituals associated with the festival are tying the *Raksha* thread, placing of the *tilak* on the forehead of the brother, offering him a sweet, while the brother in return offers her a gift and avows her protection. Rakhi symbolises the **pious bond** between brothers and sisters.

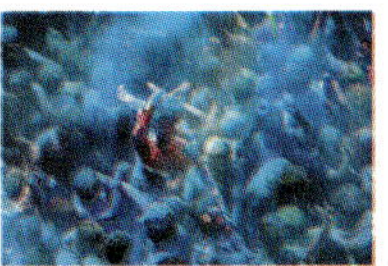

Dhanteras also known as Dhana-Trayodashi, is celebrated on the 13th day of *Krishna-Paksha* of the month of Ashvin. It falls one or two days before Deepawali and is another festival popular in different parts of the country. Dhanteras is associated with the rituals of worship of Goddess Lakshmi. Devotees also venerate Yama the Lord of Death, by lightning of *diyas* (earthen lamps) called the *Yama ka Diya.* Besides Dhanvantari the god of medicine is also venerated. Cleaning of the houses and purchase of utensils or metal objects are some common customs that are associated with this festival.

Like other Hindu festivals, different legends are associated with it. It is believed that on this day Dhanvantri the God of medicine and Ayurveda, emerged out of the *Amrit Manthan* holding the book of Ayurveda and the *amrit kalash* (a pot containing the elixir of immortality). It is also believed that Goddess Lakshmi the goddess of wealth and prosperity, also emerged from the churning of the ocean on this day. Hence the festival is associated with veneration of the two deities. Further, as per traditional belief, lack of cleanliness and darkness would dissuade the goddess of wealth from entering a household and hence emerged the customary practice of cleaning of the house and lighting of the *diyas*.

Another legend associated with Dhanteras is that of lord Yama. As per the story of the legend, there were predictions that king Hima's son would die from a snake bite on the 4th day after his marriage. When this day arrived, the wife of the young prince did not allow him to sleep and instead engaged her throughout the night and day in stories and songs. She also lit several *diyas* and placed gold and silver jewellery and coins in the room. Yama entered the room in the guise of a snake but owing to the bright light from the numerous *diyas* and the dazzle of the coins and ornaments, could not see clearly and kept sitting near the pile of the coins, engrossed in the stories. As the day passed away, the snake returned back sparing the life of the prince. Thus emerged the tradition of the lighting of *Yama ka diya,* which was to ward off death and to pray for a long life.

The next day to Dhanteras and the day before Deepawali is referred to as **Narak Chaturdashi** and is associated with the legend of the slaying of the *asura* Narakasura by Lord Krishna. The festival of *dhanteras* signifies **material well-being**, **prosperity**, **good health and long life**. Thus, it involves the propitiation of deities considered to be endowers of these attributes and wishes.

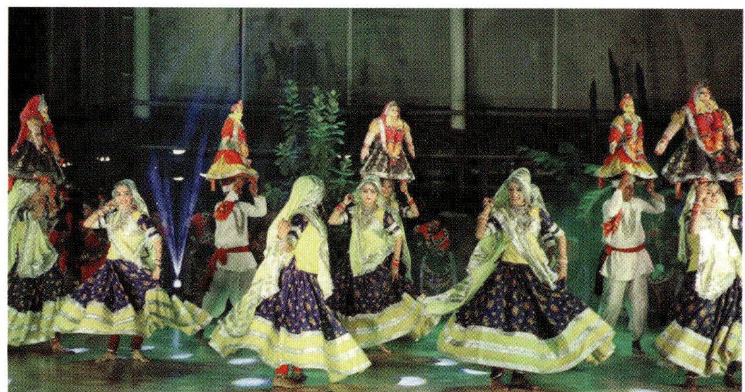

23.20: Gangaur dance performance on the occasion of Gangaur festival in obeisance of Lord Shiva and Goddess Gauri; dancers carrying overhead, deity idols in the form of dolls — Courtesy, Madhya Pradesh Tourism Board

The **Gangaur** festival is popular in Northern and Central India and particularly in the state of Rajasthan. The term Gangaur comprises of *Gan* and *Gaur*; the former term refers to **Lord Shiva** and the latter to **Goddess Gauri**, the consort of Lord Shiva. Besides, it is also celebrated in Haryana, Uttar Pradesh, Madhya Pradesh and parts of West Bengal, Gujarat and Maharashtra. In the southern states of Andhra Pradesh and Telangana, it is also known as Saubhagya Gauri Vratam. The first day of the month of Chaitra (the day following Holi) marks the arrival of Gangaur, which is celebrated over a period of 18 days. It is especially popular among the women folk who pray to Goddess Gauri for marital **well-being, health and long life of their husbands** or to be betrothed to a good husband, in case they are unmarried. It is also a festival associated with **spring harvest**. Preparation of clay idols of Shiva and Gauri, their ritual worship, observing a fast, *vrat katha* recitals (recital of the legend associated with the festival') fasting and other customs are also associated with it. A colourful fair is also held on this occasion.

Chhath is a unique and ancient festival, which is dedicated to the **Sun God**, the sustainer of life, wherein the devotees pray to him for overall well-being and thank him for the bounties of life endowed by his beneficence. It is popular in the states of Bihar, Jharkhand, Eastern Uttar Pradesh and parts of Nepal. In recent times, owing to the migration of people from these regions to other cities, the festival is also celebrated on a community level in metropolises like Delhi, Mumbai, Kolkata and other places.

Chhath is observed on the 6th day of *Shukla Paksha* of the Kartika month. This also happens to be the 6th day from the festival of Deepawali. The entire festival is spread over four days. The first day is *Nahay-Khay,* or taking a holy dip in the river Ganga (or other river bodies), followed by having food. Cleaning

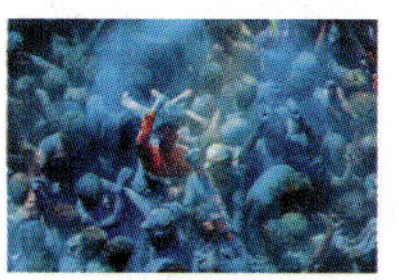

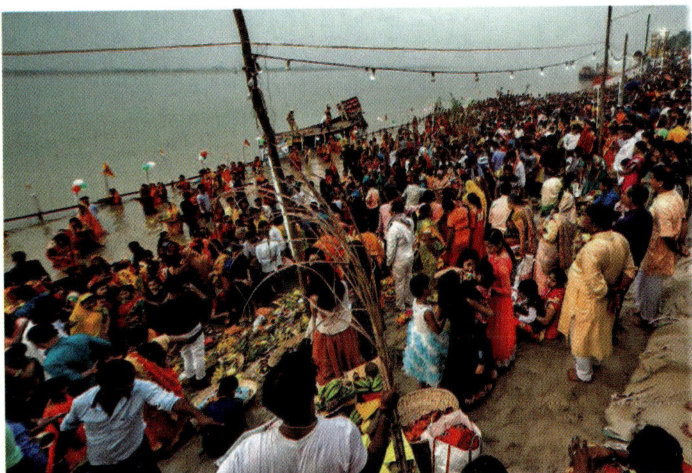

23.21: Celebration of Chhath festival on the banks of river Ganga at Patna. Devotees offering early morning *arghya* on the concluding fourth day of the festival — Courtesy, Bihar Tourism

of the house, the surroundings and the bathing *ghats* of the river is another custom associated with this day. The second day of *Khairna* involves fasting till dusk without having water. This is followed by the offering of the *Khairna prasad* (offering to the gods) comprising of traditional jaggery-laden *kheer* and *puri/roti* (wheat bread) and then breaking the fast. Post having this *prasad,* starts another stringent fast of one and a half days (till the morning of fourth day) where no food or even water is consumed. The fast is often observed by the women folk. On the third day, *Pehla Araghya/Arghya* or the first offering to the setting sun is made while standing in a water body. The rituals of the day also involve worship of the goddess **Chhathi Maiya** who is considered a form of Devi Prakriti, a sister of the Sun God. Singing songs in her praise and other rituals are a part of the day's custom. On the next day, the 2nd *arghya* takes place which incorporates ritual worship of the rising Sun God and offering of water, fruits, grains and other items to the Sun god while facing eastwards (towards the early morning sun). The devotees stand in knee or waist-deep water in the river Ganga or other sacred rivers and water bodies. Post this ritual, the devotees break their fast with a bit of water and some *prasad* which is referred to as the *paran*.

The tradition of Chhath is very ancient and as per some accounts owes its origin to Sri Rama and Sita observing a fast in honour of Sun God on their return to Ayodhya. Some legends associate it with the traditions of fasting and charity of Karna (the great Mahabharata warrior) who is considered the *Surya-Putra* (son of the Sun God). The custom of fasting and worshipping a Vedic deity Sun, without any element of idol worship, also associates this festival with **early Vedic practices**. Overall, Chhath is a festival that is in harmony with **nature**. It is also considered eco-friendly and bereft of any environmental externalities, which are otherwise associated with other festivals like Deepawali or those involving idol immersions. Chhath also i**ntegrates the society**, as it transcends the differences of caste and social hierarchy thus creating a **community bond**.

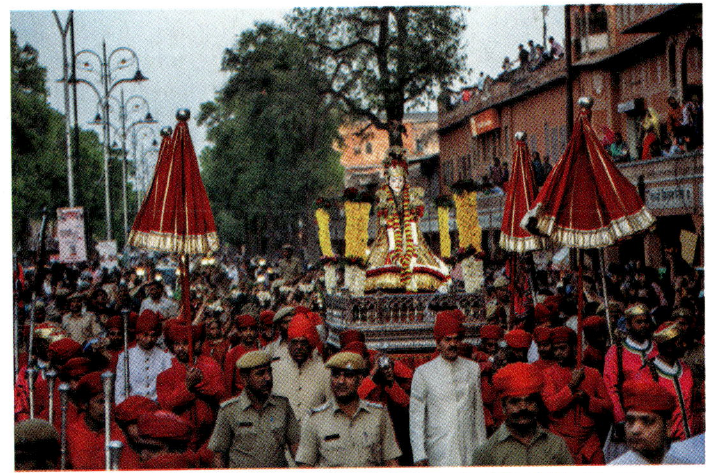

23.22: A procession being taken out of Teej Mata on the occasion of Teej at Jaipur, Rajasthan — Courtesy, Rajasthan Tourism

Teej is a festival associated with the arrival of the monsoon and is particularly popular in the northern and western parts of the country. Literally, Teej refers to the 'third day' which falls on the ascending or descending phase of the moon. The festival of Teej which is also referred to as the *Haratalika* or *Hariyali Teej*, falls on the third day after the new moon in the month of *Shravan* (July-August). The festival is celebrated largely by women who keep fast and also pray to Goddess Parvati/Gauri for their matrimonial well-being or desire for a suitable husband, as this day marks the union of Parvati with Lord Shiva after her long penance. Singing, dancing, applying henna on their hands, and meeting and greeting each other, are some traditions associated with this festival. Flying of kites by boys in some parts of the country is also popular. Overall, it is a festival of celebration of the **joy of the arrival of the monsoons** which brings new life to nature.

Some other important festivals of Hinduism are:

Hanuman Jayanti which marks the birth of lord Hanuman and entails rituals of worship and veneration of the deity. It falls on Purnima (full moon day) of *Chaitra* month;

Akshaya Tritiya, observed on the third day of the *Shukla Paksha* of *Vaisakha* (April-May), is considered an auspicious day for marriages, new ventures etc.;

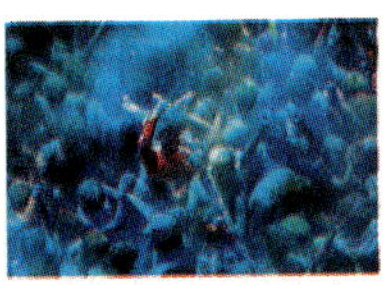

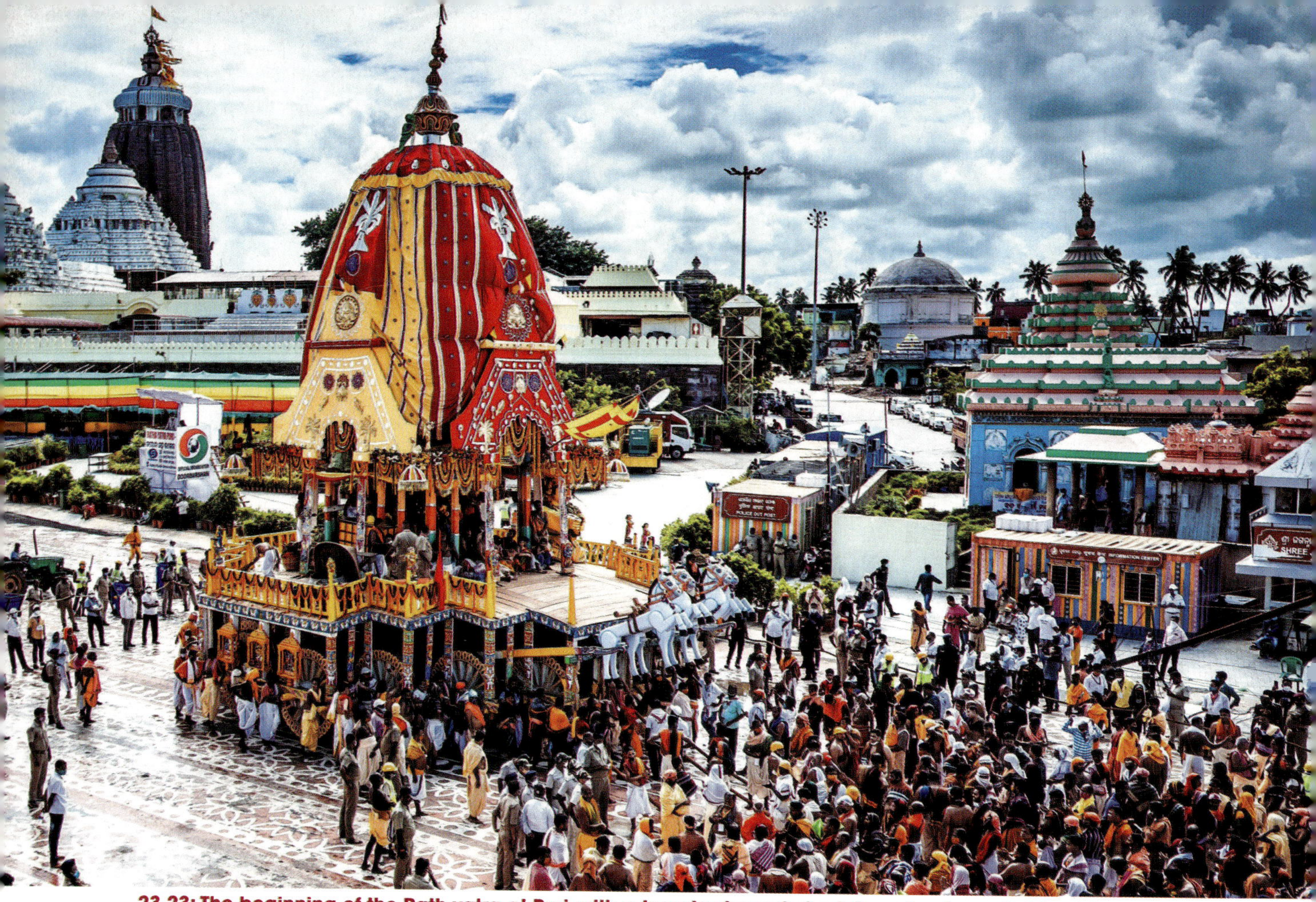

23.23: The beginning of the Rath yatra at Puri, with a temple-shaped chariot made of wood of Lord Jagannatha; in background is the centuries old Jagannatha temple of Puri — Courtesy, Department of Tourism Odisha

Rath Yatra, is a famous chariot festival of Puri in Odisha that involves the moving of the idols of Lord Jagannath, Balabhadra and Subhadra in large wooden chariots. It is celebrated in the *Shukla-Paksha* of the month of *Ashadha* (June-July) and is a centuries-old tradition finding references in Purana and even in accounts of European travellers of the 13th century;

Guru Purnima, a festival of the veneration of the gurus (teachers) and seers which falls on the full moon day (*Purnima*) of the month of *Ashadha* (June–July);

Nag Panchami-involves the worship/veneration of the *nagas* or snakes. It falls on the 5th day of *Shukla-paksha* of *Shravana* month;

Vishwakarma Puja, a festival of veneration of lord Vishwakarma, a divine architect and God of engineering, which is popular in East India;

Pitru Paksha, the 2nd fortnight of the Bhadrapada month is a period to pay homage to the ancestors and is considered an inauspicious period for marriages, festivity or new ventures. **Mahalaya** is the last day of the Pitru-Paksha which also marks the beginning of the *Devi-Paksha* or the *Durga Puja* period;

Karwa Chauth, popular in northern and western India, the festival is celebrated on the 4th day after the full moon in the month of *Kartik*. The festival is observed by married women who undertake a fast without water and food for the day and pray for the well-being and long life of their husbands.

Bhai Dooj, similar to Raksha Bandhan, the festival celebrates the love of a brother and sister where a sister prays for the well-being of the brother. It usually falls on the 2nd day after Deepawali.

Islamic religious festivals in India

Eid-ul-Fitr, also referred to as Eid–al–Fitr or simply Eid, is one of the major Islamic festivals. It is celebrated by the Muslims after the end of the holy month of *Ramadan* (the ninth month of the Islamic calendar) during which the Muslims fast from dawn to dusk without food or water. It is believed that the holy Quran was revealed to the prophet Muhammad during the month of Ramadan and hence fasting during the month is considered pious and Eid marks the end of this period of austerity and piousness.

The festival is held on the first day of the month of *Shawwal* that is once the new crescent moon has been sighted. Eid is marked by the offering of community prayers (*namaz*), at mosques or other open spaces. This is followed by the greeting of family and friends with remarks of *Eid Mubarak*, offering of gifts to each other and *Eidi* (cash gift) to children. Holding traditional fairs of Eid, performing acts of charity

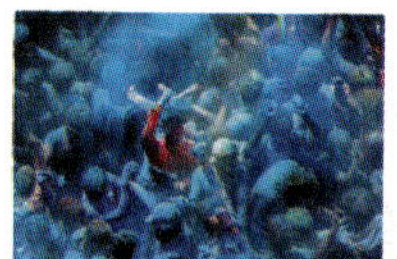

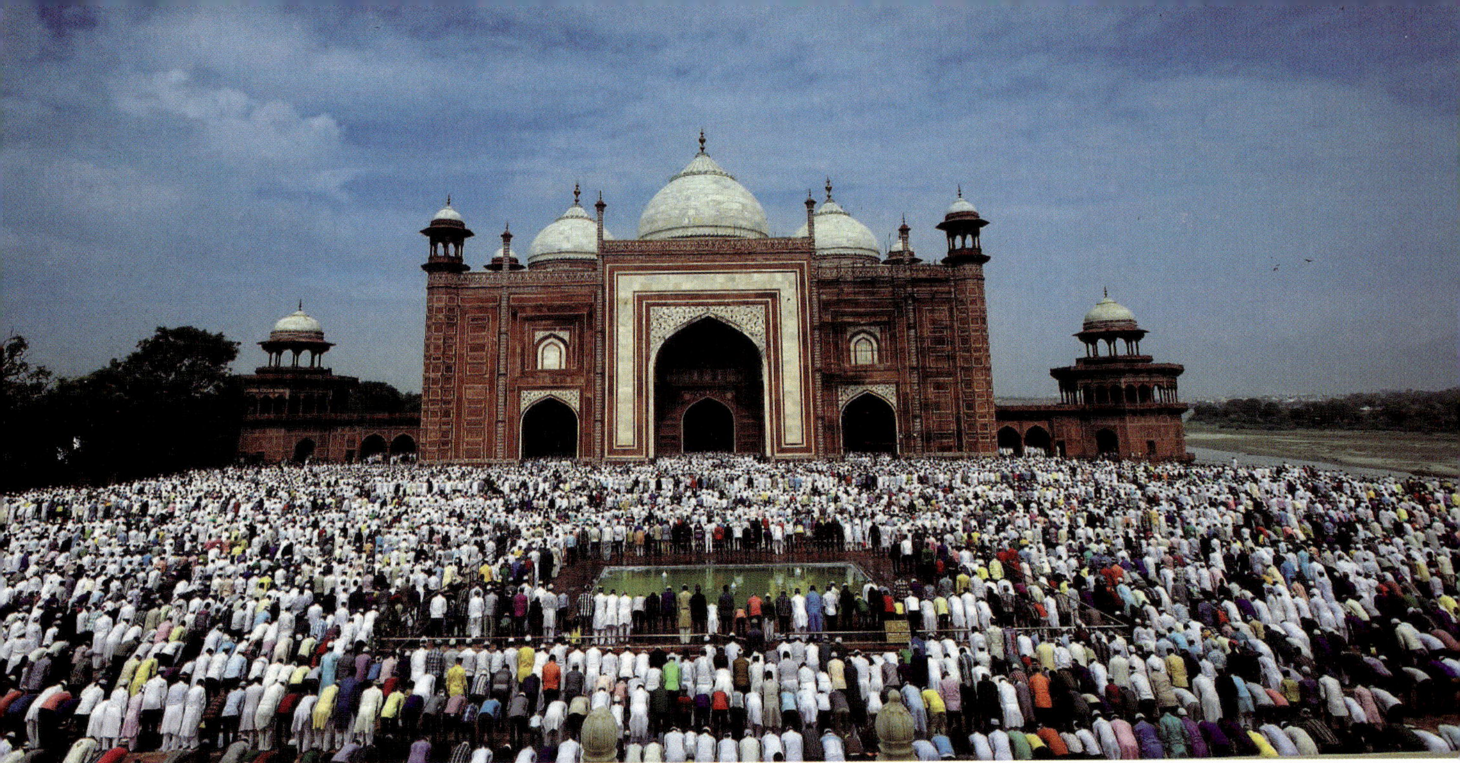

23.24: Namaz being offered on the occasion of Eid at mosque at Taj Mahal — Courtesy, Directorate of Uttar Pradesh Tourism

(*Eid Zakat*) and holding community feasts are some of the common customs which are associated with the festival. Traditional dishes, *sewaiyaan* of Eid, and sumptuous meals, mark the feast of most of the households.

As per some scholars, Eid is said to have originated with the migration of Prophet Muhammad from Mecca to Medina. The festival signifies the **gratitude of the devotees to Allah for his kindness** and for **giving them strength to bear the fast** during the holy month. Besides, they also pray to Allah for f**orgiveness for any sins** they may have committed during the year.

Eid-ul-Zuha, or **Eid-al-Adha** also referred to as **Bakrid**, is another important festival of the Muslims. It falls on the 10th day of the month of *Dhu-al-Hijja* (the 12th month of the Islamic calendar). The festival entails the custom of the sacrifice of a goat or a *bakr*. As a tradition, a part of the sacrificial meat is consumed by the family while some is distributed amongst the poor. Friends and relatives meet and greet each other.

The legend associated with this festival is that Ibrahim, a faithful prophet of Allah, when asked to sacrifice his son (Ismail) showed his willingness to do so as a mark of devotion. But God accepted the sacrifice of a ram instead of his son, sparing the life of the latter. Thus, the festival **commemorates the devotion of the prophet Ibrahim** and inspires devout Muslims to inculcate this devotion.

Muharram is the first month of the Islamic calendar. The 10th day of this month, also referred to as the Day of Ashura, is considered as a day of mourning amongst Muslims. On this day (61 A.H. of the Islamic calendar or 680 CE) marks the martyrdom of **Hussain-ibn-Ali** or Imam Hussain (grandson of Prophet Muhammad) in the battle of Karbala. Prayers are offered on this day. Muslims fast or eat sparingly, avoid entertainment till the afternoon and undertake charity. Processions of Muharram commemorating the battle of Karbala and the sacrifice of the Prophet's grandson are some other common events of this day.

Fundamental Islamic Beliefs and Features of Islam in India

Islam is one of the major religions of the world. With 1.7 billion followers it has the second largest following in the world. It has its origin in the teachings of the **Quran** revealed by God (Allah) to the **Prophet Muhammad** (570 CE to 632 CE). The religion had its origin in **Mecca** in the 7th century CE. By the 8th century, it had spread to the entire Arabian Peninsula and from the Iberian Peninsula in the west (covering portions of Portugal and Spain) to the Indus River in the east.

Islamic Faith and Fundamental Beliefs: Islam is a monotheistic religion that believes in only one God or Allah (the incomparable one) with Prophet Muhammad as his last messenger. It advocates universal brotherhood, love and equality of mankind, as key tenets of its teachings and prohibits idolism and deity worship. The five pillars of Islam are at the core of Islamic religious beliefs. These include:

Shahda – or belief in one God or Allah with Muhammad as his messenger and the last prophet.

Namaz – or offering of prayer to God five times a day.

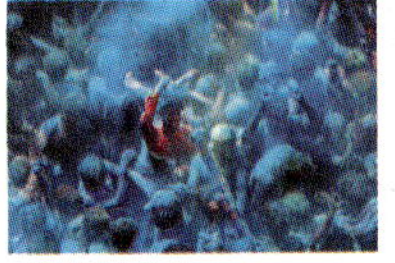

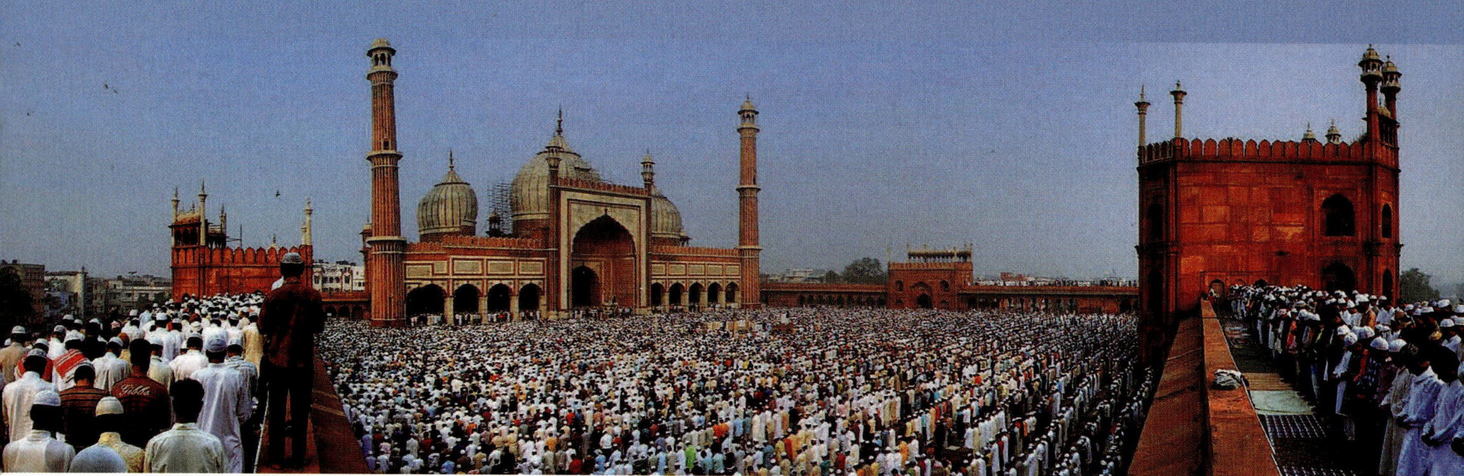

23.25: A panoramic image of namaz being offered on the occasion of Eid at Jama Masjid, Delhi — Wikimedia Commons

Roza – keeping of compulsory fast in the holy month of Ramadan.

Zakat – giving charity as an obligation to the extent of 2.5% of one's yearly savings to the needy.

Hajj – To take the pilgrimage to **Mecca** once in a person's lifetime for those who can afford to do so physically as well as financially.

Islam also believes in earlier prophets, viz. **Abraham, Moses**, and **Jesus,** but believes that **Prophet Muhammad** was the last messenger or prophet of God. It also believes in the doctrine that the world will come to an end on the Last Day or the *Yawm–al-Qiyamah*, (day of judgement or resurrection) when everybody will be accountable for their deeds.

Scriptures in Islam: The Islamic faith is based on the Holy Quran which is believed to contain the revelations of God to the Prophet Muhammad. It contains 114 verses or *Surahs* and 6236 verses or *ayats* which cover varied subjects. The next important source of Islamic belief is the *Hadith* or the *Sunnah*. These are the traditions of the Prophet as to what he did or said or approved regarding various subjects, which were compiled by his companions. Thus, *Sunnah* plays an important role in the interpretation of the Quran. The Islamic law or Sharia covers different aspects of personal as well as social life.

Sects in Islam: The Shias and the Sunnis are the two main sects of Muslims with the Sunnis comprising the majority (85%–90%). The Shias consider Ali who was the son-in-law of Prophet Muhammad as the rightful *Khalifah* (Caliph) and does not believe in Abu Bakr, Umar, and Usman who were the first three Caliphs in which the Sunnis believe.

Islam in India: Islam is believed to have first come to India in the 7th century CE along with the Arab traders who came to the Malabar coast. Islam also spread to Sindh and parts of Gujarat through the Arabic traders and later due to the Arabic conquest of Sind in the early 8th century. However, large scale Islamic influence and presence only happened after the Turkic invasion and establishment of the Delhi Sultanate in the late 12th and 13th century CE. With the establishment of the Mughal dynasty in the 16th century in large parts of India, Islamic influence also spread in India.

As per the 2011 census, there are 172.2 million Muslims in India and constitute 14.2% of the Indian population. They are the second largest religious group in India after the Hindus. The Indian Muslims are largely the followers of *Hanafi Madhab* (school) which is one of the main Sunni Orthodox schools. Some Muslims in Kerala are also the followers of the *Shafi Madhab*.

Festivals of Christianity in India

Good Friday: Considered as one of the most important of Christian events, Good Friday marks the occasion of the **crucifixion** of **Jesus Christ**. It usually occurs in the month of March or April. As per the Biblical accounts, Jesus was betrayed by his own disciple Judas for 30 pieces of silver and arrested by the Roman soldiers. Later he was tried for blasphemy for claiming himself to be the son of God and for other crimes. Jesus was sentenced to death by the Roman leader Pontius Pilate. On this day at Calvary (near Jerusalem) he was nailed on the cross, hung up and thus condemned to die.

Good Friday is observed as a day of penance and sorrow for the entire Christian community. The day is marked with prayers and fasting. It is believed that Jesus endured extreme pain and suffering to atone for the sins of humanity. Thus, this day **signifies the sacrifice of Jesus Christ and is a day for humanity to remember this and reflect on his teachings.**

Easter is a day of great significance in the Christian community. As per Biblical belief, three days after Jesus was crucified, he was again **resurrected**. This day is celebrated as the day of Easter. Falling in the season of spring (March-April), Easter is celebrated on the first Sunday after the first full moon following the spring equinox. In India, Easter is popular in different parts of the country particularly in the states of Kerala, Goa, Maharashtra, and Northeastern states, besides Pondicherry and other cities having a sizeable Christian population.

As per the Biblical account in the New Testament, after crucifixion, Jesus was buried in a tomb. However, on the third day of his burial, he was resurrected. The event is considered one of the paramount beliefs in the Christian faith thus making it one of the most important festivals of the community. The entire

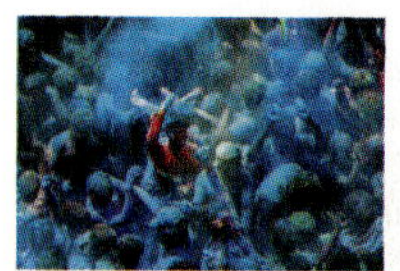

week before the day of Easter is considered the **Holy Week**. The preceding Sunday, as per Western Christian accounts, is referred to as the **Palm Sunday**, marking the entry of Jesus Christ in Jerusalem. The Wednesday falling in the week also referred to as **Spy Wednesday**, marks the betrayal of Jesus. The Thursday referred to as **Maundy Thursday** is the day to commemorate Maundy or foot washing of the saints by Jesus, as well as the **Last Supper** of Jesus with his disciples. The **Good Friday** commemorates his crucifixion and the week ends with the joyous **Easter Sunday**.

Easter is celebrated as a festival of great happiness and gaiety. People meet and greet family and friends. The day is marked with Easter prayers, celebrations and feasts. The custom of decorated Easter eggs and Easter bunny is also popular in different parts of the world as well as in India. With spring arrives new life and the resurrection of Jesus is also a manifestation of the arising of new life. Easter eggs are said to represent the emergence of new life while the bunny is said to signify innocence. Overall, **Easter symbolises the Christian belief in hope, new life and salvation,** reflected in the resurrection of Jesus Christ.

Fundamental Beliefs of Christianity and Features of Christianity in India

Christianity originated nearly 2,000 years ago and is based on the life and teachings of Jesus Christ. Today, it is the largest religion in the world with over 2.4 billion followers or roughly a third of the world's population. In India, there are around 28.7 million Christians (as per the 2011 census).

Christian Faith and Fundamental Beliefs: Christianity is a **monotheistic** religion that believes in the existence of only one God. It believes in the **Holy Trinity**, the Father, the Son, and the Holy Spirit (Holy Ghost). The God appears as the three forms, but all the three are the manifestation of the same God. While the Father is unbegotten or unborn, the Son is born from the Father and the Holy Spirit proceeds from the Father. Jesus Christ is considered as the messenger or the Son of God. He is considered to be a prophet in human form who spread the message of God and was a saviour of mankind. He endured suffering and crucifixion to save mankind from sin and to grant salvation to those who believed in him. While his suffering and death symbolise the human form in which he appeared, he was resurrected from the dead signifying his Godliness. Thus, the death and resurrection of Jesus offer hope to the sinning humanity for salvation, if they reconcile to God. Christians also consider God to be omniscient, omnipotent, omnipresent, just, loving, eternal, holy and sinless and that He is knowable through His Son Jesus Christ.

Scriptures in Christianity: The Holy Bible is the sacred text of Christians which comprises the Old Testament and the New Testament, the two major sections. The Old Testament written in the Hebrew text is considered to contain information about the creation of the World. It is sacred to both Jews and Christians alike. The life and teachings of Jesus Christ are contained in the New Testament and form the core of the Christian faith. The teachings of Jesus Christ are compiled from the Gospels or the written accounts of Jesus's life and teachings. There are four Gospels that are considered canonical and are included in the Bible. These are the Gospels of Mathew, Mark, Luke, and John.

Sects in Christianity: Christianity is divided into several sects, the most important of which are the Roman Catholics and the Protestants. Originally, the Christian religion was referred to as the Catholic religion with the Roman Pope as its head. However, differences among the Christians led to the splitting of the Church into the Western Roman Catholic and Eastern Orthodox groups. Further, in the 16th century, owing to the numerous reforms advocated by Martin Luther King, the emergence of the Protestant School of Christianity took place. Besides, there also exist other sects, such as Oriental Orthodoxy, Restorationism and Church of the East besides smaller sects.

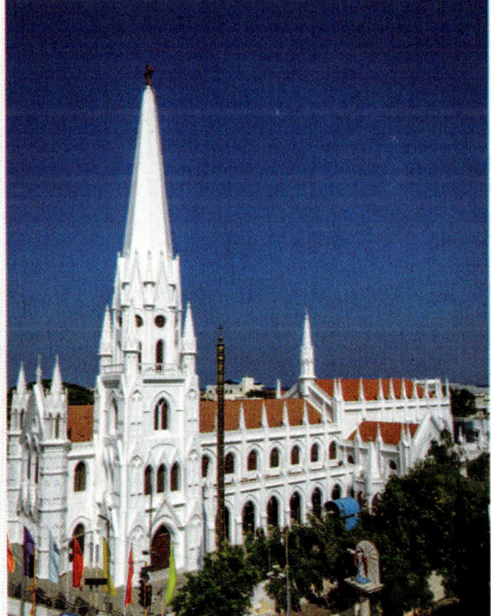

23.26: Santhome Cathedral or Cathedral of Saint Thomas in Chennai, where the tomb of Saint Thomas, the apostle who preached in India in the 1st century CE, is believed to be located — Courtesy, Tamil Nadu Tourism Development Corporation

Christianity in India: With nearly 28.7 million followers (as per the 2011 Census), Christianity has the third largest following in India after Hinduism and Islam. As per a section of scholars, **Christianity came to India in the 1st century CE** itself. It is believed that Thomas the Apostle came to India on the Malabar coast in Kerala in 52 CE. However, scholars generally believe that Christianity was fully established in the Malabar region in India by the 6th-7th century CE. Concerted Christian missionary activities started in India only after the arrival of St. Francis Xavier (mid-16th century) followed by other Christian missionaries. Substantial spread of Christianity eventually took place during the British rule, particularly in the 19th and the 20th centuries.

Christians in India are followers of different sects and churches. These include the followers of the **Roman Catholic Church** (in Goa, Malabar coast, and other parts), the **Syrian Church** (mostly in South India), the **Protestant Missions** (parts of South India), the **Church of North India,** and the **Church of South India,** besides others.

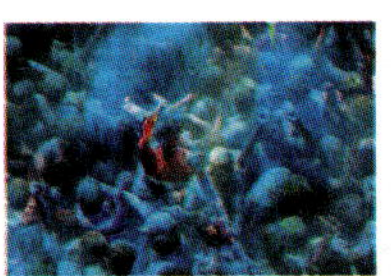

Jain festivals in India

Mahavir Jayanti or **Mahavir Janam Kalyanak** is the most important of the Jain festivals. Besides it, there are other significant festivals centred on the events in the life of the Tirthankaras, or associated with the Jain principles of purification of the soul. The former categories of festivals are associated with the *Panch Kalyanaka* or the five events associated with the life of a Tirthankara. These include *Garbha Kalyanaka* (entry of the soul in the womb), *Janam Kalyanaka* (the birth), *Diksa Kalyanaka* (taking a vow of asceticism and renunciation of worldly possessions), *Keval-jnan Kalyanaka* (acquisition of the absolute knowledge) and *Nirvana Kalyanaka* (attainment of Nirvana and liberation from the mortal form). Besides, there are festivals associated with religious rituals undertaken with the intention of purifying the soul and eliminating the accumulated karma. These are undertaken in terms of the Jain philosophy of *Samvara* and *Nirjara*. A salient aspect of Jain festivals is that these are largely centred in the period of *Chaturmasa* or the period of four months of the monsoons when the Jain monks are supposed to reside in one place, unlike the remaining part of the year, when they are prohibited from stay at a place for more than a month.

Paryushan or **Das Lakshana** is a major festival in Jainism which is centred around forgiveness and compassion. It falls in the period of August and September (*Shravan-Bhadrapad*) and is celebrated by both the Digambar Jains (who refer to it as *Das Lakshana* and celebrate it for 10 days), as well as Shwetambaras (who refer to it as *Paryushan* and celebrate it for 8 days). This festival is aimed at the purification of the soul and thus attainment of salvation. Fasting, meditations, prayers, listening to the talks of the Jain monks, recital of the accounts of the lives of the Tirthankaras from *Kalpasutra*, and talks from the *Tattvartha Sutra* are some of the activities associated with this festival. The five vows of the Jain ethical code which include *Ahimsa* (Non-violence), *satya* (truth), *asteya* (non–stealing), *brahmacharya* (chastity) and *aparigraha* (non-possession), are also emphasised.

Another activity of this festival is *Pratikraman*, a long meditation that is a reflection on one's sins and repentance thereof. This is followed by the ritual of *Michhami Dukkadam,* which is seeking forgiveness from others for any conscious or unconscious wrong of theirs. The festival ends with *Samvatsari* or *Kshamavani* when people gather and celebrate the seeking of forgiveness. The **festival signifies the Jain philosophy of non-violence**, **compassion and self-purification**, as a means of salvation.

The other important Jain festivals are:

Deepawali, when lord Mahavir is believed to have attained Moksha;

The Ashtahnika Parv which is celebrated for a period of eight days, three times a year in the months of *Kartik*, *Phalgun* and *Asadh*;

Gyana Panchami which is celebrated on the fifth day of the *Kartik* month and observed as the day of knowledge when the holy scriptures are worshipped;

Pausha Dashmi is celebrated on the 10th day of Krishna Paksha of Pausha and marks the event of the *Janma Kalyanaka* of Parshavanath, the 23rd Tirthankara;

Mahamastakabhisheka is a unique festival which is held only once every 12 years. The festival is centred around the sage Bahubali and entails paying homage to him. The anointing of the 18-metre-high standing statue of lord Bahubali at Shravanabelagola in Karnataka is the highlight of this festival. The next *Mahamastakabhisheka* is to take place in 2030.

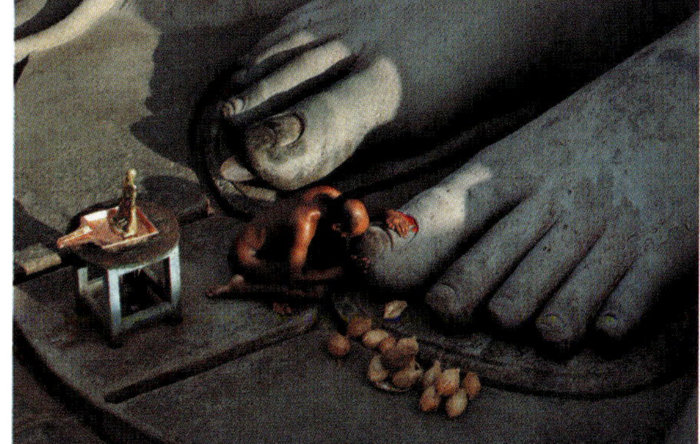

23.27: *Samarpan*: A Jain devotee praying at the feet of Lord Bahubali at the statue at Shravanabelagola — Courtesy, Karnataka State Tourism Development Corporation

Buddhist festivals in India

The birth of lord Buddha which is celebrated on the occasion of **Buddha Purnima** is the most important of the Buddhist festival. However, a number of other festivals are also celebrated by different sects and Buddhist communities.

Magha Puja Day is the next most important of the Buddhist festivals after the Buddha Purnima. It is observed on the full moon day of the *Magha* (the third lunar month). It is believed that on this day Lord Buddha had delivered a discourse to 1250 of his first disciples who had congregated and also gave a personal ordination to them (initiation). Thus, this event marked the creation of a large community

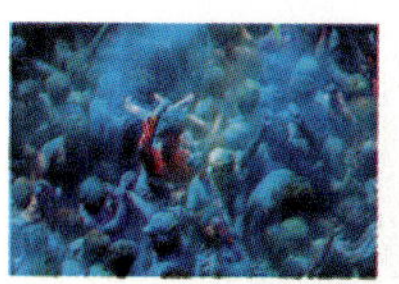

of Buddhist followers. The day is also a celebration of the creation of the ideal community or Buddhist Sangha; hence it is also known as the Sangha Day.

Dharma Day or **Asalaha/Asalha Puja Day** falls on the full moon day (Purnima) of the month of *Asadha*. It is believed that on this day lord Buddha delivered his first sermon at Deer Park at Sarnath, to his former monk associates who thus became his first disciples. This day is thus associated with the event of *Dharma Chakra Pravartana*, one of the four important events of lord Buddha's life. Offering prayers to lord Buddha, listening to sermons, recitals from the Buddhist scriptures and charity are some activities associated with this festival.

The other important Buddhist festivals are:

Ullambana festival or the **Ghost festival** falls on the 15th day of the 7th lunar month and is associated with the belief that in this period, the spirits of the deceased come out of the lower realm. The living pays homage to their deceased ancestors in this festival and prays for their salvation;

Pavarana day is celebrated on the Purnima (full moon day) of Ashvin month. It marks the end of the three months of *Vassa* (the period of three months of retreat during rains). On this day the Buddhist monks ought to come to the Sangha (Buddhist community) and confess and atone for any sins that were committed by him in the period of *Vassa*;

Losar festival which is popular in Ladakh celebrates the arrival of the Tibetan New Year;

Hemis festival is popular in the Hemis monastery of Ladakh and marks the birth of Padmasambhava. It owes its origins to the Tibetan Buddhism traditions. It is also notable for the Hemis Gompa fair which takes place.

Sikh festivals

Among the Sikh festivals, the most important is indeed the **Gurupurabs** (see earlier section of Gurupurabs), while **Baisakhi** (see section on 'Harvest festivals') and Hola Mohalla are other important festivals associated with the community.

The festival of **Hola Mohalla** is held on the 1st day of the lunar month of *Chet* (*Chaitra*) and this usually falls after the day of Holi. The tradition of this festival was established by Guru Gobind Singh, the 10th Sikh Guru. Originally celebrated at Anandpur Sahib, it is now celebrated in different Gurudwaras the world over.

While the word *Hola* is a masculine form of Holi, Mohalla is a word which means an 'organised procession in the form of any army column'. The word Hola Mohalla is said to signify a 'mock fight'. The festival is marked with processions in the form of an army-type column with war drums and other arms, moving from one Gurudwara to another. The festival continues for three days and features a display of weapons, mock battles etc. Performances of tent pegging, bareback horse riding, martial arts, besides other events of bravery, are held. Kirtans, listening to music and poetry are also a part of the festival.

Zoroastrian festivals in India

The Zoroastrian religion is followed by the Parsi community of India. It celebrates a variety of festivals ranging from the new year to those marking the advent of a new season, from the observance of the birth and death anniversary of the Prophet Zarathustra to those associated with religious rites and ceremonies. Among its main festivals are the Parsi New Year Nouroz or **Jamshedi Nouroz** (see section on 'New Year Festivals'), the **Pateti festival**, the **Gahambars**, **Khordad Sal** (see sections of festivals associated with the birth of Prophets) and **Zarthost No Deeso**.

Zoroastrianism: Features and its Presence in India

Zoroastrianism, among the oldest of the living religions of the world, had its origin in Persia in the teachings of Zoroaster (or Zarathustra) in around 700–600 BCE. Some scholars believe it to be an older religion and ascribe an earlier date around 1500–1000 BCE to Zarathustra and hence to the origin of Zoroastrianism. The followers of this faith are less than 150,000 in number and are largely concentrated in Iran and India. The teachings of Parsis are contained in their Holy Book **Zend Avestha**.

The Zoroaster faith believes in a single God or **Ahura Mazda**. However, it also believes in a concept of duality based on constant strife between the forces of good (represented by Ahura Mazda) and of the evil **Angra Mainyu** (or **Ahriman**). Human beings have the choice to follow the good forces or the evil ones, but on the **Day of the Judgment**, they have to account for their deeds and will go to heaven or hell depending on their deeds.

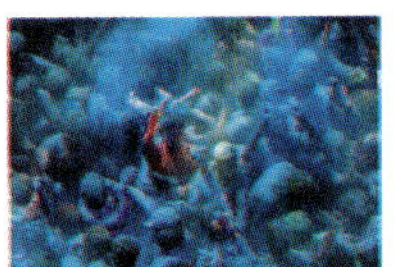

The Zoroasters' place of worship is the **Fire Temple**, as fire is considered to be the son of Ahura Mazda. A unique practice of this faith is disposing of the dead by excarnation (neither by cremation nor by burial). It involves placing the dead in stone-enclosed circular structures called *Dakhma* (tower of silence) for the corpse to be eaten by vultures or other such carrion birds.

As a religion, Zoroastrianism, among the oldest of faiths, has also influenced other religious thoughts, particularly of Christianity, as seen from the teachings in the Old Testament.

Due to the persecution of Zoroasters in the 7th and 8th centuries CE, pursuant to the Arab conquest of Islam, there was a migration of Zoroasters to India. The community settled in the region around Gujarat and is referred to as **Parsis**. Today, they are less than 50,000 in number and their population is believed to be dwindling further.

Pateti is the festival of repentance. It is observed on the last day of the year as per the Parsi calendar. Prayers are offered in the fire temple and thereafter Parsis reflect on their past years' actions and sins. It is believed that through their repentance and rites, their sins are consigned to the holy fire and they start afresh for the next year. Wearing new clothes, a feast of celebration, cleaning and decoration of the houses and wishing each other *Pateti Mubarak* are some of the features of this festival.

The Gahambars/Gahanbars are the six seasonal festivals that were supposed to mark the beginning of the six seasons of the year. However, due to the system of the lunar calendar which is not in sync with the annual solar cycle, the six Gahambars are now irregularly spaced in different parts of the year. These are also associated with the six primordial creations of the Ahura Mazda which are known as *Amesha Spentas* through whom the other creations came into existence which included the sky, the waters, the earth, plant life, animal life, and humankind. The Gahambars include;

Maidyozarem Gahambar, a mid-spring event in April or May;

Maid Yaoi-Shema Gahambar marks the midsummer festivities, of June or July;

Paitishahema Gahambar, the annual harvest festival of September;

Ayathrem Gahambar celebrates herding time in October;

Maidyarem Gahambar, a winter event held in December or January;

Hamaspathmaidyem Gahambar which means the middle path of all Seasons or soul festivals and takes place in March.

Zarthost No Deeso is the observation of the death anniversary of Prophet Zoroaster. This falls in the month of June, on the *Khorshed roz*, (11th day), *Dae mah* (10th month) as per the Parsi calendar. The Parsis visit the Fire Temple and offer special prayers. The day is marked with mourning, besides discourses on the life and works of the Prophet.

Judaism and festivals in India

Judaism, an ancient religion of the world, has its presence in India for more than two millennia. Although only a small number of Jewish people remain in India, yet the Jewish festivals have become a part of the assimilative culture of India. Among the most important of the Jewish festivals of India are Sabbath, Pesach or Passover, Jewish New Year, Yom Kippur, Feast of Tabernacle, Purim and Hannukaa.

Judaism: Features and Presence in India

Judaism is an ancient **monotheistic religion** that is nearly 3000 (or more) years old. It traces its origin to the Abrahamic religion of the Middle East which also influenced the religious thought of Christianity and later Islam. However, Judaism in the present form owes its origin to teachings revealed to **Moses** by God on Mount Sinai, referred to as the **Ten Commandments.** It is among the oldest of world religions with nearly 14–15 million followers, mostly in Israel and North America.

Jewish Faith and Salient Aspects of Religion: As a monotheistic religion, Judaism believes in only one God called Yahweh. Its basic tenets of faith are based on the Ten Commandments which are considered the Word of God and are sacrosanct. The *Torah* is the religious text of the Jewish people which is also a part of the larger text called the *Tanakh* or the Hebrew Bible. It is also referred to as the Old Testament in Christianity. The Jews also believe in the concept of the Day of Judgment, when the world comes to an end and when everybody will be answerable for one's deeds. Their place of worship is called the **Synagogue**.

Sects in Judaism: There are three main sects of Judaism; Orthodox Judaism, Conservative Judaism, and Reform Judaism. Orthodox Judaism believes that the Torah and Jewish religious laws (*Halakha*) are divine and must be followed. The Reform and Conservative Judaism are more liberal than Orthodox Judaism. Conservative Judaism follows a more traditional path than Reform Judaism and is a sort of middle position between Orthodox and Reform groups.

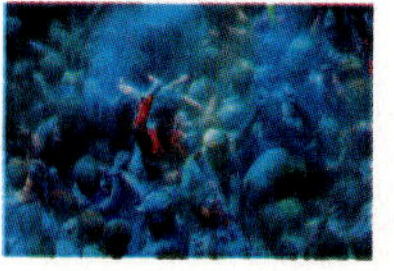

Judaism in India: Jews are believed to have been in India for nearly 2500 years. These include five sects of Jews which are;

The Cochin Jews are believed to have arrived with the merchants of King Solomon. Based on the region of settlement or presence, some other categories of Jews are the Chennai Jews, the Nagercoil Jews, and the Jews of Goa.

The **Bene Israel** (or Children of Israel) are the most numerous. These are Marathi-speaking Jews. They are said to have come to India from Pakistan after partition.

The **Baghdadis** are Jews who came to India from Baghdad nearly 250 years ago and settled around Mumbai and Pune.

The **Bnei Menashe** are communities of Mizo and Kuki tribesmen in Manipur and Mizoram. They claim to be the descendants of one of the 10 lost tribes of the Jews.

Bene Ephraim is a small community of Telugu-speaking Jews (Telugu Jews).

The Jews were one of the earliest of the faiths of non-Indian origin to arrive and settle in India. Their presence in this country has been marked by an absence of antisemitism (hostility/prejudice to the Jews). Over the centuries, they have practised the Jewish faith in peace, with gradual assimilation of the local languages and customs, leading to their integration in the assimilative culture of India. With the creation of the state of Israel, a large number of Indian Jews have migrated and today their population in India is estimated only to be around 5000.

Pesach or Passover considered the most important of the Jewish festivals, takes place on the first day of the month of Nisan (March-April). It marks the liberation of the people of Israel from the Pharaohs of Egypt and is also referred to as the 'Festival of Freedom'. It is celebrated with the Jewish feast of *Seder*.

Rosh Hashanah is the Jewish New Year which is celebrated in the month of *Tisheri* (September-October). Celebrations continue for the next 10 days till the festival of Yom Kippur. These 10 days are also called the 'Days of Awe'.

Yom Kippur is the Day of Atonement and is considered the most solemn day for the Jewish people. It is celebrated 10 days after the New Year and is marked with prayers, contemplation, repentance and seeking forgiveness from God.

Shavuot or the 'Festival of Weeks' takes place seven weeks after the festival of freedom. It symbolises spiritual liberation or the feast of revelation. It is believed that on this day the faithful got the holy book Torah on Mount Sinai. The synagogues are decorated and the Ten Commandments are read.

Besides the above are, **Purim**-the 'Festival of Merrymaking', **Hanukah** – the Festival of Lights, and **Sukkot** – the Festival of Thanks Giving.

Tribal Festivals

A variety of tribal festivals are popular in India which is home to numerous indigenous tribes. These may be related to their religious belief, worship of nature, festivals associated with the harvest or with the seasons. Some are also associated with births and deaths or other events of social life. All of the festivals exemplify the unique and varied culture of the tribes of India.

Sammakka Sarlamma Jatra or the **Medaram Jatra** is celebrated in the state of Telangana in Tadvai Mandal in Mulugu district. The festival is in veneration of the Hindu tribal goddess. The rituals are conducted by the priests of the **Koya tribe**, in accordance with Koya customs and traditions. It is also said to commemorate the fight of a mother and daughter, Sammakka and Saralamma with the reigning rulers, against an unjust law. The festival attracts a large number of tribal and other non-tribal devotees as well. As per some estimates, nearly 12 million people had gathered in this festival in 2012 making it the second largest congregation after the Kumbh and among the largest of the tribals festivals.

Karam festival or **Karma** is one of the most important tribal festivals and is held in the month of *Bhado* (August-September). It is celebrated in the states of Jharkhand, Bihar, Bengal, Odisha, Chattisgarh, Assam and Madhya Pradesh by different tribal groups such as **Baiga**, **Bagal**, **Oraon**, **Munda Lohra**, **Korwa** and others. It is dedicated to Karam-Devta, the deity of power and youth, and is also associated with health and good harvest.

Sarhul festival of Jharkhand is a spring festival that is marked by the worship of *Sarhul* or *Sal* tree which is considered to be auspicious to the people of the **Ho tribe** in the region. It is celebrated for three days in the month of *Chaitra* and also marks the beginning of the tribal new year.

Bhagoria festival celebrated by the **Bhil** and **Bhilala** tribes of the Jhabua and Alirajpur districts in the state of Madhya Pradesh is another spring festival of the tribals and usually takes place in the month of March. It also marks the celebration of the harvest.

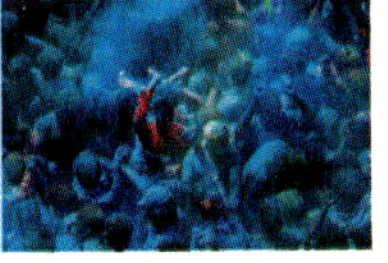

Bastar Dussehra is an important tribal festival celebrated by the tribes of Bastar in Chattisgarh. The festival is marked by the worship of the local tribal deity **Danteshwari.**

Thisam Phanit, one of the major festivals of the **Tangkhuls** and the **Naga** tribes of Manipur, is observed for a period of 12 days at the end of January every year. It is a ritualistic festival aimed to bid farewell to the spirit of the dead.

Harvest Festivals

For centuries, India has been a society dependent substantially on agriculture, which has led to the evolution of a variety of festivals associated with harvest in different parts of the country. These festivals celebrate the bounty of nature, for this is the basis of food security for human civilisation as well as for the sustenance of social life. Besides, in a land endowed with great geographical diversity and different weather patterns, these festivals also mark the transition in the solar cycle and welcome the different seasons. Rituals and propitiation of the gods and nature, festivities marked with music and dance, fairs and other celebrations, are some integral elements of the harvest festivals. Although these festivals have emanated in the rural-agrarian society, migrations to cities and other cross-cultural permeations have carried these festivals even to the bustling cities of today. Among the most prominent of these harvest festivals are **Makar Sankranti**, **Lohri**, **Baisakhi**, **Onam**, **Pongal** and **Magh Bihu**.

Makar Sankranti, a festival popular in North India, literally means, the **transition of the Sun in the zodiac (*Sankranti*) of Capricorn (*makar*)**. Thus, the festival marks the beginning of the journey of the Sun in the northern hemisphere (*Uttarayan)* as it enters the constellation Capricorn from the constellation Sagittarius (*dhanu*). In a way, it also marks the beginning of the end of the winters and the starting of the auspicious six months of *Uttarayan* for the Hindus, who pay obeisance to the Sun God whose beneficence makes a good harvest possible. As a festival associated with agriculture, it marks the celebration of the winter harvest. Making specific dishes such as *til ke laddo* (sweet sesame balls), *chikki* (sesame sweat-meat), *Khichdi* (a dish of rice and lentils) and other delicacies etc., is quite popular. These are often made using the produce of the season. Fairs referred to as *Magha-mela* (fair of the month of *Magha*) are also organised near the river banks. Taking a dip in the holy water of the Ganges or other rivers and praying to the Sun God, is considered auspicious. The flying of kites is another popular activity which is organised.

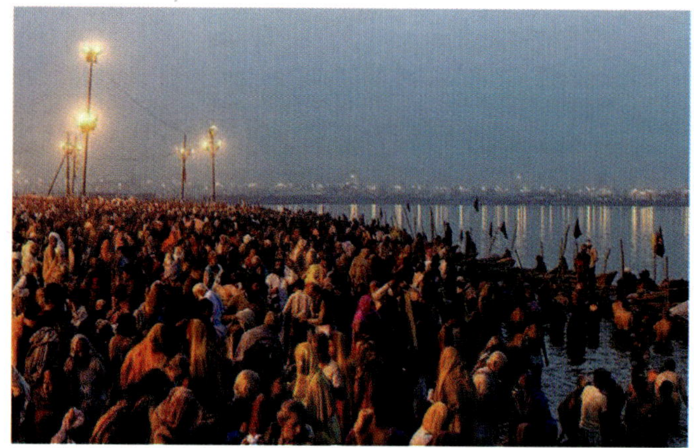

23.28: Holy dip in the River Ganga on the occasion of Makar Sankranti — Wikimedia Commons

The festival is known by different names and regional variations in the customs and practices are observed in different parts of the country. This includes *Uttarain* in Jammu, *Maghi Sangrand* in Punjab, *Maghi Sajji* in Himachal Pradesh, *Ghughuti* in Uttarakhand, *Dahi-Chura* or *Til-Sakarat* in Bihar (named after the dish of *Dahi Chura*), *Poush Sankranti* in West Bengal, *Magh Bihu* Assam, Uttarayana in Gujarat, *Sukarat* in central India, *Pongal* in Tamil Nadu and *Makar Sankranti/Sankranti* in other parts of the country. The festival is also observed in Nepal (*Sankranti*), Thailand (*Songkran*), Myanmar (*Thingyan*) and Cambodia (*Mohan Songkran*). The festival usually falls on the 14th of January in the Gregorian calendar and the 15th of January in the leap years.

Lohri, a festival popular in the community of Sikhs and Hindus of Punjab, is a celebration of the winter harvest of the Rabi crops. The festival which falls on the 13th of January is also an indication of the end of the winters and the beginning of the northward journey of the sun. The festival is marked with the organization of large community bonfires in the evening of the festival day, where some of the items of winter produce are offered to the fire. These include typical items such as corn, ground nuts, sugarcane, *gajak*, *jaggery*, *rewari*, etc. which are then had as *prasad*/blessings of the Lohri goddess. Traditional song and dance (of Bhangra and Gidda) is also organised around the bonfire, while people exchange greetings and gifts with friends and family members. This folk festival is also associated with the tale of Dulla Bhatti, a Punjabi folk hero as he is the central theme of many of the Lohri songs.

The **Bihu festivals** of Assam are a set of unique festivals which are associated with agriculture and harvest. These include a set of three festivals, the **Magh Bihu**, the **Bohag Bihu** and the **Kongali** or the

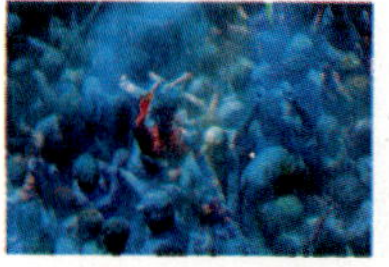

Kati Bihu. The **Magh Bihu** or the Bhogali Bihu is celebrated in Assam around the 14th of January. It is a harvest festival which also marks the winter solstice. It is celebrated by people of all religions, castes and tribes of the region. The festival marks the end of the period of harvest and thus the produce of the season is to the brim at this point in time. Accordingly, it is also known as Bhogali Bihu (*bhog*: feast) and the festival is associated with feasts and festivities which last for a week. The celebrations also involve singing and dancing to the beats of *dhol* (drum).

The **Bohag** or the **Rongali** Bihu, is celebrated usually on the 14th of April and is considered amongst the most important of the Bihu festivals. It is a spring festival that is associated with the beginning of the agricultural season and the preparation of the agricultural fields. It also marks the beginning of the Assamese New Year. The festival aims to cherish the process of cultivation and to pray for bountiful agricultural produce. The customs and festivities associated with it last for a week with different days being dedicated to different traditional practices viz. worship of the cow and the cattle, celebration of the new year with new clothes and festivities and the worship of the deities and seeking the blessing of the elders etc.. The celebrations also include; the singing of folk songs, the traditional Bihu dance and a variety of games.

Kati Bihu, or the Kongali Bihu (Kartik Bihu), is celebrated in October. This is a festival that is associated with the protection of the crops and worship of plants and is an animistic festival. As the food at this time of year is less, it is also referred to as the Kongali Bihu (*Kongal*–poor) and is more sombre than the other two Bihus. The festival involves lighting of the earthen lamps with mustard oil and placing them in the evenings in the agricultural fields as well as in front of the *Tulsi* (holy Basil) plants and elsewhere, for a whole month. It is believed that such practices help control the number of insects and agricultural pests that, attracted by the light, fall into it. Thus, it helps in preserving the agricultural produce. The worship of the goddess Lakshmi (goddess of wealth) is also performed by the Hindus.

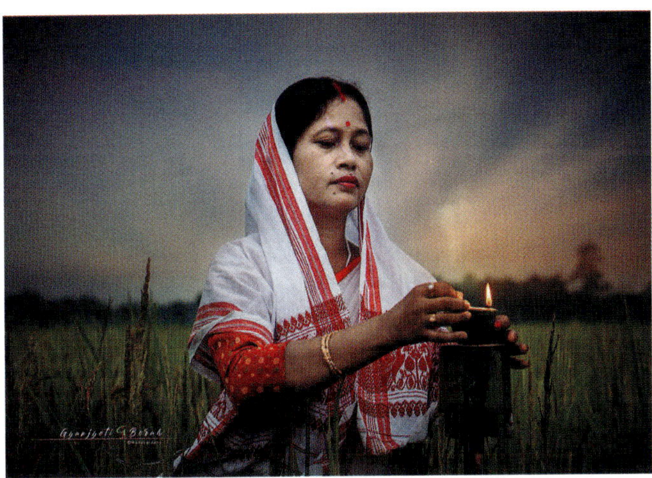

23.29: A woman lighting an earthen lamp in an agricultural field on the occasion of Kati Bihu — Wikimedia Commons

Baisakhi, another important harvest festival of Punjab, is celebrated on the 1st day of the month of *Baisakh*. This is also the 1st day of Punjabi New Year and that of the traditional Hindu calendar and falls on the 13th to 14th of April. The festival has centuries-old historical tradition. The third Sikh Guru, Guru Amar Das chose to celebrate it as one of the three important festivals of the region. Later it was on this day the that *Khalsa Panth* was established by Guru Gobind Singh, the 10th Sikh guru. Baisakhi is also the time when the Rabi crops are harvested in Punjab. The celebrations are marked with decorations of the Gurudwaras, holding of community Baisakhi fairs, people wearing new clothes, gathering, greeting and socializing. Song dance and martial arts performances are also commonplace in the festival. Besides Punjab, where it is celebrated as Baisakhi, this day is also celebrated in other parts of the country with different traditions and names as the new year day. These include Jammu, Haryana, Himachal Pradesh, Uttar Pradesh (as *Satwahi*), Bihar (as *Jur Sital* or Maithali new year), West Bengal (as *Pohela Boisakh*), Assam (as *Bohag Bihu*) and Odisha (as *Pana Sankranti*), Tamil Nadu (*Puthandu*), Karnataka (as *Bishu*), Kerala (as *Vishu*).

Pongal, a harvest festival, is one of the most important festivals of Tamil Nadu and adjoining regions. It is also associated with *Makar Sankranti* or the transition of the sun in the *Makar* zodiac and its northward (*Uttarayan*) journey. The festival of Pongal is celebrated around the 14th or the 15th of January. It also marks the beginning of the third Tamil month of *Thai* and hence it is also known as Thai Pongal. Celebrated over a period of four days, the festival involves rituals and paying obeisance to the different elements of nature that are associated with agriculture. The first day referred to as the *Bhogi Pongal*, is for worshipping the god of rain. The second day *Surya Pongal* is considered the most auspicious, where the Pongal sweet is made and offered to the Sun god. On the third day of *Mattu Pongal*, the cow and other cattle are venerated.

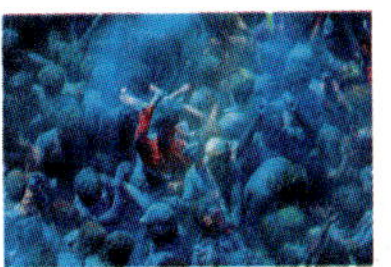

These are bathed and painted, their horns are polished and they are garlanded/decorated with flowers. On the fourth day, referred to as the *Kanum Pongal*, traditional meal of coloured rice is prepared.

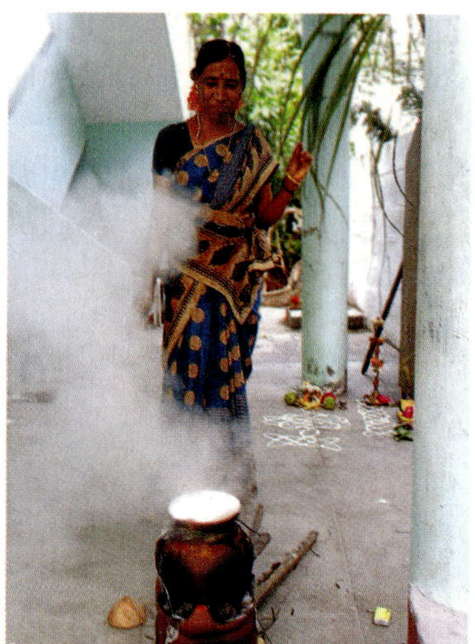

23.30: Traditional preparation of Pongal dish — Wikimedia Commons

The very word 'Pongal' means to 'boil' or to 'overflow' and refers to the traditional dish of rice which is boiled along with milk and jaggery and offered to the deities. This is then taken as their blessing (*prasad*). Decoration of houses and temples with rice powder artworks called *kolam*, meeting and greeting family, friends and relatives and exchanging gifts, are some other features of this popular festival.

Onam, a major festival of Kerala, is celebrated in the Malayalam month of *Chingam* (around August–September). The festival is observed for a period of 10 days and is associated with ritual worship and a variety of celebrations, including different cultural events, feasts and festivities. Essentially a harvest festival, it also has mythological significance. The festival involves the worship of lord Padmanabhan (a form of Lord Vishnu) and the celebration of the return of the mythical king Bali or Mahabali or Maveli. As per the mythological tale associated with the story of the *Vamana* avatar, Bali, an *asura* king, was sent to the nether world (*patal*) by Lord Vishnu who was incarnated as a *Vamana*. However, considering his righteousness and empathy for his subjects, he was granted the right to visit his subjects once a year on this day. Thus, the festival marks the day of the return of this popular king who is welcomed by the subjects.

Of the 10 days of the festival, the first day (referred to as *Atham*) and the last day (*Thiruvonam*) are the most important. The day of *Atham* marks the beginning of the festivities. Ritual worship at the temple of lord Vishnu, floral decorations, a variety of dances such as *Theyyam* (ritual dance), *Pulikali* (tiger dance) and other cultural performances take place. Holding colourful parades, the snake boat race (*Vallamkali*), and martial arts performances, are some of the other activities associated with this 10-day festival. *Onam Sadya* or the Onam feast, comprising several traditional dishes which are served on banana leaves, is another salient aspect of this joyous festival.

New Year Festivals

India is a land of diverse traditions. This is also reflected in the system of calendars and the observation of the first day of the year or the new year day. This varies from the region to region depending on whether the region follows a solar calendar, a lunar calendar or a luni-solar calendar. Many regions of the country follow the solar calendar system where the year corresponds to the movement of the earth around the sun. For regions such as Punjab, Assam, West Bengal, Odisha, Tamil Nadu and Kerala which follow this calendar, the new year falls in the month of **Vaisakha**. This usually occurs around the 14th–15th of April and usually remains the same every year.

In the regions of Maharashtra, Andhra Pradesh, Telangana, and Karnataka, the months are lunar, i.e., the months are based on the monthly cycles of the moon. For such regions, **Chaitra** is considered as the first month of the year.

The traditional Hindu calendar also referred to as the *panchangam* is a lunisolar calendar where the months are based on the lunar cycle but the year is based on the movement of the earth around the sun with the adjustment of a lunar month every three years. This calendar, such as the one based on Shaka and the Bikram Samvat, has the New Year in the season of spring. Some of the New Year's festivals popular in different parts of the country are briefly described here.

Ugadi, also known as *Samvatsaradi,* is the New Year day of **Kannada** and **Telugu** communities and is observed in the states of Andhra Pradesh, Telangana, Karnataka and Goa. It is celebrated on the **First day of *Chaitra*** as per the lunisolar calendar system. This usually falls late in the month of March or early April. Visiting temples, wearing new clothes, preparing the traditional dish *Pachadi*, and decorating the houses with colourful patterns and mango leaves *torans*, are some of the practices associated with this festival.

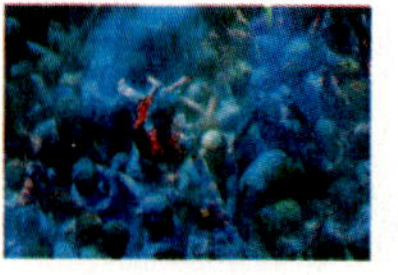

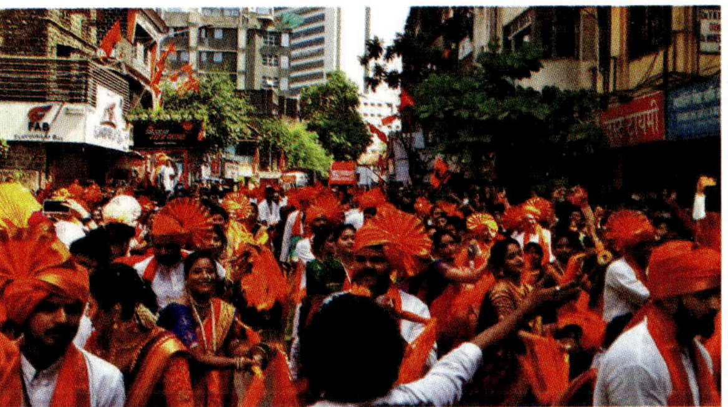

23.31: A celebratory procession on the occasion of Gudi Padwa at Girgaum in Mumbai — Courtesy, Maharashtra Tourism Development Corporation

Gudi Padwa is the New Year festival of **Maharashtra**, **Goa**, and **Konkan** region. This is also celebrated on the **1st day of** ***Chaitra*** as per the lunisolar calendar system where months are lunar. It also marks the beginning of the spring season. Houses are decorated with *rangoli* (colourful floor decorations) and a *Gudi Dvaja* is hoisted. It has a piece of cloth hoisted as a flag with an upturned copper vessel. Taking out of processions on the street, festive dancing and preparing traditional foods are some of the other events and activities that mark the occasion.

Chaitra Navaratri refers to the auspicious period of the first nine days in the month of *Chaitra* (March–April). This also marks the beginning of new year in the region of **Uttar Pradesh**, **Bihar**, **Jharkhand**, **Madhya Pradesh**, **Chattisgarh** and parts of **Delhi**. The period is also celebrated by worshipping different forms of the Goddess Durga, with the 9th day being celebrated as Ram Navami. The first of the nine days marks the beginning of the new year. The followers of the traditional Hindu calendar as per the Vikram Samvat, observe 1st day of Chaitra as the day of the new year.

Rongali Bihu: Amidst the three Bihu festivals of **Assam**, the Rongali Bihu is considered the most important and is celebrated as the New Year day. As per the solar calendar system, it is observed in the month of Baisakh and falls around the **15th of April**. It is also known as the Bohag Bihu, as the first Assamese month is known as *Bohag*. It marks the arrival of spring and is also an agricultural festival. The celebrations take place over seven days. There are specific days dedicated to the cattle, preparation of traditional dishes, worship of household deities and taking care of agricultural equipment. A day is also dedicated to textiles and another day dedicated to domestic animals, besides the last day to the celebratory Bihu dance.

Vishu marks the beginning of the new year in **Kerala**, and it also celebrates the beginning of the new harvest year. Based on the solar calendar system, the festival falls in **mid-April** (**14th-15th April**). This is also the first day of the month of *Medam* as per the Malayalam calendar and marks the onset of spring. The festival is associated with *Vishukkani*, a tradition where the different types of colourful and auspicious items are gathered in a cauldron and viewed as the first thing in the morning. These include the golden blossoming flowers of Indian laburnum, money, silver, mirror, cloth, rice, coconut, and other fruits and items considered auspicious, besides the image of the deity Sri Krishna. It is believed that on this day the *asura* Naakasura was slayed by Sri Krishna. Meeting and greeting loved ones and worshipping the deities are other traditions of this festival. Wearing of new clothes, the traditional feast of *sadhya* and fireworks are also associated with Vishu.

Puthandu is the Tamil New Year and is celebrated on the first day of the month of *Chittirai* as per the **Tamil** calendar. It falls in mid-April i.e. **13th-14th of April**, as do the new years of Baisakh in North, Central and parts of East India and Vishu in Kerala. To celebrate the New Year, people clean their households, wear new and traditional clothes, pay respect to elders and seek their blessings, besides they bring home sweets, fruits, flowers and other items considered auspicious. Worshipping the deities, offering to the deities of *Pongal* dish, and having a traditional vegetarian meal are some of the other customs associated with this day.

Poila Baisakh, or **Naba Barsha**, is the New Year day in West Bengal and also in some parts of North East. It is celebrated in mid-April usually around the **14th** or **15th** of April (as are the festivals of Baisakh, Vishu and Puthandu celebrated). *Poila* literally means first and *Baisakh* is the first month of the year. The word *naba-barsha* means new-year, thus signifying the 1st day of the year/new year. The festival is celebrated with people wearing traditional clothes, greeting each other with *shubho nob barsha* and cooking special traditional dishes. Besides, fairs and processions are also organised with people singing and dancing folk songs.

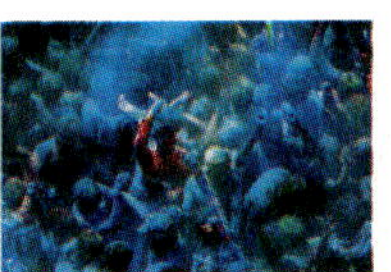

Pana Sankranti is the new year of Odisha which occurs on the **13th–14th of April** every year. This corresponds to the 1st day of the Odia month of *Mesha* which is equivalent to the month of *Vaisakha*. People visit the temples of lord Jagannatha and other deities, fairs and processions are organised, besides, traditional dishes are prepared. A special sweet drink called *Pana* is prepared and shared which is also believed to have given the name to this festival. The festival also marks the beginning of the new agricultural year.

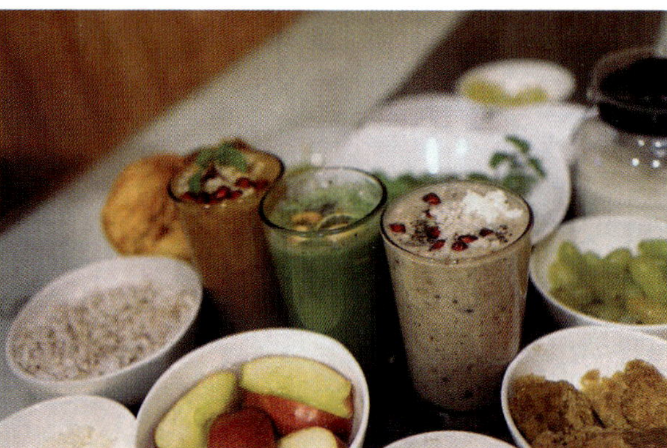

23.32: Bael Pana, fruits and other dishes offered on the occasion of Pana Sankranti — Courtesy, Department of Tourism, Odisha

Vaisakhi/Baisakhi is the Punjabi new year day as well as the harvest festival. It falls on the first solar month Baisakh/Vaisakh of the Punjabi calendar and is celebrated on the **13th–14th of April**. (see harvest festival Baisakhi for details). It marks the beginning of New Year for a large section of the population in North India, specially in the states of Punjab, Haryana, Jammu and parts of Delhi.

Navroz/Nowruz is the new-year's day of the ***Parsi*** community. It is based on the lunar calendar system and usually falls in **mid-August**. Parsis wear their traditional attire, visit the fire temple and perform the ritual worship of their divine deity *Ahura Mazda* so as to purify their mind, body and soul. Besides, they meet and greet family and friends and also undertake works of charity on this day.

Bestu Varas, or the Gujarati New Year, is celebrated on the **day after Deepawali**. The traditional Vikram Samvat Hindu calendar which is followed in the region considers the month of Kartik as the first month of the year. This usually occurs in the period of late October-November. The *Kartik Shukla Paksha Pratipada* or the first day of the ascending phase of the Kartik month is considered the beginning of the New Year.

Besides the above, some other New Year festivals include *Navreh* of Kashmir, *Losar* of Ladakh, *Mesha Sankranti* of Uttarakhand, *Jur Sital* of Mithila region (North Bihar), *Lhosar* of Sikkim, *Sajibu Chairoba* of Manipur, *Buisu* of Tripura, *Sangken* of Arunachal Pradesh.

Calendars In India

The word 'calendar' has its origin in the Roman word *calends/kalends* which means a method of distributing time into certain periods. Thus, a calendar is understood to be a measure/reckoning of time that keeps its record in terms of divisions called years, months, weeks and days. Since ancient times, different civilisations have adopted different methodologies for tracking time. Usually, it has been based on the movement of the earth and the moon. A year has been taken as the time for one revolution of the earth around the sun while the month is usually taken as the time for one revolution of the moon around the earth (in lunar month calendars). A day is the period of rotation of the earth on its axis. Thus, years, months, and days are natural units or measures of time, while further subdivisions of time as hours, minutes, and seconds are artificial/man-made. However, many variations in these systems of measurement exist which are manifested in the different calendar systems.

The system of calendar and measurement of time plays an important role in the determination of the day of celebration of the religious, harvest as well as the secular festivals.

In India, the most common calendar systems used are:

(*a*) The **Gregorian** calendar (Solar calendar)

(*b*) The **Saka** calendar (luni-solar calendar) and

(*c*) The **Vikram Samvat** calendar (lunar)

Besides these, regional variations such as the Bengali calendar, Tamil calendar, and others also exist. *Hijri* or the Islamic calendar (lunar calendar) is another important calendar system that is followed by the Muslim community.

The Gregorian Calendar

This is a solar calendar with a year comprising **365 days**. The entire year is divided into **twelve months of 30/31 days** (except February). Hence, the months are longer than the mean lunar months of 29.5 days. The calendar is said to commence from the year of the birth of Jesus Christ, also referred to as Anno Domini (the year of Christ) (AD) which is now referred to as the Common Era (CE).

This calendar was introduced in 1582 CE by **Pope Gregory XIII** who made modifications to the then-in-vogue **Julian calendar** and brought about a 0.002% correction in the length of the year. Its objective was to bring the calendar in consonance with the equinoxes and the solstices. The Gregorian calendar is the most widely used calendar worldwide and followed in India too, although it is not the designated official calendar.

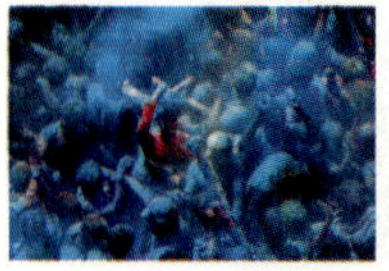

Gregorian Calendar: Facts of Interest

A solar year comprises 365 days, 5 hours, 49 minutes, and 12 seconds or 365. 2425 days. The earlier Julian calendar which was commonly used prior to 1582 (the year of introduction of Gregorian calendar) took the length of the year to be 365.25 days. This difference meant that in every 400 years, the Julian calendar calculated 3 more days to have occurred. As a result, the solstices and equinoxes were not in synchronisation with the days of the calendar. Pope Gregory XIII's reform reduced the number of leap years in 400 years from the earlier 100 to 97. Thus, every year divisible by 4 was to be a leap year, but the centuries were not leap years, except those divisible by 400. Thus, year 1900 was not a leap year but year 2000 was. When the new calendar was introduced in 1582, it had been in vogue for the last 1300 years (since the council of Nicaea of the Church in 325 CE). As a result, there were 10 days extra in the Julian calendar. These 10 days were skipped in the year 1582, which did not have dates October 5 to October 14.

The Saka Calendar

The Saka calendar is the **national calendar of India**. It starts in **78 CE** and is a **lunisolar calendar**. Here, while the year is solar consisting of 365 days, the months are lunar. The calendar begins on the **22nd March** which coincides with the 1st day of the first month *Chaitra* of the Saka calendar. The leap year begins on the 21st of March. Thus, the year begins with the spring equinox. The months of the year are (*i*) *Chaitra* (*ii*) *Vaisakha* (*iii*) *Jyeshtha* (*iv*) *Asadha* (*v*) *Shravana* (*vi*) *Bhadrapada* (*Bhadra/Bhado*) (*vii*) *Ashwin* (*viii*) *Kartika* (*ix*) *Agrahayana/Marghasirsa* (*x*) *Pausha* (*xi*) *Magha* and (*xii*) *Phalguna*.

The months of *Vaisakha* to *Bhadrapad* have 31 days each, while in the leap year, *Chaitra* month also has 31 days. The remaining six months have 30 days each. Months are also divided into two lunar phases *Shukla Paksha* (phase of ascendency of the moon) and *Krishna Paksha* (phase of descendency of the moon).

The Saka calendar was adopted as the national calendar in 1957 by the Government of India. It is used alongside the Gregorian calendar in various official works.

The Vikram Samvat Calendar

This calendar is based on **Vikram Samvat** which commences in 56 BCE. It is a lunar calendar. The year is of 354 days while the 12 months are lunar. The deficit of 11 days is made up by adding an extra month called '*Adhika Masa*' after a cycle of 2.71 years (approximately 32.5 months). The name of the months is the same as in the Saka calendar. The year begins on the first day of the new moon in the month of *Chaitra*, which is in March–April.

Secular Festivals and Celebrations

Reposited in the religious customs and practices, the traditions of India have given rise to a variety of festivals over the period of several centuries. However, some festivals have emerged also from the socio-cultural practices of different regions which are secular in nature or an offshoot of some religious custom or practice. Besides, with the independence of the country and the establishment of the Republic of India, emerged the national traditions of Independence Day and Republic Day celebrations. These celebrations are a reflection of the national ethos and also encapsulate the diverse culture of the country. The secular festivals and celebrations are a comparatively recent addition to the bouquet of Indian festivals and signify the evolving cultural tapestry of the land and its people.

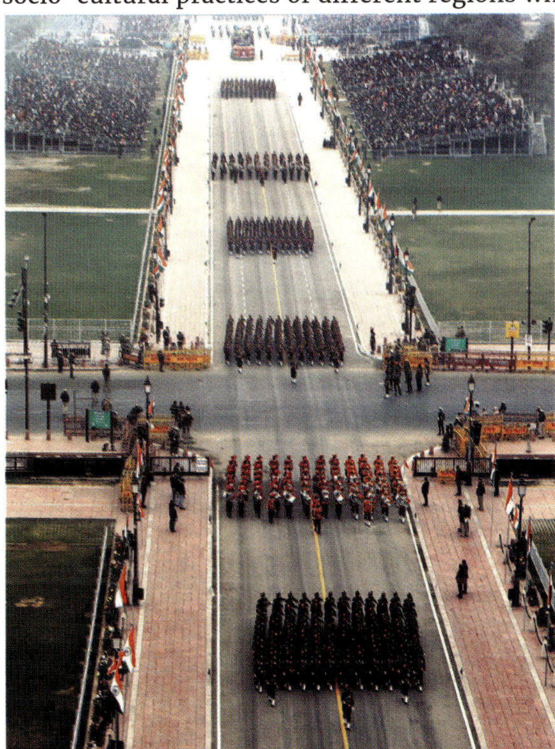

23.33: An aerial view of the 2023 Republic Day Parade on Kartavya Path, New Delhi — Courtesy, Ministry of Defence

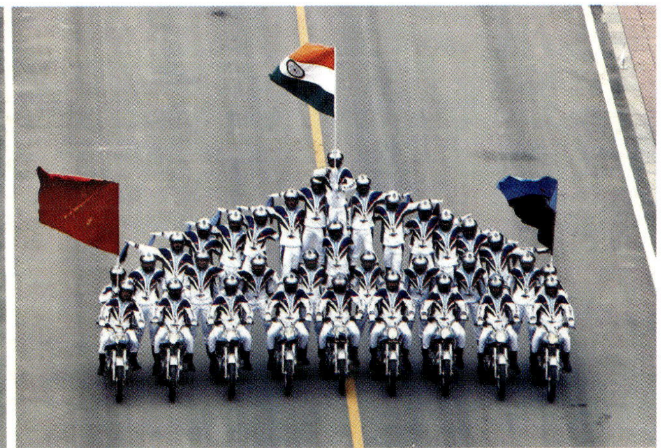

23.34: An acrobatic motorcycle formation in the 2023 Republic Day Parade — Courtesy, Ministry of Defence

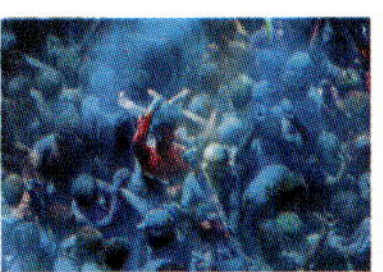

Republic Day Celebrations

Republic Day celebrations is one of the most important celebrations for our nation. A day of great significance for the country, Republic Day symbolises the emergence of the democratic republic of India. On the **26th of January, 1950**, came into effect the Constitution of India, replacing the Government of India Act 1935, thus marking the emergence of the Indian republic from the erstwhile British imperialism. The day is celebrated with the unfurling of the Indian tricolour by the President of India in New Delhi and by the Governors of the states in the state capitals.

Honouring of the martyrs at the Amar Jawan Jyoti at India Gate by the Prime Minister and a 21 gun-salute, is followed by the unfurling of the national flag by the President and the singing of the national anthem. Another highlight of the Republic Day celebrations is the ceremonious parade by different contingents of the armed forces at Rajpath (now Kartavya Path) in New Delhi. The parade moves from the Rashtrapati Bhavan on Raisina Hill and goes down the Kartavya path to the India Gate offering a salute to the President. This is followed by a showcasing of the country's defence capability and a display of the socio-cultural ethos of the nation through, the tableaus of the states and other performances. Giving bravery awards to the soldiers and to children (for displaying exemplary courage) and the flypast in formation by the air force pilots, are some other highlights of this national event.

The Republic Day celebrations also take place in different parts of the country including the national capital, the state capitals, the cities, the smaller towns and villages. Different functions are organised to celebrate this day in government establishments and private institutions as well as in schools and colleges. These celebrations, besides being a socio-cultural manifestation of the country, signify the unity and integrity of the nation making it truly a national festival.

Beating of Retreat

It is a ceremony held on the 29th of January which marks the **end of the Republic Day festivities**. The bands of all the three wings of the armed forces perform on this day. This special performance takes place at the Vijay Chowk, with the Rashtrapati Bhavan in the background and flanked by North and South Blocks. The President of India and other dignitaries grace the occasion.

Traditionally, beating of retreat symbolises the end of the war/day's battle and the return of the forces to camps to the beats of the drums, trumpets and bugles. In India, the ceremony of Beating Retreat was started in 1955, with bands of the three wings of armed forces performing. Since 2016 the bands of the Central Armed Police Forces and Delhi Police also participate. The performance begins with the arrival of the President with bodyguards and his/her welcome with a fanfare of trumpets. This is followed by the national anthem. The bands perform a variety of marching songs and tunes and usually end with the playing of the patriotic song, *Sare jahan se Accha*.

Desert Festival is celebrated in Jaisalmer in the **1st week of February**. This festival is a mix of cultural events, camel races, camel polo matches and various other competitions. Referred to as the *Maru Mahotsav*, the festival is organised in the sand dunes of the Sam desert near Jaisalmer. The festival is three days of cultural extravaganza with fairs, songs and dance and performances of the ballads

23.35: Rehearsals of the 'Beating of the Retreat' function at Vijay Chowk with the backdrop of North Block (right) South Block (left) and Rashtrapati Bhavan — Courtesy, Ministry of Defence

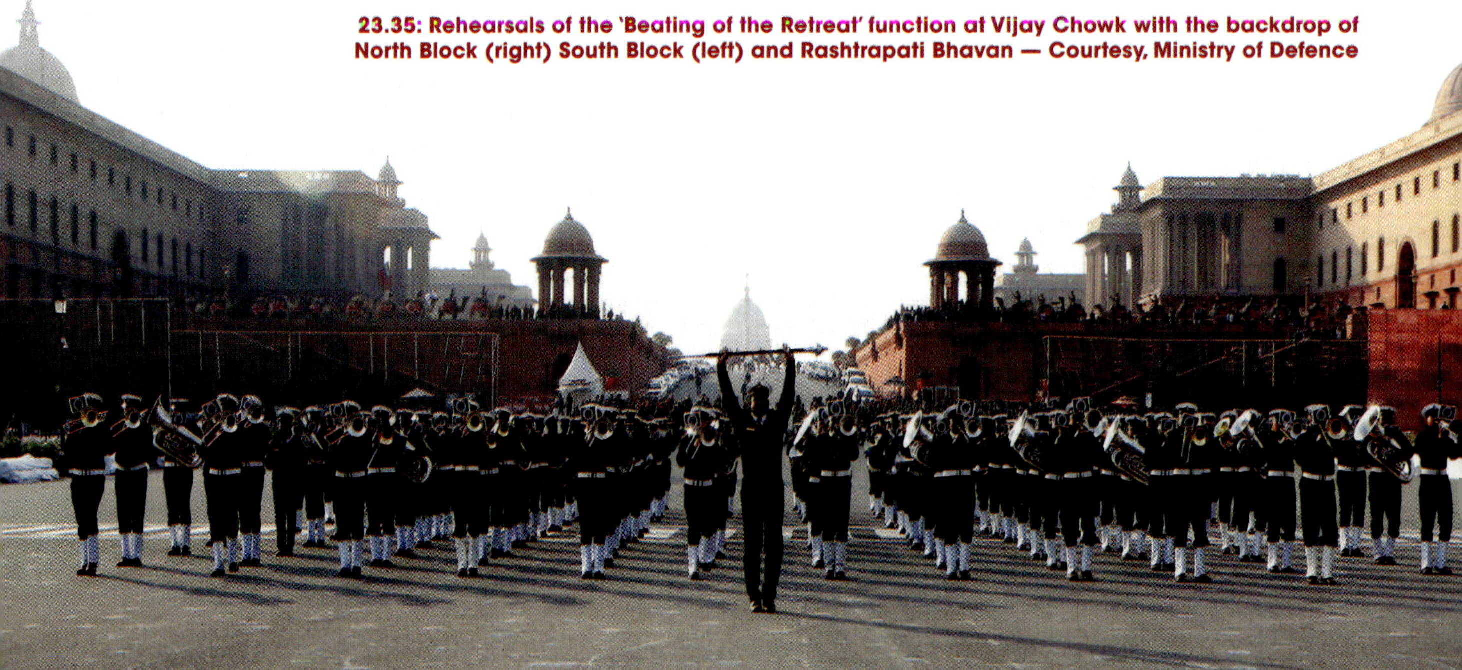

of the folklore of the region. A variety of traditional artists including puppeteers, acrobats, folk performers, gair and fire dancers, *Kalbelia* and *Ghoomar* artists and snake charmers also perform during it. Local handicrafts, jewellery, textiles and artefacts are also a part of the fair. Competitions of unorthodox events such as 'tying of turban', 'longest moustache' and 'Mr. Desert', impart uniqueness to the event. A 'tug of war' contest with foreign tourists and Indians, adds to the fun. Overall, it is a festival showcasing the regional culture and is marked with fun and gaiety.

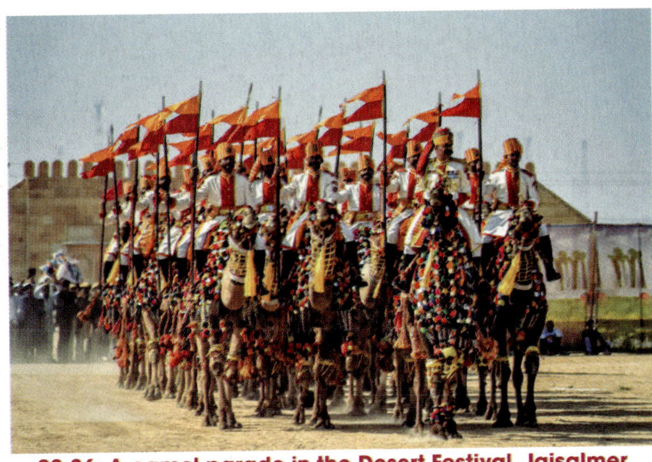

23.36: A camel parade in the Desert Festival, Jaisalmer, Rajasthan — Courtesy, Rajasthan Tourism

Khajuraho Festival is a festival of dances organised in Khajuraho, Madhya Pradesh, in the backdrop of the world-famous Khajuraho temples. The one-week festival is organised in the month of **February** (usually between the 20th to 26th of February). The festival showcases the richness of Indian Classical dances in an open air format in the backdrop of the world famous Khajuraho temples.

Independence Day, observed on the **15th of August**, is another occasion which transcends the boundaries of region, divisions of religion, language and customs. The day symbolises India's struggle for independence and the sacrifices of the martyrs and the freedom fighters. The hoisting of the Tricolour at the Red Fort by the prime minister and at the state capitals by the chief ministers, marks the beginning of the celebrations. Hoisting of the national flag at different government and private establishments, organisation of cultural programmes based on the theme of our independence, playing of patriotic songs, talks on the values and significance of independence and other activities mark the occasion. Like Republic Day, this day also signifies the freedom, unity and integrity of India.

Phoolwalon Ki Sair or **Sair-e-Gul-Faro-shan**, which literally means the procession of flowers, is the annual **Festival of Flowers** which is held in **Old Delhi** and also in **Mehrauli** region. The festival is held in the month of **September** after the end of the rainy season and is celebrated by different communities. *Pankhas* which are large palm leaf fans, are decorated with a variety of flowers and taken out in a procession to the *dargah* of Khwaja Bakhtiar Kaki. A procession is also taken to the temple of Jog Maya. The processions include dancers, people playing clarinets and other instruments, with florists and others carrying large fans made of flowers.

The festival is said to have a history of around two hundred years. It is believed to have been started as thanksgiving in the early 19th century by Begum Hazrat Mahal, queen of the then Mughal emperor Akbarshah when their son was released from British imprisonment. Although the festival was discontinued by the British in 1942, but was again revived in 1962 and continues to remain emblematic of communal harmony.

Batkama or **Bathukamma** is a **floral festival** celebrated by **Hindu women** in the **Telangana region**. The festival is observed in the period of *Sarada Navaratri* which is also the period of Durga Puja and continues for nine days. A variety of seasonal flowers are arranged in concentric layers to create the shape of a temple gopuram. Bathukamma is considered to be a festival of life and is in reverence to goddess Gauri who is considered the giver of life. It's a women centric festival where women dress in traditional clothes and prepare the floral Bathukamma as a folk art. The festival also symbolises the celebration of feminity.

Goa carnival also known as the **Carnaval** is an annual festival that takes place in the weeks leading to Lent (Lent: a period of 40 days of fasting and abstinence that begins six and a half weeks before Easter). The fest includes a parade, musical performances, dance competitions, food festivals and cultural displays. The parade which passes through the streets and roads of different towns of Goa is the highlight of the event. It incorporates different floats, dancers, musicians and other artists all dressed in colourful costumes. The parade is led by King Momo who is presumed to be the king of the carnival (a person is nominated as mythical king King Momo every year). The carnival which has been in vogue since 1965, is indeed one of the most important events of the Goan calendar. It makes Goa come alive while showcasing its culture and traditions in an atmosphere of fun and gaiety and is also a major tourist attraction.

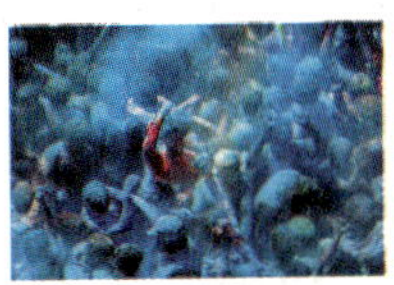

Some other important cultural festivals celebrated in different parts of the country are as follows:

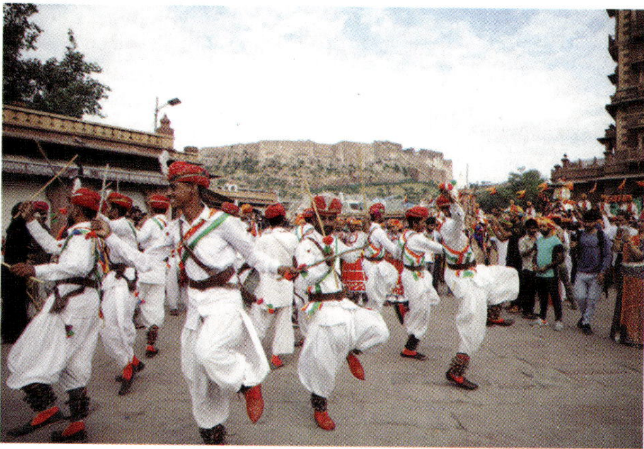

23.37: Marwar Festival Jodhpur; Mehrangarh fort in the background — Courtesy, Rajasthan Tourism

Ladakh Festival is organised in September and represents a blend of the Muslim and Buddhist cultures of the region. The mask dances of the region are the highlight of the festival.

Marwar Festival, also known as Maand, is a festival of Music and dance held in Jodhpur in the months of September-October to commemorate the valour of its warriors. The festival is held in the backdrop of the Umaid Bhawan Palace (in Jodhpur), Mandore and Mehrangarh fort. Show of camels and polo are also a part of the festival.

Rajgir Mahotsav is a music, dance and cultural festival organised for three days in **November** at Rajgir in Bihar.

Konark Dance Festival held in December, celebrates folk and classical dances from across the country in the backdrop of the famous Sun temple at Konark.

Hornbill Festival of music and dance of the ethnic tribes of Nagaland is organised for 10 days in December in Kohima.

Mammallapuram Dance Festival is organised in Mammallapuram (Mahabalipuram), in Tamil Nadu over a period of 30 days in December and January. It showcases the classical dances of the country.

Nishagandhi Dance Festival organised in Thiruvananthapuram, Kerala since 2013. It brings classical dancers across the country on a common platform.

Thyagaraja Aradhana or the **Thyagaraja music festival** is held in the month of *Pausa/Pusha* (December-January) in honour of the great 19th-century saint composer Tyagraja to mark his death anniversary. The festival takes place at Thiruvaiyaru (in Thanjavur) in Tamil Nadu and also in other states where the musicians render the *Pancharatna Kritis* of Thyagaraja.

Raan Utsav, a two to three-month-long cultural cum tourism festival which takes place in the Rann of Kutch, Gujarat from December to February, showcasing the music, dance and crafts of the region and also incorporating carnivals and other programmes.

International Kite Festival or Uttarayan celebrated on the occasion of Makar Sankranti (14th January) at the Sabarmati Riverfront in Ahmedabad, Gujarat, sees thousands of domestic and international participants flying a variety of kites.

Bodh Mahotsav held at Bodhgaya in the month of January, is a cultural festival that showcases the song and dance performances of various national as well as international artists. Besides bringing out the element of spirituality associated with the holy Buddhist site, it also showcases the regional culture of the state of Bihar.

Hampi Utsav, a music and dance festival, is organised in the backdrop of the ruins of Hampi, Karnataka, for three days in January. It is considered to be the oldest cultural festival continued since the time of the Vijayanagar Empire.

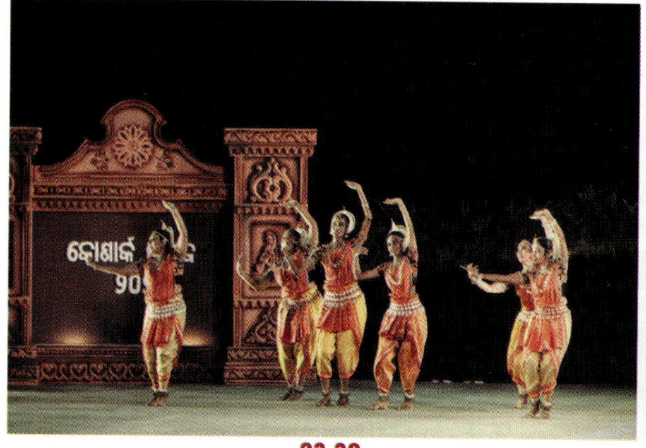

23.38

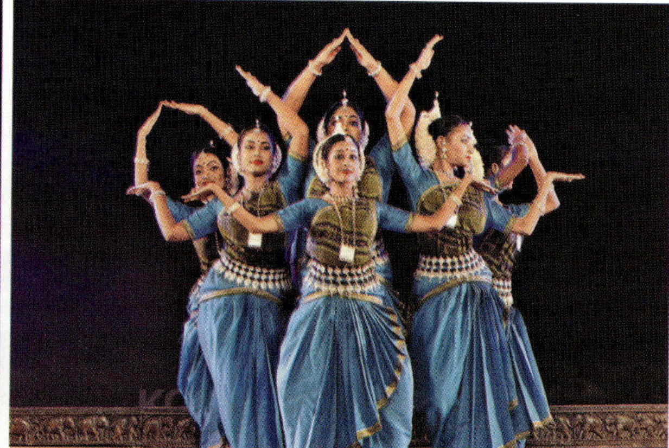

23.39

23.38 & 23.39: Dance performances at the Konark Dance Festival — Courtesy, Department of Tourism, Odisha

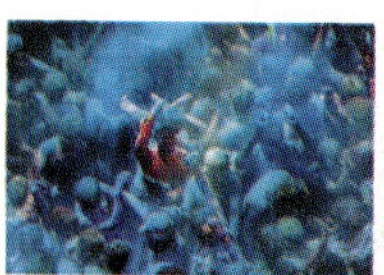

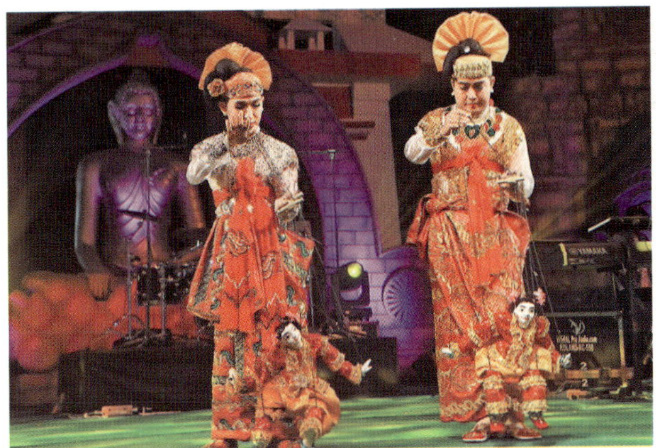

23.40

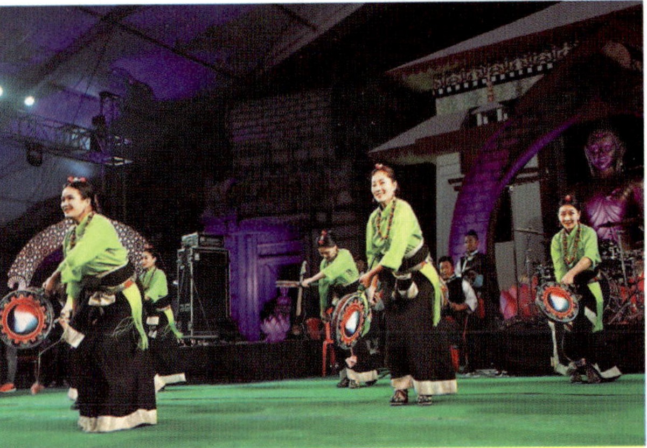

23.41

23.40 & 23.41: Puppet show and dance performance by international artists at Bodh Mahotsav at Bodh Gaya — Courtesy, Bihar Tourism

Qila Raipur sports festival which is also known as 'Rural Olympics' is held annually in February in Qila Raipur in Punjab. It showcases varied competitions such as, cart racing, athletics, tug of war and a variety of other rural sports in Punjab.

International Sand Art Festival is held at Chandrabhaga beach near Konark along with the Konark dance festival. It showcases sand arts created by eminent artists of this craft who are from India and several other countries. It is another unique festival which is gradually garnering international acclaim.

FAIRS OF INDIA

Fairs are occasions and events of human congregations which are held on account of diverse factors ranging from religious to social and from agrarian to economic. In India, referred to as *mela*, which literally means a gathering, or 'to meet', fairs have been a significant event of human activity since ancient times. Reference to *Magh Mela*, a fair of the month of *Magha*, is found in Puranic and earlier literature.

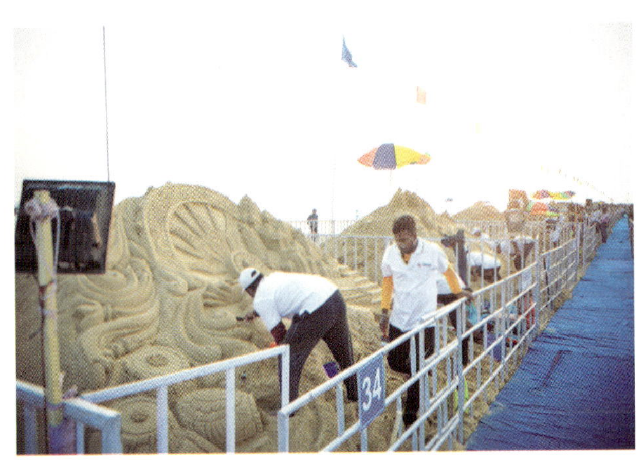

23.42: Artist at work at International Sand Art Festival at Chandrabhaga beach, Konark, Odisha — Courtesy, Department of Tourism, Odisha

Today, each region and state of India celebrates scores of regional and local fairs. Besides being reflective of the regional traditions, customs and practices, they have also emerged as important events of economic activities while supplementing the tourism industry. Fairs are also a significant expression of different tangible and intangible elements of culture, ranging from religion and customs to arts and crafts and from music and dance to agriculture and commerce. They are also a crucial occasion of community interactions and bonding. Like festivals, they truly showcase the diverse regional culture of India. Some of the more prominent and popular Indian fairs are described here.

Kumbh Mela is considered as the largest peaceful congregation of humanity on earth. Kumbh is a culmination of religious faith and fervour. The festive assembly is centred around the practice of taking a holy dip in a sacred river at certain very auspicious occasions. As per the traditional Hindu belief, the act is considered to absolve one of the past sins and endow spiritual liberation to the devotee.

There are four widely recognised Kumbhs. Based on astrological auspicious timings, these are held in rotation in four holy places, usually after three to four years and once in 12 years in a particular place. Kumbh congregation also takes place in the 6th year of the previous congregation and is referred to as the Ardha Kumbha. These Kumbhs are;

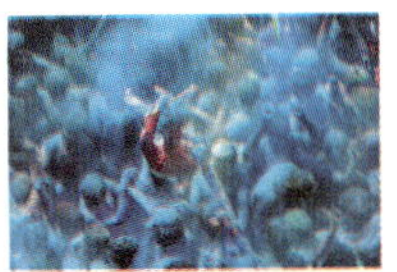

The **Prayag Kumbh** which takes place at the confluence of the Ganga, the Jamuna and the mythical Saraswati River in Prayagraj (erstwhile Allahabad).

The **Haridwar Kumbh**, which takes place on the bank of the Ganga at Haridwar;

The **Nashik Trimbakeshwar Simhastha** which is held on the banks of the Godavari River at Nashik; and

The **Ujjain Simhastha** which is held at the banks of the Shipra River at Ujjain.

Kumbh literally means a pitcher, and signifies the pitcher containing the nectar of immortality which emerged from the 'churning of the ocean' as per the mythological legends. In the scuffle between the *devas* and the *asuras* to take control of the pitcher, some of the nectar is believed to have fallen on the four spots which became holy and are focal points of this grand religious gathering. On certain auspicious occasions, the water at these spots is believed to return to its primordial nectar-like property and hence imparts the immense religious significance associated with the Kumbhs. As per some accounts, although the significance of taking a holy dip at Kumbh, is contained in the ancient scriptures, the practice of an organised Kumbh congregation at these spots began due to the efforts of Adi Shankaracharya in the 8th century CE.

In the modern form, the Kumbhs, besides being a holy congregation of ascetic monks and lay devotees, are also an occasion for religious discourse and discussions, besides for other cultural activities and events. With the Kumbhs being organised at four different places, each has its uniqueness and adds to the cultural diversity of this festival. The organisation of traditional fairs and the establishment of a virtual township to support the gathering of millions are some other poignant features of this religious fair. As per the estimates in official records, more than 200 million visitors came over a period of several weeks to the 2019 Kumbh at Prayagraj, with nearly 50 million congregating on the most auspicious day of bathing. Another feature of these Kumbhs is the gathering of *sadhus* (monks and ascetics) of the different *akharas* (bands of monks which number to thirteen). The group of such monks gather from all

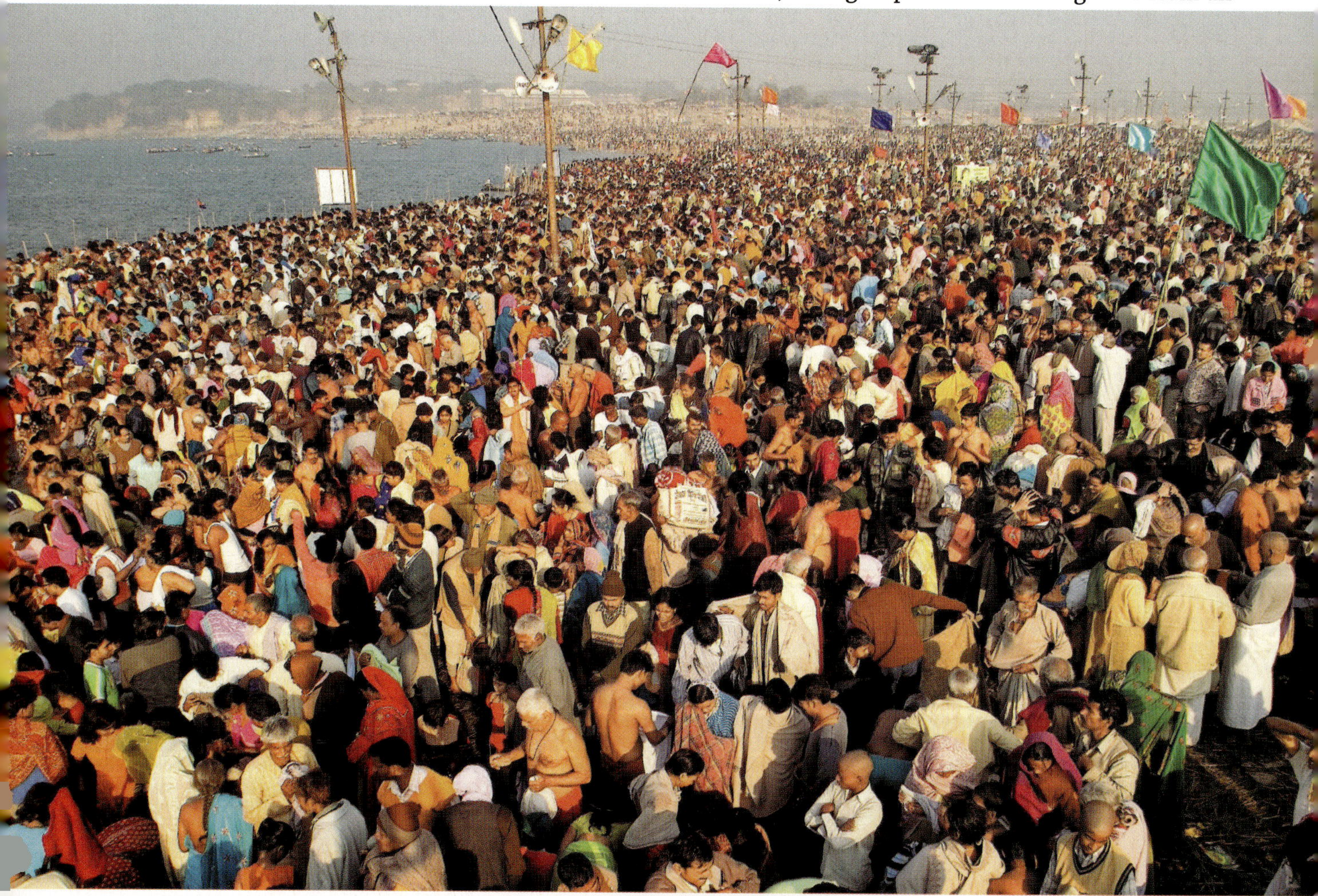

23.43: An unending sea of people gathered for a holy dip on the confluence of the rivers at Prayagraj Kumbh — Courtesy, Directorate of Uttar Pradesh Tourism

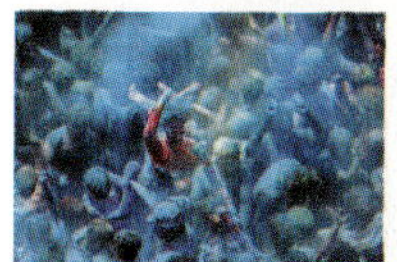

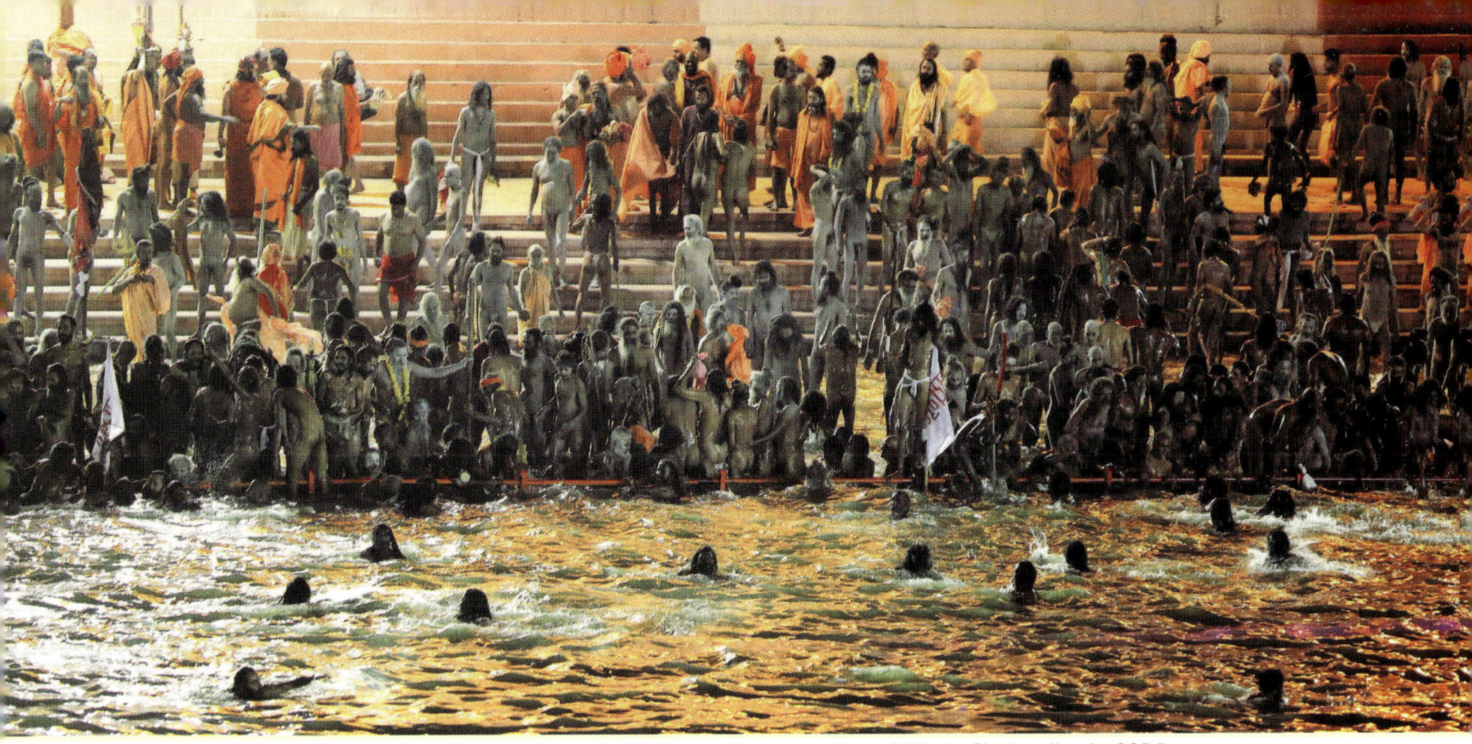

23.44: A throng of sadhus taking a holy dip on the occasion of Ujjain Simhastha in 2016 — Courtesy, Madhya Pradesh Tourism Board

parts of the country, making it one of the largest gathering of monks and religious leaders of all forms and sects of Hinduism. In the year 2017, the **UNESCO** included the Kumbh Mela in the **Representative List of the Intangible Cultural Heritage of Humanity**.

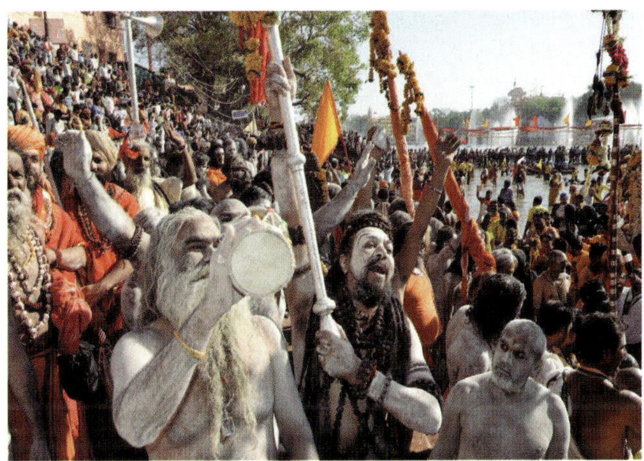

23.45: Jubilant sadhus with bodies smeared with holy ash, ready for a holy dip on the occasion of Ujjain Simhasta in 2016 — Courtesy, Madhya Pradesh Tourism Board

Ganga Sagar Mela is the next biggest congregation after the Kumbh ela. It is another religious gathering which takes place on the island of Ganga Sagar in the Bay of Bengal. This is the location of the confluence of the holy river Ganga with the waters of the Bay of Bengal. This fair is held every year on the 14th or the 15th of January on the auspicious day of Makar Sankranti. A large number of Hindu pilgrims gather on this island to take a holy dip at the confluence and offer prayers. As per official estimates, around 5.1 million people congregated at Gangasagar in 2023.

As per the mythological belief attached to it, King Bhagirath prayed to Lord Shiva for the descent of Ganga from the heavens so that her confluence with the mighty Sagar (ocean) could redeem the soul of his ancestors. The congregation at this place is said to find reference in ancient scriptures, and in the 15th century the efforts of Swami Ramananda culminated in the beginning of this pilgrimage.

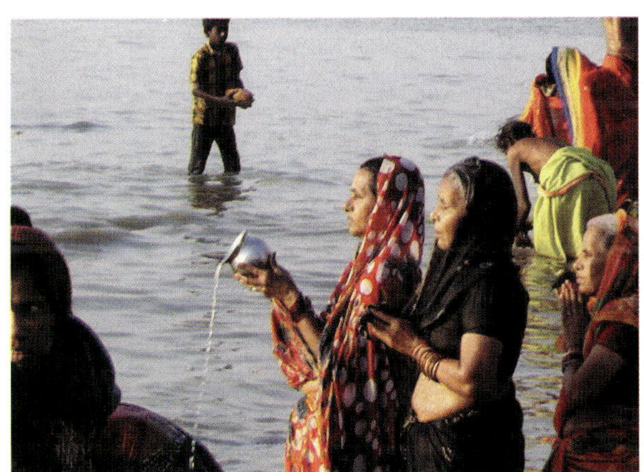

23.46: Ritual obeisance at Ganga Sagar island

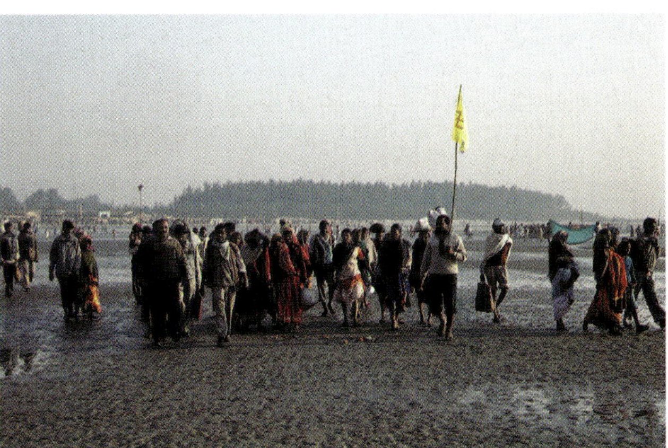

23.47: Devotees at Ganga Sagar island

— Courtesy, Department of Tourism, West Bengal

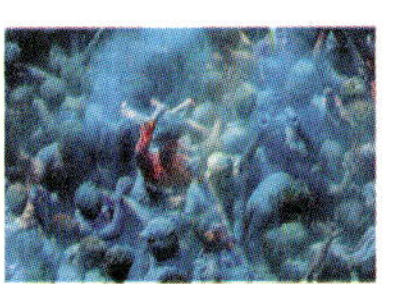

Magh Mela refers to the religious congregation and fair that takes place annually in the month of *Magha* (usually January) at *Triveni Sangam* (the confluence of the rivers of Ganga, Jamuna and Saraswati) at Prayagraj (Allahabad). Once in 12 years, when the astrological position of Jupiter, Sun and Moon are auspicious, then the occasion partakes the character of a Kumbh. Devotees take a ritual bath and pray for penance for their sins. The day of *Makar Sankranti* which marks the beginning of the fair is considered very auspicious, while the day of *Mouni Amavashya* is another occasion for the devotees to throng for the holy dip. The festival ends with Maha Shivaratri. As per scholars, the tradition of Magha Mela is very ancient with reference to it being found in Mahabharata, Puranas other scriptures.

The congregation also inspires a large community fair at the venue with tent cities and pontoon bridges lining the banks of the rivers. Religious leaders from different parts of the country and various akharas also take part in it. Marking the occasion are religious discourses, cultural programmes, and various economic and other commercial activities which are directly associated with the festival or support it. Several million people throng this great spiritual fair which continues for nearly six weeks and makes it only a marginally lesser version of the Kumbh.

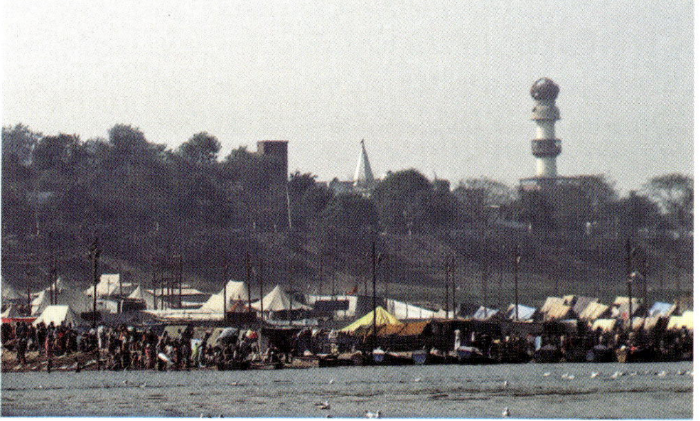

23.48: A city of tents and other temporary shelters which spring up on the occasion of Magha Mela at Prayagraj — photograph by Madhukar Kumar Bhagat

Pushkar Mela held in **Pushkar** in **Rajasthan** is one of the largest **fairs of camels and other livestock**. The event is held annually for a period of five days in the month of *Kartik* (October–November). Hindu devotees also take a holy dip in the Pushkar lake and pay obeisance to Lord Brahma (the creator among the Holy Trinity) whose temple stands in Pushkar. Different cultural events, and competitions such as *mataka phod* (breaking the pot), tug of war, 'longest moustache' etc. are added attractions. Thus, apart from the activity of buying and selling livestock which remains the primary basis of this fair, many religious and cultural attractions also make this fair a tourist destination. As per official estimates, nearly 2,00,000 visitors come to this fair.

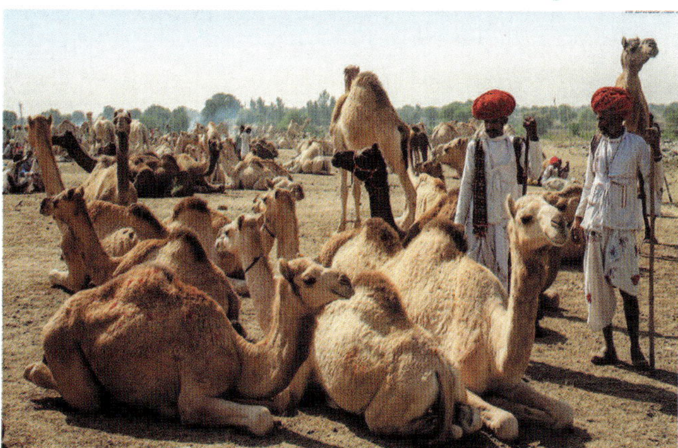

23.49: Camels at display at Pushkar Camel Fair, Rajasthan — Courtesy, Rajasthan Tourism

Sonepur Mela is the largest cattle fair of Asia. Held in Sonepur, Bihar, on the confluence of rivers Ganga and Gandak, the fair is organised annually in the month of *Kartik* (usually in November-December) and continues for nearly a month. As the fair takes place on the auspicious occasion of *Kartik Purnima*, it is also a time for the Hindu devotees to take a holy dip at the confluence of the rivers and offer prayers at the famous **Harihar Nath** temple. As per legends, this temple was established by lord Rama at the confluence of the rivers during his visit to Mithila. However, the current Harihar Nath temple is said to be built in the medieval period. It also lends the name *Harihar Kshetra Mela* to the fair.

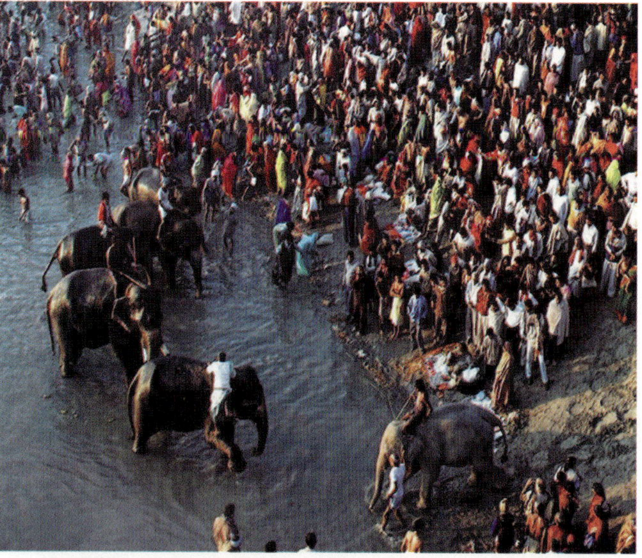

23.50: Sonepur Mela; devotees taking a holy dip at the confluence of the rivers Ganga and Gandak; elephants being given a bath by their handlers — Courtesy, Bihar Tourism

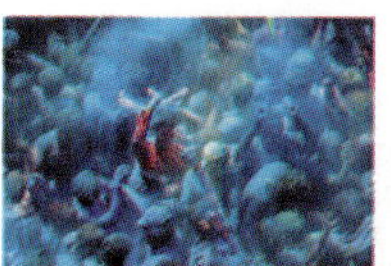

For centuries, the Sonepur Mela has seen a wide array of animals being traded which included farm animals, cattle, ponies, horses, goats, dogs, birds poultry, even elephants and occasional camel. The fair is believed to be in vogue since the Vedic period, where historically, traders from different regions of the country converged for this month-long trade. Apart from the animal fair, shops of a wide variety of goods, ranging from furniture to weapons, from garments to toys, and from jewellery to handicrafts come up. Now a variety of cultural programmes are also organised. The fair has also emerged as a significant religious occasion for the Hindu devotees.

Nagaur Mela is another popular cattle fair, which is held at Nagaur, in Rajasthan in the months of January and February. Among the largest of cattle fairs of the state, a wide variety of animals ranging from bullocks, horses and camels are traded. Competitions like turban tying, longest moustache, tug of war and a variety of cultural programmes, are the added attractions. Besides sale of the regional textiles, handicrafts, local spices and other items is also quite popular in the makeshift villages that come up during the fair.

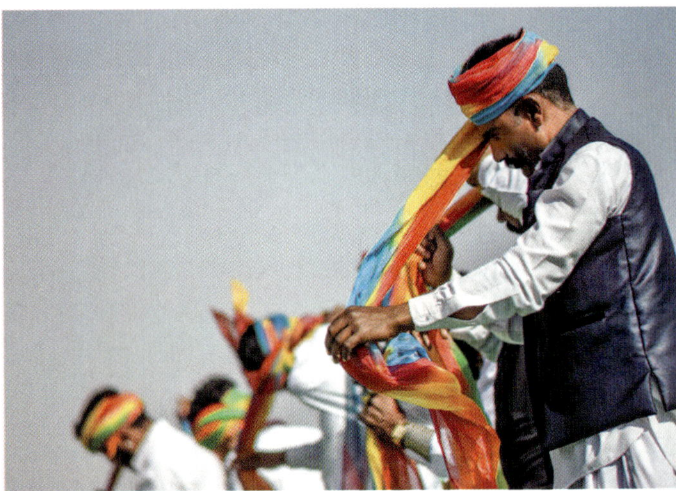

23.51: Turban tying competition — Courtesy, Rajasthan Tourism

Surajkund Crafts Fair or the Surajkund Mela as it is known, is among the largest of international fairs of crafts. It elicits participation from master craftsmen from different states of India and from other countries. The fair takes place annually in the first fortnight of February at Surajkund in Haryana, near Delhi. Started in 1987, traditional craftsmen, including painters, weavers, sculptors and other artists come up with a variety of crafts which are made of textile, metal, bamboo, glass and stones. The fair is visited every year by nearly 1.2 million visitors, including 2,00,000 foreigners, and is definitely among the most popular of the modern fairs.

Taj Mahotsav held at Shilpgram near the eastern gate of Taj Mahal in Agra, is a fair cum fest organised for a period of 10 days to two weeks every February. The event showcases the work of hundreds of artisans and craftsmen from different parts of India. The products range from wood & stone carvings from Tamil Nadu to bamboo and cane work from the Northeastern states, from papier-mache from Kashmir to brassware from Moradabad in Uttar Pradesh, from carpets from Gujarat and Kashmir to silk and *zari* work from Varanasi, besides other traditional crafts from different parts of the country. The fair also showcases the different cuisines of India and the music and dance of the different regions. A road procession that features elephants and camels imitating the victory procession of the Mughals with trumpet players, drums, folk dancers etc. marks the beginning of the event and also showcases the local culture.

Besides, there are other popular regional fairs of India that are related to religious festivals and deities, tribal customs and practices, traditional crafts and products of arts. These include;

Ambubachi mela held at Kamkhya temple in Assam for a period of three days during the monsoons in the Assamese month of Ahar (mid-June);

The **Baneshwar fair**, a tribal fair held in Dungarpur in Rajasthan in Magh (January-February) for a period of two weeks;

The **Nauchandi fair** of Meerut, Uttar Pradesh, which has a tradition of several hundred years, takes place for a month after Holi, showcasing the regional craft such as Lucknow's *chikan* work, the brassware of Moradabad, footwear of Agra, silk sarees of Varanasi, besides other products, local delicacies etc.

Madhavpura Ghed (fair) held in Madhavpura near Porbandar in Gujarat for five days (March–April), celebrates the marriage of Lord Sri Krishna with Rukmani. It showcases the local crafts and cuisines besides cultural performances of artists.

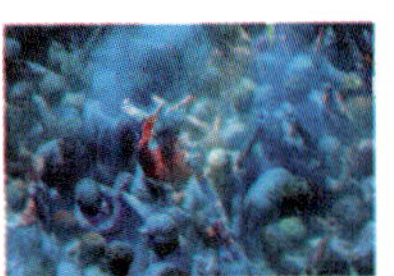

PICTURE GALLERY

Prayagraj Kumbh

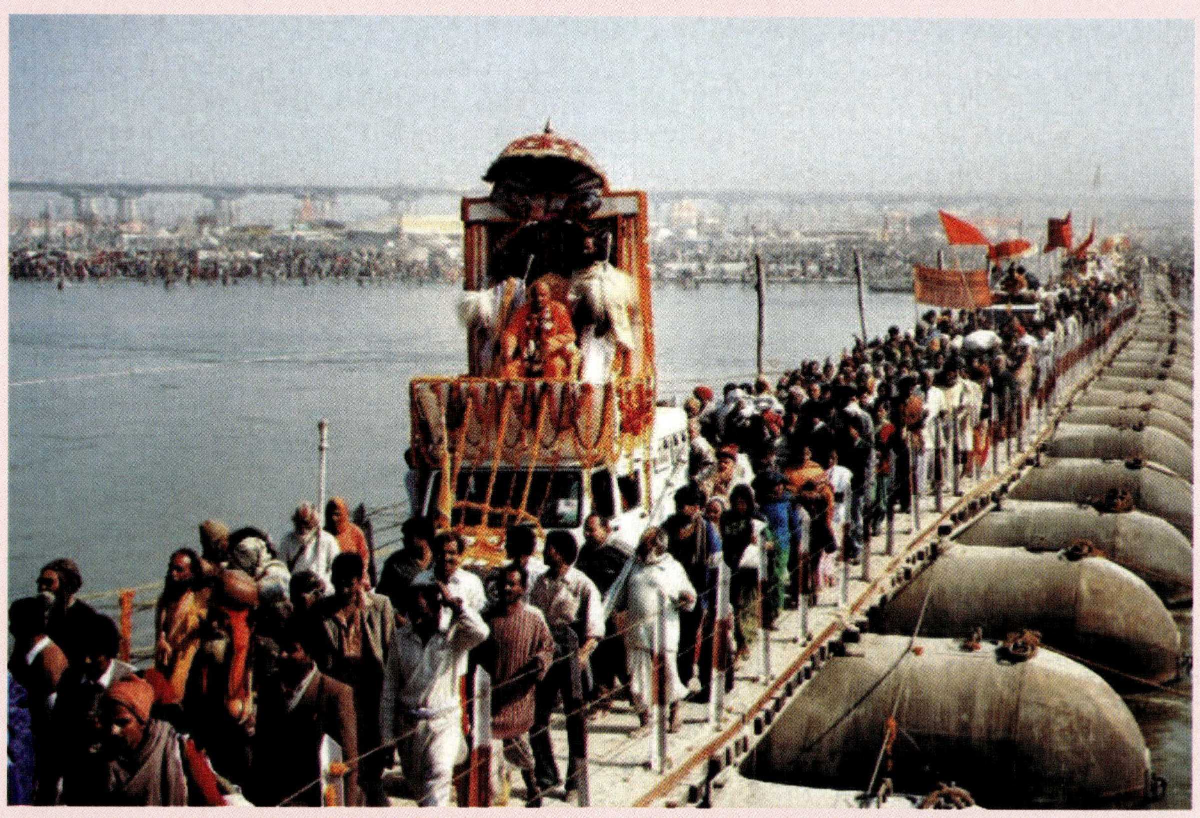

23.52: A retinue of *akhadas* led by their Mahant crossing a pontoon bridge

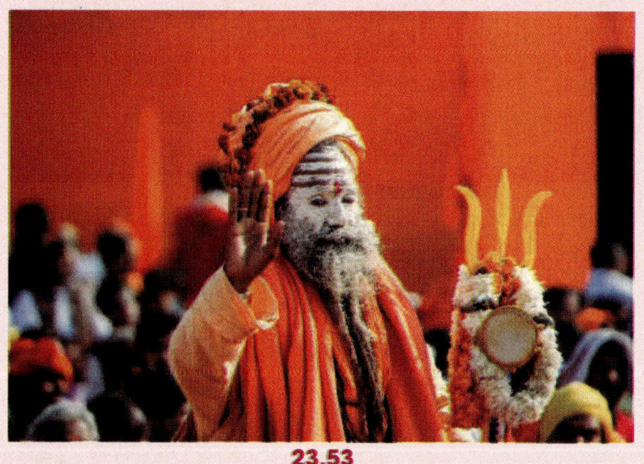

23.53

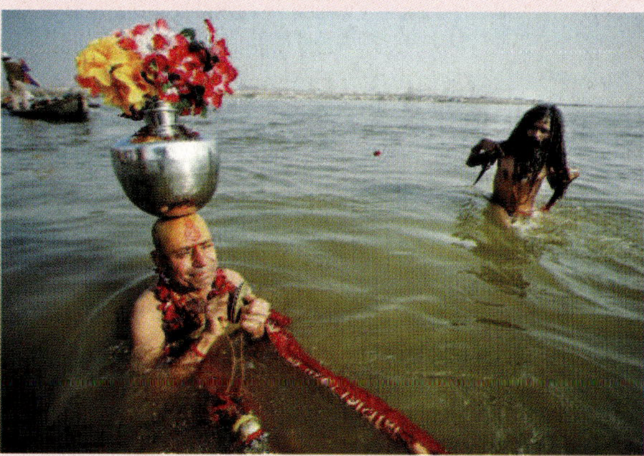

23.54

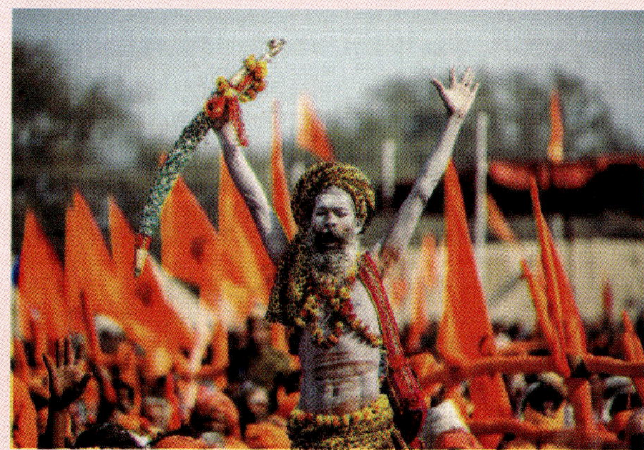

23.55

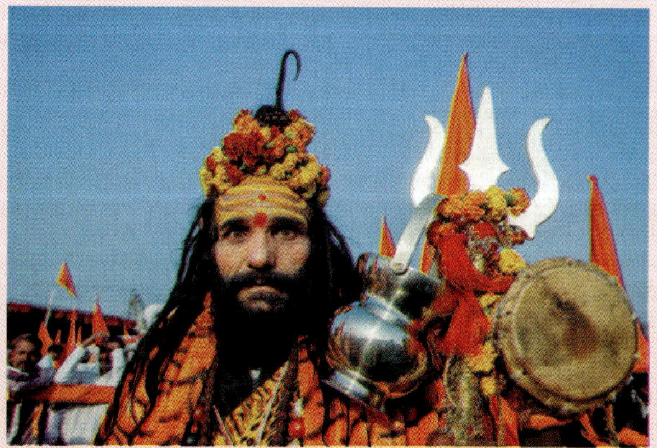

23.56

23.52, 23.53, 23.54, 23.55 and 23.56: Sadhus at Prayagraj Kumbh
— Pictures : Courtesy, Directorate of Uttar Pradesh Tourism

Ujjain Simhasta: 2016

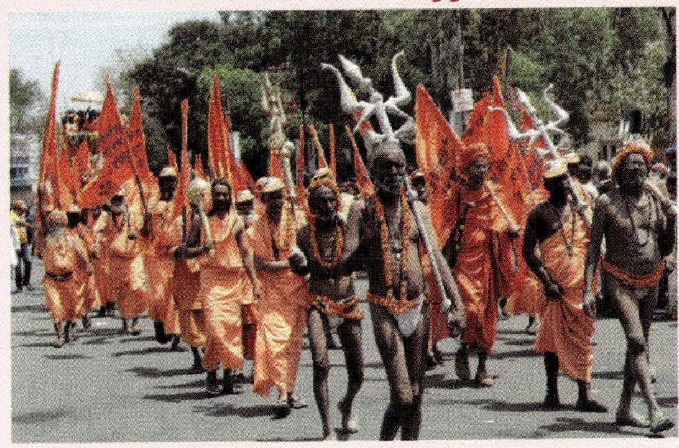

23.57: A procession of sadhus and seers

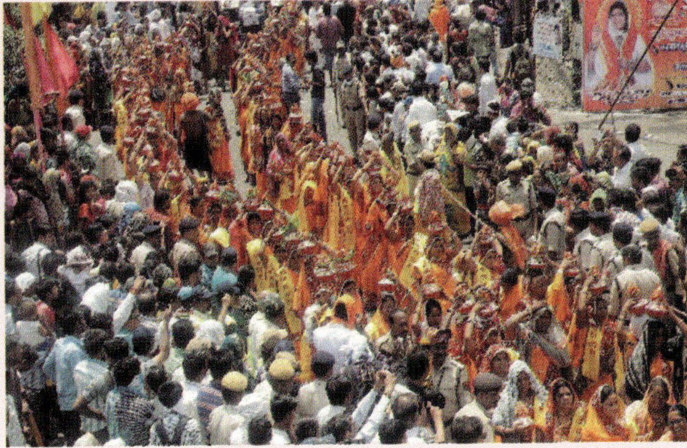

23.58: Women devotees proceeding for ritual worship with pots on their head

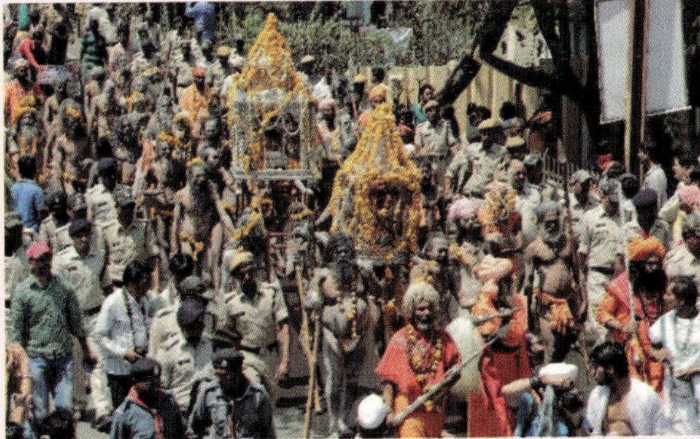

23.59: A procession of sadhus with idols of deities

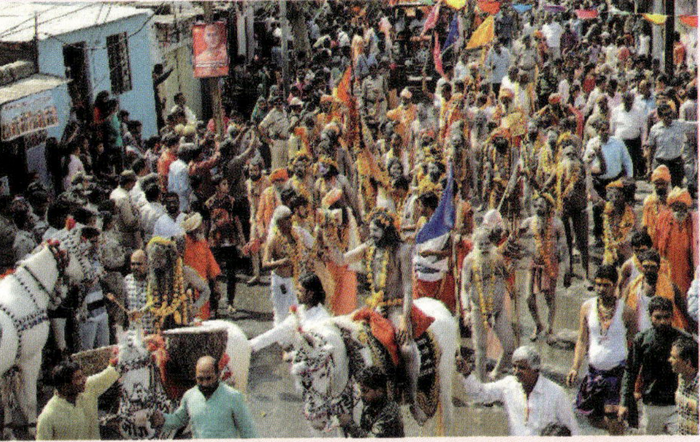

23.60: An order of sadhus proceeding to the Ghats

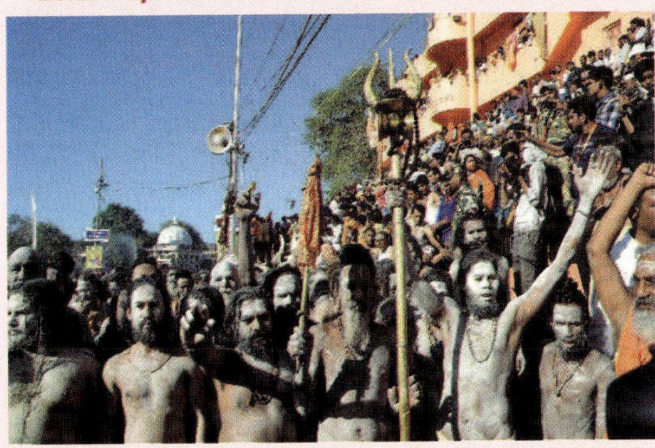

23.61: Sadhus of a sect awaiting their turn for a holy dip

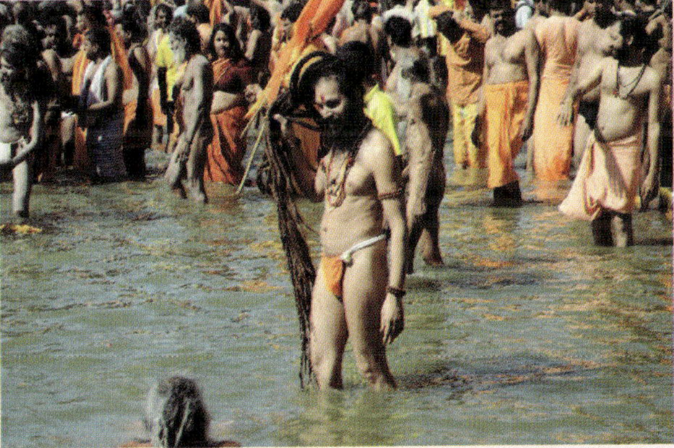

23.62: And finally the dip and the delight

— Pictures : Courtesy, Madhya Pradesh Tourism Board

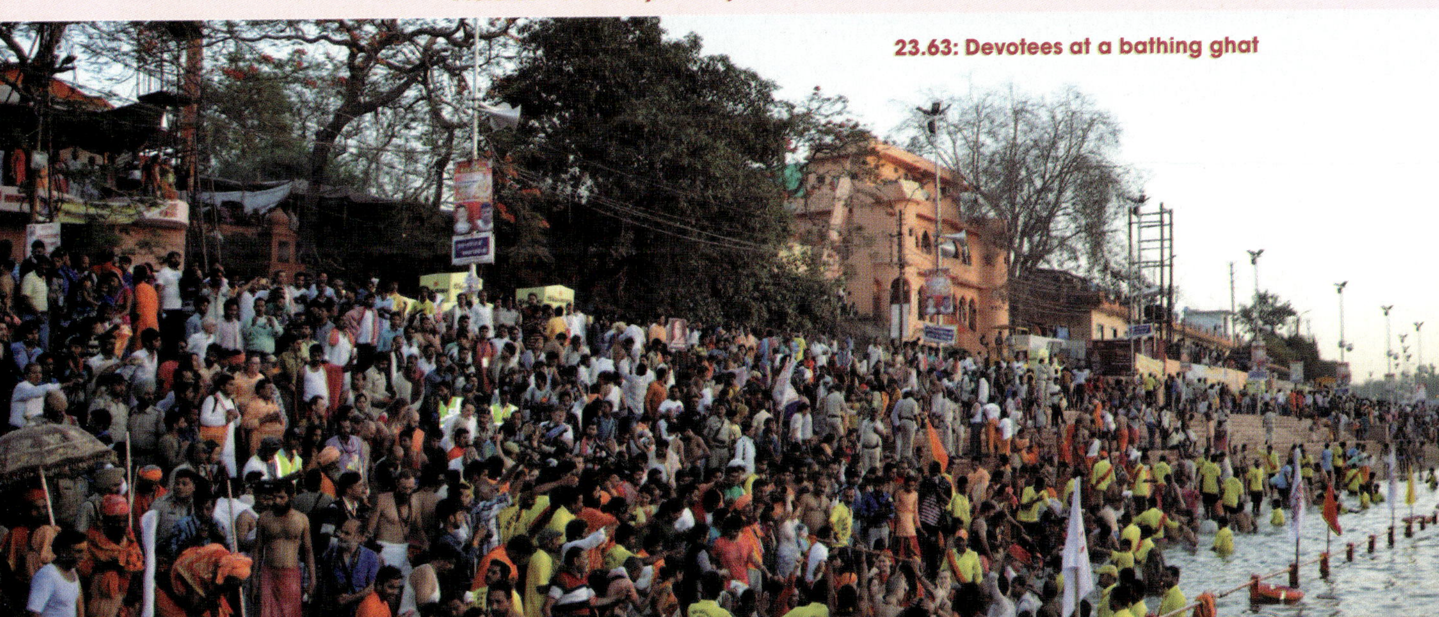

23.63: Devotees at a bathing ghat

Rang Panchami at Indore

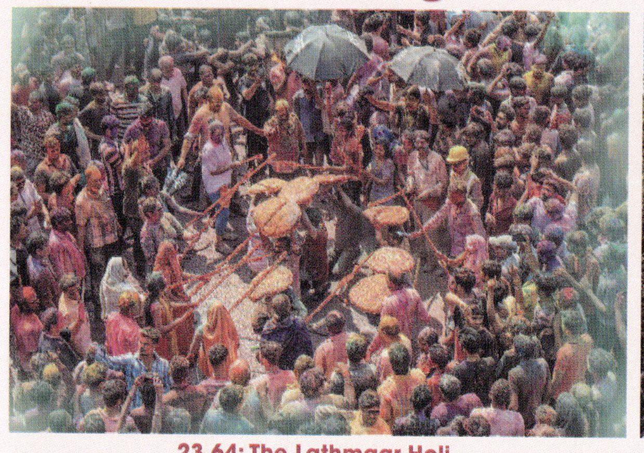

23.64: The Lathmaar Holi

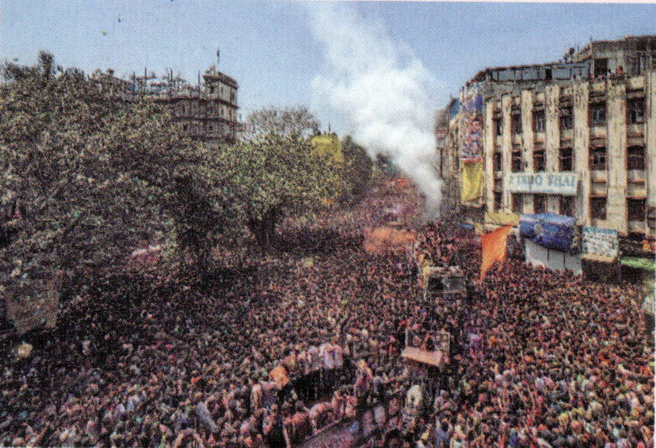

23.65: The sea of people

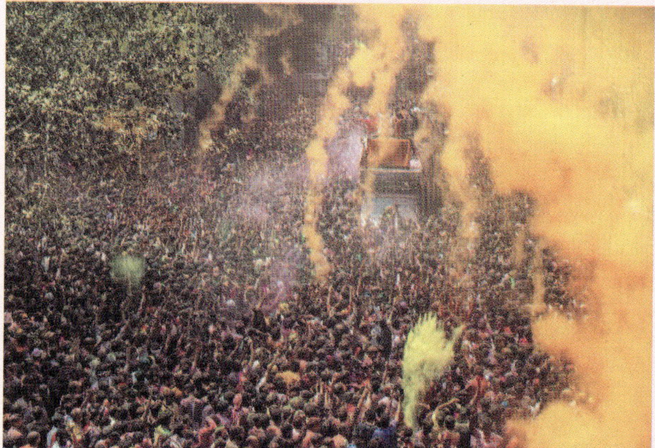

23.66: A cloud of colours

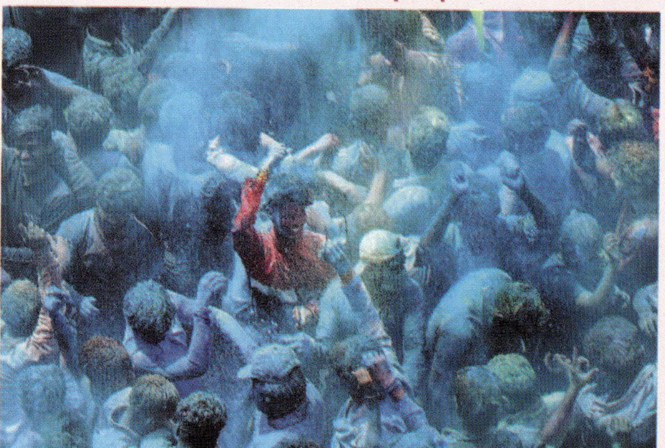

23.67: Misty blue

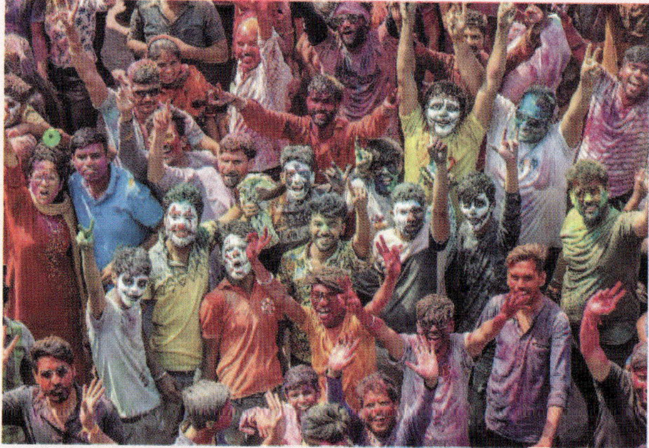

23.68: The colour of delight

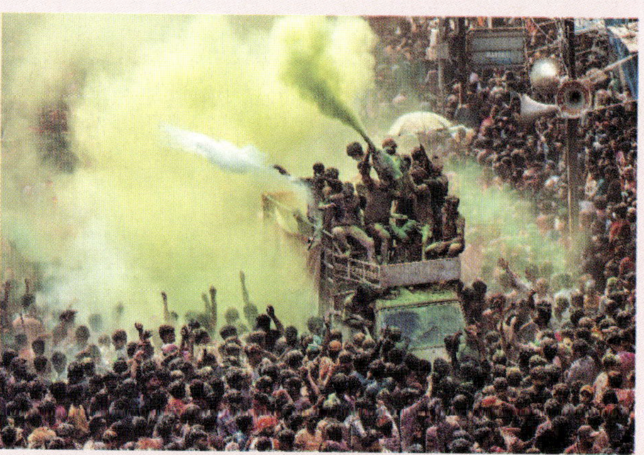

23.69: Its raining colours

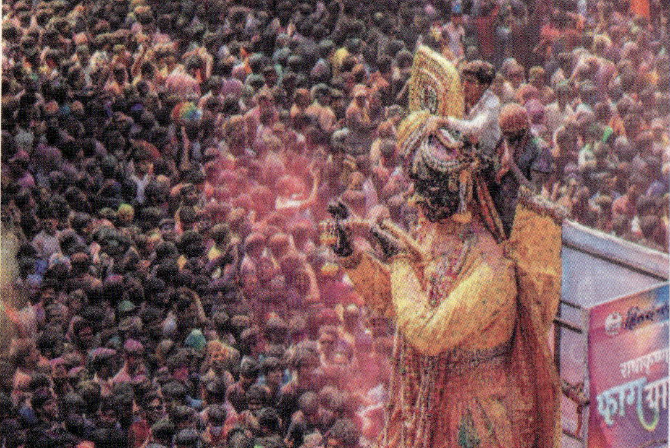

23.70: The deity blesses

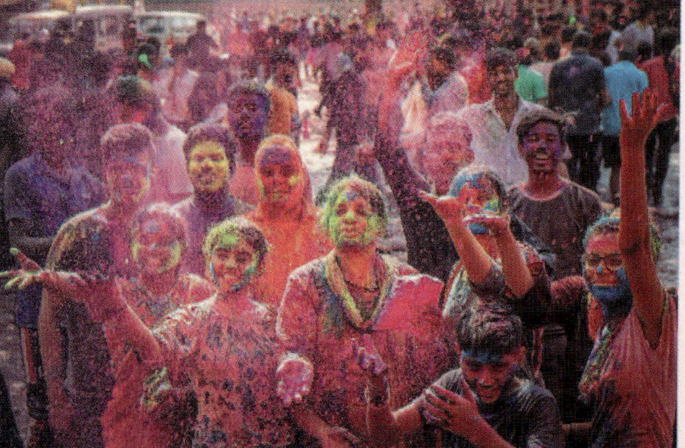

23.71: The festival of joy

— Pictures : Courtesy, Madhya Pradesh Tourism Board

Deepotsav Ayodhya

23.72: Image of Lord Ram, Lakshmana, Sita and Hanuman created by *diyas*

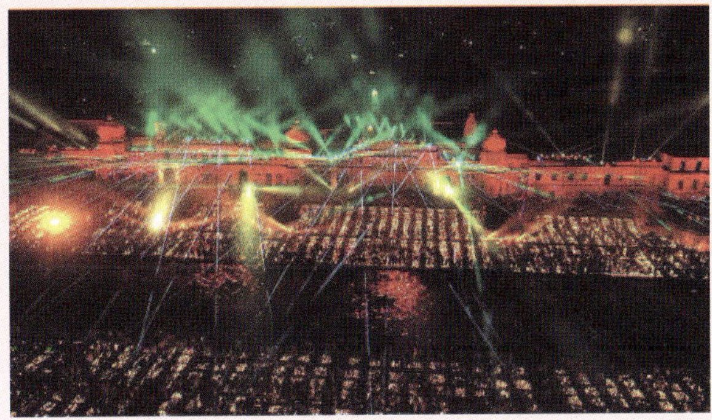

23.73: Diyas and laser show on Deepotsav on the banks of the river Sarayu

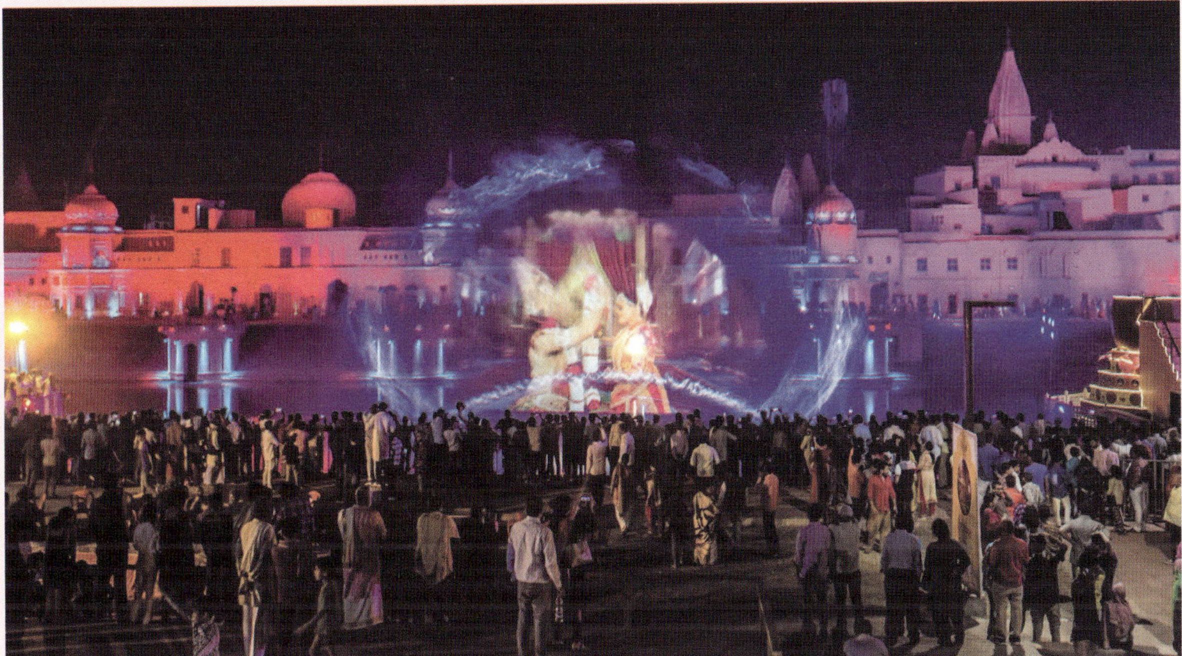

23.74

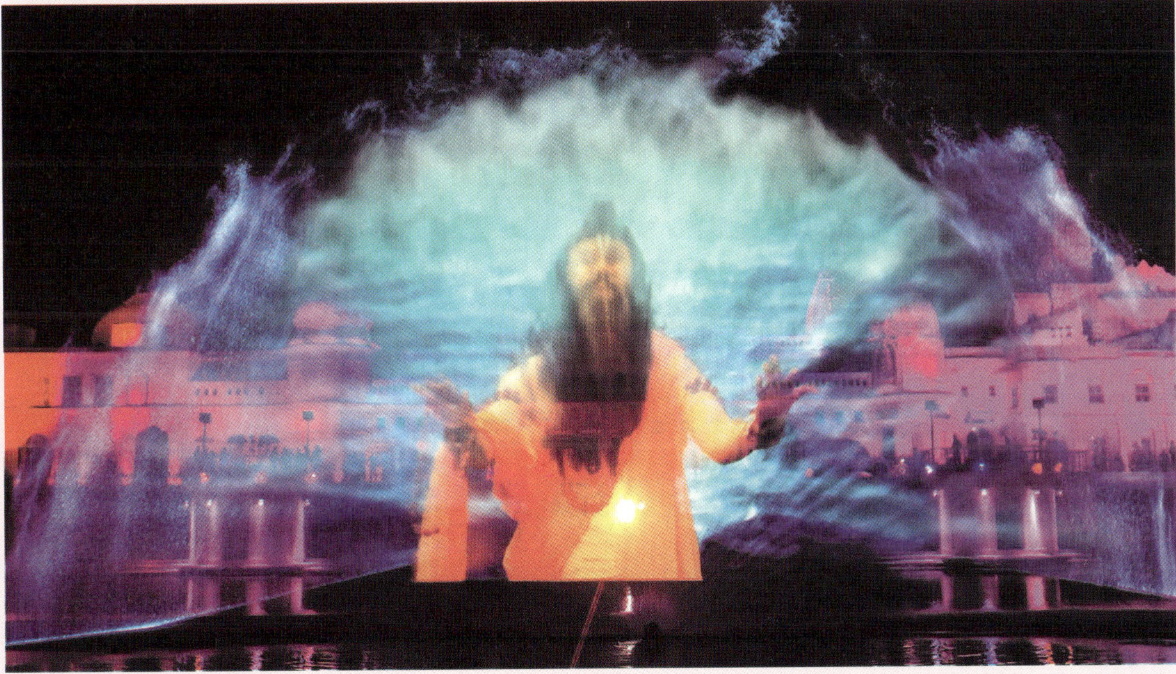

23.75

Laser-show depicting events from Ramayana on the occasion of Deepotsav on Choti Deepawali 2019 in Ayodhya — Pictures : Courtesy, Directorate of Uttar Pradesh Tourism

Janmashtami–Krishnotsav Celebrations at Vrindavan

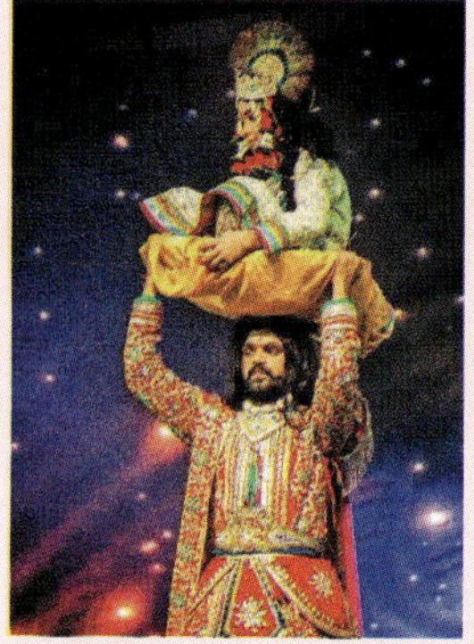
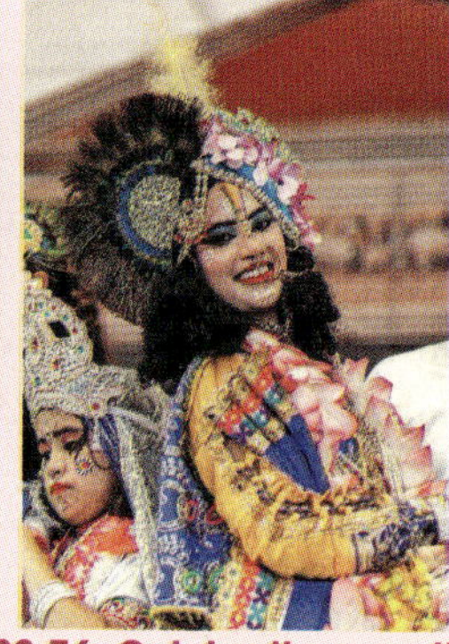
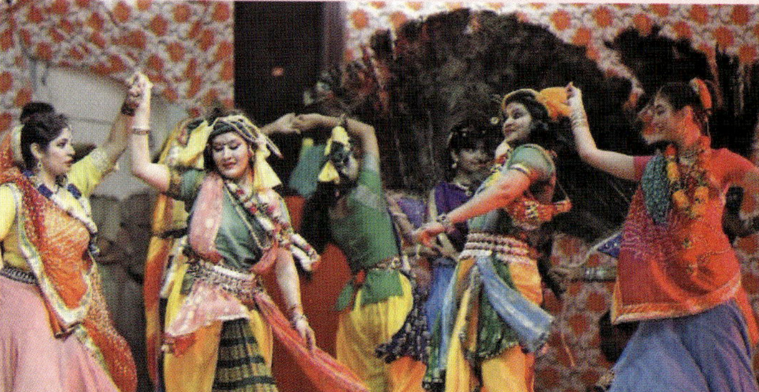

23.76: Celebrations on the occasion of Janmastami at Vrinadavan

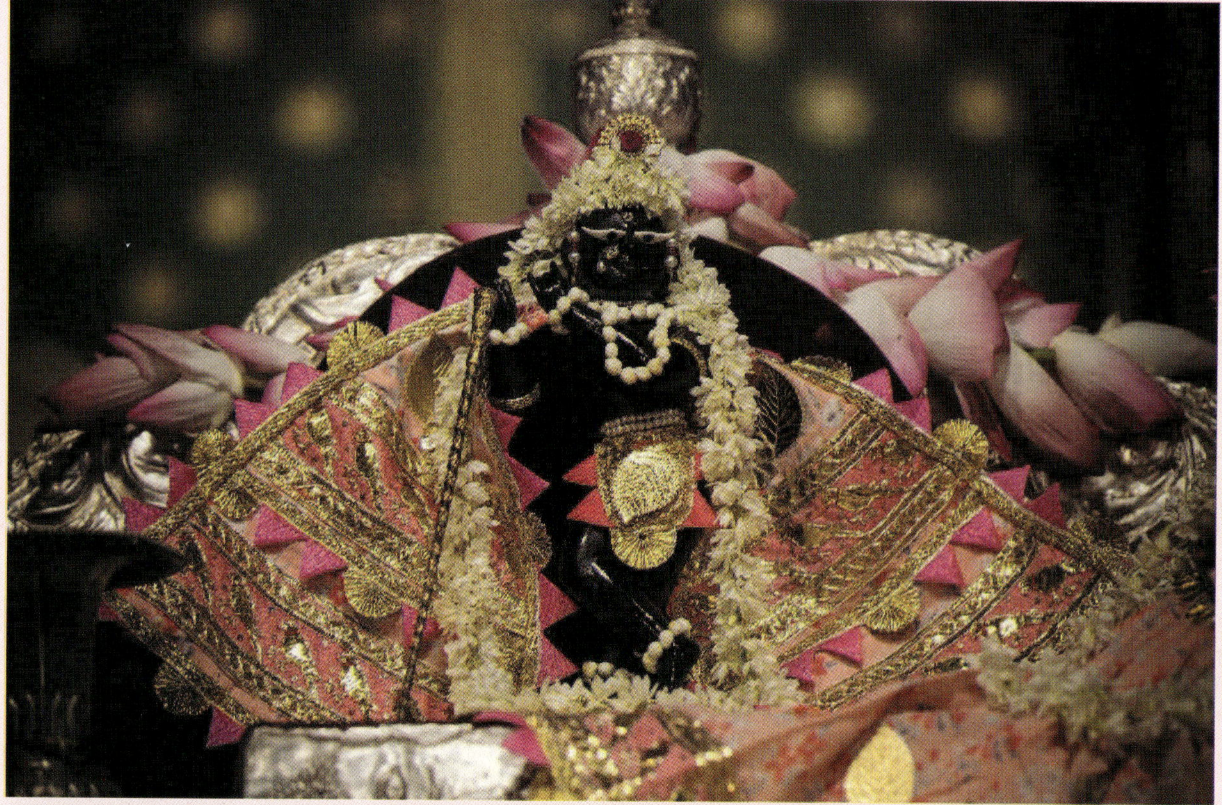

23.77: A decorated idol of child Sri Krishna

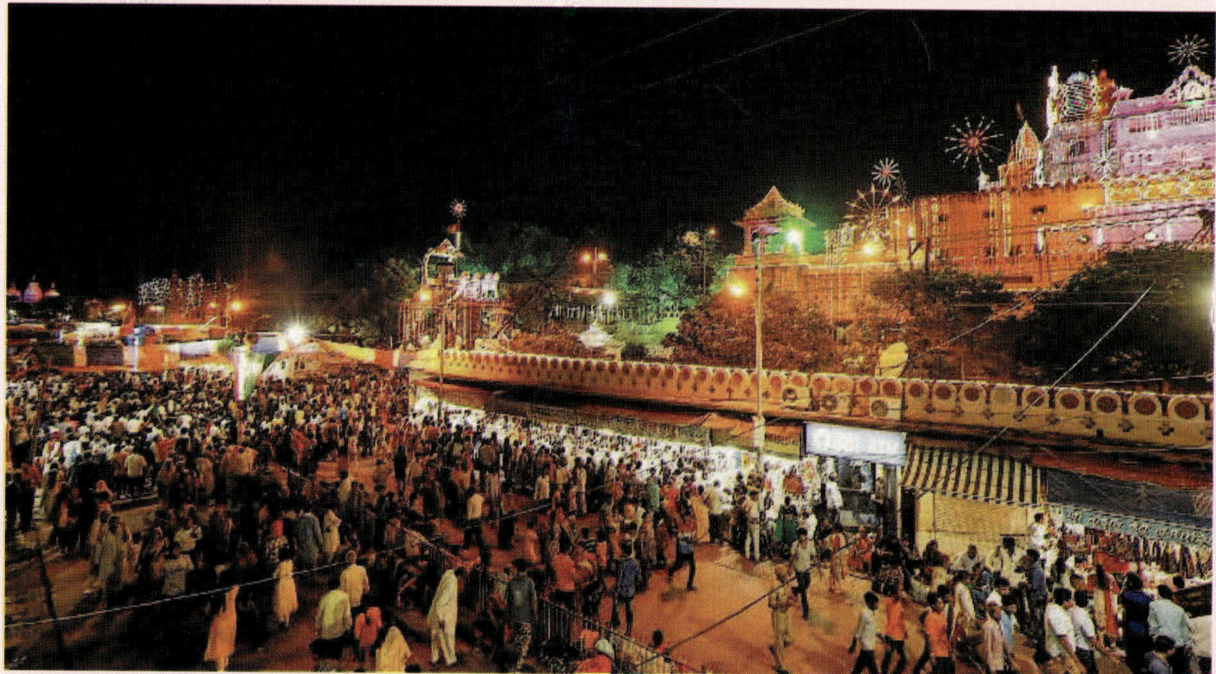

23.78: A fair and decorated temple at Vrindavan on the occasion of Janmashtami
— Pictures : Courtesy, Directorate of Uttar Pradesh Tourism

The Rath Yatra at Puri

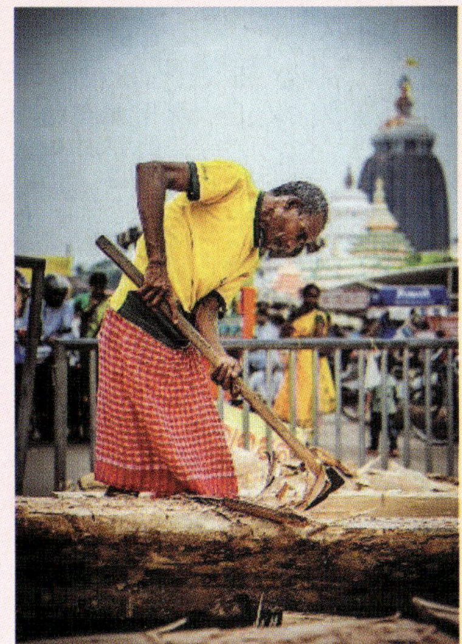

23.79: The beginning of making of the Ratha using special wood from specific tress

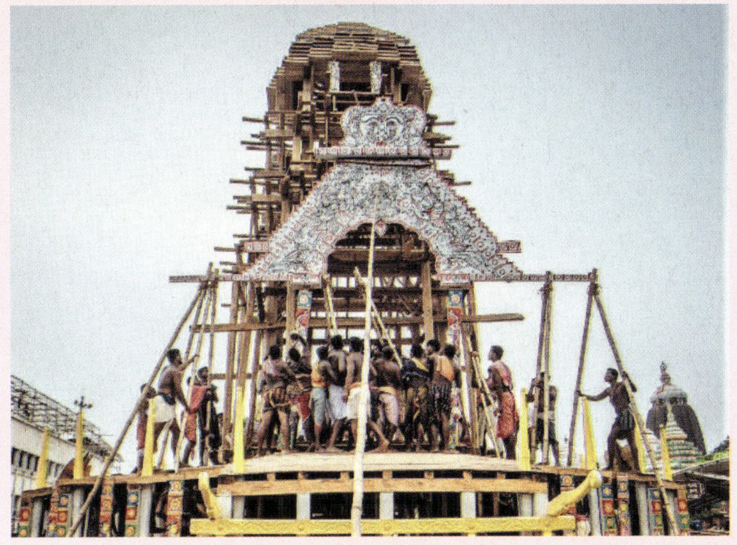

23.80: The frame of the Ratha being constructed

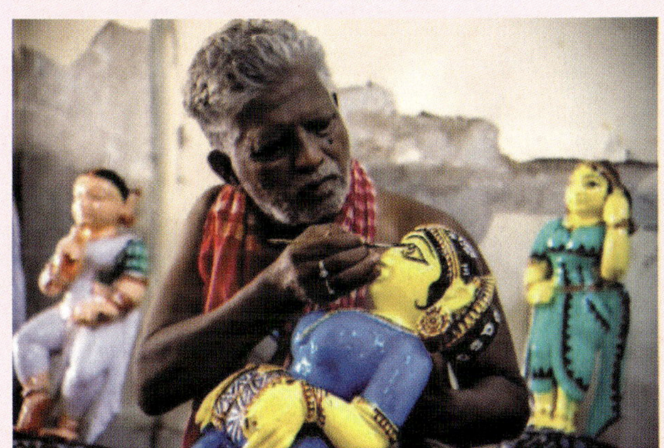

23.81

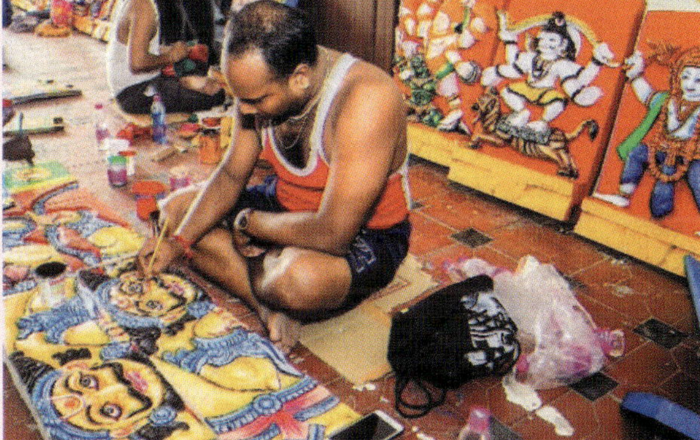

23.82

23.81 & 23.82: Decorative idols and Pattachitra being prepared

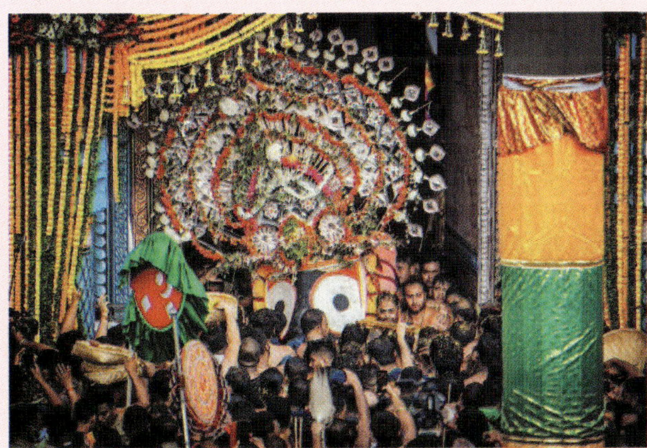

23.83: The deity placed in the Ratha

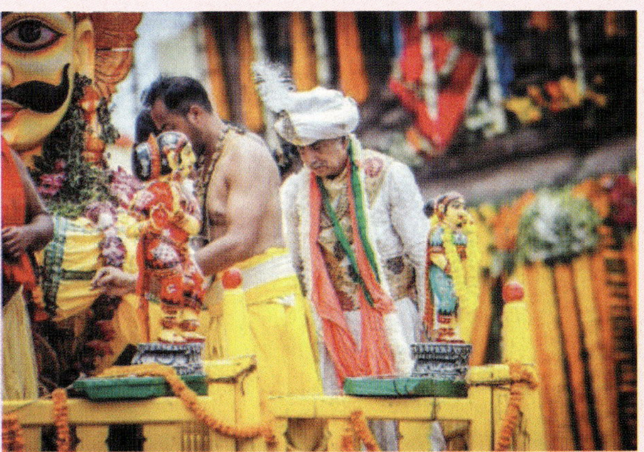

23.84: Final touches and rituals
— Pictures : Courtesy, Department of Tourism, Odisha

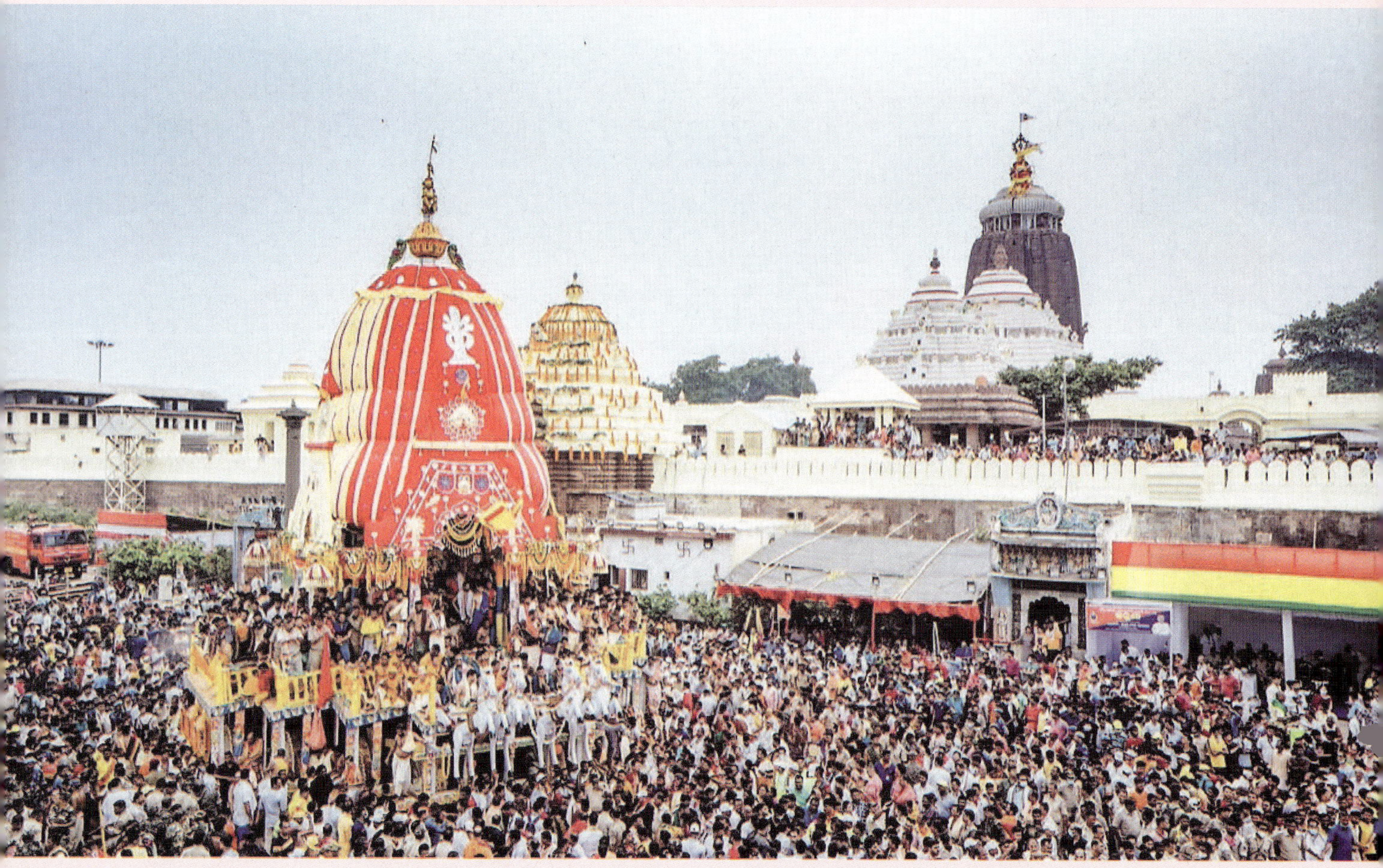

23.85: The Rathyatra begins - Courtesy, Department of Tourism, Odisha

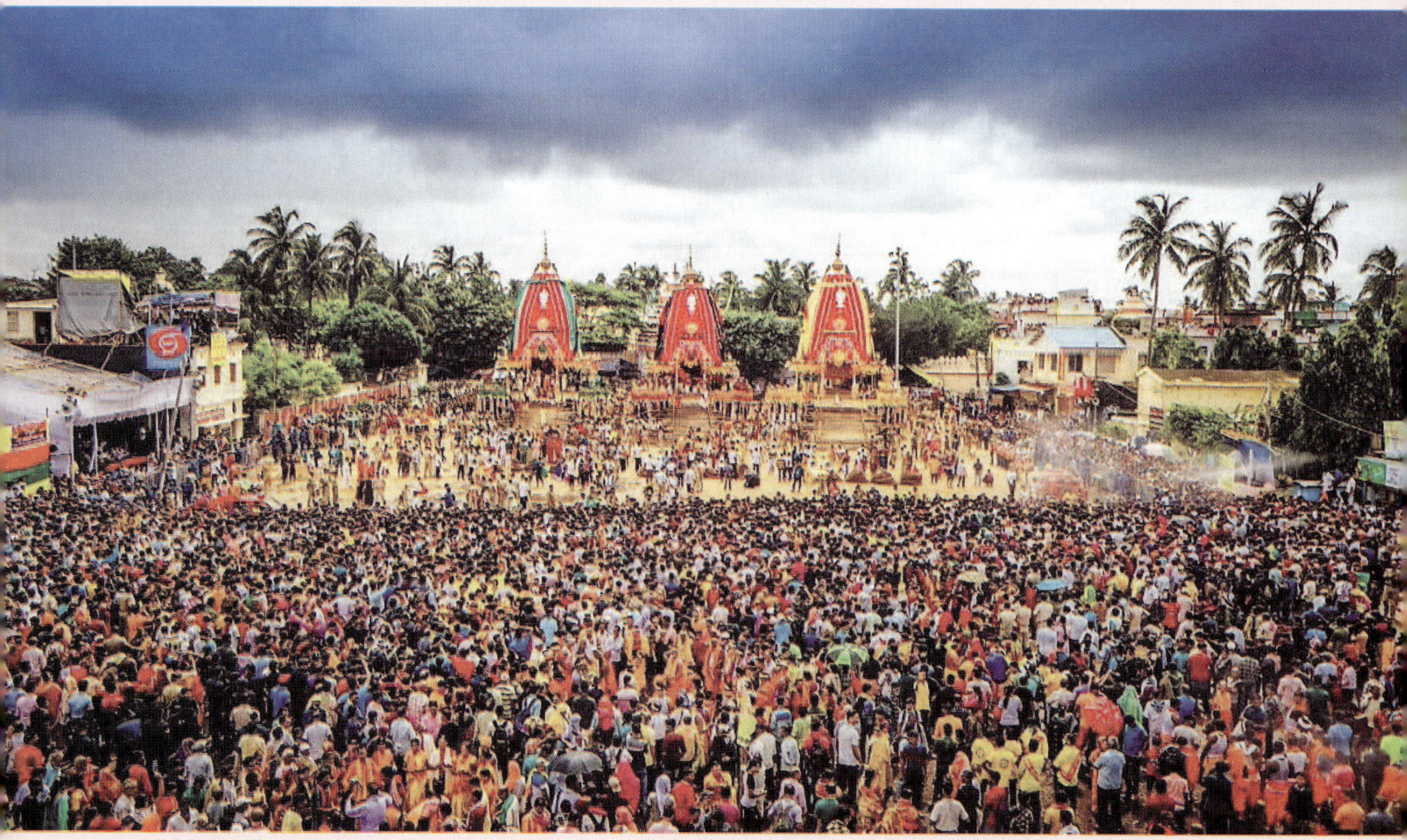

23.86: The three Rathas of Lord Jagannatha, Lord Balabhadra and Subhadra offering *darshana* to the devotees - Courtesy, Department of Tourism, Odisha

Durga Puja Festival

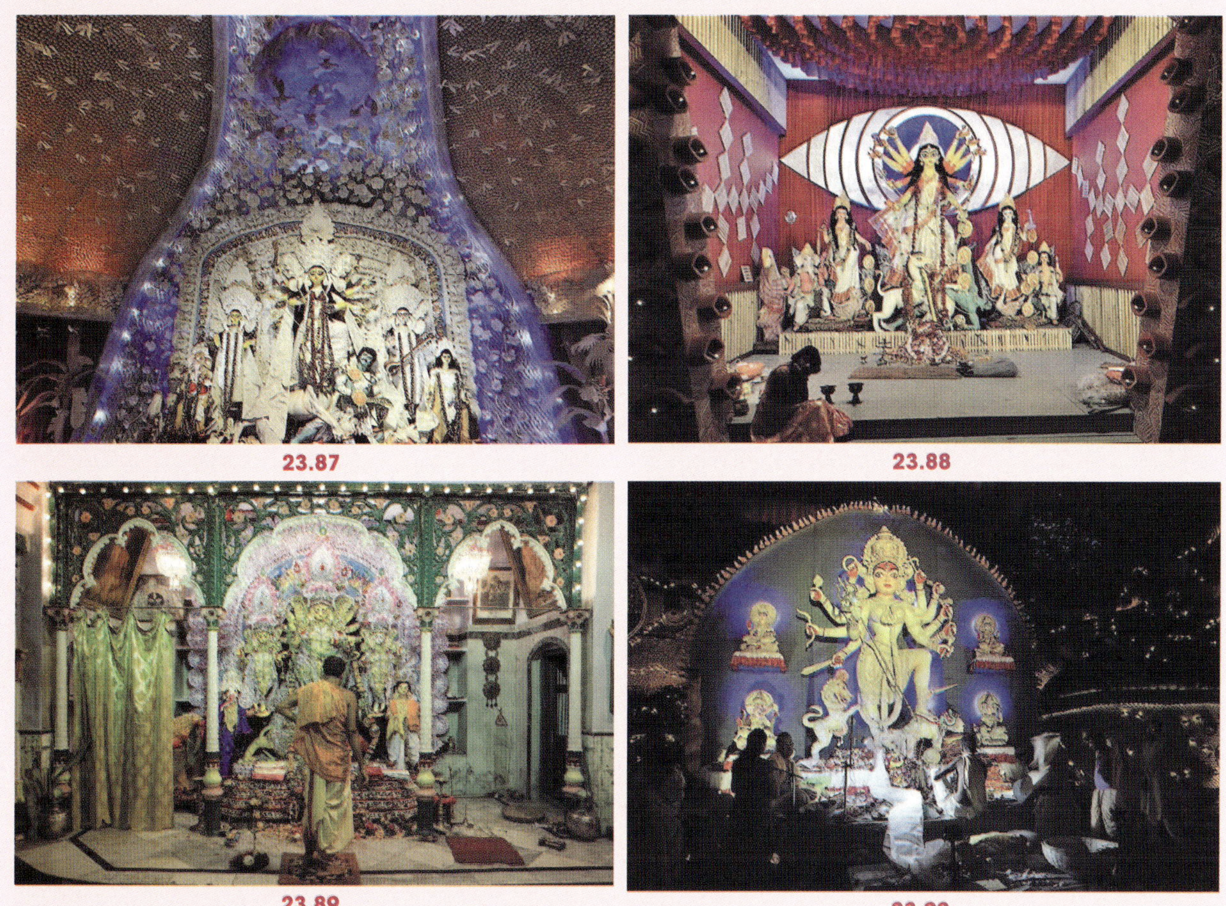

23.87 23.88

23.89 23.90

Durga Puja Celebrations at Kolkata, a UNESCO Intangible Cultural Heritage of humanity

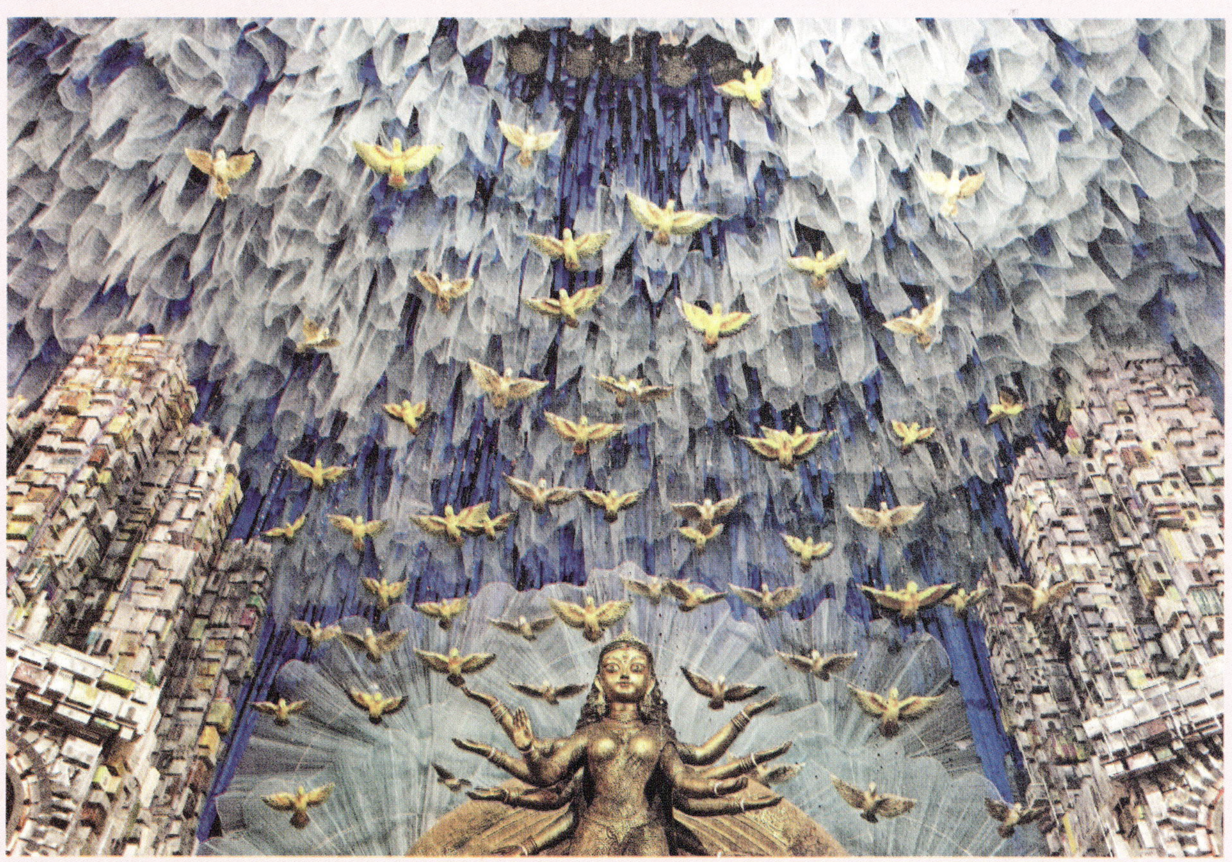

23.91: Durga Puja Celebrations at Kolkata, a UNESCO Intangible Cultural Heritage of humanity — Pictures : Courtesy, Department of Tourism, West Bengal

Teej Festival

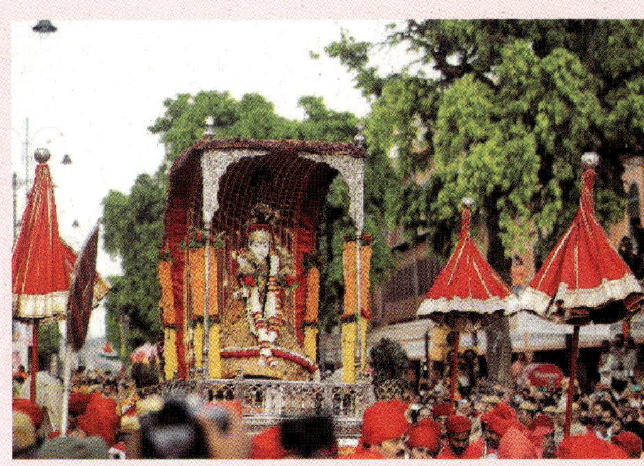

23.92

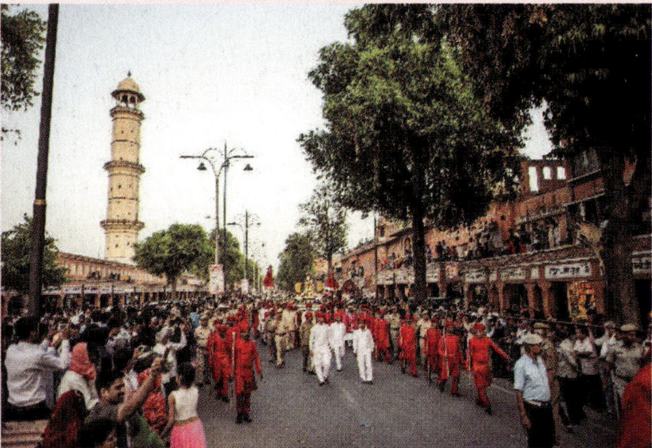

23.93

23.92& 23.93: Teej Mata Procession on occasion of Teej in Jaipur — Pictures : Courtesy, Rajasthan Tourism

Secular Festivals

Konark Dance Festival

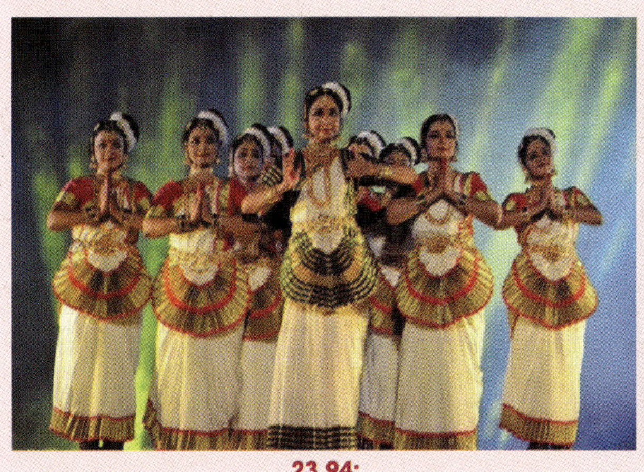

23.94:

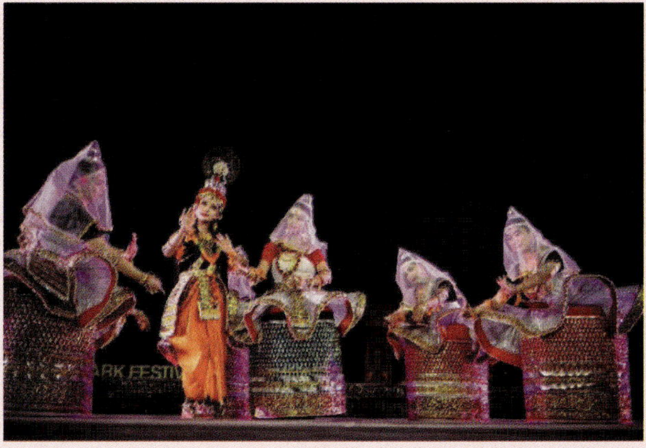

23.95:

Different dance performances at the Konark Dance Festival

International Sand Art Festival

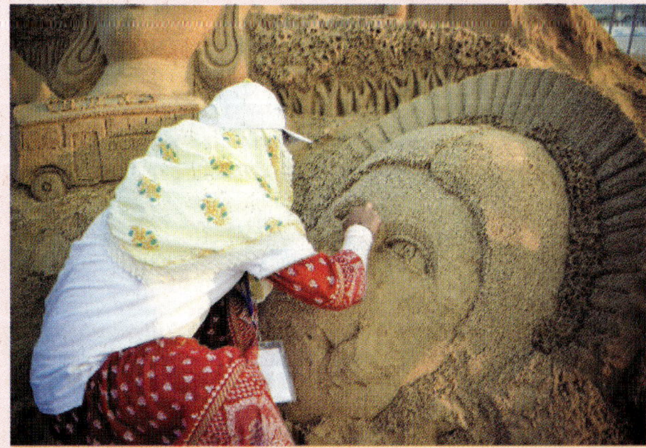

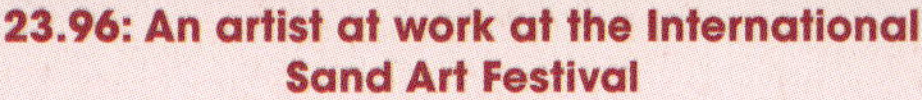

23.96: An artist at work at the International Sand Art Festival

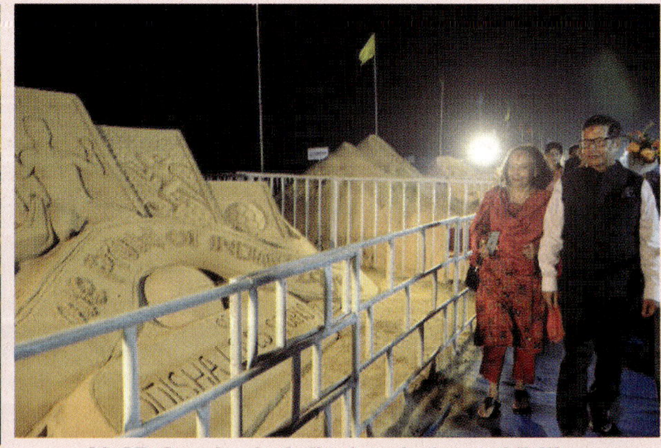

23.97: Sand art at display during exhibition

Bodh Mahotsav at Bodh Gaya

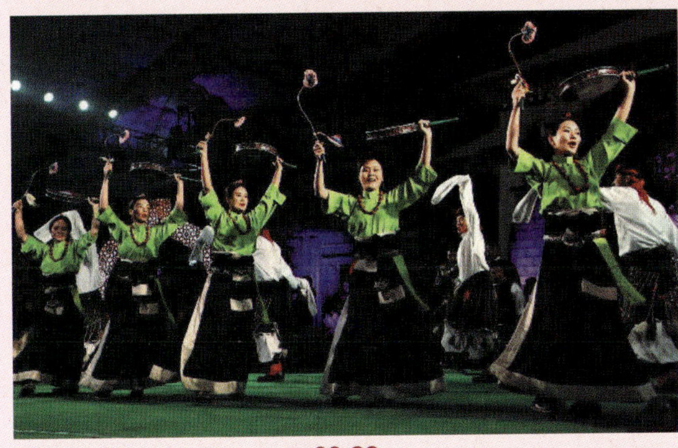

23.98

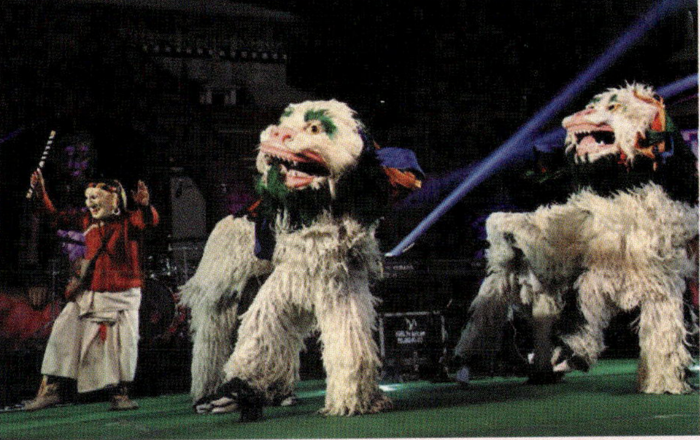

23.99

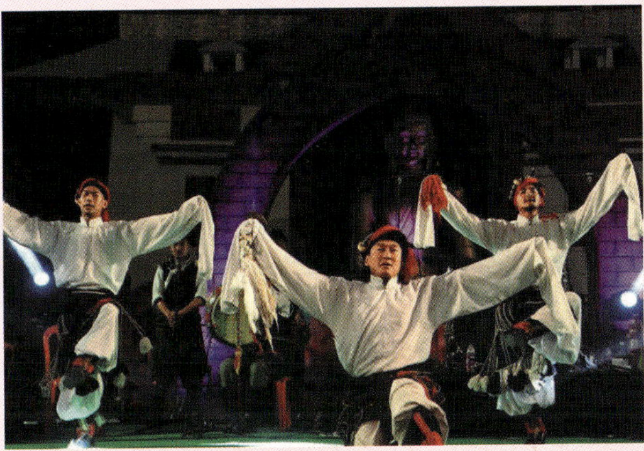

23.100

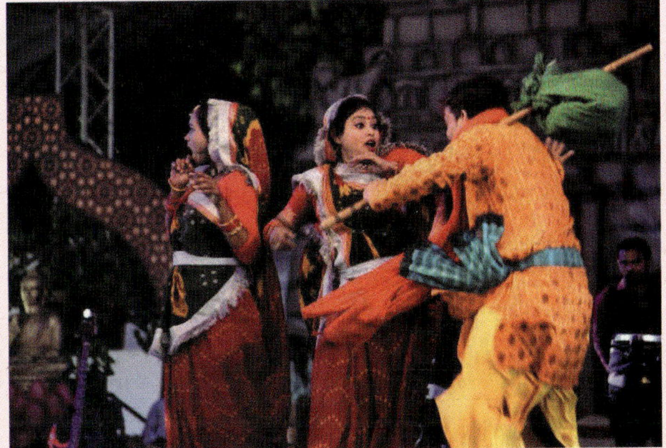

23.101

23.98 to 23.101: Performance by international and national artists at the Bodh Mahotsav at Bodh Gaya, Bihar — Courtesy, Bihar Tourism

Rajgir Mahotsav, Bihar

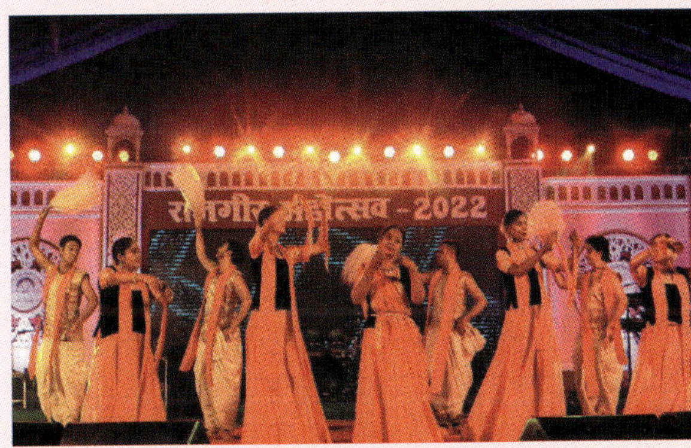

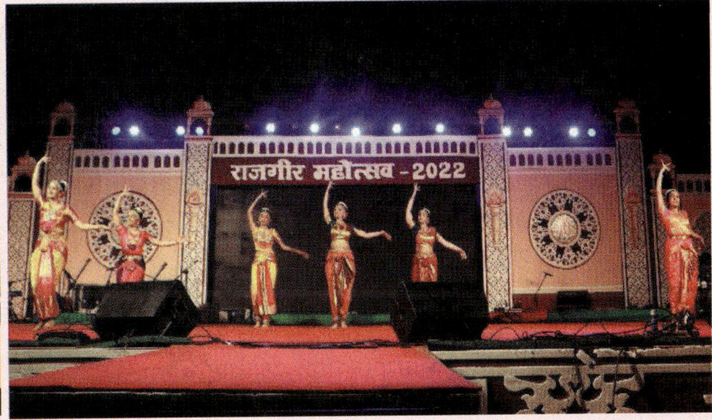

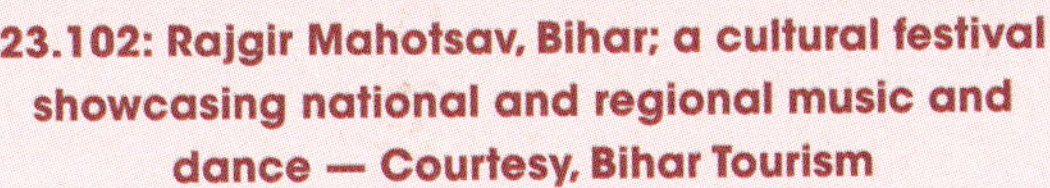

23.102: Rajgir Mahotsav, Bihar; a cultural festival showcasing national and regional music and dance — Courtesy, Bihar Tourism

23.103: Rajgir Mahotsav, Bihar; a cultural festival showcasing national and regional music and dance — Courtesy, Bihar Tourism

The Desert and Marwar Festivals

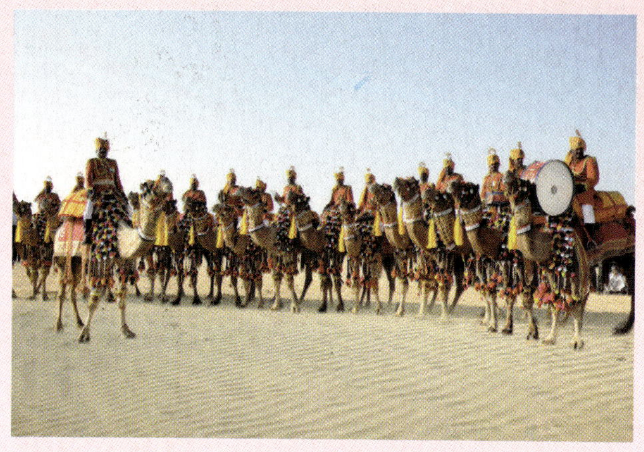

23.104: Performance by a band at the Desert Festival, Jaisalmer

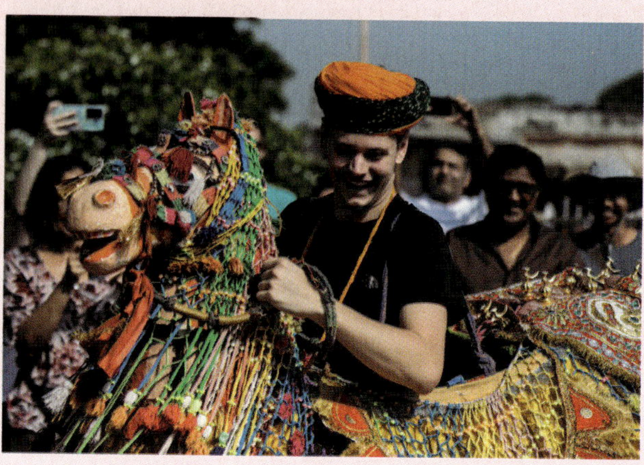

23.105: A tourist participating in the dummy horse dance at the festival

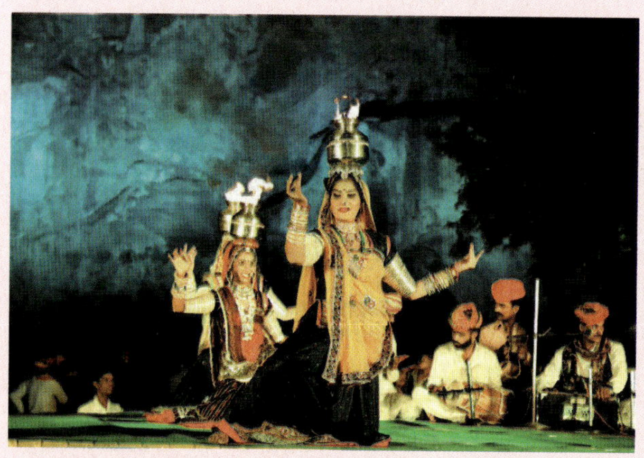

23.106: Dance with flaming overhead pots, a musical-dance programme at Marwar Festival, Jodhpur

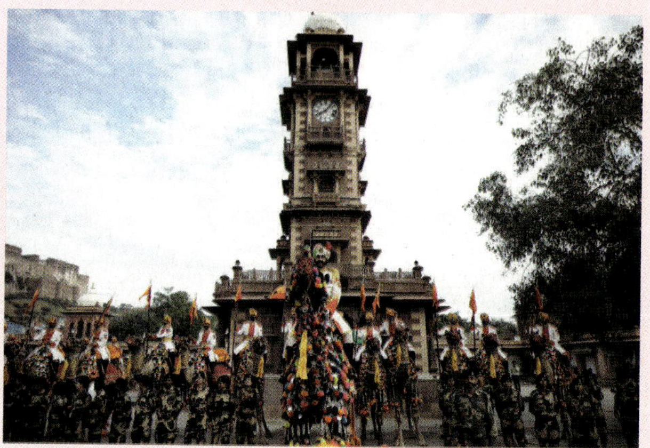

23.107: Guard of Honour, at Marwar Festival, Jodhpur

— Courtesy, , Rajasthan Tourism

Modern Indian Architecture

> *Architecture is sculpture with gestures of human occupation.*
>
> — Charles Correa
>
> *House is a grain, like a small sapling in the bio-diverse wild forest.*
>
> — B.V. Doshi

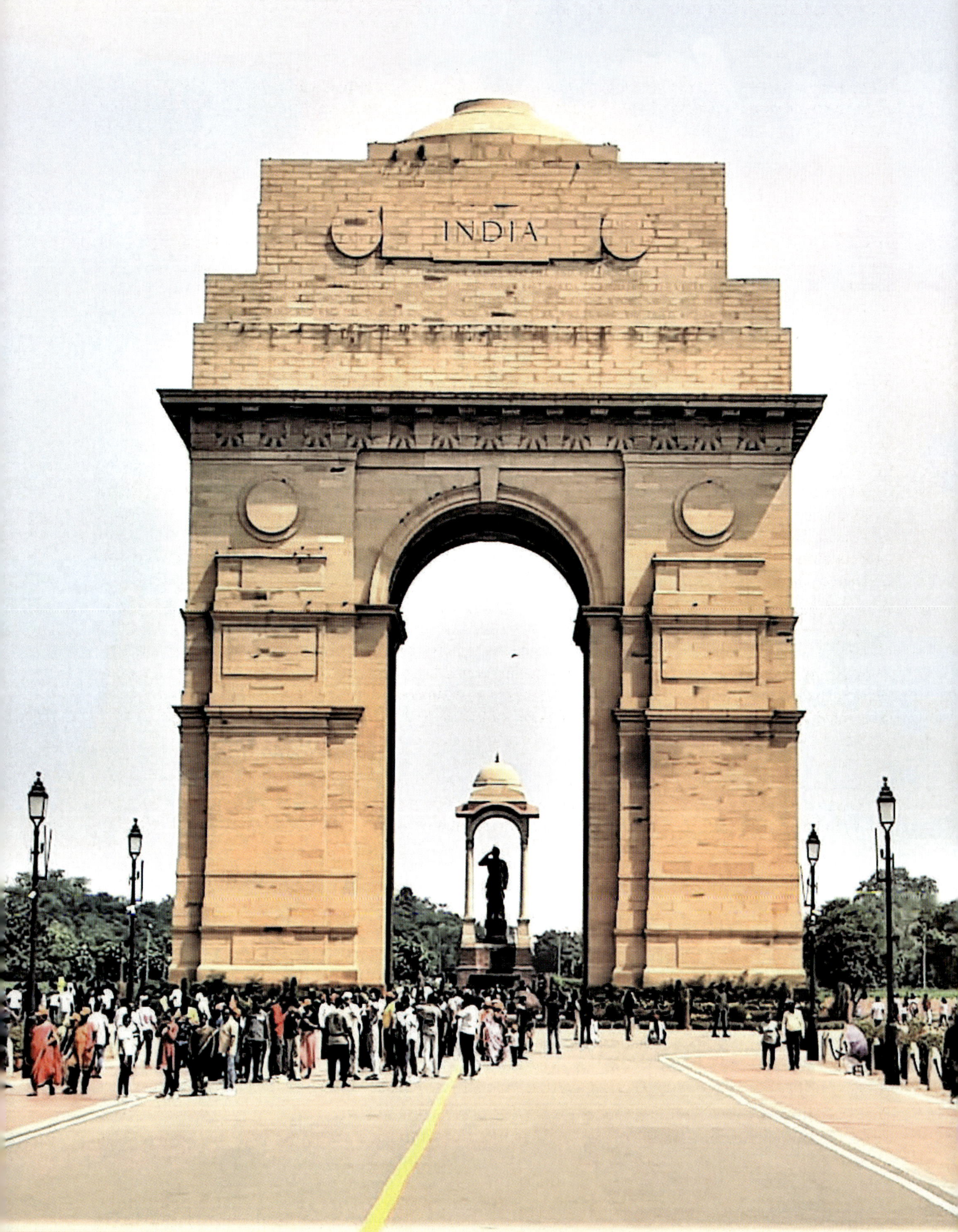

24.1: India Gate — photograph by Madhukar K Bhagat

EVOLUTION OF MODERN ARCHITECTURE IN INDIA

Introduction

Architecture is one of the most visible and significant tangible elements of culture which also leaves an enduring legacy on the sands of time. It reflects the evolution of the science, engineering, craftsmanship and other disciplines of the age. It is shaped by the needs of society as well as its taste and in turn, influences the societal aesthetics as well. Building large or small monuments, which define the architecture of an age, are also resource-intensive measures. Hence the dominating architectural achievements of an age are invariably influenced by the political authority and are also a reflection of the authority and the history of the land.

The period of Indian history from the late 18th century onwards, saw a steady decline in the power of the Mughal dynasty and other Indian rulers. In different parts of the country, European colonial powers established their political authority. This sounded the death knell for the Mughal dynasty and the Islamic rule which was already in its waning phase post the reign of Aurangzeb. With this came to an end the chapter of Indo-Islamic architecture. It also marked the beginning of what is referred to as the **Colonial architecture**.

Although the British authority vested over the largest part of the Indian territory, the Portuguese, French, Dutch, and Danish too, had smaller regions of a stronghold. Thus, the period of the last 250–300 years saw varied influences on Indian architecture in different regions of the country. This could be **Neo-Classical, Romanesque, Victorian, Gothic** influence or an altogether new **Indo-Saracenic** style as in British structures. **Iberian** and **Baroque** influences were seen in the Portuguese structures, as seen in Goa. The French introduced the Cartesian grid plan architecture in Pondicherry (now Puducherry). For the colonial masters, introducing new architectural forms was a statement of their authority besides, it was also a matter of practical convenience for them. The European styles also influenced the local tastes and absorbed indigenous elements to suit the local environment. Thus, varied European architectural influences found space and growth in India and evolved over a period of time.

Post-independence, Indian architecture initially suffered from a hangover of the colonial era. Later, it was inspired by the modern architectural movements in Europe and America. The growth of modern cities like Chandigarh allowed the development of newer architectural styles based on indigenous needs and sensitivity. These were examples of modern architecture which are still evolving. While the dense metropolises like Mumbai have experienced vertical growth with towering structures looming on the skyline, areas of central Delhi also referred to as Lutyens' Delhi, still maintain a stately old-world plan and architectural charm. In the emerging new metropolises bursting to the seams under the strain of the burgeoning population, space efficiency, cost and utility are the determinants of modern architecture, besides aesthetics and safety. Modern cities and the changing society are constantly upping the size and scale of new structures. For many of these, energy efficiency and green architecture are other priority considerations of architectural design. Truly, Indian architecture has changed with times and is evolving with the times.

COLONIAL ARCHITECTURE

The Portuguese Colonial Architecture

The first colonial power in India, the Portuguese came to Goa as merchants in 1498 and remained there for the next 450 years. They were also the very first European power to introduce colonial architecture on the Indian landscape. The long Portuguese rule had a predominant effect on the architecture of the state. The early Portuguese architecture which is still found in plenty was inspired by the Iberian Style and Baroque architecture, a part of the Renaissance architecture of Europe. These were seen in the medieval colonial churches and houses of Goa. The Basilica of Bom Jesus, Se Cathedral, Church of St. Francis of Assisi, Our Lady of Immaculate Conception Church, and Reis Magos Fort in Goa, were glorious examples of this architecture of the 17th century to 18th century (see chapter Chapter 9 on 'Medieval Architecture').

Some later examples of modern church architecture in Goa include the **Mae De Deus Church** (literal meaning 'mother of god') which was established in 1873 in Saligao. It has a unique Neo-Gothic style of architecture and is perhaps the only church of Goa of this style. With a pristine white exterior in a picturesque countryside setting, the church gives the impression of a fairytale castle. **Our Lady of the Lourdes Church** established in 1913 in Utorda, a relatively smaller church, depicts Neo-Roman style

architecture. **St. John Baptist Church**, in Benaulim, is another of the modern Portuguese churches. Established in 1956, it is known for its elegant altars and galleries with a modern white-washed exterior façade.

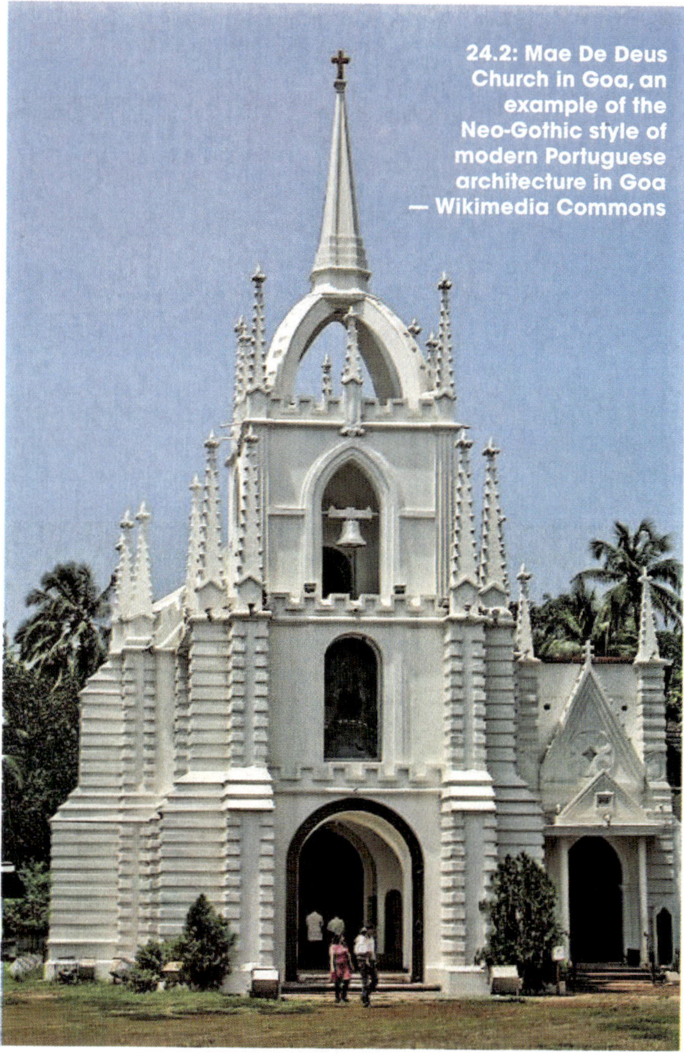
24.2: Mae De Deus Church in Goa, an example of the Neo-Gothic style of modern Portuguese architecture in Goa — Wikimedia Commons

Another repository of this architectural style is the **old mansions** and houses of Goa. Reflective of the Portuguese residential architecture, many of these date from the 17th to 19th century and are found in rural Goa, particularly in areas of Loutolim and Chandor. With covered porches and verandahs overlooking the street, large *balcoes* (balconies) terracotta tiled roofs, wrought iron grills etc. these are reminiscent of the old-world charm. Many of them even had their own dance rooms and mini-chapels. Among the famous of such mansions are, **Salvador Costa Mansion** (19th century, Loutolim), **Solar Dos Colacos Mansion** (near Mandovi river between Old Goa and Panjim) which displays a Baroque style of architecture, **Mascarenhas Mansion** (Anjuna, North Goa) which is especially noteworthy for its characteristic *balcoes* and light tinted glass and **Vivian Coutinho Mansion**. Perhaps the oldest amongst these is the **Menezes Braganza/Braganza house** which is said to be nearly 350 years old. Made of laterite, the house with a Portuguese-style outer façade has two wings and 24 windows. A large ballroom with a coat of arms, gifted by the Portuguese king more than three centuries ago, is another special feature of the house.

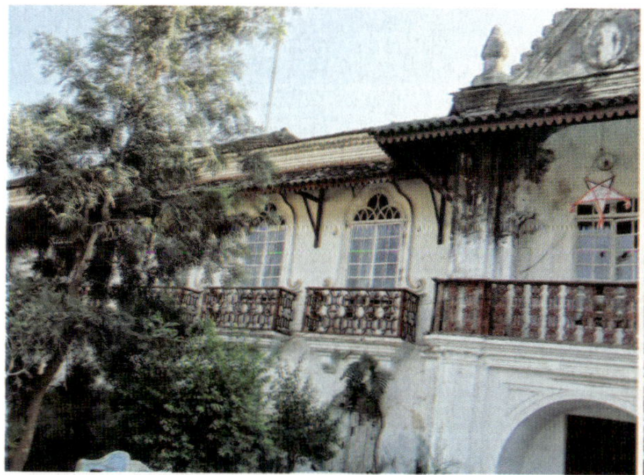

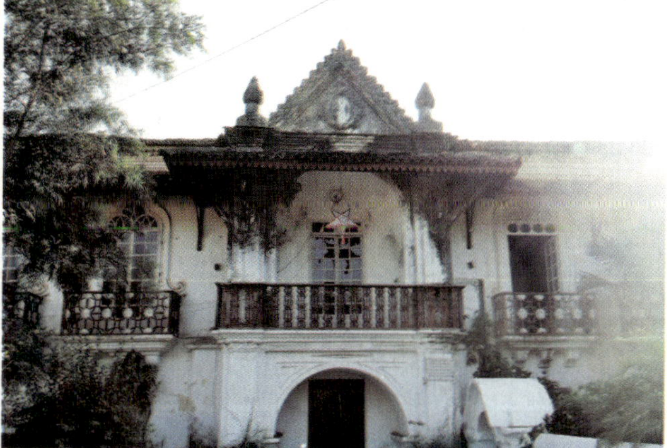

24.3 & 24.4: The 350-year-old Braganza mansion, the right-wing (left photo) and main entrance (right photo); with large balcoes, beautiful windows and wrought iron grill railings — photograph by Madhukar K Bhagat

Dutch Colonial Architecture

After the Portuguese, the **Dutch** were another important colonial power to establish their presence in India. The Dutch started trading in India in the early 17th century and remained in India for nearly 200 years. They colonised areas in Ahmedabad, Surat, Bharuch, and Kochi which they took over from the Portuguese. Besides they had a significant presence in Masulipatnam (present-day Machilipatnam in

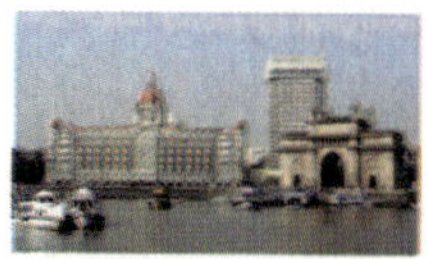

Andhra Pradesh). The Dutch architecture is visible in a variety of surviving structures which include the Dutch Factory (built in 1630 in Bharuch), a cemetery in Ahmedabad, and **Mattancherry Palace** in Kochi which was originally built by the Portuguese. **David Hall Residence** the former residence of Dutch commanders in Kochi, and the Fort at Kochi beach, the tomb of Susanna Anna Maria at Chinsurah (Hooghly district) in West Bengal are some other examples of Dutch architecture in India. However, after their loss in the Travancore Dutch War in 1741, their power in India substantially diminished. As such there is little Dutch architecture belonging to the 19th century or beyond which can be considered as part of the modern colonial architecture. Similarly, the **Danish** who had a presence only in the 16th and 17th centuries, made little impression in the later phase of Indian colonial architecture.

French Colonial Architecture

The French, another colonial power, established their trading centre in Pondicherry in 1674 and continued to remain in occupation till the 1950s before it became a union territory of India. Through the four centuries of French presence, Pondicherry (now Puducherry) became a major centre of repository of French culture with its architecture preserved even now. This is visible in the part of the town referred to as the French quarters. This area of the city has a layout characterised by a **Cartesian grid plan** with main roads and avenues that are perpendicular to each other.

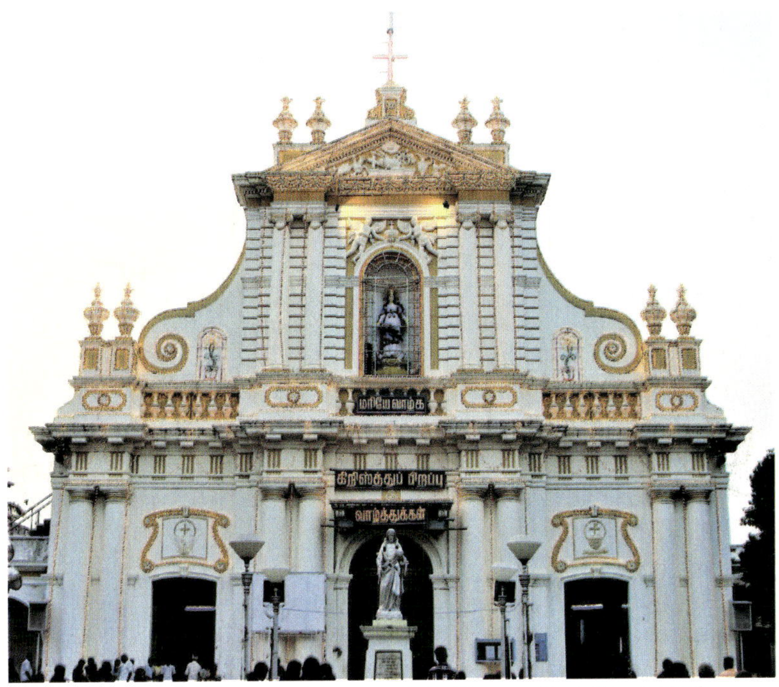

24.5: The Cathedral of Immaculate Conception, decorated on Christmas Eve; one of the oldest churches of Puducherry — photograph by Madhukar K Bhagat

French architecture is best visible in the churches of Pondicherry and the various old houses in the French quarters. Among the most prominent examples of the churches, are the **Basilica of Sacred Heart of Jesus** (built in 1907) and **Eglise de Notre Dame de Lourdes** (located in Villianur; built in 1866) both of which display Gothic revival architecture. **Eglise De Notre Dame des Anges** (Our Lady of Angels Church; 1887) was built in Greco-Roman architecture, while the **Cathedral of Immaculate Conception** (1791) is the oldest of all and has Herrerian-Gothic style of architecture.

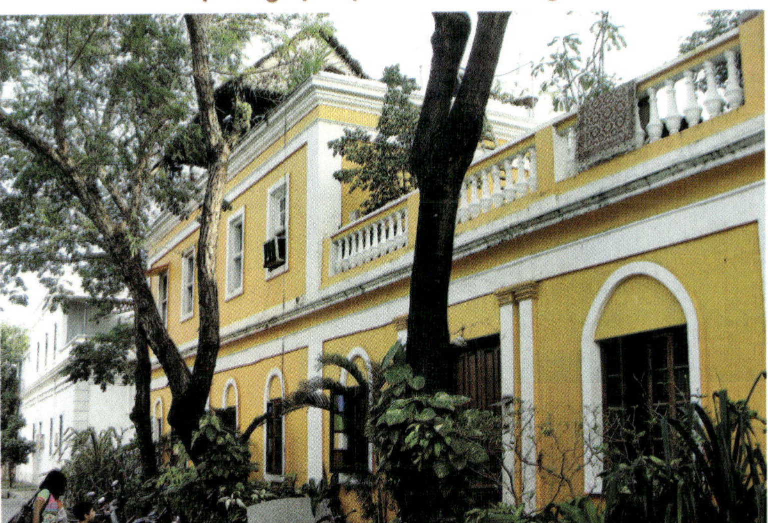

24.6: A bright-coloured villa in the French Quarters, with long windows and stained glass, bearing typical French architecture seen in such French mansions at Puducherry — photograph by Madhukar K Bhagat

The French houses which are typically colonial-styled villa, are characterized by large compound walls with courtyards, circular arched gates, columns and stucco designs. Long French windows and ornate balconies with vertical cast iron grills are some other poignant features of these.

British Colonial Architecture

The British presence in India

The British came to India in the early 16th century and remained in India for nearly 450 years. In the process they left a profound impact on the society, polity, economy and culture of the land. The British

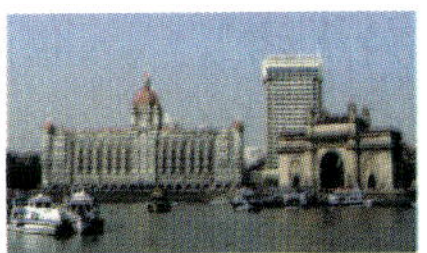

East India Company was created in 1600 with exclusive rights granted by the English crown to explore the trade of spices, cotton and other products. It got a *firman* in 1613 from the then-Mughal emperor Jahangir to set up a factory in Surat, thus marking the beginning of the British presence in India. In the first 150 years, this presence was largely as a trading company. However, their influence and presence in India increased gradually.

In the Battle of Plassey in 1757, the Company forces defeated the Nawab of Bengal, Siraj-ud-Daulah. Later they acquired the *Diwani* of Bengal in 1765 from the Mughal emperor and therefore the rights to collect revenue. Thus, they established a significant presence as well as a reasonable political control in India. Their authority in India grew from mere trading rights to territorial rights.

With the suppression of the revolt of 1857 (also referred to as the First War of Independence) and the passage of the Government of India Act of 1858, the political authority was completely transferred to the British crown. This was the third phase of the British presence in India. Henceforth its influence permeated almost every part of the country and every aspect of socio-political life, whether as a direct rule or indirect influence, till India became independent in 1947.

Different phases and styles of British colonial architecture

Indian architecture was one of the significant elements of tangible culture which the nearly two centuries of British rule greatly influenced. This was a cultural element that evolved squarely out of the **needs** of the colonial masters as well as their desire to **stamp a mark of the ruler** on the land on which they established their political authority. British Colonial architecture developed in different phases and in different cities and towns. Among the earliest to develop were the port cities. To begin with, the need for constructing a variety of structures arose on account of practical and security considerations in the port cities from where the British carried their trade. The Company and its officials had the emergent need for structures to fulfil the requirements of trading, basic administration, security, housing and other social needs. Accordingly in the **early phase** of the East India Company in the 17th-18th century, colonial architecture emerged in the forts, warehouses, residential houses, churches and other monuments.

Later in the 18th and 19th centuries, with the Company taking over the administration in several provinces, the demands of administration and hence of the infrastructure requirements became more complex. This marked the **next phase** of British architecture. After 1858, India came under direct British rule in the 19th and 20th centuries. New cities and towns developed. Rail lines were laid to connect different parts of the country to establish administrative control as well as transfer the raw materials and finished goods from the hinterland to the ports and vice-versa. There was an increasing need for the establishment of government administrative complexes, military complexes, large residential complexes, public infrastructure, railways and transport infrastructure, besides commemorative monuments and other structures. This was reflected in the changing landscape, emerging monuments and evolving architecture. This was the **final phase** of British architecture in India which continued in the 19th and 20th centuries till India's independence.

The **British Colonial architecture** was not a singular style but a mix of different styles of European architecture. These different styles flourished in different phases of their presence in the country. Further, British architecture could not remain untouched by indigenous architecture and the demands placed on it by environmental and social factors. Over a period of time, it also incorporated elements of Mughal architecture and indigenous Indian elements to evolve into a fusion of new styles. Among the popular styles of the British colonial architecture were the Gothic, Renaissance, Baroque, Neo-Classical, Neo-Gothic, Victorian and the Indo-Saracenic styles.

European Architectural Styles in India and their Features

Gothic architecture was a style that developed in medieval Europe, particularly in the 12th to 16th centuries, and was visible in structures such as churches, cathedrals, castles, palaces, town halls and others. It evolved from the Romanesque and was succeeded by the Renaissance architecture. Its identifying features include its **pointed arches** (curving sides of the arch meet at a sharp angle), **ribbed vault**, (curved area of the roof such as in a passage having rib-like structures), flying buttresses (arched structures supporting the wall), detailed tracery (architectural device of division of a window of a screen or panel into different sections of varying proportion) and stained-glass work besides other features.

Renaissance architecture developed around the 14th to 16th century in Florence in Italy and spread to different parts of Europe. It was a revivalist form of architecture that aimed at the conscious revival of the elements of architecture of ancient Greece and Rome. The architecture laid special emphasis on the geometry of the structures and on symmetry

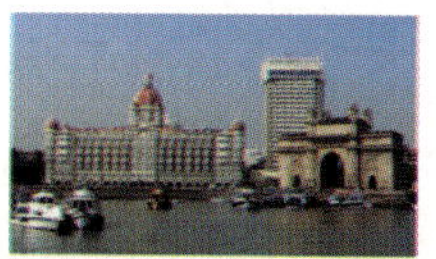

and proportion. **Hemispherical domes, semi-circular arches** and **orderly placed columns** were inter-alia others some of the poignant features of this style. Its influence can be seen in monuments such as the Rashtrapati Niwas (erstwhile Viceregal Lodge) in Shimla.

Baroque architecture developed in the 17th century in Italy and spread to the larger parts of Europe. It was a style which was known for its **grandness** and **decorative elements**. It emanated from the earlier Renaissance architecture whereby it retained its fundamental elements including the domes and colonnades (a passage with a long sequence of columns as a part of a building or free-standing). However, it made them more **dramatic** and added **greater elements of decoration** including sculptures and paintings. This was one of the earliest forms of European architecture that came to India and is seen in the Portuguese structures of Goa such as in the Basilica of Bom Jesus and other churches, besides in old houses such as the Braganza mansion. This architecture is also seen in some of the churches in Daman and Diu, Pondicherry and Kerala.

Neoclassical architecture was another **revivalist** school of architecture (also referred to as Classical Revival architecture) that began as a movement in Italy and France in the mid-18th century and later spread to other parts of Europe. It aimed at the revival of the classical architecture of ancient Greece and Rome. Although the Renaissance and Baroque styles also aimed at the revival/incorporation of the elements of classical architecture, Neoclassical aimed at **purging** the **excess decoration** and other elements that had seeped into styles like Baroque and return to a purer Classical style with emphasis on contextual needs. It focused on s**implicity of design** and on **geometry,** rather than ornamentation. In India, this style was seen in many important structures such as the Government House and the Indian Museum in Calcutta (Kolkata) and The Town Hall and the Elphinstone Circle in Bombay (Mumbai).

Neo-Gothic also known as the Victorian Gothic or the Gothic Revival style evolved from the earlier Gothic style in the 17th century but became popular in the 19th century largely in England. Later it caught up in style in the Western world and remained popular till the late 19th century. The style was also quite popular in India, particularly in the city of Bombay, where several buildings, monuments and public infrastructure were developed in the mid to late 19th century. The Neo-Gothic structures in India were characterized by **high-pitched roofs, pointed arches** and **detailed decorations** as seen in the finials, lancet windows (tall narrow windows with pointed arches) hood moulds (hood-shaped external projection over a door or window to keep away rainwater) besides other architectural elements. The Chhatrapati Shivaji Terminus building, the Municipal Corporation of Mumbai building, and the Maharashtra Police Headquarters building are some spectacular examples of this form of architecture.

Indo-Saracenic style was an admixture of the Indo-Islamic style and the then-in-vogue European syles in India. The style emanated during British Rule in India in the latter half of the 19th century and became popular in the 1880s and continued well in the 20th century. The word 'Indo' refers to the Indian, while 'Saracen' was a term of reference of the Europeans for the Muslims. Thus, the architecture while dwelling on the basic layout and plan of the then extant Neoclassical and Neo-Gothic architecture incorporated elements from the Indo-Islamic architecture of the Mughal school. Elements of Indo-Islamic like domes, *chhatris*, *jalis,* arches etc. were incorporated into European architecture. The idea was to create a British imperialistic style of India which could be a stamp of their authority as rulers of the land akin to the erstwhile Mughals. Many public structures and some private ones were developed in this style including; the Victoria Memorial in Calcutta, the Madras High Court, Victoria Hall in Madras, The Gateway of India, The Prince of Wales Museum, the Taj Mahal Palace Hotel in Bombay, The President's House, the North and South Block secretariat buildings in New Delhi, besides many others.

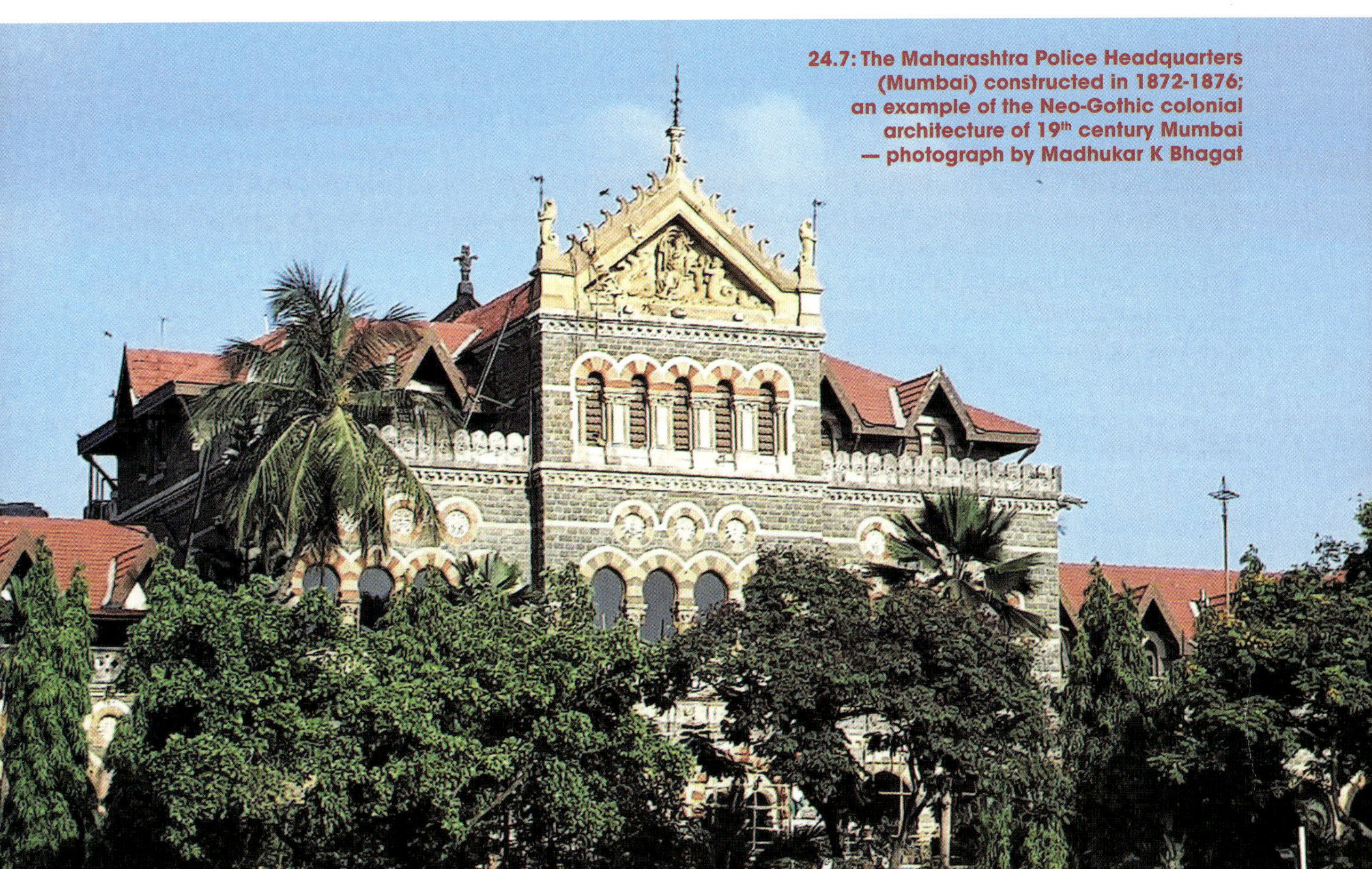

24.7: The Maharashtra Police Headquarters (Mumbai) constructed in 1872-1876; an example of the Neo-Gothic colonial architecture of 19th century Mumbai — photograph by Madhukar K Bhagat

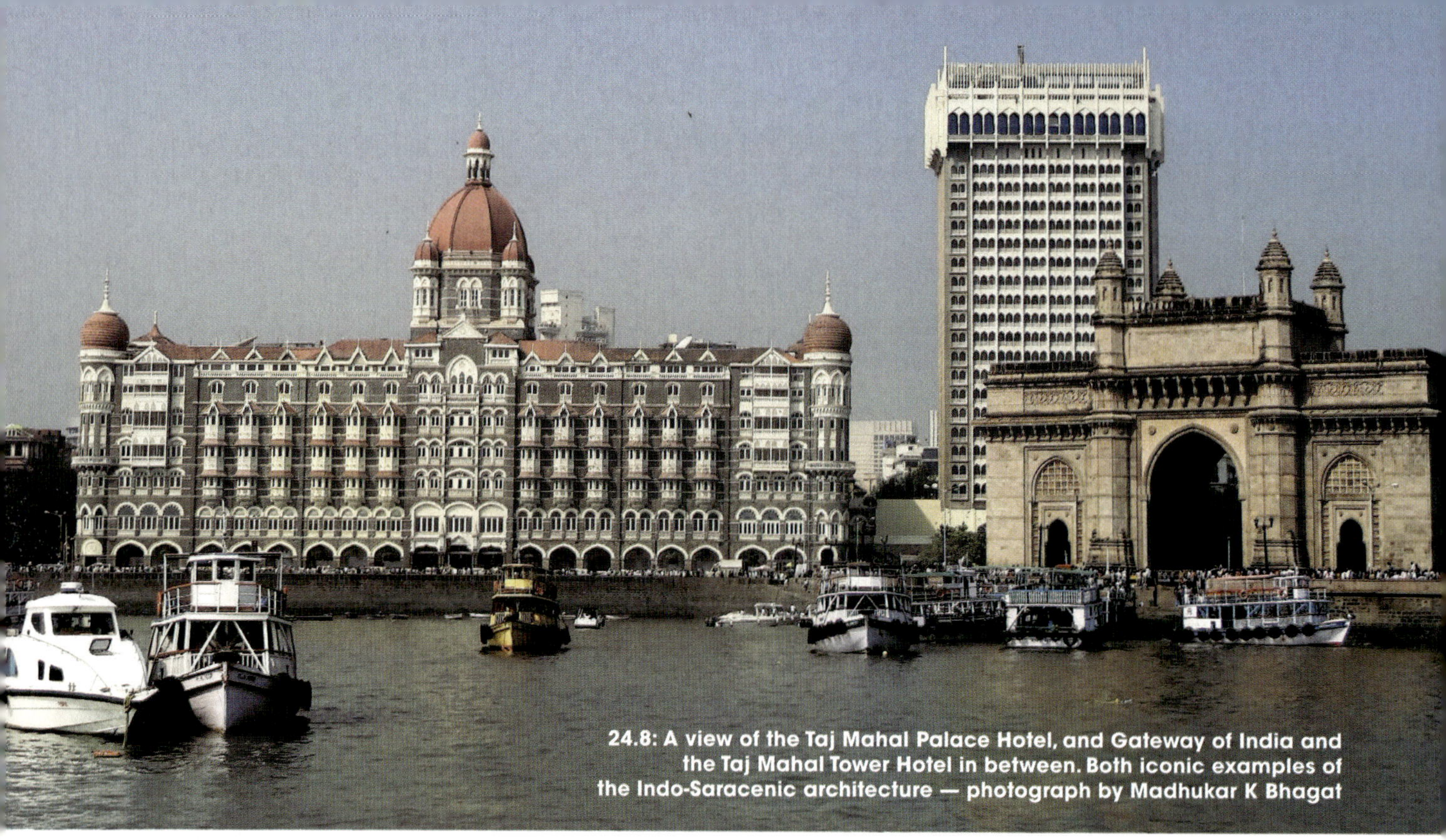

24.8: A view of the Taj Mahal Palace Hotel, and Gateway of India and the Taj Mahal Tower Hotel in between. Both iconic examples of the Indo-Saracenic architecture — photograph by Madhukar K Bhagat

Victorian architecture, a broad category of architecture, was a mix of different revivalist architectural styles popular in the 2nd half of the 19th century. The name emanates from the reign of Queen Victoria (1837 to 1901) and from the practice of classifying architectural styles as per the name of the reigning monarch. It spread to different parts of the world. In India, the Neo–Gothic also referred to as the Indo-Gothic and Indo-Saracenic were its prominent architectural styles. These incorporated different elements of Neoclassical, Gothic, Persian, and the indigenous Indian elements as well. Some of its features included pointed arches, large windows, thinner walls (than the previous Islamic style), domed roofs, etc. in rather large and encompassing structures. It also incorporated the use of modern construction techniques such as iron and steel, bricks along with stones, and later concrete. Several structures of this category were constructed in Mumbai, Kolkata and Chennai including the likes of Victoria Memorial, and Raj Bhavan in Kolkata, Victoria Terminus and Gateway of India in Mumbai, Madras High Court in Chennai besides others.

The port cities and the Presidency towns

The colonial structures and monuments came up first in the port cities of Madras (Chennai), Calcutta (Kolkata) and Bombay (Mumbai) from where the trade of the company was carried out. Later, they were to become the centres of administration known as the **Presidency towns**. As new emerging economic centres and the centres of political power of the Company, they grew rapidly and became the most populous of Indian cities by the turn of the 19th century. The first of the structures at these centres were in the form of forts. The Company's settlements, factories and mercantile offices were fortified as a protection against the other competing colonial powers. Thus, came up **Fort St. George in Madras** (built 1639-1644) the oldest British structure in India, **Fort William in Calcutta** (built 1696-1706 & 1758-1781) and **Fort in Bombay** (first Built in 1665 and expanded in 1715-1722). As centres of administration of the Company and later of the Crown, they were headed by a governor and required a sizeable presence of British officials. This necessitated a variety of public infrastructure and other office complexes. This included administrative offices, courthouses, mercantile offices, warehouses, agency offices for shipping, banking establishments, markets/bazaars, municipal halls, and educational institutions. With the new cities, new buildings, institutions, urban spaces and new architecture also developed.

Colonial architecture also flourished in the adjoining regions. While the fort areas were the exclusive preserve of the British, areas also developed around it for the settlement of the native population. This catered to the needs of the merchants, artisans, workers and others who had dealt with the Company and the British merchants. In the vicinity, there also came up the houses of the rich Indian merchants, agents and middlemen. These were large traditional courtyard houses, particularly in the vicinity of the *bazaars.* Such native settlements were referred to as the **Black town** while the British settlement was referred to the **White town**, a segregation which remained as sharp even in the times to come.

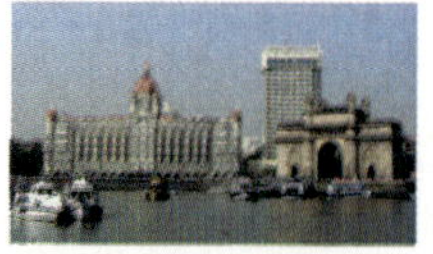

Post the rebellion of 1857 the British had become extremely wary and security conscious. There was a growing realization to better defend the towns. The British cleared the pastures/ grasslands and agricultural fields around older towns and built areas called **'Civil Lines'** which were urban spaces exclusively/substantially for the British. **Cantonments** were also developed in many towns which were areas where the Indian troops were stationed under the Command of European officers and were also considered as a safe enclave. These areas were characterized by wide roads/ streets, large bungalows with gardens, space for the barracks, parade grounds and churches. They were also seen as the models of urban settlements as compared to the dense and crowded Indian towns. Thus, came up new standards of urban town planning and infrastructure.

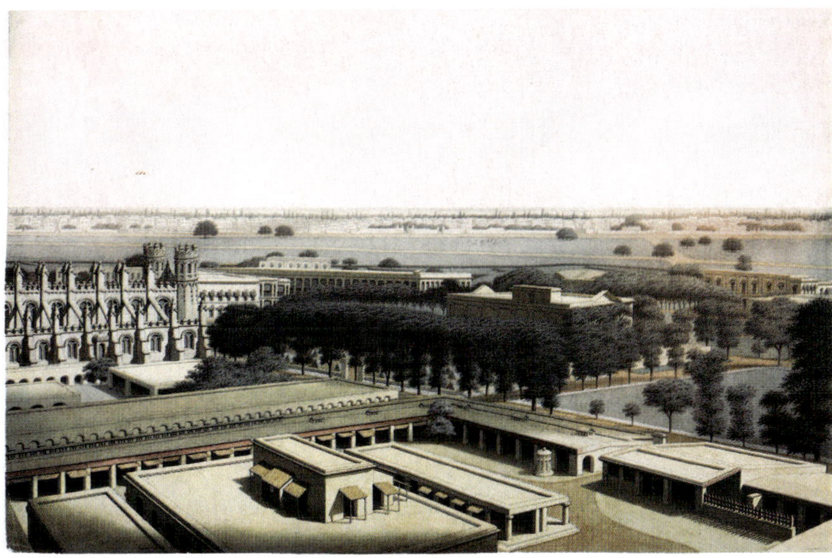

24.9: Fort William in 1828 on the banks of river Hooghly, a painting by William Wood in the British Library displaying the architecture — Wikimedia Commons

The capitals of the early British empire

Calcutta was the first capital of the Company and then of the British Empire in India and it remained to be so from 1772 to 1911. Warren Hastings, the first Governor-General of India, established here (in 1772), the Supreme Court of Justice and the Supreme Revenue Administration, thus making it the capital of the Company's administration. The other important offices were also transferred from Murshidabad, the then capital of the Nawabs in Bengal. Many important buildings and structures were built; some of which still exist and reveal the architecture of this period. The **Writers' Building** in Calcutta (established 1777-1780) was one such administrative office that functioned as the headquarters of the East India Company and later of the British Raj and continues to function as the office of the Chief Minister of West Bengal. It had a **Greco-Roman** style of architecture with prominent Corinthian columns.

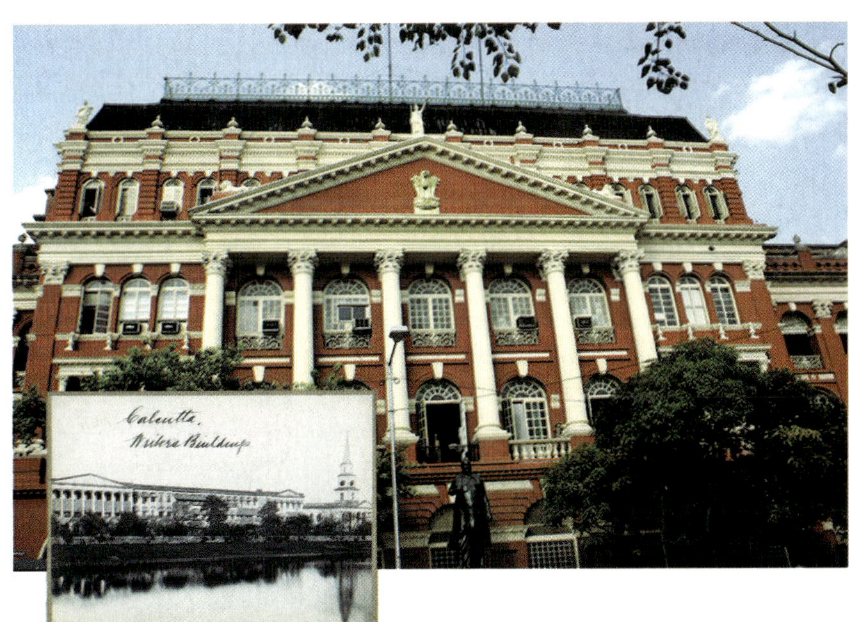

24.10: The Writers' Building, Kolkata, an administrative headquarter of the East India Company from late 18th century and now the office of the Chief Minister of West Bengal; an older image of the Writers' Building superimposed on the bottom left corner of the photo — Courtesy, Department of Tourism, West Bengal

In 1803, another important structure referred to as the **Government House** was established which was the residence of the Governor General of India. This was a massive residential palace that was meant to convey colonial authority. This was later to serve as the residence of the Viceroy of India and post-independence as that of the Governor of West Bengal (now referred to as Raj

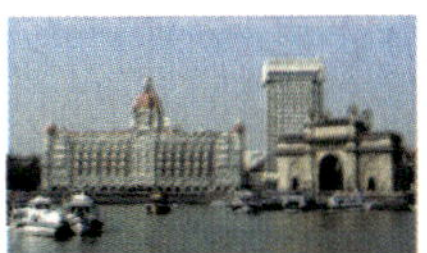

Bhavan). It was built with a **neoclassical** architecture with baroque overtones. The structure is characterized by a central core with four radiating wings, a large central dome, and a majestic portico on the front entrance which is supported by tall pillars. The structure also has several arched doors and windows highlighting the monument's elevation.

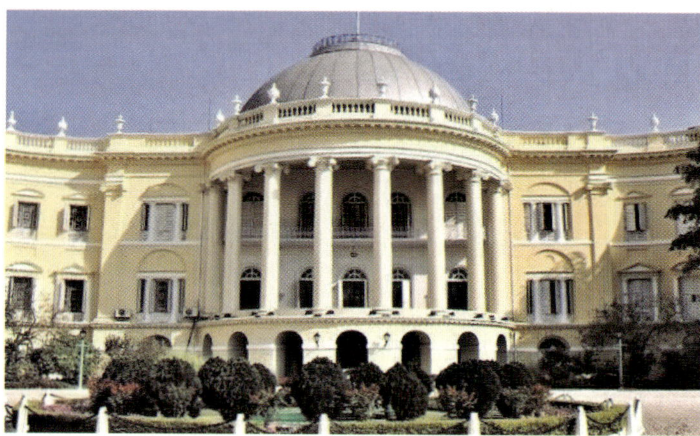

24.11: The South Front Façade of the Raj Bhavan Kolkata — Courtesy, Department of Tourism, West Bengal

In the last decade of the 18th and the first few decades of the 19th century, a variety of structures and public infrastructure of Calcutta developed, thus bringing to life a range of colonial architecture in India. Among the important structures of the 19th century Calcutta, included the **Indian Museum** (founded 1814) then known as the Imperial Museum which had a neoclassical architecture. The **Metcalfe Hall** (established 1840-1844) had a white notable appearance with a surrounding colonnade and Corinthian columns. The **Calcutta High Court** (established 1862), had Neo-Gothic architecture with a striking red appearance with several prominent arches and columns. Among the notable non-British structure was the **Marble Palace** built in 1835 by Raja Rajendra Mullick, a wealthy Bengali businessman, having a penchant for art collection. The building has a **neoclassical style** with fluted Corinthian columns and also has a large open courtyard with an adjacent *thakur-dalan* (place of worship) in the traditional Bengali style. Thus, it incorporated colonial as well as Indian architectural features.

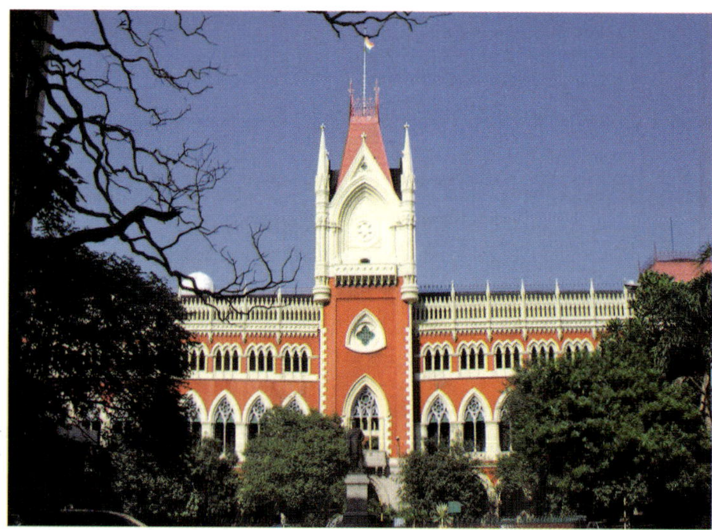

24.12: The Calcutta High Court, a 19th century Neo-Gothic architecture — Courtesy, Department of Tourism, West Bengal

But the monument of Kolkata that best symbolizes the British architecture of the period is the iconic **Victoria Memorial**. Conceived by Lord Curzon as a memorial to Queen Victoria (who passed away in 1901), the foundation of this grand monument was laid in 1904 and was eventually completed in 1921. An example of Indo-Saracenic architecture, its use of the white Makrana marble (of which the Taj Mahal is also made), the grand central dome, the four corner domes and the subsidiary four octagonal domed *chatris*, are reminiscent of the Mughal architecture. Its colonnade and the triumphal archway entrance are some elements of

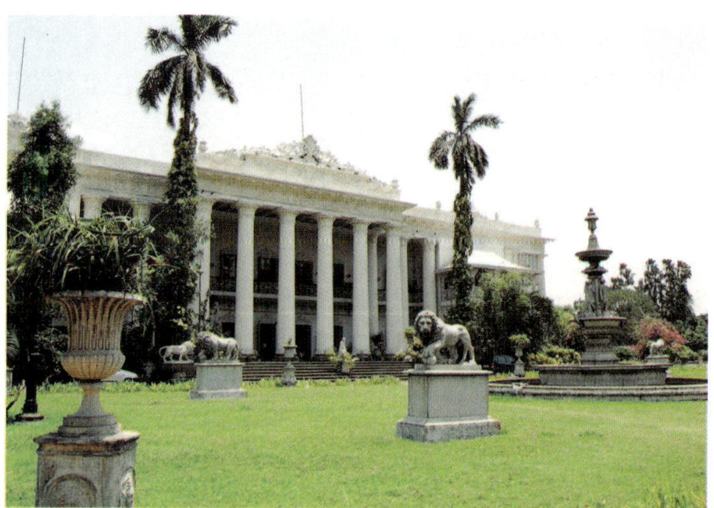

24.13: The Marble Palace, a private residence of an Indian businessman of the 19th century, built as per the European Style of architecture — Courtesy, Department of Tourism, West Bengal

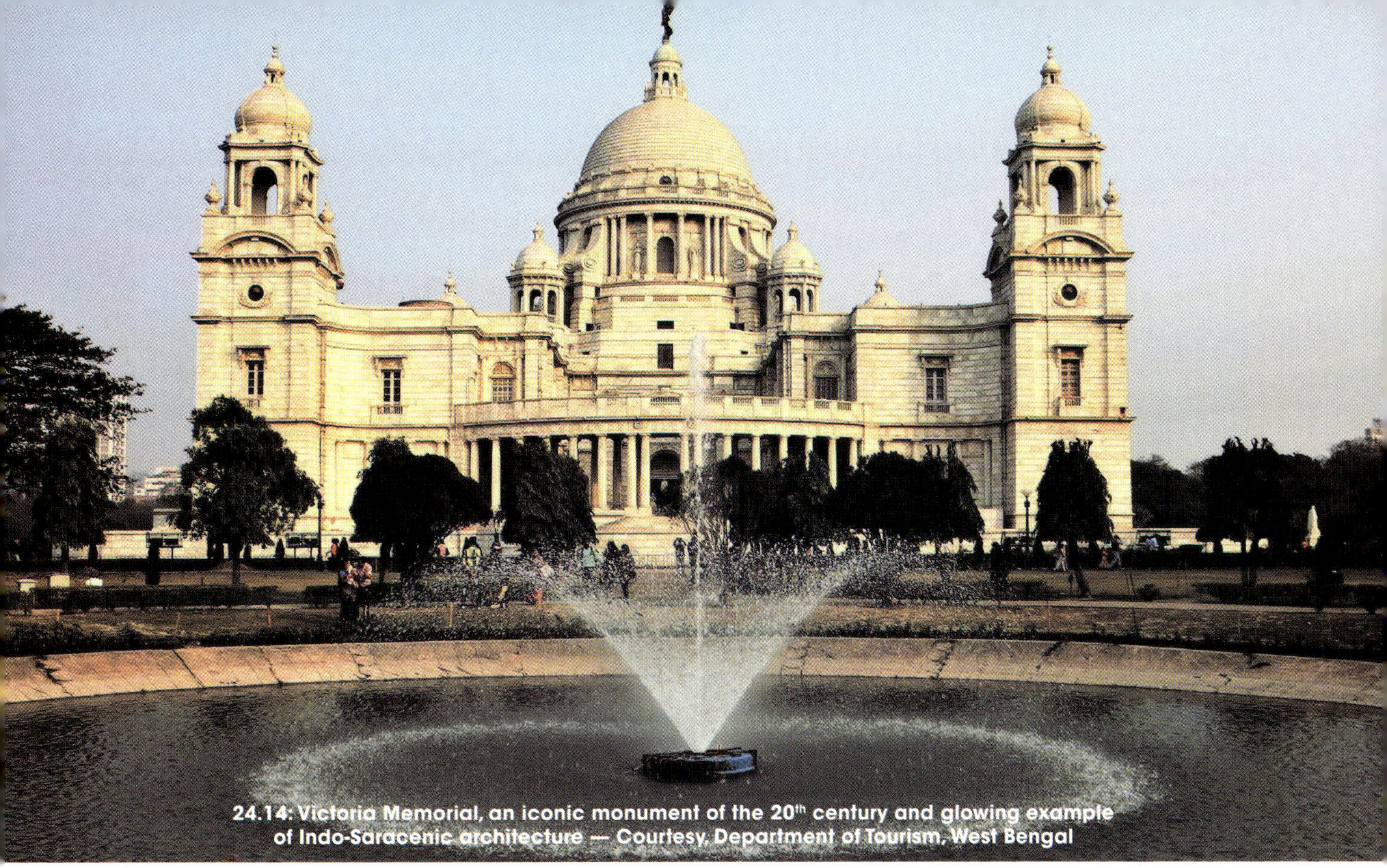

24.14: Victoria Memorial, an iconic monument of the 20th century and glowing example of Indo-Saracenic architecture — Courtesy, Department of Tourism, West Bengal

European architecture. Atop the central dome is the bronze statue of the 'Angel of Victory'. The height of the large dome is nearly 184 feet and the whole structure is of nearly 338 feet by 228 feet. It is located amidst a sprawling 64 acres of gardens. The architect of the Victoria Memorial was William Emerson. The monument also serves as a museum and houses a rich collection of paintings, sculptures, treatises, illustrated books, armoury, antiques and other items in its nearly 25 large galleries.

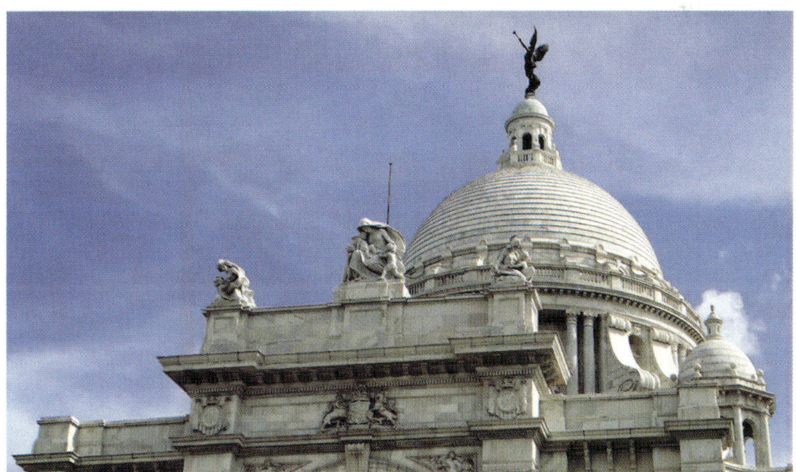

24.15: A closer view of the central dome of Victoria Memorial with the bronze idol of the Angel of Victory atop and other marble sculptures in the front façade — Courtesy, Department of Tourism, West Bengal

Shimla, the summer capital

In 1864, Shimla was declared as the summer capital of British India. This implied the shifting of the entire British administration from Calcutta to Shimla for a few months to escape the summer heat of the Gangetic Plains. Besides, it later also became the summer headquarters of the Commander in Chief of British India and also of the regional government of Punjab. This necessitated a sizeable administrative presence and the establishment of several government buildings, residences, a marketplace, a library, a church

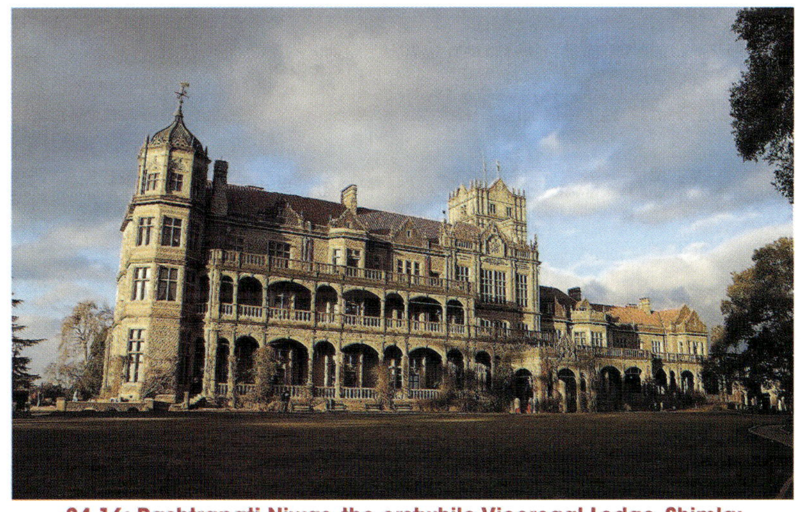

24.16: Rashtrapati Niwas, the erstwhile Viceregal Lodge, Shimla; an iconic British architecture and a venue of several important meetings and conferences — Wikimedia Commons

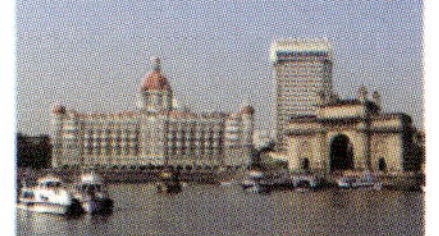

and other structures in the hill town. This included the iconic **Viceregal Lodge** (now known as the Rashtrapati Niwas) the residence of the Viceroy in Shimla which was built from 1880-1888. The monument, which has been the venue of several important accords and treaties, has a mix of **English Renaissance architecture** and other architectural styles and also reflects elements of Scottish highland castles. Built of blue-grey stone masonry, the structure is noted for its elaborate woodwork. Another notable monument of Shimla is the **Christ Church**. Constructed in 1857, it is the second oldest British church in India. It has **Neo-Gothic architecture** and is known for its stained-glass work. The **Gaiety Theatre** (established 1887; having Gothic-Revival architecture), **Gorton Castle** (1904; Neo-Gothic architecture), and **Shimla Town Hall** (1910) are some other 19th-century- early 20th-century colonial structures.

The Presidency towns

Madras and Bombay the two other Presidency towns that were the regional centres of power also witnessed substantial development of city infrastructure. These included structures ranging from office complexes to courts from museums to railway stations and from marketplaces to churches.

Madras was one of the earliest centres where the British had established trading. Post the defeat of the French in the Battle of Wandiwash (1760-1761) the British presence in Madras was substantially strengthened and thus administrative and trade activities increased ushering a new phase of colonial architecture. Several office complexes and other structures came up beyond Fort George. Among the prominent set of structures of this period was the **Government Museum Buildings** (Egmore), which were constructed from 1789-1890. Most of these structures were in the Indo-Saracenic style. Among these, the most notable is the circular structure of the **Museum Theatre** which has a red façade dominated by high arches. The **Chepauk Palace** (1764) and the **Amir Mahal** (1807) which was the residential palace of the nawab of Arkot, were built in the Indo-Saracenic style. These were early examples of Indian nobility coming up with European architecture. Among the most prominent churches of this period are the **St. Andrews Church** (1821) which has a Neo-Classical design and **Anderson Church** (1845). The **Madras School of Art** the oldest of such art schools came up in 1850. It had the Indo-Saracenic style. Later, this became the Government School of Arts. The **Madras High Court** (established in 1862, current structure built from 1888-1892) is another prominent structure in the Indo-Saracenic style with a striking red brick appearance. The **Senate House** (1874-1879) where currently the University of Madras is located is considered one of the oldest and best examples of the Indo-Saracenic style. It was designed by Robert

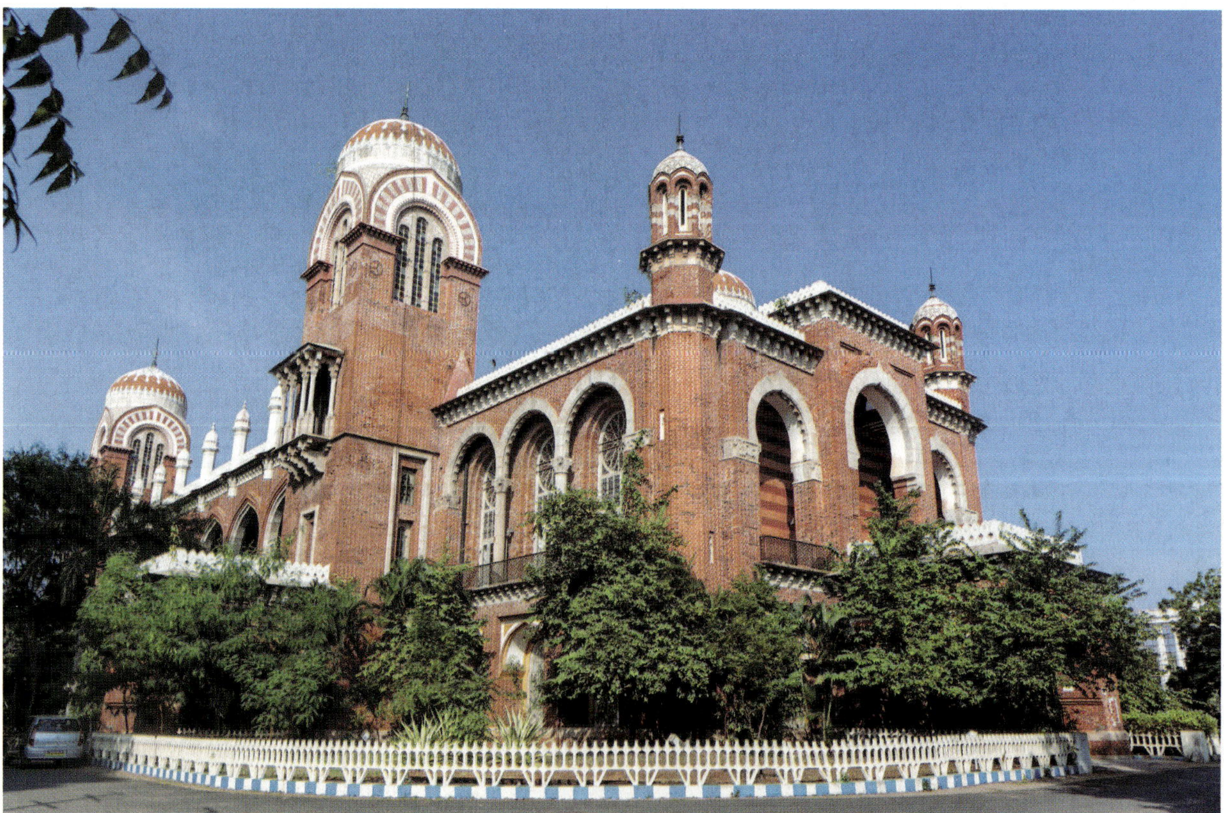

24.17: The Senate House, University of Madras, in Chennai, one of the prominent examples of Indo-Saracenic architecture — Courtesy, Tamil Nadu Tourism Development Corporation

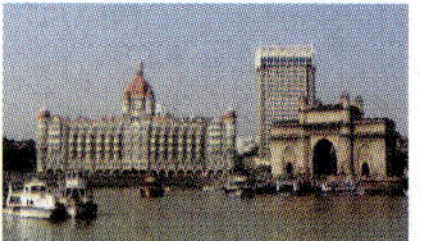

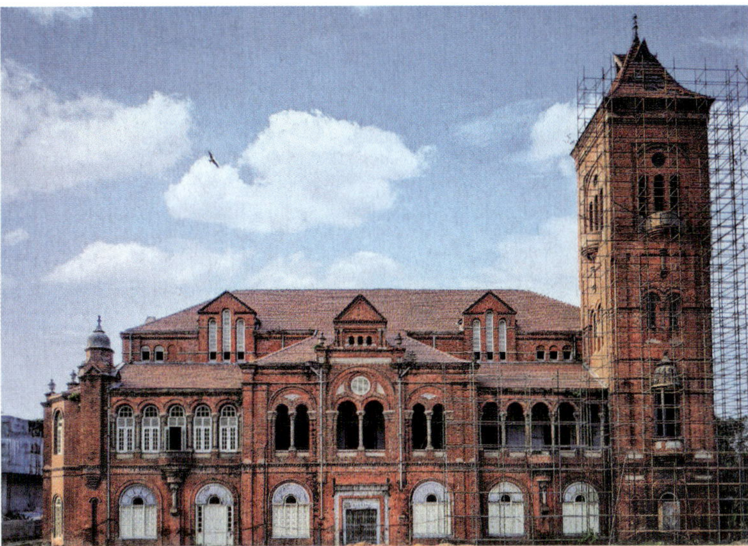
24.18: Victoria Hall, Chennai, a town hall with Indo Saracenic design — Courtesy, Tamil Nadu Tourism Development Corporation

Chisholm, one of the early pioneers of 19th century Indo-Saracenic architecture. Among its noteworthy features is its bright red brick look with well-proportioned features, its high great hall of Senate House, besides its stained-glass windows.

The Madras Central railway station (Chennai Railway Station; established in 1873) which has Gothic Revival architecture the **General Post-office** (1884) of Victorian-Gothic architecture, are among the public utilities incorporating new architectural style. The **Victoria Hall** (1888-1890) which was built to commemorate the golden jubilee of Queen Victoria was a public hall built with the contribution of different people as a trust. Designed by Robert Chisholm, it was another magnificent example of Indo-Saracenic architecture having Romanesque features.

Among the prominent early 20th century architectures are the **National Art Gallery** (1906; Indo-Saracenic style), **Egmore Railway Station** (1908; Indo-Saracenic style), and the **Rippon Building** (1913; Neo-Classical style). The latter which presently houses the Greater Chennai Corporation with its all-white appearance and a central clock tower, has a distinct appearance different from the red brick Indo-Saracenic structures of this period.

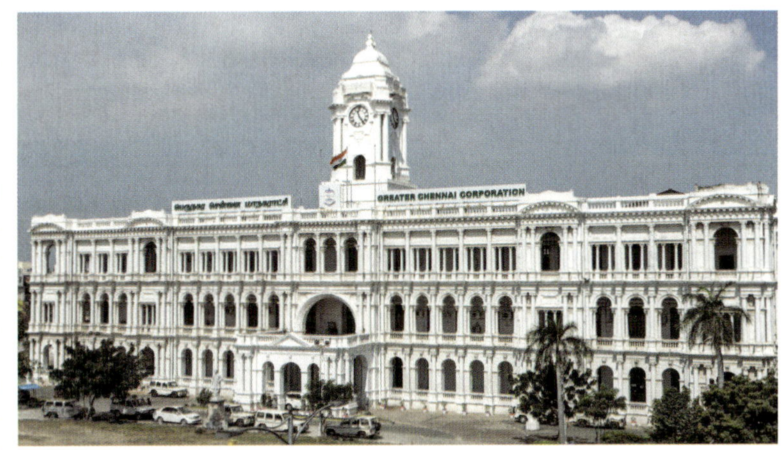

24.19: The Ripon Building, Chennai: A Neo-Classical architecture having an all-white appearance and a central clock tower — Courtesy, Tamil Nadu Tourism Development Corporation

Bombay (now **Mumbai**) the other Presidency town, developed as one of the most important ports of the country catering to nearly half of the overseas trade. The demand for cotton and the trade of opium fueled its economy. This brought in a class of Indian capitalists from diverse communities, besides the presence of the British, the supporting middlemen, artisans and labourers. As the population pressure and demand for space increased, the seven islands of Bombay were joined to form a singular land mass gradually developing into one big city.

Like in the other Presidency towns, one of the earliest structures was Fort George (named in honour of King George III of the United Kingdom), which was built in 1769 in the area now known as Fort in Mumbai. The fort itself was later demolished in 1862. Over a period of time, Bombay witnessed the growth of several colonial structures that displayed three prominent architectural styles; The Neo-Classical, the Neo-Gothic and the Indo-Saracenic.

Among these, the **Neo-Classical** was the earliest style of Mumbai's colonial architecture which is visible in structures such as the Town Hall and the Elphinstone Circle. Built in 1833 the **Asiatic Society of Mumbai Town Hall**, or simply the Town Hall, is a large all-white 100 feet tall structure with a span of 200 feet. Inspired by the Greek and Roman styles the structure has a large Grecian-style portico standing on eight tall pillars and is approached by a flight of majestic steps. Another famous monument of this style was the **Elphinstone Circle** (renamed after independence later as the Horniman Circle) which was built in 1869 as a part of the redevelopment of Bombay. This was an impressive arcade and a commercial structure that enclosed a circular garden in its centre. The buildings had a uniform-covered design to shield the shoppers/visitors from the sun and rain of the city.

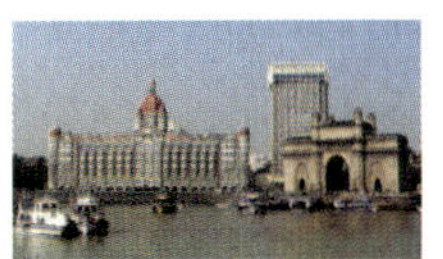

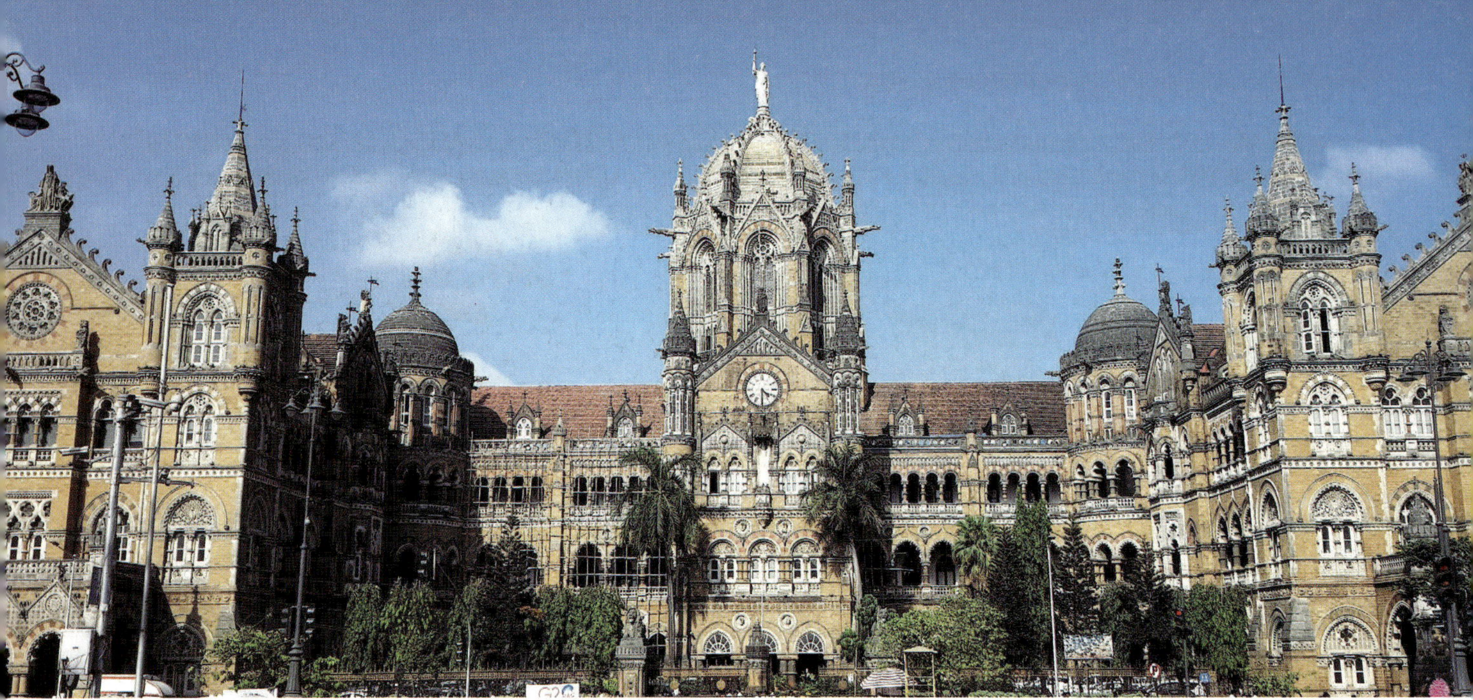

24.20: Chhatrapati Shivaji Maharaj Terminus, Mumbai, a glorious example of the Neo-Gothic architectural style along with influences of the Indo-Saracenic architecture — photograph by Madhukar K Bhagat

The **Neo-Gothic** structures came up in the period of 1860s to 1880s. These were characterised by their high-pitched roofs pointed arches and elements of detailed decoration. These included the **Bombay High Court** (established 1862), the **University of Mumbai Library** and the **Rajabai Clock Tower** (1878) at the Fort Campus, The **Elphinstone College** (1860-1875), the **Maharashtra Police Headquarters** building (formerly Royal Alfred Sailors' Home; 1872-1876), **Esplanade Mansion** (known as Watson's hotel; 1867-1869; a cast iron framed structure), besides others.

The most famous and spectacular example of the Neo-Gothic monument of Mumbai is indeed the **Chhatrapati Shivaji Maharaj Terminus**, formerly the Victoria Terminus, which was also the headquarters of the Great Indian Peninsular Company. The monument designed by architect F. W. Stevens was started in 1878 and completed in 1887 to commemorate 50 years of rule of Queen Victoria. Architecturally, it combines the elements of **Neo–Gothic/ Victorian Gothic Revival Architecture**, which is seen in the form of its pointed arches tall spires and intricate decoration as well as some elements of the **Indo-Saracenic,** particularly its large domes. In 2004 it was also included in the list of **UNESCO World Heritage Site**.

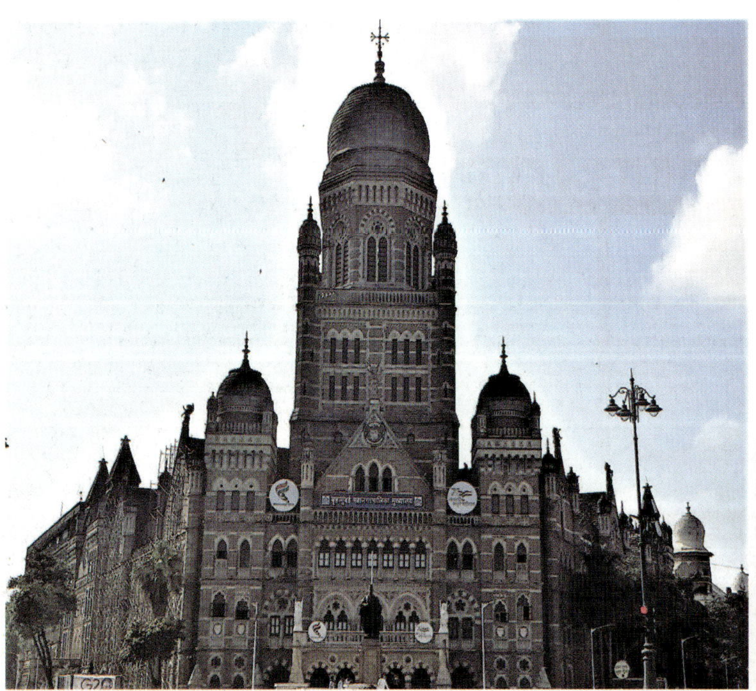

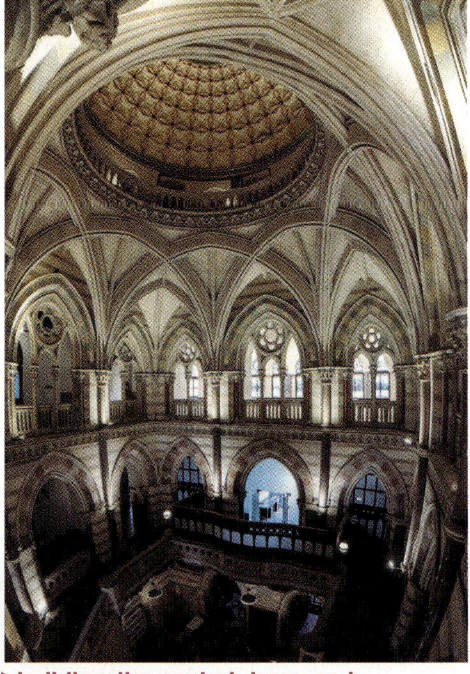

24.21 & 24.22: Brihan Mumbai Municipal Corporation (BMC) building, the central dome and the interiors of the BMC building — photographs by Madhukar K Bhagat

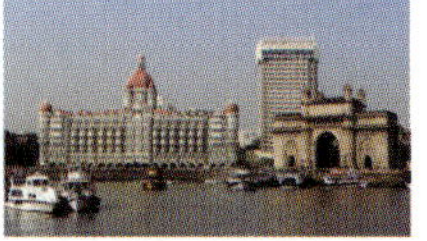

The **building of the Municipal Corporation of Mumbai** which is adjacent to the Chhatrapati Shivaji Maharaj Terminus, is yet another grand example of Victorian Gothic architecture. Its key features include the tall tower, the high central dome and a unique V-shaped plan facing two different streets with the front face of the structure at the junction of the streets.

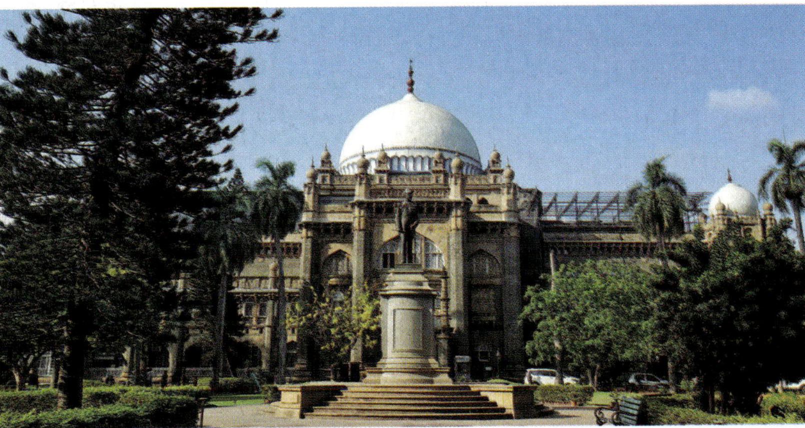

24.23: Chhatrapati Shivaji Maharaj Vastu Sangrahalaya, the erstwhile Prince of Wales Museum, a glorious example of the 20th century Indo-Saracenic architecture in Mumbai — photograph by Madhukar K Bhagat

In the 20th century, came the new architectural style of **Indo-Saracenic** which combined the European elements with elements of Indo-Islamic architecture such as the domes, the *chhatris* and the arches. Among the most magnificent monuments of this style in Mumbai is the **Chhatrapati Shivaji Maharaj Vastu Sangrahalaya** (earlier known as the Prince of Wales Museum) which was built in 1910. The structure has a prominent porch above which is a large tiled dome supported on a lotus petal base. Several miniature domes surround the main dome and they all end in finials, reminiscent of the Mughal architecture.

Another famous example of this style is the **Gateway of India**. It is an arched monument that was built to commemorate the arrival of King George V and Queen Mary to India in 1911. The memorial was designed by architect George Wittet and was completed in 1924. The structure comprises four turrets and large arched entrances. It is made of grey basalt and concrete. Architecturally, it draws features from the Islamic style of the 16th century Gujarat. Over the period of a century, it has remained one of the most iconic monuments of India, where the dignitaries arriving from the Arabian Sea would be given a ceremonial welcome. The last British troops leaving India in 1948 also passed through it.

Another iconic structure of this style is the **Taj Mahal Palace Hotel** in Colaba Mumbai, which was built in 1903, a couple of decades earlier than the adjacent Gateway of India. Built by the noted industrialist **Jamshedji Tata** and designed by Indian architects Sitaram Khanderao Vaidya and D. N. Mirza, it was truly symbolic of the Indian enterprise. Among the most poignant of its architectural features is the 240-foot-high red dome with four smaller domes on the corners. The front elevation is also marked with arches and beautifully designed jutting-out oriel windows.

Mumbai was witness to another style of architecture in the 20th century referred to as the **Art Deco**. This style prevalent in the world architecture in the early 20th century was an evolution of another type of architecture namely the Art Nouveau. The Art Deco movement in Mumbai further adopted Indian elements to emerge as another unique style called the Deco-Saracenic architecture. The style also touched on different aspects of architecture, particularly the interiors, and experimented with a variety of construction materials. Although the structures of this style are often less noted, several Art Deco structures came up in the pre-independence period in Mumbai, including, the **Regal Cinema**, buildings around the Oval Maidan and Marine Drive, **Soona Mahal**, **Keval Mahal** and others. The Victorian Gothic and Art Deco Ensembles of Mumbai have also been included in the **World Heritage List of UNESCO.**

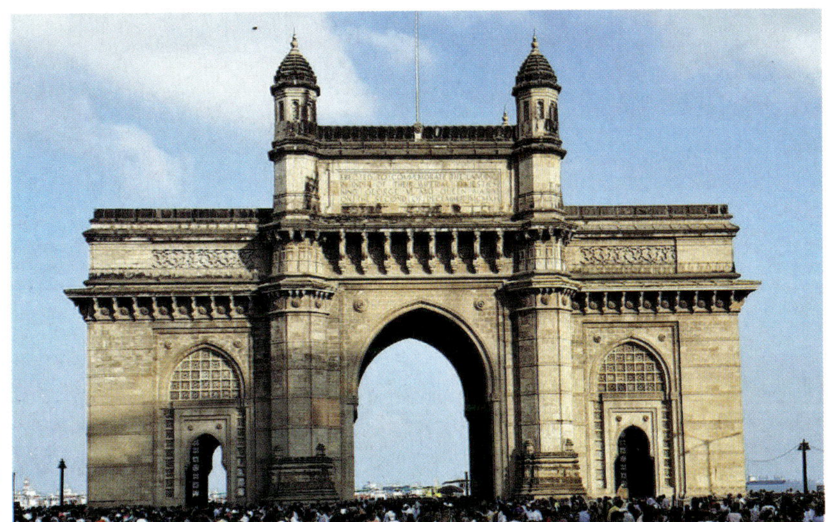

24.24: The Gateway of India, an iconic monument and an example of Indo-Saracenic architecture; a ceremonial gateway of the past and a popular tourist destination of the day — photograph by Madhukar K Bhagat

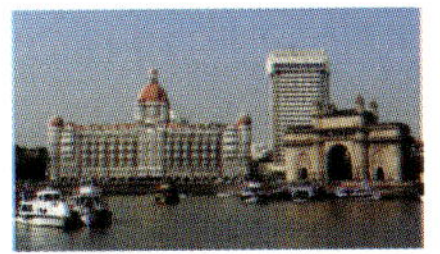

New Delhi, the New Capital

After the partition of Bengal in 1905 and the subsequent nationalist movement which compelled the reunification of Bengal, the British were wary of the growing antipathy towards foreign rule, especially amongst Bengal's elite. In the **Delhi Durbar** (a grand assembly) held in **December 1911** to mark the **coronation of King George V**, a decision was taken to shift the capital from Calcutta to Delhi. This was also in keeping with the historical significance of Delhi as the capital city of several dynasties including the Mughals. The foundation of the new capital was laid on 12th December 1911 by King George V. The work of construction of the new capital began in full earnest only after the First World War and the capital area of New Delhi was completed in 1931.

With the decision to shift the capital to New Delhi, another chapter was added to the colonial architecture of the 20th century. A new city was designed and many grand monuments were constructed which became the symbol of the British Raj in India. Amongst the most iconic of these structures include the **Rashtrapati Bhavan** (the erstwhile Viceroy's House), **the Secretarial complex of North and South Blocks**, the war memorial now referred to as the **India Gate,** the **Indian Parliament,** the **Connaught Place,** the **Eastern and Western Courts**, besides others. The new capital complex was designed by the British architects **Edwin Lutyens** and **Herbert Baker**. Sri Tej Singh Malik was the chief engineer and Sardar Sobha Singh was the civil contractor of a large part of this complex. **Robert Tor Russell,** another prominent architect, designed the Connaught Place and the Eastern and Western Courts. The structures were examples of the **Indo-Saracenic** and other architectural styles.

The city of New Delhi was envisioned and designed by Lutyens in line with the design of many great capitals of the world such as Washington DC, Paris and Rome. It was planned to have broad long avenues, with adjoining lawns and gardens. These were to be punctuated with important structures and monuments and end in a grand monument symbolic of the power of the British Crown. This design view materialised in what is referred to as the Central Vista portion of the so-called Lutyens' Delhi. The Kingsway (later known as Rajpath and now Kartavya Path) ran from East to West with several lawns adjoining it. On its eastern end was a large hexagon with a grand memorial alike the Arc de Triumph of Paris, which is known as the **India Gate**. This was in the direction of Purana Qila, the erstwhile centre of power in the medieval period. Thus, the Kingsway was akin to a symbolic inter-connection between Delhi's old and new centres of power. On either side of the Kingsway were roads connected at precise angles to it and lined with government and public buildings. The Kingsway on its western side ended on the Raisina Hill. Two secretariats, the **North** and the **South Blocks** were planned atop it. On the western end of this grand avenue atop the Raisina Hill and flanked by the North and South Blocks, was the **Viceroy's House** (now the Rashtrapati Bhavan) which was the seat of the British power.

The plans of the city of New Delhi were finalized in 1913, envisioning a royal capital that could accommodate nearly 60000 people. Several gardens, bungalows, markets, public infrastructure, roads, a railway station, and other buildings were planned and constructed. It took nearly 20 years for its completion. On 13th February 1931, the Viceroy of India inaugurated New Delhi. The city was designed as an imperial capital with grandiose architecture reflective of the belief that the sun would never set on the British empire. In less than two decades thereafter, the British left India.

The Rashtrapati Bhavan

The Viceroy's Residence, the symbol of the imperial authority, was indeed the grandest element of this architectural plan and its crowning glory. Spread over a 320-acre Presidential Estate, the imposing structure has 340 rooms in its main building and includes the official residence, reception rooms, offices, guest rooms, large Mughal-style presidential gardens, open spaces and courtyards besides staff quarters, utilities, guard rooms etc., within its perimeter wall. As per accounts, 27000 workers were employed for its construction which began in 1914 and continued till 1927. For a British empire at its zenith of power, it was planned as the world's largest and grandest of imperial residences.

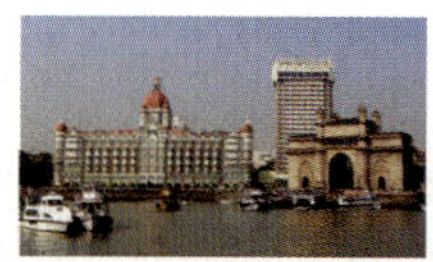

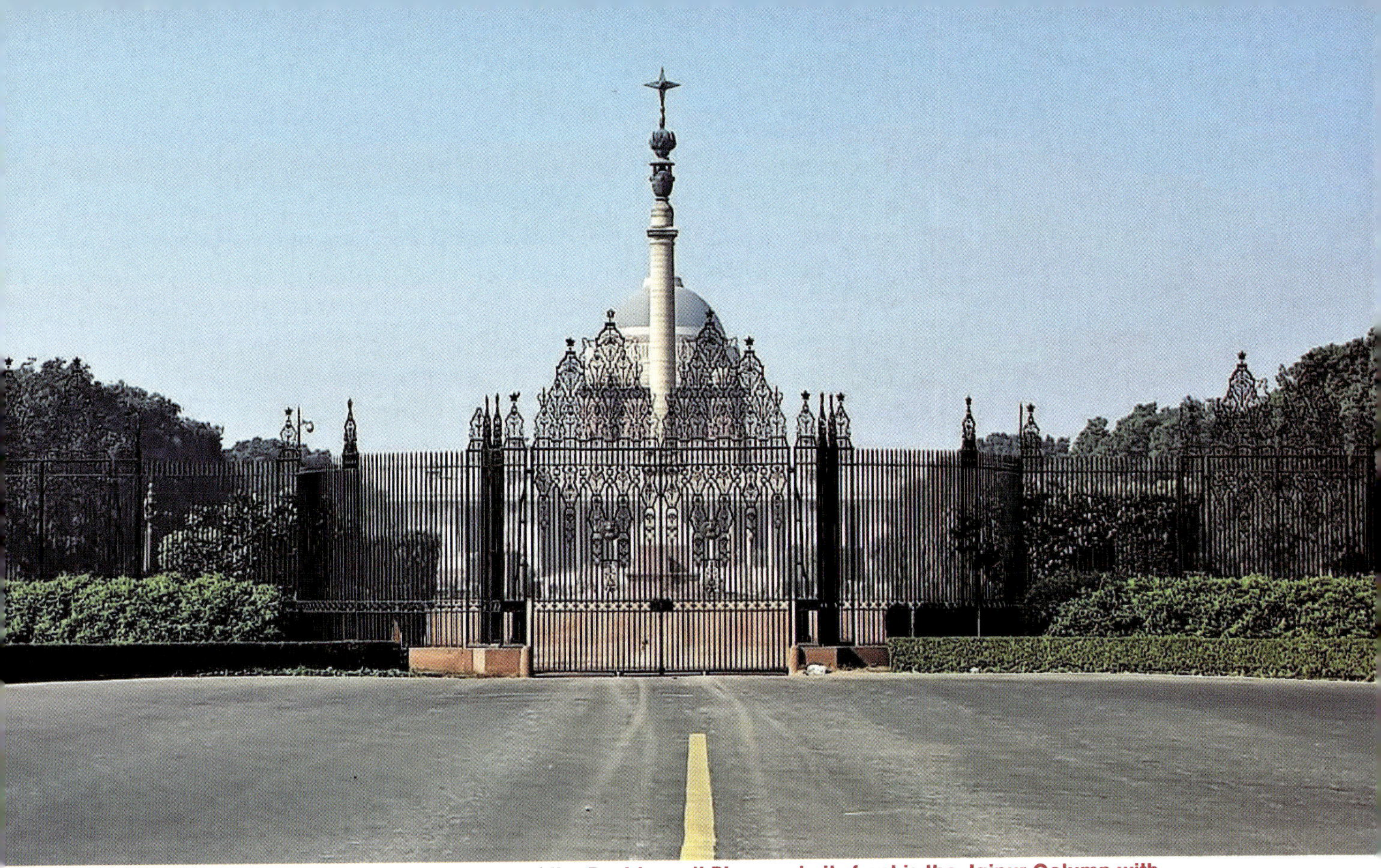

24.25: The majestic front entrance of the Rashtrapati Bhavan; in its front is the Jaipur Column with a glass star atop. In the foreground is the ornate wrought iron gate also designed by Lutyens — photograph by Madhukar K Bhagat

Designed by Lutyens, the structure is said by experts to have **European architectural elements with Indo-Saracenic design**. Some experts refer to it as an example of Imperial architecture. It is said that Lutyens wanted the design to be primarily of European architecture but owing to the growing resentment to the British rule, the Viceroy emphasized on incorporation of Indian elements in it. Thus, were incorporated Indian features such as the *chhatris* (the small domed pavilions), the *chajjas* (dripstones), and the *jalis* (lattice screens). The large dome which is nearly twice the height of the main structure but compliments the large span of the façade is said to be inspired by the dome of Grand Stupa at Sanchi as well as the Pantheon at Rome. The most visible and significant element of its architecture which is completely Indian, was the use of red and buff (yellowish beige) stones in the structure. The Jaipur Column with a star placed in the front courtyard of the monument, sprawling Mughal-styled gardens, carved stone elephants and metallic cobras around a fountain in the south court, were some other Indian elements which are merged with the European architectural elements.

A notable element in the precincts of the Rashtrapati Bhavan is a buff sandstone column standing in the foreground which was inspired by the Trojan's Column in Rome. The 145-foot-tall column referred to as the Jaipur Column has atop it a bronze lotus and a six-pointed glass star. Though the column was also designed by Lutyens, it was erected under the aegis of the Maharaja of Jaipur, to whom originally belonged a substantial portion of the land on which New Delhi was built, and who had offered to sponsor the column to commemorate the Delhi Durbar and the building of new capital.

The **Secretariat complex** of **North and South Blocks** was designed by Herbert Baker. These two buildings were placed on either side of the east-west axis formed by the Kingsway (now Kartavya Path) on a large plaza on the Raisina hill. Both the structures have a symmetrical design as if a reflection of each other

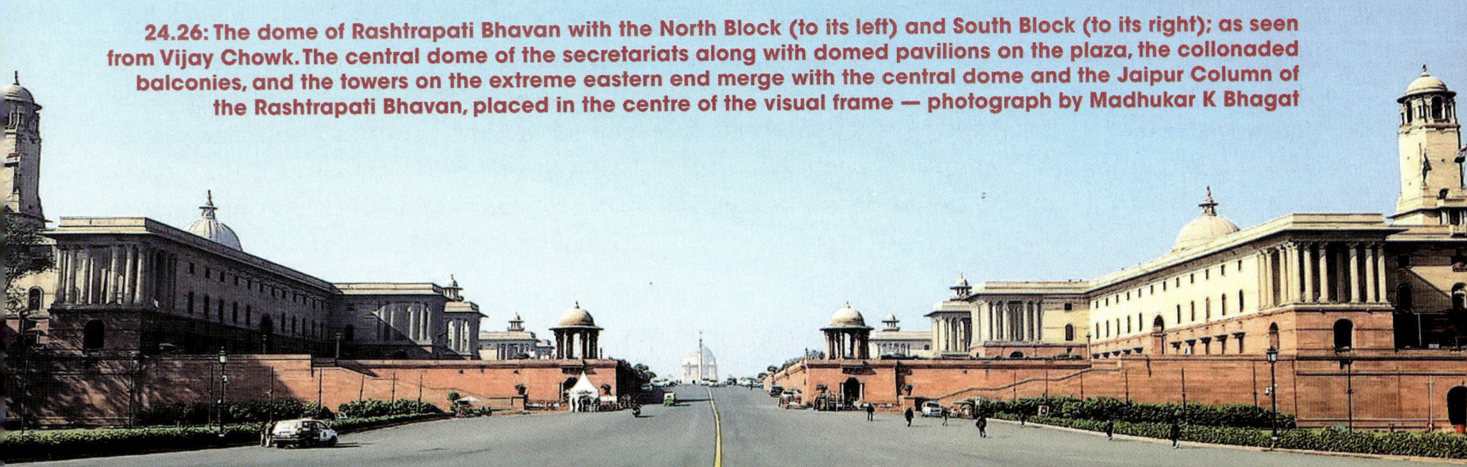

24.26: The dome of Rashtrapati Bhavan with the North Block (to its left) and South Block (to its right); as seen from Vijay Chowk. The central dome of the secretariats along with domed pavilions on the plaza, the collonaded balconies, and the towers on the extreme eastern end merge with the central dome and the Jaipur Column of the Rashtrapati Bhavan, placed in the centre of the visual frame — photograph by Madhukar K Bhagat

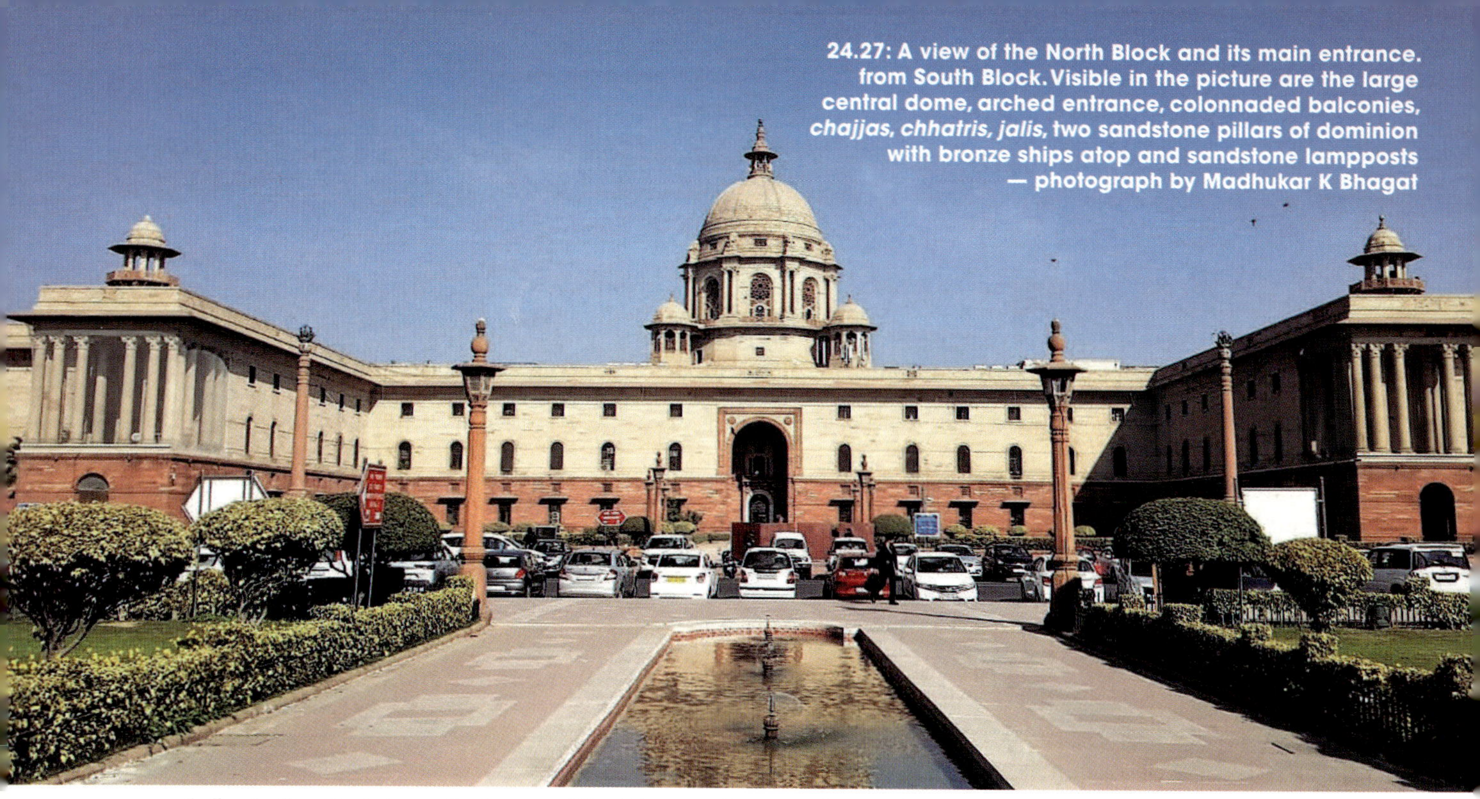

24.27: A view of the North Block and its main entrance. from South Block. Visible in the picture are the large central dome, arched entrance, colonnaded balconies, *chajjas, chhatris, jalis*, two sandstone pillars of dominion with bronze ships atop and sandstone lampposts — photograph by Madhukar K Bhagat

and flank the Rashtrapati Bhavan (the Viceroys's house) creating a large façade formed by the three mammoth structures. The two buildings of the Secretariat complex were designed in **Indo-Saracenic Revival architecture**. Among the poignant features of its architectural design is its giant central dome surrounded by smaller domes/cupolas. A collonaded balcony on its north-south wings with *chatris* atop is yet another noticeable feature. Together with these, the domed pavilions on the exterior of its plaza and tower capped with a cupola at the eastern end, visually harmonise with the central dome of the Rashtrapati Bhavan, creating the impression of a singular sprawling central structure looming imposingly over the Raisina Hill with stretched out limbs.

A unique feature of the design of the Viceroys' House and the two Secretariat buildings is that the former is visible from a distance when one approaches from the Kingsway (now Kartavya Path) but gets hidden behind the Raisina Hill as one approaches the base of the hill (presently called the Vijay Chowk). Only a part of the dome remains visible at this point (see picture earlier). The design of Viceroy's house which was made by Lutyens is believed not to have factored the problem caused by the steep slope of the hill. It is said that Lutyens wanted the slope to be reduced for the grand structure to be continuously visible throughout the approach from the India Gate side. However, this would have meant that the flat land/plaza available between the North and South blocks would have to be substantially reduced in size. This was completely unacceptable to Baker, the architect of the Secretariat buildings. The latter had his way in the design, thus creating a visual anomaly.

The secretariat buildings also saw a merger of European and Indian architectural elements. The Baroque-styled dome, the semicircular arches and the Corinthian columns were drawn

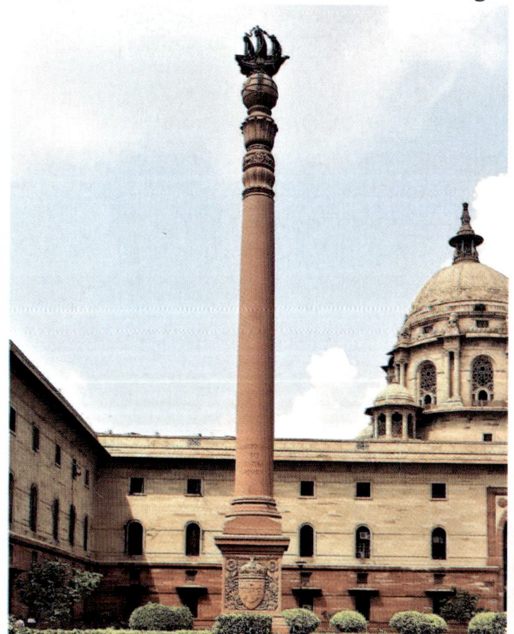

24.28: The Column of Dominion of Australia with a bronze ship atop in front of North Block

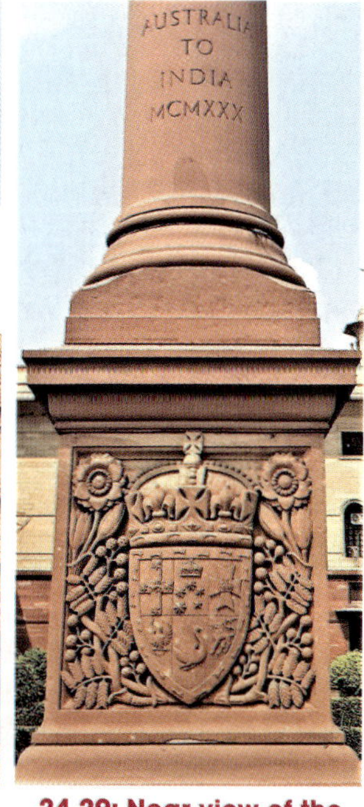

24.29: Near view of the Coat of Arms at the base, with 'Australia to India MCMXXX' (MCMXXX-1930) inscribed in the middle of the pillar

— photographs by Madhukar K Bhagat

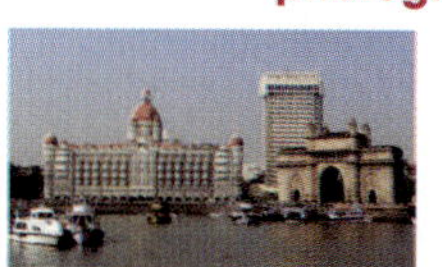

from European architecture. The use of red and buff sandstone with a red sandstone broad base for outer walls, *chhatris*, *chajjas* and *jalis* of sandstone on the terraces carved elephants and lotuses, were some of the notable Indian elements integrated in the design. The main entrance of the secretariat has a Mughal architecture-style gateway similar to that in Humayun's Tomb. It has a large gateway frame with a smaller arched gateway.

In the front entrance of the North and South blocks are two sandstone columns (a total of four columns). These are the **'Columns of Dominion'** which were ceremonial gifts to India from, Australia, Canada, New Zealand, and South Africa, the dominions of Britain. The columns are topped by bronze ships symbolic of Britain's maritime traditions. They are placed on a replica of the Ashokan Capital that has a lotus motif placed above a wheel, flanked by a horse and bull.

The structures of the North and South Blocks were meant to be official complexes and continue to be. These were designed with four levels and a staggering 4,000 rooms in a labyrinth of corridors running into kilometres. They were also connected with an internal tunnel. Today, they house the most important ministries of the government; The Prime Minister's Office, the Ministry of Defence, the Ministry of External Affairs (in the South Block) and the Ministry of Finance and the Ministry of Home Affairs (in the North Block).

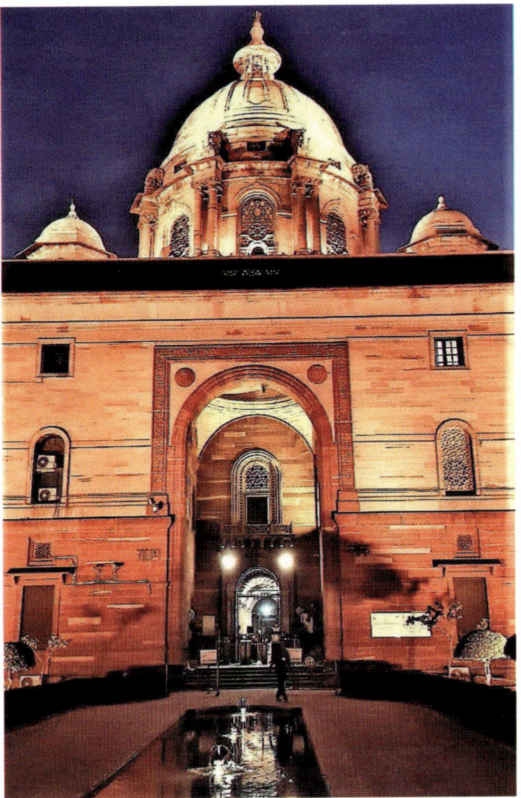

24.30: The main entrance of the South Block with a large framed doorway and arched entrance lit up in the night. Large central dome, *jali* window and fountain in the foreground, are other visible architectural elements — photograph by Madhukar K Bhagat

The India Gate is another of the iconic monuments on the eastern periphery of the main east-west axis, which was earlier the King's Way. It was designed to be The 'All India War Memorial' what the Arc du Triomphe was to the Champs Élysées in Paris. The monument serves as a memorial to nearly 90000 Indian soldiers who lost their lives in the First World War on different frontiers and also in the Third Afghan War. The names of these soldiers are inscribed on the uprights of the arch. Further, it now also serves as a memorial to Indian soldiers who laid their lives in later wars. It also has the name inscribed of the soldiers awarded the Param Vir Chakra, (India's highest military decoration).

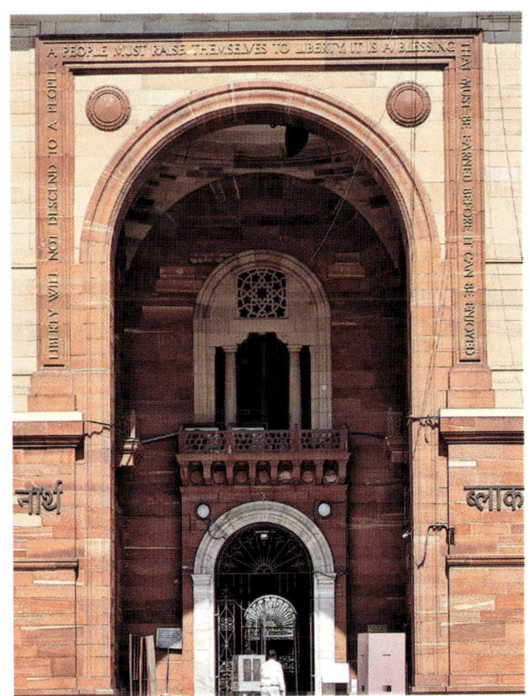

24.31: North block main entrance gate with the inscription on top; *"Liberty will not descend to a people. A people must raise itself to liberty: It is a blessing that must be earned before it can be enjoyed"* — photograph by Madhukar K Bhagat

The monument designed by Lutyens is nearly 138 feet tall and is made of buff sandstone. It has a relatively plain façade with clear lines as compared to the Rashtrapati Bhavan and the Secretariat buildings. Designed like a tall arch, it is topped with a shallow dome. A bowl on the dome and a bowl below the arch were placed, where oil was ceremonially burnt on the anniversary of the inauguration. While the top bowl was rarely lit up, the bottom bowl was replaced with an eternal flame in 1972 and is known as the *Amar Jawan Jyoti* (Flame of the Immortal Soldier).

Further beyond the India Gate is a domed canopy standing on four tall columns in a pool of water. Like India Gate, the structure is made of buff sandstone. It is said that an ornate pavilion at Mahabalipuram was the inspiration of Lutyens for this structure. This was built to commemorate King George V whose standing marble statue was installed here. This statue was later

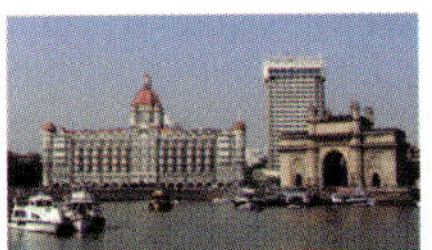

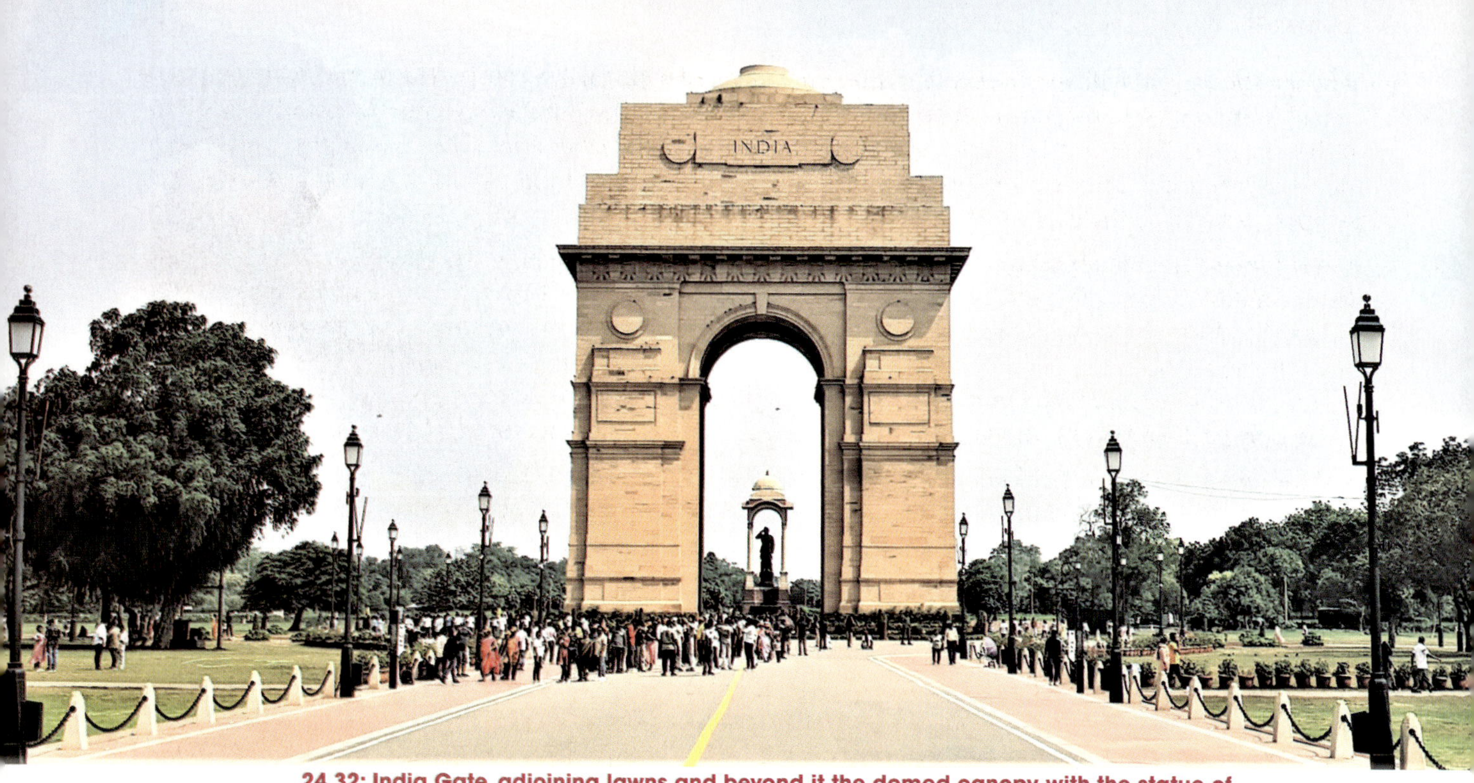

24.32: India Gate, adjoining lawns and beyond it the domed canopy with the statue of Netaji Subhash Chandra Bose; a view from Kartavya Path — photograph by Madhukar K Bhagat

shifted to Coronation Park in 1968 and in 2022 a statue of Netaji Subhas Chandra Bose was installed here to mark his 125th birth anniversary.

Besides reminding the country of the valour of the soldiers, today it serves as a monument where the Prime Minister and other dignitaries pay their homage to the martyrs on ceremonial occasions like Republic Day. Besides, it has also developed as a very popular tourist destination and come up as a spot for people to voice their opinion and even protests.

The **Indian Parliament** or the Imperial Legislative Council, which was later to be known as the **Sansad Bhavan**, was not a part of the original plan of the Central Vista in Lutyens Delhi. After the Morely Minto Reforms of 1919, the Indian representation to the Viceroy's council rose substantially and thus emerged the need for a structure that could accommodate hundreds of council members. Accordingly, in 1921, the foundation of the Indian Parliament was laid by the Duke of Connaught and in 1927 the building was inaugurated by Lord Irwin, the Viceroy.

The Parliament was designed by **Lutyens** and **Baker** and is located on the northern side of the King's Way east-west axis near the foot of Raisina Hill (now called the Vijay Chowk). This is the only structure that breaks the symmetry of design on the North and South of the King's Way (now Kartavya Path). It is designed as a circular ringed structure on the outside with a collonaded verandah circumnavigating it and has a large diameter of 560 feet. The two-floor structure rests on a red sandstone platform and is mainly made of buff sandstone. The interior has a circular central hall which is topped with a dome. Three semicircular chambers are placed on the periphery of the central hall, with the remaining space in

24.33: The old Indian Parliament, now renamed as the Samvidhan Bhavan, a view from Vijay Chowk — photograph by Madhukar K Bhagat

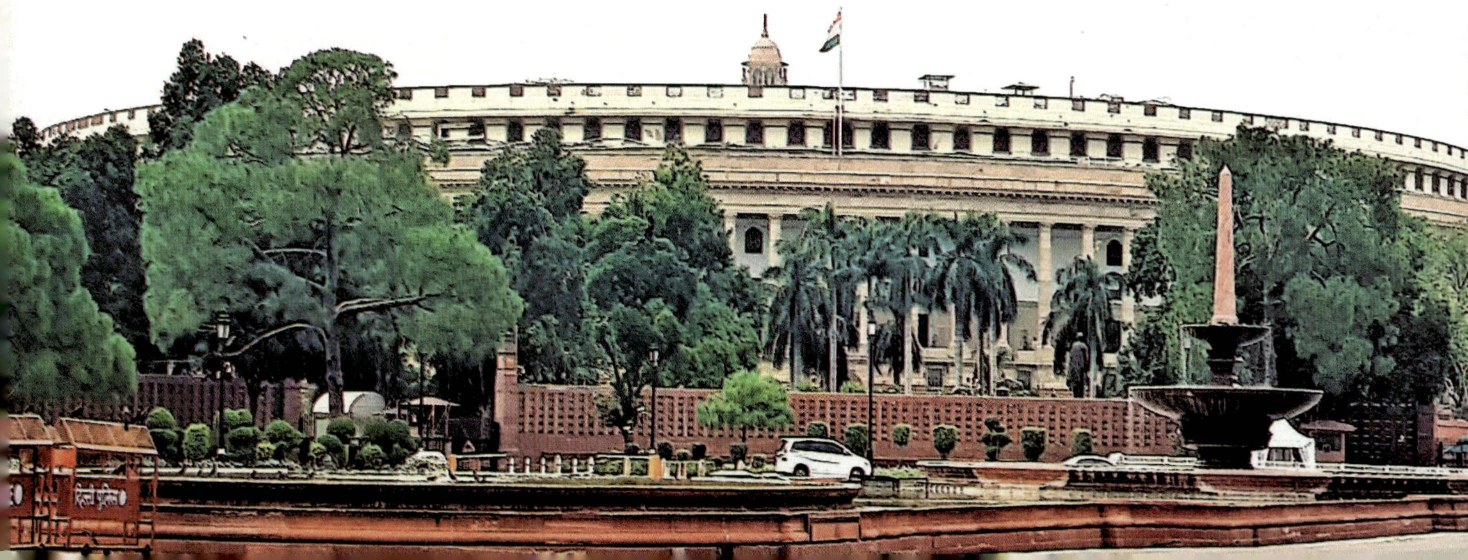

between the central hall and the semicircular ones covered with garden courts. The architecture employs a combination of European as well as Indian elements. While the European elements include the dome of the central hall, the semi-circular arched windows and the tall columns of the verandahs, the distinct Indo-Saracenic features are the geometric patterns that comprise the *jalis* of the boundary wall, the parapets, as well as the capitals that support the portico roof.

In the pre-independence period, the three semi-circular chambers housed the Chamber of Princes, the Council of States, and the Legislative Assembly. After India's independence, these chambers provided for the Rajya Sabha (the Upper House), the Lok Sabha (the House of the People) and the Parliament Library. The central hall was used as a venue for joint sessions of both houses of Parliament and for the address of both houses by the President of India or visiting dignitaries of other countries. Post the construction of the new parliament of India in 2023, this structure has been renamed as the *Samvidhan Sadan*.

Besides the above, the other important British architectures of this period include the **Connaught Place**, the **Eastern Court** and the **Western Court**, the **Teen Murti Bhavan**, the **Cathedral Church of Redemption**, and the **Cathedral of Sacred Heart**. Among these, the most iconic is indeed the **Connaught Place**, a marketplace and a central business district of Delhi. Designed by **Robert Tor Russel**, it was constructed in the period 1929-1933. The circular market complex has Georgian architecture which is said to be inspired by the Royal Crescent of Bath. The market complex is designed with two concentric circles, creating thereby, the Inner Circle, the Middle Circle and the Outer Circle for the market with seven radial roads. The structure itself is of two floors with the colonnaded ground floor serving as a marketplace while the upper floor was for residential purposes. Nearly a century later, it continues to remain a bustling marketplace and central business district it was designed to be.

The **Teen Murti Bhavan**, formerly the Flagstaff House, built in 1930, is another notable British architecture of this period. Designed by **Robert Tor Russel**, it has a signature appearance of white stone and stucco. It has an arched entrance, recessed windows, cylindrical columns at the entrance and a pillared verandah in the rear. It has a symmetrical composition and elements of Georgian architecture of the 18th-19th century. It was built as the residence of the Commander in Chief of the British armed forces in India and post-independent also served as the residence of the first Prime Minister of India. Today it serves as *Pradhan Mantri Sangrahalaya* (museum of the Prime Ministers of India).

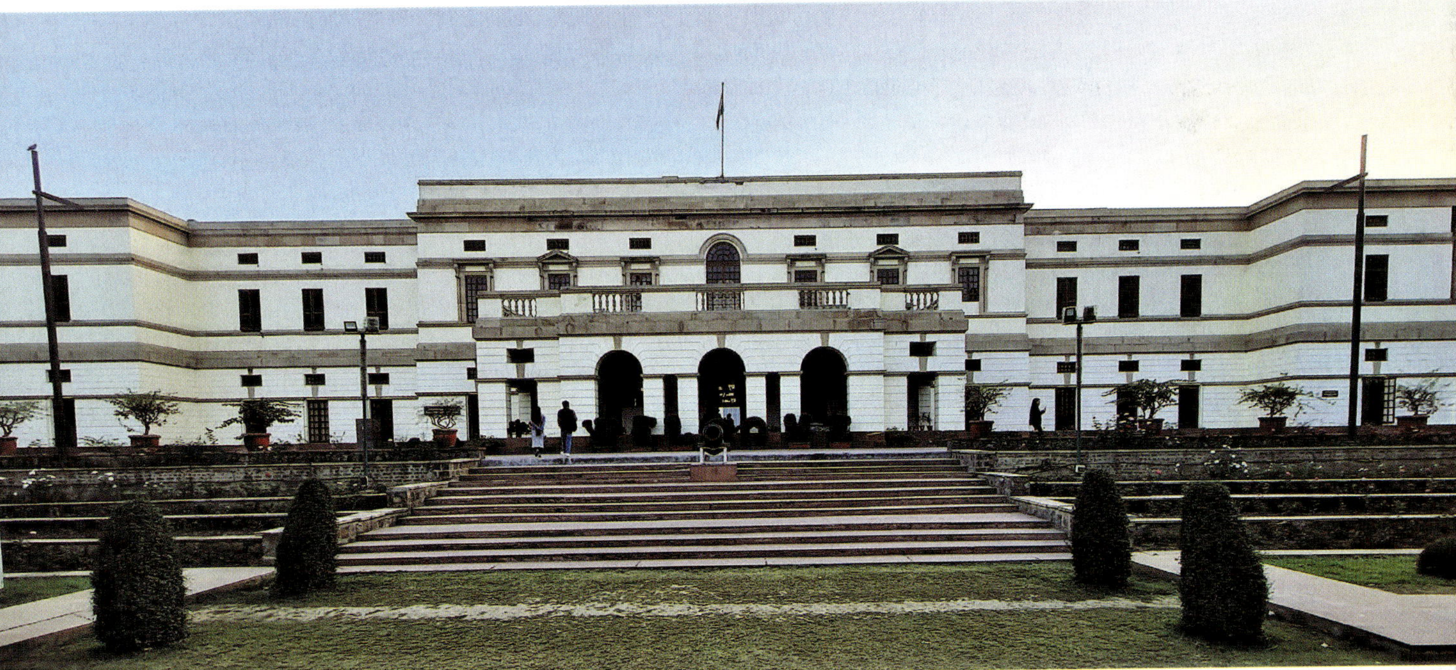

24.34: The Teen Murti Bhavan, erstwhile Flagstaff House and the residence of the Commander in Chief of British armed forces in India and later the residence of the first Prime Minister of independent India; an example of British Georgian architecture with highly symmetrical composition — photograph by Madhukar K Bhagat

The **Western** and **Eastern Courts** at the Queen's Way (now Janpath) were also designed by Robert Tor Russel. Meant to be hostels for the legislators, the two structures on the opposite side of the Janpath and facing each other have a distinct white appearance with an arcaded look. Designed on two floors, the

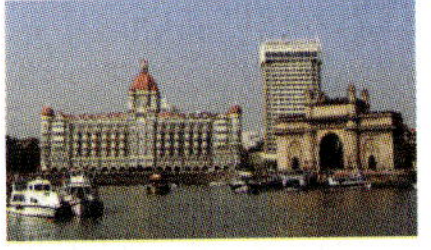

long verandah with tall Tuscan columns, provide them a distinctive appearance. These are also said to be among the best works of Russel. While the Eastern Court now has Telegerpah, MTNL and other offices, the Western Court continues to be a guest house for legislators.

The palaces of the princely states

With the formation of the Chamber of Princes in 1921, there was the need to provide space to the rulers of various Indian states who could then build a residential building in New Delhi. An area called Princess Park was conceived around India Gate. This space was provided next to the India Gate hexagon to the larger principalities and powerful states like Hyderabad, Baroda, Bikaner, Jaipur and Patiala and on roads radiating from the India Gate Hexagon to the smaller states. The latter included those of Jaisalmer, Travancore, Dholpur etc. Hence, there emerged several Indian structures in the new capital city that were the palaces of the princely states.

Among the grandest of the palaces of the princely states is the **Hyderabad House** located in a wedge-shaped land and facing the hexagon of India Gate and two streets emerging from it (presently adjacent to Ashok Road). The palace is said to have been built at an estimated cost of around 15 million rupees in 1926. It was then an astronomical amount; however, it could well be afforded by the Nizam of Hyderabad, considered one of the richest men in the world then. The structure was designed by Lutyens and was shaped like a butterfly with its two wings facing the two streets emerging from the India Gate Hexagon. The overall design is **Indo-Saracenic** and a blend of European architecture and Indian features. The large dome above the entrance hall of the palace is similar to that of the Rashtrapati Bhavan and is said to be inspired by the Great Stupa at Sanchi. Its carved sandstone *jalis* of the façade are quite similar to the *jalis* at the Red Fort. The palace has 36 rooms, broad sweeping staircases, marble fireplaces and floors decorated with rich patterns. Post-independence the property was taken over by the Government of India and presently it serves as a State Guest house and a venue for hosting meetings with foreign dignitaries.

Adjacent to the Hyderabad House is another magnificent palace called the **Baroda House**, which was also designed by Lutyens with a butterfly shape. It has a large central dome and has a similar **Indo-Saracenic architecture** with a central dome inspired by the Great Sanchi Stupa. However, it has less of Indian features and more Anglo-Saxon elements such as large French windows with semi-circular arches; a portico; and unornamented Doric columns. It is made of buff sandstone and presently the headquarters of the Northern Railways is located in it.

The **Jaipur House** located at the end of the Kartavyapath and on opposite end of the India Gate, was designed by Charles Blomfield. It too has a butterfly-shaped architecture, which has a large central dome, and two wings with European and Indian features. It presently houses the National Gallery of Modern Art.

Jodhpur House, **Bikaner House** and **Patiala House** were the other large princely palaces constructed during this period. These too reflect a blend of European and Indian architectural elements. The lesser principalities also had some palaces built including, the **Jaisalmer House, Dholpur House** and **Travancore House**.

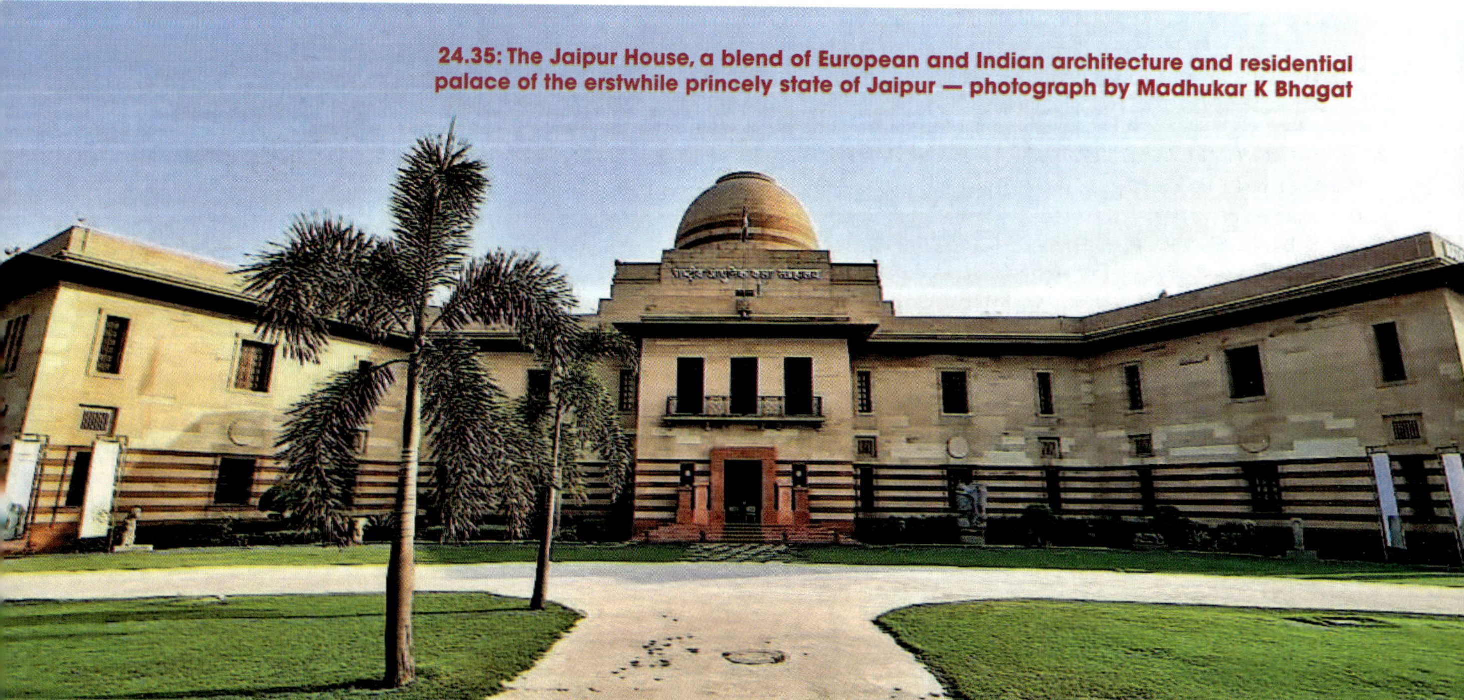

24.35: The Jaipur House, a blend of European and Indian architecture and residential palace of the erstwhile princely state of Jaipur — photograph by Madhukar K Bhagat

Although the most important of the British architecture in Delhi came in the 20th century, some churches and other monuments also came up in the 19th century. This includes the **St. James' Church** which was built in 1836. It has Renaissance Revival architecture and its features include a central octagonal dome, three porticoed porches elaborate stained glass windows etc. Another, Church of this period is **St. Stephen Church** which was built in 1862. It has Gothic architecture with Romanesque features and is known for its stained-glass windows. The **Central Baptist Church** is the oldest of the churches of Delhi (early 19th century) and has a typical European architecture of the time. Another notable church of this period is the **Cathedral Church of Redemption** located to the east of the Parliament House and the Rashtrapati Bhavan. It was founded in 1927 by Lord Irwin and completed in 1931. Also called the Viceroy's church, it is known for its high arches and beautiful dome with a relatively simple and elegant overall design.

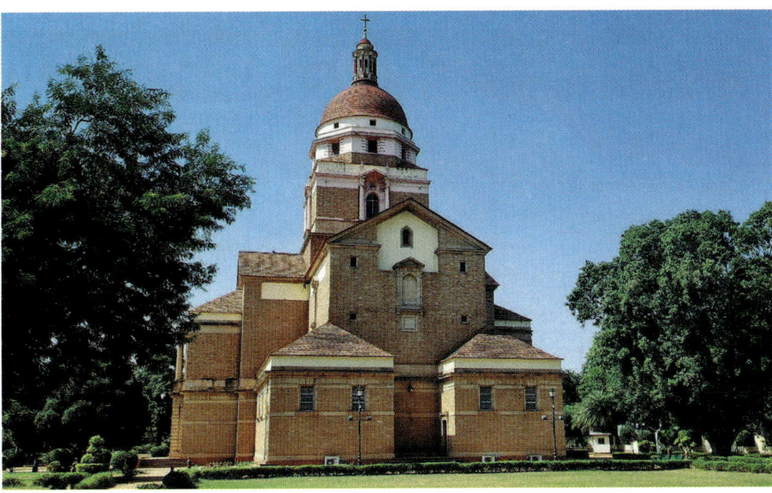

24.36: The Cathedral Church of Redemption, also known as the Viceroy's church in New Delhi — photograph by Madhukar K Bhagat

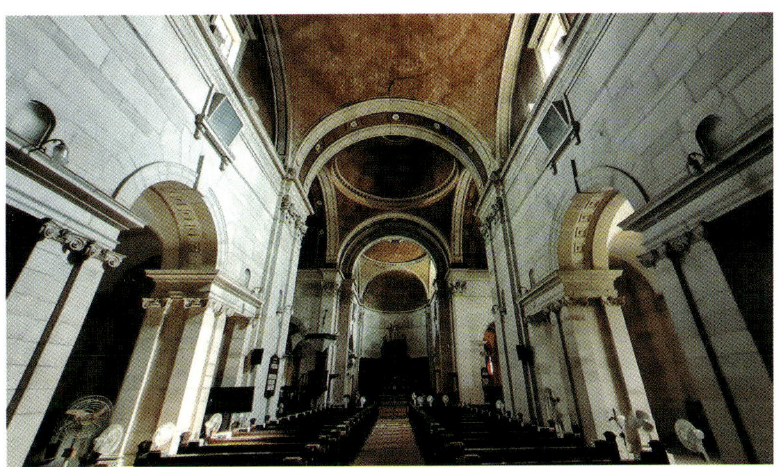

24.37: The interiors of the church revealing its arches and dome — photograph by Madhukar K Bhagat

Besides the above national and provincial capitals, the colonial architecture could permeate as well in other cities such as Agra, Bangalore, Hyderabad, Nagpur, Allahabad, Kanpur, Lucknow, Patna, Lahore, Karachi (latter two now in Pakistan) and many other smaller towns. The establishment of hill stations and resorts such as at Mussorie, Nainital, Shimla, Darjeeling, Ooty and others led to the development of the hill architecture.

Besides the grand palaces, large official complexes and monuments that became the face of British architecture, what also developed were residential colonies, smaller offices, residences, dak bungalows and other structures. Many of these are still littered across different towns and cities. Several railway establishments, railway stations, military cantonments, civil-lines offices in districts, tea estates, churches, museums, art galleries etc., were some other places where pre-independence British architecture found expression. These were structures more connected with the daily lives of the people and less grandiose than the royal residences, and the stately official complexes. Thus, British colonial architecture permeated the social hierarchy and the geographical spread of the country.

INDIAN ARCHITECTURE IN PRE-INDEPENDENCE

The pre-independence period also witnessed the growth of architecture in Indian establishments. These were visible in the palaces of the Maharajahs, the residences of the nobility, as well as in the ordinary houses of the common folks and other structures. While for the common people, traditional Indian architecture continued to rule the roost, the influence of British/European architecture was quite visible in the palaces and residences of the Maharajas and the nobility. Many rulers of the princely states were inspired by the grandeur of colonial architecture or wanted to emulate it. Several wealthy Indian families and zamindars also adopted European architecture and had European firms and architects designing their private mansions. Some glorious examples of these indeed came in New Delhi in the first half of the 20th century (as discussed above). But many exemplary palaces also came up in other cities and towns. Among the grandest of the late 19th century and early 20th century, Indian palaces were; the **Umaid Bhavan Place** of Jodhpur, the **Rambagh Palace** of Jaipur, the **Bangalore Palace** (in Bengaluru), the **Amba Vilas** or the Mysuru Palace (Mysuru), the **Lalitha Mahal** Palace (Mysuru), **Falaknuma Palace** of Hyderabad, **Cooch Behar Palace** (Cooch Behar) and **Laxmi Vilas Palace** (Baroda), besides others.

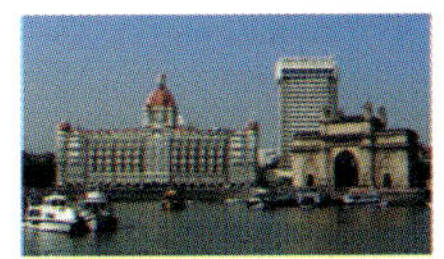

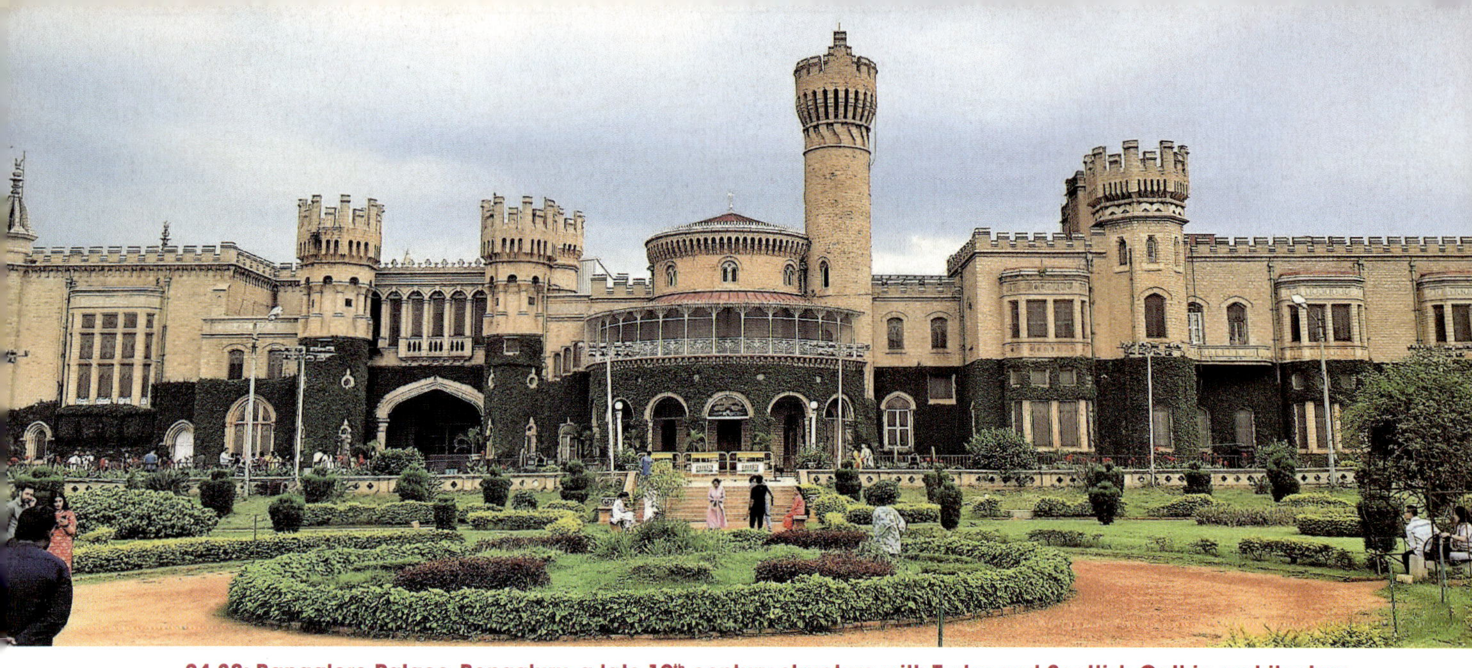

24.38: Bangalore Palace, Bengaluru, a late 19th century structure with Tudor and Scottish Gothic architecture — photograph by Madhukar K Bhagat

The **Umaid Bhawan Palace** of Jodhpur which is considered one of the largest private residences of the world with 347 rooms is indeed a statement of royal opulence. Started by Maharaja Umaid Singh of Jodhpur (in 1929) as a project to provide some work to the famine-stricken farmers and population of the city, it took a long 14 years for completion. The imposing structure designed by Henry Vaughan Lanchester (a contemporary of Lutyens) has an **Indo-Saracenic** design resembling the structures of New Delhi. Besides, elements of Classical Revival and Western Art Deco are also seen. The sandstone structure with the golden dune colour, is especially notable for its double vaulted 103 feet high dome which also has a sky-blue inner dome. Presently, it serves as a hotel and a museum besides as a private residence of the erstwhile Maharaja.

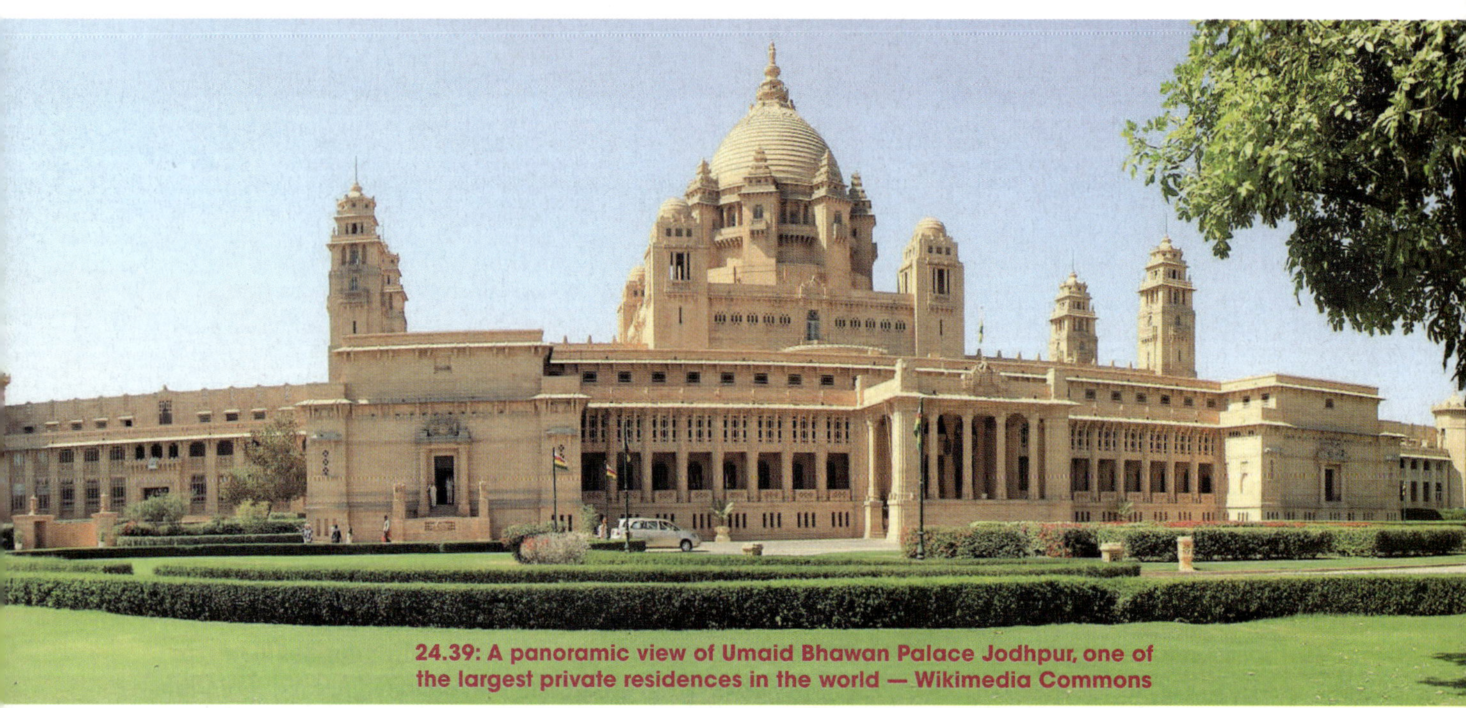

24.39: A panoramic view of Umaid Bhawan Palace Jodhpur, one of the largest private residences in the world — Wikimedia Commons

The **Amba Vilas Palace**, Mysuru, also known as the Mysore Maharajah Palace, is the royal residence of the Wadiyar dynasty of Mysore and was constructed between 1897 and 1912. It was designed by British architect Henry Irwin and is another glorious example of **Indo-Saracenic architecture**. The palace has a mix of features, including the traditional Hindu architecture of the region, Rajput and Islamic styles, besides Gothic architecture. The three-storey structure is capped with a tower having five storeys. Its beautiful arches and pink domes are some of its other striking features. The palace is also the centre of the famous 'Mysore Dasara' and is a popular tourist destination.

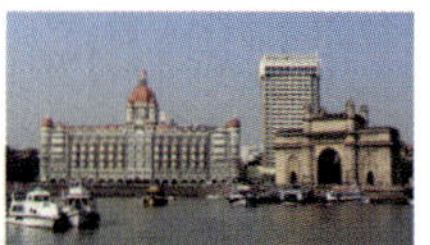

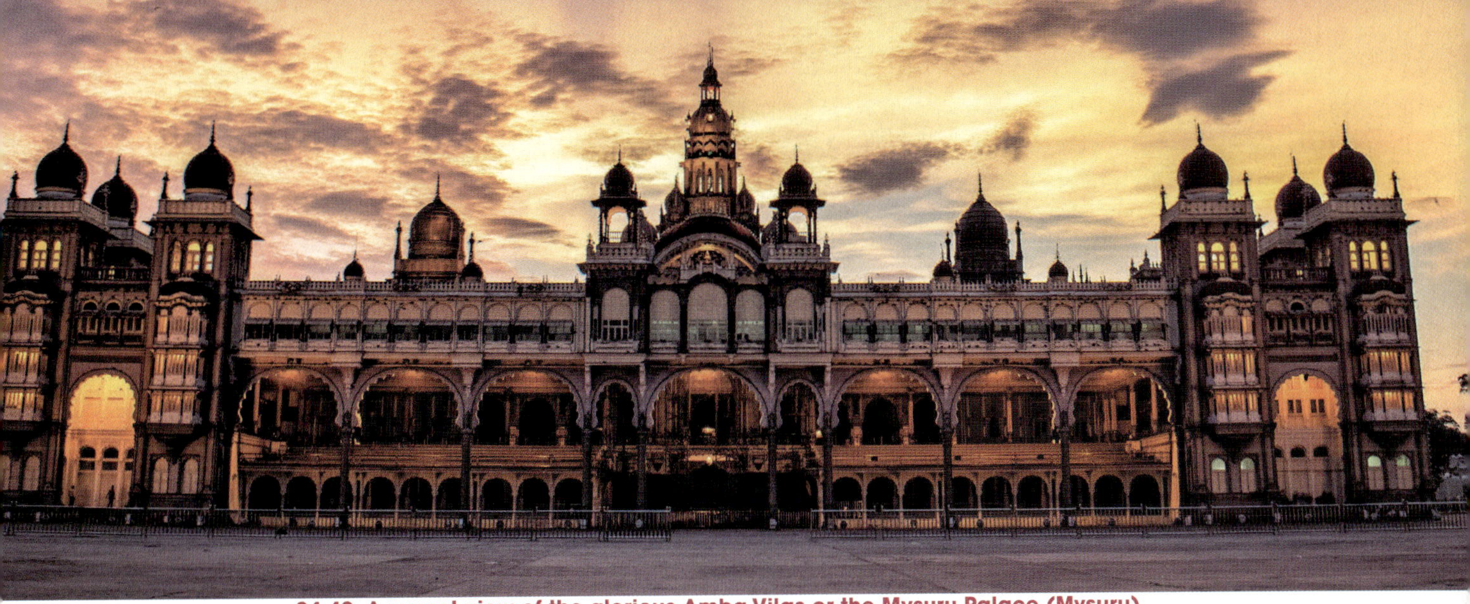

24.40: A sunset view of the glorious Amba Vilas or the Mysuru Palace (Mysuru) — Courtesy, Karnataka State Tourism Development Corporation

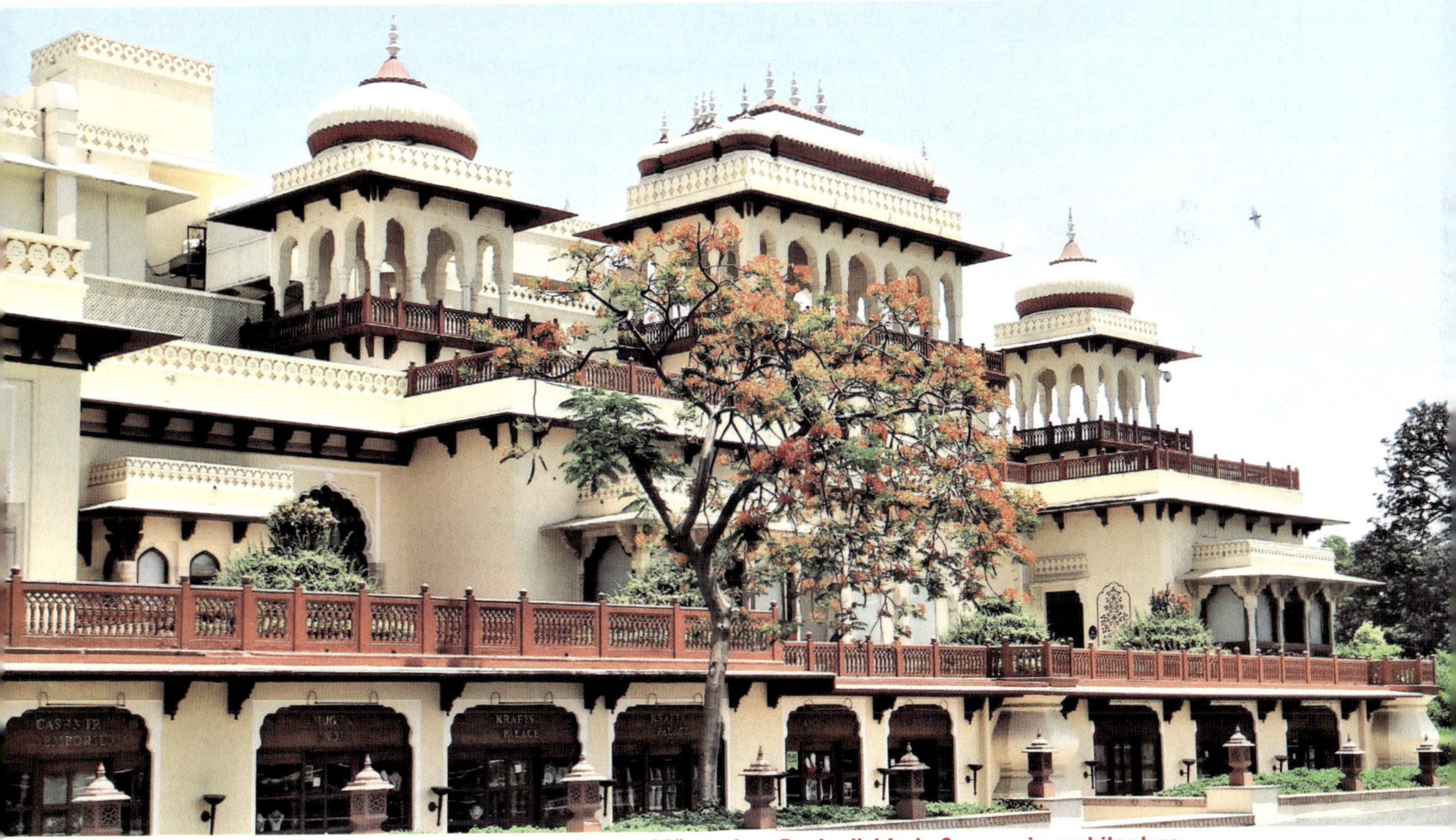

24.41: Rambagh Palace Jaipur, a 20th-century Revivalist Indo-Saracenic architecture, and an example of late Rajput architecture — photograph by Madhukar K Bhagat

POST INDEPENDENCE ARCHITECTURE

The Challenge to Modern Architecture

The independence of India ushered in a new dawn and new challenges for the country. The discipline of architecture, which has a significant bearing on the lives of the people, was no exception to it. The ancient and medieval architecture is remembered more for the grand temples, the great palaces, the imposing forts and other iconic monuments of the past. They indeed reflect the glory of a bygone era. However, these monuments had only a limited interconnect with the daily lives of the common people. The architecture of the commoners of this era is less known and hardly emphasized. The modern British architecture apart from the royal viceregal lodges and the stately secretarial buildings did bring in some elements of the architecture of the masses in the form of the civil lines, the railways, the district offices and other public infrastructure. Besides, some elements of modern construction techniques were incorporated and modern materials also started to be used. However, this was limited largely to fulfilling the needs of the British administration rather than offering a solution to the needs of the common people.

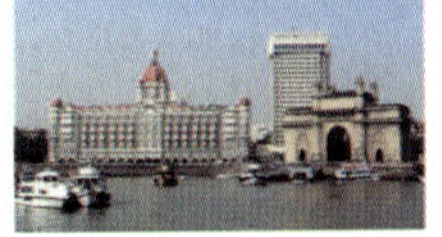

As such, on the eve of India's independence, and for the decades later, Indian architecture faced one of the greater challenges of a growing nation. The landscape of the country was changing from rural to urban. The demand for a new kind of civic and urban infrastructure was rising on account of growing industrialization and changing demography. But above all, there was the pressing demand for housing for the common folks and the teeming millions that had been neglected by the state, perhaps in the past several centuries. Developing low-cost housing, incorporating new technologies, adoption of new materials and developing a style of architecture that could suit the Indian society, culture and environment, were some challenges of post-independence architecture.

Thus, Indian architecture needed to develop a new ethos that could assimilate modern ideas as well as cater to emerging challenges. In the initial years of independence, Indian architecture was caught between two architectural schools of thought, the **Revivalists** and the **Modernists**. While the Revivalists believed in continuing the past architectural tradition, the Modernists wanted to emulate the modern European and American architectural movement. The former was less conscious of the changing times and how ill-suited the colonial architecture was for a country grappling with huge demand and grave socio-economic problems. The architectural vision of the latter on the other hand incorporated lesser consideration of the indigenous elements. Hence, for some time after post-independence, Indian architecture faced a **challenge of evolution**.

Architectural Movements of Post-Independence

The architecture of Chandigarh; designing new cities for India

An important leap in Indian architecture took place in the design of Chandigarh, the capital city of the then state of Punjab. Founded in 1952, it is said to be the dream city of the first Prime Minister of India, Jawaharlal Nehru and it soon came to symbolise the modern architecture of independent India. The chief architect of this project was **Le Corbusier**, a Swiss-French architect. Pierre Jeanneret, Jane Drew and Maxwell Fry were the other associate architects.

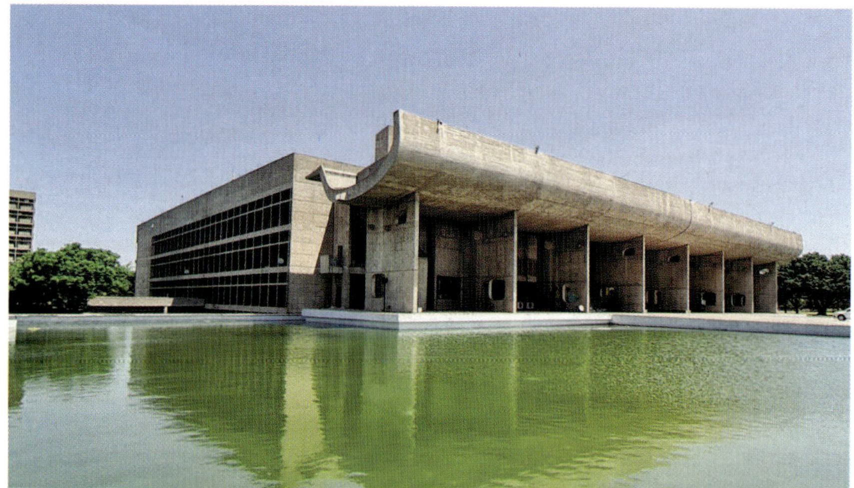

24.42: The Palace of Assembly Chandigarh, a significant architecture of the Capitol Complex of Chandigarh; in view sun breakers and atop it a sickle-shaped rooftop rainwater harvesting system which feeds to the pond below; an unplastered exposed concrete design of the structures by Le Corbusier emphasised on modernism and minimalism in architectural movement — photograph by Madhukar K Bhagat

Located near the foothills of the Shivaliks, the city of Chandigarh was envisaged in the master plan as a post-war 'garden city'. It incorporated the vision of Corbusier of light, space and greenery. The city was conceived with an overall rectangular shape with a grid-iron pattern for roads for faster movement of traffic. Using the metaphor of a human being in the plan, the city was divided into three sections. The topmost or **head** contained the **capitol complex** comprising the political, judicial, and administrative buildings. The **middle portion** or the body housed the residential, educational, and commercial complexes with the commercial complex being at the metaphorical **heart**,

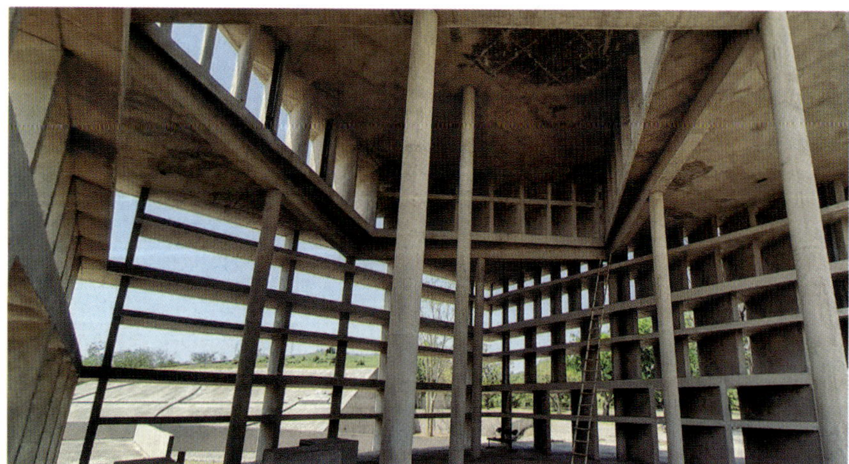

24.43: The Hall of Shadows at the Capitol Complex Chandigarh, an inside view of the open structure that prohibits the entry of sunlight at all times and at all angles; designed by Le Corbusier to show his study and understanding of Sun and its movement; the north side (from which the photo is taken) is open as sunlight never reaches this latitude from the north side; partially visible behind is the Geometric Hill lying in full sunlight — photograph by Madhukar K Bhagat

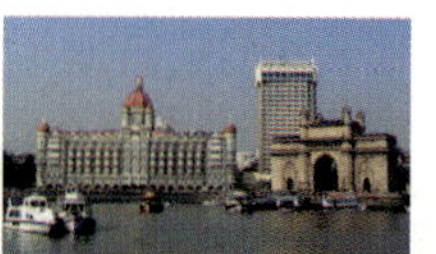

and the arms which were perpendicular to the main axis, had academic and leisure facilities. The **lower portion** or feet consisted of the industrial complex and the railway station.

The city was further divided into sectors in a concept analogous to Indian *mohallas*, or community clusters. Each sector measured roughly 800 metres to 1200 metres with a green strip running north to south and a commercial road running east to west bisecting it. Roads and streets were planned in eight categories in order of diminishing hierarchy (V1 to V8), with V1 representing the arterial roads connecting cities, V2 being the urban city roads, while the V7 being the pedestrian path and V8 the cycling tracks. The sectors were designed to be self-sufficient with community and shopping facilities accessible within them. Sector 17 remains the hub of activities with the large commercial centre, district courts, inter-state bus terminus and parade ground.

In July 2016, **the Chandigarh Capitol Complex** was declared a **UNESCO World Heritage Site** under the inscription of '*Architectural work of Le Corbusier, an outstanding contribution to the modern movement*'. Located in sector 1 and spread over an area of nearly 100 acres, it comprises the **Palace of Assembly** (Legislative Assembly), the **Secretariat Building**, and the **High Court**. Besides, it also includes four poignant monuments; the **Open Hand Monument**, the **Geometric Hill**, the **Tower of Shadows** and the **Martyr's Monument**. Overall, the city of Chandigarh serves as an architectural template for the modern city movement which requires integrating the pressures of housing and commerce, the challenges of modern transport and traffic with the need for a breathing city, green spaces and demands of a growing population.

The low-cost mass housing

Another significant architectural movement was the development of **low-cost, environment-friendly, sustainable architecture** which was pioneered by **Laurie Baker**, a British-born Indian architect. He was renowned for conceiving the low-cost mass housing architecture in the villages and coasts of Kerala in the 70s and later. Having earlier lived in the Himalayas (in Pithoragarh, Uttarakhand) for nearly 15 years and absorbing the penchant of the hill people for environment friendliness and optimization of local resources besides also being deeply inspired by Mahatma Gandhi's philosophy of simplicity, he integrated local resources, environmental concerns and minimalism in developing sustainable mass housing concept.

Significant/notable monuments and structures of Independent India

The latter half of the 20th century also witnessed some notable structures by some renowned architects. These reflected the assimilation of past architectural trends as well as the evolution of new trends in the form of modernist movements. The **Supreme Court** building, whose foundation was laid in 1954, was a prominent structure of the 50s which incorporated the architectural ethos of the previous decades. It was designed by Ganesh Bhikaji Deolalikar in a manner to symbolise the scales of justice. The central beam of the building represents the central beam of the scale with two wings on either side representing the two beams of the scale. With a high dome (90 feet) and collonaded verandahs, it borrows features of 20th-century British Indian architecture and merges with the pre-independence structures of Lutyens New Delhi.

Vidhan Soudha Bengaluru, the largest legislative chamber of India, marks a modern revival of Dravidian architecture. Designed by B. R. Manickam and built in 1956, it borrows features of the temple architecture of the erstwhile medieval dynasties of Chalukyas, Hoysalas and the Vijaynagar Empire. The grand architecture has a front face of nearly 700 feet, a width of 350 feet and is 175 feet tall, endowing it a

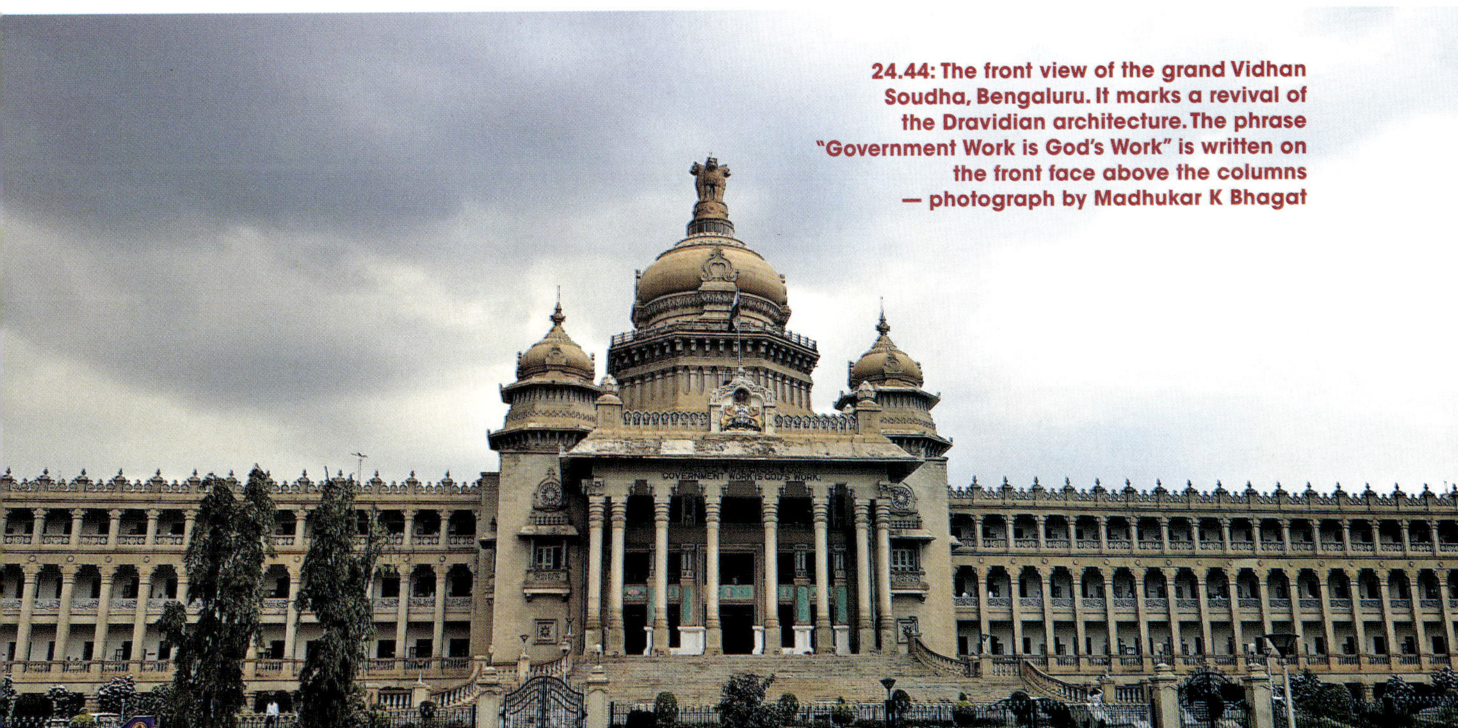

24.44: The front view of the grand Vidhan Soudha, Bengaluru. It marks a revival of the Dravidian architecture. The phrase "Government Work is God's Work" is written on the front face above the columns — photograph by Madhukar K Bhagat

pleasing proportionality. The structure, largely made of granite, can be accessed from four sides and has four domes in its corners. Its imposing front facade with 12 granite columns is approached by a flight of 45 stairs. A large central dome (60 feet in height) is crowned with a replica of the Lion Capital (the State emblem of the country).

Modernist architecture

The decades of the 60s and 70s also witnessed a movement of modernist architecture. These reflected the changing ethos and the emerging needs of modern structures. Some of the notable architectures and structures in this category include institutional buildings of IIM Ahmedabad (1961) by Louis Kahn, IIT Delhi (1961), by Jugal Kishore, IIT Kanpur by Achyut Kanvinde (1963) and IIM Bangalore (1972) by B.V. Doshi. The architecture of **IIM Ahmedabad** incorporates extensive use of red bricks with structures in different geometric shapes, long corridors and supporting arches. It merges modern architectural trends with the indigenous local traditions. The structures of **IIT Delhi** were made of exposed concrete, with the hyperbolic paraboloid roof of the main administration building, emblematic of its modernist architecture. The architecture of **IIT Kanpur** combines modernity with greater openness. With the linking corridors and spaces penetrating through the structures, it integrates the environmental factors (in hot weather conditions) by providing shady and breezy structures. The modernist structures of **IIM Bangalore** also incorporate elements from the structures of Fatehpur Sikri and the temples of Madurai. Its stone architecture is complemented with green spaces. The network of long corridors, courtyards with gardens skylights and pergolas (arched garden structures with a framework for climbing plants), provide for a living and breathing campus. **The Hall of Nations** at Pragati Maidan New Delhi (1972) by Raj Rewal was another unique and modern architecture. It was a large-scale spatial structure in concrete that incorporated Indian innovation in design and execution and took modern Indian architecture to the world stage.

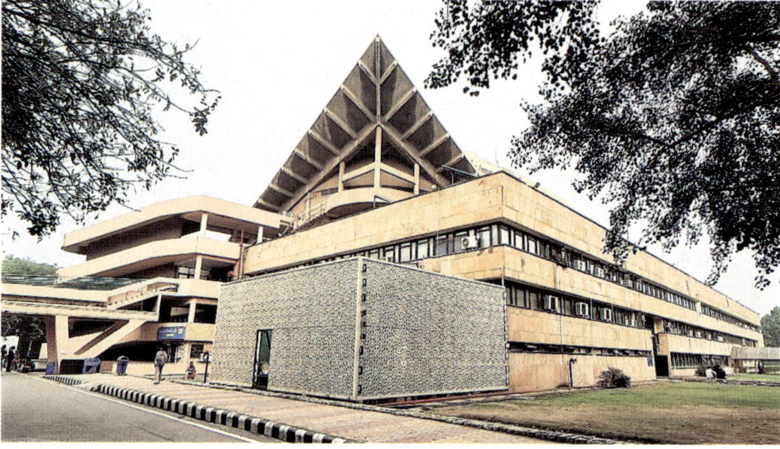

24.45: IIT Delhi, a modernist architecture with exposed concrete and hyperbolic paraboloid roof — photograph by Madhukar K Bhagat

Among the notable **architectures of the 80s and 90s** were; the Lotus Temple (1986) at New Delhi by Fariborz Sahba, Jawahar Kala Kendra (1992) in Jaipur and Vidhan Bhawan (1996) in Bhopal by Charles Correa. The **Lotus Temple,** a Bahai house of worship, that allows entry to the worshippers of all faiths, is

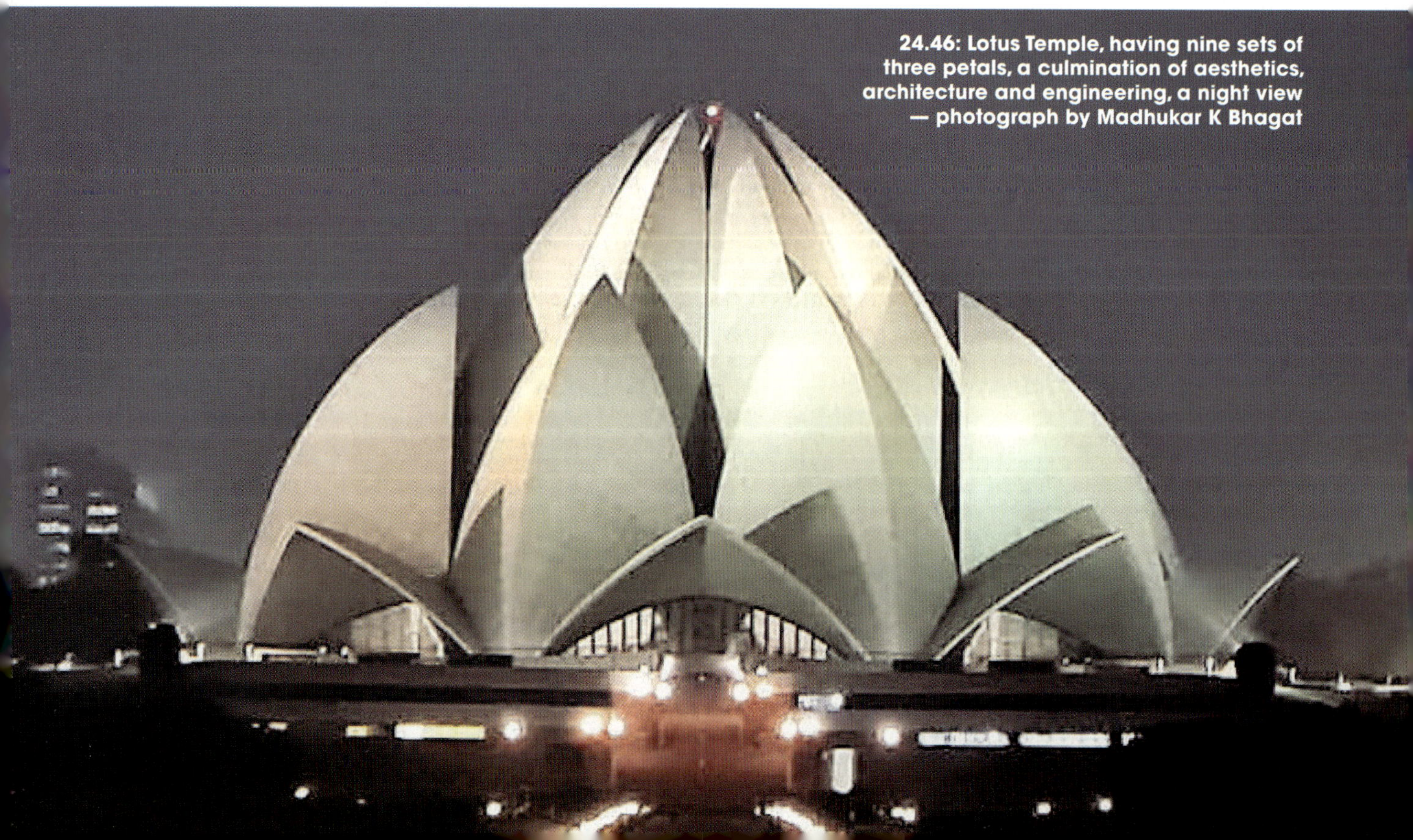

24.46: Lotus Temple, having nine sets of three petals, a culmination of aesthetics, architecture and engineering, a night view — photograph by Madhukar K Bhagat

also designed like a lotus. Its 27 petals clad with marble, are arranged in clusters of three along its nine sides, with entry possible from any of the nine sides to its central hall. An innovative and a marvel of architecture, it accommodates nearly 1300 people in its spacious central hall. The **Jawahar Kala Kendra** draws inspiration from the original plan of Jaipur which is based on the principles of ancient Vaastu Shastra. The architectural plan of the Kendra is based on nine adjoining squares with the central square left vacant as a courtyard. The specific design is based on *Navagraha Mandal* where the design is symbolic of the cosmos with each square representing a planet. The red façade of the structure has a resemblance to the fort structures with no windows on its face. The **Vidhan Bhavan of Bhopal**, another of Correa's works draws inspiration from the concept of Mandala and the Stupa of Sanchi. Located on the edge of a hill with a circular approach to the top the legislative house has a circular design with a large dome resembling the Sanchi Stupa but placed asymmetrically. Rather than designing the Vidhan Bhawan as a monolith, its architecture is unique; for it combines a series of interconnected spaces that still fulfil the role and functions required to be discharged by the structure.

The **Matrimandir,** Auroville, is indeed a unique architecture in all respects. Designed in 1968 by Roger Anger (a French architect) its foundation was laid in 1971 and the construction was completed in 2008.

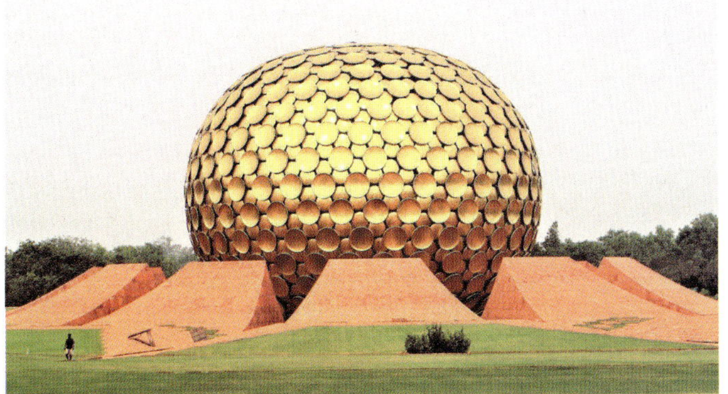

24.47: The Matrimandir at Auroville near Puducherry, a temple designed as a gigantic geodesic dome with a meditation centre within — photograph by Madhukar K Bhagat

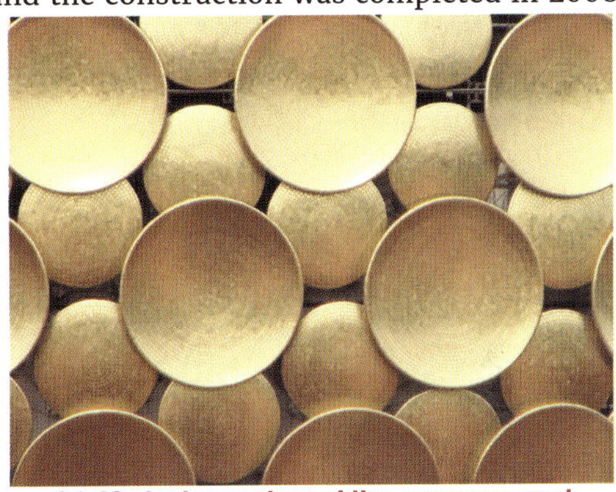

24.48: A closer view of the concave and convex layers of golden discs — photograph by Madhukar K Bhagat

Structurally the temple is a geodesic dome or a flattened sphere. It is covered with golden discs that impart it a glowing outward radiance. The large dome is supported by 12 petal-like red structures. The monument represents a cosmic egg. Its central dome includes a large meditation chamber which is located in the upper hemisphere and is illumined by a giant glass globe reflecting inside the sun's rays. A processional path runs around the chamber. The Matrimandir (or the Temple of the Mother) is inspired by the vision of the Mother (of Aurobindo Ashram, Puducherry). It is considered to be the soul of the city and the area adjoining it is referred to as 'peace'.

Some of the other salient architectures of the 20th century are as follows:

The **Indian Coffee House** (1958), Thiruvananthapuram, designed by Charles Correa, is classified as a neo-vernacular architecture. It has a striking red cylindrical appearance running upwards like a spiral with *jalis* to allow light and air;

India International Centre (1962) New Delhi, designed by **Joseph Allen Stein**, presents a low-profile architecture that creates an informal atmosphere that merges the three separate wings of the centres, each having a different profile, with the adjoining environment;

The Asian Games Village Complex (1980-1982) by Raj Rewal was a large community housing project initially designed for the Asian Games athletes and later made available to the public. It was a venture in low-rise and high-density housing, with several blocks interlinked with streets and pedestrians, with open spaces, commercial and recreational areas, while ensuring a sense of enclosure as well as continuity;

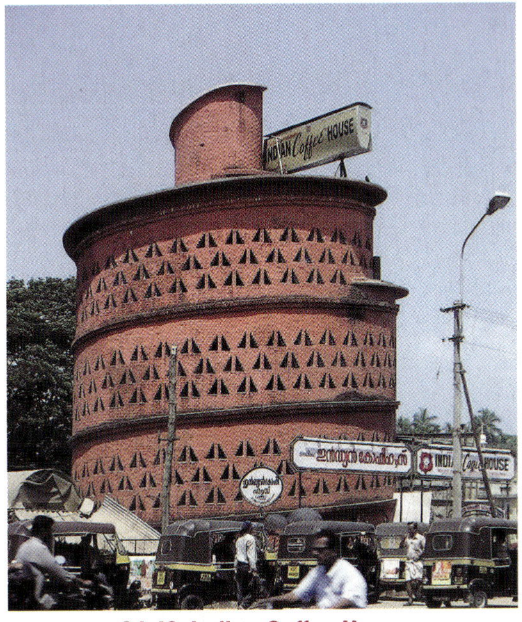

24.49: Indian Coffee House Thiruvananthapuram, a unique spiralling cylindrical structure with *jalis*, merging vernacular with modern architecture — Wikimedia Commons

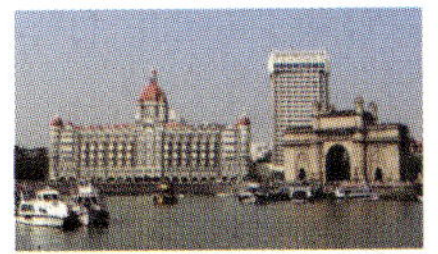

Amdavad ni Gufa (1992), Ahmedabad by Balkrishna Doshi, a partially underground art gallery housing M.F. Hussain artworks, which boasts of multiple interconnected circular and elliptical subterranean spaces with dome-like roofs supported by tree-like columns;

Rajkumari Ratnavati Girls School, Jaisalmer, has a distinctive architecture to withstand the harsh desert conditions. Made of the local yellow sandstone, it has an oval shape with a hollow interior that serves as a courtyard. It has a design to permit winds, especially through the *jalis* in the wall thus withstanding the desert heat.

21st CENTURY ARCHITECTURE

The architectural landscape of 21st-century India has witnessed some grand monuments and some modern architecture. The challenge to this phase of architecture has been manyfold. Indeed, the pressure of the burgeoning population, the demand for economic/cost-effective structures and taking into account the huge diversities of region, weather, culture, local needs etc.,continues. To add to it, are the demands of 'green architecture', manifested in the need for low energy consumption buildings and the use of environment-friendly materials and technology. The changing needs and taste of the people are another salient consideration. But entering into a new century, what is also palpable is the search for an Indian identity in a field otherwise influenced by Western ethos and developments. In this quest, modern architecture has often taken inspiration from ancient and medieval designs while at times it has redefined modernity in the Indian context. Some significant architectural monuments and developments are identified here.

The Central Vistas Redevelopment

Redefining the administrative New Delhi: Over a century ago, when New Delhi was developed as the new capital of the country, the areas adjoining the east-west axis (Kingsway, later called Rajpath and now Kartavyapath) were developed as the focal centre of British administration. Beginning from the Viceroy's House in the west (now the Rashtrapati Bhavan) and ending with the India Gate (in the east) a long corridor and adjoining areas to its north and south (also called the Central Vistas) were developed to house the most important offices and the corridors of power. Presently, these include the Rashtrapati Bhavan, the secretarial complex of the North and South Blocks, the Indian Parliament, besides different buildings where various ministries and other organisations function.

A century has taken a toll on some of these structures, while the changing times have put additional demand on many which they were not designed for. The need for more office space, the call for the development of modern infrastructure and other factors led the government to take a decision, to **redevelop Central Vista** along the nearly three-kilometre-long east-west axis. The objective of the project is to **develop new infrastructure** to cater to the needs of the legislature and administration while **restoring or maintaining the original symmetry** along this corridor. While some new structures are to come up, some of the existing structures are to be repurposed. The most important among the new structures are indeed the **new parliament** building and an ensemble of **new secretariat buildings.** The entire project which is likely to be completed in the period 2020-2026 is perhaps among the most significant and ambitious architectural projects of the 21st century.

The **New Parliament of India**, a part of the **Central Vistas Redevelopment project**, already stands completed and was inaugurated in September 2023. Located in a triangular plot of land, the new structure is akin to a large triangle with its vertices chamfered to impart a hexagonal shape, with three long and three short sides. The structure is almost equal in size to the earlier Parliament structure (now called *Samvidhan Bhavan*). It too has a similar two-colour, red and buff sandstone appearance, as its adjoining predecessor. It is designed with a much larger and modern, Lok Sabha chamber (capacity of 888 seats) and Rajya Sabha chamber (capacity of 384 seats). This is to accommodate an increase in the size of the houses in the future on account of a possible delimitation of the current Parliament seats. The structure dispenses with the central hall, a feature of the earlier parliament building. In case of a joint session, the Lok Sabha chamber is designed to accommodate 1272 members.

Designed by the Bimal Patel-led company HCP Design Planning and Management Pvt. Ltd., the New Parliament incorporates elements from the erstwhile Parliament and other structures of the Central Vista. Besides it also incorporates elements from the architectural styles of different parts of the country. It has three main entrance gates christened as the *Gyan Dwar* (the knowledge gate), the *Shakti Dwar* (the power gate) and the *Karma Dwar* (the action gate). These main entrances and the three other entrances

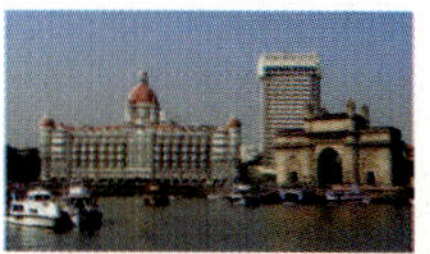

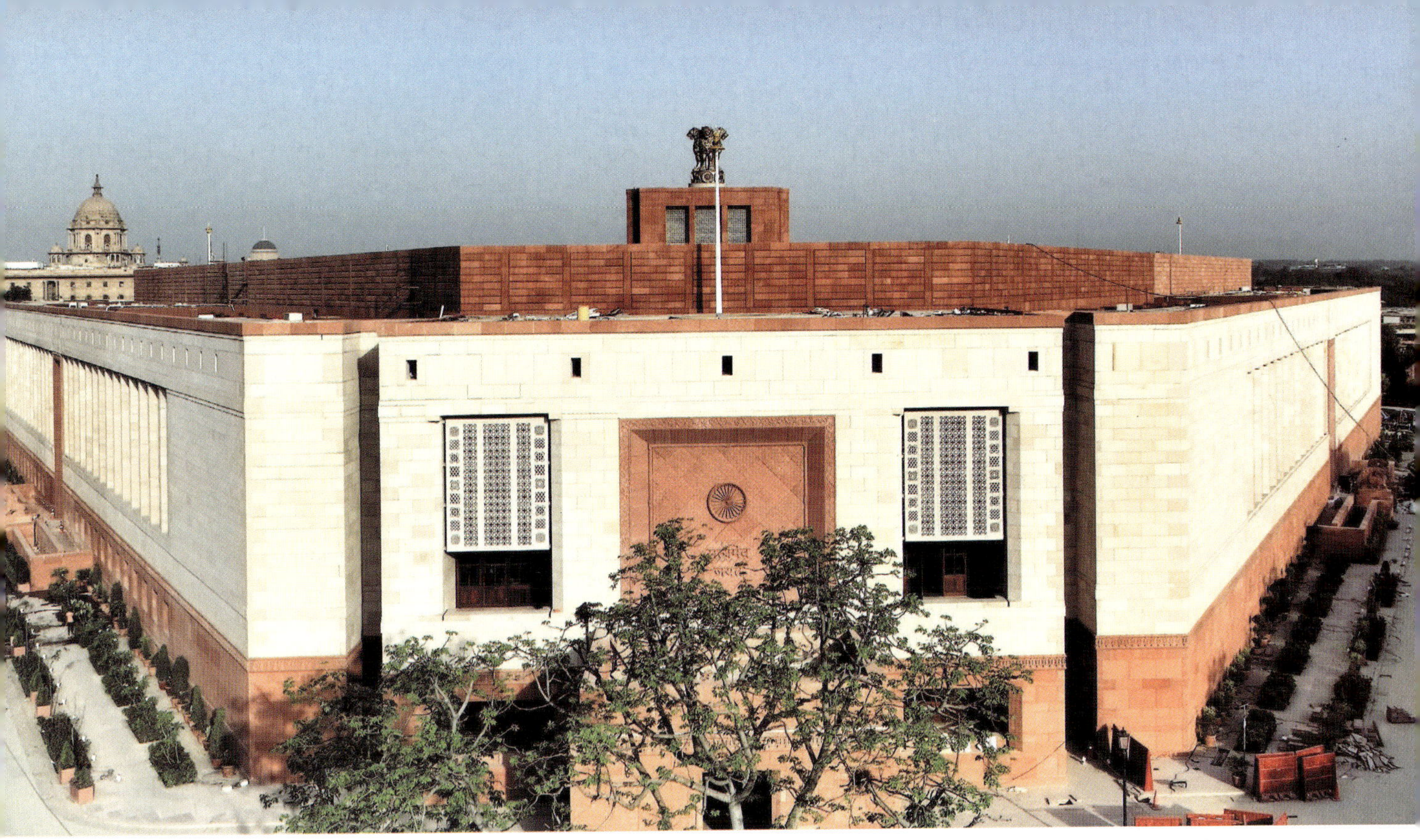

24.50: The New Parliament; in view the front face and two adjoining long sides of the hexagonal structure — Courtesy, Ministry of Parliamentary Affairs

have different guardian creatures, viz. *Gaja* (elephant), *Ashwa* (horse) *Garuda* (king of birds), *Makar* (crocodile), *Shardul* (lion) and *Hans* (swan) each symbolizing different attributes. The use of sandstone *jalis* to permit natural lights, interior design and decoration based on the national symbols and national bird peacock, are some other salient features of its design. The inner courtyard is planted with a banyan tree, the national tree of India. The new Parliament also encloses a variety of artwork showcasing India's regional culture. The structure is also a platinum-rated green building.

Among the 21st-century structures, a few unique architectures that stand out are that of the Pradhan Mantri Sangrahalaya (2022) and the Bharat Mandapam (2023). Located within the premise of Teen Murti Bhavan, New Delhi, Block 2, of the **Pradhan Mantri Sangrahalaya** (Prime Ministers' Museum) is an amalgamation of modernism and symbolism. The structure's external edifice is designed as several layers of flaps which are symbolic of India's Prime Ministers and the citizens. These give the appearance of a palm/hand which upholds the crowning feature of the structure, the Ashoka Chakra, a symbol of Indian nationhood and also embodying perpetual motion and continuity. The structure also serves as a canvas of light and sound show and has modernistic interiors with expansive galleries befitting a futuristic museum.

24.51: The Pradhan Mantri Sangrahalaya (Block 2), merging symbolism and modernity — photograph by Madhukar K Bhagat

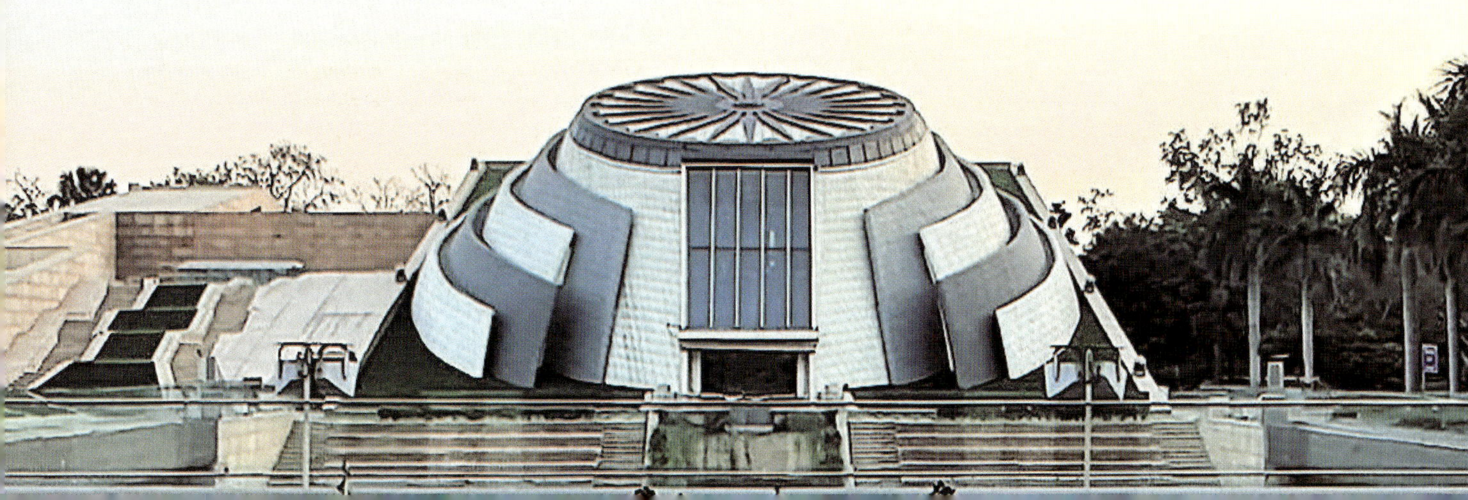

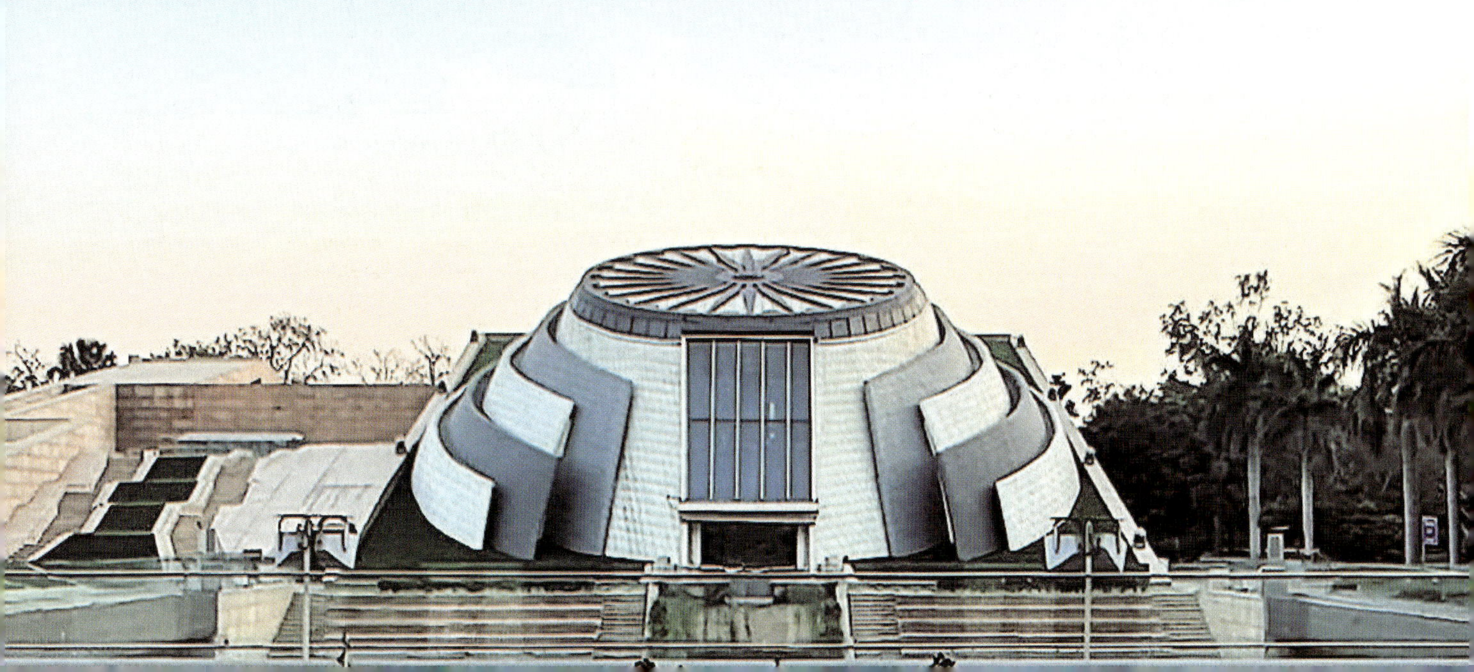

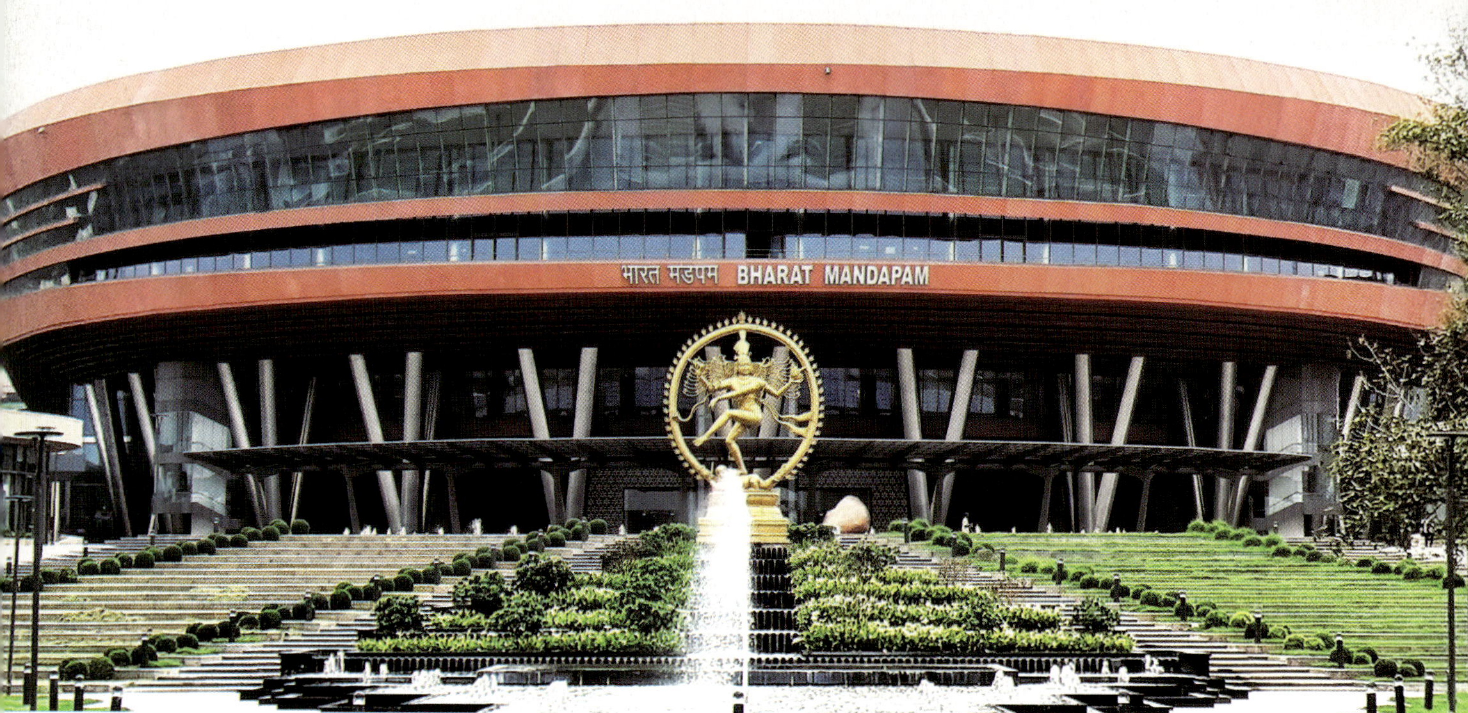

24.52: The Bharat Mandapam, located in Pragati Maidan, New Delhi; a sculpture of Natraj in the foreground, and behind it (on its left) is a large conch shell (light pink) placed on the ground which inspires the elliptical shape of the structure; a confluence of ancient traditions and modern architecture — photograph by Madhukar K Bhagat

The Bharat Mandapam located in Pragati Maidan, New Delhi, is an international exhibition cum convention centre of scale and grandeur unmatched. A centrepiece of the Pragati Maidan Complex, the architecture draws roots from the concept of *Anubhav Mandapam*, a pavilion for public ceremonies, an idea conceived by Basaveshvara/Basavanna, a philosopher, poet and social reformer of the 12th century. Its elliptical shape which is free from angularities is inspired by the elegant form of a conch shell and also from the fluid flow of Yamuna river, near the banks of which the structure is constructed. Standing on the location of the erstwhile Hall of Nations, the project is spread in nearly 123 acres. It comprises modernistic architecture with state of art display space, including a majestic plenary hall of 7000 people capacity and an amphitheatre that can seat nearly 3000. Thus, the architecture draws inspiration from the culture and traditions of the land while weaving it with modern technology.

The Skyscrapers and High-rises: The Changing Skyline of the Modern Cities

The story of modern Indian architecture of the 21st century is indeed incomplete without the account of the skyscrapers and high-rises that dot the skyline of the modern metropolises. While there is no watertight definition of a high-rise or a skyscraper, buildings that are 7 to 10 storeys tall (above 75 feet or 23 metres) are usually referred to as a high-rise while those above 100 metres (150 metres by some standards) or more than 33 storey buildings are reckoned as a skyscraper. The desire to soar high in the sky is an age-old fantasy of humans. It was partially made possible in the earlier centuries by the towering *minars* (like the Qutab Minar) or the *gopurams* and the *shikharas* of the lofty temples. However, these were not the abode of the commoners. The genre of high-rises and skyscrapers is generally considered a modern architectural feature made possible due to new technology and inventions such as lifts and escalators and lighter and stronger construction materials like high tensile steel and reinforced concrete etc. The changing demography of the cities, urban pressure and a cultural shift has enabled the mushrooming of such structures in modern metropolises.

In India, the earliest of high rises came up in the metropolises of Chennai (the LIC Building, 12 storeys-54 metres, 1959), Mumbai (Usha Kiran building, 25 storeys-80 metres, 1961), Kolkata (Tata Centre, 1963, 18 storeys-79.2 metres) and Delhi (Vikas Minar, 23 storeys-80 metres, 1976). Post economic liberalization and particularly in the new millennium, urban conglomerates such as Mumbai and Greater Mumbai,

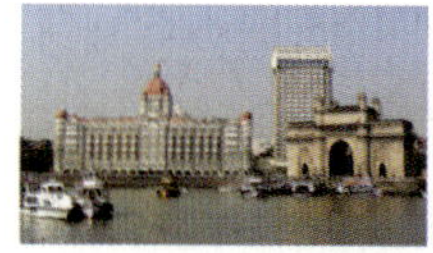

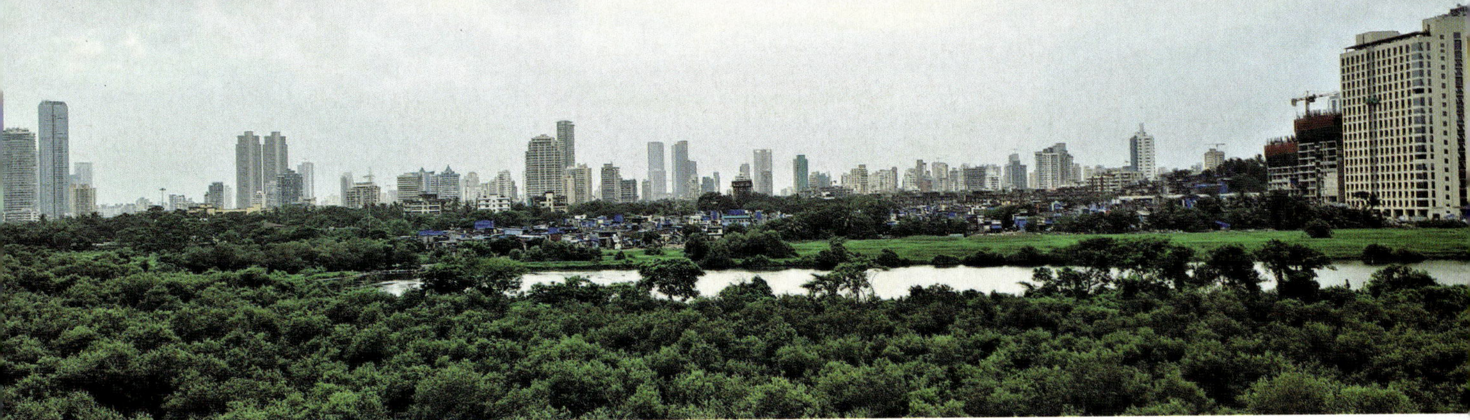

24.53: The changing skyline of Mumbai with the skyscrapers competing with the *chawls* and the green cover for the limited urban space available; a trend that challenges the sustainability of modern metropolises. A view from Eastern Expressway, Mumbai — photograph by Madhukar K Bhagat

the National Capital Region (including New Delhi, Noida, Greater Noida, and Gurugram), besides cities like Chennai, Bengaluru, Hyderabad, Pune and Ahmedabad have witnessed a boom in such structures. Among the tallest buildings of today are those in Mumbai, and include skyscrapers like **Palais Royale** (Mumbai, Worli, 88 storeys-320 metres, 2024), **Lokhandwala Minerva** (Mumbai, Mahalaxmi, 78 floors- 301 metres, 2023) besides others. 'The 42' in Kolkata (268 metres, 2019), the 'Supernova Minerva' in Noida, the Raheja Revanta in Gurugram, the SPR City in Chennai, and the CNTC Presidential Tower in Pune, are among the highest of skyscrapers in other cities. Today, India has more than 2600 high rises and above 200 skyscrapers, with Mumbai much ahead of other cities in this race to pierce the sky.

But why has the skyline of these cities changed? The increasing economic activities and job opportunities have changed the demographics of these cities, fueling a migration of population from the rural to the urban conglomerates and leading to the emergence of modern and sprawling suburbs. The increasing need for housing, the demand for new commercial and institutional space, and the pressure on urban land accompanied by the increasing wealth of individuals and enterprises, have manifested in the vertical growth of the cities. But besides crucial urban space, these high-rises also offer modern amenities, comfort of living, ease of access to workspace and commercial space, leisure amenities, security and a community life. Sustainability and incorporation of green and modern technology to make the habitat safer and more secure is another factor of consideration. Above all, there is a change in the culture of habitat and work. The high rises that sprung earlier as a necessity borne out of space crunch, have transitioned from being a convenience to becoming a luxury. At times, they have become a symbol of status that is only affordable by the noveau-rich and the uber-rich.

The culture of high rises is now substantially assimilated in the cities of today and their presence can be said to be ubiquitous, despite its consequences. The higher the pressure on land and the greater the economic prosperity, the more is the acceptance of the skyscrapers. Slowly and steadily, the culture of high rises has grown and now it is here to stay. The architecture of these modern megaliths is also steadily undergoing evolution. While the earliest of the buildings were often built in the modernist style with a block/rectangular tower-like appearance and exposed concrete look, the modern skyscrapers display a variety of designs. With cladding of steel, aluminium and glass, these are gleaming structures kissing the rays of the sun. Multi-use designs (viz. residential, commercial and institutional) green spaces and landscaped gardens, varied amenities of entertainment and recreation, energy-efficient designs, and digital access control, are some features that are regularly seen in modern structures.

The shape and aesthetics too have undergone tremendous evolution. Apart from the single block monoliths in vogue, twin towers connected through bridges are increasingly becoming popular (viz. The Imperial at Tardeo Mumbai, Lokhandwala Minerva, at Mumbai), an ensemble of towers (like World One, World View and World Crest at Lower Parel, Mumbai) also occasionally features on the city skyline. Apart from the earlier rectangular or square plan, the modern buildings are also displaying a variety of structures ranging from circles to ovals, to a combination of geometric shapes. Certain towers are even designed with emblematic architecture. The Namaste Tower, Mumbai (310 metres) is designed with its two hotel wings appearing like a clasped hand which is greeting in the *namaste* gesture. Thus,

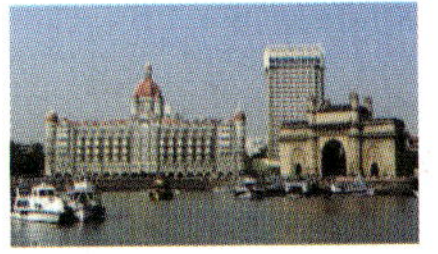

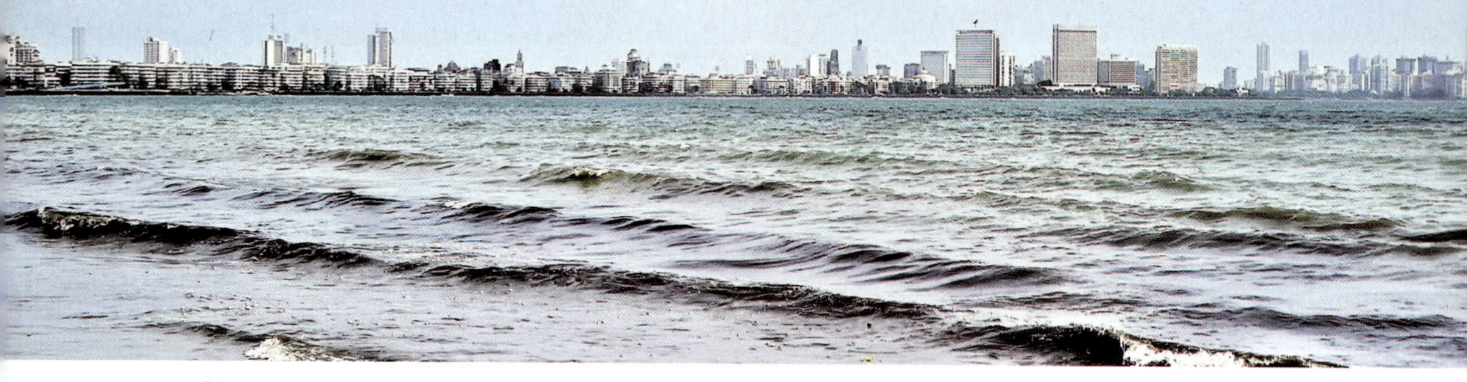

24.54: Mumbai skyline, pierced by skyscrapers and high rises, as seen from Girgaon Chowpatty; an image symbolic of the high-rise architecture of the modern cities — photograph by Madhukar K Bhagat

it incorporates a culture of welcome in its architecture suited to the service industry of hotels. The Cybertecture Egg, a 13-storey commercial building (in Bandra Kurla complex, Mumbai) has a unique architecture akin to an egg. It as well combines green technology such as wind turbines, photovoltaic panels and a greywater recycling system. The proposed Naga Tower at GIFT city Gandhi Nagar, with its hood-like appearance, is said to be a modernist architectural interpretation of a cobra (*naga*) which is described as the 'guardian of the city'. Besides the above, many novel architectural designs are in the offing and projects are in various stages of completion.

Modern Indian architecture is still grappling with the problem of urban housing and mass housing for suburban and rural areas. There is no let up from the rural to urban migration and the immense population pressure which the modern cities face. Besides the continuing sociological and economic challenges, the environmental stress emanating from factors like the changing weather pattern has emerged as a daunting challenge. Quite like other elements of culture, architecture is also responsive to these challenges and demands of time. Its dynamism also factors in the changing social needs and tastes. In its journey of evolution, the state of the economy and the growth of technology and engineering have a crucial bearing. The challenge of sustainability as well as affordability is likely to be some other determinants of the future. But from a cultural perspective, developing an Indian ethos and coming up with modern architecture that is connected to the local/regional environment and roots, is what is going to define modern Indian architecture.

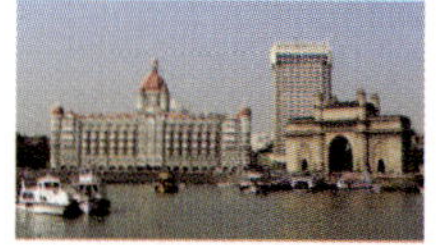

PICTURE GALLERY

INDO-SARACENIC ARCHITECTURE OF THE 20th CENTURY

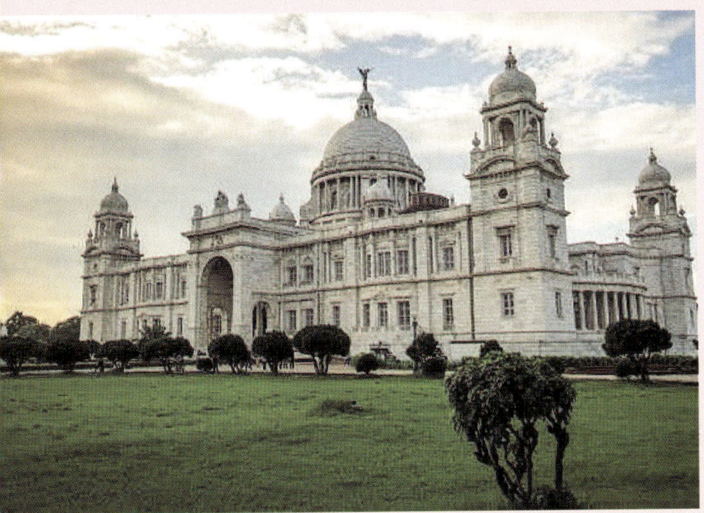

24.55

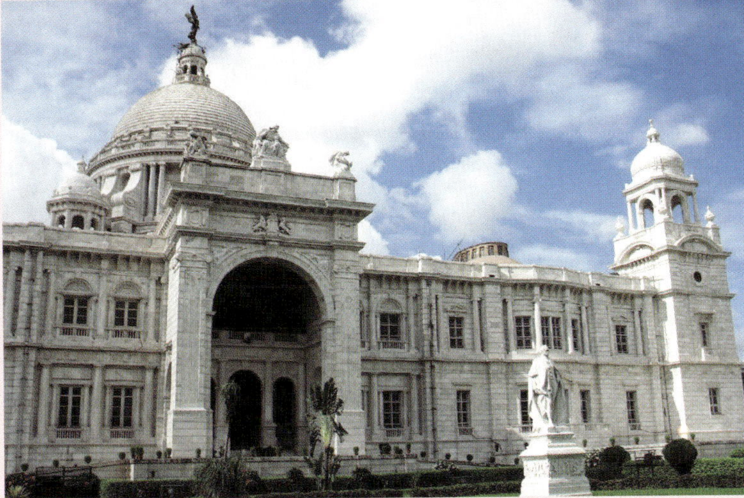

24.56

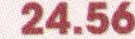

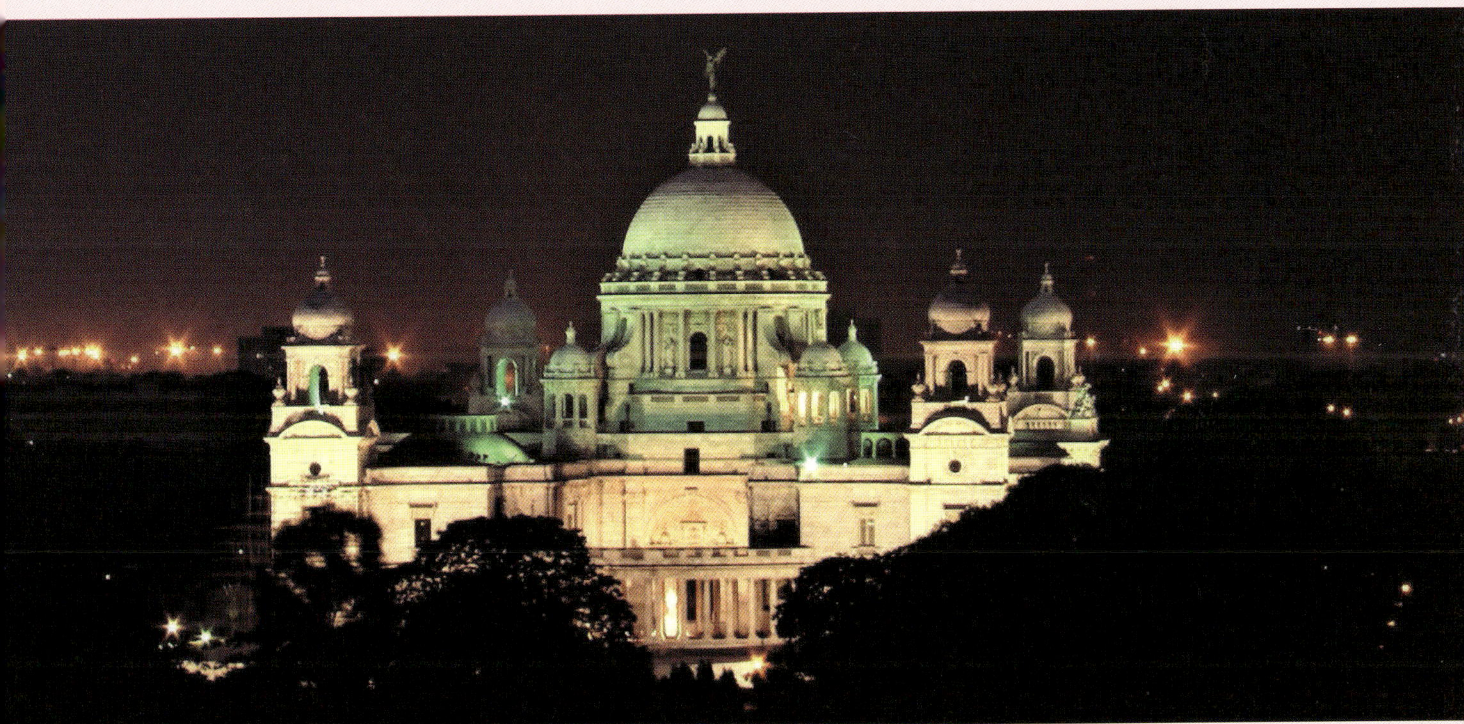

24.57

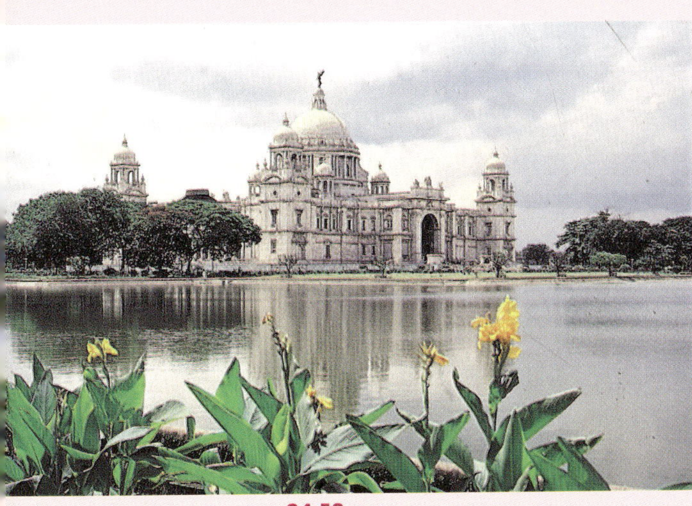

24.58

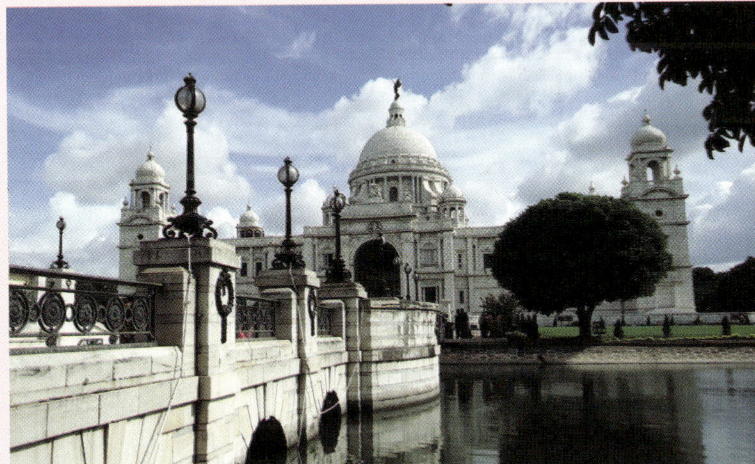

24.59

24.55 - 24.59: Victoria Memorial, Kolkata: an epitome of Indo-Saracenic architecture — Courtesy, Department of Tourism, West Bengal

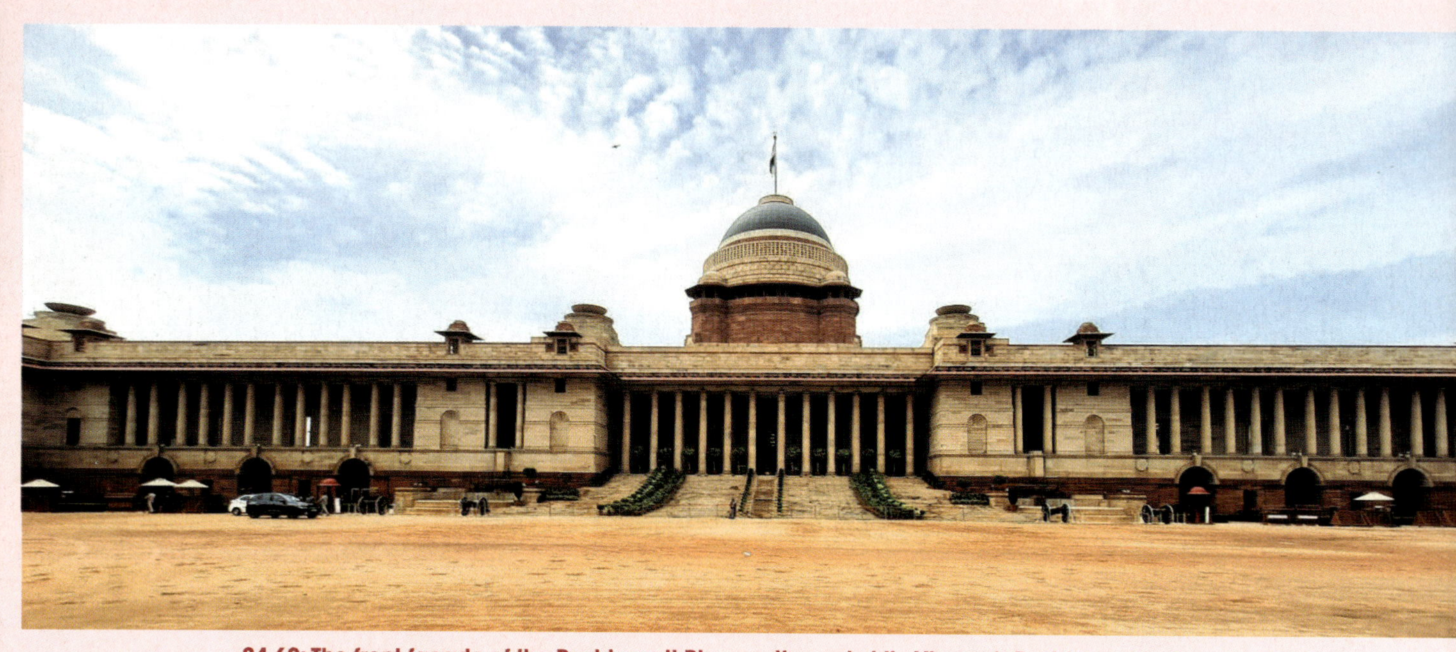

24.60: The front facade of the Rashtrapati Bhavan, the erstwhile Viceroy's Residence, designed as the grandest royal residence of its time, incorporating European architectural elements with Indo-Saracenic design. In view, the large forecourt, the imposing central dome, the Tuscan pillars, the chatris and the royal approach staircase, built in red sandstone (bottom) and buff sandstone.
— photograph by Madhukar K Bhagat

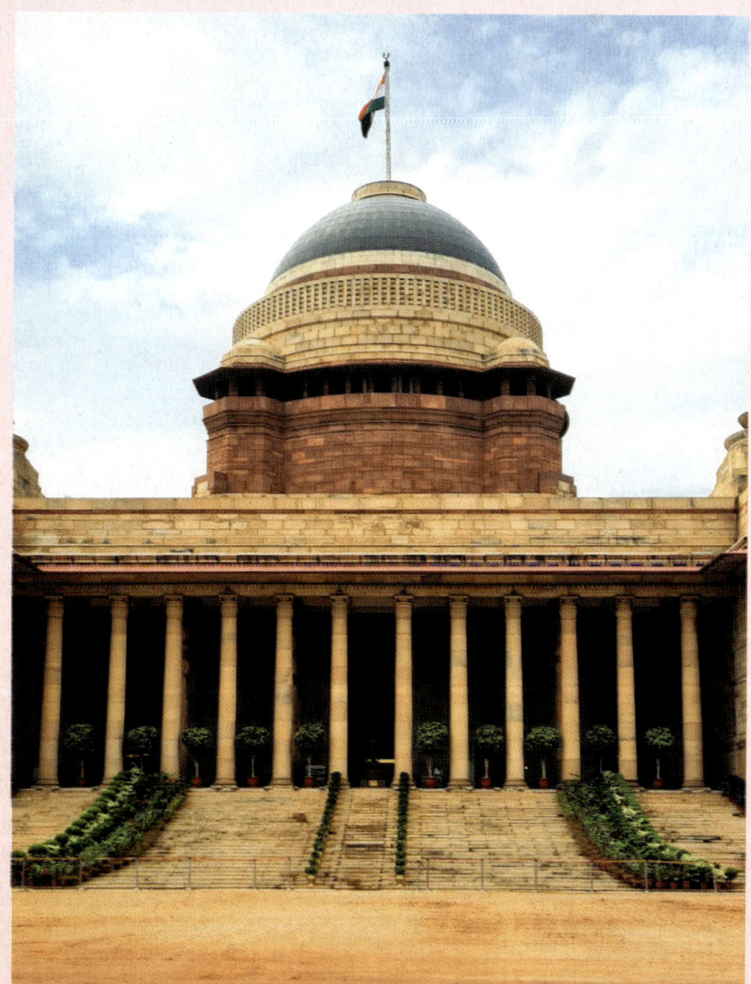

24.61: A close view of the central dome of the Rashtrapati Bhavan, incorporating the design of a circumnavigating balcony and railing atop; features seen in the Sanchi stupa and inspired by it
— photograph by Madhukar K Bhagat

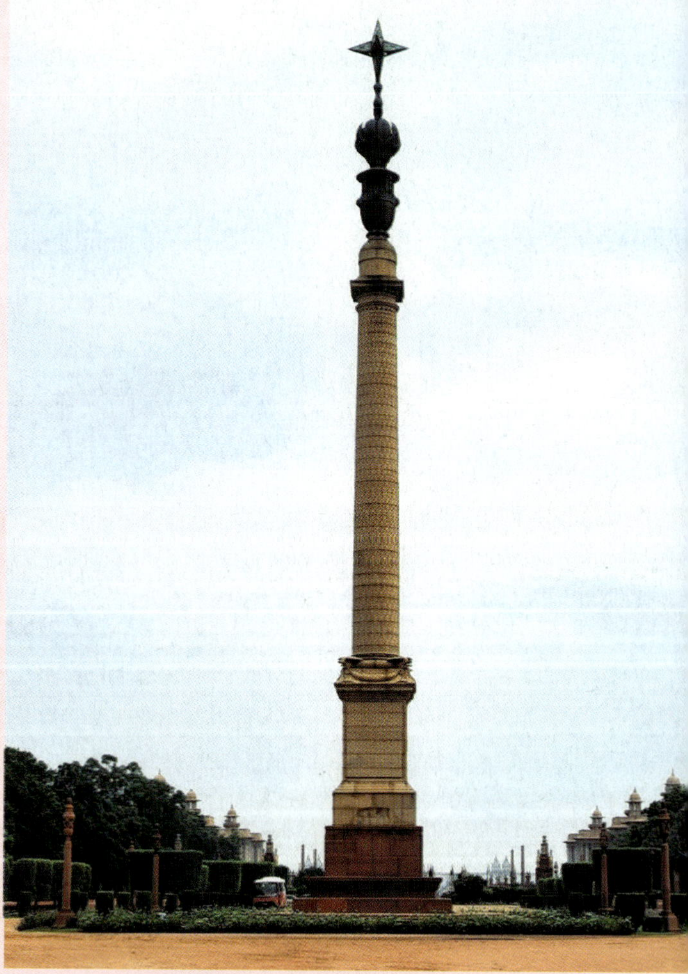

24.62: A close view of the Jaipur Column with a bronze lotus and a six-pointed glass star atop
— photograph by Madhukar K Bhagat

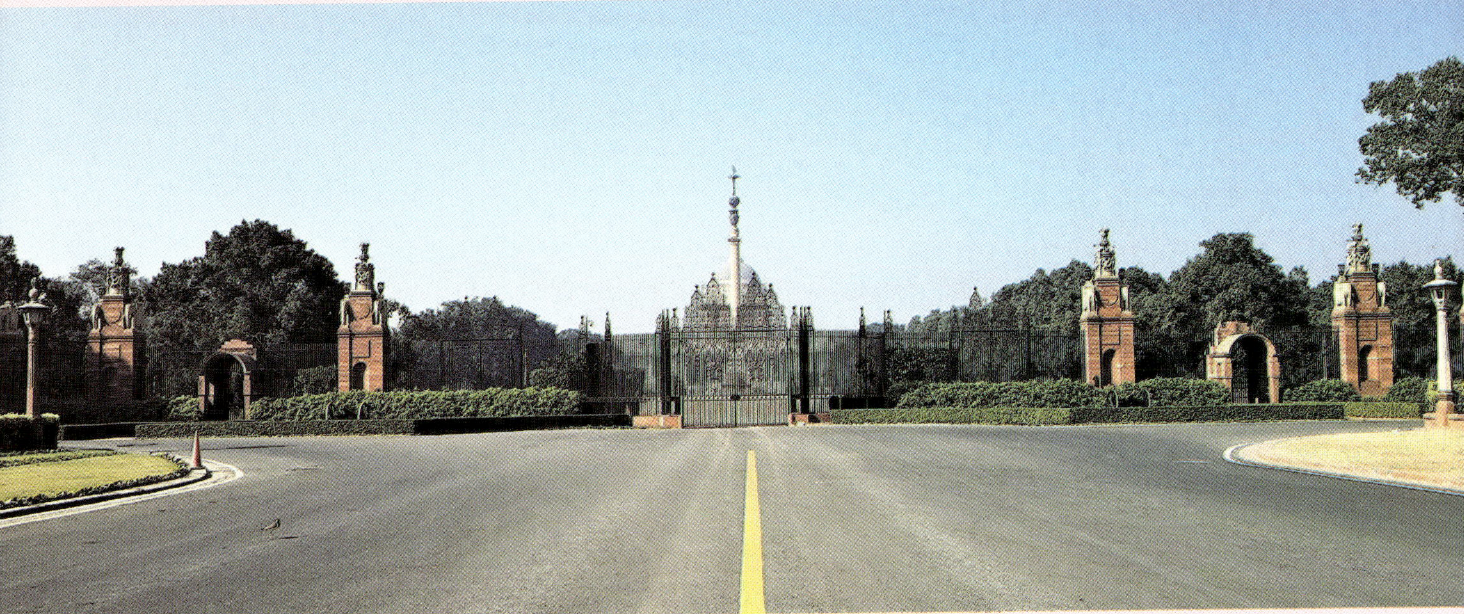

24.63: Panoramic view of the Rashtrapati Bhavan (President's House), in view, the Jaipur Column, the ornate gate and stone pillars with elephant sculptures and Lion Capital atop; on a bright and clear day, picture from Kartavya Path; a grand example of Indo Saracenic architecture — photograph by Madhukar K Bhagat

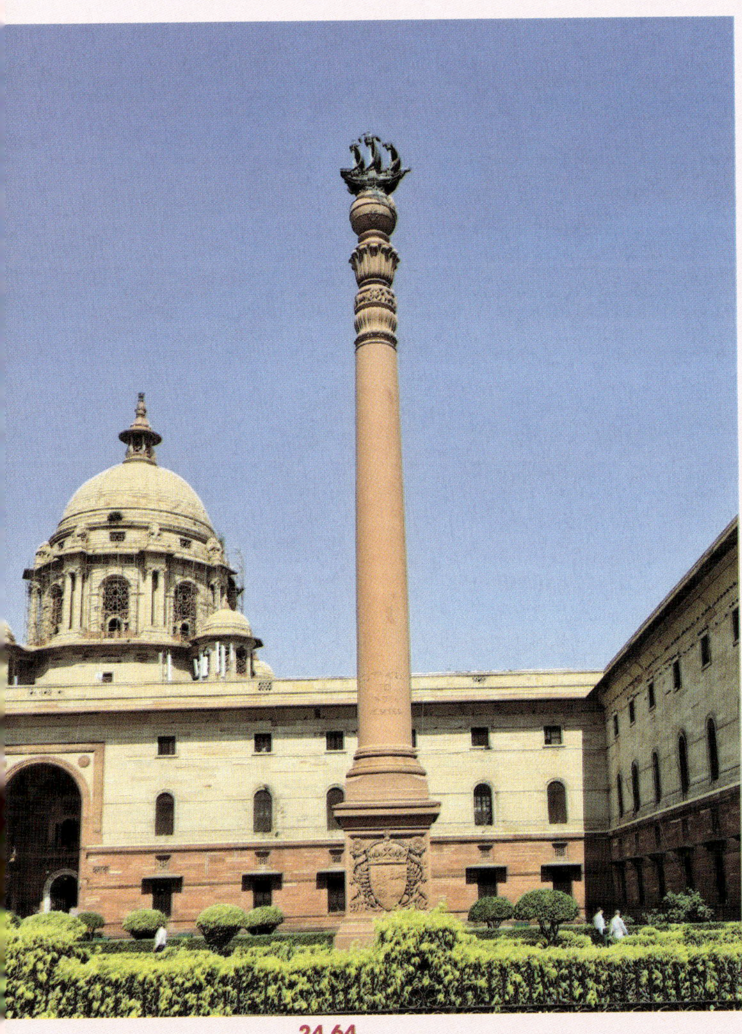

24.64

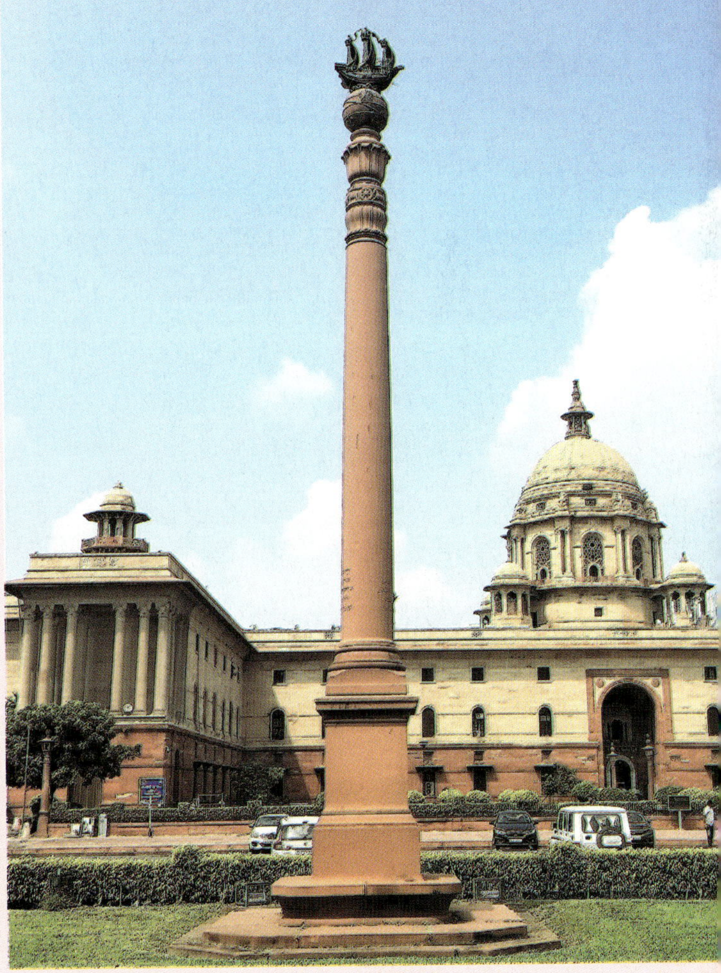

24.65

24.64 & 24.65: The Dominion Pillar of South Africa (Left; front view) in front of North Block, and the Dominion Pillar of Canada (right; rear view) in front of South Block; a part of the ensemble of four Dominion Pillars placed before the Secretariats; a ceremonial gift to British India from the Commonwealth nations. The pillars display a coat of arms at the bottom, a lotus capital at the top and a bronze ship above it, signifying Britain's maritime tradition — photograph by Madhukar K Bhagat

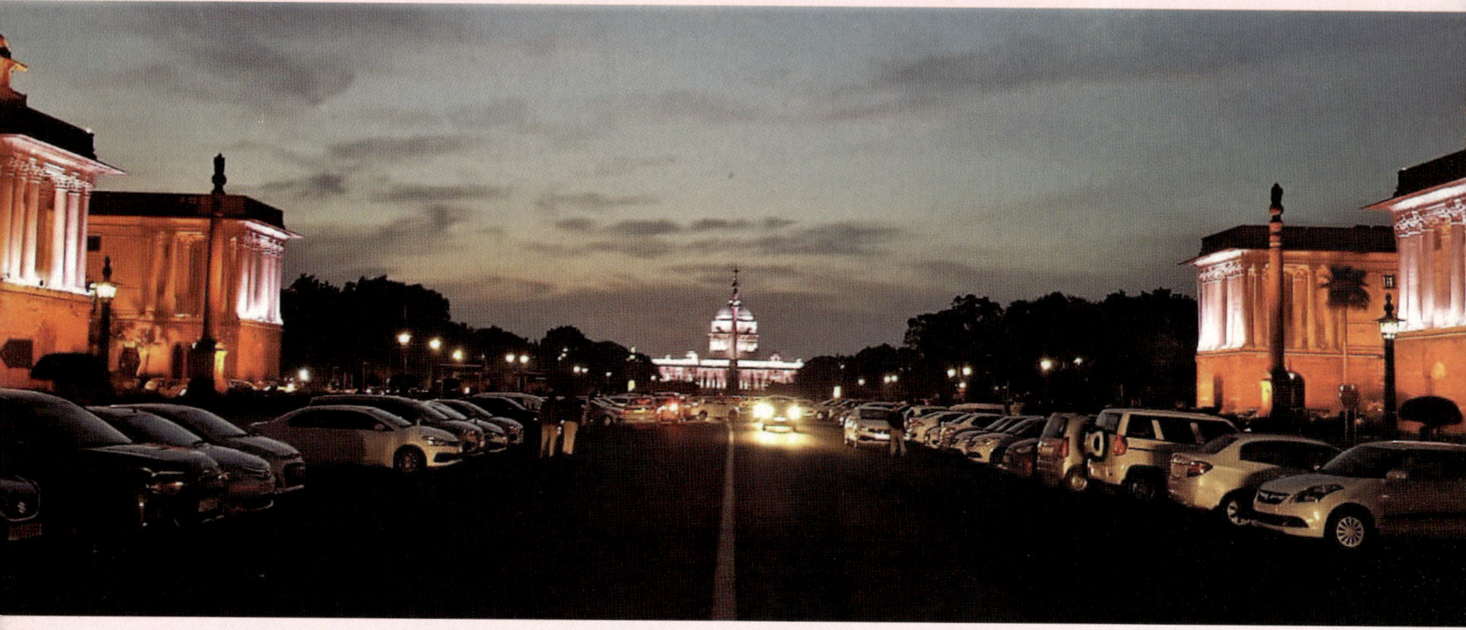

24.66: A busy night at the North and South block; a view from the Kartavya Path of the lit-up President House and the Secretariats — photograph by Madhukar K Bhagat

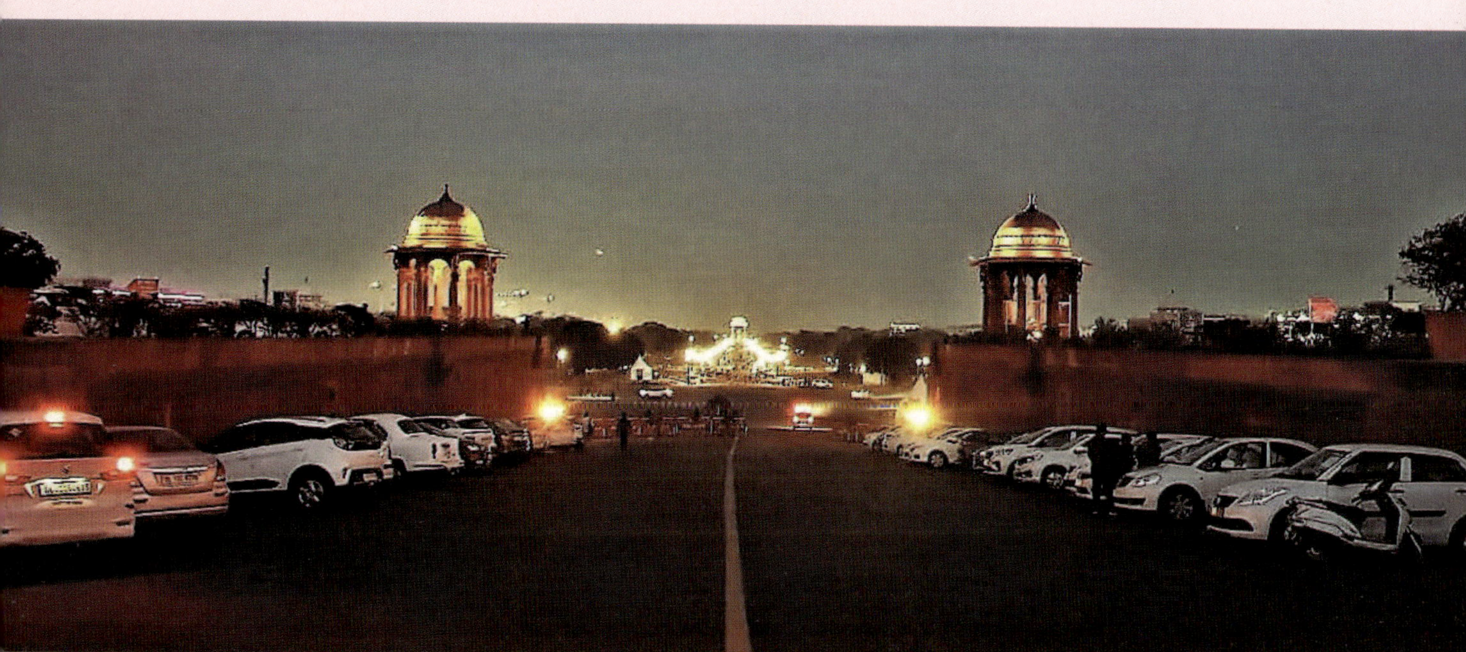

24.67: The gleaming lights of the Kartavya Path, India Gate at a distance; a view from the plaza in between the two Secretariat blocks — photograph by Madhukar K Bhagat

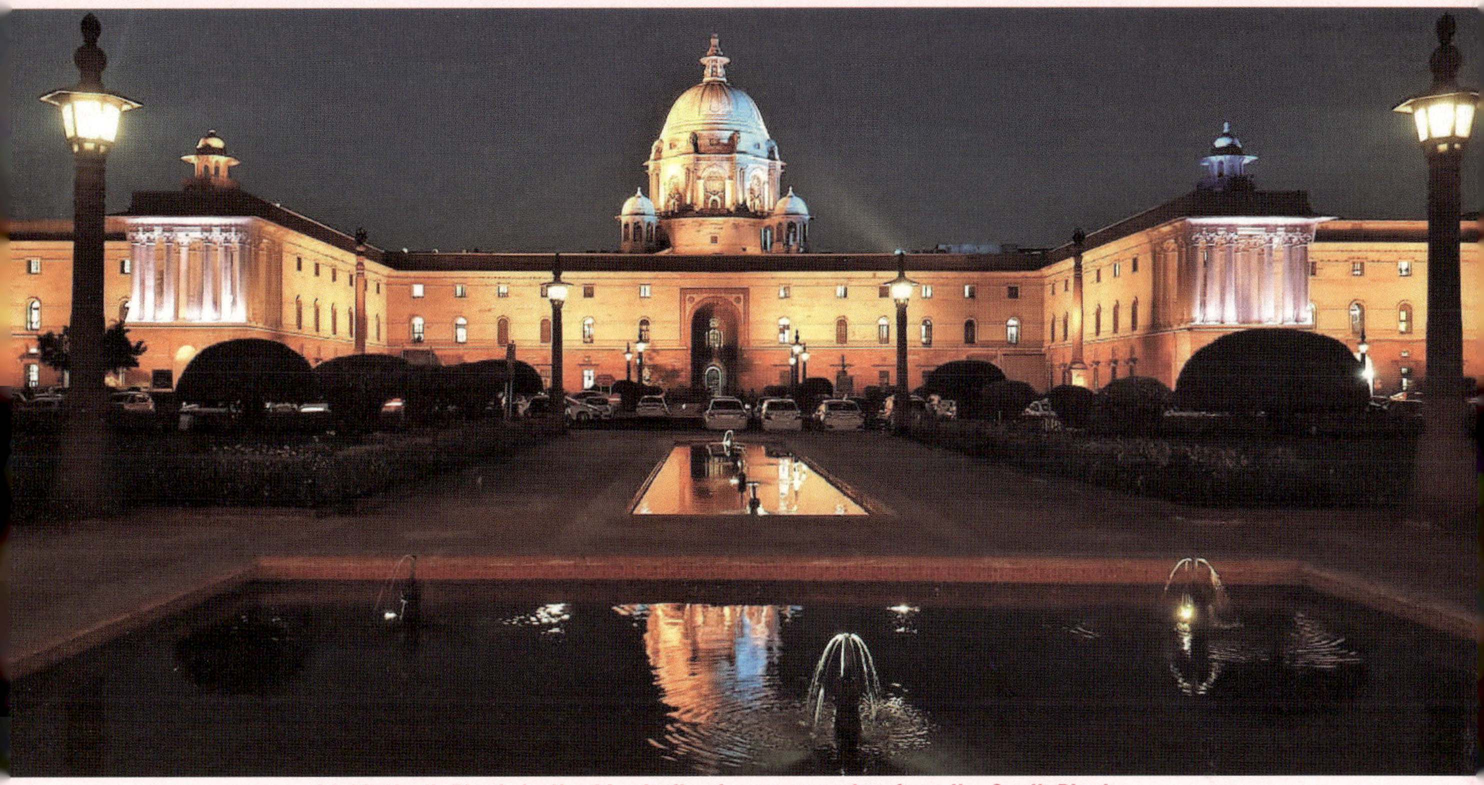

24.68: North Block, bathed in shafts of orange, a view from the South Block — photograph by Madhukar K Bhagat

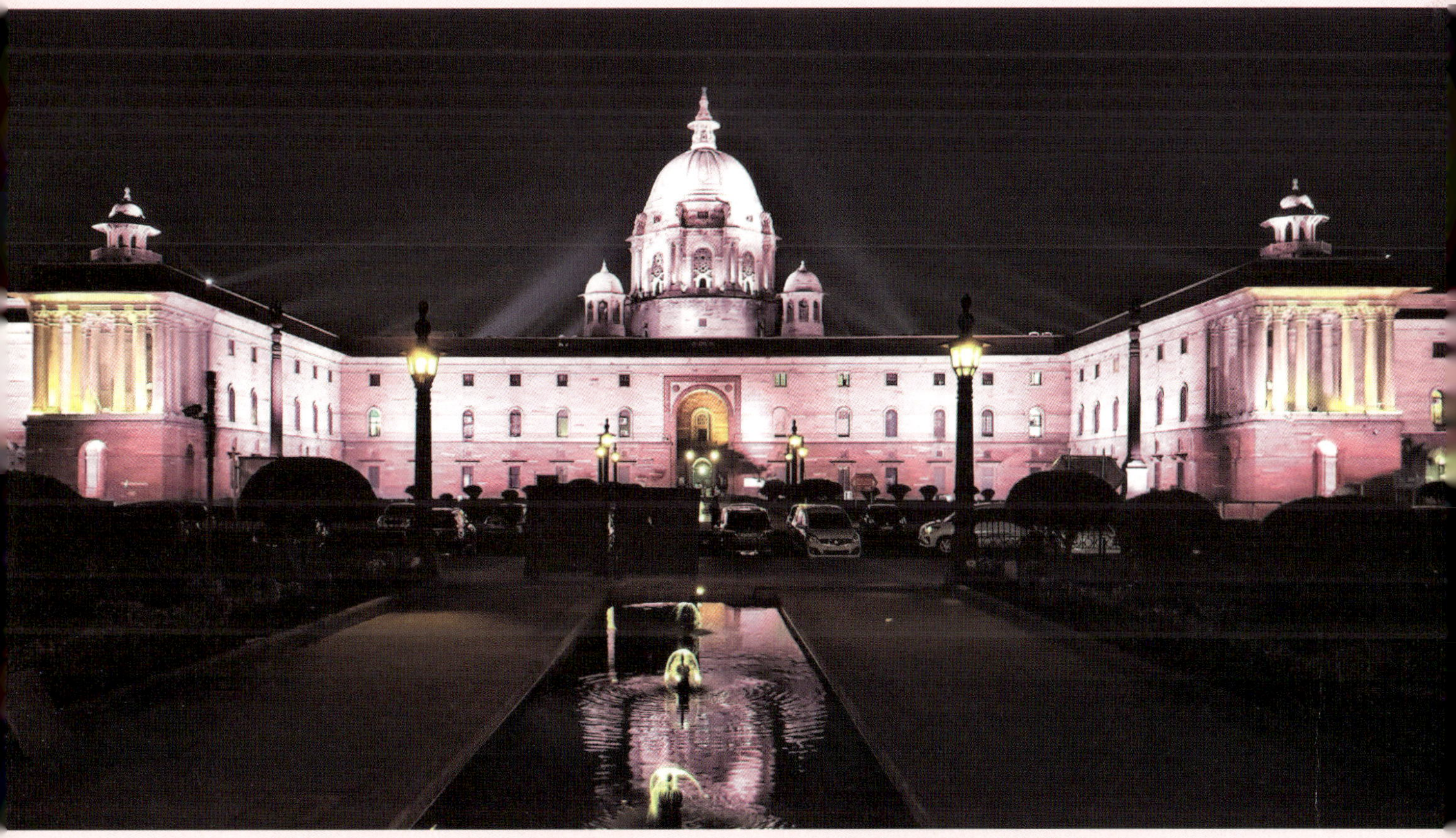

24.69: Glowing in pink, South Block, a night view from the fountains of North Block — photograph by Madhukar K Bhagat

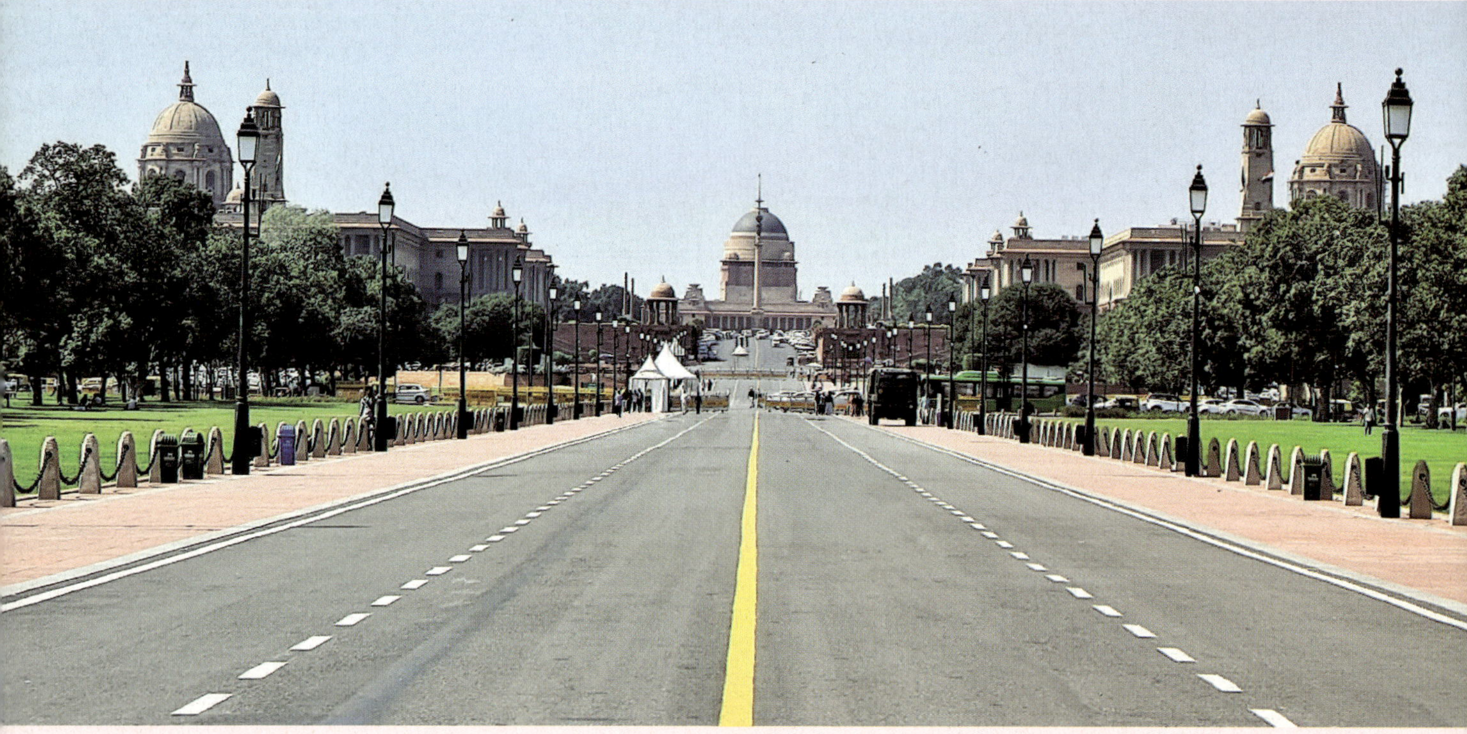

24.70

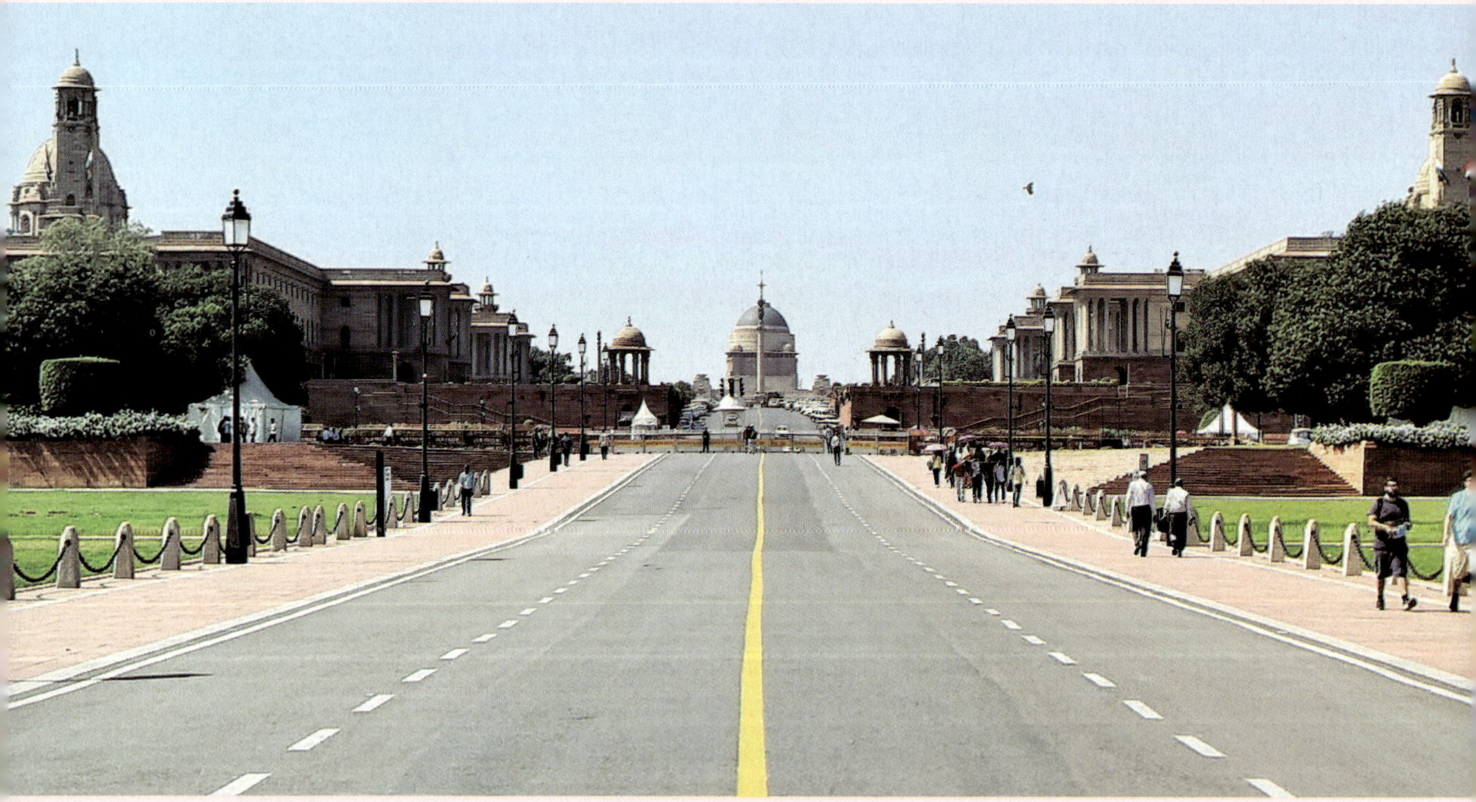

24.71

24.70 & 24.71: A view of the Rashtrapati Bhavan North Block and South Block ensemble from afar on the Kartavya Path (picture above). The base of the Rashtrapati Bhavan including the Tuscan columns, are in full view. However, on moving more towards Vijay Chowk, the base of the Raisina Hill blocks the view of the Rashtrapati Bhavan and only the large dome remains visible (picture below). This was an error in Lutyens's design. While Lutyens wanted the slope of Raisina Hill to be reduced substantially to allow for an unhindered view of the structure designed by him, Baker, who designed the two Secretariat buildings, objected to it as the flat land (plaza) available between the two buildings would have to be considerably reduced creating a functional anomaly in his design. The latter's objections were upheld, but the visual anomaly of Rashtrapati Bhavan remains — photographs by Madhukar K Bhagat

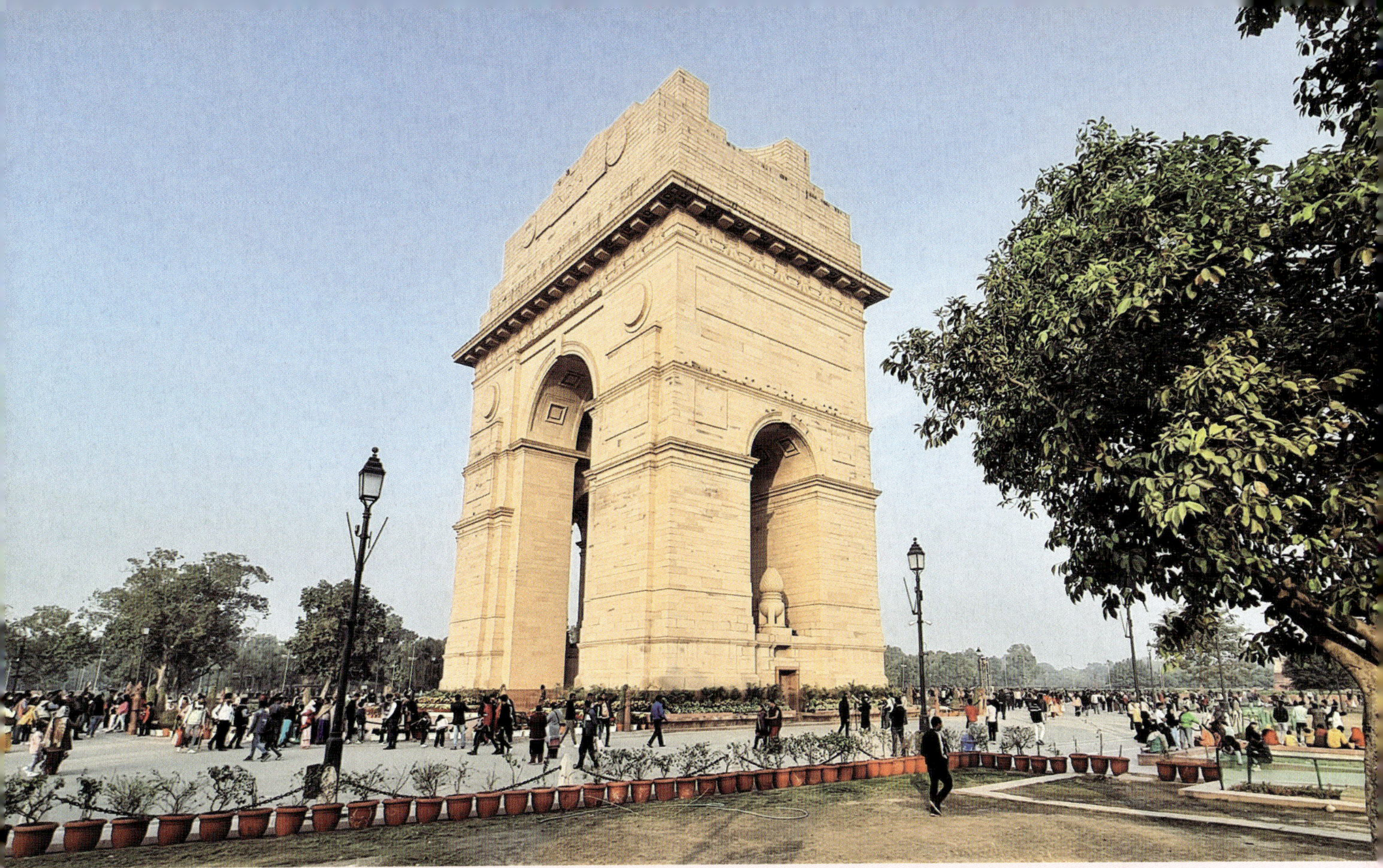

24.72: India Gate and adjoining lawns; an isometric view revealing the side-face architectural features, the front as well as the side-face uprights of the arch carry the names of the martyred soldiers — photograph by Madhukar K Bhagat

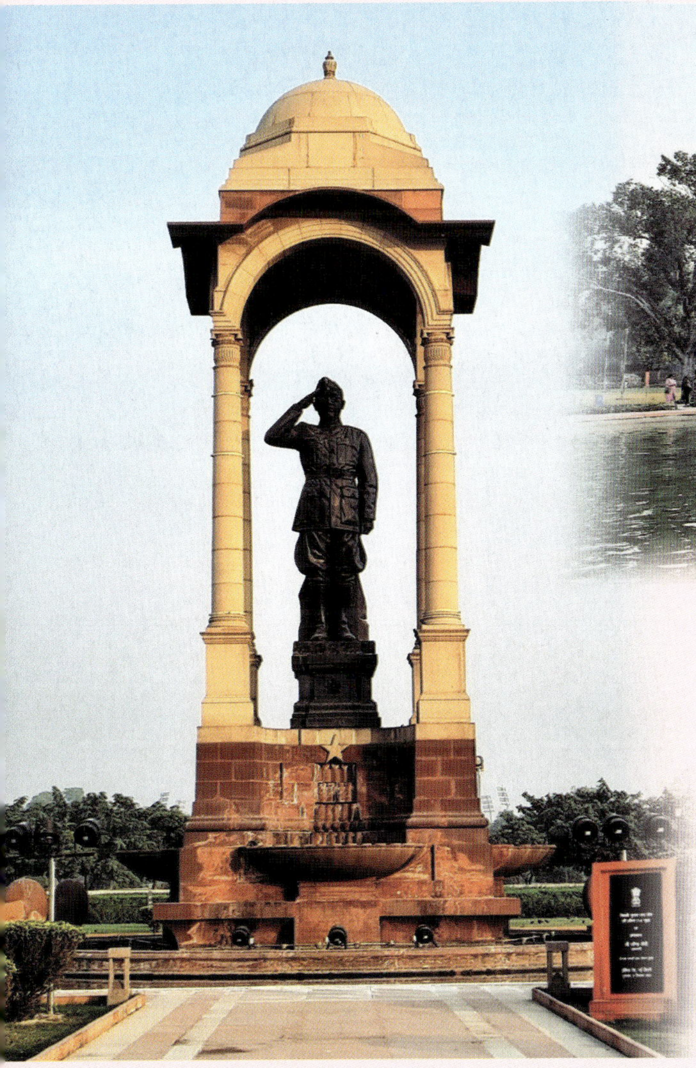

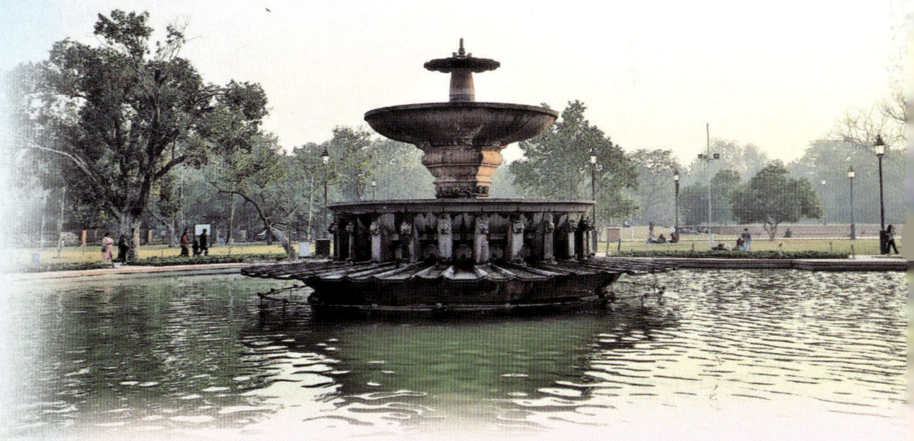

24.73: A beautiful stone fountain standing in a pool of water at India Gate lawns — photograph by Madhukar K Bhagat

24.74: The domed canopy at India Gate which earlier had the statue of King George V, now has the statue of Netaji Subhas Chandra Bose (since 2022). The canopy with four tall columns stands in a pool of water and was inspired by the ornate pavilions of Mahabalipuram — photograph by Madhukar K Bhagat

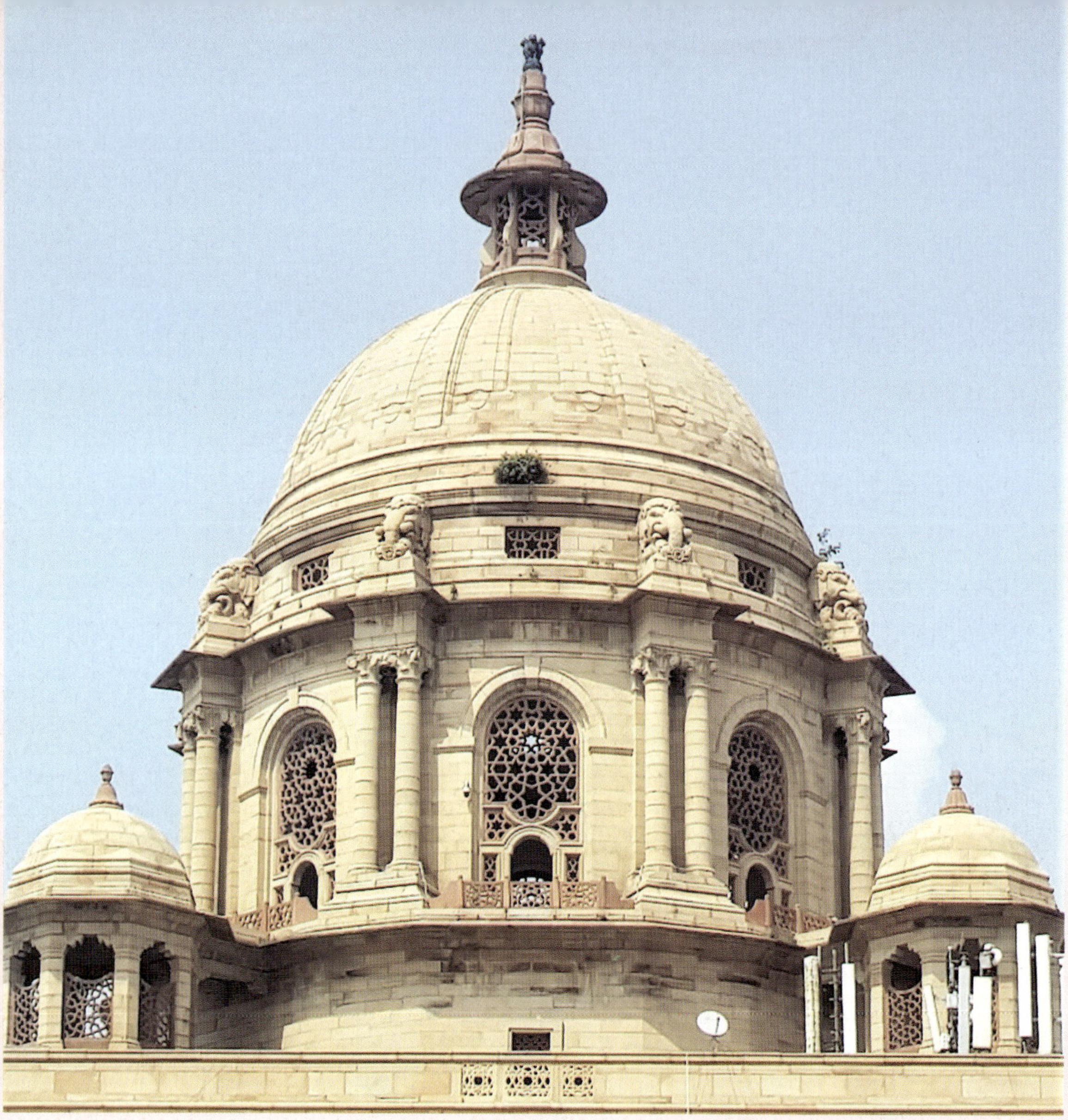

24.75: The central dome of North Block with adjoining *chhatris*; The dome has a cupola atop with an inverted and blooming lotus stone finial which ends in a Lion Capital (made of black stone). Arched doors lead to projected balconies. The central dome along with the adjoining *chhatris* has intricately carved stone *jalis* revealing various geometrical shapes. The hemispherical dome is supported by columns with double pillars, which end in a cuboidal capital with a *chajja* (overhanging dripstone). Above it is a sculpture of an elephant's head and trunk. This along with the *jalis*, *chhatris* and *chajjas*, constitutes the Indian elements in this Baroque-style dome of this Indo-Saracenic British architecture — photograph by Madhukar K Bhagat

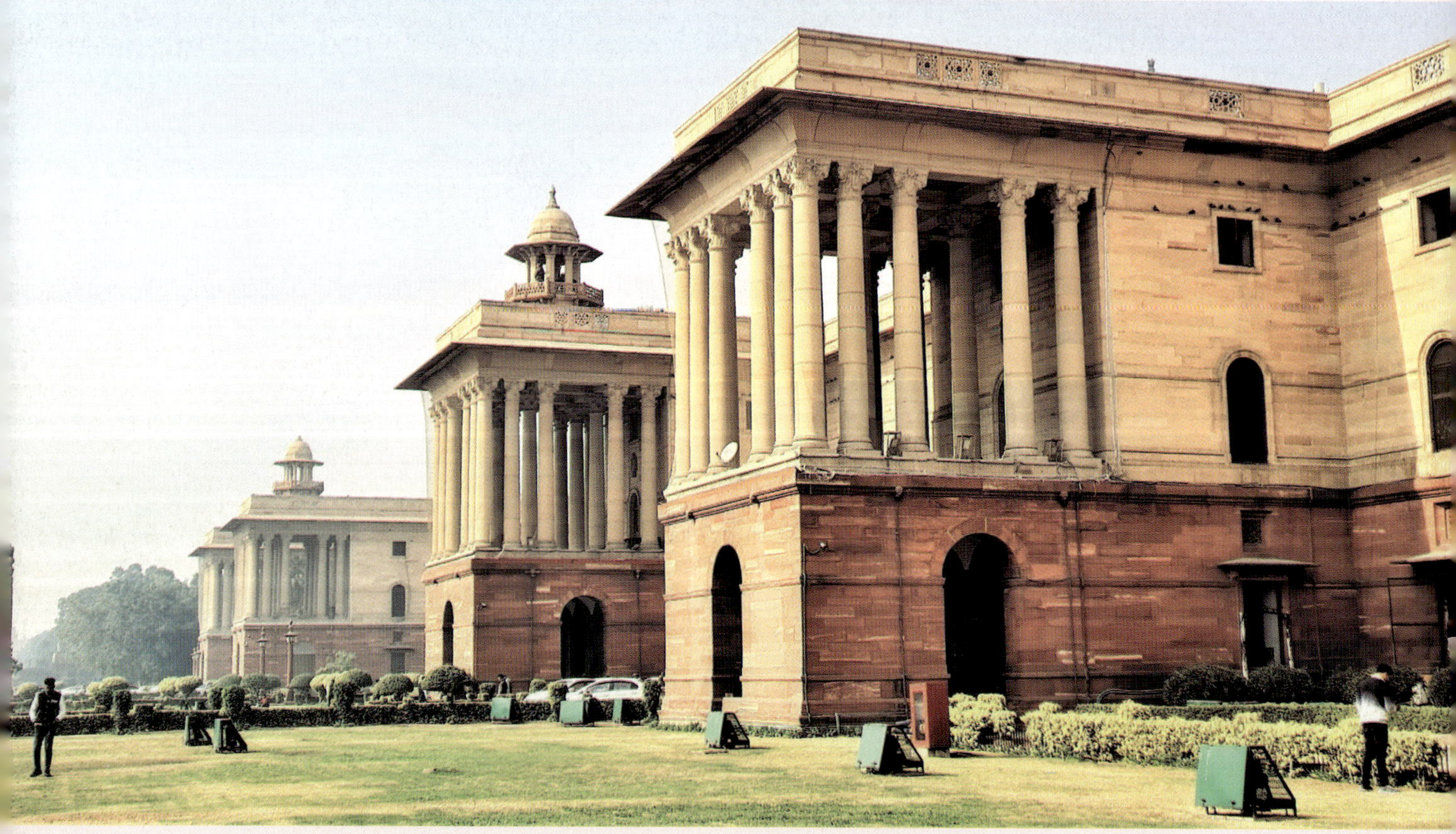

24.76: The colonnaded balconies of the North Block; in view are the 'Pillars of Dominion' (extreme left of the picture), large arched gateways and windows and the *chhatris* atop — photograph by Madhukar K Bhagat

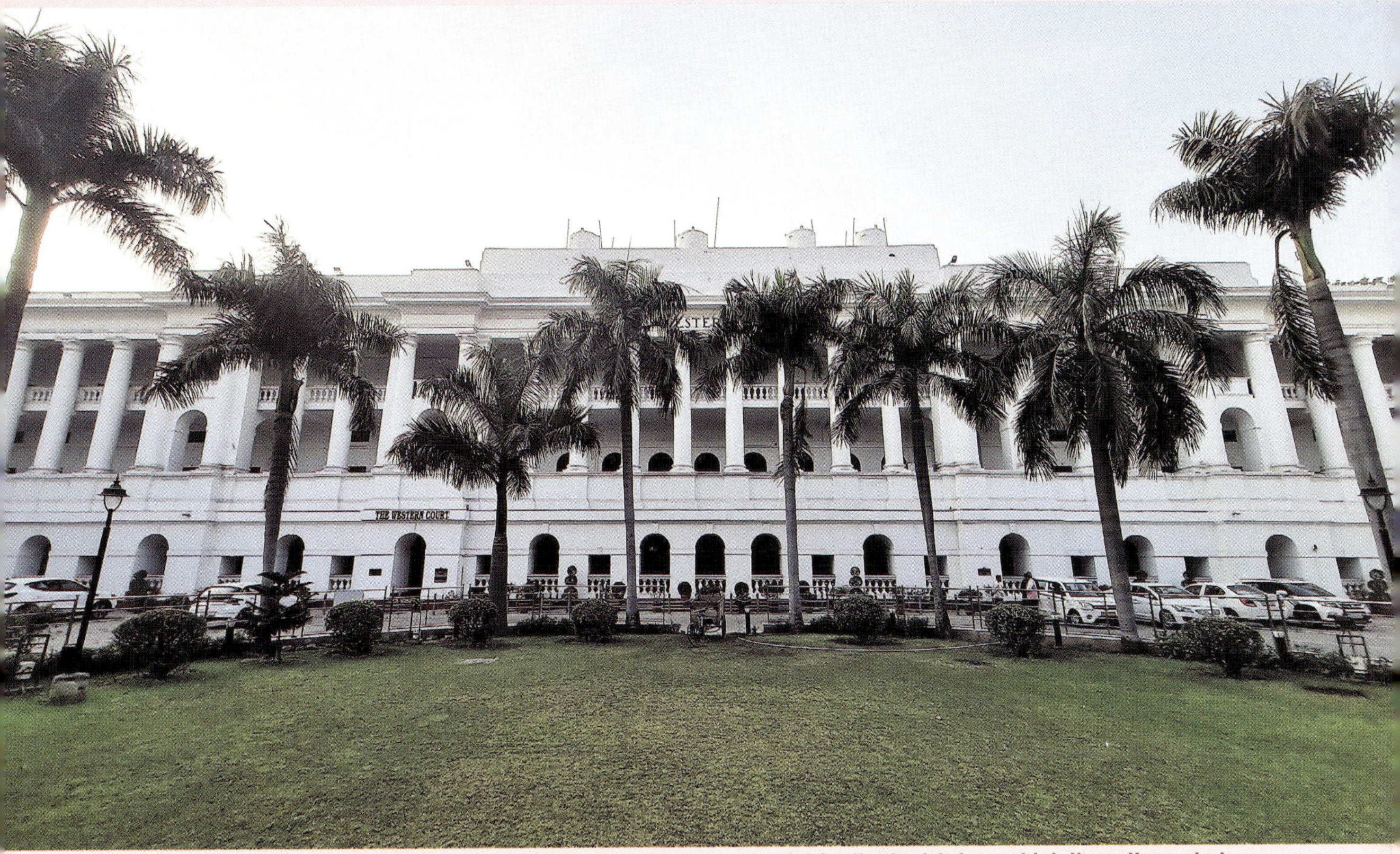

24.77: The Western Court, designed by Robert Tor Russel as a hostel for the legislators, which it continues to be. With a long verandah, tall Tuscan columns, and an overall white appearance, it has a distinctive identity — photograph by Madhukar K Bhagat

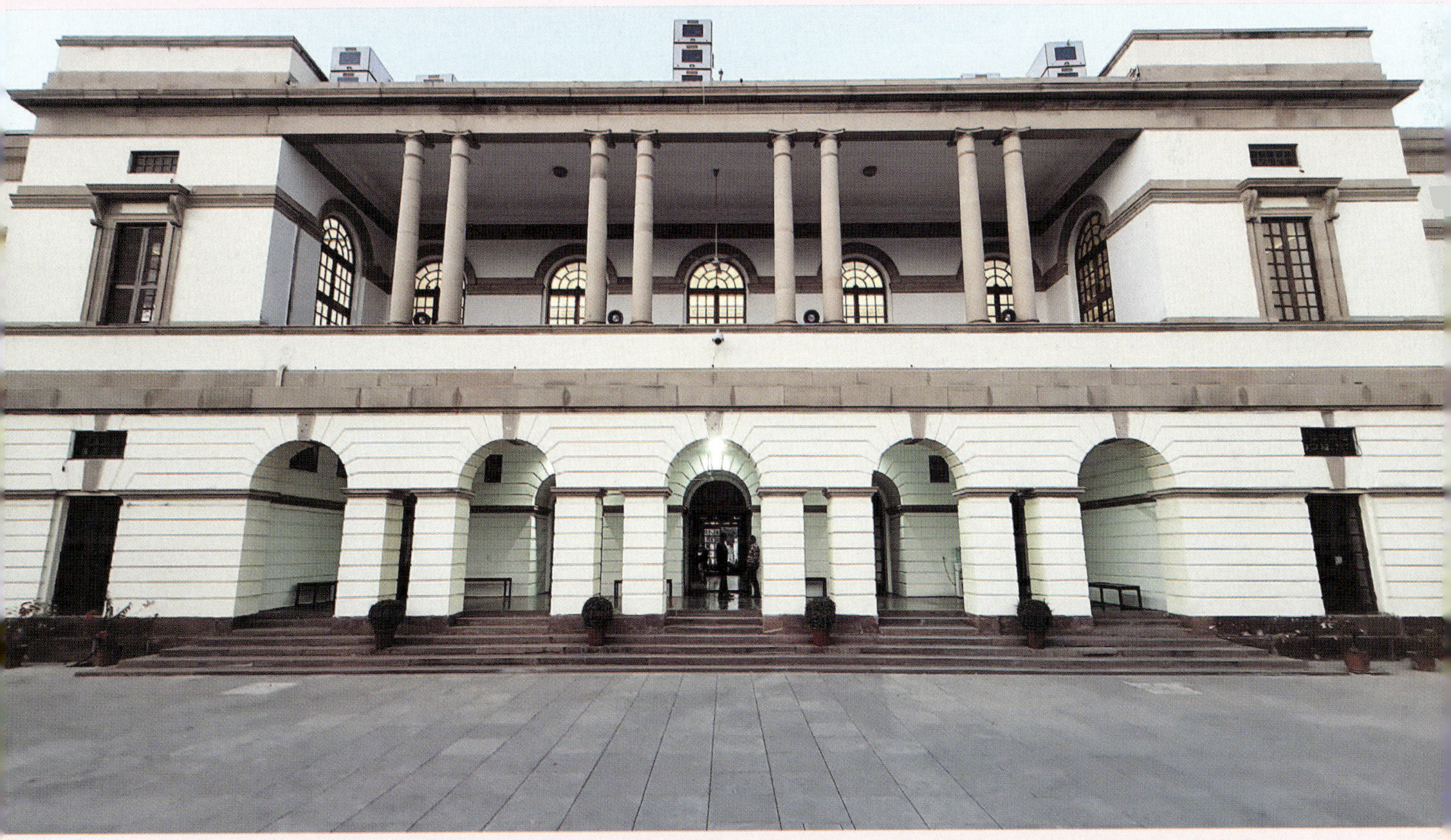

24.78: A view of the rear side of the Teen Murti Bhavan, in view, its veranda with columns and arched windows; erstwhile Flagstaff House and the residence of Commander in Chief of British armed forces in India; an example of British Georgian architecture with highly symmetrical composition — photograph by Madhukar K Bhagat

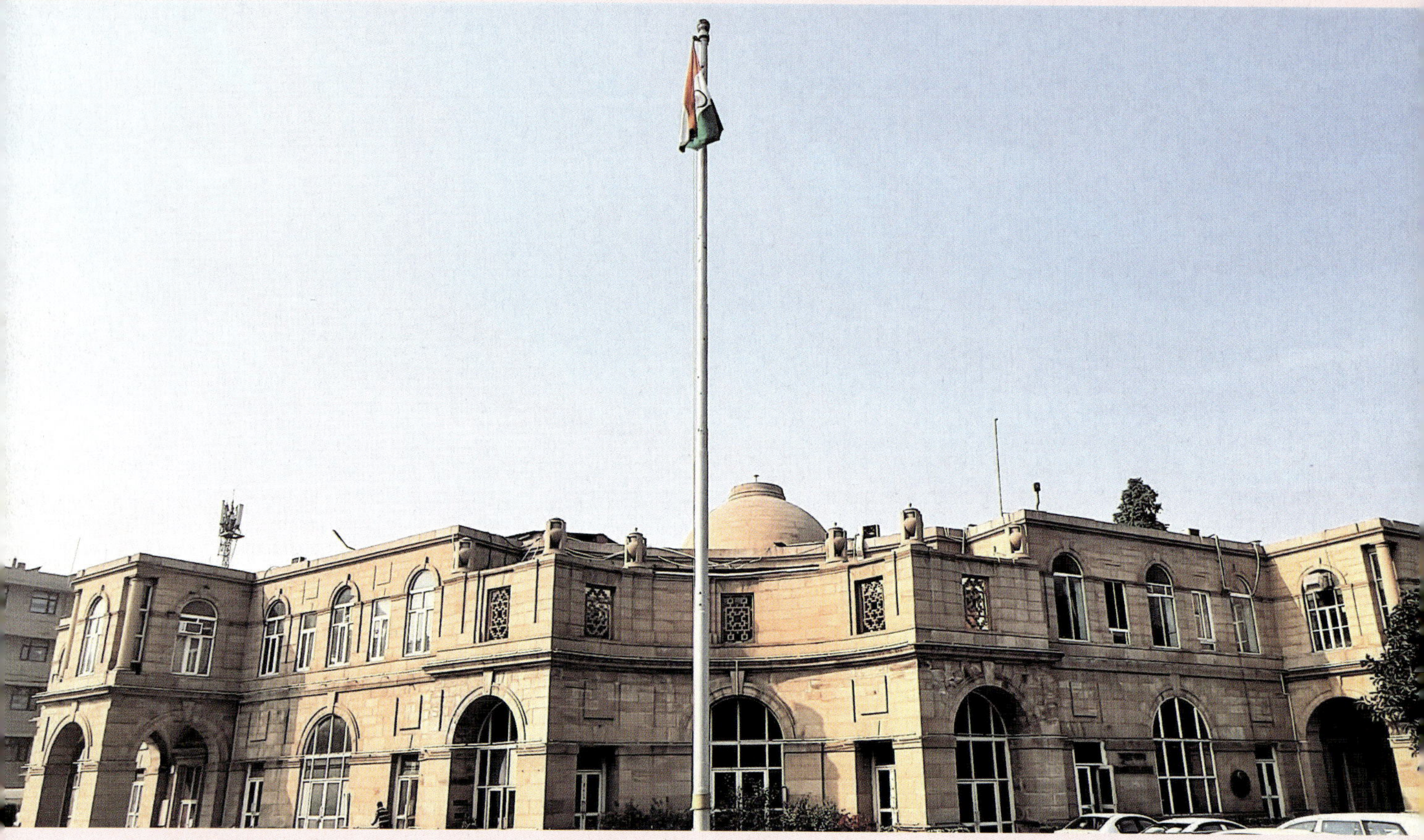

24.79: Baroda House, one of the residential palaces of the princely states, now serves as the headquarters of the Northern Railways. An overall Indo-Saracenic architecture, it has a distinctive butterfly shape with side wings radiating out. Anglo-Saxon elements such as large French windows with semi-circular arches and other features merge with the central dome inspired by the Great Sanchi Stupa — photograph by Madhukar K Bhagat

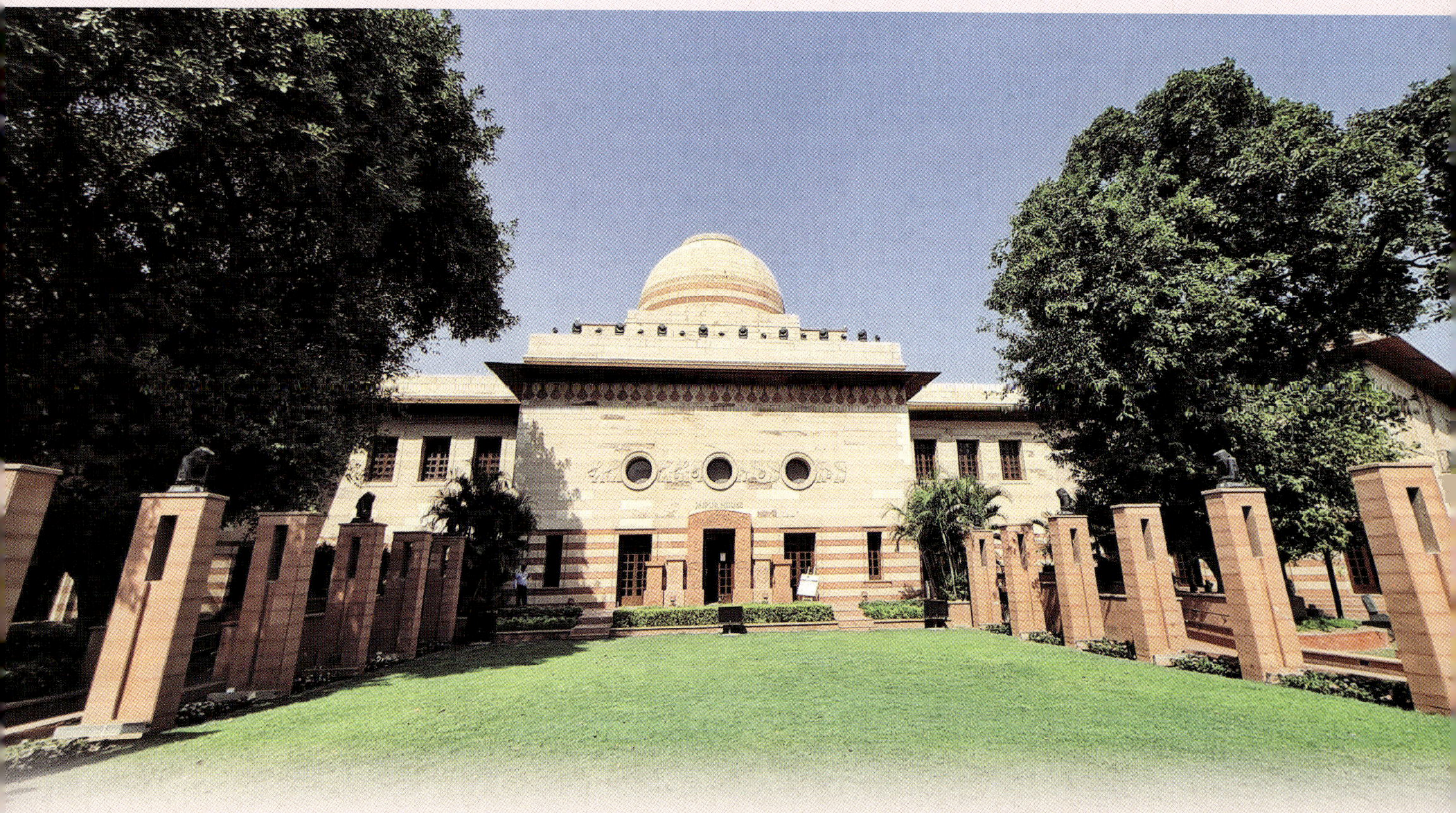

24.80: A view of the rear side of Jaipur House (near India gate), an example of the architecture of the Princely States of pre-independence which incorporated Indo-Saracenic architectural features; has a distinctive central dome inspired by the Great Sanchi Stupa — photograph by Madhukar K Bhagat

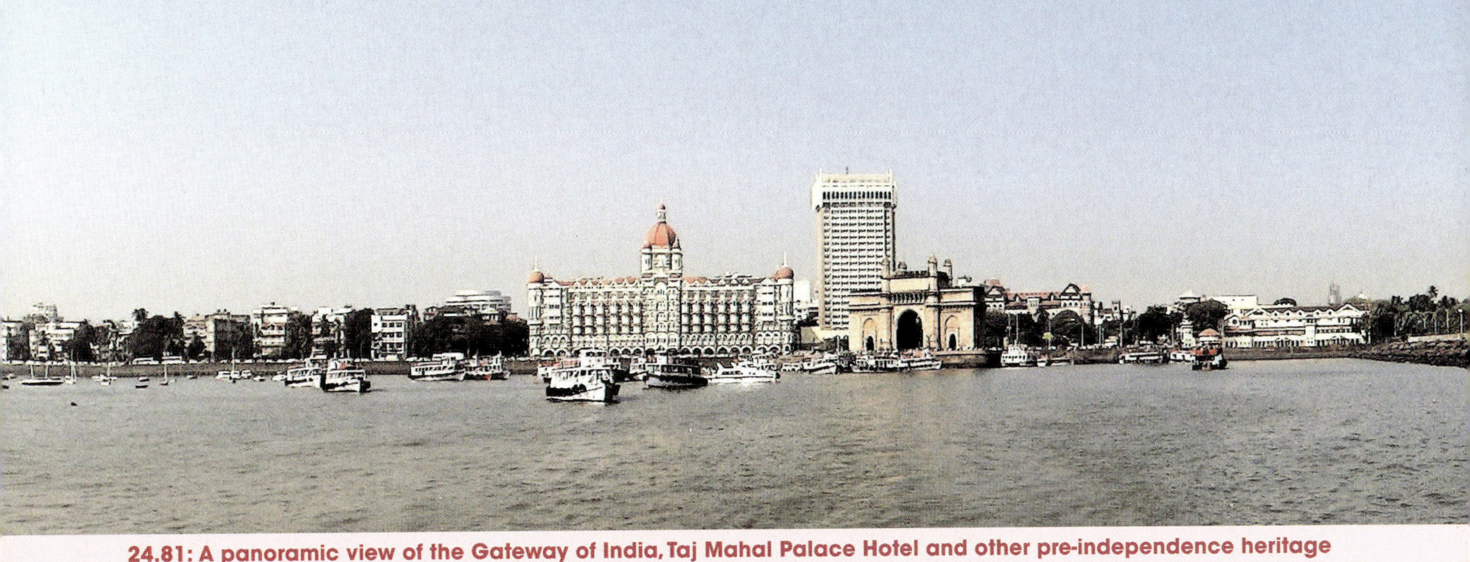

24.81: A panoramic view of the Gateway of India, Taj Mahal Palace Hotel and other pre-independence heritage structures that define the skyline, a view from the Elephanta Island ferry — photograph by Madhukar K Bhagat

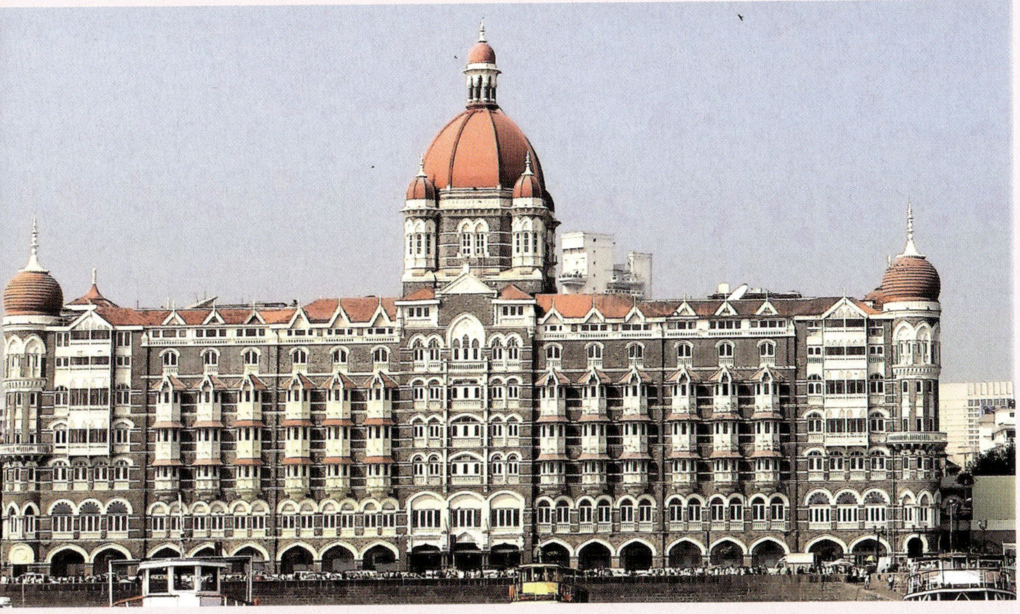

24.82: A closer view at the iconic Taj Mahal Palace Hotel, an Indo-Saracenic architecture designed by Indian architects and made by Indian industrialist Jamshedji Tata; the structure predates the adjoining Gateway of India — photograph by Madhukar K Bhagat

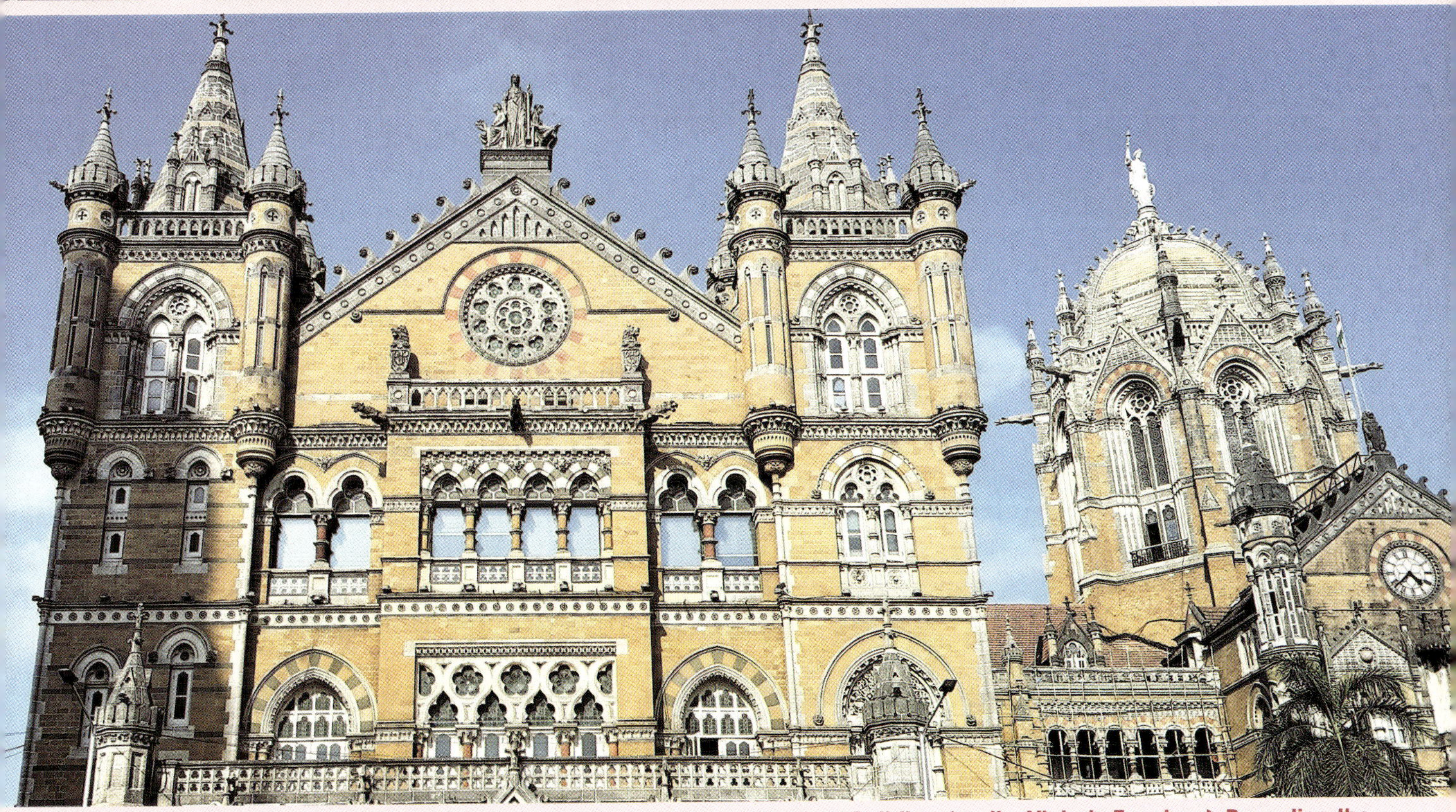

24.83: A near view of the right wing of the Chhatrapati Shivaji Terminus Building (earlier Victoria Terminus). Revealing the elements of the rich Neo-Gothic architecture, including the tall spires, pointed arches, decorated windows, ornate balconies etc., also having some elements of Indo-Saracenic architecture — photograph by Madhukar K Bhagat

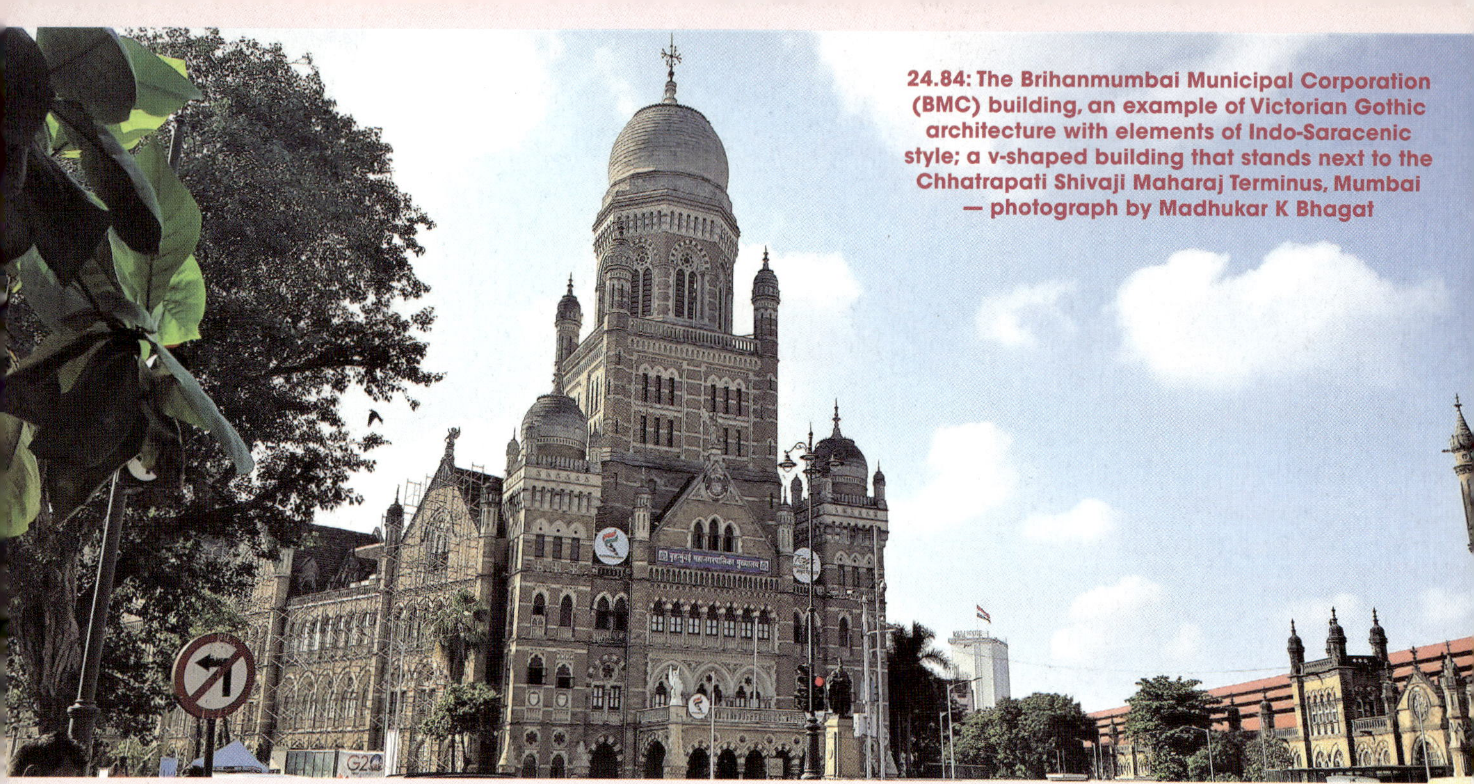

24.84: The Brihanmumbai Municipal Corporation (BMC) building, an example of Victorian Gothic architecture with elements of Indo-Saracenic style; a v-shaped building that stands next to the Chhatrapati Shivaji Maharaj Terminus, Mumbai — photograph by Madhukar K Bhagat

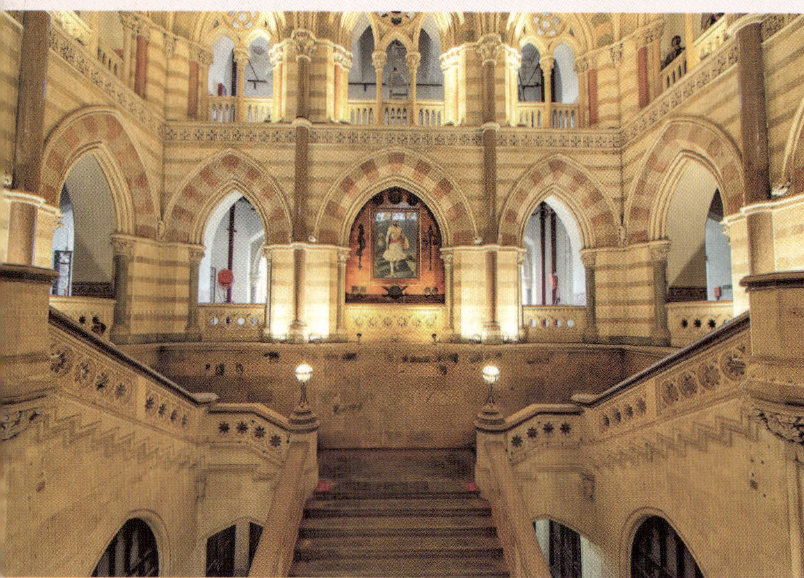

24.85: The majestic central staircase and side wings, corridors with cusped arches; a view of the internal structure of BMC building — Courtesy, Maharashtra Tourism Development Corporation

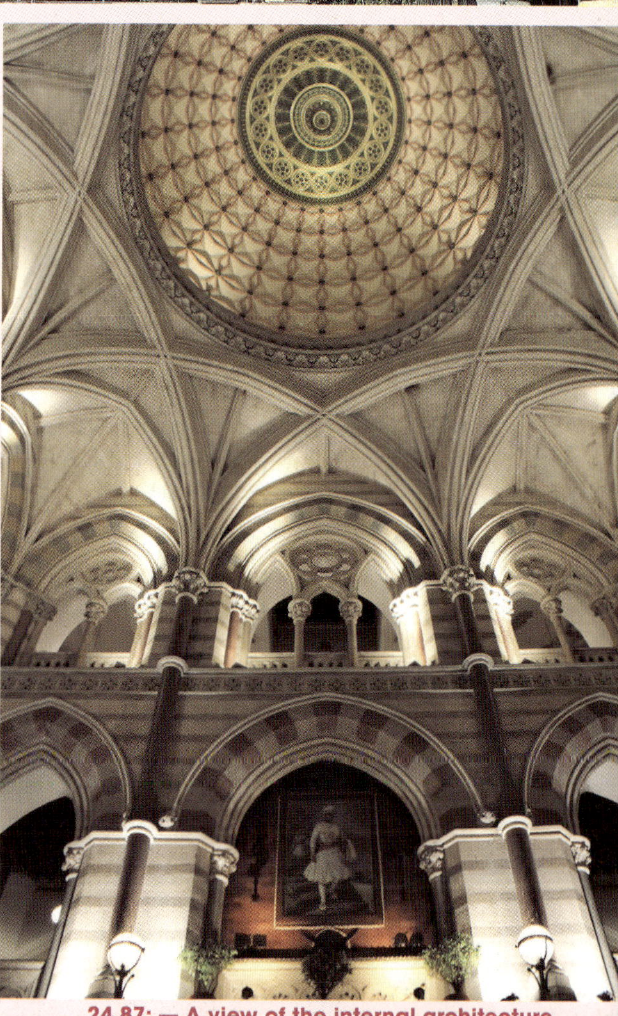

24.87: — A view of the internal architecture of the BMC building — Courtesy, Maharashtra Tourism Development Corporation

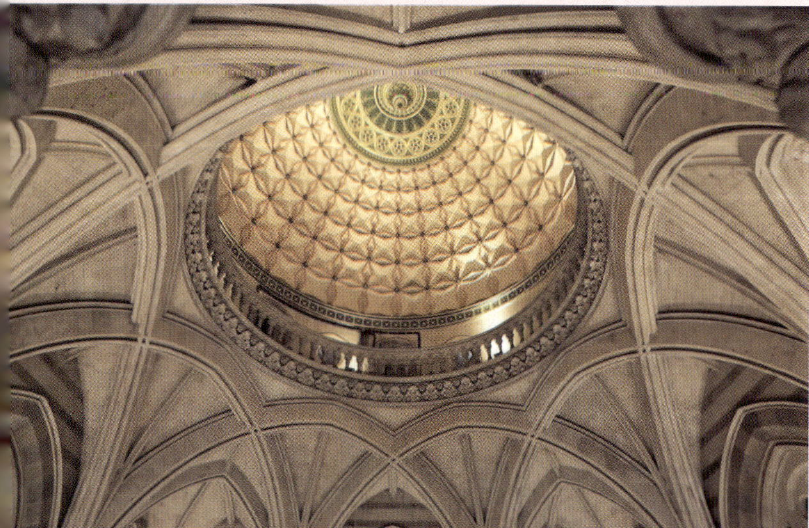

24.86: The central dome BMC building, the grand central dome with circular gallery and supporting structures — Courtesy, Maharashtra Tourism Development Corporation

24.88: The winged lion-like creatures, guardians of the building — Courtesy, Maharashtra Tourism Development Corporation

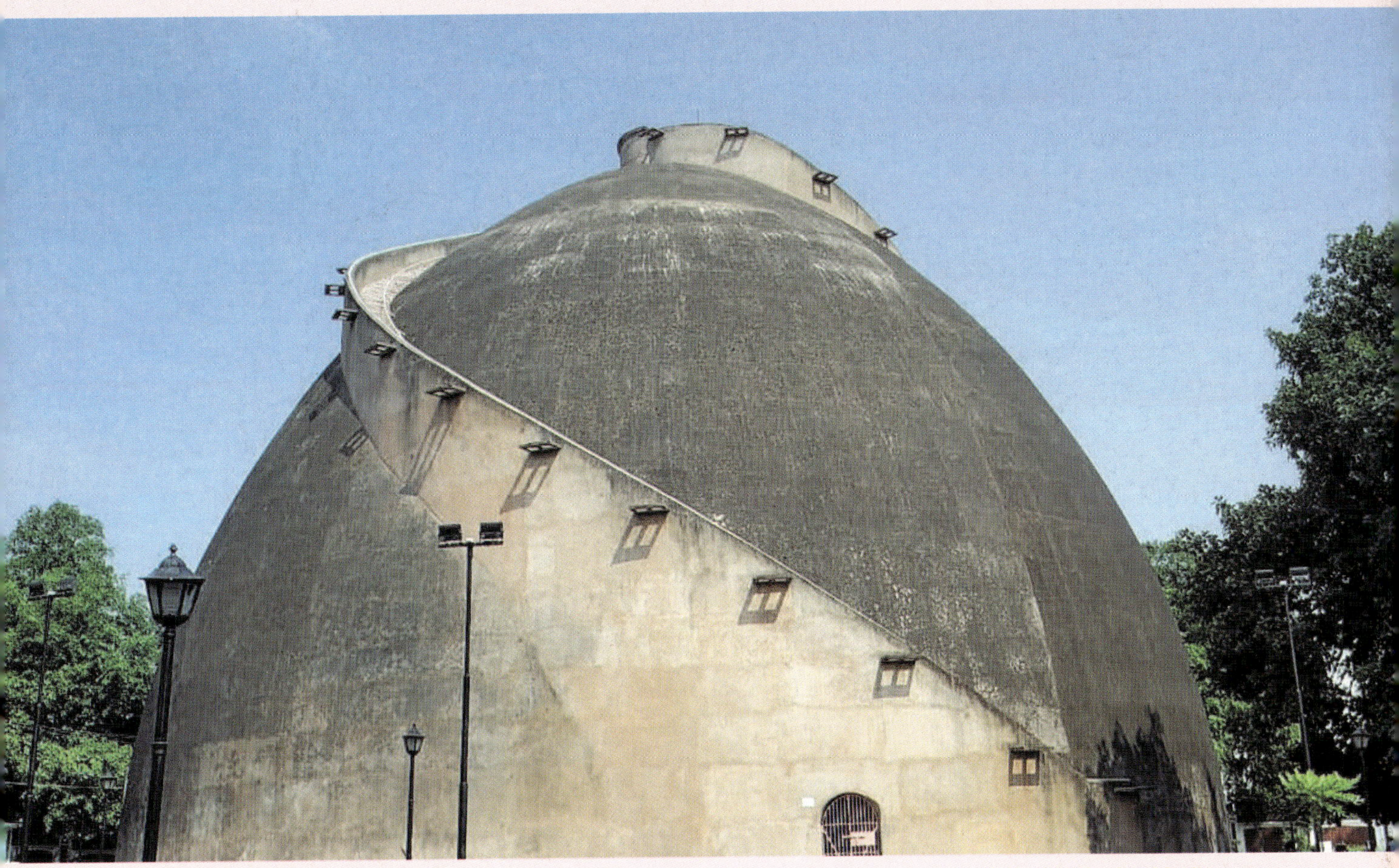

24.89: Golghar, on the banks of river Ganga at Patna, Bihar; a large granary built in 1786 by East India Companies' Bengal Army, post the 1770 great famine of Bengal and other famines in the region; the stupa-like structure has a hollow pillarless interior with thick walls and a spiral staircase for grain sacks to be taken to the top and unloaded through a hole; a prominent tourist spot now — photograph by Madhukar K Bhagat

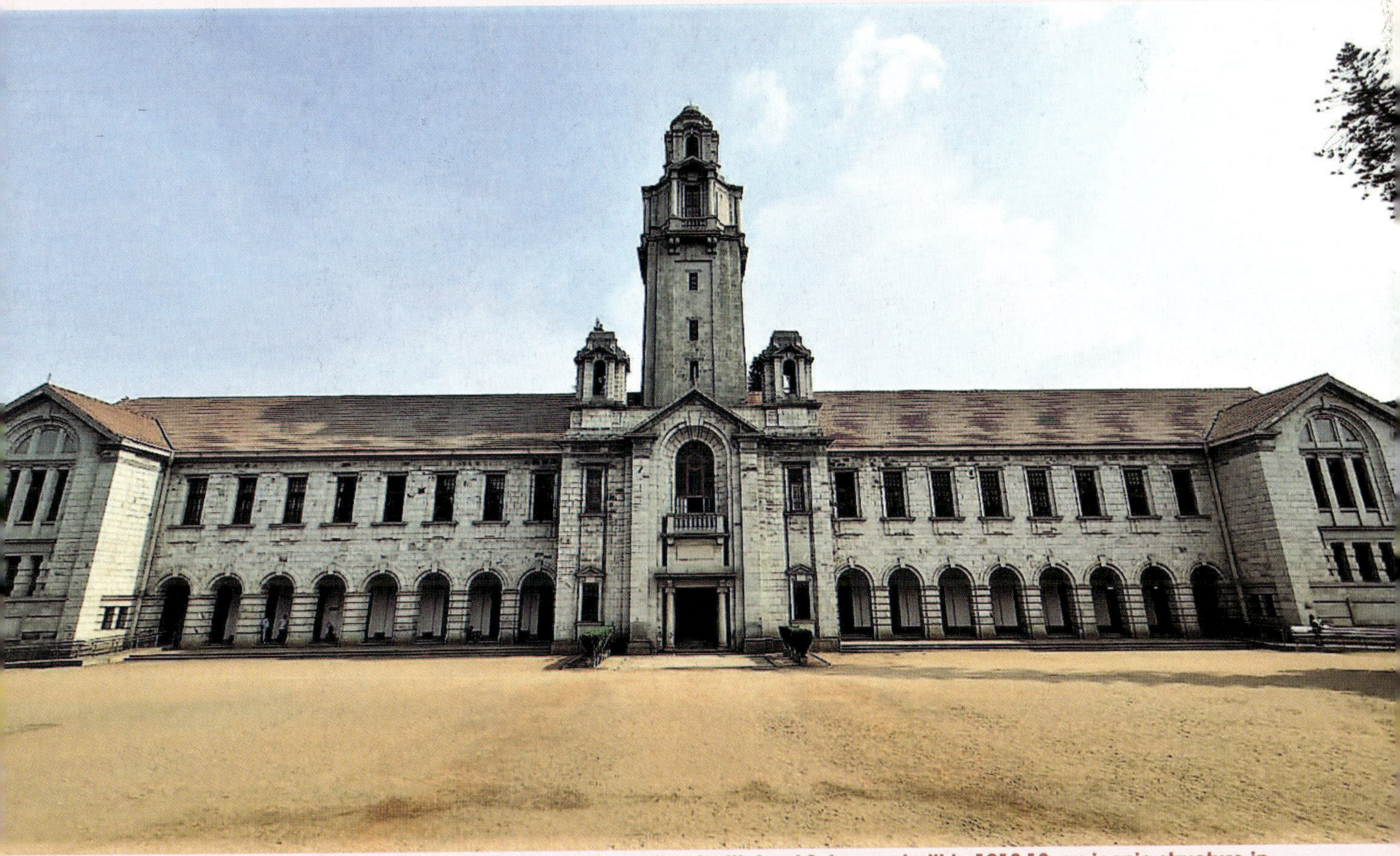

24.90: The main building and central tower of the Indian Institute of Sciences, built in 1912-13; an iconic structure in Classical style, offering a grand look to an institution of pre-eminence — photograph by Madhukar K Bhagat

PORT BLAIR AND ROSS ISLAND: ANDAMAN

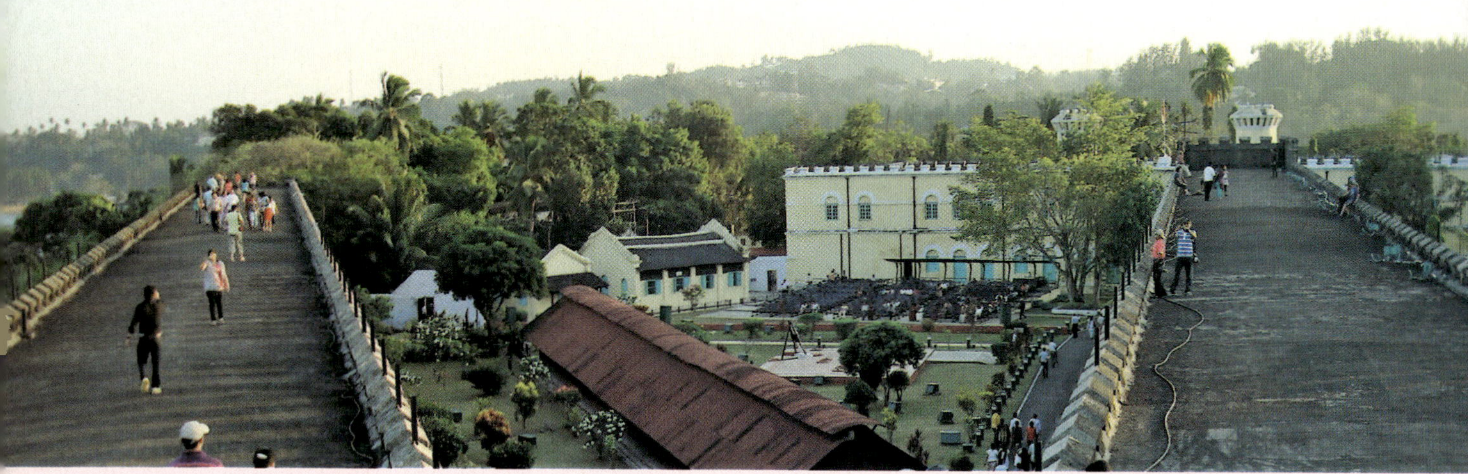

24.91: The two surviving wings of the cellular jail at Port Blair which was established as a penal settlement of the British in 1858. A view from the central watch tower. The jail was designed with seven wings radiating from a central tower guarded by a sentry. The front of a wing faced the back of another wing, thus precluding any form of eye contact or communication between the inmates of different wings. Over the years, the structures of Port Blair and the nearby Ross Island which served as the headquarters of the British troops in the Island, have come to symbolize British tyranny and were also known as *Kala Pani*
— photograph by Madhukar K Bhagat

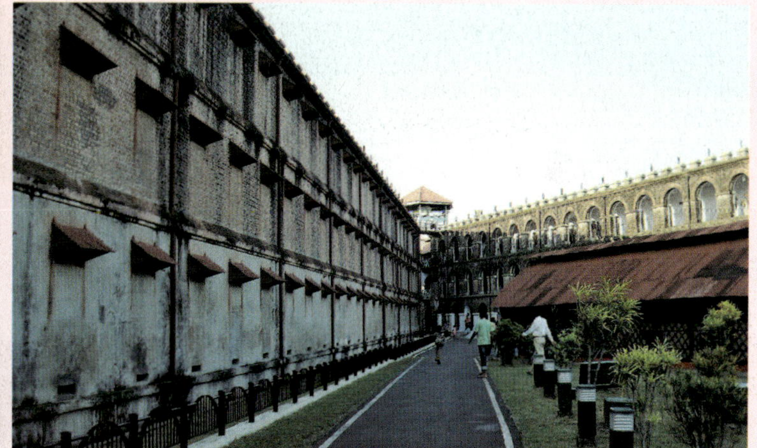

24.92

24.93

24.92 & 24.93: The view of the front and the rear of the wings of the Cellular Jail at Port Blair with the central watch tower in view (left). A model of the jail displaying all the seven wings (right)
— photographs by Madhukar K Bhagat

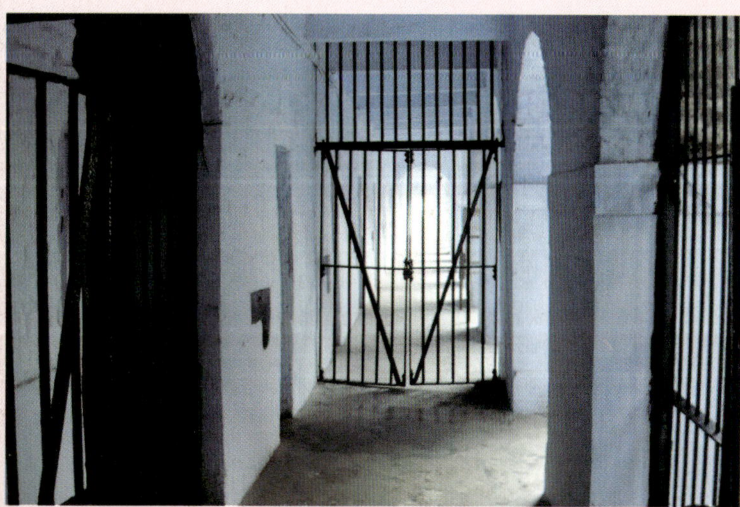

24.94: The long corridors housing the jail cells

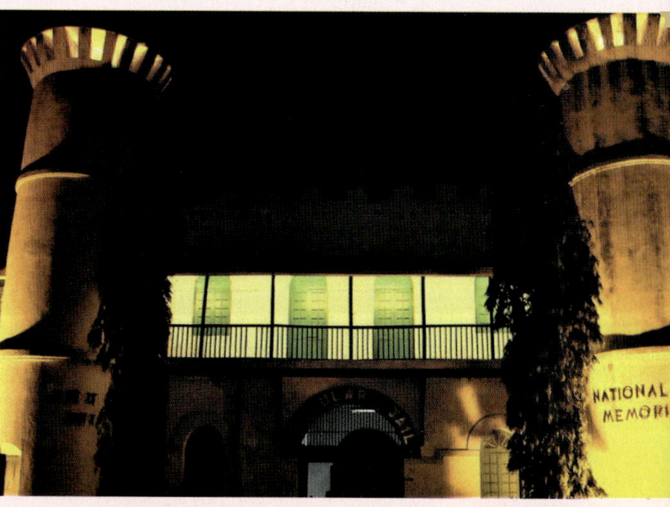

24.95: The main entrance to the jail (night view)

— photographs by Madhukar K Bhagat

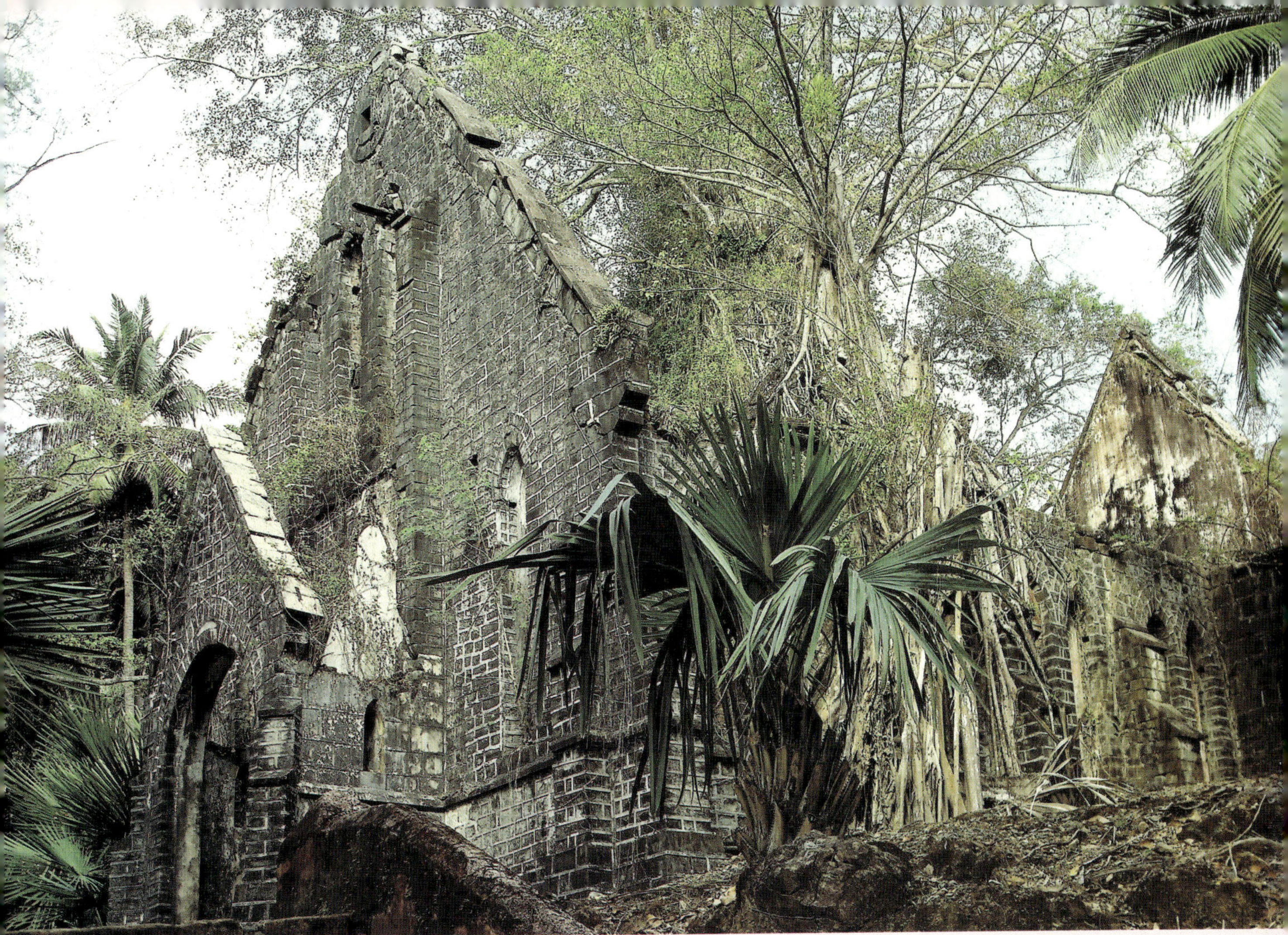

24.96: The remains of a Presbyterian Church of the late 19th century at Ross Island, the erstwhile headquarters of the British Commissioner in the Andamans. The island was renamed as the Netaji Subhash Chandra Bose Island in 2018 — photograph by Madhukar K Bhagat

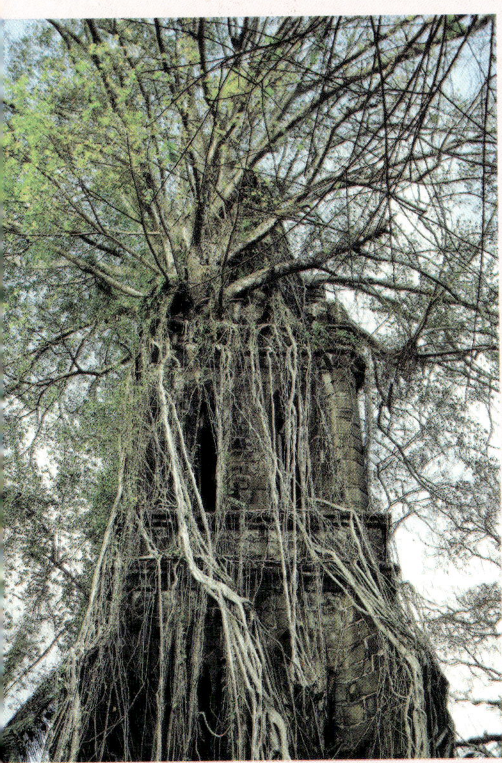

24.97: The tower of the Presbyterian Church, fully engulfed by a giant banyan tree, emblematic of the change and decline of the British power and nature reclaiming what was originally its.

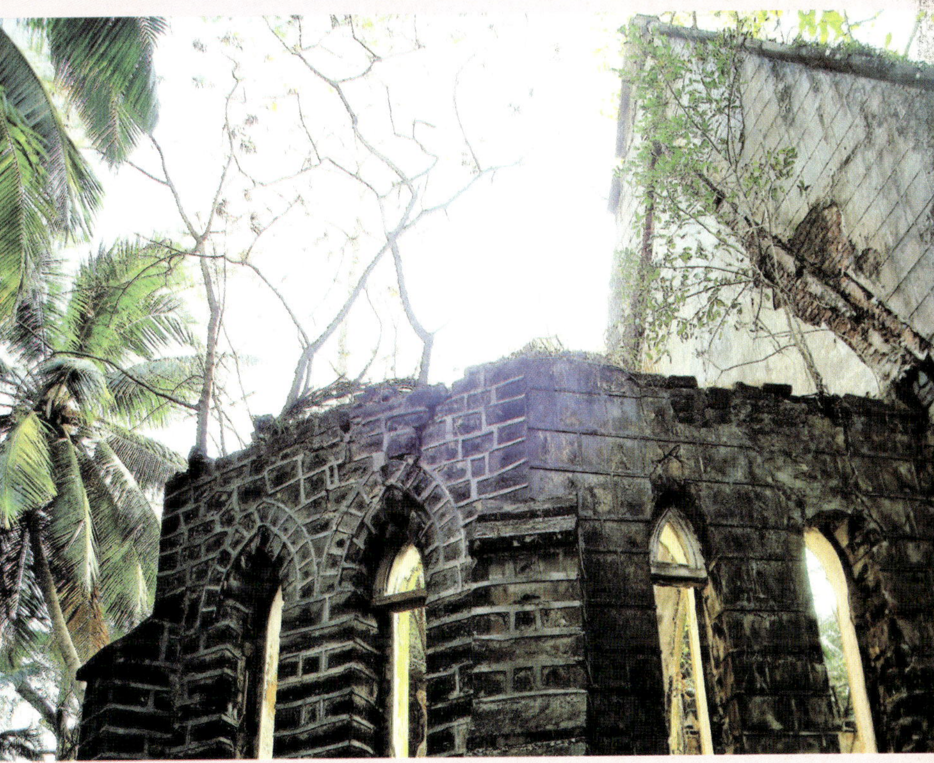

24.98: The tall and slender church windows which would have once been fitted with tinted glass and would have glowed in the sunlight, now lie barren and decaying.

— photographs by Madhukar K Bhagat

POST-INDEPENDENCE ARCHITECTURE

Capitol Complex of Chandigarh: A UNESCO World Heritage Site and a New Architectural Movement of Independent India

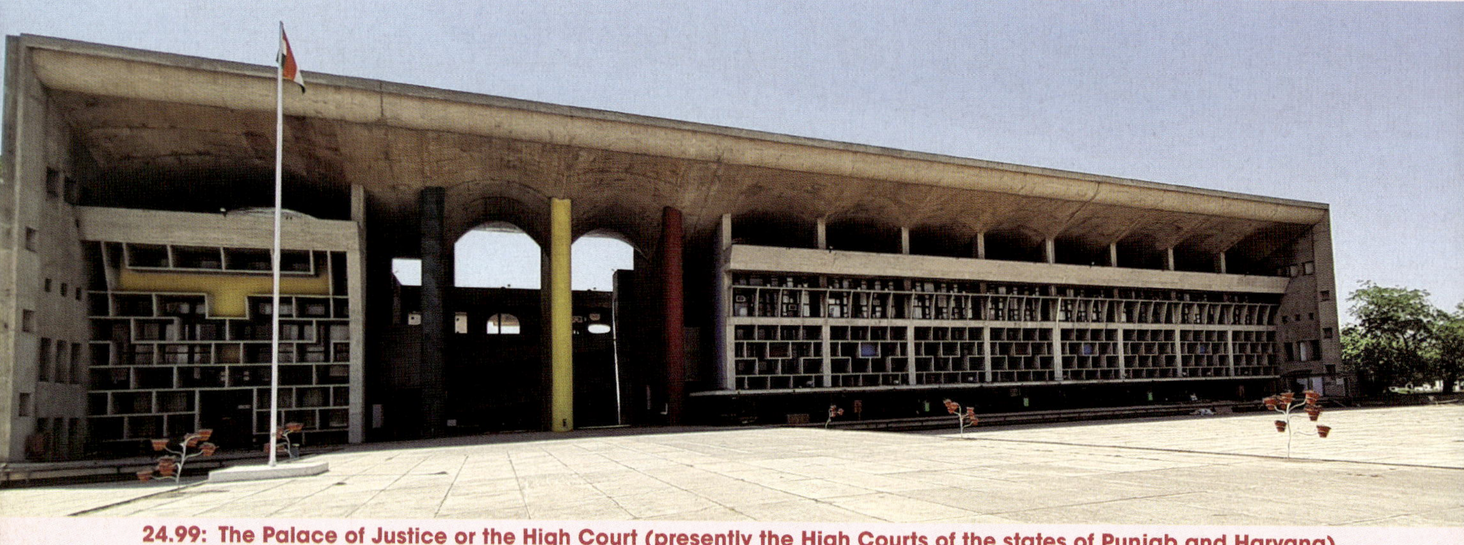

24.99: The Palace of Justice or the High Court (presently the High Courts of the states of Punjab and Haryana)

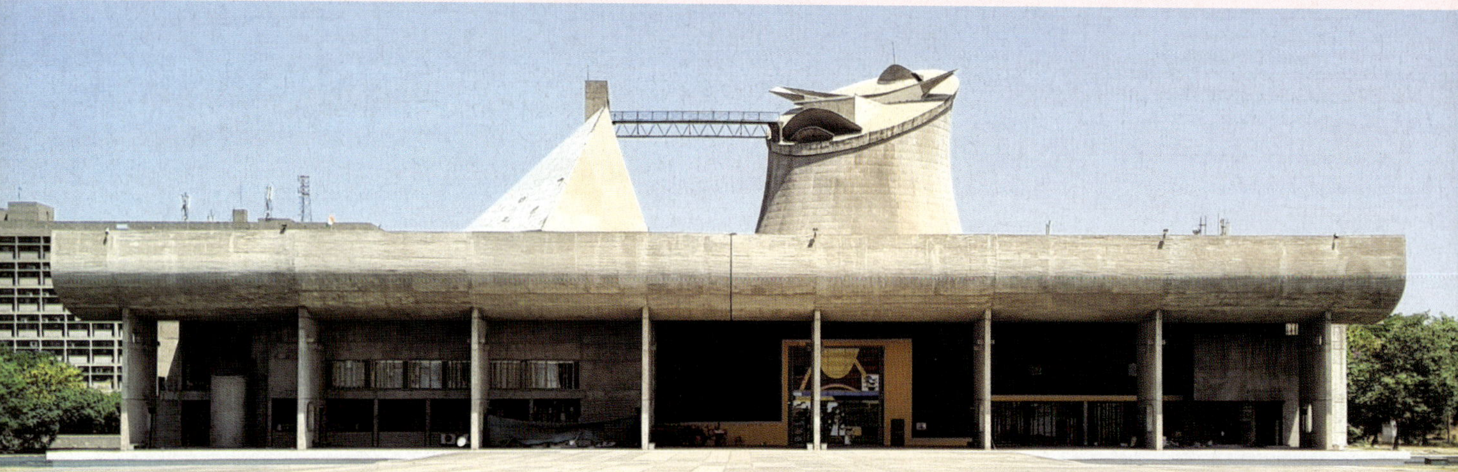

24.100: The front view of the Palace of Assembly (presently houses the assemblies of the states of Punjab and Haryana); visible in front are the structures which are sun breakers, along with the rainwater harvesting system (that collects water in the adjoining pond) they are designed to cut heat; in view the Secretariat behind it.

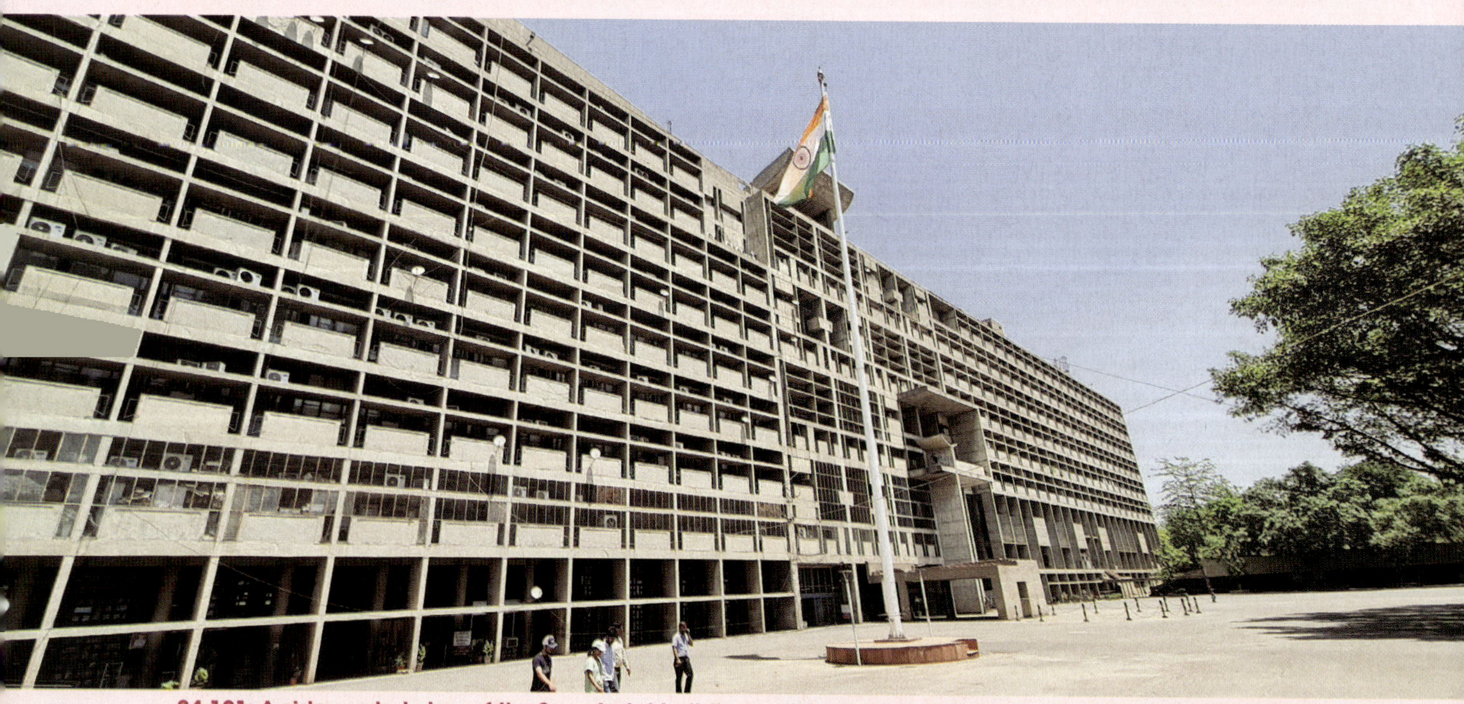

24.101: A side-angled view of the Secretariat building on the Capitol Complex; an unplastered exposed concrete design of the structures by Le Corbusier emphasising modernism and minimalism in architectural movement; Above photographs by Madhukar K Bhagat

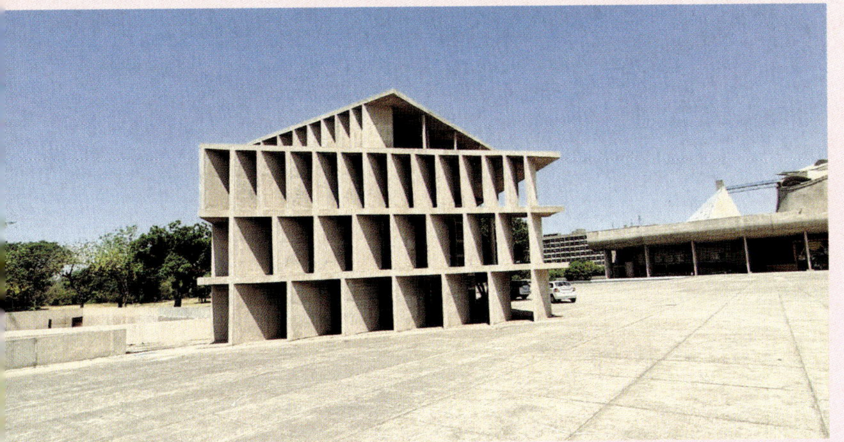

24.102: The Hall of Shadows, designed to cut off the sunshine from all angles at all times, bright sunlight is seen on the angled projections which cut the light forming sharp shadows; an open structure that served as a study displaying the understanding of the Sun and its movement; behind it are the assembly and the secretariat complex.
— photograph by Madhukar K Bhagat

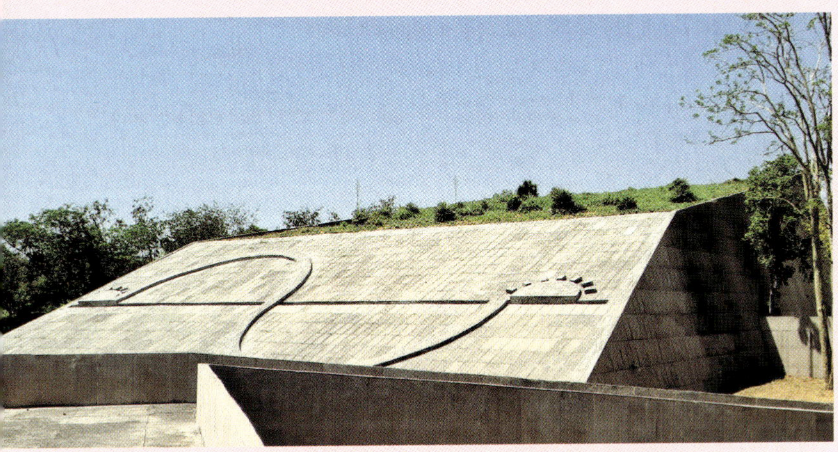

24.103: The Geometric Hill (as seen from the Hall of Shadows), has the carved imagery of a diurnal cycle, symbolic of the movement of the Sun and the flow of time
— photograph by Madhukar K Bhagat

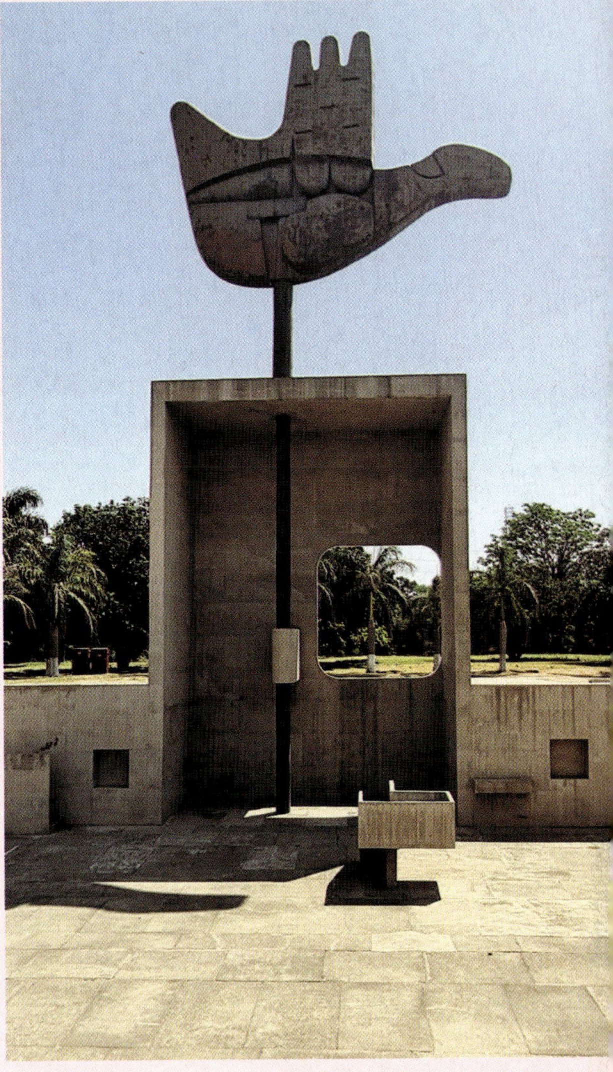

24.104: The Open Hand Monument and its internal mechanism, which enables its rotation with the wind; designed by Le Corbusier as a symbol of peace and reconciliation; today it also serves as an emblem of the Government of Chandigarh
— photograph by Madhukar K Bhagat

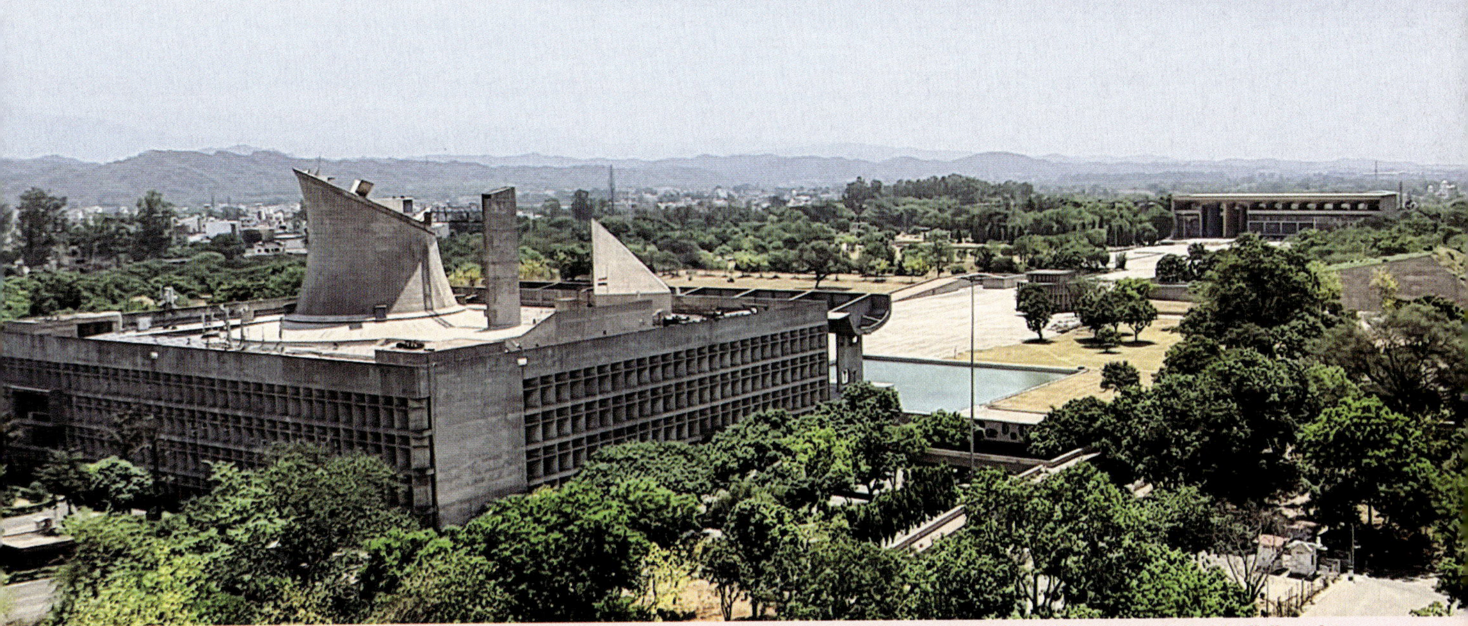

24.105: A panoramic view of the Capitol Complex of Chandigarh, as seen from the top of the Secretariat building; in view is the Palace of Assembly, while at the far end lies the Palace of Justice and on the right side of the picture the Geometric Hill; Sivalik hills on foothills of which the city of Chandigarh was designed are seen on the far horizon
— photograph by Madhukar K Bhagat

Lotus Temple: New Delhi

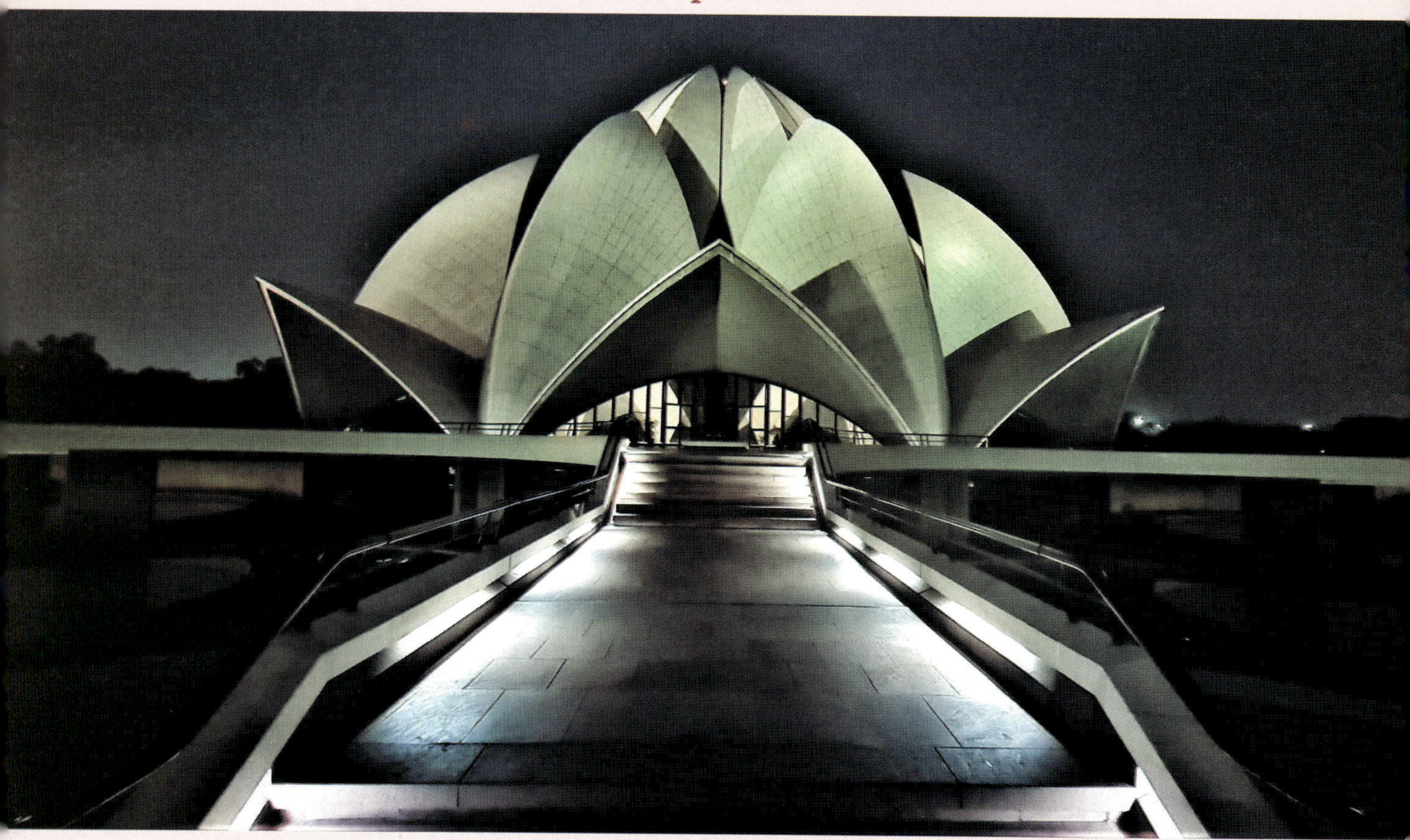

24.106: Lotus Temple, bathed in light, a view at night from the central steps. A unique architecture designed like a lotus with nine sets of three petals each — photograph by Madhukar K Bhagat

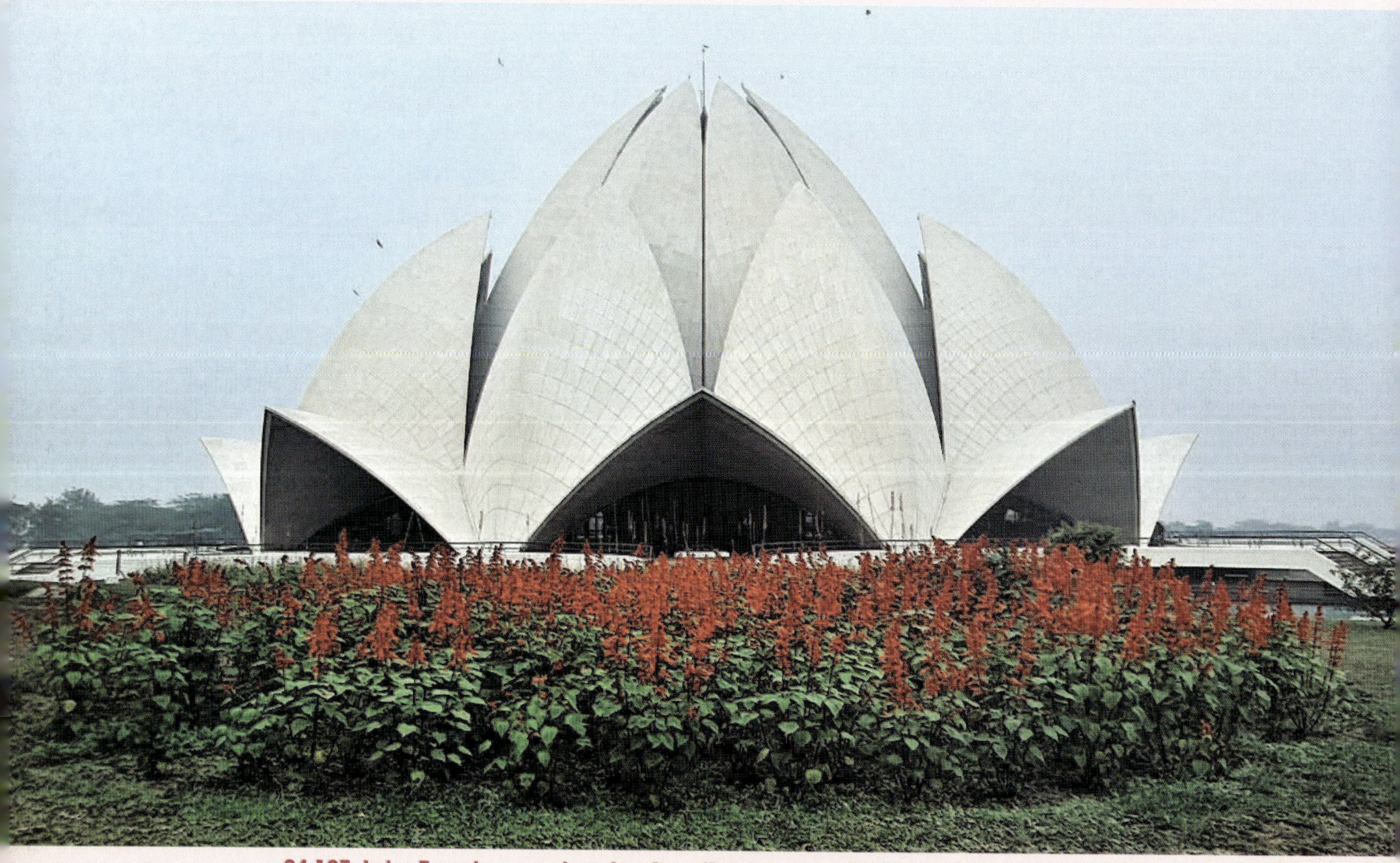

24.107: Lotus Temple, a garden view from the rear side of the symmetrical structure — photograph by Madhukar K Bhagat

Vidhan Soudha, Bengaluru and the New Parliament in New Delhi

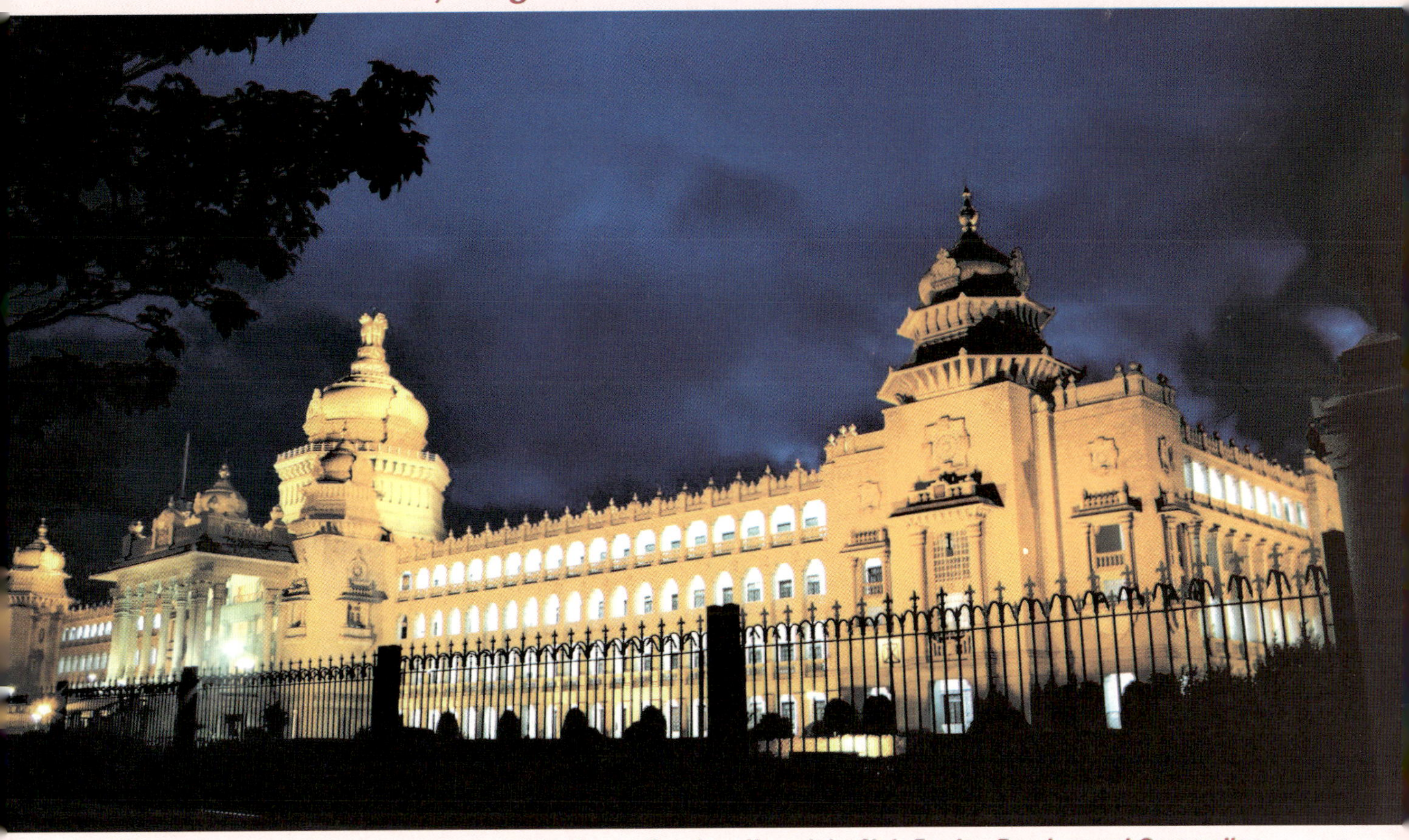

24.108: Vidhan Soudha, Bengaluru, a night view — Courtesy, Karnataka State Tourism Development Corporation

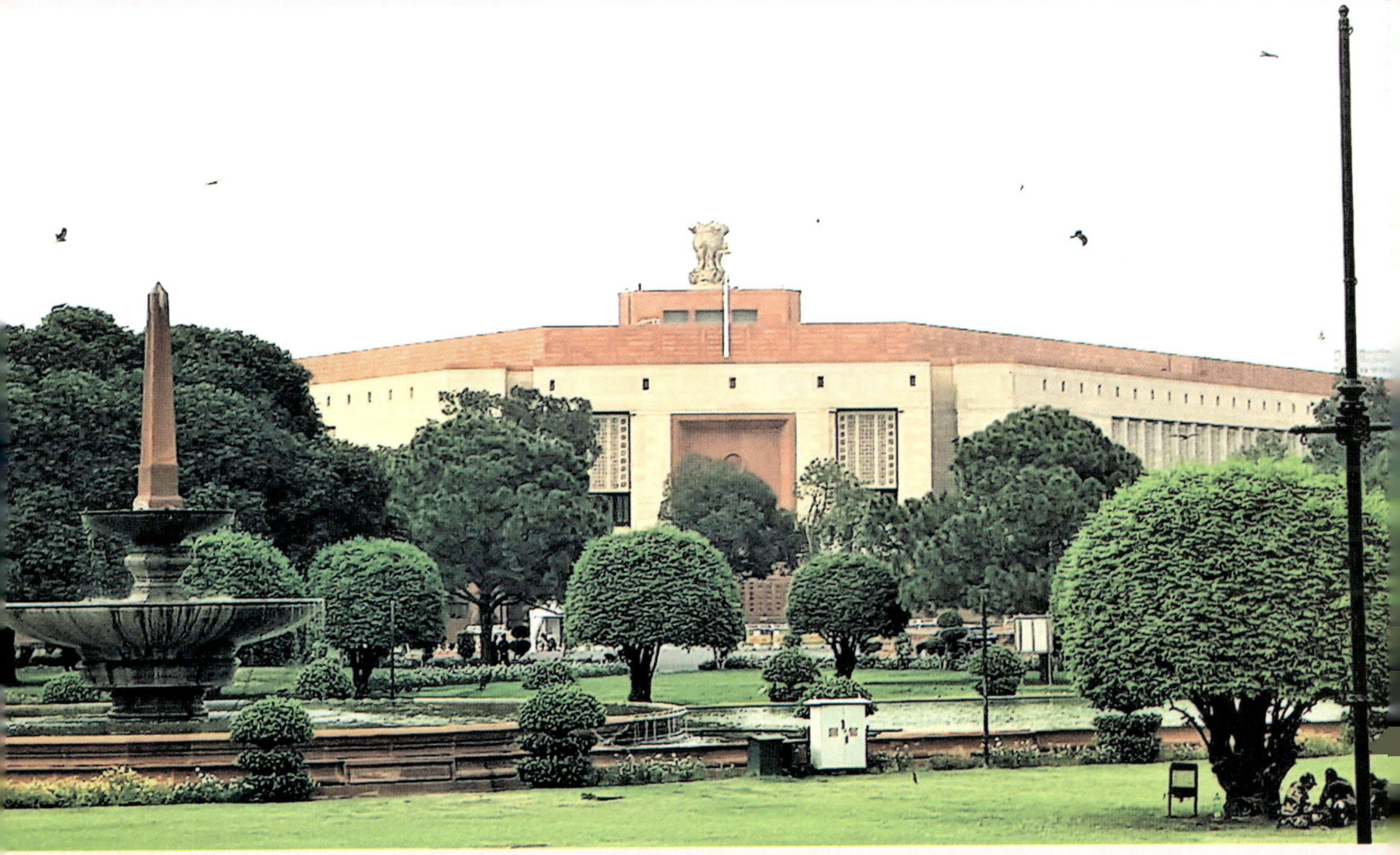

24.109: New Parliament, a view from the lawns near Vijay Chowk
— photograph by Madhukar K Bhagat

PHOTO/PICTURE CREDITS

(The numbers 14.1, 14.2, 15.3, ... etc. denotes the number of the captioned photographs.)

Chapter 14 Cultural Eras: Modern India

(a) Photographs by Madhukar K Bhagat (author) 14.1, 14.2, 14.4, 14.12, 14.16, 14.17, 14.18, 14.21, 14.22, 14.24, 14.25, 14.28

(b) Photographs-Courtesy, Department of Post 14.9, 14.14, 14.15, 14.19,

(c) Links of copyright free photographs from Wikimedia Commons/Wikipedia

Source: Achchum Padhippum by Ma. Sa. Sambandhan 1980
https://commons.wikimedia.org/wiki/File:Luso_Tamil_Catechism_Lisbon_1554.JPG 14.3

Author Sita Ram, Collection British Library
https://commons.wikimedia.org/wiki/Category:1810s_paintings_from_India#/media/File The_Chowk,_and_the_main_street_of_Patna,_1814-15.jpg 14.5

Author, The Illustrated Times
https://commons.wikimedia.org/wiki/File:The_Sepoy_revolt_at_Meerut.jpg 14.6

Source: Sir Syed Album, by Khaliq Ahmad Nizami, published by Idara-I Adabiyat, Delhi, 1983.
https://commons.wikimedia.org/wiki/File:Muhammadansocialreformer.jpg 14.7

Source: SRINVANTU Magazine, April 2017
(http://srinvantu.com/https://en.wikipedia.org/wiki/Kesari_(Marathi_newspaper)#/media/ File:KESARI.jpg 14.8

Author, Sastri, Sibnath, 1847-1919
https://commons.wikimedia.org/wiki/File:Michael_Madhusudan_Dutta.jpg 14.13
https://upload.wikimedia.org/wikipedia/commons/4/4d/Constitution_of_India.jpg 14.20

(d) Photographs with permission from State Tourism Boards, Government Departments and Sangeet Natak Akademi

Courtesy, Department of Tourism, West Bengal 14.10, 14.11
Courtesy, Madhya Pradesh Tourism Board 14.26
Courtesy, Sangeet Natak Akademi 14.23, 14.27,

Chapter 15 Socio-Religious Reforms and Reformers in Modern India

(a) Photographs by Madhukar K Bhagat (author) 15.7, 15.9, 15.12, 15.16,

(b) Photographs: Courtesy, Department of Post 15.2, 15.5, 15.6, 15.8, 15.10, 15.13, 15.14, 15.15, 15.18, 15.19, 15.20, 15.21

(c) Links of copyright free photographs from Wikimedia Commons/Wikipedia

https://en.wikipedia.org/wiki/File:Swami_Vivekananda-1893-09-signed.jpg 15.1
https://commons.wikimedia.org/wiki/File:Debendranath_Tagore.jpg 15.3
https://en.wikipedia.org/wiki/Keshub_Chandra_Sen#/media/File:Keshub_Chunder_ Sen_(1838-1884).jpg 15.4
https://commons.wikimedia.org/wiki/File:Annie_Besant,_LoC.jpg 15.11
https://upload.wikimedia.org/wikipedia/commons/c/c1/Syed_Ahmed_Khan.jpg 15.17

Chapter 16 Paintings in Modern India

(a) Photographs by Madhukar K Bhagat (author)

16.1, 16.2, 16.7, 16.8, 16.10, 16.12-16.18, 16.23, 16.24-16.28, 16.30-52, 16.54-16.64, 16.66-16.74

(b) Links of copyright free photographs from Wikimedia Commons/Wikipedia

Author Thomas and William Daniell
https://en.wikipedia.org/wiki/Thomas_Daniell#/media/File:Daniell_Taje_Mahel3.JPG 16.3

Author Thomas and William Daniell
https://en.wikipedia.org/wiki/Thomas_Daniell#/media/File:Thomas_Daniell_-_Ruins_of_the _Naurattan,_Sasaram,_Bihar_-_Google_Art_Project.jpg 16.4

Author George Chinnery
https://en.wikipedia.org/wiki/File:Chinnery,_Indian_Herdsman_on_a_Bank.jpg#metadata 16.5

Edwin Benny, 3rd Collection
https://en.wikipedia.org/wiki/Company_style#/media/File:Group_of_Courtesans,_northern_ India,_19th_century.jpg 16.6

Author Sewak Ram
https://commons.wikimedia.org/wiki/Category:1800s_paintings_from_India#/media/File:Durga_Puja,_1809_watercolour_painting_in_Patna_Style.jpg 16.9
Artist Raja Ravi Varma
https://en.wikipedia.org/wiki/Galaxy_of_Musicians#/media/File:Raja_Ravi_Varma,_Galaxy_of_Musicians.jpg 16.11
Artist Abanindranath Tagore
https://en.wikipedia.org/wiki/Bharat_Mata_(painting)#/media/File:Bharat_Mata_by_Abanindranath_Tagore.jpg 16.19
Author Gaganendranath Tagore
https://commons.wikimedia.org/wiki/Category:Paintings_by_Gaganendranath_Tagore#/media/File:Gaganendranath_Tagore_-_Dwarkapuri.jpg 16.21
Author Gaganendranath Tagore
https://commons.wikimedia.org/wiki/Category:Paintings_by_Gaganendranath_Tagore#/media/File:Gaganendranath_Tagore_-_City_in_the_Night,_1925.jpg 16.22
Collection Victoria Memorial
https://en.wikipedia.org/wiki/Abanindranath_Tagore#/media/File:Abanindranath_Tagore_-_The_Passing_of_Shah_Jahan,_1902.jpg 16.29
Author Will
https://en.wikipedia.org/wiki/Kalighat_painting#/media/File:The_demon_ravana_fighting_with_the_ape_hanuman,_1880,_kalighat_school.jpg 16.53
Author Rangan Datta
https://commons.wikimedia.org/wiki/File:Cherial_1.jpg 16.65

Chapter 17 Music in Modern India

(a) Photographs by Madhukar K Bhagat (author) 17.12, 17.15–17.21, 17.47

(b) Photographs: Courtesy, Department of Post 17.1, 17.3, 17.4, 17.5, 17.7–17.10, 17.24–17.27, 17.29, 17.56, 17.58–17.62, 17.64–17.68, 17.70–17.79

(c) Links of copyright free photographs from Wikimedia Commons/Wikipedia

https://en.wikipedia.org/wiki/Abdul_Karim_Khan#/media/File:Abdul_Karim_Khan.jpg 17.2
Author Chandraprabha Cinetone
https://commons.wikimedia.org/wiki/File:Ms_subbulakshmi.jpg 17.6
Author suyash.dwivedi
https://commons.wikimedia.org/wiki/File:Pandit_Jasraj_at_Bhopal_2015.jpg 17.11
Author adil 113
https://commons.wikimedia.org/wiki/File:A_Mohan_Veena,_string_musical_instruments_of_India.jpg 17.13
MET Museum
https://en.wikipedia.org/wiki/Sitar#/media/File:Sitar3.jpg 17.14
Author Sven.petersen
https://commons.wikimedia.org/wiki/File:Ghatam.jpg 17.22
Author Prof. Rafiqul Islam
https://en.wikipedia.org/wiki/Allauddin_Khan#/media/File:Ustad_Alauddin_Khan_Full_1.jpg 17.23
Author Tiwaribharat
https://commons.wikimedia.org/wiki/File:Amjad_Ali_Khan_bharat-s-tiwari-photography-IMG_3786_Dember_23,_2018.jpg 17.28
Author Shrimali Vijay
https://upload.wikimedia.org/wikipedia/commons/f/f3/Pandit_shivkumar_sharma.jpg 17.30
Author Emma Dusepo
https://commons.wikimedia.org/wiki/File:Thumbi_2.jpg 17.31
Credit line: The Crosby Brown Collection of Musical Instruments, 1889
https://commons.wikimedia.org/wiki/File:Ranasringa_MET_89.4.161_slide.jpg 17.33
Author Adil 113
https://en.wikipedia.org/wiki/Dholak#/media/File:Dholak_dhol_drum,_one_of_many_percussion_instruments_of_South_Asia.jpg 17.34
Author Ihsanwayfarer
https://en.wikipedia.org/wiki/Alghoza#/media/File:Rajasthan_Folk_Music.jpg 17.35
Author Vamsivadrevu
https://en.wikipedia.org/wiki/Bansuri#/media/File:All_scales_of_Bansuris_in_a_set.jpg 17.36
Author Pebble101
https://en.wikipedia.org/wiki/List_of_Indian_musical_instruments#/media/File:Anchor_Shaped_Sarinda.jpg 17.38
Author Kuruman
https://en.wikipedia.org/wiki/Dhak_(instrument)#/media/File:Dhak_at_Dhakeshwari_Temple.jpg 17.39

User: Abhi Kal
https://en.wikipedia.org/wiki/Gogona#/media/File:%E0%A6%97%E0%A6%97%E0%A6%A3%E0%A6%BE.JPG 17.40
Author Abhi Kal
https://en.wikipedia.org/wiki/Xutuli#/media/File:Xutuli (Assamese_%E0%A6%B8%E0%A7%81%E0%A6% A4% E0%A7%81%E0%A6%B2%E0%A6%BF).JPG 17.41
Author Diamond Oina
https://en.wikipedia.org/wiki/Pena_(musical_instrument)#/media/File:%22PENA%22_a_musical_instrument.jpg 17.42
Author Diamond Oina
https://commons.wikimedia.org/wiki/File:%22PENA%22_a_musical_instrument.jpg 17.43
Author Bogman
https://en.wikipedia.org/wiki/Tangmuri#/media/File:Tangmuri_player_2.jpg 17.44
Author Aniruddha Buragohain
https://commons.wikimedia.org/wiki/File:Khuti_taal.jpg 17.46
Author Donkey335
https://en.wikipedia.org/wiki/Ghumot#/media/File:Ghumot_in_Goa.jpg 17.48
Author Martin spaink
https://en.wikipedia.org/wiki/Tanpura#/media/File:Tanjore-style_Carnatic_tambura.JPG 17.51
Author Mullookkaaran
https://en.wikipedia.org/wiki/Idakka#/media/File:Edakka_-_Idakka_-_Edaykka.JPG 17.54
Author Praveenp
https://en.wikipedia.org/wiki/Villu_Paatu#/media/File:Villu_patt.JPG 17.55
Author Unknown
https://en.wikipedia.org/wiki/K._L._Saigal#/media/File:Saigal_1938.jpghttps://en.wikipedia.org/wiki/K._L._Saigal#/
media/File:Saigal_1938.jpg 17.57
LataRamdas.jpg
https://en.wikipedia.org/wiki/Lata_Mangeshkar#/media/File:Lata_Mangeshkar_black-and-white.jpg 17.63
Mehboob Productions
https://en.wikipedia.org/wiki/File:Begum_Akhtar_(1942).jpg 17.69

(d) **Photographs: Courtesy, State Tourism Boards**

Madhya Pradesh Tourism Board 17.49

(e) **Photographs: Courtesy, Sangeet Natak Akademi** 17.32, 17.37, 17.45, 17.50, 17.52, 17.53, 17.80-17.97

Chapter 18 Dances in Modern India

(a) **Links of copyright free photographs from Wikimedia Commons/Wikipedia**

author Felix Francis
https://en.wikipedia.org/wiki/Kathak#/media/File:Shovana_Narayan.jpg 18.2
Author https://flickr.com/photos/payalam
https://en.wikipedia.org/wiki/Kathak#/media/File:Kathak_3511900193_986f6440f6_b_retouched.jpg 18.3
Author Dipjyotidipankarsattriya
https://commons.wikimedia.org/wiki/Category:Sattriya#/media/File:Bishnu_Sattriya.jpg 18.7
Author https://www.flickr.com/photos/matsukin
https://en.wikipedia.org/wiki/Manipuri_Raas_Leela#/media/File:Rasa_Lila_in_Manipuri_dance_style.jpg 18.10
Author ImpuMozhi at English Wikipedia
https://en.wikipedia.org/wiki/Bharatanatyam#/media/File:Rukmini_Dev.jpg 18.12
Author Augustus Binu/facebook
https://en.wikipedia.org/wiki/Kuchipudi#/media/File:Kuchipudi_Performer_DS.jpg 18.17
Author Gokul Krishna Raja
https://en.wikipedia.org/wiki/Kathakali#/media/File:Shree_Krishnan_by_FACT_Jayadeva_Varma.jpg 18.18
Author Gokul Krishna Raja
https://en.wikipedia.org/wiki/Kathakali#/media/File:Hanuman_by_FACT_Jayadeva_Varma.jpg 18.19
Author Nomu420
https://commons.wikimedia.org/wiki/File:Mohini_01.JPG 18.21
Author Ramesh Lalwani
https://commons.wikimedia.org/wiki/File:Sirmauri_Nati_Himachal.jpg 18.23
Author Lokesh negi
https://commons.wikimedia.org/wiki/File:Kayang_At_Mt._piri.jpg 18.24
Author Kalpana
https://en.wikipedia.org/wiki/Ghoomar#/media/File:Ghoomar.jpg 18.31
Author Ramesh Lalwani
https://en.wikipedia.org/wiki/Charkula#/media/File:Charkula_Dance.jpg 18.33
Author Amitsah8888
https://en.wikipedia.org/wiki/Chholiya#/media/File:Cholliyar.jpg 18.34

Author Sumitsurai
https://en.wikipedia.org/wiki/Matki_dance#/media/File:Jal_Mahotsav_Dance.jpg 18.37
Author Pankaj Oudhia
https://en.wikipedia.org/wiki/Raut_Nacha#/media/File:Raut_Nacha.jpg 18.39
Author Dev
https://en.wikipedia.org/wiki/Jhijhiya#/media/File:Women_performing_Jhijhiya_dance.jpg 18.42
Author Bipul Rabha
https://en.wikipedia.org/wiki/Folk_dances_of_Assam#/media/File:Bhortal_Dance.jpeg 18.50
Author Ramesh Lalwani
https://upload.wikimedia.org/wikipedia/commons/9/97/Lavani_Dancer.jpg 18.57
Author Ramesh Lalwani
https://en.wikipedia.org/wiki/Fugdi#/media/File:Fugdi_Dancers_from_South_Goa.jpg 18.58
Author Sukanto Debnath
https://en.wikipedia.org/wiki/Burra_katha#/media/File:India_village_musicians.jpg 18.59
Original source from Flickr
https://en.wikipedia.org/wiki/Folk_arts_of_Karnataka#/media/File:Mahila_Dollu_Kunita.jpg 18.60
Author Jasinth M V
https://commons.wikimedia.org/wiki/File:Bali_theyyam,_Payyannur.jpg 18.61

(b) Photographs: Courtesy, Department of Post 18.16

(c) Photographs: Courtesy, State Tourism Boards

Department of Tourism, Odisha 18.4, 18.5, 18.56
Tamil Nadu Tourism Development Corporation 18.14, 18.15, 18.61, 18.63
Jammu and Kashmir Tourism Development Corporation 18.22
Rajasthan Tourism 18.26-18.30
Madhya Pradesh Tourism Board 18.38
Department of Tourism, West Bengal 18.44-18.47

(d) Photographs: Courtesy, Sangeet Natak Akademi 18.1, 18.6, 18.8, 18.9, 18.11, 18.13, 18.20, 18.25, 18.32, 18.35, 18.36, 18.40, 18.41, 18.43, 18.48, 18.49, 18.51- 18.55, 18.62

Chapter 19 Indian Textiles and Handicrafts

(a) Photographs by Madhukar K Bhagat (author) 19.1, 19.2, 19.3, 19.5, 19.6, 19.8, 19.12-19.18, 19.23-19.32, 19.35-19.39, 19.44, 19.45, 19.48, 19.52, 19.60, 19.62-19.64, 19.71, 19.72, 19.74, 19.75, 19.81, 19.82, 19.85-19.88, 19.90, 19.92-19.96, 19.107-19.112

(b) Department of Post 19.83

(c) Links of copyright free photographs from Wikimedia Commons/Wikipedia

Author Naveed Akhtar
https://en.wikipedia.org/wiki/Himroo#/media/File:Himrooshawl.jpg 19.11
Author Alfred Barlow
https://en.wikipedia.org/wiki/Warp_and_weft#/media/File:Warp_and_weft_2.jpg 19.19
Author Pearson Scott Foresman
https://en.wikipedia.org/wiki/Warp_and_weft#/media/File:Loom_(PSF).png 19.20
Los Angeles County Museum of Art
https://commons.wikimedia.org/wiki/File:Chamba_Rumal_with_Scenes_of_Gopis_Adoring_Krishna_LACMA_M.71.1.40.jpg 19.40
Author Shibu Bh
https://en.wikipedia.org/wiki/Embroidery_of_India#/media/File:Modern_Naksi_kantha.jpg 19.42
Author Priya, source Pinterest
https://en.wikipedia.org/wiki/Embroidery_of_India#/media/File:Kasuti_embroidery.jpg 19.43
Author unknown
https://en.wikipedia.org/wiki/Kamaladevi_Chattopadhyay#/media/File:Kamaladevi_Chattopadhyay.png 19.49
Author Vassil
https://en.wikipedia.org/wiki/Kundan#/media/File:British_Museum_The_Islamic_world_ 19.50
Necklace_Kundan_India_21022019_7703.jpg
https://en.wikipedia.org/wiki/Filigree#/media/File:Cuttack_Tarkasi_(silver_filigree)_pendant_&_ear_rings.jpg 19.51
Author unknown
https://commons.wikimedia.org/wiki/Category:Bidriware#/media/File:Bidriware_cup_and_lid,_ca_1850_V&A_Museum.jpg 19.53
Author Sankoswal
https://en.wikipedia.org/wiki/Khurja_pottery#/media/File:Khurja_Pottery.jpg 19.54
Author Aishik Rehman
https://en.wikipedia.org/wiki/Nizamabad_black_clay_pottery#/media/File:Nizamabad_black_clay_pottery.png 19.57

Author Mythcollector
https://en.wikipedia.org/wiki/Longpi#/media/File:Lori_Ham.png 19.58
Author VinPrasad
https://commons.wikimedia.org/wiki/File:Khavda_pottery_from_Ludia_village_in_Gujarat.jpg; 19.59
Author Daderot
https://www.wikidata.org/wiki/Q6894977#/media/File:Indian_mojari,_19th_century,_red_velvet_with_gold_embroidery_and_sequins_-_Bata_Shoe_Museum_-_DSC00132.JPG 19.65
Author prashant
https://en.wikipedia.org/wiki/Kolhapuri_chappal#/media/File:Kolh 19.66
Author http//gaatha.com
https://en.wikipedia.org/wiki/Kashmiri_handicrafts#/media/File:Kmrwalnut.jpg 19.73
Author Ricce
https://en.wikipedia.org/wiki/Sandalwood#/media/File:Ganesh_in_legno_di_sandalo.jpg 19.76
Author Pratheeps
https://commons.wikimedia.org/wiki/File:Wooden_toys.JPG 19.91

(d) Photographs: Courtesy, State Tourism Boards

Department of Tourism, West Bengal 19.4, 19.7, 19.61, 19.67, 19.114
Madhya Pradesh Tourism Board 19.9, 19.10, 19.21, 19.22, 19.33, 19.34, 19.46, 19.47, 19.100, 19.101
Rajasthan Tourism Development Corporation 19.55, 19.56
Directorate of Uttar Pradesh Tourism 19.68, 19.69, 19.84, 19.119-19.128
Bihar Tourism 19.70
Tamil Nadu Tourism Development Corporation 19.77-19.79, 19.89, 19.97-19.99, 19.102-19.106
Maharashtra Tourism Development Corporation 19.80, 19.113
Department of Tourism, Odisha 19.115-19.118

Chapter 20 Language and Literature of Modern India

(a) Photographs by Madhukar K Bhagat (author) 20.13, 20.21-20.27, 20.29, 20.30, 20.34, 20.35

(b) Photographs: Courtesy, Department of Post 20.1, 20.5-20.9, 20.11, 20.14-20.20, 20.28, 20.31-20.33, 20.36-20.78

(c) Photographs from copyright free links (Wikimedia Commons)

Internet identifier: ramtanulahiribra00sastiala
https://en.wikipedia.org/wiki/Dinabandhu_Mitra#/media/File:Dinobandhu_Mitra.jpg 20.10
https://commons.wikimedia.org/wiki/File:Gitanjali_11_title_page.jpg 20.12

(d) Maps: Courtesy, Census Commissioner, Government of India 20.2, 20.3, 20.4

Chapter 21 Folk and Modern Theatre of India

(a) Photographs by Madhukar K Bhagat (author) 21.21

(b) Photographs: Courtesy, Department of Post 21.31, 21.32, 21.36, 21.42, 21.44, 21.47, 21.49, 21.50

(c) Photographs from copyright free links (Wikimedia Commons)

Author Rosehubwiki, Kuber Patel
https://commons.wikimedia.org/wiki/File:Ramnnagar_Varanasi_Ramlila.jpg 21.4
https://www.wikiwand.com/en/Nautanki#Media/File:DevendraSharma_PunditSharma.png 21.5
Author Vinayak.Razdan
https://commons.wikimedia.org/wiki/File:Bhand_Pather.jpg 21.8
Author Swang Opera
https://en.wikipedia.org/wiki/File:Swang_%27Raja_Vikramaditya%27_in_Mandi_House_SRC_New_Delhi.jpg 21.9
https://commons.wikimedia.org/wiki/File:Sutradhar_in_Bhaona.jpeg 21.10
Author Suyash Dwivedi
https://commons.wikimedia.org/wiki/File:Bhavai_Gujrat_(2).jpg 21.11
Author Varsha Deshpande
https://commons.wikimedia.org/wiki/File:A_scene_from_Dashavatara_folk_theatre_in_Konkan_region_of_Maharashtra_state_in_India.jpg 21.12
Author Jean Pierre Dalbera
https://commons.wikimedia.org/wiki/File:Krishnanattam_(th%C3%A9%C3%A2tre_rituel_du_Kerala).jpg 21.18
Author Sivavkm
https://commons.wikimedia.org/wiki/File:Mudiyettu_at_Kezhoor_kavu_02-02-2013_2-04-33.JPG 21.19

Author Ed and Eddie from Palo Alto, USA
https://commons.wikimedia.org/wiki/File:SFOperaHouse3_(8189967590).jpg 21.30
Unknown author
https://commons.wikimedia.org/wiki/File:Nabanna_Bengali_theatre_scene.png 21.33
Author Homen Biswas
https://commons.wikimedia.org/wiki/File:Laksminath_Bezbaruah.jpg 21.34
Author Prateek Pattanaik
https://commons.wikimedia.org/wiki/File:Kabichandra_Kali_Charan_Patnaik_(Kalicharan_Patnaik).jpg 21.35
https://www.wikiwand.com/en/articles/Mumbai_Gujarati_Natak_Company 21.37
Unknown author
https://commons.wikimedia.org/wiki/File:Bapulal_Nayak_ane_Jaishankar_Sundari_in_1901.jpg 21.38
User: phantomiyer
https://commons.wikimedia.org/wiki/File:Sankaradas_Swami.jpg 21.39
https://commons.wikimedia.org/wiki/File:Drama_Scene.jpg 21.40
Author unknown
https://upload.wikimedia.org/wikipedia/en/a/ab/Vedam_Venkataraya_Sastry.jpg 21.41
User DatBot
https://en.wikipedia.org/wiki/File:Kalyanam_Raghuramaiah.jpg 21.43
Source: Sree Chitra Art Gallery
https://commons.wikimedia.org/wiki/File:Kerala_Varma_Valiya_Koil_Thampuran_Changanassery_Lakshmipuram_Palace.jpg 21.45
Public domain
https://commons.wikimedia.org/wiki/File:CVs60thbirthday.png 21.46

(d) Photographs: Courtesy, State Tourism Boards

Karnataka Tourism Development Corporation 21.1, 21.2, 21.13, 21.14
Department of Tourism, West Bengal 21.6, 21.7
Tamil Nadu Tourism Development Corporation 21.15, 21.16

(e) Photographs: Courtesy, Sangeet Natak Akademi 21.3, 21.17, 21.20, 21.22-21.29

(f) Photographs: Courtesy, National School of Drama 21.51, 21.52

Chapter 22 Indian Cinema

(a) Photographs by Madhukar K Bhagat (author) 22.88, 22.90-22.92

(b) Photographs: Courtesy, Department of Post 22.1-22.3, 22.8- 22.20, 22.23-22.30, 22.32, 22.34, 22.36-22.39, 22.43, 22.46- 22.48, 22.50, 22.53, 22.55-22.60, 22.61, 22.63-22.68, 22.70, 22.71, 22.73, 22.76

(c) Photographs from copyright free links (Wikimedia Commons)

Author unknown
https://commons.wikimedia.org/wiki/File:Ardeshir_Irani_recording_Alam_Ara,_1931.jpg 22.5
Author unknown
https://en.wikipedia.org/wiki/Alam_Ara#/media/File:Alam_Ara_poster,_1931.jpg 22.6
Author unknown
https://en.wikipedia.org/wiki/V._Shantaram#/media/File:V._Shantaram.jpg 22.7
Author film producer
https://en.wikipedia.org/wiki/Pran_(actor)#/media/File:Pran_Actor.JPG 22.31
Author Studio Harcourt
https://en.wikipedia.org/wiki/Cinema_of_India#/media/File:BACHCHAN_Amitabh_03-24x30-2009b.jpg 22.33
Authors Sudhir Vasudev Nandgaonkar, Chaitanya Kunte, Madhav Imarate
https://commons.wikimedia.org/wiki/File:Savkari_Pash_(1925).jpg 22.35
Author Imperial Film Company
https://en.wikipedia.org/wiki/Kalidas_(film)#/media/File:Kalidas_1931_Songbook.JPG 22.41
Author unknown
https://en.wikipedia.org/wiki/R._Nataraja_Mudaliar#/media/File:R._Nataraja_Mudaliar.jpg 22.42
Author calcuttaweb.com
https://en.wikipedia.org/wiki/Cinema_of_India#/media/File:Dena_paona_1931.jpg 22.44
Author unknown
https://en.wikipedia.org/wiki/Bilwamangal#/media/File:Billwamangal.jpg 22.45
Author unknown
https://en.wikipedia.org/wiki/Pramathesh_Barua#/media/File:P.C._Barua_and_Jamuna_-_Bengali_version_of_Devdas_(1935).jpg 22.49

Author Bimal Roy
https://upload.wikimedia.org/wikipedia/commons/7/7f/Suchitra_Sen.jpg 22.51
Harendra Nath Chattopadhay Productions
https://en.wikipedia.org/wiki/Uttam_Kumar#/media/File:Uttam_Kumar_Indrani_(1958).png 22.52
Author unknown
https://en.wikipedia.org/wiki/Raithu_Bidda#/media/File:Raitu_Bidda_1939.JPG 22.54
Author Kundoosi
https://en.wikipedia.org/wiki/Savitri_(actress)#/media/File:Savitri_Actress.jpg 22.62
Author Joy Varghese
https://commons.wikimedia.org/wiki/File:Vigathakumaran.jpg 22.72
Author Sagar Movi-tone
https://en.wikipedia.org/wiki/Narsinh_Mehta_%28film%29 22.77

(d) **Photographs: Courtesy, NFDC-National Film Archives of India, (Pune)** 22.4, 22.40, 22.69, 22.74, 22.75, 22.78-22.87, 22.89, 22.93-22.105

(e) **Photographs: Courtesy, Directorate of Film Festivals** 22.21, 22.22

Chapter 23 Festivals & Fairs in Modern India

(a) **Photographs by Madhukar K Bhagat (author)** 23.1, 23.8, 23.9, 23.16, 23.18, 23.19, 23.48

(b) **Photographs from copyright free links (Wikimedia Commons)**
Author Shakti
https://en.wikipedia.org/wiki/Vijayadashami#/media/File:F%C3%AAte_de_Dusshera.jpg 23.6
Author NatePowell
https://en.wikipedia.org/wiki/Ganesh_Chaturthi#/media/File:Lalbaugh_Ganesha.jpg 23.14
Author Chris
https://en.wikipedia.org/wiki/Ganesh_Chaturthi#/media/File:Anant_Chaturdashi.jpg 23.15
Author Nimitnigam
https://commons.wikimedia.org/wiki/File:Jama_Maszid.jpg 23.25
Author Abhay12253
https://en.wikipedia.org/wiki/Makar_Sankranti#/media/File:Photo_of_makar_sankranti_devootees.jpg 23.28
Author Gjbhd
https://www.wikidata.org/wiki/Q67907801#/media/File:Kati_Bihu_Assamese_.jpg 23.29
Author Saral Shots
https://en.wikipedia.org/wiki/Pongal_(festival)#/media/File:Pongal_fest.jpg 23.30

(c) **Photographs: Courtesy, State Tourism Boards**
Department of Tourism, West Bengal 23.7, 23.46, 23.47, 23.87-23.91
Karnataka State Tourism Development Corporation 23.10, 23.11, 23.27
Maharashtra Tourism Development Corporation 23.31,
Madhya Pradesh Tourism Board 23.4, 23.5, 23.20, 23.44, 23.45, 23.57-23.63, 23.64-23.71
Rajasthan Tourism 23.22, 23.36, 23.37, 23.49, 23.51, 23.92, 23.93, 23.104-23.107
Bihar Tourism 23.17, 23.21, 23.40, 23.41, 23.50, 23.98-23.103
Directorate of Uttar Pradesh Tourism 23.2, 23.3, 23.12, 23.13, 23.24, 23.43, 23.52-23.56, 23.72-23.78
Tamil Nadu Tourism Development Corporation 23.26
Department of Tourism, Odisha 23.23, 23.32, 23.38, 23.39, 23.42, 23.79-23.86, 23.94-23.97

(d) **Photographs: Courtesy, Ministry of Defence** 23.33, 23.34, 23.35

Chapter 24 Modern Indian Architecture

(a) **Photographs by Madhukar K Bhagat (author)** 24.1, 24.3-24.8, 24.20-24.38, 24.41, 24.42-24.48, 24.51- 24.54, 24.60- 24.84, 24.89-24.107, 24.109

(b) **Photographs from copyright free links (Wikimedia Commons)**
Author Anurag Jain
https://commons.wikimedia.org/wiki/File:M%C3%A3e_de_Deus_Parish_Church.jpg 24.2
Source British Library
https://commons.wikimedia.org/wiki/File:Fortwilliam1828.jpg 24.9
Author ptwo, Allahabad, India
https://commons.wikimedia.org/wiki/File:Rashtrapati_Niwas,_Shimla.jpg 24.16
Author Sambit04126
https://commons.wikimedia.org/wiki/File:Umaid_Bhawan_Palace.jpg 24.39
Author Soman
https://commons.wikimedia.org/wiki/File:Tvdnindiancoffeehouse_(89).JPG 24.49

(c)	**Photographs: Courtesy, State Tourism Boards**	
	Department of Tourism, West Bengal	24.10-24.15, 24.55-24.59,
	Tamil Nadu Tourism Development Corporation	24.17-24.19
	Karnataka State Tourism Development Corporation	24.40, 24.105, 24.108
	Maharashtra Tourism Development Corporation	24.85-24.88
(d)	**Courtesy, Ministry of Parliamentary Affairs**	24.50

Bibliography and References

Books

General Culture and Cultural History of India

- The History and Culture of the Indian People Volume VIII: The Maratha Supremacy
- The History and Culture of the Indian People, Volume IX: British Paramountcy and the Indian Renaissance; Part-I
- The History and Culture of the Indian People, Volume X: British Paramountcy and the Indian Renaissance; Part-II
- The History and Culture of the Indian People, Volume XI: Struggle for Freedom
- Themes in Indian history, Part III: NCERT
- Our Pasts volume III: NCERT
- An Introduction to Indian Art, Part I: NCERT
- An Introduction to Indian Art, Part II: NCERT
- Living Craft Traditions of India: NCERT
- Bhartiya Sanskriti Ke Char Adhyay: Ramdhari Singh Dinkar
- The National Culture of India: S. Abid Hussain
- The Cultural Heritage of India, Volume 4, & Volume 5: The Ramakrishna Mission Institute of Culture
- Indian Heritage Art and Culture: Madhukar Kumar Bhagat
- Gitanjali by : Gurudev Rabindra Nath Tagore
- India of My Dreams: Mahatma Gandhi
- Rashtrapati Bhavan and Central Vista: INTACH Delhi Chapter

Official Publications of the Government of India

- The Constitution of India
- Language Atlas of India-2011; A publication of Registrar General and Census Commissioner of India
- Treasures: a publication of the National Museum, New Delhi
- The Art of Puppetry (booklet): Centre for Cultural Resource and Training
- Telugu Drama and Stage: Sangeet Natak Akademi
- Gallery of Musical Instruments: Sangeet Natak Akademi
- State Awards for Films-1954: Ministry of Information and Broadcasting

Websites

- Articles on Wikipedia
- Articles on Encyclopaedia Britannica
- Centre for Cultural Resource and Training: https://ccrtindia.gov.in/
- UNESCO; World Heritage Convention: https://whc.unesco.org/en/convention/
- Indian Culture; https://indianculture.gov.in/
- Raag Hindustani, Demystifying Indian Classical Music: https://raag-hindustani.com/Notes.html
- Indian Postage stamps, Department of Post; https://postagestamps.gov.in/Stamps.aspx
- Registered GI of India: https://ipindia.gov.in/registered-gls.htm
- National School of Drama: https://nsd.gov.in/delhi/
- The Film and Television Institute of India (FTII): https://www.ftii.ac.in/p/about-ftii
- Websites of State Governments of India

Articles in Journals and Newspapers

- *Communication Through Public Stage: A Study in 19th Century Bengali Theatre* by Moloy Rakshit: Global Media Journal-Indian Edition/ISSN 2249-5835; December 2013
- *Tamil drama in colonial Madras: the Parsi theatre connection by* Kathryn Hansen: South Asian History and Culture, DOI: 10.1080/19472498.2020.1816414
- *Assamese Theatre by Daisy Bhattacharjee* : International Journal of Science and Research (IJSR) ISSN: 2319-7064 SJIF (2019): 7.583